Microsoft
Windows® 2000
Professional
Resource
Kit

PUBLISHED BY
Microsoft Press
A Division of Microsoft Corporation
One Microsoft Way
Redmond, Washington 98052-6399

on Data
rce Kit / Microsoft Corporation.

) 2. Operating systems (Computers) I. Microsoft

005.4'4769--dc21   99-088818

Printed and bound in the United States of America.

9 10 11 12 13   QWT   7 6 5 4 3 2

Distributed in Canada by H.B. Fenn and Company Ltd.

A CIP catalogue record for this book is available from the British Library.

Microsoft Press books are available through booksellers and distributors worldwide. For further information about international editions, contact your local Microsoft Corporation office or contact Microsoft Press International directly at fax (425) 936-7329. Visit our Web site at www.microsoft.com/mspress. Send comments to *rkinput@microsoft.com*.

Active Accessibility, Active Channel, Active Client, Active Desktop, Active Directory, ActiveMovie, ActiveX, Authenticode, BackOffice, DirectAnimation, DirectPlay, DirectShow, DirectSound, DirectX, DoubleSpace, DriveSpace, FrontPage, Georgia, Hotmail, IntelliMirror, IntelliSense, JScript, Links, Microsoft, Microsoft Press, MSDN, MS-DOS, MSN, Natural, NetMeeting, NetShow, OpenType, Outlook, PowerPoint, Sidewalk, Slate, Starts Here, TrueImage, Verdana, Visual Basic, Visual C++, Visual InterDev, Visual J++, Visual Studio, WebBot, Win32, Windows, Windows Media, and Windows NT are either registered trademarks or trademarks of Microsoft Corporation in the United States and/or other countries. NT is a trademark of Northern Telecom Limited. Other product and company names mentioned herein may be the trademarks of their respective owners.

Any RFC excerpts are subject to the following statement:
Copyright © The Internet Society (1999). All Rights Reserved. This document and translations of it may be copied and furnished to others, and derivative works that comment on or otherwise explain it or assist in its implementation may be prepared, copied, published and distributed, in whole or in part, without restriction of any kind, provided that the above copyright notice and this paragraph are included on all such copies and derivative works. However, this document itself may not be modified in any way, such as by removing the copyright notice or references to the Internet Society or other Internet organizations, except as needed for the purpose of developing Internet standards in which case the procedures for copyrights defined in the Internet Standards process must be followed, or as required to translate it into languages other than English. The limited permissions granted above are perpetual and will not be revoked by the Internet Society or its successors or assigns. This document and the information contained herein is provided on an "AS IS" basis and THE INTERNET SOCIETY AND THE INTERNET ENGINEERING TASK FORCE DISCLAIMS ALL WARRANTIES, EXPRESS OR IMPLIED, INCLUDING BUT NOT LIMITED TO ANY WARRANTY THAT THE USE OF THE INFORMATION HEREIN WILL NOT INFRINGE ANY RIGHTS OR ANY IMPLIED WARRANTIES OF MERCHANTABILITY OR FITNESS FOR A PARTICULAR PURPOSE.

Information in this document, including URL and other Internet Web site references, is subject to change without notice. The example companies, organizations, products, people, and events depicted herein are fictitious. No association with any real company, organization, product, person, or event is intended or should be inferred.

Acquisitions Editor: Juliana Aldous
Project Editor: Maureen Williams Zimmerman

Part No. 097-0008636

Thank you to those who contributed to this book:

Department Manager: Ken Western
Documentation Manager: Martin DelRe
Resource Kit Program Manager: Martin Holladay

Windows 2000 Professional Resource Kit

Technical Writing Lead: Pilar Orozco Ackerman
Writers: Chris Aschauer, Ross Carter, Phyllis Collier, Rick DeJarnette, Vincent Edd, Kristen Gill,
Bill Gruber, Lou Gomm, Kristin King, Paulette McKay,
Pilar Orozco Ackerman, Shira Paul, Renee Smith, Susan Stevenson,
Carol Troup, Audrey Wehba, Mark Wilkinson

Editing Manager: Kate O'Leary
Book Editing Leads: Kristen Gill, Uma Kukathas, Paulette McKay
Developmental Editors: Sandra Faucett, Minette Layne, Chris McKitterick,
Gary W. Moore, Susan Sarrafan, Peter Tysver, Scot Yonan, Todd Young
Copy Editors: Scott Somohano, Mary Rose Sliwoski, Sigrid Strom,
Debbie Uyeshiro, Thelma Warren, Todd Young
Glossary: Daniel Bell

Online Writing Leads: June Blender, Maureen Carmichael, Peter Costantini
Online Writers: Michael Bates, Rick DeJarnette, Jay French, Lola Gunter,
Margaret Plumley, Chris Revelle, Audrey Wehba
Online Editing Lead: Neil Orint
Online Editors: Chris McKitterick, Paulette McKay

Resource Kit Tools Software Developers: Dan Grube,
Michael Hawkins, Darryl Wood, Zeyong Xu
Documentation Tools Software Developers: Ryan Farber, Mark Pengra

Production Lead: Jason Hershey
Production Specialist: Lori Robinson

Indexing Leads: Veronica Maier, Kumud Dwivedi
Indexers: Diana Rain, Tony Ross

Lead Graphic Designer: Flora Goldthwaite
Designer: Chris Blanton

Lead Production Artist: Gabriel Varela
Production Artists: Blaine Dollard, Amy Shear

Test Lead: Jonathan Fricke
Testers: Brian Klauber, Jeremy Sullivan

Windows 2000 Lab Manager: Edward Lafferty
Administrators: Dave Meyer, Dean Prince, Robert Thingwold, Frank Zamarron
Lab Partners: Cisco Systems, Inc., Compaq, Inc.,
Hewlett-Packard Corporation, Intel Corporation

A special recognition to the following technical experts for their exceptional contributions:
Darrell Gorter, Joseph Dadzie

A special thanks to the following technical experts who contributed to and supported this effort:
Linda Apsley, Lowell Allen III, Brandon Allsop, Starr Andersen, Brian Aust, Adam Bargmeyer, Doug Barlow, Jason Bellis, Noury Bernard-Hasan, June Blender, Bill Blomgren, Richard Bond, Chris Brown, Dick Brown, Peter Brundrett, Andrea Burns, Felipe Cabrera, Eric Carmel, Laura Carmichael, Phillip Carver, Daniel Chan, Charlie Chase, Yuying Chen, Frank Chidsey, John Claugherty, Marion Cole, Wayne Cook, Debie Courtney, Scott Cousens, Mark Croft, Nathaniel Crum, Trudy Culbreth Brassell, Joseph Dadzie, Simon Daniels, Joseph Davies, JD Davis, Anthony DeMarco, Michael Dennis, Bo Downey, David Eitelbach, Mike Fenelon, Chris Frediani, Bob Fruth, Mark Galioto, Marsha Gladney, David Golds, Fabian Gramer, Randy Grandle, Timothy Green, Darrell Gorter, Todd Hafer, Rich Hagemeyer, Josh Helm, Janice Hertz, Greg Hinkel, Eugene Ho, Anne Hopkins, Stephen Hui, John Hunter, Bob Hyman, Michael Jacquet, Babak Jahromi, Romano Jerez, Jeramy Jones, Nikhil Joshi, Mark Kenworthy, Jim Klima, Ivan Kreslin, Karen Krueger, Diane LaCaze, Bruce Langworthy, Mark Larusso, Jason Leznek, Jimin Li, John Lim, Steve Lipner, Daniel Lovinger, Don Lundman, Russ Madlener, Aaron Massey, Dave Massy, Michael McCartney, Lonny McMichael, Wayne Melvin, George Menzel, Dennis Morgan, Greg Nichols, Vivek Nirkhe, Larry Ockene, Steve Olsson, Shishir Pardikar, Theodore Parker, Will Parkerson, Dave Parsons, Annie Pearson, Rick Plant, Charles Porter, Sandeep Prabhu, Kartik Raghavan, Sankar Ramasubramanian, Michael Raschko, Randy Reeder, Aaron Reynolds, Jeff Robison, Lynn Roe, Steve Rowe, Louise Rudnicki, Jason Rush, Andy Ruth, Jeffrey Saathoff, Walter Schmidt, Kate Seekings, David Sheldon, Muhunthan Sivapragasam, Chris Slemp, James Slonsky, Steve Smaller, Erick Smith, Jonathan V. Smith, Carla Sornson, Sandy Spinrad, Sundar Srinivasan Michael Stokes, Todd Stout, Sriram Subramanian, Ryan Taylor, Bogdan Tepordei, Rob Trace, Catharine van Ingen, Bob Watson, Tammy White, James Wilson, Roland Winkler, Jon Wojan, Peter Wong, Craig Zhou

Contents

PART 3   System Configuration and Management

PART 4   Network Configuration and Management

PART 6   Performance Monitoring

PART 7　Troubleshooting

PART 8   Appendixes

Introduction

Welcome to the *Microsoft® Windows® 2000 Professional Resource Kit*.

The *Windows 2000 Professional Resource Kit* consists of this guide and a compact disc (CD) containing tools, additional reference materials, and an online version of the *Microsoft® Windows® 2000 Server Resource Kit Deployment Planning Guide*. Supplements to the *Windows 2000 Professional Resource Kit* will be released as new information becomes available, and updates and information will be available on the Web on an ongoing basis.

This guide is a comprehensive technical resource for installing, configuring, and supporting Microsoft® Windows® 2000 Professional in either a Microsoft® Windows® 2000 Server environment or other environments. It provides task-based information for automating installations as well as for customizing and configuring Windows 2000 Professional to suit your needs. To help you solve problems, this guide contains extensive troubleshooting information and a troubleshooting quick guide that points you to answers for common problems.

Document Conventions

The following style conventions and terminology are used throughout this guide.

Element	Meaning
bold font	Characters that you type exactly as shown, including commands and switches. User interface elements are also bold.
Italic font	Variables for which you supply a specific value. For example, Filename.ext could refer to any valid file name for the case in question.
`Monospace font`	Code samples.
`%SystemRoot%`	The folder in which Windows 2000 is installed.

Reader Alert	Meaning
Tip	Alerts you to supplementary information that is not essential to the completion of the task at hand.
Note	Alerts you to supplementary information.
Important	Alerts you to supplementary information that is essential to the completion of a task.
Caution	Alerts you to possible data loss, breaches of security, or other more serious problems.
Warning	Alerts you that failure to take or avoid a specific action might result in physical harm to you or to the hardware.

Resource Kit Compact Disc

The *Windows 2000 Professional Resource Kit* companion CD includes a wide variety of tools and resources that help you work more efficiently with Windows 2000 Professional.

Note The tools on the CD are designed and tested for the U.S. version of Microsoft® Windows® 2000. Use of these tools on other versions of Windows 2000 or on versions of Microsoft® Windows NT® can cause unpredictable results.

The *Resource Kit* companion CD contains the following:

Windows 2000 Professional Resource Kit Tools and Tools Help Over 200 software tools, tools documentation, and other resources that enhance Windows 2000. Use the tools to manage the Active Directory™ directory service, administer security features, work with the registry, automate recurring tasks, and perform many other important tasks. Use Tools Help documentation to discover and learn how to use these administrative tools.

Windows 2000 Server Resource Kit Deployment Planning Guide Online
An HTML Help version of the print book. The *Deployment Planning Guide* provides both rollout planning guidelines and strategies for deploying the various technologies that make up Windows 2000. This guide provides critical decision points and technical information that help you determine the scope, sequence, and processes for your deployment. The guide also provides step-by-step procedures for automating both server and client installations.

Windows 2000 Resource Kit References A set of HTML Help references:

- **Error and Event Messages Help** contains most of the error and event messages generated by Windows 2000. With each message comes a detailed explanation and a suggested user action.

- **Technical Reference to the Registry** provides detailed descriptions of Windows 2000 registry content, such as the subtrees, keys, subkeys, and entries that advanced users want to know about, including many entries that cannot be changed by using Windows 2000 tools or programming interfaces.

- **Performance Counter Reference** describes all performance objects and counters provided for use with tools in the Performance snap-in of Windows 2000. Use this reference to learn how monitoring counter values can assist you in diagnosing problems or detecting bottlenecks in your system.

- **Group Policy Reference** provides detailed descriptions of the Group Policy settings in Windows 2000. These descriptions explain the effect of enabling, disabling, or not configuring each policy, as well as explanations of how related policies interact.

Resource Kit Support Policy

The software supplied in the *Windows 2000 Professional Resource Kit* is not supported. Microsoft does not guarantee the performance of the *Windows 2000 Server Resource Kit* tools, response times for answering questions, or bug fixes to the tools. However, Microsoft does provide a way for customers who purchase the *Windows 2000 Professional Resource Kit* to report bugs and receive possible fixes for their issues. You can do this by sending e-mail to rkinput@microsoft.com. This e-mail address is only for issues related to *Windows 2000 Professional Resource Kit*. For issues related to the Windows 2000 operating system, please refer to the support information included with your product.

P A R T   1

Overview

In This Part

CHAPTER 1

Introducing Windows 2000 Professional

Microsoft® Windows® 2000 Professional is the most reliable operating system for business computers. It combines the best business features of Microsoft® Windows® 98 with the reliability, security, and manageability of Microsoft® Windows NT® version 4.0.

In This Chapter

Related Information in the Resource Kit

- For more information about the advantages of using Windows 2000 Professional in a Microsoft® Windows® 2000 Server environment, see "Using Windows 2000 Professional with Windows 2000 Server" in this book.

- For more information about managing Windows 2000 Professional in Windows 2000 Server environments, see "Introduction to Desktop Management" in the *Windows 2000 Server Resource Kit Distributed Systems Guide*.

Quick Guide to Using Windows 2000 Professional

This quick guide points you to chapters in this book that cover the new and improved features that make Windows 2000 Professional reliable, secure, and easy to use and manage.

What benefits does Windows 2000 Professional provide to users and administrators?

Windows 2000 Professional is reliable, built for mobile users, easy to use, and easy to manage. It provides better browser integration and a platform for developing Web applications, enabling your business for the Internet.

- See "Overview" later in this chapter.
- See Part 1, "Overview" in this book.

How is Windows 2000 Professional easier to deploy?

For the first time, Windows 2000 Professional provides migration paths for upgrading computers from Microsoft® Windows® 95 and Windows 98 to a Windows operating system that is based on Windows NT technology. It includes an updated wizard, Setup Manager, that makes it easier to create setup scripts and distribution points for installation files. There are more and improved tools to choose from to customize and automate installations, such as an improved version of System Preparation Utility tool (Sysprep.exe) for image-based installations and the new Remote OS Installation that allows administrators to centralize and quickly duplicate Windows 2000 Professional installations from one desktop computer to another.

- See "Deployment and Installation" later in this chapter.
- See Part 2, "Deployment and Installation" in this book.

How is it easier to manage and support Windows 2000 Professional desktops in my organization?

Windows 2000 Professional is easier to manage with the Microsoft® Management Console (MMC), Windows Script Host (WSH), support for self-repairing applications, and comprehensive system, application, and driver protection. If you use Windows 2000 Professional with Windows 2000 Server, you can take advantage of the IntelliMirror™ technology for managing desktops from a central location.

- See "Configuration and Management" later in this chapter.
- See "Using Windows 2000 Professional with Windows 2000 Server" in this book.
- See Part 3, "System Configuration and Management" in this book.

What new features help simplify setting up and administering corporate networks?

Windows 2000 Professional provides improved autoconfiguration of both intranet and Internet setups. It combines networking (intranet and Internet) and dial-up connectivity functions into the new Network and Dial-Up Connections folder in Control Panel. Windows 2000 Professional can automatically create an intranet for you, so that all of the computers on your intranet can "talk to each other" within minutes by using Automatic Private IP Addressing (APIPA). Other networking improvements include better name resolution, network security, and TCP performance.

- See "Networking" later in this chapter.
- See Part 4, "Network Configuration and Management" in this book.

How can my existing environment coexist with Windows 2000 Professional?

Windows 2000 Professional can coexist with earlier versions of Windows (Microsoft® Windows® 3.*x*, Windows 95, Windows 98, Microsoft® Windows NT® Workstation version 4.0, or Microsoft® Windows NT® Server version 4.0) or third-party environments such as Netware, UNIX, IBM mainframe, or Macintosh. NetWare interoperability is provided through Client Services for NetWare, NWLink, and Novell Client 32 version 4.51, UNIX interoperability is provided through an add-on pack called Windows Services for UNIX. Macintosh interoperability is provided by File Server for Macintosh, which allows Macintosh clients to use TCP/IP (AFP over IP) to share files and to access shares on a Windows 2000 Server–based computer.

- See "Interoperability" later in this chapter.
- See Part 5, "Network Interoperability" in this book.

How can I monitor performance and perform preventive maintenance of my Windows 2000 Professional system?

Window 2000 Professional includes the Performance console to assess available memory, observe the effects of memory shortage, and monitor the file system cache. There are also new tools for monitoring processor activity, identifying bottleneck issues, and tuning disk performance.

- See "Performance Monitoring" later in this chapter.
- See Part 6, "Performance Monitoring" in this book.

How do I solve problems when they arise?

Microsoft® Windows® 2000 Professional provides tools you can use to resolve problems that might occur. Windows Professional also includes a wide range of troubleshooters that help you solve many common problems.

- See "Troubleshooting" later in this chapter.
- See Part 7, "Troubleshooting" in this book.

How does Windows 2000 Professional make computers more accessible?
Windows 2000 Professional provides users with special needs better access to programs and applications with features such as hot keys, sound events, and Narrator, a text-to-speech tool. Windows 2000 Professional also supports the Human Interface Device (HID) firmware specification for specialized input and output devices.

- See "Accessibility" later in this chapter.

- See Appendix A, "Accessibility for People with Disabilities" in this book.

Overview

Businesses today require reliability, security, and manageability with simplicity of use. Windows 2000 Professional goes beyond the reliability and security provided in Windows NT 4.0 and extends the ease-of-use of Windows 98.

Reliable

Windows 2000 Professional is built on the reliability of Windows NT technology, which makes it significantly more reliable than either Windows 95 or Windows 98. In Windows NT, each application runs in its own memory space, so when an application crashes, it does not bring down the entire system.

Windows File Protection

In addition to the way it allocates memory to applications, Windows 2000 Professional includes a built-in safeguard called Windows File Protection. This feature prevents system files, which are critical to the operating system, from being deleted or altered by users or applications.

Windows File Protection can also repair system files if one is deleted or altered. It detects the change, retrieves a correct version of the file from a cache, and restores it to the system file folder.

Windows Installer

In the past, if users incorrectly installed or uninstalled an application, or changed a file by accident, they could destabilize their entire system. In Windows 2000 Professional, when a user makes a mistake, applications repair themselves.

Windows Installer is the technology in Windows 2000 Professional that enables self-healing applications. With Windows Installer,, if installing or deleting an application, or even a part of an application, causes a problem, Windows Installer fixes it. For example, if a newly installed application has a dynamic-link library (DLL) with an identical name to another application's DLL, Windows Installer stores them in different folders.

To further ensure that applications work correctly with Windows 2000 Professional, Microsoft created an application certification program with business customers and independent software vendors (ISVs). To be certified, an application must meet technical reliability criteria, such as minimizing DLL conflicts, providing self-repairing installation, and maintaining user settings.

Dynamic System Configuration

Windows 2000 Professional reduces the number of restarts by improving how new hardware and software is installed. With Plug and Play, Windows 2000 Professional lets users easily add hardware devices such as scanners, DVD players, and speakers without restarting. It automatically recognizes and adapts to hardware changes, automatically configuring new hardware devices, and therefore minimizing user error.

To further reduce the need to restart, Microsoft created a program to certify hardware drivers. Drivers that meet Windows 2000 certification requirements do not need to be restarted after installation. Certified drivers are tested and digitally signed by Microsoft. If Windows 2000 Professional detects a driver that Microsoft has not digitally signed, it warns users about the risk before they install it on their system.

Performance

Windows 2000 Professional performs better than Windows NT Workstation or Windows 98. Users can run more programs and perform more tasks at the same time because it is completely based on a 32-bit architecture. Adding more memory makes Windows 2000 Professional run even faster. Windows 2000 Professional supports up to 4 gigabytes (GB) of RAM and up to two-way symmetric multiprocessing. Achieving this level of performance in Windows 98, even if you add more memory, is not possible.

Easy to Use and Maintain

Windows 2000 Professional has an improved user interface, provides a new interface for managing network connections, supports interoperability with other networks, has wizards that assist in the completion of common tasks, and has a broader set of tools for flexible deployment.

Easy to Use Desktop Interface

Windows 2000 Professional refines the look and design of the desktop. Improved windows provide quicker access to information, whether it is on the computer, a network, or the Internet. Wizard improvements help users accomplish difficult tasks faster. Screen clutter is reduced because only the most frequently used items are displayed on the Start menu. Dialog box improvements help users save time by automatically completing words as they type them and by displaying the most recently used lists.

Customizable Toolbars Users can add one or more customizable toolbars to the taskbar for single-click access to the Internet, the desktop, and programs. For example, users can use the Quick Launch toolbar to open a Microsoft® Internet Explorer window or read e-mail.

Show Desktop Button Switching between open windows and the desktop is easy with the new Show Desktop button, located on the taskbar.

My Documents and My Pictures Folders My Documents provides a convenient default storage location for personal files and folders. My Documents contains the My Pictures folder, a convenient place for to store photos, scanned images, faxes, and bitmaps.

Multilingual Support Regardless of which language version of Windows 2000 Professional is installed, users can write, edit, view, and print content in all supported languages. Windows 2000 Professional detects and installs any necessary fonts or symbols to view multilingual information.

Accessibility Tools The user can use the Accessibility Settings wizard to adapt Windows options to specific needs and preferences. Magnifier enlarges a portion of the screen for easier viewing, which can be useful for people who have impaired vision. Narrator uses text-to-speech technology to read the contents of the screen. On-Screen Keyboard makes it possible for those with limited dexterity to type by using a pointing device (such as a mouse) or a single-switch input device.

Networking

You can easily integrate Windows 2000 Professional with your existing networking infrastructure. It can coexist with earlier versions of Windows (Microsoft® Windows® 3.*x*, Windows 95, Windows 98, Windows NT Workstation 4.0, or Windows NT Server 4.0) or third-party environments such as UNIX, Novell Netware, IBM host systems, or Macintosh. UNIX interoperability is provided through an add-on pack called Windows Services for UNIX. Macintosh interoperability is provided by a number of services including File Server for Macintosh, which allows Macintosh clients to use TCP/IP (AFP over IP) to share files and to access shares on a Windows 2000 Server–based computer.

Windows 2000 Professional also has built-in peer-to-peer support for Windows 95, Windows 98, and Windows NT Workstation, enabling interoperability between Windows 2000 Professional and earlier versions of Windows.

Security

Windows 2000 Professional is a highly secure operating system. Based on the security system built into Windows NT, it allows users and administrators to select the appropriate level of protection for their information and applications, whether they are exchanging or storing information on individual computers, the network, an intranet, or the Internet.

With Encrypting File System (EFS), Windows 2000 Professional protects data on a computer's hard drive. EFS, which is part of the NTFS file system, encrypts each file with a randomly generated key. The encryption and decryption processes are transparent to the user.

With support for Kerberos v5 authentication, Windows 2000 Professional protects your corporate network or intranet. Kerberos v5 authentication protects data by tracking and verifying each user's activity on a network. Windows 2000 Professional safeguards even the most sensitive communications exchanged over a public network with its support for public keys, Layer 2 Tunneling Protocol (L2TP), and smart cards. Smart cards require a combination of credentials such as a user name and password instead on relying on a single factor to authenticate a user.

Desktop Management

Windows 2000 Professional simplifies desktop management. Numerous wizards and troubleshooters help end-users perform routine and challenging tasks, reduce the time desktop managers spend helping them, and reduce the number of calls to Help desk. The Hardware Wizard helps users add, configure, remove, troubleshoot, or upgrade peripherals. The Network Connection Wizard lets users start network connections wherever they are.

Windows 2000 Professional gives desktop managers more control over individual desktops. With IntelliMirror™ management technology, based on the Active Directory™ directory service, administrators can easily manage and back up users' data. IntelliMirror, allows desktop managers to apply policies to user data, desktop settings, and software. These policies travel with users, allowing them to work in the same environment on different computers. IntelliMirror requires Windows 2000 Server.

For global companies, Windows 2000 Professional offers comprehensive multilanguage support. Because of its implementation of Unicode 2, Windows 2000 Professional can display documents in over 60 languages. If users receive documents written using an Arabic font, they can view it and edit it without installing additional fonts or language support. To further enhance multilanguage support, Microsoft offers a separate multilanguage version of Windows 2000 Professional, which provides up to 24 localized language versions of the Windows user interface. A user can log on to any computer and view the interface in the preferred language. Microsoft also provides separate language versions of Windows 2000 Professional in more than 20 languages.

Deployment

Whether you are upgrading from previous versions of Windows or installing on clean computers, Windows 2000 Professional provides deployment tools to make the process more efficient, and thus less costly. The System Preparation tool allows administrators to use imaging techniques to roll out Windows 2000 Professional. By rerunning a portion of setup on each computer, characteristics that are unique to that computer can be set even though it has been installed from a single image. Using Remote Installation Services (RIS) desktop managers can start and configure a computer.

Built for Mobile Users

Windows 2000 Professional is built for mobile users with features such as Advanced Configuration and Power Interface (ACPI), hibernation, power schemes, Smart Battery, offline files and folders, Synchronization Manager, Internet Explorer 5 Web page caching, virtual private networking technology, and improved hardware support.

Advanced Configuration and Power Interface

Windows 2000 Professional manages portable computer power so users can work longer. Support for Advanced Configuration and Power Interface (ACPI) in Windows 2000 Professional lets users put a portable computer running Windows 2000 Professional into Hibernate mode, which quickly shuts down the system without shutting down applications. It then lets them restart the system in the same state. It also supports Smart Battery, which gives users a detailed picture of a battery's life and settings, so they can reduce power to some functions.

Offline Files and Folders

With Windows 2000 Professional, mobile users can stay productive offline, and reconnect to the network quickly. The Windows 2000 Professional mobile computing features keep files up-to-date and let users work offline as if they were still connected.

The offline files and folder feature mirrors how documents are stored on the network. The Synchronization Manager compares and updates offline files and folders whenever the portable computer is reconnected. Internet Explorer 5 saves Web pages with all their graphics and links for viewing from the cache, so users can browse Internet information offline.

Improved connection wizards and support for advanced security and networking protocols let business users dial up to the Internet or to a virtual private network (VPN) from any location. When they connect to the Internet through a network, Windows 2000 Professional automatically locates the correct proxy server and configures Internet Explorer 5 to connect through it.

Hardware Support

Windows 2000 Professional supports more than 11,000 hardware devices, including support for removable storage devices such as digital video discs (DVDs) and Device Bay.

Windows 2000 Professional works with such a large number of devices because it supports the latest hardware standards, including universal serial bus (USB), Infrared Data Association (IrDA) protocols for wireless communication, and Institute of Electrical and Electronics Engineers (IEEE) 1394 for devices that require ever faster data transfer. Advanced Plug and Play technology eliminates the time users previously spent manually configuring and restarting each time they added a device or docked a portable computer.

Internet Ready

With Internet Explorer 5 built in, Internet connection sharing, and support for Dynamic HTML (DHTML) and DHTML Behaviors in Internet Explorer 5, Windows 2000 Professional is Internet-ready.

Browser Integration

Windows 2000 Professional offers users an easy way to connect and work on the Internet, whether at the office, at home, or even offline. Internet Explorer 5 is designed to save time on tasks users do most often: searching and keeping track of information, whether on their hard disk, an intranet, or the Internet.

With the Search bar, users can search faster and get exactly where they want to go. They can choose whether to search Web pages, addresses, or businesses and which search engine to use. With the integrated History bar, users can find their way back to information they browsed in the past, whether it was on a Web site, intranet site, or network or local folder.

Internet Connection Sharing

Windows 2000 Professional helps small businesses and other business to connect to the Internet by enabling several computers to share a single connection to the Internet at the same time. Internet connection sharing supports dial-up or broadband connections. With Internet connection sharing, a single computer can provide network address translation and name resolution for all computers on the network.

Development Platform

With support for Dynamic HTML (DHTML) and DHTML Behaviors in Internet Explorer 5, developers can rapidly build rich applications with attributes that can be easily replicated and tested on multiple sites. Developers can invent new ways to create, exchange, and display information using Extensible Markup Language (XML).

When Windows 2000 Professional is combined with the integrated Web and communication services built into Windows 2000 Server, developers can create scalable end-to-end e-commerce solutions.

Deployment and Installation

Windows 2000 Professional provides migration paths for most of the earlier versions of Windows, including Windows 95, Windows 98, and Windows NT Workstation 4.0. The enhancements in the Setup program, as well as the new and improved tools for customizing and automating an installation, make the operating system easier to install on individual computers or deploy to several computers in your organization.

Setup Program

The Windows 2000 Professional Setup program provides enhancements to the installation process compared to previous versions of the operating system. Some of the most important enhancements are the integration of the Plug and Play technology introduced with Windows 95 and Windows 98 and compatibility check options that allow you to verify that your hardware and software is compatible with Windows 2000 Professional before you start the installation process.

Support for Plug and Play Devices

Windows® 2000 now supports Plug and Play technology. Plug and Play automatically guides the interaction of the operating system, basic input/output system (BIOS), devices, and device drivers. Plug and Play is an enhanced implementation that extends the existing Windows NT® 4.0 input/output (I/O) structure to support Plug and Play and power management.

Compatibility Check Options

Windows 2000 Professional Setup comes with a compatibility-mode option that can be used prior to installation to examine hardware and software for known problems that might be encountered during the Setup process. It creates a report to help you determine if any hardware files or upgrade packs are needed to successfully run Windows 2000 Professional. You can print this report or save it as a file for later review.

For more information about Windows 2000 Professional Setup, see "Installing Windows 2000 Professional" in this book.

Custom and Automated Installations

Windows 2000 Professional supports enhanced deployment in the enterprise by giving administrators a variety of tools to automate installation. The process of upgrading from an earlier version of the Windows operating system or applying a service pack has also been streamlined.

By creating automated installation scripts, administrators can eliminate the need to personally visit users to configure their workstations. Traditionally, scripts have been difficult to create and required extensive research and troubleshooting to work properly. Even the most skilled script writers often could not fully automate every aspect of setup because not all setup functionality could be easily scripted. For example, installing sound cards could not be scripted.

Windows 2000 Professional includes support for automated installation scripts, such as the following:

Nearly Every Aspect of Installation Can Be Scripted.   The new answer file format in Windows 2000 Professional allows you to customize and automated more components, including modems, sound cards, time zones and other aspects traditionally difficult to script. Windows 2000 Professional also supports several new tools that help administrators to make systems unique, such as setting static IP addresses or using a list of computer names.

Installation Can Be Completed with No User Interaction.   Previously it was difficult to completely hide installation options from users—such as the product ID page. Every aspect of Windows 2000 Professional can be installed without user interaction.

Easier to Create Scripts.   Using a new graphical tool, called Setup Manager, administrators can more easily create installation scripts. Setup Manager takes care of many traditionally challenging tasks, such as using correct syntax, and eliminates typographical errors, which often cause scripts to not work properly. Setup Manager also allows you to create or import UDF files, which are files used to apply unique settings to desktops, such as computer names and static IP addresses.

Scripts Are More Reliable.   The setup process has been improved so that it does not stop installation if a noncritical device (for example, a modem) does not install properly. Windows 2000 Professional also supports better reporting mechanisms so administrators can troubleshoot installations that did not go as planned.

For more information about how to customize and automate Windows 2000 Professional installations, see "Customizing and Automating Installations" in this book.

Configuration and Management

A key issue for managing desktops includes centralizing computer control, managing multiple hardware and software configurations, and managing configuration changes.

If you have Windows 2000 Server in your organization, you can leverage its technologies to centralize control, increase the availability of resources, and minimize the cost of configuring and managing changes on Windows 2000 Professional–based desktops through Group Policy-based change and configuration management.

Even if you don't have Windows 2000 Server in your organization, you can take advantage of a variety of tools that Windows 2000 Professional introduces that work on any type of network, such as the Microsoft Management Console (MMC), Windows Management Instrumentation (WMI), and Security Templates. MMC consolidates various administrative tasks to manage many of the hardware, software, and networking components of Windows 2000 Professional into a single user interface.

Configuration and Management Tools

Windows 2000 Professional provides better tools for managing and configuring desktop computers. All of the new configuration and management tools are listed here. In the Configuration and Management chapter, you'll find details about general management tools and how to use features such as Group Policy. For details about new features in a specific area, such as hardware management, printing, or fonts, see other chapters in this book.

Add/Remove Programs

The new user interface and wizard make it easy to install programs, get detailed information about program usage, and remove program elements from the hard disk.

Administrative Tools

Administrative Tools, which are available through Control Panel, is the central repository for tools such as Computer Management, Event Viewer, Local Security, and Services.

Color Management System

Image Color Management (ICM) 2.0 ensures that colors are retained between the input and output devices (such as monitors, printers, and platforms) that support ICM 2.0.

Fonts

Support for OpenType fonts combines TrueType and Type 1 fonts in a unified registry. OpenType fonts are secured by using public key signatures, which ensures that fonts are authentic and are not corrupted.

Hardware Tab and Troubleshoot Option in Properties Page

A separate **Hardware** tab is provided in the properties page for **Sounds and Multimedia**, **Mouse**, **Display**, and **Fax**. The new **Troubleshoot** option on this tab helps you detect problems with these devices.

Hardware Wizard

You can use the new Add/Remove Hardware Wizard to add, troubleshoot, uninstall, and unplug devices.

Multilanguage Support

This feature allows users to read and write documents in more than one language.

Network and Dial-up Connections Icon

The Network Connection Wizard, Network Protocol, and Network Adapter configurations are now under Network and Dial-up Connections in Control Panel.

Phone and Modem Options

You can use **Phone and Modem Options** in Control Panel to configure Telephony API (TAPI) devices and reconfigure installed modems. Only members of the Administrators group can make changes to these configuration settings.

Power Options Icon

You can use **Power Options** in Control Panel to reduce the power consumption of individual devices or of the entire system. You can either choose a power scheme (collection of settings that manages the power usage of the computer) that is provided with Windows 2000 Professional, or create your own power scheme.

Printers

You can use the new Add Printer Wizard for easy installation.

Scanners and Cameras

This new option in Control Panel manages scanners and digital camera devices.

Scheduled Tasks Icon

You can use the new Maintenance wizard to schedule tasks.

System Icon in Control Panel

The **System Properties** page now includes a **Network Identification** tab, **Hardware** tab, **User Profiles** tab, and **Advanced** tab. The **Advanced** tab allows you to configure performance options, environment variables, and startup and recovery settings.

Users and Passwords

Going to **Users and Passwords** in Control Panel is the fastest, easiest way to set up user accounts, assign permissions, and configure logon options.

For an overview of tools and methods for managing Windows 2000 Professional, see "Introduction to Configuration and Management" in this book.

Files, Folders, and Search Methods

Microsoft® Windows® 2000 Professional makes it easier for users to find and store files and folders, and for administrators to manage file storage and access. By using new tools such as Group Policy, Indexing Service, and Offline Files, you can prevent users from accessing required system files, enable powerful searches, and prevent network problems from affecting user productivity.

There are a few significant changes from Windows 98 and Windows NT Workstation 4.0 that affect the way files and folders are stored, viewed, and accessed in the Windows Explorer user interface for Windows 2000 Professional. This section describes these changes.

My Network Places   My Network Places, which was previously named Network Neighborhood, now provides a comprehensive list of all the shared computers, files and folders, printers, and other resources on the network or networks to which a computer connects.

My Computer   My Computer now lists the storage devices available to the computer and provides access to Control Panel. Control Panel has become the central repository for tools, such as Network and Dial-up Connections and Scheduled Tasks.

My Documents and My Pictures   The contents of My Documents are stored on a per-user basis. A new subfolder in My Documents, called My Pictures, is the default location for storing graphic images, such as digital camera pictures.

Offline Files and Folders   Users can work on files even if the network resource is unavailable. Changes made to files can be automatically synchronized on the server when the network connection is restored.

System Files Hidden by Default   By default, files with system and hidden attributes do not appear in Windows Explorer windows, such as My Computer. This prevents users from inadvertently deleting or modifying required system files.

Indexing Service   You can search for files and folders based on their content, author, size, or other attributes. Indexing Service is available for files stored on the hard disk drive and shared network drives.

AutoComplete   AutoComplete caches previously typed addresses and file names so that when you begin to type an address or file name, Windows 2000 Professional displays entries similar to what you entered. AutoComplete works throughout the Windows 2000 Professional user interface, including in dialog boxes (such as **Run** and **Map Network Drive**), and in Windows Explorer.

Mobile Computing

Many mobile users want to use the same computer as they move from one geographical location to the next, but that might require them to use a different configuration. For example, sometimes they might need to connect through a high-speed connection and at other times through a low-speed connection or dial-up line. Each of these uses requires a different desktop configuration. Windows 2000 Professional provides the features to meet these and other requirements.

If you use Windows 2000 Professional with Windows 2000 Server, you can use roaming profiles to support roaming users. A roaming user requires the ability to move from computer to computer throughout an organization. Although a roaming user logs on to different computers, the computers are usually connected to a network through a high-speed connection or LAN connection.

Multimedia

The new Sounds and Multimedia tool available in Control Panel lets you easily install, configure, and troubleshoot multimedia hardware. You can also create and deploy custom sound schemes and browser configurations to optimize the multimedia capabilities of your workstations.

Windows 2000 Professional supports the latest multimedia hardware, such as the Accelerated Graphics Port (AGP), DVD devices, and digital video cameras. Windows 2000 Professional also supports a wide range of Human Interface Devices (HIDs) and other peripherals connected through the universal serial bus (USB) or an IEEE 1394 port.

For more information about managing multimedia devices and sounds, see "Multimedia" in this book.

Telephony and Conferencing

Windows 2000 Professional provides support for telephony and conferencing applications in a variety of telecommunications environments, including device support for modems, network adapters, and other telecommunications devices used by applications.

Telephony support has steadily evolved from its introduction in Microsoft® Windows® 95, which was the first operating system to include Telephony Application Programming Interface, also known as Telephony API (TAPI) support. In Windows 2000 Professional, Microsoft builds upon this initial Telephony support by making improvements in the following areas:

TAPI 3.0. Function calls made by TAPI provide the foundation for the deployment of telephony and conferencing applications. TAPI abstracts the details of the underlying telecommunications network, allowing applications and devices to use a single command set. TAPI-enabled applications and devices can operate in a variety of telecommunications environments, including traditional analog-switched networks, Private Branch Exchange (PBX) phone networks, and Integrated Services Digital Network (ISDN). TAPI further expands telecommunications support through IP-based telephony, enabling telecommunications functions through a private intranet or over the Internet.

NetMeeting 3.0. NetMeeting 3.0 is an application included with Windows 2000 Professional that provides conferencing capabilities within an intranet or to users on the Internet. NetMeeting 3.0 provides point-to-point audio and video conferencing, data conferencing, text chat, whiteboard, and file transfer features. In addition, NetMeeting 3.0 provides the following improvements:

- Improved user interface facilitates use, and provides additional features, such as picture-in-picture and compact views.

- Remote Desktop Sharing allows viewing and control of a remote computer in a separate window.

- Enhanced security protects data transferred during text-chat, whiteboard, shared programs, and data conferences.

Phone Dialer. Phone Dialer in Windows 2000 Professional is a TAPI-enabled application that can be used to place audio and video calls. The version of Phone Dialer supplied with Windows NT 4.0 was limited to voice calling onto private and public-switched telephone networks. Windows 2000 Professional Phone Dialer also supports point-to-point and multipoint audio and video conferencing over a private intranet or over the Internet.

Security

Windows 2000 Professional has stronger local and network security compared to Windows NT Workstation 4.0 and Windows 95 or Windows 98. It supports security over public networks by using a public key security infrastructure. This allows users to authenticate the origin of information they receive. It also allows for secure Internet connections and transactions.

You can now more easily create a virtual private network to securely connect computers over the Internet. Windows 2000 Professional supports the following scalable security technologies: Kerberos v5 protocol, smart card authentication, public key cryptography, and Internet Protocol security (IPSec).

Point-to-Point Tunneling Protocol (PPTP) was available in Windows NT Workstation 4.0; in addition, Windows 2000 Professional contains innovations for local security through the new Encrypting File System (EFS). EFS allows users to transparently encrypt individual files or entire folders.

Kerberos Authentication   Kerberos, an industry-standard network-authentication protocol, makes it possible for users to log on to the network by providing their credentials one time. Windows 2000 Professional implements Kerberos authentication based on Request for Comments (RFC) 1510 and supports Novell NetWare, UNIX, HP-UX, LINUX, SGI IRIX, and Sun Solaris.

Smart Card Authentication   Windows 2000 Professional supports Kerberos authentication for using other security infrastructures and devices such as smart cards. Rather than relying on a single factor to authenticate the user's credentials, multifactor authentication relies on a combination of credentials, such as a user name/password combination and a smart card.

For more information about the configuring security in Windows 2000 Professional, see "Security" in this book.

Printing

Windows 2000 Professional includes Image Color Management (ICM) 2.0, which ensures that colors are retained between input and output devices, such as monitors, printers, and platforms, that support ICM 2.0. You can use the new Add Printer Wizard for easy installation of printer devices.

For more information about printing, see "Printing" in this book.

Scanners and Cameras

Microsoft® Windows® 2000 Professional supports a wide range of scanners and cameras, and has been optimized to produce more accurate reproductions of images and their colors. For example, IrTran-P is provided to enable easier transfer of image information from digital cameras to computers and pushbutton scanning simplifies acquiring images.

The new Scanners and Cameras option in Control Panel manages installing, configuring, and troubleshooting scanners, digital still cameras, and the latest digital video cameras.

For more information about configuring your scanner or camera and understanding imaging architecture, see "Scanners and Cameras" in this book.

Fonts

Microsoft® Windows® 2000 Professional supports a wide range of fonts and font types, allowing for high-quality printed and displayed text while supporting a wide range of printing devices. It includes a new universal font format, OpenType®, which combines the TrueType® and Type 1 font technologies.

With Windows 2000 Professional, it is easier to install fonts, their integrity is ensured by public key signatures, and they are used more efficiently, resulting in faster printing.

For more information about installing, managing, and embedding fonts in documents, see "Fonts" in this book.

File Systems

In Windows 2000 Professional, you can use four types of file systems on readable/writable disks: the NTFS file system and three file allocation table (FAT) file systems: FAT12, FAT16 and FAT32.The version of NTFS included with Windows 2000 Professional offers several enhancements over previous versions of NTFS, as well as features not available with FAT.

Windows 2000 Professional also supports two types of file systems on CD-ROM and digital video disk (DVD) media: Compact Disc File System (CDFS) and Universal Disk Format (UDF). The structures of the volumes formatted by each of these file systems, as well as the way each file system organizes data on the disk, are significantly different.

For more information about these file systems, how to choose the appropriate one, and using file system tools to manage files and folders on NTFS volumes, see "File Systems" in this book.

Removable Storage and Backup

Microsoft® Windows® 2000 Professional includes a feature called Removable Storage that you can use to manage the data that is stored on your system. Use the Microsoft Management Console (MMC) Removable Storage snap-in for managing the Removable Storage service.

Removable Storage provides services that allow both system administrators and applications to use, share, and manage removable media devices, such as tape drives and robotic storage libraries. Removable Storage provides a single interface for managing the data that is stored on stand-alone drives and in storage libraries, and it allocates media to applications.

Removable Storage provides a single set of application programming interfaces (APIs) that allow applications to catalog all removable media (except floppy disks and similar small-capacity media), such as disk, tape, and optical media, which are either stored on shelves (offline) or in libraries (online). Also, by disguising the complexities of underlying robotic library systems, Removable Storage both lowers the costs of developing and operating storage applications and provides consistency to customers who purchase these applications.

Removable Storage eliminates the need for independent software vendors (ISVs) to develop customized solutions to support these devices on a per-device basis. More importantly, Removable Storage enables multiple applications to share expensive removable media storage devices. This allows the focus of storage applications to be directed to customer features rather than hardware issues.

Removable Storage uses media pools to organize media. Media pools control access to media; group media by their use; allow media to be shared across applications; and allow such sharing to be tracked.

Because backing up the data on your system is one of the most important aspects of data management, Windows 2000 Professional also includes Backup, a tool that uses Removable Storage technology to ensure that up-to-date copies of your data can be readily restored.

Backup allows you to schedule backup jobs on local and remote computers. Review the options for backing up data that this tool provides, and note some important differences between it and the backup tool that is included with Microsoft® Windows NT® 4.0.

For more information about Removable Storage and Backup, see "Removable Storage and Backup" in this book.

Device Management

A new, separate **Hardware** tab is provided for Sounds and Multimedia, Mouse, Display, and Fax. The new **Troubleshoot** button on the **Hardware** tab helps detect problems with these devices.

For more information about configuring and managing hardware and other devices, see "Device Management" and "Power Management" in this book.

Power Management

Windows 2000 Professional has new, more advanced power options. For more information about power management options, see "Device Management" and "Power Management" in this book.

For more information about using power management options on portable computers, see "Mobile Computing" in this book.

Networking

The Windows 2000 Professional Setup program automatically creates a typical network configuration (called a connection) for each network adapter, which users are free to customize. Each connection includes Client for Microsoft Networks, File and Printer Sharing for Microsoft Networks, and the Transmission Control Protocol/Internet Protocol (TCP/IP) with Dynamic Host Configuration Protocol (DHCP) enabled.

Users can modify the default network connection to suit their needs by using Network and Dial-up Connections in Control Panel.

Local and Remote Network Connections

In Windows 2000 Professional, connectivity to the Internet as well as to local and remote networks is configured with the Microsoft® Windows® 2000 Professional Network and Dial-up Connections.

Network and Dial-up Connections improves upon the dial-up networking functionality in Microsoft® Windows® 98 and Microsoft® Windows NT® version 4.0 by providing improved autoconfiguration of networking components and devices, and a single folder in which to configure all networking options. Network and Dial-up Connections combines functionality found in Windows 98 and Windows NT 4.0 Dial-up Networking, with features that were formerly configured in the Network Control Panel, such as network protocol and service configuration.

Table 1.1 demonstrates how networking support in Windows 2000 Professional has improved upon Windows NT 4.0 and Windows 98.

Table 1.1   Comparing Networking Support

Windows 2000 Professional	Windows NT 4.0	Windows 98
Network and Dial-up Connections installed by default	Must install Remote Access Service (RAS).	Dial-up Networking installed by default, but must install Dial-up Server to create incoming connectivity.
Modem detected and configured by Plug and Play.	Must install modem in Modems in Control Panel.	Modem detected and configured by Plug and Play.
COM port detected and enumerated by Plug and Play.	Must configure COM port.	COM port detected and enumerated by Plug and Play.
Protocol change does not require restart.	Restart when RAS is installed or protocol changes.	Protocol change requires restart.

continued

Table 1.1   **Comparing Networking Support** *(continued)*

Windows 2000 Professional	Windows NT 4.0	Windows 98
Virtual private network (VPN) connections can be configured to automatically dial a connection to the Internet service provider (ISP) before establishing the VPN connection.	VPN connections require activating two connections.	VPN connections require activating two connections.

You can also use other tools, such as local Group Policy and Connection Manager, to manage networking connections in your organization.

For more information about the Network and Dial-up Connections feature, which includes a remote networking scenario, see "Local and Remote Network Connections" in this book.

Windows 2000 TCP/IP

TCP/IP in Windows 2000 Professional builds upon the networking strengths found in Windows NT Workstation 4.0 and Microsoft® Windows® 98. These improvements result in a scalable networking platform that can be implemented in a variety of environments, from a branch office configuration, to a powerful workstation within a multidomain enterprise. The improvements made in Windows 2000 Professional can be categorized into five areas:

Address Assignment and IP Packet Handling.   Windows 2000 Professional makes setting up branch office configurations easier because of two new features: Automatic Private IP Addressing and Internet Connection Sharing.

Automatic Private IP Addressing (APIPA) assigns an IP address and subnet mask to a Windows 2000 Professional–based computer if a DHCP server is not available. You can connect to other networks through *Internet Connection Sharing (ICS)*, which translates private IP addresses to a single public IP address, which can access other intranets or the Internet.

Name Resolution.   Windows 2000 Professional includes several modifications to its IP address/name resolution process to make it an Internet-ready client. DNS is the default name resolution method for the Windows 2000 Production environment, replacing NetBIOS as the default name management method for Windows-based domains. A number of additional improvements have been made in DNS, including support for an extended character set (RFC 2181), client-side caching, connection-specific domain names, and improved performance through subnet prioritization.

IP Security. Windows 2000 Professional provides network security through the implementation of *IP security* (IPSec). IPSec is a set of rules and protocols defined by the Internet Engineering Task Force (IETF) that provide encryption, data authentication, and data integrity at the packet level. Local and domain-based IPSec policies can be created to implement IP security.

Quality of Service. As multimedia-rich applications such as video conferencing and video-on-demand become more pervasive within a network, the issues of network bandwidth and the quality of data transmission become more critical. Windows 2000 Professional addresses this through its implementation of *Quality of Service (QoS)*, a set of specifications that determine a multimedia or qualitative application's network requirements. Windows 2000 Professional also implements the *Resource Reservation Protocol (RSVP)*, which allows an application or service to reserve a specific amount of bandwidth needed for data transmission.

TCP Performance. Windows 2000 Professional includes enhancements to TCP that improve the performance of TCP/IP-based networks. *Larger default TCP receive window size* increases performance on high-speed networks. *Window scaling*, as documented in RFC 1323, allows the use of a very large TCP receive window in high-bandwidth, high-delay environments. To improve performance in high-loss environments such as the Internet, *selective acknowledgments (SACKs)* enables a receiving host to selectively acknowledge only the data it has received.

For more information about configuring TCP/IP in Windows 2000 Professional, see "TCP/IP in Windows 2000 Professional" in this book.

Windows 2000 Professional on Microsoft Networks

The improvements made in Windows 2000 Professional can be categorized into three areas:

Directory Services. A directory service provides information about objects in a network environment, including user and computer accounts and shared resources such as printers and directories. Active Directory™ is the directory service that is included with Windows 2000; it offers an extensible, scalable directory service with hierarchical views and distributed security. Active Directory stores information such as user names, passwords, and phone numbers in a structured database called a *data store* which is represented by objects with *attributes* or *properties*. For example, a user account is an object in the directory and the user's name, password, and phone number are attributes of that user.

Active Directory is available only on Windows 2000 Server domain controllers, although an Active Directory domain can span multiple servers and support heterogeneous clients, including Windows NT version 4.0, Windows 95 and Windows 98, and UNIX–based workstations.

Account Authentication. Windows 2000 uses Kerberos security as the default authentication method for domain and local access. The Kerberos v5 authentication protocol is an industry-supported distributed security protocol based on Internet standard security.

Windows 2000 also supports NTLM security as a method for account authentication. NTLM is used as the account authentication method in Windows NT domains.

Policy Handling. In a Windows NT domain, administrators use system policy to control the user work environment and to enforce system configuration settings. In a Windows 2000 Server domain, Group Policy settings are the administrator's primary method for enabling centralized change and configuration management. A domain administrator can create Group Policy settings at a Windows 2000–based domain controller to create a specific system configuration for a particular group of users and computers. Group policy can be used to:

- Enable IntelliMirror™ management technologies to automatically install assigned applications and provide location independence for roaming users.
- Permit desktop customization and lockdown.
- Configure security policies.

Group Policy settings can also be created locally for individual workstations, and for customized environments that differ from the domain's.

Interoperability

Windows 2000 Server can coexist with your current environment, whether it is an earlier version of Windows (Microsoft® Windows® 3.*x*, Windows 95, Windows 98, Windows NT Workstation 4.0, or Windows NT Server 4.0) or a third-party environment such as UNIX, IBM mainframe, or Macintosh. UNIX interoperability is provided through an add-on pack called Windows Services for UNIX. The add-on pack provides support for Network File System (NFS), password synchronization, a UNIX command shell, and a collection of UNIX tools. The add-on pack also supports Network Information Service (NIS). Telnet services (for remote access and administration) are included in Windows 2000 as well as in the add-on pack. Macintosh interoperability is provided by File Server for Macintosh, which allows Macintosh clients to use TCP/IP (AFP over IP) to share files and to access shares on a Windows 2000–based Server computer.

NetWare Interoperability

Windows 2000 Professional uses Client Service for NetWare and the NWLink protocol to provide connectivity between Windows 2000 Professional and servers running Novell Directory Services (NDS) or NetWare bindery-based servers. NWLink is the Microsoft equivalent to the IPX/SPX protocol.

On computers running Windows 95, Windows 98, or Windows NT 4.0 Workstation, it is necessary to remove Novell Client 32 before upgrading the operating system to something other than Windows 2000, and then reinstall and reconfigure Novell Client 32 after the upgrade.

When using Windows 2000 Professional, you can leave Novell Client 32 on the operating system while upgrading from Windows 95, Windows 98, or Windows NT Workstation 4.0. Windows 2000 Professional upgrades computers running versions of Novell Client 32 earlier than version 4.7. During the upgrade to Windows 2000 Professional, Novell Client 32 version 4.51 is installed. This process allows for a seamless upgrade of Novell Client 32 with no loss in functionality.

UNIX Interoperability

Microsoft® Windows® Services for UNIX 2.0 provides a set of additional features to Windows NT 4.0 and Windows 2000 that allows for greater interoperability with existing UNIX servers in the enterprise. Services for UNIX 2.0 provides fully supported and fully integrated interoperability components that allow customers to integrate Windows NT 4.0 and Windows 2000 operating systems into their existing UNIX environments. It also provides manageability components that enable customer organizations to simplify network administration and account management across both platforms.

The add-on pack Services for UNIX version 2.0 adds to Services for UNIX version 1.0 the following new capabilities:

- Two-way password synchronization between Windows NT 4.0 and UNIX.

- Administration of Services for UNIX through Microsoft Management Console (MMC).

- Gateway for NFS allows client computers running Windows 95, Windows 98, Windows NT Workstation, or Windows 2000 Professional access to NFS shared files.

- Network File System (NFS) version 3.0 support.

- Network Information Service (NIS) support.

- Additional UNIX tools support.
- Migration wizard to migrate NIS source files to Active Directory™ directory service on a Windows 2000–based server configured as a domain controller.
- Username Mapping Server.
- ActiveState Perl engine.

Interoperability with IBM Host Systems

You can integrate the management and troubleshooting of Windows 2000 Professional with IBM host systems by using Windows 2000 Professional with Microsoft SNA Server to directly access IBM host systems. Microsoft SNA Server is Microsoft's solution to integrating personal computer-based clients and servers with IBM host systems. It is also possible to directly connect to an IBM host system without using a gateway like Microsoft SNA Server. This requires the IBM host to support and be configured for either TN3270 or TN5250 telnet access, and then to use host-emulation software that supports direct connection without going through a gateway.

For more information about interoperability between Windows 2000 Professional and IBM host systems, see "Interoperability with IBM Host Systems" in this book.

Performance Monitoring

Monitoring the performance of your Windows 2000 Professional system is an important part of a preventive maintenance program. Monitoring enables you to obtain performance data useful in diagnosing system problems and in planning for future system resources demands, such as CPU, disk, and memory subsystems. Windows 2000 Professional provides the user with several performance-monitoring tools to accomplish these tasks.

For more information about how performance monitoring works, which tools are used when, and how it can help you diagnose problems and prepare for anticipated changes in system workload, see "Overview of Performance Monitoring" in this book.

Evaluating Memory and Cache Usage

Windows 2000 Professional provides several tools, including the Performance console, to assess available memory and to observe the effects of memory shortage, a common cause of poor computer performance. You can also monitor the effectiveness of the current file system cache. In addition, Windows 2000 Professional offers tools to investigate memory problems caused by applications that have not been optimized.

For more information about monitoring the system's use of memory and cache, as well as evaluating the results, see "Evaluating Memory and Cache Usage" in this book.

Analyzing Processor Activity

Windows 2000 Professional offers tools that enable you to monitor processor activity and determine whether a busy processor is efficiently handling its workload or if it might be overwhelmed. These tools use performance counters to measure processing activity and can help identify bottleneck issues that, if resolved, can improve overall system performance.

For more information about monitoring and evaluating processor performance, as well as determining factors that might improve performance, see "Analyzing Processor Activity" in this book.

Examining and Tuning Disk Performance

In Windows 2000 Professional, the disk subsystem handles the storage and movement of programs and data on your system. As disks are several orders of magnitude slower than memory, their performance has a major impact on your system's overall responsiveness. You can use tools that use disk-specific performance counters that enable you to measure disk activity and throughput, determine which programs are putting the greatest demand on your disk system, and develop strategies to improve disk performance.

For more information about analyzing and improving the performance of the disk subsystem, see "Examining and Tuning Disk Performance" in this book.

Troubleshooting

Having a problem? Windows 2000 Professional includes use a wide range of troubleshooters and tools that you can use to solve problems. You can also use the troubleshooting quick guide provided in this book for using these tools and other methods to solve problems.

Troubleshooters

You can use the troubleshooters included in Windows 2000 Professional to help you solve many common computer problems. For instance, if you're having difficulty setting up a new printer, the Print troubleshooter can walk you through the process step by step.

▶ **To open troubleshooters in Windows 2000 Professional Help**

1. Click the **Start** button, and then click **Help**.

2. On the **Contents** tab, click **Troubleshooting and Maintenance**, and then click **Use the interactive troubleshooters**.

Quick Guide to Troubleshooting Windows 2000 Professional

In addition to the troubleshooters, you can use the Quick Guide to Troubleshooting Windows 2000 Professional provided in this book for rapid access to comprehensive troubleshooting information for common problems. This quick guide points you to chapters throughout this book which cover troubleshooting information for specific technologies and types of problems.

For more information about troubleshooting Windows 2000 Professional, see "Troubleshooting" in this book.

Troubleshooting Tools and Strategies

Twenty of the most useful tools for diagnosing and resolving problems are discussed in detail in the *Microsoft® Windows® 2000 Professional Resource Kit*. These tools, including both command-line and Windows-based programs, cover such wide-ranging topics as startup problems, system file and drivers issues, application difficulties, networking problems, system recovery, system maintenance, and updates. They give the user the ability to, at a minimum, gather diagnostic information useful to technical-support personnel. Often, these tools can help you resolve the problem on the spot. In addition, the "Troubleshooting Tools and Strategies" chapter outlines useful strategies for troubleshooting problems, and provides some common troubleshooting procedures not found in the other chapters in this book.

For more information about the strategies, tools, and common procedures used in troubleshooting problems with Windows 2000 Professional, see "Troubleshooting Tools and Strategies" in this book.

Disk Concepts and Troubleshooting

Understanding how disks work and what configuration options Windows 2000 Professional offers for disk systems is critical for resolving disk-related problems. There are two disk configuration options available: basic disk and dynamic disk. Understanding the implications of either choice, and what tools and techniques are available in each scheme to resolve problems, are necessary skills for the Windows 2000 Professional user. In addition, a thorough grasp of fundamental disk structures, such as the master boot record and the boot sector, is very helpful when troubleshooting disk problems. This knowledge is especially helpful when problems, such as disk corruption and virus infection, prevent the system from recognizing a particular volume or even starting.

For more information about fundamental disk structures, disk configuration options, and troubleshooting disk problems, see "Disk Concepts and Troubleshooting" in this book.

Windows 2000 Professional Stop Messages

Windows 2000 Professional is the most resilient, robust, and dependable version of Windows available. However, in circumstances when an error condition from which the system cannot recover is detected, Windows 2000 Professional generates a full-screen, character-based error message. If the error detected was due to hardware failure, a hardware malfunction message is displayed. If the error detected was caused by a problem affecting the kernel, such as a faulty device driver, damaged memory, or corrupted system files, a Stop message is displayed. The usability of the information displayed on-screen has been improved in Windows 2000 Professional, and now offers troubleshooting suggestions to help resolve the problem that caused the detected error condition.

For more information about hardware malfunction and Stop messages, including a general troubleshooting overview for these types of messages, as well as a thorough troubleshooting discussion of 12 Stop messages a user might encounter, see "Windows 2000 Stop Messages" in this book.

Accessibility

Windows 2000 Professional provides new and customizable accessibility features that provide users with disabilities better access to the programs and applications they need. For example, these new features allow you to:

Override Defaults for Multiple-User Customized Settings. Administrators can set a wider range of accessibility and other options for groups by using Control Panel, Accessibility wizard, and Utility Manager.

Quickly and Easily Navigate Windows 2000 Professional. Special features, such as hot keys and Active Desktop™, facilitate access to objects on the desktop, Windows Explorer, other servers on the network, or Internet Explorer 5. These features also give quick access to Windows 2000 Professional and help users open folders and create their individualized settings.

Use a Wider Range of Assistive Technology. With Microsoft® Active Accessibility®, applications work more effectively with system extensions, applications, devices, and other third-party add-on accessibility aids, such as speech-recognition products. Invisible to the user, Active Accessibility is integrated into the Windows 2000 Professional operating system.

Use Human Interface Devices. Windows 2000 Professional supports the Human Interface Device (HID) firmware specification, a new standard for input and output devices such as drawing tablets, keyboards, universal serial bus (USB) speakers, and other devices designed to improve accessibility.

Customize Input Methods. Windows 2000 Professional has expanded configurations of keyboards, including On-Screen Keyboard, special mouse settings, and other options, allowing users to customize their user-interface (UI) schemes.

Configure Options Through a Single Entry Point. Located on the **Start** menu, **Accessibility wizard** is a tool that allows administrators and users to set up their computers quickly with the most commonly used features to suit individual needs.

Magnify a Portion of the Screen for an Enlarged Display. Several built-in, limited-use features, such as Magnifier, make it possible for users to work free from their customary assistive devices.

Maneuver Within Windows 2000 Professional. Utility Manager, personalized keyboard options, and keyboard shortcuts assist users with their work in applications.

Set Sound Options to Suit Individualized Hearing Needs. In addition to customizable features, such as volume adjustment and multimedia options, several accessibility features, such as ShowSounds and SoundSentry, give people with hearing impairments control of their audio environment.

Set Options for Users with Vision Requirements. Specialized features include Narrator, a text-to-speech tool that is built into Windows 2000 Professional, ToggleKeys, a feature that gives audio cues when the user presses certain locking keys; and event cues under **Sounds and Multimedia** in Control Panel.

Use Keyboard Filters to Customize Keys to Aid Various Cognitive, Hearing, Mobility, and Vision Needs.
The FilterKeys feature adjusts keyboard response time and ignores accidental pressing of keys.

Assign Contrast, Color, Timing, and Sizing Schemes for Screen Elements.
Expanded ranges of screen elements, such as high-visibility mouse pointers, high-contrast color schemes, and Accessibility Wizard give users options that suit their needs and preferences.

For more information about the accessibility features in Windows 2000 Professional, see "Accessibility for People with Disabilities" in this book.

Where to Find More Information in this Book

Table 1.2 provides a reference to the new and improved features and technologies discussed in this book and tells you where to find information for configuring and supporting those features and technologies.

Table 1.2   Topics in Part 3 of the Windows 2000 Professional Resource Kit

Technology	Chapter
Access control lists (ACLs)	Security (Chapter 13)
Active Directory searches	Managing Files, Folders, and Search Methods (Chapter 9)
Administrative Tools	Introduction to Configuration and Management (Chapter 7)
Audio	Multimedia (Chapter 11)
Backup	Removable Storage and Backup (Chapter 18)
Bus technologies	Power Management (Chapter 20)
Cameras	Scanners and Cameras (Chapter 15)
Character sets	Fonts (Chapter 16)
Code pages	Fonts (Chapter 16)
Compact disc file system	File Systems (Chapter 17)
Control Panel	Introduction to Configuration and Management (Chapter 7)
Desktop options (including policies)	Customizing the Desktop (Chapter 8)
Digital audio	Power Management (Chapter 20)
Disk formats	File Systems (Chapter 17)
Drivers	Power Management (Chapter 20)
Digital video disc (DVD)	Multimedia (Chapter 11)
Encryption	Security (Chapter 13)

(continued)

Table 1.2   Topics in Part 3 of the Windows 2000 Professional Resource Kit *(continued)*

Technology	Chapter
File system and tools	File Systems (Chapter 17)
Fonts: installing, managing	Fonts (Chapter 16)
Group Policy (overview)	Introduction to Configuration and Management (Chapter 7)
Hardware on portable computers	Mobile Computing (Chapter 10)
Hardware policies	Power Management (Chapter 20)
Human Interface Device (HID)	Power Management (Chapter 20)
IEEE 1394 support	Power Management (Chapter 20)
Image Color Management (ICM)	Scanners and Cameras (Chapter 15)
Indexing Service	Managing Files, Folders, and Search Methods (Chapter 9)
IrTran-P	Scanners and Cameras (Chapter 15)
Managing users and groups	Introduction to Configuration and Management (Chapter 7)
Microsoft® Management Console (MMC)	Introduction to Configuration and Management (Chapter 7)
Multiple display support	Power Management (Chapter 20)
Multiple monitors	Device Management (Chapter 19)
NetMeeting 3.0	Telephony and Conferencing (Chapter 12)
Offline files and folders	Managing Files, Folders, and Search Methods (Chapter 9)
Offline files on portable computers	Mobile Computing (Chapter 10)
Passwords	Security (Chapter 13)
PC Card, CardBus, and smart cards	Power Management (Chapter 20)
PC Cards	Device Management (Chapter 19)
PC Cards for portable computers	Mobile Computing (Chapter 10)
Phone Dialer	Telephony and Conferencing (Chapter 12)
Plug and Play	Device Management (Chapter 19) and Power Management (Chapter 20)
Portable computers	Mobile Computing (Chapter 10)
Power management	Power Management (Chapter 20)

continued

Table 1.2   Topics in Part 3 of the Windows 2000 Professional Resource Kit *(continued)*

Technology	Chapter
Power management (for portable computers)	Mobile Computing (Chapter 10)
Printers: installing, configuring, managing	Printing (Chapter 14)
Redirection (on portable computers)	Mobile Computing (Chapter 10)
Remote hardware management	Power Management (Chapter 20)
Roaming user profiles and folders	Mobile Computing (Chapter 10)
Security and Group Policy	Security (Chapter 13)
Security considerations for portable computers	Mobile Computing (Chapter 10)
Still image devices	Power Management (Chapter 20)
Storage (Removable)	Removable Storage and Backup (Chapter 18)
Telephony API (TAPI) 3.0	Telephony and Conferencing (Chapter 12)
User groups	Security (Chapter 13)
Video	Multimedia (Chapter 11)
Video capture	Power Management (Chapter 20)

Additional Resources

- For more information about Windows 2000 Professional, see the *Getting Started Guide* included in the Windows 2000 Professional packaging.

- For more information about features new to Windows 2000 Professional, see *Introducing Windows 2000 Professional* by Jerry Honeycutt, 1999, Redmond: Microsoft Press.

- For more information about features new to Windows 2000 Server, see *Introducing Microsoft Windows 2000 Server* by Tony Northrup, 1999, Redmond: Microsoft Press.

C H A P T E R   2

Using Windows 2000 Professional with Windows 2000 Server

Microsoft® Windows® 2000 Professional provides a desktop operating system for business users and administrators that is reliable and easy to install, use, and maintain, regardless of the type of network in which it is deployed. Using Windows 2000 Professional with Microsoft® Windows® 2000 Server greatly extends the level of support that you can provide to your users. It allows you to centrally deploy and manage the operating system; it provides a stronger security and networking infrastructure; and it extends interoperability with other environments such as Novell NetWare and UNIX.

In This Chapter

Related Information in the Windows 2000 Resource Kit

- For an introduction about managing Windows 2000 Professional Desktops in a Windows 2000 Server and other environments, see "Introduction to Configuration and Management" in this book.

- For more information about managing Windows 2000 Professional Desktops in a Windows 2000 Server environment, see the *Microsoft® Windows® 2000 Server Resource Kit Distributed Systems Guide*.

Quick Guide to Using Windows 2000 Professional with Windows 2000 Server

Use this quick guide to find out how using Windows 2000 Professional in a Windows 2000 Server–based environment allows you to centrally deploy and manage Windows 2000 Professional and to review the added benefits that you gain for security, networking, and interoperability.

 How can I deploy customized Windows 2000 Professional installations from a central location?

You can use the Remote Installation Services (RIS) feature in Windows 2000 Server to standardize a Windows 2000 Professional installation and to allow users to install it from a central location. Users simply connect to the custom installation on a server configured with RIS.

- See "Centralized Deployment" in this chapter.

- See "Customizing and Automating Installations" in this book.

 How can I centrally manage desktops in my organization?

Using the Windows 2000 Server IntelliMirror™ management technologies, administrators can have total control over users' data, client applications, and system settings. This reduces helpdesk calls and ensures that end users do not inadvertently damage their systems. More importantly, it helps ensure that users always have access to the data, applications, and settings that they need to do their jobs—even when working from another computer.

- See "Centralized Administration" in this chapter.

- See "Introduction to Configuration and Management" in this book.

How can I control access to sensitive data and provide stronger authorization with mutual client and server authentication?

With Windows 2000 Server, administrators have more precise administration of network traffic by granting specific rights to Active Directory™ directory service containers. Windows 2000 Server also provides stronger security mechanisms for authenticating users. Kerberos v5 is the default authentication protocol in Windows 2000 Server; it includes mutual client and server authentication and reduced server load while connections are being established.

- See "Advanced Security" in this chapter.

- See "Security" in this book.

What networking features in Windows 2000 Server support Windows 2000 Professional client computers?

Although Windows 2000 Professional can take advantage of many of the latest networking technology and protocols on any network, Windows 2000 Server provides a complete Windows 2000 networking solution, including the Windows 2000 implementation of Domain Name System (DNS), Dynamic Host Configuration Protocol (DHCP), and Quality of Service (QoS) as well as Windows Internet Name Service (WINS) support for interoperability with previous versions of Windows, such as Microsoft® Windows® 95 and Microsoft® Windows NT® version 4.0.

- See "Robust Networking Infrastructure" in this chapter.
- See Part 4, "Network Configuration and Management" and Part 5 "Network Interoperability" in this book.

What Windows 2000 Server features extend interoperability with other networks?

The core Microsoft® Windows® 2000 technology for interoperability is the Windows 2000 implementation of Transmission Control Protocol/Internet Protocol (TCP/IP). Windows 2000 Professional allows you to provide interoperability with earlier versions of Windows and third-party networks. With Windows 2000 Server you can extend interoperability through add-on packs such as Services for UNIX and File Server for Macintosh.

- See "Interoperability with Other Networks" in this chapter.
- See Part 5, "Network Interoperability" in this book.

Centralized Deployment

With Windows 2000 Server, you can use the RIS change and configuration management feature to deploy Windows 2000 Professional from a central location. This enables users to connect to a Windows 2000 Server configured for RIS and choose customized installation options as shown in Figure 2.1.

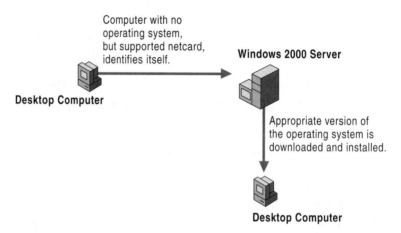

Figure 2.1   Installing Windows 2000 Professional from a RIS Server.

RIS uses the Pre-Boot eXecution Environment (PXE) Dynamic Host Configuration Protocol (DHCP)-based remote startup technology to connect to a Remote Installation Services (RIS) server and start the installation process. The RIS server provides the network equivalent of a CD-based installation and preconfigured installation images.

RIS is used during initial startup before the operating system loads. RIS supports clients without an installed operating system or computers that need to have the operating system restored. RIS allows hardware connected through a LAN to find a networked RIS server and request a new copy of Windows 2000 Professional that is appropriately configured for the user and computer. RIS cannot be used to upgrade an existing operating system.

Table 2.1 shows the Windows 2000 features you need to use RIS.

Table 2.1   Windows 2000 Features Needed to Use RIS

Technology	Purpose
Windows 2000 DHCP	Assigns an IP address to a remote boot–enabled client computer prior to contacting a server running RIS.
Windows 2000 DNS	Resolves computer names from TCP/IP addresses.
Group Policy	Defines the users and computers eligible (or ineligible) for a specific desktop configuration.
Active Directory	Locates client computers and RIS servers and stores the Group Policy objects that define what resources a user or computer can or cannot access.
RIS	Manages and distributes Windows 2000 Professional image files to clients enabled for remote startup.

Using RIS servers to deploy and upgrade operating systems throughout a company reduces the costs incurred by either preinstalling the client computer or physically installing the operating system on each client. Automatically installing the operating system by using RIS and Group Policy can reduce the staff support overhead for adding new computers to a network and reinstalling operating systems.

Use a RIS server as a remote source. The following are descriptions of these two methods.

CD-Equivalent Installation   This is similar to setting up a client computer that directly uses the unattended installation options available on the Windows 2000 Professional operating system CD. The source files, however, reside across the network on available Windows 2000–based servers rather than on a local CD.

Preconfigured Desktop Image Installation   This allows you to reproduce a working copy of a corporate desktop configuration, including operating system configurations, desktop customizations, and locally installed software. After the reproduced image is configured, it is stored on RIS servers. On request, the server downloads these images to new computers.

Note   The new computer does not need to have identical hardware to the computer on which the image was created. Windows 2000 Professional support for Plug and Play can adjust for hardware differences.

It is important that your DHCP, DNS, and Active Directory servers are configured appropriately to work with RIS. These services can be installed either on individual servers or the same server and must be active and available to use RIS. RIS uses these components to detect client computer requests for service.

For more information about DHCP technology and its use, see "Determining Network Connectivity Strategies" in the *Microsoft® Windows® 2000 Server Resource Kit Deployment Planning Guide* and "Dynamic Host Configuration Protocol" in the *Microsoft® Windows® 2000 Server Resource Kit TCP/IP Core Networking Guide*. For more information about DNS technology, see "Introduction to DNS" in the *TCP/IP Core Networking Guide*. For more information about Remote OS Installation, see "Remote OS Installation" in the *Distributed Systems Guide*.

Centralized Administration

A key advantage of using Windows 2000 Professional with Windows 2000 Server is that Active Directory and change and configuration management features allow you to centrally manage desktop installations and configurations. Table 2.2 summarizes the management features that are available by using Windows 2000 Professional with and without Windows 2000 Server Active Directory.

Table 2.2   Comparison of Management Features for Windows 2000 Professional with and without Windows 2000 Server

Management Feature	Windows 2000 Professional without Windows 2000 Server	Windows 2000 Professional with Windows 2000 Server, Active Directory, and Group Policy
Administrative Templates (registry-based settings)	Yes	Yes
Security settings	Yes	Yes
Software Installation and Maintenance (Assign and Publish)	No	Yes
Remote Installation Service (RIS)	No	Yes
Unattended installation	Yes	Yes
Windows Installer Service	Yes	Yes
Sysprep	Yes	Yes
Scripts	Yes	Yes
Folder redirection	No	Yes
Microsoft® Internet Explorer maintenance	Yes	Yes
User profiles	Yes	Yes
Roaming user profiles	No	Yes

Active Directory

The process that makes directory information useful and available to users, software applications, and third-party services in a network environment is called a *directory service*. Active Directory is a directory service.

Note A directory service includes both the directory information and the services that make that information useful.

The main functions of a directory service are the following:

- Replicate directory information to make it available to all users in the network and to overcome failures.
- Partition directory information into multiple stores to store a large number of objects.
- Enforce security policies defined by the administrator.

Active Directory makes centralized administration possible in Windows 2000. Active Directory offers an extensible, scalable directory service with hierarchical views and distributed security. Active Directory stores information such as user names, passwords, and phone numbers in a structured database called a *data store* which is represented by objects with *attributes* or *properties*. For example, a user account is an object in the directory and the user's name, password, and phone number are attributes of that user.

Active Directory gives network administrators and end users access to a directory service that provides the following features:

Flexible Querying Users and administrators can use the global catalog to find any object on the network using any attribute of that object. For example, you can find users by their first name, last name, e-mail address, office location, or other attribute of their user account.

Flexible Administration An access control list (ACL), or permissions, protects access to objects in Active Directory. An ACL determines who can view and use objects, and specifies how objects can be used. You can grant access to an entire object or to each attribute of an object. For example, you can grant all users access to view names and office telephone numbers of all users on the network, but restrict access to any other attributes, such as home telephone numbers and other personal information.

Delegation of Authority   Active Directory security supports both inheritance and delegation of authority. Inheritance makes an object's specific permission set available to all of its child objects. Administrators can use delegation of authority to grant specific administrative rights for containers and subtrees to other individuals and groups. By using delegation of authority, instead of granting administrators authority over large parts of the network, you can assign them to precise areas of the network.

Information Replication   Within a domain the directory is replicated, or copied, to each server running Active Directory. If the domain contains multiple Active Directory servers (or *domain controllers*), the directory is replicated to multiple servers. Each domain controller stores and maintains a complete copy of the domain's directory. Replication of this directory provides fault tolerance, load balancing, and more reliable data availability.

Information Partitioning   With Active Directory, the directory of each domain stores information about only the objects located in that domain instead of using one massive store. By enabling multiple domains, trees, and forests, Active Directory scales to suit the smallest and largest organizations. Both small and large organizations benefit from smaller domains that are easy to administer, but large companies can easily add to their Active Directory environment by configuring multiple domains.

Directory Extensibility   Active Directory has an extensible schema, which means that administrators can add new object types to the directory and new attributes to existing object types. For example, you can add a *purchase authority* attribute to the *user* object type, and then store each user's purchase authority limit as part of the user's account.

DNS Integration   DNS is a set of protocols and services used throughout the Internet and other Transmission Control Protocol/Internet Protocol (TCP/IP) networks to provide name registration and name-to-address resolution services. This enables identification and connection to computers and users on TCP/IP networks. Active Directory uses DNS as its location mechanism and supports DNS dynamic update protocol.

Interoperation with Other Directories In addition to DNS, Active Directory supports other industry standards, such as Lightweight Directory Access Protocol (LDAP) version 2 and version 3, and Name Service Provider Interface (NSPI). LDAP, the core protocol of Active Directory, is an industry-standard directory service protocol, enabling Active Directory to share information with any other directory service that supports LDAP. Active Directory support for NSPI, which is used by Microsoft® Exchange 4.0 and later clients, provides complete backward compatibility with those products. By supporting these standards, Active Directory can expand its services across multiple namespaces, and process information and resources from the Internet, other operating systems, and other directories.

Full Backward Compatibility Active Directory supports and works with Windows NT 4.0 and earlier. Servers running Windows NT can operate with each other within a domain. Active Directory domain controllers appear to earlier-version clients as Windows NT Server 4.0 domain controllers.

Change and Configuration Management

Change and configuration management reduces the total cost of ownership (TCO) and managing change in network environments. After you install Windows 2000, you can use Group Policy to manage computing environments for groups of users and computers. This significantly reduces the need for administrators to visit desktops for application or operating system installations, updates, or to repair unauthorized or unexpected configuration changes.

Change and configuration management consists of two features, IntelliMirror and RIS. IntelliMirror in turn consists of the User Data Management, Software Installation and Maintenance, and User Settings features. Figure 2.2 shows the benefits and technologies for each of these features.

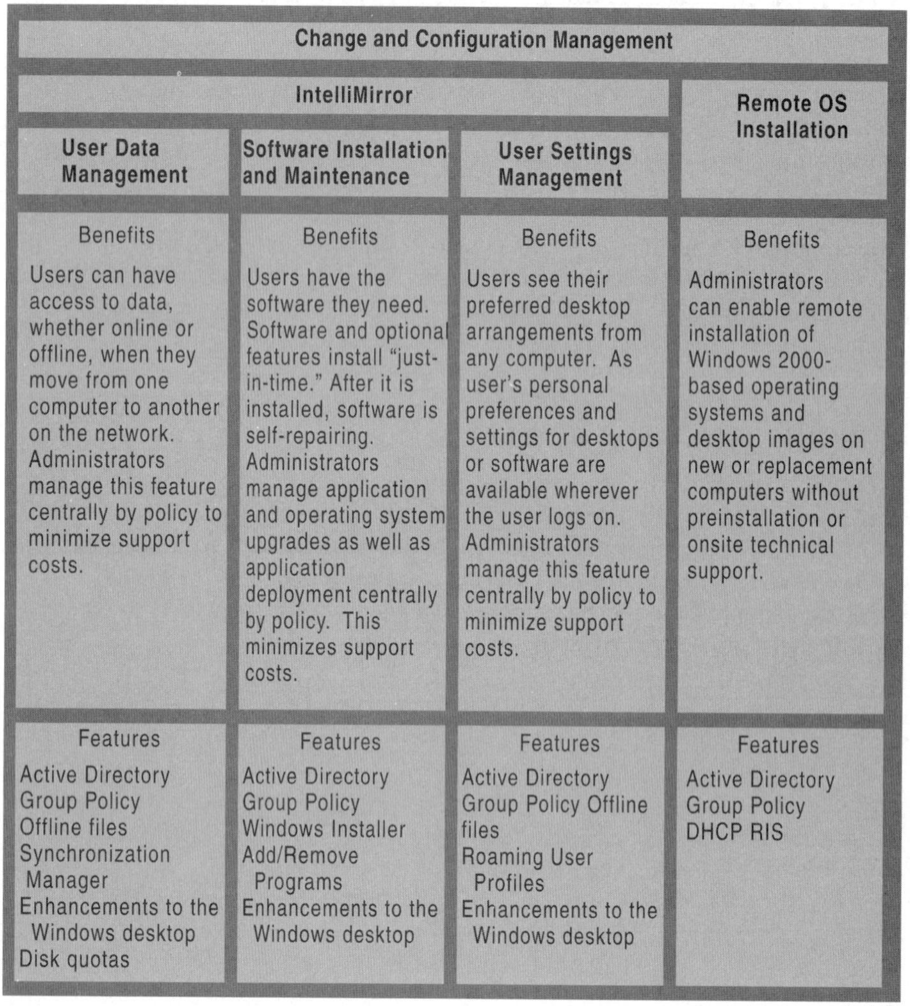

Change and Configuration Management			
IntelliMirror			**Remote OS Installation**
User Data Management	**Software Installation and Maintenance**	**User Settings Management**	
Benefits	Benefits	Benefits	Benefits
Users can have access to data, whether online or offline, when they move from one computer to another on the network. Administrators manage this feature centrally by policy to minimize support costs.	Users have the software they need. Software and optional features install "just-in-time." After it is installed, software is self-repairing. Administrators manage application and operating system upgrades as well as application deployment centrally by policy. This minimizes support costs.	Users see their preferred desktop arrangements from any computer. As user's personal preferences and settings for desktops or software are available wherever the user logs on. Administrators manage this feature centrally by policy to minimize support costs.	Administrators can enable remote installation of Windows 2000-based operating systems and desktop images on new or replacement computers without preinstallation or onsite technical support.
Features	Features	Features	Features
Active Directory Group Policy Offline files Synchronization Manager Enhancements to the Windows desktop Disk quotas	Active Directory Group Policy Windows Installer Add/Remove Programs Enhancements to the Windows desktop	Active Directory Group Policy Offline files Roaming User Profiles Enhancements to the Windows desktop	Active Directory Group Policy DHCP RIS

Figure 2.2   Change and Configuration Management Features

By using the standard change and configuration management features with Windows 2000 Professional and Windows 2000 Server together, you can:

- Log on to any computer in the domain and access your personal desktop configuration including data, applications, and preference settings.

- Quickly find your data files and access network files even if the network is offline.

- Centrally define settings for groups of users and computers and rely on the system to enforce those settings.

- Quickly replace a computer and automatically regenerate its settings, data, applications, preferences, and administrative policies.

- Centrally install, update, and remove software, eliminating the need for user intervention and onsite support.

- Configure a computer running Windows 2000 Server with RIS to allow PXE-enabled client computers to connect and install Windows 2000 Professional.

For more information about using the change and configuration management features from the perspective of a Windows 2000 Professional administrator, see "Introduction to Configuration and Management" in this book. For a thorough description of configuring and using Windows 2000 Server change and configuration management features, see the *Distributed Systems Guide*.

IntelliMirror

IntelliMirror is a set of Windows 2000 features used for desktop change and configuration management. Taking advantage of different features in both server and client, IntelliMirror enables data, applications, and settings to follow roaming users.

With IntelliMirror management technologies, administrators can have total control over client data, applications, and system settings. This helps reduce the need for technical support, and ensures that users do not inadvertently damage their systems. More importantly, it helps ensure that users always have access to needed data, applications, and settings.

At the core of IntelliMirror are three features:

- User Data Management
- Software Installation and Maintenance
- User Settings Management

You can use these features separately or together. When fully deployed, IntelliMirror uses Active Directory and Group Policy to provide policy-based management of users' desktops. You can centrally defined policy settings based on criteria such as business roles, group memberships, and location.

Note Client computers that are running Microsoft® Windows® 95, Microsoft® Windows® 98, and Microsoft® Windows NT® version 4.0 or earlier cannot use IntelliMirror technologies.

User Data Management

User Data Management technologies include Active Directory, Group Policy, Offline Files, and Folder Redirection. These technologies ensure that data is protected, available offline, and available from any computer on the network.

User data can follow the user whether the user is online and connected to the network or the user is offline in a stand-alone state. The user's data follows the user because Windows 2000 can store the data in specified network locations while making the data appear local to the user. You can configure which files and folders are available manually, set them up on a per-user basis, or configure them by using Group Policy settings.

By using the Offline Files feature of User Data Management, you ensure that the items that users create, such as files and documents, are easily accessible and readily available. If users take their work home or on the road, they still have access to their files. The network files that a user works with when online are automatically cached on that user's computer and available when he or she is offline. The master version of the file is stored on a server. When users reconnect to the network, any files that they have worked on are synchronized with the network version. For more information about using Offline Files, see "Managing Files, Folders, and Search Methods" in this book.

By using the Folder Redirection feature, you can redirect specific user data folders, such as My Documents, to a network location using Group Policy settings, and then make this location available to users for offline use. When a user saves a file to My Documents, the file is actually saved on the network location, and the local computer is synchronized with the network copy. This synchronization occurs in the background and is transparent to the user.

Because user files are redirected to a server, you can protect the centrally stored version of the data. If user data is lost on a local computer because a hard disk drive fails, you can restore that data from the network.

Software Installation and Maintenance

Use Software Installation and Maintenance to manage the installation, configuration, repair, upgrade, and removal of software, including applications and service packs.

Software Installation and Maintenance provides software installation and automatic repair of software to groups of users and computers. By using Software Installation and Maintenance, you can define Group Policy settings that specify which applications a user can use, regardless of which computer the user logs on to; you can also set how software files update and synchronize on a per-computer or per-user basis. You can assign software to a user or computer, or you can publish applications to a user.

Assigned Applications   Assigned applications appear to be installed on the user's computer; the user sees shortcuts for the applications on the desktop or **Start** menu. Registry entries are made and shortcuts are placed on the desktop or the **Start** menu, but the software is not installed until the first time a user selects the software. Use this method to deploy software that is resilient and available regardless of user actions; if the user removes the software, it is installed again the next time the user selects it.

Published Applications   Published applications do not appear to be installed on the user's computer; there is no evidence of the application on the desktop. Published applications are installed by using Add/Remove Programs in Control Panel. Use this method for managing software that is not necessary for a user to perform a job.

When you deploy applications by either assigning or publishing them, you can update them from the server. When the user logs on to the client computer, any new applications or updates are installed. For more information about Software Installation and Maintenance features of IntelliMirror, see "Software Installation and Maintenance" in the *Distributed Systems Guide*.

User Settings Management

User Settings Management is used to configure Group Policy settings that are applied to the operating system, desktop environment, and software for each user. These include language settings, custom dictionaries, accessibility options, desktop configurations, and other user preferences and restrictions.

By using User Settings Management, you can centrally define computing environments for organized groups of users and computers; you can also grant or deny users the ability to further customize their computing environments, such as style and default settings.

For more information about using User Settings Management, see "Introduction to Configuration and Management" in this book.

Group Policy

You can use Group Policy to have any level of control for managing desktops. You can choose to centrally manage a wide variety of settings, to control options such as desktop settings and the applications available to the user, or you can allow an open environment to enable users to modify their own desktops and install any application.

The Microsoft Management Console (MMC) Group Policy snap-in is used configure Group Policy settings. The settings are storedGroup Policy objects, which you associate with specific Active Directory container sites, domains, or organizational units. Group Policy settings can be filtered by using memberships in security groups. Table 2.3 lists the components of Group Policy.

Table 2.3   Group Policy Components

Component	Description
Administrative Templates	Establish registry-based policy (equivalent to System Policy in Microsoft® Windows NT® Server 4.0).
Security Settings	Establish security settings for domains, computers, and users.
Software Installation	Assign or publish applications.
Internet Explorer Maintenance	Administer Internet Explorer after deployment.
Scripts	Log on or log off users and start up or shut down computers.
Folder Redirection	Redirect folders and files to the network.

Group Policy and its extensions provide a unified replacement for many of the functions of the System Policy Editor in Windows NT 4.0.

Table 2.4 lists some of the ways in which you can control a user's work environment by enforcing system configuration settings for all computers that are using Group Policy and the equivalent tools used in Windows NT Server 4.0.

Table 2.4   Group Policy Administrative Tools

Task	Windows 2000 Tool	Windows NT 4.0 Tool
Set policies for users and computers in a network.	Group Policy, accessed through Active Directory Sites and Services.	Not available
Set policies for users and computers in a domain.	Group Policy, accessed through Active Directory Users and Computers.	System Policy Editor
Set policies for users and computers in an organizational unit.	Group Policy, accessed through Active Directory Users and Computers.	Not available
Edit the security descriptor for Apply Group Policy.	Security Groups.	**System Policy Editor**
Manage software.	Software Installation snap-in, accessed through the Group Policy snap-in.	Systems Management Server

For more information about Group Policy settings, the order in which Group Policy settings can be processed, and how to filter and block Group Policy inheritance, see "Group Policy" in the *Distributed Systems Guide*. For more information about using Group Policy on computers running Windows 2000 Professional, see "Introduction to Configuration and Management" in this book.

Support for Roaming and Mobile Users

Using Windows 2000 Professional with Windows 2000 Server allows you to provide an even richer support for roaming and mobile users. Roaming users need to move from computer to computer while keeping a single desktop configuration. Although a roaming user logs on to different computers, they are usually connected to a network through a high-speed or LAN connection.

Mobile users need different desktop configurations as they move from one location to another. For example, a mobile user might require one network configuration that supports high-speed connections at headquarters and another for low-speed or dial-up lines at a branch office.

Using Windows 2000 Professional with Windows 2000 Server allows a roaming or mobile user to use a single profile when logging on to the network, while moving from computer to computer (roaming user) or among different locations (mobile user).

In Windows 2000, user profiles define customized desktop configurations, which include individual display settings, network and printer connections, and other specified settings. There are three types of user profiles—local, roaming, and mandatory.

Local user profiles are available on Windows 2000 Professional, regardless of the network being used. When a user logs on to the network for the first time, a local user profile is created and stored on a local hard disk. Users can modify their own local user profiles. Any changes the user makes to the local user profile are specific to the computer where the changes were made.

Because local profiles are specific to the local computer, they cannot support the needs of roaming and mobile users. With Windows 2000 Server, you can support these users by creating roaming user profiles and mandatory user profiles.

These types of user profiles are created by a server administrator and stored on computers running Windows 2000 Server. Changes made by a user to a roaming profile are updated and kept on the server. Only server administrators can make changes to mandatory user profiles.

Roaming user profiles allow users to wander among computers within a corporate network. With roaming user profiles, a user can log on to any computer that is running Windows 2000 within the user's domain. After logging on, all of the user settings and documents stored on the server in the roaming user profile are copied to the local computer. A user can run applications, modify documents, and work on the computer normally until logging off. When a user logs off, the user profile is copied to a server. When the user logs on to another computer, all of that user's profile information is copied to the second computer. This profile is available every time a user logs on to any computer on the domain.

A mandatory user profile is a special kind of roaming profile that specifies particular settings for an individual or an entire group of users. A mandatory profile is not updated when the user logs off. It is created by a server administrator, assigned to one or more users for job-specific functions, and downloaded to the desktop each time the user logs on.

For more information about how to setup and manage roaming user profiles, see "Introduction to Desktop Management" in the *Distributed Systems Guide*.

Advanced Security

When using Windows 2000 Professional in a Windows 2000 Server–based environment, you can take advantage of Windows 2000 Server distributed security features that provide you with flexibility to delegate account administration, strong authentication with the Kerberos v5 protocol, network security at the domain level with Internet Protocol security (IPSec), and public-key security technology.

Because security in Windows 2000 Server is integrated with Active Directory, administrators have precise administration of the network by granting specific rights to Active Directory containers. In Windows 2000 Server, the Kerberos v5 protocol is the default mechanism for authentication and access control. It provides a common protocol that enables a single-account database to access all services in a mixed environment.The Kerberos v5 protocol is an Internet security standard with mutual authentication of client and server and provides server load balancing during the authentication process. Kerberos v5 is implemented for a variety of systems and provides a single authentication service in a distributed network.

The Kerberos v5 protocol is a "shared-secret" authentication protocol in which the user and the authentication service both know the user's password or the one-way encrypted password. The Kerberos protocol defines the interactions between a client and a network authentication service known as a Key Distribution Center (KDC). Windows 2000 implements a KDC as the authentication service on each domain controller. The KDC uses Active Directory as the account database for users and groups. The initial Windows NT domain logon is provided by the WinLogon single sign-on architecture. Initial Kerberos-protocol authentication is integrated with WinLogon. Windows 2000 Server also provides other mechanisms for authentication, such as smart cards and NTLM for compatibility with other versions of Windows.

For more information about security at the domain level, see the *Distributed Systems Guide*. For more information about the security features available in Windows 2000 Professional, see "Security" in this book.

Many Windows 2000 Server security features use public key technology as well as certificates to provide authentication, integrity, confidentiality, and nonrepudiation for network and information security. Public key security in Windows 2000 is based on industry-standard public key technologies, such as the Diffie-Hellman Key Agreement algorithm, the RSA public key algorithms developed by RSA Data Security, and the Digital Signature Algorithm. Windows 2000 security also makes use of the industry-standard, X.509 version 3 digital certificates that are issued by trusted certification authorities. For more information about the public key technologies used in Windows 2000, see the *Distributed Systems Guide*.

Windows 2000 incorporates Internet Protocol security (IPSec) for data protection of network traffic. IPSec is a suite of protocols that allow secure, encrypted communication between two computers over an insecure network. The encryption is applied at the IP network layer, so it is transparent to most applications that use specific protocols for network communication. IPSec provides end-to-end security, meaning that the IP packets are encrypted by the sending computer, are unreadable while they are being transmitted, and can be decrypted only by the recipient computer. For more information about IPSec, see "Internet Protocol Security" in the *Microsoft® Windows® 2000 Server Resource Kit TCP/IP Core Networking Guide*.

Robust Networking Infrastructure

Windows 2000 Professional makes configuring and using networking technology easier with features such as Network and Dial-up Connections. It also includes numerous networking features to take advantage of the latest TCP/IP networking innovations and standards, such as Layer Two Tunneling Protocol (L2TP), Internet Protocol security (IPSec), Internet Connection Sharing, Quality of Service (QoS), and dynamic multi-link dialing. For more information about Network and Dial-up Connections, see "Local and Remote Network Connections" in this book.

When using Windows 2000 Professional with Windows 2000 Server, you can take advantage of many server-based networking features and services, such as the Windows 2000 implementations of DNS, and the WINS name-resolution services that provide interoperability with previous versions of Windows. For more information about the networking features included with Windows 2000 Server, see the *TCP/IP Core Networking Guide*. For more information about the networking features in Windows 2000 Professional, see Part 4, "Network Configuration and Management" and Part 5 "Network Interoperability" in this book

Windows 2000 DNS

Domain Name System (DNS) is the default naming system for Internet Protocol (IP)–based networks. It enables users to use hierarchical, display names to easily locate computers and other resources on an IP network. Using Windows 2000 Professional with Windows 2000 Server allows you to take advantage of the new features and enhancements in the Windows 2000 implementation.

Windows 2000 DNS is compliant with standard DNS as described in the Request for Comments (RFC) documents of the Internet Engineering Task Force (IETF). Because Windows 2000 DNS is RFC-compliant, it provides interoperability with most of the other DNS server implementations, such as those DNS servers that use the Berkeley Internet Name Domain (BIND) software.

The Windows 2000 implementation of DNS has several new features and improvements over Windows NT 4.0, including the following:

Support for Active Directory as a Locator Service for Domain Controllers

DNS is required to locate Active Directory objects. You can also use a third-party DNS server implementation solution to support Active Directory deployment.

Integration with Active Directory   You can integrate DNS zones into Active Directory to provide increased fault tolerance and security. Every Active Directory–integrated zone is replicated among all domain controllers within the Active Directory domain. All DNS servers running on these domain controllers can act as primary servers for the zone, accepting dynamic updates. Active Directory replicates on a per-property basis, propagating only relevant changes.

Support for Dynamic Updates   The DNS service allows client computers to dynamically update their resource records in DNS. This improves DNS administration by reducing the time needed to manually manage zone records. The dynamic update feature can be used in conjunction with Dynamic Host Configuration Protocol (DHCP) to update resource records when a computer's IP address is changed. Computers running Windows 2000 can send dynamic updates.

Support for Aging and Scavenging Records   The DNS service can scan and remove records that are no longer needed records. When enabled, this feature can prevent stale records from remaining in the DNS.

Support for Secure Dynamic Updates in Active Directory–Integrated Zones
You can configure Active Directory–integrated zones for secure dynamic update so that only authorized users can make changes to a zone or record.

Easier Administration   The DNS console for managing the DNS service offers an improved graphical user interface (GUI) over Windows NT 4.0. Windows 2000 Server provides several new configuration wizards and tools to help you manage and support DNS servers and clients on your network.

Administration from the Command Prompt   You can use the command-line tool Dnscmd.exe for most tasks that you can perform from the DNS console, such as:

- Creating, deleting, and viewing zones and records
- Resetting server and zone properties
- Performing routine administrative operations, such as:
    - Updating the zone
    - Reloading the zone
    - Refreshing the zone
    - Writing the zone back to a file or Active Directory
    - Pausing and resuming the zone
    - Clearing the cache
    - Stopping and starting the DNS service
    - Viewing statistics

You can also use Dnscmd.exe to write scripts for remote administration. For more information about Dnscmd.exe, see Windows 2000 Support Tools Help. For information about installing and using the Windows 2000 Support Tools and Support Tools Help, see the file Sreadme.doc in the directory Support\Tools on the Windows 2000 operating system CD.

Enhanced Name Resolution   The Windows 2000 DNS resolver tries to resolve names with DNS before trying to use Network Basic Input/Output System (NetBIOS). Also, it can query different servers based on the adapters to which they are assigned.

Enhanced Caching and Negative Caching   You can view and flush the resolver cache by using the command-line tool Ipconfig, and you can flush the server cache from within the DNS console. Also, the resolver performs negative caching, which remembers that a name or type of record does not exist. Negative caching reduces lookup time when the user queries for a name that the resolver has already determined does not exist.

Additional Client Enhancements   The cache can be preloaded with Hosts file entries (a file that contains a mapping of computer names to IP addresses). Also, the resolver server list can be dynamically reordered to prioritize responsive DNS servers.

Support for DNS in Mixed Environments   If all of the computers on your network are running Windows 2000, you do not need any WINS servers. Even in a mixed environment, you do not need to configure WINS on your Windows 2000–based clients if you have configured WINS lookup. By using WINS lookup, you can direct a Windows 2000 DNS server to query WINS for name resolution, so that DNS clients can look up the names and IP addresses of WINS clients.

Interoperability with Other DNS Server Implementations   Because the Windows 2000 DNS server is RFC-compliant, it works with other DNS server implementations, such as BIND.

Integration with Other Network Services   The Windows 2000 DNS server is integrated with DHCP and WINS.

Incremental Zone Transfer   In addition to performing full zone transfers (sending a copy of the entire zone), the DNS server can send and receive incremental zone transfers, in which only changes to the zone are transferred. This can reduce the amount of time and bandwidth required for zone transfers.

For information about DNS and the Windows 2000 implementation of DNS, see "Introduction to DNS" and "Windows 2000 DNS" in the *TCP/IP Core Networking Guide*.

Windows 2000 DHCP

Dynamic Host Configuration Protocol (DHCP) is a TCP/IP standard that reduces the complexity and administrative overhead of managing network client IP address configuration. Windows 2000 Server provides the DHCP service, which enables a computer to function as a DHCP server and to configure DHCP-enabled client computers on your network. DHCP runs on a server, enabling the automatic, centralized management of IP addresses and other TCP/IP configuration settings for client computers on your network. The DHCP service also provides integration with Active Directory and the DNS service, enhanced monitoring and statistical reporting for DHCP servers, vendor-specific options and user-class support, multicast address allocation, and rogue DHCP server detection.

DHCP simplifies the administrative management of IP address configuration by automating address configuration for network clients. A DHCP server is any computer running the DHCP service. The DHCP server automatically allocates IP addresses and related TCP/IP configuration settings to DHCP-enabled clients on the network.

Every interface on a TCP/IP-based network must have a unique IP address to access the network and its resources. Without DHCP, IP configuration must be done manually for new computers, for computers moving from one subnet to another, and for computers that have been removed from the network.

By deploying DHCP in a network, this process is automated and centrally managed. The DHCP server maintains a pool of IP addresses and leases an address to any DHCP-enabled client when it logs on to the network. Because the IP addresses are dynamic (leased) rather than static (permanently assigned), addresses no longer in use are automatically returned to the pool for reallocation.

The DHCP service for Windows 2000 Server is based on IETF standards, and DHCP specifications are defined in RFCs. The following RFCs specify the core DHCP standards that Microsoft supports with its DHCP service:

- RFC 2131: Dynamic Host Configuration Protocol (replaces RFC 1541)
- RFC 2132: DHCP Options and BOOTP Vendor Extensions

For more information about the Windows 2000 DHCP support, see "Dynamic Host Configuration Protocol" in the *TCP/IP Core Networking Guide*.

Quality of Service

Quality of Service (QoS) facilitates the deployment of media-rich applications, such as video conferencing and IP telephony, without adversely affecting network throughput. Windows 2000 QoS also improves the performance of mission-critical software such as Enterprise Resource Planning (ERP) applications. Windows 2000 supports the QoS Admission Control Service, a policy mechanism that offers the ability to centrally designate how, when, and by whom network resources are used on a per-subnet basis. QoS is an emerging technology, with standards that are being developed and revised based on customer feedback and industry-wide cooperation.

QoS is a set of methods and processes that a service-based organization implements to maintain a specific level of quality. In the context of networking, QoS refers to a combination of mechanisms that provide a specific quality level to application traffic on a network or on multiple networks. Implementing QoS means combining a set of IETF-defined technologies to alleviate the problems caused by shared network resources and finite bandwidth.

QoS provides two distinct benefits:

- A mechanism for applications to request service quality parameters, such as low network delay.
- Higher levels of administrative control over congested subnet bandwidth resources.

Implementing QoS enables administrators to make the most efficient use of subnet bandwidth when deploying resource-intensive applications. A QoS-enabled network provides guarantees for sufficient resources; this gives a congested, shared network segment a level of service approaching that of a private network. Different classes of applications have varying degrees of tolerance for delay in network throughput. A QoS guarantee ensures that an application can transmit data in an acceptable way, in an acceptable time frame so that the transmission is not delayed, distorted, or lost.

To uphold such guarantees, QoS requires cooperation from the sending and receiving hosts (end nodes), the data link layer (open systems interconnection reference model [OSI] model layer 2) devices (switches), the network layer (OSI model layer 3) devices (routers), and any wide area network (WAN) links in between. Without QoS, each of these network devices treats all data equally and provides service on a first-come, first-served basis. In addition, an application must have some level of QoS awareness so that it can request bandwidth and other resources from the network.

The efficient use and allocation of bandwidth is critical for productivity. Real-time applications, media-rich applications, and Enterprise Resource Planning applications require a large amount of uninterrupted bandwidth and can strain existing network resources. When traffic is heavy, overall performance degrades and results in traffic delay and packet loss. This degradation causes problems with video conferencing, real-time audio, and interactive communication, causing distortion of voices and images. Because media-rich applications use large quantities of bandwidth, traditional mission-critical applications suffer from the lack of available resources. QoS provides a delivery system for network traffic that guarantees limited delays and data loss.

It is important to realize that QoS cannot create bandwidth; it can only efficiently partition bandwidth based on different parameters.

For information about the Windows 2000 implementation of QoS, see "Quality of Service" in the *TCP/IP Core Networking Guide*.

WINS

While Windows 2000 uses Domain Name System (DNS) as its primary method for matching a host name to its IP address, Windows 2000 also supports Windows Internet Name Service (WINS) for matching a NetBIOS name to its IP address. WINS is the name resolution system used for Windows NT Server 4.0 and earlier operating systems.

Windows 2000 DNS uses hierarchical fully qualified domain names (FQDNs) rather than the flat NetBIOS naming conventions supported by WINS. However, WINS provides an important service for network administrators with heterogeneous systems that support clients running older operating systems, such as Windows 95 and Windows NT 4.0. These systems do support DNS name resolution but do not support dynamic updates to DNS records.

For more information about WINS, see "Windows Internet Name Service" in the *TCP/IP Core Networking Guide*.

Interoperability with Other Networks

Using Windows 2000 Server with Windows 2000 Professional computers provides greater interoperability with existing UNIX, Novell NetWare, Windows NT Server 4.0, and Macintosh networks than is possible by using only Windows 2000 Professional.

Industry-Standard Features Windows 2000 supports Lightweight Directory Access Protocol (LDAP) for interoperability with third-party directory services, DNS for domain name resolution with other DNS-enabled networks, and Kerberos v5 for authentication interoperability.

Coexistence with Existing Operating Systems   Windows 2000 Server can coexist with your current environment, whether it is an earlier version of Windows (Microsoft® Windows® 3.*x*, Windows 95, Windows 98, or Windows NT 4.0) or a third-party environments such as UNIX, IBM mainframes, Novell NetWare, or Macintosh. UNIX interoperability is provided through an add-on pack called Windows Services for UNIX. The add-on pack provides support for network file system (NFS), password synchronization, a UNIX command shell, and a collection of UNIX tools. The add-on pack also supports Network Information Service (NIS). Telnet services (for remote access and administration) are included in Windows 2000 as well as in the add-on pack. NetWare interoperability is provided through the NWLink IPX/SPX-Compatible protocol and the Client Service for NetWare or Gateway Service for NetWare components. Macintosh interoperability is through File Server for Macintosh, which allows Macintosh clients to use TCP/IP (AFP over IP) to share files and to access shares on a Windows 2000 Server computer.

Additional Resources

- For more information about Windows 2000, see the *Getting Started Guide.*
- For more information about features new to Windows 2000 Professional, see *Introducing Windows 2000 Professional* by Jerry Honeycutt, 1999, Redmond: Microsoft Press.
- *Introducing Microsoft Windows 2000 Server* by Tony Northrup, 1999, Redmond: Microsoft Press.

P A R T 2

Deployment and Installation

In This Part

C H A P T E R   3

Deploying Windows 2000 Professional

Deploying Microsoft® Windows® 2000 Professional requires thorough planning and an understanding of how to map the needs of your organization to the features that Windows 2000 Professional provides. While this chapter focuses on planning issues for the enterprise organization doing wide scale deployments, small to mid-size organizations can also find useful information suitable for smaller-scale deployments. Use this overview of the deployment process to develop and implement a plan for a successful deployment.

In This Chapter

Related Information in the Windows 2000 Professional Resource Kit

- For more information about how to install Windows 2000 Professional, see "Installing Windows 2000 Professional" in this book.

- For more information about how to use the Windows 2000 tools and methods for customizing and automating an installation, see "Customizing and Automating Installations" in this book.

Related Information in the Windows 2000 Server Resource Kit

- For a thorough discussion on deployment planning, and for more information about assessing your current network infrastructure, and client connectivity strategies, see the *Microsoft® Windows® 2000 Server Resource Kit Deployment Planning Guide.*

Quick Guide to Deploying Windows 2000 Professional

Use this quick guide to follow the steps you need to plan your Windows 2000 Professional deployment.

Assess your needs and map them to Windows 2000 Professional features.

The first step in the deployment process is to identify user needs in your organization and map those needs to the features and benefits that Windows 2000 Professional provides. This allows you to determine when and how to implement features in your organizations.

- See "Mapping Your Needs to Windows 2000 Professional" later in this chapter.

Define and plan your project.

After you have determined the project management structure you will use for planning your deployment, it is time to start addressing the details of your plan.

- See "Planning Your Deployment" later in this chapter.

Assess your current client configuration and determine the preferred configuration.

To determine a preferred client configuration you need to first assess user needs. After you have identified the preferred configuration you can create client computer standards that will make client systems more manageable.

- See "Determining a Preferred Client Configuration" later in this chapter.

Assess your current network infrastructure.

Before you deploy Microsoft Windows 2000 Professional in your organization, you should prepare your network. Your first step is to document the current state of your network.

- See "Assessing Your Current Network Infrastructure" later in this chapter.

Determine a client connectivity strategy.

To ensure that clients can connect reliably and efficiently, you need to determine your Windows 2000 Professional connectivity strategy before you begin your implementation.

- See "Determining a Client Connectivity Strategy" later in this chapter.

Determine implementation methods.

At this step of your deployment planning you need to determine how to implement, or deploy, the preferred client configuration. To do this you select your installation processes.

- See "Determining Implementation Methods" later in this chapter.

Test your deployment plan.

Early in deployment planning you need to prepare a test plan so you can test your design as it is developed. A plan includes the specific types of tests, specific areas to be tested, test success criteria, and information about the resources (hardware, software, and people) required for testing.

- See "Testing Your Deployment Plan" later in this chapter.

Conduct a pilot.

The pilot is the last major step before your full-scale deployment of Windows 2000 Professional, the rollout. During the pilot, you test your design in a controlled real-world environment in which users perform their normal business tasks using the new features.

- See "Conducting a Pilot" in later this chapter.

Prepare for the production rollout.

Use what you have learned from the pilot to prepare for your rollout of Windows 2000 Professional to your entire organization.

- See "Preparing for the Rollout" later in this chapter.

Mapping Your Needs to Windows 2000 Professional

The first step in the deployment process is to assess user needs in your organization and map those needs to the features and benefits that Windows 2000 Professional provides. This will allow you to determine when and how to implement features in your organization.

Assessing user needs means identifying the types of features and applications your users require, such as e-mail, connectivity to the Internet, multimedia applications such as Microsoft® NetMeeting®, and so on.

To obtain this data, you can solicit feedback from users and management on the type of applications, features, and services they need. You can then use this data to determine the best client configurations for your organization. For example, you can determine how to group users, decide on the amount of disk space they need, and estimate how network traffic might increase if they require applications that use a lot of network bandwidth, and so on.For additional detail on defining company needs, see "Introducing Windows 2000 Deployment Planning" in the *Deployment Planning Guide.*

Planning Your Deployment

Planning your deployment of Windows 2000 Professional includes the following primary tasks:

- Defining project scope and objectives
- Assembling your project team
- Assessing and documenting your current computing environment
- Establishing standards and guidelines
- Creating a testing environment
- Creating a master project plan and associated documents

Defining Project Scope and Objectives

When you begin the project, start preparations by identifying your organization's objectives. By keeping business objectives in mind while creating the project objectives, you ensure that your project aligns with the long-term vision of your organization. The project objectives need to answer the following questions:

- What is the business problem?
- How will the business change with the new Windows 2000 Professional client configuration?
- How does the Windows 2000 Professional client implementation interact with other enterprise infrastructure functions?
- What is the long-term goal of the project?

When you document your project scope, indicate the areas, functions, and environments that your Windows 2000 implementation will cover. The scope defines which features the team will deploy to meet your organization's business needs and project objectives. The project scope needs to be specific, realistically achievable, and include a time frame for delivery.

The project scope is the document that will be your baseline for creating a functional specification, described later in this section.

Example Project Objectives

The following example describes business problems for a fictitious company and resulting project objectives.

Business Problems

The IT department is receiving increased pressure from the business units to account for and manage aggregated IT costs on an enterprisewide basis. In reviewing these costs, it is apparent that a lack of standardization is costing a lot of money. For example, help desk staffing has grown disproportionately large due to the variety of operating systems, applications, hardware configurations, and the resultant complex mixture of skills necessary to support such an environment.

Project Goals

The IT department is viewed as a business partner and facilitator. The IT department will drive technology enhancements that help the business change to be more profitable and responsive to requests from the business units to deploy new hardware and software. This will be accomplished without great expense and with high efficiency.

To reach this goal, the IT department views standardization of their desktop computing infrastructure environment as paramount. The IT department has a long-term goal of a desktop environment that will be as reliable as the telephone system. Additionally, when problems do arise with the desktop, they will be quick and easy to fix.

Example Project Scope

The IT department will deliver functionality and value incrementally, rather than try to do one or two very large projects that address all opportunity areas. The focus of the first version of the preferred desktop environment will be called the Enterprise Desktop project. The major focus areas will be as follows:

- Identify two desktop hardware configurations and three portable computer hardware configurations that will become the standards. Supplement existing purchasing processes so that any exceptions to these standards will require special approval.
- Develop one or more standard baseline configurations that will be loaded on all new standard desktops and portable computers.

- Develop an automated, hands-free tool set that enables IT staff to quickly install baseline configurations on standard desktop and portable computers using Windows 2000 Professional System Preparation tool and a disk imaging tool.

- Develop and implement change control and release management mechanisms that will be used to deploy the new environment and upgrade it in a more manageable fashion over time. The first iteration of the standard desktop environment will be called Version 1.0.

It is essential that this functionality be delivered rapidly, as there is great pressure to show value quickly. The Enterprise Desktop Version 1.0 project is targeted to begin rollout by end of June 2000. This date is firm. It might be that some desired functionality would need to be deferred so that Version 1.0 can be released by end of June.

Assembling Your Project Team

A small team of three to eight people with shared responsibilities is recommended. Each member needs to have a deep technical knowledge of Windows 2000 Professional and an understanding of the business. This will help reduce overhead that inhibits communications and give each member a direct role in defining the goals for the project.

Your project team needs to be a team of peers and include the areas of responsibility shown in Table 3.1. It is not necessary for these roles to be filled by separate team members.

Table 3.1   Project Team Roles and Responsibilities

Position	Tasks
Project Management	Manages the preferred client configuration specification.
	Manages the project schedule and resource allocation.
	Drives all critical trade-off decisions
Customer Advocate (Customer is not the end user in this context, the customer *pays* for the solution.)	Acts as the customer advocate for the team and the team advocate for the customer.
	Drives features versus schedule trade-offs.
	Develops business case.
	Develops, maintains, and executes communications plan.

(continued)

Table 3.1   Project Team Roles and Responsibilities *(continued)*

Position	Tasks
Implementation	Builds automated setup process.
	Participates in preferred desktop design, focusing on physical design.
	Configures and customizes preferred desktop.
Testing	Develops testing strategy and plans to ensure all issues are known.
	Responsible for periodically building the preferred client using the automated setup process developed by the implementation team member.
End User Advocate	Acts as end user advocate to the team and team advocate to the end user.
	Participate in preferred desktop design.
IT Deployment/Support Management (IT deployment is responsible for actually deploying the preferred desktop.)	Acts as technical support and IT deployment advocate to team and team advocate to technical support and IT deployment.
	Participates in preferred desktop design focusing on management, support, and deployment aspects.
	Trains help desk personnel on Windows 2000 Professional issues.

It is also important that one or more team members have expertise in networking and line-of-business (LOB) applications.

Assessing and Documenting Your Current Computing Environment

Before you design your Windows 2000 Professional deployment, you need to understand your current computing environment. Documenting your existing computing environment will help you understand your organization's structure and how it supports your users, and it will help you design your deployment plan. Diagrams are a useful way to deal with complex concepts such as network layout. Where appropriate, create these diagrams and include them in your project plan documentation.

Some of the areas to address include the following:

Business Organization and Geographical Requirements Describe the location and organization of your business units. Are large groups of employees located in widely separated geographic areas or are they all located in close proximity to each other? Are your business units closely related, or do they have significantly different needs and requirements?

Application Requirements   Conduct a complete inventory of the applications that are used in your organization. Include all custom (in-house) applications. As you are documenting your computing environment, also note the different tasks for which employees use computers and note how the change to Windows 2000 Professional will affect their work. For example, if employees are using an old line-of-business application that is reliant upon certain Open Database Connectivity (ODBC) driver versions, the line-of-business application needs to be tested to ensure that it will work.

Technology Architecture   When documenting your network architecture, be sure to include topology, size, type, and traffic patterns. Any significant changes you plan to make to your technology architecture, such as hardware, networking, and services, needs to be illustrated in high-level diagrams.

Interoperability   Determine which users need access to various applications and data and how they currently obtain access to these. How will access change with Windows 2000 Professional?

Current and Future IT Standards   Over time, the network and application standards in many organizations become fragmented or obsolete. This is common in organizations that have merged with or acquired other companies. Disparate systems, built over a wide time frame, designed by different people, and often geographically separated, are a potential risk to a successful deployment. An audit of existing systems contributes to the success of the deployment team.

Establishing Standards and Guidelines

Many organizations find that establishing Windows 2000 Professional standards and guidelines can save time and money. This is because a standard environment reduces the potential for too many configuration combinations, making administrative and architectural workloads more efficient. Base these standards on how employees use their computers. For example, an employee doing computer-aided design has higher requirements than an employee using general office applications.

For best results, establish standard configurations for your client computers. Include guidelines for minimum and recommended values for CPU, RAM, and hard disks, as well as for accessories such as CD-ROM drives and uninterruptible power supplies.

Establish the standard software configurations that are used in your organization. Include guidelines for how you distribute, support, and restrict the use of this software.

Establish guidelines for the network operating systems and protocols that are used in your organization. Include standard configurations for all network components (such as routers, hubs, and repeaters). Establish guidelines for supporting and maintaining these configurations.

Identify requirements for meeting current operational standards or aligning with operational goals. For example, how will user data be backed up? How will troubleshooting be performed? How will new applications be deployed? Describe processes and solutions for satisfying current or future operational standards.

Creating a Testing Environment

Test your Windows 2000 Professional deployment design in a lab before you deploy. For enterprise deployments, you will need to also conduct a pilot before you deploy to your entire organization. See "Conducting a Pilot" later in this chapter.

In the early planning stages, you will need to select testing sites and assess hardware requirements. As soon as your lab is operational you can use the lab to better understand the product, prove concepts, and validate solutions. Expect the lab to evolve as the project progresses.

In general, provide as much detail as possible in your test plan documents so that your test and deployment teams have all the information they need to be successful. Describe the scope, objectives, methodology, schedule, and resources (hardware, software, personnel, training, and tools) in your test plan. Individual subteams need to create their own test plans for their areas of technical expertise and write test cases. Test cases describe how the testing is to be done. This makes it possible to replicate and compare test results.

You need to test applications for compatibility with Windows 2000 Professional. Start by testing features that are mission-critical to your organization and whose design choice would be expensive and time-consuming to change.

Include a plan to escalate any issues that arise to the person most able to resolve the situation. A clear escalation process helps the team focus on the solution and take immediate corrective action.

For more information about setting up a test lab, see "Building a Windows 2000 Test Lab" in the *Deployment Planning Guide.*

Creating a Master Project Plan

The master project plan includes three major documents:

- Functional specification—the preferred client configuration and the deployment process for this configuration.
- Project plan—the activities and deliverables necessary to deliver the design described in the functional specification.
- Master project schedule—dates for when the preferred client solution will be developed, tested, and deployed.

The functional specification is the basis of your deployment design. Your Windows 2000 Professional client specification incorporates the prioritized set of user requirements, a proof of concept demonstration of the client configuration, and an implementation plan. It details the operating system features that you will implement, and how they will be configured and deployed. All of these elements need to align with the scope and objectives of the deployment project.

Describe the different types of users, the key tasks they perform, how these tasks are currently performed, and how performance can be improved in the new client environment. If yours is a large organization with multiple sites, or an international organization, you need to detail your geographical issues.

When these three documents are approved they form the baseline from which you begin to implement your deployment plan. In most cases the team will need to modify some initial assumptions and plans as the project moves forward. The team needs to be willing to move forward even though some unknowns exist, adding details as the project progresses.

The project manager owns the deployment plan and is responsible for updating its tasks, resources, and dates during implementation

It is recommended you also include the following documents in your master project plan:

Communications Strategy

A good communications strategy plays a very important but often overlooked role in the success of your project. An effective communications strategy identifies the needs of several types of audiences, such as executive management, project teams, IT organization, and users at all levels. Keeping people informed keeps them involved.

In addition to keeping interested parties informed, your communications strategy needs to include internal marketing that sells the Windows 2000 Professional client solution. Communicating what the new client change will do for the user, the department, and the company, especially when the new client configuration represents a big change, will greatly increase the likelihood of a successful deployment.

Education and Training Plan

Educate your users about Windows 2000 Professional features and functions before you begin deployment. You might also want to provide formal training and develop a feedback mechanism.

Your existing user environment will largely determine what training is needed. Project constraints (time, budget, and so on) will determine the vehicle that is used. Users familiar with Microsoft® Windows® 95, Microsoft® Windows® 98 or Microsoft® Windows NT® Workstation 4.0 will likely require very little training. New users or users transitioning from another operating system will require some training, even if it is nothing more than going through the Introducing Windows 2000 Professional wizard.

Microsoft Official Curriculum (MOC) for Microsoft Windows 2000 Professional offers computer professionals training to deploy, administer, and support Windows 2000 Professional. For more information about MOC for Windows 2000, see the Microsoft Official Curriculum link on the Web resources page at http://windows.microsoft.com/windows2000/reskit/webresources.

Risk Assessment

When you plan to deploy an operating system, plan for the unexpected. Even the best deployment plans can be affected by changes in business needs, economics, user requirements, or disruptions such as power outages or storms.

A well thought-out and proactive risk management plan can help you:

Reduce the likelihood that a risk factor will actually occur. If only one person on your staff fully understands your security infrastructure, losing that person in the middle of the deployment could have serious repercussions. You can reduce the risk by training a backup for each key expert and keeping documentation up-to-date and accessible.

Reduce the magnitude of loss if a risk occurs. If you suspect that your Windows 2000 Professional deployment project has been under-budgeted, you might be able to identify several backup sources to cover unexpected expenses.

Change the consequences of a risk. A sudden reorganization, business acquisition, or divestiture in the middle of a deployment can seriously disrupt your plans. If you have established a process for making abrupt changes, you can meet the challenge with little or no impact to the project schedule.

Be prepared to mitigate risk during your deployment. When you mitigate risk you are asking the following questions regarding that risk:

- How can this be resolved?

- Are the mitigation factors suitable? Will option 'A' or 'B' be acceptable?

- Would it be too costly or time consuming?

- Are we taking into account realistically what the chances are for this risk to become real?

For example, a company might identify as a risk that some MS-DOS applications might not work with Windows 2000 Professional. To mitigate that risk they will include in their schedule the task to identify critical MS-DOS applications and have them tested within a specified timeframe.

A risk management plan helps you identify potential risks before they occur and prepares you for a quick response if they do occur.

Test Plan

The test plan outlines the strategy the team will use to test the deployment design. It includes the specific types of tests, specific areas to be tested, test success criteria, and information about the resources (hardware, software, and people) required to test. When testing software and hardware be sure to start by assembling the resources available from Microsoft and any third-party vendors of the products you will be testing. For hardware testing, be sure to start with the Hardware Compatibility List (HCL), located on the Web Resources page at http://windows.microsoft.com/windows2000/reskit/webresources. You also need to go to each application and hardware vendor to identify any issues or updates specific to Windows 2000 Professional. This step takes some diligence, but it will save significant amounts of testing and solution development time.

Pilot Plan

The pilot is the first opportunity to deploy your new client configuration in a production environment. In many cases, the success of the pilot will determine how quickly the rest of the deployment will proceed. The team needs to plan a full solution test if at all possible, including all deployment processes. The pilot will almost certainly uncover technical and process problems. Planning time after the pilot that allows the team to discover and resolve any problems that arise during the pilot will reduce many of the risks inherent in any infrastructure deployment project. It is advisable to plan to freeze the client solution specification after the pilot.

For additional information about the planning aspect of your deployment, see "Planning for Deployment" in the *Deployment Planning Guide.*

Determining a Preferred Client Configuration

Users in large organizations typically have a wide variety of skill levels. They use a variety of applications and hardware, and often work in widely distributed locations. Numerous studies have identified these diverse usage patterns and a lack of client configuration standards as among the most significant factors behind rising IT support costs. This section will help you define basic client configuration standards that serve the needs of your users.

Assessing Your Current Client Configuration

Planning client computer standards requires both technical and organizational knowledge. You must understand your current computing environment and identify the needs of both your users and your organization. You must also decide which Windows 2000 Professional capabilities you want to enable and then document the changes needed to meet your goals. To determine a preferred client configuration you need to assess the following:

- Users and their computing requirements.
- Applications and application requirements.
- Hardware and software requirements.
- Significant support issues and solutions.

Based on your research and an understanding of the new client features in Windows 2000 Professional, you can plan your configuration standards.

Defining User Types

Large organizations have many different types of users. The following are some of the things that influence a user's pattern of computer usage:

- The organizational unit (OU) to which the user belongs (such as accounting, engineering, or marketing).
- The type of work the user performs (technical, executive, or administrative support, for example).
- Where the user performs his or her work (such as in an office, from a remote location, or at a shared computer).
- The degree of autonomy the user requires to do his or her job.
- The amount and type of support the user requires.

In addition, it is also important to notice whether the user is:

Roaming   Many users move from one computer to another. Roaming users typically do not take a computer with them when they move from one location to another; instead, they use the computer at the location where they are working. Receptionists or bank tellers who often work at several different desks are examples of roaming users.

Mobile   A growing number of workers travel regularly and perform their work using a portable computer. While traveling, they are frequently disconnected from the network, and often connect to the network using low-bandwidth connections. Sales people and consultants are frequently in the mobile user category.

Remote   Remote users differ from mobile users because they generally connect to the network from a fixed location, such as a branch or home office that often involves a slow or intermittent network link.

Task-based   Users who require a computer to perform a specific, limited set of tasks, such as entering orders. The task-based user might only require a computer running Terminal Services. Receptionists and bank tellers are examples of task-based users.

Knowledge-based   Users, such as engineers, lawyers, graphic designers, and programmers, who place the greatest demands on their computers, often require specialized applications and customized configurations.

Assessing Software Standards

To develop your client application standards, address the following questions regarding operating systems, generic commercial applications such as word processing software, and line-of-business applications that have been developed internally to perform tasks such as client management or order fulfillment.

- What software is mandatory for your organization?
- What software is required for a particular job or business unit?
- What software is optional for the organization, business units, or workers who perform a particular type of job?
- How often do software requirements at your organization change?
- Who determines which software is used—throughout the organization and in specific workgroups?
- How is software customized?
- How is software distributed?
- How is software configured?
- How do you install new client software?

- How do you upgrade existing software?
- How do you pilot or evaluate new software?

At the same time, decide which software to deploy with Windows 2000 Professional—and how to deploy it. Software that is not installed along with the operating system can be made available to users on an as-needed basis.

Basic Users

Basic users might require a standardized configuration of the operating system and the minimum number of corporate-standard applications, such as e-mail and word processing, along with the specific applications they need to do their job (for example, an order entry application). However, basic users would not be permitted to install optional applications, and more complex application features, such as pivot tables in spreadsheet applications, can be disabled.

Advanced Users

Advanced users frequently require advanced operating system features such as the ability to create personal network shares. They also commonly require additional optional applications and features, which they can install as needed. However, you can still prevent them from installing unapproved applications.

Defining Hardware Standards

The applications that your users need to perform their jobs determine your company's hardware requirements. However, planning hardware budgets generally involves longer lead times than planning for software upgrades. Therefore, plan carefully and allow enough time to provide your users with the computer hardware they need when they need it.

The following are some of the questions you might ask regarding your organization's clients:

- How fast are the processors in your current client desktop computers? How fast are the processors in your portable computers?
- How fast is the network connectivity for your current clients (including portable computers that are network connected and modem connected)?
- How much RAM and hard disk space do they have?
- Are Windows 2000 Professional drivers available for current network adapters and other peripherals?
- What file systems do they use?
- Are current computers running other operating systems that need to be upgraded, or do you need to perform clean installations?
- Can current computers use remote boot technology? Do they have remote boot-compatible network adapters? Can they use a remote boot floppy disk?

- Will you be using network shares to store user data and configuration data?

- Who is responsible for backing up the user's data?

- How do you bring new computers into your organization? How do you stage new hardware? Does the original equipment manufacturer preinstall applications? Do you remove any preinstalled software from new hardware and then reinstall it according to your own standards?

- How do you replace failed hardware? If a hard disk fails, how do you replace it? How do you replace or restore the operating system? How do you replace or restore applications? How do you replace or restore the user's data?

- Do you have security requirements for data on the hard disk? Do you use any form of data encryption?

- Do your computers have multiple configurations? For example, does a portable computer have one set of hardware features for when it is in a docking station (including a network adapter) and another hardware profile for when it is undocked (and using a high-speed modem rather than a network adapter)?

- How long do you spend troubleshooting a hardware problem before you replace the computer and restore a standard operating system and application environment?

For each class of users in your organization, define a standard type of computer that can meet current and anticipated processing needs for two years at a minimum. In addition, try to reduce the number of different hardware configurations that you support to improve your ability to support users and also reduce client support costs.

Conducting a Hardware and Software Inventory

If you have not already done so, conduct hardware and software inventories of all servers and client computers in use on your network. Document all routers, printers, modems, and other hardware, such as redundant array of independent disks (RAID) arrays and Routing and Remote Access Service (RRAS) server hardware. Be sure that you include such details as basic input/output system (BIOS) settings and the configuration of any peripheral devices such as printers, scanners, and input devices. Record driver versions and other software and firmware information.

Your software inventory needs to list all applications found on all computers, and include version numbers (or date and time stamp data) of dynamic- link libraries (DLLs) associated with the applications on your system. Remember to document any service packs you might have applied to your operating system or applications. You can use scripts and a variety of third-party applications to obtain this information from Windows and Windows NT networks that use Windows Management Instrumentation (WMI).

Identifying Significant Support Issues

Understanding your current support issues can help you improve client configuration standards and reduce support costs. Some questions to address include the following:

- What are the top 10 support issues?

  List them and develop action plans to reduce their frequency.

- How often do users "break" their configuration by attempting to change settings (such as video drivers) and other configuration options?

  If the frequency of configuration problems is unacceptably high, you might want to restrict users' ability to change their operating system configuration.

- How often do users "break" their configuration by attempting to either add or remove applications incorrectly?

  If the frequency of this problem is unacceptably high, you might want to restrict their ability to install or uninstall applications.

- Do users install unauthorized software on their computers?

  If this is a problem in your organization, institute corporate policies on whether unauthorized software is allowed. Even if you allow users to bring unauthorized software into the organization, define the types of software to allow and the licensing rules by which users must abide.

- Has the data on clients been secured? Does it need to be?

  Most organizations will want to define security measures for corporate data. The amount of security varies by the type of data involved (financial data or trade secrets require one level of security, public relations releases require another level, for example). You might also want to define who is responsible for security (users versus IT, for example) depending on the type of data.

- How much time does your help desk spend trying to fix a broken configuration before they reinstall or reset the basic configuration?

  If you do not have time limits on support calls for broken configurations, consider instituting limits. Also, evaluate Windows 2000 Professional features that can be used to back up user data and install or reinstall the operating system and applications. These new features can affect the length of support calls. For example, if it is easier to reinstall a desktop and data than to troubleshoot a broken configuration, you can significantly reduce the length of your average support call.

Your answers to these and other support questions will help you determine which Windows 2000 Professional features and configuration options to implement.

Determining Your Preferred Client Configuration

Whether you choose to accept the Windows 2000 Professional defaults or implement your own configuration preferences, it is recommended that you evaluate Windows 2000 Professional configuration options according to the following criteria:

- Are they easy to learn?
- Are they efficient to use?
- Are they easy to remember?
- Can they help address your top help desk issues or concerns?
- Do they reduce the number of user errors?

The following techniques might help you to determine a preferred client configuration to best meet the needs of your users:

Focus groups   Bring groups of users together for focused discussions about what they like and dislike about their computer configurations, and what changes might make them more productive.

Observational research   Watch users while they work on their computers.

Field research   Talk to administrators at other organizations about what they have learned.

Expert reviews   Study the research that exists about user interface design and user productivity.

User surveys   Create a questionnaire and through e-mail or your organization's intranet you can obtain feedback from a broad range of users on their preferences.

A prioritized list of user requirements needs to guide the development of the preferred client configuration. After the entire deployment team has had an opportunity to go through training on Windows 2000 Professional, the team needs to understand the features well enough to map them to the specific user requirements.

Assessing Your Current Network Infrastructure

Asses your network infrastructure by identifying existing network protocols, speed of network links (network bandwidth), and whether or not there is a Windows 2000 Server network infrastructure in place when you install Windows 2000 Professional.

Table 3.2 lists key planning issues related to assessing your network infrastructure and describes how these issues affect your plan.

Table 3.2 Key Planning Issues for Assessing the Network Infrastructure

Issue	Effect on your plan
Network protocols	Network protocols determine how you customize network protocol and associated adapter parameters in several networking sections in the answer file, such as the [NetAdapter], [NetProtocols], and [NetServices] sections.
Network bandwith	The amount of network bandwidth available affects your choice of installation tool and method. For example, in locations that do not have a highbandwidth connection to a network server, using a CD-ROM or other local method of installing Windows 2000 Professional (executing Winnt.exe or Winnt32.exe at the command prompt on each computer) is probably the best option. For users with high-bandwidth network connections, but whose computers do not have a remote boot–compliant network card or remote-boot CD ROM, a network-based image duplication or manual installation method will be the next best option.
Windows 2000 Server network infrastructure	Having an existing Windows 2000 Server infrastructure in place affects the range of tools you can use to automate and customize installations. For example, if you have a Windows 2000 Server computer configured as a RIS server, you can use Remote OS Installation to image and automatically distributed customized images of a Windows 2000 Professional installation to users.

Documenting Your Network Infrastructure

While you are documenting your current network environment, take special note of areas where you are currently experiencing problems. If you stabilize your network before deploying a new operating system, deployment and troubleshooting will be easier, and you can have increased confidence in the upgraded network.

When documenting your network infrastructure, you are obtaining both hardware data to document your infrastructure's physical structure and software data to document the existence and configuration of the protocols in use on your network. You also need to document the logical organization of your network, name and address resolution methods, and the existence and configuration of services used. Documenting the location of your network sites and the available bandwidth between them will also assist you in deciding whether to perform push or on-demand installations when you upgrade or migrate to Windows 2000 Professional.

Developing a physical and logical diagram of your network will help you organize the information you gather in an understandable and intuitive manner.

Physical Network Diagram

The physical diagram presents the following information about your existing network:

- Details of physical communication links, such as cable length, grade, and approximation of the physical paths of the wiring, analog, and ISDN lines.
- Servers, with computer name, IP address (if static), server role, and domain membership. A server can operate in many roles, including primary or backup domain controller, Dynamic Host Configuration Protocol (DHCP) service server, Domain Name System (DNS) server, Windows Internet Name Service (WINS) server, print server, router, and application or file server.
- Location of devices such as printers, hubs, switches, modems, routers and bridges, and proxy servers that are on the network.
- Wide area network (WAN) communication links (analog and ISDN) and the available bandwidth between sites. This might be an approximation or the actual measured capacity.

Document firmware version, throughput, and any special configuration requirements for any devices on the network. If you assign static IP addresses to any of these devices, record them.

Logical Network Diagram

The logical diagram shows the network architecture, including the following information:

- Domain architecture, including the existing domain hierarchy, names, and addressing scheme.
- Server roles, including primary or backup domain controllers, DHCP service servers, or WINS servers.
- Trust relationships, including representations of transitive, one-way, and two-way trust relationships.

Network Configuration

In general, document these areas of your network configuration:

- Name resolution services
- IP addressing methods and service configurations
- Remote and dial-up networking
- Bandwidth issues

Include these additional areas in your current infrastructure assessment:

- File, print, and Web servers
- Line-of-business applications
- Directory service architecture
- Security

Incorporate Plans for Future Network Changes

Determine if there are any current plans for increasing network capacity or adding networking features and functions. For example, is there a major network upgrade planned that would coincide with the planned Windows 2000 Professional rollout? Is there any planning being done to add new user services such as instant messaging or videoconferencing? These plans will affect your deployment strategies.

For additional details on documenting your current environment, see "Preparing Your Network Infrastructure for Windows 2000," "Determining Network Connectivity Strategies," and "Using Systems Management Server to Analyze Your Network Infrastructure" in the *Deployment Planning Guide*.

Determining a Client Connectivity Strategy

Networks vary in size and type depending on their function. How clients connect to the network depends upon where they are located. Some examples include:

- Internal clients are physically located within the corporate infrastructure. Internal clients can use a variety of different network media, such as asynchronous transfer mode (ATM), Ethernet, or Token Ring.
- External clients are remote from the corporate network infrastructure and require Routing and Remote Access or virtual private networking.

Clients need to be able to connect to a variety of resources. These resources can include file and print servers, database servers such as Microsoft® SQL Server™, Microsoft® Exchange servers, and internal Web servers.

Overview of Client Connectivity

When you connect computers running Windows 2000 Professional to a local area network, the Windows 2000 Professional operating system detects your network adapter and creates a local area connection for you. It appears, like all other connection types, in the Network and Dial-up Connections folder, which is accessed from Control Panel. By default, a local area connection is the only type of connection that is automatically activated. Dial-up connections are not activated by the system. They require a manual configuration using the Network Connection wizard located in the Network and Dial-up Connections folder in Control Panel.

If you make changes to your network, you can modify the settings of an existing local area connection to reflect those changes. These changes can be in one of the following forms:

- Protocols such as static IP address changes
- Domain Name System (DNS) or Windows Internet Name Service (WINS) configurations
- Services

By means of the **Status** dialog box, you can view connection information for a local area connection such as connection duration, speed, amount of data transmitted and received, and the diagnostic tools available for a particular connection. You can also add a status icon for the local area connection in the Windows taskbar.

If you install a new LAN device on your client, the next time you start Windows 2000 Professional, a new local area connection icon appears in the Network and Dial-up Connections folder. For portable computers, you can add a Personal Computer Memory Card International Association (PCMCIA) slot, or PC card network adapter while the computer is on, and the local area connection icon is immediately added to the folder without restarting the computer.

You can configure network components used by your local network connection with the **Properties** menu option. Network components are the clients, services, and protocols you use to communicate with servers on your network after you are connected to a server. The components you can configure and their functions are as follows:

- Services, such as file and printer sharing.
- Protocols, such as Transmission Control Protocol/Internet Protocol (TCP/IP).
- Clients, such as Gateway Services for NetWare and Client Services for NetWare.

For more information about configuring local area connection properties, see Windows 2000 Professional Help.

You can configure settings for multiple LAN adapters through the **Advanced Settings** menu option for the local area connection in the Network and Dial-up Connections folder. Using this option, you can modify the order of adapters that are used by a connection, and the adapter's associated clients, services, and protocols.

Windows 2000 Professional Services and Protocols

TCP/IP is the standard network protocol used by Windows 2000 Professional. If a client needs to access file and print resources from NetWare or Macintosh servers, Microsoft supplies either the protocol necessary for connectivity on these networks or a compatible protocol for these environments. An example of such a compatible protocol is NWLink, which is the Microsoft implementation of Novell IPX/SPX protocol.

You can install Services for Macintosh, which includes the AppleTalk protocol on client computers that need access to Macintosh resources. Macintosh clients can also access file servers by running TCP/IP.

Windows 2000 Professional attempts network connectivity with remote servers using network protocols in the order of the local area connection specified by the user in the **Advanced Settings** dialog box. Install and enable only the protocols that you need. For instance, if you only need TCP/IP, but have IPX loaded as well, it generates unnecessary IPX and Service Advertising Protocol (SAP) network traffic.

TCP/IP Network Clients

Clients on a TCP/IP network can have an IP address assigned to them either statically, by the network administrator, or dynamically, by the Dynamic Host Configuration Protocol (DHCP) server.

Windows 2000 uses a new DNS service called DNS dynamic update. It is used as the namespace provider whether the client is using DHCP or static IP addresses. In previous Windows networks, WINS was used in conjunction with DHCP, allowing hosts to dynamically register their NetBIOS name and IP address in the WINS database. You still need WINS if you have any clients on your network that are running Windows NT Workstation, Windows 95, Windows 98, or Microsoft® Windows® 3.1, because these clients use the NetBIOS name resolution method. It is recommended that you upgrade all NetBIOS clients to DNS dynamic update, but plan to support both DNS and WINS for some period of time.

Using Microsoft DNS on your network offers the following advantages:

- Provides interoperability with other DNS servers, such as Novell NDS and UNIX Bind.

- Integrates with and is required for the support of Active Directory.

- Integrates with other networking services, such as WINS and DHCP.

- Allows clients to update resource records by dynamically registering their DNS names and IP addresses.

- Supports incremental zone transfers between servers.

- Supports new resource record types including the Services Locator and asynchronous transfer mode addresses records.

Before you install TCP/IP on a system, determine whether the client will receive static or dynamic IP addresses. Identify whether the hosts on your network are using DHCP or if your IP addresses are statically assigned.

DHCP

Using the Dynamic Host Configuration Protocol (DHCP) allows a client to receive an IP address automatically. This helps avoid configuration errors caused by the need to manually type in values at each computer. Also, DHCP helps prevent address conflicts that occur when a previously assigned IP address is reused to configure a new computer on the network. In addition, the DHCP lease renewal process helps assure that where client configurations need to be updated often (such as users with mobile or portable computers who change locations frequently), these changes can be made efficiently and automatically. Finally, deploying DHCP in a network allows a much more efficient use and management of your organization's address space, because addresses that are no longer used by devices are reintroduced in the address pool and reallocated to other clients.

To enable DHCP, a client simply needs to have the **Obtain an IP address automatically** radio button selected in the **TCP/IP Properties** property sheet, which is accessible through the **Local Area Connection** icon. This option is enabled by default when a Windows 95, Windows 98, Windows NT, or Windows 2000 Professional client is initially installed, so if you are using DHCP, you do not need to manually set your IP configuration.

The benefits of using DHCP are as follows:

- You do not have to manually change the IP settings when a client, such as a roaming user, travels throughout the network. The client is automatically given a new IP address no matter which subnet it reconnects to, as long as a DHCP server is accessible from each of those subnets.

- There is no need to manually configure settings for DNS or WINS. The DHCP server can give these settings to the client, as long as the DHCP server has been configured to issue such information to DHCP clients. To enable this option on the client, simply select the **Obtain DNS server address automatically** option button.

- There are no conflicts caused by duplicate IP addresses.

Static Addresses

If your IP addresses are assigned statically, you have the following information available:

- The IP address and subnet mask for each network adapter installed in the client.

- The IP address for the default gateway.

- Whether or not the client is participating in DNS or WINS.

- If the client is participating in DNS, the name of the DNS domain that the client is currently part of, and the IP addresses of the primary and backup DNS servers.

- If the client is participating in WINS, the IP addresses for the primary and backup WINS servers.

IPX Network Clients

Windows 2000 Professional clients can operate with NetWare servers by using Client Services for NetWare or Gateway Services for NetWare.

If there are servers on the network that use Novell NetWare operating systems, Windows clients can use Client Services for NetWare to connect directly to the server, or they can connect indirectly to a Windows 2000–based server that is running Gateway Services for NetWare.

The following steps are required to gain client access to NetWare resources:

1. Install Client Services for NetWare. This allows you to make direct connections to NetWare resources. The NetBIOS NWLink protocol is installed when Client Services for NetWare is installed. This is the Microsoft version of the IPX protocol, and supports connectivity between systems running Windows 2000 Server and systems running NetWare 4.*x* and earlier.

2. Connect to NetWare volumes. After installing the services listed previously, you can connect to a NetWare volume by clicking **My Network Places** on the desktop.

3. Connect to NetWare file and print resources. You can add a NetWare printer in a Windows 95 or later client by going to the Printer folders in the **Settings** menu, and follow the Printer Installation wizard. You can add NetWare printers in the wizard by typing in the name of the printer in normal Universal Naming Convention (UNC) format.

Gateway Services for NetWare

You can install Gateway Services for NetWare on a Windows 2000–based server to enable it to act as a gateway. Clients can then connect to NetWare resources without running NWLink, using TCP/IP only. The server runs Gateway Services for NetWare and NWLink, linking the client to the NetWare server. This service is included with Windows 2000 Server.

File and Print Services for NetWare

The File and Print Services for NetWare service is a separate product and enables a Windows 2000–based server to provide file and print services directly to a NetWare server and compatible client computers. Resources connected through this service appear to NetWare clients like any NetWare server and clients can gain access to volumes, files, and printers on the server. No changes or additions to the NetWare client software are necessary.

Client Services for NetWare

The Client Services for NetWare service enables client computers to make direct connections to file and printer resources on NetWare servers running NetWare 2.*x*, 3.*x*, or 4.*x*. You can use Client Services for NetWare to gain access to servers running either Novell Directory Services or bindery security. This service is included with Windows 95, Windows 98, Windows NT, and Windows 2000 Professional.

For information about advanced client connectivity and remote network connection methods, see "Defining a Client Connectivity Strategy" in the *Deployment Planning Guide*. For additional details on TCP/IP features in Windows 2000 Professional and information about how to configure TCP/IP, see the chapter "TCP/IP in Windows 2000 Professional" in this book.

Determining Implementation Methods

Windows 2000 Professional includes tools that provide you with the flexibility to choose a method of deployment that will best help you achieve your specific technical and business goals, and meet the needs of your network infrastructure.

Determining Your Installation Processes

There are two basic approaches to deploying Windows 2000 Professional to existing computers; the first is to upgrade the existing operating system, and the second is to run a "clean" installation.

Upgrade

Windows 2000 Professional Setup includes the ability to upgrade Windows 95, Windows 98, and Windows NT Workstation version 3.51 and version 4.0. After an upgrade the user's operating system settings, applications, and data are preserved.

Clean Installation

There are two methods of running setup using the clean installation method:

- The operating system is installed on a computer system with a newly formatted hard disk drive or into a different directory from the existing operating system. After setup is complete, the user's data must be restored and applications must be reinstalled.

- The operating system is copied using a third-party disk-image copying tool, along with applications and settings, to the hard disk drive as part of a hard disk drive image. This is often referred to as disk-image copying. After disk-image copying is completed, the user's data must be restored.

If you are deploying new computers, have them preconfigured and tested prior to deployment. This will remove any potential issues with hardware and configuration incompatibilities or discrepancies.

Minimizing the Costs of Implementation

You might determine that a Windows 2000 Professional deployment project is an opportune time to implement best management practices, taking advantage of the features of Windows 2000 Professional that enable improved management and lower total cost of ownership (TCO).

Using Disk-image Copying

If your existing environment has a standardized hardware base, then a clean install using disk-image copying is the recommended method to deploy Windows 2000 Professional. It can provide the most effective, lowest cost method to deploy a standardized image of Windows 2000 Professional and applications.

In many cases, this method of deployment is cost-effective because it reduces the number of hours necessary to both install and configure the operating system and applications for each computer significantly. Disk-image copying allows the full desktop to be deployed in one pass: operating system, applications, and settings. In addition to this, planning and preparation for the installation process is reduced. Using disk-image copying ensures that each system has a standard directory structure, a best practice that typically enables ongoing change and configuration management. Backing up local end user data and settings is the most significant cost of using the disk-image copying method, and needs to be taken into consideration when evaluating this deployment method.

Windows 95 or Windows 98

Organizations with a Windows 95 or Windows 98 environment will find that a clean install is the most cost-effective method for deploying Windows 2000 Professional. A clean install increases the success rate of setup and reduces the complexity of your environment. A clean install eliminates the potential software configuration issues that often arise due to users installing software and making configuration changes over time. Customers with a well-managed, homogeneous Windows 95 or Windows 98 environment need to create a lab environment that will allow them to develop, test, evaluate, and refine an upgrade process that can then be implemented on production systems.

You will also need to test your applications based on Windows 95 or Windows 98 and determine if there are any issues that need to be addressed. Create a plan for addressing these issues in the lab environment prior to rollout. You can find information about Windows 2000 product compatibility on the Web Resources page at http://windows.microsoft.com/windows2000/reskit/webresources.

Windows NT Workstation 4.0 and Windows NT Workstation 3.51

If your existing environment consists of either Windows NT Workstation 4.0 or Windows NT Workstation 3.51, then upgrade is the most cost-effective method for deploying Windows 2000 Professional. However, if third-party network components, anti-virus programs, computer manufacturer developed utilities like power management utilities, or software digital video disc (DVD) decoders are installed on your clients, it might be necessary to perform a clean install. You might also develop a process to uninstall the components before installing Windows 2000 Professional.

Testing Your Deployment Plan

A key factor in the success of your Windows 2000 Professional project is thorough testing based on realistic scenarios. Realistic scenarios require a test environment that simulates your production environment as much as possible. In this test environment, members of the planning team can verify their assumptions, uncover deployment problems, and optimize the deployment design, as well as improve their understanding of the technology. Such activities reduce the risk of errors and minimize downtime in the production environment during and after deployment.

Creating a Test Environment

A test environment encompasses all the locations that support testing without risk to your corporate network. Many large organizations distribute their test environments across numerous physical, or even geographical, locations for testing in various technical, business, or political contexts. The following factors influence the decisions you make about your test environment:

- Your testing methodology
- Features and components you test
- Personnel who perform the testing

A test environment might include one or more labs, and a lab might include one or more locations. The lab needs to be a network that is designed solely for testing and is isolated from the corporate network.

When you select personnel to perform testing in the lab be sure to include end users. Having end users test the planned configuration will prove to be invaluable for uncovering problems and determining training needs. These users can also become advocates for the deployment.

Simulating the Client Computer Environment

This section covers some considerations for designing a lab to test Windows 2000 Professional. The issues presented here might not apply to all Windows 2000 Professional implementations. Focus on the considerations that apply to your design.

Client Computer Hardware

Include at least one client computer for each vendor and model that is to run Windows 2000 Professional in your production environment. If your organization uses portable computers, docking stations, or port replicators, be sure to include those vendors and models as well. Be sure to obtain an updated BIOS that is compatible with Windows 2000 Professional.

It is recommended that you develop a standard hardware configuration for Windows 2000 Professional as part of your deployment project. Your lab testing can help you define and refine a standard configuration. As you define hardware configurations, verify that the components are compatible with Windows 2000 Professional. For example, you might need to verify compatibility for the following components:

- Universal Serial Bus (USB) adapters
- Compact disc and DVD drives
- Sound adapters
- Network adapters
- Video adapters
- Small computer system interface (SCSI) adapters
- Mass storage controllers
- Removable storage devices
- Pointing devices (mice, trackballs, tablets)
- Keyboards

To determine compatibility, look up the components on the Microsoft Hardware Compatibility List (HCL). For information about the HCL, see the Microsoft Windows Hardware Compatibility List link on the Web Resources page at http://windows.microsoft.com/windows2000/reskit/webresources.com. Search with the keyword "HCL." The HCL includes all the hardware that Microsoft supports. If your hardware is not on the list, contact the vendor to find out if there is a driver. If your components use 16-bit drivers, you need to obtain a 32-bit driver.

You can also use Windows 2000 Professional Setup to check for hardware compatibility. Run Setup in check-upgrade-only mode to obtain log files that indicate hardware and software incompatibilities and device drivers that need to be updated. Use the following command line format for check-upgrade-only mode:

```
winnt32 /checkupgradeonly
```

On computers running Windows 95 or Windows 98, the log file, called Upgrade.txt, is located in the Windows installation folder. On systems running Windows NT, the log file is called Winnt32.log and is located in the installation folder.

If updated device drivers for your devices are not included with Windows 2000 Professional, contact the vendor to obtain an updated driver.

After you decide on the standard hardware configuration, inventory the computers in your production environment to determine which ones need to be upgraded before you deploy Windows 2000 Professional.

Note   As previously discussed, it is very important that you obtain an updated BIOS that is compatible with Windows 2000 Professional. Be sure to test your client computers to ensure Windows 2000 compatibility.

Network Connectivity

Provide connectivity to the same types of networks that you use in the production environment, such as a local area network (LAN), a wide area network (WAN), or the Internet.

If you plan to use Routing and Remote Access or a proxy network service in the production environment, include these types of connections in the lab.

Server-based Services

Configure servers for the services used in the production environment. For example, include the following services:

- DNS, WINS, and DHCP
- Directory services (such as X.500 and NetWare)
- File sharing
- Network printing
- Server-based line-of-business applications, both centralized and decentralized

Remember to provide for the following administrative services:

- Remote operating system installation
- Server-based application deployment
- Tools for managing client computers (SMS, for example)

Domain Authentication

If your organization uses, or plans to use, domain authentication, simulate your authentication configuration in the lab. If you are migrating from Windows NT 4.0 to Microsoft® Windows® 2000 Server, plan for authentication in the mixed environment that will occur during the phased rollout.

Network Management Services

Include network services used in your environment, such as Simple Network Management Protocol (SNMP).

Network Protocols

Use the protocols you plan to use in the production environment. Verify the protocols you use on client computers before connecting them to the production network.

Applications

You need licenses for and access to the software for all applications, stand-alone or server-based, that are to be supported on Windows 2000 Professional computers.

Peripherals

Include a representative sample of the types of peripherals, such as printers and scanners, used in the production environment.

Server Platform Interoperability

Simulate the server platforms to be accessed by Windows 2000 Professional computers. If you have a separate server lab, consider connecting the client computer lab to it instead of installing servers in the client computer lab. You might need to establish connectivity to the following systems:

- Windows 2000 Server
- Windows NT 4.0 or earlier
- Mainframes supporting 3270 emulation
- UNIX
- Other network operating systems

Desktop Configurations

As part of your testing, you might decide to evaluate standard client configurations. Lab tests can provide information for recommending specific configurations to management. If you decide to perform this type of evaluative testing, include side-by-side comparisons of different configurations.

Plan to have enough computers of the same make and model to allow for the side-by-side evaluations. Evaluate client configurations based on performance, ease of use, stability, hardware and software compatibility, functionality, and security model.

Performance

Use the lab to start evaluating the impact on your network traffic by testing for changes in baseline traffic patterns without user activity. For more information about performance concepts and monitoring tools, see "Overview to Performance Monitoring" in this book.

Production Network Connectivity

Your client computer lab needs to be isolated from the corporate network. If you need to provide a connection from the lab to the corporate network, plan how you will use routers to separate the two networks.

For detailed information about setting up a test lab, see "Building a Windows 2000 Test Lab" in the *Deployment Planning Guide.*

Conducting a Pilot

After you verify your Windows 2000 Professional design in your test environment, you need to test it in your production environment with a limited number of users. A pilot reduces your risk of encountering problems during your full-scale deployment.

The primary purposes of a pilot are to demonstrate that your design works in the production environment as you expected and that it meets your organization's business requirements. A secondary purpose is that the pilot gives the installation team a chance to practice and refine the deployment process.

The pilot provides an opportunity for users to give you feedback about how features work. Use this feedback to resolve any issues or to create a contingency plan. The feedback can also help you determine the level of support you are likely to need after full deployment. Ultimately, the pilot leads to a decision to proceed with a full deployment or to slow down so you can resolve problems that might jeopardize your deployment.

The primary steps for conducting your pilot are:

- Select the pilot group.
- Prepare users and sites.
- Conduct the pilot.
- Support and monitor the pilot.
- Obtain feedback and evaluate the results.

Selecting the Pilot Group

Choosing the pilot group and the start date of the pilot deployment is one of the most important tasks of the Windows 2000 Professional deployment project. One of your primary goals needs to be to build and test version one of your preferred client configuration, take time to learn from the experience, and then make the necessary adjustments for the actual deployment. Ideally, the pilot group will be representative of the larger group you are targeting, but this is not important enough to delay the project. Regardless of the group you choose for the pilot deployment, the lessons that are learned and the skills that are developed during the pilot in most cases will apply more generally to the wider deployment.

The pilot group you select will determine the specifics of many other tasks you need to perform, such as identifying applications and hardware that must be tested, the specific design of the desktop, and the target date for completion of the deployment.

The size of the pilot group needs to be small enough to minimize risk and large enough to test the logistics and scalability of your process. The size will also depend on the larger scope of your project. If your entire deployment project is 50 general business users, then a pilot of 5 is enough. For a group of 1,000 users, a pilot group of at least 25 users will ensure that your processes are tested. In general, it is best to keep the pilot group between 25 and 100 users.

Consider the following when choosing the pilot group:

- Selecting the pilot group is the "critical path" in the project, meaning that it directly affects the project schedule. Many other tasks are dependent on the choice you make.

- Ideally the group will be technically representative of the overall project scope. This includes hardware and software in use.

- To minimize risk in the pilot, avoid groups that will be focused on business critical tasks during the pilot deployment. For example, you need to avoid the accounting department during the end of your company's fiscal year.

After selecting the pilot group, the End User Advocate needs to select an influential end user representative from the pilot group to add to the project team. An influential end user is the "computer expert" in the group, the person that group members go to for peer technical support or computer advice. These influential end users will provide essential feedback on all aspects of the project, particularly the desktop design, user training, and communications to the other users in the pilot group.

Preparing Users and Sites

The pilot process includes the following logistical and planning activities. Many of these activities can and should take place concurrently with other planning, design, and testing processes. Be sure to include these activities in the project plan as appropriate.

- Develop the pilot user communication, training, and support plans.
- Conduct pilot department site survey of equipment and software.
- Procure any additional hardware required to bring the computers up to the minimum project standards.
- Purchase any additional software and deployment tools required for the pilot.
- Determine who will perform the deployment.
- Determine the installation process and the number of systems that can be installed per day using the process. Start with a conservative number and adjust the schedule as the pilot progresses.
- Create a specific user-by-user implementation schedule. Determine when the deployment will start and the time of day that the installations will occur. Notify the users of the specific downtime requirements.
- Set up the installation server with the appropriate configuration files and setup scripts.
- Have the users reset the complementary metal oxide semiconductor (CMOS), screen saver, and application passwords.
- Line up administrative access to reset passwords, user IDs, and so on, as necessary during deployment.
- Create a support and feedback mechanism plan. Determine the escalation path for problem resolution.
- Train the installation team on the configuration and installation process.

As you develop the checklist of logistics, consider your goals for the pilot rollout and the factors that define its success. For example, you might set a percentage for successful upgrades or for automated installations that, if achieved, would indicate that the rollout had been successful. Or you might set a threshold of end-user downtime. If downtime stays below this threshold, another indicator of success has been met. Document these goals and criteria, so that the project team can monitor performance against them during the rollout.

Conducting and Monitoring the Pilot

As you conduct the pilot rollout, you might find that certain tasks take more or less time than expected, that some tasks need to be added, or that some tasks can be left out. Be prepared to modify the pilot rollout schedule to account for such changes, and use the pilot schedule for projecting the final rollout timetable.

The following is a summary of the tasks involved in conducting the pilot rollout:

- Conduct virus, disk scan, and defragmentation tasks on the target hard disk drives.
- Conduct the file and configuration backup per your installation plan.
- Perform the automated installation process you created and tested.
- Have your technicians on-site for the initial installations to document the process and problems and to support the users.

Your team needs to continually monitor the pilot including the following:

- The time and all measurable factors in the installation process, including the number of attempted installations, the number of successful installations, and the elapsed time for each installation.
- Network bottlenecks and areas that need to be tuned.
- Application performance.

Although monitoring tools provide much information, it also helps to visit the pilot site periodically. Talking with users frequently uncovers issues that might otherwise go unnoticed. Be sure to check problem reports frequently and look for trends.

Continue to monitor the pilot installation for a week to make sure that everything continues to run smoothly. Make note of improvements to the installation, training, or support, where appropriate.

During the pilot, assess risks to the project. For example, look for the following:

- Scope changes
- Cost increases
- Interoperability problems
- Unanticipated downtime

For more information about conducting a pilot, see "Conducting Your Windows 2000 Pilot" in the *Deployment Planning Guide.*

Preparing for the Rollout

The rollout is the final phase of your deployment, when Windows 2000 Professional is implemented throughout your organization. Rollout is a production activity, which means any potential problems encountered during the rollout can adversely affect productivity and subsequently profitability. A well-designed rollout plan is essential for making your deployment a positive experience for all users.

Your pilot process will have simulated on a smaller scale the process for rolling out Windows 20000 Professional to your entire organization. The results of the pilot installation provide the basis for developing a final plan for rollout. Your preparation for the production rollout begins with the evaluation of the pilot results.

Evaluating the Pilot Results

The final part of the pilot rollout involves collecting and summarizing the data and feedback from the users to help plan for the production rollout. The project team needs to use this data to make any necessary adjustments to the planning and installation process. Tasks to perform during this phase include:

- Survey members of the pilot user group about their satisfaction with the installation process and ask for their suggestions on what might have been done better. Ask them to also evaluate the level of training and support provided.

- Survey the pilot implementation team to collect ideas for improvement to the planning and installation process.

- Compare your installation results against goals and evaluation criteria for this process.

- Create a checklist of open issues that must be resolved prior to the final rollout. Assign to individual team members the actions for solving problems or making improvements.

If the pilot program did not run smoothly or if user feedback was poor, you might find it necessary to conduct additional pilot installations.

As necessary, modify and retest the configuration and installation procedures. Document any changes made to the installation process that address improvements, problems, or other support requirements.

Finalizing the Rollout Plan

Using information about the actual time and resource requirements of the pilot rollout, the project team can make projections scaled to the organizationwide scope of the final rollout. You can then create the deployment schedule and budget the resources in terms of personnel and tools required to meet the rollout schedule. If additional resources are required, they need to be identified and acquired at this time. Include in your rollout plan a support plan and training plan.

When finalizing your rollout plan perform the following tasks:

- Determine the number of computers involved in the final deployment and the time required to upgrade or install Window 2000 Professional on each.
- List the resources needed to complete the process within the schedule.
- Identify any additional personnel needed for the deployment processes, and associated training requirements.
- Present a formal budget for the organizationwide implementation.

When deploying Windows 2000 Professional in an enterprise organization, you will want to employ automated installation methods. Include in your rollout plan a description of your enterprisewide automated installation methodology. Microsoft® Systems Management Server (SMS) can help you perform the following tasks:

- Selecting computers that are equipped for Windows 2000 and that you are ready to support.
- Distributing Windows 2000 source files to all sites, including remote sites and sites without technical support staff.
- Monitoring the distribution to all sites.
- Securely providing enough operating system rights to do the upgrade.
- Automatically initiating the installation of the software package with the possibility of allowing the user to control the timing.
- Resolving problems related to the distributions or installations.
- Reporting on the rate and success of deployment.

SMS provides tools for upgrading your current computers but not for the installation of new computers that do not have an operating system already installed.

C H A P T E R   4

Installing Windows 2000 Professional

One of the key steps for a successful rollout of Microsoft® Windows® 2000 Professional is installing the operating system on a stand-alone computer. This provides you with a thorough and practical understanding of the setup process and helps you prevent any setup-related problems before an organization-wide rollout. You can refer to this chapter for technical details on installation requirements, preparatory steps, installation methods, post-installation considerations, and troubleshooting information for the setup process.

In This Chapter

Related Information in the Windows 2000 Professional Resource Kit

- For information about customizing and automating Windows 2000 Professional installations, see "Customizing and Automating Installations" in this book.

- For detailed information about troubleshooting Windows 2000 Professional, see "Troubleshooting Tools and Strategies" in this book.

Quick Guide

Use this quick guide to plan your Windows 2000 installation.

Plan your installation.

This section provides planning guidelines to ensure an easier installation or upgrade. Topics discussed are:, Choosing an Upgrade or a Clean Installation, Common Planning Issues, Planning a Clean Installation, Planning an Upgrade, and Planning a Multiple-Boot Configuration.

- See "Planning Your Installation" later in this chapter.

Run Setup.

When you understand the planning issues that affect installation, you're ready to begin installing or upgrading Windows 2000 Professional. This section leads you through the Setup process.

- See "Running Setup" later in this chapter.

Perform post-installation tasks.

After Setup has finished, you might need to perform additional tasks to complete the installation or upgrade, such as creating user accounts, joining an existing domain or workgroup, or creating emergency repair disks.

- See "Post-Installation Tasks" later in this chapter.

What's New

The Windows 2000 Professional installation and upgrade procedures have been enhanced from previous versions of the operating system. The following is a brief description of these enhancements.

Support for Plug and Play Devices

Microsoft® Windows® 2000 now supports Plug and Play technology. A Plug and Play system requires the interaction of the operating system, basic input/output system (BIOS), devices, and device drivers. Windows 2000 Plug and Play is an enhanced implementation which extends the existing Microsoft® Windows NT® version 4.0 input/output (I/O) structure to support Plug and Play and power management. For more information about Plug and Play, see "Device Management" in this book.

Compatibility Check Options

Windows 2000 Professional Setup comes with a compatibility-mode option that can be used before installing Windows 2000 Professional to examine hardware and software for known problems that might be encountered during the Setup process. It creates a report to determine which hardware files and any upgrade packs are needed to successfully run Windows 2000. This report can be sent to a printer or saved to a file for later review. You can also get a downloadable version of this compatibility check option by using the Windows 2000 Readiness Analyzer link on the Windows 2000 Web Resources Page at: http://windows.microsoft.com/windows2000/reskit/webresources.

Planning Your Installation

Although Windows 2000 Professional is easy to install, the Setup process can be complicated if you are not prepared. Getting all the aspects of the installation correct the first time can be a challenge and requires careful planning. This section gives you the information needed to successfully install and set up Windows 2000 Professional.

When planning to set up Windows 2000 Professional, you need to consider a number of issues, including:

- Whether to upgrade or perform a clean installation.
- Whether to use a multiple-boot configuration with other operating systems.
- When and how to back up critical files.
- Checking minimum hardware requirements.
- Checking hardware and software compatibility.
- Disabling services that might impede Setup's ability to properly install and configure Windows 2000 Professional.

Checklist for Preparing to Run Setup

Use the checklist in Table 4.1 to verify that you have completed the necessary preparatory steps before setting up Windows 2000.

Table 4.1   Windows 2000 Professional Setup Checklist

Step	Reference in this Chapter
Check system requirements: Review the minimum system requirements.	"Checking Hardware Requirements"
Record information: Computer name. Workgroup or domain name. IP address (if on a network without a DHCP server).	"Obtaining Network Information"
Back up your data.	"Backing up Your Files"
Choosing between an upgrade or a clean installation: Decide whether to upgrade your existing operating system or to perform a new installation.	"Choosing an Upgrade or a Clean Installation"
Multiple-boot considerations: Do you want the ability to choose between operating systems every time you start your computer?	"Planning a Multiple-Boot Configuration"
Creating disk partitions: Do you need to create disk partitions or make changes to your existing disk partitions?	"Disk Partition Options" in "Planning Your Installation"
File system considerations: Is the more powerful Windows 2000 NTFS file system your best choice?	"Choosing a File System" in "Planning Your Installation"
Network Connection: Do you want to connect your computer to a network?	"Post-Installation Tasks"
Select the installation method.	"Running Setup"

Choosing an Upgrade or a Clean Installation

Before beginning Windows 2000 Professional Setup, decide whether to upgrade your current operating system or to install a fresh copy of Windows 2000 Professional. When you begin Setup from an earlier version of Windows, you are asked to choose between upgrading or installing a new copy of Windows 2000.

During an upgrade, Setup replaces the existing Windows operating system files, but preserves your existing user and application settings. Some applications might not be compatible with Windows 2000 and, therefore, might not function properly after an upgrade. Windows 2000 Professional upgrades from the following operating systems:

- Microsoft® Windows® 95
- Microsoft® Windows® 98
- Microsoft® Windows NT® Workstation version 3.51
- Microsoft® Windows NT® Workstation version 4.0

You can choose to upgrade your existing operating system if:

- You are already using a previous version of Windows that can be upgraded to Windows 2000 Professional.
- You want to replace your existing operating system with Windows 2000 Professional.

During a clean installation of Windows 2000 Professional, Setup installs the operating system files in a new folder. If you are currently using an operating system that does not support an upgrade, such as Microsoft® Windows® 3.1 or OS/2, you must install a new copy of Windows 2000 Professional and then reinstall all your applications, as well as reset your personal preferences, such as application settings and Windows settings.

You need to perform a clean installation of Windows 2000 Professional if the following are true:

- You have no operating system on your computer.
- Your current operating system does not support an upgrade.
- You have an existing operating system, but you don't want to keep your existing files or settings. That is, you want a clean installation.
- You have more than one partition, and you want to have a multiple-boot configuration using both Windows 2000 Professional and your current operating system. For more information about planning a multiple-boot configuration, see "Planning a Multiple-boot Configuration" later in this chapter.

Obtaining Network Information

If your computer will not participate on a network, skip this section.

First, you need to decide whether your computer is joining a domain or a workgroup. If you don't know which option to choose, or if your computer won't be connected to a network, select the Workgroup option. (You can join a domain after you install Windows 2000 Professional.) If you select the Domain option, ask your network administrator to create a new computer account in that Domain, or to reset your existing account.

If your computer is currently connected to a network, you need to find out the following information from your network administrator before you begin Setup:

- Name of your computer.
- Name of the workgroup or domain.
- TCP/IP address of your computer, if your network doesn't have a Dynamic Host Configuration Protocol (DHCP) server.

If you want to connect to a network during Setup, you must have the correct hardware installed on your computer and be connected by a network adapter and cable.

Backing Up Your Files

If you're upgrading from a previous version of Windows, it is recommended that you back up your important files. If you're performing a clean installation, you must back up any files you want to keep, or they will be lost. You can back up files to a disk or other backup media, or to another computer on your network.

How you back up your files depends on your current operating system. If you're using Windows 95 or Windows 98, you might need to install the Windows Backup program. If you're using Microsoft® Windows NT® version 3.51 or Windows NT 4.0, Windows Backup is installed by default. You must have a tape drive installed to use the Backup tool in Windows NT 4.0 and earlier.

For more information about installing or using Windows Backup, see your current version of Windows Help.

Checking Hardware Requirements

Table 4.2 shows the minimum and recommended hardware requirements for installing and running Windows 2000 Professional.

Table 4.2   Windows 2000 Hardware Requirements

Minimum Requirements	Recommended Requirements
Intel Pentium or compatible 133 MHz or higher processor. Windows 2000 Professional supports single and dual CPU systems.	Intel Pentium II or compatible 300 MHz or higher processor.
32 MB of RAM.	64 MB (4 GB maximum).
2-GB hard disk with 650 MB free disk space. (Additional disk is required if installing over the network).	2 GB of free space.
VGA-compatible or higher monitor.	SVGA Plug and Play Monitor.
Keyboard, mouse or other pointing device.	Keyboard, mouse or other pointing device.
CD-ROM or DVD drive (required for compact disc installation).	CD-ROM or DVD drive 12x or faster.
Network adapter (required for network installation).	Network adapter.

Checking the BIOS

A basic input/output system (BIOS) is a set of instructions stored on a ROM chip inside x86 and compatible computers, which handles all input/output (I/O) functions.

Before upgrading to Windows 2000 Professional, check the BIOS on the portable or desktop computer to see that is has an updated BIOS. If the BIOS is not compatible, obtain an updated BIOS from the manufacturer.

If your system does not have Advanced Configuration and Power Interface (ACPI) functionality during installation, you might need to update the BIOS. However, to get ACPI functionality after Windows 2000 is installed, you are required to do another installation. You can, however, upgrade your existing installation.

Important Microsoft does not provide technical support for BIOS upgrades. Contact the manufacturer for BIOS upgrade instructions.

For more information about BIOS issues, see the Hardware Update link on the Web Resources page at: http://windows.microsoft.com/windows2000 /reskit/webresources

Checking Hardware and Software Compatibility

Ensure that the hardware on the target computer meets the minimum requirements mentioned earlier and that the individual components are listed in the Hardware Compatibility List (HCL). This list is available on the Windows 2000 Professional operating system CD (which contains the devices that were compliant with Windows 2000 Professional at the time of shipping) or, for the most up-to-date information, see the HCL link on the Web Resources page at http://windows.microsoft.com/windows2000/reskit/webresources

If you have hardware devices that are not listed in the HCL, check with the manufacturer of the device to see if an updated driver is available.

You can also check for potential incompatible hardware and software by using the Check Upgrade or Check Upgrade only mode that can be run as a switch with winnt32.exe. The Check Upgrade mode provides a report prior to installing Windows 2000 so that you can install Windows 2000–compliant drivers or remove unsupported applications or devices.

Hardware Compatibility List

The Windows 2000 Professional Hardware Compatibility List (HCL) is a list of hardware devices that have successfully passed the Hardware Compatibility Tests (HCT). Installing Windows 2000 on a computer that has hardware that is not listed in the HCL might cause the installation to fail.

Note Windows 2000 Professional supports only those items listed on the Hardware Compatibility List (HCL). If your device is not listed on the HCL, it might still function, but it is not supported. For devices that do not function under Windows 2000 Professional, you must contact the hardware manufacturer and ask if there is a Windows 2000 compatible driver for the device in question. If you have a program that uses 16-bit drivers, you will have to install 32-bit Windows 2000–compatible drivers from the manufacturer to ensure functionality with Windows 2000 Professional after the upgrade or installation. A copy of the HCL, which lists supported components at the time of shipping, resides on the Windows 2000 Professional operating system CD. It can also be found by means of the Hardware Compatibility List link on the Web Resources page at: http://windows.microsoft.com/windows2000/reskit/webresources

---

Using Check Upgrade Only Mode

The Setup procedure for Windows 2000 Professional includes a "Check Upgrade Only" mode, which can be used to test the upgrade prior to a real upgrade. This produces a report that flags potential problems that might be encountered during the actual upgrade, such as hardware compatibility issues or software that might otherwise not be migrated during the upgrade. Figure 4.1 shows the Windows 2000 Check Upgrade tool.

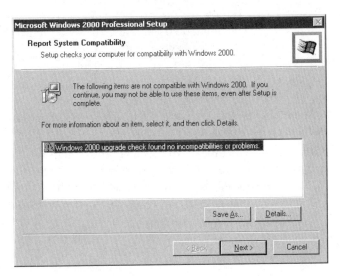

Figure 4.1   Check Upgrade Tool

- The format used from Windows 95 and Windows 98 is **Winnt32 /checkupgradeonly**. The report is saved to **%windir%\upgrade.txt**. You can change this location if you want.

- The format used from Windows NT Workstation 4.0 and 3.51 is also**Winnt32 /checkupgradeonly**. The report is saved to **%windir%\win32.log.**

On Windows 95 and Windows 98, the Check Upgrade Only mode also supports scripting that allows compatibility data to be stored from each computer to a central location for later analysis.

The Upgrade Report is a summary of potential hardware and software upgrade issues. The entries in the report include:

- **MS-DOS Configuration**. Entries in Autoexec.bat and Config.sys that are incompatible with Windows 2000. These entries might be associated with older hardware and software that is incompatible with Windows 2000. It also suggests that more technical information is provided in the Setupact.log file, located in the Windows folder.

- **Plug and Play Hardware**. Hardware that might not be supported by Windows 2000 without additional files. The report refers the administrator to the Windows Hardware Compatibility List (HCL).

- **Software Incompatible with Windows 2000**. Upgrade packs are required for some programs because they do not support Windows 2000, or because they can introduce problems with Windows 2000 Control Panel. Before upgrading to Windows 2000, gain disk space by using Add/Remove Programs in Control Panel to remove programs not being used.

- **Software to Reinstall**. Upgrade packs are recommended for programs because they use different files and settings in Windows 2000. If an upgrade cannot be obtained, remove the program before upgrading by using Add/Remove Programs in Control Panel. After upgrading to Windows 2000 Professional, reinstall or upgrade the program.

The Upgrade Report also displays links to Microsoft Windows 2000 Web sites, including the Hardware Compatibility List, and Add/Remove Programs in Control Panel where appropriate.

The last screen also contains **Save As** and **Print** buttons. If you click the **Next** button, the program uninstalls itself from memory, and verification is finished.

Incompatibility Preventing an Upgrade

If an incompatibility prevents the upgrade from continuing, a wizard appears to inform the user. The user can view details about the incompatibility, if available. Unless the incompatible application has support for fixing the problem by means of the **Have Disk** button, the user must exit the upgrade and fix the problem before rerunning Winnt32.

Incompatibility Warning During an Upgrade

If the incompatibility does not prevent a successful upgrade to Windows 2000, the user is warned that this application might not function correctly with Windows 2000. Even so, the user can continue with the upgrade. The **Have Disk** button is also supported in this case.

For more information about hardware compatibility issues and Windows 2000, see the Windows 2000 Professional Upgrade link on the Web Resources page at: http://windows.microsoft.com/windows2000/reskit/webresources or http://www.microsoft.com/hcl/.

Planning a Clean Installation

A clean installation of Windows 2000 Professional is one that does not use any settings from an existing operating system, or one that is installed onto a computer with no existing operating system.

It is highly recommended that you install Windows 2000 on its own partition. Installing Windows 2000 Professional on the same partition as the existing operating system for a multiple-boot configuration is not supported and causes the other operating system to function improperly.

During Setup, you can either create a new partition out of unused disk space or format an existing partition. If your computer contains a single partition that uses all of the hard drive, and an older operating system already resides there, you have two options:

1. Upgrade the current operating system (Windows 95, Windows 98, and Windows NT Workstation 3.51 or 4.0 only) to Windows 2000 Professional.

2. Back up your data, reformat your partition, and then perform a clean installation of Windows 2000 Professional.

A clean installation of Windows 2000 supports the FAT and NTFS file systems. A clean installation can be performed from a bootable CD-ROM (if your CD-ROM drive supports starting from a CD-ROM), from a setup floppy with CD-ROM, from the network, or by running Winnt32.exe from the command line of an existing Windows 95, Windows 98, or Windows NT Workstation operating system (for multiple boot configurations).

The method you choose for running Setup depends on your current configuration and whether you are performing a clean install or an upgrade. The following section is a guide to choosing the appropriate method.

Disk Partition Options

Disk partitioning is a way of dividing your hard disk so that each section functions as a separate unit. You can create a partition to organize information (for example, to back up data) or to dual-boot with another operating system. When you create partitions on a disk, you divide the disk into one or more areas that can be formatted for use by a file system, such as FAT or NTFS.

Note If you're performing a new installation from an existing operating system, Windows 2000 Professional Setup automatically selects an appropriate disk partition, unless you click **Advanced Options** during setup and specify otherwise. A hard disk can contain up to four partitions.

Configuring Disk Partitions

Depending on your existing hard disk configuration, you have the following options during setup:

- If the hard disk is unpartitioned, you can create and size the Windows 2000 Professional partition.

- If the existing partition is large enough, you can install Windows 2000 Professional on that partition.

- If the existing partition is too small but you have adequate unpartitioned space, you can create a new Windows 2000 Professional partition in that space.

- If the hard disk has an existing partition, you can delete it to create more unpartitioned disk space for the Windows 2000 Professional partition. Keep in mind that deleting an existing partition also erases any data on that partition.

Important Before you change file systems on a partition or delete a partition, back up the information on that partition, because reformatting or deleting a partition deletes all existing data on that partition.

If you're setting up a dual-boot configuration of Windows 2000 Professional, it's important to install Windows 2000 Professional on its own partition. Installing Windows 2000 Professional on the same partition as another operating system might cause Setup to overwrite files installed by the other operating system.

Sizing Disk Partitions

It is recommended that you install Windows 2000 Professional on a 2 gigabyte (GB) or larger partition. Although Windows 2000 Professional requires a minimum of 650 megabytes (MB) of free disk space for installation, using a larger installation partition provides flexibility for adding future updates, operating system tools, and other files.

During setup, you only need to create and size the partition on which you want to install Windows 2000 Professional. After Windows 2000 Professional is installed, you can use Disk Management to make changes or create new partitions on your hard disk.

For more information about Disk Management, see Windows 2000 Professional Help.

Converting vs. Reformatting Existing Disk Partitions

Before you run Setup, you must decide whether you want to keep, convert, or reformat an existing partition. The default option for an existing partition is to keep the existing file system intact, thus preserving all files on that partition.

If you decide to convert or reformat, select an appropriate file system (NTFS, FAT16, or FAT32). The following guidelines will help you decide.

Note You must uncompress any DriveSpace or DoubleSpace volumes from previous operating systems before upgrading to Windows 2000 Professional.

Converting an Existing Partition to NTFS

You can convert an existing partition to NTFS during setup to make use of Windows 2000 Professional security. You can also convert file systems from FAT or FAT32 to NTFS at any time after setup by using Convert.exe.

This option preserves your existing files, but only if Windows 2000 Professional has access to files on that partition. Use this option if:

- You want to take advantage of NTFS features, such as security, disk compression, and so on.
- You aren't dual-booting with another operating system that needs access to that partition.

For more information about dual-booting, see "Planning a Multiple-Boot Configuration" later in this chapter.

Note NTFS is the recommended file system for Windows 2000. However, there are specific reasons that you might want to use another file system. If you format a partition with NTFS, only Windows 2000 can gain access to files subsequently created on that partition. If you plan to access files from other operating systems (including Microsoft® MS-DOS®), it is best to install a FAT file system.

Reformatting an Existing Partition

Reformatting a partition erases all existing files on that partition. Make sure to back up your files before you reformat a partition.

Choosing a File System

Windows 2000 Professional supports the FAT16, FAT32, and NTFS file systems. To take advantage of the full potential of Windows 2000 Professional, it is recommended that you use the NTFS file system. NTFS has all the basic capabilities of FAT16 and FAT32, with the added advantage of advanced storage features such as compression, improved security, and larger partitions and file sizes.

There are many advantages to using NTFS. Among these are:

- Increased robustness—NTFS is a transactional file system and can automatically recover from many errors.
- Increased security—access to files can be secured, and files and folders can be encrypted.
- Support for large media.
- Support for large hard disks, up to 2 terabytes (TB). The maximum drive size for NTFS is much greater than that for FAT, and as drive size increases, performance with NTFS doesn't degrade as it does with FAT.
- Faster access.

Windows 2000 NTFS has been improved over Windows NT 4.0 NTFS with such features as:

- Encryption—Can be used to protect the contents of individual files from unauthorized use.
- Volume extension—Volumes can now be extended without having to restart the computer.
- Disk Quotas—Administrators can allocate the amount of disk space for individual users on a per-user basis.
- Distributed Link Tracking—Can be used to preserve shortcuts when files are moved from one volume to another or to a different computer.
- Mount points—Can be used to place another volume onto an NTFS folder, avoiding the use of additional drive letters.
- Full text and property indexing—Allows fast searching and retrieval of files and documents.

Tip If you do not plan to use a multiple-boot configuration, format your partitions as Windows 2000 partitions with NTFS.

In Windows NT 4.0, you can only access an NTFS drive from within the Windows NT 4.0 operating system. This made repairing or fixing the NTFS partition a difficult task. The only solution was to reinstall Windows NT 4.0 to access the NTFS volume, or to run the repair process, both time-consuming processes.

With Windows 2000 Professional, by using the Recovery Console, the administrator can read and write to the NTFS volume by using the four Windows 2000 Professional boot floppy disks or by starting from the Windows 2000 operating system CD. This gives administrators the ability to copy and delete system files and to repair the system.

Note By default, only an administrator account can access an NTFS volume by using the Recovery Console (RCC), as they are required to log on to the system before accessing the hard drives.

For more information about RCC, see "Troubleshooting Tools and Strategies" in this book.

You might want to run Windows 2000 with another operating system on your computer, such as MS-DOS or Windows 95. If this is the case, you might also want to take advantage of the file system features built into each of the operating systems. To manage different file systems on one computer, you might have to create or delete partitions on your hard disks.

If you want to use the integrated security features built into the Windows 2000 NTFS file system or any other features of NTFS, you'll need one partition formatted with NTFS.

Windows 2000 Professional provides support for existing Windows 95 or Windows 98 file systems, including FAT16 and FAT32 file systems. Users have the option to convert to the Windows 2000 NTFS file system.

Caution Compressed Windows 95 or Windows 98 drives cannot be upgraded, and need to be uncompressed before upgrading to Windows 2000 Professional.

If you also want to use MS-DOS on your system, you need another partition formatted with FAT, which is the MS-DOS operating system's native file system. MS-DOS cannot recognize data on an NTFS partition.

Important The primary active partition on your system must be formatted with a file system recognizable by all the operating systems running on that computer (you can have four primary partitions, but the active one is the one that starts all the operating systems). The number of file systems present on your system doesn't necessarily indicate the number of operating systems in use. For example, Windows 2000 Professional can be installed on a FAT partition. This lets you maintain your MS-DOS system, as well as run Windows 2000 Professional. In this case, two operating systems can be used with just one file system.

File System Accessibility

Table 4.3 describes the different file systems that are accessible by Windows 2000 Professional as well as other operating systems, such as MS-DOS, Windows 95, Windows 98, and OS/2.

Table 4.3   Windows 2000 Supported File Systems

NTFS	FAT16	FAT32
A computer running Windows 2000 has full access to a Windows NT 4.0 or 3.51 NTFS volume. A computer running Windows NT Workstation 4.0 with Service Pack 5 can access a Windows 2000 NTFS volume. Other operating systems cannot access a Windows 2000 NTFS volume in a multiple-boot configuration on the same computer.	Local access available through MS-DOS, all versions of Windows and Windows NT Workstation, Windows 2000, Windows 95, Windows 98, and OS/2.	Local access available only through Windows 95 OSR2, Windows 98, and Windows 2000.

File System Limitations

Table 4.4 describes the size and domain limitations of each file system.

Table 4.4   File System Limitations

NTFS	FAT	FAT32
Minimum volume size is approximately 10 MB.	Volumes from floppy disk size up to 4 GB.	Volumes from 512 MB to 2 TB.
Recommended practical maximum for volumes is 2 TB (terabytes). Can't be used on floppy disks.	Does not support domains.	In Windows 2000, you can format a FAT32 volume only up to 32 GB.
File size limited only by size of volume.	Maximum file size 2 GB.	Maximum file size 4 GB.

Planning an Upgrade

Windows 2000 Professional has the ability to upgrade from all of the following operating systems:

- Windows NT Workstation 4.0
- Windows NT Workstation 3.51
- Windows 98
- Windows 95

Upgrades are *not* supported from the following operating systems:

- Microsoft® Windows® 3.*x*, including Microsoft® Windows® for Workgroups.
- Versions of Windows NT Workstation earlier than version 3.51.
- Microsoft® BackOffice® Small Business Server.
- Non-Microsoft operating systems.

Planning the Upgrade From Windows 95 or Windows 98 to Windows 2000 Professional

Upgrading from Windows 95 or Windows 98 to Windows 2000 Professional might require some additional planning due to the differences in the registry structure, as well as differences in how software developers structure their application setup procedures.

Prior to upgrading from Windows 95 or Windows 98 to Windows 2000 Professional, make sure that you meet the minimum hardware requirements mentioned in "Planning Your Installation" earlier in this chapter. Also, for information on upgrade issues with Windows 95 or Windows 98, check the Hardware Update link on the Web Resources page at: http://windows.microsoft.com/windows2000/reskit/webresources.

Hardware Compatibility With Windows 95 and Windows 98

The Windows 2000 upgrade does not migrate drivers from Windows 95 or Windows 98 to Windows 2000. If the driver doesn't exist in Windows 2000, you might need to download a Windows 2000 driver to have available during Setup. Virtually no Windows 95 and Windows 98 drivers are compatible with Windows 2000.

Older, 16-bit device drivers for Windows 95 and Windows 98 and Windows 3.*x* were based on the virtual device driver (V*x*D) model. The V*x*D model is not supported in Windows 2000 Professional. Device drivers in Windows 95 and Windows 98 do not work in Windows 2000. Either Windows 2000 has its own device drivers for these devices, or new ones need to be downloaded.

Many updated drivers ship with the Windows 2000 Professional operating system CD. However, when critical device drivers, such as hard-drive controllers, are not compatible with Windows 2000 Professional and cannot be found on the CD or elsewhere, the Setup program aborts the upgrade until updated drivers are obtained.

The upgrade process stores the system files for Windows 2000 Professional in the existing Windows 95 or Windows 98 system directory, while deleting all the old Windows 95 and Windows 98 files that were originally in the directory.

Software Compatibility With Windows 95 and Windows 98

System tools in Windows 95 and Windows 98, such as ScanDisk, Defragger, and DriveSpace, do not upgrade to Windows 2000 Professional. Also, third-party network clients do not upgrade to Windows 2000, so new drivers must be acquired to complete the upgrade.

Note Novell has included an upgrade for their Client32 on the Windows 2000 Professional operating system CDROM. The upgrade detects and automatically upgrades a previous version of Client32 during the upgrade to Windows 2000 Professional. For the latest Client32 upgrade, see the Novell Web site at http://www.Novell.com.

Some applications written for Windows 95 or Windows 98 might not run properly on computers running Windows 2000 Professional without some modification.

For example, applications can:

- Maintain registry data in different locations. Windows 95 and Windows 98 store this data in different locations than Windows 2000 or Windows NT 4.0 and earlier.

- Make calls to Windows 95 or Windows 98–specific application programming interfaces.

- Install different files when installed on Windows 95 or Windows 98 than when installed on Windows 2000 or Windows NT 4.0 and earlier.

There are three ways to overcome these problems:

- Reinstall the applications after the upgrade. This step is only applicable to applications that are compatible with Windows 2000 Professional.

- Create a new Windows 2000 Professional–based standard configuration with compatible versions of the applications.

- Use migration dynamic-link libraries (DLLs) for each application that is not migrated during the upgrade.

For more information about migration DLLs, visit the Software Development Kit (SDK) information in the MSDN Library link on the Web Resources page at: http://windows.microsoft.com/windows2000/reskit/webresources.

Software vendors and corporate developers can use migration DLLs that move registry keys, install new versions of files, or move files within the file system. These migration DLLs are used by Windows 2000 Setup to resolve these incompatibilities. Setup calls these DLLs to update the application installation. The migration DLL mechanism is fully extensible.

Migration DLLs have four basic functions:

- Replace or upgrade Windows 95 or Windows 98–specific files with Windows 2000 Professional–compatible files.

- Move Windows 95 or Windows 98 application- and user-specific settings (that Setup did not already move) to their proper locations in Windows 2000 Professional.

- Map Windows 95 or Windows 98–specific registry subkeys to the appropriate Windows 2000 Professional locations.

- Provide Upgrade Packs. If you upgrade from Windows 95 or Windows 98, during setup you have the option of providing upgrade packs that modify your existing software. Upgrade packs are available from the appropriate software vendors.

Organizations with proprietary applications might want to consider writing their own migration DLLs for in-house applications.

Note For more information about writing migration DLLs, see the Windows 2000 Software Development Kit (SDK) link on the Web Resources page at: http://windows.microsoft.com/windows2000/reskit/webresources.

Removing Applications From Windows 95 and Windows 98

If you have applications that have been identified by the Check Upgrade tool as incompatible, you must remove the conflicting applications before installing Windows 2000.

In most situations, the supported operating systems will upgrades smoothly to Windows 2000 Professional. However, each operating system requires a different approach to ensure a smooth upgrade. For example, you might want to use migration DLLs for upgrading certain Windows 95 or Windows 98 applications that are not compatible with Windows 2000 Professional.

Running Winnt32.exe from within Windows NT Workstation 3.51 or 4.0 , Windows 95, or Windows 98 enables Windows 2000 to detect the current operating system and give you the option to upgrade or to do a clean installation. Upgrading from a previous operating system allows you to retain most of your system and network settings, preferences, and applications. If you decide to do a clean installation on a separate partition, your previous operating system remains intact and functional. In this case, Windows 2000 is completely separate from your earlier operating system and does not migrate any of your earlier settings.

For upgrades from any of the supported operating systems, Windows 2000 can be formatted to use either FAT16 or NTFS and can convert both FAT16 and FAT32 partitions to NTFS. You can upgrade by running Winnt32.exe from within the existing operating system, connecting to a network share and running Winnt32.exe, or by inserting the Windows 2000 Professional operating system CD and having it do an Autorun.

For upgrades from Windows NT Workstation 4.0 and 3.51, most applications will migrate. Certain proprietary applications, such as applications that were custom-made for your business, will not migrate.

Planning an Upgrade From Windows NT Workstation 4.0 or 3.51 to Windows 2000 Professional

Windows NT Workstation 4.0 and 3.51 provide the easiest upgrade path to Windows 2000 Professional because they share a common operating system structure and core features, such as:

- Registry structure.
- Supported file systems.
- Same security concepts.
- Similar device driver requirements.

Upgrading from Windows NT Workstation 4.0 or 3.51 is fairly straightforward, and most upgrades do not require significant preparation.

Windows NT Workstation 3.51–based computers must have networking installed before the upgrade. If you do not have networking installed and have never installed networking, do not upgrade or you will not be able to log on to Windows 2000.

If you are upgrading Windows NT Workstation 3.x–based computers, you must first upgrade the older computers to Windows NT Workstation 3.51, and then apply Service Pack 5 prior to upgrading to Windows 2000 Professional.

If you are upgrading or installing Windows 2000 on a Windows NT Workstation 4.0–based computer that is currently using NTFS, the installation process automatically upgrades the file system to Windows 2000 NTFS without prompting. This happens even after installation, and there is no way to avoid this.

If you are installing or upgrading to Windows 2000 and the file system is currently FAT or FAT32, you are asked if you want to upgrade to the NTFS file system.

Hardware Compatibility With Windows NT Workstation 4.0 and 3.51

Some hardware devices that functioned successfully on Windows NT Workstation 4.0 work on Windows 2000 Professional; however, it is best to run the Check Upgrade mode to check for driver compatibility issues prior to upgrading the operating system. Some third-party drivers that worked on Windows NT Workstation 4.0 might require updated drivers for Windows 2000 from the manufacturer for that specific device. The NTFS file system that was used in Windows NT 4.0 is transparently updated during the upgrade to Windows 2000 Professional NTFS. Advance work on the test computer typically eliminates any issues concerning deployment or upgrade of Windows NT Workstation 4.0 or 3.51.

Software Compatibility With Windows NT Workstation 4.0 and 3.51

Because Windows NT Workstation 4.0 and 3.51 share common attributes with Windows 2000 Professional, almost all applications that run on Windows NT Workstation 4.0 and 3.51 run without modification on Windows 2000 Professional. However, there are a few application incompatibilities between Windows NT Workstation 4.0 and Windows 2000. One example is antivirus software. Due to changes between the version of NTFS included with Windows NT 4.0 and the version of NTFS included with Windows 2000, file system filters used by antivirus software no longer function between the two file systems. Another example is third-party networking software (such as third-party TCP/IP or IPX/SPX protocol stacks) originally written for Windows NT Workstation 4.0.

Important   You must remove any virus-scanners and third-party network services or client software before starting the Windows 2000 Professional Setup program.

Even though the upgrade from Windows NT is easier than upgrading from Windows 95 or Windows 98, be aware that the following features and applications cannot be properly upgraded:

- Applications that depend on file system filters, for example antivirus software, disk tools, and disk quota software.
- Custom power management solutions and tools. Windows 2000 support for Advanced Configuration and Power Interface (ACPI) and Advanced Power Management (APM) replaces these. Remove the custom tools and solutions before upgrading.

- Custom Plug and Play solutions. These are no longer necessary, because Windows 2000 provides full Plug and Play support. Remove the custom solutions before upgrading.
- Fault tolerant options such as Disk mirrors.
- Third-party network clients and services.
- Uninterruptible power supplies.

For more information about Windows 2000 Professional hardware compatibility, see the Windows Upgrade link on the Web Resources page at: http://windows.microsoft.com/windows2000/reskit/webresources.

–Or–

Contact the software vendor to determine the availability of Windows 2000–compatible upgrades.

Removing Applications From Windows NT Workstation 4.0

The following procedure enables you to remove conflicting applications from Windows NT Workstation 4.0.

1. On the Windows NT Workstation 4.0 desktop, from the **Start** menu, click **Settings** and **Control Panel**.
2. In **Control Panel**, double click **Add/Remove Programs**.
3. In the **Add/Remove Programs** dialog box, select the application you want to remove, and then click **Add/Remove**. This removes the application from the operating system.

Planning a Multiple-Boot Configuration

Windows 2000 Professional can be configured to start with multiple operating systems, such as Windows 2000, Windows NT 4.0 and earlier, Windows 95, Windows 98, Windows 3.*x*, MS-DOS, and OS/2. This is called a dual-boot or multiple-boot configuration. This section discusses configuration details for when Windows 2000 Professional resides with another operating system on the same computer.

Windows 2000 Professional can have a multiple-boot configuration with the following operating systems:

- Windows NT Workstation 3.51 or 4.0
- Windows 95 or Windows 98

- Microsoft® Windows® 3.1 or Microsoft® Windows® for Workgroups version 3.11

- MS-DOS

- OS/2

To set up a dual- or multiple-boot configuration, you must use a separate partition for each operating system. See "Disk Partition Options" earlier in this chapter.

When running Windows 2000 Professional Setup, you can use Winnt32 or Autorun from the Windows 2000 Professional operating system CD to select a folder on an unused partition.

Before You Set up a Multiple-Boot Configuration

If you want to set up a dual-boot or multiple-boot configuration to make available Windows 2000 Professional and another operating system that does not support NTFS (such as MS-DOS or Windows 98) on your computer, first review the following precautions:

- Each operating system must be installed on a separate partition. Installing Windows 2000 Professional on the same partition that contains another operating system is not supported.

- Because you're performing a new installation of Windows 2000 Professional, you must reinstall any programs, such as word-processing or e-mail software, after setup is complete.

- Use a FAT file system for dual-boot configurations. Although using NTFS in a dual-boot configuration is supported, it introduces additional complexity into the choice of file systems. For more information about using NTFS with a dual-boot configuration, see "Setup and Startup" in this book.

- To set up a multiple-boot configuration between MS-DOS or Windows 95 and Windows 2000 Professional, install Windows 2000 Professional last. Otherwise, important files needed to start Windows 2000 Professional might be overwritten.

- For a dual-boot configuration of Windows 2000 Professional with Windows 95 or MS-DOS, the primary partition must be formatted as FAT.

- For a dual-boot configuration with Windows 95 OSR2 or Windows 98, the primary partition must be formatted as FAT or FAT32, not NTFS.

- If you install Windows 2000 Professional on a computer that already has a dual-boot configuration with OS/2 and MS-DOS, Windows 2000 Professional Setup configures your system so that you can dual-boot between Windows 2000 Professional and the operating system (MS-DOS or OS/2) you most recently used before running Windows 2000 Professional Setup.

- Don't install Windows 2000 on a compressed drive unless the drive was compressed with the NTFS file system compression tool.

- It isn't necessary to uncompress DriveSpace or DoubleSpace volumes if you plan to use a dual-boot configuration with Windows 95 or Windows 98. However, the compressed volume won't be available while you are running Windows 2000, and the hard disk drive cannot be compressed if you are starting Setup from within Windows 95, Windows 98, or MS-DOS.

- Windows 95 or Windows 98 might reconfigure hardware settings the first time you use them, which can cause problems if you want a multiple-boot configuration with Windows 2000 Professional.

- If you want your programs to run on both operating systems on a dual-boot computer, you need to install them from within each operating system. You can't share programs across operating systems.

- If the dual-boot computer is part of a Windows NT 4.0 or Windows 2000 domain, each installation of Windows NT Workstation or Windows 2000 Professional must have a different computer name.

- If you're using NTFS and you want a multiple-boot configuration with Windows NT Workstation, you must upgrade to Windows NT Workstation 4.0 SP4 or later before continuing with the Windows 2000 Professional installation.

For more information, see "Setup and Startup" in this book.

Running Setup

How you start Setup depends on whether you are performing an upgrade on your current operating system or installing a new copy of Windows 2000 Professional. To help determine your installation method, see "Choosing an Upgrade or a Clean Installation" earlier in this chapter. The following section guides you through your chosen installation path.

Using Winnt32.exe to Upgrade to Windows 2000 Professional

Upgrading from Windows NT Workstation 4.0 and 3.51, Windows 98, and Windows 95 must be done from within the existing operating system by using Winnt32.exe. To launch Setup from within an operating system, run Winnt32.exe from the command prompt, as well as any additional command-line options you might need.

Setup detects your previous operating system, and then prompts you to upgrade to Windows 2000. During the upgrade, the Setup Wizard detects and installs Windows 2000 drivers for your devices, and then it creates a report on devices that cannot be upgraded so that you can be sure your hardware and software are compatible with Windows 2000 Professional.

The following sections give detailed descriptions of the upgrade process for Windows NT Workstation 4.0 and 3.51, as well as Windows 95 and Windows 98.

Note Running Winnt.exe, performing a network installation, starting from the Windows 2000 Professional operating system CD, or using the four boot floppy disks performs a clean installation and does not allow you to upgrade. **You must be inside the existing operating system to upgrade.**

Running Winnt32.exe from the command prompt installs or upgrades Windows 2000 Professional from a previous version of Windows 95, Windows 98, or Windows NT Workstation 4.0 and 3.51.

Note In this chapter, Winnt.exe and Winnt32.exe are also referred to as Setup.

Running Setup to Upgrade an Existing Microsoft Windows Operating System

You can run the **winnt32** command at a Windows 95, Windows 98, or Windows NT Workstation 4.0 and earlier command prompt.

The syntax of the Winnt32 command is as follows:

winnt32 [/s:sourcepath] [**/tempdrive**:drive_letter] [**/unattend**[num]:[answer_file]] [**/copydir**:folder_name] [**/copysource**:folder_name] [**/cmd**:command_line] [**/debug**[level]:[filename]] [**/udf**:id[,UDF_file]] [**/syspart**:drive_letter] [**/checkupgradeonly**] [**/cmdcons**] [**/m**:folder_name] [**/makelocalsource**] [**/noreboot**]

Table 4.5 describes the Winnt32.exe command switches in more detail.

Table 4.5   Winnt32.exe Command Switches

Switch	Meaning
/s:sourcepath	Specifies the location of the Windows 2000 Professional files. To simultaneously copy files from multiple servers, specify multiple **/s** sources. To copy files from a particular server more quickly (depending on your local hardware), specify the same source multiple times.
/tempdrive:drive_letter	Directs Setup to place temporary files on the specified drive and to install Windows 2000 on that drive.
/unattend[num]: [answer_file]	Performs a new installation in unattended mode, using an answer file for user settings, rather than using settings from the previous installation. The **num** variable is the number of seconds between when Setup finishes copying the files and when Setup restarts. You can use **num** only on a computer running Windows 2000 Professional. The **answer_file** variable is the name of the answer file.
/copydir:folder_name	Creates an additional folder within the folder that contains the Windows 2000 Professional files. For example, if the source folder contains a Private_drivers folder that has modifications just for your site, you can type **winnt32 /copydir:Private_drivers** to have Setup copy that folder to your Windows 2000 Professional folder (C:\Winnt\Private_drivers). You can use the **/copydir** switch to create as many folders as you like. Replaces the **/r** switch.
/copysource:folder_name	Temporarily creates an additional folder within the folder that contains the Windows 2000 files. For example, if the source folder contains a Private_drivers folder that has modifications just for your site, you can type **winnt32 /copysource:Private_drivers** to have Setup copy that folder to your Windows 2000 Professional folder and then use its files during Setup (C:\Winnt\Private_drivers). Unlike folders created by the **/copydir** switch, folders created by using **/copysource** are deleted after Setup completes.
/cmd:command_line	Instructs Setup to carry out a specific command before the final phase of setup; that is, after your computer has restarted twice and after Setup has collected the necessary configuration information, but before setup is complete.
/debug[level]**:**[filename]	Creates a debug log at the specified level. The default creates a log file (C:\Winnt32.log) that has the level set to 2 (Warning).

(continued)

Table 4.5   Winnt32.exe Command Switches *(continued)*

Switch	Meaning
/udf:id[,UDF_file]	Indicates an identifier (id) that Setup uses to specify how a Uniqueness Database (UDF) file modifies an answer file (see the **/unattend** entry). The UDF overrides values in the answer file, and the identifier determines which values in the UDF file are used. For example, /udf:RAS_user,Our_company.udb overrides settings specified for the identifier RAS_user in the Our_company.udb file. If no UDF_file is specified, Setup prompts the user to insert a disk that contains the $Unique$.udb file.
/syspart:*drive_letter*	Specifies that you can copy Setup startup files to a hard disk, mark the disk as active, and then install the disk into another computer. When you start that computer, it automatically starts with the next phase of the Setup. You must always use the **/tempdrive** switch with the **/syspart** switch.
	The **/syspart** switch for Winnt32.exe only runs from a computer that already has Windows NT 3.51, Windows NT 4.0, or Windows 2000 installed on it. It cannot be run on Windows 95 or Windows 98.
/checkupgradeonly	Checks your computer for upgrade compatibility with Windows 2000. For Windows 95 or Windows 98 upgrades, Setup creates a report named Upgrade.txt in the Windows installation folder. For Windows NT 3.51 or 4.0 upgrades, it saves the report to the Winnt32.log in the installation folder.
/cmdcons	Adds to the operating system selection screen a Recovery Console option for repairing a failed installation. It is only used post-setup.
/m:*folder_name*	Specifies that Setup must copy replacement files from an alternate location. Instructs Setup to look in the alternate location first and, if files are present, use them instead of the files from the default location.
/makelocalsource	Instructs Setup to copy all installation source files to your local hard disk. Use **/makelocalsource** when installing from a CD-ROM to provide installation files when the CD-ROM is not available later in the installation.
/noreboot	Instructs Setup to not restart the computer after the file copy phase of **winnt32** is completed so that you can carry out another command.

Upgrading from Windows 95 or Windows 98

Upgrading from Windows 95 or Windows 98 to Windows 2000 Professional might require additional planning because of the differences in the registry structure and differences in how software developers structure their application setup procedures.

Also, while in Windows 95 or Windows 98 you do not need an account to access the operating system, in Windows 2000 Professional you are required to have an existing account, or you need to create an account during the upgrade. In this situation, if you do not already have an account set up on the Windows 95 or Windows 98–based computer, set up an account on the Windows 95 or Windows 98–based computer prior to upgrading to Windows 2000 Professional. This way, the Windows 95 or Windows 98 account migrated when you upgrade to Windows 2000 Professional. Prior to upgrading from Windows 95 or Windows 98 to Windows 2000 Professional, make sure that you meet the minimum hardware requirements. See "Checking Hardware Requirements" earlier in this chapter.

The following steps lead you through an upgrade from Windows 95 or Windows 98 to Windows 2000.

1. When the Windows 2000 Professional operating system CD is inserted, the Autorun.inf program runs the installation SplashScreen, and then the installation procedure is initiated. The installer detects your current operating system version and, if the version on the CD is later, it asks if you want to upgrade. If the installation version is earlier than the installed version, you must perform a clean installation, and you cannot upgrade.

2. At this point, Setup asks whether you want to install Windows 2000 Professional to a new directory, or upgrade an existing version of Windows.

   Figure 4.2 shows the Windows 2000 Professional Setup Wizard screen.

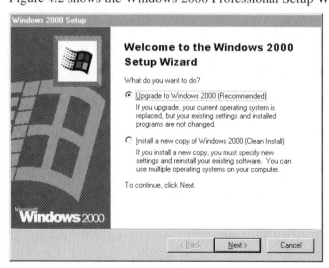

Figure 4.2   Windows 2000 Professional Setup Screen

3. Next you see the **Windows 2000 Professional End User License Agreement** (EULA) screen, shown in Figure 4.3. If you agree with the terms provided, select **I accept this agreement** to continue the installation. You have **Next** and **Back** buttons to move between screens.

Figure 4.3   Windows 2000 Professional End User License Agreement Screen

4. After the License Agreement screen, you see the **Windows 2000 Professional Upgrade Preparation** screen, shown in Figure 4.4.

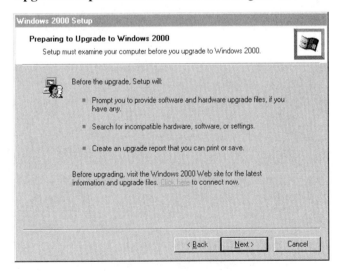

Figure 4.4   Upgrade Preparation Screen

5. The next screen is the **Windows 2000 Professional Product Key**, shown in Figure 4.5, where you are asked to enter the product key that came with your version of Windows 2000 Professional.

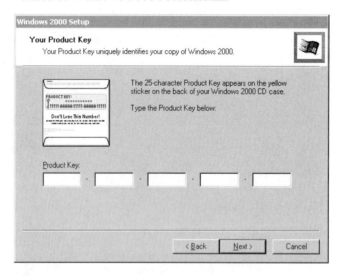

Figure 4.5   Windows 2000 Professional Product ID Screen

6. After entering the product key, clicking **Next** begins the hardware-detection phase of Setup. Setup detects the hardware on your system for the upgrade report.

7. After the hardware-detection phase has completed, the next screen prompts you to provide upgrade packs. These can be either migration DLLs or upgrade files. If you choose **YES**, a screen appears asking you to add the available upgrade packs. If **NO**, click **Next**.

8. Next you are presented with the option to **upgrade to the NTFS file system**. The Setup screen observes that, although this option provides added file security, reliability, and more efficient use of disk space, that you should not use it if you are planning to use Windows 2000 Professional with another operating system, such as MS-DOS or Windows 95 or Windows 98. In other words, don't convert the drive to NTFS if you want to be able to have a dual-boot configuration with Windows 95 or Windows 98 or MS-DOS and want access to all partitions from both operating systems. For more information on dual booting, see "Planning a Multiple-Boot Configuration" earlier in this chapter. This conversion is only for FAT or FAT32 drives and only applies to the drive where the operating system files reside.

9. On systems that have hardware components with drivers that are known to not be Windows 2000–compatible, and software programs that cause problems or failures during the upgrade, you might be halted at this point with a message that one or more devices or programs will be disabled if you continue.

10. After you make these choices, the installer copies the necessary files to your computer's hard drive. This typically takes several minutes.

11. When it is done, the computer needs to restart. You can choose to have it restart automatically, or you can do this manually. When it restarts, a new item appears in the **Boot Manager** startup menu, followed by several text-mode screens.

12. You are prompted right before the first logon to enter a password for all user accounts you had on Windows 95 or Windows 98. If you had user profiles enabled, accounts are created for all users who log on to the computer. If you did not have user profiles enabled, only the current user account and the administrator account are created. All accounts are set to the password you select. They can be changed by means of **Users and Passwords** in **Control Panel**.

Upgrading Windows NT Workstation 4.0 from CD

The following procedure describes upgrading your existing Windows NT Workstation 4.0 operating system to Windows 2000 Professional.

1. Start your computer by running your current operating system, and then insert the Windows 2000 Professional operating system CD-ROM into your CD-ROM drive.

2. If Windows NT 4.0 does not detect the CD, from the **Start** menu, and then click **Run**. At the prompt, type the following command, replacing *D* with the letter assigned to your CD drive:

D:\i386\winnt32.exe

and then press **Enter**.

–Or–

Run **Setup** from the root of the CD-ROM.

3. The **Windows 2000 Professional Setup screen** appears, asking if you want to upgrade your existing operating system or perform a clean installation of Windows 2000 Professional, as shown in Figure 4.6.

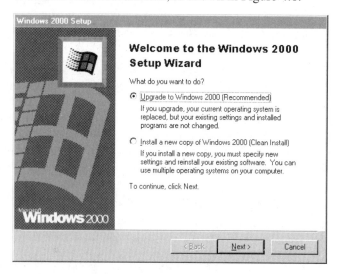

Figure 4.6   Windows 2000 Professional Setup Screen

4. The **Licensing Agreement** screen is next. If you agree with the terms, select **I accept this agreement** to continue. You have **Next** and **Back** buttons to navigate between screens, as shown in Figure 4.7.

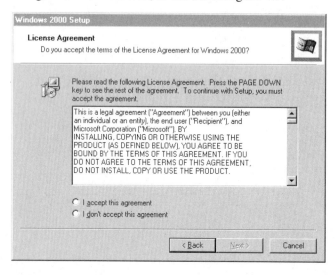

Figure 4.7   Windows 2000 Professional End User License Agreement Screen

5. The next screen is the **Windows 2000 Professional Product Key**, shown in Figure 4.8, where you are asked to enter the product key that came with your version of Windows 2000 Professional.

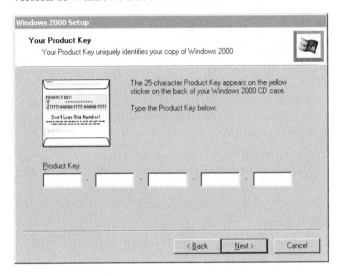

Figure 4.8   Windows 2000 Professional Product Key Screen

6. After entering the product key, Setup runs a compatibility check, which checks the computer for incompatible devices and applications.

7. Next, Setup begins copying installation files to the hard drive, as shown in Figure 4.9.

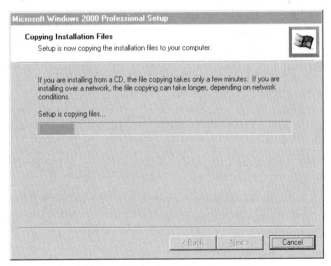

Figure 4.9   Copying Installation Files Screen

8. After the installation files are copied, Setup initializes your Windows 2000 configuration. The computer then restarts.

9. After Setup restarts the computer, you see a blue text screen, and then Setup begins to load the hard-drive controller drivers, search for earlier versions of the Windows operating system, and copy the remaining Setup files to the installation folders. When this is complete, Setup restarts.

10. After Setup restarts, the graphical user interface (GUI) mode of Setup begins. Next, the **Installing devices** screen appears and detects your computer hardware devices, such as the mouse and keyboard, followed by the **Network Settings** screen, which installs the default network components. This can take several minutes.

11. Next, the **Components** screen installs and configures default components, such as Component Services Accessories and Utilities, and Fax Service.

During the final stage of the installation, Windows 2000 Setup completes the following:

- Installs Start menu items
- Registers components
- Saves settings
- Removes temporary files

At this point, Setup is complete. For further information about setting up an account, joining a workgroup, or joining a domain, see "Post-Installation Tasks" later in this chapter.

When the computer restarts, the **Welcome to Windows** screen appears, prompting you to press CTRL+ALT+DELETE to log on.

Upgrading Windows NT Workstation 3.51 From CD

To begin your upgrade from Windows NT Workstation 3.51, start your computer by running your current operating system, and then insert the Windows 2000 Professional operating system CD into your CD-ROM drive.

Note Make sure that you have networking installed before starting the upgrade.

---

1. In **Program Manager**, click **File**, and then click **Run**. At the prompt, type the following command, replacing *D* with the letter of your CD-ROM drive:

   D:**\i386\winnt32.exe**

2. Press ENTER.

3. Follow steps 3 through 11 of the procedure, "Upgrading Windows NT 4.0 Workstation from CD."

Running Setup for a Clean Installation of Windows 2000 Professional

To begin installing Windows 2000 Professional on your computer, run the Windows 2000 Setup program. For a clean installation on *x*86-based computers, run Winnt.exe from an MS-DOS prompt.

Note If you are using Winnt.exe to start Setup, it is highly recommended that you load Smartdrv.exe or other disk-caching software before beginning Setup.

Winnt.exe Command Syntax

Running Winnt.exe performs a clean installation of Windows 2000 Professional. You can run the Winnt.exe command at an MS-DOS, Windows 3.1, or Windows for Workgroups 3.11 command prompt. Winnt.exe command switches are shown in Table 4.6.

The syntax of the Winnt.exe command is as follows:

winnt [/**s**[:sourcepath]] [/**t**[:tempdrive]] [/**u**[:answer file]] [/**udf**:id[,UDF_file]]

[/**r**:folder] [/**r**[x]:folder] [/**e**:command] [/**a**]

Table 4.6   Winnt.exe Command Switches

Switch	Meaning
/**s**:*sourcepath*	Specifies the source location of the Windows 2000 Professional installation files. The location must be a full path in the form *x:\[path]* or *\\server\share[\path]*. The default is the current folder. To simultaneously copy files from multiple servers, specify multiple /**s** sources.
/**t**:*tempdrive*	Specifies a drive to contain temporary Setup files. If you don't specify a location, Setup attempts to locate a drive for you, and then uses the partition with the most free space.
/**udf**:**id**[,UDF_file]	Indicates an identifier (id) that Setup uses to specify how a Uniqueness Database File (UDF) modifies an answer file (see /**u**). The /**udf** switch overrides values in the answer file, and the identifier determines which values in the UDF files are used. If no UDF_file is specified, Setup prompts you to insert a disk that contains the $Unique$.udb file.
/**a**	Enables accessibility options.
/**u**[:*answer file*]	Performs unattended Setup using an answer file (requires /**s**). The answer file provides answers to some or all of the prompts you normally respond to during Setup.

(continued)

Table 4.6   Winnt.exe Command Switches *(continued)*

Switch	Meaning
/r:*folder*	Specifies an optional folder to be installed. The folder remains after Setup finishes. Use additional /r switches to install additional folders.
/r[x]:*folder*	Specifies an optional folder to be copied. The folder is deleted after Setup finishes.
/E	Specifies a command to be carried out at the end of the GUI-mode portion of Setup.

Performing a New Installation by Using the Setup Startup Disks

The following procedure describes installing Windows 2000 Professional by using the four Setup floppy disks.

Before you begin Installing Windows 2000 Professional by using the Setup startup disks, make sure your BIOS is set to start from the floppy drive, then the hard disk drive. For example, Boot Sequence A, C (A being your floppy drive, C being your hard drive).

1. With your computer turned off, insert the Windows 2000 Professional Setup startup disk #1 into your floppy disk drive.

2. Start your computer.

3. When your computer starts from the floppy drive, the Windows 2000 Professional Setup screen appears as blue text.

4. Setup inspects your computer's hardware configuration, and then begins to install the Setup and driver files. After a short time, it asks you to insert startup disk #2.

5. After startup disk #2 is inserted, Setup continues to install files needed for installation. Insert startup disk #3 when prompted, and then startup disk #4 when prompted.

6. Startup disk #4 will finish loading the driver files. After all the files are installed, the Welcome to Windows 2000 Professional Setup screen appears, asking you to chose from the following three options:

   - To Setup Windows 2000 Professional now, press ENTER.

   - To repair a Windows 2000 Professional installation, press R.

   - To quit Setup without installing Windows 2000 Professional, press F3.

   Pressing ENTER continues installation.

7. Next, a blue text screen version of the License Agreement appears. Read the License Agreement, and then press F8 if you agree to the terms to continue the installation.

8. The **Windows 2000 Professional Setup** screen appears and welcomes you to Setup, and then a second screen appears with the following options:

   - To Setup Windows 2000 on the selected partition, press ENTER.

   - If you have unpartitioned space on your hard drive, Setup asks if you want to create a partition in the unpartitioned space. Press C to select this option.

   - To delete the selected partition, press D.

9. If you elected to install Windows 2000 Professional on a FAT partition, Setup asks if you want to leave the current file system intact, format the partition as FAT16, convert the existing file system to NTFS, or format the partition using the NTFS file system.

10. Next, Setup examines the existing hard disks, and then copies the files needed to complete the installation of Windows 2000 Professional. After files are copied, the computer restarts.

11. When the computer finishes restarting, the **Windows 2000 GUI mode Setup Wizard** screen appears. Setup then proceeds to detect and install devices such as the mouse and keyboard. This can take several minutes.

12. The next screen that appears is the regional options screen. At this point, you can customize your installation of Windows 2000 Professional for such settings as locale, number format, currency, time, date, and language.

13. The **Personalize your Software** screen follows. You are asked to type in your name and the name of your organization.

14. The next screen is the **Product ID** screen, where you are required to enter the 25-character product key that appears on the CD case.

15. Next is the **Computer Name and Password** screen. You can either accept the default name that Setup generates, or you can give the computer a different name. You are also asked for an administrative password. You can leave this empty, but it is not recommended.

16. The **Date and Time** settings screen asks you to set the correct date and time for your computer.

17. Next is the **Network Settings** screen. Windows 2000 Professional detects your network settings, and then asks if you want to use Typical or Custom settings. Typical will set default network settings such as File and Print for Microsoft Networks, Client for Microsoft Networks, and TCP/IP protocol using DHCP. Custom settings gives you the ability to choose the network components that you require for your network environment.

18. The **Workgroup or Computer Domain** screen is where you add your computer to a workgroup or join a domain.

19. Next is the **Installing Components** screen, where Windows 2000 Professional Setup installs the operating system components. This can take a few minutes.

20. During the final stage of installation, Windows 2000 Setup completes the following:

   - Installs Start menu items
   - Registers components
   - Saves settings
   - Removes temporary files

Setup is now complete. For further information about setting up accounts, joining a workgroup, or joining a domain, see "Post-Installation Tasks" later in this chapter.

Performing a Clean Installation From the CD-ROM

You can perform a clean installation of Windows 2000 Professional from within an existing Windows 95, Windows 98, Windows NT Workstation 4.0, or Windows NT Workstation 3.51 operating system by using Winnt32.exe. From within Windows 3.*x* or MS-DOS, use Winnt.exe.

1. Start your computer by inserting the Windows 2000 Professional operating system CD into your CD-ROM drive.

2. If Windows automatically detects the CD, click **Install Windows 2000**, and Setup begins automatically.

   If Windows doesn't automatically detect the CD, start Setup from the **Run** command prompt.

   - In Windows 95, Windows 98, or Windows NT Workstation 4.0, from the **Start**, click **Run**.
   - In Windows NT Workstation 3.51 or Windows 3.1, in **Program Manager**, click **File**, and then click **Run**.

Note   You can also run Setup.exe from the root of the CD.

---

3. At the command prompt, type the following command, replacing *D* with the letter of your CD-ROM drive:

   D:\i386\winnt32.exe

   If you're using Windows 3.1 or starting from MS-DOS, type the following command at the prompt, replacing *D* with the letter of your CD-ROM drive:

   D:\i386\winnt.exe

The procedure from the CD is the same as performing a clean installation by using the four startup disks. After you start the installation, refer to "Performing a New Installation by Using the Setup Startup Disks" in "Running Setup for a Clean Installation of Windows 2000 Professional" earlier in this chapter.

Performing a Clean Installation From a Network Connection

Using your existing operating system, establish your connection to the shared network folder that contains the Setup files. You can also use an MS-DOS or network installation disk containing network client software to connect to the network server. (Make sure disk caching software, such as Smartdrv, is loaded.) The syntax is:

\\servername\sharename\i386\winnt.exe

The procedure for a network installation is the same as for performing a clean installation by using the four startup disks. After you start the installation, refer to "Performing a New Installation by Using the Setup Startup Disks" in "Running Setup for a Clean Installation of Windows 2000 Professional" earlier in this chapter.

Adding Additional Components

After Setup has finished, you can install optional components. In Windows 2000 Professional, components that were optional with Windows NT 4.0 or earlier and Windows 95 or Windows 98 are now automatically installed by Setup, such as Notepad, Paint, and some network-related components. To support the installation of these optional components, Windows 2000 Setup provides a mechanism that allows any number of these components to be installed on a stand-alone computer after setup has finished.

If you want to install additional components from within Windows 2000 Professional, you can use the Add/Remove Programs in Control Panel. After you click the **Add/Remove Windows Components** icon, a screen appears, giving a list of components. These include:

- Indexing Service
- Internet Information Services
- Management and Monitoring Tools
- Message Queuing Services

- Networking Services
- Other Network File and Print Services
- Script Debugger

Note If you want to install or remove components after Setup has finished, you must have administrator privileges.

Figure 4.10 shows the optional components available for Windows 2000 Professional.

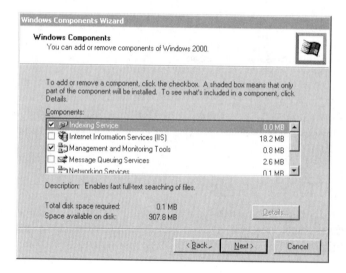

Figure 4.10   Windows 2000 Professional Optional Components

Some components contain subcomponents. These can be viewed by clicking the **Details** button, located on the **Windows Components Wizard** dialog box. Figure 4.11 shows the subcomponents of the Microsoft® Internet Information Services (IIS) component.

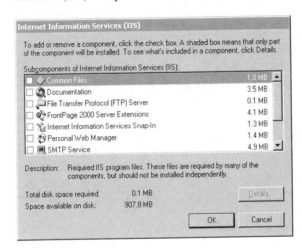

Figure 4.11   IIS Details

You can add or remove additional components by using the Add/Remove Programs facility, which can be accessed in **Control Panel**.

After choosing the optional components you want, you are asked to restart the computer to complete the configuration.

Post-Installation Tasks

After completing the installation process on a stand-alone computer, you must log on to the operating system as an administrator to create new accounts, join a workgroup or domain, or create an emergency repair disk.

Logging on to Windows 2000 Professional

When your computer restarts after installation, log on to Windows 2000 Professional for the first time.

On a clean installation of Windows 2000, you are prompted to automatically log on with a user name generated by Setup. If you choose to do this, a user account is created with the suggested name, and you are automatically logged on every time you start the computer.

▶ **To log on to Windows 2000 Professional by using the Administrator account**

1. In the **Log on to Windows 2000** dialog box, type the Administrator password that you created during Setup.

2. Press ENTER.

Note If your system automatically logs you on, but you prefer a standard logon process, you can configure that option through the **Users and Passwords** icon in Control Panel. Double-click **Users and Passwords**, and then select that **Users must enter a user name and password to use this computer** check box.

Joining a Workgroup

A *workgroup* is one or more computers with the same workgroup name. Any user can join a workgroup. If you won't be working on a network, specify that you want to join a workgroup. To join a workgroup, you must provide an existing or new workgroup name, or you can use the workgroup name that Windows 2000 Professional suggests during Setup.

Joining a Domain

A *domain* is a collection of computers defined by a network administrator for security and administrative purposes. Check with your network administrator to see if you need to join a domain.

Joining a domain during Setup requires a computer account in the domain you want to join. If you're upgrading from Windows NT Workstation, Setup uses your existing computer account. Otherwise, you'll be asked to provide a new computer account. Ask your network administrator to create a computer account before you begin Setup. Or, if you have the appropriate privileges, you can create the account during Setup, and then join the domain. To join a domain during Setup, you need to provide your Domain user name and password.

Note A *computer account* differs from your user account in that it identifies your computer to the domain, but a *user account* identifies you to your computer.

If you have difficulty joining a domain during Setup, join a workgroup instead, and then join the domain after you finish installing Windows 2000 Professional.

If you're joining a domain, the Network Identification wizard appears before you can log on to Windows 2000 Professional to help you connect your computer to a network.

Creating a User Account

Your user account identifies your user name and password, the groups of which you're a member, which network resources you have access to, and your personal files and settings. Each person who regularly uses the computer needs a user account. A user name and a password, both of which the user types when logging on to the computer, identify the user account. You can create individual user accounts after logging on to the computer as Administrator.

Note Windows 2000 Professional has two types of user accounts: *domain user accounts* and *local user accounts*. With a domain user account, a user can log on to the domain to gain access to network resources. With a local user account, a user logs on to a specific computer to gain access to resources only on that computer. If you're not sure which account you need, check with your network administrator. Domain user accounts are created by network administrators and need to be added to local groups; they cannot be created on the local computers.

Creating an Emergency Repair Disk

After a successful installation of Windows 2000 Professional, it's a good idea to create an emergency repair disk in case of a future system failure. For more information about creating an emergency repair disk (ERD), see "Troubleshooting Tools and Strategies" in this book.

Additional Resources

- For more information about Windows 2000 Professional Setup, see Windows 2000 Help.

- For more information about Windows 2000 Professional Setup, see the Pro1.txt and Pro2.txt files in the \Setuptxt folder on the Windows 2000 Professional operating system CD.

- For more information about Windows 2000 Professional hardware support, see the Hardware Update link on the Web Resources page at: http://windows.microsoft.com/windows2000/reskit/webresources.

- For more information about Windows 2000 Compatibility and BIOS issues, see the Windows 2000 Upgrade link on the Web Resources page at: http://windows.microsoft.com/windows2000/reskit/webresources.

C H A P T E R   5

Customizing and Automating Installations

In an organization with a large number of computers, it is more cost effective to automate the installation of Microsoft® Windows® 2000 Professional than it is to use the standard interactive Setup program to install it manually on individual computers. Windows 2000 Professional includes methods and tools that allow you to add specific components and applications to your installation and to distribute that customized installation to the end-user with little or no intervention. In Windows 2000 Professional, you customize your installation by using answer files and by adding files and applications of your choice to a distribution folder. There are a variety of tools that you can use to distribute customized Windows 2000 Professional installations to destination computers. The method you use depends on your current environment and needs.

In This Chapter

Related Information in the Resource Kit

- For more information about installing Windows 2000 Professional on a stand-alone computer, see "Installing Windows 2000 Professional" in this book.

- For more information about creating answer files, see "Sample Answer Files for Windows 2000 Professional Setup" in this book.

- For more information about planning Microsoft® Windows® 2000 deployments, see the *Microsoft® Windows® 2000 Server Resource Kit Deployment Planning Guide*.

Quick Guide to Customizing and Automating Installations

Windows 2000 Professional provides tools and methods for customizing and automating installations to meet a range of user requirements and software and hardware configurations. Use this guide to understand the steps in the customization and automation process and to choose the best tool and method for your needs.

Understand the process and tools for customizing and automating an installation.

Familiarize yourself with the steps involved in customizing and automating a Windows 2000 Professional installation. Determine the best methods and tools to use for installing Windows 2000 Professional and Microsoft® Windows® 95, Microsoft® Windows® 98, or Microsoft® Windows NT® version 4.0.

- See "Overview of Customizing and Automating Installations " in this chapter.

Plan for the most appropriate method to customize and automate your installation.

Plan your installation by conducting an inventory of your existing computers; assessing your network infrastructure; and determining your organization's user types, requirements, and preferences. You must know, for example, the number of computers in your organization; their existing software and hardware configurations; whether applications are required or optional; protocols and network speed; and whether or not there is a Windows 2000 Server infrastructure in place when you deploy Windows 2000 Professional. Choose the appropriate tools and methods for your existing environment.

- See "Step 1: Plan" in this chapter.

Prepare for a successful customized and automated installation.

Prepare for your installation: find the information you need; verify that you have the required hardware and software; set up a distribution folder; and create an answer file.

- See "Step 2: Prepare" in this chapter.

Modify the answer file and populate the distribution folder.

Add entries in the answer file to automate specific tasks during installation. Populate the distribution folder by adding files, programs, and applications of your choice. These can include mass storage device drivers, Plug and Play device drivers, and applications.

- See "Step 3: Customize" in this chapter.

Distribute your customized installation files and start Setup on the destination computers.

Run Setup in unattended mode (Winnt.exe or Winnt32.exe with the **/u** switch) on individual computers, over the network, or on a master computer to create a master installation. If you are not automating the installation individually on each computer, you can choose one of the imaging tools (System Preparation tool [Sysprep] or Remote Installation Services [RIS]) or a network management tool (Microsoft® Systems Management Server) to distribute your customized installation files and start Setup on the destination computer.

- See "Step 4: Deploy" in this chapter.

Overview of Customizing and Automating Installations

In large organizations which support hundreds or even thousands of desktop computers, it is expensive and inefficient to install the operating system manually on each computer, and to answer every question Setup asks. In this environment, it is often necessary to automate the installation process. Different software and hardware configurations and varying user needs also make it necessary to customize installations.

An *automated installation* involves running Setup with minimal or no user interaction. Questions asked when Setup is running, are answered by an answer file. An *answer file* or *script file* is a text file with a specific format that contains predefined settings and information used by Setup. It can also contain optional information or instructions for running programs and applications.

A *custom installation* is a modification of a standard Windows 2000 Professional installation that supports specific hardware and software configurations and meets specific user needs. To customize an installation, modify the answer file to provide Setup with specific answers and instructions and add specific custom files, applications, and programs to the distribution folder.

Customization and Automation Process

The process for customizing and automating a Windows 2000 Professional installation includes the following steps:

1. Plan

   Gather the data you need to choose the appropriate tool for installing the operating system in your organization. As you plan for the installation, determine types of users and their needs; conduct an inventory of existing clients and assess your network infrastructure.

2. Prepare

   Gather all necessary information, verify that you have the software and hardware that you need, create a distribution folder, and create an answer file.

3. Customize

   Add devices, drivers, applications, Help files, support information, and other components of your choice.

4. Deploy

   Deploy the operating system in an automated fashion using the tool you chose in step 1.

Each of these steps is described in detail in this chapter. Figure 5.1 illustrates the entire process.

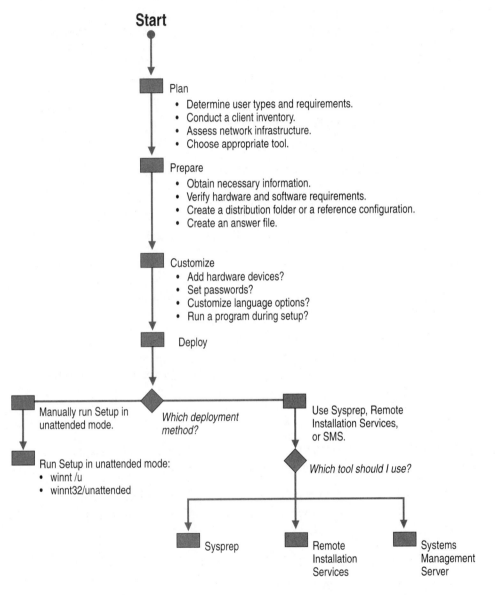

Figure 5.1   Generic Method for Automating and Customizing Installations

What's New

Windows 2000 Professional introduces many new features that simplify the process of customizing and automating an installation. It also includes enhancements to existing features in other versions of Windows, making it easier, more efficient, and less expensive to customize, automate, and deploy an installation of the operating system. Some of the most important features and benefits of Windows 2000 Professional include the following:

Setup Manager, for more efficient creation of answer files. Setup Manager is a wizard that guides you through the process of creating a custom answer file. You can use it to set many of the answer file parameters that customize and automate an installation. Using this tool also minimizes data-entry errors that are more likely to happen when using a text editor to create the answer file.

Greater choice of tools and methods. Windows 2000 Professional provides customization and automation tools and methods. Choose from either an improved version of the traditional unattended installation method or from new imaging tools, such as Remote Installation Services (RIS) and the System Preparation Tool (Sysprep). Your choice depends on the specific needs of users in your organization, your computer configurations and models, your existing network infrastructure, and the number of computers participating in the customization and automation process.

Easier to customize components. With Windows 2000 Professional you can customize nearly all installation components, including installing modems, installing sound cards, presetting passwords, presetting time zones, detecting display options, and automatically converting file allocation table (FAT16/FAT32) file systems to NTFS. You can also automate computer-specific information, such as setting static IP addresses or using a list of computer names.

Automatic application installation. Windows 2000 Professional enables you to conveniently install applications during the automation process.

Flexibility in your choice of hardware. You can install devices on computers running Windows 2000 Professional that do not have built-in support in the operating system.

Audit capability. Windows 2000 Professional allows you audit and test installations.

Methods and Tools for Customizing and Automating Installations

The primary methods and tools available for automating and customizing Windows 2000 Professional installations are the following.

Unattended installations using Winnt.exe and Winnt32.exe.   Unattended installations allow administrators to completely or partially automate installation of Windows 2000 Professional on multiple computers, requiring minimal user input.

Disk duplication using Sysprep.exe.   Disk duplication, or imaging, is a method for duplicating a configuration to multiple destination computers. The destination computers might be part of a network or nonnetworked. Sysprep works on computers that have similar hardware configurations with identical hardware controllers and hardware abstraction layers (HALs) as the source computer.

Remote Installations using Remote Installation Services.   Remote installation allows you to perform clean installations of Windows 2000 Professional on clients that are part of a Microsoft® Windows® 2000 Server–based network and that are properly configured to support RIS. With this technology, clients use a RIS server to start remotely and to install Windows 2000 Professional and applications.

Electronic distribution using Systems Management Server or third-party software management software.
Microsoft® Systems Management Server version 2.0 provides tools that allows administrators to centrally deploy and manage Windows 2000 Professional.

Feature Comparison with Previous Versions of Windows

Depending on whether you are upgrading from Windows 95, Windows 98, or Microsoft® Windows NT® Workstation version 4.0, you might be familiar with the customization and automation tools available in Windows 2000 Professional.

Windows 95

Use Table 5.1 to compare the customization tools used for Windows 95 with those prescribed for Windows 2000 Professional.

Table 5.1   Comparison of Customization Tools for Windows 95 and Windows 2000 Professional

Windows 95	Windows 2000 Professional
Use NetSetup to create answer files.	Use Setup Manager to create answer files.
You can perform unattended installations but no support is provided for: ▪ Third-party drivers. ▪ Multiple network adapters. ▪ Microsoft® Internet Explorer and Proxy services. ▪ Selection of components (Notepad).	You can perform unattended installations with added support allowing the following: ▪ Plug and Play drivers can be added to the distribution folder for automation. ▪ Multiple network adapters can be configured. ▪ Internet Explorer and proxy services with answer files or IEAK.ins files can be configured. Support is also provided for selection of components.
Create an answer file in Msbatch.inf format by using NetSetup.	Create an answer file in Unattend.txt format by using Setup Manager or a text editor, such as Notepad.
Use Msbatch.inf to customize system settings, force Setup options, and copy additional files.	Use answer files in Unattended.txt format to customize system settings, force Setup options, and copy additional files.
Use NetSetup to prepare a network server to run Setup.exe on client computers.	Use Setup Manager to create a distribution folder and copy the Windows 2000 Professional installation files and optional components. – Or – Use Remote Installation Services (RIS). – Or – Use Systems Management Server (SMS).
Add device drivers by using a trial and error process.	Add device drivers by using the distribution folder and answer files.
Use Automate.inf to create answer files that include the Windows 95 Accessibility Options.	Accessibility options are installed by default.
Use Netdet.ini to detect components on NetWare networks.	Use the [NetProtocols], [params.MS_NWIPX], and related sections in the answer file to detect components on NetWare networks.
Use Wrkgrp.ini to specify a list of workgroups that users can join.	Use the [Identification] section in the answer file to specify a list of workgroups that users can join.
Use System policies and user profiles to customize the desktop contents and restrict users' abilities to change configurations.	Use Group Policy to customize the desktop contents and restrict users' abilities to change configurations.

Windows 98

Use Table 5.2 to compare the customization tools used for Windows 98 with those prescribed for Windows 2000 Professional.

Table 5.2   Comparison of Customization Methods for Windows 98 and Windows 2000 Professional

Windows 98	Windows 2000 Professional
Use Microsoft Batch 98 to create Setup scripts.	Use Setup Manager to create answer files.
You can perform unattended installations but no support is provided for: ▪ Third-party drivers. ▪ Multiple network adapters. ▪ Microsoft® Internet Explorer and Proxy services. ▪ Selection of components (Notepad).	You can perform unattended installations with added support allowing the following: ▪ Plug and Play drivers can be added to the distribution folder for automation. ▪ Multiple network adapters can be configured. ▪ Internet Explorer and proxy services with answer files or IEAK.ins files can be configured. Support is also provided for selection of components.
Use Msbatch.inf to customize system settings, force Setup options, and copy additional files.	Use answer files in Unattended.txt format to customize system settings, force Setup options, and copy additional files.
To install the operating system over the network, use a simple drag-and-drop solution: copy the Windows 98 CAB files to an installation point on a network server.	To install the operating system over the network, use Setup Manager to create a distribution folder and copy the Windows 2000 Professional installation files and optional components to that central installation point. – Or – Use Remote Installation Services (RIS). – Or – Use Systems Management Server.
Use INF Installer (Infinst.exe) to add device drivers.	Use the distribution folder, the [MassStorageDrivers] and [OEMBootFiles] sections in the answer file, and Txtsetup.oem file to add device drivers.
Use Preptool to duplicate (image) custom Windows 98 installations.	Use Sysprep to duplicate (image) custom Windows 2000 Professional installations.
Use Microsoft Batch 98 to generate a script with the Windows 98 accessibility options.	Accessibility options are installed by default.
Use Netdet.ini to detect components on NetWare networks.	Use the [NetProtocols], [params.MS_NWIPX], and related sections in the answer file to detect components on NetWare networks.
Use Wrkgrp.ini to specify a list of workgroups that users can join.	Use the [Identification] section in the answer file to specify a list of workgroups that users can join.
Use System policies and user profiles to customize the desktop contents and restrict users' abilities to change configurations.	Use Group Policy to customize the desktop contents and restrict users' abilities to change configurations.
Use Apps.inf to automate upgrades from Windows 95 to Windows 98.	Use Setup in unattended mode or Systems Management Server to automate upgrades from Windows 98 to Windows 2000 Professional.

Windows NT Workstation 4.0

If you are upgrading from Windows NT Workstation 4.0, refer to Table 5.3 to compare the customization methods you used to the methods available in Windows 2000 Professional.

Table 5.3   Comparison of Customization Methods for Windows NT Workstation 4.0 and Windows 2000 Professional

Windows NT Workstation 4.0	Windows 2000 Professional
Use Setup Manager to create Setup scripts.	Use the improved version of Setup Manager to create answer files.
You can perform unattended installations but no support is provided for: • Third-party drivers. • Multiple network adapters. • Microsoft® Internet Explorer and Proxy services. • Selection of components (Notepad).	You can perform unattended installations with added support allowing the following: • Plug and Play drivers can be added to the distribution folder for automation. • Multiple network adapters can be configured. • Internet Explorer and proxy services with answer files or IEAK.ins files can be configured. Support is also provided for selection of components.
Sysprep.exe is used to replicate model computer configurations to destination computers with exactly the same hardware. • There is no support for regional options. • Sysprep.exe is available only with a signed license. • There is no support for configuring network and domain components.	Enhanced Sysprep.exe is used to replicate model computer configurations to destination computers with diverse hardware. The hardware controller and HAL must still be identical on the destination computers. • Sysprep.exe can be used for networked computers. • Support is provided for regional options and multiple languages. • Sysprep.exe is integrated with the operating system; no license is required.

Step 1: Plan

Effective planning helps minimize the time and effort spent in deploying Windows 2000 Professional. Planning for a custom and automated installation is critical for a successful installation. During this step of the process, you gather the data you need to choose the appropriate tool for installing the operating system in a way that best suits organization. As you plan for the installation, you must determine types of users and their needs; conduct an inventory of existing clients and assess your network infrastructure.

For an overview about how to plan Windows 2000 Professional deployment and installations, see "Deploying Windows 2000 Professional" in this book. For a thorough discussion about this subject, see the chapters under "Network Infrastructure Prerequisites" in the *Deployment Planning Guide.*

User Types and Requirements

Assess the requirements of your users and define user types. User requirements and types are important factors in deciding what to customize and how to conduct an automated installation. For example, if a group of users needs a specific application, you must add it to the distribution folder or customize the answer file so that Setup installs it as part of the unattended installation.

There are many ways to classify user types. Some criteria include the level of computer knowledge (such as beginning, intermediate, or advanced); location (such as on-site, roaming, or remote); job function (such as members of marketing, research, or customer service departments), or job categories (such as manager, project lead, or individual contributor).

For example, after you have classified users into groups or types by computer knowledge, you determine how many and what choices you give a particular group in an installation. You want to allow less knowledgeable or task-oriented users to make few or no choices during installation. Advanced users might require additional choices during installation. So then in this case you might decide to have two different answer files—one for beginner users and another for those with more experience.

User requirements might also include language (English or Spanish), regional options (country/region and time zone), and applications (line-of-business applications, spreadsheets, word-processing applications).

Table 5.4 lists key planning issues related to user requirements and types and describes how these issues might affect your plan.

Table 5.4   Key Planning Issues for User Types and Requirements

Issue	Effect on Your Plan
User types	User types affect the how you customize the Setup wizard, what security settings you use, network configuration, and so on. Examples of sections in the answer file that depend on user types include [URL] and [Components], which contain the parameters that define the settings for the Windows 2000 browser and components (such as Calculator, CD Player, and desktop wallpaper).
Language and regional options requirements	Language and regional requirements determine how to customize language and regional options in the [RegionalSettings] section of the answer file.
Application requirements	Application requirements for your users affect how you populate the distribution folder and how you modify the answer file. Determine which applications are required, which are optional, and which ones have to be advertised only to specific users. If Windows 2000 Professional is used in a Windows 2000 Server–based network, determine if applications will be deployed using Group Policy. If an application, must be part of an installation, automate the installation of applications by using Cmdlines.txt, the [GuiRunOnce] section of the answer file or Sysdiff. If the applications must be advertised later, use Windows Installer.
	The use of Windows Installer is beyond the scope of this chapter. For more information, see Windows 2000 Professional Help.

Conduct an Inventory of Clients

Conduct an inventory of your existing clients to determine the number of clients, types of existing desktop operating systems, and types of hardware configurations in your organization. Table 5.5 lists key planning issues related to conducting an inventory and explains how these issues affect your plan.

Table 5.5   Key Planning Issues for Conducting an Inventory

Issue	Effect on Your Plan
Types of desktop operating system	What desktop operating systems are used—whether Windows 95, Windows 98, Windows NT Workstation 4.0, and so on—determine whether you perform an upgrade or a clean installation. Some tools, such as Systems Management Server, can only be used to upgrade existing Windows operating systems. Windows 3.*x* clients cannot be upgraded to Windows 2000 Professional; you must perform a clean installation.
Number of clients	The number of computers you have has an impact on your choice of tool for automating an installation. For example, if you have a large number of computers, Sysprep, RIS, or Systems Management Server are good choices. For a small number of computers, using the Winnt.exe or Winnt32.exe programs in unattended mode (with the **/u** or **/unattend** switch, respectively) alone might be sufficient.
Types of hardware configuration	Hardware configurations affect your choice of tool for automating an installation and which hardware devices must be added to the distribution folder and specified in the answer file.
	For an example of the effect of hardware configuration on your **choice of tool**, consider that if you choose to use Sysprep, all computers (master computer and destination computers) must have the same HAL, Advanced Configuration and Power Interface (ACPI), and mass storage devices.
	For an example of the effect of hardware configuration on your **migration path**, consider the difference between keeping existing hardware and buying new hardware.
	For an example of the effect of hardware configuration on your **adding hardware devices** to the distribution folder and specifying then in the answer file, consider mass storage devices such as SCSI hard drives. Windows 2000 Professional Setup detects and installs most hardware devices automatically. However, to install a SCSI device that is not supported by Windows 2000 Professional during the text-mode phase of Setup, you must add the driver files for that SCSI device and its Textsetup.oem file to the distribution folder (OEM subfolder) and you must modify the [MassStorageDrivers] section of the answer file with the appropriate driver entries.
Software and hardware compatibility	Ensure that the hardware on the target computer meets the minimum requirements mentioned earlier and that the individual components are listed in the Hardware Compatibility List (HCL). For more information, see the HCL link on the Web Resources page at http://windows.microsoft.com/windows2000/reskit/webresources

Assess Your Network Infrastructure

Assess your network infrastructure by identifying existing network protocols, speed of network links (network bandwidth), and whether or not there is a Windows 2000 Server–based network infrastructure in place when you install Windows 2000 Professional.

Table 5.6 lists key planning issues related to assessing your network infrastructure and describes how these issues affect your plan.

Table 5.6   Key Planning Issues for Assessing the Network Infrastructure

Issue	Effect on Your Plan
Network infrastructure	Network protocols determine how you customize network protocol and associated adapter parameters in several networking sections of the answer file, such as the [NetAdapter], [NetProtocols], and [NetServices] sections.
Network bandwith	The amount of network bandwidth available affects your choice of installation tool and method. For example, in locations that do not have a high-bandwidth connection to a network server, using a CD-ROM drive or other local method of installing Windows 2000 Professional (carrying out **winnt or winnt32** at the command prompt on each computer) is probably the best option. For users with high-bandwidth network connections, but whose computers do not have a remote boot–compliant network adapter or a computer that can be started from a CD, a network-based image duplication or manual installation method is the next best option.
Windows 2000 Server network infrastructure	Having an existing Windows 2000 Server infrastructure in place affects the range of tools you can use to automate and customize installations. For example, if you have a Windows 2000 Server–based computer configured as a RIS server, you can use RIS to image and automatically distribute customized images of a Windows 2000 Professional installation to users.

Choose the Appropriate Tool

Choose the appropriate tools and methods for your existing environment based on the information you gathered in your plan as explained in the previous sections. Table 5.7 provides guidelines to help you choose the appropriate tool for your particular environment.

Table 5.7   Guidelines for When to Use a Tool for Customizing and Automating Installations

Tool	When to Use
Winnt.exe or Winnt32.exe	Use Winnt.exe when running Setup on Microsoft® MS-DOS® or Microsoft® Windows® 3.1–based clients. Perform an automated installation by specifying the **/u** switch and using an answer file. Use this tool locally on each computer or remotely over the network.
	Use Winnt32.exe when upgrading Windows 95, Windows 98, Windows NT Workstation 4.0, or beta versions of Windows 2000 to Windows 2000 Professional. Perform an automated installation by specifying the **/unattend** switch. Use this tool to run Setup locally on each computer, remotely over the network, for a clean installation, or for an upgrade.
	These tools are appropriate for installing Windows 2000 Professional on a large number of clients with different hardware and software configurations.
	The major advantage of these tools is their flexibility. When you run the commands manually, the disadvantage is that you must use them on each computer individually. The disadvantage of this tool is that you must install applications individually on each computer.
Sysprep	Use Sysprep to install an identical configuration, including applications, on multiple computers. Sysprep allows you to duplicate a custom image based on a Windows 2000 Professional installation from a master computer to destination computers. Both the master and destination computers must have similar hardware and software configurations. The master computer and the destination computers must have the same HAL and mass storage device controllers.
	You can also use Sysprep if you have slow network links, in which case you can burn the image of the master computer on CDs and use the CDs to distribute the customized installation.
	You can use Sysprep for clean installations only, not for upgrades.
Remote Installation Services (RIS)	Use RIS when you want to standardize a Windows 2000 Professional configuration on new computers or on computers with an existing operating system that you can replace with Windows 2000 Professional. With RIS you can create two types of media: CDs or images.
	RIS uses the Pre-Boot eXecution environment (PXE) to initiate a Windows 2000 Professional installation from a RIS server computer and then install the operating system on a client's hard disk.
	The major advantage of RIS is that it allows you to standardize your Windows 2000 Professional installation, enables you to customize and control the end-user installation (you can configure the end-user Setup wizard with specific choices that can be controlled by using Group Policy), and gives you a choice of media to distribute the software.
	You can use RIS for clean installations only, not for upgrades.
Systems Management Server	Use Systems Management Server to perform managed upgrades of Windows 2000 Professional to multiple computers, especially those that are geographically dispersed.
	The primary advantage of upgrading by using Systems Management Server is that you can maintain centralized control of the upgrade process. For example, you can control when upgrades take place, which computers to upgrade, and how to apply network constraints.
	You can use Systems Management Server for upgrades of Windows–based clients only, not for clean installations.

Where Do You Find These Tools and Related Information?

Table 5.8 provides the locations of the tools and related information.

Table 5.8   Where to Find the Windows 2000 Professional Installation Tools

Tool/Information	Go To
Winnt.exe	\i386
Winnt32.exe	\i386
Sysprep.exe	Support\Tools\deploy.cab on the Windows 2000 Professional operating system CD
Syspart	Support\Tools\deploy.cab on the Windows 2000 Professional operating system CD
RIS for Remote Installation Services	Included in Microsoft Windows 2000 Server under Administrative Tools.
Systems Management Server	Systems Management Server product CD.
Sysdiff	Microsoft OEM System Builder Web site at: http://oem.microsoft.com/
Setup Manager	Support\Tools\deploy.cab on the Windows 2000 operating system CD
Sample answer files	"Sample Answer Files for Windows 2000 Professional Setup" later in this book
Windows 2000 product family CDs	General packaging
Microsoft Windows 2000 Guide to Unattended Setup (Unattend.doc)	Support\Tools\deploy.cab on the Windows 2000 operating system CD

Step 2: Prepare

To prepare for a custom and automated installation, perform the following steps.

1. Get all the necessary information.
2. Verify that you have the hardware and software you need.
3. Create a distribution folder.
4. Create an answer file.

The following sections explain what you must do to accomplish these tasks.

Get the Necessary Information

Table 5.9 provides a checklist of the information you need to get before automating and customizing an installation.

Table 5.9   Checklist for Preparing to Customize and Automate an Installation

Information	Reference
Obtain latest installation information.	Relnotes.txt and Read1st.txt on the Windows 2000 Professional operating system CD.
Understand the Windows 2000 setup process.	"Setup and Startup" in this book.
Verify hardware compatibility.	For the most up-to-date list of supported hardware, see the Hardware Compatibility List link on the Web Resources page at http://windows.microsoft.com /windows2000/reskit/webresources
	For a version that was accurate as of the date Windows 2000 Professional was released, see Windows 2000 Professional operating system CD in *drive*:\Support\Hcl.txt.
Choose between performing an upgrade of your existing operating system and performing a clean installation.	"Installing Windows 2000 Professional" in this book.
Back up your data.	"Installing Windows 2000 Professional" earlier in this book.
Consider issues for multiple-boot configurations: Do you want to be able to choose between different operating systems each time you start your computer?	"Installing Windows 2000 Professional" in this book.
Create disk partitions: Do you have to create disk partitions or make changes to your existing disk partitions?	"Installing Windows 2000 Professional" in this book and "Sysprep" later in this chapter.
Decide what components are required for your customization: Choose what hardware, drivers, applications, and optional files you want to add to the distribution folder.	"Step 3: Customize" later in this chapter.
If you are running Winnt.exe or Winnt32.exe over the network: Select network connectivity, bootable floppy disks, or a bootable compact disc to connect to the distribution share that contains the installation files.	"Running Setup from the Operating System CD" in this chapter.

Verify Hardware and Software Requirements

Table 5.10 provides a checklist of the hardware and software you need to customize and automate an installation.

Table 5.10   Checklist of Hardware and Software Requirements for Customizing and Automating an Installation

Hardware and Software Requirements	Reference
If you are using Sysprep:	"Sysprep" later in this chapter.
• **Master (reference) computer.** This is the computer on which you install Windows 2000 Professional customized to your specifications. Use the installation on this master computer to generate the image that is used to install Windows 2000 Professional on the destination computers.	
• **Destination computers.** These are the computers to which you distribute the installation of Windows 2000 Professional from the master image.	
• **Disk-duplicating equipment or software.** You must have third-party hard disk–duplicating tools such as Ghost or PowerQuest drive image software to generate the master image for distribution to the destination computers.	
If you are using RIS:	"Remote Installation Services" later in this chapter.
• **A Windows 2000 Server computer configured as RIS server.** This configuration requires the Dynamic Host Configuration Protocol (DHCP), a Domain Name System (DNS) server, Active Directory, a RIS server, and Group Policy.	*Microsoft® Windows® 2000 Server Resource Kit Distributed Systems Guide.*
If you are using Systems Management Server:	"Using Systems Management Server" later in this chapter.
• **Systems Management Server software** configured on a Windows 2000 Server computer.	*Microsoft® Systems Management Server Resource Kit.*

Create a Distribution Folder

A *distribution folder* is a hierarchical folder structure that contains the Windows 2000 installation files, as well as any device drivers and other files that are required to customize and automate an installation. You can create one or many distribution folders. Distribution folders typically reside on a server to which the destination computers on which you want to install Windows 2000 Professional can connect.

One of the most important advantages of using a distribution folder is that it provides a consistent environment for installing Windows 2000 Professional on multiple computers. You can use the same distribution folder for all computers with the same processor platform. For example, if you are installing Windows 2000 on different models of computers with same processor platform, all your answer files can reference the same distribution folder, provided it contains the necessary drivers for all models. Then, if a hardware component changes, you can place the new drivers in the subfolder, rather than change the answer file.

To help load balance the servers and make the file-copy phase of Windows 2000 Setup faster for computers already running Windows 95, Windows 98, Windows NT Workstation 4.0, or Windows 2000, you can create distribution folders on multiple servers. You can then run Winnt32.exe with up to eight source file locations.

Distribution Folder Structure

Figure 5.2 shows the distribution folder structure that you must create and the relative location of each subfolder.

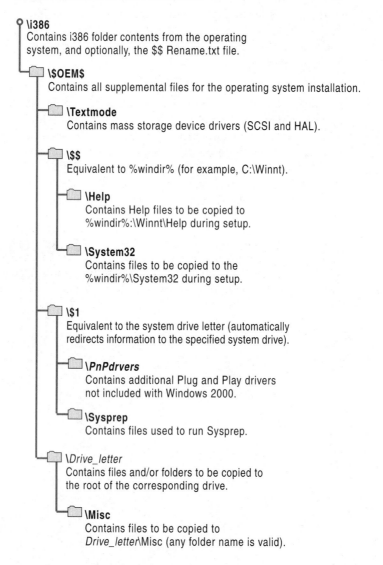

\i386
Contains i386 folder contents from the operating system, and optionally, the $$ Rename.txt file.

\OEM
Contains all supplemental files for the operating system installation.

\Textmode
Contains mass storage device drivers (SCSI and HAL).

\$$
Equivalent to %windir% (for example, C:\Winnt).

\Help
Contains Help files to be copied to %windir%:\Winnt\Help during setup.

\System32
Contains files to be copied to the %windir%\System32 during setup.

\$1
Equivalent to the system drive letter (automatically redirects information to the specified system drive).

\PnPdrvers
Contains additional Plug and Play drivers not included with Windows 2000.

\Sysprep
Contains files used to run Sysprep.

\Drive_letter
Contains files and/or folders to be copied to the root of the corresponding drive.

\Misc
Contains files to be copied to Drive_letter\Misc (any folder name is valid).

Figure 5.2   Distribution Folder Structure

\i386 Folder

This folder is the distribution folder. You create it at the root of the distribution server (the server on which the distribution folder is located) by copying the contents of \i386 on the Windows 2000 Professional operating system CD to the distribution folder. The \i386 folder includes the following files and folders.

$$Rename.txt File

The $$Rename.txt file contains a list of files that Setup uses during the installation process to convert specified file names from short to long. Each subfolder in the distribution folder that contains file names that you want to convert from long to short must have its own $$Rename.txt file.

\OEM

This folder, which you create in the distribution folder as a subfolder of the \i386 folder, contains all the additional files required to complete the installation. If you use the OemFilesPath key in the [Unattended] section of the answer file, you can create the \OEM folder outside the distribution folder.

You can instruct Setup to automatically copy directories, standard 8.3 format files, and any tools required for your automated installation to the \OEM subfolder.

One of the additional files that you can add to the \OEM subfolder is Cmdlines.txt. This file contains a list of commands that Setup carries out during its GUI mode. These commands can, for example, run an INF file, an application installation command, Sysdiff.exe, or another executable file. For more information about the Cmdlines.txt file, see "Adding Applications" in this chapter.

Note   In this chapter, the GUI phase of Setup is referred to as "GUI mode," and the text phase of Setup is referred to as "text mode."

As long as Setup finds the \OEM subfolder in the root of the distribution folder, it copies all the files found in this directory to the temporary directory that is created during the text phase of Setup.

\OEM\Textmode

This folder contains the hardware-dependent files that Setup Loader and text-mode Setup install on the destination computer during text-mode setup. These files can include original equipment manufacturer (OEM) HALs; mass storage device drivers; and Txtsetup.oem, which directs the loading and installing of these components.

Be sure to list the Txtsetup.oem file and all the files placed in this folder (HALs and drivers) in the [OEMBootFiles] section of Unattend.txt.

\$OEM\$\\$\$

The \$OEM\$\\$\$ subfolder is equivalent to the *%systemroot%* or *%windir%* environment variables. The subfolder contains additional files that you want copied to the subfolders of the Windows 2000 Professional installation directory. The structure of this subfolder must match the structure of a standard Windows 2000 Professional installation, where \$OEM\$\\$\$ matches *%systemroot%* or *%windir%* (for example, C:\winnt), \$OEM\$\\$\$\System32 matches *%windir%*\System32, and so on. Each subfolder must contain the files that need to be copied to the corresponding system folder on the destination computer.

\$OEM\$\\$\$\Help

This subfolder contains the OEM Help files to be copied to C:\Winnt\Help during setup.

\$OEM\$\\$\$\System32

This subfolder contains files to be copied to the C:\Winnt\System32 folder during setup.

\$OEM\$\\$1

This folder is equivalent to the *SystemDrive* environment variable. For example, if the operating system is installed on drive C, \$OEM\$\\$1 refers back to drive C. The use of a variable makes it possible to rearrange drive letters without creating errors in applications that point to a hard-coded drive letter.

\$OEM\$\\$1*PnPdrvrs*

This folder contains additional Plug and Play drivers not included with Windows 2000. You can replace *PnPdrvrs* with an name of your own choosing with eight or fewer characters.

Note   This folder replaces the Display and Net folders used in Windows NT Workstation 4.0.

\$OEM\$\\$1\Sysprep

This subfolder contains the files required to run the Sysprep tool. For more information about Sysprep, see "Sysprep" later in this chapter.

\OEM*Drive_letter*

Each \$OEM$*Drive_letter* folder contains a subfolder structure that is copied to the root of the corresponding drive in the destination computer during text-mode Setup. For example, files you put in an \$OEM$\C folder are copied to the root of drive C. You can also create subfolders in these folders. For example, \$OEM$\D\Misc creates a \Misc folder on drive D.

Files that must be renamed need to be listed in $$Rename.txt. Note that the files in these subfolders must have short file names.

Creating a Distribution Folder

The easiest way to create a distribution folder is by using Setup Manager, a tool that is available on the Windows 2000 Professional operating system CD.

Follow these steps to create a distribution folder manually:

▶ **To create a distribution folder**

1. Connect to the network server on which you want to create the distribution folder.

2. Create an \i386 folder on the distribution share of the network server.

   To help differentiate between multiple distribution shares for the different editions of Windows 2000 (Windows 2000 Professional, Windows 2000 Server, and Microsoft® Windows® 2000 Advanced Server), choose another name for this folder. If you plan to use localized language versions of Windows 2000 for international branches of your organization, create separate distribution shares for each localized version.

3. Copy the contents of the \i386 folder from the Windows 2000 Professional operating system CD to the folder that you created.

4. In the folder that you created, create a subfolder named \OEM.

   The \OEM subfolder provides the necessary folder structure for supplemental files to be copied to the destination computer during setup. These files include drivers, tools, applications, and any other files required for deployment of Windows 2000 Professional within your organization.

The following information is provided to help make the creation of the distribution folders easier and faster.

Copying a Folder to the System Drive of the Computer

You can copy an additional folder to the system drive during the customization process. For example, you might want to copy a folder containing additional device drivers.

▶ **To copy a folder to the system drive**

1. In the \$OEM$ subfolder of the distribution share, create a subfolder called \$1. This folder maps to *SystemDrive*, the destination drive for the Windows 2000 installation.

2. In the \$1 folder, copy the folder containing the files.

3. Verify that the following statement is in the Unattend.txt answer file:

    ```
    OemPreinstall = Yes
    ```

Important The OemPreinstall = Yes statement is required if you are using the \OEM folder to add any more files to the system.

Create an Answer File

An answer file or Setup script is a text file that follows a specific format and syntax with all the information Setup must have to customize and automate an installation. The Setup program uses this customized script to answer all the questions it asks when it runs in interactive mode without requiring user input.

The answer file is usually named Unattend.txt, but you can use other names. Any valid file name—for example, Comp1.txt, Install.txt, and Setup.txt—can be used, as long as the name is correctly specified in the Setup command. The use of differentiated names for multiple versions of an answer file allows you to build and use as many unique answer files as you need to maintain different scripted installations for different parts of your organization. Note that answer files are also used by other programs such as Sysprep, which uses the optional Sysprep.inf file.

The answer file tells Setup how to interact with the distribution folders and files you have created. For example, in the [Unattended] section of the answer file, there is an "OEMPreinstall" entry that tells Setup to copy the OEM subfolders from the distribution folders to the destination computer.

You can create an answer file by using two tools:

- The Setup Manager wizard to create it automatically.

- A text editor such as Notepad to create it manually.

You can create the answer file from scratch or modify an existing one.

Using the Setup Manager Wizard

The Setup Manager wizard is available on the Windows 2000 Professional operating system CD in the Deploy.cab file of the Support\Tools folder. The Setup Manager wizard helps you create and modify an answer file by providing prompts for the information that is required for the answer file and then creating it. The Setup Manager wizard can create a new answer file, import an existing answer file for modification, or create a new file based on the configuration of the computer on which it is running.

The following is a list of parameters that can be configured with the Setup Manager wizard in the order in which they are presented. The Setup Manager wizard then generates the results as answer file keys.

Set user interaction.   This sets the level of user interaction that is appropriate during the setup process.

Set default user information.   Specify an organization or user name.

Define computer names.   When an administrator enters multiple names during the setup process, Setup Manager automatically generates the UDF file that is required in order to add those unique names to each system during setup. If the administrator imports names from a text file, Setup Manager converts each name to a UDF file. The administrator can also set an option to generate unique machine names.

Set an administrator password.   The administrator can set an administrative password and hide it from users. The Setup Manager wizard can also be set to prompt the user for the administrative password during setup.

Display settings.   The administrator can automatically set the display color depth, screen area, and refresh frequency display settings.

Configure network settings.   Any custom network-setting option that can be configured from the desktop can be configured remotely using the Setup Manager Wizard. The interface for setting network settings in the wizard is the same interface that the user sees on their desktop. Using Setup Manager the administrator can also join computers to a domain or workgroup, or automatically create accounts in the domain.

Set time zone and regional options.   Set the correct time zone using the same property sheet that a user would access to change the time zone locally. Specify regional options such as date, time, numbers, character sets, and keyboard layout.

Set Internet Explorer 5 settings. The administrator can use Setup Manager to carry out the basic setup for Internet connections, such as connecting to proxy servers. If the organization wishes to customize the browser, the administrator can use Setup Manager to access the customization tool that is part of the Internet Explorer Administration Kit available from www.microsoft.com/windows/ieak.

Set telephony settings. Set telephony properties such as area codes and dialing rules.

Add Cmdlines.txt files. These files are used to install additional components, such as applications. For example, the administrator can add the command line to run office setup by including the command line for office setup in the cmdlines.txt file.

Create an installation folder. Use the default installation folder, \\winnt, to generate a unique folder during setup or to set a custom folder.

Install printers. Set up multiple printers as part of the installation process.

Add commands to the Run Once section. Set up commands that run automatically the first time a user logs on. These may include running an application setup program, running a resource kit tool, or changing security settings.

Run commands at the end of setup. Specify commands that run at the end of the setup process and before users log onto the system, such as launching an application setup file.

Copy additional files. Specify additional files to be copied to the user's desktop, such as device-driver libraries. The administrator can also use Setup Manager to specify where these files are copied.

Create a distribution folder. Create a distribution folder on the network that includes the required Windows source files. You can also add files that you want to copy or supply additional device drivers for use with Windows.

Setup Manager cannot perform the following functions:

- Specify system components, such as Internet Information Services.
- Create Txtsetup.oem files.
- Create subfolders in the distribution folder.

Table 5.11 describes some of the most common answer file specifications that are created by Setup Manager.

Table 5.11 Answer File Specifications Created by Setup Manager

Specification	Purpose
Installation path	Specifies the desired path on the destination computer in which to install Windows 2000 Server.
Upgrade option	Specifies whether to upgrade from Windows 95 or Windows 98, Windows NT Workstation 4.0, or Windows 2000.
Destination computer name	Specifies the user name, organization name, and computer name to apply to the destination computer.
Product ID	Specifies the product identification number obtained from the product documentation.
Workgroup or domain	Specifies the name of the workgroup or domain to which the computer belongs.
Time zone	Specifies the time zone for the computer.
Network configuration information	Specifies the network adapter type and configuration with network protocols.

Answer File Format

To create the answer file manually, use a text editor such as Notepad. In general, an answer file consists of section headers, parameters, and values for those parameters. Although most section headers are predefined, you can also define additional section headers. Note that you do not have to specify all possible parameters in the answer file if the installation does not require them. Invalid parameter values generate errors or result in incorrect behavior after Setup. The answer file format is as follows:

```
[section1]
;
;  Section contains keys and the corresponding
;  values for those keys/parameters.
;  keys and values are separated by ' = ' signs
;  Values that have spaces in them usually require double quotes
;  "" around them
;
key = value
 [section2]
key = value
 .
```

Step 3: Customize

When you have created a distribution folder and an answer file, you can start customizing the installation by adding devices, drivers, applications, Help files, support information, and other components of your choice. Depending on what you want to customize, perform either or both of the following tasks:

- Add entries in the answer file to provide specific instructions to be carried out by Setup during installation.

- Populate the distribution folder by adding to it the files, programs, and applications of your choice. These can include mass storage devices, Plug and Play devices, and applications.

You can customize features and components in Windows 2000 Professional. The examples provided cover the following:

- Adding hardware devices, including storage devices, Plug and Play devices, and hardware abstraction layers (HALs).

- Setting passwords for local user accounts. You can also force all users or certain users to change their passwords when they log on after an upgrade from Windows 95 or Windows 98.

- Setting options for language and multilingual support and key descriptions for other regional options such as language-specific keyboard layouts.

- Setting time zones.

- Specifying display settings to ensure that Setup automatically detects the display resolution on a portable computer.

- Specifying file system settings to automatically convert FAT16/FAT 32 file systems to NTFS during installation.

- Specifying BIOS settings to force Setup to use the computer's BIOS to start the computer.

- Using the $$Rename.txt file to automatically convert short file names to long file names.

- Adding applications during the GUI-mode phase of Setup (using Cmdlines.txt), when the user logs on for the first time (using [GuiRunOnce]), using batch files, and packaging applications to be used with the Windows Installer Service.

There are a many Windows 2000 Professional features that you can customize after installation, such as wallpaper, screen saver settings, Active Desktop, custom toolbars and taskbars, and new **Start** and **Programs** menus options. For more information about post-installation customization, see "Introduction to Configuration and Management" and "Customizing the Desktop" in this book.

Adding Hardware Devices

This section details the steps you take to add hardware devices, including:

- Mass storage devices
- Plug and Play devices
- HALs

For the most up-to-date information about hardware devices with Windows 2000, see the Windows Driver and Hardware Development Web site link on the Web Resources page at http://windows.microsoft.com/windows2000/reskit /webresources

Mass Storage Devices

In Windows 2000 Professional, Plug and Play installs most hardware devices, which can be loaded later in the setup process. However, mass storage devices, such as hard disks, must be properly installed for full Plug and Play support to be available during the GUI mode of Setup. For this reason, the installation of mass storage devices is handled differently from that of other hardware devices.

Note   It is not necessary to specify a device if it is already supported by Windows 2000.

To add SCSI devices during text-mode Setup—that is, before full Plug and Play support is available—you must provide a Txtsetup.oem file that describes how Setup needs to install the particular SCSI device. For more information about Txtsetup.oem, see the Microsoft® Windows® 2000 Device Driver Kit.

▶ **To install a mass storage device**

1. In the distribution folder, create the Textmode subfolder in the \OEM subfolder.

2. In the Textmode subfolder, copy the following files, which you obtain from the device vendor (replace the word *Driver* with the appropriate driver name):

   - *Driver*.sys
   - *Driver*.dll
   - *Driver*.inf

- *Driver*.cat
- Txtsetup.oem

Note You must also copy the driver files to the *<PnPdrvrs>* location that you specified for the OemPnPDriversPath parameter in the answer file. For example:

\$OEM$\$1*<PnPdrvrs>**<Storage>*

Some drivers, such as SCSI miniport drivers, might not include a DLL file.

---

3. In the answer file, create a [MassStorageDrivers] section, and include the driver entries that you want to include. For example, a possible entry in the [MassStorageDrivers] section might be the following:

"Adaptec 2940..." = "OEM"

Information for this section can be obtained from the Txtsetup.oem file, which is provided by the hardware manufacturer.

4. In the answer file, create an [OEMBootFiles] section, and include a list of the files in the OEM\Textmode folder. For example, a possible entry to the [OEMBootFiles] section might be the following:

```
[OEMBootFiles]
Driver.sys
Driver.dll
Driver.inf
Txtsetup.oem
```

Where *Driver* is the driver name.

5. In the Txtsetup.oem file, verify that a section named [HardwareIds.Scsi.*yyyyy*] exists. If it does not, create it following this format:

```
[HardwareIds.scsi. yyyy]
id = "xxxxx" , "yyyyy"
```

where *xxxxx* is the device identifier and *yyyyy* is the device service name. For example, for the Symc810 driver, which has a device ID of PCI\VEN_1000&DEV_0001, you create this section:

```
[HardwareIds.scsi.symc810]
id = "PCI\VEN_1000&DEV_0001" , "symc810"
```

Plug and Play Devices

Plug and Play device drivers that are not included on the Windows 2000 Professional operating system CD can easily be added by following the steps in this section. This method works for all Plug and Play device drivers. You can also use this method for updating drivers.

▶ **To add Plug and Play devices**

1. In the \OEM subfolder of the distribution folder, create a subfolder for any special Plug and Play drivers and their INF files, for example:

   OEM\$1\PnPDrvrs

2. In the answer file, edit the [Unattend] key for Plug and Play, adding the path to the list of Plug and Play search drives, for example:

   OEMPnPDriversPath = "PnPDrvrs"

To maintain the folders so that they can accommodate future device drivers, create subfolders for potential device drivers. By dividing the folders into subfolders, you can store device driver files by device type, rather than having all device driver files in one folder. Suggested subfolders types include Audio, Modem, Net, Print, Storage, Video, and Other. An Other folder can give you the flexibility to store new hardware devices that might not be currently known.

If the PnPDrvs folder contains the subfolders Audio, Modem, and Net, the answer file must contain the following line:

   OEMPnPDriversPath = "PnPDrvs\Audio;PnPDrvs\Modem;PnPDrvs\Net"

Note The specified folder is created at the root of the system drive and remains there after setup is complete.

Driver Signatures

If you intend to use any updated drivers, you must first verify that they are properly signed. If they are not, those drivers might not be installed. To verify that drivers are properly signed, contact the vendor.

Driver Signing Policy

In the answer file, the DriverSigningPolicy key in the [Unattended] section specifies how nonsigned drivers are processed during installation.

Important Microsoft strongly advises against using **DriverSigningPolicy = Ignore** unless you have fully tested the device driver in your environment and are sure that it works properly. Using unsigned drivers increases the risk of device driver problems that can effect the performance or stability of your computer.

If you are using **DriverSigningPolicy = Ignore** and you attempt to install a newer, unsigned copy of a driver that is protected by Windows 2000 Professional, the policy level is automatically updated to **Warn**.

For more information about driver signing policy, see Unattend.doc in Support\Tools\Deploy.cab on the Windows 2000 Professional operating system CD.

Hardware Abstraction Layers

To specify HALs for installation, you must have a Txtsetup.oem file and the HAL files, which the vendor provides. Use the same Txtsetup.oem file if you are installing mass storage device drivers. Only one Txtsetup.oem file can be used, so if you have to install HALs and mass storage device drivers, combine entries into one file.

To use third-party drivers, you must make appropriate changes to the answer file. For more information about answer file parameters and syntax, see Unattend.doc in Support\Tools\Deploy.cab on the Windows 2000 Professional operating system CD.

▶ **To install a HAL**

1. If you have not already done so, create a Textmode subfolder in the \OEM folder.

2. Copy the files that you receive from the device vendor to the Textmode subfolder.

3. In the answer file, edit the [Unattend] section for the HAL, adding any drivers that you want to install. For example, type the following:

```
[Unattend]
Computertype = "HALDescription   ", OEM
```

   Information for the *HALDescription* can be obtained from the [Computer] section of the Txtsetup.oem file from the driver provider.

4. In the answer file, create an [OEMBootFiles] section, and enter the names of the files in the \OEM\Textmode folder.

Setting Passwords

When upgrading from Windows 95 or Windows 98, you can customize your answer files to set passwords for all local user accounts and to force all users or specific users to change their passwords when they first log on. You can also set passwords for the local Administrator account.

Table 5.12 describes the types of passwords that you can set in an answer file:

Table 5.12   Types of Passwords That Can Be Set in an Answer File

Section in Answer File	Key	Usage
[Win9xUpg]	DefaultPassword	Used to automatically set a password for all local accounts created when upgrading from Windows 95 or Windows 98 to Windows 2000 Professional.
[Win9xUpg]	ForcePassword	Used to force users for all local accounts to change their passwords when they log on for the first time after upgrading from Windows 95 or Windows 98 to Windows 2000 Professional.
[Win9xUpg]	UserPassword	Used to force specific users to change their passwords on their local accounts when they log on for the first time after upgrading from Windows 95 or Windows 98 to Windows 2000 Professional.
[GuiUnattended]	AdminPassword	Used to automatically set the password for the local Administrator account.

Setting Passwords on All Local Accounts

For Windows 95 or Windows 98 upgrades, you can customize your answer file to set all local account passwords to a default value.

▶ **To set passwords on all local accounts**

- In your answer file, add the following entry in the [Win9xUpg] section:

```
[Win9xUpg]
DefaultPassword = "password"
```

where *password* is the default password you want to set for all local users.

Note If a local account must be created for a user without a UserPassword entry and no DefaultPassword is specified, Setup creates a random password. After the first restart, the user is prompted to enter a password.

Forcing All Users to Change Local Account Passwords When Upgrading from Windows 95 or Windows 98

For upgrades from Windows 95 or Windows 98, you can customize your answer file to require all users to change their passwords on their local accounts when they log on for the first time. When a user logs on for the first time, he or she is notified that his or her current password has expired and that a new one must be supplied.

▶ **To force users to change their password after an upgrade from Windows 95 or Windows 98**

   ▪ In your answer file, add the following entry in the [Win9xUpg] section:

   ```
   [Win9xUpg]
   ForcePasswordChange = "Yes"
   ```

Creating Passwords for Specific Local Accounts When Upgrading from Windows 95 or Windows 98

For Windows 95 or Windows 98 upgrades, you can customize your answer file to create passwords for specific local accounts. Because Windows 95 and Windows 98 passwords cannot be migrated during the upgrade, Setup must create passwords for local accounts during the upgrade process. Using this key, the administrator can predetermine those passwords for specific users. If a local account needs to be created for a user without a preset value for the UserPassword entry and no value is specified for DefaultPassword, Setup creates a random password.

▶ **To force a user to create a new password after an upgrade from Windows 95 or Windows 98**

   ▪ In the answer file, add the following entry in the [Win9xUpg] section:

   ```
   [Win9xUpg]
   UserPassword = user,password [,user,password......]
   ```

Customizing Language and Regional Options

You can customize the [RegionalSettings] section of your answer file to specify the regional options listed in Table 5.13

Note To use this section of your answer file, you must add, as a minimum, the **/copysource:lang** switch to Winnt32.exe or the **/rx:lang** switch to Winnt.exe. This enables you to copy the appropriate language files to the hard disk. For example, if you are only interested in Korean settings while installing a U.S. version of Windows 2000 Professional, you can specify /copysource:lang\kor if starting from Winnt32.exe.

When specifying OemPreinstall = Yes and not providing values for the [RegionalSettings] section, set OEMSkipRegional = 1 in the [GuiUnattended] section of the answer file to ensure that Setup completes without prompting for regional option information.

Table 5.13   Customizing Regional Options

Key in [RegionalSettings]	Usage
InputLocale	Used to specify the input locale and keyboard layout combinations to be installed on the computer. The first keyboard layout specified is the default layout for the installation. The specified combinations must be supported by one of the language groups defined by using either the LanguageGroup key or the default language group for the language version of Windows 2000 Professional being installed. If an available language group does not support the combination specified, the default combination is used for the installation. This key is ignored if the Language key is specified.
Language	Used to specify the language and locale to be installed on the computer. This language must be supported by one of the language groups specified by using the LanguageGroup key. If an available language group does not support the locale, the default language for the Windows 2000 Professional version being installed is used.
	If this key is specified, the SystemLocale, UserLocale, and InputLocale keys are ignored.
LanguageGroup	Used to specify the supported language group to be installed on the computer. If this key is specified, it provides default settings for SystemLocale, InputLocale, and UserLocale keys.
	For a list of the supported language group IDs, see the LanguageGroup heading in the Unattend.doc provided in \Support\Tools\Deploy.cab on the Windows 2000 Professional operating system CD

(continued)

Table 5.13   Customizing Regional Options *(continued)*

Key in [RegionalSettings]	Usage
SystemLocale	Used to enable localized applications to run and display menus and dialog boxes in the local language.
UserLocale	Used to key control the settings for numbers, time, currency, and dates.

Note   A list of valid locales and their language groups is available at the Global Software Development Web site link on the Web Resources page at http://windows.microsoft.com/windows2000/reskit/webresources.

Note   Any settings specified here are *not* kept if Sysprep is run on the computer.

▶   **To use [RegionalSettings] for multilingual support during Mini-Setup**

1. Create a subfolder named \i386 under \$OEM$\$1\Sysprep\ in the distribution folder.

2. At the command prompt, type the following to copy files from \i386 of the Windows 2000 Professional operating system CD to the \i386 directory in the Sysprep folder:

```
*.nl?
kbd*.dl?
*.fo?
agt*.dl?
agt*.hl?
conime.ex?
wbcache.*
noise.*
wbdbase.*
infosoft.dl?
f3ahvoas.dl?
sylfaen.tt_
c_is*.dl_
\Lang\...
```

Note   You can also use Setup Manager to add the necessary files and folders to the \i386 subfolder.

3. In Sysprep.inf, add the InstallFilesPath key to the [Unattended] section:

```
InstallFilesPath = %systemdrive%\Sysprep\i386
```

For more information about the InstallFilesPath key, see Unattend.doc provided in Support\Tools\Deploy.cab on the Windows 2000 Professional operating system CD.

Note   The \i386 subfolder and its contents are only required if the end user needs language support from one of the language groups provided in that folder.

The \i386 subfolder is deleted after the Mini-Setup wizard has been run on the end user's computer. If you perform an audit, or if a reseller further customizes the computer, you must recreate \Sysprep\i386 and then rerun Sysprep.exe before the image is installed to allow the end-user to specify the necessary regional options.

Presetting Time Zones

You can specify the time zone of the computers in your organization by using the TimeZone key in the [GuiUnattended] section of your answer file or the Sysprep.inf file. If the TimeZone key is not present, the user is prompted for a time zone specification during setup.

▶ **To preset time zones**

- In your answer file, add the following entry in the [GuiUnattended] section:

```
[GuiUnattended]
TimeZone = "index"
```

where *index* specifies the time zone of the computer.

For a list of valid TimeZone indixes, see Unattend.doc in Support\Tools \Deploy.cab on the Windows 2000 Professional operating system CD.

Detecting Video Mode for Portable Computer Displays

You can customize the [Display] section answer file to ensure that Setup automatically detects the display resolution on a portable computer. Specify the optimal settings (you must know what the valid settings are) for the keys listed in Table 5.14. If the settings that you specify are not valid, Setup finds the closest match to the selected settings, but they might not be optimal.

Table 5.14   Customizing Display Settings

Key in [Display]	Usage
BitsPerPel	Specifies the valid bits per pixel for the graphics device being installed. For example, a value of 8 (2^8) implies 256 colors; a value of 16 implies 65,536 colors.
Vrefresh	Specifies a valid refresh rate for the graphics device being installed.
Xresolution	Specifies a valid x resolution for the graphics device being installed.
Yresolution	Specifies a valid y resolution for the graphics device being installed.

▶ **To ensure the video mode is properly detected by Setup**

1. Check that the computer BIOS supports the set of Video ACPI extensions.

2. Check that the drivers for the video cards and displays are included in the \$1\PnPdrvrs path.

3. In the [Unattended] section of the answer file, set the OemPnPDriversPath key to the \$1\PnPdrvrs path.

4. In the [Display] section of the answer file, set the optimal settings for your portable computer.

For the most up-to-date information about hardware devices with Windows 2000 Professional, see the Windows Driver and Hardware Development link on the Web Resources page at http://windows.microsoft.com/windows2000 /reskit/webresources/

Automatically Converting FAT16 and FAT32 to NTFS

You can customize the [Unattended] section of your answer file to convert FAT16 and FAT32 file systems automatically to NTFS.

▶ **To automatically convert FAT16 and FAT32 partitions to NTFS**

- In your answer file, add the following entry in the [Unattend] section:

```
[Unattended]
FileSystem = ConvertNTFS
```

When the FileSystem key is specified, Setup automatically converts your drive just before the GUI mode of Setup starts.

Note The FileSystem = ConvertNTFS key and value do not work in Sysprep.inf.

For more information about the differences between the NTFS, FAT16, and FAT32 file systems, see "File Systems" in this book.

Converting Short File Names to Long File Names

If you are starting Setup from MS-DOS, you can convert short file names to long names by creating a file called $$Rename.txt and putting that file in the subfolder of the distribution folder that also contains the files that you want to convert. If you are starting Setup from any other operating system, they are converted automatically.

Setup uses the list of files that you specify in $$Rename.txt to convert short names to long names during the installation process. You must include a $$Renamte.txt file in each subfolder that contains

The $$Rename.txt file changes short file names to long file names during Setup. $$Rename.txt lists all of the files in a particular folder that must be renamed. Each folder that contains short file names to be renamed must contain its own version of $$Rename.txt.

▶   **To convert short file names to long file names**

- Create a $$Rename.txt file following this syntax:

```
[section_name_1]
short_name_1 = "long_name_1"
short_name_2 = "long_name_2"

short_name_x = "long_name_x"

[section_name_2]
short_name_1 = "long_name_1"
short_name_2 = "long_name_2"

short_name_x = "long_name_x"
```

Where:

section_name_x is the path to the subfolder that contains the files. A section does not have to be named, or it can have a backslash (\) as a name, which indicates that the section contains the names of the files or subfolders that are in the root of the drive.

short_name_x is the name of the file or subfolder within this subfolder to be renamed. The name must *not* be enclosed in quotation marks.

long_name_x is the new name of the file or subfolder. This name must be enclosed in quotation marks if it contains spaces or commas.

Tip   If you are using MS-DOS to start the installation, and your MS-DOS-based tools cannot copy folders with path names longer than 64 characters, use short file names for the folders and then use $$Rename.txt to rename them later.

Adding Applications

There are several methods from which you can choose to add applications to your installation:

- Using Cmdlines.txt to add applications during the GUI mode of Setup.

- Installing applications when the user logs on for the first time by customizing the [GuiRunOnce] section of the answer file.

- Using batch files.

- Using Windows Installer.

- Using the Sysdiff tool to install applications that don't have an automated installation routine.

Using Cmdlines.txt

The Cmdlines.txt file contains the commands that GUI mode runs when installing optional components, such as applications that must be installed immediately after Windows 2000 Professional is installed. If you plan to use Cmdlines.txt, place it in the OEM subfolder of the distribution folder. If you are using Sysprep, place Cmdlines.txt in the OEM\$1\Sysprep subfolder.

Use Cmdlines.txt under following conditions:

- You are installing from the \OEM subfolder of the distribution folder.

- The application that you are installing:

  - Does not configure itself for multiple users (for example, Microsoft® Office 95).

  - Is designed to be installed by one user and to replicate user-specific information.

The syntax for Cmdlines.txt is as follows:

```
[Commands]
"<command_1>"
"<command_2>"
        .
        .
"<command_x>"
```

Keys are defined as follows:

- "<command_1>", "<command_2>", ... "<command_x>" refer to the commands that you want to run (and the order in which you want to run them) when GUI mode calls Cmdlines.txt. Note that all commands must be in quotation marks.

When you use Cmdlines.txt, be aware of the following:

- When the commands in Cmdlines.txt are carried out during setup, there is no logged-on user and there is no guaranteed network connectivity. Therefore, user-specific information is written to the default user registry, and all users receive that information.

- Cmdlines.txt requires that you place the files that you must have to run an application or tool in directories that you can access during the setup process, which means that the files must be on the hard disk.

Important Applications that can be set up by using Windows Installer cannot be added using Cmdlines.txt.

▶ **To specify a Cmdlines.txt file during the mini-Setup portion of Sysprep**

1. Create a Sysprep.inf file to be used by Sysprep. This is a requirement and cannot by bypassed. The Sysprep.inf file must be named Sysprep.inf and be located in the folder Sysprep from the root of the volume that contains the folder *%SystemRoot%*.

2. Place the following entry in the [Unattended] section of the Sysprep.inf file:

   ```
   InstallFilesPath = drive:\path
   ```

   where:

   <path> is any folder you want to use. Microsoft recommends that *<drive>* be the volume containing the *%SystemRoot%* folder.

3. Create the folder *drive:\path*. You can use any folder name you want, but it must match the location that you specified in Sysprep.inf.

4. In the *drive:\path* folder, create a folder named oem, and then place the Cmdlines.txt file in this folder. This file is processed at the end of the mini-Setup wizard, before saving any settings.

Using the [GuiRunOnce] Section of the Answer File

The [GuiRunOnce] section of the answer file contains a list of commands that run the first time a user logs on to the computer after Setup has run. For example, you enter the following line to the [GuiRunOnce] section to start the application installation program automatically.

```
[GuiRunOnce]
"%systemdrive%\appfolder\appinstall -quiet"
```

If you plan to use the [GuiRunOnce] section to initiate an installation, there are some additional factors to take into consideration.

If the application forces a restart, determine whether there is a way to suppress the restart.

This is important because any time the system restarts, all previous entries in the [GuiRunOnce] section are lost. If the system restarts before completing entries previously listed in the [GuiRunOnce] section, the remaining items are not run. If there is no way within the application to suppress a restart, you can try to repackage the application into a Windows Installer package. There are third-party products that provide this functionality.

Windows 2000 includes Veritas WinINSTALL Limited Edition (LE), a repackaging tool for Windows Installer. You can use WinINSTALL LE to efficiently repackage pre-Windows Installer applications into packages that can be distributed with Windows Installer. For more information about WinINSTALL LE, see the Valueadd\3rdparty\Mgmt\Winstle folder on the Windows 2000 Professional operating system CD.

For more information about Windows Installer packaging, see "Using Windows Installer Service" later in this chapter.

Important If you are adding an application to multiple localized language versions of Windows 2000 Professional, it is recommended that you test the repackaged application on the localized versions to ensure that the files are copied to the correct locations and the required registry entries are written appropriately.

If an application requires a Windows Explorer shell to install, the [GuiRunOnce] section does not work because the shell is not loaded when the Run and RunOnce commands are carried out.

Check with the application vendor to determine whether an update or patch is available that can address this situation for the application installation. If not, repackage the application as a Windows Installer package or use another means of distribution.

Applications that use the same type of installation mechanism might not run properly if a /wait switch is not used.

This can happen when an application installation is running and starts another process. When Setup is still running, initiating another process and closing an active one might cause the next routine listed in the RunOnce registry entries to start. Because more than one instance of the installation mechanism is running, the second application usually fails.

Using Application Installation Programs

The preferred method for adding an application is to use the installation routine supplied with the application. You can do this if the application that you are adding can run in *quiet* mode (that is, without user intervention) by using a **/q** or **/s** switch. For a list of switches supported by the installation mechanism, see the application Help file or documentation.

The following is an example of a line that you can place in the [GuiRunOnce] section to initiate the unattended installation of an application by using its own installation program:

```
<path to setup>\Setup.exe /q
```

Setup parameters vary between applications. For example, the **l** parameter included in some applications is useful when you want to create a log file to monitor the installation. Some applications have commands that can keep them from restarting automatically. These commands are useful in helping to control application installations with a minimal number of restarts.

Make sure that you check with the application vendor for information, instructions, tools, and best practices information before you install any application.

Important   You must meet the licensing requirements for any application that you install, regardless of how you install it.

Using a Batch File to Control How Multiple Applications Are Installed

If you want to control how multiple applications are installed, you can create a batch file that contains the individual installation commands and uses the **Start** command with the **/wait** switch. This method ensures that your applications install sequentially and that each application is fully installed before the next application begins its installation routine. The batch file is then run from the [GuiRunOnce] section.

The following procedure explains how to create the batch file, install the application, and remove all references to the batch file after the installation is complete.

▶ **To install applications using a batch file**

1. Create the batch file containing lines similar to the following example:

```
Start /wait <path to 1st application>\Setup <switches>
Start /wait <path to 2nd application>\Setup <switches>
Quit
```

where:

<path> is the path to the executable file that starts the installation. This path must be available during Setup.

Setup is the name of the executable file that starts the installation.

<switches> are any available quiet-mode switches appropriate for the application that you want to install.

2. Copy the batch file to the distribution folders or another location to which you have access during setup.

3. With *<file name>*.bat as the name of the batch file, include an entry in the [GuiRunOnce] section of the answer file to run the batch file, as is done in the following example. This example assumes that the batch file was copied to the Sysprep folder on the local hard disk drive, though it can be in any location to which Setup has access during an installation.

```
[GuiRunOnce]
"%systemdrive%\sysprep\<file name>.bat"= "<path-1>\Command-1.exe"
"<path-n>\Command-n.exe"
"%systemdrive%\sysprep\sysprep.exe -quiet"
```

where:

<path-1>\Command-1.exe and *<path-n>\Command-n.exe* are fully qualified paths to additional applications or tool installations or configuration tools. This can also be a path to another batch file. These paths must be available during setup.

Using Windows Installer Service

Windows Installer Service is a Windows 2000 Professional component that standardizes the way applications are installed on multiple computers.

When you install applications without using Windows Installer Service, every application must have its own setup executable file or script. Each application has to ensure that the proper installation rules (for example, rules for creating file versions) are followed. This is because the application setup was not an integral part of the operating system development, so no central reference for installation rules exists.

Windows Installer Service implements all the proper Setup rules in the operating system itself. To follow those rules, applications must be described in a standard format known as a Windows Installer package. The data file containing the format information is known as the *Windows Installer package file* and has an .msi file name extension. Windows Installer Service uses the Windows Installer package file to install the application.

Windows Installer Terminology

The following terms are used to describe the installation process that uses Windows Installer technology:

Resource. A file, registry entry, shortcut, or other element that an installer typically delivers to a computer.

Component. A collection of files, registry entries, and other resources that are installed or uninstalled as a unit. When a particular component is selected for installation or removal, all of the resources in that component are either installed or removed.

Feature. The granular pieces of an application that a user can choose to install. Features typically represent the functional features of the application itself.

Product. A single product, such as Microsoft® Office. Products contain one or more features.

Windows Installer Package File

The package file is a database format that is optimized for installation performance. Generally, this file describes the relationships between features, components, and resources for a specific product.

The Windows Installer package file is typically located in the root folder of the Windows 2000 Professional operating system CD or network image, alongside the product files. The product files can exist as compressed files known as cabinet (CAB) files (which have a .cab file name extension). Each product has its own package file. During installation, Windows Installer Service opens the package file for the product and uses the information inside the Windows Installer package to determine which installation operations must be performed for that product.

Sysdiff Tool

The preferred method for automating application installation is to use their own scripting and installation routines. However, you can install applications that do not support this by using the Sysdiff tool. To perform the various steps to add applications, run Sysdiff in several different modes. In **/snap** mode, Sysdiff.exe takes a "snapshot" of a clean Windows 2000 Professional computer, and then the applications are installed. A *clean* copy of Windows 2000 Professional is an installation of Windows 2000 Professional that has not been modified and has not had additional software installed on it. Use Sysdiff in **/diff** mode to record all the changes that the application installation made to the computer (INI files, the registry, and so on).

Sysdiff creates a difference file or package that includes all the files and settings that you must install with applications on a clean copy of Windows 2000 Professional. Running Sysdiff in **/apply** or **/inf** mode applies the package to the clean Windows 2000 Professional installation.

Sysdiff generates the \$OEM$ folder structure in 8.3 file name format for maximum compatibility with OEM preinstallation environments and methods. It places $$Rename.txt in the appropriate folder.

Sysdiff Parameters

The Sysdiff switches are listed in this section. The sections that follow discuss each switch in greater detail. Sysdiff syntax is as follows:

```
sysdiff [/snap | /diff | /apply | /dump | /inf]
        [/log:Log_file]
        [/m]
        [/?]
        [/dsp]
        [/p]
        [/q]
        [/c:"comment"]
        Snapshot_file
        Sysdiff_file
        Dump_file
        Oem_root
```

where:

- **/snap**, **/diff**, **/apply**, **/dump**, **/inf** are the modes available. You must specify one of these switches, because this switch determines the Sysdiff mode and specifies how Sysdiff proceeds.

- *Log_file* is the name of an optional log file to which Sysdiff writes information describing its actions (used only in **/snap** and **/diff** modes).

- **/m** is a switch that remaps file changes during the creation of a Sysdiff package so that they appear as Default User files. (Used only in **/apply** and **/inf** modes.)

- **/?** is a switch that calls the Help file.

- **/dsp** is a switch that instructs Sysdiff to not generate the distribution share point that **sysdiff /inf** normally generates because the files already exist in the appropriate folders on the destination computer. (Used only in **/inf** mode.)

- **/p** is a switch that instructs Sysdiff to not scan all folders and files on the computer for changes. Instead, Sysdiff only scans files in the *UserProfile* folder. (Used in **/snap** and **/diff** modes.)

- **/q** is a switch that instructs Sysdiff to run in unattended (quiet) setup mode.

- *"comment"* is the name you give to the Sysdiff package as it appears in an onscreen message during setup. (Used in **/diff** mode only.) This comment must contain only the names of the applications being added.

- *Snapshot_file* is any valid Microsoft® Win32® file name. (Used in **/snap** and **/diff** modes only.) A snapshot of the system is recorded in this file.

- *Sysdiff_file* is any valid Win32 file name. (Not used in **/snap** mode.) The specified file is the output of Sysdiff and can be applied to a Windows 2000 Professional installation by using **sysdiff /apply** or **sysdiff /inf** modes.

- *Dump_file* is a Win32 path to a text file that is created to contain the dump. (Used in **/dump** mode only.) A dump file is used for diagnostic purposes.

- *Oem_root* is the Win32 path of a folder. (Used in **/inf** mode only.) The \OEM structure is created in this folder, and the INF file is placed in this folder and named *Sysdiff_file*.inf.

Figure 5.3 shows the sequence of steps for using Sysdiff to add applications. The sections that follow discuss each step in greater detail.

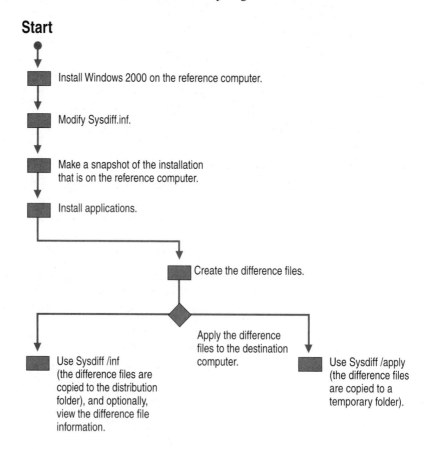

Start

Install Windows 2000 on the reference computer.

Modify Sysdiff.inf.

Make a snapshot of the installation that is on the reference computer.

Install applications.

Create the difference files.

Apply the difference files to the destination computer.

Use Sysdiff /inf (the difference files are copied to the distribution folder), and optionally, view the difference file information.

Use Sysdiff /apply (the difference files are copied to a temporary folder).

Figure 5.3   Sysdiff Overview

Sysdiff is used in as many as six different steps to add applications during installation. The following sections explain these steps.

Step 1: Install Windows 2000 Professional on the Reference Computer

Before you add applications by using Sysdiff, you must install a clean copy of Windows 2000 Professional on your reference computer.

Important Do not make any changes to Windows 2000 Professional on the reference computer before you run Sysdiff.

Step 2: Modify the Sysdiff.inf File

You can exclude items from the Sysdiff snapshot by modifying the Sysdiff.inf file. When Sysdiff runs in **/snap** or **/diff** mode, it looks for the Sysdiff.inf file in the same folder that contains Sysdiff.exe. This file contains information that Sysdiff uses to exclude certain files and registry entries from snapshots or difference files. To modify the Sysdiff.inf file, follow the instructions in the file.

Step 3: Make a Snapshot of the Clean System

Sysdiff **/snap** takes a snapshot of a clean system. A *clean system* is a reference computer that is running Windows 2000 Professional but has no applications installed.

Run Sysdiff in **/snap** mode to create the snapshot for later difference files.

The syntax for this command is as follows:

```
sysdiff /snap [/log:Log_file] Snapshot_file
```

where:

Log_file is the optional name of a log file to which Sysdiff writes information describing its actions. The log file is not used in **/apply** or **/dump** modes.

Snapshot_file is any valid Win32 file name. A snapshot of the system is recorded in this file.

Step 4: Create the Difference Files

After you install applications on the reference computer, run Sysdiff with the **/diff** switch to determine the differences between the new system state of the computer and the earlier, clean system snapshot. The result is a Sysdiff difference file package that contains a description of the INI file changes, registry changes, and other changes (including the application files themselves, which can make Sysdiff packages quite large). You can then apply these changes to another Windows 2000 Professional installation, duplicating the changes made to the reference computer.

Important If you change any of the system's settings after you create the snapshot, you must recreate the snapshot file before you create the difference file.

The syntax for this command is as follows:

```
sysdiff /diff [/log:Log_file] Snapshot_file Sysdiff_file
    /c:"comment"
```

where:

Log_file is the optional name of a log file to which Sysdiff writes information describing its actions. The log file is not used in **/apply** or **/dump** modes.

Snapshot_file is a file generated by an earlier invocation of **sysdiff /snap** on the same Windows 2000 Professional installation. (Sysdiff fails if *Snapshot_file* is from a different Windows 2000 Professional installation.)

Sysdiff_file is any valid Win32 file name. The specified file is the output of Sysdiff, and you can apply it to a Windows 2000 Professional installation by using Sysdiff **/apply** or Sysdiff **/inf**.

"comment" is the name you give to the Sysdiff package. This name appears in a screen message during setup. (Used in **/diff** mode only.) This comment can contain only the names of the applications being added.

Important Do not try to quit Sysdiff until a message appears informing you that the difference package has been created. If you quit before this message appears, Sysdiff fails.

Step 5: View Difference File Information (Optional)

You can also run Sysdiff in **/dump** mode, which is a special mode for diagnostic purposes. The output of this command is a text file containing a readable form of the contents of a Sysdiff package.

The syntax for this command is as follows:

```
sysdiff /dump Sysdiff_file Dump_file
```

where:

Sysdiff_file is a Win32 path to a file that is created in **/diff** mode.

Dump_file is a Win32 path to a text file that is created to contain the dump.

Step 6: Apply Difference Files

After you create at least one snapshot on your reference computer and at least one difference file based on that snapshot, you have a Sysdiff package file that can be applied to multiple destination computers during Setup. Two Sysdiff modes can have difference files applied: Sysdiff **/apply** and Sysdiff **/inf**.

Sysdiff /apply

You can apply Sysdiff packages during setup if the Sysdiff package is available on the hard disk and the correct switch is specified. When a Sysdiff package is applied, Sysdiff copies each file from the package to its final location on the hard disk.

Setup starts Sysdiff in **/apply** mode to apply a difference file to a Windows 2000 Professional installation. You must specify **/m** when running Sysdiff in **/apply** mode. You can specify one or more Sysdiff switches in the Cmdlines.txt file.

The syntax for this command is as follows:

```
sysdiff /apply /m Sysdiff_file
```

where:

/m   remaps file changes to the user profile (*UserProfile*) during the creation of a Sysdiff package so that they appear as Default User files. The **/m** switch is required when running Sysdiff in either **/apply** or **/inf** modes.

Sysdiff_file   specifies the file that was generated by carrying out **sysdiff /diff**.

Important   The *SystemRoot* folder must be located in the same position as it was on the system that generated the difference file. That is, if you generate a Sysdiff package on a Windows 2000 Professional installation in C:\Winnt, that Sysdiff package can be applied on other computers only if they are running Windows 2000 Professional installed in C:\Winnt.

Sysdiff /inf

Running Sysdiff **/inf** also allows Setup to install applications, but in this mode, the Sysdiff package does not contain the actual application files. Instead, Sysdiff determines the files that the application placed on the reference computer and their locations. Sysdiff then copies these files to the corresponding folders in the distribution folder. By including only information that refers to a location for the application files, the Sysdiff package can be much smaller.

Running Sysdiff **/inf** creates the following files, folders, and settings:

- **\OEM\Cmdlines.txt**
- **\OEM*Package*.inf** *Package* represents the Sysdiff package file name.
- **\OEM*C**Programs*** *C* represents the drive where the newly installed application is stored, and *Programs* represents the folder.

Rather than creating the distribution folder manually, you can use Sysdiff to generate an Inf and \$OEM$ folder structure from the Sysdiff file. The Inf folder contains registry and INI file settings. The \$OEM$ folder structure is created during an early phase of Setup. The application files have already been copied to the hard disk when the GUI mode of Setup begins. This allows greater flexibility in applying changes.

Running Sysdiff in **/inf** mode creates an INF file that instructs Setup to make the INI file and registry changes contained in the Sysdiff package and also to generate an \$OEM$ folder structure for file changes contained in the Sysdiff package. The folder structure is created using only file names in 8.3 format. The $$Rename.txt files throughout the tree contain mappings from file names in 8.3 format to long file names where necessary. These $$Rename.txt files are used during later phases of Setup.

The syntax for using **/inf** mode is as follows:

```
sysdiff /inf /m Sysdiff_file Oem_root
```

where:

/m remaps file changes during the creation of a Sysdiff package so that the files appear as Default User files. The **/m** parameter is required when running Sysdiff in **/apply** or **/inf** modes.

Sysdiff_file is the Win32 path to a file that was created by running Sysdiff in **/diff** mode. The name of this file must be no more than eight characters long.

Oem_root is the Win32 path of a folder. The \OEM structure is created in this folder, and the INF file is copied there and named Sysdiff_file.inf.

Step 4: Deploy

After you have customized your answer file and the distribution folder with the appropriate files, you need to decide how to deploy the operating system. See the deployment step in this section that corresponds to the tool you chose to use for your installation.

Unattended Installations

An unattended installation is a hands-free method of installing Windows 2000 Professional that is convenient and flexible and does not require additional tools. Unattended installations are done on a computer-by-computer basis.

This section explains how to use the Winnt32.exe and Winnt.exe commands; it also provides step-by-step instructions for running Setup on different operating systems and platforms, including the following:

- Using Winnt.exe to run Setup on MS-DOS, Windows 3.1, or Windows for Workgroups–based computers.
- Using Winnt32.exe to run Setup on Windows 95, Windows 98, Windows NT Workstation 4.0, or Windows 2000 Professional–based computers.
- Running Setup from the operating system CD.

Note When you run Setup in unattended mode on a computer with multiple hard disks or partitions, specify the exact location of the destination hard drive or partition where you are installing. Use the **Winnt /t** or **Winnt32 /tempdrive** switch to specify the destination. If you use the CD Boot method, add AutoPartition = 1 to the [Data] section of the Winnt.sif file to specify the location. With CD Boot, Setup installs to the first logical partition that it finds with sufficient disk space. Your computer must have a minimum of 1 GB of free space and at least a 2-GB partition.

▶ **To run Setup in unattended mode**

- At the command prompt type:

    winnt /u

    –Or–

    winnt32 /unattend

Table 5.15 shows when to use these.

Table 5.15   Using the Setup Commands with an Answer File

Setup Command	Upgrade	Clean Installation
Winnt.exe	No	Yes
Winnt32.exe	Yes	Yes

When you run the Setup program, it installs Windows 2000 Professional in three phases:

- File-copy
- Text-mode
- GUI-mode

File copy   Setup copies the Windows 2000 Professional program files and any additional files that you specify from the distribution folder to the computer's hard disk.

Text mode   Setup identifies the basic hardware in the computer (such as the microprocessor and motherboard type, hard disk controllers, file systems, and memory), installs the base operating system required to continue with Setup, and creates any folders that you specify.

GUI mode   Setup configures the computer's hardware (audio, video, and so on), configures the network settings, prompts you to provide an Administrator password, and allows you to personalize the installation. If you use Sysprep, the Setup program goes through another phase called Mini-Setup. This phase is a subset of the regular GUI mode of Setup and is only enabled on computers on which Sysprep has been run. Mini-Setup is used only to prompt for user-specific information, to redetect new hardware, and to regenerate System IDs.

Using the Winnt32.exe and Winnt.exe Programs

To install Windows 2000, run the appropriate Windows 2000 Setup program, either Winnt.exe or Winnt32.exe.

Note   In this chapter, Winnt.exe and Winnt32.exe are both referred to as Setup.

Winnt32.exe   Use Winnt32.exe for a clean installation or upgrade on a computer running Windows NT version 4.0, Windows 95, or Windows 98.

Winnt.exe   Use Winnt.exe for a clean installation on a computer running MS-DOS or Windows 3.*x*. Upgrades of these operating systems are not supported.

Caution   Before upgrading to the Windows 2000 operating system, restart the computer if you have just upgraded any applications.

Winnt32.exe Command Syntax

```
Winnt32
[/checkupgradeonly]
[/cmd:command_line]
[/cmdcons]
[/copydir:folder_name]
[/copysource:folder_name]
[/debug[level][:file_name]]
[/m:folder_name]
[/makelocalsource]
[/noreboot]
[/s:sourcepath]
[/syspart:drive_letter]
[/tempdrive:drive_letter]
[/udf:ID[,UDB_file]]
[/unattend]
[/unattend[seconds][:answer_file]]
```

Where:

/checkupgradeonly

Checks the current operating system for upgrade compatibility with
Windows 2000. This is simply a verification and does not install
Windows 2000.

/cmd:command_line

Specifies a command to be carried out after the graphical user interface (GUI)
portion of Setup finishes. The command occurs before Setup is complete and
after Setup has restarted your computer and collected the necessary
configuration information. For example, this option can run Cmdlines.txt,
which usually specifies the applications to be installed immediately after Setup
completes.

/cmdcons

Adds a Recovery Console option for repairing a failed installation.

/copydir:folder_name

Creates a subfolder within the folder that contains the Windows 2000 files. For
example, if the source folder contains a Private_drivers folder that has
modifications just for your site, you can type **/copydir:private_drivers** to
copy that folder to your Windows 2000 folder. You can use the **/copydir**
option multiple times.

/copysource:folder_name

Temporarily creates a subfolder within the folder that contains the
Windows 2000 files. For example, if the source folder contains a
Private_drivers folder that has modifications just for your site, type
/copysource:private_drivers to have Setup copy that folder to your
Windows 2000 folder and use its files during Setup. Unlike the **/copydir**
option, folders created by using **/copysource** are deleted when Setup finishes.

/debug[*level*][*:file_name*]

Creates a debug log at the level specified. When you use the default setting, the program creates a log file (*%windir%*\Winnt32.log) that has a warning level of 2. The warning levels for the log file are as follows: 0 = severe errors, 1=errors, 2 = warnings, 3 = information, and 4 = detailed information for debugging. Each level also includes the levels below it.

/m:*folder_name*

Instructs Setup to copy replacement files from an alternate location. It directs Setup to look at the alternate location first and to copy the files from that location (if they files are present) instead of from the default location.

/makelocalsource

Instructs Setup to copy all installation source files to your local hard disk. Use **/makelocalsource** to obtain installation files if you begin installation from a CD and the CD becomes unavailable during the installation.

/noreboot

Instructs Setup to not restart the computer after the file copy phase of Winnt32 is complete so that you can execute another command.

/s:*sourcepath*

Specifies the source location of the Windows 2000 files. The default is the current folder. To copy files simultaneously from multiple servers, you can specify up to eight sources. For example:

```
winnt32 /s:server1 … /s:server8
```

Windows 2000 can use up to eight **/s** switches to point to other distribution servers as source locations for installation to the destination computer. This functionality speeds up the file copy phase of Setup to the destination computer and provides additional load balancing capability to the distribution servers from which Setup can be run. For example:

```
path to distribution folder 1\winnt32 [/unattend] [:path\answer.txt]
[/s:path to distribution folder 2] [/s:path to distribution folder 3]
[/s:path to distribution folder 4]
```

/syspart:*drive_letter*

Specifies that you can copy Setup startup files to a hard disk, mark the disk as active, and install the disk in another computer. When you start that computer, Setup automatically starts at the next phase. Remember the following points when you use this switch:

- You must always use the **/syspart** option with the **/tempdrive** option.

- Both **/syspart** and **/tempdrive** must point to the same partition of a secondary hard disk.

- You must install Windows 2000 on the primary partition of the secondary hard disk.

- You can use the **/syspart** switch only from a computer that is running Windows NT 3.51, Windows NT 4.0, or Windows 2000. You cannot use this switch from a computer that is running Windows 95 or Windows 98.

/tempdrive:_drive_letter_

Directs Setup to place temporary files on the specified partition and to install Windows 2000 on that partition. Remember the following points as you use this switch:

- You must always use the **/tempdrive** option with the **/syspart** option.

- Both **/tempdrive** and **/syspart** must point to the same partition of a secondary hard disk.

- You must install Windows 2000 on the primary partition of the secondary hard disk.

/udf:_ID_[,_UDB_file_]

Indicates an identifier that Setup uses to specify how a Uniqueness Database File (UDB) modifies an answer file (see the **/unattend** option). The UDB file overrides values in the answer file, and the identifier determines which values in the UDB file are used. For example, **/udf:Roaming_user,Our_company.udb** overrides settings specified for the identifier **Roaming_user** in the **Our_company.udb** file. If you do not specify a UDB file, Setup prompts you to insert a disk that contains the file $_Unique_$.udb.

/unattend

Upgrades your previous version of Windows by using unattended Setup mode. All user settings are taken from the previous installation so that no user intervention is required during Setup.

Important   Using the **/unattend** switch to automate Setup affirms that you have read and accepted the End User License Agreement (EULA) for Windows 2000. Before using this switch to install Windows 2000 on behalf of an organization other than your own, you must confirm that the end user (whether an individual or a single entity) has received, read, and accepted the terms of the Windows 2000 EULA. Original equipment manufacturers (OEMs) may not specify this key on computers being sold to end users.

/unattend[*seconds*][*:answer_file*]

Installs Windows 2000 without using prompts that require user interaction; instead, Setup obtains the information it needs from an answer file that you prepare in advance. For more information about answer files, see "Sample Answer Files for Unattended Setup," in this book.

Include *seconds* only if you are upgrading from Windows NT 4.0. *Seconds* specifies the delay, in seconds, between when Setup finishes copying the files and when system setup begins.

Winnt.exe Command Syntax

```
Winnt
[/E: command]
[/R: folder_name]
[/Rx: folder_name]
[/S: sourcepath]
[/T[: tempdrive]]
[/U[: answer_file]]
[/udf: ID[, UDB_file]
[/A:]
```

/E:*command*

Specifies a command to be carried out after the GUI portion of Setup finishes. For example, this option can run Cmdlines.txt, which usually specifies the applications to be installed immediately after Setup completes.

/R:*folder_name*

Creates a subfolder within the folder that contains the Windows 2000 files. For example, if the source folder contains a Private_drivers folder that has modifications just for your site, type **/R:private_drivers** to copy that folder to your Windows 2000 folder. You can use the **/R** option multiple times.

/Rx:*folder_name*

Temporarily creates a subfolder within the folder that contains the Windows 2000 files. For example, if the source folder contains a Private_drivers folder that has modifications just for your site, you can type **/Rx:private_drivers** to have Setup copy that folder to your Windows 2000 folder and use its files during Setup. Unlike the **/R** option, folders created by using **/Rx** are deleted when Setup finishes.

/S:*sourcepath*

Specifies the source location of the Windows 2000 files. The location must be a full path of the form *Drive_letter*:*Path* or *Server**Share**Path*. The default is the current folder.

/T:*tempdrive*

Directs Setup to place temporary files on the specified drive and to install Windows 2000 on that drive. If you do not specify a location, Setup attempts to locate a drive for you.

/U:_answer_file_

Installs Windows 2000 without using prompts that require user interaction; instead, Setup obtains the information it needs from an answer file that you prepare in advance. For more information about answer files, see "Sample Answer Files for Windows 2000 Professional" in this book. This requires **/S**.

/udf:_ID_[,_UDB_file_]

Indicates an identifier that Setup uses to specify how a UDB modifies an answer file. The UDB file overrides values in the answer file, and the identifier determines which values in the UDB file are used. For example, **/udf:Roaming_user,Our_company.udb** overrides settings specified for the identifier **Roaming_user** in the file **Our_company.udb**. If you do not specify a UDB file, Setup prompts you to insert a disk that contains the file $_Unique_$.udb.

/A

Enables accessibility options.

Running Setup on Windows 95, Windows 98, Windows NT Workstation 4.0, or Windows 2000 Professional–based Computers

Use Winnt32.exe to start Windows 2000 Professional Setup from computers running Windows 95, Windows 98, Windows NT Workstation 4.0, or Windows 2000 Professional.

▶ **To run Setup in unattended mode from Windows 95, Windows 98, Windows NT Workstation 4.0, or Windows 2000 Professional**

- At the command prompt, type:

```
winnt32 /unattend:answer_file /s:install_source
[/syspart:target_drive] [/tempdrive:target_drive] [t]
```

The following is an example of how Winnt32.exe can be used:

```
<path to source>\i386\Winnt32.exe /s:<path to source>\i386
/unattend:<path to answer file>\Unattend.txt
```

where:

- _<path to source>_ and _<path to answer file>_ are fully qualified Uniform Naming Convention (UNC) or drive-letter references to the locations of the Windows 2000 Professional source files and of the answer file.

Running Setup on MS-DOS, Windows 3.1, or Windows for Workgroups–based Computers

Use Winnt.exe to start Windows 2000 Professional Setup from computers running MS-DOS, Windows 3.1, or Windows for Workgroups. Run Winnt.exe from the MS-DOS command prompt.

▶ **To run Setup in unattended mode from MS-DOS, Windows 3.1, or Windows for Workgroups**

- At the command prompt, type:

    winnt **/u:**<*answer file*> **/s:**<*install source*> **/t:**<*target drive*>

The following is an example of how Winnt.exe can be used:

    <*path to source*>\i386\Winnt.exe **/s:**<*path to source*>\i386 **/u:**<*path to answer file*>\Unattend.txt

where:

- <*path to source*> and <*path to answer file*> are fully qualified UNC or drive-letter references to the locations of the Windows 2000 Professional source files and of the answer file.

Note Winnt.exe can only be run on computers that are running MS-DOS or Windows 3.*x*.

Running Setup from the Operating System CD

To run Windows 2000 Professional Setup in unattended mode from the Windows 2000 Professional operating system CD, the following conditions must be met:

- The computer must support starting from the CD-ROM drive—El Torito No Emulation CD boot support.

- The answer file must be named Winnt.sif and be on a floppy disk to be inserted when the computer starts from the CD.

- The answer file must contain a [Data] section with the required keys specified.

System Preparation Tool

The System Preparation tool, Sysprep.exe, is an imaging method that you can use to install identical configurations on multiple computers. You can also use Sysprep to customize and automate Mini-Setup and to audit computers. There is no limit to the number of times that you can use Sysprep.

On a master computer, install Windows 2000 Professional and any applications that you want installed on your destination computers. Then run Sysprep to transfer the image to the other computers. Sysprep prepares the hard disk on the master computer for duplication to other computers and then runs a third-party disk-imaging process. The major advantage of Sysprep installation is speed. The image can be packaged and compressed; only the files required for the specific configuration are created as part of the image.

To use Sysprep, your master and destination computers must have identical HALs, Advanced Configuration and Power Interface (ACPI) support, and mass storage controller devices. Windows 2000 Professional automatically detects Plug and Play devices, and Sysprep redetects and reenumerates the devices on the system when the computer is turned on after Sysprep has run. This means that Plug and Play devices, such as network adapters, modems, video adapters, and sound cards, do not have to be the same on the master and destination computers. Additional Plug and Play drivers that you might require on other systems are also created. The image can also be copied to a CD and distributed to remote sites that have slow links.

Note Because the master and destination computers are required to have identical HALs, ACPI support, and mass storage devices, you might be required to maintain multiple images for your environment.

Important When performing disk duplication, check with your software vendor to make sure that you are not violating the licensing agreement for installation of the software that you want to duplicate.

Overview of the Sysprep Process

The following steps describe the process of preparing a master computer to use for disk duplication.

1. Install Windows 2000 Professional on a computer that has hardware similar to the destination computers. While preparing the computer, do not join it to a domain, and keep the local administrative password blank.

2. Configure the computer. Log on as the administrator, and then install and customize Windows 2000 Professional and associated applications. These might include productivity applications, such as Microsoft® Office, business-specific applications, and other applications or settings that you want included in a common configuration for all clients.

3. Validate the image. Run an audit, based on your criteria, to verify that the image configuration is correct. Remove residual information, including anything left behind from audit and event logs.

4. Prepare the image for duplication. When you are confident that the computer is configured exactly as you want, you are ready to prepare the system for duplication. You accomplish this by running Sysprep with the optional Sysprep.inf file, described later in this chapter. When Sysprep has been run, the computer shuts down automatically or indicates that it is safe to shut down.

5. Duplicate. The computer hard disk is triggered to run Plug and Play detection, create new security identifiers (SIDs), and run the Mini-Setup wizard the next time the system is started. You can duplicate or create an image of the system by using hardware or software. The next time Windows 2000 Professional is started from this master computer or from any destination computer created from this image, the system detects and reenumerates the Plug and Play devices to complete the installation and configuration on the destination computer.

Important Components that depend on the Active Directory™ directory service cannot be duplicated.

Sysprep Components

Run Sysprep.exe manually or configure Setup to run Sysprep.exe automatically by using the [GuiRunOnce] section of the answer file. The files Sysprep.exe and Setupcl.exe must be located in a Sysprep folder at the root of the system drive (*%SystemDrive%*\Sysprep\). To place the files in the correct location during an automated Setup, add these files to your distribution folders under the OEM\$1\Sysprep subfolder. For more information about this subfolder, see "Create a Distribution Folder" earlier in this chapter.

These files prepare the operating system for duplication and start the Mini-Setup wizard. You can also include an optional answer file, Sysprep.inf, in the Sysprep folder. Sysprep.inf contains default parameters that you can use to provide consistent responses where they are appropriate. This limits the requirement for user input, and reduces potential user errors. You can also place the Sysprep.inf file on a floppy disk to insert after the Windows startup screen appears to allow further customization at the location of the destination computer. The floppy disk drive is read when the "Please Wait…" Mini-Setup wizard screen appears. When the Mini-Setup wizard has successfully completed its tasks, the system restarts a final time, the Sysprep folder and all of its contents are deleted, and the system is ready for the user to log on.

The Sysprep files are defined in the following sections.

Sysprep.exe

Sysprep.exe has the following optional parameters:

- *quiet*. Runs Sysprep without displaying on-screen messages.
- *nosidgen*. Runs Sysprep without regenerating SIDs that are already on the system. This is useful if you do not intend to duplicate the computer on which you are running Sysprep.
- *reboot*. Automatically restarts the computer after Sysprep shuts it down. This eliminates the need to manually turn on the computer again.

Sysprep.inf

Sysprep.inf is an answer file that is used to automate the Mini-Setup process. It uses the same INI file syntax and key names (for supported keys) as the Setup answer file. Place the Sysprep.inf file in the *%SystemDrive%*\Sysprep folder or on a floppy disk. If you use a floppy disk, insert it into the floppy disk drive after the Windows startup screen appears. Note that if you do not include Sysprep.inf when running Sysprep, the Mini-Setup wizard requires user input at each customization screen.

Note If you provided a Sysprep.inf file on the master computer and want to individually change Sysprep.inf on each destination computer, use the floppy disk method.

The following is an example of a Sysprep.inf file:

```
[Unattended]
;Prompt the user to accept the EULA.
OemSkipEula=No
;Use Sysprep's default and regenerate the page file for the system
;to accommodate potential differences in available RAM.
KeepPageFile=0
;Provide the location for additional language support files that
;might be required in a global organization.
InstallFilesPath=%systemdrive%\Sysprep\i386

[GuiUnattended]
;Specify a non-null administrator password.
;Any password supplied here only takes effect if the original source
;for the image (master computer) specified a non-null password.
;Otherwise, the password used on the master computer is
;the password used on this computer. This can only be changed by
;logging on as local administrator and manually changing the password.
AdminPassword=""
;Set the time zone
TimeZone=20
;Skip the Welcome screen when the system boots.
OemSkipWelcome=1
;Do not skip the regional options dialog box so that the user can
indicate
;which regional options apply to them.
OemSkipRegional=0

[UserData]
;Prepopulate user information for the system
FullName="Authorized User"
OrgName="Organization Name"
ComputerName=XYZ_Computer1

[Identification]
;Join the computer to the domain ITDOMAIN
JoinDomain=ITDOMAIN

[Networking]
;Bind the default protocols and services to the (s) network adapter
used.
;in this computer.
InstallDefaultComponents=Yes
```

Note You can change the administrative password using Sysprep.inf only if the existing administrative password is null. This is also true if you want to change the administrator password by using the Sysprep GUI.

For more information about answer file parameters and syntax, see Unattend.doc in Support\Tools\Deploy.cab on the Windows 2000 Professional operating system CD. In Windows 98, Windows NT, or Windows 2000 Professional, use Windows Explorer to extract this document. In Windows 95 and earlier, or in MS-DOS, use the **Extract** command to access the file.

Setupcl.exe

Setupcl.exe does the following:

- Regenerates new SIDs for the computer
- Starts the Mini-Setup wizard

Mini-Setup Wizard

The Mini-Setup wizard starts the first time that a computer starts from a disk that has been duplicated when using Sysprep. The wizard gathers information that is required to further customize the destination computer. If you do not use Sysprep.inf, or if you leave some sections of the file blank, the Mini-Setup wizard displays screens for which no answer was provided. The possible screens include the following:

- Welcome to Windows 2000 Professional Setup wizard (always shown)
- EULA (always shown)
- Regional options (can be hidden)
- User name and company (can be hidden)
- Product key (always shown unless you prepopulate this information for the user)
- Computer name and administrator password (can be hidden)
- TAPI settings (displayed only if a modem or a new modem device exists on the computer)
- Date and time settings (can be hidden)
- Networking settings (can be hidden)
- Workgroup or computer domain

Optional information appears unless you prepopulate answers for the end user by using the Sysprep.inf file. For more information about the Sysprep.inf file, see Unattend.doc in Support\Tools\Deploy.cab on the Windows 2000 Professional operating system CD.

To bypass these screens, specify certain parameters within Sysprep.inf. These parameters are listed in Table 5.16.

Note Because Setup detects optimal settings for display devices, you no longer see the "Display Settings" screen when Setup or the Mini-Setup wizard are running. You can specify the settings in the [Display] section either in the answer file that is used for your master computer or in the Sysprep.inf file used for your destination computer. If settings in the [Display] section are in the answer file that is used for your master computer, Sysprep retains those settings unless Sysprep.inf contains different settings or unless a video adapter or monitor is detected that requires settings different from those of the master computer.

Table 5.16   Parameters in Sysprep.inf for Bypassing the Mini-Setup Wizard

Parameter	Section

Regional options	`[RegionalSettings]`
	`– Or –`
	`[GuiUnattended]`
	`OemSkipRegional=1`

User name and company	`[UserData]`
	`FullName="User Name"`
	`OrgName="Organization Name"`

Computer name and administrator password	`[UserData]`
	`ComputerName=W2B32054`
	`[GuiUnattended]`
	`AdminPassword=""`

TAPI settings	`[TapiLocation]` `AreaCode=425`
Network settings	`[Networking]`

Server licensing (server only)	`[LicenseFilePrintData]`
	`AutoMode = PerServer`
	`AutoUsers = 5`

Time zone selection	`[GuiUnattended]` `TimeZone=<desired time zone index>`

Running Sysprep.exe

You can run Sysprep manually or automatically. This section lists the requirements for running Sysprep and procedures for running it manually or automatically.

Requirements to Run Sysprep

To use Sysprep, the following requirements must be met:

- The master and destination computers must have compatible HALs. For example, HAL Advanced Processor Interrupt Controller (APIC) and HAL MPs (multiprocessor systems) are compatible, whereas HAL PIC (Programmable Interrupt Controller) is not compatible with either HAL APIC or HAL MPs.

- The mass storage controllers (IDE or SCSI) must be identical between the master and destination computers.

- Plug and Play devices such as modems, sound cards, network adapters, and video cards do not have to be the same, but drivers for those devices should be available.

- Third-party software or disk-duplicating hardware devices are required. These products create binary images of a computer's hard disk and either duplicate the image to another hard disk or store the image in a file on a separate disk.

- The size of the hard disk on the destination computer must be at least the same size as the hard disk on the master computer. If the destination computer has a larger hard disk, the difference is not included in the primary partition. However, you can use the ExtendOemPartition key in the Sysprep.inf file to extend the primary partition if it was formatted as NTFS.

Running Sysprep

After you install Windows 2000 Professional, you can use Sysprep to prepare the system for transfer to other similarly configured computers. To run Sysprep manually, first install Windows 2000 Professional, configure the system, and install the applications. Then run Sysprep without the –**reboot** command-line switch. After the system shuts down, duplicate the image of the drive to the similarly configured computers.

When users start up their duplicated computers for the first time, the Mini-Setup wizard runs, allowing the users to customize their systems. You can also preassign all or some of the Sysprep configuration parameters by using Sysprep.inf. The Sysprep folder (which contains Sysprep.exe and Setupcl.exe) is automatically deleted after Mini-Setup is completed.

▶ **To prepare a Windows 2000 Professional installation for duplication**

1. From the **Start** menu, click **Run**, and then type:

   cmd

2. At the command prompt, change to the root folder of drive C, and then type:

   md sysprep

3. Insert the Windows 2000 Professional operating system CD into the appropriate CD-ROM drive. Open the Deploy.cab file in the folder Support\Tools.

4. Copy Sysprep.exe and Setupcl.exe to the Sysprep folder.

   If you are using Sysprep.inf, copy this file to the Sysprep folder. Sysprep.exe, Setupcl.exe, and Sysprep.inf must be in the same folder for Sysprep to function properly.

5. At the command prompt, change to the Sysprep folder by typing:

   cd sysprep

6. At the command prompt, type one of the following, as required:

   sysprep /optional_parameter

7. If the –**reboot** command-line switch was not specified, perform the following:

   When a message requesting that you shut down the computer appears, from the **Start** menu, click **Shut Down**. You are now ready to use a third-party disk-imaging tool to create an image of the installation.

Note You can add a Cmdlines.txt file to the Sysprep folder, to be processed by Setup. This file is used to run post-setup commands, including commands for application installation.

Using Sysprep with Nonnetworked Computers

Even if you don't have a network, you can still install Windows 2000 Professional and various applications on destination computers, one computer at a time.

▶ **To install Windows 2000 Professional on nonnetworked computers**

1. Choose a setup method, and then start Setup.

2. Add custom information and additional files.

3. Install applications. If you have no applications to install, skip this step.

   Important Each destination computer must have a CD-ROM drive.

Step 1: Choose a Setup Method and Then Start Setup

Setup can typically be started from an MS-DOS bootable floppy disk, from the Windows 2000 Professional Setup floppy disks, from the hard disk of the destination computer (if it has an operating system installed), or from the CD-ROM drive. CD Boot is available only with computers that support starting from the CD-ROM drive by using the El Torito No Emulation Mode CD Boot specification. Choose from the methods provided later in this section.

▶ **To install from the Setup floppy disks**

1. Start the computer using the Windows 2000 Professional Setup floppy disks.

2. When Setup is complete, you're ready to add applications and run Sysprep.

   For more information about how to install applications, see "Step 3: Customize" earlier in this chapter.

▶ **To install from MS-DOS or Windows 3.*x***

1. Make sure that the drivers required for the CD-ROM drive are available on the disk or the drive and that they are loaded correctly.

2. Start the computer.

3. Change to the distribution folder and, at the command prompt, type:

   winnt /s:*install_source* **/u:Unattend.txt**

   where:

   install_source is the location of the Windows 2000 Professional files.

   Unattend.txt is the answer file, which contains answers to installation questions that you want to automate.

   For more information about Unattend.txt, see Unattend.doc in Support\Tools\Deploy.cab on the Windows 2000 Professional operating system CD.

4. When Setup is complete, you can add applications and run Sysprep.

   For more information about how to install applications, see "Step 3: Customize" earlier in this chapter.

▶ **To install from Windows 95, Windows 98, or Windows NT Workstation 4.0**

1. Start the computer.

2. From the **Start** menu, click **Run**, and then type:

   *<path to distribution folder>***winnt32 /unattend:Unattend.txt**

   where:

   ▪ Unattend.txt is the answer file, which contains answers to installation questions that you want to automate.

3. When Setup is complete, you're ready to add applications and run Sysprep to prepare for creating an image.

For instructions about how to install applications, see "Step 3: Customize" earlier in this chapter.

Note To ensure a clean installation, make sure that you do not install Windows 2000 Professional as an upgrade.

Before you use CD Boot, make sure that the following conditions are met:

- Your computer has El Torito No Emulation CD Boot support.
- The answer file is called Winnt.sif and is located on a floppy disk.
- The answer file contains a [Data] section with the required keys.

Note The **/udf** switch cannot be used with the CD Boot method.

▶ **To install by using CD Boot**

1. Start the computer from the Windows 2000 Professional operating system CD. Setup begins automatically.

2. When Setup displays the message that it is examining the hardware configuration, insert the floppy disk containing the Winnt.sif file.

3. When the floppy drive light goes off, remove the floppy disk. Setup begins copying files to the hard disk.

   For more information about how to install applications, see "Step 3: Customize" ealier in this chapter.

Step 2: Add Customized Information and Components

During this step, you can add customized information (such as your company's name) and components (such as custom help files and documentation).

▶ **To add customized information and components**

- Create a file called Oeminfo.ini and copy it to the %SystemRoot%\System32 folder. The *SystemRoot* folder is usually C:\Winnt.

Step 3: Install Applications

After Windows 2000 Professional installation is complete, install any applications that you want to include with the computer. If you don't have any applications to install, you can skip this step.

▶ **To install applications**

1. After the computer restarts, log on to Windows 2000 Professional as an administrator, leaving the password field blank.

2. Install any applications that your user has requested.

Using Sysprep to Extend Disk Partitions

When installing Windows 2000 Professional, you might find it necessary to extend the partition of the destination computer. You can use Sysprep with the appropriate entries in the answer file to extend an NTFS partition. You might want to do this to do the following:

- Create images that can be extended into larger disk partitions to take full advantage of hard disks that might have more space than the original hard disk on the master computer.

- Create images on smaller hard disks.

Review the steps that follow and choose the method that works best for you based on the tools that you are using to create an image of the operating system.

Caution Make sure that you do not accidentally delete the files Pagefile.sys, Setupapi.log, and Hyberfil.sys (if applicable) when modifying the image. These files are recreated when the Mini-Setup wizard runs on the destination computer. Deleting these files on an active system can cause the system to function improperly.

When used in an answer file, the ExtendOemPartition key causes Setup to extend the destination partition into any available unpartitioned space that physically follows it on the disk.

The values for ExtendOemPartition are 0, 1, and *<extra size in MB>*

where:

- 0 Setup does not extend the partition.

- 1 Setup extends the partition to fill out the hard disk.

- *<extra size in MB>* Setup increases the current partition size by this amount.

Note ExtendOemPartition automatically leaves the last cylinder on the hard disk free to allow dynamic disk support.

ExtendOemPartition can be set to a number other than 1 to indicate a specific disk size for extending the hard disk in addition to the current space used. This is useful if more than one partition is requested on a computer.

Important Only NTFS partitions can be extended. If the destination partition you plan to extend is FAT or FAT32, set FileSystem = ConvertNTFS in the answer file to convert the partition. Setup does not extend FAT16 and FAT32 partitions.

ExtendOemPartition can be used with both the Unattend.txt and Sysprep.inf Setup files.

When used in Sysprep.inf for imaged computers, the destination computer's hard disk must be the same size or larger than the master computer's hard disk.

The partition to be extended must have available, unpartitioned space following it to allow the extension.

▶   **To extend a hard disk partition when using a third-party imaging product or a hardware imaging device that supports NTFS used by Windows 2000 Professional**

1. Create a partition on the master computer hard disk that is just large enough to install Windows 2000 Professional with all the components and applications that you intend to add. This helps keep the size of the master image file to a minimum.

2. Include FileSystem=ConvertNTFS in the [Unattended] section of the answer file that creates the master image. You do not need to include ExtendOemPartition because you want to maintain the smallest possible image size.

Note ConvertNTFS does not work in Sysprep.inf because this is a text mode–only function and Sysprep does not go through text mode.

---

3. In the [Unattended] section of Sysprep.inf, include the statement:

```
ExtendOemPartition = 1
```

Or additional size in megabytes to extend the partition.

4. Install Windows 2000 Professional on the master computer. Sysprep shuts down the system automatically.

5. Generate the image.

6. Place the image on the destination computer where the destination computer has the same size system partition as the master computer.

7. Restart the destination computer.

When you place the master image on a destination computer, drive C is converted when the computer is turned on. The computer then restarts and starts Mini-Setup. During Mini-Setup, Windows extends drive C to the rest of the unpartitioned space on the hard disk in an almost instantaneous process. The destination computer then restarts again, and the end user can log on and begin using Windows 2000 Professional.

The Mini-Setup wizard starts and the partition is extended.

▶ **To extend a hard disk partition when using an imaging product that does not support NTFS used by Windows 2000 Professional**

1. In the [Unattended] section of Sysprep.inf, include the statement:

```
ExtendOemPartition = 1
```

Or additional size in megabytes to extend the partition.

2. Convert short file names using Cmdlines.txt

3. Run Sysprep.

The following occurs when you restart the destination computer:

- The computer initially starts in conversion mode to convert the system partition on the destination computer to NTFS.

- The computer automatically restarts.

- The Mini-Setup wizard starts, and the partition is extended almost instantaneously.

Reducing the Number of Master Images

With Sysprep you can minimize the number of images you need to use for preinstalling Windows 2000 Professional from multi-processor (MP) to uni-processor (UP) computers or from UP to MP computers. However, this onlys work for APIC or ACPI APIC computers.

Note More interrupts are available with APIC systems than with Processor Interrupt Controller (PIC) uni-processor systems. As a result, your computers:

- Will have faster response times.

- Will be able to support more hardware devices than PIC HALs.

There are two methods for creating images that you can use between MP and UP systems. Each method has advantages and disadvantages associated with it, as outline in the following sections. Choose the method that works best for you and your preinstallation environment.

Table 5.17 illustrates the compatibility of computers based on their HAL type. One image is required for each compatibility group.

Table 5.17   HAL Compatibility

Compatibility	ACPI PIC	ACPI APIC UP	ACPI APIC MP	Non-ACPI UP PIC	Non-ACPI APIC UP	Non-ACPI APIC MP
ACPI PIC	x					
ACPI APIC UP		x	x			
ACPI APIC MP		x	x			
Non-ACPI APIC UP					x	x
Non-ACPI UP PIC				x		
Non-ACPI APIC MP					x	x

Multiprocessor to Uniprocessor

For this process, the image is created on an multiprocessor master computer. This image can be used on other multiprocessor computers or on uniprocessor computers.

Important This image can only be used in one of the following configurations depending on the HAL type you are using:

- From an ACPI APIC MP-based master computer for use on other ACPI APIC MP or ACPI APIC UP-based computers.

- From a non-ACPI APIC MP-based master computer for use on other non-ACPI APIC MP or non-ACPI APIC UP-based computers.

▶ **To create an multiprocessor to uniprocessor image**

1. Copy the Mp2up.inf and associated Mp2up files to the location you are using for your Plug and Play device drivers in your distribution folders, for example, \$OEM$\$1\Sysprep\Hal.

Note For System Builders, the necessary Mp2up files can be downloaded from the Microsoft OEM System Builder Web site link on the Web Resources page at http://windows.microsoft.com/windows2000/reskit/webresources

---

2. In Sysprep.inf, add:

```
[Unattended]
UpdateUPHAL = "hwid,%SystemDrive%\Sysprep\Hal\Mp2up.inf"
```

where:

- *hwid* is either MPS_UP or ACPI APIC_UP.

3. Install Windows 2000 Professional from the distribution folders to an multiprocessor computer.

4. Run Sysprep with the Sysprep.inf created in step 2.

5. Image the computer.

6. Place the image on comparable destination computers.

Advantage   You can create a single entry in the Sysprep.inf which then prompts Windows 2000 Professional to determine, after Mini-Setup is complete, if a single processor or if multiple processors are running and to then use the correct kernel files.

Disadvantage   This process requires that, when you create the master image, you include each of the Mp2up.inf files and other related Mp2up files in the distribution folders.

Uniprocessor to Multiprocessor

For this process, the image is created on a uniprocessor master computer with an APIC HAL. This image can then be used on computers with compatible hardware, including the HAL, to be used between either APIC UP HALs or APIC MP HALs.

Important   This image can only be used in one of the following configurations depending on the HAL type you are using:

- From an ACPI APIC UP-based master computer for use on other ACPI APIC UP or ACPI APIC MP-based computers.

- From a non-ACPI APIC UP-based master computer for use on other non-ACPI APIC UP or non-ACPI APIC MP-based computers.

▶ **To create the uniprocessor to multiprocessor image**

1. Install Windows 2000 Professional on a uniprocessor computer.

2. Run Sysprep.

3. Create the image of the computer.

4. In Sysprep.inf, add:

```
[Unattended]
UpdateHAL = "hwid,%windir%\inf\hal.inf"
```

where:

- *hwid* is either MPS_MP or ACPI APIC_MP.

5. Place the image on comparable destination computers.

6. On multiprocessory computers, use the Sysprep.inf file created in step 4 to replace all previous Sysprep.inf files.

   You can use any tools you normally use to manipulate files on the hard disk when creating new computers from an image.

Advantage You do not have to install the Mp2up files on the computer.

Disadvantage Before the computers can be shipped, the Sysprep.inf file must be replaced depending on the type of computer being shipped: uniprocessor or multiprocessor.

Remote Installation Services

Remote Installation Services (RIS) allows a client computer to connect to a Windows 2000 Server network to initiate an automated installation on that client computer.

The RIS process enables administrators to perform most of the work of installing the operating system by having the following configurations in place:

- Defining how the operating system is to be configured for each group of users.

- Limiting users to the operating system configurations determined to be appropriate.

- Guiding the user through a successful operating system installation by predetermining which installation options, if any, the end user can modify.

Table 5.18 describes the major RIS components and the individuals who work with each component.

Table 5.18   RIS Components and Users

Component	Description	User
Remote Installation Services Setup (Risetup.exe)	Sets up the RIS server.	Server administrator
Remote Installation Services Administrator	Configures Group Policy settings relating to RIS.	Server administrator
Remote Installation Preparation wizard (Riprep.exe)	Creates operating system images and installs them on the RIS server. You can also use Riprep.exe to create application images to install applications with the operating system.	Desktop administrator
Remote Installation Services boot disk (Rbfg.exe)	Creates the bootable floppy disk required to install RIS-based operating systems on certain client computers.	Desktop administrator
Client Installation wizard (Oschooser.exe)	Selects the RIS image that the user must install. This wizard is used on the client computer.	End user

The following sections discuss how to plan for RIS from a client perspective and how to use the Remote Installation Preparation wizard, the Remote Installation Services boot disk, and the Client Installation wizard. For more information about how to use the server components, see the *Distributed Systems Guide*.

During the initial startup sequence, the client computer connects to a Windows 2000–based server computer configured with RIS. The server subsequently installs Windows 2000 Professional on the client computer, as shown in Figure 5.4.

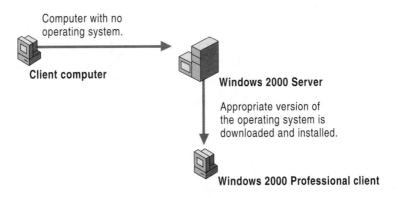

Figure 5.4   Installing Windows 2000 from a RIS Server

RIS allows the administrator to configure Windows 2000 Professional and any applications for a single group of users, and then to apply this configuration when installing the operating system on client computers. For users, the result is a simplified and timely installation and configuration of their computer and a more rapid return to productivity if a hardware failure occurs.

Administrators have two options when using RIS:

CD-based installation The CD-based option is similar to setting up a workstation directly from the Windows 2000 Professional operating system CD; however, the source files reside across the network on available RIS servers.

Sysprep imaging installation The Sysprep imaging option allows a network administrator to clone a standard desktop configuration, complete with operating system configurations and desktop customizations. After installing and configuring Windows 2000, its services, and any standard applications on a workstation, the network administrator runs a wizard that prepares the installation image and replicates it to available RIS servers. Remote boot–enabled client computers can then request to install that image locally from the RIS servers on the network.

The BIOS of the client computer or a special remote boot disk can initiate a network service boot. When a network service boot is requested, DHCP provides an IP address for the client computer, and the client can then download the Client Installation wizard. At this point, the wizard prompts the user to log on, and, depending on the user's credentials or security group membership, displays a menu that offers appropriate customized unattended operating system installation options. (The network administrator uses Group Policy settings to determine which installation options are available to a user, based on the policy defined for that user at the client computer that initiated the network service boot request.)

If you have a Windows 2000 Server infrastructure with RIS installed and a client computer with the appropriate hardware, you can install Windows 2000 Professional and any applications on that client computer, remotely and automatically.

For more information about installing and configuring RIS on a server computer that supplies the installation images, see "Remote OS Installation" in the *Distributed Systems Guide*.

For more information about how to plan for installing and upgrading client systems using RIS, see "Applying Change and Configuration Management" and "Automating Client Installation and Upgrade" in the *Microsoft® Windows® 2000 Server Resource Kit Deployment Planning Guide*.

Terminology

To better understand Remote Installation Services, it is necessary to know these terms:

A *remote boot-enabled client computer* is a computer that meets the PC98 version 0.6 or later design specification and includes a Pre-Boot eXecution Environment (PXE) remote-boot ROM.

A *RIS server computer* is a computer running Windows 2000 Server with RIS installed and configured.

PXE is a Dynamic Host Configuration Protocol (DHCP)–based technology that client computers use to start up remotely over the network and install Windows 2000 Professional from a RIS server.

A *boot ROM* is a BIOS-oriented chip on a network adapter that is responsible for initiating the sequence to start the client computer remotely.

Planning for Client Configuration with Remote Installation Services

Figure 5.5 illustrates the major steps for configuring RIS.

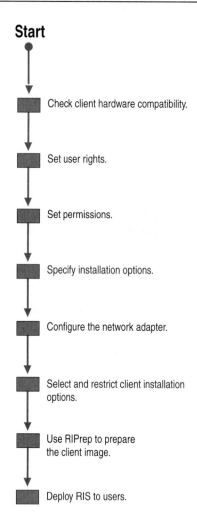

Figure 5.5   Planning Steps for RIS

To ensure that a remote installation can proceed successfully, prepare the client computer for installation from a RIS server by completing the following tasks. Table 5.19 lists the tasks that the server administrator performs on a RIS server versus those that the desktop administrator performs on the client.

Table 5.19 Tasks for Preparing a Client Computer for a Remote Installation

Task	Description	User
Verify that the client hardware meets requirements.	The client computer must meet the requirements for Windows 2000 Professional installation and have a bootable network adapter or be enabled for remote startup. All computers that meet the PC98 0.6 and later design specification include a PXE remote-boot ROM for RIS. For client computers that do not contain a PXE ROM, use the Remote Installation boot disk to create a floppy disk that initiates the RIS process.	Desktop administrator
Set user rights on a domain controller or member server running RIS.	The user account used to install an operating system on the client computer must have **Logon as a Batch Job** user rights. Use Group Policy to grant users or administrators **Logon as a Batch Job** rights.	Server administrator
Set required permissions on the RIS server.	If users are allowed to use RIS to install an operating system on client computers, those users need correct permissions for creating computer accounts within the domain, specifically the Organizational Unit container specified in the Advanced Settings on the RIS Server. Use **Active Directory Users and Computers** to set permissions on a container that allows users to use RIS to install an operating system on their own computers.	Server administrator
Specify installation options on the RIS server.	On the RIS server you can use Group Policy settings to restrict the installation options and the operating-system images that are available to users during remote installation. To restrict images, set access control permissions on the folders containing the installation images.	Server administrator
Configure the network adapter on the client computer.	You must configure the network adapter of the client computer as the primary startup device within the system BIOS. This allows the client computer to request a network service startup from the RIS server on the network.	Desktop administrator

Using the Remote Installation Preparation Wizard

The Remote Installation Preparation wizard provides the ability to prepare a Windows 2000 Professional installation, including locally installed applications and specific configuration settings, and to replicate that image to an available RIS server on the network. The wizard feature currently supports replication of a **single disk single partition (Drive C only)** Windows 2000 Professional installation. This means that the operating system and the applications included with the standard installation must reside on drive C before running the wizard.

First, use the RIS feature to remotely install the Windows 2000 Professional operating system on a client computer. After the operating system is installed, you can install any application, including in-house business applications. You can then configure the installation to adhere to company policies. For example, you might define specific screen colors, set the background bitmap to a company logo, and set intranet proxy server settings within Internet Explorer. After the workstation is configured and has been tested, you can run the Remote Installation Preparation wizard from the RIS server.

The destination computer (that is, the computer that installs the image) does not need to have identical hardware as that of the computer that was used to create the image. However, the Hardware Abstraction Layer (HAL) drivers must be the same (for example, they both must be ACPI-based or both must be non-ACPI-based). In many cases, workstation class computers do not require unique HAL drivers as server class computers do. During image installation, the wizard features use Plug and Play to detect differences between hardware on the source and the destination computers.

▶ **To run the Remote Installation Preparation wizard**

1. Install the standard Windows 2000 Professional operating system from a RIS server on a client computer that supports RIS.

2. Install any applications locally on the client computer. Configure the client computer with any specific corporate standard desktop settings. Be sure the client installation is correct. After the image is replicated to the RIS server, you cannot modify its configuration.

3. Connect to the RIS server where you want to replicate this image. In the **Run** dialog box, type:

   \\RISservername\Reminst\Admin\Riprep.exe

   where:

   RISservername is the computer name of the RIS server where you want to replicate this image.

   Reminst is the Remote Installation Share that is created when you installed the RIS service on the server.

   Admin is the folder that contains the file Riprep.exe that launches the remote installation.

When you connect to the RIS server, the Remote Installation Preparation wizard starts.

4. Enter the name of the RIS server where you want to replicate the contents of the client hard disk. By default, the RIS server from which the wizard is being run is filled in automatically.

5. Type the name of the folder on the RIS server where this image is to be copied. The image is created automatically in the RemoteInstall\setup*OS Language*\Images folder.

6. When prompted, provide a description and help text describing this image. These are displayed to users during operating system image selection. Provide enough information to allow a user to distinguish between images.

7. After you complete the Remote Installation Preparation wizard, review your selections on the summary screen that is displayed.

8. After you review the summary screen, click **Next.** The image preparation and replication process begin. The system is prepared and files are copied to the RIS server. Once the replication of the image completes, any DHCP PXE-based remote-boot enabled client computer, including clients using the Remote Installation Services startup disk, can select the image within the Client Installation wizard for a local installation.

Using the Remote Installation Services Boot Disk

You can use the Remote Installation Services boot disk with client computers that do not contain a remote boot–enabled ROM. The startup disk simulates the PXE startup process for computers that lack a formal remote boot ROM. The boot disk is analogous to a boot ROM, which uses the floppy disk drive to install the operating system from the RIS server.

Insert the remote boot disk into the client computer during the startup process. The RIS remote boot disk can be used with a variety of supported Peripheral Component Interconnect (PCI)–based network adapters. For more information about PCI-based network adapters, see the Windows 2000 Hardware Compatibility List (HCL) link on the Web Resources page at http://windows.microsoft.com/windows2000/reskit/webresources.

Using the Client Installation Wizard

Unless you configured the RIS server to provide a CD-based image for unattended installation, users use the Client Installation wizard, a text-based tool that guides the user through the remote operating system installation process.

When a remote boot-enabled client computer is turned on for the first time, the user is prompted to press **F12** to initiate the download of the Client Installation wizard. After the wizard is downloaded to the client computer, the Welcome screen appears. In response to the welcome, the user is prompted to log on to the network with an existing user account, password, and logon domain. After the logon process is established, RIS checks to see what installation options the user has access to based on Group Policy settings. The Client Installation wizard presents a menu with the appropriate installation options tailored to that user. RIS has been configured so that a user is not presented with installation options by default; rather, the **Automatic setup** option is chosen automatically. For an administrator-based account, all installation and maintenance options are displayed.

The installation process is initiated when the user selects one of the operating system images. Figure 5.6 illustrates the sequence that a user follows when installing a remote operating system by using the default Client Installation wizard screens.

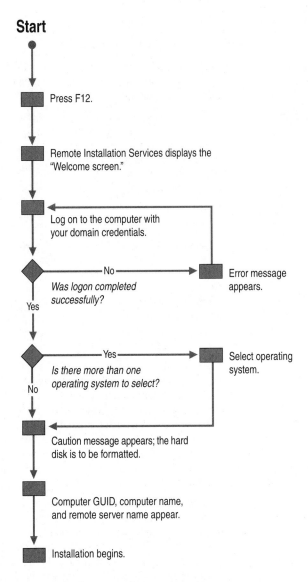

Start

Press F12.

Remote Installation Services displays the "Welcome screen."

Log on to the computer with your domain credentials.

Was logon completed successfully?

No → Error message appears.

Yes

Is there more than one operating system to select?

Yes → Select operating system.

No

Caution message appears; the hard disk is to be formatted.

Computer GUID, computer name, and remote server name appear.

Installation begins.

Figure 5.6   Default Client Installation Wizard

Table 5.20 describes the Client Installation wizard screens that are downloaded when a remote boot–enabled client is started for the first time. The file names and any customization information are also listed.

Table 5.20   Client Installation Wizard Screens

Screen	Description and Customization
Welcome screen (Welcome.osc)	Welcomes the user. You can customize the welcome screen with a specific company message or information to users before they install the operating system.
Logon screen (Login.osc)	Requires a user to log on. The user logs on to the network by using an existing user account, password, and domain. After the user successfully logs on, RIS uses these credentials to determine which installation options to display on the Setup Options screen. If the process is not successful and the logon account, password, or domain are not recognized, the user is prompted to log on again.
Setup Options screen (Choice.osc)	Displays installation options to the user, including: **Automatic**. Provides the easiest operating system installation path. If there is already a computer account object in Active Directory with a GUID that matches the client's GUID, the existing computer account is reused. If a matching GUID is not found in Active Directory, the client is named based on the automatic naming format configured in the properties of the RIS server, and a new computer account is created in the location specified by the RIS server. **Custom**. Allows users to override the automatic computer naming process, as well as the default location within Active Directory where client computer account objects are created. The Custom Setup option is similar to the automatic option, but it can be used to set up a client for a subsequent user (for example, to install an operating system on a client within the enterprise) before delivery to a user. If either the computer name or computer location is left blank on the Custom Setup screen, the automatic name or location is used. **Restart a Previous Setup Attempt**. Restarts the operating system installation process by using the information entered during the previous attempt. If the installation process fails or network connectivity is disrupted during the initial text-mode phase of setup (before completing the file copy phase), a Restart Setup command is available for optional display to the user the next time the computer is started. **Maintenance and Troubleshooting**. Provides access to maintenance and troubleshooting tools, such as system flash BIOS updates and computer diagnostic tools, that can be used prior to operating system installation. The degree to which this screen and its options are displayed is controlled by means of RIS Group Policy settings.

continued

Table 5.20   Client Installation Wizard Screens *(continued)*

Screen	Description and Customization
Error screen (Dupauto.osc)	Instructs the user to contact the network administrator. If a duplicate GUID is found in Active Directory, the user is presented with this screen.
Operating system choice screen (Oschoice.osc)	Displays the list of operating system images on the RIS server that are available to the logged-on user. If only one image is available for the user to install, that image is selected and the user does not see this screen.
Caution screen (Warning.osc)	Displays a warning message that the hard disk is formatted. The user is cautioned that an operating system is about to be installed on the computer, a process which requires the hard disk to be repartitioned and formatted, erasing all data currently on the disk.
Summary screen (Install.osc)	Displays information about the computer including computer name, computer GUID, and the RIS server to be used for downloading the image. Pressing any key begins the installation process.
	At this point, the RIS server has created a computer account object in Active Directory for the computer and can look up the computer and its computer name and other settings if the computer is reinstalled.
	If you were running the Client Installation wizard to prestage the computer for another user, you can now shut down the computer and return it to the end user. The end user must reset password permissions on the newly created computer account object in Active Directory.

After the summary screen appears, the user exits the Client Installation wizard and proceeds to the automated installation process. This is similar to the installation process of installing from a CD, but it is automated and occurs while the operating system files are stored on the RIS server. Depending on the speed of your network and the load on the RIS server, this process can be much faster than an installation from a CD-ROM drive.

Caution   All data is erased from your hard disk drive when you install a new operating system.

Microsoft Systems Management Server

Microsoft® Systems Management Server 2.0 provides tools that allows administrators to centrally deploy and manage software in an organization. These tools are especially useful in large organizations with complex environments because they provide hardware and software inventory collection; software distribution and installation; and software metering, diagnostics, and troubleshooting.

This section provides a brief overview of how you can use Systems Management Server to perform an automated upgrade of the existing Windows operating systems on your client computers to Windows 2000 Professional.

For more information on the functionality that Systems Management Server provides for deploying and managing Windows 2000, see "Using Systems Management Server to Deploy Windows 2000" in the *Deployment Planning Guide*. For comprehensive information about Systems Management Server, see the *Microsoft® Systems Management Server Resource Kit*.

Overview of Systems Management Server

Systems Management Server allows administrators to centrally manage all desktop computers in an organization. It supports all Windows-based 16-bit and 32-bit desktops, from Windows 3.1 to Windows 2000 Professional, whether operating in Windows NT, NetWare 3.1, or NetWare NDS environments. Systems Management Server can be used as a stand-alone desktop management system or as a desktop management component within an integrated enterprise management solution Its key features are summarized here.

Hardware and Software Inventory—Systems Management Server uses Windows Management Instrumentation (WMI) and new version resource information software scanners to upload a wealth of detailed hardware and software inventory information into a Microsoft® SQL Server™-based repository. This provides administrators with a dynamic, efficient mechanism for getting hardware and software information on every application on every desktop computer. Additionally, a new compliance-comparative database tool has been added that evaluates inventory after it is collected and generates reports on compliance status.

Software Distribution and Installation—Using Systems Management Server, administrators can deploy both the operating system and applications. Software distribution is now rules-based, and distribution destinations are dynamically evaluated. It is also fully integrated with inventory management to allow sophisticated targeting. Systems Management Server first performs a query of software inventory and collection information, then targets an audience, and finally deploys software to that audience according to administrator-defined rules.

For example, if a new user joins a user group, software is now automatically sent to them according to the Group Policy of the user's group. With Systems Management Server, you can distribute an application immediately if a situation requires it, roll back an application, and uninstall software automatically when a user moves to a different department.

Software Metering—Administrators often require tools to track software usage by users, groups, workstations, time, or license quota. Systems Management Server 2.0 can monitor, analyze, and if required, control the use of applications on servers and workstations. These tools provide administrators with varying levels of control, ranging from simple alerts to the ability to prevent applications from running.

Diagnostics and Troubleshooting—In addition to reporting on the current state of a workstation or server and providing remote control facilities, Systems Management Server provides a range of advanced diagnostic tools such as the following: a network monitor with real-time and post-capture experts to analyze network conditions and performance; a server HealthMon tool that tracks critical performance information on a Windows 2000 Server; and the Microsoft®BackOffice® family of applications.

Distributing Windows 2000 Professional with Systems Management Server

This section describes how Systems Management Server-based software distribution proceeds from the perspective of users of client computers in your organization. For information about how administrators should plan for and undertake Windows 2000 Professional deployment by using Systems Management Server, see "Using Systems Management Server to Deploy Windows 2000" in the *Deployment Planning Guide*.

Software distribution starts with Systems Management Server packages that the administrator creates. These packages contain the source files for the program being installed and the details that direct the software distribution process. Instead of creating a package, administrators can use a preformatted file called a *package definition file* that contains all the information necessary to create a package. Systems Management Server 2.0 provides a package definition file for Windows 2000 Professional installation. The packages or package definition files reside at a distribution point, which is a shared directory from which client computers can access the files.

The administrator alerts users about the Systems Management Server package by creating an advertisement. An advertisement specifies what program is available to client computers, which computers will receive the advertisement, and when the program is scheduled for installation. Depending on how the advertisement is defined, it can grant users control over the scheduling of the package, it can run in privileged mode so that you do not have to give privileges to users, or it might operate without any intervention from the user.

Figure 5.7 shows the software distribution process.

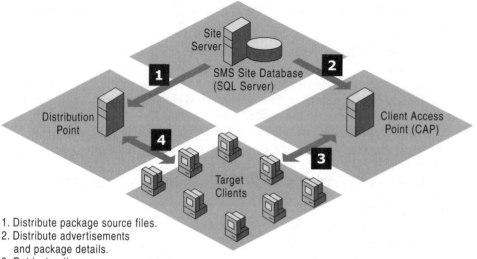

1. Distribute package source files.
2. Distribute advertisements
   and package details.
3. Get instructions.
4. Run programs.

Figure 5.7   Systems Management Server Software Distribution Process

Typically, administrators give users advance notice of the upgrade. When users are notified of an impending upgrade, it is a good idea for users to get any training they might require, perform backups, prepare any programs they are responsible for, and make sure all their documents are closed.

During a Windows 2000 Professional upgrade, the computer must be restarted several times. If this can occur automatically, the entire upgrade can be accomplished without input from users. Typically, administrators consider it good practice not to allow user input during package installations in order to reduce inconvenience to the user and limit the potential for problems during upgrade. The packages themselves contain passwords, file locations, and other information a user must typically provide in an attended installation. Even if the process does involve the user, the administrator can define the packages to proceed so that users do not have to choose between complex options.

For packages that are scheduled to run overnight or over a weekend, Windows 95–based or Windows 98–based client computers must have a user logged on for the upgrade to start automatically. In this case, users might want to use a secure screen saver to prevent others from using their computers while they are away. Windows NT Workstation 4.0–based client computers do not require that a user be logged on for the advertisements to start. Users who maintain a boot password on their computers must temporarily disable their boot passwords for the upgrade. If this is not possible, someone must be present during the upgrade.

For more information about the specific procedures and strategies involved in Systems Management Server deployment of Windows 2000 Professional in your organization, see "Using Systems Management Server to Deploy Windows 2000" in the *Deployment Planning Guide*.

Additional Resources

- For more information about the answer file parameters, see Unattend.doc file provided in Support\Tools\Deploy.cab on the Windows 2000 Professional operating system CD. You can either use Windows Explorer or run the Extract.exe command to extract and view the Unattend.doc file.

- For the latest information about Windows 2000 Professional, see the Windows 2000 Professional link on the Web Resources page at http://windows.microsoft.com/windows2000/reskit/webresources.

- For more information about deployment tools and methods, see http://www.microsoft.com.

C H A P T E R   6

Setup and Startup

Understanding the Microsoft® Windows® 2000 Professional startup process, how startup interacts with the registry, Plug and Play device detection, and multiple-boot operating systems, can help you optimize your system and effectively troubleshoot problems when they occur.

In This Chapter

Related Information in the Resource Kit

- For more information about Plug and Play, see "Device Management" in this book.

- For more information about Advanced Configuration and Power Interface (ACPI), see "Power Management" in this book.

- For more information about registry settings, see the Technical Reference to the Windows 2000 Registry (Regentry.chm) on the *Microsoft® Windows® 2000 Resource Kit* companion CD.

Quick Guide to Setup and Startup

Understanding the Setup and startup processes in Windows 2000 Professional is important to maintaining your system. Use this quick guide to understand the steps involved in setting up and starting up Windows 2000 Professional, including how the devices are detected, how to configure your computer with multiple operating systems, how to update Windows 2000 Professional with service packs, and how to troubleshoot related problems.

Review the Phases of Setup

Review a brief description of how boot drivers and Plug and Play devices are loaded during the text-mode and graphical user interface (GUI)-mode phases of Setup, as well as a description of the Setup log files. An understanding of the Setup process can help you troubleshoot any problems you encounter during Setup.

- See "Phases of Setup" in this chapter.

Understand the steps involved in starting Windows 2000 Professional.

Understanding the system startup procedure allows you to troubleshoot problems with installing and starting Windows 2000 Professional.

- See "Windows 2000 Professional Startup Process" in this chapter

Understand how Windows 2000 Professional detects Plug and Play devices.

An understanding of how Windows 2000 Professional detects and loads Plug and Play devices can give you a better understanding of how these devices are detected and configured during Setup and help you troubleshoot any problems that might occur.

- See "Plug and Play Device Detection" in this chapter.

Configure your computer to create a multiple-boot system by using Windows 2000 Professional with other operating systems.

Review the procedures and considerations for setting up a multiple-boot configuration. Review the detailed description about how to set up a multiple-boot system by using Windows 2000 Professional with Microsoft® Windows NT® 4.0, Microsoft® Windows® 95, Microsoft® Windows® 98, and Microsoft® MS-DOS®.

- See "Installing a Multiple-Boot Operating System" in this chapter.

Install service packs with Windows 2000 Professional.

Learn how service packs are added to Windows 2000 Professional and how Service Pack installation has changed since Windows NT 4.0.

- See "Installing Service Packs" in this chapter.

Remove Windows 2000 Professional from your computer

If you have problems during Setup or if Windows 2000 Professional does not run, you might need to remove the operating system from the computer. Review details about how to remove the operating system and the associated files.

- See "Removing Windows 2000 Professional from Your Computer" in this chapter.

Troubleshoot Windows 2000 Professional Setup

Review some of the problems that can occur during Windows 2000 Professional Setup and the steps you can take to troubleshoot them.

- See "Troubleshooting Windows 2000 Professional Setup" in this chapter.

Phases of Setup

When you are installing or upgrading Windows 2000 Professional, follow the three general Setup phases, including: the Setup Loader phase, which is used to begin the installation process; text-mode Setup, which is the text-based portion of Setup and is characterized by a blue background; and GUI-mode Setup, which is the final phase of Setup and is distinguished by a Windows graphical interface and wizard page.

Setup Loader

The Setup Loader phase of Setup is usually initiated by running Winnt.exe or Winnt32.exe from the command line. You can also initiate Setup Loader by starting the computer from the Windows 2000 operating system CD. Setup copies the installation files and Setupldr from the CD to the hard drive and creates or modifies Boot.ini (in multiple-boot configurations in which either Windows NT 4.0 or Windows 2000 is previously installed). Setupldr is a variant of Ntldr, which initiates the installation process when it is called by the bootstrap loader and loads Ntbootdd.sys and Ntdetect.com. These files perform initial hardware detection and then pass control to the kernel, which is loaded along with the boot drivers and the drivers for the hard drive controller(s). Setupldr also changes the boot sector to point to Setupldr.

This phase of Setup also gathers information to create a small unattended file. This file answers some of the questions that are asked later in the Setup process so that it can be run with minimal involvement.

For more information about using Winnt.exe and Winnt32.exe, see "Installing Windows 2000 Professional" in this book.

Text-Mode Setup

The text-mode phase of Setup is a mini-kernel mode phase that is started by a special session manager called Usetup.exe, which is located in the folder i386. The text-mode phase is also identified by its character-based screen with a blue background. During this phase, Setup completes the following tasks:

- Determines the basic hardware installed (such as the CPU, motherboard type, and hard disk controllers).
- Examines the hard disks.
- Creates the registry and file systems.
- Performs limited Plug and Play detection.
- Partitions and formats the drive for the file system or converts to an NTFS file system when you upgrade from Windows NT 4.0 Workstation.
- Checks that there is adequate disk space for the installation and checks for minimum system requirements, such as memory and hard disk drive space.
- Copies most installation files to the Windows 2000 installation folder to begin the GUI-mode phase of Setup.

GUI-Mode Setup

After the text-mode phase of Setup is complete, the computer restarts, and the GUI-mode phase of Setup begins. GUI-mode is identified by a graphical user interface (GUI) and the Setup wizard, which begins with the End-User License Agreement (EULA) and **Product ID** dialog box.

Note When you use Winnt32.exe or Autorun.exe, the EULA and **Product ID** dialog box appear during the Setup loader phase.

Setup performs the following tasks during the GUI-mode phase:

- Detects and installs devices found on the computer.
- Configures each device, and installs and configures networking components.
- Installs any optional components.
- Copies the remaining installation files that were not copied during the text-mode phase of Setup.

- Writes the Setup log files to the installation directory. The Setup log files are as follows:

  - Setupact.log, which contains information about all the files copied during setup.

  - Setuperr.log, which contains information about any errors that were encountered during Setup.

  - Setupapi.log, which contains information about the device driver files that were copied during Setup.

  - Setuplog.txt, which contains additional information about the device driver files that were copied during Setup.

Note The log files that are created during Setup can be used to help troubleshoot any installation problems that you might encounter. Double-click a log file to read it, or open it by using Notepad or a word processing application.

When GUI-mode has completed these tasks, it starts the operating system and presents the Winlogon screen. This stage of Setup is recoverable; if Setup halts, it can restart and continue where it left off.

During a clean installation of Windows 2000 Professional, Setup now prompts you to provide a user account and logon information. If you are upgrading from Windows 95 or Windows 98, Setup prompts you to supply password information.

Note On a new installation, you are prompted for an Administrator password; you can also personalize the installation, for example, by customizing Regional Options, Accessibility Options, and Network and Dial-up Connections settings.

Windows 2000 Professional Startup Process

The Windows 2000 startup process is similar to the startup process for Windows NT 4.0 but is significantly different from other operating systems. In MS-DOS, Windows 95, and Windows 98, the computer loads the IO.sys file followed by Msdos.sys and Command.com. However, in Windows 2000, these files only exist on computers that have multiple-boot configurations with Windows 95, Windows 98, or MS-DOS.

The following list describes the startup sequence on a computer running Windows 2000 Professional:

- Power-on self test (POST)

- Initial startup process

- Bootstrap loader process

- Operating system selection (if the computer has a multiple-boot configuration)
- Hardware detection
- Hardware configuration selection (if you are using more than one hardware profile)
- Kernel loading
- Operating system logon process

Note The system startup sequence only applies to a system that is started from a reboot or a power off state. This sequence does not apply to a system that is turned on from a hibernated state.

This startup sequence applies to all versions of Windows 2000.

Power-on Self Test

When a computer is started or reset, it runs the power-on self test (POST), which determines the amount of memory in the computer and checks that required hardware devices, such as the keyboard, are present and functioning. After the POST sequence, adapters that have their own basic input/output system (BIOS) run individual POST routines.

Note Some adapters (for example, some video adapters) run their POST sequence before the memory and device check, which runs during the initial POST.

Starting the Computer

After the computer finishes the POST, the system BIOS attempts to start an operating system. The sequence that the BIOS follows depends on the BIOS configuration. For example, if the BIOS search order is set to A and then C (A, C), the BIOS searches the floppy disk drive for a bootable disk. If drive A contains a bootable floppy disk, the BIOS loads its first sector (the partition boot sector) into memory. If the floppy disk is not bootable, the following error message appears.

```
Non-system disk or disk error
Replace and press any key when ready
```

If the BIOS does not find a floppy disk in the drive, it then searches for the active partition on the hard disk drive. If there is no system partition on the first hard disk, the master boot record (MBR) displays one of the following errors:

- Invalid partition table
- Error loading operating system
- Missing operating system

When the active partition of the hard drive is found, the system BIOS reads the MBR and loads it into memory. The MBR then scans the partition table for the system partition information. When the system partition information has been read, it loads sector 0 of the system partition into memory and starts it.

Note   Sector 0 of the system partition can be a utility, a diagnostic program, or a partition boot sector that contains the startup code for the operating system.

The system partition must be on the first physical disk and contain the system startup files listed in Table 6.1.

Table 6.1   Windows 2000 Startup Files

File Name	Location
Ntldr	Root of startup disk
Boot.ini	Root of startup disk
Bootsect.dos	Root of startup disk (on multiple-boot systems)
Ntdetect.com	Root of startup disk
Hyberfil.sys	%Systemdrive%
Ntbootdd.sys	Root of startup disk (for SCSI and some large IDE drives)
Ntoskrnl.exe	%SystemRoot%\System32
Hal.dll	%SystemRoot%\System32
System key	%SystemRoot%\System32\Config
Device drivers	%SystemRoot%\System32\Drivers
Cdldr	Root of startup disk

Note   If the name of the path in Boot.ini uses small computer system interface (SCSI) syntax, the Ntbootdd.sys must be in the root folder of the system partition.

The boot partition can be on the same partition as the system partition, on a different partition, or on a different hard disk.

For the most part, the MBR is independent of the operating system. For example, the MBR can start Windows NT, Windows 95, Windows 98, MS-DOS, Microsoft® Windows® 3.*x*, and Windows 2000 Professional. However, after boot sector 0 has been loaded into memory, the partition boot sector is dependent on both the operating system and the file system. The Windows 2000 partition boot sector performs the following functions:

- Reads the file system to find the bootstrap loader.
- Loads the bootstrap loader into memory.
- Starts the bootstrap loader.

Bootstrap Loader Process

Ntldr loads the operating system files from the boot partition. If you have a multiple-boot configuration, you are prompted to choose an operating system.

Ntldr controls the operating system selection and the hardware detection process before passing control to the Windows 2000 kernel. Ntldr must be in the root folder of the startup disk.

Ntldr performs the following steps:

- Sets the processor to run in 32-bit flat memory mode. When you first start a computer, it runs in real mode, which is similar to an 8088 or 8086 CPU. Because Ntldr is a 32-bit program, it must switch the processor to 32-bit mode so that it can continue to load the operating system.

- Starts the NTFS file system or the file allocation table (FAT) 16 or 32 file system. The code to access the appropriate file system is built into Ntldr.

- Reads Boot.ini, which displays the operating selections on the boot loader screen. If you select an operating system other than Windows 2000 Professional, Ntldr loads and passes control to the Bootsect.dos file, and the selected operating system starts. If you select Windows 2000 Professional, Ntldr starts Ntdetect.com, which gathers information about the computer hardware.

- Asks you to choose a hardware profile if you have one or more hardware profiles on your computer.

- Loads and passes the information from Ntdetect.com to Ntoskrnl.exe, starting the startup screen.

Operating System Selection

Boot.ini contains the list of available operating systems. Each entry includes the path to the boot partition for the operating system, the string to display in the boot loader screen, and optional parameters. Boot.ini supports starting multiple versions of Windows 2000, as well as starting other operating systems, such as Windows 95, Windows 98, Windows NT 4.0, MS-DOS, and OS/2.

When you install Windows 2000, Setup places Boot.ini at the root of the system partition.

The following is a sample Boot.ini file:

```
[boot loader]
timeout=30
default=multi(0)disk(0)rdisk(0)partition(1)\WINNT
[operating systems]
multi(0)disk(0)rdisk(0)partition(1)\winnt= "Microsoft Windows 2000
Professional" /fastdetect
C:\="Windows 98"
```

The information displayed on the boot loader screen is based on the contents of Boot.ini, such as in the following example:

```
Please select the operating system to start:

Microsoft Windows 2000 Professional
Microsoft Windows 98

Use ↑ and ↓ to move the highlight to your choice.
Please Enter to choose.
Seconds until highlighted choice will be started automatically: 29

For troubleshooting and advanced startup options for Windows 2000, press
F8.
```

The first operating system listed is the default. In this configuration, if you do not select an operating system before the timer reaches 0, Windows 2000 Professional is started.

Hardware Detection

After you select the operating system, Ntdetect.com detects the hardware, gathers a list of the currently installed hardware components, and passes the information to Ntldr.

Ntdetect.com detects the following components:

- Computer ID
- Bus/adapter type
- Video adapter
- Keyboard
- Communications ports
- Floppy disks
- Mouse or other pointing devices
- Parallel ports

Selecting a Hardware Configuration

During the Ntdetect phase, if you have multiple hardware configurations, the following information appears:

```
Hardware Profile/Configuration Recovery Menu
This menu allows you to select a hardware profile
to be used when Windows 2000 is started.
```

Note Profiles are only necessary under non–Plug and Play conditions. Plug and Play negates the need for profiles.

The bootstrap loader pauses for a few seconds or until you press Enter. If you have only one hardware profile, Windows 2000 Professional uses the default settings.

Windows 2000 Professional automatically uses the default settings if you do not select a hardware profile. When the default configuration is used, the bootstrap loader uses the registry information that Windows 2000 Professional saved at the completion of the last shutdown. After you select a hardware profile, Ntdetect.com passes control back to Ntldr.

Loading and Initializing the Kernel

During the next phase, Ntldr loads the kernel and the hardware abstraction layer (HAL) into memory. Next the bootstrap loader loads the registry key HKEY_LOCAL_MACHINE\SYSTEM from the folder %SystemRoot%\system32\Config\System. Ntldr creates the control set that it uses to initialize the computer. The loader uses the control set identified by the default value unless you choose the **Last Known Good Configuration** from the Hardware Profiles screen.

The kernel initiates the Windows 2000 Professional screen, and the Starting Up progress bar is displayed. When the status bar completes, Ntoskrnl prepares the network information.

The kernel uses the information that was passed from the boot loader to create the HKEY_LOCAL_MACHINE\HARDWARE key, which contains the hardware data that is collected at system startup. The data includes information about various hardware components on the motherboard and the system interrupts allocated by each device.

The kernel then creates the Clone control set, which is a copy that points to the Current control set. The Clone control set represents the state of the computer during configuration and is not changed or modified.

Logging On to the Operating System

The Windows subsystem automatically starts Winlogon.exe, which starts the Local Security Administration. The **Begin Logon** dialog box appears. Windows 2000 might still be initializing network device drivers, but you can log on.

The Service Controller searches the registry for services that are configured to load automatically. Autoload services have a Start value of 0x2 in the subkey HKEY_LOCAL_MACHINE\SYSTEM\CurrentControlSet\Services*DriverName*. The services that are loaded during this phase are loaded in parallel and so are loaded based on their dependencies. The dependencies are described in the **DependOnGroup** and **DependOnService** entries in the subkey HKEY_LOCAL_MACHINE\SYSTEM\CurrentControlSet\Services*DriverName*.

Note   Windows 2000 startup is not considered complete until a user successfully logs on to the system. After a user logs on, the Clone control set is copied to the LastKnownGood control set.

Understanding the Boot.ini Naming Convention

Windows 2000 uses the Advanced Reduced Instruction Set Computing (RISC) naming convention to define the path to a Windows 2000 installation.

Using ARC Pathnames

The Advanced RISC Computing (ARC) pathnames in Boot.ini point to the location of the boot partition for all Windows 2000 installations. A single line in Boot.ini represents each installation. During the startup process, the boot loader screen prompts you to choose an installation.

The ARC names in the file Boot.ini are similar to the following:

- Multi(W)disk(X)rdisk(Y)partition(Z)\%systemroot%
- Scsi(W)disk(X)rdisk(Y)partition(Z)\%systemroot%
- Signature(8b467c12)disk(1)rdisk(0)partition(2)%systemroot%="description"

Windows 2000 Professional can use any of these formats in Boot.ini to locate the *SystemRoot* directory.

Multi Syntax

This form of the ARC pathname is referred to as Multi. On Microsoft® Windows NT® version 3.1, Multi syntax was only valid for Integrated Device Electronics (IDE), Enhanced Integrated Drive Electronics (EIDE), and Enhanced Small Device Interface (ESDI) disks. In Microsoft® Windows NT® version 3.5 and later (including Windows 2000), it is also valid for small computer system interface (SCSI) disks. It is not used with Windows 95 or Windows 98.

The Multi syntax instructs Windows 2000 Professional to rely on the system BIOS to load system files. This means that Ntldr is using interrupt (INT) 13 BIOS calls to find and load Ntoskrnl.exe and any other files it needs to start the system.

The following is an example of the Multi syntax :

```
multi(W)disk(X)rdisk(Y)partiton(Z)
```

Table 6.2 describes the parameters used in the Multi syntax:

Table 6.2   Multi Syntax Parameter Variables

Parameter	Multi Parameter Definitions
W	The number of the adapter, usually 0.
X	Always 0.
Y	The number for the disk on the adapter, usually between 0 and 3.
Z	The partition number. All partitions that are in use receive a number. Primary partitions are numbered before logical drives.
	The first valid number for Z is 1; W, X, and Y start at 0.

In theory, the Multi syntax can start Windows 2000 from any disk. However, this requires that all connected disks use the INT 13, and the system BIOS usually identifies only one disk adapter with INT13. For this reason, you can only use the Multi syntax to start Windows 2000 Professional from either of the two disks on the primary IDE or SCSI device or on the secondary IDE or SCSI device.

The use of the Multi syntax depends on the type of adapter that your computer uses. For example:

- On IDE adapters, the Multi syntax works for up to four disks: two on primary and two on secondary IDE channels.

- On SCSI adapters, the Multi syntax works for the first two disks on the first SCSI adapter (the adapter whose BIOS loads first).

- With both SCSI and IDE adapters, the Multi syntax works for only the IDE disks on the first adapter.

SCSI Syntax

The SCSI syntax tells Windows 2000 Professional to load a SCSI device driver to access the boot partition.

The SCSI syntax is as follows:

```
scsi(W)disk(X)rdisk(Y)partition(Z)
```

Table 6.3 defines the parameters used in the SCSI syntax:

Table 6.3   SCSI Syntax Parameters

Parameter	SCSI Parameter Definitions
W	The controller that is found.
X	The number of the physical disk attached to the computer.
Y	The SCSI logical unit number (LUN) of the disk that contains the boot partition. This is typically 0.
Z	The partition number. All partitions that are in use receive a number. Primary partitions are numbered before logical drives. The first valid number for Z is 1; W, X, and Y start at 0.

Signature Syntax

The Signature syntax is equivalent to the SCSI syntax but is used instead to support the Plug and Play architecture in Windows 2000. Because Windows 2000 is a Plug and Play operating system, the SCSI controller number instance might vary each time you start Windows 2000, especially if you add new SCSI controller hardware after Setup.

The Signature syntax instructs Ntldr to locate the drive with a disk signature that matches the value in the parentheses, regardless of which SCSI controller number that the drive is connected to.

The naming format in Boot.ini starts with Signature syntax. For example:

```
signature(8b467c12)disk(1)rdisk(0)partition(2)\winnt="description"
```

The Signature syntax is used only if one of the following conditions exists:

- The partition on which you installed Windows 2000 is larger than 7.8 gigabytes (GB) in size, or the ending cylinder number is higher than 1024 for that partition, and the system BIOS or boot controller BIOS does not support Extended INT13.

- The drive on which you installed Windows 2000 is connected to a SCSI controller whose BIOS is disabled, so INT13 BIOS calls cannot be used during the startup process.

The Signature value is extracted from the MBR. This unique hexadecimal number is either written to the MBR during the text-mode portion of Setup or by a previous installation of Windows NT 4.0 or earlier.

Ntbootdd.sys

Ntbootdd.sys is a copy of the SCSI device driver and resides on the system partition. Ntbootdd.sys is used when using the SCSI or Signature syntax in the file Boot.ini.

Additionally, if you have multiple SCSI controllers that use different device drivers, include only the controllers that are controlled by Ntbootdd.sys when determining the value of the W parameter. For example, if you have an Adaptec 2940 controller (which uses Aic78xx.sys) and an Adaptec 1542 controller (which uses Aha154x.sys), the value of W is always 0. Ntbootdd.sys changes in the following situations:

- If you load Windows 2000 Professional from a disk on the Adaptec 2940 controller, Ntbootdd.sys is a copy of Aic78xx.sys.

- If you load Windows 2000 Professional from a disk on the Adaptec 1542 controller, Ntbootdd.sys is a copy of Aha154x.sys.

Editing Boot.ini

When you install Windows 2000 Professional, Boot.ini sets the system and hidden attributes for you. You can edit the time-out and default parameters in Boot.ini by using the System option in Control Panel.

Important Back up the original Boot.ini file before making any changes.

To view Boot.ini, you must be able to view hidden files in My Computer.

▶ **To show hidden files in My Computer**

1. On the **Tools** menu, click **Folder Options,** and then click the **View** tab.

2. Clear **Hide protected operating system files**.

3. Click **OK**.

To edit the file Boot.ini, you can use Windows Explorer and double-click Boot.ini, or you can open any text editor to edit the file.

If you change the path to the Windows 2000 boot partition, edit the entries for both the default path and the operating system path. If you change only one, a new choice is added to the boot loader screen with the default designator next to it.

Driver Cabinet File

A cabinet (.cab) file is a compressed file that contains other distribution files, such as drivers and system files. Drivers are placed in a single .cab file on the Windows 2000 operating system CD. This driver .cab is used by both Setup and other system components that need to install drivers. The .cab file contains approximately 3000 files and is installed at:

%windir%\Driver Cache\<platform>\driver.cab

The list of files is in Drvindex.inf. To view the .cab file, use Windows Explorer.

The benefits of using a .cab file include the following:

- Does not require administrators to use a Setup CD to install new devices on the computer.

- Does not require you to log on with local admin rights to install new hardware as long as the device is present in the .cab file and digitally signed. You can override this by deleting the .cab file from the drive.

- Reduces the amount of bandwidth and installation time that is required for network installations. (Winnt32.exe and Winnt.exe copy a single file instead of many smaller files.)

- Provides a simple way to install printer drivers. Administrators do not need to have the Windows 2000 CD to install printer drivers because most printer manufactures use Microsoft core printer drivers. For mobile users, the printer drivers are always available for quick printing.

- Enables remote install services clients to install drivers for new devices locally. It also allows the Remote Installation feature to support different hardware between the source computer used to create the image and the destination computer installing that image. For more information about Remote Installation Services, see "Customizing and Automating Installations" in this book.

When a driver file is needed, Setup checks the Drvindex.inf file to see if the file is listed. If the file is listed and the .cab file is on your computer, Setup tries to copy the file from the .cab file. If a signed driver file is found in the driver cache directory and has the same name as the needed file, Setup uses this file instead of the one contained in the .cab file. If the required file does not exist in the directory of the .cab, the installation path is searched. If that fails, Setup prompts you to supply the required file.

Plug and Play Device Detection

Plug and Play is a combination of the system BIOS, hardware devices, system resources, device drivers, and operating system software. This combination provides dynamic installation and configuration of new system hardware components and Plug and Play devices that require little or no manual intervention. For more information about the Windows 2000 implementation of Plug and Play, see "Device Management" in this book.

System BIOS

The basic input/output system (BIOS) starts the computer by providing a basic set of instructions. It performs all necessary startup tasks, including POST and starting an operating system from a floppy disk or hard disk. The BIOS uses a library of interrupt handlers to provide the operating system with an interface to the underlying hardware. For instance, each time a key is pressed, the CPU performs an interrupt to read that key. This is similar for other input/output devices, such as serial and parallel ports, video cards, sound cards, hard disk controllers, and so on. Some older computers cannot cooperate with modern hardware because the operating system cannot call a BIOS routine to use it. You can solve this problem by replacing the BIOS with a newer one that supports your hardware or by installing a device driver for the hardware.

How the BIOS interacts with Plug and Play devices varies, depending on whether the system BIOS or the operating system is responsible for configuring the hardware device. Taking this into consideration, you have three possible scenarios:

Only the initial program load or boot devices are controlled by the BIOS

Initial program load (IPL) devices are required to start the system. They can be embedded on the system board or on added devices.

This scenario also supports dynamic configuration, where a non-boot device, such as a PCMCIA card, is installed while the power is on. Each time the system is started in a dynamic configuration, the devices are reexamined. In theory, the assigned resources can be rearranged at restart whether devices have been added or removed.

All devices are configured by the BIOS

If **Enable Plug and Play operating system** is disabled and the device has a static configuration, you can not remove the device without turning off the system. In addition, you must first turn off the system before you remove almost any device. The exceptions are external port devices and bus types that are Plug and Play by nature, such as universal serial bus (USB) and IEEE 1394.

No devices are configured by the BIOS

In the Advanced Configuration and Power Interface (ACPI) of Windows 98 and Windows 2000, the operating system configures almost all devices. The exceptions are those devices that are needed to start the operating system and bus types that handle it on their own, such as Peripheral Component Interconnect (PCI), USB, and IEEE 1394.

System Resources

System resources are made up of the BIOS, interrupt request lines (IRQs), direct memory access (DMA), input/output (I/O) port addresses, and reserved memory. They allow the individual hardware components to signal and gain access to the CPU without conflicting with other hardware devices. Before Plug and Play, each resource had to be configured manually, which could be difficult.

The Plug and Play Manager determines the hardware resources requested by each device (for example, I/O ports, IRQs, DMA channels, and memory locations) and assigns them appropriately. The Plug and Play Manager can reconfigure resource assignments when necessary, such as when a new device is added that requires resources that are already in use. It can also maintain ISA detection and configuration that is non–Plug and Play.

IRQs

IRQs are channels or switches that are used by hardware devices to signal the CPU. The traditional architecture has 16 IRQs, some of which are used for onboard devices such as the system clock, keyboard, and mouse. The remaining IRQs can be used by expansion cards that are added to the computer.

When you have used all your IRQs, you can share them. In addition, methods have been devised that do not require IRQs. Some new bus types, such as USB and IEEE 1394, require at least one IRQ for the bus controller itself because they reside over the PCI bus. It is possible to share available IRQs, On ACPI systems, all PCI devices can share IRQ 9 by default. Most of the problems created by sharing IRQs are related to bandwidth. To share IRQs, the system places these IRQs on a stack and manages them in first in, first out (FIFO) fashion. The more sharing, the longer it takes to traverse the stack and the more opportunity for time-outs and other problems.

I/O Port Address

After a device signals the CPU by using its assigned IRQ, the device needs to pass information between it and the CPU. This is done through memory. An I/O port address is an area of memory that is reserved by the device to pass required information to the device driver, which in turn passes the information to the CPU. These are not linear memory locations but numerical pointers or representations of physical memory locations. On each hardware device, a read-only memory (ROM) chip stores a collection of device descriptors as hardware registers or on the PCI bus, as the configuration memory space. I/O port addresses serve as a special "lens" that isolates one register from another. There are 65,535 of these ports available in current systems, but as with IRQs, the ports are already reserved for specific devices. In addition, I/O ports can be segregated according to bus type, with some I/O addresses reserved for PCI and others for ISA.

DMA

The device can access physical memory either through the CPU or by bypassing the CPU entirely. Direct memory access (DMA) channels allow devices to write to physical memory without placing a load on the CPU. There are usually eight DMA channels; existing devices reserve a number of channels, leaving approximately five channels free to be used with additional devices. The exception is the PCI bus, in which the DMA is replaced by bus mastering.

Detecting Plug and Play Devices

The Plug and Play detection process in Windows 2000 works similarly to Plug and Play in Windows 98. Each device that is attached to the computer is identified when Windows 2000 Professional starts. Devices that are not required to start the computer remain inactive until the operating system has started.

After identifying each device, Plug and Play determines the system resources that each device requires, stores the configuration in memory, and assigns those resources to the device. After the devices have been configured, Plug and Play identifies and loads the drivers that each device requires.

Plug and Play continues to provide an interface between the system and the device drivers, which consist of I/O routines, Interrupt Request Packets (IRPs), driver entry points, and the registry. In addition, Plug and Play handles power management events and hardware detection, such as removing a portable computer from a docking station or adding or removing a hardware device. Plug and Play also allows applications to control certain power management events.

For more information about Plug and Play devices, see "Device Management" in this book. For more information about power management, see "Power Management" in this book.

Building the Device Tree

The device tree contains information about the devices attached to the system. The operating system uses information from drivers and other components to build this tree when the computer starts, and it updates the tree as devices are added or removed. The device tree is hierarchical, with devices on a bus represented as subcomponents of the bus adapter or controller.

▶ **To view the hierarchy of devices in the device tree**

- In Device Manager, click the **View** menu, and then click **Devices by connection**.

Figure 6.1 shows the structure of the device tree.

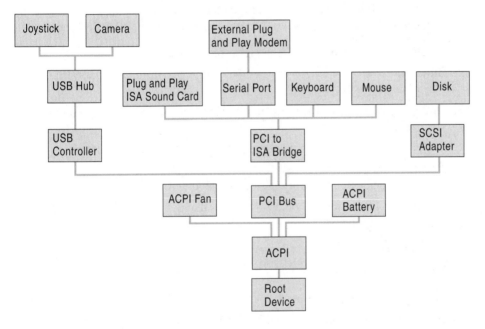

Figure 6.1   Device Tree Structure

Each node of the device tree is a device node, which consists of the device objects for the drivers and internal information maintained by the operating system.

The hierarchy of the device tree reflects the structure in which the devices are attached to the computer. The operating system uses this hierarchy as it manages the devices. For example, if a user requests to unplug the USB controller from the computer represented in Figure 6.1, the Plug and Play Manager asks the drivers for the USB controller to remove the controller, and the Plug and Play Manager queries the drivers for any descendants of the controller. The Plug and Play Manager determines that this action would cause the USB hub, the joystick, and the camera to become unplugged.

Plug and Play Detection on Non-ACPI Systems

Before installing Windows 2000 on a non-ACPI system, disable **Plug and Play Operating System** support in the system BIOS.

When a non-ACPI computer is started, Plug and Play is configured by the system BIOS and not the operating system. The BIOS performs the following steps:

1. Isolates any Plug and Play ISA devices for configuration.
2. Builds a *resource allocation map* of the resources consumed by non-Plug and Play devices.
3. Optionally maintains a list of the previous resource configuration in non-volatile storage or memory.
4. Selects and enables the input and output devices that are required during the startup process.
6. Initializes the device ROM if the device encountered is a boot device.
7. Allocates conflict-free resources to devices that have not yet been configured.
8. Activates all devices.
9. Initializes any option ROMs that have been encountered.
10. Starts the bootstrap loader.

One requirement of Plug and Play is the ability to isolate individual cards for configuration. PCI cards are isolated by the PCI architecture itself. Because the original ISA specification provided no method for isolating one card from another, either the operating system or the system BIOS can perform these steps.

The detection process remains largely unchanged under the ACPI architecture, except that on an ACPI system, the operating system and not the BIOS is responsible for device detection and configuration.

Plug and Play Detection on ACPI Systems

ACPI combines and enhances both Plug and Play and power management. On an ACPI computer, Plug and Play is configured by the operating system and not the system BIOS.

In the following example, a user installs a Plug and Play USB joystick into a USB hub on a USB host controller. The USB hub is a Plug and Play bus device because it can have other devices attached to it. In this example, the USB supports hot-plug notification, and the function driver for the USB is notified that its subcomponents have changed. The operating system performs the following steps:

1. The function driver for the device determines that there is a new device on its bus.

2. The function driver for the bus device notifies the Plug and Play Manager that its set of devices has changed.

3. The Plug and Play Manager queries the drivers for the bus for the current device tree.

4. The Plug and Play Manager sends an Interrupt Request Packet (IRP) to the device stack for the bus asking for the current list of devices on the bus.

5. When the main driver of the USB hub (the USB host controller class or miniclass driver pair) completes the IRP, the IRP travels back through the device stack by means of any completion routines registered by the hub drivers.

   When the Plug and Play Manager has the current list of devices on the bus, it determines if any devices have been added or removed. In this example, there is one new device, and the only driver that is configured for the joystick is the main USB hub driver. Any optional bus filter drivers are also present in the device stack.

6. The Plug and Play Manager gathers information about the new device and begins configuring the device.

7. The Plug and Play Manager checks the registry to determine if the device has been installed on this computer before.

8. The Plug and Play Manager stores information about the device in the registry.

9. The kernel-mode Plug and Play Manager attempts to find and load the function and filter drivers for the device, if any exist.

10. The Plug and Play Manager assigns resources to the device, if needed, and issues an IRP to start the device.

For more information about device detection during Setup, see the Driver Development Kits (DDKs) link on the Web Resources page at http://windows.microsoft.com/windows2000/resourcekit/webresources.

Installing a Multiple-Boot Operating System

You can configure Windows 2000 Professional to start with other operating systems, such as Windows 2000 Server, Windows NT, Windows 95, Windows 98, Windows 3.*x*, MS-DOS, and OS/2. This section discusses how you can set up Windows 2000 Professional as a multiple-boot system with the following operating systems:

- Windows NT 4.0 and Windows NT 3.51
- Windows 95 or Windows 98
- MS-DOS or Windows 3.*x*

Important Each operating system in a multiple-boot configuration must reside in its own partition. Windows 2000 Professional does not support a multiple-boot system that shares the same partition with another operating system.

Multiple-Boot Considerations

Before you set up a multiple-boot configuration between Windows 2000 and another operating system, you need to consider certain precautions, as described in Table 6.4.

Table 6.4   Multiple Boot Considerations

Operating System Combinations	Considerations
Windows 2000 and Windows NT 4.0	Install operating systems on different partitions. Apply Windows NT 4.0 Service Pack 4.
	Install applications while running each operating system.
Windows 2000 and Windows 95	Install operating systems on different partitions.
	Install applications while running each operating system.
	Ensure that the active partition is formatted as FAT16.
Windows 2000 and Windows 98	Install operating systems on different partitions.
	Install applications while running each operating system.
	Ensure that the active partition is formatted as FAT16 or FAT32.
Windows 2000 and Windows 3.*x*	Install operating systems on different partitions.
	Install applications while running each operating system.
	Ensure that the active partition is formatted as FAT16.
Windows 2000 and MS-DOS	Install operating systems on different partitions.
	Install applications while running each operating system.
	Ensure that the active partition is formatted as FAT16.

If you need a multiple-boot configuration between Windows 2000 and Windows NT, Windows 95, or Windows 98, install the applications while you are running each of the operating systems to ensure that the applications are included in the registry for all the operating systems.

File System Considerations

Each operating system in a multiple-boot configuration can use one or more file systems to organize data on partitions. Operating systems that use the same file systems can share volumes, so a user can see files in shared partitions from different operating systems.

For more information about the NTFS and FAT file systems, see "File Systems" in this book.

Additional file system considerations include:

- NTFS partitions are not available to users running Windows 95, Windows 98, Windows 3.*x*, or MS-DOS.
- A computer that is configured with Windows 2000, Windows NT, Windows 95, and Windows 98 can see long file names on a FAT16 volume.

Windows 2000 Professional Multiple-Boot Configurations

Windows 2000 Professional can support multiple-boot configurations between one or more instances of Windows 2000 and additional operating systems in separate partitions on the same computer.

This section describes the configuration details involved when you start Windows 2000 Professional with MS-DOS.

Bootsect.dos

Bootsect.dos is a file with the hidden, system, and read-only attributes that Ntldr uses when the computer is configured to start MS-DOS, Windows 3.*x*, and Windows 95 or Windows 98.

If there is an existing MS-DOS-based operating system, Windows 2000 Setup copies the boot sector on the active partition of the computer to Bootsect.dos and replaces the original boot sector on the active partition with its own boot sector.

When the computer is started, the active partition that contains the boot sector code starts Ntldr, which loads and displays the boot loader screen from Boot.ini. From the boot loader screen you can choose to start Windows 2000 Professional or another operating system.

If you select an operating system other than Windows 2000 Professional, Windows NT 4.0, or Windows NT 3.51, Ntldr loads ands passes control to Bootsect.dos, which then loads the other operating system.

Configuring a Multiple-Boot System with MS-DOS

If you are going to set up Windows 2000 with a multiple-boot system that includes MS-DOS, it's a good idea to install MS-DOS before installing Windows 2000 Professional. If MS-DOS is installed after Windows 2000, the boot sector is overwritten with the MS-DOS boot sector and you can no longer start Windows 2000 Professional.

If you have already installed Windows 2000 Professional and you want to install MS-DOS on another partition, you can install MS-DOS and then restore the Windows 2000 boot sector by using the Emergency Repair Disk (ERD). For more information about repairing the boot sector, see "Troubleshooting Tools and Strategies" in this book.

Configuring a Multiple-Boot System with Windows 95, Windows 98, or Windows NT 4.0.

You can configure Windows 2000 Professional as a multiple-boot system with Windows 2000 Server, Windows NT 4.0, Windows 95, or Windows 98.

If you plan to set up a multiple-boot system with Windows 95, Windows 98, or Windows NT 4.0, install Windows 95 or Windows 98 before installing Windows NT or Windows 2000 because Windows 95 and Windows 98 sometimes replace the Windows 2000 Professional boot sector with their own boot sector.

Configuring a Multiple-Boot System with Windows 2000 Professional, Windows NT, Windows 95 or Windows 98, and MS-DOS

You can configure a computer with a multiple-boot system that includes MS-DOS, Windows 95 or Windows 98, Windows NT, and Windows 2000 Professional, if each operating system resides in its own partition. You need to install the systems in the following order:

- MS-DOS
- Windows 95 or Windows 98
- Windows NT
- Windows 2000 Professional

If you are already running a multiple-boot system with Windows 2000 Professional and MS-DOS, you can install Windows 95 or Windows 98.

▶ **To install Windows 95 or Windows 98 after installing MS-DOS**

1. From the **Start** menu, click **Shut Down**.

2. In the **Shut Down Windows** box, click **Restart** and then click **OK**. The boot loader screen appears.

3. Under **Please select the operating system to start**, select **MS-DOS**.

4. Install Windows 95 or Windows 98 in a separate partition, following the standard installation procedures.

After the Windows 95 or Windows 98 installation has finished, restart the computer. With Windows 95, you need to run the Windows 2000 Professional repair process, and then replace the Windows 95 boot sector with the Windows 2000 boot sector. The Windows 2000 boot loader screen allows you to choose between Windows 2000 Professional and MS-DOS. If you choose MS-DOS, Windows 95 or Windows 98 starts. For more information about editing the boot loader menu, see the section "Editing Boot.ini" earlier in this chapter.

Installing Service Packs

Windows 2000 Professional makes it easier for administrators to add service packs through a process called *slipstreaming,* in which the service pack is added directly to the operating system's distribution share during installation.

Windows 2000 Professional also eliminates the need to reinstall components that were applied before a service pack was installed. In the past, when service packs were applied, many previously installed components had to be reinstalled. Windows 2000 Professional provides the following solutions to service pack installation.

When Windows 2000 Professional is installed from a network share, the appropriate files from the service pack are installed without having to manually apply the service pack after the installation.

To apply a new service pack, use Update.exe with the **/slip** switch to copy over the existing Windows 2000 files with the updated service pack files. Some of the key files that update during this process include:

- New Layout.inf, Dosnet.inf, and Txtsetup.sif files, which have the updated checksums for all the service pack files. These files need additional entries if any additional files have been added.

- A new driver .cab if the drivers in the cabinet file have been changed.

  If you apply a service pack to a single computer running Windows 2000, you must reapply the service pack to add another service, unless you are updating from a network share that supports service pack slipstreaming.

Removing Windows 2000 Professional from Your Computer

Important Before removing Windows 2000 Professional from your computer, make sure to back up all important data.

Before removing Windows 2000 Professional, make sure you know where Windows 2000 Professional is installed, what you want to remove, and how your hard disk is partitioned and formatted. The following sections describe how to remove Windows 2000 from your computer:

- "Removing Windows 2000 Professional from the Boot Sequence"
- "Removing a Primary NTFS Partition"
- "Removing Windows 2000 Professional Files"

Note If the hard disk contains a partition using the NTFS file system, remove this partition from within Windows 2000 before removing Windows 2000 from the boot sequence.

Removing Windows 2000 from the Boot Sequence

You can remove the Windows 2000 boot sector from your computer in two ways.

You can use an MS-DOS boot floppy to start MS-DOS, and then type:

sys c:

This command replaces the Windows 2000 boot sector with the MS-DOS boot sector and allows your computer to start MS-DOS. The following files remain in the root and %SystemRoot% folder and can be deleted after you perform this operation:

- Hyberfil.sys (located in %Systemdrive%)
- Pagefile.sys (located in %Systemdrive%)
- Boot.ini
- Ntldr
- Ntdetect.com
- Ntbootdd.sys

You can also start your computer with a Windows 95 or Windows 98 bootable floppy disk and use the **sys c:** command to return to your original configuration.

You can leave the Windows 2000 boot sector on the disk and start MS-DOS without being prompted by changing the startup operating system and time-out value.

▶ **To change the startup operating system and time-out value**

1. Click the **Start** button, point to **Settings**, and then click **Control Panel**.

2. In **Control Panel**, double-click the **System** icon, click the **Advanced** tab, and then click **Startup and Recovery**.

3. Click the **Default operating system** list, and then select **MS-DOS**.

4. In the **Display list of operating systems for \<n\> Seconds** box, type or select **0** (zero).

Note If the primary partition was converted to NTFS, to return to starting MS-DOS automatically, reformat the drive and reinstall MS-DOS.

Removing a Primary NTFS Partition

Modifying the primary, bootable NTFS partition does not typically succeed for the following reasons:

- MS-DOS versions 5.0 and 6.0 do not recognize an NTFS partition. The MS-DOS program Fdisk reports an NTFS partition as an OS/2 high-performance file system (HPFS) partition.

- You cannot modify or delete an NTFS partition from within an existing partition.

To delete or modify a primary NTFS partition, use any of the following methods:

- Start MS-DOS by using a Windows 95 or Windows 98 boot disk, then run Fdisk and delete the non-MS-DOS partition.

- Run the Windows 2000 installation from floppy disks or the Windows 2000 operating system CD. Choose **D** to remove the partition when you are prompted.

Removing Windows 2000 Professional Files

Caution Make sure you back up all important data before removing the Windows 2000 files from the computer.

You can delete the following Windows 2000 Professional folders to free additional disk space:

- Program Files
- Documents and Settings
- Winnt
- Debug

Note The folder name for Winnt might vary.

Troubleshooting Windows 2000 Professional Setup

Windows 2000 provides valuable troubleshooting tools that can be used to resolve problems that might occur during Setup. This section discusses how to create Setup and startup disks as well as some frequently asked questions about common Setup problems.

Creating the Startup Disks

To prepare for a system failure on a computer that you cannot start from the operating system CD, you need to create floppy disks that can start the computer.

Note Before starting a computer by using the Windows 2000 operating system CD or the floppy disks, try starting the computer in safe mode. For more information, see "Troubleshooting Tools and Strategies" in this book.

After you start the computer by using the floppy disks, you can then use the Recovery Console or an Emergency Repair Disk (if you have prepared one).

Note   You can create floppy disks for starting a disabled system by using the Windows 2000 operating system CD on any computer running a version of Windows or MS-DOS. You need four blank, formatted, 3.5-inch, 1.44-MB floppy disks. Label them Startup Disk One, Startup Disk Two, Startup Disk Three, and Startup Disk Four.

Disks created from the Windows 2000 Server operating system CD cannot be used with Windows 2000 Professional.

▶ **To create floppy disks for starting the system**

1. Insert a blank, formatted, 1.44-MB disk into the floppy disk drive on a computer that is running any version of Windows or MS-DOS.

2. Insert the Windows 2000 Professional operating system CD into the CD-ROM drive.

3. Click **Start**, and then click **Run**.

4. In the **Open** box, type

   d:\bootdisk\makeboot.exe a:

   where **d:** is the drive letter assigned to your CD-ROM drive.

5. Click **OK**.

6. Follow the screen prompts to finish the installation.

Media Errors

If the CD-ROM drive does not work, replace it. For a list of drives that are supported for use with Windows 2000 Professional, see the Hardware Compatibility List (HCL) link on the Web Resources page at http://windows.microsoft.com/windows2000/reskit/webresources.

Try another installation method, such as copying the source files from the CD-ROM to the hard drive or installing over the network.

If you are unable to copy from the CD-ROM, test the CD-ROM on another computer. If possible, use the CD-ROM on the other computer, use a different CD, or copy the installation folder i386 to the hard drive of the computer that works, and then copy the folder to the computer that had the media errors. To request a replacement CD, contact the vendor.

Disk Errors

If you receive the error **Not enough disk space for installation,** use the Setup program to create a partition by using the existing free space on the hard disk or, if you do not have enough space, you may have to delete files on the target partition to make room for the installation. You can delete and create partitions as needed to obtain a partition that has enough disk space to install Windows 2000 Professional.

Other Common Setup Problems

If Windows 2000 does not start, make sure that all the hardware that is installed on the computer is being detected. Check that all hardware is listed on the HCL. Only devices that are listed on the HCL have passed testing for compatibility with Windows 2000 Professional.

Stop messages

If you are installing Windows 2000 and you encounter a Stop message, check the HCL to determine if the computer and its components are supported with Windows 2000 Professional. Reduce the number of hardware components by removing nonessential devices. For more information, see "Windows 2000 Stop Messages" in this book.

Setup stops during text mode

Although text-mode Setup does not execute any code, it does rely on access to the devices on the system. It is important on both ACPI and non-ACPI systems to verify that any legacy device IRQ requirements have been set in the BIOS to **Reserved for ISA**. If possible, avoid legacy boot devices on ACPI systems because these settings cannot be reliably determined by the ACPI system. This can make the building of the device tree inaccurate, causing problems that are very hard to track.

For non-ACPI systems, verify that the **Plug and Play operating system** option has been disabled in the BIOS. If it has not been disabled, your operating system might read and write to the hardware registers.

Setup stops during GUI mode

During GUI-mode Setup, the computer might stop responding; if this happens, restart the computer and Setup attempts to resume from where it stopped responding. You can usually isolate these failures to one of the following locations:

- Device detection. At the beginning of the GUI-mode phase of Setup, Plug and Play runs to detect all the devices on the system. This involves external code called class installers. These class installers check the hardware settings on the computer to determine which devices are present. The system can sometimes stop responding during this phase.

- OC Manager. The OC Manager (OCM) is a Setup component that allows the integration of external components, such as server applications, into the Setup process. As with device detection, this phase can cause the system to stop responding.

- Computer configuration. This is one of the last phases of Setup and involves the registration of OLE control dynamic-link libraries (DLLs). It is possible for Setup to stop responding during this phase as well.

For more information about the Setup process see "Phases of Setup" earlier in this chapter.

For more information about Troubleshooting Windows 2000 Professional, see "Troubleshooting Tools and Strategies" in this book.

P A R T   3

System Configuration and Management

In This Part

C H A P T E R 7

Introduction to Configuration and Management

Microsoft® Windows® 2000 Professional introduces new configuration and management tools, such as Microsoft Management Console (MMC), Group Policy, and more administrative tools. When you use Windows 2000 Professional with Microsoft® Windows® 2000 Server, you can centralize control of workstations easily and effectively.

In This Chapter

Related Information in the Resource Kit

- For more information about Group Policy settings, see "Group Policy Reference" on the *Microsoft® Windows® 2000 Resource Kit* companion CD.

- For more information about using Group Policy, see "Group Policy" and "Introduction to Desktop Management" in the *Microsoft® Windows® 2000 Server Resource Kit Distributed Systems Guide*.

- For more information about defining and setting configuration standards, see "Defining Client Administration and Configuration Standards" and "Applying Change and Configuration Management" in the *Microsoft® Windows® 2000 Server Resource Kit Deployment Planning Guide*.

Quick Guide to Workstation Configuration and Management

Use this quick guide to find information in this chapter about configuration management. Windows 2000 Professional is designed to simplify administration. Understanding the available tools can help you effectively manage Windows 2000 Professional–based workstations.

Learn about new configuration and management tools.

Review descriptions of new technologies that are available to administrators.

- See "What's New" in this chapter.

Powerful features are available with Windows 2000 Server.

Windows 2000 Professional workstations are easier to use when features such as IntelliMirror™, Change and Configuration Management, and Group Policy are centrally managed.

- See "Managing Windows 2000 Professional in a Windows 2000 Server Environment" in this chapter.

Using Windows 2000 Professional in Microsoft® Windows NT®, UNIX, and Novell NetWare environments.

Learn about considerations for managing Windows 2000 Professional in environments that are not exclusively Windows 2000 Server environments.

- See "Managing Windows 2000 Professional in a Non-Windows 2000 Environment" in this chapter.

Manage workstations by using Group Policy

Know how Group Policy works and how to leverage its power in your organization.

Set up user profiles, rights, and permissions.

Use user profiles and access permissions to successfully configure and manage Windows 2000 Professional systems.

- See "Managing Users and Groups" in this chapter.

Use administrator tools.

Use tools, such as Microsoft Management Console (MMC), Administrative Tools, and Control Panel to configure and manage Windows 2000 Professional systems. Learn what tools can be used in Microsoft® Windows® 98 and Microsoft® Windows NT® 4.0 Workstation.

- See "Management Tools" in this chapter.

Create, view, and edit documents in multiple languages.

The Windows 2000 Professional multilanguage option offers users the ability to easily view and edit documents in more than one language at a time. Learn how to upgrade to the multilanguage version of Windows 2000 Professional, which product fits your needs, and how the multilanguage option can benefit your organization.

- See "Managing Windows 2000 Professional in a Multilanguage Environment" in this chapter.

Configure new tools for users with special needs.

The Accessibility wizard, Utility Manager, On-Screen Keyboard, Narrator, and other options make it easier than ever to configure accessibility options.

- See "Making Windows 2000 Professional More Accessible" in this chapter.

Find out more about related topics.

Learn where to find more information about the topics in this chapter.

- See "Additional Resources" later in this chapter.

What's New

Windows 2000 Professional provides better tools for managing and configuring workstations. All of the new configuration and management tools are listed here. In this chapter, you'll find details about general management tools and how to use features such as Group Policy. For details about new features in a specific area, such as hardware management, printing, or fonts, see other chapters in this book.

Add/Remove Programs

The new user interface and wizard make it easy to install programs, get detailed information about program usage, and remove program elements from the hard disk.

Administrative Tools

Administrative Tools, which are available through Control Panel, is the central repository for tools such as Computer Management, Event Viewer, Local Security, and Services.

Color Management System

Image Color Management (ICM) 2.0 ensures that colors are retained between the input and output devices (such as monitors, printers, and platforms) that support ICM 2.0.

Fonts

Support for OpenType fonts combines TrueType and Type 1 fonts in a unified registry. OpenType fonts are secured by using public key signatures, which ensures that fonts are authentic and are not corrupted.

Hardware Tab and Troubleshoot Option in Properties Pages

A separate **Hardware** tab is provided in the properties pages for **Sounds and Multimedia**, **Mouse**, **Display**, and **Fax**. The new **Troubleshoot** option on this tab helps you detect problems with these devices.

Hardware Wizard

You can use the new hardware wizard to add, troubleshoot, uninstall, and unplug devices.

Multilanguage Support

This feature provides the ability to read and write documents in more than one language.

Network And Dial-Up Connections Icon

The Network Connection wizard, Network Protocol, and Network Adapter configurations are now under Network and Dial-up Connections in Control Panel.

Phone And Modem Options

You can use **Phone and Modem Options** in Control Panel to configure TAPI devices and reconfigure installed modems. Only members of the Administrators group can make changes to these configuration settings.

Power Options Icon

You can use **Power Options** in Control Panel to reduce the power consumption of individual devices or of the entire system. You can either choose a power scheme (collection of settings that manages the power usage of the computer) that is provided with Windows 2000 or create your own power scheme.

Printers

You can use the new Add Printer wizard for easy installation.

Scanners and Cameras

This new option in Control Panel manages scanners and digital camera devices.

Scheduled Tasks Icon

You can use the new Maintenance wizard to schedule tasks.

System Icon in Control Panel

The **System Properties** page now includes a **Network Identification** tab, **Hardware** tab, **User Profiles** tab, and **Advanced** tab. The **Advanced** tab allows you to configure performance options, environment variables, and startup and recovery settings.

Users and Passwords

Going to **Users and Passwords** in Control Panel is the fastest, easiest way to set up user accounts, assign permissions, and configure logon options.

Managing Windows 2000 Professional in a Windows 2000 Server Environment

When you use Windows 2000 Professional with Windows 2000 Server, you can centrally manage workstations by using change and configuration management features. Change and configuration management is a set of Windows 2000 features that simplifies basic tasks such as the following:

- Installing an initial operating system on a new computer.
- Managing how software is deployed and installed on personal computers to ensure that users have the software that they require to perform their jobs.
- Managing the configuration of each user's desktop.
- Replacing computers.

In this chapter, the focus of the discussion is managing the configuration of the user desktop and replacing computers. For more information about the other Change and Configuration Management features, see "Using Windows 2000 Professional and Windows 2000 Server" in this book.

Change and Configuration Management

Change and configuration management includes User Data Management, Software Installation and Maintenance, and User Settings Management, which are collectively known as the *IntelliMirror* management technologies.

IntelliMirror features increase the availability of the user's computing environment by storing information, settings, and applications.

By using change and configuration management features, you can perform the following tasks:

- Define computing environment settings centrally for both groups of users and groups of computers and enforce those settings.

- Allow users to log on to any computer on the network and have the same computing environment available to them, including access to data, applications, and preference settings.

- Replace a computer quickly and then regenerate its settings, thus restoring data, applications, preferences, and Group Policy settings.

IntelliMirror

IntelliMirror technologies can help you manage user and computer information and settings. IntelliMirror uses Group Policy and *Active Directory*™ directory service to manage computers using centrally defined settings that are based on user business roles, group memberships, and locations. Depending on the requirements of your organization, you can use the three IntelliMirror features listed earlier either separately or together.

User Data Management

A user's data can follow the user while he or she is online and connected to the network or is offline in a stand-alone state because Windows 2000 can store the data in specified network locations and still make it appear local to the user. You can manually configure which files and folders are available, set them up on a per-user basis, or configure them through Group Policy.

User Data Management technologies include Group Policy, Offline Files, Folder Redirection, and Synchronization Manager. These technologies ensure that data is protected, is available offline, and is available from any computer on the network.

For more information about User Data Management, see "Applying Change and Configuration Management" in the *Deployment Planning Guide*.

User Settings Management

You use User Settings Management to set Group Policy settings that define customizations and restrictions that are applied to the operating system, desktop environment, and software for each user. These restrictions include language settings, custom dictionaries, accessibility, desktop configurations, and other user preferences and restrictions.

User Settings Management allows you to centrally define computing environments for organized groups of users and computers and allows or prevents users from making any further customization. When users have the appropriate permissions, they can customize the style and default settings of their computing environment to suit their needs and work habits.

You use IntelliMirror features to restore user settings if a computer fails and to ensure that desktop settings follow the user if he or she logs on to another computer. The settings follow users because IntelliMirror uses Group Policy and roaming user profiles to store all important user settings.

Settings contain three types of information:

- Vital settings, which are set by the user and administrator.
- Temporary settings.
- Local computer settings.

When you manage user settings with roaming user profiles and compatible applications, you ensure that only vital settings are retained and that temporary and local computer settings are dynamically regenerated as required. This ensures that users have the same settings on any Windows 2000–based computer on the network in which they log on.

Note The information in this chapter refers to technologies that support IntelliMirror on computers running Windows 2000 Professional within a Windows 2000 Server environment. Client computers that are running Microsoft® Windows® 95, Windows 98, or Microsoft® Windows NT® version 4.0 or earlier cannot use these IntelliMirror technologies.

Comparison of Local Features and Windows 2000 Server Features

Table 7.1 compares the management features that are available when a Windows 2000 Professional–based computer is not part of a Windows 2000 Server network and when it is part of a Windows 2000 Server network.

Table 7.1   Comparison of Local and Network Management Features Available in Windows 2000 Professional

Management Feature	Windows 2000 Professional, Managed Locally	Windows 2000 Professional with Windows 2000 Server, Active Directory, and Group Policy
Administrative Templates (registry-based settings)	Available	Available
Security settings	Available	Available
Software installation and maintenance (Assign and Publish)	Not available	Available
Remote installation	Not available	Available
Unattended install	Available	Available
Sysprep	Available	Available
Scripts	Available	Available
Folder redirection	Not available	Available
Internet Explorer maintenance	Available	Available
User profiles	Available	Available
Roaming user profiles	Not available	Available

You can use all of the Group Policy snap-ins on a local computer that you can use when Group Policy is focused on an Active Directory container. However, the following activities require Windows 2000 Server, an Active Directory infrastructure, and a client running Windows 2000:

- Software installation and maintenance, that is, the ability to centrally manage software for groups of users and computers.

- Remote user data and settings management, including folder redirection, which allows special folders to be redirected to the network.

- Installation of the operating system on a remote computer.

For more information about change and configuration options, see "Applying Change and Configuration Management" in the *Deployment Planning Guide*.

Managing Windows 2000 Professional in a Non-Windows 2000 Environment

You can install Windows 2000 Professional on clients in a Windows NT 4.0 Server, Novell NetWare, or UNIX network.

You can use local Group Policy settings to manage Windows 2000 Professional–based workstations outside a Windows 2000 Server Active Directory network. However, this is not the preferred method of implementing Group Policy. For more information, see "Group Policy" later in this chapter.

Windows NT 4.0 Server Environments

Using Windows 2000 Professional in a Microsoft® Windows® NT 4.0 Server environment, you can remotely administer the Windows 2000 Professional–based client either by using Microsoft Management Console (MMC) or by using standard Windows NT 4.0 Server administrative tools. You can integrate Windows 2000 Professional–based systems into an existing set of Windows NT–based management tools and procedures. These tools are as follows:

Event Viewer   You can gain access to the Event, Security, and Application logs of Windows 2000 Professional–based workstations remotely by using Windows NT 4.0 Event Viewer. Management applications that process Windows NT–based event logs, such as Seagate Manage Exec, are also compatible with Windows 2000 Professional–based workstations.

Performance Monitor   You can view Performance Monitor on Windows NT 4.0–based servers and workstations remotely from Windows 2000 Professional–based workstations.

Server Manager   Server Manager views Windows 2000 Professional-based workstations just as it does Windows NT 4.0–based workstations. All Server Manager administrative options are available for Windows 2000 Professional–based systems. By using Server Manager, a remote administrator can view system users and shares and set in-use files and replication settings, as well as start, stop, and pause Windows 2000 Professional services.

Novell NetWare Environments

Many of the Windows 2000 Professional capabilities are based on industry-wide standards, so that organizations using Novell NetWare servers can experience the same levels of time and resource savings as organizations using Windows 2000–based servers. For example, Windows 2000 Professional supports Web-based Enterprise Management (WBEM), an industry initiative that establishes management infrastructure standards and provides a way to combine information from various hardware and software management systems. Deployment and configuration tools include capabilities specific to deploying Windows 2000 Professional in a Novell NetWare environment running ManageWise.

WBEM specifies standards for a unifying architecture that allows access to data from a variety of underlying technologies and platforms and presents that data in a consistent fashion. Management applications can then use this information to create solutions that reduce the maintenance and life cycle costs of managing an enterprise network. WBEM is based on the Common Information Model schema —an industry standard driven by the Desktop Management Task Force.

Microsoft Windows Management Instrumentation (WMI) is the Microsoft implementation of WBEM. WMI provides a consistent and descriptive model of the configuration, status and operational aspects of Windows 2000 Professional. Used in conjunction with other management services provided in Windows 2000 Professional, WMI can simplify the task of developing well-integrated management applications. WMI event notifications are passed to standard WBEM management tools. WMI also allows a management application to configure a device. A management application might have to reconfigure a device as a response to a driver-raised event or data that is collected by the management application.

In order to use Novell's Zero Effort Network (Z.E.N. Works), you must first register Windows 2000 Professional with Z.E.N. Works; then a workstation record is imported into Novell Directory Services (NDS). The workstation is registered by running WSRED32.exe either from a command line or from a logon script. An example of the logon script code that detects Windows 2000 and runs the correct registry program is as follows:

```
IF " %PLATFORM" =" WINDOWS_NT" THEN BEGIN
#F:\PUBLIC\WSREG32.EXE
END
```

After the workstation is registered, it can be imported into NDS by using NWADMN32.exe. Click **Tools**, click **Import Workstation**, and then select the **Windows 2000 Workstations** container.

You can administer Windows 2000 Professional by using the standard Z.E.N. Works tools. You can use the Network application launcher (NAL.exe) to prepare software distributions, and you can run the Remote Control application by starting the Novell Remote Control Agent. To do this, in Control Panel, click the **Services** shortcut icon.

UNIX Environments

You can use Windows 2000 Professional on a Unix network. You have many management options that are based on industry standard protocols, such as Simple Network Management Protocol (SNMP) and Telnet.

Standards-based Management

Windows 2000 Professional provides full support for SNMP, a standards-based TCP/IP network management protocol that is implemented in many UNIX environments. With SNMP support, you can easily manage systems that are running Windows 2000 Professional by using a UNIX-based SNMP management suite sold by independent software vendors.

Telnet Client and Server

By using Telnet you can remotely log on to and execute commands on a Windows 2000 Professional–based or UNIX-based system. The Telnet client included with Windows 2000 Professional is character and console–based and is enhanced for advanced remote management capabilities.

Another new feature found in the Windows 2000 Telnet client is the NTLM authentication support. With this feature, a Windows 2000 Telnet client can log on to a Windows 2000 Telnet server that uses NTLM authentication.

Managing Users and Groups

Windows 2000 allows you to manage user accounts and passwords. It also provides you with tools such as the Local Users and Groups management tool, security for users, and user and computer profiles.

Setting Up User Accounts

A local user account gives a user access to resources that are located only on the computer where you create the account. Local user accounts are stored in the security database of the computer where you create them.

Overview of Users and Passwords

Users and Passwords in Control Panel simplifies adding and removing local user accounts, adding and removing users from groups, and working with passwords. It also provides access to certificate management and secure boot settings.

When the Windows 2000 Professional–based computer is connected to a Windows NT or Windows 2000 Server domain, you can use **Users and Passwords** to add and remove domain user accounts to local groups.

When the Windows 2000 Professional–based computer is not connected to a domain, you can use **Users and Passwords** to add and remove local user accounts and assign users to a local group.

In addition, you can specify whether users can log on automatically each time the computer starts. You enable this feature on the **Users** tab by clearing the **Users must enter a user name and password to use this computer** check box. **Users and Passwords** is not available on Windows 2000 Server or when Windows 2000 Professional is running in Terminal Services mode.

Note You must log on as an administrator or be a member of the Administrators group to add and delete user accounts, assign users to a local group, and change user passwords.

To add users to more than one group or create groups, use the Local Users and Groups MMC snap-in that is available by going to **Users and Passwords** in Control Panel and clicking **Advanced** on the **Advanced** tab.

Users and Passwords allows you to create or change the password for local user accounts, which is necessary when you create a new local user account or when a local user forgets his or her password.

To improve the security of user passwords, the password should contain at least two of the following elements: uppercase letters, lowercase letters, numbers, and punctuation. The longer the password and the more of these elements it contains, the more secure it is.

You can use Group Policy settings to enforce password requirements such as minimum length and expiration time. However, domain controller Group Policy settings override local computer configuration and local user configuration Group Policy settings.

For more information about using Group Policy, see "Group Policy" later in this chapter. For more information about using Local Users and Groups to manage certificates and secure boot settings, see Windows 2000 Professional Help.

Local Users and Groups

The Local Users and Groups MMC snap-in gives you more control setting up and maintaining local user accounts. It is similar to User Manager in Windows NT 4.0 Workstation.

With Local Users and Groups you can assign profiles, add and edit users and groups, assign users to more than one group, and set or modify password restrictions. You can also add a domain user to any local group. This is helpful for assigning domain user accounts to the local Administrators group. This allows domain user account members to have administrator rights on the local computer without giving them administrator rights on the domain.

To gain access to Local Users and Groups, start MMC and then add the Local Users and Group snap-in; or open **Users and Passwords** in Control Panel, click the **Advanced** tab, and then click **Advanced**.

You should review the information about security settings for Windows 2000 before you create or modify user accounts and groups. For more information about security settings, see "Security" in this book.

Security for Users and Groups

To effectively manage users of Windows 2000 Professional, it is important to understand how user rights are defined and set, how privileges and logon rights are granted, and how to change these settings.

User rights are assigned by using the Group Policy MMC snap-in. After you have started MMC and opened the Group Policy snap-in, in the console tree pane under Local Computer Policy/Computer Configuration/Windows Settings/Security Settings/Local Policies, locate the User Rights Assignment folder.

For more detailed information about planning security, see "Security" in this book. For more information about using MMC and Group Policy, see "Group Policy" later in this chapter. For information about configuring security options, see Windows 2000 Professional Help.

User Rights

You can assign specific rights to group accounts or to individual user accounts. These rights authorize users to perform specific actions, such as logging on to a system interactively or backing up files and directories. User rights are different from permissions; user rights apply to user accounts, permissions are attached to objects.

Although user rights can apply to individual user accounts, user rights are best administered on a group account basis. A user who is a member of one or more groups, inherits rights associated with that group. You can simplify user account administration by assigning user rights to groups rather than to individual users. When all users in a group require the same user rights, you can assign the set of user rights once to the group, rather than repeatedly assigning the same set of user rights to each user account.

User rights that are assigned to a group apply to all members of the group. If a user is a member of multiple groups, the user's rights are cumulative, which means that the user has more than one set of rights. Occasionally, some logon rights assigned to one group might conflict with rights assigned to another group. However, this is generally not the case. To remove rights from a user, remove the user from the group that has those rights.

There are two types of user rights:

Privileges. A right that is assigned to a user and specifies allowable actions on the network. An example of a privilege is the right to back up files and directories.

Logon rights. A right that is assigned to a user and specifies the ways in which a user can log on to a system. An example of a logon right is the right to log on to a system locally.

Privileges

To ease the task of user account administration, you should assign privileges primarily to group accounts, rather than to individual user accounts. When you assign privileges to a group account, users are assigned those privileges when they become a member of that group. This method of administering privileges is easier than assigning individual privileges to each user account when the account is created.

Some of these privileges can override permissions set on an object. For example, a user logged on to a domain account as a member of the Backup Operators group has the right to perform backup operations for all domain servers. However, this requires the ability to read all files on those servers, even files for which their owners have set permissions that explicitly deny access to all users, including members of the Backup Operators group. A user right, in this case, the right to perform a backup, takes precedence over all file and directory permissions.

The following list shows the privileges that you can assign to a user by setting user rights. You can manage these privileges by using settings in the MMC Group Policy console in the console tree pane under Local Computer\Windows Settings\Security Settings\Local Policies\User Rights Assignment.

- Act as part of the operating system
- Add workstations to a domain
- Back up files and directories
- Bypass traverse checking
- Change the system time
- Create a token object
- Create permanent shared objects
- Create a pagefile
- Debug programs
- Enable trusted for delegation on user and computer accounts
- Force shutdown from a remote system
- Generate security audits
- Increase quotas
- Increase scheduling priority
- Load and unload device drivers
- Lock pages in memory
- Manage auditing and security log
- Modify firmware environment values
- Profile a single process
- Profile system performance
- Replace a process-level token
- Restore files and directories
- Shut down the system
- Take ownership of files or other objects
- Unlock a laptop

For detailed descriptions of these privileges and for information about using Group Policy to manage security settings, see "Security" in this book.

Logon Rights

The special user account called "LocalSystem" has almost all available privileges and logon rights assigned to it because all processes that are running as part of the operating system are associated with this account, and these processes require a complete set of user rights. The logon rights of the local system user account are as follows:

- Log on locally
- Log on as a batch job
- Log on as a service
- Deny access to this computer from the network
- Deny logon as a batch job
- Deny logon as a service
- Deny local logon

For more information about logon rights, see "Security" in this book.

User Profile Types

In Windows 2000 Professional, user profiles automatically create and maintain the desktop settings for each user's work environment on the local computer. A user profile is created for each user when the user logs on to a computer for the first time.

User profiles include all user-specific settings of a user's Windows 2000 Professional environment, including program items, screen colors, network connections, printer connections, mouse settings, window size and position, and desktop preferences.

User profiles provide several advantages to users. For example, when users log on to their workstations, they receive the desktop settings as they existed when they logged off. Also, when several users log on to the same computer, each receives a customized desktop.

There are three types of user profiles, which are as follows:

Local User Profile This profile is automatically created the first time a user logs on to the computer, and it is stored on the computer's local hard drive. Any changes made to the local user profile are specific to the computer where the change was made.

Roaming User Profile You, as the administrator, create this profile, and store it on a network server. This profile is available when a user logs on to any computer on the network. Any changes made to roaming user profiles are automatically updated on the server when the user logs off.

Mandatory User Profile   Mandatory user profiles are stored on a network server and are downloaded each time the user logs on. This profile does not update when the user logs off. It is useful for situations where consistent or job-specific settings are needed Only administrators can make changes to mandatory user profiles. If the mandatory user profile is unavailable, the user cannot log on.

Important   Group policy settings take precedence over user settings.

For more information about roaming user profiles and mandatory user profiles, see "Defining Client Administration and Configuration Standards" in the *Deployment Planning Guide*.

Creating User Profiles

When you install Windows 2000 Professional, a user profile is created on the *%SystemDrive%*\Documents and Settings partition.

When a user logs on to a Windows 2000 Professional–based computer, the name of the folder that is created is derived from the user account name, and, if necessary, the user account name is appended with the name of the local computer or domain that is applicable to the user who is logging on.

The user account name in Windows NT 4.0 Server is in NetBIOS format, such as *<domain>*\jeffsmith. In Windows 2000 Server, you can specify user accounts in the NetBIOS format, or you can use the user principal name (UPN) format. An example of a UPN format is jeffsmith@*<domain>*.com.

If the NetBIOS name is *<domain>*\jeffsmith, the user ID is jeffsmith. If the UPN is jeffsmith@*<domain>*.com, the user ID also is jeffsmith. The user ID portion of the UPN and the user ID portion of the NetBIOS name usually are the same. However, they might not be the same, as shown in the following example:

```
NetBIOS name: <domain>\jeffsmith
User principal name: jeffreysmith@<domain>.com
```

Whether the user logs on to a local account or to an account from a domain, if the *%UserProfile%* folder does not contain a folder with the name of the user who is logging on (in this case jeffsmith), a folder with that name is created and the path is recorded in the registry of the user who is associated with the profile. The folder that is created as a result is the following:

```
%SystemDrive%:\Documents and Settings\jeffsmith
```

If another user with the NetBIOS name jeffsmith logs on, another folder is created, but it is created with the name of the local computer or domain in which the user's account originates. The folder that is created as a result is the following:

`%SystemDrive%:\Documents and Settings\jeffsmith.NEWDOMAIN.`

Or, if the user account is established on the local computer, the folder that is created as a result is the following:

`%SystemDrive%:\Documents and Settings\jeffsmith.LOCALBOX.`

If another user with an account name jeffsmith logs on to the same Windows 2000 Professional–based computer from an identically named source (either a domain or local computer) and the SIDs of the two accounts are not the same, a new folder is created with an extension indicating how many times the user account name was used. This occurs when the user accounts are re-created and the user logs on to the same computer, as shown in the following example:

- For the first user: *%SystemDrive%*:\Documents and Settings\jeffsmith [NEWDOMAIN].000

- For the second user: *%SystemDrive%*:\Documents and Settings\jeffsmith [NEWDOMAIN].001

For more information about setting and changing local profiles, see Windows 2000 Professional Help.

Upgrading User Profiles from Previous Versions of Windows

The naming convention for user profile folders in Windows 2000 is different from the naming convention that is used in Microsoft Windows NT 4.0 and earlier versions of Windows. There is a new location for user profile folders in Windows 2000 and also a new way to create subfolders for individual user profiles.

If you upgrade from Windows NT, the user profile folders are stored in the same location as in Windows NT. This location is as follows:

`%SystemRoot%\Profiles`

When you upgrade to Windows 2000 from Windows 95 or Windows 98, a new folder for user profiles is created on the same partition as the Windows 2000 installation:

`%SystemDrive%:\Documents and Settings`

Note: The appropriate path to the user profiles folder is represented as *%UserProfile%*.

Group Policy

Group Policy settings allow you to define the customizations and restrictions applied to the operating system, desktop environment, and applications for users, such as language settings, custom dictionaries, accessibility, desktop configurations, and other user preferences and restrictions. You can use Group Policy settings to grant and deny users the ability to customize their own computing environments.

For centralized control of workstations, you should apply Group Policy settings by using Active Directory tools. In addition, each computer has one local Group Policy object that can be used outside an Active Directory domain. When you use Group Policy with Active Directory, you can precisely adjust Group Policy settings on computers and users by using security groups to filter Group Policy objects.

Important You cannot use security groups to filter Group Policy objects when you use local Group Policy on an individual computer.

This section compares Windows NT 4.0 Workstation System Policy Editor with Windows 2000 Professional Group Policy, describes how to set Group Policy settings on individual workstations, alerts you to migration issues when you move individual workstations to a Windows 2000 Server network, describes where local Group Policy settings are stored and how they are enforced, and points you to resources where you can find more information about Group Policy in a Windows 2000 Server environment.

It is important to understand the difference between local Group Policy, which is set on an individual computer, and centrally managed Group Policy, which is implemented by using Windows 2000 Server with Active Directory. The following sections primarily describe how to use local Group Policy settings on a computer that is not managed by Windows 2000 Server.

Important Group policy settings take precedence over user settings.

For more information about planning and deploying Windows 2000 Server Active Directory and Group Policy, see "Active Directory Logical Structure" and "Group Policy" in the *Distributed Systems Guide*.

Note The Microsoft® Internet Explorer Administration Kit 4.0 in the *Microsoft® Internet Explorer 4.0 Resource Kit* is used to control some desktop configuration settings on Windows 95 or Windows 98. You should not use Microsoft® Internet Explorer Administration Kit 5 to configure Group Policy on computers that are running Windows 2000 Professional. You should use Group Policy only to control configuration options.

Using Local Group Policy on Individual Computers

Although it is not recommended in large organizations, there might be instances when you need to deploy Group Policy on computers that are not managed in a Windows 2000 Server Active Directory domain.

On a computer running Windows 2000 Professional, local Group Policy objects are located at \%SystemRoot%\System32\GroupPolicy. You can use the following sets of Group Policy settings when the Group Policy snap-in is used on the local computer:

Security settings. Defines security settings only for the local computer, not for a domain or network.

Administrative Templates. These Group Policy settings allow you to set more than 450 operating system behaviors.

Scripts. Allows you to specify scripts to automate what happens at computer startup and shutdown and when the user logs on and off.

For more information about the Group Policy settings you can set in these categories, see the chapters in this book about the type of configuration setting in which you are interested. For example, to learn about Group Policy settings that affect desktop settings, see "Customizing the Desktop" in this book. For complete details about specific Group Policy settings, use the **Explain** tab on the **Properties** page of each Group Policy setting; or refer to "Group Policy Reference" on the *Windows 2000 Resource Kit* companion CD.

To manage Group Policy on local computers, you must have administrative rights on those computers. You can open the Group Policy snap-in by using one of the following procedures.

▶ **To gain access to Group Policy snap-in on the local computer**

1. From the **Start** menu, click **Run**, and then type:

   MMC

2. Click **OK**.

3. In the **Console** menu of the MMC window, click **Add/Remove Snap-in**.

4. On the **Stand-alone** tab, click **Add**.

5. In the **Add Snap-in** dialog box, click **Group Policy**, and then click **Add**.

6. When the **Select Group Policy Object** dialog box appears, click **Local Computer** to edit the local Group Policy object.

7. Click **Finish**.

8. Click **Close**, and then click **OK**. The Group Policy snap-in opens with its focus on the local Group Policy object.

If you want to open the Group Policy snap-in for setting Group Policy on a remote computer, you must do it when the extension is added to an MMC console file or do it as a command line option.

Note To use the Group Policy snap-in on a remote computer, you must have administrative rights on both computers and the remote computer must be part of the namespace.

▶ **To gain access to Group Policy snap-in on remote computers**

1. On the **Start menu**, click **Run**, and type:

   MMC

   –Or–

   Open an existing saved console (such as Console1.mmc).

2. In the **Console** menu of the MMC window, click **Add/Remove Snap-in**.

3. On the **Stand-alone** tab, of the **Add/Remove Snap-in** dialog box, click **Add**.

4. In the **Add Standalone Snap-in** dialog box, click **Group Policy**, and then click **Add**. The **Group Policy Object** option in the **Select Group Policy Object** dialog box is, by default, set to **Local Computer**.

5. Click **Browse**.

6. On the **Computers** tab, select the **Another computer** option.

7. Either type in the name of the remote computer, or click **Browse** to locate the remote computer. You can use the **Look in** drop-down list box to select the domains to which you have access.

Note The Security Settings extension does not support remote management for local policy in Windows 2000.

Computer Name Formats

The supported computer name formats are as follows:

- NetBIOS names, for example, *%ComputerName%*.
- DNS-style, for example, *%ComputerName*.Microsoft.com%*.

Starting the Group Policy Snap-in by Using Command Line Options

The Group Policy snap-in can be started with either of the following two command line switches.

Gpcomputer Command Line Switch

You can use the **gpcomputer** command line switch by using either the NetBIOS name or the DNS name of the destination computer.

The NetBIOS Syntax is as follows:

```
gpedit.msc/gpcomputer:"computername"
```

The DNS syntax is as follows:

```
gpedit.msc /gpcomputer:computername.microsoft.com
```

Gpobject Command Line Switch

You can use the **gpobject** command line switch with an Active Directory Services Interface (ADSI) path. The syntax for this command line switch is as follows:

```
/gpobject:"ADSI path"
```

This is illustrated in the following example:

```
gpedit.msc/gpobject:"LDAP://CN={GUID of the
GPO},CN=Policies,CN=System,DC=microsoft,DC=com"
```

For these command line options to work with a saved console file, you must select the check box titled **Allow the focus of the Group Policy snap-ins to be changed when launching from the command line. This only applies if you save the console.** The Gpedit.msc file is saved with this option on.

Security Considerations

Local Group Policy does not allow you to apply security filters or to have multiple sets of Group Policy objects, unlike Active Directory–based Group Policy objects. You can, however, set Discretionary Access Control Lists (DACLs) on the %SystemRoot%\System32\GroupPolicy folder so that specified groups are either affected or are not affected by the settings contained within the local Group Policy object. This option is useful if you have to control and administer computers that are used in situations such as kiosk environments, where the computer is not connected to a local area network (LAN). Unlike Group Policy administered from Active Directory, the local Group Policy object uses only the Read attribute, which makes it possible for the local Group Policy object to affect ordinary users but not local administrators. The local administrator can first set the policy settings he or she wants and then set the DACLs to the local Group Policy object directory so that administrators as a group no longer have Read access. For the administrator to make subsequent changes to the local Group Policy object, he or she must first take ownership of the directory to give him or herself Read access, make the changes, and then remove Read access.

Important After you make changes to the Group Policy object, remember to remove Read access for the group in which you are a member. If you fail to remove Read access, it can be difficult, if not impossible, to gain access to the Group Policy object.

Setting Local Group Policy Settings

You can apply local Group Policy settings to the computer configuration or to the user configuration.

Computer Configuration Includes all computer-related Group Policy settings that specify operating system behavior, desktop behavior, application settings, security settings, computer-assigned application options, and computer startup and shutdown scripts. Computer-related Group Policy settings are applied when the operating system initializes and during the periodic refresh cycle.

User Configuration Includes all user-related Group Policy settings that specify operating system behavior, desktop settings, application settings, security settings, assigned and published applications options, user logon and logoff scripts, and folder redirection options. User-related Group Policy settings are applied when a user logs on to the computer and during the periodic refresh cycle.

By default Group Policy settings are set to **Not Configured**. You can choose to select the **Enable** or **Disable** option for each Group Policy setting.

Note If you use local Group Policy settings initially and then make the computer a member of a domain that has Group Policy settings implemented, local Group Policy settings are processed first, and domain-based Group Policy settings are processed next. If there is a conflict between the settings, the domain Group Policy setting prevails. However, if a computer subsequently leaves the domain, local Group Policy settings reapply.

Important If you deploy Windows 2000 Professional in an unmanaged environment and later want to move Windows 2000 Professional computers into a managed Active Directory domain, you might have to reinstall the operating system and applications to ensure that unauthorized changes have not been made to the system configuration.

If a local Group Policy setting is configured for **Enabled** or **Disabled** and the Active Directory Group Policy setting is set to **Not Configured**, the local Group Policy setting prevails on that computer.

Viewing Group Policy Settings

You can view the Group Policy settings in effect on a computer by using the GPResult.exe file that is available on the *Microsoft® Windows® 2000 Professional Resource Kit* companion CD. This tool gives you information about both domain and local Group Policy settings.

This command-line tool displays information about the Group Policy settings on the computer and the user who is logged on.

GPResult.exe provides the following general information.

Operating System
- Type (Professional, Server, Domain Controller).
- Build number and Service Pack details.
- Whether Terminal Services is installed and, if so, the mode it is using.

User Information

- User name and location in Active Directory (if applicable).
- Domain name and type (Windows 2000 or Windows NT).
- Site name.
- Whether the user has a local or roaming profile and location of the profile.
- Security group membership.
- Security privileges.

Computer Information

- Computer name and location in Active Directory (if applicable).
- Domain name and type (Windows 2000 or Windows NT).
- Site name.

GPResult also provides the following information about Group Policy:

- The last time Group Policy was applied and the domain controller that applied the Group Policy, both for the user and for the computer.
- The complete list of applied Group Policy objects and their details, including a summary of the extensions that each Group Policy object contains.
- Registry settings that were applied and their details.
- Folders that are redirected and their details.
- Software management information with details about assigned and published applications.
- Disk quota information.
- Internet protocol security settings.
- Scripts.

Note Gpresult.exe does not display information about Internet Explorer Maintenance Group Policy settings.

Extensions to the Group Policy Snap-in

The Group Policy snap-in includes several snap-in extensions. A Group Policy snap-in extension can extend either or both of the User or Computer Configuration nodes in either the Windows Settings node or the Software Settings node. Most of the snap-in extensions extend both of these nodes, but frequently with different options. The local Group Policy snap-in extensions include the following components:

Administrative Templates   These include registry-based Group Policy settings, which you use to mandate the registry settings that govern the behavior and appearance of the desktop, including the operating system components and applications. Administrative templates are stored in the Gptext.dll file.

Security Settings   You can use the Security Settings extension to define security configuration for computers. You can define local computer, domain, and network security settings. Security settings are stored in the Wsecedit.dll file.

Scripts   You can use scripts to automate computer start up and shut down and the user logon and logoff process. For these purposes, you can use Windows Script Host to include Microsoft® Visual Basic® Scripting Edition programming system (VBScript), and Microsoft® JScript® programming system type scripts. Scripts are stored in the Gptext.dll file.

The following snap-ins are available only in an Active Directory domain.

Software Installation   You use the Software Installation snap-in to centrally manage software in your organization. You can assign and publish software for groups of users and computers. The software installation snap-in is stored in the Appmgr.dll file.

Folder Redirection   The Folder Redirection snap-in allows you to redirect special folders to the network. Folder redirection information is stored in the Fde.dll file.

Internet Explorer Maintenance   Use Internet Explorer Maintenance to define and manage Internet Explorer Group Policy settings.

Administrative Templates

The Administrative Templates folder contains Group Policy settings that manage a variety of Windows 2000 features, components, and services. The settings are stored in an administrative template (.adm) file.

The .adm file is a text file that consists of a hierarchy of categories and subcategories that together define how the options are displayed through the Group Policy snap-in user interface. It also indicates the registry locations of a particular selection, specifies any options or restrictions (in values) that are associated with the selection, and in some cases, specifies a default value to use if a selection is activated.

Windows 2000 includes three .adm files—System.adm, Inetres.adm, and conf.adm—which contain all the settings initially displayed in the Administrative Templates node. The Administrative Templates node of the Group Policy snap-in can be extended by using custom .adm files. However, unlike other Group Policy snap-in extensions, it is not extensible by an MMC snap-in extension.

Local Group Policy Objects

A local Group Policy object exists on every computer, and, by default, only nodes under Security Settings are configured; settings in other parts of the local Group Policy object's namespace are set to **Not Configured**. The local Group Policy object is stored in %SystemRoot%\System32\GroupPolicy, and it has the following ACL permissions:

- Administrators: full control
- Operating system: full control
- User: read

Gpt.ini File

At the root of each Group Policy template folder is a file called Gpt.ini. For local Group Policy objects, the Gpt.ini file stores information that indicates the following:

- Which client-side extensions of the Group Policy snap-in contain User or Computer data in the Group Policy object.
- Whether the User or Computer portion is disabled.
- Version number of the Group Policy snap-in extension that created the Group Policy object.

The local Group Policy object Gpt.ini file can contain the following information.

GPCUserExtensionNames   This includes a list of globally unique identifiers (GUIDs) that tells the client-side engine which client-side extensions have User data in the Group Policy object. The format is the following:

[{*<GUID of client-side extension>*}{*<GUID of MMC extension>*}{*<GUID of second MMC extension if appropriate>*}][repeat first section as appropriate]

GPCMachineExtensionNames   This includes a list of GUIDs that tells the client-side engine which client-side extensions have Computer data in the Group Policy object.

Options   This refers to Group Policy object options such as User portion disabled or Computer portion disabled.

GPCFunctionalityVersion   This is the version number of the Group Policy extension tool that created the Group Policy object.

Group Policy Folder

The local Group Policy folder contains the following subfolders:

Adm

Contains the .adm files for the Group Policy template.

User

Includes the Registry.pol file, which contains the registry settings that apply to users. When a user logs on to the computer, the Registry.pol file downloads and applies to the HKEY_CURRENT_USER portion of the registry. The User folder contains the following subfolders:

- **Microsoft\IEAK** contains settings for the Internet Explorer Maintenance snap-in.
- **Scripts\Logoff** contains scripts that run when the user logs off the computer.
- **Scripts\Logon** contains scripts that run when the user logs on to the computer.

Machine

Includes the Registry.pol file, which contains the registry settings that apply to the computer. When the computer initializes, the Registry.pol file downloads and applies to the HKEY_LOCAL_MACHINE portion of the registry. The Machine folder contains the following subfolders:

- **Microsoft\Windows NT\SecEdit** contains the security settings file Gpttmpl.inf.
- **Scripts\Shutdown** contains scripts that run when the computer shuts down.
- **Scripts\Startup** contains scripts that run when the computer starts up.

Note The User and Machine folders are created when Windows 2000 Professional is installed. Other folders are created as Group Policy settings are set.

Registry.pol Files

The Administrative Templates extension of Group Policy saves information in the Group Policy template in Registry.pol files. These files contain the customized registry settings that you specify (by using the Group Policy snap-in) to be applied to the Machine (HKLM) or User (HKCU) portion of the registry. The Windows 2000 Registry.pol file is analogous to the Windows 95 or Windows 98 Config.pol file and the Windows NT 4.0 NTConfig.pol file.

Note The format of the .pol files in the Group Policy template differs from that of previous versions of Windows NT and Windows 95 operating systems.

Two Registry.pol files are created and stored in the Group Policy template, one for **Computer Configuration**, which is stored in the **\Machine** subdirectory, and one for **User Configuration**, which is stored in the **\User** subdirectory.

The .pol files that are created by Windows NT 4.0 and Windows 95 can be applied only to the operating system on which they were created. The .pol file produced by the Windows NT 4.0 System Policy Editor is a binary file, whereas the Registry.pol file produced by Administrative Templates node of the Group Policy snap-in is a text file with embedded binary strings.

To view the effect of a Registry.pol file on a Windows 2000 Professional workstation, use Gpresult.exe /s or Gpresult.exe /v after the Registry.pol file is applied.

For more information about Registry.pol files, see the Microsoft Platform SDK link the Web Resources page at http://windows.microsoft.com/windows2000 /reskit/webresources.

System Policy Editor

Although System Policy Editor (Poledit.exe) is largely replaced by Group Policy, it is still useful in some circumstances, such as the following:

For Managing Computers That Are Running Windows 95 or Windows 98

You must run the Windows 2000 version of System Policy Editor locally on computers running Windows 98 or Windows 95 to create Config.pol files that are compatible with the local operating system.

For Managing Computers That Are Running Windows NT 4.0 Workstation or Windows NT 4.0 Server

These computers also need their own version of the .pol file (Ntconfig.pol).

For Managing Windows 2000–based Computers That Are Not Connected to a Windows 2000 Server Network

A Windows 2000–based computer that is not joined to any domain is not subject to Group Policy settings by way of Active Directory. The only Group Policy settings that apply to such a computer are those associated with local Group Policy, which contains settings that are applied to that computer and all of its users.

It is possible to provide settings for multiple users by using System Policy Editor to create an Ntconfig.pol file. For information about distributing the Ntconfig.pol file, see the "Implementing Profiles and Policies for Windows NT 4.0" link on the Web Resources page at http://windows.microsoft.com/windows2000 /reskit/webresources.

You should use only the Group Policy settings that are intended for use with Windows 2000 Professional (System.adm, Inetres.adm, and Conf.adm), which install by default with the Group Policy snap-in. To prepare these files for use with System Policy Editor, remove the #if ver constructs from the files. Otherwise, the policy settings will not display in the file.

Note   You can use Windows 2000 .adm files only in the System Policy Editor (Poledit.exe) that is included with all versions of Windows 2000 Server

---

Although earlier versions of System Policy Editor work only with ASCII-encoded .adm files, Group Policy in Windows 2000 also supports Unicode-encoded .adm files.

Windows NT 4.0 and Windows 2000 Policy Comparison

Windows NT 4.0 introduced the System Policy Editor (Poledit.exe), a tool that you use to specify user and computer configurations that it stores in the Windows NT registry. With the System Policy Editor, you control the user work environment and enforce system configuration settings for all domain computers running Windows NT 4.0 Workstation or Windows NT 4.0 Server. System Policy settings are registry settings that define the behavior of various components of the desktop environment.

In Windows 2000, you can create a specific desktop configuration for a particular group of users and computers by using the Group Policy snap-in. For Windows 2000–based clients, the Group Policy snap-in almost entirely supersedes the System Policy Editor. It allows management of desktop configurations for large, possibly nested, and even overlapping groups of computers and users. Group Policy objects that are not local work by being linked to any number of sites, domains, or organizational units in Active Directory.

System Policy in Windows NT 4.0, Windows 95, and Windows 98

The System Policy settings you specify with System Policy Editor (Poledit.exe) have these characteristics:

- They are applied to domains.
- They can be further controlled by user membership in security groups.
- They are not secure. They can be changed by a user with the registry editor (Regedit.exe).
- They overwrite user preferences.
- They persist in users' profiles, sometimes beyond their useful lives. After a registry setting is set using Windows NT 4.0 System Policy, the setting persists until the specified policy setting is reversed or the user edits the registry.
- They are limited to administratively mandated desktop behavior that is based on registry settings.

With more than 110 security-related settings and more than 450 registry-based settings, Windows 2000 Group Policy provides you with a broad range of options for managing the user's computing environment. Windows 2000 Group Policy has these characteristics:

- It can be based on Active Directory or defined locally.
- It can be extended by using MMC or .adm files.
- It stores settings in a secure location.
- It does not overwrite user preferences.
- It does not leave settings in the users' profiles when the effective policy is changed.
- It can be applied to users or computers in a specified Active Directory container (sites, domains, and organizational units).
- It can be further controlled by user or computer membership in security groups.
- It can be used to configure many types of security settings.
- It can be used to apply logon, logoff, startup, and shutdown scripts.
- It can be used to install and maintain software.
- It can be used to redirect folders (such as My Documents and Application Data).
- It can be used to perform maintenance on Internet Explorer.

System policy settings are applied to the user and the computer when the user logs on, whereas Group Policy settings are applied to the computer when the computer starts and to the user when the user logs on. Also, Group Policy settings refresh every 90 minutes by default, with a 30 minute offset.

For more information about setting local security Group Policy settings, see "Security" in this book. For more information about using Group Policy settings see "Group Policy" in the *Distributed Systems Guide*; or refer to "Group Policy Reference" on the *Windows 2000 Resource Kit* companion CD.

Migrating from Windows NT 4.0 to Windows 2000

The effect of persistent registry settings in Windows NT 4.0 can be problematic when a user's group membership changes. An advantage of Windows 2000 Group Policy is that this does not occur. This is because in Windows 2000, registry settings that are written to the following two, secure registry locations are removed when a Group Policy object no longer applies:

- \Software\Policies
- \Software\Microsoft\Windows \CurrentVersion\Policies

If you deploy Windows 2000 Professional in an unmanaged environment and later want to move Windows 2000 Professional computers into a managed Active Directory domain, you might have to reinstall the operating system and applications to ensure that unauthorized changes have not been made to the system configuration.

If a local Group Policy setting is configured for **Enabled** or **Disabled** and the Active Directory Group Policy setting is set to **Not Configured**, the local Group Policy setting prevails on that computer.

For more information about using Windows 2000 Professional in Active Directory environments, see "Introducing Windows 2000 Deployment Planning" in the *Deployment Planning Guide*.

Management Tools

Windows 2000 Professional has a variety of tools for administrators, including MMC, tools in the Administrative Tools folder, System Tools, Control Panel, scripts, environment variables, Windows Update, and Windows Management Instrumentation.

Microsoft Management Console

Microsoft Management Console (MMC) is a tool you use to create, save, and open collections of administrative tools, called consoles. Consoles contain items such as snap-ins, extension snap-ins, monitor controls, tasks, wizards, and documentation required to manage many of the hardware, software, and networking components of the Windows 2000 Professional–based system. You can add items to an existing MMC console, or you can create new consoles and configure them to administer a specific system component. If you want to do so, you can save and distribute consoles. To start MMC, on the **Start** menu, click **Run**, and then type **MMC**.

After you open the default console, you can the add snap-ins you use frequently and save the console. Console files are saved as *.msc files. To start a saved console, type the name of the console on the **Run** line.

The following snap-ins are available by default with Windows 2000 Professional:

- ActiveX® Control
- Certificates
- Component Services
- Computer Management
- Device Manager
- Disk Defragmenter

- Disk Management
- Event Viewer
- Fax Service Management
- Folder
- Group Policy
- Indexing Service
- IP security policy management
- Link to Web Address
- Local Users and Groups
- Performance Logs and Alerts
- Removable Storage and Management
- Security Configuration and Analysis
- Security Templates
- Services
- Shared Folders
- System Information
- WMI Control

For more information about the functions each snap-in provides, see the Windows 2000 Professional MMC Help. To view MMC topics, start Help from MMC. Help for MMC topics is not available by from the **Start** menu of Windows 2000 Professional.

Administrative Tools

The Administrative Tools folder, in Control Panel, contains shortcuts to tools you can use frequently. With the exception of **Data Sources (ODBC)** and **Telnet Server Administration** icons in Administrative Tools, all of the shortcuts start MMC consoles. The following is a list of the available tools.

Component Services With the Component Services administrative tool, you can configure and administer Component Object Model (COM) components applications. You can use the Component Services administrative tool to perform administrative tasks such as configuring your system, installing applications, and configuring and monitoring services used by your applications.

Computer Management   You can use Computer Management to manage local or remote computers using a single, consolidated desktop tool. It combines several Windows 2000 administration tools into a single console tree, which provides easy access to a specific computer's administrative properties and tools. Use Computer Management to do the following:

- Monitor system events such as logon times and application errors.
- Create and manage shares.
- View a list of users connected to a local or remote computer.
- Start and stop system services such as Task Scheduler and Spooler.
- Set properties for storage devices.
- View device configurations and add new device drivers.
- Manage server applications and services such as the Domain Name System (DNS) service or the Dynamic Host Configuration Protocol (DHCP) service.

Note   You must be a member of the Administrators group to take full advantage of Computer Management.

Data Sources (ODBC)   Data Sources (ODBC) adds, deletes, or sets up data sources with user data source names (DSNs). These data sources are local to a computer and are accessible only by the current user.

Event Viewer   Using the event logs in Event Viewer, you can gather information about hardware, software, and system problems and monitor Windows 2000 security events. Windows 2000 records events in three kinds of logs:

- **Application log**: Contains events logged by applications or programs. For example, a database program might record a file error in the application log. The application developer decides which events to record.
- **System log**: Contains events logged by the Windows 2000 system components. For example, if a driver or other system component fails to load during startup, this is recorded in the system log. The event types logged by system components are predetermined.
- **Security log**: Can record security events such as valid and invalid logon attempts, as well as events related to resource use, such as creating, opening, or deleting files. An administrator can specify what events are recorded in the security log. For example, if you have enabled logon auditing, attempts to log on to the system are recorded in the security log.

Local Security Policy   The Security Settings node allows a security administrator to configure security levels assigned to a Group Policy object or local computer policy. You can do this after importing or applying a security template or instead of importing or applying a security template.

Performance   Performance Logs and Alerts contains features for logging counter and event trace data and for generating performance alerts. With counter logs, you can record data about hardware usage and the activity of system services from local or remote computers. Logging can occur manually on demand, or automatically according to a user-defined schedule. Continuous logging, subject to file-size or duration limits, is also available. You can view logged data by using the System Monitor display, or you can export the data to a spreadsheet program or database to analyze it and generate a report. Trace logs record data when activities, such as a disk input/output error or a page fault occurs. When an event occurs, the provider sends the data to the log service.

Note   The Performance snap-in combines the System Monitor snap-in and the Performance Logs and Alerts snap-in.

Services   By using Services, you can start, stop, pause, or resume services on remote and local computers and configure startup and recovery options. You can also enable or disable services for a particular hardware profile.

Telnet Server Administration   Telnet provides user support for the Telnet protocol, a remote access protocol you can use to log on to a remote computer, network device, or private TCP/IP network. To display help for Telnet, type **Telnet** at a command prompt, and then type **Help**.

Using Administrative Tools to Manage Remote Windows 2000-based Servers

Many of the administration tools included in Windows 2000 are used to manage the operating-system components common to all Windows 2000–based computers —such as installed services, hard disks, or event logs—and are installed by default for all versions of Windows 2000. You can use these tools to manage and configure many commonly used operating-system settings on remote Windows 2000–based computers.

To manage remote servers from a computer running Windows 2000 Professional, you can install the Windows 2000 administration tools that are included on the Windows 2000 Server and Microsoft® Windows® 2000 Advanced Server installation CDs. These tools are MMC snap-ins that include Active Directory Users and Computers, Distributed file system, and other snap-ins that are not available in Windows 2000 Professional.

▶ **To install Windows 2000 administration tools on a local computer**

1. In the i386 folder on the Windows 2000 Server or Windows 2000 Advanced Server installation CD, double-click the AdminPak.msi file.

2. Under **Target folder location,** type a destination or click **Find Target** to view locations.

3. Run the Windows 2000 Administration Tools Setup wizard.

Using Terminal Services to Manage Remote Computers

If you can connect to the computer you want to administer — either via a LAN connection or a dial-up connection — you can view the administrator's desktop. Windows 2000 Server and Windows 2000 Advanced Server include Terminal Services, a set of software services that provide remote access to the server desktop from a client computer.

Essentially, the server desktop user interface appears in an application window on the client computer; keyboard and mouse clicks are sent to the server and are processed there. By using a Terminal Services client to connect to a Windows 2000–based server (domain controller), you can run any applications — including all administration tools — that reside on the server just as though you were logged on at the server.

Windows 2000 Server and Windows 2000 Advanced Server include the ability to install Terminal Services for remote administration only. This special mode allows up to two concurrent Terminal Services client connections to the server and does not require a Terminal Services Licensing server to be installed on the network.

On client computers, install the appropriate Terminal Services client software to connect to the server. Terminal Services allows you access to a local desktop session on the server from a window on your client computer. You have access to all of the administrative tools and applications on the server computer, and the tools function the same as if you were sitting at the local computer.

▶ **To install Terminal Services for remote administration**

1. In Control Panel, click Add/Remove Programs.

2. In the dialog box, click Add/Remove Windows Components.

3. In the Windows Components wizard, under **Components**, select the Terminal Services check box, and then click Next. You do not have to enable Terminal Services Licensing when you enable Terminal Services in remote administration mode. A maximum of two concurrent connections are automatically allowed on a server running Terminal Services in remote administration mode.

4. On the Terminal Services Setup page, click Remote Administration Mode, and then click Next.

5. When you are prompted to do so, click Finish.

System Tools

Windows 2000 offers a number of system tools. By using these tools, you can perform many necessary system tasks, such as backing up or defragmenting a hard disk and performing schedules tasks or other functions.

To gain access to System Tools, from the **Start** menu, point to **Programs** and then **Accessories**, and then click **System Tools**. The following tools are available:

Backup   Use Backup to create a copy of data on the hard disk drive, and then use this copy to restore lost or damaged data. Clicking Backup starts an interface that gives you access to the Windows 2000 Backup and Recovery Tools wizards.

Character Map   Use Character Map to copy and paste special characters into documents, such as the trademark symbol, special mathematical characters, or a character from the character set of another language.

Disk Cleanup   This tool helps clear space on the hard disk drive. Disk Cleanup searches the drive, and then shows the temporary files, Internet cache files, and unnecessary program files that you can safely delete. You can direct Disk Cleanup to delete some or all of those files.

Disk Defregmenter   This tool rearranges files, programs, and unused space on the hard disk so that programs run faster and files open more quickly.

Note   Disk Defragmenter is also available in the Computer Management snap-in under **Storage**.

Getting Started   This starts the online version of "Getting Started," which introduces the user to Windows 2000 Professional. Topics include learning how to install Windows 2000, how to use the desktop, and new features. Topics also include how to connect to a network and answers to frequently asked questions.

Scheduled Tasks   Schedule any script, program, or document to run at a convenient time. Scheduled Tasks starts each time Windows 2000 starts and runs in the background. By using the Scheduled Task wizard, you can schedule a task to run daily, weekly, or monthly, change the schedule for a task, and customize how a task runs at a scheduled time. When you click **Scheduled Tasks**, a Windows Explorer window opens and gives you access to the wizard and to any saved scheduled tasks.

System Information   System Information collects and displays the computer's configuration information. It includes a System Summary, Hardware Resources, Components, Software Environment, Internet Explorer 5, and Applications (Microsoft® Office 2000 only).

Note   System Information is a snap-in that opens in MMC. It displays the same system information that is available through the Computer Management snap-in.

For more information about using these tools, see Windows 2000 Professional Help or MMC Help.

Control Panel

Control Panel is the central location for system configuration changes. To reduce clutter and provide easier access to some options, certain tools are no longer located in Control Panel. Table 7.2 lists the feature or function, how to gain access to it from Control Panel or another location, and where the feature or function is located in earlier versions of Windows.

To view a detailed description of each Control Panel item, click **Details** on the **View** menu in Control Panel. For additional information about any Control Panel item, see Windows 2000 Help.

Table 7.2   Tasks in Control Panel

Feature or Function	Location in Windows 2000 Professional	Location in Windows 98	Location in Windows NT 4.0 Workstation
Add/Delete Users	Users and Passwords	Control Panel/Users	In User Manager on the **Start/Programs/Admin istrative Tools** menu.
Administrative Tools	**Programs** menu (if enabled) or Control Panel	System Tools\Programs\Accessories	On **Start/Programs** menu.
Console (MS–DOS)	Programs/Accessories/Command Prompt	Programs/MS DOS prompt	Under **Console** in Control Panel
Device configuration	Control Panel/System/Hardware/Device Manager option	Control Panel/System Device Manager tab	Under **Devices** in Control Panel.
Dial-up connections	Control Panel/Network and Dial-up Connections	Control Panel/Modems	Under **Modem** in Control Panel.

(continued)

Table 7.2 Tasks in Control Panel *(continued)*

Feature or Function	Location in Windows 2000 Professional	Location in Windows 98	Location in Windows NT 4.0 Workstation
Display options: Plus! property page	Control Panel/Display/Effects property page	Control Panel/Display/Plus!	On the **Plus!** tab under **Display** in Control Panel.
Game Controllers	Control Panel/Game Controllers	Control Panel/Game Controllers	On the **Devices** tab under **Multimedia** in Control Panel.
Hardware installation	Control Panel/Add/Remove Hardware	Control Panel/Add New Hardware	The **Hardware** tab of the property page for the device.
Modem configuration	Control Panel/Phone and Modem Options	Control Panel/Modems	Under **Modems** in Control Panel.
Multimedia	Control Panel/Sounds and Multimedia	Control Panel/Multimedia	Under **Multimedia** in Control Panel.
Network configuration	Control Panel/Network and Dial-up Connections	Control Panel/Network	Under **Network** in Control Panel.
Network Connections	Control Panel/Network and Dial-up Connections	My Computer and My Network Places	Under **Network** in Control Panel.
ODBC Data Sources	Administrative Tools	Control Panel/32bit ODBC	In Control Panel.
Passwords	Control Panel/Users and Passwords	Control Panel/Passwords or Users	In User Manager on the **Start/Programs/Administrative Tools** menu.
PC Card (PCMCIA)	Control Panel/Add/Remove Hardware	Control Panel/System/Device Manager tab	Under **PC Card (PCMCIA)** in Control Panel.
Ports	Control Panel\Phone and Modem Options	Control Panel/Modems/Connection tab of device	Under **Ports** in Control Panel.
Scanners and Cameras	Control Panel\Scanners and Cameras	Not available	Not available.
Scheduled Tasks	Control Panel/Scheduled Tasks	My Computer	Services/Schedule.

(continued)

Table 7.2   Tasks in Control Panel *(continued)*

Feature or Function	Location in Windows 2000 Professional	Location in Windows 98	Location in Windows NT 4.0 Workstation
SCSI Adapters	Control Panel/System/Hardware tab/Device Manager option	Control Panel/System/Device Manager tab	Under **SCSI Adapters** in Control Panel.
Services	Control Panel\Administrative Tools	Control Panel\Services	Under **Services** in Control Panel.
Sounds	Control Panel\Sounds and Multimedia	Control Panel\Sounds	Under **Sounds** in Control Panel.
Tape Devices	System/Hardware property page/Device Manager option	Control Panel/System//Device Manager tab	Under **Tape Devices** in Control Panel.
Telephony	Control Panel\Phone and Modem Options	Control Panel\Telephony	Under **Telephony** in Control Panel.
UPS	Control Panel\Power Options	Control Panel\Power Management	Under **UPS** in Control Panel.

You can use Group Policy settings to restrict access to Control Panel. Table 7.3 is a list of some of the Group Policy settings that affect Control Panel and a brief description of each policy. For additional information, right-click the policy in MMC, click **Properties**, and then click the **Explain** tab; or see "Group Policy Reference" on the *Microsoft® Windows® 2000 Resource Kit* companion CD.

Table 7.3   Group Policy Settings That Affect Control Panel

Group Policy Setting	Location	Description
Disable programs on Settings menu	Local Computer Policy\User Configuration\Administrative Templates\Start Menu & Taskbar.	Prevents any programs on the **Start/Settings** menu from running.
Disable Control Panel	Local Computer Policy\User Configuration\Administrative Templates\Start Menu & Taskbar.	Disables all Control Panel programs. This policy prevents Control.exe, the program file for Control Panel, from starting. As a result, users cannot start Control Panel or run any Control Panel programs.
Show only specified Control Panel applets	User Configuration\Administrative Templates\Control Panel	Hides all Control Panel programs and folders except those specified in this setting. This setting removes all Control Panel programs (such as Network) and folders (such as Fonts) from the Control Panel window and the **Start** menu. It removes Control Panel programs you have added to your system, as well the Control Panel programs that are included in Windows 2000. The only programs that are displayed in Control Panel are those you specify in this setting.
Hide specified Control Panel applets	User Configuration\Administrative Templates\Control Panel	This policy removes Control Panel programs (such as Display) and folders (such as Fonts) from the Control Panel window and the **Start** menu. It can remove Control Panel programs you have added to your system, as well Control Panel programs that are included in Windows 2000.

Caution   If you enable either **Show only specified Control Panel applets** or **Hide specified Control Panel applets**, users still have access to all Control Panel programs from Help.

Scripts

You can use Windows Script Host and Group Policy to manage scripts. Windows 2000 supports the following scripting areas:

- Computer Management
- Printer Management
- Page File
- Service Management
- Network Configuration
- Device Management
- Process Management

- Thread Management
- Event Log Management
- User Management
- Security
- File System
- Application Management

Windows Script Host

Windows Script Host enables you to run scripts directly in Windows 2000 by clicking a script file on the Windows desktop or by typing the name of a script file at the command prompt. Just like Internet Explorer 5, Windows Script Host serves as a controller of ActiveX scripting engines. Unlike Internet Explorer 5, however, Windows Script Host has very low memory requirements and is ideal for both interactive and noninteractive scripting needs such as logon scripting and administrative scripting.

Windows Script Host supports scripts written in VBScript or JScript. When a script is run from the Windows desktop or from the command prompt, the script host reads and passes the specified script file contents to the registered script engine. The scripting engine uses file extensions (.vbs for VBScript, .js for JScript) to identify the script instead of using the SCRIPT tag (which is used in HTML). This way, the script writer doesn't have to be familiar with the exact programmatic ID (ProgID) of various script engines. The script host itself maintains a mapping of script extensions to ProgIDs and uses the Windows association model to start the appropriate engine for a given script.

There are two versions of the Windows Script Host: a Microsoft® Windows®-based version (Wscript.exe) that provides a Windows-based property sheet for setting script properties and a command prompt-based version (Cscript.exe) that provides command line switches for setting script properties. You can run one of these by typing either **Wscript.exe** or **Cscript.exe** at the command prompt.

Using Group Policy to Run Scripts

The Scripts extensions of Group Policy allows you to assign scripts to run when the computer starts or shuts down or when users log on or off their computers.

The names of scripts and their command lines (in the form of registry keys and values) are stored in the Registry.pol file, as described earlier in this chapter.

The following five script types exist:

- Group Policy logon scripts
- Group Policy logoff scripts

- Group Policy startup scripts
- Group Policy shutdown scripts
- Legacy logon scripts (those specified on the User object). Because Windows Script Host supports scripts written in either VBScript or JavaScript, you can enter a command line entry such as CheckBios.vbs in the logon script path of the user object.

By default, each of these script types runs asynchronously, and the window is hidden.

Note Consider carefully how to use scripts if you have a mixed environment that includes Windows NT 4.0, Windows 95, Windows 98, and Windows 2000–based clients. The Windows 2000–based and the Windows 98–based clients properly run .vbs and .js scripts. To run .vbs and .js scripts on Windows NT 4.0–based and Windows 95–based clients, you must embed the scripts in batch (.bat) files. The scripts continue to run in a normal window. A policy exists that allows for scripts to be run as hidden or minimized. You can also install Windows Script Host on Windows NT 4.0–based and Windows 95–based clients.

Table 7.4 describes the Group Policy options that control the behavior of scripts.

Table 7.4   Group Policy Options That Control Script Behavior

Group Policy Setting	Location	Description
Run logon scripts synchronously	Computer Configuration\Administrative Templates\System\Logon	When this option is enabled, the system waits until the script finishes running before it starts Windows Explorer. An equivalent option for this is available under the User Configuration node. The setting you specify in the Computer Configuration node has precedence over the one set in the User Configuration node.
Run startup scripts asynchronously	Computer Configuration\Administrative Templates\System\Logon	By default, startup scripts run synchronously and hidden, which means the user cannot log on until the scripts complete. In some organizations, you might want the scripts to run asynchronously because they can take a long time to complete. This policy allows the you to change the default behavior.
Run startup scripts visible	Computer Configuration\Administrative Templates\System\Logon	If you enable this option, startup scripts run in a command window.
Run shutdown scripts visible	Computer Configuration\Administrative Templates\System\Logon	If you enable this option, shutdown scripts run in a command window.

(continued)

Table 7.4   Group Policy Options That Control Script Behavior *(continued)*

Group Policy Setting	Location	Description
Maximum wait time for Group Policy scripts	Computer Configuration\Administrative Templates\System\Logon	This policy setting allows you to change the default script timeout period. (By default, scripts time out after 600 seconds). The range is 0 sconds to 32000 seconds.
Run logon scripts synchronously	User Configuration\Administrative Templates\System\Logon/Log off	When you enable this option, Windows waits for the scripts to finish running before it starts Windows Explorer. Note that an equivalent option for this is available under the Computer Configuration node. The setting you specify in the Computer Configuration node has precedence over the one set in the User Configuration node.
Run legacy logon scripts hidden	User Configuration\Administrative Templates\System\Logon/Log off	If you enable this option, legacy logon scripts run in hidden mode.
Run logon scripts visible	User Configuration\Administrative Templates\System\Logon/Log off	If you enable this option, logon scripts run in a command window.
Run logoff scripts visible	User Configuration\Administrative Templates\System\Logon/Log off	If you enable this option, logoff scripts run in a command window.

Scripts that run hidden (and to a lesser degree minimized) can cause an errant script or one that prompts for user input to wait for 600 seconds. This is the default wait time value and can be changed by using Group Policy. During this time, the system appears to stop responding. If this is a script that is running in a minimized window and the user selects the window, the script stops running.

Changing System Environment Variables

Environment variables specify the computer's search path, directory for temporary files, and other similar information.

Windows NT 4.0 requires specific information to find programs, to allocate memory space for some programs to run, and to control various programs. You can view this information—called the system and user environment variables—in Control Panel. Under the **System** icon in Control Panel, click the **Advanced** tab , and then click **Environment Variables**. These environment variables are similar to those that you can set in the MS–DOS operating system, such as Path and Temp.

User environment variables can be different for each user of a particular computer. They include any environment variables you define or variables that are defined by applications, such as the path where application files are located.

System environment variables are defined by Windows 2000 Professional and are the same no matter what user is logged on at the computer. If you are logged on as a member of the Administrators group, you can add new variables or change the values.

After you change any environment variables, Windows 2000 Professional saves the new values in the registry so they are available automatically the next time the computer starts.

If any conflict exists between environment variables, Windows 2000 Professional resolves the conflict in this way:

- System environment variables are set first.
- User environment variables are set next and override conflicting system variables.
- Variables that are defined in Autoexec.bat are set last, but they do not override conflicting system or user environment variables.

Note Path settings, unlike other environment variables, are cumulative. The full path that you see when you type **path** at the command prompt is created by appending the path that is contained in Autoexec.bat to the paths that are defined in the **System Properties** sheet under **System** in Control Panel.

Windows Update

You can download system enhancements such as drivers, service packs, and new functions specifically selected to work with your personal computer from the Windows Update Web site. You can gain access to Windows Update by clicking **Windows Update** on the **Start** menu. With Windows Update, users can choose to scan their personal computers to receive a list of software applications that are specific to their computer's hardware and software configuration.

You can use the **Disable and remove links to Windows Update** Group Policy setting to prevent connections to the Windows Update Web site. This policy is located in the Group Policy console under User Configuration\AdministrativeTemplates\Start Menu & Taskbar.

For additional information, right-click the policy in MMC, click **Properties**, and then click the **Explain** tab; or see "Group Policy Reference" on the *Microsoft® Windows® 2000 Resource Kit* companion CD.

Windows Management Instrumentation

Windows Management Instrumentation (WMI) is the Microsoft implementation of Web-Based Enterprise Management (WBEM), an initiative to establish standards for gaining access to and sharing management information over an enterprise network. WMI is WBEM-compliant and provides integrated support for the Common Information Model (CIM), the data model that describes the objects that exist in a management environment.

WMI includes a CIM-compliant object repository, which is the database of object definitions, and the CIM Object Manager, which handles the collection and manipulation of objects in the repository and gathers information from the WMI providers. WMI providers act as intermediaries between components of the operating system and applications. For example, the registry provider draws information from the registry; the SNMP provider provides data and events from SNMP devices.

For more information about WMI, see Windows 2000 Professional Help and the *Deployment Planning Guide*.

Managing Windows 2000 Professional in a Multilanguage Environment

Windows 2000 Professional makes the process of deploying and supporting Windows 2000 across language boundaries easier and more flexible. To meet the needs of global businesses, Microsoft offers the following products:

- Microsoft® Windows® 2000 Professional English Version
- Translated editions of Windows 2000 Professional (available in 24 languages)
- Microsoft® Windows® 2000 Professional MultiLanguage Version

Table 7.5 compares the multilanguage support provided by each edition of Windows 2000 Professional.

Table 7.5   Multilanguage Support Provided by Windows 2000

Features and Benefits	English Version of Windows 2000 Professional	Translated Version of Windows 2000 Professional	Multilanguage Version of Windows 2000 Professional
Features for users	User can enter, view, and print data in more than 60 languages.	User can view a translated user interface (menus, help files, dialog boxes and folder names). User can enter, view, and print data in more than 60 languages.	User can switch the user interface, (menus, help files, and dialog boxes) to a preferred language. User can enter, view, and print data in more than 60 languages.
Benefits for Administrators	Provides support for working with documents in other languages.	Provides native-language user environment. Provides support for working with documents in other languages.	Provides flexibility for meeting the needs of a multilingual user base. Requires management of only one operating system code base for the entire organization

The Microsoft MultiLanguage technology consists of two elements: multilingual editing and viewing and the multilanguage user interface that comes with Windows 2000 Professional MultiLanguage Edition.

Multilingual Editing and Viewing Features

The multilingual editing and viewing features allow users to view and edit information in more than 60 languages. For example, a user with the English version of Windows 2000 Professional can work with a Japanese document without requiring a Japanese version of Windows 2000. This feature is part of all editions of Windows 2000 Professional and Windows 2000 Server, including both the English and the translated editions. This function is ideal for users who only occasionally need to communicate in another language. The ability to edit, process, and view documents in multiple languages is possible because of several components of the Windows 2000 Professional architecture, as described in the following sections.

Unicode Support

Windows 2000 Professional uses Unicode version 2.1 as its base character encoding. Unicode is an international standard that represents the characters that are in common use in the world's major languages. The benefit of Unicode is that it allows for unambiguous, plaintext representation of data, which simplifies sharing of data in a mixed platform environment.

National Language Support API

National Language Support in Windows 2000 Professional consists of a set of system tables that provide the following information:

- Locale information such as date, time, number, or currency format or translated names of countries and regions, languages, or days of the month and week.

- Character mapping tables that map local character encodings (ANSI or OEM) to Unicode.

- Keyboard layout information.

- Character typing information.

- Sorting information.

With Windows 2000 Professional, users can change their system settings to reflect those of their chosen locale through the **Regional Options** in Control Panel.

Multilingual API

The multilingual API contains functions to process text input and display—for example, changing the keyboard layout tables or the fonts used to display text. It also handles text layout issues, such as vertical text for Japanese or right-to-left text containing ligatures for Arabic. Applications that use these APIs contain basic, transparent support for creating mixed-language documents.

Resource Files

With Windows 2000 Professional, information that changes from language to language, such as menu text, dialog boxes and Help text, is stored in separate, language-specific resource files. This allows the system code to be shared by all language editions of Windows 2000 Professional—the only change from edition to edition are the translated resources.

Windows 2000 Professional MultiLanguage Version

Windows 2000 Professional MultiLanguage Version is designed with a single worldwide executable file that supports most European and East Asian languages, as well as languages such as Arabic and Hebrew. Instead of deploying a different translated version of Windows for each language that your organization needs, you can deploy Windows 2000 with the MultiLanguage Pack to all international users. The worldwide executable file makes multilanguage set ups much easier because there are few differences in set up routines, registry settings, and component configurations. The single worldwide executable file also streamlines the development and deployment of customized solutions.

The multilanguage version of Windows 2000 offers the following features:

- Supports multilingual editing of documents.

- Allows you to deploy different language user interfaces within your environment.

- Allows users who speak different languages to share workstations.

- Decreases the cost of implementing and maintaining multiple language environments.

Windows 2000 Professional MultiLanguage Version is available to Microsoft Open License Program (MOLP/Open), Select, and Enterprise agreement customers only. For more information about these programs, see the Licensing Programs for Enterprises link the Web Resources page at http://windows.microsoft.com/windows2000/reskit/webresources.

Windows 2000 Professional MultiLanguage Version provides an extra level of multilanguage support by allowing users to change the language of the operating system user interface. This means the user can log on to a workstation and use the Windows 2000 Professional user interface in any of the 24 languages that ship translated editions—provided that the appropriate language files are installed. Additionally, users can edit and view documents in more than 60 languages.

Upgrading to the Multilanguage Version

You can only upgrade to the multilanguage version from international English version of Windows. If you want to replace any other language version of Windows with Windows 2000 Professional MultiLanguage Version, you must perform a clean installation of Windows 2000 Professional MultiLanguage Version.

There are additional version restrictions that you need to be aware of when you are planning an upgrade to the multilanguage version. Table 7.6 provides version compatibility guidelines.

Table 7.6   MultiLanguage Version Upgrade Restrictions

Version of Windows Operating System	Availability of Upgrade Option
Windows 3.x	Not available
Windows for Workgroups	Not available
Windows NT 3.51 Workstation	Available
Windows NT 4.0 Workstation	Available
Windows 95	Available
Windows 98	Available
Windows 2000 Professional	Available
Windows NT 4.0 Terminal Server	Not available
Windows NT 4.0 Enterprise Edition	Not available

Files and Language Groups

Two distinct collections of language files are necessary for user interface language support in Windows 2000 Professional MultiLanguage Version:

- Language groups, which contain all of the necessary fonts and other files that are necessary to process and display a particular group of languages.

- Windows 2000 Professional MultiLanguage Version files that provide the language content for the user interface and help system.

For each user interface language that you install, Windows 2000 Professional MultiLanguage Version also requires that you install the relevant language group. For example, to use the German user interface, you must first install the Western Europe and United States language group.

You can install and uninstall Windows 2000 language groups during Windows 2000 setup and, after Windows 2000 setup, under **Regional Options** in Control Panel. Installing and removing Windows 2000 Professional MultiLanguage Version files is a separate process from installing language groups.

Disk Space Requirements

Each additional language group that you choose to support on a single computer requires additional disk space. Table 7.7 displays the approximate amount of space required for each language group.

Table 7.7   Approximate Disk Space Required for Language Groups

Language Group	Space Required in Megabytes (MB) (estimated)
Arabic	1.6
Armenian	11.5
Baltic	1
Central European	1.2
Chinese, Simplified	32.5
Chinese, Traditional	13.5
Cyrillic	1.2
Georgian	5.8
Greek	1
Hebrew	1.4
Indic	0.25
Japanese	58
Korean	29.4

(continued)

Table 7.7   Approximate Disk Space Required for Language Groups *(continued)*

Language Group	Space Required in Megabytes (MB) (estimated)
Thai	3.9
Turkic	0.9
Vietnamese	0.5
Western Europe and United States	10.1

Note A number of files (primarily fonts and keyboard layouts) are shared by several language groups. Therefore, if you install multiple language groups, the total amount of space required might be slightly less than a sum of table values.

In addition, allow up to 45 MB of disk space for installation of Windows 2000 Professional MultiLanguage Version files for each user interface language you choose to install.

Setting Up Windows 2000 Professional MultiLanguage Version

To install Windows 2000 Professional MultiLanguage Version, you must first set up Windows 2000 and then set up Windows 2000 Professional MultiLanguage Version files.

If you install the necessary language groups during Windows 2000 setup (before you install the corresponding Windows 2000 Professional MultiLanguage Version files), you avoid the need to swap CD-ROMs when you install Windows 2000 Professional MultiLanguage Version.

The default user interface language (that is, the language applied to all new user accounts created on the computer) is determined when you set up Windows 2000 Professional MultiLanguage Version. You can change the default user interface or add or remove user interface languages using the Muisetup.exe file.

Note Adding and removing languages using Muisetup.exe affects only Windows 2000 Professional MultiLanguage Version files. To add or remove the files associated with language groups, use **Regional Options** in Control Panel.

For more information about automating the set up of Windows 2000, see "Automating Server Installation and Upgrade" and "Using Systems Management Server to Deploy Windows 2000" in the *Deploymen Planning Guide*.

For more information about installing and maintaining Windows 2000 Professional MultiLanguage Version software in Windows 2000 Server environments and Group Policy considerations, see the "Software Installation and Maintenance" in the *Distributed Systems Guide*.

Using Group Policy to Manage User Interface Languages

Using Windows 2000 Professional MultiLanguage Version to reduce the number of client configurations in the organization can greatly simplify the job of administering clients. However, enabling all users to change the user interface language on their computer can add unnecessary complexity to the environment. For this reason, you might want to restrict some users' ability to change their user interface language. You can do this by using Group Policy settings from the User Configuration node of the Group Policy snap-in.

If you apply multilanguage Group Policy settings to a local computer by using local Group Policy, the local Group Policy object affects all users of that computer because there is no way to filter local Group Policy objects for individual users.

For more information about Windows 2000 Professional MultiLanguage Version, see the Windows 2000 Professional MultiLanguage Support link on the Web Resources page at http://windows.microsoft.com/windows2000 /reskit/webresources.

Making Windows 2000 Professional More Accessible

Making software accessible means that you give equal access to all users, including users with cognitive, hearing, physical, or visual disabilities. Windows 2000 Professional makes computers more usable through a flexible, customizable user interface, alternative input and output methods, and better visibility of screen elements.

You can use several built-in technologies and Windows Explorer options to configure user's computers with the accessibility features that users need. These features are as follows:

Tools You can set a wider range of accessibility and other options for groups by configuring the settings in **Accessibility Options** in Control Panel, Accessibility wizard, and Utility Manager.

Navigation Features Features, such as hot keys and Active Desktop™, allow users to gain access to desktop icons, Windows Explorer, servers on a network, or Internet Explorer. They give users quick access to Windows and help users open folders and create their individualized settings. Keyboard shortcuts and personalized keyboard options assist users in working with programs and applications.

Active Accessibility With Active Accessibility®, applications work more effectively with system extensions, programs, devices, and other third-party accessibility aids, such as speech recognition systems. Active Accessibility upgrades are invisible to the user.

Customized Input Methods On-Screen Keyboard, special mouse settings, and other options, allow users to customize their user interface input schemes.

Accessibility Wizard The Accessibility wizard allows you to quickly customize user's computers with the features that they use most often.

Enlarged Display Magnifier makes it possible for users to view the display in a larger format.

Sound Options Sound options allow you to customize volume adjustment and multimedia options and use ShowSounds and SoundSentry to give users with hearing impairments control of their audio environment.

Visual Aids Windows 2000 offers several visual aids which help users who have special visual needs. For example, you can use Narrator to convert text to speech, set ToggleKeys to play audio cues when the user presses certain keys; and configure sounds for events in **Sounds and Multimedia** in Control Panel.

Keyboard Filters The FilterKeys feature adjusts keyboard response time and ignores accidental key-strokes.

Contrast, Color, Timing, and Sizing Schemes High-visibility mouse pointers, high-contrast color schemes, and the Accessibility wizard give users options that suit their needs and preference.

Third-Party Hardware Devices The SerialKeys feature, designed for users who are unable to use standard user interface options, allows users to attach an alternative input device through the computer's serial port.

For more information about using and configuring accessibility features, see the appendix, "Accessibility for People with Disabilities" in this book.

Enabling Third-Party Hardware Devices

Some users with disabilities might need additional tools for daily use. The Microsoft Active Accessibility (MSAA) application programming interface (API) allows additional accessibility aides to work with Windows user interface elements such as toolbars, menus, text, and graphics.

You can install smaller or larger keyboards, eye-gaze pointing devices, sip-and-puff systems that are controlled by breathing, and augmentative communication devices, which are designed to control a speech synthesizer for users who are nonverbal.

For more information about hardware and software for users with accessibility needs, see the Microsoft Accessibility link on the Web Resources page at http://windows.microsoft.com/windows2000/reskit/webresources.

Group Policy and Accessibility Options

Some Group Policy settings can limit the ability to change accessibility options. Table 7.8 lists some of the Group Policy settings that can affect accessibility options:

Table 7.8   Group Policy Settings That Can Affect Accessibility Options

Group Policy Setting	Location in Group Policy Console	Description
Disable changing accessibility settings	User Configuration\Administrative Templates\Windows Components\Internet Explorer	Prevents users from changing accessibility settings. If you enable this setting, the **Accessibility** option on the **General** tab in the **Internet Options** dialog box in the user interface appears dimmed. If you disable this setting or do not configure it, users can change accessibility settings, such as overriding fonts and colors on Web pages. You do not have to enable this setting if you use the **Disable the General Page Group Policy** setting (located under User Configuration\Administrative Templates\Windows Components\Internet Explorer\Internet Control Panel) because the **Disable the General page** setting removes the **General** tab from the user interface.
Disable the General page	User Configuration\Administrative Templates\Windows Components\Internet Explorer\Internet Control Panel	Removes the **General** tab from the user interface in the **Internet Options** dialog box. If you enable this setting, users cannot see and change settings for the home page, the cache, history, Web page appearance, or accessibility. If you disable this policy setting or do not configure it, users can see and change these settings.
Show only specified control panel applets	User Configuration\Administrative Templates\Control Panel	Hides all Control Panel programs and folders except those specified in this policy.
Hide specified control panel applets	User Configuration\Administrative Templates\Control Panel	Hides specified Control Panel programs and folders.
Disable Control Panel	User Configuration\Administrative Templates\Start Menu & Taskbar	Disables all Control Panel programs.

C H A P T E R   8

Customizing the Desktop

Microsoft® Windows® 2000 Professional provides users with more options to tailor the desktop user interface and gives administrators better tools to enforce standards within their organizations. Using features such as Active Desktop, custom toolbars and taskbars, and new **Start** and **Programs** menus options, you can customize the user interface to help increase your productivity. Using Group Policy settings, administrators can enforce standards and prevent inappropriate use of features such as wallpaper and screen saver settings.

Before you read this chapter, read "Introduction to Configuration and Management" in this book, particularly the sections on Group Policy and profiles.

If you plan to deploy Windows 2000 Professional in a Microsoft® Windows® 2000 Server network, read the related server documentation listed below.

In This Chapter

Quick Guide to Customizing the Desktop

Use this quick guide to locate information about customizing the desktop. You will find information about the new customization features available in Windows 2000, information about customizing desktops in different ways and in differing environments, and ideas to help you resolve any problems you may have with customization.

Learn about new features related to desktop customization.

Building on the Microsoft® Windows® 98 and Microsoft® Windows NT® Workstation version 4.0 user interface, Windows 2000 Professional introduces new features to help users stay organized and efficiently access the programs they need. Group Policy settings give administrators more control over the user interface.

- See "Overview of Desktop Customization and Configuration" later in this chapter.

Define desktop configuration standards.

Desktop configuration standards can lower the total cost of ownership of Windows 2000 Professional computers. Learn how to define standards in your organization.

- See "Defining Desktop Administration Standards" later in this chapter.

Customize Windows 2000 Professional on a Windows 2000 Server network.

Implementing centralized custom desktop configurations is easy when you use the Group Policy functionality of Windows 2000 Server and Active Directory™.

- See "Implementing Custom Desktops in a Windows 2000 Server Network" later in this chapter.

Customize Windows 2000 Professional desktops independent of a Windows 2000 server network.

Even when your Windows 2000 Professional users are connected to UNIX, NetWare, or Windows NT 4.0 Server networks, you can implement custom desktops by applying Group Policy settings to the user's computer.

- See "Implementing Custom Desktop Configurations in Non–Windows 2000 Server Networks" later in this chapter.

Control the features users can access and set.

Use Group Policy and System Policy Editor to control the Windows user interface within your organization.

- See "Using Group Policy Settings for Desktop Control" later in this chapter.

Provide quick access to programs and folders.

Create custom shortcuts and program icons on desktops for immediate access to frequently used programs, folders, and files.

- See "Desktop Shortcuts and Icons" later in this chapter.

View Web content on the desktop.

With Active Desktop, you can give users up-to-the-minute access to Web content directly from the desktop.

- See "Active Desktop and Wallpaper Settings" later in this chapter.

Access commands and programs from the Start menu.

Customize the **Start** and **Programs** menus to help users find what they need quickly, prevent users from changing or accessing operating system functions, or provide access to custom programs, folders, and files.

- See "Start and Programs Menus" later in this chapter.

Provide quick access to frequently used functions.

Design and distribute custom toolbars and taskbars to your users.

- See "Customizing the Taskbar and Toolbars" later in this chapter.

Limit access to display options.

Use Group Policy settings to prevent users from changing display options, such as wallpaper settings.

- See "Limiting Access to Display Options" later in this chapter.

Control use of screen savers.

Use Group Policy settings to prevent or control the use of screen savers.

- See "Screen Saver Group Policy Settings" later in this chapter.

Restore the original configuration.

Reset modified settings back to the default Windows 2000 Professional settings.

- See "Restoring the Original Configuration" later in this chapter.

Specify an alternate user interface.

Choose your own custom user interface rather than the default Windows 2000 Explorer user interface program.

- See "Choosing a New User Interface" later in this chapter.

Solve desktop problems.

If you experience problems with the Windows 2000 Professional desktop, you can troubleshoot to determine possible solutions.

- See "Troubleshooting" later in this chapter.

Overview of Desktop Customization and Configuration

You can customize various aspects of the desktop—such as toolbars, shortcuts, wallpaper, Active Desktop, and screen savers—to meet a workgroup's specific needs. By effectively managing elements such as Favorites, shortcuts, network connections, and Active Desktop items, you can ensure that the most current information gets to the people who need it most.

You can use desktop customization to:

- Enforce standards within your organization.
- Limit the ability of users to access and modify operating system settings.
- Increase productivity by providing quick access to frequently used programs, files, and intranet sites.
- Allow the preferences and settings of workgroup members to be in effect on any computer they use.
- Create a similar user interface across your workgroup to reduce training and support expenses.

What's New

Several new Windows 2000 Professional features can increase productivity for both users and administrators.

As discussed in "Introduction to Configuration and Management" in this book, Microsoft® Windows® 2000 implements Group Policy as a replacement for System Policy. Even if you don't have a Windows 2000 Server network, you can use Group Policy settings on local computers to manage desktops in your organization.

Windows 98 and Windows NT Workstation version 4.0 users will notice some features have moved to new locations in Windows 2000. For a comprehensive, alphabetical list of components and their new locations, see Windows 2000 Professional Help.

The following list describes desktop features new to both Windows 98 and Windows NT Workstation users.

Accessibility options   Enhancements include new wizard, magnifier, narrator, and on-screen keyboard.

Expanded menus   The contents of Control Panel, My Documents, Network and Dial-Up Connections, and Printers are automatically displayed as submenus from the **Start** menu.

Help improvements   Help is a separate window that now includes common tasks, troubleshooter topics, and Favorites.

Indexing service   Allows context-sensitive searches on local drive and network resources.

Keyboard underscores hidden   Keyboard shortcuts on menus are hidden by default.

Personalized menus   Infrequently used items on the **Programs** menu are hidden. Allow the mouse pointer to pause on the double arrows at the bottom of the menu to reveal hidden items.

The following list describes desktop features new to Windows NT Workstation users only.

Active Desktop   HTML elements can now be displayed on the desktop. (This feature is not new for Windows NT Workstation users who also run Microsoft® Internet Explorer 4.0 or later.)

Administrative Tools hidden by default   You can access Administrative Tools in Control Panel, or, to display Administrative Tools on the **Programs** menu, right-click the taskbar, click **Properties**, click the **Advanced** tab, and then select the **Display Administrative Tools** check box.

Favorites folder available on Start menu   You can choose to display the Favorites folder on the **Start** menu, providing fast, easy access to printers, Web sites, documents, folders, and other computers on the network.

My Documents folder now on Desktop   Shortcut to My Documents now appears on the desktop above My Computer.

Quick Launch bar   Easily access files, folders, and programs from the Quick Launch bar. You can add frequently accessed items and remove infrequently accessed items.

Show Desktop icon Click this icon on the Quick Launch bar to quickly minimize all open windows.

Taskbar and toolbars Create and modify toolbars for quick access to frequently used Web sites and programs. Modify the taskbar by adding and removing elements to suit your needs.

Customizing the Windows 2000 Professional Desktop

Whether you use Windows 2000 Professional at home, in a small to medium-size business, or in a worldwide enterprise organization, you can benefit from the features that provide the ability to customize the desktop user interface.

Use the Quick Guide to find the topics you need, from learning how to define standards to configuring or controlling use of the Active Desktop. Within this chapter you'll find all the information you need to perform advanced customization techniques, including a list of Group Policy settings that affect each type of desktop feature. For comprehensive listings of related documentation, see "Related Information in the Windows 2000 Professional Resource Kit" and "Related Information in the Windows 2000 Server Resource Kit" earlier in the chapter and "Additional Resources" at the end of the chapter.

Note Many organizations want to create custom configurations of their Internet and intranet browser software. For more information about customizing and managing Microsoft® Internet Explorer 5, see the Microsoft® Internet Explorer Administration Kit link on the Web Resources page at http://windows.microsoft.com/windows2000/reskit/webresources.

Windows 2000 includes a Group Policy snap-in to configure and manage Internet Explorer 5, called Internet Explorer Maintenance.

Defining Desktop Administration Standards

Setting standards within your organization can reduce support and training costs. Read this section to learn about guidelines for setting standards for desktop configurations.

Every organization has unique user computing requirements. Windows 2000 allows you to create standard operating environments, including user interface standards, based on the needs of your organization.

Whether you choose to accept the Windows 2000 defaults or implement your own user interface preferences, Microsoft recommends that you evaluate Windows 2000 configuration options according to the following criteria:

- Are they easy to learn?
- Are they efficient to use?
- Are they easy to remember?
- Can they help address your top help desk issues or concerns?
- Do they reduce the number of user errors?

Although few organizations need to research these questions in as much depth as a software manufacturer such as Microsoft, the following techniques might help you configure Windows 2000 to best meet the needs of your users:

- *Focus groups.* Bring groups of users together for focused discussions about what they like and dislike about their computer configurations, and what changes could make them more productive.
- *Observational research.* Watch users while they work on their computers.
- *Field research.* Talk to administrators at other organizations about what they have learned.
- *Expert reviews.* Study the research that exists about user interface design and user productivity.

Consider how much or how little you want to control the user interface. Basic users who have less experience with computers might need highly customized systems to maximize their productivity and to minimize their ability to make potentially harmful changes to their systems.

Advanced users who frequently run demanding programs that require special configuration options, or are disconnected from the network, might need to be given greater control over their own systems.

For more information about defining and setting configuration standards, see "Defining Client Administration and Configuration Standards" and "Applying Change and Configuration Management" in the *Deployment Planning Guide*, and "Introduction to Desktop Management" in the *Distributed Systems Guide*.

Implementing Custom Desktops in a Windows 2000 Server Network

When Windows 2000 Professional is part of a Windows 2000 Server network running Active Directory, powerful administrative functions—such as Group Policy and change and configuration management—are available to customize and control the desktop.

Use Group Policy to set and enforce Group Policy settings on multiple workstations from a central location. There are more than 550 Group Policy settings, including those that help prevent users from making potentially counter-productive changes to their computers. You can optimize the desktop for the specific needs of each workgroup or department in your organization.

For more information about Group Policy, see "Using Group Policy Settings for Desktop Control" later in this chapter.

Change and Configuration Management features include User Data Management, Software Installation and Maintenance, and User Settings Management, which are collectively known as the *IntelliMirror*™ management technologies. IntelliMirror and Remote OS Installation are the Windows 2000 Change and Configuration Management technology set.

IntelliMirror features increase the availability of the user's computer and computing environment by intelligently storing information, settings, and programs. Remote OS Installation installs Windows 2000 Professional operating system and desktop images on new or replacement computers without on-site technical support. When you combine IntelliMirror and Remote OS Installation throughout your organization, you create a system that makes computer replacement easier.

You can use Change and Configuration Management features to perform the following functions:

- Define computing environment settings centrally for both groups of users and computers. Then you can rely on Windows 2000 to enforce those settings.

- Make it possible for users to log on to any computer on their network and have the same computing environment, including access to their data, programs, and preference settings.

- Enable users to find all their data files and network files quickly, even when they are working offline. Offline files are cached locally and are synchronized with the server.

- Manage software installation, updates, and removal, all from a central location. Programs can also repair themselves if a user inadvertently removes key files.

- Replace a computer quickly and then regenerate its settings, restoring data, programs, preferences, and administrative policies.
- Allow workstations enabled with Preboot Execution Environment (PXE)–based remote boot technology to install an operating system on the local hard disk drive automatically.

Microsoft® Systems Management Server also provides change and configuration management services. You can use Systems Management Server in combination with IntelliMirror and Remote OS Installation.

For information about the benefits of combining these technologies, see "Introduction to Desktop Management" in the *Distributed Systems Guide*. For more information about deploying Windows 2000 Professional with Windows 2000 Server, see the *Deployment Planning Guide*.

Implementing Custom Desktop Configurations in Non–Windows 2000 Server Networks

You can deploy custom desktop configuration in UNIX, Novell NetWare, and Windows NT 4.0 Server networks using System Policy Editor or by applying Group Policy settings locally on each computer.

For more information about using Group Policy and System Policy Editor with Windows 2000 Professional, see "Introduction to Configuration and Management" in this book.

Using Group Policy Settings for Desktop Control

Group Policy settings should be enforced using Windows 2000 Server and Active Directory. However, when necessary, you can use Group Policy locally to control desktop settings and configuration options such as:

- Wallpaper and screen saver settings.
- **Start** and **Programs** menu options.
- Display properties.

The following sections discuss many of the user interface options you can configure, as well as the Group Policy settings that might affect those options. Options that are not set by Group Policy can be configured by the user and are saved in the user's profile. However, when Group Policy settings are in effect, they take precedence over user-implemented configurations.

Overall, there are more than 550 different Group Policy settings, and the best way to see all the different options is to study an installed version of Windows 2000 Professional. For more information about Group Policy settings and using Group Policy in non–Windows 2000 Server networks, see "Introduction to Configuration and Management" in this book and "Group Policy" in the Distributed Systems Guide.

Applying Group Policy Settings to Multiple Users of the Same Computer

If you want to enforce Group Policy settings in a non–Windows 2000 Server network and want different settings for each user of the same computer, you need to use System Policy Editor. For more information about using System Policy Editor, see "Introduction to Configuration and Management" in this book.

Applying Group Policy Settings to the Desktop

Most of the local computer Group Policy settings that control desktop functions are configured under the User Configuration\Administrative Templates node in Group Policy. As illustrated in Figure 8.1, Group Policy settings are located in the following folders: Start Menu & Taskbar, Desktop, Desktop\Active Desktop, and Control Panel\Display.

To open Group Policy, click **Start**, click **Run**, type **gpedit.msc**, and then click **OK**.

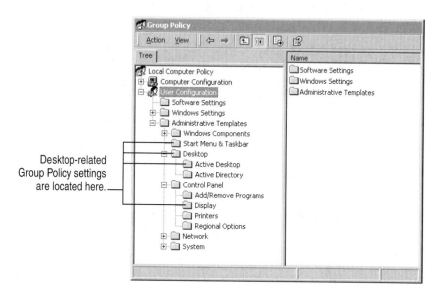

Figure 8.1   Location of Group Policy Settings for Customizing the Desktop

For detailed descriptions of each Group Policy setting, right-click the setting in Group Policy, click **Properties**, and then click the **Explain** tab. Some of the desktop local computer Group Policy settings are discussed later in this chapter. For a more comprehensive description of Group Policy settings, refer to the Group Policy Reference on the *Windows 2000 Resource Kit* companion CD.

Desktop Shortcuts and Icons

You can create shortcuts to programs, files, folders, and Web sites on the desktop to provide fast access to frequently used information and programs. Windows 2000 provides shortcuts for My Documents, My Network Places, and Internet Explorer. Using local Group Policy settings, you can prevent access to the standard Windows 2000 shortcuts or hide all the icons on a desktop.

For more information about creating and using shortcuts, see Windows 2000 Professional Help.

Group Policy Settings That Affect Desktop Icons

You can set Group Policy settings to hide desktop icons. The policies listed in Table 8.1 are located in the Group Policy snap-in under Local Computer Policy\User Configuration\Administrative Templates\Desktop.

Table 8.1   Group Policy Settings That Can Affect Desktop Icons

Group Policy Setting	Description
Hide all icons on Desktop	Removes all menus, folders, and icons from the desktop.
Hide My Documents icon on desktop	Removes the My Documents icon from the desktop. Note: The My Documents folder cannot be deleted.
	See also the "Start and Programs Menus" section later in this chapter for the **Remove Documents menu from Start Menu Group** Policy setting.
Hide My Network Places icon on desktop	Removes the My Network Places icon from the desktop.
Hide Internet Explorer icon on desktop	Removes the Internet Explorer icon from the desktop.

You can use Group Policy settings to determine the method Windows 2000 Professional uses to search for the target of a shortcut. The Group Policy settings listed in Table 8.2 are located in the Group Policy snap-in under Local Computer Policy\User Configuration\Administrative Templates\Start Menu & Taskbar.

Table 8.2   Group Policy Settings That Can Affect Shortcut Search Methods

Group Policy Setting	Description
Do not use the search-based method when resolving shell shortcuts	Prevents comprehensive search of NTFS partition to locate target file.
Do not use the tracking-based method when resolving shell shortcuts	Prevents system from using NTFS target file ID to search for files.

Active Desktop and Wallpaper Settings

Active Desktop for Windows 2000 Professional uses Web, HTTP, and HTML components—such as Web sites, Microsoft® ActiveX® Controls, and floating frames, along with traditional Microsoft® Win32® presentation services—to enhance the Windows user interface.

Active Desktop incorporates Microsoft Internet Explorer with HTML Web browser technology to enable browsing and viewing information, along with new features such as subscriptions that allow the desktop to automatically receive information from network servers on TCP/IP networks.

Using Active Desktop, you can:

- Add Web content to desktops from the Internet or your intranet.
- Use subscriptions to regularly update content.
- Browse the Active Desktop Gallery to choose sites.
- Lock down Active Directory elements to prevent changes.

Considerations for Using Active Desktop

The advantage of using Active Desktop is to provide users with immediate access to the most current information. You need to review the type of information your workgroups need and consider the best method of delivery. Active desktop works best when time-critical information, such as a stock ticker or inventory counter, is needed.

You can choose to disable Active Desktop on general installations, but give users the ability to enable it as they choose.

▶ **To disable Active Desktop without using Group Policy**

1. Right-click an empty area on the desktop, point to **Active Desktop**, and then click **Customize My Desktop**.

2. Clear the **Show Web content on my Active Desktop** check box.

Using an HTML File as Wallpaper

You can display an HTML file as wallpaper when Active Desktop is enabled. The HTML page can be on your local computer or on a network drive, but it cannot point to a URL on your intranet or on the World Wide Web. You can save a file from the Internet or intranet to your hard disk drive by displaying the page in your browser, selecting **Save As** from the **File** menu, and saving it to your local hard disk drive.

▶ **To use an HTML file as the Active Desktop wallpaper**

1. Right-click the desktop, and then click **Properties**.

2. On the **Background** tab, click **Browse,** and then navigate to the location of the HTML file you want to use.

Note If you select a .bmp file for Windows 2000 Professional background wallpaper and then choose to use Active Desktop wallpaper, the Active Desktop runs in the foreground, covering up the system wallpaper. When you press CTRL+ALT+DELETE, Active Desktop is disabled and the system wallpaper (the specified .bmp file) is displayed. This behavior is normal.

Using Graphics and HTML Pages as Active Desktop Items

You can add an HTML page, or a JPEG or GIF graphics file, as an item on the Active Desktop. In a corporate intranet, for example, you might want to add a frequently-used HTML form, such as a sales order, for faster access by sales personnel. You might add an animated GIF of your corporate logo to make it easier for users to copy and paste the logo into letters, spreadsheets, or Web pages.

The Microsoft Active Desktop Gallery on the World Wide Web contains Active Desktop items, such as MSN Investor Tickers and Java clocks, that you can download. To use these items, visit the Active Desktop Gallery Web site at http://www.microsoft.com/.

▶ **To add an item to the Active Desktop**

1. Right-click the Active Desktop, point to **Active Desktop**, and then click **New Desktop Item**.

2. Click **Visit Gallery** to select an item from the Microsoft Active Desktop Gallery. Otherwise, type or browse the path to the HTML page or graphic file that you want to display as an Active Desktop item.

Locking Down an Active Desktop Configuration

You can prevent changes to an Active Desktop configuration without using Group Policy.

▶   **To lock Active Desktop settings**

- Right-click the desktop, point to **Active Desktop**, and then click **Lock Desktop Items**.

Group Policy Settings That Affect Active Desktop

As with most Group Policy settings, Active Desktop policy settings can have multiple effects. For example, if you set the Enable Active Desktop Group Policy to **Enable**, users cannot disable Active Desktop. When you right-click the desktop and point to **Active Desktop**, the **Show Web Content** command is unavailable; when you right-click the desktop, click **Properties**, and then click the **Web** tab, the **Show Web content on my Active Desktop** check box is unavailable; and on the **General** tab of Folder Options in Control Panel, the **Use Windows classic desktop** option is unavailable.

Other Group Policy settings you enforce can affect how Active Desktop Group Policy settings work. For additional information, right-click the Group Policy setting, click **Properties**, and then click the **Explain** tab, or refer to the Group Policy Reference on the *Windows 2000 Resource Kit* companion CD.

The Group Policy settings listed in Table 8.3 are located in the Group Policy snap-in under Local Computer Policy\User Configuration\Administrative Templates\Desktop\Active Desktop.

Table 8.3   Group Policy Settings That Can Affect Active Desktop

Group Policy Setting	Description
Enable Active Desktop	Prevents users from disabling Active Desktop.
Disable Active Desktop	Prevents users from enabling Active Desktop.
Disable all items	Removes all Active Desktop items from the desktop, but does not disable Active Desktop.
Prohibit changes	A comprehensive Group Policy setting that locks down an established Active Desktop configuration.
Prohibit adding items	Prevents adding Web pages or pictures from the Internet or intranet.
Prohibit deleting items	Prevents removing Web content from Active Desktop items.
Prohibit editing items	Prevents changing the properties on Web content desktop items.
Prohibit closing items	Prevents Active Desktop items from closing.
Add/Delete items	Add or delete specific Web-based items or shortcuts to the desktop each time the Group Policy setting is refreshed.
Active Desktop Wallpaper	Prevents changes to the wallpaper image.
Allow only bitmapped wallpaper	Prevents the use of JPEG, GIF, PNG, or HTML wallpaper files.

Start and Programs Menus

For many users, the **Start** and **Programs** menus are the central repository for frequently used programs and files. You can customize the contents of the **Start** menu and the **Programs** menu—simply drag items to easily add, remove, and reorder links to programs, files, and folders. A shortcut menu appears when you right-click an item.

In Windows 2000 Professional, you can display certain components, such as Control Panel, as subfolders directly from the **Start** menu rather than in a new window. For more information about changing the display of components from the **Start** menu, see "Procedures for Customizing the Start Menu" later in this chapter.

Personalized menus are another new feature of Windows 2000 Professional. Enabled by default, the system keeps track of the most frequently used items on the **Programs** menu (and its submenus) and displays only those items when you activate the menu. To expand the menu to see all of the items that are available, allow the mouse pointer to pause on the double arrows at the bottom of the menu (as seen in Figure 8.2) to display infrequently used items (as seen in Figure 8.3).

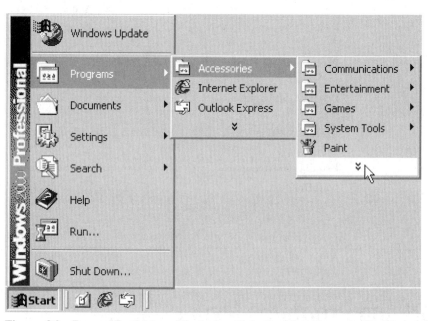

Figure 8.2   Personalized Menu Displaying Only the Most Recently Used Items

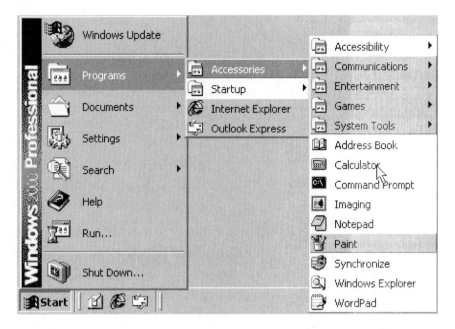

Figure 8.3   Personalized Menu Expanded to Display Infrequently Used Items

For more information about Personalized Menus, see "Procedures for Using Personalized Menus" later in this chapter.

Personalized menus are also available in Internet Explorer 5 and Microsoft® Office 2000 programs. Enabling and disabling personalized menus in Windows 2000 does not affect personalized menus in other programs.

Administrators can use Group Policy settings to restrict access to the **Start** and **Programs** menus. Some of these Group Policy settings are described later in this chapter.

Considerations for Customizing the Start and Programs Menus

When customizing the **Start** and **Programs** menus, you need to consider the following:

- Add the folders, documents, and programs that your workgroup uses most frequently to the **Start** menu. You also might want to add some of these items to the Windows taskbar, to the Quick Launch toolbar, or to new toolbars that you create. See "Customizing the Taskbar and Toolbars" later in this chapter.

- Add all of your workgroup's custom program groups and programs to the **Programs** menu. You can reorganize the **Programs** menu and add custom program groups to suit the specific needs of your workgroup. For example, you might want to create a program group called "Inventory" that contains only the inventory programs specific to your workgroup.

- If your workgroup accesses distributed applications that use the Distributed Component Object Model (DCOM), you might want to customize program shortcuts to point to the appropriate local component or to a component on a network server.

- Consider how much control you want your users to have. Use local computer Group Policy settings if a greater degree of control is necessary and you don't have a Windows 2000 Server Active Directory network.

Customizing the Start and Programs Menus for All Users

You can add shortcuts to frequently used programs, files, folders, or Web sites to the **Start** or **Programs** menus for every user who logs on to the computer, or for individual users.

▶ **To add and remove Start and Programs menu items for all users**

1. Right-click **Start**, and then click **Open All Users**.

2. Add items to and remove items from the **Start** menu, or double-click **Programs** to add items to and remove items from the **Programs** menu.

Procedures for Customizing the Programs Menu

The items that appear on the **Programs** menu are arranged alphabetically by default. You can add, remove, and reorder items.

▶ **To add items to or remove items from the Programs menu**

1. Click **Start**, point to **Settings**, and then click **Taskbar & Start Menu**.

2. Click the **Advanced** tab, and then do one of the following:

   - To add an item, click **Add**, and then follow the instructions in the Create Shortcut wizard.

   - To remove an item, click **Remove**, click the item you want to remove, and then click **Remove**.

▶ **To reorder items on the Programs menu**

1. Click **Start**, and then point to **Programs**.

2. Click the item you want to move, and then drag it to the new location.

▶ **To alphabetize items on the Programs menu**

1. Click **Start**, point to **Settings**, and then click **Taskbar & Start Menu**.

2. Click the **Advanced** tab, and then click **Re-sort**.

Procedures for Customizing the Start Menu

You can add and remove items from the **Start** menu, or change their order.

▶ **To add an item to the Start menu**

- Drag the item's icon to the **Start** button.

▶ **To remove an item from the Start menu**

- Click **Start**, right-click the item you want to remove, and then click **Delete**.

▶ **To reorder the items on the Start menu**

- Click **Start**, click the item you want to move, and then drag it to the new location.

▶ **To add Administrative Tools to the Start menu**

1. Click **Start**, point to **Settings**, and then click **Taskbar & Start Menu**.
2. Click the **Advanced** tab, and then select the **Display Administrative Tools** check box.

▶ **To add the Favorites folder to the Start menu**

1. Click **Start**, point to **Settings**, and then click **Taskbar & Start Menu**.
2. Click the **Advanced** tab, and then select the **Display Favorites** check box.

▶ **To add the Logoff command to the Start menu**

1. Click **Start**, point to **Settings**, and then click **Taskbar & Start Menu**.
2. Click the **Advanced** tab, and then select the **Display Logoff** check box.

▶ **To display the contents of subfolders on the Start menu**

1. Click **Start**, point to **Settings**, and then click **Taskbar & Start Menu**.
2. Click the **Advanced** tab, and then select the **Expand Control Panel**, **Expand My Documents**, **Expand Network and Dial-up Connections**, and **Expand Printers** check boxes.

▶ **To display the contents of the Programs menu in a scrolling list**

1. Click **Start**, point to **Settings**, and then click **Taskbar & Start Menu**.
2. Click the **Advanced** tab, and then select the **Scroll the Programs menu** check box.

Procedures for Using Personalized Menus

Personalized Menus hides infrequently used items from the **Programs** menu. The Personalized Menus option in Windows 2000 is different from the Personalized Favorites Menu setting in Internet Explorer 5 and the Personalized Menus and Toolbars options in Microsoft Office 2000 programs.

In Windows 2000, you cannot customize how Personalized Menus works; the option is either enabled or disabled. By default, Personalized Menus is enabled.

▶ **To disable Personalized Menus in Windows 2000 without using Group Policy**

1. Click **Start**, point to **Settings**, and then click **Taskbar & Start Menu**.
2. On the **General** tab, clear the **Use Personalized Menus** check box.

Note If you disable personalized menus in the Accessibility Wizard, the **Use Personalized Menus** check box is cleared, but the option remains available.

▶ **To enable Personalized menus for Internet Explorer 5**

1. On the **Tools** menu, click **Internet Options**.
2. On the **Advanced** tab, select the **Enable Personalized Favorites Menu** check box.

Group Policy Settings That Affect the Start Menu

You can use Group Policy settings or a combination of Group Policy settings to control access to the **Start** menu. Table 8.4 lists and describes each Group Policy setting that can affect the **Start** menu.

Other Group Policy settings you enforce can affect how the **Start** menu Group Policy settings work. For additional information, right-click the Group Policy setting, click **Properties**, and then click the **Explain** tab, or refer to the Group Policy Reference on the *Windows 2000 Resource Kit* companion CD.

The Group Policy settings listed in Table 8.4 are located in the Group Policy snap-in under Local Computer Policy\User Configuration\Administrative Templates\Start Menu & Taskbar.

Table 8.4   Group Policy Settings That Can Affect the Start Menu

Group Policy Setting	Description
Remove user's folders from the Start Menu	Hides all user-specific folders from the **Start** menu. Use in conjunction with folder redirection Group Policy settings.
Remove common program groups from Start Menu	Removes items in the All Users profile from the **Programs** menu on the **Start** menu.
Remove Documents menu from Start Menu	Hides the Documents folder from the **Start** menu.
Remove Favorites menu from Start Menu	Prevents users from adding the **Favorites** menu to the **Start** menu.
Remove Help menu from Start Menu	Removes the **Help** option from the **Start** menu, but does not disable Help files from running.
Remove Run menu from Start Menu	Removes the ability to execute programs from the **Run** option on the **Start** menu, Task Manager, or by pressing **Application key + R**.
Add Logoff to the Start Menu	Adds the **Logoff** option to the **Start** menu and prevents users from removing the **Logoff** option from the **Start** menu.
Disable Logoff on the Start Menu	Removes ability to log off from Windows from the **Start** Menu.
Disable and remove the Shut Down command	Prevents shutting down Windows using the standard shutdown user interface.
Disable drag-and-drop context menus on the Start Menu	Prevents users from modifying the **Start** menu by dragging and dropping items. Other methods of customizing the **Start** menu are still enabled.
Disable changes to Taskbar and Start Menu Settings	Removes the **Taskbar & Start Menu** item from the **Settings** submenu.
Disable personalized menus	All menus items appear in default Windows 2000 order.
Disable user tracking	Prevents the system from remembering the programs run, paths followed, and documents used. Usually used in conjunction with the **Disable personalized menus** Group Policy setting.
Maximum number of recent documents	Specifies the number of shortcuts displayed on the **Documents** submenu.
Add "Run in Separate Memory Space" check box to Run dialog box	Allows 16-bit programs to run in a dedicated Virtual DOS Machine (VDM) process.
Gray unavailable Windows Installer programs Start Menu shortcuts	Displays partially installed programs in gray text on the **Start** Menu.

Customizing the Taskbar and Toolbars

Toolbars provide quick access to frequently used functions in programs and utilities such as Internet Explorer, My Computer, My Network Places, the Recycle Bin, and Windows Explorer. Toolbars can be added to the Taskbar (docked) or can float on the desktop (undocked). They can be positioned and resized. The Quick Launch bar, located to the right of the **Start** button by default, provides easy access to frequently used programs.

Figure 8.4 illustrates the Windows 2000 taskbar and toolbars that can be displayed at the bottom of the desktop.

Figure 8.4   Taskbar and Toolbars on the Windows 2000 Professional Desktop

Considerations for Customizing the Taskbar and Toolbars

When you customize the Windows taskbar or Quick Launch toolbar, or create new toolbars, consider the following:

- Decide which files, folders, programs, and Internet shortcuts your workgroup uses most frequently.

- Determine the best method of presentation for your workgroup. For example, if your workgroup consists of writers working on a specific Microsoft® Word document, you might want to create a shortcut to Microsoft Word or to that document on the Quick Launch toolbar. If your workgroup regularly accesses a folder of related files, programs, or Internet shortcuts, you might want to create a toolbar containing the contents of that folder and place it on the Windows taskbar or as a floating toolbar on the desktop.

- Before you create new toolbars, you need to group the files, programs, and Internet shortcuts that your workgroup uses most frequently into one or more appropriately named folders. A new toolbar consists of the contents of a folder on a local or network drive; Windows 2000 uses the folder name for the toolbar name.

Configuring the Taskbar and Toolbars

You can simplify a user's or workgroup's access to files, programs, and Internet shortcuts by:

- Enabling one or more of the Address, Links, Desktop, and Quick Launch toolbars on the taskbar.
- Customizing the Windows taskbar.
- Customizing the Quick Launch toolbar.
- Creating a new toolbar.
- Adding a floating toolbar to the Active Desktop.
- Removing a folder or toolbar from the Windows taskbar.
- Adding or removing titles and text from taskbar items.

Procedures for Customizing the Taskbar and Toolbars

Use the following procedures to customize the Windows taskbar and Quick Launch toolbar and to create new toolbars.

▶ **To add an Address box to the taskbar**

- Right-click anywhere on the taskbar, point to **Toolbars**, and then click **Address**.

▶ **To add the contents of the Links folder to the taskbar**

- Right-click anywhere on the taskbar, point to **Toolbars**, and then click **Links**.

▶ **To add all desktop icons to the taskbar**

- Right-click anywhere on the taskbar, point to **Toolbars**, and then click **Desktop**.

▶ **To add the Quick Launch toolbar to the taskbar**

- Right-click anywhere on the taskbar, point to **Toolbars**, and then click **Quick Launch**.

▶ **To customize the Windows 2000 Quick Launch toolbar**

- Drag a file, folder, program, or Internet shortcut from My Computer or Windows Explorer to the Quick Launch toolbar.

▶ **To create a new toolbar**

You create a new toolbar by pointing to a folder. The new toolbar will contain icons representing shortcuts to the contents of that folder—files, subfolders, programs, and Internet shortcuts. The name of the toolbar will be the same as the name of the folder.

1. Right-click the Windows taskbar, point to **Toolbars**, and then click **New Toolbar**.

2. In the **New Toolbar** dialog box, select the folder for which you want to create a toolbar, and then click **OK**. Windows 2000 adds the folder as a new toolbar, named for that folder, to the Windows taskbar.

Tip The easiest way to create a new toolbar on the Windows taskbar is to drag a folder from My Computer or Windows Explorer onto the taskbar. If you want to add the new toolbar as a floating toolbar on the desktop, drag the toolbar from the taskbar to the desktop.

▶ **To add a floating toolbar to the desktop**

- Drag the toolbar from the Windows taskbar to the desktop.

▶ **To remove a folder or toolbar from the Windows taskbar**

- On the Windows taskbar, right-click the toolbar name, and then click **Close**.

▶ **To add or remove titles and text from taskbar items**

- Right-click a clear area on the Windows taskbar, and then click **Show Text** or **Show Title**.

Group Policy Settings That Affect the Taskbar and Toolbars

You can use Group Policy settings or a combination of Group Policy settings to control access to the taskbar and toolbar options. Table 8.5 and Table 8.6 list and describe each Group Policy setting.

Other Group Policy settings you enforce can affect taskbar Group Policy settings. For additional information, right-click the Group Policy setting, click **Properties**, and then click the **Explain** tab, or refer to the Group Policy Reference on the *Windows 2000 Resource Kit* companion CD.

The Group Policy settings listed in Table 8.5 are located in the Group Policy snap-in under Local Computer Policy\User Configuration\Administrative Templates\Start Menu & Taskbar.

Table 8.5   Group Policy Settings That Can Affect the Taskbar

Group Policy Setting	Description
Disable changes to Taskbar and Start Menu Settings	Removes the **Taskbar & Start Menu** item from the **Settings** submenu.
Disable context menus for the taskbar	Hides menus that appear when users right-click the taskbar.

The Group Policy settings listed in Table 8.6 are located in the Group Policy snap-in under Local Computer Policy\User Configuration\Administrative Templates\Desktop.

Table 8.6   Group Policy Settings That Can Affect Toolbars and the Taskbar

Group Policy Setting	Description
Disable adding, dragging, dropping and closing the Taskbar's toolbars	Prevents ability to customize toolbars.
Disable adjusting desktop toolbars	Prevents resizing or repositioning toolbars.
Don't save settings at exit	Prevents window and taskbar positions from being saved when user logs off.

Limiting Access to Display Options

As in previous versions of Windows, most display options are configured through Display in Control Panel. Using Group Policy settings, you can restrict some or all of the access to the display options.

Group Policy Settings That Affect the Desktop Display

You can use Group Policy settings or a combination of Group Policy settings to control access to display properties. Table 8.7 lists and describes each Group Policy setting.

Other Group Policy settings you enforce can affect display settings. For additional information, right-click the Group Policy setting, click **Properties**, and then click the **Explain** tab, or refer to the Group Policy Reference on the *Windows 2000 Resource Kit* companion CD.

The Group Policy settings listed in Table 8.7 are located in the Group Policy snap-in under Local Computer Policy\User Configuration\Administrative Templates\Control Panel\Display.

Table 8.7   Group Policy Settings That Can Affect the Desktop Display

Group Policy Setting	Description
Disable Display in Control Panel	Error message appears when Display is run from Control Panel.
Hide Background tab	Removes the **Background** tab from Display in Control Panel.
Disable Change wallpaper setting	All options on the **Background** tab of Display in Control Panel are disabled.
Hide Appearance tab	Removes the **Appearance** tab from Display in Control Panel.
Hide Settings tab	Removes the **Settings** tab from Display in Control Panel.

Screen Saver Group Policy Settings

You can enable Group Policy settings that control whether users use screen savers and whether they can change screen saver properties. Table 8.8 lists and describes each Group Policy setting.

Other Group Policy settings you enforce can affect screen saver Group Policy settings. For additional information, right-click the Group Policy setting, click **Properties**, and then click the **Explain** tab, or refer to the Group Policy Reference on the *Windows 2000 Resource Kit* companion CD.

The Group Policy settings listed in Table 8.8 are located in the Group Policy snap-in under Local Computer Policy\User Configuration\Administrative Templates\Control Panel\Display.

Table 8.8   Group Policy Settings That Can Affect Screen Saver Functionality

Group Policy Setting	Description
Hide screen saver tab	Removes **Screen Saver** tab from Display in Control Panel.
No screen saver	Enable to prevent any screen savers from running.
Screen saver executable name	Specifies the screen saver for the user's desktop and prevents changes.
Password protect the screen saver	Enable to set passwords on all screen savers. Disable to prevent passwords from being used on all screen savers.

Restoring the Original Configuration

When several users work on the same computer and you allow changes to the taskbar and window positions, consider using the following Group Policy setting to restore the desktop to the configuration in effect at logon. Table 8.9 lists and describes the **Don't save settings on exit** Group Policy setting.

Other Group Policy settings you enforce can affect how this Group policy setting works.. For additional information, right-click the Group Policy setting, and then click the **Explain** tab, or refer to the Group Policy Reference on the *Windows 2000 Resource Kit* companion CD.

The Group Policy setting listed in Table 8.9 is located in the Group Policy snap-in under Local Computer Policy\User Configuration\Administrative Templates\Desktop.

Table 8.9   Group Policy Setting to Restore the Original Configuration

Group Policy Setting	Description
Don't save settings at exit	Prevents window and taskbar positions from being saved when user logs off.

Choosing a New User Interface

The Explorer program (Explorer.exe file) is the source of the Windows user interface. You can use the **Custom user interface** Group Policy setting to specify an alternate interface. If you enable this setting, the system starts the interface you specify instead of the Explorer.exe file.

To use this setting, copy your interface program to a network share or to your system drive. Then, enable this setting in Local Computer Policy\User Configuration\System, and type the name of the interface program, including the file name extension, in the **Shell name** text box. If the interface program file is not located in a folder specified in the Path environment variable for your system, enter the fully qualified path to the file.

If you disable this policy or do not configure it, the policy is ignored and the system displays the Explorer interface.

Troubleshooting

When the desktop doesn't behave as you expect, you can run the Gpresult.exe file on the workstation to view local and domain Group Policy settings currently in effect. Certain Group Policy settings override other Group Policy settings, some disable user interface elements, others leave user interface elements intact but disabled. Become familiar with the Group Policy settings used in your organization and refer to the Group Policy Reference on the *Windows 2000 Resource Kit* companion CD or the **Explain** tab to understand the effects of each Group Policy setting.

Two of the most common desktop-related issues are listed below.

Personalized menus doesn't seem to be working

To enable Windows 2000 personalized menus, click **Start**, point to **Settings**, and then click **Taskbar & Start Menu**. On the **General** tab, make sure personalized folders has not been disabled by Group Policy on the Local Computer.

You cannot change or modify the personalized menus algorithm; the option is either enabled or disabled.

Use the following steps to verify that personalized menus is working.

1. Create a new shortcut item on the **Programs** menu.
2. In the **Date/Time Properties** dialog box, add one day to the current date.
3. Shut down and restart Windows 2000 Professional.
4. Open the **Programs** menu to see if the item is hidden. If the item is hidden, continue to step 5. If the item appears, return to step 2.
5. Reset the current date and remove the test shortcut.

My desktop turns white and I receive an error message when I start Windows 2000 Professional

When you upgrade to Windows 2000 Professional from Windows 98 using a Web page as wallpaper, the **Show Web content on my Active Desktop** and **My Current Home Page** check boxes are selected on the **Web** tab of the **Display Properties** dialog box. The error message appears when the connection to the home page cannot be established.

To disable the **Show Web content on my Active Desktop** option, right-click the desktop, click **Properties**, click the **Web** tab, and clear the **Show Web content on my Active Desktop** check box.

Additional Resources

- For more information about the new location and name of a feature from a previous version of Windows, see the Windows 2000 Professional Help.

- For more information about using Group Policy, go to http://windows.microsoft.com, click the **Windows 2000 Professional** or **Windows 2000 Server Family** link, and then search by using the term Group Policy.

- For more information about using Internet Explorer 5, see the *Microsoft® Windows® 2000 Server Resource Kit Internet Explorer Guide*.

- For more information about using Group Policy, see "Introduction to Configuration and Management" in this book.

- For more information about Group Policy settings, see the Group Policy reference on the *Microsoft® Windows® 2000 Resource Kit* companion CD.

- For more information about using Group Policy, see "Group Policy" and "Introduction to Desktop Management" in the *Microsoft® Windows® 2000 Server Resource Kit Distributed Systems Guide*.

- For more information about managing the Windows 2000 Professional desktop in a Windows 2000 Server environment, see "Introduction to Desktop Management" in the *Distributed Systems Guide*.

- For more information about defining and setting configuration standards, see "Defining Client Administration and Configuration Standards" and "Applying Change and Configuration Management" in the *Microsoft® Windows® 2000 Server Resource Kit Deployment Planning Guide*.

C H A P T E R   9

Managing Files, Folders, and Search Methods

Microsoft® Windows® 2000 Professional makes it easier for users to find and store files and folders, and for administrators to manage file storage and access. By using new tools, such as Group Policy, Indexing Service, and Offline Files, you can prevent users from accessing required system files, enable powerful searches, and prevent network problems from affecting user productivity.

In This Chapter

Related Information in the Resource Kit

- For more information about using Group Policy, see "Introduction to Configuration and Management" in this book.

- For more information about file and folder security, see "Security" in this book.

- For more information about Active Directory™, Group Policy, and IntelliMirror™, and defining and setting configuration standards see the *Microsoft® Windows® 2000 Server Resource Kit Distributed Systems Guide* and the *Microsoft® Windows® 2000 Server Resource Kit Deployment Planning Guide*.

Quick Guide to Files, Folders, and Search Methods

Use this quick guide to obtain an overview of what Windows 2000 Professional offers you for managing files, folders, and search methods. Then pinpoint the features you want to use for effectively managing your process.

Learn new ways to access, view, and store files and folders.

Windows 2000 Professional introduces new features for locating, viewing, and storing files and folders.

- See "What's New" later in this chapter.

View and access files and folders.

Windows Explorer provides several ways to access and view files and folders on the local computer and network resources. This section describes how to customize and use Group Policy to control user interface options.

- See "Working with Files and Folders" later in this chapter.

Set preferences for viewing folders.

Customize and set Group Policy settings to control folder views.

- See "Customizing Folders" later in this chapter.

Manage Offline Files and Folders.

Users can cache network files and folders to their hard disk drive for use when network resources are unavailable. Learn how to manage the cache and set Group Policy settings that affect the functionality of Offline Files.

- See "Using Offline Files and Folders" later in this chapter.

Understand the new search methods.

The new Active Directory search method (available on a Microsoft® Windows® 2000 Server network) and the powerful Indexing Service make it easier to find files and folders on the network and local drives. Distribute custom Active Directory search files and learn what Group Policy settings are available to control searches.

- See "Searching for Files, Folders, and Network Resources" later in this chapter.

Resolve questions about how files and folder searches work.

Find help with problems and answers to common questions about finding files and using the Windows Explorer user interface.

- See "Troubleshooting" later in this chapter.

What's New

There are a few significant changes from Microsoft® Windows® 98 and Microsoft® Windows NT® Workstation version 4.0 that affect the way files and folders are stored, viewed, and accessed in the Windows Explorer user interface for Windows 2000 Professional. This section describes these changes.

My Network Places My Network Places, which was previously named Network Neighborhood, now provides a comprehensive list of all the shared computers, files and folders, printers, and other resources on the network or networks that a computer connects to.

My Computer My Computer now lists the storage devices available to the computer and provides access to Control Panel. Control Panel has become the central repository for utilities, such as Network and Dial-up Connections and Scheduled Tasks.

My Documents and My Pictures The contents of My Documents are stored on a per-user basis. A new subfolder in My Documents, called My Pictures, is the default location for storing graphic images, such as digital camera pictures.

Offline Files and Folders Users can work on files even if the network resource is unavailable. Changes made to files can be automatically synchronized on the server when the network connection is restored.

System Files Hidden by Default By default, files with system and hidden attributes do not appear in Windows Explorer windows, such as My Computer. This prevents users from inadvertently deleting or modifying required system files.

Indexing Service You can search for files and folders based on their content, author, size, or other attributes. Indexing Service is available for files stored on the hard disk drive and shared network drives.

AutoComplete AutoComplete caches previously typed addresses and file names so that when you begin to type an address or file name, Windows 2000 displays entries similar to what you entered. AutoComplete works throughout the Windows 2000 user interface, including in dialog boxes (such as **Run** and **Map Network Drive**) and in Windows Explorer.

Windows 2000 Server Network Advantages

When you use Windows 2000 Professional on a Windows 2000 Server Active Directory network, two new features are available: IntelliMirror and Active Directory.

With IntelliMirror, users' documents can be stored, or mirrored, on a centrally managed server. This feature allows users to log on to any computer in the network and obtain access to their documents and files from that computer.

Active Directory allows users to search for network resources by specifying attributes of the object they need, such as a printer capable of printing in color.

For more information about Active Directory and IntelliMirror, see the *Distributed Systems Guide* and the *Deployment Planning Guide*.

This chapter describes Group Policy objects that affect working with files, folders, and search methods. Group Policy can be set on the local computer, but it is recommended that Group Policy be administered centrally using a Windows 2000 Server network. For more information about Group Policy, see "Group Policy" in the *Distributed Systems Guide*.

Working with Files and Folders

This section describes changes to how files are accessed, methods for customizing the Windows Explorer user interface, and policies you can set to control how the interface works.

My Computer

My Computer provides access to local drives, mapped network drives, and Control Panel. System folders, such as Network and Dial-up Connections, Scheduled Tasks, and Printers, are now available through Control Panel.

By using the Address bar, you can quickly access other desktop shortcuts, such as My Network Places, the Recycle Bin, and Internet Explorer.

By default, when you open My Computer, you do not see the Folders Explorer Bar, which displays folders in a hierarchical relationship in a pane on the left side of the user interface.

To display the folders, you can choose **Explorer Bar** from the **View** menu and then select **Folders**. Enabling the Folders option is only in effect until you close My Computer. The next time you open My Computer the folders do not display until you choose the option again.

You can configure Windows 2000 Professional to show the Explorer Bar every time you open My Computer. To do this, use the following procedure:

▶ **To permanently display the Explorer Bar in My Computer**

1. In My Computer, click the **Tools** menu, and then click **Folder Options**.

2. Click the **File Types** tab, and then under **Registered file types**, click **Folder** (the extension is **N/A**).

3. Click **Advanced**.

4. Under **Actions**, click **Explore**, and then click **Set Default**.

My Documents and My Pictures

New to Windows NT 4.0 users is the My Documents folder, which is the default location for storing user documents and files. Windows 98 users will notice a new location for the My Documents folder. It is stored with other user profile settings in the Documents and Settings folder. Users who share computers cannot read each other's documents.

A subfolder of My Documents that is called My Pictures provides a place to store graphics and digital images from sources such as digital cameras. With Web View enabled, you can view images by using thumbnails (see Figure 9.1) or full screen previews, zoom in and out, pan left and right, scroll up and down, and print images.

Figure 9.1 My Pictures Window Displaying Thumbnails View

If the picture or image is stored on a drive that uses the NTFS file system, you can enter and view text descriptions of picture attributes, such as title, subject description, or category. Additional columns can also be displayed in the folder.

For more information about changing folder views and using Web view, see "Customizing Folders" later in this chapter.

My Documents is a system folder that cannot be deleted. However, you can rename the desktop shortcut, rename the folder, and redirect the My Documents folder to a network location by using Group Policy.

Note If you upgrade to Windows 2000 from a Windows 98 workstation that had redirected the My Documents folder, Windows 2000 Professional redirects My Documents to the same location.

▶ **To change the location of the My Documents folder**

1. Right-click **My Documents** on the desktop, and then click **Properties**.

2. Under **Target folder location**, type a destination, or click **Find Target** to view locations (see Figure 9.2).

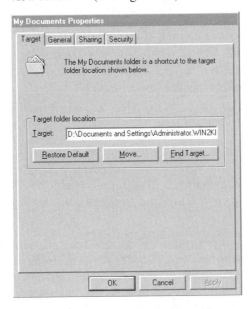

Figure 9.2   Target Tab of the My Documents Properties Dialog Box

Group Policy Settings That Affect My Documents

You can use a Group Policy setting or a combination of Group Policy settings to control the My Documents folder. On a Windows 2000 Server, Group Policy has a special Folder Redirection component. For more information about using Group Policy with Windows 2000 Server, see "Group Policy" and "Introduction to Desktop Management" in the *Distributed Systems Guide*.

Table 9.1 lists some of the Group Policy settings that affect My Documents and provides a brief description of each. Before you change a Group Policy setting, you should be familiar with using Group Policy and with using Microsoft® Management Console (MMC). To make changes to these settings, you must log on as a member of the Administrators group. You can find these Group Policy settings by using the Group Policy MMC snap-in and then following this path:

Local Computer Policy\User Configuration\Administrative Templates\Desktop

Table 9.1   Group Policy Settings That Affect My Documents

Group Policy Setting	Description
Hide My Documents icon on desktop	Removes the My Documents icon from the desktop, Windows Explorer, and the **Open** dialog box.
Prohibit user from changing My Documents path	Disables the **Target** box in the **My Documents Properties** dialog box.

For additional information about Group Policy settings, including a more complete description of each setting, follow the preceding path to the Group Policy setting, right-click the Group Policy setting, click **Properties**, and then click the **Explain** tab, or refer to the Group Policy Reference on the *Microsoft® Windows® 2000 Resource Kit* companion CD.

My Network Places

My Network Places replaces the Network Neighborhood feature that you used in both Windows 98 and Windows NT Workstation 4.0. In the My Network Places window, you can double-click **Computers Near Me** to quickly access files and folders on other computers in your workgroup or double-click **Entire Network** to search more widely.

The Add Network Place wizard, also available in My Network Places, guides users through connecting to a shared folder, a Web folder (not a Web site), or an FTP site. Users can specify alternate credentials for automatic access to Web folders and FTP sites. Users can provide friendly names for shortcuts that display in My Network Places. Network resources can be added to the **Favorites** menu.

When you open a document on a network resource, a folder shortcut is automatically created in My Network Places.

Note Mapped network drives do not appear in My Network Places.

Group Policy Settings That Affect My Network Places

You can use a Group Policy setting or a combination of Group Policy settings to control the functioning of the My Network Places folder. For example, with Group Policy on a Windows 2000 Server, an administrator can specify the connections that are displayed in a user's My Network Places folder. For more information about using Group Policy with Windows 2000 Server, see "Group Policy" and "Introduction to Desktop Management" in the *Distributed Systems Guide*.

Table 9.2 and Table 9.3 list some of the Group Policy settings that affect My Network Places and provide a brief description of each. Before you change a Group Policy setting, you should be familiar with using Group Policy and MMC snap-ins. To make changes to these settings, you must log on as a member of the Administrators group. You can find the Group Policy settings that Table 9.2 lists by using the Group Policy MMC snap-in and then following this path:

Local Computer Policy\User Configuration\Administrative Templates\Desktop.

Table 9.2   Group Policy Settings That Affect My Network Places and Desktop Icons

Group Policy Setting	Description
Hide My Network Places icon on desktop	Removes the My Network Places icon from the desktop. This Group Policy setting only affects the desktop icon. It does not prevent users from connecting to the network or browsing for shared computers on the network.
Do not add shares from recently opened documents to My Network Places	Prevents a connection from being saved if it was established by opening files on remote shares.
Hide all icons on Desktop	Removes all icons and shortcuts, including My Network Places, from the desktop.

You can find the Group Policy settings that Table 9.3 lists by using the Group Policy MMC snap-in and then following this path:

User Configuration\Administrative Templates\Windows Components \Windows Explorer.

Table 9.3   Group Policy Settings That Affect My Network Places

Group Policy Setting	Description
No "Computers Near Me" in My Network Places	Removes computers in the user's workgroup from lists of network resources.
No "Entire Network" in My Network Places	Removes all computers outside the user's workgroup from lists of network resources.
Remove "Map Network Drive" and "Disconnect Network Drive"	Prevents using My Network Places to connect to other computers or to close existing connections.

For additional information about Group Policy settings, including a more complete description of each setting, follow the preceding paths to the Group Policy setting, right-click the Group Policy setting, click **Properties**, and then click the **Explain** tab, or refer to the Group Policy Reference on the *Microsoft® Windows® 2000 Resource Kit* companion CD.

Windows Explorer

In Windows 2000 Professional, Windows Explorer is located in the Accessories folder. Using Windows Explorer, you can easily add, remove, reorder, and size columns by right-clicking any column heading.

By default, the My Documents folder is selected when Windows Explorer opens. You can change the focus to My Computer.

▶ **To open Windows Explorer with My Computer selected**

1. Click **Start**, point to **Programs**, point to **Accessories**, right-click **Windows Explorer**, and then click **Properties**.

2. On the **Shortcut** tab, type the following text in the **Target** box:

   `%SystemRoot%\explorer.exe /e,::{20D04FE0-3AEA-1069-A2D8-08002B30309D}`

▶ **To restore Windows Explorer to the default My Documents view**

1. Click **Start**, point to **Programs**, point to **Accessories**, right-click **Windows Explorer**, and then click **Properties**.

2. On the **Shortcut** tab, type the following text in the **Target** box:

   `%SystemRoot%\explorer.exe /e,::{450D8FBA-AD25-11D0-98A8-0800361B1103}`

Command Line Switches for Windows Explorer

You can control the functionality of Windows Explorer by using the command-line switches listed in Table 9.4.

Use the following syntax:

```
EXPLORER.EXE [/n][/e][,/root,<object>][[,/select],<sub object>]
```

Table 9.4   Command-Line Switches to Control Windows Explorer

Command-Line Switch	Description
/n	Opens a new window in single-paned (My Computer) view for each item selected, even if the new window duplicates a window that is already open.
/e	Uses Windows Explorer view. Windows Explorer view is similar to File Manager in Windows version 3.x. Note that the default view is Open view.
/root,<object>	Specifies the root level of the specified view. The default is to use the normal namespace root (the desktop). Whatever is specified is the root for the display.
/select,<sub object>	Specifies the folder to receive the initial focus. If **/select** is used, the parent folder is opened and the specified object is selected.

The following examples illustrate how you can use command-line switches to modify the way you view folders and objects in Windows Explorer:

To view objects on **\\<server name>** only:

```
explorer /e,/root,\\<server name>
```

To view the C:\Windows folder and select Calc.exe:

```
explorer /select,c:\windows\calc.exe
```

Group Policy Settings That Affect Windows Explorer

You can use a Group Policy setting or a combination of Group Policy settings to control the functioning of Windows Explorer. For more information about using Group Policy with Windows 2000 Server, see "Group Policy" and "Introduction to Desktop Management" in the *Distributed Systems Guide*.

Table 9.5 lists some of the Group Policy settings that affect Windows Explorer and provides a brief description of each. Before you change a Group Policy setting, you should be familiar with using Group Policy and MMC snap-ins. To make changes to these settings, you must log on as a member of the Administrators group. You can find these Group Policy settings by using the Group Policy MMC snap-in and then following this path:

Local Computer Policy\User Configuration\Administrative Templates \Windows Components\Windows Explorer

Table 9.5   Group Policy Settings That Affect Windows Explorer

Group Policy Setting	Description
Enable Classic Shell	Disables Active Desktop, Web View, Thumbnails view, and single-click mouse option. User interface looks and acts like Windows NT 4.0.
Remove File menu from Windows Explorer	Hides the **File** menu in My Computer and Windows Explorer. Does not disable other methods of performing the same tasks.
Remove "Map Network Drive" and "Disconnect Network Drive"	Prevents you from using Windows Explorer and My Network Places to connect to or disconnect from other computers.
Remove Search button from Windows Explorer	Hides the **Search** button in Windows Explorer but shows it in Internet Explorer and on the **Start** menu.
Disable Windows Explorer's default context menu	Prevents shortcut menus from appearing when you right-click items in Windows Explorer.
Hides the Manage item on the Windows Explorer context menu	Prevents the Compmgmt.msc file from running when you choose the **Manage** command in Windows Explorer or shortcut menus in My Computer.
Hide these specified drives in My Computer	Removes icons that represent selected disk drives from My Computer and Windows Explorer.
Prevent access to drives from My Computer	Prevents viewing content on selected drives in My Computer, Windows Explorer, and My Network Places. Disables the **Run** command, the **Map Network Drive** dialog box, and the **Dir** command at the command prompt.
Disable UI to change menu animation setting	Disables the option that animates the movement of windows, menus, and lists.
Disable UI to change keyboard navigation indicator setting	Disables the **Hide keyboard navigation indicators until I use the Alt key** check box on the **Effects** tab of **Display** in Control Panel.

(continued)

Table 9.5   Group Policy Settings That Affect Windows Explorer *(continued)*

Group Policy Setting	Description
Disable DFS tab	Removes the **DFS** tab from the **Properties** dialog box when you right-click a folder in Windows Explorer or in other programs that use the Windows Explorer browser, such as My Computer. As a result, users cannot use this tab to view or change the properties of the Distributed file system shares that are available from their computer.
No "Computers Near Me" in My Network Places	Prevents computers in the user's workgroup or domain from appearing in My Network Places or Windows Explorer.
No "Entire Network" in My Network Places	Prevents any computer that is outside the user's workgroup from appearing as network resources in My Network Places or Windows Explorer.

For additional information about Group Policy settings, including a more complete description of each setting, right-click the Group Policy setting, click **Properties**, and then click the **Explain** tab, or refer to the Group Policy Reference on the *Microsoft® Windows® 2000 Resource Kit* companion CD.

Customizing Folders

Windows 2000 Professional offers new options for using Windows Explorer to view folders and new ways to set your viewing preferences. Two new ways to customize folder views in Windows Explorer are as follows: choosing **Folder Options** from the **Tools** menu or using the Customize This Folder wizard.

Setting Folder Options

All the options for customizing folder views and preferences are found in **Folder Options** on the **Tools** menu. Folder Options has four tabs: General, View, File Types, and Offline Files.

You use the **General** tab to configure Active Desktop and Web view. You can also configure whether new windows open as you browse folders and whether you single-click or double-click to select items.

The **View** tab is the primary location for setting folder options. The options that are available on the **View** tab of the **Folder Options** dialog box are shown in Figure 9.3.

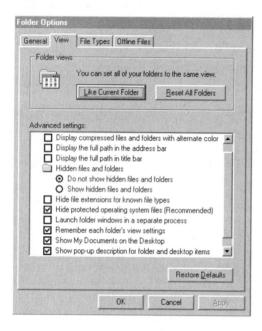

Figure 9.3 **The View Tab of the Folder Options Dialog Box**

For more information about setting options on the **View** tab and the **File Types** tab, see Windows 2000 Professional Help.

For more information about using the **Offline Files** tab, see "Using Offline Files and Folders" later in this chapter.

Using the Customize This Folder Wizard

The Customize This Folder wizard allows you to choose and edit folder templates, preview and set the background picture, define colors for the file name and background, and add a comment for the folder that can be viewed when an HTML template is used to display folder contents. The wizard creates a hidden Desktop.ini file and a hidden folder containing the folder settings.

Using the Customize This Folder Wizard

1. In My Computer or Windows Explorer, click the folder you want to customize.

2. Click the **View** menu, and then click **Customize This Folder**.

Using Web View with the Wizard

Enable Web view on the **General** tab of the **Folder Options** dialog box. With Web view enabled, use the Customize This Folder wizard to set the folder's background to any image file format, such as .bmp, .jpg, .gif, .tif, .dib, .png, .art, and .xif files. The background image is seen by anyone who accesses the folder.

Web view works by applying HTML templates to folder views. Some of the default folder templates are stored in %WinDir%\web and are hidden files. For example, the Folder.htt file is the template that is applied to most folders. Be careful not to delete or move these files.

Note In Windows 98, you could enable Web content for individual folders. In Windows 2000, Web content is either enabled or disabled for all folders.

Understanding Saved Views and Browsing Folders

In Windows 2000 Professional, the view you use is not always permanently saved in Windows Explorer. You can control whether the views you use are saved permanently or temporarily by using the **Remember each folder's view settings** check box on the **View** tab of the **Folder Options** dialog box (see figure 9.3).

By default the **Remember each folder's view settings** option is enabled. When you choose to leave this setting enabled, the following happens:

- The changes you make to a folder's view is automatically saved when you close the folder.
- The view you use to view one folder is not applied to other folders.
- When you open a folder, it opens in the view you used when you last viewed it.

When you clear the check box for **Remember each folder's view settings**, the following happens:

- When you start Windows Explorer, the first folder you view displays in the folder's saved view. Windows Explorer holds that view in temporary memory and applies it to all the folders that you visit while Windows Explorer remains open unless you manually alter the view.
- As you browse to other folders (after the initial folder is opened), the saved view for each folder is ignored, and when you quit Windows Explorer, the folder view that you have been using to view multiple folders is deleted from temporary memory.
- The next time you open Windows Explorer, once again, it is the saved view of the first folder you open that determines how you view multiple folders.

Setting All Folders to the Same View

Some users want to have all their Windows Explorer folders set to the same view. In Windows 2000 Professional, the default setting is that any change made to a folder's view is automatically saved when you close the folder and is not applied to other folders. However, you can set all folders to the same view by using the **Folder Options** command as described in the following procedure.

▶ **To set all folders to the same view**

1. In My Computer or Windows Explorer, set the view to your preference.

2. On the **Tools** menu, click **Folder Options**.

3. In the **Folder Options** dialog box, click the **View** tab.

4. Under **Folder Views**, click **Like Current Folder**.

Important The **Remember each folder's view settings** check box on the **View** tab of the **Folder Options** dialog box (see Figure 9.3) affects how the view settings of individual folders are applied and saved. For more information about the impact of clearing this check box, see "Understanding Saved Views and Browsing Folders" earlier in this chapter.

Group Policy Settings That Affect Folders

You can use Group Policy settings to control how folders are used.

Table 9.6 lists some of the Group Policy settings that affect folders and provides a brief description of each. Before you change a Group Policy setting, you should be familiar with using Group Policy and MMC snap-ins. To make changes to these settings, you must log on as a member of the Administrators group. You can find these Group Policy settings by using the Group Policy MMC snap-in and then following this path:

User Configuration\Administrative Templates\Windows Components\Windows Explorer.

Table 9.6   Group Policy Settings That Affect Folders

Group Policy Setting	Description
Remove the Folder Options menu item from the Tools menu	Disables the **Folder Options** command on the **Tools** menu. Properties on folders cannot be set.
Enable Classic Shell	Disables Active Desktop, Web View, Thumbnails view, and single-click mouse action. User interface looks and acts like Windows NT 4.0.

For additional information about Group Policy settings, including a more complete description of each setting, follow the preceding path to the Group Policy setting, right-click the Group Policy setting, click **Properties**, and then click the **Explain** tab, or refer to the Group Policy Reference on the *Microsoft® Windows® 2000 Resource Kit* companion CD.

Using Offline Files and Folders

Offline Files provides access to network files and folders from a local disk when the network is unavailable. This feature is particularly useful when access to information is critical, when network connections are unstable and nonpermanent, and when you are using mobile computers. This section discusses how Offline Files works and how to manage computers using Offline Files.

For specific information about using Offline Files with mobile computers, see "Mobile Computing" in this book.

Overview of Offline Files and Folders

Any shared file or folder on a Microsoft network can be made available offline. You can make files available from any computer that supports server message block (SMB)--based File and Printer Sharing, including Microsoft® Windows® 95, Windows 98, and Windows NT 4.0. Offline Files is not available on Novell NetWare networks or when Windows 2000 is running Terminal Services.

Files specified for offline use are stored, or cached, in a database on the hard disk drive of the local computer. If the network resource becomes unavailable, notification appears in the status area. Changes made to the file while offline are saved locally and then synchronized when the network resource is available.

Offline files and information about them are stored in a database in a hidden system folder (%systemroot%\CSC). The database emulates the network resource while it is offline so that files are accessed as though the network resource is still available.

The Offline Files Folder is created when files are requested offline and provides a view of the files stored in the database.

Caution If the network resource is online, renaming files in the Offline Files Folder takes effect immediately on the network resource.

▶ **To access Offline Files configuration options**

1. In My Computer or Windows Explorer, click a folder.

2. On the **Tools** menu, click **Folder Options**.

3. Click the **Offline Files** tab.

Note If there is already an Offline Files shortcut on your desktop, you can skip the following procedure and access the Offline Files Folder by double-clicking the desktop shortcut to Offline Files.

▶ **To access the Offline Files Folder**

1. In My Computer of Windows Explorer, click a folder.

2. On the **Tools** menu, click **Folder Options**.

3. Click the **Offline Files** tab.

4. Click **View Files**.

Making Files Available Offline

Files are cached to the computer that requests them in one of two ways: automatic caching or manual caching. Automatic caching occurs when a specific file in a folder has been opened, but only if the network server indicates that the contents of the share should be automatically cached. Automatically cached files are marked as **Temporarily Available Offline** in the Offline Files Folder because they can be removed from the cache as the cache fills up. There is no guarantee that an automatically cached file will be available when offline. Automatic caching does not cache all the files in a folder.

Files are manually cached when a computer specifically requests, or pins, a particular file or folder on the network to be available offline. Files and folders are pinned by selecting the file or folder and clicking **Make Available Offline** on the **File** menu. Manually cached files are marked as **Always available offline** in the Offline Files Folder. The icon representing the file or folder updates to depict its offline status.

In Windows 2000 Professional, when a folder is shared, **Manual Caching for Documents** setting is enabled by default. To change the setting so that documents are automatically cached, right-click the folder, click **Sharing**, and then click **Caching**. In the **Setting** box, click **Automatic Caching for Documents**. You can also choose to disable caching.

Note You can also manually pin files and folders that have been configured for automatic caching.

By default, the following files types cannot be cached:

```
*.SLM; *.MDB; *.LDB; *.MDW; *.MDE; *.PST; *.DB?
```

You can override the default settings by using the **Files not cached** Group Policy setting. Any file types you specify in the Group Policy setting override the default files types not usually cached. For example, if you specify that only *.txt files cannot be cached, all other file types become available for caching. .

The default cache size for automatically cached offline files is 10 percent of the total disk space of the hard disk drive. You can change the default (specify a value between 0 and 100 percent) on the **Offline Files** tab of the **Folder Options** dialog box (accessed by clicking **Folder Options** on the **Tools** menu). This setting does not affect the cache for manually cached files. You can store up to 2 gigabytes (GB) of manually cached files per computer if you have that much space available.

More About the Offline Files Database

The database containing information about Offline Files resides in the hidden system folder, or directory, called %systemroot%\CSC. The name CSC refers to client side caching. The CSC directory contains all offline files requested by any user on the computer.

Files in the CSC directory are not encrypted, nor is encryption preserved, but file permissions and system permissions on the file are preserved. Therefore, a Microsoft® Word document created by Peter Tysver, given a password, and saved to a share on which only he has Full user rights, cannot be opened from the CSC directory by Renee Smith, because she has neither the share rights to open the file nor the password required to open the file in Microsoft Word.

To open or view the files in the CSC directory, you must log on as a member of the Administrators group. Because file encryption is not preserved, it is possible to log on as an administrator and to open files and view their content from the CSC directory by using a program such as Notepad. Users who share computers need to be aware that sensitive information can be viewed by anyone who is a member of the Administrators group.

Note On a FAT file system or a FAT file system converted to NTFS, users might be able to read information that is cached in the %systemroot%\CSC directory. This includes offline files requested by another user on the same computer.

It is very important not to move or delete files directly from the CSC directory. For more information about moving the cache folder and deleting files from the cache, see "Managing Offline Files" later in this chapter.

Reconnecting to the Network Resource

When a network share becomes available after being offline (for example, a server goes offline and is then brought back online, or a mobile computer is disconnected from the network and then reconnected), the network share is automatically available when three conditions are met:

- No offline files from that network share are open on the user's computer.
- No offline files from that network share have changes that need to be synchronized.
- The network connection is not considered a slow link.

When all these conditions are satisfied and a user opens a file on the network share, the user is automatically working online on that network share. Any changes that a user makes is saved to the file on the network share and to the file that is cached in the Offline Files Folder. When any of these conditions are not satisfied and a user opens a file on the network share, the user is still working offline even though the network share is available. Any changes the user makes are saved only to the offline version of the file.

For more information about reconnecting over slow links or with mobile computers, see "Mobile Computing" in this book.

Synchronizing Files and Folders

It is important to understand how synchronization works between the locally cached version and the network resource version of a file. There are several ways to initiate synchronization, and, depending on the method you choose and the options you've enabled, either a full or quick synchronization of the files occurs.

When full synchronization occurs, the most current version of every *cached* network file is cached to the local drive. A quick synchronization is faster, but might not provide the most current version of every network file that has been made available offline. However, a quick synchronization does ensure that a complete version of every file is available.

There are several options that control how files are synchronized when the network resource becomes available. You can choose to synchronize:

- Automatically at logon.
- Automatically at logoff.
- Manually at any time.
- When the computer is idle for a specified amount of time.
- Automatically at specified times.

▶ **To configure synchronization**

1. Click **Start**, point to **Programs**, point to **Accessories**, and then click **Synchronize**.

2. Click **Setup**.

3. Use the **Logon/Logoff**, **On Idle**, and **Scheduled** tabs to configure options.

Note Synchronization works only for the user who is currently logged on.

You can also start synchronization from Windows Explorer by clicking the **Tools** menu and then clicking **Synchronize**.

In order for synchronization to work, the network resources must be online or available for reconnection. Depending on how the synchronization is executed, offline changes might or might not be sent to the network resource and new versions of cached files might or might not be downloaded. In cases where a *quick* or *partial* synchronization occurs, data is copied from the network only to ensure availability while offline. When a *full* synchronization occurs, newer versions of files on the network are located and cached. Table 9.7 describes what kind of synchronization occurs when each method is used.

Table 9.7   Description of Synchronization Options and How Files are Cached

Synchronization commands and options	Send offline changes to the network resource?	Receive cached files from the network resource?
Automatically synchronize the selected items when I log on to my computer	Yes	No
Synchronize all offline files before logging off is enabled	Yes	Fully
Synchronize all offline files before logging off is disabled	No	Partially
Synchronize the selected items while my computer is idle	Yes	Partially
Scheduled	Yes	Fully
Clicking **Synchronize** from the **Start** menu or on the **Tools** menu	Yes	Fully
Clicking **Synchronize** on the **File** menu	Yes	Fully
Clicking **Make Available Offline** on the **File** menu	No	Partially
From the Offline Files icon in the Status area of the task bar	Yes	No

If the network resource version of a file and the locally cached version of the file are different, you can choose one of the following options in the **Resolve file conflicts** dialog box.

- *Keep both versions.* Saves the version on my computer to the network as *<filename>(username vX)*.doc, where *filename* is the name of the file, *username* is my user name, and *X* is the version number.

- *Keep only the version on my computer.* Replaces the network version.

- *Keep only the network version.* Replaces the version on my computer.

You are given the option to view each individual file. The date and time the files were saved is provided.

Using Offline Files on Mobile Computers

Offline files are particularly useful for mobile computer users. For more information about using offline files on mobile computers, such as synchronizing with a slow link and preventing synchronization when running on battery power, see "Mobile Computing" in this book.

Managing Offline Files

There are several different options you can use to delete files and folders no longer needed for offline use. It is important to understand how, where, and when to delete files, so that no changes are lost and files needed offline are still available.

Deleting Files and Folders

It is very important that nothing is deleted or moved directly from the %systemroot%\CSC folder. When you need to remove all the files in the folder, see "Deleting All the Offline Files and Folders in the Cache" later in this chapter.

Remember, if you are working with files in the Offline Files Folder when the network resource is *online*, you are working *directly* on the network computer. When you rename or modify files from this location, the changes are immediately saved both in the Offline Files Folder and on the network resource.

There are two methods for safely removing offline files from the cache without affecting network files or folders. You can choose to delete files from the Offline Files Folder or click the **Delete Files** button on the **Offline Files** tab of the **Folder Options** dialog box (accessed by clicking **Folder Options** on the **Tools** menu).

Deleting Files from the Offline Files Folder

You can open the Offline Files Folder and delete files directly from the list of offline files. This allows you to delete individual files regardless of where they are located on the network or which folder they are contained in. When you delete a file this way, the file is removed from the cache regardless of whether it was manually cached (pinned) or whether it was automatically cached.

Note Deleting files and folders from the cache does not delete the network copy of the file or folder.

If an offline folder is manually cached and you delete any or all offline files in the folder, the folder remains pinned and all files in the folder are cached the next time a full synchronization occurs.

▶ **To delete files from the cache using the Offline Files Folder**

1. Click a folder, and on the **Tools** menu, click **Folder Options**.

2. On the **Offline Files** tab, click **View Files**.

3. Click the file you want to delete and on the **File** menu, click **Delete**.

Using the Delete Files Function

You can delete all files on a network share using the **Delete Files** button on the **Offline Files** tab of the **Folder Options** dialog box (accessed by clicking **Folder Options** on the **Tools** menu). This method allows you to delete every file in a network share and to distinguish between automatically cached files (temporarily available offline) and manually cached files (always available offline).

If you delete manually cached folders this way, the folders and the files in them are no longer pinned. To make those files or folders available offline again, you need to pin the files or folders. When you delete automatically cached files this way, you only need to open the files to make them temporarily available offline.

Note Deleting files and folders from the cache does not delete the network copy of the file or folder.

▶ **To delete files from the cache on a network share**

1. Click a shared network folder and then on the **Tools** menu, click **Folder Options**.

2. On the **Offline Files** tab, click **Delete Files**.

3. In the **Confirm File Delete** dialog box, select the shared folders containing the offline files you want to delete.

4. Click **Delete only the temporary offline versions** if you want to delete files that have been automatically cached. Click **Delete both the temporary offline versions and the versions that are always available offline** if you want to delete files that have been automatically cached and files that have been manually cached (pinned).

Note Files are also deleted from the cache whenever an offline file is deleted through any usual user path, such as Windows Explorer, My Computer, the **Run** dialog box, or the Command Prompt. When users verify that they want to delete a file, the file is removed from the cache. This is not an effective way to clean up the cache because it also deletes files in the shared network folder.

Deleting All the Offline Files and Folders in the Cache

You can delete all the offline files stored in the %systemroot%\CSC folder by using a process known as *reinitializing* the cache. This method deletes all offline files from the Offline Files Folder and resets the Offline Files database. If any files in the cache have changed and have not been synchronized with the network versions, the changes are lost when the cache is reinitialized. You must restart the computer after the cache is reinitialized.

▶ **To reinitialize the Offline Files cache**

1. Click a folder, and then on the **Tools** menu, click **Folder Options**.

2. Click the **Offline Files** tab.

3. Press CTRL+SHIFT, and then click **Delete Files**.

4. Restart the computer.

Caution You cannot undo the effects of reinitialization. After the cache is reinitialized all offline files are permanently removed from the computer.

Moving the Cache

The only way to safely move the hidden system folder (%systemroot%\CSC) is by using the Offline Files Cache Mover (Cachemov.exe) tool available on the *Windows 2000 Resource Kit* companion CD. You can move the cache database to another location on a fixed disk only.

For more information about using the Offline Files Cache Mover tool, see *Windows 2000 Resource Kit* Tools Help on the *Windows 2000 Resource Kit* companion CD.

Policy Settings That Affect Offline Files

You can use a Group Policy setting or a combination of Group Policy settings to control the functionality of the Offline Files feature. For more information about using Group Policy with Windows 2000 Server, see "Group Policy" and "Introduction to Desktop Management" in the *Distributed Systems Guide*.

Table 9.8 lists some of the Group Policy settings that affect Offline Files and provides a brief description of each. Before you change a Group Policy setting, you should be familiar with using Group Policy and MMC snap-ins. To make changes to these settings, you must log on as a member of the Administrators group. You can find these Group Policy settings by using the Group Policy MMC snap-in and then following this path:

Local Computer Policy\User Configuration\Administrative Templates \Network\Offline Files.

Note   These Group Policy settings appear in the User Configuration folders. If Group Policy settings are also configured in the Computer Configuration folders, the setting in Computer Configuration takes precedence over the setting in User Configuration.

Table 9.8   Group Policy Settings in User Configuration That Affect Offline Files

Group Policy Setting	Description
Disable user configuration of Offline Files	Removes the **Offline Files** tab from the **Folder Options** dialog box. It also removes the **Settings** command from the **Offline Files** shortcut menu and disables the **Settings** button in the **Offline Files Status** dialog box. As a result, users cannot view or change the options on the **Offline Files** tab or in the **Offline Files** dialog box.
Synchronize all offline files before logging off	Determines whether offline files are fully synchronized when users log off. Disables the option on the **Offline Files** tab in the **Folder Options** dialog box.

(continued)

Table 9.8   Group Policy Settings in User Configuration That Affect Offline Files *(continued)*

Group Policy Setting	Description
Action on server disconnect	Determines whether network files remain available if the computer is suddenly disconnected from the server hosting the files. Also disables the **When a network connection is lost** option on the **Offline Files** tab in the **Folder Options** dialog box.
Nondefault server disconnect actions	Determines how computers respond when they are disconnected from particular offline file servers. This Group Policy setting overrides the default response, a user-specified response, and the response specified in the **Action on server disconnect** Group Policy setting.
Disable "Make Available Offline"	Removes the **Make Available Offline** command from the user interface.
Prevent use of Offline Files folder	Disables the **View Files** button on the **Offline Files** tab in the **Folder Options** dialog box.
Disable reminder balloons	Hides the reminder balloons that would appear above the **Offline Files** icon in the status area.
Reminder balloon frequency	Determines how often reminder balloons appear.
Initial reminder balloon lifetime	Determines how long the first reminder balloon for a network status change is displayed.
Reminder balloon lifetime	Determines how long updated reminder balloons are displayed.
Event logging level	Determines which events the Offline Files feature records in the event log.

All the Group Policy settings that are available in the User Configuration folder are also available in the Computer Configuration folder. The Group Policy settings listed in Table 9.9 are only used as Computer Configuration settings. You can find the Computer Configuration Group Policy settings by using the Group Policy snap-in and then following this path:

Local Computer Policy\Computer Configuration\Administrative Templates \Network\Offline Files.

Note If a Group Policy setting is configured in both locations, the Computer Configuration setting takes precedence.

Table 9.9   Group Policy Settings in Computer Configuration That Affect Offline Files

Group Policy Setting	Description
Default cache size	Limits the percentage of the computer's disk space that can be used to store automatically cached offline files.
Files not cached	Lets you exclude certain types of files from automatic and manual caching for offline use. *Warning*: See "Making Files Available Offline" earlier in this chapter.
Administratively assigned offline files	Lists network files and folders that are always available for offline use. Makes the specified files and folders available offline to users of the computer.
At logoff, delete local copy of user's offline files	Deletes local copies of the user's offline files when the user logs off. This Group Policy setting specifies that automatically and manually cached offline files are retained only while the user is logged on to the computer. When the user logs off, the system deletes all local copies of offline files.

For additional information about Group Policy settings, including a more complete description of each setting, right-click the Group Policy setting, click **Properties**, and then click the **Explain** tab, or refer to the Group Policy Reference on the *Microsoft® Windows® 2000 Resource Kit* companion CD.

Searching for Files, Folders, and Network Resources

Windows 2000 Professional makes it easy to search for files, folders, and resources using the new Windows Explorer user interface, the Search Assistant, and Indexing Service.

Navigating through Windows Explorer in Windows 2000 Professional is similar to using a Web browser. Forward and Back buttons, a History folder, an Address bar, custom views, and the Search Assistant have been added to all windows accessed through My Computer, My Network Places, My Documents, the **Search** command on the **Start** menu, and in Windows Explorer windows.

When you use Windows 2000 Professional on a Windows 2000 Server Active Directory domain, you can search the directory by specifying attributes for the resource you want. For example, you can search for printers capable of printing double-sided pages. For more information about using Active Directory, see "Using Active Directory to Search for Network Resources" later in this chapter.

Finding Files and Folders

Windows 2000 offers a number of ways to find files or folders. Each method provides access to the Search Assistant, History folder, and Indexing Service on the local computer.

You can search for files and folders in the following ways:

- On the **Start** menu, point to **Search** and then click **For Files or Folders**, **On the Internet**, **For People**, or in an Active Directory domain, **For Printers**.
- On the **Start** menu, point to **Programs**, point to **Accessories**, and then click **Windows Explorer**.
- On the desktop, double-click **My Documents**, **My Computer**, or **My Network Places**.

Group Policy Setting That Affects Searching for Files and Folders

You can use a Group Policy setting to control how you search for files and folders. Table 9.10 lists a Group Policy setting that affects how you search for files and folders and provides a brief description of it. Before you change a Group Policy setting, you should be familiar with using Group Policy and MMC snap-ins. To make changes to this setting, you must log on as a member of the Administrators group. You can find this Group Policy setting by using the Group Policy MMC snap-in and then following this path:

Local Computer Policy\User Configuration\Administrative Templates \Start Menu & Taskbar.

Table 9.10   Group Policy Setting That Affects Searching for Files and Folders

Group Policy Setting	Description
Remove Search menu from Start menu	Removes the **Search** menu from the **Start** menu and shortcut menus, and disables the use of the F3 and Application key+F keystrokes.

Saving and Opening Files

Among the new features of Windows 2000 Professional are the new **Save As** and **Open** dialog boxes.

In the left pane, shortcuts to the History folder, the Desktop, My Documents, My Computer, and My Network Places provide easy access to these locations. You can customize the appearance of the right pane by choosing to view Large Icons, Small Icons, List, Details, or Thumbnails.

In addition, Windows 2000 provides a list of recently used files in the **File name** box. When you begin typing in the **File name** box, files with names similar to the characters you type appear. You can choose from the list or continue typing to create a new file name.

Figure 9.4 illustrates the new features of the **Open** and **Save As** dialog boxes.

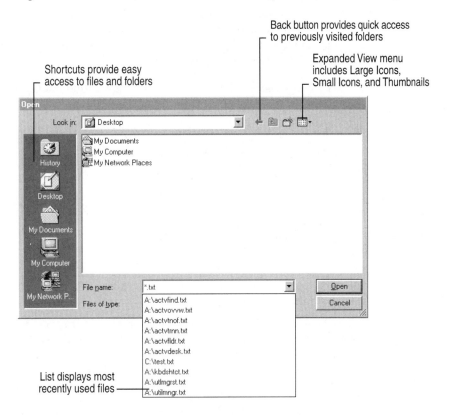

Figure 9.4   New Features of the Open and Save As Dialog Boxes

Group Policy Settings That Affect Saving and Opening Files

You can use Group Policy settings to control how you save and open files. Table 9.11 lists Group Policy settings that affect how you save and open files and provides a brief description of each. Before you change a Group Policy setting, you should be familiar with using Group Policy and MMC snap-ins. To make changes to these settings, you must log on as a member of the Administrators group. You can find these Group Policy settings by using the Group Policy MMC snap-in and then following this path:

User Configuration\Administrative Templates\Windows Components \Windows Explorer.

Table 9.11   Group Policy Settings That Affect Saving and Opening Files

Group Policy Setting	Description
Hide these specified drives in My Computer	Removes the icons representing selected disk drives from My Computer. Also, the drive letters representing the selected drives do not appear in the standard **Open** dialog box.
Prevent access to drives from My Computer	Prevents users from using My Computer to gain access to the content of selected drives.

Using the History Folder

The Windows 2000 Professional History folder integrates Web links and network shares, so that no matter from where you view the History folder, you have access to everywhere you've been. You can choose to view the History folder by using the following filters: **By Date**, **By Site**, **By Most Visited**, or **By Order Visited Today**.

The History view, which you selected from the toolbar in Windows Explorer, tracks the history of all Web sites and now tracks the history of all documents you've opened. You can sort by location, date used, or search the history list itself, using option buttons.

Group Policy Settings That Affect the History Folder

Table 9.12 lists Group Policy settings that affect the History folder and provides a brief description of each. Before you change a Group Policy setting, you should be familiar with using Group Policy and MMC snap-ins. To make changes to these settings, you must log on as a member of the Administrators group. You can find these Group Policy settings by using the Group Policy MMC snap-in and then following this path:

Local Computer Policy\User Configuration\Administrative Templates \Start Menu & Taskbar.

Table 9.12   Group Policy Settings That Affect the History Folder

Group Policy Setting	Description
Do not keep history of recently opened documents	Prevents shortcuts to documents from appearing on the **Documents** submenu (accessed by clicking **Start** and then pointing to **Documents**).
Clear history of recently opened documents on exit	Deletes the contents of the **Documents** submenu on the **Start** menu when the user logs off.

Connecting to Network Shares

Windows 2000 Professional allows you to map drives directly to shared subfolders on the network. For example, in previous versions of Windows, you mapped drives to *servername**sharename*. In Windows 2000, you can map drives to *servername**sharename**subsharenname*.

You can use the Add Network Place wizard to connect to frequently accessed network resources. Mapped network drives do not appear in My Network Places. To view mapped drives, use My Computer or the Address bar as shown in the Figure 9.5.

Figure 9.5   Mapped Drive as Viewed on the Address Bar in My Network Places

Group Policy Setting That Affects My Network Places

Table 9.13 lists a Group Policy setting that affects the History folder and provides a brief description of it. Before you change a Group Policy setting, you should be familiar with using Group Policy and MMC snap-ins. To make changes to this setting, you must log on as a member of the Administrators group. You can find this Group Policy setting by using the Group Policy MMC snap-in and then following this path:

Local Computer Policy\User Configuration\Administrative Templates\Desktop.

Table 9.13   Group Policy Setting That Affects My Network Places

Group Policy Setting	Description
Do not add shares of recently opened documents to My Network Places	Prevents the system from adding a connection to shared folders accessed through My Network Places.

You can find the Group Policy settings listed in Table 9.14 by using the Group Policy MMC snap-in and then following this path:

User Configuration\Administrative Templates\Windows Components \Windows Explorer.

Table 9.14   Group Policy Settings That Affect My Network Places

Group Policy Setting	Description
Remove "Map Network Drive" and "Disconnect Network Drive"	Prevents users from using Windows Explorer or My Network Places to connect to other computers or to close existing connections.
No "Entire Network" in My Network Places	Removes all computers outside the user's workgroup from lists of network resources in Windows Explorer and My Network Places.
No "Computers Near Me" in My Network Places	Removes computers in the user's workgroup and domain from lists of network resources in Windows Explorer and My Network Places.

Using Indexing Service

Indexing Service is a Windows 2000 service that extracts information from a set of documents and organizes it in a way that makes it quick and easy to access that information through the Windows 2000 Search Assistant, the Indexing Service query form, or a Web browser. This information can include text from within a document (its *contents*), and the characteristics and parameters of the document (its *properties*), such as the author's name. After the index is created, you can search, or *query* the index for documents that contain key words, phrases, or properties. For example, you can run a query for all documents containing the word "product" or you can run a query for all Microsoft Office documents written by a specific author. Indexing Service returns a list of all documents that meet the search criteria.

Indexing Service can index the following types of documents in several languages:

- HTML
- Text
- Microsoft Office 95 and later
- Internet mail and news
- Any other document for which a document filter is available

Indexing Service automatically stores all the index information in the System or the Web catalogs.

▶ **To enable Indexing Service on a local computer**

1. Click **Start**, point to **Search**, and then click **For Files or Folders**.

2. In the left pane of the **Search Results** dialog box (see Figure 9.6), click the **Search Options** link, and then click the **Indexing Service** link.

3. Click **Yes, enable Indexing Service and run when my computer is idle**.

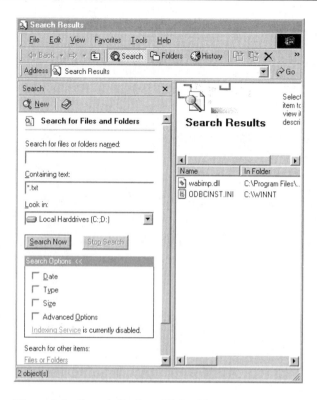

Figure 9.6   Search Options Dialog Box

Indexing Service is designed to run continuously and requires little maintenance. After it is set up, all operations are automatic, including index creation, index updating, and crash recovery if there is a power failure.

For more information about Indexing Service, see "Administering Indexing Service" in the Microsoft Management Console (MMC) Help file. Other topics in the MMC Help file explain how the Indexing Service works and how to conduct searches.

Group Policy Setting That Affects Indexing Service

Table 9.15 lists a Group Policy setting that controls users' access to Indexing Service and provides a brief description it. Before you change a Group Policy setting, you should be familiar with using Group Policy and MMC snap-ins. To make changes to this setting, you must log on as a member of the Administrators group. You can find this Group Policy setting by using the Group Policy MMC snap-in and then following this path:

User Configuration\Administrative Templates\Windows Components \Microsoft Management Console\Restricted/Permitted snap-ins

Table 9.15   Group Policy Setting That Affects Indexing Service

Group Policy Setting	Description
Indexing Service	Permits or prohibits users from gaining access to the **Indexing Service** snap-in.

Using Active Directory to Search for Network Resources

When Windows 2000 Professional is connected to a Windows 2000 Server using Active Directory, you can search the directory for resources such as computers, printers, people, and shared folders, as long as the resource is *published* in the Active Directory.

To help users locate resources quickly, you can create custom Active Directory searches and distribute query directory search (*.qds) files to workgroups or organizational units.

Active Directory contains objects and each object is assigned specific attributes. For example, if a printer is capable of printing double-sided pages, the Active Directory administrator can specify that attribute for the printer in the Active Directory. When a user searches for printers capable of printing double-sided, the search returns all printers with that attribute. If the administrator chooses not to give the printer that attribute, even if it is capable of that function, the printer wouldn't be found by searching only for that attribute.

For more information about Active Directory, see the *Windows 2000 Server Resource Kit*.

Important To search using Active Directory, the computer must be part of a Windows 2000 Server Active Directory domain.

Searching for Printers

To search for printers in an Active Directory domain, click **Start**, point to **Search**, and then click **For Printers**. If **For Printers** does not appear on the **Search** menu, your computer is not connected to an Active Directory domain.

Searching for People

In an Active Directory domain, click **Start**, point to **Search**, and click **For People** to start an Active Directory search. You can also specify to use an Internet search service in the **Look in** box. If you are not in an Active Directory domain, **Active Directory** does not appear as an option in the **Look in** box.

Searching for Computers

When you use Windows 2000 Professional in an Active Directory domain, you can search for computers two ways: using NetBIOS or using Active Directory. It is important to understand the difference between the two methods.

In previous versions of Windows, any time you specify a search for computers, the computer executes a NetBIOS search. If the computer you search for is logged on to the network, you can connect to it and view its shared folders. Figure 9.7 illustrates the results of a NetBIOS search and the available shares on the computer that was found.

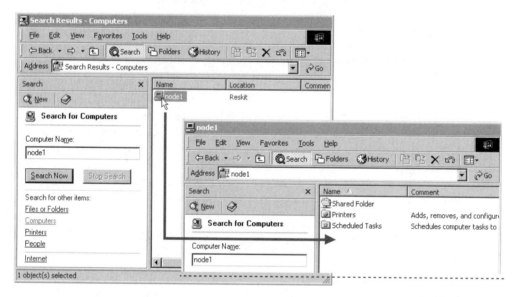

Figure 9.7   NetBIOS Search Results Displaying Available Shares

▶ **To search for computers using NetBIOS**

1. Click **Start**, point to **Search**, and then click **For Files or Folders**.
2. In the left pane, click the **Computers** link.

In an Active Directory network search, computers in the directory are represented by objects. You can locate an object even when it is disconnected from the network. Therefore, when you double-click the icon representing a computer found using an Active Directory search, only the properties for that computer are displayed, as shown in the Figure 9.8. The actual computer and its available shares are not available from an Active Directory search. To access shares in an Active Directory domain, the shares must be published and you must know the name of the share.

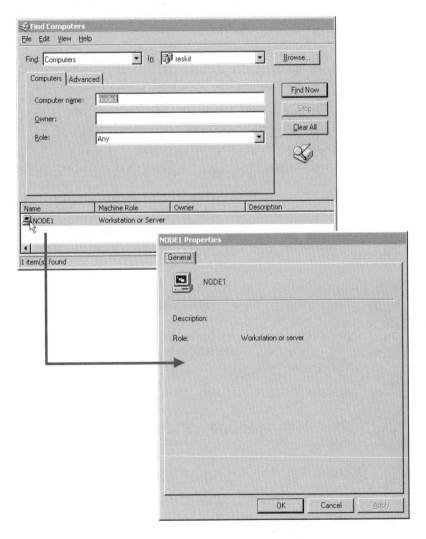

Figure 9.8   Active Directory Search Results Displaying the Computer's Properties

▶ **To search for computers using Active Directory**

1. In My Network Places, double-click **Entire Network**.

2. Do one of the following:

   ▪ If Web View is enabled, click the **entire contents** link, and then double-click **Directory**.

   ▪ If Web View is not enabled, double-click **Directory**.

3. Right-click the object representing an Active Directory domain, and then click **Find**.

4. In the **Find** box, click **Computers**.

Note   You might need to specify an object in the **In** box.

Searching for Shared Files and Folders

To access files and folders in an Active Directory domain, the Active Directory administrator must first publish them. Folders that are shared but not published do not appear in the Search Results window. If you search for a computer by using Active Directory, you can not view or access any shared folders residing on that computer. You must execute a NetBIOS search to view shares. For more information about NetBIOS searches, see "Searching for Computers" earlier in this chapter.

You can use the Search Assistant in Active Directory to locate shared folders, but you must specify the exact folder name. You cannot browse a list of shared folders. To find a shared folder in Active Directory, open the Search Assistant, and in the **Find** box, click **Shared Folders**. Then, in the **Named** box on the **Shared Folders** tab, type the shared folder name.

Group Policy Settings That Affect Active Directory

Table 9.16 lists Group Policy settings that affect Active Directory searches and provides a brief description of each. Before you change a Group Policy setting, you should be familiar with using Group Policy and MMC snap-ins. To make changes to these settings, you must log on as a member of the Administrators group. You can find these Group Policy settings by using the Group Policy MMC snap-in and then following this path:

Local Computer Policy\User Configuration\Administrative Templates \Desktop\Active Directory.

Table 9.16   Group Policy Settings That Affect Active Directory

Group Policy Setting	Description
Maximum size of Active Directory searches	Specifies the maximum number of objects returned on an Active Directory search. Use to protect the network and the domain controller from the effect of expansive searches.
Enable filter in Find dialog box	Displays a filter bar above the results of an Active Directory search, so additional filters can be applied.
Hide Active Directory Folder	Removes the Active Directory folder from My Network Places.

Preventing Access to System Files

Windows 2000 Professional provides new ways to help prevent users from deleting or modifying operating system and hidden files. By default, hidden files and folders and system files do not display in Windows Explorer windows or search results views.

To view system files, clear the **Hide protected operating system files (Recommended)** check box on the **View** tab of the **Folder Options** dialog box (accessed by clicking **Folder Options** on the **Tools** menu).

To view hidden files and folders, select the **Show hidden files and folders** option on the **View** tab of the **Folder Options** dialog box (accessed by clicking **Folder Options** on the **Tools** menu).

Group Policy Setting That Prevents Access to System Files

Table 9.17 lists a Group Policy setting that prevents access to system files and provides a brief description of it. You can use this Group Policy setting to prevent users from changing the setting that hides system and hidden files and folders.

Before you change a Group Policy setting, you should be familiar with using Group Policy and MMC snap-ins. To make changes to this setting, you must log on as a member of the Administrators group. You can find this Group Policy setting by using the Group Policy MMC snap-in and then following this path:

User Configuration\Administrative Templates\Windows Components \Windows Explorer.

Table 9.17   Group Policy Setting That Prevents Access to System Files

Group Policy Setting	Description
Remove the Folder Options menu item from the Tools menu	Removes the **Folder Options** command from all Windows Explorer menus and removes the Folder Options icon from Control Panel.

Troubleshooting

The following topics are frequently asked questions about working with files, folders, and search methods. For more general information about troubleshooting in Windows 2000 Professional, see "Troubleshooting Tools and Strategies"in this book.

Why is nothing listed in the relevance column in my search results window?

The Relevance column is used only when Indexing Service is enabled and you search for a word, phrase, or other content. The *relevance* of an item represents a ranking that indicates how closely the content in the file matches the text you searched for. In Figure 9.9, the Relevance column of the Search Results window is blank, indicating that Indexing Service is not enabled or that a content search was not performed.

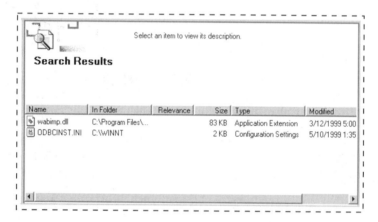

Figure 9.9   The Relevance Column in the Search Results Window

Why can't I view system files, such as my Swap file?

By default, Windows 2000 hides files with attributes of System and Hidden. You can enable the **Show hidden files and folders** setting on the **View** tab in the **Folder Options** dialog box to view hidden files. To see files with both the Hidden and System attributes, you must also disable the **Hide protected operating system files (Recommended)** option on the **View** tab in the **Folder Options** dialog box. To access the **Folder Options** dialog box, click **Folder Options** on the **Tools** menu.

Why can't I see shared folders on the network?

You are probably using an Active Directory search. In an Active Directory search for computers, you can only see the properties of the computer, not the available shares. Execute a NetBIOS search instead. See "Using Active Directory to Search for Network Resources" earlier in this chapter.

How do I recover deleted Administrative Tools shortcuts?

Unlike previous versions of Windows, you can delete shortcuts to programs in the Administrative Tools folder in Control Panel.

If you delete a shortcut, you can restore it from the Recycle Bin. If the shortcut is no longer in Recycle Bin, you can add it to the Administrative Tools folder using the information in Table 9.18.

▶ **To add a shortcut to Administrative Tools**

1. Open Administrative Tools in Control Panel.

2. On the **File** menu, point to **New**, and then click **Shortcut**.

3. Use Table 9.18 to find the value to type in the **Type the location of the item** box.

4. Click **Next**.

5. Use Table 9.18 to find the proper name of the tool and type it in the **Type a name for this shortcut** box.

6. Click **Finish**.

7. Follow the steps in the procedure that follows Table 9.18.

Table 9.18   Name, Description, and Location of Administrative Tools Files in Windows 2000 Professional

Tool Name	Tool Description	Tool File Name and Location
Component Services	Configures and manages Component Services applications.	%SystemRoot%\system32\com\comexp.msc
Computer Management	Starts and stops services, manages disks, and provides access to other system tools to manage local and remote computers.	%SystemRoot%\system32\compmgmt.msc /s
Data Sources (ODBC)	Adds, removes, and configures Open Database Connectivity (ODBC) data sources and drivers.	%SystemRoot%\system32\odbcad32.exe
Event Viewer	Displays and allows configuration of monitoring and troubleshooting messages from Windows and other programs.	%SystemRoot%\system32\eventvwr.msc /s
Local Security Policy	Displays and allows configuration of security levels assigned to a Group Policy object or local computer Group Policy setting.	%SystemRoot%\system32\secpol.msc /s
Performance	Displays graphs of system performance and configures data logs and alerts.	%SystemRoot%\system32\perfmon.msc /s

(continued)

Table 9.18   Name, Description, and Location of Administrative Tools Files in Windows 2000 Professional *(continued)*

Tool Name	Tool Description	Tool File Name and Location
Component Services	Configures and manages Component Services applications.	%SystemRoot%\system32\com\comexp.msc
Services	Start, stop, pause, or resume services on remote and local computers, and configure startup and recovery options.	%SystemRoot%\system32\services.msc /s
Telnet Server Administration	View and modify telnet server settings and connections.	%SystemRoot%\system32\tlntadmn.exe

The following procedure changes the **Start in** location so the program can find necessary associated files. The **Start in** location is the same for all tools described in Table 9.18.

▶ **To Specify the Start in location**

1. Click the shortcut, and then on the **File** menu, click **Properties**.

2. In the **Start in** box on the **Shortcut** tab, type the following:

    %HomeDrive%%HomePath%

Additional Resources

- For more information about the new location and name of a feature from a previous version of Windows, see Windows 2000 Professional Help.

- For more information about using the registry, see the Technical Reference to the Windows 2000 Registry on the *Windows 2000 Resource Kit* companion CD.

CHAPTER 10

Mobile Computing

This chapter describes how to configure and administer Microsoft®
Windows® 2000 for mobile users. This includes hardware, power management,
and security on portable computers, as well as Windows 2000 features and tools
that are relevant to portable computer users. In addition, this chapter covers
administrative issues that are relevant to roaming users if your organization uses
roaming user profiles or folder redirection. Although remote network connectivity
is an important aspect of mobile computing, this chapter does not discuss network
connections.

In This Chapter

Related Information in the Windows 2000 Professional Resource Kit

- For more information about remote networking, see "Local and Remote
  Network Connections" in this book.

- For more information about IntelliMirror™ management technologies such as
  Offline Files, folder redirection, and roaming user profiles, see "Introducing
  Configuration and Management" in this book.

Related Information in the Windows 2000 Server Resource Kit

- For more information about IntelliMirror™ management technologies such as
  Offline Files, folder redirection, and roaming user profiles, see "Introduction
  to Desktop Management" in the *Microsoft® Windows® 2000 Server Resource
  Kit Distributed Systems Guide*

Mobile Computing Quick Guide

The following list is a brief summary of the mobile computing topics and tasks that are covered in this chapter. Use it to quickly find the information or task you are seeking.

Verifying the configuration of a portable computer.

Before you put a portable computer into service, you need to be sure that you have properly configured the software and hardware as well as any Windows 2000 features or components.

- See "Setting Up a Portable Computer" in this chapter.

Gaining access to network files and folders while working offline.

Portable computer users who frequently use their computers while they are away from the office can continue working with shared network files and folders even though they are not connected to the network. The feature that enables this, known as Offline Files, also synchronizes differences between the offline and online versions of folders and files.

- See "Configuring Offline Files on a Portable Computer" in this chapter.
- See "Managing Files, Folders, and Search Methods" in this book.

Conserving battery power.

Portable computers often rely on battery power. Use Windows 2000 power management features to optimize battery use by configuring power schemes, standby settings, hibernation settings, and battery alerts.

- See "Configuring Power Management" in this chapter.
- See "Hardware Management" in this book.

Removing and swapping devices.

Knowing when it is safe to change device configurations is as important as knowing how. If you are adding or removing PC Cards, or docking and undocking a portable computer, you need to know how dynamic Plug and Play is implemented in Windows 2000.

- See "Managing Hardware on Portable Computers" in this chapter.
- See "Hardware Management" in this book.

Ensuring that a portable computer is secure.

Avoiding unauthorized access is the cornerstone of a secure system. However, you also need to maximize file and folder security, and minimize the risk of theft when it comes to a portable computer.

- See "Security Considerations for Portable Computers" in this chapter.
- See "Security" in this book.

Providing a consistent user environment for roaming users.

If you deploy Windows 2000 Professional with Microsoft® Windows® 2000 Server, you can use roaming user profiles and folder redirection to ensure that users have a consistent desktop environment regardless what computer they are logged onto in the organization.

- See "Configuring Roaming User Profiles and Folder Redirection" in this chapter.
- See "Managing Files, Folders, and Search Methods" in this book.

Identifying potential hardware incompatibilities with portable computers.

Some devices exhibit unexpected behavior when they are installed on portable computers. Knowing how particular devices impact some types of portable computers can help you avoid hardware configuration problems.

- See "Hardware Issues Related to Portable Computers" in this chapter.
- See "Hardware Management" in this book.
- See "Device Management" in this book.

What's New

Microsoft® Windows® 2000 has several new features that are designed specifically for mobile users. In addition, several features in Microsoft® Windows NT® version 4.0 and Microsoft® Windows® 98 have been enhanced, providing even more functionality for mobile users. All of these new features and feature improvements are discussed in this chapter.

Offline Files Offline Files, one of the IntelliMirror™ technologies, stores information in a cache on a local drive so users can access shared files and folders when they work offline. When they reconnect to the network, Offline Files synchronizes the files stored on the local drive with the files on the network.

Hibernate mode During hibernate mode, a computer's current system state is saved to the hard disk and then the computer is turned off. When a user starts a computer after putting it into hibernate mode, it restarts any programs that were running when the computer entered hibernate mode and restores all network connections

ACPI and APM support Windows 2000 supports the Advanced Configuration and Power Interface (ACPI) specification, which takes over system configuration and power management from the Plug and Play Basic Input/Output System (BIOS). Windows 2000 also supports the Advanced Power Management (APM) 1.2 specification by taking over the power management from an APM 1.2 BIOS.

Management of power to disks and monitors You can configure Windows 2000 to turn off the power to a monitor or a hard disk even if the portable computer does not have an ACPI-based or an APM-based BIOS.

Standby mode (APM and ACPI only) All ACPI-based and some APM-based computers allow you to put a computer into standby mode. In this state, Windows 2000 puts the monitor, hard disk, and other hardware into a low power state but does not save the computer's current system state as it does in hibernate mode.

Battery management (APM and ACPI only) Windows 2000 Professional provides several new battery management features, including improved battery metering, dual battery support, and the ability to designate different power down options depending on whether your portable computer is powered by battery or alternating current.

Dynamic configuration of PC Cards If your portable computer has an ACPI-based BIOS, you can insert and remove PC Cards and Windows 2000 detects and configures them without your needing to restart the computer.

Hot and warm docking or undocking During Setup, Windows 2000 creates two hardware profiles for portable computers: one for when the portable computer is docked and one for when it is undocked. This, along with dynamic Plug and Play support, allows users to dock and undock from the Windows 2000 **Start** menu without turning off their computer.

Hot swapping of Integrated Drive Electronics (IDE) and floppy disk drives
Dynamic Plug and Play support allows you to remove or swap devices such as floppy drives, DVD or CD drives, and hard drives without shutting down or restarting the computer.

Folder redirection Folder redirection allows you to direct the contents of a folder to an alternate location on a server or a network share. When folder redirection is applied to folders such as My Documents, the redirection is transparent to the user.

Table 10.1 displays the new features that are implemented in Windows 2000 and compares them to the features in Microsoft® Windows® 95, Microsoft® Windows® 98, and Microsoft® Windows NT® 4.0.

Table 10.1   Comparison of Windows 2000 Mobile User Profile Computing Features

Windows 2000 Feature	Windows 95	Windows 98	Windows NT 4.0
Offline Files and synchronization	--	--	--
Briefcase	X	X	X
Hibernate mode	--	--	--
Manage power to hard disks and monitors	--	X	--
Standby mode (APM and ACPI only)	X	X	--
Battery management (APM and ACPI only)	--	X	--
Dynamic configuration of PC Cards	--	X	--
Hot docking and undocking of portable computers	--	X	--
Hot swapping of IDE and floppy devices	--	--	--
ACPI support	--	X	--
APM support	--	X	--
Folder redirection	--	--	--
Roaming user profiles	--	X	X

Setting Up a Portable Computer

This section identifies critical operating system components, properties, and features you need to configure before you put a portable computer into service. The information in this section is meant to be used as an administrative checklist. Use it as a quality assurance tool to help ensure that you have addressed the major configuration issues pertinent to portable computers. In-depth configuration information is provided in subsequent sections of this chapter.

Check BIOS Compatibility

If a portable computer has an ACPI-based BIOS, use the Hardware Compatibility List (HCL) to verify that it is compliant with the newest ACPI standard. If it is not, upgrade the BIOS to the newest version that is compatible with the ACPI standard. If you flash an ACPI-based BIOS on to your portable computer after you have installed Windows 2000 and your old BIOS was not ACPI-based, you need to reinstall Windows 2000. For more information about the HCL, see the Hardware Compatibility List link on the Web Resources page at http://windows.microsoft.com/windows2000/reskit/webresources. For more information about upgrading the BIOS in a portable computer, see the Hardware Update link on the Web Resources page at

If a portable computer has an APM-based BIOS, run the Apmstat support tool to determine whether the BIOS has any known problems. If it has no known problems and you want to use APM to manage power on your portable computer, you must manually enable APM by using Power Options in Control Panel. You can install Apmstat by running Setup.exe, which is located in the Support\Tools folder on the Windows 2000 Professional operating system CD.

Establish Group Memberships

If you are configuring a portable computer for someone who travels frequently, add this person to the Power Users group. This allows the user to install, uninstall, and configure software and Plug and Play hardware if a device fails or software needs to be reinstalled while he or she is not connected to the network. All other types of users should be members of the Users group, which does not allow them to install, uninstall, or configure software and hardware. In general, no users should be members of the Administrators group unless they need to install, uninstall, and configure non-Plug and Play hardware and drivers.

Verify Hardware Configuration

After you finish installing hardware on a portable computer, verify that all of the devices are operational when the computer is docked and undocked. Be sure to test the devices, as well as the docking and undocking functionality, as a member of the Power Users and the Users group. This testing is necessary because some printers, scanners, and ISDN adapters can be fully installed only by a member of the Administrators group; when these devices are installed by members of the Power Users or Users group, the devices might not be fully installed. Also, verify that the properties are set correctly for both the Docked Profile and the Undocked Profile.

Configure Power Management Options

Hibernate support and APM support are not enabled by default when you install Windows 2000. If you want to use these features, and your portable computer supports them, you must manually enable them by using Power Options in Control Panel. Also, hibernate mode must be entered manually unless the computer has an ACPI-based or APM-based BIOS that supports automatic hibernation.

Verify that the power scheme is appropriate for the end-user environment. Power schemes define how power is managed on a computer. The most useful power schemes for portable computers are Portable/Laptop, Presentation, and Max Battery. Using the Portable/Laptop power scheme might not be the best configuration. By default, it powers down the monitor after 15 minutes, which could be undesirable if the portable computer is primarily used for presentations. Using the Presentation scheme is best when a user is giving a presentation and it is imperative that the computer not enter standby mode. However, Presentation does not preserve battery power. Max Battery preserves battery life by putting the computer into standby mode or hibernate mode after the computer has been idle for a relatively short period of time. This is useful if the user does not mind frequently resuming the computer from standby mode or hibernate mode.

Install All Software

Be sure that all software and software components (for example, add-ins and spell check tools) are installed locally and run locally on the portable computer. You should not have any partially installed programs or distributed (COM+) programs installed on a portable computer that is frequently used offline. Install all software for personal digital assistants (PDA) as a member of the Administrators group because some PDA software cannot be installed by members of the Power Users group. Finally, members of both the Users and the Power Users group cannot use the Internet Connection Wizard to configure an internet connection; this must be done by a member of the Administrators group.

Configure Offline Content

Enable and configure file-storing settings on the server or network share for the files and folders that you want to make available offline. This is particularly important for folders such as My Documents if you have redirected them to a network share or a server. Also, make sure you have configured all offline files settings, including synchronization settings, on the portable computer.

If user is using an e-mail program or a Web browser, be sure to configure the e-mail program and the Web browser for offline content.

Configure Security

Because portable computers are vulnerable to theft, format all hard drives as NTFS and apply the appropriate permissions to files and folders that contain sensitive data. Also, encrypt files and folders that contain sensitive data, and require users to use strong passwords for logging on both locally and on the network.

Configure User Profiles and Folder Redirection

Do not use roaming user profiles or folder redirection if the portable computer is rarely connected to the network or is remotely connected to the network most of the time. These features are more suited to roaming desktop users or portable computer users who are connected directly to a network a majority of the time.

Configuring Offline Files for Portable Computers

Offline Files gives users access to files and folders that are on network shares even when they are disconnected from the network. It does this by storing the network version of files and folders on the local hard disk. When users are not connected to the network, they have access to the offline version of the files and folders as though they were connected to the network. When they reconnect to the network, the stored files and folders are synchronized with the network versions of the files. This section discusses configuration issues you need to consider when you are using offline files on a portable computer. For more information about configuring offline files and synchronization, see "Managing Files, Folders, and Search Methods" in this book.

Configuring Files on a Network Share for Offline Use

Before you can have access to the files on a shared network folder offline, you must specify how the files in the folder are stored in a cache on the client computer (in this case, the user's portable computer). For non-executable files, such as word processing documents, spreadsheets, and bitmaps, there are two options for storing files:

- Automatic caching
- Manual caching

Automatic caching makes a file available offline (creates a locally stored copy of the file) when a user opens the file on their portable computer. Automatically stored files might not always be available in the cache because Windows 2000 might remove (purge) them from the cache when the cache becomes full. Windows 2000 selects files for purging on the basis of how often they are used. Automatic caching is the most useful when you have an unreliable or unpredictable network connection. For example, if a user is working on an automatically stored file and the portable computer gets disconnected from the network, the user can continue working on the file without interruption because the file has been automatically stored on the portable computer. If a user requires that a file be available offline all of the time, the user should mark the file as **Always available offline** by using Windows Explorer or My Computer. For more information about making files available offline, see "Pinning Files and Folders for Offline Use" later in this chapter.

Manual caching makes a file or a folder available offline, but only when it is manually marked ("pinned"), on the user's computer. A manually stored file or folder that is not pinned on the user's computer is not available offline. Manual caching is useful for users who need access to a file or folder all of the time or for users who need access to entire folders, especially when the folder contains documents that have been created by or modified by other people. For example, manual caching works well for someone who frequently uses their portable computer away from their office without a network connection but who still needs access to a large number of files on the network. In this case, you can manually pin folders on the user's portable computer, and then those folders are available to the user when he or she is away from their office. Automatic caching is not ideal in this case because the files in the network folder are not locally stored unless the portable computer user opens each of them while the portable computer is connected to the network share.

▶ **To configure automatic or manual caching on a shared network folder**

1. Right-click the shared folder you want to configure, and then click **Sharing**.

2. In the folder properties dialog box, click **Caching**.

3. In the **Setting** drop-down box, select the type of storing (caching) you want.

Note You can also choose **Automatic caching for programs**, which is useful if a user runs programs from the network. This option stores a copy of a network program on the user's hard disk so they can run the program when they are offline. However, portable computer users need to be careful when they use this feature because only the program files that are executed get stored on the local computer. For example, if you run Microsoft® Word from a network share but you do not use the spell checking tool, the spell checking tool is not stored. If you then run Word when you are offline and you try to run the spell checking tool, the tool is not available. To avoid this problem, you can load all of your programs and all associated tools locally on a portable computer and not use the **Automatic caching for programs** option.

Pinning Files and Folders for Offline Use

If you choose manual caching for offline files, you must pin the file or folder on the user's portable computer. When you pin a file or folder, a copy of the file or folder is copied to the local cache on the portable computer. By default, all users have permission to pin files and folders. However, you can use Group Policy to change this default behavior.

▶ **To manually pin a file or folder**

1. While you are connected to the network, select the shared network folder or file you want to make available offline.

2. On the **File** menu, click **Make available offline**.

Note You can manually pin a folder or a file even when the folder or file has been configured for automatic caching. In this case, pinning forces the file or folder to be stored. Therefore, pinning has precedence over automatic caching.

When you manually pin a folder that contains subfolders, you are prompted to choose whether you want to make subfolders available offline or whether you want to make only the contents of the folder available offline. You can change this behavior by using administrative templates in Group Policy so that subfolders are always made available offline.

▶ **To make subfolders always available offline when a folder is manually pinned**

1. From the **Start** menu, click **Run**.

2. Type:

   gpedit.msc

3. Press ENTER.

4. In the console tree pane of the Group Policy console, under **Computer Configuration**, open the Administrative Templates folder, and then open the Network folder.

5. Click the Offline Files folder.

6. In the details pane, double-click **Subfolders always available offline**.

7. In the **Properties** dialog box, click **Enabled**.

You can also pin folders using the administrative templates in Group Policy. Along with other Group Policy settings, this is the best way to ensure that folders and their contents are always available offline.

▶   **To pin folders using Group Policy**

1. From the **Start** menu, click **Run**.

2. Type:

   gpedit.msc

3. Press ENTER.

4. In the view pane of the Group Policy console, under **Computer Configuration**, open the Administrative Templates folder and then open the Network folder.

5. Click the Offline Files folder.

6. In the details pane, double-click **Administratively assigned offline files**.

7. In the **Properties** dialog box, click **Enabled**, and then click **Show**.

8. In the **Show Contents** dialog box, click **Add**.

9. Enter the Universal Naming Convention (UNC) path for any folder or file you want to administratively pin. Do not enter a value for these folders. You can use environment variables in the paths.

When you administratively pin a folder using Group Policy, all files and subfolders within that folder are made available offline. As a consequence, the **Make available offline** menu item that appears when you right-click a shared folder or file is checked and disabled. This prevents users from manually unpinning administratively pinned files and folders, although they can still pin and unpin folders and files that have not been administratively pinned.

Users can delete offline files in the Offline Files folder even though they have been administratively pinned. However, the deleted files and folders are-stored the next time Group Policy updates policies on the computer (by default, every 90 minutes, although you can change this). Also, users can still enable, disable, and configure offline files unless you administratively restrict a user's ability to configure offline files, which you also can do by using administrative templates in Group Policy.

▶   **To prevent users from configuring offline files**

1. From the **Start** menu, click **Run**.

2. Type:

   gpedit.msc

3. Press ENTER.

4. In the view pane of the Group Policy console, under **Computer Configuration**, open the Administrative Templates folder and then open the Network folder.

5. Click the Offline Files folder.

6. In the details pane, double-click **Disable user configuration of Offline Files**.

7. In the **Disable user configuration of Offline Files Properties** dialog box, click **Enable**.

Be careful how you implement this policy. Preventing users from configuring offline files might not be appropriate for all portable computer users. For example, if a portable computer is frequently disconnected from the network and a user needs to reconfigure offline files, he or she is unable to do so. Administratively pinning folders might be enough to ensure that specific folders are always available offline and do not get unpinned or deleted from the cache by a user.

Configuring Options for Offline Files

A general overview of Offline Files options is presented earlier in this book. (See "Managing Files, Folders, and Search Methods.") Two of those options are particularly relevant to portable computer users: the size of the cache and the way Offline Files behave when network connections are disconnected.

Offline Files allows you to configure the amount of disk space that is used to store offline files (in other words, you can configure the size of the local cache). This option only affects offline files that are stored automatically; it does not affect offline files that are stored manually. Because disk space is often limited on a portable computer, you might want to modify this value if you are relying on automatic caching. By default, the value is set at 10 percent of disk size.

For manually stored files, the cache size is limited only by available disk space, up to a maximum value of 2 gigabytes (GB). This can be a problem if you are using manual caching and disk space is limited. In this case, you might want to limit the number of folders you manually store or change some folders from manual caching to automatic caching.

▶ **To change the size of the Offline Files cache**

1. In Windows Explorer, open any folder that contains offline files

2. On the **Tools** menu, click **Folder Options**.

3. In the folder options dialog box, click the **Offline Files** tab.

4. Under **Amount of disk space to use for temporary offline files**, move the slider to change the cache size.

Offline Files also allows you to configure how lost network connections are handled. There are two options: **Notify me and begin working offline**, or **Never allow my computer to go offline**. The first option, which is the default, gives users access to offline files and folders when a connection is lost or when a connection is intentionally disabled or disconnected (for example, when a portable computer is undocked). The second option should be used carefully with portable computers because it prevents user access to offline files, whether a network connection is lost or is intentionally disabled or disconnected. In other words, if you choose the second option with a portable computer and a user disconnects the portable computer from the network, the user does not have access to any offline files. The offline files are essentially disabled. The following procedure describes how to change the way Offline Files is handled when a network connection is lost.

▶ **To change the way Offline Files is handled when network connections are lost**

1. In Windows Explorer, open any folder that contains offline files.

2. On the **Tools** menu, click **Folder Options**.

3. In the folder options dialog box, click the **Offline Files** tab.

4. Click **Advanced**, and then choose either **Notify me and begin working offline** or **Never allow my computer to go offline**.

For portable computers that are frequently disconnected from the network, **Notify me and begin working offline** is the preferable setting. Because it is the system default for Offline Files, you should not have to change this option.

Configuring Synchronization for Offline Files

Synchronization ensures that any changes that are made to offline files and folders are propagated back to the network and that any changes that have occurred on the network are propagated to the user's computer. A general overview of synchronization options is presented earlier in this book. (See "Managing Files, Folders and Search Methods.") This section discusses synchronization features and options that relate specifically to portable computers.

Configuring Synchronization for Battery-Powered Computers

In order for synchronization to occur, the hard disk on a user's portable computer must be powered up so that files can be copied from the network to the local cache and files in the local cache can be copied to the network. This might not be an optimum use of power for a portable computer when it is running on battery power. Fortunately, there are configuration options that allow you to control whether synchronization occurs when a computer is running on battery power.

Enabling Synchronization During Idle

By default, offline files are not synchronized when a computer is in an idle state and it is using battery power. This is because portable computers rely on a low-power idle state to conserve battery power and you might not want to waste battery power synchronizing files. You can change this so that synchronization occurs when the computer is on idle even when the computer is running on battery power.

▶ **To enable synchronization during idle when running on battery power**

1. From the **Start** menu, point to **Programs** point to **Accessories**, and then click **Synchronize**.

2. In the **Items to Synchronize** dialog box, click **Setup**.

3. In the **Synchronization Settings** dialog box, click the **On Idle** tab, and then click **Advanced**.

4. In the **Idle Settings** dialog box, click the **Prevent synchronization when my computer is running on battery power** check box to clear it.

Preventing Scheduled Synchronization

You can also schedule synchronization for specific days and times. Because a scheduled synchronization is often a low-priority task that consumes power, Windows 2000 allows you to prevent scheduled synchronization from running when a computer is operating under battery power.

▶ **To prevent scheduled synchronization when the computer is running on battery power**

1. From the **Start** menu, point to **Programs** and then **Accessories**, and then click **Synchronize**.

2. In the **Items to Synchronize** dialog box, click **Setup**.

3. In the **Synchronization Settings** dialog box, click the **Scheduled** tab.

4. Click a scheduled task, and then click **Edit**.

5. On the **Settings** tab, under **Power Management**, click the **Don't start the task if the computer is running on batteries** check box.

If a scheduled synchronization is in progress and a portable computer is shifted from alternating current power to battery power, you can have Windows 2000 cancel synchronization. This might occur if scheduled synchronization starts on a docked portable computer that is using a wireless network connection and the user performs a hot-undock.

▶ **To stop scheduled synchronization when the computer is running on battery power**

1. From the **Start** menu, point to **Programs** and then **Accessories**, and then click **Synchronize**.

2. In the **Items to Synchronize** dialog box, click **Setup**.

3. In the **Synchronization Settings** dialog box, click the **Scheduled** tab.

4. Click a scheduled task, and then click **Edit**.

5. On the **Settings** tab, under **Power Management**, click the **Stop the task if battery mode begins** check box.

Enabling Automatic Connection During Scheduled Synchronization

If a computer is not connected to a network when scheduled synchronization occurs, you can configure Windows 2000 to connect so that synchronization can occur. This might not be desirable for portable computer users, especially if they frequently use the portable computer while it is disconnected from the network. In this case, Windows 2000 attempts to connect to the designated network, detects that the computer is not connected to the network, and then informs the user that the network is not available. By default, Windows 2000 does not connect if there is no network connection at the time of synchronization.

▶ **To enable automatic connection for scheduled synchronization**

1. From the **Start** menu, point to **Programs** point to **Accessories**, and then click **Synchronize**.

2. In the **Items to Synchronize** dialog box, click **Setup**.

3. In the **Synchronization Settings** dialog box, click the **Scheduled** tab.

4. Under **Current synchronization tasks**, click a scheduled task, and then click **Edit**.

5. On the **Synchronization Items** tab, click the **If my computer is not connected when this scheduled synchronization begins, automatically connect for me** check box.

Note You can also enable automatic connection during scheduled synchronization when you first schedule the synchronization.

Synchronizing Over a Slow Link

Windows 2000 does not provide a system-wide definition or threshold for a slow link; rather, Windows 2000 allows every system component to define a slow link in terms of its own capabilities and requirements. For example, one component might define a slow link as 28.8 kilobits per second (Kbps), while another might define it as 56 Kbps. For Offline Files and synchronization, a slow link is defined as any connection that operates at 64 Kbps or slower, which is the speed of a single-channel Integrated Services Digital Network (ISDN) connection. Therefore, most modem connections through telephone lines are considered slow link connections with regard to offline files synchronization. This is important because synchronization behaves differently depending on whether the network connection is considered a slow link or not.

A slow link connection affects synchronization two ways: it prevents the automatic transition of shared network folders to an online state, and it prevents newly added files from being pulled from the network share to the user's computer during synchronization. This behavior is not configurable, but it is important to know how the behavior affects portable computer users.

Transitioning from an Offline State to an Online State

After a network share has been offline to a user (for example, a server goes offline and is then brought back online, or a user undocks their portable computer and then docks it), it becomes available online for the user if three conditions are met:

- No offline files from that network share are open on the user's computer.

- None of the offline files from that network share have changes that need to be synchronized.

- The network connection is not considered a slow link.

When all of these conditions are satisfied and a user opens a file on the network share, the user is working online on that network share. Any changes that the user makes are saved to the file on the network share as well as to the file that is stored in the Offline Files folder. When any one of these conditions is not met and a user opens a file on the network share, the user is still working offline, even though the network share is available. Any changes that the user makes are saved only to the offline version of the file.

When a user first connects to a network over a slow link connection, the user also is working offline on any shared network folders, even though the folders are available. To start working online with a shared network folder, the user must synchronize the shared network folder. Synchronization shifts the folder to an online state and pushes any offline files that have changed to the shared network folder. It does not pull files on the shared network folder to the Offline Files folder. To do this, the user must perform a second synchronization, which pulls files that have changed from the network share to the Offline Files folder.

Note When you are using a slow link connection, a second synchronization does not pull newly created files from the network share to the Offline Files folder. To make new files on the network share available offline during a slow link connection you must manually pin the files.

Making Network Shares Available Without Synchronization

As discussed in the previous section, slow link connections can prevent a network share from coming online even though the network share is available. Although you can bring the network share online by synchronizing it, this method might not be ideal—for example, when a user's portable computer is disconnected from the network and the user requires access to a file on a shared network folder that has been made available offline, a file to which the user has made several changes offline but is not ready to synchronize with the network share. Another example is when a user is in a hurry and does not want to take the time to synchronize files— the user wants only to connect to the network, get the new file from the network share, and then log off. Windows 2000 provides a way of doing this.

▶ **To make a folder available online without synchronizing offline files**

1. In the System Tray, click the **Offline Files** icon to open the **Offline Files Status** dialog box.

2. Click the **Work online without synchronizing changes** check box.

Note The Offline Files icon appears in the System Tray when users are working offline.

Managing the Offline Files Folder

Portable computer users who frequently work offline might end up with hundreds of files stored in the Offline Files folder on their hard disk. Because many of these files might be out-of-date, rarely used, or no longer needed offline, you might want to delete them from the Offline Files folder (the cache) in order to maximize the available disk space. You might also want to delete files in the Offline Files folder if a network share has been deleted or is no longer available. In addition to deleting individual files, you can reinitialize the Offline Files cache, which deletes the entire contents of the Offline Files folder. Reinitializing the Offline Files cache is useful when you transfer a computer to a new user or when a user has been working offline with sensitive or proprietary documents and you want to ensure that they are no longer available offline or that they are not in the cache.

Deleting Files

There are two methods for safely removing offline files from the cache without affecting network files or folders. You can open the Offline Files folder and delete files directly from the list of offline files. This method of cleaning up the cache allows you to delete individual files regardless of where they are located on the network or of the folder in which they are contained. Also, when you delete a file this way, the file is removed from the cache regardless of whether it was manually or automatically stored.

If you remove a file from the cache and its parent folder is pinned, the file is copied to the cache the next time you synchronize offline files.

▶ **To delete files from the cache by using the Offline Files folder**

1. In Windows Explorer, open a shared network folder.

2. On the **Tools** menu, click **Folder Options**.

3. In the **Folder Options** dialog box, click the **Offline Files** tab, and then click **View Files**.

4. Click the file you want to delete, and then on the **File** menu, click **Delete**.

You can also delete files on a network-share basis. This method allows you to delete batches of files according to the shared folder in which they are contained. This method also allows you to distinguish between automatically stored files and manually stored files. If you delete manually stored folders this way, the folders and the files in them are no longer be pinned. To make these files or folders available offline again, you must pin the files or folders. When you delete automatically stored files this way, you only need to open the files to make them available offline.

▶ **To delete files from the cache on a network share basis**

1. In Windows Explorer, open a shared network folder.

2. On the **Tools** menu, click **Folder Options**.

3. In the **Folder Options** dialog box, click the **Offline Files** tab, and then click **Delete Files**.

4. In the **Confirm File Delete** dialog box, select the shared folders that contain the offline files that you want to delete.

5. Click the **Delete only the temporary offline versions** check box if you want to delete only the files that have been automatically stored. Click the **Delete both the temporary offline versions and the versions that are always available offline** check box if you want to delete files that have been automatically stored and files that have been manually stored.

Note Files are also deleted from the cache whenever an offline file is deleted through any usual user path, such as Windows Explorer, My Computer, the **Run** dialog box, or the command prompt. As soon as the user verifies that he or she wants to delete the file, the file is removed from the cache. This is not an effective way to clean up the cache because it also deletes files in the shared network folder.

Reinitializing the Cache

Reinitializing the Offline Files cache deletes all of the offline files from the Offline Files folder, and it resets the system's Offline Files database. If there are files in the cache that have changed and have not been synchronized with the network versions, the changes are lost when you reinitialize the cache. Also, this procedure requires that you restart the computer after the cache is reinitialized.

▶ **To reinitialize the Offline Files cache**

1. In Windows Explorer, open a shared network folder.

2. On the **Tools** menu, click **Folder Options**.

3. In the **Folder Options** dialog box, click the **Offline Files** tab.

4. Press CTRL + SHIFT, and then click **Delete Files**.

Caution You cannot undo the effects of reinitialization. After the cache is reinitialized, all offline files are permanently removed from the computer.

Configuring Power Management

Power management allows you to configure how a computer consumes energy. In Windows 2000, power management is based on the ACPI architecture implementation, which is based on the OnNow design initiative for power management. The OnNow design initiative is a comprehensive, system-wide approach to system and device power control based on a group of new specifications. The ACPI architecture gives the operating system complete control of power use on the computer. Windows 2000 also supports some implementations of the APM architecture. However, APM does not give Windows 2000 control of the power being used by devices (that is, power that is controlled by the BIOS), and your ability to manage power is more limited with APM-based computers than it is with ACPI-based computers.

Even if you do not have an APM-based or an ACPI-based computer, Windows 2000 allows you to manage some aspects of power consumption. For example, depending on the capabilities of your hardware, you can power down disks, turn off power to monitors, and put the computer into hibernate mode.

This section discusses power management in Windows 2000. It includes procedures for configuring and using power management as well as procedures for identifying whether your computer is ACPI-based, APM-based, or neither.

ACPI Power Management

Windows 2000 directs power management through the ACPI system. Unlike previous approaches to power management, ACPI manages power for the entire system, including all system devices and peripherals. To make this possible, the operating system must direct power to the computer. Older power management architectures, such as APM, do not do this. For these systems, the BIOS controls the power state of system devices. However, ACPI makes it possible for the operating system to coordinate power management activities at all levels and define the power-state transitions for the system.

With ACPI power management, the computer has the ability to function as follows:

- The computer is be ready for immediate use when the user turns it on.

- The computer appears to be off when not in use, but it can still respond to wakeup events. Wakeup events can occur when a device receives input, such as a telephone ringing, or when software requests that the computer wake up at a predetermined time (for example, to download e-mail so it is ready in the morning).

- The system can change how software responds when the power state of the computer changes. The operating system and applications work together intelligently to operate the computer and deliver effective power management according to the user's current actions. Applications do not keep the computer busy unnecessarily; instead, they proactively participate in shutting down the computer to conserve energy and reduce noise.

- All devices can participate in the power management scheme, whether the device was originally installed when Windows 2000 was installed or it was added as a peripheral after Windows 2000 was installed.

Figure 10.1 shows the components of the ACPI system.

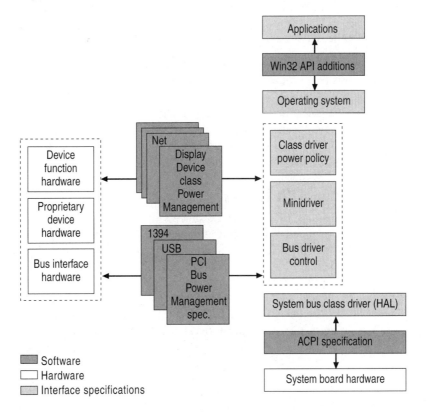

Figure 10.1   ACPI System Components

Applications that were developed before ACPI was available were designed with the assumption that the computer is always fully powered while the application is running. Such applications can inadvertently keep the system from entering a lower power state. In addition, these applications can fail if the computer enters standby mode or hibernate mode and then wakes up.

Managing Power with ACPI

In ACPI, power policy is based on the end user's preferences, the application requirements, and the system hardware capabilities. In other words, although Windows 2000 supports ACPI, applications need to be designed to work with ACPI power management and Plug and Play to make the entire process seamless.

The operating system controls energy use by putting the computer into a low-power state (for example, standby mode) when the computer is not in use. What determines how to save energy and when to go into a low-power state is referred to as the operating system's power policy. Power policy is distributed throughout the system, with system components acting as policy owners. For example, the operating system itself is the policy owner for determining when the computer should go into standby mode and hibernation mode and how to operate the processor to obtain energy conservation and meet thermal and audible noise goals.

There is also a policy owner for each device class on the computer. The policy owner for a particular device class is the component that is aware of how the device is used by the end user and the applications. This is generally a high-level component and in most cases a Win32 Driver Model (WDM) class driver. Each policy owner must manage power appropriately for its class and work consistently with the operating system's policy for putting the computer into a low-power state such as standby mode or hibernate mode.

How ACPI Works

For the ACPI system to be successful, Windows 2000 must be aware of how power management features integrate throughout the computer. This is done through the ACPI implementation, which is based on the OnNow design initiative. This feature is a system interface that provides a standard way of controlling the power management and Plug and Play functions of the computer hardware. ACPI allows the operating system to automatically turn on and turn off standard devices, such as CD-ROMs, network adapters, hard disk drives, and printers, as well as consumer devices that are connected to the computer, such as video recording and play-back devices, televisions, telephones, and stereo phonograph and CD players.

For a system to be completely OnNow capable, the system BIOS must support ACPI. The BIOS plays an important role in the ACPI by working with Windows 2000 to perform the necessary initialization processing and handoff during startup and when the working (full power) state is resumed from standby mode or hibernate mode. Figure 10.2 is an overview of the ACPI.

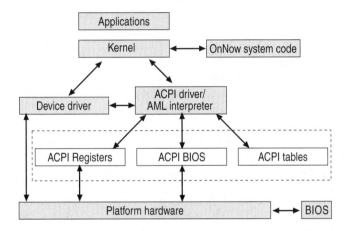

Figure 10.2   Overview of the ACPI

The ACPI specification has two parts: configuration (Plug and Play), and power management. ACPI gives Windows 2000 and the device drivers full control over power management. The BIOS provides Windows 2000 with access to the hardware controls for controlling power in the system. Windows 2000 and the device drivers, which are aware of the system's active state, determine when to turn off devices that are not in use and when to put the entire system into standby or hibernate mode.

Because power management is controlled by the operating system, there is a single user interface for managing power that works on all ACPI computers and simplifies the experience for the end user. ACPI also provides details to the operating system about system capability and sources of events. For example, an ACPI computer and operating system can do the following:

- Be sure the screen does not turn off in the middle of a presentation.

- Allow the machine to "wake" at a specified time to perform a task but not turn on the monitor and drives needlessly.

- Allow the user to choose what the power and reset buttons on the computer do to the operating system. You can configure the power button so that it does not shut down the computer. Instead, it puts the computer into standby mode.

How APM Works

In contrast to ACPI, there is the APM BIOS version 1.2 specification. With APM, the BIOS controls system power management. The BIOS has timers that monitor most interrupts and the data that is being transmitted through the input/output (I/O) port. When the timer for a device exceeds a value set in the BIOS setup, the BIOS turns off the device. When the system-wide timer exceeds some value set in the BIOS, the BIOS sends a message to Windows 2000 to put the entire computer in a low-power state. Windows 2000 then verifies that the computer is ready to be placed into standby mode or hibernate mode, and it tells the BIOS to do so. The APM BIOS is also responsible for monitoring the battery status and requesting a low power state if the battery is getting low. In general, APM has the following limitations:

Inconsistent user interfaces.   Each BIOS has its own user interface and its own power management behavior. This means every computer operates differently—users have to be retrained on each computer.

Reasons for suspend are not known.   Because of the architecture of the APM BIOS interface, the APM BIOS cannot inform Windows 2000 that a request is a response to the user pushing a sleep button, to the BIOS sensing that the system is idle, or to the battery running out of power. As a result, Windows 2000 must always honor this suspend request and attempt to put the computer into low-power state—even if the computer is not idle. For this reason, it is recommended that you set the BIOS time-out settings to a very large value or turn them off.

Devices might be turned off at inappropriate times.   By monitoring I/O ports and interrupts, the BIOS is essentially trying to determine what the user and the applications are doing. Although this often works, there are many scenarios in which the response of the BIOS is incorrect—for example, the BIOS turns off or slows down a computer when it is in use (such as a screen saver turning on in the middle of a presentation), or the BIOS does not turn off a truly idle computer.

BIOS detects activity only on devices that are residing on the motherboard.
The BIOS cannot detect devices that are not on the motherboard, such as USB devices and IEEE 1394 devices. As a result, the system might appear to the BIOS as if it were not in use, even if one or more of these off-motherboard devices actually is in use.

In addition to these general limitations, there are several limitations specific to Windows 2000:

- Windows 2000 only supports the following APM features: battery status, suspend, resume, and hibernate. It does not support other APM features such as timer wake up, wake-on-local area network (LAN), or wake-on-ring.

- APM is supported only on portable computers.

- APM is not supported in the Windows 2000 Server family of products.

- APM does not work with multiprocessor systems.

In the following section, APM and how you can configure APM so that it works with Windows 2000 Professional are discussed.

BIOS Compatibility and Configuration

To use ACPI-based or APM-based power management features with Windows 2000 Professional, the ACPI-based BIOS on your computer must be fully ACPI-compliant, or the APM-based BIOS on your computer must be compatible with Windows 2000. In addition, you must configure an APM-based BIOS in order for power management to work properly with Windows 2000.

Checking ACPI Compliance

During setup, Windows 2000 determines which hardware abstraction layer (HAL) to install on a computer. This determination is based on whether a computer has a compliant ACPI BIOS or not. If it does, the ACPI HAL is installed and you are able to use the ACPI power management features; if it doesn't, an older HAL is installed and the ACPI power management features are not available.

Note In general, the HAL directs information from the operating system and device drivers to specific devices. ACPI-based computers require an ACPI HAL. Non-ACPI-based computers require an older HAL.

To determine which HAL to install, Windows 2000 performs the following procedures during setup:

1. Windows 2000 checks the ACPI BIOS tables that are generated during startup. These tables list the devices that are installed on the computer and their power management capabilities.

   If this information is missing or if the information is in the wrong form, an older HAL is installed.

2. If the tables are correct, Setup checks whether the BIOS is known to be incompatible or non-compliant with the ACPI standard.

   If the BIOS is incompatible, an older HAL is installed.

3. If the BIOS is not on the incompatible BIOS list, Setup looks at the BIOS date.

   If the BIOS is not on the incompatible BIOS list and the BIOS date is later than 1/1/99, Windows 2000 accepts it, and the ACPI HAL is installed.

4. If the BIOS is not on the incompatible BIOS list and the BIOS date is earlier than 1/1/99, Setup looks for a compatible BIOS.

If the BIOS is on the compatible BIOS list, an ACPI HAL is installed.

If the BIOS is not on the list, an older HAL is installed.

You can check a computer's BIOS compatibility on the Microsoft Windows Hardware Compatibility List (HCL) Web site. For more information about the HCL, see the Hardware Compatibility List link on the Web Resources page at http://windows.microsoft.com/windows2000/reskit/webresources. If you have already installed Windows 2000, you can check to see whether the computer is operating in ACPI mode by following this procedure.

▶ **To determine whether Windows 2000 is running in ACPI mode**

1. From the **Start** menu, point to **Settings**, and then click **Control Panel**.

2. Double-click **Administrative Tools**, and then double-click **Computer Management**.

3. In the view pane, click **Device Manager**.

4. In the details pane, click **System devices**.

   If **Microsoft ACPI-Compliant System** is listed under **System devices**, the computer is operating in ACPI mode.

If you have an ACPI BIOS but Windows 2000 didn't install in ACPI mode, you might have a non-compliant ACPI BIOS. Check your computer manufacturer's Web site to see whether a more recent ACPI BIOS version is available. If one is available, you have an older HAL installed on your computer, and you flash a new BIOS version on to your computer, you must reinstall Windows 2000. Reinstalling Windows 2000 is the only way to replace an older HAL with an ACPI HAL. For more information about upgrading the BIOS in a portable computer, see the Hardware Update link on the Web Resources page at http://windows.microsoft.com/windows2000/reskit/webresources.

▶ **To determine which hardware abstraction layer is installed**

1. Find Hal.dll (which located in %SystemRoot%\system32).

2. Click the file, and on the **File** menu, click **Properties**.

3. In the **hal.dll Properties** dialog box, click the **Version** tab.

4. On the **Version** tab, in the **Other version information** box, in the **Item name** pane, click **Original Filename**.

5. Look under **Value**.

If **halacpi.dll** is listed, an ACPI HAL is installed on the computer. If **hal.dll** is listed, a previous HAL is installed.

Note ACPI functionality is new, and features are being added by BIOS manufacturers and system manufacturers. If functionality is missing that you believe should exist, if you are experiencing unusual behavior with a BIOS that is dated later than 1/1/99 or a BIOS that is listed on the compatible BIOS list, verify with the computer manufacturer that you have the most current BIOS revision installed on the computer.

Checking APM BIOS Compatibility

Windows 2000 supports APM version 1.2 on portable computers, but the computer must have a compatible APM BIOS for APM features to work properly. Windows 2000 determines whether a BIOS is APM-compatible during setup. On the basis of this determination, Windows 2000 does one of the following:

- Installs APM support (Ntapm.sys and Apmbatt.sys) and enables APM if the computer's BIOS is found on the auto-enable APM list. APM is fully functional after Setup completes.

- Does not install or enable APM support if the computer's BIOS is found on the disable APM list. APM does not work reliably, and it should not be used on the computer, or data loss might occur.

- Installs APM support but does not enable APM support if the computer's BIOS is not on the auto-enable APM list or the disable APM list. APM might work properly, but you have to enable APM in the Windows 2000 graphical user interface (GUI) for APM to be enabled. (See "Enabling and Configuring APM" in later this chapter.)

Important APM must be enabled in the BIOS before Windows 2000 is installed. If APM is disabled in the BIOS before installation, Windows 2000 does not install power management support even if the APM BIOS is on the auto-enable APM list.

If APM is not enabled after you install Windows 2000, either the computer's BIOS is on the disable APM list, or it is not on either the disable APM list or the auto-enable APM list. You can determine this by running the Apmstat.exe tool, which is part of the Windows 2000 Support Tools. The Windows 2000 Support Tools are included on the Windows 2000 Professional operating system CD.

▶ **To install the Windows 2000 Support Tools**

- Run Setup.exe, which is located in the Support\Tools folder on the Windows 2000 Professional operating system CD.

  The Apmstat.exe tool must be run from the command line. It has one command line switch (**-v**), which indicates that you want the tool to run in verbose mode. You do not need to run the tool with the **-v** switch in order to determine APM BIOS compatibility.

▶ **To check APM BIOS compatibility by using Apmstat.exe**

1. From the **Start** menu, point to **Programs** and then **Accessories**, and then click **Command Prompt**.

2. Type:

   apmstat

3. Press ENTER.

If Apmstat.exe reports that an APM BIOS is known to be incompatible or that an APM BIOS is known to have problems, you must not attempt to circumvent Windows 2000 Setup by forcing it to install APM support. This might cause a computer behave erratically, and it might result in the loss of data. In addition, if an APM BIOS is known to be incompatible, make sure that APM is disabled in the BIOS.

If Apmstat.exe reports that an APM BIOS is not known to be compatible and it is not known to be incompatible, you might still be able to use APM, but you need to enable and configure APM in order for it to work effectively on your computer.

Enabling and Configuring APM

APM must be enabled before you can use it. However, you can only enable APM if Windows 2000 installed APM support during setup. You can verify whether APM support is installed by using Device Manager. Enabling APM does not require that you restart the computer; however, disabling APM does require it.

▶ **To verify that APM support is installed on a computer**

1. From the **Start** menu, point to **Settings**, and then click **Control Panel**.

2. Double-click **Administrative Tools**, and then double-click **Computer Management**.

3. In the view pane of Computer Management, click **Device Manager**.

4. On the **View** menu, click **Show hidden devices**.

   If **NT Apm/Legacy Support** is present in the details pane, APM support is installed.

▶ **To enable APM**

1. From the **Start** menu, point to **Settings**, and then click **Control Panel**.

2. Double-click **Power Options**.

3. In the **Power Options Properties** dialog box, click the **APM** tab.

4. On the **APM** tab, in the **Advanced Power Management** check box, click **Enable Advanced Power Management support?**

Note The **APM** tab is present only if an APM BIOS is detected that is either APM 1.2 compliant or might not be APM 1.2 compliant but might work. It is not reccomended that you enable APM support on a computer that has a BIOS that is not APM compliant. If you experience problems after enabling APM support, disable APM and contact the computer manufacturer for an updated BIOS. In addition, the APM tab is not present if a computer has multiple processors because Windows 2000 does not install APM support on multiprocessor computers.

You can verify that APM is enabled and running by looking at the **Shut Down Windows** dialog box. This procedure only works on computers that have a non-ACPI BIOS

▶ **To verify that APM is running on a computer**

1. Click **Start**, and then click **Shutdown**.

2. In the **Shut Down Windows** dialog box, under **What do you want the computer to do?**, look for **Stand by**. If it is present, APM is running.

Although Windows 2000 supports APM, you might have to configure two settings in the APM BIOS before APM works properly. First, configure BIOS time-outs to the longest possible time or disable them. This allows the operating system rather than the BIOS to control time-outs. Be aware that some APM BIOSs turn off or refuse to function if all time-outs are disabled, so it might be better to set time-outs to the maximum allowed time rather than disabling them. Second, make sure that screen blanking is turned off in the BIOS. Screen blanking reduces power to the display, which causes the display to appear as though the computer is shut down. Normally, activating a pointing device wakes the system and restores power to the display. However, USB and other external pointing devices do not wake the system, and power is not restored to the display. You can usually turn off screen blanking in the BIOS by disabling the time-out for the display or by setting the time-out to the maximum value.

Finally, do not use a supplemental video card with a portable computer if you are using APM. Only use the video card that is included with the portable computer. The APM BIOS might not detect a video card that is added to the system or a video card that is in a docking station. If the adapter is not discovered by the APM BIOS, suspend does not work.

Power Management Options

Whether you have an ACPI-based or an APM-based computer, you must enable or configure the power management options; otherwise, they do not function properly. This includes choosing and configuring a power scheme, enabling hibernate mode and the battery status indicator, and configuring the power button and the battery alarms.

Configuring Power Schemes

Power schemes allow you to configure how and when a computer turns off devices or enters a suspend state. For example, you can set individual power-down settings for the monitor and the hard disk. (Depending on the computer's hardware capability, you might be able to configure these settings even if the computer is not ACPI-enabled or APM-enabled.) If the computer is ACPI-enabled or APM-enabled, you are also able to configure power-down settings for standby mode and hibernate mode, although you must first enable hibernate mode or it is not available. (For information about how to do this, see "Hibernation and Standby" later in this chapter.) ACPI and APM also allow you to configure these settings separately depending on whether the computer is powered by alternating current or a battery. There are six default power schemes: Home/Office Desk, Portable/Laptop, Presentation, Always On, Minimal Power Management, and Max Battery. You can customize any scheme or add new schemes to fit a specific situation.

You need to configure the power scheme for a portable computer because the default power scheme is Home/Office Desk, which does not optimize battery power. The power scheme might also need to be changed according to how the computer is used. The Presentation scheme is useful because it prevents the computer from entering standby mode or hibernate mode.

▶ **To configure power schemes**

1. From the **Start** menu, point to **Settings**, and then click **Control Panel**.
2. Double-click **Power Options**.
3. In the **Power Options Properties** dialog box, click the **Power Schemes** tab.
4. Select a power scheme, and then change any of the settings you want.

Hibernate Mode and Standby Mode

When a computer enters hibernate mode, the current state of the computer is saved to disk and the power to the computer is turned off. When a computer resumes from hibernation, it reads the state data from the disk and restores the system as it was before it entered hibernate mode. Software programs are restarted, and network connections are restored.

Hibernate mode must be enabled; by default, it is disabled. If a computer is not ACPI-enabled or APM-enabled, you are able only to enter hibernate mode manually. You are not able to set the computer to autohibernate after a certain time. ACPI-enabled and APM-enabled computers are able to enter hibernate mode automatically. Resuming from hibernate mode requires users to enter a user name and a password. This setting cannot be changed.

Because the contents of the computer's memory are written to disk when it enters hibernate mode, you must have at least as much available disk space as you have random access memory (RAM) installed on your computer.

▶ **To enable hibernate mode**

1. From the **Start** menu, point to **Settings**, and then click **Control Panel**.

2. Double-click **Power Options**.

3. In the **Power Options Properties** dialog box, click the **Hibernate** tab.

4. Click **Enable hibernate support**.

Note You must have the proper hardware to use hibernate mode. If the **Hibernate** tab is not available, the computer does not support hibernation.

When a computer enters standby mode, the computer's state is not saved to a disk; rather, it puts the computer in a low-power state. When a computer resumes from standby mode, full power is restored to devices. If the power is interrupted when the computer is in standby mode, data might be lost. You do not have to enable standby mode in order for it to be available. It is available automatically on ACPI-enabled and APM-enabled computers. It is not available on non-ACPI-based or non-APM-based computers.

You can have the computer prompt the user for a user name and password after it resumes from standby. This is enabled by default.

▶ **To disable password protection when resuming from standby mode**

1. From the **Start** menu, point to **Settings**, and then click **Control Panel**.

2. Double-click **Power Options**.

3. In the **Power Options Properties** dialog box, click the **Advanced** tab.

4. Click the **Prompt for password when computer goes off standby** check box to clear it.

Hibernate Mode or Standby Mode and the Group Policy Refresh Interval

Group Policy allows you to configure the policy refresh interval, which controls how often policies are applied on the computer. By default, the refresh interval is 90 minutes, although it can be set to any value between 0 minutes and 64,800 minutes. In addition to the refresh interval, you can set an interval offset, which is a random period of time that is applied to the refresh interval. The interval offset randomizes the refresh interval and prevents clients with the same refresh interval from simultaneously requesting policy updates, which can overload the server. By default, the interval offset is 30 minutes, which means a random time between 0 minutes and 30 minutes is applied to the refresh interval.

In some cases, Group Policy refresh settings can prevent a computer from entering hibernate mode or standby mode. This is because a policy update resets the hibernation or standby timer (just like moving the mouse or pressing a key on the keyboard). For example, if a computer is configured so that it enters hibernate mode or standby mode after being idle for 45 minutes but the Group Policy refresh interval is set at 30 minutes, the hibernation or standby timer never reaches 45 minutes. To ensure that the standby timer does not reach 45 minutes, set the Group Policy refresh interval so that it is greater than the hibernation setting or standby setting in Power Options. You can also configure Group Policy so that it does not apply settings while the computer is running. The descriptions of the procedures follow.

▶ **To change Group Policy refresh interval and interval offset for User Configuration settings**

1. From the **Start** menu, click **Run**, and then type:

   gpedit.msc

2. Press ENTER.

3. In the view pane of Group Policy, under User Configuration, open the Administrative Templates folder, and then open the System folder.

4. Click **Group Policy**.

5. In the details pane, double-click **Group Policy refresh interval for users**.

6. In the **Group Policy refresh interval for users Properties** dialog box, click **Enabled**.

7. Change the settings for the refresh interval and the interval offset.

▶ **To change Group Policy refresh interval and interval offset for Computer Configuration settings**

1. From the **Start** menu, click **Run**, and then type:

   gpedit.msc

2. Press ENTER.

3. In the view pane of Group Policy, under Computer Configuration, open the Administrative Templates folder, and then open the System folder.

4. Click **Group Policy**.

5. In the details pane, double-click **Group Policy refresh interval for computers**.

6. In the **Group Policy refresh interval for users Properties** dialog box, click **Enabled**.

7. Change the settings for the refresh interval and the interval offset.

▶ **To disable policy updates while a computer is running**

1. From the **Start** menu, click **Run**, and then type:

   gpedit.msc

2. Press ENTER.

3. In the view pane of Group Policy, under Computer Configuration, open the Administrative Templates folder, and then open the System folder.

4. Click **Group Policy**.

5. In the details pane, double-click **Disable background refresh of Group Policy**.

6. In the **Disable background refresh of Group Policy Properties** dialog box, click **Enabled**.

Operation During Commercial Air Travel

Some commercial airlines might request that you turn off portable computers during portions of a flight, such as takeoff and landing. To comply with this request, users must turn off their computer completely.

A computer might appear to be turned off while it is in either standby or hibernate mode. However, the operating system might automatically reactivate itself to run certain preprogrammed tasks or to conserve battery power. To prevent this from occurring during air travel, be certain that users shut down their computer completely when it is not in use. For more information about shutting down a computer, see Windows 2000 Professional Help.

In addition, if a computer is equipped with a cellular modem, users must ensure that this modem is completely turned off during air travel as required by Federal Communication Commission regulations.

Important Failure to comply with these requirements could lead to civil or criminal penalties.

Battery Monitoring and Management

Battery monitoring and management is only available on ACPI-enabled and APM-enabled computers. Windows 2000 can manage batteries that have a Smart Battery subsystem interface or a Control Method Battery (CMBatt) interface. Windows 2000 can also monitor multiple batteries.

You must enable the battery status icon in order for it to appear on the taskbar. This icon gives users direct access to the power meter so that they can monitor the battery level.

▶ **To add the battery status icon to the taskbar**

1. From the **Start** menu, point to **Settings**, and then click **Control Panel**.
2. Double-click **Power Options**.
3. In the **Power Options Properties** dialog box, click the **Advanced** tab.
4. Click the **Always show icon on the taskbar** check box.

You can also configure the battery meter so that it displays the status of multiple batteries if your portable computer uses multiple batteries.

▶ **To configure the battery meter for multiple battery computers**

1. From the **Start** menu, point to **Settings**, and then click **Control Panel**.
2. Double-click **Power Options**.
3. In the **Power Options Properties** dialog box, click the **Power Meter** tab.
4. Click **Show details for each battery**.

You can also set alarms to indicate low battery and critical battery levels. You can set the alarm to be a notification (visual or audible), a change in power state (standby, hibernate, shutdown), or the execution of a program.

▶ **To configure alarms**

1. From the **Start** menu, point to **Settings**, and then click **Control Panel**.

2. Double-click **Power Options**.

3. In the **Power Options Properties** dialog box, click the **Alarms** tab.

4. Drag the sliders to change the battery level at which a low-battery alarm and a critical-battery alarm are activated.

5. Click **Alarm Action** to configure the actions you want taken when an alarm is activated. You must configure alarm actions separately for low-battery and critical-battery actions.

Power Button Behavior

ACPI-enabled computers allow you to change how the power button behaves when you press it. There are three options: **Power Off**, **Standby**, and **Hibernate**. By default, none of these options are assigned to the power button. If you change the power button functionality to **Standby** or to **Hibernate**, the computer enters the specified modes when the user presses the power button. To resume from these modes, the user also presses the power button. If you change the power button functionality to **Power Off**, the computer immediately powers down when the user presses the power button. This type of power down is not the same as shutting down the computer by clicking **Shut down** from the **Start** menu. Using the **Shut down** command prompts users to save data (if necessary) and then flushes the hard drive cache. When the **Power Down** option is set, and the user presses the power button, the hard drive cache is not flushed and the user is not prompted to save data (even if there are open documents or files).

▶ **To change power button functionality**

1. From the **Start** menu, point to **Settings**, and then click **Control Panel**.

2. Double-click **Power Options**.

3. In the **Power Options Properties** dialog box, click the **Advanced** tab.

4. Under **When I press the power button on my computer**, select the power button functionality you want.

Caution Setting power button functionality to **Power Off** could result in the loss of data if files or documents are open when a user presses the power off button. The **Power Off** option is a quick and fast method of turning off power to the computer. It is not the recommended method for powering down a portable computer. The recommended method is to use the **Shut down** command on the **Start** button.

Wake-On Technology

"Wake-On" technology allows individual devices to resume for certain actions without requiring the rest of the system to start up. Windows 2000 supports Wake-On features such as wake-on-ring and wake-on-LAN, but only on ACPI-based computers. Windows 2000 does not support wake-on-LAN or wake-on-ring if the PC Cards you are trying to wake require CardBus technology.

Hiding Power Options

You can prevent users from configuring power options by specifying Control Panel settings in Group Policy. You can disable Control Panel entirely, hide specific Control Panel tools, and show specific Control Panel applets. Hiding the Power Options tool can be beneficial if you have configured power options and it is imperative that users not change those options. However, if you hide **Power Options**, users have no method for reconfiguring power management settings if something needs to be changed while they are away from the office. For example, portable computer users frequently use the Portable/Laptop scheme, but when they use the portable computer for a presentation, they should switch to the Presentation scheme to prevent the portable computer from turning off the display or entering standby mode or hibernate mode. Users are not able to change power schemes, or any other power option, if Power Options is not available.

▶   **To hide Power Options by using Group Policy settings**

1. From the **Start** menu, click **Run**, and then type:

   gpedit.msc

2. Press ENTER.

3. In the view pane of Group Policy, under User Configuration, open the Administrative Templates folder.

4. Click the Control Panel folder.

5. In the details pane, double-click **Hide specified control panel applets**.

6. In the **Hide specified control panel applets Properties** dialog box, click **Enabled**, and then click **Show**.

7. In the **Show Contents** dialog box, click **Add**.

8. In the **Add Item** dialog box, type:

   power options

9. Click **OK**.

   Power Options should show up under **List of disallowed Control Panel applets** in the **Show Contents** dialog box.

▶ **To disable the Control Panel by using Group Policy settings**

1. From the Start menu, click Run, and then type:

   gpedit.msc

2. Press ENTER.

3. In the view pane of Group Policy, under User Configuration, open the Administrative Templates folder.

4. Click the Control Panel folder.

5. In the details pane, double-click **Disable Control Panel**.

6. In the **Disable Control Panel Properties** dialog box, click **Enabled**.

Important   Disabling **Control Panel** in Group Policy prevents Control.exe from starting. This removes **Control Panel** from the **Start** menu and removes the Control Panel folder from Windows Explorer.

Managing Hardware on Portable Computers

The Plug and Play support in Windows 2000 allows the operating system to configure devices quickly without requiring you to restart the computer. As a consequence, you can add or remove a device from the computer while it is running; and Windows 2000 allocates resources, loads the appropriate device drivers, and enables the device. Full Plug and Play support is useful for portable computers because the device configuration frequently changes to accommodate the user's environment (docked or undocked) and the user's needs (work remotely online, or work offline). For portable computers that are ACPI enabled, Plug and Play makes the following functionality possible:

- Hot docking and undocking.
- Hot swapping of Integrated Drive Electronics (IDE) devices in device bays, such as hard drives, floppy drives, and CD-ROM drives.
- Automatic creation of docked and undocked hardware profiles.
- Dynamic configuration of PC Cards and CardBus cards without restarting the computer.

This section discusses the functionality presented in the preceding list and also hardware management issues such as surprise removal. For more information about installing, configuring, and troubleshooting devices, see "Device Management" in this book. For more information about hardware management, including power management and Plug and Play, see "Hardware Management" in this book.

Note Full Plug and Play support is possible only if both the device and the device drivers support Plug and Play and the computer is ACPI-based. For computers that are not ACPI-based, Plug and Play recognizes hardware changes, but only after the computer is restarted.

Hardware Profiles

Windows 2000 uses hardware profiles to determine what drivers to load when the system hardware changes. Hardware profiles are an important feature for portable computers that use a docking station. Windows 2000 uses one hardware profile to load drivers when the portable computer is docked and another when the computer is undocked. Windows 2000 automatically creates these two hardware profiles for portable computers.

The profiles are created when Windows 2000 queries the BIOS for a dock serial ID and then assigns names for the docked and undocked configurations. By default, the docked and undocked profiles are called Undocked Profile and Docked Profile. If a portable computer is fully Plug and Play–compliant, you do not need to use any other hardware profiles except these. Also, you do not have to designate which profile to use when the computer starts. The computer is aware of the docked or undocked state and chooses the appropriate profile.

If a portable computer is not fully Plug and Play–compliant, you might need to create a new hardware profile. You can then configure the profile by enabling and disabling devices.

▶ **To create a new hardware profile**

1. From the **Start** menu, point to **Settings**, and then click **Control Panel**.
2. Double-click **System**.
3. On the **Hardware** tab, click **Hardware Profiles**.
4. Under **Available hardware profiles**, click a profile, and then click **Copy**.
5. In the **Copy Profile** dialog box, enter a name for the new profile.

▶ **To configure a hardware profile**

1. From the **Start** menu, point to **Settings**, and then click **Control Panel**.

2. Double-click **System**.

3. On the **Hardware** tab, click **Device Manager**.

4. Double-click the device you want to add or remove from the hardware profile, and then under **Device usage** select the setting you want.

Note Do not reconfigure the Docked Profile or the Undocked Profile if your system is Plug and Play-compliant.

Dynamic Device Configuration

Dynamic device configuration allows portable computer users to add or remove PC Cards and IDE devices without restarting the computer. However, this is possible only if the device and the device drivers support Plug and Play and the computer is ACPI-enabled. For computers that are not ACPI-enabled, Plug and Play support recognizes hardware changes, but only after the computer is restarted.

PC Card Devices and CardBus Devices

In Windows 2000, Plug and Play support for the PC Card socket is enabled for CardBus devices and PC Card devices. To take advantage of Plug and Play, a PC Card device or a CardBus device must contain the information that Windows 2000 can use to create a unique device ID for the card. This is called the card information structure (CIS). If a CIS is present, Windows 2000 configures the device, loads the appropriate drivers, and enables the device without requiring you to restart the computer. If the computer is not ACPI-based and the device and its drivers are Plug and Play–compliant, this happens after you restart the computer.

You can implement PC Card device drivers and CardBus device drivers in three possible scenarios:

- A standard Plug and Play device driver for PC Card (the preferred driver) can handle dynamic configuration and removal and receive configuration information from the operating system without knowledge of the card in the PC Card bus. The recommended choices are NDIS version 5.x drivers for network adapters and miniport drivers for Small Computer System Interface (SCSI) cards.

- Generic Windows 2000 device drivers are supported automatically for such devices as modems and disk drives. If the card contains complete configuration information, the operating system initializes the device and passes configuration information to the driver.

- Manufacturer-supplied drivers are required for device classes that Windows 2000 does not natively support.

If Windows 2000 includes supporting drivers for the PC Card device or CardBus device, installation and configuration should be automatic. Otherwise, you might be prompted for the device drivers. Also, device drivers (saved in .cab files) are installed on the hard drive during setup. You do not need the Windows 2000 operating system CD to install drivers that are included with Windows 2000.

Although Windows 2000 dynamically configures PC Card devices and CardBus devices, notify Windows 2000 before you remove these types of devices from the computer. This notification, which tells Windows 2000 to stop the device, ensures that your system remains stable. You can stop devices by using **Add/Remove Hardware** in Control Panel.

▶ **To stop a PC Card or CardBus device**

1. From the **Start** menu, point to **Settings**, and then click **Control Panel**.
2. Double-click **Add/Remove Hardware**, and then click **Next**.
3. Click **Uninstall/Unplug a device**, and then click **Next**.
4. Click **Unplug/Eject a device**, and then click **Next**.
5. Select the device you want to remove, and then click **Next**.
6. Confirm that you want to remove the device by clicking **Next**.
7. Click **Finish**.

You can also stop a device by clicking the **Unplug/Eject** icon on the taskbar. The icon appears by default whenever a PC Card device or CardBus device is installed. You can hide the icon by configuring the properties of the icon.

▶ **To hide the Unplug/Eject icon in the taskbar**

1. Right-click the **PC Card** icon in the taskbar, and then click **Properties**.
2. In the **Unplug or Eject Hardware** dialog box, clear the the **Show Unplug/Eject** icon check box on the taskbar.

IDE Devices

Windows 2000 supports hot swapping of IDE devices such as floppy drives, CD-ROM drives, and hard drives. As with PC Card devices, this is only available if the computer is ACPI-enabled. Non-ACPI-enabled computers can swap IDE devices, but to do so requires restarting the computer. Also, you should stop IDE devices by clicking the **Unplug/Eject** icon or **Add/Remove Hardware** in Control Panel before you swap them or remove them.

Important Some ACPI-enabled machines may not be fully ACPI compliant or support the ability to hot swap mass storage IDE-based devices without rebooting. In these cases, removing an IDE-based device without first shutting down the computer could physically damage the device.

Docking and Undocking

There are three methods of docking and undocking a portable computer: cold, warm, and hot. A cold dock or undock means that the computer has been shut down before it is inserted into or removed from the docking station. A warm dock or undock means the computer has been put into standby mode before it is inserted into or removed from the docking station. A hot dock or undock means that the computer is running, with or without programs and documents open, when it is inserted into or removed from the docking station.

Caution Do not undock portable computers while they are in hibernate mode. Hibernate mode saves the system's state to a file, including the current hardware configuration. When a computer resumes from hibernate mode and the actual hardware configuration is different from the hardware configuration at the time it went into hibernate mode, errors result and the system might behave erratically.

Hot Docking and Undocking

There is only one way to perform a hot dock. But there are two ways a user can perform a hot undock—by using the **Eject PC** command in the Windows 2000 user interface, or by physically removing the portable computer from the docking station using whatever mechanism the docking station provides. The latter method is not recommended.

Note Hot docking and hot undocking can only be performed on computers that are ACPI-enabled.

▶ **To perform a hot dock**

- While the computer is running, insert it into the docking station.

▶ **To perform a hot undock**

- From the **Start** menu, click **Eject PC**, and then eject or remove the computer from the docking station. The **Eject PC** command appears only if a computer is ACPI-enabled.

You can also use Group Policy to disable hot docking, in which case the **Eject PC** command does not appear, not even on ACPI-based computers. For more information about using Group Policy, see "Undocking Portable Computers" later in this chapter.

Warm Docking and Undocking

Windows 2000 adheres to the ACPI specification in terms of warm docking and undocking. If a portable computer supports warm undocking, the **Eject PC** command instructs Windows 2000 to unload the device drivers for the devices in the docking station and then put the computer into standby mode. After the computer enters standby mode, the user can undock the computer. The original equipment manufacturer (OEM) can help you determine whether the BIOS in a portable computer supports warm undocking.

Important You cannot manually put the computer into standby mode or hibernate mode and then undock. This is because Windows 2000 does not unload the device drivers for devices in the docking station when standby mode or hibernate mode are activated manually or through a timer event.

Some manufacturers use warm undocking as an alternative to hot undocking if low battery power is detected. In these cases, when a user attempts a hot undock using the **Eject PC** command and the system detects that there is insufficient battery power to maintain the system after it undocks, Windows 2000 checks the BIOS to see if it supports warm undocking. If it does, the device drivers for the devices in the docking station are unloaded and the computer is put into standby mode.

There is only one way to perform a warm dock.

▶ **To perform a warm dock**

- While the computer is in standby mode, insert it in the docking station.

Likewise, there is only one way to perform a warm undock.

▶ **To perform a warm undock**

1. From the **Start** menu, click **Eject PC**.

2. After the computer enters standby mode, remove or eject the computer from the docking station.

Note   Warm undocking can only be performed on computers that are ACPI-enabled and that have a BIOS that supports warm undocking functionality.

Cold Docking and Undocking

Cold docking means that the computer is completely shut down before it is docked or undocked. Cold docking and undocking should be used if you have a non-ACPI-based computer, including an APM-based computer. Also, when you shut down the computer before a cold dock or undock, you must use the **Shut down** command, not the **Hibernate** command or **Stand by** command.

▶ **To perform a cold dock**

• While the computer is shut down, insert it into the docking station.

▶ **To perform a cold undock**

• While the computer is shut down, remove or eject it from the docking station.

Surprise Removals

A *surprise removal* is when a PC Card or CardBus device is removed from a portable computer while the computer is running and Windows 2000 is not notified before the device is removed. ACPI-based computers can usually recover from surprise removals because ACPI allows Windows 2000 to dynamically reconfigure hardware. However, surprise removals are not recommended. Instead, stop a device, and then remove it.

▶ **To stop a device**

1. Double-click the **Unplug/Eject** icon on the taskbar.

2. In the **Unplug or Eject Hardware** dialog box, select the device you want to stop, and then click **Stop**.

3. Remove, eject, or unplug the device from the computer.

Surprise removal can also occur when a computer is running and someone undocks it without first using the **Eject PC** command. Or it can occur when someone puts a portable computer into standby mode or hibernate mode and then physically removes the computer from the docking station without first shutting down the computer.

Warning Removing a portable computer without using the **Eject PC** command is not supported in Windows 2000 and can result in hardware damage and data loss. To avoid this, use the **Eject PC** command to perform a hot undock, or shut down the system and perform a cold undock. Undocking a portable computer while it is in standby mode or hibernate mode is also not supported in Windows 2000. Although doing this might not incur hardware damage, it is likely to result in data loss and system instability. To avoid this situation, use the hot undock or cold undock procedures described in the preceding sections.

Security Considerations for Portable Computers

Because portable computers are vulnerable to theft, it is important that you secure a portable computer and the data on it with as many Windows 2000 security features as possible. In general, hard drives format to use NTFS so that permissions can be set and encryption (EFS) enabled on files and folders. Add the users of portable computers to the Power Users group so that they have maximum control of the computer without having full control of the system. Users should use strong passwords for logging on to their network and administrators should use strong passwords for the local administrator account. Use Group Policy settings as much as possible to restrict access to the computer and any data on it. For more information about these security features, see "Security," "Managing Files, Folders, and Search Methods," and "File Systems" in this book. In this section, the discussion focuses on security considerations that are relevant to portable computers, including undocking privileges, BIOS security, and security for offline files.

Undocking Portable Computers

Portable computers can be undocked in any one of the following ways depending on the type of docking station, the type of portable computer, and the permissions and Group Policy settings that have been implemented on the computer.

- While the portable computer is shut down and the power is off, someone physically ejects it or removes it from the docking station (a cold undock).

- While the portable computer is running, someone physically ejects it or removes it from the docking station (a surprise removal).

- While the portable computer is running, someone uses the **Eject PC** command in Windows 2000 Professional to eject the computer from the docking station (a hot undock).

Each of these undocking methods relies on a different security mechanism to restrict undocking. Some of these security mechanisms are configurable, and some are not.

Undock Notifications

Depending on how a portable computer is undocked, Windows 2000 might or might not receive notification. Depending on how the notification is reported, Windows 2000 might or might not be able to authorize the undock event.

When someone shuts down a portable computer and physically ejects or removes it from its docking station, Windows 2000 is not notified that the computer is being undocked (that is, turned off). In this case, the only security that restricts undocking is physical security (for example, a keyed lock on the docking station or a cable connected between the docking station and the portable computer).

When someone physically ejects or removes a portable computer from its docking station without first shutting down Windows 2000 or turning off the portable computer, the BIOS notifies Windows 2000 that the portable computer has been undocked. This notification is initiated in kernel mode. When an undock notification is initiated in kernel mode, Windows 2000 does not perform a security check to determine whether there are any restrictions (for example, Group Policy settings) that affect the removal of the computer. In other words, Windows 2000 performs no security check. In this case, the only security mechanism that restricts undocking is physical security.

When someone uses **Eject PC** in Windows 2000 Professional to eject or remove a portable computer from a docking station, Windows 2000 is notified that the computer is being undocked. This notification is initiated in user mode. When an undock notification is initiated in user mode, Windows 2000 performs a security check to determine whether there are any undocking restrictions.

Setting Undock Permissions

You can choose a local Group Policy setting that controls who has docking privileges on a portable computer. If a user has the undocking privilege, he or she is able to use the **Eject PC** command. If the user does not have the undocking privilege, the **Eject PC** command is not available. However, any program can call the application programming interface (API) that controls the **Eject PC** command, which means that any program can have its own button or menu item that tries to eject a portable computer. If a user tries to use such a button or menu item and doesn't have the undocking privilege, the command fails, but the user is not notified about why it failed.

▶ **To set undocking privileges by using Group Policy**

1. From the **Start** menu, click **Run**, and then type::

   gpedit.msc

2. Press ENTER.

3. In the view pane of Group Policy, under **Computer Configuration**, open the **Windows Settings** folder, **Security Settings**, and the **Local Policies** folder.

4. Click the User Rights Assignment folder.

5. In the details pane, double-click **Remove computer from docking station**.

6. In the **Local Security Policy Setting** dialog box, under **Local Policy Setting**, clear the check box next to any user or group that you do not want to have the undocking privilege. If you want to add users and groups to the list, click **Add**.

Note This procedure restricts undocking only when a user attempts to undock a portable computer by using the **Eject PC** command.

By default, undocking privileges are granted to everyone during clean installs of Windows 2000 and during upgrades from Windows 95, Windows 98, and Windows NT 4.0. In these cases, you must use the preceding procedure if you want to prevent users from undocking.

BIOS Security

Some computers allow you to implement system security or device security at the BIOS level. Equipment manufacturers usually implement this type of security by requiring a password at startup while the BIOS is loading. If the user enters an incorrect password, the BIOS does not finish loading and the computer does not start; or the BIOS might finish loading, but it does not transfer control of the computer to Windows 2000. Although this type of security is designed to control access to the computer at startup, it might also control access when the computer resumes from a low power state such as standby mode or hibernate mode. In these cases, users might have to enter the BIOS password when the system resumes from either standby or hibernate mode.

If you want to implement BIOS security on a portable computer, contact the portable computer manufacturer to verify that it operates properly with the standby and hibernate features of Windows 2000. Also be aware that BIOS security can supercede Windows 2000 security insofar as it prevents Windows 2000 from taking control of the computer or various other devices.

Offline Files

Offline files use two types of security to ensure that offline files are secure. The first type of security protects the Offline Files folder, including the Offline Files database and the stored offline files, from unauthorized access. The second type of security ensures that offline files and folders behave like their network counterparts with regard to user rights.

Protecting the Offline Files Folder

Offline files are stored (cached) in the Offline Files folder. This folder is machine-centric not user-centric, which means that there is only one Offline Files folder for each computer and all offline files are stored in this folder. By default, this folder is protected by administrator-level permissions so that unauthorized users cannot view the contents. However, these permissions are only applied to the folder if the folder is located on a drive that is formatted to use NTFS. (A warning notifies you of this when you first cache an offline file on a FAT or FAT32 drive.)

Maintaining File and Folder Permissions

In addition to the protection afforded by the permissions on the actual Offline Files folder, offline files and folders retain the permissions set specifically on them when they were on the network share. This type of security is important if multiple users use a single computer. For example, if John creates a file on a network share, changes its permissions so that only he has access to the file, and then makes the file available offline, another user who tries to open the offline version of the file on John's computer is denied access just as if he or she tried to open the file directly on the network share.

This type of security is applied to offline files independent of the formatting of the user's hard disk. In other words, if you set permissions on a file on a network share that is formatted to use NTFS and you make that file available offline on a computer that has a FAT or FAT32 drive, the permissions carry over to the offline version of the file, even though the drive is formatted to use FAT or FAT32.

Note Offline files and folders do not retain encryption. If a user encrypts a file or folder on a network share using EFS and then makes the file or folder available offline, the offline version of the file or folder is not encrypted with EFS.

Also, you cannot encrypt the Offline Files folder by using EFS. It is a system folder, and system folders cannot be encrypted.

Folder Redirection and Configuring Roaming User Profiles

Roaming user profiles make it possible for users to use different computers within the corporate network and still retain a consistent desktop. With a roaming user profile, a user can log on to any computer that is running Windows 2000 within the user's domain. When the user logs on to a computer, all of the settings and documents the user stored on the server in the roaming user profile are copied to the local computer. Users can run applications, modify documents, and work on the computer as they would if the user profile existed on the local computer. When a user logs off, the user profile is copied to the server. When the user logs on to another computer, all of that user's profile information is then copied to the second computer.

Roaming user profiles depend on many of the IntelliMirror technologies to specify the information that is available for the user who is assigned a roaming user profile. You use roaming user profiles primarily to preserve the user's customizations because the My Documents folder is often redirected to another share.

You can use roaming user profiles together with Remote OS Installation and Software Installation and Maintenance when you replace a computer. If a computer system fails and loses its data, you can use Remote OS Installation to install Windows 2000 Professional, use Software Installation and Maintenance to restore applications, and use roaming user profiles to restore critical information. Because a network copy of the data exists, you can easily reestablish links to critical information.

You must configure roaming user profiles on the server; you cannot configure roaming user profiles on Windows 2000 Professional.

Folder redirection allows you to redirect the path of a local folder to a server location. Users can work with individual or shared documents on a secure server as if the folders were on the local drive.

You can not only redirect the My Documents folder, including the My Pictures subfolder, you can also redirect to a network location: the Desktop, Application Data, and **Start** menu folders. All of these folders are where the user is likely to store data. These folders are located in the Documents and Settings user profile folder on the local computer.

You can also combine folder redirection and roaming user profiles to increase performance for roaming users and mobile users. Besides the improved availability and backup benefits of having the data on the network, users also have performance gains with low-speed network connections and subsequent logon sessions. Because only some of their documents are copied, these users experience performance gains when their profiles are copied from the server. Not all of the data in the user profile is transferred to the desktop each time a user logs on—only the data that the user requires is transferred.

You must configure folder redirection on the server; you cannot set folder redirection on Windows 2000 Professional.

Hardware Issues Related to Portable Computers

Some hardware is not compatible with Windows 2000. This section identifies specific devices and device types that have known compatibility problems with Windows 2000 or that have conflicts and limitations when they are used with Windows 2000.

Infrared Devices

Windows 2000 supports the IrTran-P image exchange protocol, which allows a computer to receive images and files from a digital camera or other digital image capture device. However, Microsoft® ActiveSync® version 3.0, the desktop synchronization technology for Microsoft® Windows® CE–based handheld computers, disables the IrTran-P service. If you have to use ActiveSync 3.0 and the IrTran-P service, toggle between the two services to use them. You can toggle these services either by using **Wireless Link** in Control Panel or by using ActiveSync 3.0.

Note By default, the IrTran-P protocol is turned on (that is, you can download images and files from a digital camera to a computer).

▶ **To toggle IrTran-P protocol on and off**

1. From the **Start** menu, point to **Settings**, click **Control Panel**, and then double-click **Wireless Link**.

2. On the **Image Transfer** tab, select the **Use Wireless Link to transfer images from a digital camera to your computer** check box to turn on the IrTran-P protocol. Clear the check box to turn off the IrTran-P protocol.

▶ **To toggle ActiveSync 3.0 on and off**

1. Open ActiveSync 3.0.

2. On the **Tools** menu, click **Options**.

3. On the **Rules** tab, select the **Open ActiveSync when my mobile device connects** check box to turn on ActiveSync. Clear the check box to turn ActiveSync off.

Windows 2000 also supports the IrDial protocol, which gives infrared devices access to the Internet and other networks by using the Point-to-Point Protocol (PPP). Cellular telephones that use IrDial do not require special installation and configuration. For example, a special modem .inf file is not necessary. This is because IrDial network connections are managed entirely through the Network and Dial-up Connections folder. The following procedure describes how to configure an IrDial connection for a cellular telephone.

▶ **To configure a connection for IrDial**

1. Double-click the connection you want to configure.

2. Click **Properties**.

3. Under **Connect Using**, select **Infrared Modem Port**, and then click **OK**.

4. Enter your user name and your password, and then click **Dial**.

For more information about infrared device configuration and **Wireless Link** in Control Panel, see Windows 2000 Professional Help, or see "Hardware Management" in this book.

Video Devices

You can use the multiple monitor feature with a docked portable computer, but only if the docking station allows you to install Peripheral Component Interconnect (PCI) or Accelerated Graphics Port (AGP) display adapters. Also, the on-board display adapter (the one that is a part of the portable computer's motherboard) must be designated as the VGA display device. This is usually not a problem, although some BIOSs allow you to choose which display adapter you want to use as the VGA device. In this case you must designate the on-board display adapter.

Windows 2000 does not support hot undocking of portable computers while they are using multiple monitors. If a portable computer is using multiple monitors and you want to perform a hot undock, you must stop using all but one of the monitors and then undock. You can do this by detaching the secondary display before performing the hot undock.

▶ **To detach a secondary monitor**

1. From the **Start** menu, point to **Settings**, click **Control Panel**, and then double-click the **Display** icon.

2. In the **Display Properties** dialog box, click the **Settings** tab, double-click the secondary monitor, and then click **Attach**.

3. Click **Apply** to detach the monitor. The secondary monitor should turn off , leaving the primary monitor running.

After you have detached the secondary monitor, you can perform a hot undock.

C H A P T E R   1 1

Multimedia

Faster hardware, new input devices, and high-speed access to the World Wide Web have created a new generation of multimedia content and applications throughout the corporate world. Microsoft® Windows® 2000 Professional makes it easier for corporate managers and network administrators to use multimedia.

In This Chapter

Related Information in the Resource Kit

- For more information about telephony, videophones, or multimedia conferencing, see "Telephony and Conferencing" in this book.

- For more information about digital video cameras, see "Scanners and Cameras" in this book.

- For more information about support for Human Interface Devices (HIDs), IEEE 1394, multiple monitor support, and the Universal Serial Bus (USB), see "Hardware Support" in this book.

- For more information about deploying custom configurations using group and local policies, see "Introduction to Configuration and Management" in this book.

Quick Guide to Multimedia

Use this guide to quickly find the information you need about using multimedia in Windows 2000 Professional.

Review the new features and devices supported in Windows 2000.

Windows 2000 combines the best of Windows 98 multimedia features with the power of Windows NT 4.0.

- See "What's New" in this chapter.

Configure and optimize workstations for multimedia.

Learn how to deploy custom multimedia environment settings, such as system sounds and browser multimedia support. Learn technical details about audio and video hardware, such as DVD drives and the Accelerated Graphics Port (AGP).

- See "Optimizing Workstations for Multimedia" in this chapter.

Create and use multimedia.

Learn about different file formats and compression, as well as how to play CDs, DVDs, or multimedia on the Web.

- See "Using Multimedia Effectively" in this chapter.

Troubleshoot problems with multimedia.

Use this section to learn how to use Troubleshooters and the Sounds and Multimedia option in Control Panel to correct problems with multimedia applications and files.

- See "Troubleshooting Multimedia" in this chapter.

What's New

The latest in multimedia and graphics improvements in Windows 2000 Professional include the following:

Accelerated Graphics Port   An Accelerated Graphics Port (AGP) is a new type of expansion slot solely for video cards. Designed by Intel and supported by Windows 2000, AGP is a dedicated bus that provides fast, high-quality video and graphics performance.

Digital Video Disc   Digital Video Discs (DVDs) provide digital, optical disc storage for audio, video, and data. A single DVD can store more than two hours of high-quality audio and video, or up to 4.7 gigabytes (GB) of data. Windows 2000 supports the DVD-Video, DVD-ROM, and DVD-RAM formats for reading and writing to DVD (writing requires third-party software). Windows 2000 supports Universal Disk Format (UDF) version 1.5.

DirectX 7.0   Windows 2000 supports Microsoft® DirectX® version 7.0, which delivers improved multimedia performance, enhanced graphics and sound, and greater ease of use over previous releases. DirectX 7.0 also offers language support for the Microsoft® Visual Basic® development system.

Human Interface Devices   Windows 2000 supports the Human Interface Device (HID) firmware specification, a new standard for input and output devices such as drawing tablets, keyboards, universal serial bus (USB) speakers, and other devices designed to improve accessibility.

IEEE 1394   The Institute of Electrical and Electronics Engineers (IEEE) has developed a standard for ports that lets you connect high-speed digital devices, such as digital video cameras. An IEEE 1394 port, often referred to as a "FireWire," provides transmission speeds of approximately 98 megabits per second (Mbps) - 393 Mbps, whereas USB provides transmission speeds of approximately 1.5 Mbps - 12 Mbps.

Multiple Monitors   Windows 2000 lets you connect up to 10 monitors to a single computer to create an extended desktop. You can display a single document or application across multiple monitors, or use each monitor to display a different document or application. For example, you can edit an HTML page on one monitor while viewing the rendered Web page on another, or stretch a Microsoft® Excel spreadsheet across several monitors to view all of the columns or rows without scrolling.

OpenGL 1.2   Windows 2000 supports the latest version of Open Graphics Library (OpenGL), providing improved performance, higher visual 3-D quality, and improved capabilities for graphics applications and development.

Universal Serial Bus   Windows 2000 supports the universal serial bus (USB) to connect to a variety of auxiliary input devices, such as drawing tablets, pointing devices, speakers, and digital video cameras.

Windows Media Player   Microsoft® Windows Media™ Player plays both stored and streaming multimedia content from a variety of formats, including Advanced Streaming Format (ASF), Windows Media Audio, MP3, and audio-video interleaved (.avi) and waveform-audio (.wav) files.

Optimizing Workstations for Multimedia

In Windows 2000, network administrators can configure workstations to optimize the multimedia experience and use group and local policies to deploy custom desktop settings or profiles.

This section also presents configuration information and technical details about AGP and DVD device support in Windows 2000 Professional.

Configuring Sounds

You can assign sounds to system and program events, such as when Windows 2000 starts or when a user logs off. You can save different combinations of event and sound pairings as custom sound schemes. You can also specify the default devices to use for playing or recording sound.

Configuring Sound Events and Sound Schemes

Use the following procedures to configure event/sound pairings and save them as custom sound schemes.

For more information about recording sounds to use for sound events or in your custom sound schemes, see "Using Multimedia Effectively" later in this chapter.

For more information about configuring multimedia hardware devices and options, see "Configuring Multimedia Devices" later in this section.

▶ **To assign sounds to system and program events**

1. In Control Panel, double-click **Sounds and Multimedia**.

2. Click the **Sounds** tab, and then in the **Sound Events** box, click the system or program event to which you want to assign a sound.

3. In the **Name** box, click the sound that you want to play when the selected event occurs.

   If the sounds that you want to play aren't listed, click **Browse** to locate the sound files on your computer or network, or select a different sound scheme from the **Scheme** box.

You can save an entire set of sound and event pairings as a custom sound scheme.

▶ **To create a sound scheme**

1. In Control Panel, double-click **Sounds and Multimedia.**

2. Click the **Sounds** tab, and then in the **Sound Events** box, click the first system or program event to which you want to assign a sound.

3. In the **Name** box, click the sound that you want to play when the selected event occurs.

   If the sounds that you want to play aren't listed, click **Browse** to locate the sound files on your computer or network, or select a different sound scheme in the **Scheme** box.

4. Repeat steps 2 and 3 until you have completed assigning event and sound pairings. Click **Save As**, and then type a name for the new sound scheme.

Configuring Preferred Playback and Recording Devices

If a workstation has multiple audio playback and recording devices, you can specify the preferred devices to use when playing or recording sound. You can also specify the default playback or recording volume for that device.

For more information about configuring a preferred device for Musical Instrument Digital Interface (MIDI) music playback, see "Playing Multimedia" later in this chapter.

▶ **To configure a preferred sound playback or recording device**

1. In Control Panel, double-click **Sounds and Multimedia**.

2. Click the **Audio** tab, and then under **Sound Playback** or **Sound Recording**, click the preferred device that this workstation should use for playing (or recording) sound.

   ▪ To specify the default playback or recording level for the selected device, click **Volume**, and then set the volume controls.

   ▪ To specify advanced properties such as the hardware acceleration level, click **Advanced**, click the **Performance** tab, and then set the properties.

Configuring Audio Performance Options

Windows 2000 lets you optimize audio playback and recording by specifying the default hardware acceleration and sample rate conversion quality.

▶ **To configure audio performance options**

1. In Control Panel, double-click **Sounds and Multimedia**.

2. Click the **Audio** tab, and then under **Sound Playback** or **Sound Recording**, click **Advanced**.

3. Click the **Performance** tab, and then under **Audio playback** or **Audio recording**, select the hardware acceleration and sample rate conversion quality settings for the workstation.

For more information about hardware acceleration, sample rate conversion quality, and other advanced audio playback and recording options, see Windows 2000 Professional Help.

Configuring the Browser

By default, Microsoft® Internet Explorer plays sounds, animations, and videos from intranet or Internet sites. However, you can disable any of these options to ensure that pages load faster or to enhance a quiet work environment. You can also configure Internet Explorer to play a specific radio station by default every time the browser starts.

▶ **To enable or disable sounds, videos, and animation from Web pages**

1. On the desktop, right-click **Internet Explorer**, and then click **Properties**.

2. Click the **Advanced** tab, and then in the **Multimedia** section, select or clear the **Play animations**, **Play sounds**, or **Play videos** check boxes.

▶ **To set a default radio station to play every time Internet Explorer starts**

1. Start Internet Explorer, and then on the **Tools** menu, click **Options**.

2. Click the **Advanced** tab.

3. In the **Multimedia** section, select the **Always show Internet Explorer (5.0 or later) Radio toolbar** check box, and then click **OK**.

4. On the **View** menu, point to **Toolbars**, and then select **Radio**.

5. On the **Radio** toolbar, click **Radio Stations**, click **Radio Station Guide**, and then select the radio station that you want to play.

Configuring Multimedia Devices

Windows 2000 supports the latest multimedia hardware, such as the Accelerated Graphics Port (AGP), DVD devices, and digital video cameras. Windows 2000 also supports a wide range of Human Interface Devices (HIDs) and other peripherals connected through the universal serial bus (USB) or an IEEE 1394 port.

For information about HIDs, IEEE 1394, multiple monitors, or USB, see "Hardware Support" in this book.

Getting Information About Multimedia Devices or Drivers

New to Windows 2000, you can view a list of installed multimedia devices, determine driver versions, perform diagnostics and more, all from one common place: the **Hardware** tab of the **Sounds and Multimedia** Control Panel option. The **Devices** list shows the audio, video, and multimedia devices installed on the workstation. When you click a device in the **Devices** list, information about that device (such as the manufacturer and operational status) is displayed under **Device Properties**.

▶ **To configure and test specific multimedia devices**

1. In Control Panel, double-click **Sounds and Multimedia**.

2. Click the **Hardware** tab, and then under **Devices**, select a device.

   ▪ To determine the properties of the device, such as the driver versions in use, click **Properties**.

   ▪ To troubleshoot that device, click **Troubleshoot**.

Overview of the Accelerated Graphics Port

An AGP is a dedicated bus that delivers improved video and graphics performance over Peripheral Component Interconnect (PCI) buses.

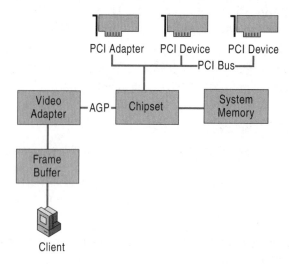

Figure 11.1   Accelerated Graphics Port Architecture

AGP has the following advantages over PCI video adapters:

- The peak bandwidth of AGP is up to four times higher than it is for PCI. AGP has higher sustained rates due to sideband addressing and split transactions.

- AGP is a dedicated bus, which reduces contention with other devices.

- AGP allows the CPU to write directly to shared system memory, which is much faster than writing directly to local memory.

- AGP can read textures from shared system memory while reading and writing other data from local memory, thereby improving performance of high-resolution 3-D scenes.

- AGP can run graphics data directly from system memory, instead of having to first move graphics data into video memory before running it.

To use an AGP video adapter, a computer must have an AGP graphics controller and a compatible chipset, such as the Pentium II LX or higher.

Overview of DVD Devices and Options

DVDs can read multiple, digitally stored data streams concurrently for playback of multimedia applications and full-length motion pictures.

Capacity of DVDs

The current capacity of a DVD starts at 4.7 gigabytes (GB). Both sides of the media can be readable and data can be layered on each side (for example, a gold layer of data can be placed above a silver layer). Lower laser power is used to read the top layer, and increased laser power allows the bottom layer to be read. Combining these two options increases the total possible capacity of a single DVD to 17 GB.

Uses of DVD Drives

A DVD drive has many uses. Although it was designed to display full-motion video, its massive storage capacity allows it to perform in other ways, including the following:

- DVD discs and devices provide cost-effective storage for large data files. In the future, DVD will allow for writable devices, opening a larger range of options.

- Because computers can achieve greater image quality than can conventional broadcast television sets, a DVD on a computer running Windows 2000 achieves even better quality than on standard DVD video player devices.

Windows 2000 supports the following DVD formats:

DVD-Video   A disc containing full-length motion pictures for playback on a computer's DVD-ROM drive, or on a home DVD-video player.

DVD-ROM   A disc containing a computer application or data that can be read by a DVD-ROM drive. A double-sided, double-layered DVD-ROM can hold up to 17 GB.

DVD-WO   A disc that supports one-time recording, similar to compact disc-recordable (CD-R). DVD-WO requires third-party software.

DVD-RAM   A disc that supports multiple recording capabilities, similar to magneto optical (MO) discs. DVD-RAM requires third-party software.

Hardware Requirements

DVD-video requires a DVD drive and a decoder (a hardware decoder card, a software decoder, or a combination of the two). DVD drives can also read data or play audio from standard CDs.

Full-motion video is stored on DVD in the Moving Pictures Experts Group (MPEG)-2 format. Because high rates of transfer are necessary to read and display full-screen, real-time data, your DVD system must have a decoder.

The following decoder cards and DVD drives are directly supported in Windows 2000:

- Toshiba Tecra 760, 780, 8000 or Portege 7010 or 7020, Toshiba Infinia
- Quadrant (Cinemaster) 1.2 and 3.0 (but not 2.0), Dell XPS series

A DVD-ready system must also include a video card capable of at least 800 x 600 x 16 bits per pixel (BPP) graphics display with Video Port Extensions (VPEs).

For more information about installing and configuring DVD devices, see Windows 2000 Professional Help.

Software Requirements

DVD technology includes several software components: MPEG-2, AC-3 (audio streaming), subpicture, two class drivers (a ROM class driver and Windows Driver Model [WDM]), UDF file system, Microsoft® DirectShow®, Microsoft® DirectDraw®, and a copyright-protection encryption key.

Figure 11.2 illustrates the Windows 2000 architecture for DVD support.

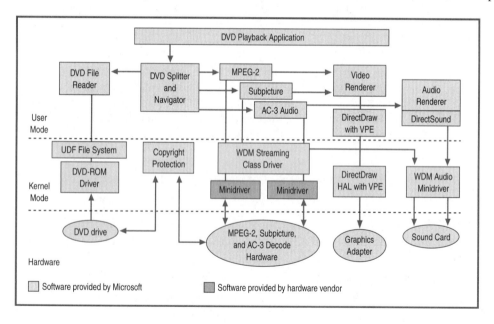

Figure 11.2   DVD Architecture

MPEG-2   MPEG-2 is a type of video compression that saves space by saving only the data that changes on the screen. Rather than storing a 640 x 480 x 12 (12-bit color depth) for each frame, only pixels that change are encoded.

Dolby Digital (AC-3)   AC-3 is a type of audio stream developed by Dolby Labs. It allows up to five separate audio channels (left and right front, left and right rear, and center) and a subwoofer channel.

Subpicture   DVDs contain a third data stream called *Subpicture*. The Subpicture stream delivers the subtitles and any other add-on data, such as system help or director's comments, which can be displayed while playing multimedia.

DVD-ROM Class Driver   Windows 2000 provides a DVD-ROM driver, which supports the DVD-ROM industry-defined command set known as the *Mt. Fuji specification*, including commands for copyright protection.

UDF File system   The file system on DVDs is the Universal Disk Format (UDF), which is a standard defined by the Optical Storage Technology Association (OSTA). UDF is compliant with the International Organization for Standardization (ISO)-13346 specification and is intended to succeed the CD-ROM File System (CDFS).

UDF supports long and Unicode file names; access control lists (ACLs); streams; reading and writing (not just mastering); and the ability to start up the computer. Windows 2000 supports UDF version 1.5, and future versions (including the UDF 2.0 draft recently approved by the OSTA) as they are released.

DirectShow   DirectShow provides support for a DVD Navigator and Splitter, proxy filters for video and audio streams, a video mixer, a video renderer, and an audio renderer. DVD movies have the equivalent of channels for the various data streams necessary to play a full-length movie. Data streams consist of not only the MPEG portion, but also digital audio, which can have Dolby surround sound and closed-captioning information. For a single video image, a DVD can provide up to eight languages and sound tracks and 32 subtitle tracks, and can support up to nine angles and eight ratings. DirectShow provides support for tracking these data streams and passing them to the proper codec.

DirectDraw HAL With VPE   Decoded video can become quite large. An MPEG-2 stream starts out at a rate of about 5–10 megabits per second (Mbps). After the stream is decoded, it can easily exceed 100 Mbps. Processing this amount of information in a continuous stream can overwhelm the PCI bus. So most of the decoding of the information is moved back to the hardware level by using dedicated MPEG decoder cards.

Support for these decoder cards is built in to DirectX, with DirectDraw's support for Video Port Extensions (VPEs). Video Port Extensions allow the MPEG stream to be written directly to the frame buffer memory of the video card from the MPEG decoder card. Data transfer occurs through a special cable that connects the video card and the decoder card at the hardware level. DirectDraw allows the data stream to be moved through the hardware layer while keeping track of such things as synchronization.

Copyright Protection Copyright protection for DVD is provided by encrypting key sectors on a disc, and then decrypting those sectors before decoding them. Microsoft provides support for both software and hardware decrypters by using a software module that enables authentication between the decoders and the DVD-ROM drives in a computer.

As part of the copyright protection scheme used for DVD, the DVD Consortium has set up eight worldwide regions, as shown in Table 11.1.

Table 11.1   DVD Regional Codes

Code	Country/Region
1	Canada, USA, United States Territories
2	Japan, Europe, South Africa, Middle East (including Egypt)
3	Southeast Asia, East Asia (including Hong Kong SAR)
4	Australia, New Zealand, Pacific Islands, Central America, Mexico, South America, Caribbean
5	Former Soviet Union, Indian Subcontinent, North Korea, Mongolia, Africa
6	China
7	(Reserved, currently unused)
8	Special international venues (including in-flight airlines, cruise ships, and so on)

Discs are playable on DVD devices in some or all of the regions according to regional codes set by the creators of the content. Microsoft provides software that responds to the regionalization codes as required by the DVD Consortium and as part of the decryption licenses.

For more information about configuring DVD devices, see Windows 2000 Professional Help.

Configuring Video Camera Devices and Options

Windows 2000 Professional supports the latest digital video cameras and other input devices attached through high-speed USB or IEEE 1394 ports.

For more information about installing and configuring digital video cameras, see "Scanners and Cameras" in this book.

Using Multimedia Effectively

Windows 2000 opens new possibilities for creating audio, video, and multimedia content and for using it more effectively on your intranet.

For more information about configuring audio, video, and multimedia devices and workstation defaults (such as audio playback level), see "Optimizing Workstations for Multimedia" earlier in this chapter.

Playing Multimedia

Windows 2000 supports a wide range of playback devices and multimedia sources, technologies, and file types. For example, you can play audio from a MIDI device, or play radio from a radio station that is broadcasting over the Web. You can play video or multimedia on DVD using DVD Player, or watch a streaming broadcast over the Web using Windows Media Player.

For more information about setting preferred devices for playing audio, see "Configuring Sounds" earlier in this chapter.

Playing CDs

You can play audio compact discs (CDs) on a CD-ROM drive or a DVD drive. (Standard CD-ROM drives cannot read DVD discs.) When you insert an audio CD into a CD drive, Windows 2000 Professional starts CD Player, as shown in Figure 11.3.

Figure 11.3   Windows 2000 CD Player

CD Player can automatically read play lists and album information when you insert a new CD. For more information about using CD Player or playing audio CDs, see Windows 2000 Professional Help.

As multimedia information is read from a CD-ROM drive, the multimedia subsystem determines what the data stream contains and then separates and routes the data accordingly.

To provide the best possible performance from CD-ROM drives, Windows 2000 includes the 32-bit CDFS for reading files from CD-ROM drives quickly and efficiently.

You can set the default volume for playing CDs or enable digital audio playback by using the following procedure.

▶ **To set CD playback options**

1. In Control Panel, double-click **Sounds and Multimedia**.

2. Click the **Hardware** tab. Under **Devices**, select the CD device, and then click **Properties**.

3. Set the volume and digital playback properties:

   ▪ Under **CD Player Volume**, set the default volume for playing audio on CD.

   ▪ Under **Digital CD Playback**, select the **Enable digital CD audio for this CD-ROM device** check box to send the playback from the CD Player to a digital device, such as USB speakers. Selecting this check box disables audio output from the headphone jack on the CD-ROM drive.

Playing Audio from MIDI Devices

Musical Instrument Digital Interface (MIDI) is a serial interface standard that allows for the connection of music synthesizers, musical instruments, and computers. The MIDI standard is based partly on hardware and partly on a description of the way in which music and sounds are encoded and communicated between MIDI devices.

MIDI is used as a development tool for musicians. Virtually all advanced music equipment supports MIDI, and MIDI offers a convenient way to precisely control the equipment.

Windows 2000 supports the General MIDI Specification to request particular instruments and sounds. This specification is an industry standard that defines how MIDI should be used, and it is supported by Microsoft and most MIDI sound-card manufacturers.

MIDI devices supported by Windows 2000 include the following:

▪ FM Synthesis

▪ Hardware Wavetable Synthesis

▪ Software Wavetable Synthesis

▪ MPU401

You can also download standard MIDI files from the Web and play them by using Windows Media Player.

▶ **To configure a preferred MIDI music playback device**

1. In Control Panel, double-click **Sounds and Multimedia**.

2. Click the **Audio** tab, and then under **MIDI Music Playback**, click the preferred device that this workstation should use for playing MIDI music.

   ▪ To specify the default playback or recording level for the selected device, click **Volume**, and then set the volume controls.

   ▪ To display information about the selected device, click **About**.

For more information about installing and configuring MIDI devices, see Windows 2000 Professional Help.

For more information about MIDI devices and the MIDI standard, see the Microsoft Knowledge Base link on the Web Resources page at: http://windows.microsoft.com/windows2000/reskit/webresources.

Playing DVDs

Windows 2000 DVD Player lets you play multimedia content and provides instant access to advanced DVD features, including movie chapters, optional closed-caption support, and choice of playback formats.

DVD Player is shown in Figure 11.4. It contains, from left to right, buttons for choosing a channel; VCR buttons for controlling playback; and menu navigation buttons for using the on-screen menu choices.

Figure 11.4   Windows 2000 DVD Player

DVD Player has only basic functionality and can be replaced by a third-party application. You can install or uninstall DVD Player from Control Panel by using the **Add/Remove Programs** option.

Note When DVD Player is started, it searches all local drives in alphabetical order, starting with C, for a folder called Video_TS. When this folder is located, the data file in it is loaded and video streaming begins. If this folder exists on a drive that comes before the preferred DVD drive, DVD Player tries to play the data in the first folder it finds.

For technical information about DVD devices and options, see "Configuring Multimedia Devices" earlier in this chapter.

Playing Multimedia From Files or the Web

You can play audio, video, or multimedia from files or from the World Wide Web as follows:

- Click a hyperlink to a source of streaming audio, video, or multimedia, such as Advanced Streaming Format (.ASF). Windows Media Player contacts the server and begins streaming the multimedia to play in real time. Because the multimedia is streamed rather than downloaded, no files are stored in your temporary Internet cache, conserving hard drive space.

- Download a nonstreaming audio, video, or multimedia file in a compatible format, such as MIDI, MP3, or .wav, and then play the file locally by using Windows Media Player.

- Use the Internet Explorer Radio toolbar to tune to a radio station that is broadcasting over the Internet.

▶ **To play a radio station over the Web or an intranet**

1. Start Internet Explorer On the **View** menu, point to **Toolbars**, and then click **Radio**.

2. On the **Radio** toolbar, click **Radio Stations**, and then select the radio station that you want to play.

If Windows Media Player is registered as the default media player, it automatically plays the streaming and nonstreaming file types shown in Table 11.2. When you open a file that has one of these extensions, either by double-clicking a file icon or clicking a link in a Web page, Windows Media Player starts.

Table 11.2   File Formats Supported by Windows Media Player

File Type	File Name Extensions
Microsoft Windows Media formats	asf, .asx, .wma, .wax
MPEG	.mpg, .mpeg, .m1v, .mp2, .mp3, .mpa, .mpe
MIDI	.mid
Apple QuickTime 1 & 2, Macintosh AIFF Resource	qt, .aif, .aifc, .aiff, .mov
UNIX formats	.au, .snd
Other formats	.avi, .wav

Windows Media Player works with the server to negotiate the most efficient allocation of bandwidth and deliver high-quality streaming media. The higher the bandwidth of your Internet connection, the higher the quality of the streaming multimedia. The best results are achieved by using high-speed connections, such as a T1 connection, or through a cable modem or digital subscriber line (DSL) line.

For more information on playing multimedia files using Windows Media Player, see the Microsoft Knowledge Base link on the Web Resources page at http://windows.microsoft.com/windows2000/reskit/webresources.

Creating Multimedia

Windows 2000 lets you record audio from a variety of input devices, and then save audio files in a variety of different formats, by using Windows Sound Recorder.

Recording Audio

If you have a microphone or other input device connected to your computer, you can record sound by using Sound Recorder as shown in Figure 11.5.

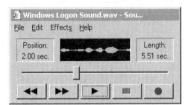

Figure 11.5   Windows 2000 Sound Recorder

Sound Recorder lets you add effects, such as echo; increase or decrease the speed or volume; and insert or mix other audio files. You can save audio files in one of three standard formats—CD quality, radio quality, or telephone quality—or you can choose a custom format to maximize compression or utilize a specific audio format (such as .au).

▶ **To select an audio format**

1. On the **Start** menu, point to **Programs**, point to **Accessories**, point to **Entertainment,** and then click **Sound Recorder**.

2. On the **File** menu, click **Properties**.

3. In the **Choose from** box, click **Recording formats**, and then click **Convert Now**.

4. In the **Format** box, click the format that you want, and then in the **Attributes** box, click the attributes (such as the sampling frequency or number of channels) available for the selected format.

For more information about audio formats and compression, see Windows Sound Recorder Help.

Mixing and Editing Audio

You can insert and combine audio files using Sound Recorder, as described in the previous section. You can mix audio input from different devices using the Windows 2000 Volume Control tool, as shown in Figure 11.6.

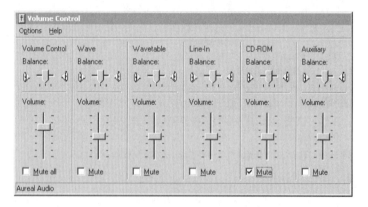

Figure 11.6 Windows 2000 Volume Control

The Volume Control tool lets you manage the different audio lines installed on a computer. An audio line consists of one or more channels of waveform-audio data coming from one origin or system resource. For example, a stereo audio line has two data channels, yet it is considered a single audio line. A mixer control can take on many different characteristics (such as controlling volume), depending on the characteristics of the associated audio line.

The number of lines that you can mix by using Volume Control depends on the number of audio source lines that the computer has, and whether they are using Volume Control for input or output.

Creating Dynamic Web Pages

You don't need multimedia authoring software to create multimedia presentations that can be broadcast over your intranet on a server computer running Windows 2000 Server. You can use HTML+Time and Extensible Markup Language (XML) multimedia elements to create interactive, multimedia Web pages.

For more information about using HTML+Time and XML to create dynamic Web pages that incorporate multimedia, see the Knowledge Base link on the Web Resources page at: http://windows.microsoft.com/windows2000 /reskit/webresources.

Using HTML+Time

You can use HTML+Time to add dynamic, interactive content to your Web pages. For example, you can create slide-show-style or multimedia presentations with synchronized text, images, audio, video, and streaming media. These presentations can be timed, interactive, or a combination of both.

HTML+Time provides an architecture that lets you extend and introduce new representations to the XML multimedia space, while taking advantage of the timing and synchronization attributes specified through HTML+Time. Custom representations can express data visualization concepts, three-dimensional models, interactive media animations, and audio and visual content.

To use HTML+Time, add HTML+Time attributes to existing HTML elements on a page. HTML+Time attributes let you specify when an element appears on a page, how long it remains displayed, and how the surrounding elements are affected.

The implementation of HTML+Time relies on Microsoft® DirectAnimation®, which enables time-varying, media-rich content and animations to be expressed in self-contained objects. These objects encapsulate both media and the behaviors that change properties of the media over time. For every HTML element associated with a timeline, you can access DirectAnimation behaviors by using scriptable properties.

Note   HTML+Time features are available as of Internet Explorer 5 and are not supported by earlier versions of the browser.

Creating Custom XML Multimedia Elements

You can also use persistent XML elements and attributes to add timing to your pages. HTML+Time supports a complete object model that extends the existing Dynamic HTML (DHTML) Document Object Model (DOM), allowing you to use properties, methods, and events to add interactivity to pages.

Custom XML multimedia elements make it easy to add multimedia to pages without having to write complex scripts. You can write one script implementing the new element and reuse it as necessary. You can further customize an element by creating properties, methods, and events associated with it.

Overview of DirectX 7.0

Windows 2000 supports DirectX version 7.0, which provides software with quick, transparent access to a broad range of peripherals, including graphics cards, audio adapters, and input devices, and delivers improved performance and enhanced graphics and sound over previous releases of DirectX.

DirectX 7.0 offers language support for the Microsoft® Visual Basic® development system. Improvements include improved 3-D graphics and sound, faster performance, easier development of 3-D sound algorithms, and easier creation of complex musical soundtracks.

DirectX provides a common set of instructions and components that accomplishes two things:

- Lets multimedia applications run on any Windows-based computer, regardless of the hardware, and ensures that products take full advantage of high-performance hardware capabilities to achieve the best possible performance.

- Provides tools to developers that simplify the creation and playback of multimedia content, while making it easier to integrate a wide range of multimedia elements.

Table 11.3 provides an overview of DirectX technologies.

Table 11.3   Overview of DirectX Technologies

DirectX Technology	Description
DirectDraw	Manipulates display modes, displays memory, and provides hardware overlay support and flipping surface support.
Microsoft® Direct3D® Immediate Mode	Enables a drawing interface for 3-D video display hardware.
Microsoft® DirectInput®	Enables support for input devices, such as joysticks, and input-output devices, such as force-feedback controllers.
Microsoft® DirectSound®	Captures, mixes and plays multiple audio signals, manages hardware voices, and enables 3-D sound effects in applications.
Microsoft® DirectPlay®	Connects games for multi-user play over the Internet, a modem link, or an intranet.
Microsoft® DirectMusic®	Creates interactive, variable music soundtracks that are streamed to DirectSound.
Microsoft® DirectShow®	Enables capture and playback of multimedia streams with Windows Media Player.

DirectX Diagnostic Tool

Windows 2000 includes the DirectX Diagnostic Tool, a utility for diagnosing problems with DirectX drivers and multimedia hardware. You can use the tool to obtain detailed system and driver information, as well as to test specific devices. The results can be reported to Microsoft Product Support Services to speed up diagnosing and resolving problems. To display the DirectX Diagnostic Tool, as shown in Figure 11.7, on the **Start** menu, click **Run**, and then type:

dxdiag

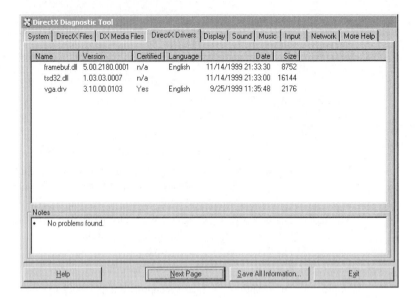

Figure 11.7   DirectX Diagnostic Tool

For more information about using the DirectX Diagnostic Tool, see the tool's Help.

DirectX Software Development Kit

The Microsoft® DirectX® 7.0 Software Development Kit (SDK) contains information for developers, including code samples, diagnostic tools, and sample applications. You can order the SDK on CD-ROM or download it from the DirectX Web site.

For more information about DirectX, or about downloading or ordering the DirectX SDK, see the Knowledge Base link on the Web Resources page at http://windows.microsoft.com/windows2000/reskit/webresources.

Troubleshooting Multimedia

Windows 2000 Professional Help includes intuitive, step-by-step Troubleshooters to help you diagnose problems with audio, video, or multimedia, including:

- Multimedia and Games Troubleshooter
- DirectX Troubleshooter
- Hardware Troubleshooter
- Display Troubleshooter
- Sound Troubleshooter

In Windows 2000 you can also troubleshoot multimedia devices using the following procedure.

▶   **To troubleshoot specific multimedia devices**

1. In Control Panel, double-click **Sounds and Multimedia**.

2. Click the **Hardware** tab, and then under **Devices**, select the device that you want to troubleshoot.

   - To determine the properties of the device, such as the driver version in use, click **Properties**.

   - To troubleshoot the device, click **Troubleshoot**.

Windows Media Player Help also contains a number of troubleshooting scenarios that can assist you in diagnosing and solving problems with playing audio, video, or multimedia.

Windows 2000 also includes the DirectX Diagnostic Tool, which you can use to obtain detailed system and driver information, as well as to test specific devices. The results can be reported to Microsoft Product Support Services to speed up diagnosing and resolving problems. To launch the DirectX Diagnostic Tool, on the **Start** menu, click **Run**, and then type:

dxdiag

Correcting Problems With Playing WAV Files

When a multimedia application is unable to play waveform-audio (WAV) files, it is usually caused by one or more of the following problems:

The Sound Card is Not Installed Properly

Make sure that the sound card settings do not conflict with other hardware. Use the **Add New Hardware** icon in Control Panel to detect your hardware and determine if you have any hardware for which the appropriate driver is not yet installed. Verify port and interrupt request (IRQ) settings.

Note If the sound card can play MIDI files, the card is probably properly installed.

The Volume Is Muted or Too Low

Check to see that the volume in **Volume Control** is not muted or set too low.

▶ **To check the volume**

- On the Windows 2000 task bar, right-click the **Volume Control** icon, and then on the shortcut menu click **Open Volume Controls**. Verify that the **Mute** check box for **Wave Balance** is not selected, or raise the volume slider for **Wave Balance** if it is too low.

Note If the **Volume Control** icon is not on the task bar, click **Start** and point to **Programs**, **Accessories**, and **Entertainment**, and then click **Volume Control**.

A Waveform-Audio Driver or Audio Codec Is Not Installed

If you are running Sound Recorder and there is no waveform-audio driver or audio codec installed, you receive an error message. In this case, make sure that the waveform-audio driver or audio codec is listed; to verify this, in Control Panel, double-click **Sounds and Multimedia** click the **Hardware** tab, and then examine the **Devices** list. Check with the manufacturer of the sound card to ensure you have the proper drivers. If you cannot find the correct audio codec or driver for the sound card in the list, connect to the manufacturer's Web site and download a current driver.

Correcting Problems With Playing MIDI Files

If a multimedia application cannot play MIDI files, it is generally the result of one or more of the following problems:

The Sound Card Is Not Installed Properly

Make sure that the sound card settings do not conflict with other hardware. Use the **Add New Hardware** option in Control Panel to detect your hardware, and determine whether you have any hardware for which the appropriate driver is not yet installed. Verify port and IRQ settings.

Note If the sound card can play WAV files, the card is probably properly installed.

The Volume Is Muted or Too Low

See "Correcting Problems With Playing WAV Files" earlier in this chapter.

A MIDI Driver Is Not Installed

If you are using Media Player and cannot play a MIDI file, there might be no MIDI driver installed. Try installing the driver that was provided with the hardware.

The Incorrect MIDI Output Device Is Selected

If the selected MIDI device is incorrect, you hear no MIDI output. Choose only External MIDI or MIDI OUT for an add-on MIDI card, or if an external MIDI device (for example, a synthesizer) is connected to the MIDI port of a sound card. For example, if you do not have an MPU-401 compatible synthesizer plugged into the MIDI port, make sure that MPU-401 is *not* selected as your default MIDI device.

▶ **To select a preferred MIDI output device**

1. In Control Panel, double-click **Sounds and Multimedia**.

2. Click the **Audio** tab.

3. Under **MIDI Music Playback**, in the **Preferred device** box, click the instrument that you want to use for MIDI music playback.

Correcting Problems With Playing a DVD Disc

Because DVD uses several pieces, the first step in troubleshooting a DVD issue is to determine which piece is not functioning correctly.

- Make sure that the DVD drive is displayed as functioning correctly in Device Manager.

- Make sure that Windows 2000 can read the data on the DVD by using Windows Explorer to see the contents of the DVD. There can be at least two folders: Video_TS and Audio_TS.

- If you are using a hardware decoder with your DVD drive, use Device Manager to verify that the decoder is working properly. To verify that your hardware decoder is supported by Windows 2000, check the Microsoft Windows Hardware Compatibility List link on the Web resources page at: http://windows.microsoft.com/windows2000/reskit/webresources.

- If you are using a software decoder with your DVD drive, use Device Manager to verify that the software decoder is working properly.

For additional help in troubleshooting problems playing DVDs, click the **Help** menu in DVD Player.

Correcting Problems With Playing an Audio CD

If a you are unable to hear an audio CD being played, it is commonly caused by one or more of the following problems:

The CD-ROM Drive Is Not Properly Installed

Place a data CD in the CD-ROM drive, and make that sure you can view the files in Windows Explorer or list the files at the command prompt. If you can, the CD-ROM drive is properly installed. If not, verify your disk drivers—Enhanced Small Device Interface (ESDI), small computer system interface (SCSI), Proprietary, MSCDEX—and then make the appropriate configuration changes so that you can view the files on a data CD.

The Volume Is Muted or Too Low

See "Correcting Problems With Playing WAV Files" earlier in this chapter.

Digital CD Audio for the CD-ROM Device Is Not Enabled

You can have Windows 2000 use digital playback of a CD audio for digital devices, such as USB speakers. This feature works only with certain CD-ROM devices. If you enable digital CD audio and encounter playback problems, such as audio skipping, or cutting in or out, your CD-ROM drive might not be compatible with digital CD audio.

▶ **To verify that the digital CD audio is enabled**

1. In Control Panel, double-click **Sounds and Multimedia.**

2. Click the **Hardware** tab. Under **Devices**, select the CD device, and then click **Properties**.

3. Under **Digital CD Playback**, select the **Enable digital CD audio for this CD-ROM device** check box to send the playback for the CD Player to a digital device, such as USB speakers. Selecting this check box disables audio output from the headphone jack on the CD-ROM drive.

The CD-ROM Is Not Connected to the Sound Card

If the CD-ROM is playing and there is no sound coming from the sound card speakers, try plugging the speakers or headphones into the audio jack on the face of the CD-ROM drive. If you hear sound, check the internal or external audio connection between the CD-ROM drive and the sound card.

Correcting Headphone Problems

If headphones are connected directly to a sound card, verify that the headphones are plugged into the line-out or audio-out connectors and not, for example, to the line-in or microphone-in connectors.

If the headphones are connected correctly and you still cannot hear audio, verify that the sound card is correctly installed by reviewing its properties.

▶ **To view sound card properties**

1. In Control Panel, double-click **Sounds and Multimedia.**

2. Click the **Hardware** tab. Under **Devices**, select your sound card or CD-ROM drive, and then click **Properties**.

3. Adjust the volume settings until you can hear output from the headphones.

Note If you have **Digital CD Playback** enabled for a CD-ROM drive, audio output from the headphone jack on the CD-ROM drive is disabled.

Additional Resources

- For more information about MIDI devices and the MIDI standard, see the Knowledge Base link on the Web Resources page at: http://windows.microsoft.com/windows2000/reskit/webresources.

- For more information about playing multimedia files using Windows Media Player, see the Knowledge Base link on the Web Resources page at: http://windows.microsoft.com/windows2000/reskit/webresources.

- For more information about using HTML+Time and XML to create dynamic Web pages that incorporate multimedia, see the Knowledge Base link on the Web Resources page at: http://windows.microsoft.com/windows2000 /reskit/webresources.

- For more information about DirectX, or on downloading or ordering the DirectX SDK, see the Knowledge Base link on the Web Resources page at: http://windows.microsoft.com/windows2000/reskit/webresources.

- For more information about DVD drives and hardware decoders supported by Windows 2000, see the Knowledge Base link on the Web Resources page at: http://windows.microsoft.com/windows2000/reskit/webresources.

C H A P T E R   1 2

Telephony and Conferencing

Microsoft® Windows® 2000 Professional provides support for telecommunications in a variety of environments, including analog modem, Integrated Services Digital Network (ISDN), Private Branch Exchange (PBX), and Internet Protocol (IP) telephony networks. Configuration details for telephony and conferencing support in Windows 2000 Professional are described in this chapter, including installation and configuration details for traditional and IP-based telephony. This chapter also provides technical details relating to modems and communications tools.

In This Chapter

Related Information in the Windows 2000 Professional Resource Kit

- For more information about installation and configuration of security certificates, see "Security" in this book.

- For more information about installing and troubleshooting hardware devices, see "Device Management" in this book.

Related Information in the Windows 2000 Server Resource Kit

- For more information about configuration of telephony and conferencing services on a computer running Microsoft® Windows® 2000 Server, see "Telephony Integration and Conferencing" in the *Microsoft® Windows® 2000 Server Resource Kit Internetworking Guide.*

- For more information about planning and deploying Group Policy on a Microsoft® Windows® 2000 domain, see "Group Policy" in the *Microsoft® Windows® 2000 Server Resource Kit Distributed Systems Guide.*

Quick Guide to Telephony and Conferencing

Use the quick guide to learn about new telephony and conferencing features and capabilities implemented in Windows 2000; to find technical information about the telephony architecture and standards; and to assist in performing installation, configuration, and troubleshooting tasks for modems, telephony interfaces, and conferencing applications.

Understand the purpose and function of telephony features and how they are implemented in your environment.

Windows 2000 Professional provides telephony and conferencing support to standard switched telephone lines through an analog modem; high-speed connectivity through ISDN modem and adapter support; telephony and conferencing support through a Private Branch Exchange (PBX); and point-to-point or multi-user conferencing support through a data network using IP telephony features. Understanding the details of the architecture of your telephony environment is needed to successfully configure your telephony client.

- See "Overview of Telephony and Conferencing" in this chapter.

Install and configure hardware drivers, TAPI support, and conferencing software.

In order to use telephony and conferencing features, a modem or network interface card must be physically installed on the computer, and drivers for the devices must be installed and configured. If a modem is to be used for telephony access, dialing locations must also be configured. For applications that use TAPI, service providers might require additional configuration, such as specification of H.323 gateways and proxies. In a client/server telephony environment, the telephony server must be specified by the **tcmsetup** command. If Microsoft® NetMeeting® 3.0 or Phone Dialer is used as the conferencing application for the Windows 2000 Professional–based computer, additional configuration of audio, video, and network features might be required.

- See "Configuring Telephony Conferencing" in this chapter.

Troubleshoot typical telephony and conferencing issues.

In order to troubleshoot telephony and conferencing issues, you must be able to determine the initial source of the problem. Use this section to determine and resolve the source of problems in modem configuration, TAPI and telephony client/server application support, and conferencing software, such as NetMeeting 3.0 and Phone Dialer.

- See "Troubleshooting" in this chapter.

Overview of Telephony and Conferencing

Windows 2000 Professional provides support for telephony and conferencing applications in a variety of telecommunications environments, including device support for modems, network adapters, and other telecommunications devices used by applications.

Function calls made by the Telephony Application Programming Interface, also known as Telephony API (TAPI), provide the foundation for the deployment of telephony and conferencing applications. TAPI abstracts the details of the underlying telecommunications network, allowing applications and devices to use a single command set. TAPI-enabled applications and devices can operate in a variety of telecommunications environments, including traditional analog switched networks, Private Branch Exchange (PBX) phone networks, and Integrated Services Digital Network (ISDN). TAPI further expands telecommunications support through the IP-based telephony, enabling telecommunications functions through a private intranet or over the Internet.

What's New

Telephony support has steadily evolved from its introduction in Microsoft® Windows® 95, which was the first operating system to bundle TAPI support. In Windows 2000 Professional, Microsoft builds upon this initial platform by making improvements in the following areas:

- TAPI 3.0
- NetMeeting 3.0
- Phone Dialer

TAPI 3.0

The Telephony Application Programming Interface, also known as Telephony API (TAPI), provides a common method for applications and devices to control the underlying communications network. TAPI was first released with Windows 95 as version 1.4, which provided a basic set of call control functions for analog modems and PBX systems, provided a common dialog for dialing rules, and introduced the Unimodem modem driver.

TAPI 2.0, released with Microsoft® Windows NT® 4.0, enhanced the basic features of TAPI 1.4. TAPI 2.0 was the first full 32-bit implementation of TAPI, providing improved processing capabilities. TAPI 2.0 introduced an expanded set of call control functions, designed specifically for call centers. TAPI 2.1 expanded the capabilities of TAPI 2.0 by adding support for client/server TAPI environments, and including support for both the Windows 95 and Microsoft® Windows® 98 platforms.

TAPI 3.0 provides the following enhancements to TAPI 2.1:

- Support for IP telephony
- Support for multiple-user conferencing
- Support for NDIS 5.0–compliant devices
- Unimodem 5 support
- Media stream control
- Compatibility with the Common Object Model (COM)

For more information about TAPI 3.0, see "Microsoft Support for CTI" later in this chapter.

NetMeeting 3.0

NetMeeting 3.0 is an application included with Windows 2000 Professional that provides conferencing capabilities within an intranet or to users on the Internet. NetMeeting provides point-to-point audio and video conferencing, data conferencing, text chat, whiteboard, and file transfer features. In addition, NetMeeting 3.0 provides the following improvements:

- Improved user interface facilitates use, and provides additional features, such as picture-in-picture and compact views.
- Remote Desktop Sharing allows viewing and control of a remote computer in a separate window.
- Enhanced security protects data transferred during text-chat, whiteboard, and shared program or data conferences.

For information about configuring NetMeeting, see "Configuring NetMeeting 3.0 later in this chapter.

Phone Dialer

Phone Dialer in Windows 2000 Professional is a TAPI-enabled application that can be used to place audio and video calls. The version of Phone Dialer supplied with Windows NT 4.0 was limited to voice calling onto private and public switched telephone networks. Windows 2000 Professional Phone Dialer additionally supports point-to-point and multipoint audio and video conferencing over a private intranet or over the Internet.

Comparison of Telephony Features

Table 12.1 lists the new features provided in Windows 2000, in comparison with Windows 98 and Windows NT 4.0.

Table 12.1   Comparison of Windows 2000 Telephony Features

Windows 2000 Telephony Feature	Windows 98	Windows NT 4.0
TAPI 3.0 Support		
TAPI version	2.1	2.0[1]
COM-compliant	no	no
Compatible with TAPI 1.4 or earlier	yes	yes
Support for H.323 conferencing	no	no
Support for multicast conferencing	no	no
Support for NDIS 4.0 WAN devices	yes	yes
Support for NDIS 5.0 WAN devices	no	no
Unimodem 5 support	no	no
Support for Media Service Providers	no	no
Phone Dialer		
Support for PSTN, PBX, ISDN dialing	yes	yes
Support for IP conferencing	no	no
Support for H.323 gateways, proxies	no	no
NetMeeting 3.0		
NetMeeting version	2.1[1]	2.1[2]
Support for H.323 conferencing	yes	yes
Program sharing	yes	yes
Remote desktop sharing	no	no
Security	no	no

[1] TAPI 2.1 provided in Windows NT Service Pack 3.0.

[2] NetMeeting 3.0 available as download from http://www.microsoft.com/windows /netmeeting/download/.

Telephony Environments

Windows 2000 Professional can provide telephony and conferencing services within a variety of communications environments. The following section describes the telephony environments that Windows 2000 Professional can operate in, including:

- Public Switched Telephone Network
- Integrated Services Digital Network
- Private Branch Exchange (PBX)
- Client/Server Telephony
- IP Telephony

Public Switched Telephone Network

Historically, most telephone connections in the world have been made through the public switched telephone network (PSTN). Most PSTN calls are transmitted digitally except while in the local loop, the part of the telephone network between the telephone and the telephone company's central switching office. Within this loop, speech from a telephone is usually transmitted in analog format.

Digital data from a computer must first be converted to analog by a modem. The modem is installed in the computer, connected to the computer by the serial port, or by a Universal Serial Bus connection. The data is converted at the receiving end by another modem, which changes the data from audio to its original data form.

Windows 2000 Professional provides basic telephony call support for modems using PSTN lines, such as dialing and call termination. Additionally, computer-based support is provided through the Hayes AT command set, as well as vendor-specific commands. Windows 2000 Professional provides device drivers for a number of internal and external analog modems, which can be automatically installed through Plug and Play, or manually installed using the Install New Device Wizard in Control Panel.

Integrated Services Digital Network

The need for high-speed telecommunications support within the existing telecommunications infrastructure has led to the development of new technologies, such as Integrated Services Digital Network (ISDN). ISDN is a digital phone service that is provided by regional and national phone companies, using existing copper telephone cabling.

To use ISDN, you need either an ISDN modem or an ISDN adapter. You might also need an NT-1 (the equivalent of the phone jack into which you plug your device) and an ISDN line from your telephone company.

ISDN modems are available in internal and external configurations. Internal ISDN modems, the more common of the two, are installed in the same manner as a network adapter card. External ISDN modems hook up to your computer through a serial port, just as regular modems do. Thus, because a serial port cannot exceed 115 kilobits per second (Kbps) (which is lower than the total effective bandwidth of the ISDN line), some throughput is lost if you are using the maximum ISDN bandwidth. An ISDN adapter, which operates at bus speed, provides the higher rate that ISDN needs. With most ISDN modems and adapters, you also need an NT-1. Some ISDN equipment comes with the NT-1 built in.

ISDN is typically supplied by the same company that supports the public switched telephone network. However, ISDN differs from analog telephone service in several ways, including:

- Data transfer rate
- Available channels per call
- Availability of service
- Cost of service
- Quality of connection

Data Transfer Rate

ISDN can provide data transfer rates of up to 128 Kbps. These speeds are slower than those of local area networks (LANs) supported by high-speed data communications technology, but faster than those of analog telephone lines. In addition to the difference in data transfer rates, ISDN calls can be established much faster than analog phone calls. While an analog modem can take up to a minute to set up a connection, you usually can start transmitting data in about two seconds with ISDN. Because ISDN is fully digital, the lengthy process of analog modems is not required.

Channels

PSTN provides a single channel, which can carry either voice or digital communications, but not both simultaneously. ISDN service is available in several configurations of multiple channels, each of which can support voice or digital communications. In addition to increasing data throughput, multiple channels eliminate the need for separate voice and data telephone lines.

Availability

PSTN is available throughout the United States.

Cost

The cost of ISDN hardware and service is higher than for PSTN modems and service.

Connection Quality

ISDN transmits data digitally and, as a result, is less susceptible to static and noise than analog transmissions. Analog modem connections must dedicate some bandwidth to error correction and retransmission. This overhead reduces the actual throughput. In contrast, an ISDN line can dedicate all its bandwidth to data transmission.

Private Branch Exchange

A Private Branch Exchange (PBX) is a private telephone switching system owned by a company or organization. The PBX is connected to a common group of PSTN lines from one or more of the telephone company's central switching offices to provide service to a number of individual phones, such as in a hotel, business, or government office. PBX solutions are available in a number of third-party hardware and software configurations, ranging from large dedicated switches, to server-based solutions, to internal cards that can be inserted into individual workstations. TAPI in Windows 2000 supports computer call control, voice mail, Caller ID, and other advanced features in conjunction with a PBX.

Client/Server Telephony

Within an organization, a computer running Windows NT Server can be configured as a telephony server, providing an interface between the PBX and TAPI-enabled workstations. For example, a LAN-based server might have multiple telephone-line connections to a local telephone switch or PBX. TAPI operations invoked at any associated client are forwarded over the LAN to the server. The server uses third-party call control between the server and the PBX to implement the client's call-control requests. Figure 12.1 shows an example of a PBX system configured with a telephony server.

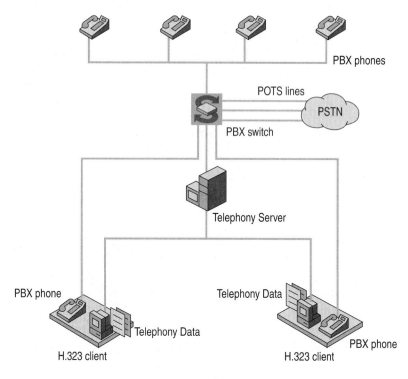

Figure 12.1   Client/Server Telephony

The server can be connected to the switch using a switch-to-host link. It is also possible for a PBX to be directly connected to the LAN on which the server and associated clients reside. Within these distributed configurations, different subconfigurations are possible, such as:

- To provide personal telephony to each desktop, the service provider can model the PBX line associated with the computer (on a desktop) as a single line device with one channel. Each client computer would have one line device available.

- Each third-party station can be modeled as a separate line device to allow applications to control calls on other stations. (In a PBX, a station is anything to which a wire leads from the PBX.) This enables the application to control calls on other stations. This solution requires that the application open each line it wants to manipulate or monitor.

Windows 2000 Professional workstations with TAPI support specify the telephony server in their configuration using the **tcmsetup** command. After it is configured, users at the Windows 2000 Professional computer can perform basic and advanced call control functions, such as placing, answering and terminating calls to the PBX or PSTN through the computer. Advanced functions, such as computer-telephony integration (CTI) functions, can be enabled through the installation of third-party telephony services that conform to TAPI 3.0 standards.

IP Telephony

IP telephony and conferencing technologies are built around simple, core concepts: A personal computer (or other device) is used to capture audio and optionally, video signals from the user (for example, by using a microphone attached to a sound card, and a video camera connected to a video capture device). This information is compressed and sent to the intended receivers over the local area network (LAN) or the Internet. At the receiving end, the signals are restored to their original form and played back for the recipient. Audio can be rendered by using speakers attached to a sound card and video by creating a window on the display of the computer.

IP telephony integrates audio and video stream control with legacy telephony functions. IP telephony in Windows 2000 is supported through the H.323 protocol and IP multicast conferencing. H.323 provides point-to-point audio and video conferencing. Support for multiple-user conferencing is provided through IP multicast conferencing. IP telephony systems can be integrated with the public telephone system through an IP-PSTN gateway, allowing users to place telephone calls from an enabled computer. Users can place audio and video calls with external users through the Internet with an H.323 proxy, allowing administrators to control host access. This IP telephony infrastructure is described in the following sections.

H.323 Protocol

H.323 is an International Telecommunication Union–Telecommunications (ITU–T) protocol that is used to provide voice and video services over data networks. At the most basic level, H.323 allows users to make point-to-point audio and video phone calls over an intranet. H.323 also supports voice-only calls to be made to conventional phones through a IP-PSTN gateway, and Internet audio-video calls to be made through a proxy server.

IP-PSTN Gateway

IP telephony permits the integration of data networks and information with the traditional public switched telephone network (PSTN) through the configuration of IP-PSTN gateways. IP-PSTN gateways are configured as part of an enterprise's IP telephony network. Client support of IP-PSTN gateways is provided through the H.323 protocol.

Figure 12.2 shows an example of a PSTN gateway.

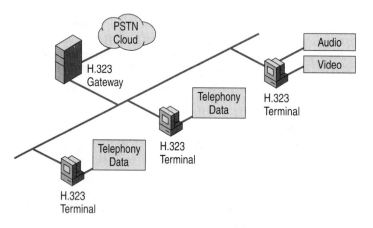

Figure 12.2   A PSTN Gateway

For example, a call from an IP telephony client to a conventional telephone would be routed on the IP network to the IP-PSTN gateway, which would translate H.323 signaling to conventional telephone signaling and route the call over the conventional telephone network to its destination.

H.323 Proxy

In enterprises where firewalls have been implemented for IP security, but IP telephony through the H.323 protocol is desired, an H.323 proxy can be used. Any IP telephony client needing to connect to users outside the firewall must specify the name or IP address of the H.323 proxy server.

IP Multicast Conferencing

The Multicast Conferencing Service Providers shipped with TAPI 3.0 provide support for IP multicast-based audio and video conferencing between multiple participants. IP multicasts support multi-user conferences using a single connection instead of multiple connections, which conserves network bandwidth.

TAPI 3.0 provides additional interfaces that TAPI-aware applications can use to access directory services, such as the Windows 2000 Site Server ILS Service.

All routers between the Windows 2000 Professional client and other conferencing participants must support IP multicasting. Windows 2000 Server provides a multicast-enabled DHCP server that can be used to allocate a unique IP address for the duration of the conference.

For more information about the installation and configuration of the Windows 2000 Site Server ILS Service, see "Telephony Integration and Conferencing" in the *Internetworking Guide*.

Microsoft Support for CTI

Support for computer-telephony integration (CTI) is built into Windows 2000 Professional. CTI support is provided in Windows 2000 Professional in the following areas:

- TAPI 3.0
- Service Providers
- NetMeeting 3.0
- Phone Dialer application

TAPI 3.0

The Telephony Application Programming Interface, also known as Telephony API (TAPI), is a set of Microsoft® Win32® function calls and Microsoft Common Object Model (COM) interfaces used by telephony applications. These function calls are processed internally by TAPI, and result in calls to service providers, which control the telephony and media hardware needed to provide the function required by the telephony application. Windows 2000 includes TAPI 3.0 and provides backward compatibility with TAPI 2.1, which was included with earlier versions of Windows. Figure 12.3 shows the architecture of TAPI.

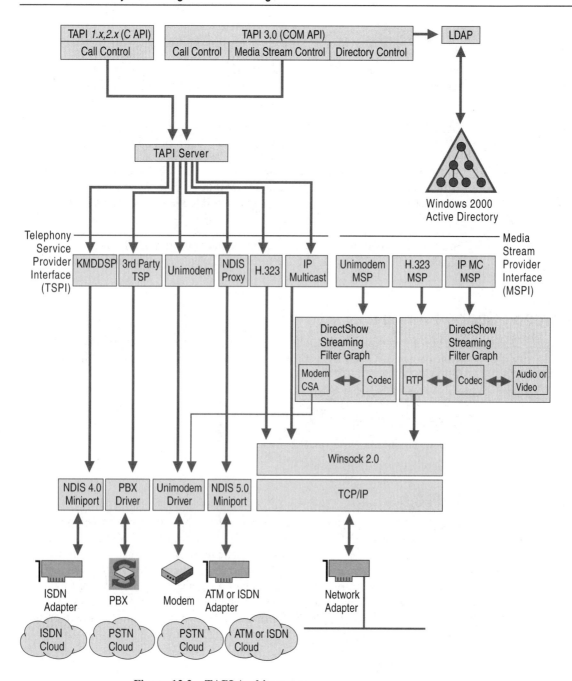

Figure 12.3   TAPI Architecture

TAPI 3.0 provides a standard method for communications applications to control telephony functions for data, fax, and voice calls. TAPI manages all signaling between a computer and a telephone network, including basic functions such as dialing, answering, and hanging up a call. It also supports supplemental services such as hold, transfer, conference, and call park, found in PBX, ISDN, and other telephone systems. The support of supplemental services varies by service provider.

In addition to support for conventional telephony, TAPI 3.0 provides support for IP telephony; that is, telecommunications through IP-based networks. TAPI 3.0 supports user-to-user and multiparty audio and video conferencing through the H.323 and IP multicast. TAPI 3.0 interfaces with user directories, such as the Site Server ILS Service, to associate user and conference objects with call information, such as IP address and computer name.

Service Providers

TAPI 3.0 supports two classes of service providers: telephony and media. Telephony Service Providers (TSPs) provide implementation of telephony signaling and connection control features, and Media Service Providers (MSPs) provide access to and control the media content associated with those connections, such as the audio and video streams of a videoconference. MSPs use the DirectShow API for efficient control and manipulation of streaming media.

For more information about Media Service Providers in TAPI, see "Telephony Integration and Conferencing" in the *Internetworking Guide.*

A Telephony Service Provider (TSP) is a dynamic-link library (DLL) that supports communications over a telephone network to one or more specific hardware devices through a set of exported service functions. The service provider responds to telephony requests sent by TAPI, and completes the basic tasks necessary to communicate over the telephone network. In this way, the service provider, in conjunction with TAPI, shields applications from the service-dependent and technology-dependent details of the telephone network communication.

The installation tool for a service provider registers the software with TAPI and associates that service provider with the hardware devices it supports. Multiple service providers can share the same device: for example, the H.323 TSP and Multicast Conferencing TSP can both use the name network interface card. Existing applications can be associated with new telephony devices, or the function of existing devices can be extended through the development and implementation of new service providers.

Table 12.2 lists the telephony and media service providers included with Windows 2000 Professional.

Table 12.2   Service Providers in Windows 2000

Service Provider	Function
H.323 TAPI Service Provider H.323 Media Service Provider	Provide voice and video services over data networks using the H.323 protocol. Support calling conventional phones through IP-PSTN gateways and Internet audio/video calls.
Multicast Conference TAPI Service Provider Multicast Conference Media Service Provider	Provides multiple-user conference support over internal intranets and the Internet.
NDIS Proxy Service Provider	Permits TAPI applications to access WAN devices, such as ISDN modems and ATM devices, using a standard NDIS 5.0 interface.
TAPI Kernel-Mode Service Provider	Provides TAPI support for NDIS 4 WAN drivers.
Unimodem 5 Service Provider	Provides device abstraction and TAPI support for a wide variety of modem devices.

Additional service providers can be obtained through third-party vendors to enable the use of their hardware with existing telephony applications, such as a PBX hardware solution.

Note To install TSPs and MSPs from third-party vendors, follow the instructions provided by the vendor.

NetMeeting 3.0

Windows 2000 Professional includes the NetMeeting 3.0 application. NetMeeting uses the NetMeeting Application Programming Interface (API) to provide telephony functions to the application. NetMeeting supports the H.323 protocol, providing point-to-point audio and video conferencing features. NetMeeting can be used separately from, or in conjunction with, TAPI 3.0 applications such as Phone Dialer. However, the two environments must be separately configured.

In addition to point-to-point audio and video call support, NetMeeting provides conferencing support. NetMeeting provides the following features for audio, video, and data conferencing:

- Multi-user whiteboard
- Text-based chat
- Program sharing
- Remote desktop sharing
- File transfer

Phone Dialer

Windows 2000 also ships with the Phone Dialer, which is a TAPI application. This can be used for basic telephony functions as well as audio and video conferencing services.

The Phone Dialer makes TAPI function calls to utilize Microsoft's Telephony Service Providers, including the H.323 and the Multicast Conference Service Providers. The Phone Dialer can also be used with Telephony Service Providers supplied by other vendors.

Configuring Telephony and Conferencing

IP telephony support is also installed during Windows 2000 Professional Setup, including the TAPI 3.0 programming interface and all telephony and media service providers. During installation, Windows 2000 Professional automatically detects, installs, and configures most Plug and Play–compliant modems, adapter cards, and other telephony devices. For devices that are not automatically configured, use the Add/Remove Hardware Wizard to install and configure legacy and Plug and Play devices that require installation information, such as the driver location. Support for telephony devices added after initial Windows 2000 Professional installation can also be provided in this manner.

For a list of supported telecommunications devices, see the Hardware Compatibility List link on the Web Resources page at http://windows.microsoft.com/windows2000/reskit/webresources.

If Windows 2000 Professional is installed over a previous version of Windows that included telephony services (such as Windows 95, Windows 98, or Windows NT 4.0), any previous versions of the TAPI programming interface are automatically upgraded to TAPI 3.0. TAPI 3.0 provides backward compatibility for TAPI 1.4 and TAPI 2.1. If provided in Windows 2000 Professional, device drivers for telecommunications hardware are also upgraded during this migration.

Configuring Modems

A modem is a communications tool that enables a computer to transmit information over a standard telephone line. With Windows 2000 Professional, you can install a modem in one of three ways:

- Plugging in your Plug and Play modem.
- Using Phone and Modem Options in Control Panel.
- Adding a modem through Add/Remove Hardware in Control Panel.

In each of these cases, the Install New Modem Wizard appears and asks if you want Windows 2000 Professional to automatically detect the modem or if you want to manually select a modem from the list of known manufacturers and modem models. If you choose the detection option, the wizard detects and then queries the modem to configure it. If it cannot detect the modem, it prompts you to select one.

After the modem has been selected, you can, if necessary, adjust its properties, such as the volume for the modem speaker, the time to wait for the remote computer to answer the call, and the maximum speed. These adjustments are made from **Phone and Modem Options** in Control Panel.

Depending on the type of modem you have, installing and configuring it might vary slightly as follows:

- If the modem supports Plug and Play, make sure it is configured to respond as a Plug and Play device, rather than manually configure resource settings. This is normally performed through a configuration application provided with the modem. Plug and Play is the preferred method of device enumeration in Windows 2000, and ensures correct configuration of the modem and its resources.

- If you install an internal legacy (non–Plug and Play) modem adapter, its built-in COM port must be configured by using the Add New Hardware wizard before it is installed by using **Phone and Modem Options** in Control Panel. In most cases, the Install New Modem Wizard does this automatically for you.

- If you are using Windows 2000 Professional PC Card (Personal Computer Memory Card International Association [PCMCIA]) drivers, Windows 2000 Professional detects and configures PC Card modem cards automatically when they are first inserted.

Note Before you install a modem, see "Modems" in the Windows 2000 Professional Readme.txt.

▶ **To install a modem by using Phone and Modem Options in Control Panel**

1. In Control Panel, double-click **Phone and Modem Options**.

2. If no modem is currently installed on your computer, the Install New Modem Wizard starts automatically and leads you through the steps for installing a modem.

   –Or–

   If you are installing an additional modem, select the **Modem** tab, then click **Add** to start the Install New Modem Wizard.

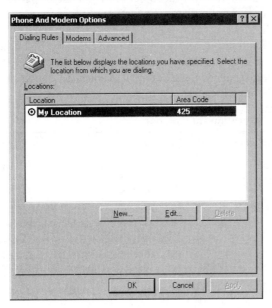

In most cases, it is best to let the Install New Modem Wizard detect the modem for you. If it cannot detect the exact manufacturer and model, the wizard picks a standard configuration that is usually compatible; your modem still functions at its maximum speed and according to factory default settings. A few advanced features, such as enabling and disabling compression, error control, and flow control, might be disabled.

Note This procedure is for both internal and external modems. PC Card modems automatically install when inserted.

For information about installing a modem if your modem is not detected or listed, or about finding a better match than a standard modem type, see "Troubleshooting Modems" later in this chapter.

Windows 2000 Professional automatically makes COM port assignments to communications ports, internal modem adapters, and PC Card modem cards according to their base I/O port addresses. For more information, see "Device Management" in this book.

Defining a Location

A location is information that the Dialing Properties tool uses to analyze telephone numbers in international format and to determine the correct sequence of numbers to be dialed. It need not correspond to a particular geographic location, but it usually does. For example, a user on a portable computer might require a dialing prefix of "9 to dial an external number from an office location, and require a dialing prefix of "*69 to disable a call waiting feature when placing calls from home. A location would be created for each dialing prefix and selected when dialing from each environment. Table 12.3 shows the information associated with a location.

Table 12.3   Location Information

Location Property	Description
Location name	A recognizable name that identifies the location.
Country/Region	The country or region for the dialing location.
Area or city code	The calling prefix for the area code
Dialing rules	Specifies what, if any, prefixes need to be dialed prior to dialing the area code and number, whether call waiting needs to be enabled or disabled, and if tone or pulse dialing method needs to be used to place the call.
Area code rules	Determines how phone numbers are dialed from the area code used in the current location to other area codes, or within the area code. For example, if your current location is area code 425, and all calls to area code 206 require the 206 area code to be omitted, then you can create a rule to enforce this whenever phone numbers are passed to TAPI.
Calling card information	Specifies the calling card type, account number, and personal identification number (PIN) to be used for the location.

The first time you set up a modem, the Install New Modem Wizard prompts you for the default dialing information about the location you usually call from (**My Location**), including your area code and country/region code. This information is stored in Dialing Properties, a communications tool that is accessible from all communications applications created for Windows 2000 Professional, and in Phone and Modems Options in Control Panel.

▶ **To set default dialing location information**

- Run the Install New Modem Wizard, and then type the area code and country/region code information in the **My Location** dialog box.

  –Or–

  Open Phone and Modem Options in the Control Panel. If the modem was configured previously, the **My Location** dialog box is displayed. Type the dialing information when prompted.

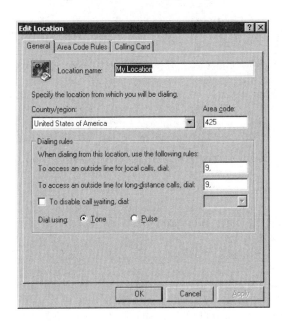

After you install the modem, more specific location information, such as calling card numbers or rules for dialing outside your local area code, can be entered by editing the fields in the **Edit Location** dialog box. Additional dialing rules can also be created from this location. For more information about configuring dialing properties, see Windows 2000 Help.

Setting Modem Properties

In the Phone and Modem Options in Control Panel, you can globally change default modem settings for all communications applications and tools created for Windows 2000 Professional. For example, if you do not want to listen to the modem speaker, you can turn it off for all tools and applications that use that modem. Alternatively, you can adjust these settings within each application.

Note For Microsoft® Windows® 3.1–based or MS-DOS®-based applications, you need to configure the modem settings within each application.

▶ **To view general properties for a modem**

1. In Control Panel, double-click **Phone and Modem Options**.

2. Select the **Modem** tab.

3. Select the desired modem or device, and then click **Properties**.

Modem settings are listed on the **General**, **Diagnostics**, and **Advanced** tabs. Table 12.4 describes the **General** settings.

Table 12.4   General Settings

Setting	Description
Port	A port is either a COM port or an LPT port to which an external modem is attached, or a COM port name that identifies an internal or PCMCIA modem. Windows 2000 Professional automatically assigns a port name (COM1, COM2, COM3, or COM4) to any device it detects. Usually, the name is adjusted only if you move an external modem from one COM port to another. For PCMCIA modem cards, the port cannot be changed.
Speaker volume	This option sets the volume for the telephone speaker, which broadcasts the dial tone, modem connection, and voices, if applicable, on the other end. To change the volume, move the slider bar to the right or left.
Maximum speed	This is the speed at which Windows 2000 Professional communicates with the modem. It is limited by the CPU speed of the computer and the speed supported by the communications port. Windows 2000 Professional selects a conservative default speed so that slower computers do not lose data during transfers.
	Set the speed lower if the faster rate causes data errors. Set it higher for faster performance. For example, 57,600 might work better than the Windows 2000 Professional default setting of 38,400 for v.32bis (14,400 bps) modems on fast computers. If applications report data errors, set a lower speed (for example, change it from 38,400 to 19,200 for v.32bis modems).
Dial control	Clear the **Wait for dial tone before dialing** option if you are making calls from a country or region other than where your modem was purchased and your modem fails to properly detect the dial tone.

Tip If you have a slower computer and an external modem, you can install a 16550A Universal Asynchronous Receiver/Transmitter (UART)–based COM port adapter to increase speeds. Some internal modems have an integrated 16550A UART adapter.

The **Diagnostics** tab provides hardware information that can be used in hardware configuration and problem determination. Table 12.5 describes the **Diagnostics** settings.

Table 12.5   Diagnostics Settings

Setting	Description
Modem Information	Displays manufacturer-specific identifying information for the modem.
Query Modem	Click the **Query Modem** button to display your modem's responses to standard AT commands sent to it. This information can be used to assist in diagnosis.
Append to Log	Windows 2000 Professional records commands and responses to and from the modem in the Modemlog.txt file in the Windows folder. If the box is not checked, Windows 2000 Professional erases the old log and records a new log at the beginning of each call. If the box is checked, Windows 2000 Professional appends new call logs to this file.
View Log	The modem log is a powerful tool for diagnosing problems, particularly with connection problems. However, the interpretation of the contents of the file requires modem documentation, technical support, and/or experience with modems. The problems diagnosed might be in the local modem, its configuration, the telephone system, the remote modem (for example, the Internet Service Provider [ISP]), or in some combination.

The **Advanced** tab of the modem dialog box allows you to override the hardware and connection settings that were configured for the modem and serial port. The **Extra initialization commands** entry box allows you to append to the standard initialization commands used to set up the modem at the start of a communications session. These can be standard AT-type commands, or commands specific to your modem or communications device. Refer to the manufacturer's documentation for a description of available commands.

The **Advanced Port Settings** button allows you to change the default configuration for the communications port used by the current modem. Table 12.6 describes the **Advanced Port** settings.

Table 12.6   Advanced Port Settings

Setting	Description
Use FIFO buffer	A serial port containing a universal asynchronous receiver/transmitter (UART) chipset allows inbound and outbound information to be stored in associated first-in, first-out (FIFO) buffers until it can be received by the computer or dispatched by the modem.
	The sizes of the inbound and outbound buffers can be enabled by checking the **Use FIFO buffers (requires 16550 compatible UART)** option. The sizes of the inbound (**Receive buffer**) and outbound (**Transmit buffer**) can be modified by using the slider bars.
	Increasing the buffer sizes in 16550 UART-compatible serial ports can improve performance in high-speed modems. However, if you experience data loss or overrun errors, try lowering the buffer sizes or disabling the FIFO buffers altogether.
COM Port Number	If Windows 2000 Professional autodetected your modem, it automatically assigned it to an available serial communications (COM) port. If you want to force the COM port assignment, select the available port here. For example, if you have three serial devices that are never used simultaneously, you can change the port settings and have all three devices share the same serial port.

Click the **Change Default Preferences** button to modify the default settings for call handling and data connection preferences. Table 12.7 describes the available settings.

Table 12.7   General Default Preferences

Setting	Description
Disconnect a call	Change the number of minutes listed in the **Disconnect a call if idle for more than x minutes** field if there is no activity on the line; for example, increase the number if you want to stay connected to a computer bulletin board even though there is no activity.
Cancel a call	Change the number of seconds listed in the **Cancel a call if not connected within x secs** field if it takes a long time to make a connection; for example, this might occur when you are making an international call and there are long delays before the call is connected.
Port speed	Determines the speed of the flow of data from the modem to the serial port. The speed is normally set correctly during modem installation; however, some modems can transfer data at a rate faster than the 115.2 Kbps supported by the standard serial ports for most computers. See your manufacturer's documentation for more details.

(continued)

Table 12.7   General Default Preferences *(continued)*

Setting	Description
Data Protocol	Enables error correction, allowing your modem to negotiate the error correction that is to be used for a communications session with another modem. Available error correction protocols are **V.42, MNP4, MNP3, MNP2** or **None**.
Compression	Select **Enable** to allow hardware-based compression. Compression boosts transmission speeds by compressing data between the modems. This feature is available on most modems. When it is enabled, modems sometimes have trouble connecting. If this occurs, select **Disable** and try again. Using modem compression can sometimes reduce performance if the data being sent is already compressed by the application.
Flow control	Select **Hardware** for all external modems to avoid loss of data. If your modem cable has RTS and CTS wires connected, you can use hardware flow control; otherwise, select **None** to use software flow control.

Default hardware settings can be changed by selecting the **Advanced** tab of the **Default Preferences** dialog box.

With hardware settings, connection settings usually correspond to what the computer on the other end is using. Therefore, do not change connection settings by using Phone and Modem Options in Control Panel. Rather, use a specific tool or application, such as HyperTerminal, to change these settings connection by connection.

Preferences include Data bits, Parity, and Stop bits. For information about these values, see Windows 2000 Help.

If you have installed an external ISDN modem, an additional **ISDN** tab is displayed. The ISDN settings must be configured before the modem can be used.

Configuring ISDN Support

Windows 2000 Professional provides built-in support for ISDN. Before configuring ISDN on a computer running Windows 2000 Professional, you need the following:

- Installed internal or external ISDN adapter.
- ISDN telephone line service at the location where you use dial-up networking to connect to the Internet.
- ISDN telephone line service at the remote location to which you want to connect, usually either your Internet Service Provider (ISP) or a remote access server.

If your ISDN adapter is Plug and Play–compatible, Windows 2000 Professional automatically installs the required support. If the ISDN adapter is not automatically installed, use the following procedure to install the device support.

▶ **To install your ISDN device**

1. In Control Panel, open **Add/Remove Hardware**.

2. In the Add/Remove Hardware Wizard, click **Next**.

3. Select **Add/Troubleshoot a device**, and then click **Next**.

4. If Windows 2000 Professional did not automatically detect the ISDN adapter, select **Add a new device**, and then click **Next**.

5. If you want Windows 2000 Professional to attempt to find the ISDN adapter, select **Yes, search for new hardware**.

    - Or -

    If you wish to manually select the ISDN adapter, select **No, I will select it from a list**, and follow the instructions.

After the device support for the ISDN adapter has been installed, you are prompted to provide the information necessary to configure ISDN support. Table 12.8 shows the information required in order to configure ISDN in Windows 2000 Professional.

Table 12.8   ISDN Configuration Information

Option	Description
Switch type	Most ISDN hardware adapters need to know what type of switch they are connected to. The switch type simply refers to the brand of equipment and software revision level that the telephone company uses to provide you with ISDN service. The switch types listed are **ESS5 (AT&T)**, **National ISDN1**, and **Northern Telecom DMS 1000**.
Service Profile Identifier (SPID)	The SPID usually consists of the telephone number with some additional digits added at the beginning and end. The SPID helps the switch understand what kind of equipment is attached to the line. If multiple devices are attached, it helps route calls to the appropriate device on the line. The SPID is generally used only within the United States and Canada.
Telephone number	In some cases, each B channel on an ISDN line has its own number, while in other cases both B channels share a single telephone number. Your telephone company tells you how many numbers are in your ISDN line. Separate numbers might be useful if you plan to take incoming calls on your ISDN line.

You can change the ISDN configuration information by performing the following steps.

▶ **To configure an ISDN adapter**

1. In Control Panel, open **System**, and then select the **Hardware** tab.

2. Click **Device Manager**.

3. Right-click the ISDN device whose settings you want to change, and select **Properties**.

4. Select the **ISDN** tab.

   Click the drop-down list box to change the switch type. To change the telephone number and SPID information, click **Configure**.

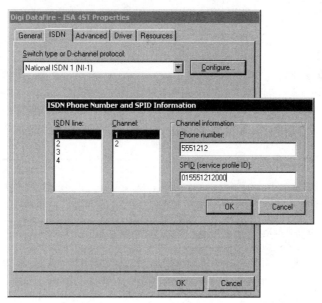

Configuring Client/Server Telephony Support

Windows 2000 Professional supports access and control of telephony features on a PBX through a telephony server. The following section describes the configuration of a Windows 2000 Professional client to access the telephony server.

The Tcmsetup tool allows you to specify the servers responsible for providing the telephony services used by the network.

▶ **To identify telephony servers to a TAPI client**

1. Log on to the client computer with an account that is a member of the Administrators group.

2. Type **tcmsetup /c telephonyserver1 [telephonyserver2]… [telephonyserverx]**

3. Click **OK**.

The switches for the **tcmsetup** command are described in Table 12.9.

Table 12.9   Tcmsetup Command Switches

Switch	Meaning
/q	Suppress message boxes during setup.
/x	Specify connection-oriented callbacks (default is connectionless).
/c telephonyserver	Set the telephony server to be used by this client to *telephonyserver*. Multiple servers can be listed, each name separated by a space.
/d	Delete the current telephony server list and disable TAPI services on this client.

The telephony client must be in the same domain as the telephony server, or must be a member of a domain that is fully trusted by the telephony server's domain.

The servers specified in the **tcmsetup** command override any previous telephony servers specified through previous instances of Tcmsetup. All servers required by the client must be specified in a single instance of the command.

The name of each telephony server is stored in the registry of the Windows 2000 Professional computer, in the key:

HKEY_LOCAL_MACHINE/Software/Microsoft/Windows/CurrentVersion/ Telephony/Providers/<servername>

The **tcmsetup** command can only be performed when logged on to the client with an account that is a member of the Administrators group. Alternatively, if you are logged on with an account in the Users or Power Users group, you can use the **runas** command to perform the **tcmsetup** command as an administrator. For example:

runas /user:mydomain\adminacct "tcmsetup /c servername"

Enter the password for the administrative account when prompted.

Configuring TAPI IP Telephony

This section discusses the procedures necessary for configuring a Windows 2000 Professional client to access IP telephony services using the H.323 protocol in an environment where an H.323 proxy or gateway is present. If your Windows 2000 Professional computer connects directly to the Internet, or an H.323 gateway is not used, this configuration is not required.

Specifying the H.323 Gateway

The H.323 protocol incorporates support for placing calls from data networks to the switched circuit PSTN network, and vice versa through an IP-PSTN gateway. The H.323 Telephony Service Provider provides support for gateway calling through the use of a static configuration option, accessible through **Phone and Modem Options** in **Control Panel**.

▶ **To specify the IP address of the IP-PSTN gateway**

1. From the **Start** menu, point to **Settings**, and then select **Control Panel**.
2. Double-click **Phone and Modem Options**.
3. Click the **Advanced** tab, and then select **Microsoft H.323 TAPI Service Provider**.
4. Click **Configure**. Select the **Use H.323 Gateway** check box, and then type the computer name or IP address of the IP-PSTN Gateway in the text box.

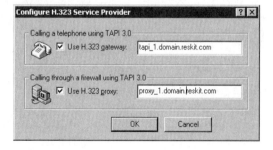

The telephony application running at the gateway must conform to ITU-T H.323 v1.0 standards.

For information about the installation and configuration of an IP-PSTN gateway, see "Telephony Integration and Conferencing" in the *Internetworking Guide*.

Specifying the H.323 Proxy

The Microsoft H.323 TSP incorporates support for firewall traversal. **Phone and Modem Options** (in Control Panel) is used to specify the inner IP address of the firewall computer. This allows calls to be made and received across the Internet.

▶ **To specify the IP address of the H.323 proxy**

1. From the **Start** menu, point to **Settings**, and then select **Control Panel**.

2. Double-click **Phone and Modem Options**.

3. Click the **Advanced** tab, and then select **Microsoft H.323 TAPI Service Provider**.

4. Click the **Configure** button. Select the **Use H.323 Proxy** check box, and then type the computer name or IP address of the inner edge of the H.323 proxy/firewall computer in the text box.

Configuring Phone Dialer

Phone Dialer is installed with the default IP telephony support. This TAPI 3.0-compliant application can be used to place and answer:

- Point-to-point audio and video calls within an intranet or the Internet.

- Multi-user audio and video conferences within a multicast-supported network.

- Telephone calls through a IP-PSTN gateway.

- Telephone calls through a modem.

For information about using Phone Dialer to place audio and video calls, see Windows 2000 Help.

By default, the Phone Dialer application is configured to work with the majority of network and hardware configurations. The following section describes the procedures to change the default configurations of Phone Dialer, if necessary.

Configuring Lines

Multiple providers, or lines, might be available with a single Windows 2000 Professional client. Default lines for each telephony application can be configured through **Options** in Phone Dialer.

▶ **To configure telephone and Internet lines to be used by Phone Dialer**

1. In Phone Dialer, select **Edit**, and then select **Options**.

2. Select the calling method by clicking the **Phone** or **Internet** button.

3. In the **Line Used For** box, select the preferred line to be used for telephone, Internet, or Internet conferencing. By default, Windows 2000 Professional automatically selects the first available line, or you can chose a default line. The lines available are:

    - *Phone*. Used to make telephone calls through a TAPI-enabled telephony server or H.323 gateway. Calls are directed to the gateway if the H.323 line is the method used for computer-to-phone calls, and an H.323 gateway is defined in **Phone and Modem Options** in Control Panel.

- *Internet.* Used for point-to-point IP-based telephone calls. Specify the network connection to be used to establish the connection.

- *Internet Conference.* Used to make multi-user telephony connections. Selected connection must support IP multicasting.

4. Click **OK**.

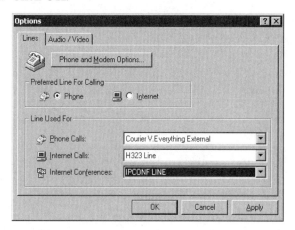

Configuring Audio and Video

When installed, Phone Dialer uses the preferred drivers for audio and video support as determined in **Multimedia** in Control Panel. If a different media device is preferred, you can override the default by using the Phone Dialer **Options** tab.

▶   **To configure audio and video settings for Phone Dialer**

1. From Phone Dialer, select **Edit**, and then select **Options**.

2. Select the **Audio/Video** tab.

3. To select the default sound device to be used, click **Sound Settings**.

4. The **Devices Used for Calling** area allows you to change the default device used for audio recording, playback, and video capture of a telephony session. Select the telephony session type in the **Line** drop-down menu.

5. Select the device to be used in the **Audio record**, **Audio playback** and **Video record** drop-down menus:

   - To allow Windows 2000 to use the default multimedia device, select **<Use Preferred Device>**.

   - To use another device, select it from the drop-down list.

6. To disable video playback, de-select the **Video Playback** check box. During a session where video playback is not required, disabling this option conserves bandwidth for low-speed connections.

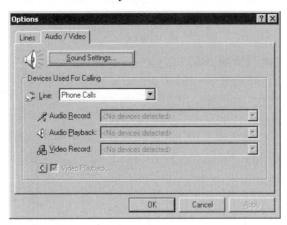

Configuring Internet Directories

Phone Dialer can access an ILS server to obtain a listing of Internet directories for contacting other users. If configured at the server, these directories appear in the **Directories** pane of Phone Dialer at program start.

You can specify additional local or Internet directories by using the **Add Directory** feature of Phone Dialer.

▶ **To add a new Internet directory**

1. From Phone Dialer, select **Edit**, and then select **Add Directory**.

2. Type or select the directory name from the **Directory Name** drop-down list box.

3. Click **Add**.

The directory name appears in the directory panel. An icon to the left of the name indicates the status of the directory. Table 12.10 describes the status and action of each directory entry.

Table 12.10   Directory Entry Information

Status	Action
Directory available ("Normal" icon)	Proceed to access directory.
Searching for directory ("Question Mark" icon)	Wait for directory query to complete.
	Click **Refresh** to re-query directory. Check for
Directory not found ("Unavailable" icon)	mistyped directory name. Directory might be busy or down. To re-query, wait, and then click **Refresh**.

Configuring Conferences

A multi-user conference can be configured from Phone Dialer, provided that the user has the permissions to create conferences. The network that is to host the conference must support both IP multicast and the Microsoft ILS Site Server Service.

▶ **To set up a multi-user conference**

1. From Phone Dialer, select the conference folder in the directory you where want to start the conference.

2. Click the **New Conference** icon.

   If the selected directory is not available, a message box is displayed indicating that the conference cannot be created. Select an available directory.

3. Complete the **Name** and **Description** fields. By default, the conference name is *<Owner>'s Conference*.

4. Under **Conference Time**, set the start and stop dates and times for the conference.

5. If your network supports them, select the desired conference scope from the **Conference Scope** list box.

   A conference scope enables the conference creator to restrict participants in a conference based on membership to a scope. A multicast scope defines the parts of the network over which multicast packets are allowed to go. A scope is used to limit packet propagation to a certain geographic area, for example, a specific building or segment within a network.

6. Click the **Permissions** tab.

7. Click **Add** to include additional attendees, or **Remove** to remove attendees.

   By default, the conference owner and Everyone are given permission to join the conference.

8. For each participant, determine conference permissions by selecting them in the **Permissions** box. The available permissions are listed below:

   - *Join Conference.* Allows a person or group to access a conference (default permission for all users).

   - *Modify Conference Properties.* Allows a person or group to change conference attributes (name, description, and start/stop date and time).

   - *Delete Conference.* Allows a person or group to cancel a scheduled conference (default permission for conference owner).

9. Click **OK**.

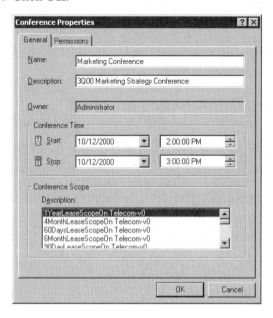

Configuring NetMeeting 3.0

The steps required to configure NetMeeting on a Windows 2000 Professional client are described in the following sections. For information about using NetMeeting to place audio, video, and data conferencing calls, see Windows 2000 Help.

Note These features can be automatically configured in a Windows 2000 domain environment using Group Policy on a Windows 2000 domain controller. For more information, see "Group Policy" in the *Distributed Systems Guide*.

NetMeeting 3.0 is installed as a default installation option of Windows 2000 Professional, located in **Start/Programs/Accessories/Communications**. In order to place audio calls with NetMeeting, you need an audio device with speakers or earphones, and a microphone. To send video with NetMeeting, you need a video capture device and camera, or a video camera that connects through the computer's parallel or USB port. A video device is not required to receive video.

Note Video devices that use a video capture card and camera use fewer of the computer's processing resources than devices that connect directly through the computer's parallel port, or USB port.

The NetMeeting Wizard collects user identification information, specifies a default directory server, configures connection settings, and optimizes audio settings. This information must be complete before NetMeeting can start. Table 12.11 lists the specific information required by the configuration wizard.

Table 12.11   NetMeeting Configuration Settings

Setting	Description
User information	Provide first and last name (required), e-mail address (required), location, and comment in the appropriate fields.
Directory	A directory server is a computer that maintains a directory of NetMeeting users in an intranet or on the Internet. Select **Log on to a directory server when NetMeeting starts** if you wish to log on to a default server when the application starts. Microsoft maintains a directory server, the Microsoft Internet Directory, which is the default selection in the **Server name** field. Other directories can be entered and selected in this field.
	If you do not want your host or name to be listed in any directories, select **Do not list my name in the directory**. Users wishing to call you must know your computer name or IP address if this option is selected.
Bandwidth	NetMeeting configures connection settings based on network bandwidth. Select the data connection speed or type that matches or closely matches your current connection: **14400 bps**, **28800 bps**, **Cable, xDSL or ISDN**, or **Local Area Network**.
Desktop configuration	Select **Put shortcut to NetMeeting on my desktop** and **Put shortcut to NetMeeting on my QuickLaunch bar** to configure your desktop options.

The user configuration settings obtained by the NetMeeting Wizard can be changed at any time in the **General** tab by selecting **Tools/Options** from the NetMeeting menu bar. NetMeeting stores all user-specific information in separate profiles for each user. The information is stored in the registry location HKEY_CURRENT_USER\Software\Microsoft\User Location Service\Client.

Configuring Audio and Video Devices

After configuration information has been collected, the NetMeeting Wizard performs a test of the computer's audio features. This test allows you to tune the playback and record volumes used in your NetMeeting sessions. You can perform the audio tests at any time by selecting **Tools/Audio Tuning Wizard** from the NetMeeting menu bar. You should to rerun this test if your audio hardware configuration changes, or if the sound environment changes, such as moving a portable computer to a noisier location. Audio settings can be further optimized by specifying options on the **Audio** tab in the **Options** dialog box. Table 12.12 describes the NetMeeting Audio Settings.

Table 12.12   NetMeeting Audio Settings

Option	Description
Enable full-duplex audio so I can speak while receiving	Full-duplex is a hardware feature that is available in many audio cards. If this feature is not supported by your audio card, the option is dimmed. Full-duplex sound cards are capable of capturing and playing audio simultaneously, while half-duplex sound cards can only do one at a time. Most modern sound cards are full-duplex.
Enable auto-gain control	Auto-gain is a sound card and driver feature that automatically adjusts the microphone volume. It is not available for all audio cards.
Automatically adjust microphone volume while in a call	If auto-gain is not supported by your audio card, this option automatically adjusts the microphone volume for improved audio
Enable DirectSound for improved audio performance	DirectSound improves audio performance by shortening the time between when audio is sent and received.
Advanced compression settings	Clicking the **Advanced** button displays the **Advanced Compression Settings** dialog box, which allows you to select an audio codec (compression/decompression algorithm). Select **Manually configure compression settings** and select the codec from the **Preferred codec for audio compression.**

Video settings are configured by selecting the **Video** tab in the **Options Properties** dialog box. This page allows you to change the size of the video window, select video quality, and to choose the device used during video sessions. Table 12.13 summarizes the available options for optimizing NetMeeting videoconferencing sessions.

Table 12.13   NetMeeting Video Settings

Option	Description
Sending and receiving video	Video transmission and reception can be turned off at NetMeeting start by clearing the **Automatically send video at the start of each call** and **Automatically receive video at the start of each call**. Disabling video reduces the amount of bandwidth required during a NetMeeting session, improving the performance of other high-bandwidth NetMeeting features such as Whiteboard or Program Sharing.

(continued)

Table 12.13   NetMeeting Video Settings *(continued)*

Option	Description
Send image size	Select **Small**, **Medium**, or **Large** to determine the size of your receive window.
Video quality	Select the desired video quality by moving the slider bar toward **Faster video** or **Better quality**. The default video quality is determined by the connection type selected.
	Faster video has improved frame rate, but a less sharp picture. Better quality video has a slower frame rate, but displays sharper images.
Video camera properties	Lists the video capture devices detected during NetMeeting configuration. You can select one camera from the list of devices shown.
	The properties of the selected video device can be modified by clicking the **Source** button. The properties available vary by manufacturer, but typical settings include brightness, contrast, and hue. Use these options to optimize the video settings.
	A video window must be displayed in order to activate this button. Select **View/My Video** from the menu bar to open a self-view.
Show mirror image in preview video window	Select this option if you want to view a mirror image of your local video.

Configuring Directory Servers

A directory server is an ILS server that provides a database of NetMeeting hosts that are currently connected to the server and have chosen to display their names. Accessing a directory server relieves users from having to manually enter the names or IP addresses of people they wish to call. Microsoft provides and maintains the Microsoft Internet Directory, which is the default directory configured in NetMeeting. In order to configure additional directory servers, perform the following steps:

▶ **To specify a directory server to place calls**

1. On the **Tools** menu, click **Options**.

2. On the **General** tab, under **Directory Settings**, in **Directory**, type or click the new directory server name.

Specifying Gatekeepers and Gateways

A *gatekeeper* is a server in a network that manages client access to telephony services. A gatekeeper provides address resolution, call routing, call logging, and other services to other computers within the local communications network, or to external users. NetMeeting can access gatekeepers and gateways that support the H.323 protocol.

▶ **To configure a gatekeeper to place calls**

1. On the **Tools** menu, click **Options**.

2. On the **General** tab, click **Advanced Calling**.

3. In the **Advanced Calling Options** dialog box, click **Use a gatekeeper to place calls**.

4. In **Gatekeeper**, type the computer name or IP address of the gatekeeper computer.

   If you log on to your organization's gatekeeper using your e-mail address, click **Log on using my account name**. Otherwise, click **Log on using my phone number**, and then type your phone number in the box.

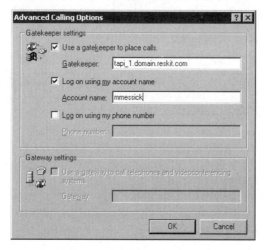

NetMeeting supports access to switched circuit PSTN networks through an H.323 gateway. In a gateway-configured environment, NetMeeting users can place telephone calls to users on public or private telephone networks.

▶ **To configure NetMeeting to access an H.323 gateway**

1. On the **Tools** menu, click **Options**.

2. On the **General** tab, click **Advanced Calling**.

3. In the **Advanced Calling Options** dialog box, under **Gateway settings**, select the **Use a gateway to call telephones and videoconferencing systems** check box.

4. In **Gateway**, type the gateway's name or IP address.

Configuring Call Security

Call Security is a new feature in NetMeeting 3.0 that provides security for data exchanged during NetMeeting chat, whiteboard, shared program, and data exchange features. Data transferred in a secured session is encrypted. Audio and video features are not secured, and are not available during a secured call. A call cannot contain both secured and nonsecured data.

NetMeeting optionally provides user authentication through certificates to verify user identity. Security certificates can support encryption, authentication, or both. NetMeeting includes a security certificate that provides encryption only. Additional security certificates can be obtained within an organization, or through a certificate authority, such as VeriSign, and are installed using the Certificates MMC snap-in. For more information about obtaining and installing additional certificates, see "Security" in this book.

Note NetMeeting only works with certificates in the Windows 2000 certificate store. Certificates obtained from browsers that use private certificate stores cannot be used with NetMeeting.

▶ **To set security options**

1. On the **Tools** menu, click **Options**.

2. On the **Security** tab, under **General**, select or clear the **I prefer to receive secure incoming calls** check box. When this option is selected, only callers making secured calls are able to contact the computer.

   - Or -

Select or clear the **I prefer to make secure outgoing calls** check box. When this option is selected, all outgoing calls will be secure. However, call security can be changed on a call-by-call basis by selecting the **Require security for this call (data only)** check box when placing a call through the **Place a call** dialog box.

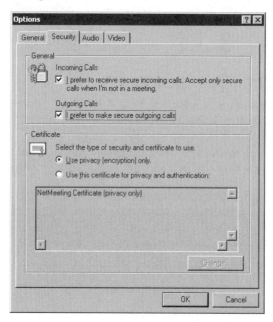

Troubleshooting

The following section describes the techniques and procedures that can be used to determine and resolve problems within telephony applications and in telephony device configuration, and H.323 and multicast conferencing.

Troubleshooting Modems

The following sections detail troubleshooting procedures for analog and ISDN modems.

An analog or ISDN modem is not listed

If your modem is not on the Windows 2000 Hardware Compatibility List (HCL) or is not detected by the Install New Hardware or Install New Modem Wizards, use one of the following procedures to install it:

- Check the modem. If it is an external modem, make sure it is turned on, and all cables are tightly connected. If the modem is internal, verify that it is properly installed.

  If the modem is a Plug and Play device, open **Device Manager** in **Control Panel** and select **Scan for hardware changes** from the **Action** menu to reinstall the modem. If the modem is a non-Plug and Play device, reinstall the modem using **Add/Remove Hardware**.

- Obtain an .inf (installation) file from the modem manufacturer specifically designed for Windows 2000. Follow the manufacturer's instructions for installing the modem in Windows 2000, or contact the modem manufacturer for assistance with this procedure.

- Install your modem as a standard modem using the Install New Modem or Install New Hardware Wizards. This option provides basic dialing and connectivity support for the modem, although manufacturer-specific features might be unavailable.

Phone Dialer cannot dial selected modem

If you cannot use Phone Dialer (or any other application) to dial your modem, verify that Windows 2000 is able to connect to it by testing the modem. In Control Panel, open **Phone and Modem Options**, and then select the **Modems** tab, then click **Properties** for the modem, then select the **Diagnostics** tab. Click the **Query Modem** button to send a set of AT commands to the modem. If the modem response is not displayed in the **Response** area, then perform the following steps to diagnose the problem:

- If an external modem is experiencing problems, make sure that the serial cable connection between the computer and the modem is secure, and that the cable is not broken or frayed.

- Verify that Windows 2000 Professional recognizes your COM ports by displaying Device Manager. Verify that the COM port is not experiencing a hardware or resource problem (identified by an exclamation point icon next to the device listing) or has been disabled (the international "No" symbol). If the connected port is listed without any additional icons, the COM port is recognized and available.

If the COM port is disabled in Device Manager, there is most likely a hardware or a configuration problem. Use the following steps to troubleshoot the problem for an external modem.

- Verify that the port is not disabled in the BIOS (also called the CMOS) setup of the computer. Refer to the documentation for your computer to obtain information about configuring options in the BIOS setup.

- Make sure there are no other adapters or devices that are configured for the same base I/O Address or IRQ as the COM port to which the modem is attached.

- Verify that the serial port is not defective. If the modem and any other serial devices fail on the COM port but work on other COM ports, and you have verified the two steps above, the serial port might be defective.

If the modem experiencing problems is internal, perform the following steps to diagnose and resolve the problem:

- If the internal modem is not Plug and Play–compatible, it might use jumpers to specify the COM port. Make sure the jumpers on the modem are configured properly. There might or might not be jumpers that allow you to set the base I/O address and IRQ to be used by the modem as well. Verify that they are properly set. Some modems use a configuration application to change these settings.

- If the modem is configured for a COM port number that is assigned to a COM port on the motherboard or a serial card (physical port), you must either set the modem to use a different COM port, or use the BIOS setup to disable the COM port with the same number as the internal modem.

- Make sure there are no other adapters or devices that are configured for the same base I/O address or IRQ as the internal modem.

- Verify that the internal modem is not defective. Also, it is often a good idea to check with the vendor of your modem to see if there is a flash upgrade available for your modem.

Troubleshooting PSTN Telephony

The following sections outline common problems and solutions for conventional (non-IP) Public Switched Telephone Network (PSTN) telephony deployment.

Computer cannot find the telephony server

If the telephony server cannot be reached through the network, for example, a user cannot "ping" the telephony server, it is possible that:

1. The telephony server is not available or has not been correctly set up. Contact the administrator of the telephony server.

2. The Tcmsetup tool has not been run. Run the Tcmsetup tool with the /c parameter to specify the correct servers.

3. The Tcmsetup tool has been run, but an incorrect telephony server was specified. Run the Tcmsetup tool with the /c parameter to specify the correct servers.

4. The Tcmsetup tool has been run multiple times, overwriting the original telephony configuration. Run the Tcmsetup tool with the /c parameter, listing all telephony severs in the single command.

5. The Tcmsetup tool has been run with the /d (delete) parameter. Run the Tcmsetup tool with the /c parameter to enable telephony services and to specify the correct server(s).

One or more client computers cannot find a line on the telephony server

If one or more client computers cannot "see" the lines of a telephony server, it might be because they are unable to be authorized for access to lines on the telephony server. When a TAPI application accesses lines on the telephony server, the user context associated with the application process is first authenticated. This means that those lines must have been configured on the server to allow access by that client. If the client cannot see lines on the telephony server, it is possible that the lines have not been configured on the server to allow access by the client. Contact the system administrator for the server.

After the lines have been configured, the new settings are not available until TAPI on the client computer restarts. The solution is to stop all client TAPI applications and restart Windows 2000 Professional. When the client applications restart, they are able to see the newly allocated lines.

An application fails to start after you have canceled the Location Information dialog box

If an application fails to start after you have canceled out of the **Location Information** dialog box, the problem might be that address translation required by TAPI applications has not been specified. This can be solved by using the **Local Information** dialog box to enter your country/region code, local area code, and pulse or tone and external line access settings.

A client cannot find a new line appearance on the server, even though the server administrator has assigned the client to the line

When you assign a currently running client to a line on the telephony server, the new settings are not available until TAPI on the client computer restarts. The solution is to stop all client TAPI applications so that TAPI shuts down. When the client applications restart, they are able to see the newly allocated lines.

Troubleshooting Conferencing Applications

Users of H.323 or multicast conferences might encounter problems connecting with other users or receiving audio or video.

Audio problems in conferencing applications

If audio problems occur in H.323 or multicast video conferences, the microphones or sound cards on the client computers might be incorrectly configured or malfunctioning.

To diagnose sound hardware on Windows 2000 Professional computers, start the Sound Recorder application by clicking **Start**, pointing to **Programs**, **Accessories**, **Entertainment**, and then clicking **Sound Recorder**, or by typing **sndrec32** at the command prompt. Make a recording of your own voice using Sound Recorder, and then play it back. If there is no sound, check if the microphone is properly plugged in.

If the Sound Recorder test works properly but you continue to have audio problems, verify the sound settings using Volume Control.

▶   **To verify sound settings through Volume Control**

1. Click **Start**, point to **Programs**, point to **Accessories**, point to **Entertainment**, and then select **Volume Control**.

2. In the **Volume Control** dialog box, select **Options**, **Properties**, and then click **Playback**. Make sure that the **Wave** and **Microphone** check boxes are selected. You might have to scroll the window in order to see these settings.

3. Click **OK**.

4. Select the **Mute** check box in the **Microphone** column if it is not checked. This prevents speech from being echoed locally (played back on the speaker's computer).

5. If the voices of all other conference participants are too loud or too quiet, adjust the **Volume Control** and/or **Wave** sliders downward or upward as needed.

6. Select **Options**, **Properties**, and then click **Recording**. Select all of the check boxes in the window at the bottom of the dialog box. (You might have to scroll the window in order to see these settings.)

7. Click **OK**.

8. Select the **Mute** check boxes in all of the columns except for the **Microphone** column if they are not already checked. Make sure that the **Mute** check box in the **Microphone** is left unchecked. This allows your speech to be sent to the conference, but prevents other sounds, including those of other conference participants, from being transmitted from your computer.

9. If other conference participants are dissatisfied with the level of sound, adjust the **Microphone** slider downward or upward as needed.

Note A single incorrectly configured computer can cause audio problems or echoes for all other conference participants.

If you continue to encounter audio problems after adjusting the sound settings, check if the affected computers have full-duplex sound cards. Full-duplex sound cards are capable of capturing and playing audio simultaneously, while half-duplex sound cards can only do one at a time. Most modern sound cards are full-duplex, but many older sound cards are only half-duplex.

To check if the sound card on your computer supports full-duplex audio, start Sound Recorder and record a speech sample for approximately 30 seconds. After this is complete, open a second instance of Sound Recorder. Play the sample you recorded using the first instance of Sound Recorder, and while this is playing, attempt to record a sample using the second instance of Sound Recorder. If the second instance of Sound Recorder is unable to properly record a sample while the first instance is recording, the sound card does not support full-duplex audio, and thus does not work with TAPI.

If sound is distorted or otherwise continues to malfunction after you attempt the above procedures, there is most likely a problem with the microphone, sound card hardware, or sound card driver. Check with the manufacturer of your sound cards to ensure that you are using the most recent Windows 2000 drivers. Also, replace the microphones and sound cards on affected computers and attempt these tests again.

Eliminating audio echo

Audio echo is a common problem with audio conferencing systems. Echo can originate in the local audio loop-back that happens when a user's microphone picks up sounds from their speakers and transmits it back to the other participants. Normal conversation can become impossible for other participants in the conference when sensitive microphones are used, speaker level is high, or the microphone and speakers are placed in close proximity to each other.

One of the easiest ways to completely eliminate audio echo is to use audio headsets. These work by eliminating the possibility of a user's microphone picking up sound that is being received from other conference participants.

A more expensive solution is to use special microphones with built-in echo-canceling capabilities. These microphones detect and cancel out echo. The main advantage to these is that users do not have to wear headsets. Echo-canceling microphones are also a necessity for conference rooms because using headphones is not a practical solution.

Video problems in conferencing applications

If the video image of an H.323 conference participant cannot be seen by the other party, or if the image of a multicast conference participant cannot be see by all of the other endpoints, the computer's video capture device might not be working properly. When using Phone Dialer, participants should be able to see their own video image whenever they participate in videoconferences. If this is not the case, run the camera troubleshooter included in Windows 2000 Help.

Audio and video problems in multicast conferences can also be caused by multicast issues. The following section describes how to diagnose these problems using the MCAST tool included in the *Microsoft® Windows® 2000 Professional Resource Kit*.

Verifying network is configured for multicast packets

If you are uncertain whether your network is configured to send and receive multicast packets, use the MCAST diagnostic tool. MCAST can send and receive multicast packets, helping you to determine which parts of your network are enabled for transmission of IP multicast packets. MCAST is supplied with the *Microsoft® Windows® 2000 Professional Resource Kit*. Install MCAST on the computer in question.

You can use MCAST in send mode to set up multicast sources at different locations on your network, and in receive mode to determine the locations at which multicast traffic from these sources is being received.

The following example shows MCAST being run as a multicast sender, on a Windows 2000 Professional–based computer:

```
MCAST /SEND /INTF:172.31.253.55 /GRPS:230.1.1.1 /INTVL:1000
/NUMPKTS:3600
```

MCAST will start sending multicast packets from the IP address 172.31.255.255 to the multicast group IP address 230.1.1.1 at the rate of 1 packet per every 1000 milliseconds. A total of 3600 packets will be sent over a one-hour period.

To run MCAST as a multicast receiver, use a command-line as follows:

```
MCAST /RECV /INTF: 172.31.255.255/GRPS:230.1.1.1
```

MCAST will start listening for multicast packets on the IP address 172.31.255.255 for the multicast group IP address 230.1.1.1. Received packets are displayed on the screen:

```
Started.... Waiting to receive packets...
Received [1]: [GOOD] SRC- 172.31.253.55 GRP- 230.1.1.1    TTL- 5 Len-
256
Received [2]: [GOOD] SRC- 172.31.253.55 GRP- 230.1.1.1    TTL- 5 Len-
256
Received [3]: [GOOD] SRC- 172.31.253.55 GRP- 230.1.1.1    TTL- 5 Len-
256
Received [4]: [GOOD] SRC- 172.31.253.55 GRP- 230.1.1.1    TTL- 5 Len-
256
Received [5]: [GOOD] SRC- 172.31.253.55 GRP- 230.1.1.1    TTL- 5 Len-
256
```

Unable to publish multicast conference invitations

If you are unable to publish multicast conference invitations, confirm with your network administrator that the Site Server ILS Service is available at your site. The Site Server ILS Service is an essential component of TAPI IP Multicast Conferencing. This server represents the meeting place where conference creators and participants go through their client software application to find the information they need to participate in a conference.

Windows 2000 Phone Dialer cannot see ILS

The Windows 2000 Phone Dialer application must know the location of the Site Server ILS Service to provide conference creation and joining facilities.

The Phone Dialer application can locate this information in Active Directory™ directory service if the following conditions are fulfilled:

- The computer running the Phone Dialer application is part of a Windows 2000 domain.
- The user is logged on using a Windows 2000 domain account.
- The ILS server location is published in Active Directory.

Using Active Directory in this way means that users do not need to know the location of the ILS server on their network or manually enter that information into their Phone Dialer application. This makes using IP Multicast Conferencing with Windows 2000 easier for the user.

Computer or user cannot access Active Directory

All of the components required to support TAPI Multicast Conferencing on a client computer are installed by default in Windows 2000 Professional. However, in order for a computer or a user to use TAPI Multicast Conferencing, they need to be added to a Windows 2000 domain. If computer or user accounts for Windows 2000 domain are not created, users cannot access Active Directory directory service and will need to add their ILS servers to the Phone Dialer application manually.

Troubleshooting NetMeeting

Although NetMeeting supports multi-user data conferencing, you can connect with only one other person at a time with audio or video functions. Other audio and video troubleshooting issues are also described in the following sections.

Cannot place a call in NetMeeting

- If you are in a network environment that uses a proxy server and are attempting to access a Web-based directory server or to contact someone on the Internet, verify that your proxy server supports NetMeeting. If the proxy supports NetMeeting, attempt to ping the directory using its DNS name or IP address to check availability.

- If a gatekeeper is used to establish calls, you might have to log on to the gatekeeper using an established alias. Contact your system administrator for details.

- Some directory names are case-sensitive; verify the correct capitalization used in a directory name before attempting to place a call.

- If you cannot place a call using a computer name, try using their IP address. If the IP address is unknown, ping the computer you are attempting to call, using the full DNS name of the host.

Audio problems in NetMeeting

If the audio functions of NetMeeting application have worked previously, and any changes have occurred in the sound card device driver (such as upgrading to a full-duplex driver) run the Audio Tuning Wizard again in order to reconfigure the NetMeeting audio settings. If running the Audio Tuning Wizard does not solve the problem, check the hardware and driver configuration, as described in "Troubleshooting H.323 Calls and Multicast Conferencing" earlier in this chapter.

Video problems in NetMeeting

- If your video capture device fails to preview video, verify that the correct display codec is selected for your video device. Select **Tools/Options** from the NetMeeting menu bar, select the **Video** tab, then click **Source** to view the codec selected for the current session. Select the correct codec, then close and restart NetMeeting.

- If another application is using the same video device selected for your NetMeeting video conference, the video functions in NetMeeting might be disabled. Select another video device or close the other application.

- If you are using the video capture functions in a dark area, some cameras cause the session to become extremely slow and unresponsive. Some video drivers provide a low-light filter option. Enable the option if available.

Additional Resources

- For more information about H.323, see the International Telecommunication Union Web site at http://www.itu.int.

CHAPTER 13

Security

It is important to protect your information and service resources from people who should not have access to them, while at the same time making those resources available to authorized users. Effective security achieves both these goals. After you understand your security needs, you can configure Microsoft® Windows® 2000 Professional to meet your goals. This chapter will help you make the most of the security technology provided with Windows 2000 Professional.

In This Chapter

Related Information in the Windows 2000 Professional Resource Kit

- For information about how security fits into Microsoft® Windows® 2000, see "Introduction to Configuration and Management" in this book.

- For information about security features of the Windows 2000 desktop, see "Customizing the Desktop" in this book.

- For information about establishing security in a network environment, including establishing secure connections, see "Local and Remote Network Connections" in this book.

Quick Guide to Security

Use this quick guide to locate information about security. You will find information about security features which are new to Windows 2000, direction on designing and implementing a security plan, ideas for making workstations secure, and detailed information about the security features of Windows 2000.

Understand what's new in security.

Learn about new features in Windows 2000 security and how those compare to available security features in older versions of Windows.

- See "What's New" later in this chapter.

Design and implement a security plan.

Designing a security plan includes setting security goals and strategies and deciding on the level of security you need. Deciding on the level of security means weighing the pros and cons of higher versus lower security. Higher security requires more administration but ensures only the right people will have access to your resources. Lower security creates a more flexible and open environment, but might not be as secure as other configurations.

- See "Planning for Security" later in this chapter.

Understand client authentication.

Windows 2000 security requires user authentication. Different authentication schemes are appropriate depending on your computing environment. Windows 2000 supports interactive logon and network authentication using Kerberos, NTLM, and smart cards, among other things.

- See "User Authentication" later in this chapter.

Understand user rights and permissions.

Windows 2000 provides permissions and user rights which enable specific, detailed management of your security environment combined with powerful group management technologies. Set rights and permissions to determine the activities and access allowed for users. Carefully setting these attributes affects how users' computers behave and how secure they are.

- See "Security Groups, User Rights, and Permissions" later in this chapter.

Understand and implement security policy.

Security policy enforces uniform security standards for groups of users. Use security policy to establish a basis of security for your environment. Different from user rights and permissions, security policy applies to all users or objects in your deployment.

- See "Security Policy" later in this chapter.

Understand and implement security templates.

Security templates provide a way to apply consistent security to multiple computers. Security templates work much like security policy, but they can be applied to any computer and provide an easy way to apply a customized set of default security settings.

- See "Security Templates" later in this chapter.

Understand and implement remote access.

Allowing users to access your network using a modem provides opportunity for more flexibility and productivity for users but also presents unusual security challenges. If you use remote access, make sure your system is configured to maintain security.

- See "Remote Access" later in this chapter.

Understand and implement Internet Protocol security.

When you send information over the Internet, Windows 2000 makes it possible for you to encrypt all information above the transmission layer, producing a secure tunnel even through insecure connections.

- See "Internet Protocol Security" later in this chapter.

Understand and implement Encrypting File System.

Data on your hard disk drive can use the Encrypting File System (EFS) to ensure that even people with access to your physical computer are unable to read the contents of your hard disk drive. EFS can be a key security feature on all computers but is particularly helpful on portable computers that are difficult to physically secure.

- See "Encrypting File System" later in this chapter.

Understand public key technology.

Public key technology allows you to encrypt data for confidentiality and use data signing for integrity. Learn how Windows 2000 uses public key technology to secure your information assets.

- See "Public Key Technology" later in this chapter.

Protect user data on portable computers.

Portable computers present special security risks. Understand what those risks are, decide how to mitigate them, and then implement a plan that will protect your portable computers, while still allowing users flexibility.

- See "Protecting User Data on Portable Computers" later in this chapter.

What's New

Table 13.1 highlights the new security features of Windows 2000, including how these new features compare to Microsoft® Windows NT® version 4.0, Microsoft® Windows® 95, and Microsoft® Windows® 98.

Table 13.1   Security Feature Comparison

Windows 2000	Windows NT 4.0	Windows 95 and Windows 98
Kerberos is provided, enabling single sign-on for network services.	No Kerberos or single sign-on support provided.	Same as Windows NT 4.0.
Encrypting File System (EFS) is supported.	No EFS provided.	Same as Windows NT 4.0.
virtual private networks (VPNs) supported using PPTP and L2TP.	PPTP supported. L2TP not supported.	Same as Windows NT 4.0.
Public Key (PK) Certificate Manager provided for public key administration.	No PK Certificate Manager provided.	Same as Windows NT 4.0.
Internet Protocol security (IPSec) provided, encrypting all information included above the transport layer.	No IPSec provided with Windows NT 4.0.	Same as Windows NT 4.0.
Auditing of security events configurable to a range of detail levels. Audited events logged for later review.	Auditing available, but on a narrower scope than provided with Windows 2000.	No auditing provided.

(continued)

Table 13.1   Security Feature Comparison *(continued)*

Windows 2000	Windows NT 4.0	Windows 95 and Windows 98
Highly configurable access control for network resources using groups, user rights, permissions, and Security Policy.	Some access control available through permissions settings.	Only user-based security using permissions.
Permissions are maintained, regardless of where a file is moved. For example, restricted files remain restricted, even when placed in a public folder.	Permissions are inherited and reapplied when files are moved to new locations.	Only user-based security. Permissions not applied to files.

Determining the identity of a user, computer, or service is critical to creating a secure environment. Only after an identity has been authenticated should authorization to use information or resources be granted. There are numerous ways to authenticate, each of which provides different advantages and disadvantages. Authentication is achieved through authentication protocols. Windows 2000 maintains and builds upon the set of authentication protocols supported by earlier versions of Windows. Table 13.2 provides a comparison of authentication protocols.

Table 13.2   Authentication Protocol Comparison

Authentication Protocol	Windows 2000	Windows NT 4.0	Windows 95 and Windows 98
Kerberos	X	O	O
NTLM v2	X	X	O
NTLM v1	X	X	X
EAP	X	O	O
MSCHAPv2	X	X	X
MSCHAP	X	X	X
CHAP	X	X	X
SPAP	X	X	X
PAP	X	X	X

Planning for Security

Although security technologies are highly advanced, effective security must combine technology with good planning for business and social practices. No matter how advanced and well implemented the technology is, it is only as good as the methods used in employing and managing it.

Implementing the appropriate security standards is a key issue for most organizations. To implement security standards, devise a security plan that applies a set of security technologies consistently to protect your organization's resources. After you have established your plan, implement the appropriate Windows 2000 Professional security features.

Consider developing a security plan that describes how you will use the features of Windows 2000 to establish a secure, usable environment. A typical security plan might include the following sections:

- **Security goals**: Describe what you are protecting.
- **Security risks**: Enumerate the types of security hazards that affect your enterprise, including what poses the threats and how significant the threats are.
- **Security strategies**: Describe the general security strategies necessary to meet the threats and mitigate the risks.
- **Security group descriptions**: Describe security groups and their relationship to one another. This section maps security policies to security groups.
- **Security Policy**: Describe Group Policy security settings, such as network password policies. Note that if you add your Windows 2000 Professional–based computer to a domain, your Security Policy settings will be affected by domain Security Policies.
- **Network logon and authentication strategies**: If you work in a networked environment, consider authentication strategies for logging on to the network and for using remote access and smart card to log on.
- **Information security strategies**: Include how you implement information security solutions, such as an encrypted file system (EFS), Internet Protocol security, and access authorization using permissions.
- **Administrative policies**: Include policies for delegation of administrative tasks and monitoring of audit logs to detect suspicious activity.
- **Public key usage policies**: Include your plans for how clients will use certification authorities for internal and external security features.

Your security plan can contain more sections, but these are suggested as a starting point. If possible, test and revise your security plans using test labs that model the computing environments for your organization. Also, conduct pilot programs to further test and refine your network security plans.

Planning for Mobile Computing

Mobile computing provides more flexibility to users, allowing them to work in a wider range of situations, increasing work potential. However, mobile computing also increases security risks.

Mobile Computing Security Threats

Because portable computers are easily stolen, there are greater physical security risks with mobile computing. If information on the hard disk drive is not encrypted with EFS, information stored on the hard disk drive, as well as any authentication information stored on the computer, might be compromised.

Another security threat when using a mobile computer is data being intercepted when it is transferred across phone lines. Users can ensure their connections are secure by using protocols to create virtual private networks.

Security Attacks

Before examining Windows 2000 security features, it is good to understand what threats security technologies address. Table 13.3 describes several types of attacks. Different attacks pose different dangers, including the loss of data confidentiality, integrity, and availability.

Creating a list similar to this in your security plan demonstrates the complexity of security problems you face and will help you establish a set of standard labels for each category of risk.

Table 13.3   Types of Attacks That Pose Security Risks in an Organization

Security Attack	Description
Identity interception	The intruder discovers the user name and password of a valid user. This can occur by a variety of methods, both social and technical.
Masquerade	An unauthorized user pretends to be a valid user. For example, a user assumes the IP address of a trusted system and uses it to gain the access rights that are granted to the impersonated device or system.
Replay attack	The intruder records a network exchange between a user and a server and plays it back at a later time to impersonate the user.
Data interception	If data is moved across the network as plaintext, unauthorized persons can monitor and capture the data.
Manipulation	The intruder causes network data to be modified or corrupted. Unencrypted network financial transactions are vulnerable to manipulation. Viruses can corrupt network data.

(continued)

Table 13.3   Types of Attacks That Pose Security Risks in an Organization
(continued)

Security Attack	Description
Repudiation	Network-based business and financial transactions are compromised if the recipient of the transaction cannot be certain who sent the message.
Macro viruses	Application-specific viruses exploit the macro language of sophisticated documents and spreadsheets.
Denial of service	The intruder floods a server with requests that consume system resources and either crash the server or prevent useful work from being done. Crashing the server sometimes provides opportunities to penetrate the system.
Malicious mobile code	This term refers to malicious code running as an auto-executed ActiveX® control or Java applet downloaded from the Internet.
Misuse of privileges	An administrator of a computing system uses full privileges over the operating system to obtain private data.
Trojan horse	This is a general term for a malicious program that masquerades as a desirable and harmless tool. For example, a screen saver that mimics a logon dialog box in order to acquire a user's name and password and then secretly sends that password to an attacker.
Social engineering attack	Sometimes breaking into a network is as simple as calling new employees, telling them you are from the IT department, and asking them to verify their password for your records.

Security Concepts

The following concepts are useful in describing security strategies under Windows 2000. All these technologies aid in creating a more secure environment, although where technology addresses a specific attack, the defense is described below.

Security Infrastructure

When planning for security in Windows 2000, it is valuable to understand how Windows 2000 provides security, as well as the environment in which you will be working.

Security Model

Windows 2000 provides security through *authentication* and *authorization*. Authentication ensures that users are who they claim to be. After a user's identity has been authenticated, that user is authorized to use network resources. Authorization is made possible by access control which uses permissions on any resource such as file systems, network files, and print shares.

Windows 2000 Professional in a Windows 2000 Server Domain Model

If you are using Windows 2000 Professional in a Microsoft® Windows® 2000 Server environment, your Windows 2000 Professional computer can join a domain. A domain is a collection of objects, such as users, computers, and groups, that share a security directory database. A domain is centered around a security authority that gates access and establishes a logical boundary. This logical boundary ensures consistent security policy and determines how objects in one domain relate to objects in other domains. Windows 2000 Professional computers that are stand-alone computers or that are members of a workgroup are not directly affected by domains.

Authentication and Its Benefits

Authentication is the first part of the Windows 2000 security model. Authentication confirms users are who they claim to be. Authentication can be completed in a variety of ways and provide a range of benefits. Windows 2000 authentication enables single sign-on to all network resources. With single sign-on, a user can log on to the client computer once, using a single password or smart card, and authenticate to any computer in the domain. Authentication in Windows 2000 is implemented by using the Kerberos v5 protocol, NTLM authentication, or the Windows NT logon feature for Windows NT 4.0 domains.

Authentication specifically prevents:

- **Masquerade attacks**: Users must prove their identity, so it is more difficult to masquerade as another.

- **Replay attacks**: Because Windows 2000 authentication protocols use timestamps, it is difficult to reuse stolen authentication information.

- **Identity interception**: Because exchanges are encrypted, intercepted identities are useless.

Two-Factor Authentication

Two-factor authentication requires users that present a physical object that encodes their identity plus a password. The most common example of two-factor authentication is the automated teller machine (ATM) that requires an ATM card that encodes the owner's identity and a personal identification number (PIN) that serves as a password.

Biometric identification is another form of two-factor authentication. A special device scans the user's handprint, thumbprint, iris, retina, or voiceprint in place of an access card. Then the user enters the equivalent of a password. This approach is expensive but it makes identity interception and masquerading very difficult.

For business enterprises, the emerging two-factor technology is the smart card. This card is the same size as an ATM card and is physically carried by the user. It contains a chip that stores a digital certificate and the user's private key. The user enters a password or PIN after inserting the card into a card reader at the client computer. Smart cards are not open to network attacks like a password can be. Smart cards use a private key and a PIN that are never on the network, and the private key never leaves the smart card, reducing the opportunities for attack. Windows 2000 directly supports smart card authentication.

Another common form of two-factor authentication is a token card. Token cards provide a token, such as a string of numbers, that changes at regular intervals. Users enter their PIN and the numbers presented on the card and they are authenticated. However, because the numbers the card presents change at a regular interval, intercepted authentication is only valid for a short time, making it minimally useful to attackers.

Single Sign-on

Authentication with Windows 2000 makes it possible for users to have access to a range of resources that might otherwise require repeated authentication. For example, without single sign-on, a user might have to provide separate passwords to log on to the local computer, to access a file or print server, to send e-mail, to use a database, and so on. Different servers can demand a change of password at different intervals, often with no reuse permitted; so a system without single sign-on might require a typical user to remember half a dozen passwords. This makes authentication an inconvenience for users, and more seriously, puts your security at risk when users begin to write down a list of current passwords.

The single sign-on strategy makes a user authenticate interactively once and then permits authenticated sign-on to other network applications and devices. These subsequent authentication events are transparent to the user.

Code Authentication

Users often download and install software on their computers. In doing so, users might inadvertently compromise your security if they download software that has been written to steal passwords, data, or other confidential information. Code authentication identifies the code publisher and determines whether the code has been modified since publication. You can configure your Web browser to refuse to run unsigned software and decide which software you will trust. Note that code authentication only ensures that the software has not been modified since it was signed, so if malicious components have been included in software before signing, these will not be detected.

Code authentication specifically prevents:

- **Macro viruses**: Macro viruses added after code signing are detected by code authentication.

- **Malicious mobile code**: You can prevent unsigned code from being installed or detect code that has inserted itself into code after that code's signing. This is an example of a Trojan horse.

Authorization

After users have been authenticated, they are granted authorization which is implemented using access control. A user who has authenticated and attempts to access a resource, such as a network file, is permitted to do so based on the permissions attached to the resource, such as read-only or read/write. Permissions implement access control in Windows 2000. You can view permissions on the **Security** tab of the property sheet of a file or folder. The list contains the names of user groups that have access to the object.

Encryption and Its Benefits

Encryption technologies can be used to assure your data is confidential.

Symmetric Key Encryption

Also called secret key encryption, symmetric key encryption uses the same key to encrypt and decrypt the data. It provides rapid processing of data and is used in many forms of data encryption for networks and file systems.

Public Key Encryption

Public key encryption has two keys, one public and one private. This technology opens up numerous security strategies and is the basis for several Windows 2000 security features including digital signing, which ensures authenticity, and encryption, which ensures secrecy. These features are dependent on a *public key infrastructure (PKI)*. For more information about PKI, see "Planning Your Public Key Infrastructure" in the *Microsoft® Windows® 2000 Server Resource Kit Deployment Planning Guide*.

Public key encryption is used in a variety of situations. For example, public key encryption is used for Web authentication by the Secure Sockets Layer (SSL) protocol.

Data Integrity

Ensuring data integrity means to protect data against malicious or accidental modification. For stored data, this means that only authorized users can edit, overwrite, or delete the data. On a network, this means that data packets are digitally signed, so tampering with the packet can be detected by the recipient. Integrity is ensured by hashing the contents of a file and then signing that hash using public key technology.

Data Confidentiality

A strategy of data confidentiality means to encrypt data before it passes through the network and to decrypt it afterward. This prevents eavesdroppers from reading the data as it travels over the network. When a packet of nonencrypted data is transmitted across a network, attackers can intercept and view it from any computer on the network. Data confidentiality uses symmetric key encryption.

Nonrepudiation

Windows 2000 uses public key technology to provide nonrepudiation. There are two parts to a nonrepudiation strategy. The first part is to establish that a message was sent by a specific user, and the second is to ensure that the message could not have been sent by anyone other than the user.

This is another application for public key technologies, and it depends upon the presence of PKI. A user's private key is used to place a digital signature on the message. If the recipient can read the message using the sender's public key, then the message could have been sent only by that user and no one else.

Nonrepudiation specifically prevents repudiation because the user, and no other party, controls the private key, so the user cannot repudiate a message signed with his or her private key.

Managing Security on Your System

Windows 2000 provides a robust set of technologies to protect your data, but you must ensure the system is running effectively and consistently. Windows 2000 provides features that help you use security technologies to achieve their intents.

Security Policy

Security policy is a subset of Group Policy. You can manage security policy on stand-alone computers, or your Group Policy can be enforced throughout a domain using Group Policy objects in Active Directory™. For more information about domainwide Group Policy objects, see the *Microsoft® Windows 2000 Server Resource Kit* and Windows 2000 Server Help.

Using security policy, you can apply explicit security settings to your computer and its security groups.

Audit Logs

Auditing user account management, along with having access to important network resources, is an important security feature. Auditing leaves a trail of network operations, showing what was attempted and by whom. Not only does this help to detect intrusion, but the logs can become legal evidence if the intruder is caught and prosecuted. Finally, finding and deleting or modifying the audit logs poses an additional time-consuming task for the sophisticated intruder, making detection and intervention easier.

Security Configuration and Analysis

Security Configuration and Analysis offers the ability to compare the security settings of a computer to a standard template, view the results, and resolve any discrepancies revealed by the analysis. You can also import a security template into a Group Policy object and apply that security profile to your computer or to many computers at once. Windows 2000 contains several predefined security templates appropriate to various levels of security and to different types of clients.

Non-software Factors Relating to Security

Although properly configuring your software contributes to secure computing, proper configuration alone will not ensure security. You must take steps to ensure the security you establish using Windows 2000 is not circumvented.

Physical Security

You must keep your computer safe from attackers. Keep your computer in a locked location when unattended, because users with direct access to computers might be able to compromise your system. Furthermore, rudimentary attacks (such as destroying your hard disk drive with a hammer) can only be prevented by physical security. Attacks on your computer do not have to be sophisticated to be effective.

User Education

It is easy for users to defeat the best laid plans through insecure practices. Writing down passwords, leaving computers unlocked, or finding other ways to circumvent the security you have put in place can quickly neutralize your security implementation. Write down effective security practices in a security policy, distribute the policy, and make your users follow it.

User education specifically prevents:

- **Identity interception**: Teaching users about what information they should and should not reveal will help prevent inadvertent security leaks to people posing as employees or other authorities.

- **Social engineering attack**: Educating users will prevent social engineering attacks, such as identity interceptions, but can also help prevent allowing unauthorized users to circumvent physical security or other such measures.

- **Ineffective passwords**: Teach users how to construct passwords that are not easy to decrypt. Any word, name, or number, regardless of whether it's spelled backward, for example, can be easily cracked using dictionary attacks. Create passwords that use symbols, numbers, and both uppercase and lowercase characters. You can attempt to prevent ineffective passwords by requiring users' passwords to meet criteria such as minimum password length using Password Policy. For more information, see "Password Policy" later in this chapter.

User Authentication

Windows 2000 Professional supports user authentication, which authenticates a user's identity. A user's authentication is the basis for granting access to network resources. Within this authentication model, the security system provides two types of authentication:

- Interactive logon, by which users confirm their identification to their local computer or network account. When using Windows 2000 Professional in a Windows 2000 Server environment, the network account is an Active Directory account.

- Network authentication, by which Windows 2000 confirms the user's identification to any network service that the user is attempting to access. To provide this type of authentication, the Windows 2000 security system includes three different authentication mechanisms: Kerberos v5, smart cards, and NTLM for compatibility with other versions of Windows.

Interactive Logon

Interactive logon confirms the user's identification to either a domain account or a local computer. This process differs, depending on the type of user account:

- With a domain account, a user logs on to the network with a password or smart card, using single sign-on credentials stored in Active Directory. By logging on with a domain account, an authorized user can access resources in the domain and any trusting domains. If a password is used to log on to a domain account, Windows 2000 uses Kerberos v5 for authentication. If a smart card is used, Windows 2000 uses Kerberos v5 authentication with certificates, unless the server is not a Windows 2000 server.

- With a local computer account, a user logs on to a local computer using credentials stored in Security Account Manager (SAM), which is the local security account database. Any workstation or member server can store local user accounts, but those accounts can only be used for access to that local computer.

Windows 2000 uses a user principal name (UPN) to identify users for interactive logon. UPNs serve the same purpose as user names and are formatted as *username@domain*.

If **Logon domain** does not appear in the dialog box provided at logon, and you want to log on to a Windows 2000 domain, you can type your user name and the Windows 2000 domain name in two ways:

- Your user principal name prefix (your user name) and your user principal name suffix (your Windows 2000 domain name), joined by the "at" sign (@). For example, user@sales.westcoast.microsoft.com.

- Your Windows 2000 domain name and your user name, separated by the backslash (\) character. For example, sales\user.

Note that the suffix in the first example is a fully-qualified DNS domain name. Your administrator might have created an alternative suffix to simplify the logon process. For example, creating a user principal name suffix of "microsoft" allows the same user to log on using the much simpler user@microsoft.com.

Smart Cards

Interactive logon can be configured to require smart card authentication for greater security.

Smart cards are credit card–sized plastic cards that contain integrated circuit chips. Smart cards are used to store users' certificates and private keys, enabling easy transport of these credentials. Smart cards can perform sophisticated public key cryptography operations, such as digital signing and key exchange.

You can deploy smart cards and smart card readers to provide stronger user authentication and security for a range of security solutions, including logging on over a network, secure Web communication, and secure e-mail.

Smart cards provide tamper-resistant authentication through onboard private key storage and processing. The private key is used in turn to provide other forms of security related to digital signatures and encryption.

For detailed procedures on implementing smart cards, see Windows 2000 Server Help.

Network Authentication

Network authentication confirms the user's identification to any network service that the user is attempting to access. To provide this type of authentication, the Windows 2000 security system supports many different authentication mechanisms, including smart cards, Kerberos v5, and NTLM for compatibility with Windows NT 4.0.

Domain account users do not see network authentication because Windows 2000 provides single sign-on support, automatically handling network authentication requests after a user has authenticated himself or herself and has been granted credentials. On the other hand, users of a local computer account must provide credentials (such as a public key certificate or a user name and password) every time they access a network resource.

Kerberos v5 Authentication

Kerberos v5 is the primary security protocol for authentication within a domain. The Kerberos v5 protocol verifies both the identity of the user and network services. This dual verification is known as mutual authentication.

The Kerberos v5 authentication mechanism issues a *ticket-granting ticket (TGT)* that is used to get *service tickets (STs)* that provide access to network services. These tickets contain encrypted data, including an encryption password that confirms the user's identity to the requested service. Except for entering an initial password or smart card credentials, the authentication process is transparent to the user. The general Kerberos Authentication process includes the following processes:

- The user on a client system, using a password or a smart card, authenticates to the Key Distribution Center (KDC). The KDC runs on each domain controller as part of Active Directory.

- The KDC issues a special ticket-granting ticket to the client. The client system uses this TGT to access the ticket-granting service (TGS), which is part of the Kerberos v5 authentication mechanism on the domain controller. The ticket-granting service then issues a service ticket to the client.

- The client presents this service ticket to the requested network service. The service ticket proves both the user's identity to the service and the service's identity to the user.

For more information about how Kerberos v5 provides authentication, see the *Windows 2000 Server Resource Kit*.

NTLM

The NTLM protocol was the default for network authentication in Windows NT 4.0 and is based on a challenge response mechanism for client authentication. It is retained in Windows 2000 for compatibility with earlier client and server versions of Windows. NTLM is also used to authenticate logons to stand-alone computers with Windows 2000.

Computers with Microsoft® Windows® 3.11, Windows 95, Windows 98, or Windows NT 4.0 will use the NTLM protocol for network authentication in Windows 2000 domains. Computers running Windows 2000 will use NTLM when authenticating to servers with Windows NT 4.0 and when accessing resources in Windows NT domain.

By default, Windows 2000 is installed in a mixed-mode network configuration, meaning a network configuration that uses any combination of Windows NT 4.0 and Windows 2000 computers. A Windows 2000 workstation or client manages the NTLM credentials entered at system logon on the client side to use when the client connects to Windows NT 4.0 servers using NTLM authentication. Support for NTLM credentials in the Windows 2000 security is the same as for Windows NT 4.0 for compatibility.

As examples, the following configurations would use NTLM as the authentication mechanism:

- A Windows 2000 Professional client authenticating to a Windows NT 4.0 domain controller.

- A Microsoft® Windows NT® Workstation 4.0 client authenticating to a Windows 2000 domain controller.

- A Windows NT Workstation 4.0 client authenticating to a Windows NT 4.0 domain controller.

- Users in a Windows NT 4.0 domain authenticating to a Windows 2000 domain.

In addition, NTLM is the authentication protocol for computers that are not participating in a domain, such as stand-alone servers and workgroups.

The NTLM authentication package in Windows 2000 supports three methods of challenge/response authentication:

- **LAN Manager (LM)**. This is the least secure form of challenge/response authentication. It is available so that computers running Windows 2000 Professional can connect in share level security mode to file shares on computers running Microsoft® Windows® for Workgroups, Windows 95, or Windows 98.

- **NTLM version 1**. This is more secure than LM challenge/response authentication. It is available so that clients running Windows 2000 Professional can connect to servers in a Windows NT domain that has at least one domain controller that is running Windows NT 4.0 Service Pack 3 or earlier.

- **NTLM version 2**. This is the most secure form of challenge/response authentication. It is used when clients running Windows 2000 Professional connect to servers in a Windows NT domain where all domain controllers have been upgraded to Windows NT 4.0 Service Pack 4 or later. It is also used when clients running Windows 2000 connect to servers running Windows NT in a Windows 2000 domain.

By default, all three challenge/response mechanisms are enabled. You can disable authentication using weaker variants by setting the LAN Manager authentication level security option in local security policy for the computer.

For more information about configuring the LAN Manager authentication level, see Group Policy Reference on the *Microsoft® Windows 2000 Professional Resource Kit* companion CD or the *Windows 2000 Server Resource Kit*.

Remote Access Logon Process

Windows 2000 supports several authentication protocols such as MS-CHAP, CHAP, and SPAP for dial-in access. Windows 2000 can be configured to support Extensible Authentication Protocol (EAP) if you want to use security devices to authenticate remote access users in conjunction with other security devices such as smart cards and certificates. EAP-transport layer security (TLS) allows users remote access by authenticating their identities using a combination of authentication vectors. When remote access users attempt to log on to a server that is using EAP-TLS, they are prompted to insert their smart card and enter their PIN during network logon authentication. If the user's PIN and smart card credentials are valid, the user is logged on and granted rights for the appropriate network user account. For more information about EAP-TLS, see "Internet Authentication Service" in the *Microsoft® Windows® 2000 Server Resource Kit Internetworking Guide*.

The remote access logon process depends primarily on server configuration to enable logon. Windows 2000 Server includes Routing and Remote Access Services which can authenticate remote access network users. Routing and Remote Access supports smart card logon authentication using the EAP-TLS extension of the Point-to-Point Protocol (PPP).

For information about adding a smart card reader to your Windows 2000 Professional computer, see Windows 2000 Professional online documentation.

For more information about Routing and Remote Access, see "Remote Access" later in this chapter.

Security Groups, User Rights, and Permissions

Security groups, user rights and permissions provide powerful security management. Management can be high-level, allowing you to manage security for numerous resources, while at the same time it can be fine-grained, allowing specific control of files and folders and user rights.

Security Groups

Windows 2000 allows you to organize users and other objects into groups for easy access permission administration. Defining security groups is a major security task. Security groups can be described according to their scope, such as Global groups or Universal groups, as well as according to their purpose, rights, and role, such as the Everyone group or the Administrators group.

The Windows 2000 security groups let you assign the same security permissions to large numbers of users. This ensures consistent security permissions across all members of a group. Using security groups to assign permissions means the access control on resources remains fairly static and easy to control and audit. Users who need access are added or removed from the appropriate security groups as needed, and the access control lists change infrequently.

How Security Groups Work

Depending on the environment you are working in, you might encounter any of the four main types of security groups:

- Domain local groups, which are best used for granting access rights to resources such as file systems or printers that are located on any computer in the domain where common access permissions are required.

- Global groups, which are used for combining users who share a common access profile based on job function or business role.

- Universal groups, which are used in larger, multi-domain organizations where there is a need to grant access to similar groups of accounts defined in multiple domains. Universal groups are used only in multiple domain trees or forests that have a global catalog.

- Computer local groups, which are security groups specific to a computer and not recognized elsewhere in the domain.

For more information about working with the four different types of groups, see the *Deployment Planning Guide*.

Permissions of Security Groups

Windows 2000 includes a number of preconfigured groups including the following:

- **Guests**: This group allows occasional or one-time users to log on to a workstation's built-in Guest account and be granted limited abilities. Members of the Guest group can also shut down the system. The built-in guest account is disabled by default.

- **Users**: Members of this group (normal authenticated users) do not have broad read/write permission as they did in Windows NT 4.0. These users have read-only permission for most parts of the system and read/write permission in their own profile folders. Users cannot read other users' data, install applications that require modification of system directories, or perform administrative tasks.

- **Power Users**: Members of this group have all the access permissions that Users and Power Users had in Windows NT 4.0. Power Users have read/write permission to other parts of the system in addition to their own profile folders. Power Users can install applications and perform many administrative tasks. If you are running applications that have not been certified for use with Windows 2000, users will need to have Power User privileges.

- **Backup Operators**: Members of this group can back up and restore files on the computer, regardless of any permissions that protect those files. They can also log on to the computer and shut it down, but they cannot change security settings.

- **Administrators**: Members of this group have total control of the desktop, allowing them to complete all tasks. Members of the Administrators group have the same level of rights and permissions they did for Windows NT 4.0. There is also a built-in administrator account that allows administration of the computer. The administrator account is the first account that is created when Windows 2000 is installed.

Prerequisites for Implementing Security Groups

Security groups are a built-in feature of Windows 2000. No special installation or prerequisite is required.

Implementing Security Groups

To create new users and place them in Security groups, use the Computer Management snap-in of MMC. For more information about creating new users, see Windows 2000 Professional Help.

User Rights

Administrators can assign specific rights to group accounts or to individual user accounts. These rights authorize users to perform specific actions, such as logging on to a system or backing up files and directories. User rights are different from permissions because user rights apply to user accounts, and permissions are attached to objects (such as printers or folders). For information about permissions, see "How Inheritance Affects Permissions" later in this chapter.

User rights can be applied to individual users or to user groups. It is simplest to apply rights to user groups because all users who belong to the group will inherit the rights you grant to the group. It is also possible to apply rights to each user, but this requires more administration because you will have to set rights for each user.

User rights that are assigned to a group are applied to all members of the group while they remain members. If a user is a member of multiple groups, the user's rights are cumulative, which means that the user has more than one set of rights. The only time that rights assigned to one group might conflict with those assigned to another is in the case of certain logon rights. In general, however, user rights assigned to one group do not conflict with the rights assigned to another group. To remove rights from a user, the administrator simply removes the user from the group.

▶ **To Assign User Rights to Groups**

1. Open the Group Policy snap-in to MMC.

2. Double-click the User right you want to assign to a group. Many user rights are in **User Rights Assignment**.

3. Click **Add**, and then enter the group or groups to which you want to grant this permission. Click **Check Names** to confirm that group names are recognized.

There are two types of user rights:

- **Privileges**: A right which is assigned to a user and specifies allowable actions on the network. An example of a privilege is the right to back up files and directories.

- **Logon rights**: A right which is assigned to a user and specifies the ways in which a user can log on to a system. An example of a logon right is the right to log on to a system locally.

Privileges

Some privileges can override permissions set on an object. For example, a user logged on to a domain account as a member of the Backup Operators group has the right to perform backup operations for all domain servers. However, this requires the ability to read all files on those servers, even files on which their owners have set permissions that explicitly deny access to all users, including members of the Backup Operators group. A user right, in this case, the right to perform a backup, takes precedence over all file and directory permissions.

Table 13.4 shows the privileges that can be assigned to a user by setting user rights. These privileges can be managed with the User Rights policy.

Table 13.4   Privileges That Can Be Assigned to a User

Privilege	Description
Act as part of the operating system	This privilege allows a process to authenticate as any user, and therefore gain access to resources under any user identity. Only low-level authentication services should require this privilege.
	The user or process that is granted this privilege might create security tokens that grant them more rights than their normal user profile provides. This includes granting themselves all access as anonymous users, which defeats attempts to audit the identity of the token's user. Do not grant this privilege unless you are certain it is needed.
	Processes that require this privilege should use the LocalSystem account, which already includes this privilege, rather than using a separate user account with this privilege specially assigned.
Add workstations to a domain	Allows the user to add a computer to a specific domain. The user specifies the domain on the computer being added, creating an object in the Computer container of Active Directory.
Back up files and directories	Allows the user to circumvent file and directory permissions to back up the system. Specifically, the privilege is similar to granting the following permissions on all files and folders on the local computer: Traverse Folder/Execute File, List Folder/Read Data, Read Attributes, Read Extended Attributes, and Read Permissions. For more information, see "Customizing the Desktop" in this book.

(continued)

Table 13.4   Privileges That Can Be Assigned to a User *(continued)*

Privilege	Description
Bypass traverse checking	Allows the user to pass through directories to which the user otherwise has no access, while navigating an object path in any Windows file system or in the registry. This privilege does not allow the user to list the contents of a directory, only to traverse directories.
Change the system time	Allows the user to set the time for the internal clock of the computer.
Create a token object	Allows a process to create a token which it can then use to get access to any local resources when the process uses NtCreateToken() or other token-creation APIs. It is recommended that processes requiring this privilege use the LocalSystem account, which already includes this privilege, rather than using a separate user account with this privilege assigned.
Create permanent shared objects	Allows a process to create a directory object in the Windows 2000 object manager. This privilege is useful to kernel-mode components that plan to extend the Windows 2000 object name space. Because components running in kernel mode already have this privilege assigned to them, it is not necessary to specifically assign this privilege.
Create a pagefile	Allows the user to create and change the size of a pagefile. This is done by specifying a paging file size for a given drive in the **Performance Options** dialog box, which is accessible through the **System Properties** dialog box.
Debug programs	Allows the user to attach a debugger to any process. This privilege provides powerful access to sensitive and critical system operating components.
Enable *Trusted for Delegation* on user and computer accounts	Allows the user to set the *Trusted for Delegation* setting on a user or computer object. The user or object that is granted this privilege must have write access to the account control flags on the user or computer object. A server process either running on a computer that is trusted for delegation or run by a user who is trusted for delegation can access resources on another computer. This uses a client's delegated credentials, as long as the client account does not have the *Account Cannot Be Delegated* account control flag set. Misuse of this privilege or of the *Trusted for Delegation* settings might make the network vulnerable to sophisticated attacks using Trojan horse programs that impersonate incoming clients and use their credentials to gain access to network resources.
Force shutdown of a remote system	Allows a user to shut down a computer from a remote location on the network.

(continued)

Table 13.4   Privileges That Can Be Assigned to a User *(continued)*

Privilege	Description
Generate security audits	Allows a process to make entries in the security log for object access auditing. The process can also generate other security audits. The security log is used to trace unauthorized system access.
Increase quotas	Allows a process with *write property* access to another process to increase the processor quota assigned to that other process. This privilege is useful for system tuning, but can be abused, as in a *denial-of-service* attack.
Increase scheduling priority	Allows a process with *write property* access to another process to increase the execution priority of that other process. A user with this privilege can change the scheduling priority of a process through Task Manager .
Load and unload device drivers	Allows a user to install and uninstall Plug and Play device drivers. Device drivers that are not Plug and Play are not affected by this privilege and can only be installed by administrators. Because device drivers run as trusted (highly-privileged) programs, this privilege might be misused to install hostile programs and give these programs destructive access to resources.
Lock pages in memory	Allows a process to keep data in physical memory, preventing the system from paging the data to virtual memory on disk. Exercising this privilege might significantly affect system performance. This privilege is obsolete and is therefore never checked.
Manage auditing and security log	Allows a user to specify object access auditing options for individual resources such as files, Active Directory objects, and registry keys. Object access auditing is not actually performed unless you have enabled it in the computerwide audit policy settings under Security Policy or under Security Policy defined in Active Directory. This privilege does not grant access to the computer-wide audit policy. A user with this privilege can also view and clear the security log from the Event Viewer.
Modify firmware environment values	Allows modification of the system environment variables, either by a user through the System Properties or by a process.
Profile a single process	Allows a user to use Windows NT and Windows 2000 performance-monitoring tools to monitor the performance of non-system processes.
Profile system performance	Allows a user to use Windows NT and Windows 2000 performance-monitoring tools to monitor the performance of system processes.

(continued)

Table 13.4   Privileges That Can Be Assigned to a User *(continued)*

Privilege	Description
Remove a computer from docking station	Allows a user to undock a portable computer with the Windows 2000 user interface.
Replace a process-level token	Allows a process to replace the default token associated with a sub-process that has been started.
Restore files and directories	Allows a user to circumvent file and directory permissions when restoring backed up files and directories, and to set any valid security principal as the owner of an object. See also the *Back up files and directories* privilege.
Shut down the system	Allows a user to shut down the local computer.
Take ownership of files or other objects	Allows a user to take ownership of any securable object in the system, including Active Directory objects, files and folders, printers, registry keys, processes, and threads.

For more information, see "Security Policy" later in this chapter.

Logon Rights

Logon rights can be assigned to a user and managed with the User Rights policy. Logon rights are assigned to users and specify the ways in which a user can log on to a system.

Table 13.5 lists and describes Windows 2000 logon rights.

Table 13.5   Windows 2000 Professional Default Logon Rights

Logon Right	Description
Access this computer from a network	Allows a user to connect to the computer over the network. By default, this privilege is granted to Administrators, Everyone, and Power Users.
Deny access to this computer	Denies a user the ability to connect to the computer over the network. By default, this privilege is not granted to anyone from the network.
Log on as a batch job	Allows a user to log on using a batch-queue facility. By default, this privilege is granted to Administrators.
Deny log on as a batch job	Denies a user the ability to log on using a batch-queue facility. By default, this privilege is granted to no one.

(continued)

Table 13.5   Windows 2000 Professional Default Logon Rights *(continued)*

Logon Right	Description
Log on as a service	Allows a security principal to log on as a service, as a way of establishing a security context. The LocalSystem account always retains the right to log on as a service. Any service that runs under a separate account must be granted this right. By default, this right is not granted to anyone.
Deny logon as a service	Denies a security principal the ability to log on as a service, as a way of establishing a security context. The LocalSystem account always retains the right to log on as a service. Any service that runs under a separate account must be granted this right. By default, this right is not granted to anyone.
Log on locally	Allows a user to log on at the computer's keyboard. By default, this right is granted to Administrators, Account Operators, Backup Operators, Print Operators, and Server Operators.
Deny log on locally	Denies a user the ability to log on at the computer's keyboard. By default, this right is granted no one.

Permissions

You can assign permissions to files or folders and determine what can be done to those resources. Note that you cannot assign *rights* to files or folders.

For information about how to set file or folder permissions, see Windows 2000 Professional Help.

▶ **To Set File or Folder Permissions**

1. Open Windows Explorer, and then locate the file or folder for which you want to set permissions.

2. Right-click the file or folder, click **Properties**, and then click the **Security** tab.

3. To set up permissions for a new group or user, click **Add**. Type the name of the group or user you want to set permissions for using the format *domainname\name*, and then click **OK** to close the dialog box.

    –Or–

    To change or remove permissions from an existing group or user, click the name of the group or user.

4. In **Permissions**, click **Allow** or **Deny** for each permission you want to allow or deny.

    –Or–

    To remove the group or user from the permissions list, click **Remove**.

How Inheritance Affects Permissions

After you set permissions on a folder, new files and subfolders created in the folder inherit these permissions unless you configure this not to happen.

▶ **To Prevent A Folder from Imposing Permissions on New Files or Folders**

1. In My Computer, right-click the folder in question, and then click **Properties**.
2. On the **Security** tab, click **Advanced**.
3. Select a permission entry from the **Permissions Entries** list, and then click **View/Edit**.
4. Select an alternate inheritance behavior from the **Apply onto** drop-down list.

▶ **To Prevent New Files or Folders from Inheriting Permissions**

1. Using **My Computer**, right-click the folder in question, and then click **Properties**.
2. On the **Security** tab, clear the **Allow inheritable permissions from parent to propagate to this object** check box.

If the check boxes appear shaded, the file or folder has inherited permissions from the parent folder. There are three ways to make changes to inherited permissions:

- Make the changes to the parent folder, and then the file or folder will inherit these permissions.
- Select the opposite permission (**Allow** or **Deny**) to override the inherited permission.
- Clear the **Allow inheritable permissions from parent to propagate to this object** check box. Now you can make changes to the permissions or remove the user or group from the permissions list. However, the file or folder will no longer inherit permissions from the parent folder.

If neither **Allow** nor **Deny** is selected for a permission, then the group or user might have obtained the permission through group membership. If the group or user has not obtained the permission through membership in another group, the group or user is implicitly denied the permission. To explicitly allow or deny the permission, click the appropriate check box.

Default Settings

The following section describes the default permissions provided to different users.

Default File System and Registry Permissions

Table 13.6 describes the default file system and registry permissions.

Table 13.6   Default Settings for User Write Access

Object	Permission	Description
HKEY_Current_User	Full Control	User's portion of the registry.
%UserProfile%	Full Control	User's Profile directory.
All Users\Documents	Read, Create File	Allows Users to create files that can subsequently be read (but not modified) by other Users.
%Windir%\Temp	Synchronize, Traverse, Add File, Add Subdir	Each computer has one temporary directory for use by service-based applications that use this directory to improve performance.
\ (Root Directory)	Not Configured during setup	No permissions are applied to the root level of the directory because the Windows 2000 ACL Inheritance model would cause any root level permissions to affect all child objects, including those outside the scope of setup.

File System Permissions for Power Users and Users

Table 13.7 describes the default access control settings that are applied to file system objects for Power Users and Users during a clean installation of the Windows 2000 operating system onto an NTFS partition. For directories, unless otherwise stated (in parentheses), the permissions apply to the directory, subdirectories, and files.

- %systemdir% refers to %windir%\system32.
- *.* refers to the files (not directories) contained in a directory.
- RX means Read and Execute.

Table 13.7   Default Access Control Settings for File System Objects

File System Object	Default Power User Permissions	Default User Permissions
c:\boot.ini	RX	None
c:\ntdetect.com	RX	None
c:\ntldr	RX	None
c:\ntbootdd.sys	RX	None
c:\autoexec.bat	Modify	RX
c:\config.sys	Modify	RX
\ProgramFiles	Modify	RX
%windir%	Modify	RX

(continued)

Table 13.7   Default Access Control Settings for File System Objects *(continued)*

File System Object	Default Power User Permissions	Default User Permissions
%windir%*.*	RX	RX
%windir%\config*.*	RX	RX
%windir%\cursors*.*	RX	RX
%windir%\Temp	Modify	Synchronize, Traverse, Add File, Add Subdir
%windir%\repair	Modify	List
%windir%\addins	Modify (Dir\Subdirs) RX (Files)	RX
%windir%\Connection Wizard	Modify (Dir\Subdirs) RX (Files)	RX
%windir%\fonts*.*	RX	RX
%windir%\help*.*	RX	RX
%windir%\inf*.*	RX	RX
%windir%\java	Modify (Dir\Subdirs) RX (Files)	RX
%windir%\media*.*	RX	RX
%windir%\msagent	Modify (Dir\Subdirs) RX (Files)	RX
%windir%\security	RX	RX
%windir%\speech	Modify (Dir\Subdirs) RX (Files)	RX
%windir%\system*.*	Read, Execute	RX
%windir%\twain_32	Modify (Dir\Subdirs) RX (Files)	RX
%windir%\Web	Modify (Dir\Subdirs) RX (Files)	RX
%systemdir%	Modify	RX
%systemdir%*.*	RX	RX
%systemdir%\config	List	List
%systemdir%\dhcp	RX	RX
%systemdir%\dllcache	None	None
%systemdir%\drivers	RX	RX
%systemdir%\CatRoot	Modify (Dir\Subdirs) RX (Files)	RX
%systemdir%\ias	Modify (Dir\Subdirs) RX (Files)	RX
%systemdir%\mui	Modify (Dir\Subdirs) RX (Files)	RX
%systemdir%\OS2*.*	RX	RX
%systemdir%\OS2 \DLL*.*	RX	RX
%systemdir%\RAS*.*	RX	RX

(continued)

Table 13.7   Default Access Control Settings for File System Objects *(continued)*

File System Object	Default Power User Permissions	Default User Permissions
%systemdir%\ShellExt	Modify (Dir\Subdirs) RX (Files)	RX
%systemdir%\Viewers *.*	RX	RX
%systemdir%\wbem	Modify (Dir\Subdirs) RX (Files)	RX
%systemdir%\wbem \mof	Modify	RX
%UserProfile%	Full Control	Full Control
All Users	Modify	Read
All Users\Documents	Modify	Read, Create File
All Users\Application Data	Modify	Read

Note that a Power User can write new files into the following directories but cannot modify the files that are installed there during text-mode setup. Furthermore, all other Power Users inherit Modify permissions on files created in these directories.

- %windir%
- %windir%\config
- %windir%\cursors
- %windir%\fonts
- %windir%\help
- %windir%\inf
- %windir%\media
- %windir%\system
- %systemdir%
- %systemdir%\OS2
- %systemdir%\OS2\DLL
- %systemdir%\RAS
- %systemdir%\Viewers

For directories designated as [Modify (Dir\Subdirs) RX (Files)], Power Users can write new files; however, other Power Users will only have read access to those files.

Registry Permissions for Power Users and Users

Table 13.8 describes the default access control settings that are applied to registry objects for Power Users and Users during a clean installation of the Windows 2000 operating system. For a given object, permissions apply to that object and all child objects unless the child object is also listed in the table.

Table 13.8   Registry Permissions for Power Users and Users

Registry Object	Default Power User Permissions	Default User Permissions
HKEY_LOCAL_MACHINE		
HKEY_LOCAL_MACHINE\SOFTWARE	Modify	Read
HKLM\SOFTWARE\Classes\helpfile	Read	Read
HKLM\SOFTWARE\Classes\.hlp	Read	Read
HKLM\SOFTWARE\Microsoft\Command Processor	Read	Read
HKLM\SOFTWARE\Microsoft\Cryptography	Read	Read
HKLM\SOFTWARE\Microsoft\Driver Signing	Read	Read
HKLM\SOFTWARE\Microsoft\EnterpriseCertificates	Read	Read
HKLM\SOFTWARE\Microsoft\Non-Driver Signing	Read	Read
HKLM\SOFTWARE\Microsoft\NetDDE	None	None
HKLM\SOFTWARE\Microsoft\Ole	Read	Read
HKLM\SOFTWARE\Microsoft\Rpc	Read	Read
HKLM\SOFTWARE\Microsoft\Secure	Read	Read
HKLM\SOFTWARE\Microsoft\SystemCertificates	Read	Read
HKLM\SOFTWARE\Microsoft\Windows\CurrentVersion\RunOnce	Read	Read
HKLM\SOFTWARE\Microsoft\Windows NT\CurrentVersion\Drivers32	Read	Read
HKLM\SOFTWARE\Microsoft\Windows NT\CurrentVersion\Font Drivers	Read	Read

continued

Table 13.8   Registry Permissions for Power Users and Users *(continued)*

Registry Object	Default Power User Permissions	Default User Permissions
HKLM\SOFTWARE\Microsoft\Windows NT\CurrentVersion \FontMapper	Read	Read
HKLM\SOFTWARE\Microsoft\Windows NT\CurrentVersion \Image File Execution Options	Read	Read
HKLM\SOFTWARE\Microsoft\Windows NT\CurrentVersion \IniFileMapping	Read	Read
HKLM\SOFTWARE\Microsoft\Windows NT\CurrentVersion \Perflib	Read (via Interactive)	Read (via Interactive)
HKLM\SOFTWARE\Microsoft\Windows NT\CurrentVersion \SeCEdit	Read	Read
HKLM\SOFTWARE\Microsoft\Windows NT\CurrentVersion \Time Zones	Read	Read
HKLM\SOFTWARE\Microsoft\Windows NT\CurrentVersion \Windows	Read	Read
HKLM\SOFTWARE\Microsoft\Windows NT\CurrentVersion \Winlogon	Read	Read
HKLM\SOFTWARE\Microsoft\Windows NT\CurrentVersion \AsrCommands	Read	Read
HKLM\SOFTWARE\Microsoft\Windows NT\CurrentVersion \Classes	Read	Read
HKLM\SOFTWARE\Microsoft\Windows NT\CurrentVersion \Console	Read	Read
HKLM\SOFTWARE\Microsoft\Windows NT\CurrentVersion \ProfileList	Read	Read
HKLM\SOFTWARE\Microsoft\Windows NT\CurrentVersion \Svchost	Read	Read
HKLM\SOFTWARE\Policies	Read	Read

continued

Table 13.8   Registry Permissions for Power Users and Users *(continued)*

Registry Object	Default Power User Permissions	Default User Permissions
HKLM\SYSTEM	Read	Read
HKLM\SYSTEM\CurrentControlSet\Control\SecurePipeServers \winreg	None	None
HKLM\SYSTEM\CurrentControlSet\Control\Session Manager \Executive	Modify	Read
HKLM\SYSTEM\CurrentControlSet\Control \TimeZoneInformation	Modify	Read
HKLM\SYSTEM\CurrentControlSet\Control\WMI\Security	None	None
HKLM\HARDWARE	Read (via Everyone)	Read (via Everyone)
HKLM\SAM	Read (via Everyone)	Read (via Everyone)
HKLM\SECURITY	None	None
HKEY_USERS		
HKEY_USERS\.DEFAULT	Read	Read
HKEY_USERS\.DEFAULT\SOFTWARE\Microsoft\NetDDE	None	None
HKEY_CURRENT_CONFIG	= HKLM\System \CurrentControlSet \HardwareProfiles \Current	
HKEY_CURRENT_USER	Full Control	Full Control
HKEY_CLASSES_ROOT	= HKLM \Software\Classes	= HKLM \Software\Classes

For more information, see the Distributed Systems Guide in the *Windows 2000 Server Resource Kit.*

Security Policy

A Security Policy object contains an extensive profile of security permissions that apply primarily to the security settings of a domain, computer, or computer desktop (rather than to users). A single Security Policy object can be applied to all of the computers in an organizational unit. Security Policy is applied when an individual computer starts up, and is periodically refreshed if changes are made without restarting.

How Security Policy Works

Stand-alone computers have Security Policy associated with them that can be modified by users with the appropriate rights. When a computer joins a domain, the domain Security Policy is applied to the local computer. Domain Security Policy will override any changes made to Security Policy at the desktop level.

For information about Security Policy and Group Policy for computers in a domain, see the *Deployment Planning Guide* and Windows 2000 Help.

Security Policy is to computers as security groups are to users. Security Policy lets you apply a single security profile to multiple computers, just as security groups let you grant a standardized set of rights to a group of users. It enforces consistency and provides easy administration.

Security Policy objects contain permissions and parameters that implement multiple types of security strategies.

Prerequisites for Implementing Local Security Policy

Security Policy is installed by default on local computers. However, Active Directory must be installed on a server before you can edit and apply domainwide Security Policy objects.

How to Implement Security Policy

To apply local Security Policy, see Windows 2000 Professional Help.

In a domain, to view a sample Security Policy, open the Group Policy snap-in in the MMC and navigate to the **Security Settings** container:

```
Local Computer Policy
  └ Computer Configuration
  └ Windows Settings
  └ Security Settings
```

Under **Security Settings** there are nine subdirectories of security policy settings. These nine groups are described later in this chapter.

Implementing Security Policy consists of creating a new Group Policy object (or modifying an existing one), enabling appropriate settings within the object, and then linking the Group Policy object to an organizational unit that contains computers in the domain.

Group Policy Considerations

Minimize the number of Group Policy objects, including Security Policy objects, that apply to users and computers. Do this first, because each computer and user Group Policy object must be loaded to a computer during startup and to user profiles at logon. Multiple Group Policy objects increase computer startup and logon time. Second, applying multiple Group Policy objects can create policy conflicts that are difficult to troubleshoot.

In general, Group Policy can be passed down from parent to child sites, domains, and organizational units. If you have assigned a specific Group Policy to a high-level parent, that Group Policy applies to all organizational units beneath the parent, including the user and computer objects in each container. For more information about inheritance of Group Policy settings, see "Defining Client Administration and Configuration Standards" in the *Deployment Planning Guide*.

Security templates (described later in this chapter) are useful as models of security settings appropriate for different types of Group Policy.

Security Policy Settings

The following are the nine groups of Security Policy features mentioned previously. They are containers located in the **Security Settings** node of a Group Policy object. Although there are some differences regarding whether you are managing Security Policy for a domain or for a local computer, in general Security Policy includes much the same thing. For a local Security Policy, find the following:

- Password Policy
- Account Lockout Policy
- Kerberos Authentication Policy
- Audit Policy
- User Rights Assignment
- Security Options
- Encrypted Data Recovery Agent
- Internet Protocol Security Policies

Some of the policy areas apply only to the scope of a domain; that is, the policy settings are domainwide. Account policies, for example, apply uniformly to all user accounts in the domain. If you cannot define different account policies for different organizational units in the same domain, the policy will affect only the account policies on member workstations and servers contained within the organizational unit (OU).

Account Policies

Account policies are the first subcategory of Security Settings. The Account policies include the following:

Password Policy You can modify password policy to meet your organization's security needs. For example, you can specify minimum password length and maximum password age. You can also require complex passwords and prevent users from reusing passwords or simple variations of passwords. Note that password policy can be applied in Active Directory as well as in your local computer's security policy. If multiple policies are set, the most restrictive policy is used.

Account Lockout Policy You can force users to be locked out after a specified number of failed logon attempts. You can also specify the period of time that accounts are frozen.

Kerberos Authentication Policy You can modify the default Kerberos settings for each domain. For example, you can set the maximum lifetime of a user ticket. Kerberos Authentication Policy is only applicable at a domain level, so no Kerberos Authentication Policy settings are available for local security policy.

The policies you choose affect the level of help desk support required for users as well as the vulnerability of your network to security breaches and attacks. For example, specifying a restrictive account lockout policy increases the potential for denial of service attacks, and setting a restrictive password policy results in increased help desk calls from users who cannot log on to the network.

In addition, specifying restrictive password policy can actually reduce the security of the network. For example, if you require passwords longer than seven characters, most users have difficulty remembering them. They might write their passwords down and leave them where an intruder can easily find them.

Local Computer Policies

The second subcategory of Security Settings is Local Computer policies. Local Computer policies include the following:

Audit Policy Windows 2000 can record a range of security event types, from a systemwide event, such as a user logging on, to an attempt by a particular user to read a specific file. Both successful and unsuccessful attempts to perform an action can be recorded.

User Rights Assignment   You can control the rights assigned to user accounts and security groups for local computers. You can specify users and security groups who have rights to perform a variety of tasks affecting security. For example, you can control access to computers from the network, who can log on locally, or who can shut down the system. You can specify who has rights to perform critical administrative tasks on the computer, such as backing up and restoring files and directories, taking ownership of files and objects, and forcing shutdown from a remote system.

Security Options   You can control a wide variety of security options for local computers. For example, you can specify policies that force users to log off when logon hours expire, disable CTRL+ALT+DEL for logon (to force smart card logon), and force computers to halt if unable to audit.

Public Key Policies

This subdivision of security settings lets you add a new Encrypted Data Recovery Agent and set up Automatic Certificate Requests. You can also manage your lists of trusted certification authorities.

Internet Protocol Security Policies

The policies in this section describe how to handle a variety of requests for Internet Protocol security (IPSec) communications. You can require secure communication, permit secure communication, or communicate without using IPSec. The predefined policies are not intended for immediate use. They provide examples of behavior for testing purposes. Network security administrators need to carefully design and assign their own custom IPSec policy to computers. For more information about working with Internet Protocol security policies, see "Internet Protocol Security" later in this chapter, or see the *Deployment Planning Guide*, the *Microsoft® Windows® 2000 Server Resource Kit Distributed Systems Guide*, or the *Internetworking Guide*.

Security Settings by Policy

The following tables list the default security settings by policy.

Account Policies

Default settings for Password Policies on a local computer are described in Table 13.9.

Table 13.9   Password Policy

Policy	Local Setting
Enforce password history	0 passwords remembered
Maximum password age	42 days
Minimum password age	0 days
Minimum password length	0 characters
Passwords must meet complexity requirements	Disabled
Store password using reversible encryption for all users in the domain	Disabled

Default settings for Account Lockout Policies on a local computer are described in Table 13.10.

Table 13.10   Account Lockout Policy

Policy	Local Setting
Account lockout duration	Not defined
Account lockout threshold	0 invalid logon attempts
Reset account lockout counter after	Not defined

Local Policies

Default settings for Audit Policies on a local computer are described in Table 13.11.

Table 13.11   Audit Policy

Policy	Local Setting
Audit account logon events	No auditing
Audit account management	No auditing
Audit directory service access	No auditing
Audit logon events	No auditing
Audit object access	No auditing
Audit policy change	No auditing
Audit privilege use	No auditing
Audit process tracking	No auditing
Audit system events	No auditing

Default settings for User Rights Assignment Policies on a local computer are described in Table 13.12.

Table 13.12   User Rights Assignment Policy

Policy	Local Setting
Access this computer from the network	Everyone
Act as part of the operating system	*<None>*
Add workstations to domain	*<None>*
Back up files and directories	Backup Operators
Bypass traverse checking	Everyone
Change the system time	Power Users
Create a pagefile	Administrators
Create a token object	*<None>*
Create permanent shared objects	*<None>*
Debug programs	Administrators
Deny access to this computer from the network	*<None>*
Deny logon as a batch job	*<None>*
Deny logon as a service	*<None>*
Deny logon locally	*<None>*
Enable computer and user accounts to be trusted for delegation	*<None>*
Force shutdown from a remote system	Administrators
Generate security audits	*<None>*
Increase quotas	Administrators
Increase scheduling priority	Administrators
Load and unload device drivers	Administrators
Lock pages in memory	*<None>*
Log on as a batch job	*<None>*
Log on as a service	*<None>*
Log on locally	*Computer Domain*\Guest
Manage auditing and security log	Administrators
Modify firmware environment values	Administrators
Profile single process	Power Users
Profile system performance	Administrators
Remove computer from docking station	Users
Replace a process level token	*<None>*
Restore files and directories	Backup Operators
Shut down the system	Users
Synchronize directory service data	*<None>*
Take ownership of files or other objects	Administrators

Note To permit users to log on to a computer, grant the user or group of users the Log *on locally* right listed above.

Default settings for Security Options Policies on a local computer are described in Table 13.13.

Table 13.13   Security Options Policy

Policy	Local Setting
Additional restrictions for anonymous connections	Rely on default permissions (none set by default)
Allow server operators to schedule tasks (domain controllers only)	Not defined
Allow system to be shut down without having to log on	Enabled
Allowed to eject removable NTFS media	Administrators
Amount of idle time required before disconnecting session	15 minutes
Audit the access of global system objects	Disabled
Audit use of Backup and Restore privilege	Disabled
Automatically log off users when logon time expires (local)	Enabled
Clear virtual memory pagefile when system shuts down	Disabled
Digitally sign client communication (always)	Disabled
Digitally sign client communication (when possible)	Enabled
Digitally sign server communication (always)	Disabled
Digitally sign server communication (when possible)	Disabled
Disable CTRL+ALT+DEL requirement for logon	Not defined
Do not display last user name in logon screen	Disabled
LAN Manager Authentication Level	Send LM and NTLM responses
Message text for users attempting to log on	*<None>*
Message title for users attempting to log on	*<None>*
Number of previous logons to cache (in case domain controller is not available)	10 logons
Prevent system maintenance of computer account password	Disabled
Prevent users from installing printer drivers	Disabled
Prompt user to change password before expiration	14 days
Recovery Console: Allow automatic administrative logon	Disabled
Recovery Console: Allow floppy copy and access to all drives and all folders	Disabled

(continued)

Table 13.13   Security Options Policy *(continued)*

Policy	Local Setting
Rename administrator account	Not defined
Rename guest account	Not defined
Restrict CD-ROM access to locally logged-on user only	Disabled
Restrict floppy access to locally logged-on user only	Disabled
Secure channel: Digitally encrypt or sign secure channel data (always)	Disabled
Secure channel: Digitally encrypt secure channel data (when possible)	Enabled
Secure channel: Digitally sign secure channel data (when possible)	Enabled
Secure channel: Require strong (Windows 2000 or later) session key	Disabled
Send unencrypted password to connect to third-party SMB servers	Disabled
Shut down system immediately if unable to log security audits	Disabled
Smart card removal behavior	No Action
Strengthen default permissions of global system objects (for example, Symbolic Links)	Enabled
Unsigned driver installation behavior	Not defined
Unsigned non-driver installation behavior	Not defined

Public Key Policies

Default settings for the Encrypted Data Recovery Agent Policy are described in Table 13.14.

Table 13.14   Encrypted Data Recovery Agent Policy

Issued To	Issued By	Expiration Date	Intended Purposes	Friendly Name	Status
Administrator	Administrator	10/8/99	File Recovery	*<None>*	*<None>*

Internet Protocol Security Policies on Local Computer

Default settings for Internet Protocol Security Policies on a local computer are described in Table 13.15.

Table 13.15   Internet Protocol Security Policies on Local Computer

Name	Description	Policy Assigned
Client (Respond Only)	Communicate normally (unsecured). Use the default response rule to negotiate with servers that request security. Only the requested protocol and port traffic with that server is secured.	No
Secure Server (Require Security)	For all IP traffic, always require security using Kerberos trust. Do not allow unsecured communication with untrusted clients.	No
Server (Request Security)	For all IP traffic, always request security using Kerberos trust. Allow unsecured communication with clients that do not respond to request.	No

Security Settings by Policy Setting

The following section lists the policies which are enabled, disabled, or not set.

Enabled

The following policies are enabled by default when you install Windows 2000 Professional on a stand-alone computer:

- Allow system to be shut down without having to log on.
- Automatically log off users when logon time expires (local).
- Digitally sign client communication (when possible).
- Secure channel: Digitally encrypt secure channel data (when possible).
- Secure channel: Digitally sign secure channel data (when possible).
- Strengthen default permissions of global system objects (for example, Symbolic Links).

Disabled

The following policies are disabled by default when you install Windows 2000 Professional on a stand-alone computer:

- Passwords must meet complexity requirements.
- Store password using reversible encryption for all users in the domain.
- Account lockout threshold.
- Audit the access of global system objects.
- Audit use of Backup and Restore privilege.
- Clear virtual memory pagefile when system shuts down.
- Digitally sign client communication (always).

- Digitally sign server communication (always).
- Digitally sign server communication (when possible).
- Do not display last user name on logon screen.
- Prevent system maintenance of computer account password.
- Prevent users from installing printer drivers.
- Recovery Console: Allow automatic administrative logon.
- Recovery Console: Allow floppy copy and access to all drives and all folders.
- Restrict CD-ROM access to locally logged-on user only.
- Restrict floppy access to locally logged-on user only.
- Secure channel: Digitally encrypt or sign secure channel data (always).
- Secure channel: Require strong (Windows 2000 or later) session key.
- Send unencrypted password to connect to third-party SMB servers.
- Shut down system immediately if unable to log security audits.
- Additional restrictions for anonymous connections.
- Message text for users attempting to log on.
- Message title for users attempting to log on.
- Smart card removal behavior.
- Audit account logon events.
- Audit account management.
- Audit logon events.
- Audit object access.
- Audit policy change.
- Audit privilege use.
- Audit process tracking.
- Audit system events.

Not Defined

By default, the following policies are not defined. This does not mean that values are not set for these parameters on the system. It just means that there is no local policy defined for these parameters.

- Account lockout duration.
- Reset account lockout counter after.
- Audit directory service access.
- Allow server operators to schedule tasks (domain controllers only).
- Disable CTRL+ALT+DEL requirement for logon.

- Rename administrator account.
- Rename guest account.
- Unsigned driver installation behavior.
- Unsigned non-driver installation behavior.

Not Granted

By default, the following policies are not granted to any particular group when you clean-install Windows 2000 Professional on a stand-alone computer:

- Act as part of the operating system.
- Add workstations to domain.
- Create a token object.
- Create permanent shared objects.
- Deny access to this computer from the network.
- Deny logon as a batch job.
- Deny logon as a service.
- Deny logon locally.
- Enable computer and user accounts to be trusted for delegation.
- Generate security audits.
- Lock pages in memory.
- Log on as a batch job.
- Log on as a service.
- Replace a process level token.
- Synchronize directory service data.

Comparison of Group Capabilities

What can an Administrator do that a Power User can't? By default, a member of the Administrators group can:

- Install the operating system.
- Install or configure hardware device drivers, although Power Users are allowed to install printer drivers.
- Install system services.
- Install Service Packs and Windows Updates.
- Upgrade the operating system.
- Repair the operating system.
- Install applications that modify Windows system files.

- Configure password policy.
- Configure audit policy.
- Manage security logs.
- Create administrative shares.
- Create administrative accounts.
- Modify groups or accounts created by other users.
- Remotely access the registry.
- Stop or start any service.
- Configure services.
- Increase quotas.
- Increase execution priorities
- Remotely shut down the system.
- Take ownership of arbitrary objects.
- Assign rights to members of the Users group.
- Override a locked computer.
- Format a hard disk drive.
- Modify systemwide environment variables
- Access the private data of members of the Users group.
- Back up and restore files.

What can a Power User do that a User can't? By default, a member of the Power Users group can:

- Create local users and groups.
- Modify users and groups that they have created.
- Create and delete nonadministrator file shares.
- Create, manage, delete, and share local printers.
- Change system time (default user right).
- Stop or start non-auto-started services.

By default, members of the Power Users group are granted the following permissions:

- Modify access to the Program Files directory.
- Modify access to many locations within the HKEY_LOCAL_MACHINE\Software registry hive.
- Write access to most system directories including %windir% and %windir%\system32.

These permissions allow members of the Power Users group to:

- Perform per-computer installation of many applications. For example, applications that do not modify Windows system files or do not modify HKEY_LOCAL_MACHINE\System.

- Run legacy applications that improperly store per-user data in per-computer locations (without receiving error messages).

Unfortunately, these permissions also allow members of the Power Users group to:

- Plant Trojan horses that, if executed by administrators or other users, can compromise system and data security.

- Make systemwide operating system and application changes that affect other users of the system.

Security Templates

A security template is a file containing security settings. Those settings can be applied to a local computer or imported to a Group Policy object in Active Directory. When you import a security template to a Group Policy object, Group Policy processes the template and makes the corresponding changes to the members of that Group Policy object, which might be users or computers. Security templates are an effective way to apply consistent security settings to a large group of computers when you cannot use domain-based Group Policy settings for one reason or another.

Windows 2000 provides a set of security templates for your use in setting up your environment. A security template is a profile of security settings thought appropriate for a specific level of security on a range of Windows 2000 computer roles, including client computer.

You can import a security template into a Group Policy object and apply it to a class of computers. You can also import the template into a personal database and use it to examine and configure the security policy of a local computer.

How Security Templates Work

Security templates provide standard security settings to use as a model for your security policies. They help you troubleshoot problems with computers whose security settings are not in compliance with policy or are unknown. Security templates are inactive until imported into a Group Policy object or the Security Configuration and Analysis snap-in to MMC.

Prerequisites for Implementing Security Templates

Security templates are a standard feature of Windows 2000. There are no prerequisites for using them. However, to ensure appropriate service levels, test security templates before applying them to your users' computers.

How to Implement Security Templates

You can edit security templates in the Security Templates snap-in to MMC.

You can use the Security Configuration and Analysis MMC snap-in to import and export templates and to compare a template to the security settings of the local computer. You can use this MMC snap-in to configure the computer to match the template.

Before you can apply templates, you must open a Security Configuration and Analysis database for your computer.

▶ **To Open a Security Database**

1. Open the Security Configuration and Analysis snap-in to MMC.
2. Right-click the Security Configuration and Analysis snap-in, and then click **Open database**.
3. Highlight a pre-existing database, and then click **Open**.

    –Or–

    Create a new database by typing a database name and clicking **Open**.
4. Highlight a template to import into the database, and then click **Open**.

After you have opened a security database and selected a security template, you can apply the security template.

▶ **To import a security template into a Group Policy object**

1. Open the Security Configuration and Analysis snap-in to MMC.
2. Right-click the Security Configuration and Analysis snap-in and select **Configure Computer Now**.
3. Highlight a security template file (*.inf), and then click **Open**.
4. Click **Browse** to specify a location for the Security Configuration error log file, and then click **OK**.

For more information about using security templates and predefined templates, see Windows 2000 Server Help.

Considerations About Security Templates

The default permissions for Windows 2000 provide a significant increase in security over previous versions of Windows NT 4.0. This default, clean-install security, is defined by the access permissions granted to three groups: Users, Power Users, and Administrators. These groups have been carefully designed for specific purposes, and should not require modifications in any but the most unusual cases.

By default, Users have an appropriate access-control policy for nonadministrative system use; Power Users are backward compatible with Windows NT 4.0 Users; and Administrators are granted full control of the system. Therefore, securing a Windows 2000–based system is largely a matter of defining the group to which the user belongs.

If your site runs only applications that are compatible with the Windows 2000 application specification, then it is possible to make all users be members of the Users group and thus achieve maximum access control security without sacrificing application functionality. If your site runs applications that are not compliant with the Windows 2000 application specification, it is likely that users will need to be Power Users in order to have the privileges necessary to run the noncompliant applications. Before considering the use of additional security templates, it is imperative that you define the level of access (User, Power User, or Administrator) that users need in order to successfully run the applications that must be supported.

Security Template Types

After you have defined user access levels using built-in groups such as User, Power User, and Administrator, the security templates can be used as follows:

Basic The Basic security templates apply the Windows 2000 default access control settings previously described. The Basic templates can be applied to a Windows NT computer that has been upgraded to Windows 2000. This will bring the upgraded computer in line with the new Windows 2000 default security settings that are applied only to clean-installed computers. The Basic templates can also be used to revert back to the defaults after making any undesirable changes.

Optional Component File Security The Optional Component templates apply default security to optional component riles that might be installed during or after Windows 2000 Setup. The Optional Component templates should be used in conjunction with the Basic Templates to restore default security to Windows 2000 system files that are installed as optional components.

Compatible   Some customers might not want their users to be Power Users in order to run applications that are not compliant with the Windows 2000 application specification. They might not want this because Power Users have additional capabilities (such as the ability to create shares) that go beyond the more liberal access control settings necessary to run legacy applications. For customers who do not want their end users to be Power Users, the Compatible template opens up the default access control policy for the Users group in a manner that is consistent with the requirements of most legacy applications. A computer that is configured with the Compatible template must not be considered a secure installation.

Secure   The Secure template focuses on making operating system and network behavior more secure by changes such as removing all members of the Power Users group and requiring more secure passwords. The secure template does not focus on securing application behavior. This template does not modify permissions, so users with the proper permissions can still use legacy applications, even though all members are removed from the Power Users group by defining the Power Users group as a restricted group.

High Secure   The High Secure template increases the security defined by several of the parameters in the secure template. For example, while the Secure template might enable SMB Packet Signing, the High Secure template would require SMB packet signing. While the Secure template might warn on the installation of unsigned drivers, the High Secure template blocks the installation of unsigned drivers. In short, the High Secure template configures many operational parameters to their extreme values without regard for performance, operational ease of use, or connectivity with clients using third-party or earlier versions of NTLM. The High Secure template also changes the default access permissions for Power Users to match those assigned to Users. This allows administrators to grant Users privileges reserved for Power Users, such as the ability to create shares, without having to give those users unnecessary access to the registry or file system. The High Secure template is primarily designed for use in an all–Windows 2000 network because the settings require Windows 2000 technology. Using High Secure templates in an environment with Windows 98 or Windows NT can cause problems.

Remote Access

Using the Routing and Remote Access service, you can connect to your network by phone. This section deals only with the remote access security features of Routing and Remote Access. Remote access by its nature is an invitation to intruders; so Windows 2000 provides multiple security features to permit authorized access while limiting opportunities for mischief.

How Remote Access Works

A client dials a remote access server on your network and is granted access to the network if:

- The request matches one of the remote access policies defined for the server.
- The user's account is enabled for remote access.
- Client/server authentication succeeds.

After the client has been identified and authorized, access to the network can be limited to specific servers, subnets, and protocol types, depending on the remote access profile of the client. Otherwise, all services typically available to a user connected to a local area network (including file and print sharing, Web server access, and messaging) are enabled by means of the remote access connection.

Authentication

Authentication establishes user identity and ensures that only the intended users will be granted remote access to your resources.

Secure User Authentication

Secure user authentication is obtained through the encrypted exchange of user credentials. This is possible with the PPP remote access protocol using either the Extensible Authentication Protocol (EAP), Microsoft Challenge Handshake Authentication Protocol (MS-CHAP) version 1 and version 2, Challenge Handshake Authentication Protocol (CHAP), or Shiva Password Authentication Protocol (SPAP) authentication protocols. The remote access server can be configured to require a secure authentication method. If the remote access client cannot perform the required secure authentication, the connection is denied.

Mutual Authentication

Mutual authentication authenticates both ends of the connection through the encrypted exchange of user credentials. This is possible with the PPP remote access protocol using either the EAP–Transport Level Security (EAP-TLS) or MS-CHAP version 2 authentication protocols. During mutual authentication, the remote access client authenticates itself to the remote access server, and then the remote access server authenticates itself to the remote access client.

It is possible for a remote access server to not request authentication from the remote access client. However, in the case of a Windows 2000 remote access client configured for only MS-CHAP version 2 or only EAP-TLS, the remote access client will force the mutual authentication of the client and server. If the remote access server does not respond to the authentication request, the connection is terminated by the client.

For more information about authentication, see "User Authentication" earlier in this chapter.

Implementing Secure Remote Access

Windows 2000 provides a channel for secure remote access using virtual private networks (VPNs).

Enabling Remote Access

To enable remote access for a Windows 2000 Professional computer, make a virtual private network (VPN) connection. For more information about how to do so, see Windows 2000 Professional Help.

To enable remote access, users must have dial-in permissions in the domain they will remotely accessing.

For more information about remote access and installing and configuring the remote access server, see Windows 2000 Server Help. For more information about remote access authentication, see "Remote Access Server" in the *Microsoft® Windows® 2000 Server Resource Kit Internetworking Guide.*

Considerations About Remote Access

Remote access permissions are ineffective if there is no appropriate remote access policy in place for the remote access server.

Windows 2000 supports the following authentication options for remote access:

- Standard Point-to-Point Protocol (PPP) challenge and response authentication methods based on user name and passwords.

  Standard PPP authentication methods offer limited security.

- Custom Extensible Authentication Protocol (EAP) authentication methods.

  EAP modules can be developed or provided by third parties to extend the authentication capabilities of PPP. For example, you can use EAP to provide stronger authentication using token cards, smart cards, biometric hardware, or one-time password systems.

- EAP Transport Layer Security (EAP-TLS) authentication based on digital certificates and smart cards.

  EAP-TLS provides strong authentication. Users' credentials are stored on tamper-proof smart cards. You can issue each user one smart card to use for all logon needs.

It is recommended that your network security plan include strategies for remote access and authentication, including the following information:

- Logon authentication strategies to be used.

- Remote access strategies by using Routing and Remote Access and virtual private networks.

- Certificate Services needed to support user logon authentication by digital certificates.

- Process and strategies to enroll users for logon authentication certificates and remote access.

- Whether to use callback with remote access, to help eliminate impersonation attacks.

Remote Access Policies on Servers

Remote Access requires there be a server configured to accept remote access requests. Such Windows 2000–based servers are governed by security policies that determine their remote access behavior. These policies establish whether a server accepts requests for remote access and, if so, during what hours of what days, what protocols are used, and what types of authentication are required.

For more information about configuring Remote Access Policies on a server, see the *Windows 2000 Deployment Planning Guide.*

Elements of Secure Remote Access

Because remote access is designed to transparently connect a remote access client to a network and its potentially sensitive data, security of remote access connections is an important consideration. Windows 2000 remote access offers a wide range of security features including secure user authentication, mutual authentication, data encryption, callback, and caller ID.

Data Encryption

Data encryption converts data sent between the remote access client and the remote access server into a form that is unreadable to eavesdroppers. Remote access data encryption only provides data encryption on the communications link between the remote access client and the remote access server. If end-to-end encryption is needed, use IPSec to create an encrypted end-to-end connection after the remote access connection has been made.

Note IPSec can also be used for encrypting a Layer Two Tunneling Protocol (L2TP) virtual private network connection. For more information, see "Virtual Private Networking" in the Windows 2000 *Internetworking Guide.*

Data encryption on a remote access connection is based on a secret encryption key known to the remote access server and remote access client. This shared secret key is generated during the user authentication process.

Data encryption is possible over dial-up remote access links when using the PPP remote access protocol and the EAP-TLS or MS-CHAP authentication protocols. The remote access server can be configured to require data encryption. If the remote access client cannot perform the required encryption, the connection attempt is rejected.

Windows 2000, Microsoft Windows NT 4.0, Windows 98, and Windows 95 remote access clients and remote access servers support the Microsoft Point-to-Point Encryption Protocol (MPPE). MPPE uses the Rivest-Shamir-Adleman (RSA) RC4 stream cipher and either 40-bit, 56-bit, or 128-bit secret keys. MPPE keys are generated from the MS-CHAP and EAP-TLS user authentication processes.

Callback

With callback, the remote access server calls the remote access client after the user credentials have been verified. Callback can be configured on the server to call the remote access client back at a number specified by the user of the remote access client during the time of the call. This allows a traveling user to dial-in and have the remote access server call them back at their current location, saving phone charges. Callback can also be configured to always call the remote access client back at a specific location, which is the secure form of callback.

Caller ID

Caller ID can be used to verify that the incoming call is coming from a specified phone number. Caller ID is configured as part of the dial-in properties of the user account. If the caller ID number of the incoming connection for that user does not match the configured caller ID, the connection is denied.

Caller ID requires that the caller's phone line, the phone system, the remote access server's phone line, and the Windows 2000 driver for the dial-up equipment all support caller ID. If a caller ID is configured for a user account and the caller ID is not being passed from the caller to the Routing and Remote Access service, then the connection is denied.

Caller ID is a feature designed to provide a higher degree of security for network that support telecommuters. The disadvantage of configuring caller ID is that the user can only dial-in from a single phone line.

Remote Access Account Lockout

The remote access account lockout feature is used to specify how many times a remote access authentication fails against a valid user account before the user is denied remote access. Remote access account lockout is especially important for remote access virtual private network (VPN) connections over the Internet. Malicious users on the Internet can attempt to access an organization intranet by sending credentials (valid user name, guessed password) during the VPN connection authentication process. During a dictionary attack, the malicious user sends hundreds or thousands of credentials by using a list of passwords based on common words or phrases. With remote access account lockout enabled, a dictionary attack is thwarted after a specified number of failed attempts.

The remote access account lockout feature does not distinguish between malicious users who attempt to access your intranet and authentic users who attempt remote access but have forgotten their current passwords. Users who have forgotten their current password typically try the passwords that they remember and, depending on the number of attempts and the MaxDenials setting, might have their accounts locked out.

If you enable the remote access account lockout feature, a malicious user can deliberately force an account to be locked out by attempting multiple authentications with the user account until the account is locked out, thereby preventing the authentic user from being able to log on.

Remote access account lockout variables include the following:

- The number of failed attempts before future attempts are denied.

  After each failed attempt, a failed attempts counter for the user account is incremented. If the user account's failed attempts counter reaches the configured maximum, future attempts to connect are denied.

  A successful authentication resets the failed attempts counter when its value is less than the configured maximum. In other words, the failed attempts counter does not accumulate beyond a successful authentication.

- How often the failed attempts counter is reset.

  You must periodically reset the failed attempts counter to prevent inadvertent lockouts due to normal mistakes by users when typing in their passwords.

The remote access account lockout feature is configured by changing settings in the Windows 2000 registry on the computer that provides the authentication. If the remote access server is configured for Windows authentication, modify the registry on the remote access server computer. If the remote access server is configured for Remote Authentication Dial-In User Service (RADIUS) authentication and Windows 2000 Internet Authentication Service (IAS) is being used, modify the registry on the IAS server computer.

To enable account lockout, you must set the MaxDenials entry in the registry (HKEY_LOCAL_MACHINE\SYSTEM\CurrentControlSet\Services\RemoteAccess\Parameters\AccountLockout) to 1 or greater. MaxDenials is the maximum number of failed attempts before the account is locked out. By default, MaxDenials is set to 0, which means that account lockout is disabled.

To modify the amount of time before the failed attempts counter is reset, you must set the ResetTime (mins) entry in the registry (HKEY_LOCAL_MACHINE\SYSTEM\CurrentControlSet\Services\RemoteAccess\Parameters\AccountLockout) to the required number of minutes. By default, ResetTime (mins) is set to 0xb40, or 2,880 minutes (48 hours).

To manually reset a user account that has been locked out before the failed attempts counter is automatically reset, delete the following registry subkey that corresponds to the user's account name:

HKEY_LOCAL_MACHINE\SYSTEM\CurrentControlSet\Services\RemoteAccess\Parameters\AccountLockout\domain name:*user name*

Note The remote access account lockout feature is not related to the **Account locked out** setting on the **Account** tab on the properties of a user account and the administration of account lockout policies using Windows 2000 group policies.

For information about how to establish secure remote access connections or for more information about VPN connections, see Windows 2000 Professional Help.

Remote Access Tunneling Protocols

Windows 2000 uses the Point-to-Point Tunneling Protocol (PPTP), Layer Two Tunneling Protocol (L2TP), and Internet Protocol security (IPSec) to create VPNs. For more detailed information about VPNs and their protocols, see the *Microsoft® Windows® 2000 Server Resource Kit Internetworking Guide*.

PPTP

The Point-to-Point Tunneling Protocol (PPTP) encapsulates Point-to-Point Protocol (PPP) frames into IP datagrams for transmission over an IP-based internetwork, such as the Internet or a private intranet. PPTP is documented in RFC 2637.

The PPTP uses a TCP connection known as the PPTP control connection to create, maintain, and terminate the tunnel and a modified version of Generic Routing Encapsulation (GRE) to encapsulate PPP frames as tunneled data. The contents of the encapsulated PPP frames can be encrypted or compressed or both.

PPTP assumes the availability of an IP internetwork between a PPTP client (a VPN client using the PPTP tunneling protocol) and a PPTP server (a VPN server using the PPTP tunneling protocol). The PPTP client might already be attached to an IP internetwork that can reach the PPTP server, or the PPTP client might have to dial into a network access server (NAS) to establish IP connectivity as in the case of dial-up Internet users.

Authentication that occurs during the creation of a PPTP-based VPN connection uses the same authentication mechanisms as PPP connections, such as Extensible Authentication Protocol (EAP), Microsoft Challenge-Handshake Authentication Protocol (MS-CHAP), CHAP, Shiva Password Authentication Protocol (SPAP), and Password Authentication Protocol (PAP). PPTP inherits encryption or compression, or both, of PPP payloads from PPP. For Windows 2000, either EAP-Transport Level Security (EAP-TLS) or MS-CHAP must be used in order for the PPP payloads to be encrypted using Microsoft Point-to-Point Encryption (MPPE).

MPPE provides only link encryption, not end-to-end encryption. End-to-end encryption is data encryption between the client application and the server hosting the resource or service being accessed by the client application. If end-to-end encryption is required, IPSec can be used to encrypt IP traffic from end-to-end after the PPTP tunnel is established.

L2TP

Layer Two Tunneling Protocol (L2TP) is a combination of PPTP and Layer 2 Forwarding (L2F), a technology proposed by Cisco Systems, Inc. Rather than having two incompatible tunneling protocols competing in the marketplace and causing customer confusion, the Internet Engineering Task Force (IETF) mandated that the two technologies be combined into a single tunneling protocol that represents the best features of PPTP and L2F. L2TP is documented in RFC 2661.

L2TP encapsulates PPP frames to be sent over IP, X.25, Frame Relay, or ATM networks. Currently, only L2TP over IP networks is defined. When sent over an IP internetwork, L2TP frames are encapsulated as User Datagram Protocol (UDP) messages. L2TP can be used as a tunneling protocol over the Internet or over private intranets.

L2TP assumes the availability of an IP internetwork between a L2TP client (a VPN client using the L2TP tunneling protocol and IPSec) and a L2TP server (a VPN server using the L2TP tunneling protocol and IPSec). The L2TP client might already be attached to an IP internetwork that can reach the L2TP server, or the L2TP client might have to dial into a NAS to establish IP connectivity as in the case of dial-up Internet users.

Authentication that occurs during the creation of L2TP tunnels must use the same authentication mechanisms as PPP connections such as EAP, MS-CHAP, CHAP, SPAP, and PAP.

For Internet-based L2TP servers, the L2TP server is an L2TP-enabled dial-up server with one interface on the external network, the Internet, and a second interface on the target private network.

Internet Protocol Security

Windows 2000 incorporates Internet Protocol security (IPSec) for data protection of network traffic. IPSec is a suite of protocols that allow secure, encrypted communication between two computers over an insecure network. The encryption is applied at the IP network layer, which means that it is transparent to most applications that use specific protocols for network communication. IPSec provides end-to-end security, meaning that the IP packets are encrypted by the sending computer, are unreadable en route, and can be decrypted only by the recipient computer. Due to a special algorithm for generating the same shared encryption key at both ends of the connection, the key does not need to be passed over the network.

IPSec Policies can be applied at a local level or at the domain level, as is the case with other parts of security policy. Experience configuring network security will help in determining what is entailed in an effective IPSec Policies.

For more information about Internet Protocol security, see "TCP/IP in Windows 2000 Professional" later in this book.

How IPSec Works

IPSec has many intricate components and options that are worthy of detailed study but at a high level the process operates in this manner:

- An application on Computer A generates outbound packets to send to Computer B across the network.
- Inside TCP/IP, the IPSec driver compares the outbound packets against IPSec filters, checking to see if the packets need to be secured. The filters are associated with a filter action in IPSec security rules. Many IPSec security rules can be inside one IPSec policy that is assigned to a computer.

- If a matched filter has to negotiate security action, Computer A begins security negotiations with Computer B, using a protocol called the Internet Key Exchange (IKE). The two computers exchange identity credentials according to the authentication method specified in the security rule. Authentication methods can be Kerberos authentication, public key certificates, or a preshared key value (much like a password). The IKE negotiation establishes two types of agreements, called *security associations*, between the two computers. One type (called the *phase I IKE SA*) specifies how the two computers trust each other and protects their negotiation. The other type is an agreement on how to protect a particular type of application communication. This consists of two SAs (called *phase II IPSec SAs*) that specify security methods and keys for each direction of communication. IKE automatically creates and refreshes a shared, secret key for each SA. The secret key is created independently at both ends without being transmitted across the network.

- The IPSec driver on Computer A signs the outgoing packets for integrity, and optionally encrypts them for confidentially using the methods agreed upon during the negotiation. It transmits the secured packets to Computer B.

Note Firewalls, routers, and servers along the network path from Computer A to Computer B do not require IPSec. They simply pass along the packets in the usual manner.

- The IPSec driver on Computer B checks the packets for integrity and decrypts their content if necessary. It then transfers the packets to the receiving application.

IPSec provides security against data manipulation, data interception, and replay attacks.

IPSec is important to strategies of data confidentiality, data integrity, and nonrepudiation.

Prerequisites for Implementing IPSec

The computers in your network need to have an IPSec security policy defined that is appropriate for your network security strategy and for the type of network communication that they perform. Computers in the same domain might be organized into groups with IPSec Policies applied to the groups. Computers in different domains might have complementary IPSec security policies to support secure network communications. For more information about using the Internet Protocol Security Policy Management snap-in and selecting an IP Policy for a workstation, see Windows 2000 Professional Help.

How to Implement IPSec

You can view the default Internet Protocol security policies in the Group Policy snap-in to MMC. The policies are listed under **IP Security Policies on Active Directory**, or under **IP Security Policies (Local Computer)**:

```
Group Policy object
 └ Computer Configuration
 └ Windows Settings
 └ Security Settings
 └ IP Security Policies on Local Computer
```

You can also view IPSec policies by using the Internet Protocol Security Policy Management snap-in to MMC. Each Internet Protocol security policy contains security rules that determine when and how traffic is protected. Right-click a policy and select **Properties**. The **Rules** tab lists the policy rules. Rules can be further decomposed into filter lists, filter actions, and additional properties.

When planning for IPSec, make the following determinations:

- Identify clients and servers to use IPSec communications.

- Identify whether client authentication is based on Kerberos trust, digital certificates, or a pre-shared key.

- Describe how each computer will initially receive the proper IPSec policy and will continue to receive policy updates.

- Describe the security rules inside each IPSec policy. Consider how Certificate Services are needed to support client authentication by digital certificates.

- Describe enrollment process and strategies to enroll computers for IPSec certificates.

For more information about Internet Protocol security, see the Windows 2000 Server Help. See also "Internet Protocol Security" in the *Microsoft® Windows® 2000 Server Resource Kit TCP/IP Core Networking Guide*.

Considerations for IPSec

IPSec provides encryption of outgoing and incoming packets, but at a cost of additional central processing unit (CPU) utilization when encryption is performed by the operating system. For many deployments, the clients and servers might have considerable CPU resources available or might have network interface cards that handle IPSec encryption, so there is no noticeable impact on performance. For servers supporting many simultaneous network connections or servers that transmit large volumes of data to other servers, the additional cost of encryption is significant. For this reason, you need to deploy IPSec wisely. Consider evaluating the effects of simulated network traffic before deploying IPSec. Testing is also important if you are using third-party hardware or software product to provide Internet Protocol security.

Windows 2000 provides device interfaces to allow hardware acceleration of IPSec per-packet encryption by intelligent network cards. Network card vendors might provide several versions of client and server cards, and might not support all combinations of IPSec security methods. Consult the product documentation for each card to be sure that it supports the security methods and the number of connections you expect in your deployment.

You can define local IPSec policy on computers that do not have domain IPSec policy assigned to them, or, if your computer is a member of a domain, domain administrators can define Internet Protocol security (IPSec) policies for each domain or organizational unit. You can configure IPSec policies to:

- Specify the levels of authentication and confidentiality required between IPSec clients.

- Specify the lowest security level at which communications are allowed to occur between IPSec-aware clients.

- Allow or prevent communications with non-IPSec-aware clients.

- Require all communications to be encrypted for confidentiality or you can allow communications in plaintext.

Consider using IPSec to provide security for the following applications:

- Peer-to-peer communications over your organization's intranet, such as legal department or executive committee communications.

- Client-server communications to protect sensitive (confidential) information stored on servers. For file share points that require user access controls, consider using IPSec to ensure that other network users cannot see the data as it is being communicated.

- Remote access (dial-up or virtual private network) communications. (For virtual private networks using IPSec with L2TP, remember to set up Security Policy to permit auto-enrollment for IPSec computer certificates. For detailed information about computer certificates for L2TP over IPSec VPN connections, see Windows 2000 Help.)

- Secure router-to-router WAN communications.

Encrypting File System

Encrypting File System (EFS) is a new feature in Microsoft Windows 2000. EFS protects sensitive data in files that are stored on disk using the NTFS file system. It uses symmetric key encryption in conjunction with *public key technology* to provide confidentiality for files. It runs as an integrated system service, which makes EFS easy to manage, difficult to attack, and transparent to the file owner and to applications. Only the owner of a protected file can open the file and work with it, just as with a normal document. Others are denied access to the protected file. However, recovery administrators (whom you can designate) have the ability to recover protected files if that becomes necessary.

How Encrypting File System Works

EFS uses an encryption attribute to designate files for EFS protection. When a file's encryption attribute is on, EFS stores the file as encrypted ciphertext. When an authorized user opens an encrypted file in an application, EFS decrypts the file in the background and provides a plaintext copy to the application. The authorized user can view or modify the file, and EFS saves any changes transparently as ciphertext. Other users are denied permission to view or modify EFS-encrypted files. EFS-protected files are bulk encrypted to provide confidentiality even from intruders who bypass EFS and attempt to read files by using low-level disk tools.

Because EFS operates in the background at the system level, applications can save temporary files as plaintext to non-EFS-protected folders and inadvertently compromise confidentiality. Therefore, encryption usually must be enforced at the folder level rather than the file level. This means that you do not encrypt individual files, but instead designate folders as EFS-protected folders. All files that are added to EFS-protected folders are encrypted automatically. To specify EFS protection for a folder, use the properties page for the folder in Windows Explorer.

EFS is supported only for the version of NTFS that is included with Windows 2000. It does not work with any other file system, including the previous versions of NTFS. For more information about EFS, see Windows 2000 Professional Help. See also "Encrypting File System" in the *Microsoft® Windows® 2000 Server Resource Kit Distributed Systems Guide.*

File Encryption and Public Key Technology

For EFS to work, the EFS user must have a valid EFS user's certificate, and at least one EFS recovery agent account must have a valid EFS recovery certificate. EFS does not require a certification authority (CA) to issue certificates because EFS automatically generates its own certificates to users and to default recovery agent accounts. The EFS private key is generated and managed by Microsoft Cryptographic Application Programming Interface (CryptoAPI) in conjunction with the base Microsoft cryptographic service provider (CSP).

When EFS encrypts a file, it does the following:

- Generates a bulk symmetric encryption key.
- Encrypts files by using the bulk encryption key.
- Encrypts the bulk encryption key by using the EFS user's public key.
- Stores the encrypted bulk key in a special field called the data decryption field (DDF), which is attached to the EFS file.

EFS can then use the user's private key to decrypt the bulk encryption key and decrypt the file as necessary. Because only the user has the private key, others cannot unlock the DDF.

In addition, EFS enables designated recovery agent accounts to decrypt and recover the file in case the user's private key is lost or damaged. For each designated recovery agent account, EFS does the following:

- Encrypts the bulk encryption key by using the public key from each recovery agent certificate.
- Stores the encrypted bulk key in a special field called the data recovery field (DRF), which is attached to the EFS file.

The data recovery field can contain information for multiple recovery agent accounts. Every time a file system operation is complete for a file, such as viewing, opening, copying, or moving the file, EFS generates and saves a new DRF with the most current public keys for the current recovery agent certificates. You can designate recovery agent accounts by configuring Encrypted Data Recovery Agents Group Policy settings.

Encrypted Data Recovery

You might want to recover encrypted files, for example, when an employee is terminated for cause or when a user's private key for EFS is damaged. You can use the command-line tool, Cipher, to recover files on a recovery computer where a current recovery agent account, certificate, and private key are located. To recover a file, a recovery administrator must log on to the recovery computer as the recovery agent account and then use Cipher to decrypt the file. Cipher only works for the recovery agent accounts that are listed in the files DRF. Cipher also only works if the private key for recovery is installed on the computer.

Encrypted Data Recovery Agent Group Policy settings are a subset of Public Key Group Policy. You can configure Encrypted Data Recovery Agent settings to designate recovery agent accounts for domains, organizational units (also known as OUs), or stand-alone computers. Trusted recovery administrators that you designate can then use the recovery agent accounts to recover EFS encrypted files for the domains or organizational units where the EFS recovery settings apply.

When Group Policy is downloaded to computers, the Encrypted Data Recovery Agent Group Policy settings contain the certificates for each designated recovery agent account within the scope of the policy. EFS uses the information in the current Encrypted Data Recovery Agent Group Policy settings to create and update DRFs. A recovery agent certificate contains the public key and information that uniquely identifies the recovery agent account.

By default, the domain Administrator's account on the first domain controller that is installed in the domain is the recovery agent account for computers that are connected to the network. On stand-alone computers, the local Administrator's account is the default EFS recovery agent account. EFS generates EFS recovery certificates automatically for default Administrator accounts.

Considerations for Encrypting File System

Keep the following considerations in mind when planning to deploy Windows 2000-based computers. You have the option to disable EFS and to designate alternate recovery agent accounts. You also need to protect recovery keys from misuse as well as to maintain archives of obsolete recovery agent certificates and private keys.

Disabling EFS for a Set of Computers   You can disable EFS for a domain, organizational unit, or stand-alone computer by applying an empty Encrypted Data Recovery Agents policy setting. Until Encrypted Data Recovery Agent settings are configured and applied through Group Policy, there is no policy, and the default recovery agents are used by EFS. However, EFS must use the recovery agents that are listed in the Encrypted Data Recovery Agents Group Policy after the settings have been configured and applied. If the policy that is applied is empty, EFS does not operate. For more information about configuring Encrypted Data Recovery Agents policy settings, see Windows 2000 Professional Help or Windows 2000 Server Help.

Designating Alternate Recovery Agents   You can configure Encrypted Data Recovery Agents policy to designate alternative recovery agents. For example, to distribute the administrative workload in your organization, you can designate alternative EFS recovery accounts for categories of computers grouped by organizational units. You might also configure Encrypted Data Recovery Agents settings for portable computers so that they use the same recovery agent certificates when they are connected to the domain and when they are operated as stand-alone computers. For more information about configuring Encrypted Data Recovery Agents policy settings, see Windows 2000 Professional Help or Windows 2000 Server Help.

Before you can designate alternate recovery agent accounts, you must deploy Windows 2000 Server and Certificate Services to issue recovery agent certificates. For more information about Certificate Services, see "Windows 2000 Certificate Services and Public Key Infrastructure" in the *Microsoft® Windows® 2000 Server Resource Kit Distributed Systems Guide.*

Securing Recovery Keys   Because recovery keys can be misused to decrypt and read files that have been encrypted by EFS users, it is recommended that you provide additional security for private keys for recovery. The first step in providing security for recovery keys is to disable default recovery accounts by exporting the recovery agent certificate and the private key to a secure medium and select the option to remove the private key from the computer. When the recovery certificate and key are exported, the key is removed from the computer. You then store the exported certificate and key in a secure location to be used later for file recovery operations. Securing private keys for recovery ensures that nobody can misuse the recover agent account to read encrypted files. This is especially important for mobile computers or other computers that are a high risk to fall into the wrong hands. For more information about how to export and secure private keys for recovery, see Windows 2000 Professional Help or Windows 2000 Server Help.

Maintaining Archives of Recovery Keys For EFS encrypted files, the recovery agent information is refreshed every time the file system performs an operation on the file (for example, when the file is opened, moved, or copied). However, if an encrypted file is dormant for a long time, the recovery agents expire. To ensure that dormant encrypted files can be recovered, maintain archives of the recovery agent certificates and private keys. To create an archive, export the certificate and its private key to a secure medium and store it in a safe location. When you export private keys, you must provide a secret password for authorizing access to the exported key. The secret key is stored in an encrypted format to protect its confidentiality.

To recover dormant files with expired recovery agent information, import the appropriate expired recovery agent certificate and private key from the archive to a recovery account on a local computer and then perform the recovery. To view recovery agent information for an encrypted file, use the **efsinfo** tool. For more information about **efsinfo**, see Windows 2000 Tools Help.

Public Key Technology

Windows 2000 includes a public key infrastructure (PKI) that can support a wide range of public key information security needs. A public key infrastructure provides the framework of services, technology, protocols, and standards that enable you to deploy and manage a strong and scalable information security system based on public key technology. The basic components of a public key infrastructure include digital certificates, certificate revocation lists, and certification authorities. Before public key cryptography can be widely used and easily managed on public networks, a public key infrastructure must be in place. Without a public key infrastructure, public key technology is not generally suitable for large-scale enterprise deployment.

The Windows 2000 public key infrastructure is based on the open standards that are recommended by the Public Key Infrastructure for X.509 Certificates (PKIX) working group of the IETF. Because Windows 2000 security is based on open standards, the security solutions you implement can operate with many standards-compliant, third-party operating systems and security products.

For more information about public key technology, see "Cryptography for Network and Information Security," "Choosing Security Solutions That Use Public Key Technology," and "Windows 2000 Certificate Services and Public Key Infrastructure" in the *Microsoft® Windows® 2000 Server Resource Kit Distributed Systems Guide*.

Overview of Public Key Security in Windows 2000

Many Windows 2000 distributed security systems use public key technology. You can deploy a wide variety of security solutions that take advantage of the benefits of public key technology.

Security Technologies That Use Public Key Technology

The following Windows 2000 distributed security systems use public key technology:

- A network logon authentication that uses the Kerberos v5 authentication protocol, including logging on with smart cards (a permitted extension to the Kerberos protocol).

- A Routing and Remote Access service that supports secure remote access to network resources. Routing and Remote Access supports the following:

  - Integration with Active Directory, the Windows 2000 directory service that makes it possible to manage remote user authentication through the use of domain network user accounts and Group Policy settings.

  - Remote Authentication Dial-In User Service (RADIUS), which makes it possible to manage remote user authentication through a variety of authentication protocols.

  - User authentication that is based on the Extensible Authentication Protocol and Transport Layer Security (EAP-TLS). Supports the authentication of users through public key certificates and the smart card logon process.

  - Confidential communication over public Internet lines by using the Layer 2 Tunneling Protocol (L2TP) and the Point-to-Point Tunneling Protocol (PPTP).

  - Remote network access and logging on through the virtual private networks and public Internet service providers.

- Microsoft® Internet Information Services, which supports Web site security through certificate mapping and secure channel communications with the Secure Sockets Layer (SSL) protocol, Transport Layer Security (TLS) protocol, and Server Gated Cryptography (SGC) protocol.

- IPSec, which supports IP-level, end-to-end authentication, integrity, anti-replay, and encrypted communication over open IP networks, including the Internet.

- Encrypting File System, which makes it possible for a user to encrypt folders and files for safekeeping and allows an administrator to recover files when the user's private key is damaged or lost.

Public key security in Windows 2000 is based on industry-standard public key technologies, such as the Diffie-Hellman Key Agreement algorithm, the RSA public key algorithms developed by RSA Data Security, and the Digital Signature Algorithm. Windows 2000 security also makes use of the industry-standard, X.509 version 3 digital certificates that are issued by the certification authorities that you choose to trust. Many Windows 2000 security features use public key technology as well as certificates to provide authentication, integrity, confidentiality, and nonrepudiation for network and information security.

Public Key Security Benefits

The Windows 2000 public key infrastructure enables you to deploy strong security solutions that use digital certificates and public key technology. Security solutions can include the following:

- Secure mail, which uses certificates and the Secure/Multipurpose Internet Mail Extensions (S/MIME) protocol to ensure the integrity, origin, and confidentiality of e-mail messages.

- Secure Web sites, which use certificates and certificate mapping to map certificates to network user accounts for controlling user rights and permissions for Web resources.

- Secure Web communications, which use certificates and the Secure Sockets Layer (SSL) and Transport Layer Security (TLS) protocols to authenticate servers, to optionally authenticate clients, and to provide confidential communications between servers and clients.

- Software code signing, which uses certificates and digital signing technology (such as Microsoft® Authenticode®) to ensure the integrity and authorship of software that is developed for distribution on an intranet or on the Internet.

- Smart card logon process, which uses certificates and private keys stored on smart cards to authenticate local and remote access network users.

- Internet Protocol security (IPSec) client authentication, which has the option to use certificates to authenticate clients for IPSec communications.

- Encrypting File System (EFS), which uses certificates for both EFS user and EFS recovery agent operations.

- Custom security solutions, which use certificates to provide confidentiality, integrity, authentication, or nonrepudiation.

Major Components of the Public Key Infrastructure

The major components of the Windows 2000 public key infrastructure include the following:

- Windows 2000 Certificate Services
- Microsoft CryptoAPI and cryptographic service providers (CSPs)

- Certificate stores
- Certificates console
- Certification authority trust model
- Certificate enrollment and renewal methods
- Public key Group Policy
- Certificate revocation lists
- Preinstalled trusted root certificates
- Smart card support

Windows 2000 Certificate Services

You can deploy Windows 2000 Server and Certificate Services to issue and manage certificates for your organization. You can also obtain Certificate Services from a variety of third-party vendors.

Windows 2000 Certificate Services support two types of Certification Authorities (CAs): enterprise CAs and stand-alone CAs. *Enterprise CAs* are integrated with Active Directory and use certificate templates to specify the types of certificates that are issued by the CA. *Stand-alone CAs* do not require Active Directory and do not use certificate templates. For more information about Certificate Services, see "Windows 2000 Certificate Services and Public Key Infrastructure" in the *Microsoft® Windows® 2000 Server Resource Kit Distributed Systems Guide*.

Microsoft CryptoAPI and Cryptographic Service Providers

Microsoft CryptoAPI provides a secure interface for the cryptographic functionality that is supplied by the installable cryptographic service provider (CSP) modules. CSPs perform all cryptographic operations and manage private keys. CSPs can be implemented in software as well as in hardware. Windows 2000 Certificate Services uses CryptoAPI and CSPs to perform all cryptographic and private key management operations. CryptoAPI and CSP services are available to all services and applications that require cryptographic services.

CSPs can be software-based, hardware-based, or a combination of both. Hardware-based cryptography and key management is more secure than software-based cryptography and key management because cryptographic operations and private keys are isolated from the operating system. However, hardware-based CSPs (such as smart card CSPs) often store only a limited number of private keys and can take a long time to generate keys.

Software CSPs usually provide more flexibility than hardware CSPs, but are somewhat less secure. Nevertheless, software-based CSPs provide ample security to meet a wide range of needs. You usually use hardware-based CSPs only for special security applications, such as for logging on with smart cards or for secure Web communications with smart cards.

Vendors can develop hardware or software CSPs that support a wide range of cryptographic operations and technologies. However, Microsoft must certify and digitally sign all CSPs. CSPs do not work in Windows 2000 unless they have been digitally signed by Microsoft.

How Private Keys Are Stored

Private keys for the Microsoft RSA-based CSPs, including the Base CSP and the Enhanced CSP, reside in the user profile under *RootDirectory*\Documents and Settings\<*username*>\Application Data\Microsoft\Crypto\RSA. In the case of a roaming user profile, the private key resides in the RSA folder on the domain controller and is downloaded to the user's computer until the user logs off or the computer is restarted.

Unlike their corresponding public keys, private keys must be protected. Therefore, all files in the RSA folder are automatically encrypted with a random, symmetric key called the *user's master key*. The user's master key is generated by the RC4 algorithm in the Base or Enhanced CSP. RC4 generates a 128-bit key for computers with the Enhanced CSP (subject to cryptography export restrictions) and a 56-bit key for computers with only the Base CSP (available for all Windows 2000 computers). The master key is generated automatically and is renewed periodically. It encrypts each file in the RSA folder automatically as the file is created.

The RSA folder must never be renamed or moved because this is the only place the CSPs look for private keys. Therefore, it is advisable to provide additional security. The administrator can provide additional file system security for users' computers or use roaming profiles.

You should protect private keys for recovery, which is critical for backup, by exporting the certificate and private key to a floppy disk or other medium, storing the floppy disk or other medium securely, and then deleting the private key from the computer. This preserves the file from a system crash and makes it unavailable for cracking. To decrypt a data file, the recovery agent administrator inserts the floppy disk or other medium and imports the certificate and private key to the recovery agent account. For more information about how to secure recovery keys, see Windows 2000 Server Help.

Protect Folder

The user's master key is encrypted automatically by the Protected Storage service and stored in the user profile under *RootDirectory*\Documents and Settings\<*username*>\Application Data\Microsoft\Protect. For a domain user who has a roaming profile, the master key resides on the domain controller and is downloaded to the user's profile on the local computer until the computer is restarted.

The user's master key is encrypted twice, and each instance of encryption is stored in one of two parts of the Protect file. The first part, the password encryption key, is produced by the Hash-Based Message Authentication Code (HMAC) and SHA1 message digest function and is a hash of:

- A symmetric encryption of the user's master key produced by 160-bit RC4.
- The user's security identifier (SID).
- The user's logon password.

The second part is to create a backup form of the master key. This is needed if the user's password changes on one computer but the keys are in the user profile on another computer, or if the administrator resets the user's password. In either case, the Protected Storage service, which cannot detect password changes, uses the backup/restore form of the master key to regenerate the password encryption key.

To create the backup form of the master key, the user's encrypted master key is sent to the Protected Storage service on the domain controller. That service uses HMAC and SHA1 again to make a hash of the master key and the domain controller's own backup master key, and sends that back to the user's computer to store in the Protect file. These transmissions are authenticated (signed and encrypted) by remote procedure calls so that the user's master key is never sent over the network as plaintext.

The domain controller's backup master key is stored on the system as a *global Local Security Authority (LSA) secret* in the HKEY_LOCAL_MACHINE/SAM key in the registry and is replicated over the network using Active Directory. (Global LSA secrets are objects provided by the LSA to enable system services to store private data securely.)

The System Certificates, RSA, and Protect folders have their system attributes set. This prevents the files in them from being encrypted by EFS, which would make them inaccessible.

System Key

You can provide another level of protection for master keys and various other secrets through use of the system key. The system key protects the following sensitive information:

- Master keys that are used to protect private keys.

- Protection keys for user account passwords stored in Active Directory.

- Protection keys for passwords stored in the registry in the local Security Accounts Manager (SAM) registry key.

- Protection keys for LSA secrets.

- The protection key for the administrator account password that is used for system recovery startup in safe mode.

For all computers in a domain, the secret key is enabled by default and all master keys and protection keys stored on a computer are encrypted with the unique 128-bit symmetric random system key. The system key must be stored in volatile memory on the operating system during system startup to unlock the password protection key. There are three ways to configure the system key for computers:

- Use a computer-generated random key as the system key and store it on the local system by using a complex obfuscation algorithm that scatters the system key throughout the registry. This option allows you to restart the computer without having to enter the system key. This is the default configuration for the system key.

- Use a computer-generated random key, but store it on a floppy disk. The system key is not stored anywhere on the local computer, and the floppy disk must be inserted for the system to start. It is inserted when prompted after Windows 2000 begins the startup sequence, but before it is available for users to log on to the system.

- Use a password to derive the system key. The password is created by the system administrator and is not stored anywhere on the computer. Windows 2000 prompts the administrator for the password when the system is in the initial startup sequence, but before the system is available for users to log on.

The system key configuration options are available from the system key dialog boxes that appear when you run **syskey**. For computers in a domain, you must be a member of the Domain Admin group to run **syskey**. For stand-alone computers, you must be logged on as the local Administrator to run **syskey**. You can configure the system key differently for each computer in the domain.

System key protection is enabled by default in each Windows 2000 domain, but you might want to change the default system key option for various computers in a domain. You also might need to enable system key protection for stand-alone computers.

Certificate Stores

The Windows 2000 certificate stores include *physical stores* and *logical stores*.

Physical certificate stores are where public key objects such as certificates, certificate revocation lists (CRLs), and certification trust lists (CTLs) are physically stored either locally in the system registry or remotely in Active Directory. Many of the public key objects in the physical stores are shared among users, services, and computers through the use of logical certificate stores.

Logical certificate stores group certificates together in logical, functional categories for users, computers, and services. Logical certificate stores contain pointers to the physical certificate stores. Use the Certificates console (an MMC snap-in) to manage certificates in certificate stores. Changes to the logical certificate stores are made to the appropriate physical stores that are located in either the system registry or Active Directory. Because you use only the logical certificate store for a user, service, or computer, you neither have to keep track of where the certificates are actually stored, nor do you have to edit the system registry to manage the certificate stores.

The use of logical certificate stores eliminates the necessity of storing duplicates of common public key objects, such as trusted root certificates, CTLs, and CRLs for users, computers, and services. Users and services share many public key policy objects in common with the local computer. The common public key objects are stored in sections of the registry of the local computer. However, some certificates, CTLs, or CRLs, are issued for use only by an individual service, user, or local computer. Therefore, users, computers, and services also have individual stores that provide a place to store certificates, CTLs, or CRLs that are not shared in common. For example, a user can request and obtain a certificate or a CRL, which appears in the individual's logical store and is physically stored in the user's unique certificate store in the registry. Such individual user certificates and CRLs are not shared with local computers or with services.

In addition, some public key objects, such as trusted root certificates and CTLs, can be distributed through Public Key Group Policy. Public key objects that are distributed through Group Policy are stored in special areas of the system registry and appear in the logical stores for users, computers, and services. When you use Group Policy, separate CTLs can be created for users and computers. The CTLs for users are not shared with services or the computer. However, the CTLs for computers are shared with users and services.

The logical certificate stores include the following categories for users, computers, and services:

- **Personal**: Contains individual certificates for the user, service, or computer. For example, when an enterprise CA issues you a User certificate, the certificate is installed in the Personal store for your user account. User certificates reside in Documents and Settings\\<*username*>\\ApplicationData \\Microsoft\\SystemCertificates\\My\\Certificates for each user profile. These certificates in the user profile are written to the user's personal store in the system registry each time the user logs on to the computer. For roaming profiles, the user's certificates are located on the domain controller so the certificates follow users when they log on to different computers in the domain.

- **Trusted Root Certification Authorities**: Contains certificates for root CAs. Certificates with a certification path to a root CA certificate are trusted by the computer for all valid purposes of the certificate.

- **Enterprise Trust**: Contains CTLs. Certificates with a certification path to a CTL are trusted by the computer for purposes specified in the CTL.

- **Intermediate Certification Authorities**: Contains certificates for CAs that are not trusted root certificates (for example, certificates of subordinate CAs), but that are required to validate certification paths. This store also contains CRLs for use by the user, service, or computer.

- **Active Directory User Object**: Contains certificates that are published in Active Directory for the user. This store appears in the Certificates console for users only, not for computers or services.

- **Request**: Contains pending or rejected certificate requests. This store appears only in the Certificates console after a certificate request has been made for the user, computer, or service.

- **SPC**: Contains certificates for software publishers that are trusted by the computer. Software that has been digitally signed by publishers with certificates in this store is downloaded without prompting the user. By default, this store is empty. When Microsoft® Internet Explorer downloads for the first time software that has been signed by a software publisher, users are prompted to choose whether they want to trust all software that is signed by this publisher. If a user chooses to trust all software signed by the publisher, the publisher's software publisher certificate (SPC) is added to the SPC store. This store appears in the Certificates console for the local computer only, not for users or services.

Certificates Console

The Certificates console is an MMC snap-in, which you can use to manage the certificate stores for users, computers, and services.

You can use the Certificates console to perform the following tasks:

- View information about certificates, such as certificate contents and the certification path.

- Import certificates into a certificate store.

- Move certificates between certificate stores.

- Export certificates and, optionally, export private keys (if key export is enabled).

- Delete certificates from certificate stores.

- Request certificates from an enterprise CA for the Personal certificate store.

For more information about how to use the Certificates console, see Certificate Manager Help.

Certification Authority Trust Model

The Windows 2000 public key infrastructure supports a hierarchical CA trust model and CTLs. To control the certificates that are trusted in the enterprise, you can deploy Windows 2000 Certificate Services to create CA trust hierarchies and you can create CTLs.

Certification Authority Hierarchies

The Windows 2000 public key infrastructure supports a hierarchical CA trust model, called the *certification hierarchy*, to provide scalability, ease of administration, and compatibility with a growing number of commercial third-party CA services and public key-aware products. In its simplest form, a *certification hierarchy* consists of a single CA. However, the hierarchy usually contains multiple CAs that have clearly defined parent-child relationships. Figure 13.1 shows some possible CA hierarchies.

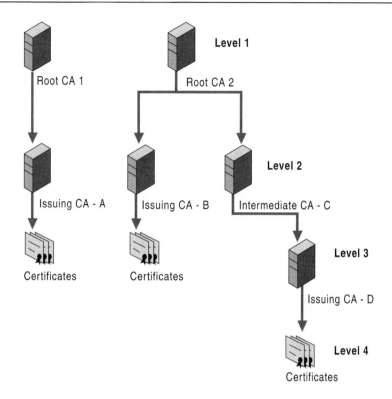

Figure 13.1   Certification Hierarchies

The CA at the top of the hierarchy is called a root CA. Root CAs are self-certified by using a self-signed CA certificate. Root CAs are the most trusted CAs in the organization, and it is recommended that they have the highest security of all. There is no requirement that all CAs in an enterprise share a common top-level CA parent or root. Although trust for CAs depends on each domain's CA trust policy, each CA in the hierarchy can be in a different domain.

Child CAs are called subordinate CAs. Subordinate CAs are certified by the parent CAs. A parent CA certifies the subordinate CA by issuing and signing the subordinate CA certificate. A subordinate CA can be either an intermediate or an issuing CA. An *intermediate CA* issues certificates only to subordinate CAs. An *issuing CA* issues certificates to users, computers, or services.

There is no restriction with regard to how deep the certification hierarchy can be. However, for many organizations, a three-level certification hierarchy (root CA, intermediate CA, and issuing CA) meets most needs.

Certification Path

A certification hierarchy forms a trust chain, called the *certification path*, from the certificate back to the root CA. Figure 13.2 illustrates a certification path for a four-level path that corresponds to the three-level CA hierarchy in Figure 13.1.

Figure 13.2   Trusted Certification Path

In the example, an EFS Recovery Agent certificate that was issued by Issuing CA-D has a certification path to Root CA 2 at the top of the path. The EFS Recovery Agent certificate is trusted because the certificate for Root CA 2 is contained in the Trusted Root Certification Authorities store.

The certification path links each certificate in the chain back to the root CA. Certificates that have a valid certification path to a root certificate that is in the Trusted Root Certification Authorities store are trusted for all purposes listed in the certificate. If the root CA's certificate for a certification path is not in the Trusted Root Certification Authorities store, the certification path is not trusted until the certificate of the root CA is added to the Trusted Root Certification Authorities store.

Before it trusts a certificate, Microsoft CryptoAPI validates the certification path from the certificate to the certificate of the root CA by checking each certificate in the path. Each certificate contains information about the parent CA that issued the certificate. CryptoAPI retrieves the certificate of each parent CA in the path from either the Intermediate Certification Authorities store or the Trusted Root Certification Authorities stores (if the certificates are present in the stores), or from an online location (such as an HTTP or LDAP address) that is specified in the certificate. If CryptoAPI discovers a problem with one of the certificates in the path, or if it cannot find a certificate, it does not trust the certification path.

When CryptoAPI retrieves a subordinate CA certificate for certificate path validation and the certificate is not located in the Intermediate Certification Authorities store, the API stores the certificate in the Intermediate Certification Authorities store for future reference. However, for computers that operate offline, such as portable computers that are used by mobile users, you might have to import subordinate CA certificates into the Intermediate Certification Authorities store to ensure that nonroot CA certificates are available to validate certification paths.

Figure 13.3 shows an example of a nontrusted certification path where the root certificate is not in the Trusted Root Certification Authorities store.

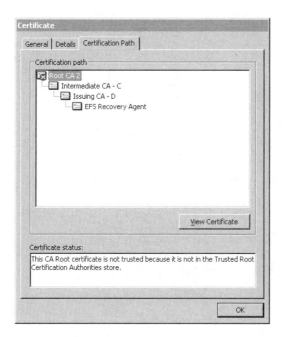

Figure 13.3   Nontrusted Certification Path

By default, certificates that are issued by trusted CAs are trusted for all of the intended purposes that are listed in the certificate. You can use the **Certificate Details** dialog box to restrict the purposes for which local certificates can be used. You can also use CTLs to establish trust for certificates and restrict the purposes for which certificates are trusted.

Certificate Trust Lists

You can use the Certificate Trust List wizard that is available from the Public Key Policy section of the Group Policy console (an MMC snap-in) to create CTLs. By using CTLs, you can choose to trust certificates that have certification paths to root CAs that are listed in the CTL. You can create CTLs for computers and users. CTLs for computers apply to all computers, users, and services within the scope of the Group Policy. However, CTLs for users apply only to users within the scope of the Group Policy. Figure 13.4 shows an example of a certification path with a CTL.

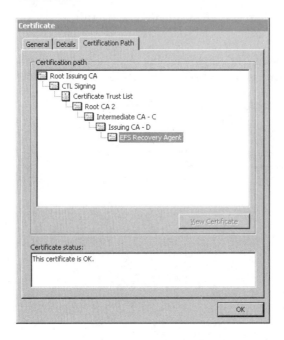

Figure 13.4   Trusted Certification Path with a CTL

In the example, the certification path from EFS Recovery Agent to Root CA 2 is identical to the certification path shown in Figure 10.3, but the certificate for Root CA 2 is not in the Trusted Root Certification Authorities store. The certification path also includes the CTL, the trust list signing certificate ("CTL Signing" in the example), and the root CA certificate that issued the signing certificate ("Root Issuing CA" in the example). The EFS Recovery Agent certificate is trusted because the certificate for Root Issuing CA (which issued the CTL Signing certificate) is contained in the Trusted Root Certification Authorities store.

A CTL must be signed by an administrator who has a valid certificate for trust list signing, such as the Administrator and Trust List Signing certificates that can be issued by enterprise CAs. By default, CTLs are valid until the trust list signing certificate expires and the CTL becomes invalid. However, to limit the time that certificates are trusted, you have the option of specifying a shorter lifetime for the CTL.

By default, members of the Domain Admins and Enterprise Admins security groups are granted permissions to enroll for Administrator and Trust List Signing certificates. To change the default certificate enrollment settings, modify the ACLs for the Administrator and Trust List Signing certificate templates.

For the CTL to be valid, the trust list signing certificate must have a certification path to a root CA in the Trusted Root Certification Authorities store. Figure 13.5 shows an example of a CTL that is invalid because the trust list signing certificate is invalid. This might be the situation because either the certification path for the trust list signing certificate does not validate to a trusted root certificate or the trust list signing certificate has expired.

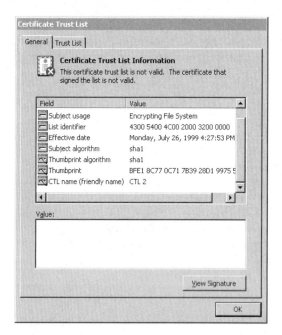

Figure 13.5   Invalid CTL

CTLs are stored in the Enterprise Trust store and you can use the Certificates console to view them.

In addition, you can use CTLs to restrict the purposes for which certificates can be used. For example, even though a certificate permits the purposes of software code signing, secure mail, and client authentication, you can use a CTL to restrict certificate use to client authentication only. CTLs are frequently used to restrict trust for certificates that are issued and managed by other organizations. For example, you might configure a CTL to trust a business partner's CA for only code signing and client authentication on an extranet that you manage.

Certificate Validation Process

Before it trusts certificates, Windows 2000 performs a validation check to ensure that certificates are valid and that they have a valid certification path. Figure 13.6 shows the basic certificate validation process.

Start

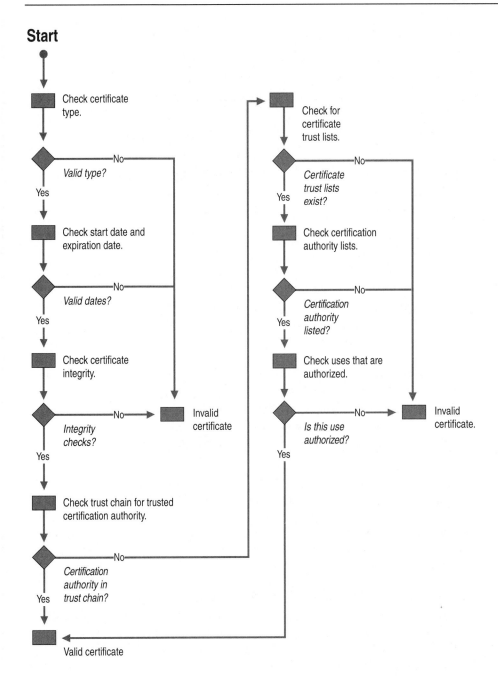

Figure 13.6   Basic Certificate Validation Process

Certificates can be invalid or are not trusted for a variety of reasons, including the following:

- The start and expiration dates are improper or expired.

- The certificate format is improper (does not conform to the X.509 version 3 standard for digital certificates).

- The information in certificate fields is improper or incomplete.

- The certificate's digital thumbprint and signature fail the integrity check, indicating that the certificate has been tampered with or corrupted.

- The certificate is listed as revoked in a published certificate revocation list.

- The issuing CA is not in either a trusted certification hierarchy or a CTL.

- The root CA for the certification path is not in the Trusted Root Certification Authorities store.

- The certificate is not permitted for the intended use as specified in a CTL.

Certificate Enrollment and Renewal Methods

Windows 2000 Certificate Services supports the following certificate enrollment and renewal methods:

- Manual certificate requests that use the Certificate Request wizard (only for Windows 2000 users, computers, and services).

- Automatic certificate requests, which use the Automatic Certificate Request Setup wizard (only for Windows 2000 computer certificates).

- Manual certificate requests that use the Web Enrollment Support pages (for Web browser users).

- Smart card enrollment, which uses the Smart Card Enrollment Station available in the Web Enrollment Support pages.

The enrollment methods and types of certificates that are supported by third-party Certificate Services depend on the features and functions of each third-party product. For more information, contact the vendor for the certificate service.

Manual Certificate Requests for Windows 2000–based Clients

You can request or renew certificates for Windows 2000 users, computers, and services by using the Certificate Request wizard that is available in the Certificates console. The Certificate Request wizard does not function unless an enterprise CA is online to process and issue certificate requests. The ACLs for the certificate templates determine which user accounts or computer accounts can enroll for the various types of certificates.

You can also use the Certificate Renewal wizard that is available in the Certificates console to renew certificates either before or after they expire. The Certificate Renewal wizard does not function unless an enterprise CA is online to process and issue certificate requests. You have the option of renewing certificates with the same private key and public key set. You must not renew certificates with the same private and public key sets if the maximum safe key lifetime would be exceeded.

Automatic Computer Certificate Enrollment and Renewal

You can use the Automatic Certificate Request Setup wizard (available from the Public Key section of the Group Policy console) to configure auto-enrollment for computer certificates. Auto-enrollment is not available for user certificates and does not function unless an enterprise CA is online to process certificate requests. You can configure auto-enrollment for Computer, Domain Controller, and IPSec certificates.

When auto-enrollment is configured, the specified certificate types are issued automatically to all computers that are within the scope of the Public Key Group Policy and to all computers that have Enroll permissions for that certificate type. Auto-enrollment certificates are issued the next time the computer logs on to the network.

For example, if you configure auto-enrollment for Computer certificates, the certificates are issued to all computers in the Domain Computers security group that are within the scope of the Public Key Group Policy. By default, all Windows 2000 computers are members of the Domain Computers security group, except for domain controllers, Routing and Remote Access servers, and Internet Authentication Service (IAS) servers. You can control which computers receive the Computer certificates by modifying the ACLs for the Computer certificate templates, for example, to grant Enroll permissions to a special security group composed of computers that you designate. Computers within the scope of the Public Key Group Policy that are members of the special security group are then issued Computer certificates the next time they log on to the network.

In addition, you also can use organizational units (OUs) and Public Key Group Policy for those OUs to restrict auto-enrollment to certain groups of computers. For example, you might create an IPSec Authentication OU that contains the Windows 2000 clients that you designate for IPSec authentication with certificates. To limit the scope of auto-enrollment for IPSec certificates, configure Public Key Group Policy and auto-enrollment for the IPSec Authentication OU.

When auto-enrollment is configured, the Computer certificates that are issued by auto-enrollment also are automatically renewed from the enterprise-issuing CA. You can also renew Computer certificates manually with the Certificate Renewal wizard or through the Certificate Services Web Enrollment Support pages.

Web Enrollment Support Pages

The Windows 2000 Certificate Services Web Enrollment Support pages are composed of Active Server Pages and ActiveX controls that provide a Web-based user interface to a CA. By default, the Web Enrollment Support pages are automatically installed on the computer where the CA is installed, but you also have the option of installing the Web Enrollment Support pages on another Windows 2000 Server computer.

You can use the Web Enrollment Support pages to perform the following tasks:

- Request and obtain a basic user certificate.
- Request and obtain other types of certificates by using advanced options.
- Request a certificate by using a certificate request file.
- Renew certificates by using a certificate renewal request file.
- Save a certificate request to a file.
- Save the issued certificate to a file.
- Check on pending certificate requests.
- Retrieve the CA's certificate.
- Retrieve the latest certificate revocation list from the CA.
- Enroll for smart card certificates on behalf of other users (for use by trusted administrators).

The Web Enrollment Support pages that are installed for stand-alone CAs are similar to the pages that are installed for enterprise CAs, but they differ in the respect that stand-alone CAs do not use certificate templates. For stand-alone CAs, all information about the certificate, including information about the requestor, must be specified in the certificate request. The Web Enrollment Support pages for stand-alone CAs support a number of types of certificates that have much of the same functionality as certificate types that are based on templates. You can deploy stand-alone CAs and Web Enrollment Support pages to issue most of the types of certificates that enterprise CAs can issue. However, certificates for logging on by using smart cards logon and for auto-enrollment require an enterprise CA to issue and renew the certificates.

The Web Enrollment Support pages work with Microsoft® Internet Explorer 4 and Microsoft® Internet Explorer 5. Use of the Microsoft Enhanced Cryptographic Provider requires Internet Explorer browsers with nonexportable cryptography. Internet Explorer browsers with exportable cryptography work only with the Microsoft Base Cryptographic Provider.

Netscape Navigator version 4.*x* and Netscape Communicator version 4.*x* work with most of the Web Enrollment Support pages. Netscape browsers do not work with the Advanced Certificate Requests form and the Smart Card Enrollment Station page because these pages use ActiveX controls. In addition, Netscape browsers use their own cryptographic security modules rather than CSPs and might not support all of the features that are available for the Microsoft CSPs.

Public Key Group Policy

Public Key settings are a subset of Group Policy. You can configure Public Key Group Policy to specify automatic enrollment for computer certificates, trusted root certificates, CTLs for computers and users, and EFS recovery agents and apply the Group Policy to sites, domains, or organizational units.

The Group Policy console is an MMC snap-in. You can use MMC to manage Public Key Group Policy for multiple sites, domains, and organizational units. You can configure Public Key Group Policy separately for users and for computers. You can use the Group Policy console to configure the following Public Key Group Policy settings for computers:

- Specify the certificates in Trusted Root Certification Authorities stores.
- Create CTLs to trust CAs and restrict the uses of certificates issued by the CAs.
- Specify automatic enrollment and renewal for computer certificates.
- Specify alternative Encrypted Data Recovery Agents for EFS.

Public Key Group Policy settings apply for computers within the scope of the Group Policy. For example, you can create an organizational unit and configure Public Key settings that apply only to the computers in that organizational unit.

You also can use the Group Policy console to configure CTLs that apply only to users within the scope of the Group Policy. For example, you can create an organizational unit and configure CTLs that apply only to the users in that organizational unit. For more information about Group Policy, see Windows 2000 Professional Help and Windows 2000 Server Help.

Certificate Revocation Lists

Windows 2000 supports industry standard X.509 version 2 CRLs. Each CA maintains a CRL for the certificates it issues and publishes the CRL-to-CRL distribution points. CRL distribution points can include Web pages, network shares, or Active Directory. An X.509 version 3 certificate usually contains the CRL distribution point for its issuing CA.

Certificate revocation checking is supported by Internet Explorer 5, Internet Information Services, and Active Directory mapping services. When revocation checking is enabled, CRLs are automatically cached on local computers to enhance revocation checking performance. If a certificate lists the CRL distribution point, the revocation checking process checks the local cache to determine whether the CRL is in the cache. If not, the revocation checking process then checks the network for the CRL. If a certificate does not list the CRL distribution point, revocation checking checks the issuing CA for a CRL, if one is available. You also can use the Web Enrollment Support pages to request the latest CRL from a CA.

When revoked certificates expire, they are removed from the next published CRL. For some large organizations with high certificate revocation rates, CRLs might become so large that it places a significant load on the network and computers during CRL publication. However, you can prevent large CRLs by deploying multiple issuing CAs to distribute the certificate load among your users and by issuing certificates with reasonably short lifetimes.

Preinstalled Trusted Root Certificates

The root CA certificates that are contained in the Trusted Root Certification Authorities store are trusted for all Windows applications that use public key certificates for security functions. Windows 2000–based computers include many preinstalled certificates in the Trusted Root Certification Authorities stores. The preinstalled trusted root certificates include root certificates from a variety of commercial CAs and Microsoft. Certificates that are issued by these trusted CAs are trusted on local computers for valid purposes. However, you might not want to trust the preinstalled root certificates, or you might want to add other certificates as trusted root certificates.

You can use the Certificates console to delete or add certificates manually for Trusted Root Certification Authorities stores on each local computer. You also can add trusted root certificates for groups of computers by using Public Key Group Policy.

In addition, you can use the Internet Explorer Administration Kit (IEAK) to create and deploy custom builds of Internet Explorer that have only the root certificates that you want for your enterprise. For example, you can create custom builds that include only a few trusted root certificates and then deploy those custom builds to groups of computers. The computers where the custom builds of Internet Explorer are installed have only the trusted root certificates that you specified. You can create different custom builds to meet the requirements of different groups in your organizations. For more information about using the IEAK, see the *Microsoft® Windows® 2000 Server Resource Kit Internet Explorer Resource Guide.*

Smart Card Support

Smart cards are credit card–sized and contain integrated circuit cards (ICCs). They can be used to store certificates and private keys and to perform public key cryptography operations, such as authentication, digital signing, and key exchange. Smart cards offer the following security enhancements and benefits:

- They provide tamper-resistant storage for protecting private keys and other forms of personal information.

- They isolate security-critical computations involving authentication, digital signatures, and key exchange from other parts of the system that do not have a specific purpose for this data.

- They enable the portability of credentials and other private information between work, home, and remote computers.

In addition, smart cards use Personal Identification Numbers (PINs) rather than passwords. The smart card is protected from misuse by the PIN, which is known only to the owner of the smart card. To use the smart card, a user inserts the card in a smart card reader that is attached to a computer and, when prompted, enters the PIN. The smart card can be used only by someone who possesses the smart card and knows the PIN.

PINs offer more protection than standard network passwords. Passwords (or derivations such as *hashes*) are sent over the network and are vulnerable to attacks. The strength of the password depends on its length, how well it is protected, and how difficult it is to guess. In contrast, PINs never travel on the network, so they cannot be stolen.

Windows 2000 supports industry standard Personal Computer/Smart Card (PC/SC)–compliant Plug and Play smart cards and smart card readers that conform to specifications that have been developed by the PC/SC Workgroup. To work with Windows 2000, a smart card must conform physically and electrically to the International Organization for Standardization (ISO) 7816-1, 7816-2, and 7816-3 standards.

Smart card readers attach to standard personal computer peripheral interfaces such as RS–232, PS/2, PCMCIA, and Universal Serial Bus (USB). Readers are considered standard Windows 2000 devices, and they carry a security descriptor and a Plug and Play identifier. Smart card readers are controlled through standard Windows device drivers and are installed and removed by using the Hardware wizard.

Windows 2000 includes drivers for various commercially available Plug and Play smart card readers that are certified to display the Windows-compatible logo. Some manufacturers might provide drivers for noncertified smart card readers that currently work with Windows 2000. Nevertheless, to ensure continued support by Microsoft, it is recommended that you purchase only those smart card readers that display the Windows-compatible logo.

The Windows 2000 CSPs includes smart card CSPs from Gemplus SCA and Schlumberger Limited. These CSPs support smart cards from the respective vendors and work with all smart card readers that display the Windows-compatible logo. The smart card CSPs store the issued certificate and the private key on the smart card.

Each smart card vendor provides software that you must install and use to initialize and configure smart cards before they can be deployed. You can use the vendor's software to configure PINs and to configure the number of PIN attempts that are allowed to occur before the smart card locks. You also can use the vendor's software to return locked smart cards to service.

For more information about smart cards, see "Choosing Security Solutions That Use Public Key Technology" in the *Microsoft® Windows® 2000 Server Resource Kit Distributed Systems Guide*.

Considerations for Public Key Security

Keep the following considerations in mind when planning to deploy Windows 2000–based computers. You have the option to deploy smart cards for higher security or to map certificates to user accounts in Active Directory. You also have the option to deploy secure mail with Microsoft® Outlook® Express.

Deploying Smart Cards

You can deploy smart cards and smart card readers to provide stronger user authentication and nonrepudiation for a range of security solutions, including logging on over a network, secure Web communication, and secure e-mail.

Smart Card Configuration Options

You have the following options when deploying smart cards:

Force Users to Use the Smart Card Logon Process   Allowing the CTRL+ALT+DEL secure logon sequence for smart card users defeats the purpose of using smart cards. During the transition to smart cards, you must enable both logon methods until users are trained and the smart card logon process has been tested for your domains. Thereafter, however, you can configure individual user accounts (but not security groups) so that the CTRL+ALT+DEL secure logon process is disabled and users are forced to use their smart cards to log on to their computers. To configure individual user accounts, use the Active Directory Users and Computers console (a snap-in to MMC).

Force Systems to Lock Upon Removal of the Smart Card   When a user walks away from a computer with an active logon session and the user fails to secure the computer by logging off or locking the computer, an intruder might use the computer for malicious purposes. If you are requiring the use of smart cards for logging on to computers, you can force the systems to lock when users remove their smart cards from the readers. Use this option as necessary to meet your security needs, especially when computers are used in an environment with easy access by the public. You can configure security options under Security Settings in Group Policy to force groups of computers to lock upon the removal of smart cards.

Deploying Secure Mail

In Windows 2000, secure mail is based on the Secure/Multipurpose Internet Mail Extensions (S/MIME) protocol, which extends the original Multipurpose Internet Mail Extensions (MIME) standard. The S/MIME standard enables the digital signing and encryption of confidential mail. Secure mail can be exchanged between S/MIME clients that run on any platform or operating system. Secure mail clients can send S/MIME messages over the Internet without regard to the types of mail servers that handle the messages between the origin of the message and the final destination, because all cryptographic functions are performed on the clients, not on the servers. Mail servers treat S/MIME messages as standard MIME. The only function of Internet mail servers is to route MIME messages; they do not alter the contents of messages in transit.

Secure Mail Clients

Microsoft supports S/MIME in the Microsoft® Outlook® 98 messaging and collaboration client as well as in Microsoft® Outlook Express version 4 and Outlook Express version 5.

Secure mail with S/MIME uses the industry-standard X.509 version 3 digital certificates and public key technology. To provide message authentication, data integrity, and nonrepudiation, secure mail clients can sign messages with the sender's private key before sending the messages. The recipients then use the sender's public key to verify the message by checking the digital signature. Clients require a valid secure mail certificate before they can send signed mail. Recipients must have a copy of the originator's secure mail certificate (which contains the public key) before they can verify the originator's signature.

In addition, secure mail clients can send and receive confidential mail. Clients generate random secret bulk (symmetric) encryption keys and use the secret key to encrypt messages for confidentiality. Then they protect the secret bulk encryption key by encrypting it with the public key of each recipient and sending the encrypted key along with the encrypted message to each recipient. Message originators must have a copy of the recipient's secure mail certificate (which contains the public key) before they can send confidential mail. Recipients use their private keys to decrypt the secret bulk encryption key; then they use the secret key to decrypt the message.

By using secure mail, senders are assured that the integrity of their messages is preserved and that only the intended recipients can read the encrypted mail. Recipients are assured that the message is genuine and originated from the sender.

The strength of the encryption cryptography that is available for secure mail clients depends on the current export or import restrictions for cryptography that are required by many governments. The actual cryptographic strength that is available to your mail clients depends on the cryptography restrictions that apply for the locality where the mail clients are deployed and for the locality where the mail clients are installed. In general, mail clients with exportable technology provide much weaker security than mail clients with nonexportable cryptography.

Trust for Secure Mail

For secure mail to work, each mail client must have a valid certificate for secure mail and each client must trust the root CA in the certification path of the other client's secure mail certificates. Certificates can be published in Lightweight Directory Access Protocol (LDAP) directories, public folders, and Web pages to facilitate the distribution of certificates and public keys. In Windows 2000, secure mail certificates are published to Active Directory for the user account that is issued a certificate. You also have the option of configuring Certificate Services to publish certificates to public folders, Web pages, or other LDAP-compliant directory services. Users with mail clients that support LDAP, such as Outlook 98 or Outlook Express, can browse directory services to locate and obtain the published certificates of others.

Secure mail clients must trust the certificates from other correspondents. You can configure secure mail for your organization to trust secure mail certificates that are issued by CAs in your organization or to trust secure mail certificates that are issued by third-party CAs. If you trust only the secure mail root CAs in your organization, secure mail communications are limited to transactions between employees. However, you can enable secure mail transactions with third parties by trusting their secure mail root CAs.

Certificate Services for Secure Mail

You can deploy Certificate Services so that it issues secure mail certificates that work with S/MIME-compliant secure mail clients such as Outlook 98 or Outlook Express. You can use the Certificate Services Web enrollment pages to enroll users and issue secure mail certificates. For more information about Certificate Services, see "Windows 2000 Certificate Services and Public Key Infrastructure" in the *Microsoft® Windows® 2000 Server Resource Kit Distributed Systems Guide*.

In addition, you can use a mail service, such as the Microsoft® Exchange Server version 5.5 client/server messaging and groupware, to provide management services for secure mail. You can deploy Exchange Server and use the Key Management server (KM server) to manage secure mail certificate enrollment for Certificate Services. You can also use KM server to provide key recovery services as described in the following section. For more information about KM Server, see Exchange Server Help and the *Microsoft® BackOffice® Resource Kit*.

Protecting User Data on Portable Computers

You can take the following steps to protect user data on portable computers in case of theft:

- Encrypt all user data with EFS.
- Configure the system key.
- Secure the private key for recovery.

Encrypting User Data

To provide EFS security for user data on a portable computer, do the following:

- Make sure the user's My Documents folder is empty, and then apply EFS protection to this folder. Therefore, all new files that are stored in the EFS-protected folder are encrypted, and all new subfolders that are created in the EFS-protected folder are protected. Users can create as many folders in My Documents as they need. If you add encrypted files to the folder, the user cannot read those files.

- Apply EFS protection for temporary folders that are used by applications. Applications work with only plaintext because EFS operates in the background. If EFS protection is not applied to the folders where the temporary files are stored, applications can save their temporary files as plaintext to the folders. You can also configure applications to store temporary files in EFS-protected folders.

- Configure NTFS file system ACLs to prevent users from creating non-EFS-protected folders and from changing EFS settings.

Configuring System Key

Use the Windows 2000 System Key (SysKey) to protect EFS private keys. SysKey uses strong encryption techniques to increase the protection of users' protected stores, including users' private keys for EFS.

▶ **To configure system key protection**

1. Type **syskey** at the command prompt. This brings up the dialog box shown in Figure 13.7.

Figure 13.7   System Key Dialog Box

After system key protection is enabled, it cannot be disabled.

2. If it is not already selected, click **Encryption Enabled**, and then click **OK**. After a reminder that you should create an updated emergency repair disk, you are presented with options for the Account Database Key as shown in Figure 13.8. The default option is a system-generated password that is stored locally.

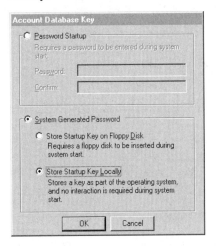

Figure 13.8   Account Database Key Dialog Box

3. Select the system key option that you want, and then click **OK**.

4. Restart the computer.

When the system restarts, you might be prompted to enter the system key, depending on the key option you chose. Windows 2000 detects the first use of the system key and generates a new random password encryption key. The password encryption key is protected with the system key, and then all account password information is strongly encrypted.

At subsequent startups:

- Windows 2000 obtains the system key, either from the locally stored key, the password entry, or insertion of a floppy disk, depending on the option you chose.

- Windows 2000 uses the system key to decrypt the master protection key.

- Windows 2000 uses the master protection key to derive the per-user account password encryption key that is then used to decrypt the password information in Active Directory or the local SAM registry key.

The **syskey** command can be used again later to change the system key storage option or to change the password.

Securing the Private Key For Recovery

It is recommended that you remove private keys for recovery agent accounts from the computers by exporting the keys to removable media and then putting the keys in locked storage. This should be done with the default recovery keys before any changes are made to recovery policy.

The Certificate Export wizard accomplishes this purpose. This wizard is available through the Certificates console. For more information about using the Certificates console and the Certificate Export wizard, see Windows 2000 Professional Help or Windows 2000 Server Help.

You must log on as Administrator, because the EFS recovery agent certificate is contained in the personal certificate store for the Administrator account. You can then use the Certificate Export wizard to export the certificate and private key to a removable medium. For information about how to export a certificate and its private key, see Certificates Help.

To delete the private key from the computer, you must select the **Delete the private key if the export is successful** check box on the Export File Format page of the wizard. When you have completed the wizard, the private key is deleted from the computer and the recovery agent certificate and private key resides in a .pfx file in the folder or drive that you have specified. Now you need to protect the .pfx file by putting it into secure storage.

▶ **To protect a .pfx file**

1. If you created the .pfx file on a floppy disk, the file is right where it should be —on a medium that can be physically removed and locked away in another location. If you did not create the .pfx file on a floppy disk, copy it to a floppy disk and delete it from your hard disk drive.

2. Remove the floppy disk and make a backup copy of the .pfx file on another floppy disk. Store both floppy disks in safes or in a secure place. One floppy disk should be stored in a secure offsite location.

You then can use the Certificates console to import the .pfx file to a recovery computer and perform recovery operations. After recovering encrypted files, secure the private key again.

Additional Resources

- For information about Active Directory, see "Active Directory" in the *Microsoft Windows 2000 Server Resource Kit Distributed Systems Guide*. Active Directory stores security data and authenticates users in a domain environment.

- For more information about security, see "Distributed Security" in the *Microsoft Windows 2000 Server Resource Kit Distributed Systems Guide*.

- For information about networking, see "Windows 2000 TCP/IP Networking" in the *Microsoft Windows 2000 Server Resource Kit Core Networking Guide*. Understanding networking is important when establishing secure connections.

CHAPTER 14

Printing

Printing is easier to use in Microsoft® Windows® 2000 and produces more consistent, higher quality results. Microsoft® Windows® 2000 Professional provides several ways to install, configure, and manage printers, each way designed to make the process more intuitive and efficient. Printing now also includes improved ways to send print jobs, including over the Internet or by using new port monitors. Most of the improvements to the Windows 2000 printing system are not obvious in the user interface, but these improvements are seen in improved performance, compatibility, and the use of automated wizards.

In This Chapter

Related Information in the Windows 2000 Professional Resource Kit

- For more information about setting permissions, see "Security" in this book. Permissions regulate printer access.

- For more information about determining a printer's location, see "TCP/IP in Windows 2000 Professional" in this book.

- For more information about Plug and Play technology, see "Device Management" in this book.

- For more information about Integrated Color Management, see "Scanners and Cameras" in this book.

Quick Guide to Printing

Use this quick guide to locate information about printing. You will find information about finding, installing, configuring, using, and managing your printers, as well as detailed information about troubleshooting printing problems.

Find a printer.

Finding printers that are directly connected to your computer is easy, but finding the right network printing device can be challenging. Windows 2000 helps you find printers based on printer attributes.

- See "Finding Printers" later in this chapter.

Install a printer.

For printers to work properly, your computer must have the proper drivers and the printer must be registered with your computer. Windows 2000 offers many ways to install a printer, emphasizing automating as many of parts of the process as possible.

- See "Installing Printers" later in this chapter.

Configure your installed printer or fax.

You can establish default behavior for a printer or fax you have installed. Some common configuration options for printers include selecting whether to print in landscape or portrait, what size paper to use, and when the printer is available. For faxes, you can set the fax cover sheet to be used and the time that jobs must be sent.

- See "Configuring Printers" later in this chapter.

Send a print job.

There are new ways to print a document when using Windows 2000. Learn about the new print options and how you can use them to improve your printing process and output. Enhancements include a reworked **Print** dialog box, enhanced color printing, enhanced UniDriver and PostScript drivers, and the Standard Port Monitor.

- See "Creating and Sending Print Jobs" later in this chapter.

Monitor and manage printers and print jobs.

Depending on your privileges, you can choose to implement security for printers, establish times when the printer can be used, establish priority for users whose print jobs must print before everyone else's, and manage some or all of the print jobs that have been sent to a printer.

- See "Monitoring and Managing Print Jobs" later in this chapter.

Troubleshoot printers.

Solve problems that arise with your printers.

- See "Troubleshooting" later in this chapter.

What's New

Windows 2000 Professional includes new features that make it easier to install, configure, and use printers. Tables 14.1 through 14.4 show the difference between features in Windows 2000 and Microsoft® Windows NT® version 4.0, Microsoft® Windows® 95, and Microsoft® Windows® 98.

Table 14.1   Printer Installation Features

Windows 2000	Windows NT 4.0	Windows 95 and Windows 98
Find a printer by entering the printer name (UNC), browsing the network, or typing a printer URL for printers with known locations. Find printers by using Search for Printers or Active Directory.	Find a printer by entering the printer name (UNC) or browse the network to find the printer.	Same as Windows NT 4.0.
Add network printers by using the Add Printer wizard or Point and Print. Point and Print automatically downloads and installs required printer drivers on the client computer.	Add a network printer by using the Add Printer wizard. Point and Print enables printing and installs drivers.	Add network printers by using the Add Printer wizard or using Point and Print. Point and Print automatically downloads printer drivers.
Add a local printer by using Plug and Play if supported by the printer or use the Add Printer wizard. You can prompt Windows 2000 to detect Plug and Play printers that use parallel connections using the Add Printer wizard.	Add a local printer by using the Add Printer wizard. No Plug and Play.	Add a local printer by using Plug and Play if supported by the printer or use the Add Printer wizard.
Point and Print available by right-clicking a printer in My Network Places, and then clicking Connect. All necessary drivers are automatically downloaded. All other Point and Print techniques available for Windows 98 are still supported.	Connect to network printers by using the Add Printer wizard.	Connect to network printers in My Network Places by using Point and Print, by entering the printer's UNC path in the printer wizard, typing the print server's path in the **Run** dialog box, or by opening the print queue using My Network Places or Windows Explorer.

Table 14.2   Printer Configuration Features

Windows 2000	Windows NT 4.0	Windows 95 and Windows 98
Printer settings configured by using Printing Preferences.	Printer settings configured by using Document Defaults.	Same as Windows NT 4.0.
Print preferences configured by using the **Layout** or **Paper/Quality** tabs.	Print preferences configured by clicking **Properties** in the **Print** dialog box.	Same as Windows NT 4.0.
Printer properties allow each user to set a unique set of persistent properties.	Default Printer properties are set by the printer administrator and appear each time a user logs on. Printer properties are not persistent per user, so users must reapply printer settings each time they print.	Same as Windows NT 4.0.

Table 14.3   Creating and Sending Print Jobs

Windows 2000	Windows NT 4.0	Windows 95 and Windows 98
Same as previous versions, plus allows Internet printing by using IPP v1.0 over HTTP connection. Allows for authentication before using printers.	Supports network printing over a LAN by using RPC, TCP/IP using Lprmon, and a variety of print port monitors for proprietary systems.	Supports network printing over a LAN by using RPC, TCP/IP using LPR, and a variety of port print monitors for proprietary systems.
Same as Windows 98, but can also drag the file to be printed to a printer shortcut on your desktop.	You can send print jobs in the following ways: ▪ Right-click the file to be printed, point to **Send to**, and then click the printer's shortcut. ▪ Right-click the file, and then click **Print**. ▪ Select **Print** from the **File** menu of the document's associated application.	Same as Windows NT 4.0. You can also create a shortcut for a printer in the Send To folder in your user profile.
UniDriver enhanced to provide font subsetting, better performance, and better handling of 2-byte fonts.	Universal driver exists, but without the optimization enhancements of the PostScript and UniDriver of Windows 2000.	Universal driver exists, but without the optimization enhancements of the PostScript and UniDriver of Windows 2000.
Supports Image Color Management (ICM) 2.0 which is improved with more color space profiles.	ICM not available.	Windows 95: ICM 1.0 available. Windows 98: ICM 2.0 available.
Internet Protocol (IP) printing is handled by the Standard TCP/IP Port Monitor. LPR is still available.	IP printing is handled by Line Printer Remote/Line Printer Daemon (LPR/LPD).	IP printing is not supported.

Table 14.4   Printing Management Features

Windows 2000	Windows NT 4.0	Windows 95 and Windows 98
Same as Windows NT 4.0, but information is also available by holding the mouse pointer over printer icons.	Double-click the printer icon to see the queue and view printing status.	Same as Windows NT 4.0.

New and improved technologies available with Windows 2000 Professional are highlighted in the following section.

Enhanced Add Printer wizard   The enhanced Add Printer wizard provides easier installation and use of a wider range of printers. The Add Printer wizard uses Active Directory™ directory service, allowing users to easily search for printers. Using Active Directory, administrators can assign users to groups that have access to certain printers, such as those in a specific locale or with specific features. This tailors the available printer list to the needs of the user and makes installing printers simpler.

Point and Print   Point and Print allows users to initiate a connection to a network printer and loads any required drivers onto the user's computer. When users know which network printer they want to use, Point and Print greatly simplifies the installation process.

Flexible, powerful network printer management   Windows 2000 supports specific, detailed printer management. For example, users in an organization's art department can be added to a group with permissions to access to a color printer, or users in Seattle can be added to a group with access to printers in Seattle, but without access to printers located elsewhere. By establishing user groups, you determine who can use certain printers and designate the security and authentication schemes required to access those resources.

Image Color Management (ICM) 2.0   ICM 2.0 ensures that colors appear as expected. Colors are accurately maintained, regardless of source, storage format, or output.

Internet printing   Internet printing enables printing throughout the world by using the Internet Printing Protocol (IPP) version 1.0.

Improved bidirectional communication   Bidirectional communication allows hardware devices to actively notify clients of problems such as paper jams or errors.

IEEE 1284.4 (DOT4) support   DOT4 support for multi-function peripherals (MFPs) transparently provides more efficient device use.

Wider printer support   Windows 2000 supports thousands of printers.

Fax printing   Windows 2000 enables sending faxes through your fax modem.

Finding Printers

A networked printer can be used by many people and allows for better resource management and flexibility. With these benefits comes the challenge of finding a printer, which is much more difficult when it is not directly connected to your computer.

When printing over a Windows 2000-based network, you can choose between printers within your local area network (LAN) and printers available on the Internet.

The Find Printer wizard supports searching Active Directory, and the Add Printer wizard supports adding Internet printers.

Active Directory allows searching on a range of printer attributes to find a printer that meets your particular needs. If subnets are being used to define sites within your organization, Active Directory can find printers that are located near the user. This is a significant advancement, because finding the closest printer has long plagued both administrators and users.

▶   **To search for nearby printers**

1. From the **Start** menu, point to **Search**, and then click **For Printers**.

2. In **Location**, type part or all of a printer location, based on the syntax that administrators have implemented for describing printer location in Active Directory, and then click **Find Now**.

   For example, if you are in Los Angeles and you want to find all printers in your deployment in the city, type "US/LAX" in **Location**, assuming this fits with the printer location syntax used for describing printer locations in Active Directory. This might return results such as:

   - US/LAX/1/101
   - US/LAX/2/103

   This would indicate that there are two printers available in Los Angeles. These results could indicate the printers are in buildings 1 and 2 and in rooms 101 and 103, if that matched the syntax that administrators applied.

Printer Locations and Active Directory

Active Directory can be used to find printers in two ways. First, you can search specific fields in the Active Directory for printers with properties you want. For example, you can search the location field to find a printer that had a specific location you want, such as New York. Second, you can use Active Directory to find printers that are well-connected to you, which typically includes those printers in your subnet. Subnets are used by Active Directory to establish areas of good connectivity, which typically means areas that are physically close. Note that good connectivity does not always mean physically close, but it typically does.

Searching Active Directory Fields

When searching for printers in large environments, you might need to use a specific format to find a printer in the location you want. Specific formats can be achieved by using a standardized format for the Location attribute of each printer, or by extending Active Directory to accommodate specific location information. Because the Location field allows for approximately 250 characters, printer locations can be described in numerous ways. For example, a printer in New York City, in Building 3, on Floor 5 can take a number of formats including:

- New York/Building 3/Floor 5
- NYC/Bldg III/Fifth floor
- NY/B3/F5

Understanding how printer location is formatted in Active Directory helps users to create searches that are more likely to yield useful results.

▶ **To search for printers with specific characteristics**

1. Double-click **My Computer**, click **Search** in the toolbar, and then click **Printers** in the **Search** window.

2. Click the **Features** tab to search using a prepared set of criteria. Use **Features** to create searches for printers using a predefined set of commonly sought features.

   –Or–

   Click the **Advanced** tab to access advanced search options. Use **Advanced** to search Active Directory using Boolean operators. You can construct complex searches based on any available criteria.

3. Enter your search criteria, and then click **Find Now**.

Active Directory returns a list of all printers that match your query. Note that when a printer has characteristics other than those listed in Active Directory, you can receive misleading search results.

Searching Active Directory Locations

You can search Active Directory locations, but to make this effective enable the following technologies:

- Location tracking enabled by Group Policy for your organization.
- A standardized location naming convention that is assigned to each site, subnet, or computer object.
- Sites based on a subnet or subnets.

If these technologies are in place, you can quickly find printers in your location.

▶ **To search for printers using Active Directory locations**

1. Double-click **My Computer**, click **Search** in the toolbar, and then click **Printers** in the **Search** window.

2. If your deployment uses location, your current location is automatically entered in the **Location** field. You can also click **Browse** to select an alternate location to find printers in other locations.

3. Enter other search criteria, if you have any, and then click **Find Now**. Active Directory returns a list of all printers that match your query. Other search criteria you might enter can include Printer Name or Model. For more information about general searching, see "Searching Active Directory Fields" earlier in this chapter.

To establish a system in which your users can search for nearby printers using subnets, your deployment must have the following:

- A directory service with more than one subnet.
- A network IP addressing scheme that roughly matches the physical layout of your enterprise.
- One or many subnet objects for each site. Create subnet objects and manage sites using Active Directory Sites and Services which is included with Microsoft® Windows® 2000 Server.

Your deployment can also use an extended schema, although in most cases, you should use location tracking rather than extend the schema. All objects in Active Directory have a base set of attributes, but this base set can be extended to accommodate the particular needs of your environment. If using an extended schema, users must construct Boolean searches using the **Advanced** tab in the **Search** dialog box. The **Advanced** tab provides the set of available Boolean operators and possible choices, when there is a limited set, such as when choosing the attribute of an Active Directory object on which to search.

Although using location tracking is typically an effective solution, as a last resort, administrators might extend the schema to include attributes such as Printer City, Printer Building, or Printer Floor. Early planning concerning how printer location is described in Active Directory will save you time later.

For more information about location tracking, see "Searching Active Directory Locations" in this chapter. For more information about setting up location tracking using sites on a Windows 2000 Server, see Windows 2000 Server Help.

Other Ways to Find Printers

You can also connect to network printers by entering their printer name (UNC) or URL. Using URLs to access printers is new to Windows 2000 and is dependent on Internet printing. You must know the UNC or URL of the printer to which you want to connect.

Plug and Play makes installing a local printer easier and is provided with Windows 2000 Professional. Finding Plug and Play printers typically is not difficult, because they must be physically plugged into your computer. For more information about installing local printers, see "Installing Local Printers" later in this chapter.

Installing Printers

Windows 2000 installs and configures printers in a several ways.

Support for Plug and Play printer devices makes it easier than ever to install printers that are attached directly to your computer. Simply attach the printer to the computer, and Windows 2000 automatically starts the Add Printer wizard. When installing printers over a network, Active Directory makes it easier to locate printers based on a range of criteria, such as the printer location or the printer's color and resolution capabilities.

Installation using Point and Print automatically downloads all required printer drivers, making installing a printer as easy as opening the print server's print queue by using My Network Places or Windows Explorer. After a print server is configured to support printers and to provide drivers to clients, users do not need to know which driver is required for the printer, or how to install the required drivers; Windows 2000 takes care of these issues for them.

If your printer and printer drivers support bidirectional communication, the device can actively report errors. If the printer is jammed or out of paper, Windows 2000 lets you know.

Installing Network Printers

There are several different ways to install network printers. Use the one that is most convenient for you.

Point and Print

Point and Print allows users to install a printer over a network. A user points to a print server by either opening its print queue by using My Network Places, by typing its path name in the **Run** dialog box on the **Start** menu, or by starting the Add Printer wizard. Windows 2000 receives printer-specific information from the server that can include:

- Printer driver files.
- The name of the server on which printer driver files are stored.
- Printer model information, which specifies which printer driver to retrieve from the Windows directory on a local computer or on the network.

▶ **To install a printer by using Point and Print**

1. Open a Network print server, then open the print server's Printers folder.
2. Right-click the printer to which you want to connect, and then click **Connect**.

Add Printer Wizard

The Add Printer wizard walks you through the steps necessary to install a printer.

▶ **To install a network printer by using the Add Printer wizard**

1. From the **Start** menu, point to **Settings**, and then click **Printers**.
2. Double-click **Add Printer**, and then follow the instructions.

Enter Printer UNCs or URLs at the Run Dialog Box

If you know the name (UNC) or the URL of the printer you want to install, this option allows for a fast, direct installation.

▶ **To install a printer by using the Run dialog box**

1. From the **Start** menu, click **Run**.
2. Type the UNC or URL of the printer, and then click **OK**.

Internet Printers

When planning to connect an Internet printer, you can view all printers available on a Microsoft Internet print server. To view these printers, enter the Internet print server's URL in Internet Explorer. Figure 14.1 is an example of a list of printers available on an Internet print server.

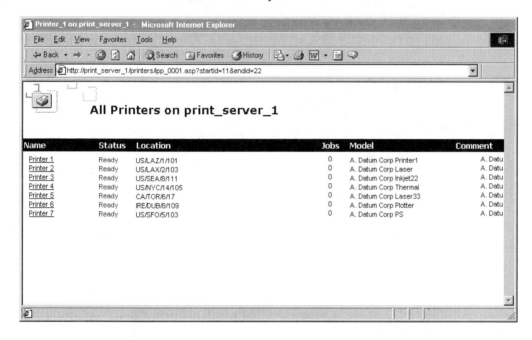

Figure 14.1   Printers Available on an Internet Print Server

For more information about any printer available on a Microsoft Internet print server, click the printer's name. This displays a page with information that can include:

- Printer model
- Location
- Comment
- Network name
- Documents in the queue
- Maximum speed
- Whether color is supported
- Whether duplexing is available
- Maximum resolution

Figure 14.2 is an example of a Web page you might find with information about a specific printer.

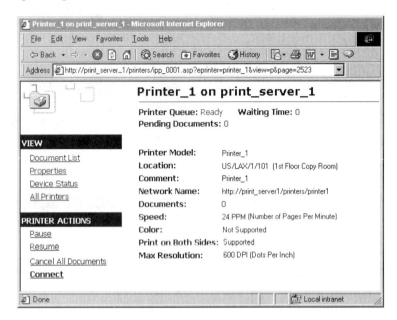

Figure 14.2   Information About a Printer on an Internet Print Server

▶ **To install an Internet printer by using the Connect button**

1. Open Internet Explorer.

2. Type the print server's URL in **Address** (for example, http://servername/printers), and then click **Go**.

3. Select the printer to which you want to connect, and then click **Connect**.

Installing Local Printers

There are several ways to install local printers. Use the one that is most convenient for you.

Add Printer Wizard

The Add Printer wizard facilitates printer setup. If you have connected a Plug and Play printer to your computer but it has not been automatically detected, you might want to use the Add Printer wizard to begin the installation process.

▶ **To install a local printer by using the Add Printer wizard**

1. From the **Start** menu, point to **Settings**, and then click **Printers**.

2. Double-click **Add Printer**, and then follow the instructions.

Plug and Play Printers

Plug and Play is a set of specifications that allows a computer to automatically detect and configure a printer and install the appropriate drivers. This installation technique is only available for printers connected directly to your computer, and is not available for networked printers.

To initiate Plug and Play printer installation, plug your printer into your computer. The printer is automatically configured in most cases. Plug and Play automatically installs the appropriate drivers and does not require you to restart your computer. If a Plug and Play printer is not automatically installed, you can manually make your computer check for Plug and Play printers by using the Add Printer wizard or by using Device Manager.

Although Windows 2000 includes drivers for many popular printers, if your printer uses a driver that is not included with Windows 2000, you will need to provide the driver. For automatically detected Plug and Play printers, if your computer does not have right driver, you are prompted to provide it.

Most Plug and Play printers use USB or parallel connections.

Automatic Detection

When supported by the printer, Windows 2000 automatically detects printers and completes the entire printer installation process, including installing the proper drivers, updating the system, and allocating resources. No user intervention or restarting is required and the printer is ready to be used immediately.

All automatically detected Plug and Play printers use Universal Serial Bus (USB) connections, Institute of Electrical and Electronics Engineers (IEEE) 1394 cables, or Infrared Data Association (IrDA) transmission.

Manual Detection

Manually-detected Plug and Play is similar to automatically-detected Plug and Play in that Windows 2000 automatically completes printer installation, but you must restart your computer to prompt the automatic installation or use the Add Hardware wizard to prompt your computer to detect the printer. Upon restarting or prompting by using the Add Hardware wizard, Windows 2000 updates your computer, allocates resources, and installs drivers. If drivers for the printer are not available, you are prompted to provide them.

Manually-detected Plug and Play printers typically use parallel or serial cables.

For more information about Plug and Play, see "Device Management" in this book.

Installing Faxes

Fax modems are automatically detected by Windows 2000, but it is recommended that you refer to the documentation provided with your fax modem for information about any other steps you must take to install your fax modem. When a fax modem is connected to your computer, Windows 2000 detects and installs the fax printer. However, if this does not happen, you can manually add a fax printer.

▶ **To add a fax printer**

1. From the **Start** menu, point to **Settings**, and then click **Control Panel**.

2. Double-click **Fax**, click the **Advanced Options** tab, and then click **Add a Fax Printer**.

3. Follow the instructions in the Add Printer wizard.

General Printer Installation Considerations

In general, printers that use USB ports are automatically-detected Plug and Play printers, whereas printers that use serial or parallel ports are not Plug and Play or are manually-detected Plug and Play printers that require that you use the Add Printer wizard to install them. To install printers, you must have administrative privileges.

Some printers require drivers that are not included with Windows 2000 Professional. If you are using a Plug and Play printer whose drivers are not included, you must use the Add Printer wizard, which allows you to provide printer drivers from sources such as floppy disk, a network share, or the printer vendor's Web site.

If Microsoft does not supply a driver for your printer, ask the printer's manufacturer for a printer driver. To ensure quality, use drivers that have passed Windows Hardware Quality Labs (WHQL) tests. Microsoft Product Support Services does not support systems with unapproved drivers. For more information about approved printer drivers, see the WHQL link on the Web Resources page at http://windows.microsoft.com/windows2000/reskit/.

You can also e-mail ntwish@microsoft.com to suggest support for a driver or feature. Please include the following information about yourself in your request:

- Name

- Business name

- Phone number or e-mail address

- Printer manufacturer
- Printer model
- Request (feature request or driver request)

Note This does not guarantee that Microsoft will write a driver for your printer.

Driver.cab File

When a Plug and Play device is installed, drivers are loaded from the Driver.cab file, if they are available.

Windows 2000 uses a cabinet file (.cab) called Driver.cab. This file is installed on Windows 2000 computers and is accessed as needed. The .cab file contains thousands of the most commonly used files, such as drivers, application extensions, and color profiles. These files enable Windows 2000 to work with a broad range of hardware devices and applications.

Installing Driver.cab as part of a standard installation of Windows 2000 avoids the need to provide the Windows 2000 operating system CD every time you want to install a new device.

Windows Update

If the drivers you need for a device are not available in the version of Windows 2000 you have installed, you might be able to get that driver from Windows Update. Windows Update updates your system with new Windows features, including device drivers and system updates.

▶ **To access Windows Update**

- From the **Start** menu, click **Windows Update**.

  –Or–

  For more information about Windows Update, see the Windows Update link on the Web Resources page at http://windows.microsoft.com/windows2000/reskit/webresources.

Operating System Exceptions

When you install a network printer on a Windows 2000 Professional-based computer, that printer might be served by a print server that is not running Windows 2000. If the printer is using a non-Windows 2000 print server, you must install additional components so the client and server computers and the printer can effectively communicate and transfer the print job.

NetWare Print Servers

To use a printer that is connected to a NetWare server, you must have a client installed on your computer such as Microsoft Client Service for NetWare or Novell's client, Novell Client 32. Such clients allow your computer to send print jobs to the NetWare server, which the server then relays to the printer.

For more information about working with NetWare, see "Interoperability with NetWare" in this book.

UNIX Print Servers

To print to a remote UNIX printer configured with Line Printer Daemon (LPD), you must first configure Windows 2000 Professional to print by using Line Printer Remote (LPR). This is done by installing Print Services for UNIX and installing and configuring a print driver to print with LPR as the printer port.

▶ **To install Print Services for UNIX**

1. In Control Panel, double-click **Network and Dial-Up Connections**.

2. On the **Advanced** menu, click **Optional Networking Components**.

3. Highlight **Other Network File and Print Services**, and then click **Details**.

4. Select **Print Services for UNIX**, and then click **OK**.

▶ **To add an LPR port**

1. In Control Panel, double-click **Printers**.

2. Double-click **Add Printer**, and then click **Next**.

3. Click **Local printer**, clear the **Automatically detect my printer** check box, and then click **Next**.

4. Click **Create a new port**, and then click **Standard TCP/IP Port**.

5. Click **Next**, and then enter the following information:

   In **Name or address of server providing LPD**, type the Domain Name System (DNS) name or Internet Protocol (IP) address of the host for the printer you are adding.

   In **Name of printer or print queue on that server**, type the name of the printer as it is identified by the host, which is either the direct-connect printer itself or the UNIX computer.

6. Follow the instructions on the screen to finish installing the TCP/IP printer.

For more information about working with UNIX, see "Interoperability with UNIX" in this book.

IBM Host Printers

IBM host printers are a component of Systems Network Architecture (SNA), which is a computer networking architecture developed by IBM. SNA provides a network structure for IBM mainframe, midrange, and personal computer systems. SNA defines a set of proprietary communication protocols and message formats for the exchange and management of data on IBM host networks.

To send print jobs to printers that are part of an SNA environment, use the Install Printer wizard to connect to the LPT port or print queue corresponding to the desired printer. Administrators must configure SNA hosts and printers to accept these connections before users can connect to them. For more information about configuring printers in a SNA environment, see the SNA documentation.

For more information about working with IBM, see "Interoperability with IBM Host Systems" in this book.

Macintosh Printers

You must have Print Server for Macintosh installed on the Windows 2000-based server that is hosting the network printer.

You also must have the port print monitor for Macintosh, Sfmmon, installed on the user's computer. The AppleTalk Port Monitor, Sfmmon.dll, transmits print jobs over the network by using the AppleTalk protocol. It also lets you send jobs to AppleTalk spoolers, regardless of the print device to which the spooler is attached.

Configuring Printers

Configure printers through Printing Preferences, shown in Figure 14.3. (Printing Preferences was called Document Defaults in Windows 98 and Microsoft® Windows NT®.) Printing Preferences is used to configure the way documents are printed, and includes the following:

- Duplexing
- Orientation
- Paper Source
- Media
- Page Order
- Pages Per Sheet
- Paper Size

Depending on the printer, different advanced options are available. Some possible advanced options include the following:

- Copy Count
- Print Quality
- Scaling
- TrueType Fonts
- PostScript Output Option
- TrueType Font Download Option
- PostScript Language Level
- Send PostScript Error Handler
- Mirrored Output
- Negative Output
- Output Destination
- Resolution Enhancement
- EconoMode
- Fit to Page
- Levels of Gray

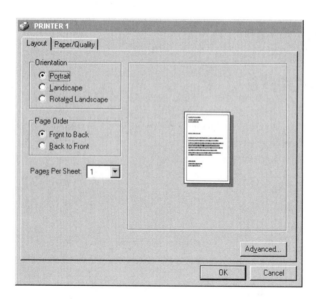

Figure 14.3   Layout Tab of Printing Preferences

▶ **To access Printing Preferences**

Click the **Layout** or **Paper/Quality** tabs in the **Print** dialog box of the program you used to create the document.

–Or–

Right-click the name of a printer in the Printers folder, and then click **Printing Preferences**.

Printing Preferences settings are maintained across different documents, allowing you to establish a standard output for all documents. Printing Preferences determine default print job settings, but you can override these defaults in the **Print** dialog box.

Configuring Fax

If you are using Windows 2000 to send faxes, you can provide information about yourself and your fax. This information includes the following:

- Your full name
- Fax number
- E-mail address
- Title
- Company
- Office location
- Department
- Home phone
- Work phone
- Address
- Billing code

Fax Service Configuration

There are several attributes about your fax service that you might want to configure first, including security settings and determining how fax jobs are stored and sent.

▶ **To configure fax service options**

1. From the **Start** menu, click **Settings**, and then click **Control Panel**.

2. Double-click **Fax**.

3. On the **Advanced Options** tab, click **Open Fax Service Management Console**.

4. Right-click **Fax Service on Local Computer**, and then click **Properties**.

5. Configure **Fax Service on Local Computer Properties**.

Using Fax Service Properties, you can configure features of your fax including the following:

- Fax retry options:
  - Number of times a fax is retried
  - Minutes between retries
  - Days an unsent fax is kept
- Whether a banner is printed at the top of each page
- Whether to use the sending device TSID
- Whether personal cover pages are allowed
- Where outgoing faxes are archived
- What the discount rate hours are in your area

The Fax Service properties page is shown in Figure 14.4.

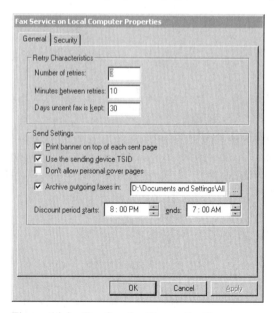

Figure 14.4   Fax Service Properties Page

Fax User Information

This information is filled in as the default for the fax coversheet when you are preparing to send a fax. The **User Information** tab is shown in Figure 14.5.

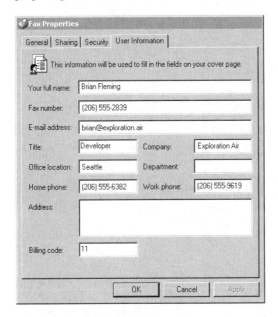

Figure 14.5   User Information Tab of the Fax Properties Dialog Box

▶ **To configure fax user information**

1. From the **Start** menu, point to **Settings**, and then click **Printers**.

2. Right-click the fax, click **Properties**, and then click the **User Information** tab.

3. Enter your information.

Fax Printing Preferences

Configure default options for sending fax jobs to a particular fax printer. By configuring fax options, you can affect the following features:

- When the fax is sent.

- The fax's printing options, including orientation, paper size, and image quality.

- Information about the sender of the fax, such as e-mail address.

▶ **Configuring fax job defaults**

1. From the **Start**, point to **Settings**, and then click **Printers**.

2. Right-click a fax printer, click **Properties**, and then click **Printing Preferences**.

3. Enter your information in the **Fax Printing Preferences** properties page.

The Fax Printing Preferences dialog box is displayed in Figure 14.6.

Figure 14.6   Fax Printing Preferences Dialog Box

The information you enter in the **Fax Properties User Information** tab and **Fax Service Properties General** tab, shown earlier, are the defaults that are offered to you by the Send Fax wizard when you prepare to send a fax. You can change these options when you prepare a fax job, but these are used as a starting point for the job.

For more information about creating and sending fax jobs, see "New Ways to Send Print Jobs" later in this chapter.

For more information about how the fax service makes fax calls, archives faxes, and determines when discount rates apply, see "Configuring Fax Service Configuration" earlier in this chapter.

Creating and Sending Print Jobs

Windows 2000 Professional supports many different ways to create and send a print job to the printer. You can send print jobs in the following ways:

- Drag the file you want to print to the printer's icon in the Printer folder. This sends the file to the printer on which you dropped the file.
- Create a shortcut for a printer, and then add it to the **Send To** menu. Right-click a file, point to **Send To**, and click the name of the printer you want to use.
- Open the file you want to print in the program you used to create the file. Click **File**, and then click **Print**.
- Right-click the file you want to print, and then click **Print**. This prints directly to the default printer, and then closes the application when the file has printed.

Modifications to the Print Dialog Box

The Windows 2000 Print dialog box includes several modifications. Figure 14.7 shows the new appearance of the Print dialog box.

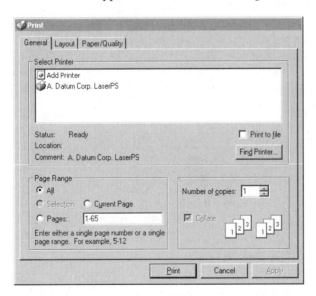

Figure 14.7   General Tab of the Print Dialog Box

The Print dialog box includes a number of improvements:

- The **Layout** and **Paper/Quality** tabs replace **Preferences**, which was available in previous versions of Windows.

- The **Find Printer** button allows browsing for printers not already installed on your computer. After you find a printer, you can use Point and Print to establish a connection with the printer and download any required drivers.

New Printer Properties Dialog Box

The new **Printer Properties** dialog box allows each user to set different properties for a printer. Because a users' printer preferences are preserved for each user, there is no need to set preferences each time the printer is used.

Enhanced Printer Drivers

Printing enhancements are made possible in large part by the Universal driver and the PostScript driver.

Universal Driver

The Universal driver has been optimized to provide higher quality and performance printing. Color printing using ICM 2.0 ensures that color images are accurately maintained. The Generic Print Description (GPD) supports minidrivers, abstracting the details of each printer's communications, thereby allowing unsupported printers to work with Windows 2000.

The Universal driver enhances font performance and capabilities. Printer font substitution results in better output, and 2-byte fonts are supported, enabling printing of extended character sets. The set of extended character fonts supported includes Latin, Greek, Cyrillic, Indic, Thai, Kana, and Hangul characters, punctuation marks, and ideographs.

The Universal driver is designed to support customization, allowing greater flexibility in the sorts of print devices that can be used with Windows 2000.

PostScript 5.0 Driver

The PostScript driver provides better performance through enhanced virtual memory management. Color printing with the PostScript driver uses ICM 2.0 ensuring that color images are faithfully maintained.

Microsoft has extended the PostScript driver to support more font formats and provide the structure for future customization.

PostScript continues to support the following:

- Support for PostScript levels 1, 2, and 3.
- ICM 2.0.
- Control over output data format, allowing for CTRL+D handling, Binary Communications Protocol (BCP), Tagged Binary Communications Protocol (TBCP), and pure binary (8-bit) channels (AppleTalk, for example).
- PPD version 4.2 and .wpd files.
- Simplified Printer Description (.spd) files.
- Tracking of virtual memory available to the printer.

Image Color Management 2.0

Image Color Management (ICM) 2.0 ensures that colors are accurately reproduced when printed. If you want to use ICM 2.0, your printer must support it. In some cases, you might want to use a third-party calibration tool to create or update a color profile for your printer. This will compensate for variations between different printers of the same type or variations that occur as a printer ages.

For more information about ICM 2.0, see "Scanners and Cameras" in this book.

New Ways to Send Print Jobs

Windows 2000 includes a number of new ways to send print jobs, including new port monitors and newly supported connection methods such as USB.

Standard Port Monitor

The new Standard Port Monitor connects clients to network printers that use the TCP/IP protocol. It replaces the LPR Port Monitor (Lprmon) as the preferred port monitor for TCP/IP printers connected directly to the network through a network adapter. The new standard port simplifies installation of most TCP/IP printers by automatically detecting the network settings needed to print. Printers connected to a UNIX or VAX host might still require Lprmon.

The Standard TCP/IP Port Monitor (SPM), which uses TCP/IP as the transport protocol, is the preferred port monitor in Windows 2000. SPM uses the Simple Network Management Protocol (SNMP) to configure and monitor the printer status. In addition to SPM, Internet printing adds a Hypertext Transport Protocol (HTTP) print provider. All port monitors that were included with Windows NT 4.0 are still present, except the Digital Network port monitor, Hewlett-Packard JetAdmin, and the Lexmark Port Monitors.

SPM communicates with network-ready printers, network adapters like Hewlett-Packard's JetDirect, and external network print servers like Intel's NetPort. SPM can support many printers on a single server and is faster and easier to configure than Lprmon.

SPM sends documents to a printer using either the RAW or LPR printing protocols. Together, these protocols support most current TCP/IP printers. Do not confuse these print protocols with the transport protocols such as TCP/IP or Data Link Control (DLC).

The RAW protocol is the default for most print devices. To send a RAW-formatted job, the print server opens a TCP stream to the printer's port 9100 (or another port number) to select connections to multiport external devices. For example, on some devices port 9101 goes to the first parallel port, 9102 goes to the second parallel port, and so on.

SPM uses the LPR protocol when you specify it during port installation or reconfiguration, or when Port 9100 protocol cannot be established.

SPM deviates from the LPR standard in two ways. First, SPM does not conform to the RFC 1179 requirement that the source TCP port lie between port 721 and port 731. SPM uses ports from the general, unreserved pool of ports (ports 1024 and above). Second, the LPR standard states that print jobs must include information about the size of the job the port monitor sends. Sending a print job with job size information requires that the port monitor spool the job twice, once to determine size, and once to send the job to the spooler. Spooling the job only once improves printing performance, so SPM sends the job to the spooler without determining the actual job size, and claims the job is a default size, regardless of the job's actual size.

SPM can send print jobs to the LPD service running on a print server. For more information about LPD, see "Print Components" later in this chapter.

Improved Status Information

SPM is compatible with RFC 1759, the standard for the Simple Network Management Protocol (SNMP). As a result, SPM can provide much more detailed status than Lprmon.

For more information about printing to devices located on other platforms, see "Operating System Exceptions" earlier in this chapter.

▶ **To configure a standard TCP/IP port by using SPM**

1. Select an installed printer, click **File**, and then click **Properties**.

2. Click the **Ports** tab, and then click **Add Port**.

3. Click **Standard TCP/IP Port**, and then click **New Port**. This starts the Add Standard TCP/IP Printer Port wizard, shown in Figure 14.8.

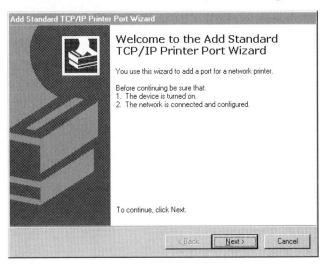

Figure 14.8   Standard TCP/IP Printer Port Wizard

4. Type a name or the IP address of a print device in the **Printer Name** or **IP Address** text box.

5. Type a host-resolvable port name, which can be any character string, in the **Port Name** text box, or use the default name that the wizard supplies, and then click **Next**.

   The system sends an SNMP **get** command to the device. An SNMP get command asks for the status of a device, so in this case, the system uses the SNMP get command to request a status information from that printer. Using the SNMP values returned from the get command, the device details are determined and the appropriate device options are displayed for further selection (for example, you can select the correct printer port).

6. If prompted by the **Additional Port Information Required** dialog box, click **Standard**, and then select one of the devices listed.

   –Or–

   Click **Custom**, and then configure the port by using the **Configure Standard TCP/IP Port Monitor** dialog box. If you do not know details of the port, use **Generic Network Card**.

   If the wizard cannot determine the protocol, it prompts you for the information. If you are not prompted, skip to step 8.

7. When prompted for the protocol, select either **RAW** or **LPR**. RAW is preferred.

   If the wizard detects that the device supports multiple ports (indicated in the Tcpmon.ini file), it prompts you to select a port.

8. Select a port from the list and finish the wizard.

   The new port is listed on the **Ports** tab of the **Properties** dialog box.

Reconfiguration

The SPM port can be reconfigured in the printer's **Properties** dialog box. Click **Configure Port** on the **Ports** tab. The SPM has its own **Configure** dialog box that appears, as shown in Figure 14.9.

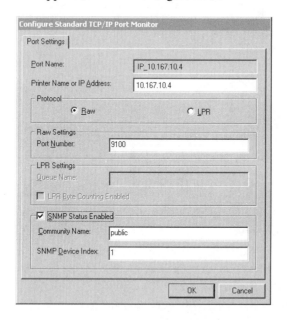

Figure 14.9   Configure Standard TCP/IP Printer Port Monitor Dialog Box

---

Caution   The Configure Standard TCP/IP Port Monitor dialog box does not verify that the options you select are correct. If they are incorrect, the port does not work. Check with the printer manufacturer to see if the device supports SNMP.

Status Reporting

Printers return status over SNMP. Since SPM is compatible with SNMP, it allows detailed status reporting when the printer provides it. Printers that are not compliant with the SNMP standard do not return status information. Therefore, when there is an error during printing, the spooler displays a general printing error or does not detect any error at all.

Internet Printing

Windows 2000 supports Internet printing. This makes it possible to use printers located anywhere in the world by sending print jobs using Hypertext Transfer Protocol (HTTP). Using Microsoft® Internet Information Services or a Web Peer Server, Windows 2000 creates a Web page that provides information about printers and provides the transport for printing over the Internet. Using the Internet, printers can be used to replace fax machines or postal mail.

Use an Internet printer as you would any other Windows 2000 installed printer.

For more information about installing an Internet printer on your computer, see "Installing Network Printers" earlier in this chapter.

For more information about managing print jobs sent by using IPP, see "Internet Printing Management" later in this chapter.

USB

Windows 2000 supports printing to Universal Serial Bus (USB) printers. USB is comprised of an external bus architecture for connecting USB-capable peripheral devices to a host computer, as well as a communication protocol that supports serial data transfers between a host system and USB-capable peripherals.

IrDA

Infrared Data Association (IrDA) is a system of exchanging information between computers using infrared transmissions that do not require a cable connection. IrDA can occur between any two devices that support IrDA (such as computers and printers). Windows 2000 supports printing using IrDA.

IrDA is a point-to-point protocol based on TCP/IP and WinSock APIs. IrDA can be used to exchange data between non-Windows devices that use the IrDA protocol. IrDA exchanges data at rates approaching those typically provided by local area network (LAN) connections.

Support for the IEEE 1284.4 (DOT4) Protocol

Windows 2000 supports DOT4, enabling Windows 2000 print servers to send data to multiple parts of a single multifunction peripheral (MFP) device. DOT4 is a driver that creates different port settings for each device function, so a device with both printing and scanning capabilities can process both types of jobs simultaneously.

DOT4 is automatically installed when a DOT4-enabled device is detected, so no installation or configuration is required.

Sending Faxes

Windows 2000 integrates sending and receiving faxes through your computer's fax modem in the same way it sets up a printer.

If your computer has a fax modem, install the modem by using the Add Printer wizard, the same as you install a printer.

When creating fax jobs, use the Send Fax wizard to provide information to send your fax. The fax wizard includes a number of pages that allow you to configure the following fax job attributes. The Send Fax wizard includes the following pages:

- Welcome page.
- Recipient and dialing information. Use this page to enter the phone number to which you want to send the fax (or multiple numbers, if desired), and special dialing rules, such as dialing 9.
- Adding a cover page. Use this page to add a cover page and note for the fax's recipient.
- Scheduling transmission. Use this page to determine when to send the fax. By scheduling transmissions, you can take advantage of lower rates during specific times of day.
- Summary page. Use this page to confirm the configuration you have chosen before sending the fax.

After you use the Send Fax wizard, Windows 2000 automatically uses the modem to send your job to the fax numbers you have specified, unless you have specified that the job is to be sent at a later time. If the fax job is not successfully sent, Windows 2000 tries sending the fax job again at regular intervals, depending on the information set in **Fax Service Properties**.

For more information about configuring Windows 2000 to send faxes, see "Configuring Fax" earlier in this chapter.

Reverse Order Printing

Windows 2000 allows printing to begin on the last page of a document and end on the first page.

▶ **To print in reverse order**

1. Open the document to be printed.
2. Click **File**, click **Print**, and then click the **Layout** tab.
3. Click **Back to Front**.
4. Click **Print** to print the document.

Number of Copies

Windows 2000 supports printing up to 10,000 copies of a document in one print job. Previously, some printers were limited to 255 copies per print job.

▶ **To select the number of copies to be printed**

1. Open the document to be printed.
2. Click **File**, and then click **Print**.
3. On the **General** tab, type a number from 1 to 10,000 in **Number of copies**.
4. Click **Print** to print the document.

Printing Multiple Pages on a Single Page

You can print multiple pages of a document on a single piece of paper. This is called *n-up printing*, and is useful when you want to conserve paper when printing a document with a small amount of information on each page.

▶ **To set the number of pages to print on one piece of paper**

1. Open the document to be printed.
2. Click **File**, click **Print**, and then click the **Layout** tab.
3. Select the number of pages to be printed on one piece of paper from the **Pages Per Sheet** box.
4. Click **Print** to print the document.

Monitoring and Managing Print Jobs

There are a range of permissions that affect how users manage printers and receive printer status.

Job Queue Security Options

Users have different levels of access to manage a printer job queue depending on their security permissions.

Users working with printer queues are typically separated into two groups:

- Administrative users: These users have Manage Printers and Manage Documents permissions. They have wide control over how the printer operates, regardless of where the print job originated.
- General users: These users have Print permissions, which include viewing general information about a printer and managing documents that they send to the printer. They cannot control other people's print jobs.

Table 14.5   Defaults Rights for Printer Users

Task	Administrative User	General User
See all jobs	X	X
Pause or resume printer operation	X	O
Pause, cancel, reschedule, or redirect any job	X	O
Pause, cancel, reschedule, or redirect own job	X	X
Restart a job from the beginning	X	X
View and change job settings such as priority and person notified upon completion	X	X
View form, paper source, page orientation, number of copies	X	X

Scheduling

Print scheduling is established by users with administrative privileges by using the printer's **Advanced** tab, which is shown in Figure 14.10.

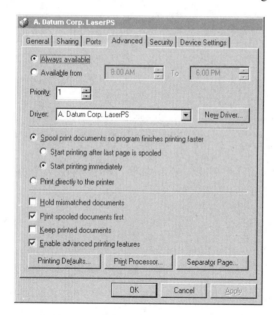

Figure 14.10   Advanced Tab of a Printer Properties Dialog Box

Users with administrative privileges can schedule printer availability, priority, and job priority. Print job priority only affects jobs in a printer's queue, not how jobs get to a print queue. Printer priority can be used to affect how print jobs reach print queues.

Printer Availability

Printer availability can be set to make the printer always available or only available during certain times of day.

Printer Priority

Printer priority determines the likelihood that a printer is chosen relative to other printers.

When adding printers, think of physical printers as the actual printers that print documents and virtual printers as representations of physical printers. You send a document to a virtual printer on the network and that print job is printed on paper by a physical printer.

Printer priority only has an effect when it is set differently for different virtual printers that correspond to the same physical printer. Setting different printer priorities for different virtual printers that correspond to different physical printers has no effect.

A few facts about printer priority:

- Higher numbers correspond to higher priorities, so priority 1 printers are of the lowest priority.
- Printer priority has no effect on job priority, so multiple jobs sent to the same virtual printer are affected by their job priority, but not by the printer's priority. Job priority can be set by viewing the properties of a job in a print queue, whereas print priority is set using the Priority field on the Advanced tab of a printer's property page.
- Printer priority is only evaluated when determining which job to complete next. A printer does not stop processing a job it is already working on, even when the spooler receives a higher priority job, directed to a higher priority printer on the same port.

▶ **To set printer priorities for multiple virtual printers**

1. Add a virtual printer using a specific port. For more information about how to add printers, see Windows 2000 Professional Help.

2. Repeat the process of adding virtual printers by using different names for the same physical printer until you have as many virtual printers as you need to accommodate your print prioritization needs.

3. Right-click a printer, click **Properties**, and set a Priority value. A greater priority value means that printer has higher, not lower priority. Repeat as necessary for other virtual printers that correspond to the same physical printer.

4. Using **Computer Management**, establish discrete groups to which you intend to add users, and associate with a printer. For more information about how to add groups, see Windows 2000 Professional Help.

5. Add groups to each virtual printer's **Security** tab and set permissions to allow specific groups to use the printer. Remember to remove other groups or disable allowing other groups to use the printer if you want to restrict access.

6. Add users to groups that correspond with the level of printer priority you want them to have. Add users to whom you want to give priority printer access to the group with permissions to use the printer that has a higher priority. Add the users intended to have lower printer priority access to the group with access to the lower priority printer. For more information about adding users to groups, see Windows 2000 Professional Help.

Caution When working with groups, it is typically better to remove the Everyone group from the printer rather than to deny access to the Everyone group and then add other groups with permitted users. This is because the Deny setting overrides any Allow settings. Therefore, if a user is a member of both the Everyone group, which is denied access to a printer, as well as the printer group you have designated allowed to use the printer, the Deny setting overrides the Allow setting.

When users install printers, they can do so based on their group membership, ensuring that the right users have the right level of priority access to printers.

▶ **To set printer priority**

1. Open **Printers**, right-click the printer whose priority you want to set, and then click **Properties**.

2. Enter a number in the **Priority** field in the **Advanced** tab of the printer's **Property** page.

Note To set printer priority, you must have Manage Printer permissions for the printer in question.

Job Priority

Job Priority is set in the print queue and determines the priority for a particular document. After a job is printing, it is not affected by other higher priority print jobs, but when a printer finishes printing a job, it first chooses the job with the highest priority and then the job submitted first.

Consider the set of jobs that you might find in a printer's queue shown in Table 14.6.

Table 14.6   Sample Jobs in a Print Queue

Job	Status	Priority
1	Printing	1
2	Spooled	10
3	Spooled	1
4	Spooled	10
5	Spooled	99

Assuming no other jobs are submitted, and no one changes the priority of their jobs, these jobs would be handled in the order shown in Table 14.7.

Table 14.7   Order in Which Jobs in Table 14.6 Are Printed

Order	Explanation
Job 1	It is in the process of printing.
Job 5	It has the highest priority
Job 2	Of the jobs of priority 10, it has been waiting the longest.
Job 4	It has the highest priority of any job remaining.
Job 3	It is the only remaining job, and it has the lowest priority.

▶ **To set job priority on an existing print job**

1. Open the print queue.

2. Double-click the job whose priority you want to set.

3. On the **General** tab, move the **Priority** slider to set the job priority.

Scheduling Faxes

You can configure your fax service to only send fax jobs at specific times, such as when lower phone rates apply. To learn how to configure your Fax Service to your specific discount periods, see "Configuring Fax Service Configuration" earlier in this chapter.

Spooler Settings

Print spooling is configured by users with administrative privileges by using the printer's **Advanced** tab. Jobs can be sent to the spooler, or sent directly to the printer. If jobs are sent to the spooler, they can be configured to start printing as soon as possible or after the final page in a job has been sent to the spooler.

When you send a print job directly to the printer, your computer renders the entire job and then transfers it directly to the printer. When you send a print job to a spooler, your computer creates the job, including meta-information about how the job must be processed, and then sends the job to the spooler. The spooler then renders the job and sends it to the printer.

Sending a job directly to the printer is good because you remove a potential point of failure in printing documents, and all print job rendering is done on your computer, affording you more control, and you don't have to wait for other jobs to complete, as you might if you were printing to a queue on a print server that was being used by many users. Conversely, rendering a print job on your computer consumes computing resources, so you might experience reduced performance or have to wait until the print job has completed before doing anything.

Sending a print job to a spooler is good because your computer does not have to render the print job, meaning your computer's resource are more completely and immediately available. Conversely, sending a print job to a spooler fails if the print server with the spooler is unavailable, and you might have to wait for other jobs to finish spooling before your job is processed.

Spoolers can be configured to send print jobs as each page is rendered and ready for printing or to wait to begin printing until the entire job has been rendered. If the spooler is configured to print each page as soon as it is rendered, there might be a long wait between each printed page, resulting in slow print production, as the printer waits for each successive page to be rendered. Printers configured to print completely spooled jobs typically print faster after the job is started, but there can be a long wait while the job is spooled. If each spooler has many users, waiting until the entire job is spooled is typically best. If each spooler has few users, printing each page as it spools might be best.

Quick Printer Status

Windows 2000 allows you quick access to basic information about printers. Letting the mouse pointer hover over a printer displays that printer's name, status, number of documents in its queue, and its location.

Internet Printing Management

Printers being hosted by Windows 2000 servers with IIS or a Peer Web Server can receive jobs sent to them over the Internet Printing Protocol. Windows 2000 Internet print servers provide information to clients about the status of jobs they have received, as well as about printers that are available.

Jobs on a server can be viewed and managed using the Internet print server's Web pages. These pages provide information about jobs that are waiting in the queue, including the job's name, status, owner, number of pages, size, and when it was submitted.

An example of the print queue provided by an Internet print server appears in Figure 14.11.

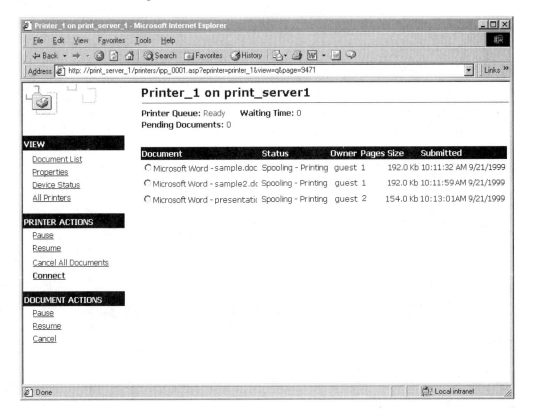

Figure 14.11   Sample Print Queue View for a Printer on an Internet Print Server

For more information about the status of a particular printer, view the printer's device status. This page can provide a range of information including the following:

- The printer's current status.

- The text the printer's display is currently presenting.

- The printer's paper tray capabilities and status. For example, this might display the approximate number of pages available in each of the printer's trays.

- The console lights currently illuminated. Console lights might include Online, Data, or Attention.

An example of a device status on a Web page provided by an Internet print server appears in Figure 14.12.

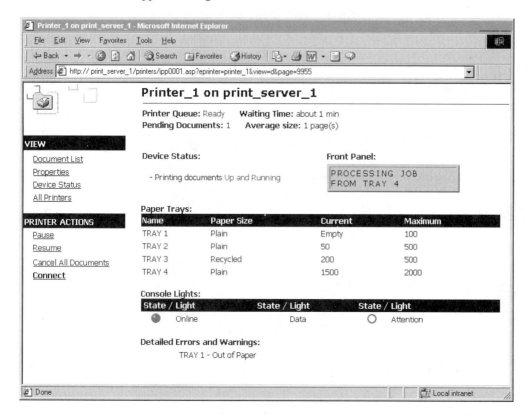

Figure 14.12   Sample Device Status for a Printer on an Internet Print Server

Printer Pooling

A printer pool associates two or more identical printers with one set of printer software. To set up such a pool, add a printer using the Add Printer wizard and assign that printer as many output ports as there are identical printers. Windows 2000 places no limit on the number of printers in a pool. When a document is sent to the printer pool, the first available printer receives and prints it. This configuration maximizes print device use while minimizing the time users wait for documents.

Efficient printer pools have the following characteristics:

- All printers in the pool are the same model.
- Printer ports can be of the same type or mixed (parallel, serial, and network).
- It is recommended that all printers be in one location. Because it is impossible to predict which printer will receive the document, keep all printers in a pool in a single location. Otherwise, users might have a hard time finding their printed document.

Note If one device within a pool stops printing, the current document is held at that device. The succeeding documents print to other devices in the pool, while the delayed document waits until the nonfunctioning printer is fixed.

Printing Concepts

When users print, the computer completes a set of steps that involve a set of components including executable files, drivers, device interfaces, and dynamic-link libraries which then work together to create printed output. Understanding how this process works will help you understand what is happening when you print a document and might help you resolve any problems that arise. Printing can be divided into the *printing process* and the *print components* that make the printing process possible. When printing to an Internet print server, the print server adds to the standard print process by creating an interface for users.

Printing Process

The printing process is divided into three groups of steps:

- Client processes
- Spooler processes
- Printer processes

These groups of broad steps include the following specific actions, represented in Figure 14.13.

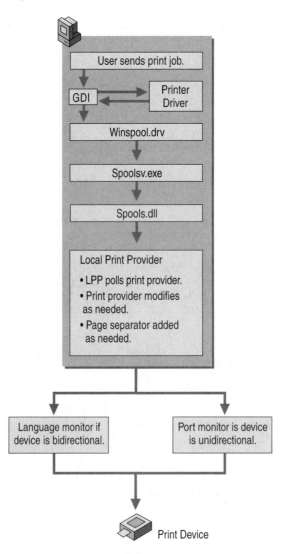

Figure 14.13   Print Process

The steps depicted in Figure 14.13 include the following:

Client Processes

- A user sends a print job from an application. The application calls the Graphics Device Interface (GDI). If print output is produced in RAW format, the GDI is not used.

- The GDI calls the printer driver for information, which the GDI uses to create a job in printer language.

- The GDI delivers the job to the spooler.

Spooler Processes

- The client side of the spooler (Winspool.drv) makes an RPC call to the server side spooler (Spoolsv.exe).

- Spoolsv.exe calls the print router (Spoolss.dll).

- The router (Spoolsv.dll) sends the print job to the local print provider (LPP) or remote print server if the job is being sent to a network printer.

- The LPP polls print processors to find one that can handle the data type of the job.

- The LPP sends the job to the print processor, which modifies the job as required to make it print properly.

- The print processor sends the job to the page separator. A separator page is added, as required.

- The job is sent to the appropriate port print monitor. If print is bidirectional, the job is first sent to the language monitor such as the Printer Job Language (PJL) monitor, and then sent on to the port monitor. If the job is unidirectional, the job is sent directly to the port monitor.

Printer Processes

The printer translates the print language into a bitmap, which it then prints.

Print Components

There are a number of components that work together to make the printing process possible. Different components are used at different times, depending on the type of print job being produced and the types of hardware being used.

Graphics Device Interface

The application calls the Graphics Device Interface (GDI) to begin the process of creating a print job. The GDI reads the driver information for the printer to get information about how to format the job. Using the document information from the application and the print device information from the printer driver, GDI renders the print job in the printer language of the printer.

Printer Drivers

Printer drivers contain information that is specific to the printer that is used. Printer drivers reside on user's computers and are used by the GDI to render print jobs.

Windows 2000 includes the most common printer drivers, but you might need to provide printer drivers for some printers. When a Windows 2000 user connects to a printer or installs a Plug and Play printer, the necessary printer drivers are loaded onto the user's computer, if they are available.

Print Spooler

The print spooler consists of a group of components, including the print router, the local and remote print provider, and the print processor. These components can reside on a computer sending a job and on a network print server receiving print jobs. The print spooler's components take the print job that the GDI has created and modify it so it has all information and formatting necessary to print correctly. If part of the spooler is on a server, the server provides the processing resources for the print job, freeing the user's computer and improving performance.

Different print servers have different spooler components. In Windows 2000, the print spooler is comprised of a router, remote print provider, local print provider, print processor, separator page processor, and port print monitors.

Print Router

The print router receives a print job and locates an available print provider that can handle the print job's protocol. For example, the router might look for a print provider designed to handle RPC print jobs or jobs transferred using HTTP. When an acceptable print provider is found, the router relays the print job from the remote print provider to the chosen local print provider, where the job is modified, if necessary, before printing.

Remote Print Providers

The remote print provider is part of the client side of the print process. The router gives control of the print job to the first remote print provider the router finds that recognizes the destination printer. A remote print provider sends the print job to the server side part of the router.

Examples of remote print providers include the Windows Network Print Provider and the Novell NetWare Remote Print Provider. When a user sends a print job to a printer on a print server, the remote print provider is on the user's computer and the local print provider is on the server, counter to how it might be perceived by users.

Local Print Providers

The local print provider receives the print job, writes it to a spool file, and keeps track of information about the job. Spooling a file to disk ensures that the job is saved and printed, even if printers are unavailable or there is a power failure. When a user sends a print job to a printer on a print server, the remote print provider is on the user's computer and the local print provider is on the server, counter to how it might be perceived by users.

The local print provider has two components that are invoked as required by the printer type and settings:

- Print processor: The print processor makes any necessary modifications to the print job. This is necessary in instances where third-party printers have special requirements. Often, no modifications are required by the print processor.

- Separator page processor: The separator page processor adds separator pages, as required. You may specify different separator pages based on your needs. Most separator pages include information such as the user and computer that created the job or the date and time the job was created.

The escape codes used in creating a separator page are listed in Table 14.6.

Table 14.8   Separator Page Escape Codes and Functions

Escape Code	Function
\	The first line of the separator file must contain only this character. The separator file interpreter considers this the separator file command delimiter.
\N	Prints the user name of the person who submitted the job.
\I	Prints the job number.
\D	Prints the date the job was printed. The time is displayed in the format specified under Regional Options in Control Panel.
\L*xxx*	Prints the string of text that appears after the \L escape code. If you were to enter \LTest, the text "Test" would appear in the separator page.
\F*pathname*	Prints the contents of the file specified by pathname, starting on an empty line. The contents of this file are copied directly to the printer without processing.
\H*nn*	Sets a printer-specific control sequence, where *nn* is a hexadecimal ASCII code sent directly to the printer. To determine the specific numbers, see your printer manual.
\W*nn*	Sets the width of the separator page. The default width is 80 characters; the maximum width is 256. Any characters beyond this width are truncated.

(continued)

Table 14.8   Separator Page Escape Codes and Functions *(continued)*

Escape Code	Function
\B\S	Prints text in single-width block characters until \U is encountered.
\E	Ejects a page from the printer. Use this code to start a new separator page or to end the separator page file. If you get an extra blank separator page when you print, remove this code from your separator page file.
\n	Skips the number of lines specified by *n* (from 0 through 9). Skipping 0 lines simply moves printing to the next line.
\B\M	Prints text in double-width block characters until \U is encountered.
\U	Turns off block character printing.

After the local print provider has passed a job through the print processor and separator page processor, it sends the job from the spooler to the appropriate port print monitor.

Port Monitors

The Local Print Provider (Localspl.dll) provided with Windows 2000 includes the Local Port Monitor and Winprint print processor. The Local Port Monitor controls the parallel and serial ports to which printers are connected, and the Standard Port Monitor (SPM) is used for most network print jobs. Other ports, such as SCSI or Ethernet, are controlled by port monitors, such as the NetWare Port Monitor or AppleTalk Port Monitor.

Windows 2000 includes port monitors which enable printing to different types of printers in different network environments. Some of the port monitors included with Windows 2000 are described in further detail below:

- The preferred network port monitor in Windows 2000 is the Standard TCP/IP Port Monitor (SPM), which uses TCP/IP as the transport protocol. SNMP is used to configure and monitor the printer ports. In addition to SPM, Internet printing adds an Hypertext Transport Protocol (HTTP) Port Monitor. All other port monitors that were included with Windows NT 4.0 are also present. For more information, see "New Ways to Send Print Jobs" earlier in this chapter.

- Local Port Monitor is the standard monitor for use with printers connected directly to your computer. If you add a printer to your computer by using a serial or parallel port (such as COM1 or LPT1), this is the monitor that is used.

- LPR Port Monitor is used to send jobs over TCP/IP from the client running Lprmon.dll to a print server running an LPD service. LPR Port Monitor can be used as an alternative to SPM to enable Internet printing, UNIX print servers, or Windows 2000 print servers over a TCP/IP network. The LPR Port Monitor is a two-part port monitor, Lprmon.dll is used on the client side and Lpr.exe is used on the server side. When a job is sent over TCP/IP, the client must have the destination address for the print server, the name of the printer, and instructions on how to print the job. The server must have Lpr.exe installed to receive the job and pass it on to the appropriate printer. Use the LPR Port Monitor if you need an RFC compliant Line Printer Remote (LPR) or to receive jobs from UNIX clients. In any other case use SPM.

- AppleTalk Port Monitor (Sfmmon.dll) is used to send jobs over the AppleTalk protocol to printers such as LaserWriters or those configured with AppleTalk or any AppleTalk spoolers. To print to LaserWriters using Windows 2000 servers, the servers must have Services for Macintosh, which includes Sfmmon.dll.

- Hewlett-Packard Network Port Monitor (Hpmon.dll) sends jobs to Hewlett-Packard network adapters. Hpmon.dll uses the DLC network protocol to communicate. Print jobs sent through Hpmon.dll cannot be sent through routers.

- PJL Monitor (Pjlmon.dll) communicates in printer job language (PJL). Any bidirectional print device that uses PJL can use the PJL language monitor.

Internet Printing

A user on a Windows 2000 computer can access information about available printers, and send jobs to those printers available on a Windows 2000 print server, or any print server that supports IPP v1.0. The process of finding an Internet printer and sending a print job to that printer includes the following steps:

1. A client connects to a Windows 2000 print server over the Internet by entering a URL.

2. The print server can require the client to provide authentication information. This helps ensure that only authorized users print documents on your printer, rather than making it available to everyone with an Internet connection.

3. After a user is authorized to access the print server, the server presents the client with Active Server Pages (ASPs) containing information about the currently available printers. Figure 14.1 shows an example of such a page.

4. Windows 2000 users can connect to any of the available printers using ASPs or get information about each printer's capabilities. Figure 14.14 shows an example of a printer's properties page, as presented by an Internet print server.

Note Only computers running Windows 95 or Windows 98 with the Internet Printing Client or computers running Windows 2000 can connect to available printers. Windows NT and and Windows 3.11 will be unable to connect.

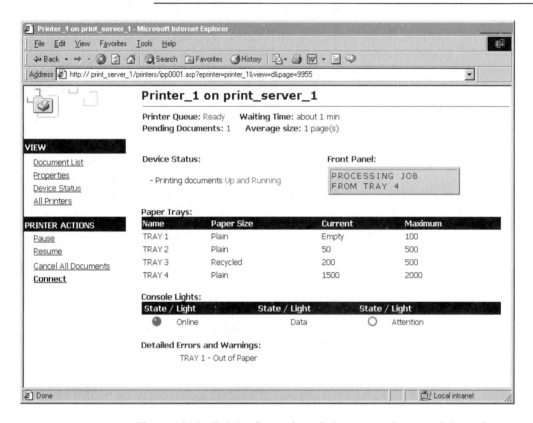

Figure 14.14   Printer Queue for a Printer on an Internet Printer Server

5. After users have connected to an Internet printer, they can print documents. Documents users print are sent using IPP v1.0 or RPC to the print server that uses RPC calls to send the job to the Internet printer of the users choice. Figure 14.15 shows potential steps included in the Internet printing process.

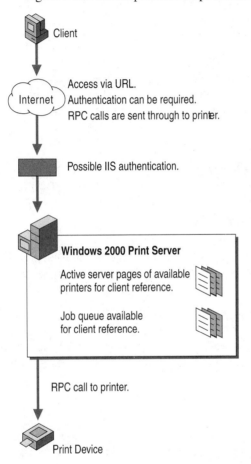

Client

Internet

Access via URL.
Authentication can be required.
RPC calls are sent through to printer.

Possible IIS authentication.

Windows 2000 Print Server

Active server pages of available
printers for client reference.

Job queue available
for client reference.

RPC call to printer.

Print Device

Figure 14.15   Internet Printing Process

Print Job Formats

Print jobs are sent in a variety of formats, each of which is suited to different computing environments.

EMF

Enhanced Metafile (EMF) is the standard format for print jobs created on Windows 2000. EMFs are very portable because the instructions for the print job are assembled on the user's computer, but processing of the print job and its instructions is completed by the spooler. Because the spooler is associated with a specific printer, EMF files can be sent to any printer that has a spooler that handles EMFs.

EMF data is created by the GDI. After an EMF job is sent to the spooler, control is returned to the user and the spooler finishes processing the job. This limits the amount of time that the user's computer is busy.

RAW

RAW is a common data type for non-Windows 2000 clients. RAW data is not modified by the spooler at all, but is sent directly to the printer.

RAW [FF Appended]

RAW [FF Appended] is exactly like the RAW data type except that a form feed character is automatically appended to the end of each print job. The last page of a RAW document does not print on a Printer Control Language (PCL) printer, so appending a form feed is necessary.

RAW [FF Auto]

RAW [FF Auto] is exactly like the RAW data type, except the spooler checks the document for a form feed character at the end of the job. If there is no form feed, the spooler adds one.

Text

Text tells the spooler that the data is ANSI text and that it must not be modified. Text is printed using the printer's default font.

Text data is composed of values from 0 to 255, each value representing a different character. This data type is based on the ANSI standard, so if the data was created with an application using another character set, it won't be printed. This is more often a problem in the extended character range, represented by values above 127.

PSCRIPT1

This data type is created by Macintosh clients printing in Level 1 monochrome PostScript. The spooler interprets the data, creates a bitmap of the page, translates the image to the printer language, and sends the information to the printer where the output is produced.

Troubleshooting Printing Problems

This troubleshooting section provides different approaches to solving printing problems. The first section describes common printing problems and their solutions. You can solve problems by matching the problems you are having to common problems encountered with printing. The second section describes the different parts of the print process. You can learn how printing works, determine where the printing problem is occurring, and fix that part of the process.

Common Printing Problems

Plug and Play printer is not automatically installing

You can instruct your computer to automatically detect and install Plug and Play printers when using the Add Printer wizard.

Windows 2000 comes with more printer drivers than ever before, but if the printer driver you need is not included with Windows 2000, your printer is not automatically installed, even if it is Plug and Play. To install such a printer, use the Add Printer wizard, and click **Have Disk** to provide the needed drivers.

If required drivers are available, you might want to restart your computer. Some printers are manually-detected Plug and Play devices, which require that you restart your computer before the printer is installed. Manually-detected Plug and Play printers typically use parallel port connections.

Cannot find a printer when searching by location

Searching by location requires that you use Windows 2000 or some other Active Directory-enabled client.

Make sure you are creating searches that match the printer location format used in your environment. For more information about printer location formats, see "Printer Locations and Active Directory" earlier in this chapter.

Bidirectional printer problem

If you encounter a problem with bidirectional printing, disable bidirectional printing and resend your print job.

▶ **To disable bidirectional printing, do the following:**

1. Click **Start**, point to **Settings**, and then click **Printers**.

2. Right-click the bidirectional printer, and then click **Properties**.

3. Click the **Ports** tab, clear **Enable bidirectional support**, and then click **OK**.

You do not have required permissions

If a printer requires security permissions, you must have the appropriate rights as provided by your user account or by a user group to which you belong.

Choose an alternate printer that does not require permissions, or that requires permissions that you have, or ask your administrator to grant you permissions to use the printer.

Bad printer port or improperly formatted data

Incorrectly configured ports can cause printing to fail. Typically, LPR ports include an IP address or a fully qualified domain name (FQDN) and let DNS resolve the address followed by a queue name. In such a situation, there can be a resolution error for the FQDN or users might enter the Windows 2000 queue name, rather than the LPD's queue name. If either of these events occur, errors such as "Bad printer port" or "Improperly formatted data" can occur.

To find out if an incorrect FQDN name is being used, review the event log for your computer for event ID 2004. Event ID 2004 indicates that the target LPD did not respond as expected, which can occur with an incorrect FQDN.

A bad printer port or improperly formatted data error can also occur if users configure their computer to print directly to the printer or to use bidirectional communication, when the hardware they are using does not support these functions.

To solve these problems with the TCP/IP port you are using for the printer, try configuring the Standard TCP/IP Port Monitor for your printer.

▶ **To configure Standard TCP/IP Port Monitor**

1. From the **Start** menu, point to **Settings**, and click **Printers**.

2. Right-click the printer whose TCP/IP port monitor you want to configure, and then click **Properties**.

3. On the **Ports** tab, click the TCP/IP Port your printer uses, and then click **Configure Port**.

The dialog box you use to configure the TCP/IP Port Monitor appears in Figure 14.16.

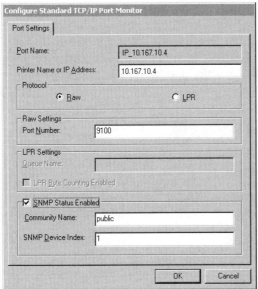

Figure 14.16   Configure Standard TCP/IP Port Monitor Dialog Box

To solve problems with the TCP/IP port you are using for a printer, try the following changes:

- Check **Port Name**, **Printer Name**, or **IP Address** in the **Configure Standard TCP/IP Port Monitor** dialog box and correct them, if necessary.

- Try toggling from one protocol to another. Some printers require you use one or the other.

- Try enabling LPR Byte Counting. Some printers required that jobs accurately represent their size. For more information about byte counting, see "New Ways to Send Print Jobs" earlier in this chapter.

Printer jobs go to the queue, but do not print

If you are using a multifunction peripheral (MFP), DOT4 might not have properly detected your print device at startup. Shut down your computer and printer, then turn on your printer followed by your computer. Typically, DOT4 now recognizes all features of your MFP.

Graphic images do not print as expected

- Disable enhanced metafile spooling (EMF).

- Try printing to the PostScript driver, if the printer supports it. If this works, the problem is with the UniDriver.

- If PostScript fails, there is a problem with the GDI or the UniDriver that is working with the application to created the print job. To verify that it is an application-related problem, try printing another document from another application.

- Try printing shorter jobs or fewer jobs at a time. You might be exceeding the print spooler's capacity.

Pages are only partially printed

- Check that there is sufficient memory to print the document.

- Pages only partially print when the page size of the document you are trying to print is bigger than the page size available for the printer to print.

- If text is missing, verify whether the missing text uses a font which is valid and is installed.

- The printer might not have adequate toner. Try replacing the printer's toner cartridge.

Printing is slow

- If the print server is taking an unusually long time to render the job, try defragmenting the server's disk and check that there is adequate space for temporary files on the hard disk.

- If you are using printer pooling to handle a large number of jobs, and print jobs are taking a long time to get to the top of queue, consider adding more printers to the pool to distribute the print jobs over a larger set of printers.

PostScript printer returns an "Out of Memory" error

To print the current document, you must allocate more memory for the printer or send smaller print jobs.

To add more PostScript memory, modify **Available PostScript Memory** on the **Device Settings** tab in **Printer Properties**. You must have Manage printer rights to change **Available PostScript Memory**.

Break large print jobs into smaller parts. For example, for a 10-page print job, you can send the first five pages in one print job and then send the last five pages in a second print job. This reduces the amount of printer memory required.

Computer stalls while printing

For local printers:

- Check that the appropriate printer driver is installed. Reinstall if necessary.
- Check for adequate space on the hard disk.

For printers on a network:

- Check that the server has enough free hard disk space.
- Try disabling EMF spooling, and send the job in RAW format.

Troubleshooting the Printing Process

There are a series of steps that take place to allow a print job to be completed. Understanding these steps and their significance will help you solve problems you encounter. These steps are as follows:

- Administrator creates a print share on a print server.
- Client system connects to the share.
- Client system creates a print job.
- Client system sends job to the print share.
- Print server receives, spools, and modifies the print job.
- Print server sends job to the printer.
- Printer interprets the job and prints it.

Administrator creates a print share on print server

This makes the printer available to the network. Necessary drivers are stored on the server for distribution to clients and the print server waits to receive jobs to be produced by the printer.

If this step is not completed properly, users might be unable to connect to the printer on the server, despite installing the printer properly.

Client system connects to the share

Using any of the Windows 2000 techniques, such as Point and Print, the Add Printer wizard, or finding the printer in My Network Places, the client connects to the printer. If necessary, appropriate drivers are downloaded to the client's computer and information about the printer is recorded.

If this step is not completed properly, the user might not locate the printer you want in the list of available printers.

Client system creates a print job

Users initiate this process by choosing to print a document. If the printer drivers are not available on the user's computer, the GDI cannot properly create the print job.

Client system sends job to the print share

A network connection between client and print server must be available.

Print server receives, spools, and modifies the print job

The print server must have enough space to accommodate print jobs.

Print server sends job to the printer

Proper port or language monitor must be available for printer type. Network connection between print server and printer must be working.

Printer interprets the job and prints it

The printer must be turned on, online, connected to the network, and functioning properly.

Troubleshooting When Printing to a Non-Windows Print Server or Printer

UNIX

If printing through a UNIX server fails, make sure that the Standard Port Monitor (SPM) or Lprmon is installed. If it is not installed, you might not be able to produce print information that is usable by the server. For more information about installing SPM, see "New Ways to Send Print Jobs" earlier in this chapter. For more information about working with UNIX, see "Operating System Exceptions" earlier in this chapter or "Interoperability with UNIX" in this book.

NetWare

If printing through a NetWare server fails, make sure that you have a client installed on your computer such as Microsoft Client Service for NetWare or Novell's client, Novell Client 32. Such clients allow your computer to send print jobs to the NetWare server, which the server then relays to the printer. If this is not installed, you might not be able to produce print information that is usable by the server. For more information, see "Operating System Exceptions" earlier in this chapter or "Interoperability with NetWare" in this book.

IBM

If printing through an IBM server fails, make sure that you have connected to the LPT port that corresponds to the printer to which you are sending the job. For more information about SPM, see "New Ways to Send Print Jobs" earlier in this chapter. If your clients need to communicate with a mainframe computer, ensure that 3270 emulation software is installed. If your clients need to communicate with an AS/400, ensure that 5250 emulation software is installed.

For more information about working with IBM servers, see "Operating System Exceptions" earlier in this chapter or "Interoperability with IBM Host Systems" in this book or for more information about working with IBM, see "Interoperability with IBM Host Systems" in this book.

Macintosh

If printing to a printer using the AppleTalk protocol fails, make sure that Services for Macintosh and the AppleTalk Port Monitor, Sfmmon, are installed on your computer.

For more information about working with Macintosh printers, see "Operating System Exceptions" earlier in this chapter.

Additional Resources

- For information about Active Directory, see chapters under "Active Directory" in the *Microsoft® Windows® 2000 Server Resolurce Kit Distributed Systems Guide*. Active Directory can be used to help users find a printer based on its attributes, such as location.

CHAPTER 15

Scanners and Cameras

Microsoft® Windows® 2000 Professional supports a wide range of scanners and cameras, and has been optimized to produce more accurate reproductions of images and their colors. For example, IrTran-P is provided to enable easier transfer of image information from digital cameras to computers and pushbutton scanning simplifies acquiring images.

In This Chapter

Related Information in the Windows 2000 Professional Resource Kit

- For more information about using printers, see "Printing" in this book.

- For more information about Plug and Play devices, see "Device Management" in this book.

Quick Guide to Scanners and Cameras

Use this quick guide to locate information about scanners or cameras. You will find information about installing and configuring scanners or cameras, information about troubleshooting problems with your scanner or camera, and detailed information about imaging architecture.

Install your scanner or camera.

The first step to using a scanner or camera is installing it on your computer.

- See "Installing Scanners and Cameras" later in this chapter.

Configure your scanner or camera.

You might need to configure your scanner or camera, depending on the type you are using. If you have an automatically detected Plug and Play scanner or camera, such as one that uses a USB connection, you might not need to configure your device. However, if you have a manually detected Plug and Play scanner or camera, a scanner that provides pushbutton scanning, or a camera that uses IrTran-P, you might need to configure the device further.

- See "Configuring Scanners and Cameras" later in this chapter.

Understand your imaging architecture.

Familiarize yourself with the Windows 2000 imaging architecture. Understanding the architecture can help you solve problems, and understand how different technologies work together to capture and manipulate images.

- See "Scanner and Camera Concepts" later in this chapter.

Troubleshoot scanners and cameras.

Solve any problems that arise with your scanner or camera.

- See "Troubleshooting" later in this chapter.

What's New

Table 15.1 describes new imaging features with Microsoft® Windows® 2000.

Table 15.1   Comparison of Imaging Features

Windows 2000	Windows NT 4.0	Windows 95/98
Image Color Management (ICM 2.0) with improved color space profiles.	ICM not available.	ICM 1.0 available for Microsoft® Windows® 95. ICM 2.0 available for Microsoft® Windows® 98.
Plug and Play available for local devices.	No Plug and Play available.	Same as Windows 2000.
Still imaging architecture adds enhanced ICM 2.0, and continues to support universal serial bus (USB) and small computer system interface (SCSI) drivers and serial ports.	Still imaging architecture provided entirely through third-party products.	Still imaging architecture is the same as Windows 2000 for Windows 98. Windows 95 supports ICM 1.0.
Standard scanner and camera control panel provided.	No standard control panel for scanners and cameras.	Same as Windows 2000.
IrTran-P is supported for image transfer, when enabled by hardware.	No IrTran-P image transfer support.	No IrTran-P image transfer support.
Expanded scanner and digital camera support through a wider range of drivers.	Microsoft® Windows NT® does not include imaging drivers.	Windows 98 includes some imaging drivers.
Support for pushbutton scanning added as a standard image acquisition technique.	Scanned images acquisition initiated through image applications such as Microsoft® Picture It!®	Same as Windows 2000 for Windows 98. No pushbutton support provided by Windows 95.

The following section describes, in greater detail, new technologies available with Windows 2000 Professional.

Easier Installation and Maintenance   Windows 2000 supports Plug and Play for easy scanner and camera installation. An enhanced hardware installation wizard walks users through configuration steps. Scanners and Cameras in Control Panel offers configuration options, as well as troubleshooting that works by means of user feedback to isolate problems and suggest solutions.

Color Matching: ICM 2.0   Image Color Management (ICM) 2.0 ensures that colors are accurately captured and stored by scanners and cameras. You must complete an initial setup of ICM 2.0 and your camera or scanner must support it. Initial setup of ICM 2.0 associates color profiles with scanners and cameras. This association can be completed either by the device vendor or the administrator, and once configured, can be modified by users with the appropriate permissions.

ICM 2.0 is mostly transparent for end-users, so when an application supports ICM 2.0, Windows 2000 uses it to produce high-quality color reproductions without requiring user intervention.

Scanner manufacturers might list their scanners as being standard RGB (sRGB) compliant (IEC 61966-2-1:1999). Most scanner vendors accurately support sRGB as the default color space, producing good colors for most users. If you require exceptionally precise color accuracy, use a third-party calibration tool to create custom profiles, and use software that operates effectively with ICM 2.0. For more information about ICM 2.0 and color profiles, see "Image Color Management 2.0" later in this chapter.

Pushbutton Scanning   Scanning can be initiated on some scanners simply by pressing a Scan button on the hardware. Pressing the button launches scanning software, scans the image, and displays the image on the computer's screen.

Pushbutton scanning is configured in Scanners and Cameras in Control Panel.

IrTran-P   Images can be transferred from cameras to Windows 2000 Professional using infrared transmissions. This makes a physical cable connection unnecessary.

Installing Scanners and Cameras

Scanners and cameras use Plug and Play and the Scanner and Camera Installation wizard to complete the installation process.

Plug and Play

Most scanners are Plug and Play devices and are installed automatically when they are connected to the user's computer. If a scanner is not installed automatically when it is connected, use the Scanner and Camera Installation wizard.

Scanner and Camera Installation Wizard

Use the Scanner and Camera Installation wizard if you have an imaging device that is not Plug and Play. If you are installing a device that is Plug and Play, but the drivers required for that device are not available on your computer, the Scanner and Camera Installation wizard prompts you to provide the drivers.

▶ **To run the Scanner and Camera Installation wizard**

1. From the **Start** menu, point to **Settings**, click **Control Panel**, and then double-click **Scanners and Cameras**.

2. Click **Add**.

The drivers provided with Windows 2000 might not be the most recent drivers available for the device you are using. For the most current drivers, visit the manufacturer's Web site.

Configuring Scanners and Cameras

Configuration of your camera or scanner is completed during Setup. For basic information about the scanner or camera, or to complete basic configuration after Setup, use Scanners and Cameras in Control Panel.

▶ **To configure basic scanner or camera properties**

1. From the **Start** menu, point to **Settings**, click **Control Panel**, and then double-click **Scanners and Cameras**.

2. Select a scanner or camera from the list, and then click **Properties**, shown in Figure 15.1

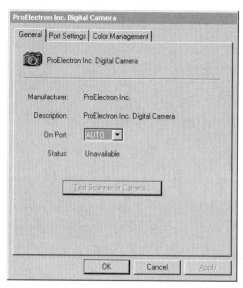

Figure 15.1   General Tab of the Digital Camera Properties Dialog Box

3. Click **Test Scanner or Camera** to test the device, or select the port the device uses from the **On Port** list.

Ports

For serial devices, the port tab displays the port being used by the scanner or camera and allows you to configure the baud rate. Change the baud rate to be faster for faster image transfer or slower to accommodate hardware limitations. Do not set the baud rate higher than the fastest speed supported by the hardware, or the image transfer will fail.

▶ **To set a serial baud rate**

1. From the **Start** menu, point to **Settings**, click **Control Panel**, and then double-click **Scanners and Cameras**.

2. Select the scanner or camera you want to configure from the list of installed scanners and cameras, and then click **Properties**.

3. Click the **Port Settings** tab, shown in Figure 15.2, and then select from the **Serial baud rate** list box.

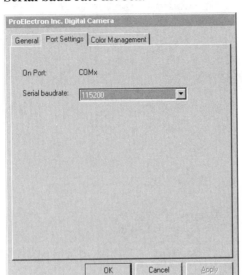

Figure 15.2   Port Settings Tab of the Digital Camera Properties Dialog Box

Image Color Management

The standard color profile for Image Color Management (ICM 2.0) on the World Wide Web, in Microsoft Windows, in Microsoft Office, and in similar display-centric workflows is sRGB, but you can add, remove, or select an alternate color profile for a device.

▶ **To add, remove, or select a color profile for a camera or scanner**

1. From the **Start** menu, point to **Settings**, and then click **Control Panel**.

2. Double-click **Scanners and Cameras**.

3. Click the device for which you want to configure color profiles, and then click **Properties**.

4. Click the **Color Management** tab, shown in Figure 15.3.

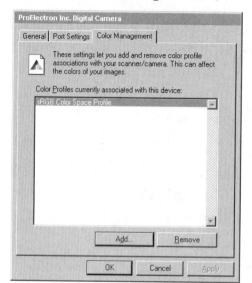

Figure 15.3 Color Management Tab of the Digital Camera Properties Dialog Box

5. To select a color profile, click the profile, and then click **OK**.

   –Or–

   Click **Add** to add a color profile.

   –Or–

   Click **Remove** to delete a color profile.

IrTran-P

IrTran-P sets up a session and sends images to Windows 2000 using infrared technology. A camera that supports IrTran-P has a Send button on it that, when pressed, causes the camera to send its stored images to Windows 2000. When the Send button is pressed, the IrTran-P server in Windows 2000 detects the connection the camera is attempting to establish, begins a session, accepts the images, and stores them in the My Pictures folder.

To use IrTran-P, you need an imaging device, typically a camera, that can produce infrared transmissions and a computer that can receive infrared transmissions. IrTran-P devices are generally self-configuring.

▶ **To configure IrTran-P devices**

1. From the **Start** menu, point to **Settings**, click **Control Panel**, and then double-click **Scanners and Cameras**.

2. Click **Wireless Device**, shown in figure 15.4.

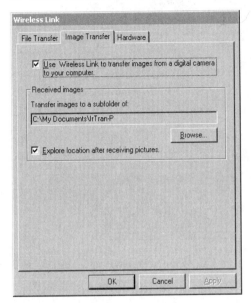

Figure 15.4   Image Transfer tab of the Wireless Link Dialog Box

3. Configure the device as necessary, and then click **OK**.

Pushbutton Scanning

Pushbutton scanning is typically configured during device installation. However, you might need to associate an application with a push button, if this is not done automatically.

▶ **To associate an application with a push button**

1. From the **Start** menu, point to **Settings**, click **Control Panel**, and then double-click **Scanners and Cameras**.

2. Select the scanner that is not working, and click **Properties**.

3. Click the **Events** tab, shown in figure 15.5, and associate an application with the pushbutton event.

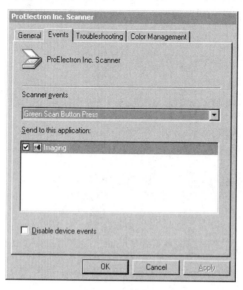

Figure 15.5   Events Tab of the Scanner Properties Dialog Box

Scanner and Camera Concepts

Scanners and cameras use a number of technologies to capture high-quality images, which are then transferred to your computer for editing and use. These technologies include the still imaging architecture, TWAIN, and ICM 2.0.

Still Imaging

Windows 2000 supports still image devices, such as scanners and cameras, by using a set of components that make up the still imaging architecture. Figure 15.6 is a graphical representation of the Windows 2000 still imaging architecture.

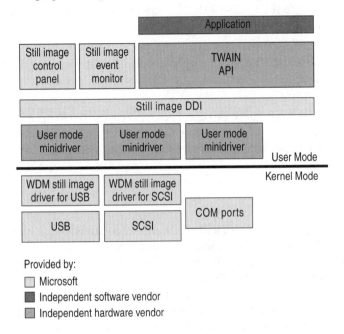

Figure 15.6   Still Imaging Architecture

The still imaging architecture is made up of the following components:

- The application layer appears at the top of the imaging architecture. Users interact directly with the application to initiate image acquisition and manipulate images.

- TWAIN or another application programming interface (API), which acquires images from a device such as a scanner or camera.

- Still scanners and cameras that support ICM 2.0 accurately, which capture still image colors, enabling accurate color information for pictures.

- Scanners and Cameras in Control Panel, which lets you add or remove scanners and cameras, configure ports and baud rates, and add, remove, or and select color profiles.

- The still image event monitor, which waits for device events, such as a user pushing the button on a scanner. When the still image event monitor detects such an event, it launches the default application associated with handling image data.

- The still image device driver interface (DDI), which communicates with devices to send commands. The DDI provides support of SCSI, parallel, serial, infrared, and USB devices. Support for Institute of Electrical and Electronics Engineers (IEEE) 1394 is incorporated using the Win32 Driver Model (WDM). Support for multifunction peripheral (MFP) devices is incorporated into the IEEE 1284.4 (DOT4) driver. For more information, see "Printing" in this book.

- User mode minidrivers are supplied by device manufacturers to implement specific DDI functionality in the manufacturer's particular hardware. User mode minidrivers inform the DDI about the specific devices capabilities, such as test or status.

- WDM still image drivers. These drivers use the Win32 Driver Model to enable delivery on USB or SCSI buses. Devices that use COM ports do not require WDM drivers. For more information, see "Hardware Management" in this book.

TWAIN

TWAIN is an API. It facilitates seamless communication between imaging devices and software, without requiring that each image device and software combination have a different driver or API implementation. Each scanner or camera has one TWAIN driver that can be used by any application designed to manipulate images. Each layer of the TWAIN architecture works with adjacent layers to pass image data from an input device, such as a camera or scanner, to an application, such as Picture It! Windows 2000 includes version 1.6.1.3 of the TWAIN source manager. The TWAIN source manager lists possible sources of imaging data, such as specific types of scanners or cameras.

TWAIN Architectural Layers

TWAIN is comprised of a number of architectural layers, each of which serve a different function in transferring an image from a scanner or camera to an application. The TWAIN layers are as follows:

- **Application layer:** An application such as Microsoft Picture It!, which is used to acquire an image from a TWAIN-compliant input device, such as a scanner or digital camera. The application requesting an image sends the request to the TWAIN data source.

- **TWAIN data source:** A software component written by a hardware vendor to translate between TWAIN commands and device driver commands. Depending on the application, the data source may present a dialog for the user to select settings on the hardware device.

- **Device driver:** The driver issues commands it receives from the TWAIN data source to the hardware to acquire an image and to check the status of the device.

- **Still image device:** The physical input device, such as a scanner or digital camera.

Image Color Management 2.0

If a user takes a photograph by using a digital camera and then loads that image onto their computer, the image should look the same on the monitor as it did when it was captured. When this same image is sent to a printer, the printed image should accurately reproduce the appearance of the colors seen by the camera and produced by the monitor.

Because different brands of monitors or printers present colors differently, it can be very difficult to produce images with accurate colors. ICM 2.0 ensures quality results by storing standard, objective color characteristics for each output device.

ICM 2.0 is an application programming interface (API) that conveniently ties together diverse technologies including scanning, capturing, displaying, and printing color pictures to yield consistent, high-quality color images without the user intervention required in the past. Color management solutions software works with profiles. Profiles are data about each device's representation of color. These profiles provide the operative information that enables the color management software to prepare an accurate color reproduction.

ICM supports international and industry standards, ensuring cross-platform compatibility. Image Color Management is based on the industry standard ICC profile, standardized Color Management Module (CMM), and the default sRGB color space (IEC 61966-2-1: 1999). Although this flexible system allows the use of any CMM, ICM uses LinoColor CMM by default. This makes Windows applications that use ICM 2.0 compatible with other platforms with respect to color management.

ICM provides ease-of-use for applications. For users who don't need to make advanced configuration choices, ICM 2.0 on Windows 2000 is set up to run transparently for printing. For users wanting to ensure color consistency with different devices and platforms, ICM provides full manual control with easy-to-use selection of alternative color profiles.

ICM has a modular, extensible architecture. Applications have the ability to support two levels of API—one that deals only in RGB, and one that works in multiple color spaces. As developers take advantage of these enhanced capabilities, advanced users are able to manage custom device profiles, work with CMYK, and select an alternate CMM for their color transformations.

ICM supports standard RGB (sRGB). Standard RGB (sRGB) complements current color management strategies by enabling a default method of handling color in the operating system and on the Internet. It efficiently provides good quality color representation and backward compatibility. Based on a calibrated colorimetric RGB color space, which is well-suited to monitors, television, scanners, digital cameras and printing systems, sRGB can be supported with minimum cost to software and hardware vendors.

Standard RGB is an international standard (IEC 61966-2-1: 1999), and is the default color space in Windows HTML, Cascading Style Sheets (CSS), .exif files which are produced by most digital cameras, and .png files. It is freely available to any software or hardware vendor. For more information about IEC 61966-2-1: 1999, see the International Electrotechnical Commission (IEC) link on the Web Resources page at http://windows.microsoft.com/windows2000/reskit/.

Standard RGB is the default color space in Windows 2000 for all color images that do not have another embedded profile or are not specifically tagged with other color information.

Table 15.2 highlights how ICM uses sRGB to handle colors when the application being used supports ICM 2.0. For example, the source might be a scanner or camera, and the destination might be a monitor or printer.

Table 15.2   Comparison of Color Profile Outcomes

	Image has source color profile	**Image has no source color profile**
Destination has color profile	Both profiles in the color mapping are used.	sRGB is used as the source profile and use the destination profile in the color mapping.
Destination has no color profile	The source profile is used and sRGB is used as the destination profile in the color mapping.	No ICM is used. Nothing is done (assume sRGB is the profile for source and destination).

Troubleshooting

The following are some of the most common problems you might encounter when using scanners or cameras and some possible solutions.

Can't Access Scanner or Digital Camera

You might need to provide scanner drivers to complete the installation. Use the Scanner and Camera Installation wizard to install or reinstall the device that is not working.

▶ **To start the Scanner and Camera Installation wizard**

1. In Control Panel, double-click **Scanners and Cameras**.

2. Click **Add**.

Alternately, if you are using a multifunction peripheral (MFP) device, Windows 2000 might not have properly detected your scanning device at startup. Shut down your computer and MFP, then turn on your MFP first, followed by your computer. This might help Windows 2000 recognize all the features of your MFP.

Finally, some older parallel port drivers that worked on Windows NT, and VXD drivers that worked on Windows 98, do not work with Windows 2000. If you are using drivers from older versions of Windows, contact the hardware manufacturer for updated drivers.

Pushbutton Scanning Fails

Pushbutton scanning most commonly fails because no applications are associated with the push button. To associate an application with the push button, see "Pushbutton Scanning" earlier in this chapter.

General Troubleshooting

Use the **Troubleshoot** button in **Scanners and Cameras Properties** to diagnose common scanner errors.

C H A P T E R   1 6

Fonts

Microsoft® Windows® 2000 supports a wide range of fonts and font types, allowing for high-quality printed and displayed text using a wide range of printing devices. Under Windows 2000, font installation is simplified, font integrity is ensured by public key signatures, and fonts are used more efficiently, resulting in faster printing.

In This Chapter

Related Information in the Windows 2000 Professional Resource Kit

- For more information about using printers, see "Printing" in this book.

Quick Guide to Fonts

Use this quick guide to locate information about fonts. You will find information about installing, managing, or embedding fonts, as well as detailed information about troubleshooting font problems.

Install fonts.

Windows 2000 comes with many of the most common fonts already installed. However, if you use special fonts, install those now.

- See "Installing Fonts" later in this chapter.

Manage your fonts.

As you use fonts with Windows 2000, you might need to remove fonts, or swap unavailable fonts with available ones.

- See "Managing Installed Fonts" later in this chapter.

Embed fonts to ensure text always appears as you intend.

You can embed fonts in a document so when it is viewed on another system, the fonts you used are included. You must have licensed fonts in order to embed them.

- See "Embedding Fonts" later in this chapter.

Troubleshoot font problems.

Solve any problems that arise with your fonts.

- See "Troubleshooting" later in this chapter.

What's New

Table 16.1 describes the differences between Microsoft® Windows NT®, Microsoft® Windows® 95, Microsoft® Windows® 98, and Windows 2000 Professional.

Table 16.1 Comparison of Font Features

Windows 2000 Professional	Windows NT 4.0	Windows 95 and Windows 98
The following font types are supported: OpenType, TrueType, raster, and vector.	The following font types are supported: TrueType, raster, and vector.	Same as Windows NT.
Font security available through public key signatures.	No security for fonts.	Same as Windows NT.
Fonts can be installed in the following ways: ■ By dragging fonts to the system fonts folder (c:\winnt\fonts, for example). ■ By installing fonts by means of Control Panel. ■ By selecting File, **Install New Fonts** when in the Fonts folder in Windows Explorer.	Fonts are installed by means of Control Panel.	Same as Windows NT
When fonts are deleted, the registry is automatically updated to reflect the changes. There is no need to run an uninstall program.	Registry must be cleaned manually when fonts are deleted.	Same as Windows NT.
Enhanced font subsetting provided by UniDriver.	No font subsetting.	Some font subsetting provided by UniDriver.

Significant new or improved features are described in the following section.

OpenType Fonts While maintaining support for raster, vector, and TrueType fonts, Windows 2000 adds support for OpenType fonts. OpenType is an extension of TrueType font technology, but also provides public key signing and extended font-specific information. As with TrueType fonts, OpenType fonts can be scaled and rotated. Therefore, fonts look good in all sizes and on all printing devices supported by Windows 2000.

Font Security OpenType fonts are now secured by using public key signatures. This ensures that fonts are authentic and have not been corrupted. Corrupted fonts might not print properly.

Easier Installation and Removal Adding and removing fonts have been simplified. To install fonts, drag the font file to the Fonts folder. To remove the font, delete it from the Fonts folder. Unlike in Windows 98 and Windows NT, you no longer have to modify the registry to properly add or remove fonts.

Improved Font Subsetting When a job is sent to a printer, the job may include information about fonts used in the document. This can significantly increase the size and complexity of the job, negatively affecting print performance. The Windows 2000 UniDriver employs font subsetting, only sending font information for characters that are actually used in the print job, rather than sending information for all characters in the font, regardless of whether the characters are used.

Installing Fonts

Windows 2000 makes font installation and management a simple task by automatically completing necessary system modifications, such as updating the registry.

There are a large number of fonts included with Windows 2000 at installation. For the list of fonts included with Windows 2000 Professional, see "Included Fonts" later in this chapter.

You can install additional fonts in the following ways:

▶ **To install a font by dragging or pasting a font file**

1. Find the font file you want to install (on a floppy disk, network share, or vendor's Web site).

2. Drag or paste the font into the \winnt\fonts directory, for example c:\winnt\fonts.

▶ **To install fonts through Control Panel**

1. From the **Start** menu, point to **Settings**, and then click **Control Panel**.

2. Double-click **Fonts**.

3. Click **File**, and then click **Install New Font**.

4. Browse your local computer or the network to find the location of the font files to be installed.

5. Select all fonts you want to install, and then click **OK**.

These installation processes install soft fonts on your computer. When you print a document, these fonts are downloaded to the printer, and then deleted from the printer's memory after the file has been printed.

Managing Installed Fonts

Fonts are managed through Fonts in Control Panel. In the Fonts folder, you can view each font's properties.

To remove a font from your system, simply delete the font from the Fonts folder. This modifies your system and updates the registry. If you attempt to view a file that contains fonts you have deleted or never installed, Windows 2000 matches the missing font to a similar font using the Font Matching Table.

For the latest information about typography at Microsoft and tools for tasks such as accessing more font information or embedding fonts, go to the Microsoft Typography link on the Web Resources page at http://windows.microsoft.com/windows2000/reskit/webresourcesEmbedding Fonts

Many fonts are widely available, and generally installed on computers. However, less common fonts might not display as expected on many computers and some computers might not have the fonts you are using.

> To address this issue, you can embed fonts in a document if your application supports font embedding. Different applications support embedding using different procedures. Refer to your application documentation for information on embedding fonts.

▶ **To embed fonts in a document using Microsoft Word 2000**

1. Open the file in which you want to embed fonts.

2. Click **File**, and then click **Save As**.

3. Click **Tools,** and then click **Embed TrueType Fonts**.

   –Or–

   Click **General Options,** and then click **Embed TrueType Fonts**.

Note You can also choose to only embed those characters of the fonts that are used by clicking **Embed characters in use only**. Some applications do not offer the option to embed fonts.

Although embedding fonts is an effective way to ensure that your fonts appear as expected, you might not want to embed fonts for the following reasons:

- If you are not certain the recipient needs the fonts. Embedding fonts can easily increase the size of files by 500 kilobytes (KB), so unless users need them, do not waste memory embedding a font.

- If you do not have the proper licensing to do so. Many fonts have special licenses associated with their use. If you embed a font with a document, you might send that font to a person who has not accepted the terms of the font's use.

Caution Never bundle fonts with applications.

Microsoft Free Font Properties Extension Utility

The Microsoft Free Font Properties Extension Utility allows you to determine the licensing status of a font. For more information about the utility, go to the Microsoft Font Properties Extension Utility link on the Web Resources page at http://windows.microsoft.com/windows2000/reskit/webresources

▶ **To View Font Embedding Rights with the Microsoft Free Font Properties Extension Utility**

1. Click a font, click **File**, and then click **Properties**.

2. Click the **Embedding** tab.

Note You must have the Microsoft Free Font Properties Extension Utility installed on your computer, or the **Embedding** tab will not be available.

Foundries permit different degrees of embedding for their fonts. To find out what sort of embedding is permitted, use the Microsoft Free Font Properties Extension Utility. The levels of embedding are described in Table 16.2.

Table 16.2   Font Embedding Levels

Font Embeddability	Description of Possible Settings
Installable embedding allowed.	Fonts can be embedded in documents and permanently installed on the remote system.
Editable embedding allowed.	Fonts can be embedded in documents, but must only be installed temporarily on the remote system.
Print & preview embedding allowed.	Fonts can be embedded in documents, but must only be installed temporarily on the remote system. Documents can only be opened as read-only.
Restricted license embedding. No Embedding allowed.	Fonts cannot be embedded in a document.

Included Fonts

There are a number of fonts that are included with Windows 2000. Although it is recommended that you always check what level of embedding is permitted by your license, embedding is often allowed with the fonts that are installed with Windows 2000, which include:

- Arial Bold Italic
- Arial Bold
- Arial Italic
- Arial
- Courier New Bold Italic
- Courier New Bold
- Courier New Italic
- Courier
- Lucida Console Bold Italic
- Lucida Console Bold
- Lucida Console Italic
- Lucida Console
- Modern
- MS Sans Serif
- MS Serif
- Roman
- Script
- Small
- Symbol
- System
- Terminal
- Times New Roman Bold Italic
- Times New Roman Bold
- Times New Roman Italic
- Times New Roman
- Wingdings

Character Set Types

Windows 2000 supports a range of character sets, which include ASCII, OEM 8-bit, ANSI, DBCS, and Unicode/ISO 10646. Character sets are formats used to compose code pages. For example, code page 1252 refers to a set of characters known as Latin I. For a complete description of all Windows 2000 supported codepages, go to the <<Microsoft Character Code Reference>> link on the Web Resources page at http://windows.microsoft.com/windows2000/reskit/webresources.

ASCII

American Standard Code for Information Interchange (ASCII) is a 7-bit character set providing 128 characters. ASCII allows for upper- and lowercase English, American English punctuation, base 10 numbers, a few control characters, and little else. Note that ASCII is the common denominator contained in all the other common character sets, making it the only means of interchanging data across all major languages without risk of character mapping loss.

OEM 8-bit

In the past, separate Original Equipment Manufacturer (OEM) code pages were created so that text-based computers could display and print line-drawing characters. These character sets are still used today for direct FAT access, and for accessing data files created by Microsoft® MS-DOS-based applications. OEM code pages typically have a three-digit label, such as CP 437 for American English.

Since each hardware manufacturer was free to set their own character standards, characters can be scrambled or lost even within the same language, if two OEM code pages have different character code points.

ANSI

Windows American National Standards Institute (ANSI) supports international characters and publishing symbols. An assortment of 256-character Windows ANSI character sets cover all the 8-bit languages supported by Windows. Windows ANSI is composed of a lower 128 characters, and an upper 128 characters. The lower 128 characters are identical to ASCII, and the upper 128 characters are different for each ANSI character set. The upper 128 contains the distinct international characters for each code page.

The European Union includes languages with more characters than a single standard code page can support, despite the fact that this code page was intended to cover all European Union font needs. Switching entirely to Unicode allows coverage of all EU languages in one character set, but the conversion is not automatic, and requires every text-related algorithm to be inspected and perhaps rewritten. As an interim solution, multiple code pages are provided for European character set needs.

DBCS

Double-byte character set (DBCS) is actually a multibyte encoding system that uses a mix of 8-bit and 16-bit characters, allowing for a wider range of characters. For example, modern writing systems used in the Far East region might require a minimum of 15,000 characters, which DBCS can accommodate. By allowing characters to be represented with two bytes, the number of possible permutations increases from 256 to 65,536, although in practice, some possible character permutations are used for special purposes, such as to indicate leading bytes or trailing bytes.

There are several DBCS character sets supported by Far East editions of Windows including Windows 95, Windows 98, and Windows NT. Leading bytes indicate that the following byte is a trailing byte of the 16-bit character unit, rather than the start of the next character. There are multiple DBCS code pages, each of which have a different leading byte and trailing byte range.

Unicode

Unicode is a 16-bit character set that contains all of the characters commonly used in information processing, including Latin, Greek, Cyrillic, Indic, Thai, Kana, and Hangul characters, punctuation marks, and ideographs. Unicode is a standard supported by members of the Unicode Consortium. Unicode is not a technology in itself, and does not solve international engineering issues.

Unicode is language-independent, helping conserve space in the character map. Characters are not assigned to specific languages, for example "a" can be used in French, German, or English. Similarly, a particular Han ideograph might map to a character used in Chinese, Japanese, or Korean. Unicode may not appear correct to viewers of a particular language because characters or ideographs are abstracted. To solve this issue, use a font that recreates a language's particular representation of the character, rather than seeking an alternate Unicode character.

Although the majority of the Unicode character space is used, approximately a third of the 64,000 possible code points are still unassigned, allowing for additional characters in the future, and for private use and compatibility issues.

Supported Code Pages

Windows 2000 supports a set of specific code pages and character sets including Windows, OEM, and ISO 8859.

Windows

Tables 16.3 and 16.4 each show a list of Windows code pages. To see the complete list of character codes and what they represent, go to the Microsoft Global Software Development: Windows Codepages link on the Web Resources page at http://windows.microsoft.com/windows2000/reskit/webresources

Table 16.3   SBCS (Single-byte Character Set) Code Pages

Code Page Number	Code Page Name
1250	Central Europe
1251	Cyrillic
1252	Latin I
1253	Greek
1254	Turkish
1255	Hebrew
1256	Arabic
1257	Baltic
1258	Vietnamese
874	Thai

Table 16.4   DBCS (Double-byte Character Set) Code Pages

Code Page Number	Code Page Name
932	Japanese Shift-JIS
936	Simplified Chinese GBK
949	Korean
950	Traditional Chinese Big5

OEM

Table 16.5 shows a list of OEM code pages. To see the complete list of character codes and what they represent, go to the <<Microsoft OEM Code Reference>> link on the Web Resources page at http://windows.microsoft.com/windows2000/reskit/webresources.

Table 16.5   Common OEM Code Pages

Code Page Number	Code Page Name
437	US
720	Arabic
737	Greek
775	Baltic
850	Western Europe
852	Central Europe
855	Cyrillic
857	Turkish
862	Hebrew
866	Cyrillic II

The code pages shown in Table 16.6 are used as both Windows ANSI and OEM code pages.

Table 16.6   Common Windows ANSI and OEM Code Pages

Code Page Number	Code Page Name
874	Thai
932	Japanese Shift-JIS
936	Simplified Chinese GBK
949	Korean
950	Traditional Chinese Big5
1258	Vietnamese

ISO 8859

Table 16.7 shows a list of ISO 8859 code pages. To see the complete list of character codes and what they represent, go to the <<Microsoft ISO 8859 Code Reference>> link on the Web Resources page at http://windows.microsoft.com/windows2000/reskit/webresources.

Table 16.7   Common ISO 8859 Code Pages

Code Page Number	Code Page Name
ISO-8859-1	Latin 1
ISO-8859-2	Latin 2
ISO-8859-3	Latin 3
ISO-8859-4	Baltic
ISO-8859-5	Cyrillic
ISO-8859-6	Arabic
ISO-8859-7	Greek
ISO-8859-8	Hebrew
ISO-8859-9	Turkish
ISO-8859-15	Latin 9

Troubleshooting Font Problems

Problems with fonts typically occur when you try to print a document. If print jobs are taking an inordinately long time to print, or if the printed result does not appear as expected, you might be having problems with your fonts. Typically, if you reinstall the fonts that are not printing as desired or if you try printing from another computer, you solve your font problems.

Font does not print correctly

Open Fonts in Control Panel, right-click the font that is not printing correctly, and then click **Properties**. Check the security information to confirm that the font has not been corrupted. Reinstall the font if corruption is present.

You can choose to reinstall the font, even if corruption is not evident based on the font's public key signature. It is possible that reinstalling the font can solve the problem, despite a lack of evidence of corruption.

When printed, font appears distorted or unreadable

Try a different font size or different font to see whether there are problems with the particular font and font size you are using.

Paste the text into another document and try to print. If the problem persists, the problem might be font specific. Reinstall the font.

Fonts are clipped when printed

Pages only partially print when the page size of the document you are trying to print is bigger than the page size available in the printer. Check to confirm that you are not sending documents that cover a larger area of paper than the printer is capable of printing to.

There might not be enough printer memory if you are printing large documents. If this is the case, increase the available virtual memory, add more RAM to the printer, or print smaller sections of the document.

Performance is slow

If you are working with an unusually large number of fonts, system performance degrades. Keeping fewer than 1,000 fonts installed on your computer at one time helps to maintain performance.

The first time you restart your computer after installing new fonts, they are added, slowing the startup process. When the computer is restarted in the future, this process is completed more quickly, due to font caching, but the process might still be slow. Enumeration of fonts can also slow your system. Font enumeration can occur when an application starts up, or when all the available fonts must be listed, such as when you select a font or open the Fonts folder.

CHAPTER 17

File Systems

Microsoft® Windows® 2000 supports four types of file systems on readable/writable disks: the NTFS file system and three file allocation table (FAT) file systems: FAT12, FAT16 and FAT32. Windows 2000 also supports two types of file systems on CD-ROM and digital video disk (DVD) media: Compact Disc File System (CDFS) and Universal Disk Format (UDF). The structures of the volumes formatted by each of these file systems, as well as the way each file system organizes data on the disk, are significantly different. The capabilities and limitations of these file systems must be reviewed to determine their comparative features.

In This Chapter

Related Information in the Resource Kit

- For more information about disks, see "Disk Concepts and Troubleshooting" in this book.

- For more information about disk storage, see "Removable Storage and Backup" in this book.

- For more information about system recovery, see "Troubleshooting Tools and Strategies" in this book.

Quick Guide to File Systems

Understanding the differences between file systems is important to configuring a system that best meets the needs of your organization. Use this Quick Guide to find information about the file systems available to users of Windows 2000 and how to implement the new features that are included with NTFS.

Understand the file systems and new file system features in Windows 2000.

Review the new features included with NTFS and the advantages of FAT32 support. Also, compare file systems details and compatibility issues.

- See "Overview of Windows 2000 File System" in this chapter.

Choose a file system.

Determine which file system or file systems provide the maximum benefit for your organization. Compare the relative advantages and disadvantages of each file system supported by Windows 2000, and the features that each offers.

- See "File System Comparisons" in this chapter.

Understand the FAT file system.

FAT32 offers enhanced features over FAT16. Review detailed information about these file systems, including the structure of FAT volumes, to determine whether they meet your needs.

- See "FAT" in this chapter.

Understand the NTFS file system.

The version of NTFS included with Windows 2000 offers several enhancements over previous versions of NTFS, as well as features not available with FAT. Review detailed information about NTFS, including the structure of NTFS volumes, to determine whether this file system best meets your needs.

- See "NTFS" in this chapter.

Understand the Compact Disc File System (CDFS).

Review the requirements for formatting CD-ROMs for use with Windows 2000.

- See "Compact Disc File System" in this chapter.

Understand the Universal Disk Format (UDF).

UDF is supported in Windows 2000 for use with removable disk media. If you are using removable media for data storage, review the details about UDF to determine whether it meets your needs.

- See "Universal Disk Format" in this chapter.

Review how Windows 2000 treats long and short file names.

Windows 2000 creates short (8.3) file names to provide MS-DOS compatibility. Review how these short file names are created and how to view the short file names created for files.

- See "Using Long File Names" in this chapter.

Use file system tools to manage files and folders on NTFS volumes.

Use the command-line tools included with Windows 2000 and the *Microsoft® Windows® 2000 Resource Kit* to manage files and folders; edit access control lists (ACLs); compress and uncompress files and folders; convert FAT volumes to NTFS; review disk space usage; and mount local volumes onto other volumes.

- See "File System Tools" in this chapter.

Overview of Windows 2000 File Systems

The file system you use with Windows 2000 determines which of the operating system's advanced features are available to you. To use a Windows 2000-based computer to startup in Microsoft® MS-DOS®, Microsoft® Windows® 3.*x*, or Microsoft® Windows® 95, use FAT16. For a multiple-boot configuration with Microsoft® Windows® 95 OSR2 or Microsoft® Windows® 98 using very large volumes, you might want to use FAT32. If you are concerned with disk security, performance, and efficiency, you might choose NTFS.

What's New

The version of NTFS that is included with Windows 2000 provides significant enhancements over previous versions. Windows 2000 also includes support for the FAT32 file system.

FAT32 support   Users of MS-DOS and Microsoft® Windows NT® version 4.0 and earlier must note that FAT32 is a new option in Windows 2000. This file system, first seen in Windows 95 OSR2 and later in Windows 98, allows FAT users to format much larger volumes than possible with FAT16, and stores files more efficiently on large volumes.

Note   FAT12, FAT16 and FAT32 are referred to synonymously as FAT unless the differences between them must be noted.

NTFS enhancements   Users of MS-DOS, Windows 95, and Windows 98 have a new, more advanced option with NTFS. NTFS, the preferred native file system for Windows 2000, is a much more sophisticated, robust, and secure file system than any of the FAT file systems. Users of Windows NT must also note the many improvements made to NTFS in Windows 2000, including the addition of encryption, disk quotas, reparse points, and so on.

Encryption   The Encrypting File System (EFS) provides the core file encryption technology used to store encrypted files on NTFS volumes. EFS keeps files safe from intruders who might gain unauthorized physical access to sensitive, stored data (for example, by stealing a portable computer or external disk drive).

Disk quotas   Windows 2000 supports disk quotas for NTFS volumes. You can use disk quotas to monitor and limit disk-space use.

Reparse points   Reparse points are new file system objects in NTFS that can be applied to NTFS files or folders. A file or folder that contains a reparse point acquires additional behavior not present in the underlying file system. Reparse points are used by many of the new storage features in Windows 2000, including volume mount points.

Volume mount points   Volume mount points are new to NTFS. Based on reparse points, volume mount points allow administrators to graft access to the root of one local volume onto the folder structure of another local volume.

Sparse files   Sparse files allow programs to create very large files but consume disk space only as needed.

Distributed link tracking   NTFS provides a link-tracking service that maintains the integrity of shortcuts to files as well as OLE links within compound documents.

File System Details

An operating system's ability to access files on a volume depends on the file system with which the volume was formatted. Table 17.1 shows the file system formats supported by various operating systems.

Table 17.1 Operating System and File System Compatibility

Operating System	File System Format
Windows 2000	NTFS
	FAT16
	FAT32
Microsoft® Windows NT® version 4.0	NTFS
	FAT16
Windows 95 OEM Service Release 2 (OSR2) and Windows 98	FAT16
	FAT32
Windows 95 (prior to version OSR2)	FAT16
MS-DOS	FAT16

You can use long and short file names in both NTFS and FAT volumes. A long file name (LFN) can be up to 255 characters long. Short file names have the 8.3 format and are compatible with MS-DOS and other legacy operating systems.

Note 8.3 format means that files can have between 1 and 8 characters in the file name. The name must start with a letter or a number and can contain any characters except the following:

```
. " / \ [ ] : ; | = , * ?  (space)
```

An 8.3 file name typically has a file name extension between one and three characters long with the same character restrictions. A period separates the file name from the file name extension.

Several special file names are reserved by the system and cannot be used for files or folders:

```
CON, AUX, COM1, COM2, COM3, COM4, LPT1, LPT2, LPT3, PRN, NUL
```

File System Comparisons

You can use FAT16, FAT32, NTFS, or a combination of file systems on a single computer, but each volume can have only one file system installed. When choosing which file system to use, you need to determine the following:

- How the computer is used (dedicated to Windows 2000 or multiple-boot).
- The number and size of locally installed hard disks.

- Security considerations.
- Interest in using advanced file system features.

Important It is recommended that you format all Windows 2000 volumes with NTFS except on computers with certain multiple-boot configurations. For more information about NTFS, see "NTFS File System" later in this chapter.

Certain file systems have limitations regarding the minimum and maximum size of volumes that they can format. Additionally, the cluster size of each file system, which depends on the size of the volume and the maximum number of clusters the file system can manage, can affect the choice of file systems.

Table 17.2 provides a comparison of FAT16, FAT32, and NTFS volume and cluster sizes.

Table 17.2   Default Cluster Sizes for Volumes with Windows 2000 File Systems

Volume size	FAT16 cluster size	FAT32 cluster size	NTFS cluster size
7 MB–16 MB	2 KB	Not supported	512 bytes
17 MB–32 MB	512 bytes	Not supported	512 bytes
33 MB–64 MB	1 KB	512 bytes	512 bytes
65 MB–128 MB	2 KB	1 KB	512 bytes
129 MB–256 MB	4 KB	2 KB	512 bytes
257 MB–512 MB	8 KB	4 KB	512 bytes
513 MB–1,024 MB	16 KB	4 KB	1 KB
1,025 MB–2 GB	32 KB	4 KB	2 KB
2 GB–4 GB	64 KB	4 KB	4 KB
4 GB–8 GB	Not supported	4 KB	4 KB
8 GB–16 GB	Not supported	8 KB	4 KB
16 GB–32 GB	Not supported	16 KB	4 KB
32 GB–2 TB	Not supported	Not supported	4 KB

The following are some file system size limitations that should also be considered:

- FAT volumes smaller than 16 megabytes (MB) are formatted as FAT12.
- FAT16 volumes larger than 2 gigabytes (GB) are not accessible from computers running MS-DOS, Windows 95, Windows 98, and many other operating systems.

- While FAT32 volumes can theoretically be as large as 2 terabytes, Windows 2000 limits the maximum size FAT32 volume that it can format to 32 GB. However, Windows 2000 can read and write to larger FAT32 volumes formatted by other operating systems.

- The implementation of FAT32 in Windows 2000 limits the maximum number of clusters on a FAT32 volume that can be mounted by Windows 2000 to 4,177,918. This is the maximum number of clusters on a FAT32 volume that can be formatted by Windows 98.

- NTFS volumes can theoretically be as large as 16 exabytes (EB), but the practical limit is 2 terabytes.

- The user can specify the cluster size when an NTFS volume is formatted. However, NTFS compression is not supported for cluster sizes larger than 4 kilobytes (KB).

Note Clusters are also known as allocation units.

Comparing FAT File Systems

The numerals in the names FAT12, FAT16, and FAT32 refer to the number of bits required for a file allocation table entry.

- FAT12 uses a 12-bit file allocation table entry (2^{12} clusters).

- FAT16 uses a 16-bit file allocation table entry (2^{16} clusters).

- FAT32 uses a 32-bit file allocation table entry. However, Windows 2000 reserves the first 4 bits of a FAT32 file allocation table entry, which means FAT32 has a theoretical maximum of 2^{28} clusters.

Note FAT12 is only used on floppy disks and on very small volumes in Windows 2000.

There are additional relative advantages and disadvantages between FAT16 and FAT32.

Advantages of FAT16

Advantages of FAT16 include:

- MS-DOS, Windows 95, Windows 98, Windows NT, Windows 2000, and some UNIX operating systems can use FAT16.

- There are many software tools that can address problems and recover data on FAT16 volumes.

- If you have a startup failure, you can start the computer by using an MS-DOS bootable floppy disk to troubleshoot the problem.

- FAT16 is efficient, in speed and storage, on volumes smaller than 256 MB.

Disadvantages of FAT16

Disadvantages of FAT16 include:

- The root folder can manage a maximum of 512 entries. The use of long file names (LFNs) can significantly reduce the number of available entries.

- FAT16 is limited to 65,536 clusters, but because certain clusters are reserved, it has a practical limit of 65,524. The largest FAT16 volume on Windows 2000 is limited to 4 GB and uses a cluster size of 64 KB. To maintain compatibility with MS-DOS, Windows 95, and Windows 98, a volume cannot be larger than 2 GB.

- FAT16 is inefficient on larger volume sizes, as the size of the cluster increases. The space allocated for storing a file is based on the size of the cluster allocation granularity, not the file size. For example, a 10-KB file stored on a 1.2-GB volume, which uses a 32-KB cluster, wastes 22 KB of disk space.

- The boot sector is not backed up.

- There is no built-in file system security or compression scheme with FAT16.

Advantages of FAT32

FAT32 has the following enhancements:

- The root folder on a FAT32 drive is an ordinary cluster chain and can be located anywhere on the volume. For this reason, FAT32 does not restrict the number of entries in the root folder.

- FAT32 uses smaller clusters (4 KB for volumes up to 8 GB), so it allocates disk space more efficiently than FAT16. Depending on the size of your files, FAT32 creates the potential for tens and even hundreds of megabytes of additional free disk space on larger volumes compared to FAT16.

- FAT32 can automatically use the backup copy of the file allocation table instead of the default copy (with FAT16, only a disk repair tool such as Chkdsk can implement the backup).

- The boot sector is automatically backed up at a specified location on the volume, so FAT32 volumes are less susceptible to single points of failure than FAT16 volumes.

Disadvantages of FAT32

Disadvantages of FAT32 include:

- The largest FAT32 volume that Windows 2000 can format is 32 GB.

- FAT32 volumes are not directly accessible from operating systems other than Windows 95 OSR2 and Windows 98.

- If you have a startup failure, you cannot start the computer by using an MS-DOS or Windows 95 (excluding version OSR2 and later) bootable floppy disk.

- There is no built-in file system security or compression scheme with FAT32.

NTFS File System

The version of NTFS included with Windows 2000 can take advantage of many advanced features not available by using other file systems. As such, using NTFS wherever possible is recommended to gain the maximum benefits from Windows 2000.

Advantages of NTFS

Formatting Windows 2000 volumes with NTFS instead of FAT allows you to use advanced features that are available only on NTFS, including the following:

- NTFS is a recoverable file system. A user seldom needs to run a disk repair program on an NTFS volume. NTFS guarantees the consistency of the volume by using standard transaction logging and recovery techniques. In the event of a system failure, NTFS uses its log file and checkpoint information to automatically restore the consistency of the file system.

- NTFS supports compression on volumes, folders, and files. Files that are compressed on an NTFS volume can be read and written by any Windows-based application without first being decompressed by another program; decompression happens automatically during the file read. The file is compressed again when it is closed or saved.

- NTFS supports all Windows 2000 file system features.

- NTFS does not restrict the number of entries in the root folder.

- Windows 2000 can format volumes up to 2 terabytes with NTFS.

- NTFS manages disk space more efficiently than FAT, using smaller clusters (4 KB for volumes up to 2 terabytes).
- The boot sector is backed up to a sector at the end of the volume.
- NTFS minimizes the number of disk accesses required to find a file.
- On NTFS volumes, you can set permissions on shares, folders, and files that specify which groups and users have access, and what level of access is permitted. NTFS file and folder permissions apply to users working on the local computer and to users accessing the file over the network from a shared folder. You can also set share permissions that operate on network shares in combination with file and folder permissions.
- NTFS supports a native encryption system, EFS, that uses symmetric key encryption in conjunction with public key technology to prevent unauthorized access to file contents.
- Reparse points enable new features such as volume mount points.
- Disk quotas can be set to limit the amount of space users can consume.
- NTFS uses a change journal to track changes made to files.
- NTFS supports distributed link tracking to maintain the integrity of shortcuts and OLE links.
- NTFS supports sparse files so that very large files can be written to disk while requiring only a small amount of storage space.

Disadvantages of NTFS

While NTFS is recommended for most Windows 2000 users, it is not appropriate in all circumstances. Disadvantages of NTFS include:

- NTFS volumes are not accessible from MS-DOS, Windows 95, or Windows 98. The advanced features of the version of NTFS included with Windows 2000 are not available in Windows NT.
- For very small volumes that contain mostly small files, the overhead of managing NTFS can cause a slight performance drop in comparison to FAT.

A former disadvantage of NTFS was accessing the NTFS-formatted system volume when corrupted or deleted system files prevented the computer from starting. In the past, it was a common requirement that Windows NT be installed to a second, separate folder to access the NTFS system volume of the first installation.

Windows 2000 resolves this problem by offering a pair of new troubleshooting tools. The first tool, known as Safe Mode, allows Windows 2000 to be started with only the basic set of device drivers and system services loaded. Safe Mode allows a system that cannot start, due to system corruption or the installation of incompatible drivers or system services, to bypass those blocking issues, enabling the local administrator to resolve the problem.

If the damage to the operating system files is severe enough that the computer cannot start even in Safe Mode, you can start the computer from either the Windows 2000 operating system CD or Setup floppy disks by using the Recovery Console. The Recovery Console is a special command-line environment that enables the administrator to copy system files from the operating system CD, fix disk errors, and otherwise troubleshoot system problems without installing a second copy of the operating system. For more information about Safe Mode and the Recovery Console, see "Troubleshooting Tools and Strategies" in this book.

Formatting the System Volume in Multiple-Boot Configurations

If you want to start another operating system, such as Windows 95, Windows 98, Microsoft® Windows® for Workgroups, or MS-DOS, use FAT16 for your system volume and the boot volumes for the other operating systems. You can use NTFS for the Windows 2000 boot volume and other volumes on the computer, if those volumes cannot be accessed by an operating system other than Windows 2000.

Performance

For small volumes, FAT16 or FAT32 might provide nominally faster access to files than NTFS because:

- The FAT structure is simpler.
- The FAT folder size is smaller for an equal number of files.
- FAT has no controls regulating whether a user can access a file or a folder; therefore, the system does not have to check that a user has access permissions to a file or folder. This advantage is minimal, however, because Windows 2000 still must determine whether the file is read-only, or whether the file is on a FAT or NTFS volume.

NTFS minimizes the number of disk accesses and time needed to find a file. In addition, if a folder is small enough to fit in the Master File Table (MFT) record, NTFS reads the entire folder when it reads its MFT record.

A FAT folder entry contains an index of the file allocation table, which identifies the cluster number for the first cluster of the folder. To view a file, FAT has to search the folder structure.

For operations performed on large folders containing both long and short file names, the speed of a FAT operation depends on the operation itself and the size of the folder. If FAT searches for a file that does not exist, it needs to search the entire folder—an operation that takes longer on a FAT structure than on the structure used by NTFS.

Several factors affect the speed with which Windows 2000 reads or writes a file:

- If a file is badly fragmented, NTFS usually requires fewer disk accesses than FAT to find all of the fragments.

- For both file systems, the default cluster size depends on the volume size, and is always a power of 2. FAT16 addresses are 16 bits, FAT32 addresses are 32 bits, and NTFS addresses are 64 bits.

- The default cluster size for a FAT16 volume is always larger than the default cluster size for either a FAT32 or an NTFS volume of the same size. The larger cluster size for a FAT16 volume, however, means that there might be less fragmentation in files on a FAT16 volume.

- With NTFS, the MFT record can entirely contain small files; FAT contains pointers to files. The file size that fits within the MFT record depends on the cluster size and the number of attributes for the file.

Maximum Size Limitations

On very large disks, the maximum size of a volume or file and the maximum number of files per volume depend on the file system used to format the volume.

Note Windows 2000 can combine noncontiguous disk areas when creating volume sets and stripe sets, but these volumes have the same maximum size limitations of a single volume.

Maximum Sizes on FAT16 Volumes

FAT16 can support a maximum of 65,524 clusters per volume. Table 17.3 lists FAT16 size limits.

Important For Windows NT and Windows 2000, the cluster size of FAT16 volumes from 2 GB through 4 GB is 64 KB, which can create compatibility issues with some applications. For example, setup programs do not compute volume free space properly on a volume with 64 KB clusters and cannot run because of a perceived lack of free space. For this reason, either NTFS or FAT32 must be used on volumes larger than 2 GB. The Format tool in Windows 2000 displays a warning and asks for a confirmation before formatting a volume with 64 KB clusters.

Table 17.3   FAT16 Size Limits

Description	Limit
Maximum file size	2^{32} minus 1 bytes
Maximum volume size	4 GB
Files per volume	2^{16}

Maximum Sizes on FAT32 Volumes

A FAT32 volume must have a minimum of 65,527 clusters. The maximum number of clusters that Windows 2000 can mount on a FAT32 volume is 4,177,918. Windows 2000 can format volumes up to 32 GB, but it can use larger volumes created by other operating systems. Table 17.4 lists FAT32 size limits.

Table 17.4   FAT32 Size Limits

Description	Limit
Maximum file size	2^{32} minus 1 bytes
Maximum volume size	32 GB (This is due to the Windows 2000 Format tool. The maximum volume size that Windows 98 can create is 127.53 GB).
Files per volume	Approximately 2^{22}

Maximum Sizes on NTFS Volumes

In theory, the maximum NTFS volume size is 2^{64} clusters. However, there are limitations to the maximum size of a volume, such as volume tables. By industry standards, volume tables are limited to 2^{32} sectors.

Sector size, another limitation, is typically 512 bytes. While sector sizes might increase in the future, the current size puts a limit on a single volume of 2 terabytes (2^{32} * 512 bytes, or 2^{41} bytes). For now, 2 terabytes is considered the practical limit for both physical and logical volumes using NTFS.

Table 17.5 lists NTFS size limits.

Table 17.5   NTFS Size Limits

Description	Limit
Maximum file size	2^{64} - 1 KB (Theoretical)
	2^{44} - 64 KB (Implementation)
Maximum volume size	2^{64} clusters (Theoretical)
	2^{32} clusters (Implementation)
Files per volume	2^{32} - 1

Controlling Access to Files and Folders

On NTFS volumes you can set access permissions on files and folders that specify which groups and users have access, and what level of access is permitted. NTFS file and folder permissions apply to users on the local computer and to users accessing the file over the network. With NTFS you can also set share permissions, which operate on shared folders in combination with file and folder permissions. File attributes (read-only, hidden, and system) also limit file access.

File and Folder Permissions

The version of NTFS included with Windows 2000 provides for inheritable permissions. In the **Properties** dialog box, on the **Security** tab, you can set the option **Allow inheritable permissions from parent to propagate to this file object**. This option is enabled by default. This feature reduces the time and input/output (I/O) work required to change the permissions of many files and subfolders. For example, suppose a user wants to change the permissions on a tree consisting of several thousand files. If the folders and subfolders inherit permissions, the user only needs to set permissions for the top-level folder.

Figure 17.1 shows the permissions listed on the **Security** tab of the **Properties** dialog box of a DOC file.

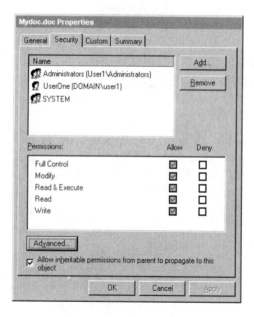

Figure 17.1   Permissions Dialog Box

Figure 17.2 shows the Permissions listed when you click **Advanced** on the
Security tab of the **Properties** dialog box.

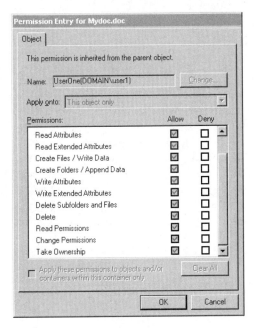

Figure 17.2   Advanced Permissions Dialog Box

Important   To preserve permissions when you copy or move files between NTFS
folders, use the Robocopy tool on the *Windows 2000 Resource Kit*
companion CD.

You can back up and restore data on FAT and NTFS volumes. However, if you
back up data from an NTFS volume and then restore it to a FAT volume, you lose
security settings and other file information specific to NTFS.

Although NTFS provides access controls to individual files and folders, users can
perform certain actions even if permissions are set on a file or folder to prevent
access. For example, you have a folder (MyFolder) containing a file (File1), and
you grant Full Control to a user for the folder MyFolder. If you specify that the
user has No Access to File1, the user can still delete File1 because the Full
Control rights in the folder allow the user to delete the contents of the folder.

To prevent files from being deleted, you must set permissions on the file itself,
and you must set permissions for the folder containing the file that won't
supercede the file's permissions. In the **Properties** dialog box, use the **Security**
tab to deny **Full Control**, but to allow **Modify**, **Read & Execute**, **Read**, and
Write permissions in place.

Anyone who has List, Read, or greater permissions in a folder can view file properties on any file in the folder, even if file permissions prevent them from seeing the contents of the file.

Share Permissions

FAT16 and FAT32 allow you to set limited file attributes but you cannot set permissions on individual files and folders. The only security available is the permissions that are set on the entire share, that affect all files and folders on that share, and that only functions over the network. After a folder is shared, you can protect the shared folder by specifying one set of share permissions for all files and subfolders of the shared folder. Share permissions are set in much the same way file and folder permissions are set in NTFS. But because share permissions apply globally to all files and folders in the share, they are significantly less versatile than the file and folder permissions used for NTFS volumes. Share permissions have no effect on users accessing the contents of a shared folder when the shared folder is on a locally-installed disk.

Share permissions apply equally to NTFS and FAT volumes. They are enforced by Windows 2000, not by the file system. However, when you move or copy a file from an NTFS to a FAT volume, permissions and other NTFS attributes are lost.

POSIX Compliance

NTFS provides Portable Operating System Interface for UNIX (POSIX) compliance, which permits UNIX programs to be ported to Windows 2000. Windows 2000 is fully compliant with the Institute of Electrical and Electronic Engineers (IEEE) standard 1003.1, which is a standard for file naming and identification.

The following POSIX-compliant features are included in NTFS:

- **Case-sensitive naming.** For example, POSIX interprets README.TXT, Readme.txt, and readme.txt as separate files.

- **Hard links.** A file can have more than one name. This allows two different file names, which can be in different folders, to point to the same data.

- **Additional time stamps.** These show when the file was last accessed or modified.

Caution   You must use POSIX-based programs to manage file names that differ only in case. You cannot use standard Windows 2000 command-line tools (such as **copy**, **del**, and **move**, or their equivalents in Windows Explorer) to manage file names that differ only in case. For example, if you type **del MyDoc.Doc** at the command prompt, both mydoc.doc and MyDoc.Doc are deleted.

FAT

The FAT file system locates the file allocation table near the beginning of the volume. FAT16 was designed for small disks and simple folder structures. FAT32 allowed users to create large volumes on large disks. Two copies of the file allocation table are stored on the volume. In the event that one copy of the file allocation table is corrupted, the other is used. The file allocation table is stored in a byte offset specified in the FAT boot sector's BIOS Parameter Block (BPB) so that the files needed to start the system can be located.

Note FAT32 can automatically implement the backup file allocation table if the primary file allocation table is damaged. FAT16 volumes require that a disk repair tool, such as Chkdsk, be used to implement the backup file allocation table.

FAT16 File System

FAT16 is included in Windows 2000 for the following reasons:

- It provides backward compatibility in the form of an upgrade path for earlier versions of Windows-compatible products.

- It is compatible with most other operating systems.

FAT16 is not recommended for volumes larger than 511 MB; when relatively small files are placed on a FAT16 volume, FAT16 manages disk space inefficiently. You cannot use FAT16 on volumes larger than 4 gigabytes (GB).

Note On volumes with fewer than 32,680 sectors, the cluster sizes can be up to 8 sectors per cluster. In this circumstance, the format program creates a 12-bit FAT. Volumes less than 16 MB are usually formatted for a 12-bit FAT, but the exact size depends on the disk geometry. The disk geometry also determines when a larger cluster size is needed because the number of clusters on the volume must fit into the number of bits used by the file system managing the volume. Therefore, you might have a 33-MB volume that has only 1 sector per cluster.

FAT12 is the original implementation of FAT and is intended for very small media. The file allocation table for FAT12 is smaller than the file allocation table for FAT16 and FAT32, because it uses less space for each entry, leaving more space for data. All 1.44-MB 3.5-inch floppy disks are formatted with FAT12.

Figure 17.3 illustrates how FAT16 maps clusters on a volume. The file allocation tables (labeled FAT1 and FAT2 in Figure 17.3) identify each cluster in the volume as one of the following:

- Unused

- Cluster in use by a file

- Bad cluster
- Last cluster in a file

Boot Sector	FAT 1	FAT 2 (Duplicate)	Root Folder	Other Folders and All Files

Figure 17.3   Organization of a FAT16 Volume

The root folder exists at a specified location and has the maximum number of available entries fixed at 512. The maximum number of entries on a floppy disk depends on the size of the disk.

Note Each folder and 8.3 file name in the root folder counts as an entry. For example, since the maximum number of entries is fixed at 512, if you have 100 folders in the root folder, you can only create 412 more files or folders in the root folder. If those folders or files use names longer than the 8.3 format, fewer files and folders can be created.

Folders contain a 32-byte entry for each file and folder they contain. The entry includes the following information:

- Name in 8.3 format (11 bytes)
- Attribute (1 byte, described later in this section)
- Create time (3 bytes)
- Create date (2 bytes)
- Last access date (2 bytes)
- Last modified time (2 bytes)
- Last modified date (2 bytes)
- Starting cluster number in the file allocation table (2 bytes)
- File size (4 bytes)

Note Three bytes in each entry are held in reserve.

In the file allocation table of a FAT16 volume, files are given the first available location on the volume. The starting cluster number is the address of the first cluster used by the file. Each cluster contains a pointer to the next cluster in the file, or an end-of-file indicator at (0xFFFF) which indicates that this cluster is the end of the file. These pointers and end-of-file indicators are shown in Figure 17.4.

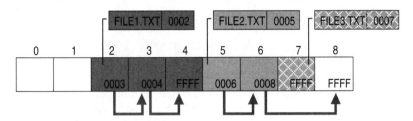

Figure 17.4   Files on a FAT Volume

Figure 17.4 shows three files in a folder. File1.txt uses three clusters. File2.txt is a fragmented file that requires three clusters. File3.txt fits in one cluster. In each case, the file allocation table entry points to the first cluster of the file.

The information in the folder is used by all operating systems that support FAT. Windows 2000 can store additional timestamps in a FAT folder entry. These timestamps show when the file was created or last accessed.

Because all entries in a folder are the same size, the attribute byte for each entry in a folder describes what kind of entry it is. For example, one bit indicates that the entry is for a subfolder and another bit marks the entry as a volume. Typically, the operating system controls the settings of these bits.

The attribute byte includes four bits that can be turned on or off by the user—archive, system, hidden, and read-only.

FAT32 File System

Support for FAT32 is new in Windows 2000. The FAT32 on-disk format and features on Windows 2000 are similar to those on Windows 95 OSR2 and Windows 98.

The size of a FAT32 cluster is determined by the system and can range in size from 1 sector (512 bytes) to 128 sectors (64 KB), incremented in powers of 2.

Note   The use of 64 KB clusters in FAT32 can lead to compatibility problems with certain programs. The maximum recommended size cluster for a FAT32 volume is 32 KB.

Since FAT32 requires 4 bytes to store cluster values, many internal and on-disk data structures have been revised or expanded. Most programs are unaffected by these changes; however, disk tools which read the on-disk format must be updated to support FAT32.

The most significant difference between FAT16 and FAT32 is the maximum number of clusters supported, which in turn affects a volume's maximum size and storage efficiency. FAT32 breaks the 4-GB volume limitation of FAT16 by extending the maximum number of clusters to over 4 million. FAT32, as implemented in Windows 2000, can mount a volume as large as 127 GB. Due to the greater number of available clusters within FAT32, each cluster can be made smaller for a particular volume, making data storage more efficient. If you have a FAT16 volume between 2 and 4 GB in size, a 64-KB cluster is used; with FAT32, volumes ranging in size between 256 MB and 8 GB use a 4-KB cluster.

The largest possible file for a FAT32 volume is 4 GB minus 2 bytes. FAT32 contains 4 bytes per cluster in the file allocation table; FAT16 contains 2 bytes per cluster; and FAT12 contains 1.5 bytes per cluster. A FAT32 volume must have at least 65,527 clusters, but no more than 4,177,918 clusters.

In Windows 2000, you cannot format FAT32 volumes greater than 32 GB. Use NTFS to format larger volumes. For more information about why it is recommended that you format all Windows 2000 volumes with NTFS, see "NTFS File System" earlier in this chapter.

Note   The Windows 2000 Fastfat driver enables you to mount and fully support a FAT32 volume larger than 32 GB that was created by another operating system.

File Names on FAT Volumes

Files created or renamed on FAT volumes use attribute bits to support LFNs in a way that does not interfere with how MS-DOS gains access to the volume.

Whenever you create a file with an LFN, Windows 2000 creates a conventional 8.3 name for the file and one or more secondary folder entries for the file, one for each set of 13 characters in the LFN. Each secondary folder entry stores a corresponding part of the LFN in Unicode. MS-DOS accesses the file by using the conventional 8.3 file name contained in the folder entry for the file.

Windows 2000 marks the secondary folder entries as part of an LFN by setting the volume ID, read-only, system, and hidden attribute bits. MS-DOS generally ignores folder entries with all these attribute bits set, so these entries are invisible to it.

Figure 17.5 shows all of the folder entries for the file Thequi~1.fox, which has a long name of The quick brown.fox. The long name is in Unicode, so each character in the name uses 2 bytes in the folder entry. The attribute field for the long-name entries has the value 0x0F. The attribute field for the short name has the value 0x20.

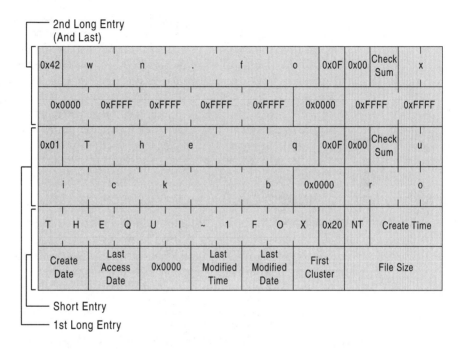

Figure 17.5   LFN on a FAT Volume

Note Windows NT and Windows 2000 do not use the same algorithm to create long and short file names as Windows 95 and Windows 98. However, on computers that use a multiple-boot process to start these operating systems, files that you create when running one operating system can be accessed when running another.

For more information about how Windows 2000 creates short file names, see "Using Long File Names" later in this chapter.

By default, Windows 2000 supports LFNs on FAT volumes. You can prevent a FAT file system from creating LFNs by setting the value of the **Win31FileSystem** registry entry (in subkey HKEY_LOCAL_MACHINE\System \CurrentControlSet\Control\FileSystem) to 1. This value prevents Windows 2000 from creating new LFNs on all FAT volumes, but it does not affect existing LFNs.

Warning Do not use a registry editor to edit the registry directly unless you have no alternative. The registry editors bypass the standard safeguards provided by administrative tools. These safeguards prevent you from entering conflicting settings or settings that are likely to degrade performance or damage your system. Editing the registry directly can have serious, unexpected consequences that can prevent the system from starting and require that you reinstall Windows 2000. To configure or customize Windows 2000, use the programs in Control Panel or Microsoft Management Console (MMC) whenever possible.

Using FAT with Windows 2000

FAT16 works the same in Windows 2000 as it does in MS-DOS, Windows 3.*x*, Windows 95, and Windows 98. FAT32 works the same in Windows 2000 as it does in Windows 95 OSR2 and Windows 98. You can install Windows 2000 on an existing FAT primary volume or logical volume. When running Windows 2000, you can move or copy files between FAT and NTFS volumes.

Note If you copy a file from an NTFS volume to a FAT volume, any NTFS-specific properties associated with that file, such as permissions, compression, encryption, and sparse file support, are permanently lost.

You cannot use Windows 2000 with any compression or partitioning software that requires disk drivers to be loaded by MS-DOS, Windows 95, or Windows 98. Therefore, you cannot use DoubleSpace®, DriveSpace®, or DriveSpace® 3 on a FAT16 primary volume or logical volume that you want to access when running Windows 2000.

NTFS

Windows 2000 includes a new version of NTFS, which provides performance, reliability, and advanced functionality not found in any version of FAT. The NTFS data structures allow you to take advantage of new features, such as storage features based on reparse points, management software, and, if the Microsoft® Windows® 2000 Professional computer is connected to a Microsoft® Windows® 2000 Server network, the Active Directory™ directory service.

NTFS also includes security features required for file servers and high-end personal computers in a corporate environment, data access control, and ownership privileges important for data integrity.

NTFS uses clusters as the fundamental unit of disk allocation. In the Disk Management snap-in, you can specify a cluster size of up to 64 KB when you format a volume. If you use the **format** command to format your NTFS volume, but do not specify a cluster size using the **/A:<size>** switch, the default values in Table 17.2 are used.

Note   Windows 2000, like Microsoft® Windows NT® version 3.51 and Windows NT 4.0, supports file compression. Since file compression is not supported on cluster sizes above 4 KB, the default NTFS cluster size for Windows 2000 never exceeds 4 KB. For more information about NTFS compression, see "Volume, Folder, and File Compression" later in this chapter.

Volume Mount Points

You can add volumes to systems without adding separate drive letters for each new volume, similar to the way Distributed file system (Dfs) links together remote network shares. Volume mount points are robust against system changes that occur when devices are added or removed from a computer.

A volume mount point can be placed in any empty folder of the host NTFS volume. The "mounting" is handled transparently to the user and applications. The version of NTFS included with Windows 2000 must be used on the host volume. However, the volume to be mounted can be formatted in any Windows 2000-accessible file system, including NTFS, FAT16, FAT32, CDFS, or UDF.

One volume can host multiple volume mount points. This allows the local administrator to easily extend the storage capacity of any particular volume on a Windows 2000 system. Users on the local system or connecting to it over a network can continue to use the same drive letter to access the volume, but multiple volumes can be in use simultaneously from that drive letter, depending on the folder used on the host. Windows 2000 automatically prevents resolution problems caused by changes in the internal device name of the target volume. A mount point is the target volume in the same way a drive letter is the target volume.

A useful example of volume mount points can be seen in the following scenario. A user recently installed Windows 2000 onto a relatively small drive C, and is concerned about unnecessary use of storage space on drive C. The user knows that the default document folder, My Documents, is on drive C, and she uses her computer extensively to create and edit digital photos, vector-based graphic art, and desktop publishing (DTP) files. Knowing that these types of documents can quickly consume a lot of disk storage space, the user creates a volume mount point to drive C under the My Documents folder called Art. Any subfolder of the Art folder actually resides on another volume, saving space on drive C.

Note You need local Administrator rights to complete this task.

▶ **To create a volume mount point under C:\My Documents**

1. If necessary, add a new hard disk to create a new volume.

2. Log on to the computer with an account that has local Administrator rights.

3. In Control Panel, double-click **Administrative Tools**.

4. In **Administrative Tools**, double-click **Computer Management**.

5. In **Computer Management**, double-click **Disk Management**.

6. If you want to use a previously existing volume as the volume mount point, skip to step 12. Otherwise, right-click in the unallocated space on the disk in which you want to create a new volume and choose **Create Partition** to start the Create Partition wizard. Follow the steps in the wizard to create an extended partition. Allocate at least as much space as you need to contain all of your art and DTP files.

   You can also create another primary partition, and then skip to step 8.

Note You do not have to use an entire extended partition for just one logical volume. Since extended partitions can contain many logical volumes, you might want to use all the remaining unallocated space for the extended partition and then allocate a portion of that for the volume to be used in this scenario. You can later create another one or more logical volumes out of the remaining free space in the extended partition.

If the disk has been upgraded to dynamic disk, you cannot see the options primary partition, extended partition, and logical volume in Disk Management. These terms only apply to basic disks. On dynamic disks you create simple volumes for this task. For more information about primary partitions, extended partitions, logical volumes, basic disks, and dynamic disks, see "Disk Concepts and Troubleshooting" in this book.

7. If you created an extended partition in step 6, right-click in the extended partition, and then choose **Create Logical Drive**. Use as much disk space for the new logical volume as you need to contain all of the games you plan to install on this computer.

8. At the **Assign Drive Letter or Path** screen of the Create Partition wizard, choose the option **Mount this volume at an empty folder that supports drive paths**, and then click **Browse**.

9. In Windows Explorer, expand drive C, navigate to the folder C:\Documents and Settings*username*\My Documents, and then click **New Folder**. In the folder name placeholder in the Explorer tree, type over the default name New Folder with the name **Art**, and then click **OK**. Click **Next** at the Create Partition wizard.

10. Format the new volume with NTFS by using the default-sized allocation units (NTFS is not required, but it is recommended). Enter a volume label for the new volume, or clear the default label in the **Volume label** text box for none. Click **Next** twice to finish the wizard. The new volume is automatically formatted after the volume is created.

11. Volumes and volume mount points can be addressed by multiple names in the file system namespace. To make the mounted volume accessible directly through a drive letter in Windows Explorer, in Disk Management, right-click the mounted volume, select **Change Drive Letter and Path**, and then click **Add** to assign a drive letter. You can also mount this volume to another folder on the same or another host volume. Click **OK** when done. Skip to step 15 of this procedure.

12. To mount previously existing volumes as a volume mount point on a folder of another volume, right-click the volume to be mounted, select **Change Drive Letter and Path**, and then click **Add**.

13. Select **Mount in the NTFS folder**, and then click **Browse**.

14. In Windows Explorer, expand drive C, navigate to the C:\Documents and Settings*username*\My Documents folder, click **New Folder**, and in the folder name placeholder in the Explorer tree, type over the default name New Folder with the name Art. Click **OK** twice to close the wizard.

15. In Windows Explorer, navigate to the C:\Documents and Settings*username*\My Documents\Art folder and create new folders such as Photos, LineArt, and DTP for the graphic arts documents.

Any bitmap files are accessed in the Photos folder on the user's computer, the volume mount point used to attach the volume to the My Documents folder on drive C directs all read and write requests to the Photos folder on the mounted volume. Any files stored in the My Documents\Art folder are stored in the root folder of the mounted volume. Any other folder created normally within Windows Explorer under the My Documents folder still resides on drive C.

Note In Windows 2000, only NTFS folders are marked as junctions to provide a mapping function from one folder name to another. NTFS files are not marked in this manner.

The tool Mountvol can identify and manage volume mount points. For more information about Mountvol, see "File System Tools" later in this chapter.

Encryption

EFS uses symmetric key encryption in conjunction with public key technology to protect files and ensure that only the owner of a file can access it. Users of EFS are issued a digital certificate with a public key and a private key pair. EFS uses the key set for the user who is logged on to the local computer where the private key is stored.

Users work with encrypted files and folders just as they do with any other files and folders. Encryption is transparent to the user who encrypted the file; the system automatically decrypts the file or folder when the user accesses. When the file is saved, encryption is reapplied. However, intruders who try to access the encrypted files or folders receive an "Access denied" message if they try to open, copy, move, or rename the encrypted file or folder.

To encrypt or decrypt a folder or file, set the encryption attribute for folders and files just as you set any other attribute. If you encrypt a folder, all files and subfolders created in the encrypted folder are automatically encrypted. It is recommended that you encrypt at the folder level.

You can also encrypt or decrypt a file or folder using the command-line tool Cipher. For quick information about an encrypted file or folder, use the *Windows 2000 Resource Kit* tool Efsinfo. For more information about Cipher or Efsinfo, see "File System Tools" later in this chapter.

Encrypting File System and Data Recovery

Data recovery is available for EFS as a part of the overall security policy for the system. For example, if you lose your file encryption certificate and associated private key (through disk failure or any other reason), data recovery is available through the designated recovery agent. The recovery agent is, by default, the local system administrator. However, if the computer is connected to a Windows 2000 Server–based network that is using Active Directory, the recovery agent role is assigned by default to the domain administrator.

EFS provides built-in data recovery by requiring that a recovery policy be in place before users can encrypt files. The recovery policy provides for a person to be designated as the recovery agent. The administrator is automatically designated as the recovery agent when logging on to the system for the first time.

The recovery agent has a special certificate and associated private key that allow data recovery for the scope of influence of the recovery policy. If you are the recovery agent, use the **export** command from the Certificates snap-in to back up the recovery certificate and associated private key to a secure location. After backing up, delete the recovery certificate from the recovery agent's personal store, not from the recovery policy. If you need to perform a recovery operation, first restore the recovery certificate and associated private key to the recovery agent's personal store by using the **import** command from the Certificates snap-in. After recovering the data, delete the recovery certificate from the recovery agent's personal store. You do not have to repeat the export process. Delete the recovery agent's recovery certificate from the computer, and keep it in a secure location as an additional security measure.

Note   The scope of influence in a domain is a site, a domain, or an organizational unit. In a workgroup, the scope of influence is the local hard disk.

The default recovery policy is configured locally for stand-alone computers. For computers on a network, the recovery policy is configured at either the domain, organizational unit, or individual computer level, and applies to all Windows 2000-based computers within the defined scope of influence. Recovery certificates are issued by a certification authority (CA) and managed by using the Certificates snap-in.

Because the Windows 2000 security subsystem handles enforcing, replicating, and caching of the recovery policy, users can implement file encryption on a system that is temporarily offline, such as a portable computer. This process is similar to logging on to the domain account using cached credentials.

Data Backup and Recovery

The main administrative tasks associated with EFS are backing up and restoring encrypted files, configuring a recovery policy, and recovering encrypted data.

Backup copies of encrypted files are also encrypted when you use a backup program designed for Windows 2000.

Data recovery refers to the process of decrypting a file without having the private key of the user who encrypted the file. When restoring encrypted data, the data remains encrypted after the restore operation.

You might need to recover data with a recovery agent if:

- A user leaves the company.
- A user loses the private key.
- A law enforcement agency makes a request.

To recover a file, the recovery agent:

- Backs up the encrypted files.
- Moves the backup copies to a secure system.
- Imports their recovery certificate and private key on that system.
- Restores the backup files.
- Decrypts the files, using Windows Explorer or the **Cipher** command.

You can use the Group Policy snap-in to define a data recovery policy for domain member servers or for stand-alone or workgroup servers. You can either request a recovery certificate, or export and import your recovery certificates.

Delegate administration of the recovery policy to a designated administrator. Although it is recommended that you limit who is authorized to recover encrypted data, allowing multiple administrators to act as recovery agents is a good idea.

Working With Encrypted Files

When you work with encrypted files and folders, keep the following in mind:

- You cannot encrypt files or folders that are compressed. First, uncompress the file or folder, and then encrypt it. On a compressed volume, uncompress folders that you want to encrypt.
- Only the user who encrypted the file can open it.
- You cannot share encrypted files.
- An encrypted file is decrypted if you copy or move the file to a FAT volume. However, a file remains encrypted when backed up by a program designed to work with Windows 2000.

- Cut and paste to move files into an encrypted folder. If you use a drag-and-drop operation, the files are not automatically encrypted in the new folder.

- System files cannot be encrypted.

- Encrypting a folder or file does not protect against deletion. Anyone with delete permission can delete encrypted folders or files.

- Temporary files created when files are being edited are encrypted if all the files are on an NTFS volume and in an encrypted folder. Encrypt the Temp folder on your hard disk to ensure that your encrypted documents remain encrypted during editing. If you create a new document or open an e-mail attachment, the file can be created as an encrypted document in the Temp folder. If you save the encrypted document to another location on an NTFS volume, it remains encrypted in the new location.

- Unless EFS is disabled by Group Policy, you can encrypt or decrypt files and folders on a remote computer that has been enabled for remote encryption. For more information, consult your domain administrator. However, If you open the encrypted file over the network, the data that is transmitted over the network is not encrypted. Other protocols, such as Secure Sockets Layer (SSL), Transport Layer Security (TLS), or IPSec must be used to encrypt data over the wire.

- A recovery policy is automatically implemented when you encrypt your first file or folder; if you lose your file encryption certificate and associated private key, a recovery agent can decrypt the file.

EFS Recommendations

- Encrypt the folder in which you save most of your documents to ensure that your personal documents are encrypted by default.

- Encrypt your Temp folder so that temporary files are automatically encrypted.

- Encrypt folders rather than individual files so that when a program creates temporary files during editing, they are encrypted.

- Use the **export** command from the Certificates snap-in to back up the file encryption certificate and associated private key on a floppy disk, and keep it in a secure location.

For more information about EFS, see "Encrypting File System" in the *Microsoft® Windows® 2000 Server Resource Kit Distributed Systems Guide*.

Sparse Files

A sparse file has an attribute that causes the I/O subsystem to allocate only meaningful (nonzero) data. Nonzero data is allocated on disk, and non-meaningful data (large strings of data composed of zeros) is not. When a sparse file is read, allocated data is returned as it was stored; non-allocated data is returned, by default, as zeros.

NTFS deallocates sparse data streams and only maintains other data as allocated. When a program accesses a sparse file, the file system yields allocated data as actual data and deallocated data as zeros.

NTFS includes full sparse file support for both compressed and uncompressed files. NTFS handles read operations on sparse files by returning allocated data and sparse data. It is possible to read a sparse file as allocated data and a range of data without retrieving the entire data set, although NTFS returns the entire data set by default.

With the sparse file attribute set, the file system can deallocate data from anywhere in the file and, when an application calls, yield the zero data by range instead of storing and returning the actual data. File system application programming interfaces (APIs) allow for the file to be copied or backed as actual bits and sparse stream ranges. The net result is efficient file system storage and access. Figure 17.6 shows how data is stored with and without the sparse file attribute set.

Without sparse file attribute set

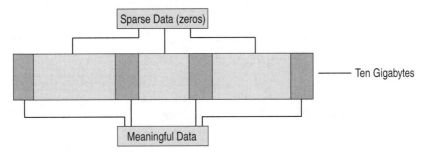

With sparse file attribute set

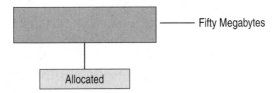

Figure 17.6   Sparse Data Storage

Important   If you copy or move a sparse file to a FAT or a non-Windows 2000 NTFS volume, the file is built to its originally specified size. If the required space is not available, the operation does not complete.

Change Journal

The change journal is a new feature of NTFS in Windows 2000 that provides a persistent log of changes made to files on a volume. NTFS uses the change journal to track information about added, deleted, and modified files for each volume. The change journal describes the nature of any changes to files on the volume. When any file or folder is created, modified, or deleted, NTFS adds a record to the change journal for that volume.

The change journal conveys significant scalability benefits to applications that might otherwise need to scan an entire volume for changes. File system indexing, replication managers, virus scanners, and incremental backup applications can benefit from using the change journal.

The change journal is much more efficient than time stamps or file notifications for determining changes in a particular namespace. Applications that normally need to rescan an entire volume to determine changes can now scan once, and subsequently refer to the change journal. The I/O cost depends on how many files have changed, not on how many files exist on the volume.

Each record in the change journal takes approximately 80-100 bytes of space, but there is a configurable maximum size that it never exceeds on disk. When this size is reached, a proportion of the oldest records are discarded.

The APIs are fully documented and can be leveraged by independent software vendors (ISVs). Microsoft uses the change journal in Windows 2000 components such as the Indexing Service. ISVs are planning to use this feature to enhance the scalability and robustness of a range of products including backup, antivirus, and auditing tools.

For more information about the change journal, see the Platform Software Development Kit (SDK) link on the Web Resource page at http://windows.microsoft.com/windows2000/reskit/webresources.

Disk Quotas

Disk quotas are tracked on a per-user, per-volume basis; users are charged *only* for the files they own. Quotas are tracked per volume, even if the volumes are different partitions on the same physical hard disk. However, if you have multiple shares on the *same* volume, the quotas apply to all shares collectively, and a user's utilization of all shares cannot exceed the assigned quota on that volume.

In the **Properties** dialog box, the **Quota** tab allows the administrator to perform the following tasks:

- Enable or disable disk quotas on a volume.
- Prevent users from saving new data when their disk quota is exceeded.
- Set the default disk quota warning level and disk quota limit assigned to new volume users.
- View disk quota information for each user from the **Quota Entries** view.

Disk quotas track and control disk space usage for volumes. Administrators can configure Windows 2000 to perform the following tasks:

- Prevent further disk space use and log an event when a user exceeds a specified disk space limit.
- Log an event when a user exceeds a specified disk space warning level.

When you enable disk quotas, you can set both the disk quota limit and the disk quota warning level. The limit specifies the amount of disk space that is allocated to a user. The warning level specifies when a user is nearing the limit. For example, you can set a user's disk quota limit to 50 megabytes (MB), and the disk quota warning level to 45 MB. The user can store no more than 50 MB of data on the volume; if more than 45 MB are stored on the volume the disk quota system can log a system event.

When you enable disk quotas for a volume, volume usage is automatically tracked for new users, but existing volume users have no disk quotas applied to them. To apply disk quotas to existing volume users, add new quota entries in the **Quota Entries** window.

For more information about setting disk quotas, see Windows 2000 Professional Help.

Disk Quotas and Free Space

Disk quotas are transparent to the user. When a user asks how much space is free on a disk, the system reports only the user's available quota allowance. If the user exceeds this allowance, the system indicates that the disk is full.

To obtain more disk space after exceeding the quota allowance, the user must do one of the following:

- Delete files.
- Have another user claim ownership of some files.
- Have the administrator increase the quota allowance.

The following conditions apply when you use disk quotas:

- Disk quotas set on a volume apply only to that volume.
- Disk quotas cannot be set on individual files or folders.
- Disk quotas are based on uncompressed file sizes. You cannot increase the amount of free space by compressing the data.
- If the computer that hosts the volume with a quota is configured as a multiple-boot system with Windows 2000 and Windows NT 4.0, the quota is not enforced and can be exceeded when it is running Windows NT 4.0. However, when that computer resumes running Windows 2000, users who exceeded their quotas must delete or move files to a different volume—that is, until they are under their limit—before they can store new files to the quota volume.
- To support disk quotas, a disk volume must be formatted with NTFS. Volumes formatted with previous versions of NTFS are upgraded automatically by Windows 2000 Setup.

- To administer quotas on a volume, you must be a member of the Administrators group on the computer where the volume resides.

- If the volume is not formatted with NTFS, or if you are not a member of the Administrators group on the local computer, the **Quota** tab is not displayed on the volume's **Properties** page.

Disk Quota Limits

The disk space used by each file is charged directly to the user who owns the file. The file owner is identified by the security identifier (SID) in the security information for the file. The total disk space charged to a user is the sum of the length of all data streams; property set streams and resident user data streams affect the user's quota. Since compressing or decompressing files does not affect the disk space reported for the files, quota settings on one volume can be compared to settings on another volume.

The following are types of disk quota limits.

Warning threshold   You can configure the system to generate a system log file entry on the computer hosting the volume with the quota when the disk space charged to the user exceeds this value. The user is not notified when this threshold is surpassed.

Hard quota   You can configure the computer hosting the volume with the quota to generate a system log file entry or deny additional disk space to the user when the disk space charged to the user exceeds this value.

NTFS automatically creates a user quota entry when a user first writes to the volume. Entries that are created automatically are assigned the default warning threshold and hard quota limit values for the volume.

Disk Quotas States

The administrator can turn quota enforcement on and off. There are three quota states, as shown in Table 17.6.

Table 17.6   Disk Quota States

State	Description
Quota disabled	Quota usage changes are not tracked, but the quota limits are not removed. In this state, performance is not affected by disk quotas. This is the default state.
Quota tracked	Quota usage changes are tracked, but quota limits are not enforced. In this state, no quota violation events are generated and no file operations fail because of disk quota violations.
Quota enforced	Quota usage changes are tracked and quota limits are enforced.

Administering Disk Quotas

Disk quotas monitor volume use to prevent users from affecting others' use of the volume. For example, if a user saves 50 MB on a volume on which each user has been allocated 50 MB of space, some of this data must be moved or deleted before additional data is written to the volume. Other users can continue to save up to 50 MB of space on that volume.

Note Disk quotas do not prevent administrators from allocating more space than is available on the disk. For example, on a 8-GB volume that is used by 100 users, each user might be allocated 100 MB of space.

Disk quotas are based on file ownership and are independent of the location of the files on the volume. If a user moves files from one folder to another on the same volume, volume space usage does not change. If the user copies the files to a different folder on the same volume, the available volume space usage against the quota for that user decreases by the number of bytes copied.

The administrator can set default quotas for the volume or for specific users on a volume. A new user receives the default quota unless the administrator established a different quota for that specific user. The administrator can view the level of quota tracking, the default quota limits, and the per-owner quota information by looking at the **Quota** tab on the **Properties** dialog box for the volume. The per-user quota information contains the user's hard quota limit, warning threshold, and quota usage.

If you do not want to use the default disk space limit and warning threshold values for a particular user, use the New Quota Entry feature to set up quota thresholds and limits before the user writes data to the volume.

User quota entries cannot be deleted if a user owns files on the volume; all files owned by that user must be deleted or moved to another volume, or ownership of the files must be transferred to another user.

Enabling Disk Quotas

When you enable quotas on a volume that already contains files, the space used by all users who have copied, saved, or taken ownership of files on the volume is calculated. The quota limit and warning level are then applied to all current users and new users. You can then disable or set different quotas for specific users. You can also set quotas for specific users who have not yet copied, saved, or taken ownership of any files on the volume.

For example, you can set a quota of 50 MB for all users of share \\Workstation1\Public, while ensuring that two users who work with larger files have a 100-MB limit. If both users have files stored on \\Workstation1\Public, open the **Properties** dialog box for that volume, click **Quota**, click **Quota entries**, select both users, right click, and then click **Properties** to set their quota limit to 100 MB. However, if either user does not have files stored on the volume, use the **Select Users** property sheet to set their quota limit higher than the default for new users.

Local and Remote Implementations

Disk quotas can be enabled on both local computers and remote computers. On local computers, quotas can limit the amount of space available to users who log on to the local computer. On remote computers, quotas can limit volume usage by remote users. The remote computer must be formatted with the version of NTFS included with Windows 2000 and be shared from the root folder of the volume. You need Administrator rights to enable, disable, or manage quotas.

You can use quotas to ensure the following:

- Disk space on public servers is not monopolized by one or a few users.
- Users do not use excessive disk space on a shared folder on your computer.
- Information technology (IT) budget dollars for mass storage are managed efficiently by making users account for the use of shared disk space, by using public disk space only for necessary files.

System files are included in the total sum of volume usage of the person who installed Windows 2000 on the local computer. When implementing disk quotas on a local volume, make sure to take into account the disk space used by these files. Depending on the free space available on the volume, you might want to set a high quota limit or no limit for the user who installed the operating system.

Auditing Disk Space Use

Enabling quotas causes a slight increase in server overhead and a slight decrease in file server performance. By periodically enabling and disabling quotas, you can take advantage of the auditing capabilities provided by Windows 2000 disk quotas without permanently affecting performance.

To create a record of the audit, save a copy of the system log data from Event Viewer to a comma-delimited file that can be read by applications such as Microsoft® Excel. These files can be useful for analyzing the data captured.

Exceeding Disk Quota Limits

When you select **Deny disk space to users exceeding quota limit** on the **Quota** tab of the **Properties** dialog box, users who exceed their limit receive an "insufficient disk space" error and cannot write additional data to the volume without deleting or moving files. Individual programs determine their own error handling for this condition. To the program, it appears that the volume is full.

By leaving this option cleared, you can allow users to exceed their limit. This is useful when you do not want to deny users access to a volume, but want to track disk space use. You can also specify whether or not to log an event to the volume host computer's system log when users exceed either their quota warning level or their quota limit.

Event Viewer builds a historical, chronological record of users who exceeded their quota warning level and quota limit, and when they exceeded them. However, it does not provide information about which users are currently over their quota warning level.

For more information about enabling disk quotas, see Windows 2000 Professional Help.

Multiple Data Streams

NTFS supports multiple data streams, in which the stream name identifies a new data attribute on the file. Each data stream is an alternate set of file attributes. Streams have separate opportunistic locks, file locks, allocation sizes, and file sizes, but files can be shared.

This feature enables data to be managed as a single unit. Using multiple data streams, a file can be associated with more than one application at a time, such as Microsoft® Word and WordPad.

Caution   When you copy an NTFS file to a FAT volume, such as a floppy disk, data streams and other attributes not supported by FAT are lost.

Distributed Link Tracking

Distributed link tracking can use a unique object identifier (ID) to locate link source files that have been moved locally on a computer or within a Windows 2000 domain. The object ID is stamped into a file when it is made the target of a shortcut or an OLE link. NTFS can maintain the integrity of its references because the objects referenced can be moved transparently. Distributed link tracking stores a file's object ID as part of its tracking information.

Distributed link tracking can resolve broken links in the following circumstances:

- The link source file has been renamed.

- The link source file has been moved within the volume, between two volumes on the same computer, or between two computers within the same Windows 2000 Server–based domain.

- The volume containing the link source file has been installed in another computer running Windows 2000 within the same Windows 2000 Server–based domain.

- The Windows 2000–based computer containing the link source file has been renamed.

- The name of the network share containing the link source file has been changed.

Volume, Folder, and File Compression

Windows 2000 supports compression on individual files, folders, and entire NTFS volumes. Files compressed on an NTFS volume can be read and written by any Windows-based application without first being decompressed by another program. Decompression occurs automatically when the file is read. The file is compressed again when it is closed or saved. Compressed files and folders have an attribute of **C** when viewed in Windows Explorer.

Only NTFS can read the compressed form of the data. When an application such as Microsoft® Word or an operating system command such as **copy** requests access to the file, the compression filter driver decompresses the file before making it available. For example, if you copy a compressed file from another Windows 2000–based computer to a compressed folder on your hard disk, the file is decompressed when read, copied, and then recompressed when saved.

This compression algorithm is similar to that used by the Windows 98 application DriveSpace 3, with one important difference—the limited functionality compresses the entire primary volume or logical volume. NTFS allows for the compression of an entire volume, of one or more folders within a volume, or even one or more files within a folder of an NTFS volume.

The compression algorithms in NTFS are designed to support cluster sizes of up to 4 KB. When the cluster size is greater than 4 KB on an NTFS volume, none of the NTFS compression functions are available.

Compressing and Decompressing Volumes, Folders, and Files

Volumes, folders and files on an NTFS volume are either compressed or decompressed. The compression state of a folder does not necessarily reflect the compression state of the files in that folder. For instance, a folder might be compressed, yet some or all the files in that folder can be decompressed if you selectively decompressed them.

You can set the compression state of folders and compress or decompress files by using Windows Explorer or the command-line program Compact.

Using Windows Explorer

With Windows Explorer, you can set the compression state of an NTFS folder without changing the compression state of existing files in that folder. If you have Read or Write permission, you can change the compression state locally or across a network. You can select individual folders or files to compress or decompress.

▶ **To set the compression state of a volume**

1. Open **Windows Explorer**. In the left pane, right-click the root folder of the volume that you want to compress or decompress.

2. Click **Properties** to display the **Properties** dialog box.

3. On the **General** tab, select or clear the **Compress drive to save disk space** check box.

4. In the **Confirm Attribute Changes** dialog box, select whether to make the compression apply only to the root folder or the entire volume, and then click **OK**.

The change to the compression attribute is applied to the files and folders you specified. If you compress the entire volume, it might take a few minutes to complete the process, depending on the size of the volume, the number of files and folders to compress, and the speed of the computer.

▶ **To set the compression state of a folder or file**

1. Open **Windows Explorer**. In the left pane, right-click the folder that you want to compress or decompress.

2. Click **Properties** to display the **Properties** dialog box.

3. On the **General** tab, click **Advanced**.

4. In the **Advanced Attributes** dialog box, select or clear the **Compress contents to save disk space** check box, and then click **OK**.

5. In the **Properties** dialog box, click **OK**.

6. If the compression state was altered for a folder, in the **Confirm Attribute Changes** dialog box, select whether to make the compression apply only to the selected folder or to all files and subfolders. Click **OK** when done.

Note Windows 2000 allows closed page files to be compressed. However, when you restart Windows 2000, the page files automatically revert to an uncompressed state. For information about page files, see the topics on virtual memory in Windows 2000 Professional Help.

You can set Windows Explorer to display alternate colors for compressed files and folders by using the following procedure:

▶ **To display alternate colors for compressed files and folders**

1. In **Windows Explorer**, click the **Tools** menu.

2. On the **Tools** menu, click **Folder Options**.

3. On the **View** tab, select the **Display compressed files and folders with alternate color** check box.

4. Click **OK** to return to **Windows Explorer**.

Using Compact

Compact is the command-line version of the compression functionality in Windows Explorer. The **compact** command displays and alters the compression of folders and files on NTFS volumes. It also displays the compression state of folders.

There are two reasons why you might want to use Compact instead of Windows Explorer:

- You can use Compact in a batch script.
- If the system fails during compression or decompression, the file or folder is marked as Compressed or Uncompressed. If the operation did not complete, Compact forces the operation to complete in the background.

Note Unlike Windows Explorer, Compact automatically compresses or decompresses any files that are not already in the compression state that you set for the folder.

For more information about Compact, see "File System Tools" later in this chapter.

Effects of Compression on Moving and Copying Files

Moving and copying files and folders on disk volumes can change their compression state. The compression state of these files and folders, and the file system in which they were created, can impact the way they are affected while being moved or copied. The compression state of an NTFS file or folder is controlled by its compression attribute.

Note The default behavior for dragging and dropping files and folders in Windows Explorer depends on the relationship between the source and the target location. If the selected item is dragged to a folder on the same volume, the item is moved. If the selected item is dragged to a folder on a different volume, the item is copied. You can force a copy by holding down the CTRL key as you drop the item to its new location. Holding down the SHIFT key as you drop the item moves it. If you right-click and drag the selected item, a context popup menu appears that allows you to select whether to copy, move, or create a shortcut to the item, or cancel the task.

Moving Files or Folders on NTFS Volumes

When you move an uncompressed file or folder to another folder, the file remains uncompressed, regardless of the compression state of the folder to which it was moved. For example, if you move an uncompressed file to a compressed folder, the file remains uncompressed after the move, as shown in Figure 17.7.

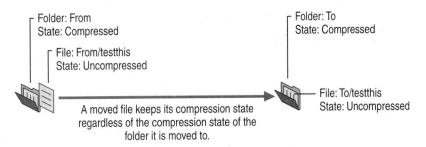

Figure 17.7   Moving an Uncompressed File to a Compressed Folder

When you move a compressed file or folder to another folder, the file remains compressed after the move, regardless of the compression state of the folder, as shown in Figure 17.8.

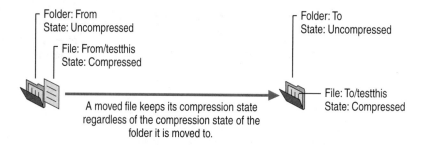

Figure 17.8   Moving a Compressed File to an Uncompressed Folder

Copying Files or Folders on NTFS Volumes

When you copy a file to a folder, the file takes on the compression attribute of the target folder. For example, if you copy a compressed file to an uncompressed folder, the file is uncompressed when it is copied to the folder, as shown in Figure 17.9.

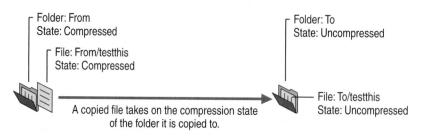

Figure 17.9   Copying a Compressed File to an Uncompressed Folder

When you copy a file to a folder that already contains a file of the same name, the copied file takes on the compression attribute of the target file, regardless of the compression state of the folder, as shown in Figure 17.10.

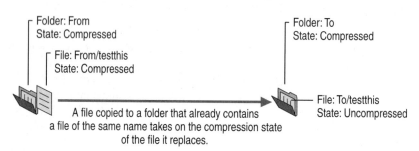

Figure 17.10   Copying a File to a Folder that Contains a File of the Same Name

Moving and Copying Files Between FAT16, FAT32, and NTFS Volumes

Like files copied between NTFS folders, files moved or copied from a FAT folder to an NTFS folder take on the compression attribute of the target folder. Because Windows 2000 supports compression only on NTFS volumes, compressed NTFS files moved or copied to a FAT volume are automatically decompressed. Similarly, compressed NTFS files copied or moved to a floppy disk are automatically decompressed.

Adding Files to an Almost Full NTFS Volume

Adding files to an NTFS volume that is almost full generates error messages indicating that there is not enough disk space to write the entire file if the file cannot be compressed, regardless of the compression in the file when it is opened. For this reason, it is possible to get a read error when you are trying to open a compressed file.

Because NTFS allocates space based on the uncompressed size of the files to be copied, if you copy files to a compressed NTFS folder that does not have enough room for the files in their uncompressed state, you receive a message indicating that there is not enough space on the disk. NTFS does not wait for the compression and writing of one file to complete before it works on subsequent files, and the system does not reclaim the unused space from compression until after the buffer is compressed.

When you run a program and save files to a compressed folder on a volume that is almost full, the success of the save depends on factors such as how much the file compresses and whether the beginning of the file compresses well.

If you cannot delete any files or do not have any files that you can compress, you can usually copy all of the files if you first copy the largest or those that compress best, such as BMP and document files. You can also copy them in smaller groups, rather than all at once.

NTFS Compression Algorithm

NTFS compression uses a 3-byte minimum search rather than the 2-byte minimum used by DoubleSpace. This search enables faster compressing and decompressing (roughly two times faster), while sacrificing only 2 percent compression for the average text file.

Each NTFS data stream contains information that indicates whether any part of the stream is compressed. Individual compressed buffers are identified by "holes" following them in the information stored for that stream. If there is a hole, NTFS automatically decompresses the preceding buffer to fill the hole.

NTFS provides real-time access to a compressed file, decompressing the file when it is opened and compressing it when it is closed. When writing a compressed file, the system reserves disk space for the uncompressed size. The system gets back unused space as each individual compression buffer is compressed.

Note Some programs do not allocate space before beginning a save operation and only display an error message when they run out of disk space.

Compression Performance

NTFS compression might cause performance degradation because a compressed NTFS file is decompressed, copied, and then recompressed as a new file, even when copied on the same computer. Similarly, on network transfers, the file is decompressed, which affects bandwidth as well as speed.

The current implementation of NTFS compression runs more efficiently on Windows 2000 Professional than on Windows 2000 Server.

The two ways to measure the performance of NTFS data compression are size and speed. You can tell how well compression works by comparing the uncompressed and compressed file and folder sizes. For more information about seeing the compressed size of folders, see "File System Tools" later in this chapter.

Other Compression Methods

Other compression tools are available to compress files on computers running Windows 2000. These tools differ from NTFS compression in the following ways:

- They usually run from either the command line or as a stand-alone application.
- Files cannot be opened when they are in a compressed state—the file must first be decompressed. When you close the file, it is saved in an uncompressed state, and you must use a program to compress it.

The *Windows 2000 Resource Kit* includes a tool called Compress, which can only be run from the command line. For more information about this and other programs, see "File System Tools" later in this chapter.

NTFS Recoverability

NTFS is a recoverable file system that guarantees the consistency of the volume by using standard transaction logging and recovery techniques. In the event of a disk corruption, NTFS runs a recovery procedure that accesses information stored in a transaction log file. The NTFS recovery procedure guarantees that the volume is restored to a consistent state. Transaction logging requires a very small amount of overhead.

NTFS ensures the integrity of all NTFS volumes by automatically performing disk recovery operations the first time a program accesses an NTFS volume after the computer is restarted following a failure.

NTFS also uses a technique called cluster remapping to minimize the effects of a bad sector on an NTFS volume.

Important If either the master boot record (MBR) or boot sector is corrupted, you might not be able to access data on the volume. For more information about recovery from errors with the MBR or the boot sector, see "Disks Concepts and Troubleshooting" in this book.

Recovering Data with NTFS

NTFS views each operation that modifies a file on a volume as a transaction, and manages each one as an integral unit. After it is started, the transaction is either completed or, in the event of a disk problem, rolled back (the NTFS volume is returned to its state before the transaction was initiated).

To ensure that a transaction can be completed or rolled back, NTFS records the suboperations of a transaction in a transaction log file before they are written to the disk. When a complete transaction is recorded in the log file, NTFS performs the suboperations of the transaction on the volume cache. After NTFS updates the cache, it commits the transaction by recording in the log file that the transaction is complete.

After a transaction is committed, NTFS ensures that the entire transaction appears on the volume, even if the disk becomes corrupted. During recovery operations, NTFS redoes each committed transaction found in the log file. Then NTFS locates in the log file the transactions that were not committed at the time of the system failure and undoes each transaction suboperation recorded in the log file. Incomplete modifications to the volume are prohibited.

Important NTFS uses transaction logging and recovery to guarantee that the volume structure is not corrupted. For this reason, all system files remain accessible after a system failure. However, user data can be lost because of a system failure or a bad sector.

Caching and Data Recovery

The cache is the area of random access memory (RAM) that contains the most recently used data. When you write data to disk, the lazy-write technique in Windows 2000 indicates that the data is written when it is still in the cache. There can also be cache memory on the disk controller, as with small computer system interface (SCSI) controllers, or on the disk unit, as with EIDE disks. The following information can help you decide whether to enable the disk or controller cache:

- Write caching improves disk performance, particularly if large amounts of data are being written to the disk.

- Control of the write-back cache is a firmware function provided by the disk manufacturer. See the documentation supplied with the disk or disk controller. You cannot configure the write-back cache from Windows 2000.

- Write caching does not impact the reliability of the file system's own metadata. NTFS instructs the disk device driver to ensure that metadata is written regardless of whether write caching is enabled. Non-metadata is written to the disk normally and can be cached.

- Read caching in the disk has no impact on file system reliability.

Cluster Remapping

In the event of a bad-sector error, NTFS automatically implements a recovery technique called cluster remapping. When Windows 2000 detects a bad-sector, NTFS dynamically remaps the cluster containing the bad sector and allocates a new cluster for the data. If the error occurred during a read, NTFS returns a read error to the calling program, and the data is lost. If the error occurs during a write, NTFS writes the data to the new cluster, and no data is lost.

NTFS puts the address of the cluster containing the bad sector in the bad cluster file so the bad sector is not reused.

Important Cluster remapping is *not* a backup alternative. Once errors are detected, the disk must be monitored closely and replaced if the detect list grows. This type of error is displayed in the System Log of Event Viewer.

FAT uses a form of cluster remapping, but only when the volume is initially formatted. If a bad sector occurs on a FAT volume after it is formatted, data stored within the associated cluster can be permanently lost. NTFS handles cluster remapping dynamically and continuously, ensuring the integrity of your data.

Converting to Windows 2000 File Systems

The on-disk format for NTFS has been enhanced in Windows 2000 to enable new functionality. The upgrade to the new version of NTFS occurs when Windows 2000 mounts an existing, locally installed NTFS volume. The upgrade is automatic and the conversion time is independent of volume size. FAT16 and FAT32 volumes can be converted to NTFS format at any time by using the Convert.exe tool.

Important The location of the MFT is different on volumes that have been converted from previous version of NTFS, so volume performance might not be as good on volumes converted from Windows NT.

You can also upgrade FAT16 and FAT32 volumes to NTFS by using the Convert tool. The conversion of a disk volume from FAT to NTFS requires a sufficient amount of available free disk space to build the NTFS disk structures. For more information about the Convert tool, see "Convert: Converts a Volume from FAT to NTFS" later in this chapter. For additional information about using Convert to convert a volume to NTFS, see the Knowledge Base link on the Web Resource page at http://windows.microsoft.com/windows2000/reskit/webresources. Search using the keywords "Convert," "NTFS," and "winnt."

Conversion Issues for NTFS and FAT Volumes

FAT and NTFS use very different on-disk structures to represent the allocation of space for files. These structures are often referred to as metadata or file system overhead. Another kind of overhead associated with FAT and NTFS is related to the fact that both file systems allocate disk space in clusters of a fixed size. The exact size of these clusters is determined at format time, and are dependent on the size of the volume. See Table 17.2 for the default cluster sizes of each file system per volume size range.

Like FAT, NTFS has a certain amount of fixed-size overhead and a certain amount of per-file overhead. To support the advanced features of NTFS, such as recoverability, security, and support for very large volumes, the NTFS metadata overhead is somewhat larger than the FAT metadata overhead. However, because NTFS clusters are smaller than FAT clusters for the same size volume, you can store more data on an NTFS volume as on a FAT volume of identical size, even without using NTFS file compression.

Convert builds the NTFS metadata by using space that FAT considers free space. Thus, if the conversion fails, the FAT representation of the user files is still valid.

NTFS Compatibility Issues

Your ability to access your NTFS volumes when you use a multiple-boot process to start up Windows NT and Windows 2000 depends on which version of Windows NT you are using. Redirected clients using NTFS volumes on file and print servers are not affected. If you are running Windows NT 4.0 Service Pack 4 or later, you can read basic volumes formatted with the new version of NTFS.

When a Windows 2000 volume is mounted on a computer running Windows NT 4.0 Service Pack 4 or later, most of the new NTFS features are not available. However, most read and write operations are permitted if they do not make use of any new NTFS features. Features affected by this configuration include the following:

- **Reparse points.** Windows NT cannot perform any operations that makes use of reparse points.

- **Disk quotas.** When running Windows NT on a multiple-boot computer that also runs Windows 2000, disk quotas implemented by Windows 2000 are ignored, allowing you to consume more disk space than is allowed by your quota.

- **Encryption.** Windows NT cannot perform any operations on files encrypted by Windows 2000.

- **Sparse files.** Windows NT cannot perform any operations on sparse files.

- **Change journal.** Windows NT ignores the change journal. No entries are logged when files are accessed.

You can only access files on NTFS volumes from Windows NT or Windows 2000. If other operating systems are installed, you must use another file system for the system and boot volumes.

Important Because NTFS data structures are not the same for Windows NT 4.0 and Windows 2000, Windows NT 4.0 disk tools such as Chkdsk and Autochk do not work on NTFS volumes formatted or upgraded by Windows 2000. These tools check the version stamp of NTFS. After installing Windows 2000, users must run the updated version of these disk tools on their NTFS volumes.

Because of these compatibility issues, using a multiple-boot process between Windows NT 4.0 and Windows 2000 is not recommended. The Windows NT 4.0 Service Pack 4 or later NTFS driver is provided only to assist in evaluating and migrating to Windows 2000.

Cleanup Operations on Windows NT Volumes

Because files on volumes formatted with the version of NTFS included with Windows 2000 can be read and written to by Windows NT 4.0 Service Pack 4 or later, Windows 2000 might need to perform cleanup operations to ensure the consistency of the data structures of a volume after it was mounted on a computer that is running Windows NT. Features affected by cleanup operations are as follows.

Disk quotas If disk quotas are turned off, Windows 2000 performs no cleanup operations. If disk quotas are turned on, Windows 2000 automatically cleans up the quota information by rebuilding the index.

If a user exceeds the disk quota while the NTFS volume is mounted by a Windows NT 4.0 Service Pack 4 or later system, and disk quotas are strictly enforced, all further disk allocations of data by that user using Windows 2000 fail. The user can still read and write data to any existing file, but cannot increase the size of a file; the user can delete and shrink files. When the user is below the assigned disk quota, disk allocations of data can resume. The same behavior occurs when a system is upgraded from Windows NT to Windows 2000 with quotas enforced.

Reparse points Because files that have reparse points cannot be accessed by computers that are running Windows NT 4.0 or earlier, no cleanup operations are necessary.

Encryption Because encrypted files cannot be accessed by computers that are running Windows NT 4.0 or earlier, no cleanup operations are necessary.

Sparse files Because sparse files cannot be accessed by computers that are running Windows NT 4.0 or earlier, no cleanup operations are necessary.

Object identifiers Windows 2000 maintains two references to the object identifier; one on the file; and one in the volume-wide object identifier index. If you delete a file that has an object identifier, Windows 2000 must scan and clean up the entry in the index.

Change journal Computers that are running Windows NT 4.0 or earlier do not log file changes in the change journal. When Windows 2000 starts, the change journals on volumes accessed by Windows NT are reset to indicate that the journal history is incomplete. Applications that use the change journal must be able to accept incomplete journals.

Master File Table and Metadata

When a volume is formatted with NTFS, an MFT file and other pieces of metadata are created. In NTFS, metadata are the files used to implement the file system structure. NTFS reserves the first 16 records of the MFT for metadata files (approximately 1 MB).

Note The data segment locations for both the MFT and the backup MFT, $Mft and $MftMirr respectively, are recorded in the boot sector. If the first MFT record is corrupted, NTFS reads the second record to find the MFT mirror file. A duplicate of the NTFS boot sector is located at the end of the volume.

For more information about the NTFS boot sector, see "Disk Concepts and Troubleshooting" in this book.

Table 17.7 describes the metadata stored in the MFT.

Table 17.7   Metadata Stored in the Master File Table

System File	File Name	MFT Record	Purpose of the File
Master file table	$Mft	0	Contains one base file record for each file and folder on an NTFS volume. If the allocation information for a file or folder is too large to fit within a single record, other file records are allocated as well.
Master file table 2	$MftMirr	1	A duplicate image of the first four records of the MFT. This file guarantees access to the MFT in case of a single-sector failure.
Log file	$LogFile	2	Contains a list of transaction steps used for NTFS recoverability. Log file size depends on the volume size and can be as large as 4 MB. It is used by Windows 2000 to restore consistency to NTFS after a system failure. For more information about the log file, see "NTFS Recoverability" earlier in this chapter.
Volume	$Volume	3	Contains information about the volume, such as the volume label and the volume version.
Attribute definitions	$AttrDef	4	A table of attribute names, numbers, and descriptions.
Root file name index	$	5	The root folder.

(continued)

Table 17.7   **Metadata Stored in the Master File Table** *(continued)*

System File	File Name	MFT Record	Purpose of the File
Cluster bitmap	$Bitmap	6	A representation of the volume showing which clusters are in use.
Boot sector	$Boot	7	Includes the BPB used to mount the volume and additional bootstrap loader code used if the volume is bootable.
Bad cluster file	$BadClus	8	Contains bad clusters for the volume.
Security file	$Secure	9	Contains unique security descriptors for all files within a volume.
Upcase table	$Upcase	10	Converts lowercase characters to matching Unicode uppercase characters.
NTFS extension file	$Extend	11	Used for various optional extensions such as quotas, reparse point data, and object identifiers.
		12–15	Reserved for future use.

The remaining records of the MFT contain the file and folder records for each file and folder on the volume.

NTFS creates a file record for each file and a folder record for each folder created on an NTFS volume. The MFT includes a separate file record for the MFT itself. These file and folder records are stored on the MFT. NTFS allocates space for each MFT record based on the cluster size of the file. The attributes of the file are written to the allocated space in the MFT. Besides file attributes, each file record contains information about the position of the file record in the MFT.

Each file usually uses one file record. However, if a file has a large number of attributes or becomes highly fragmented, it might need more than one file record. If this is the case, the first record for the file, the base file record, stores the location of the other file records required by the file. Small files and folders (typically 1,500 bytes or smaller) are entirely contained within the file's MFT record. Figure 17.11 shows the contents of an MFT record for a small file or folder.

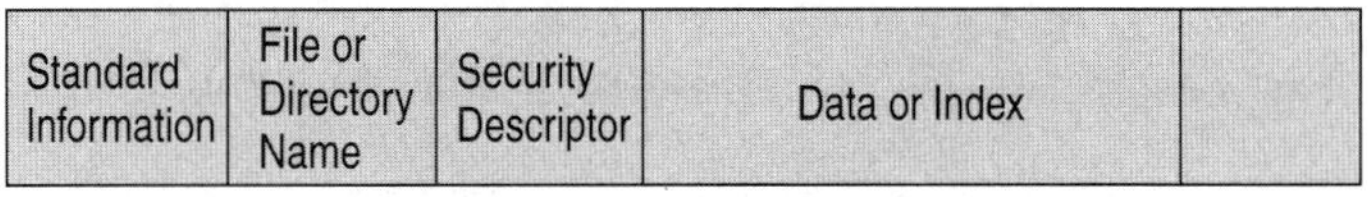

Figure 17.11   MFT Record for a Small File or Folder

Folder records contain index information. Small folder records reside entirely within the MFT structure, while large folders are organized into B-tree structures and have records with pointers to external clusters that contain folder entries that cannot be contained within the MFT structure.

NTFS File Attributes

Every allocated sector on an NTFS volume belongs to a file. Even the file system metadata is part of a file. NTFS views each file (or folder) as a set of file attributes. Elements such as the file name, its security information, and even its data, are all file attributes. Each attribute is identified by an attribute type code and, optionally, an attribute name.

When a file's attributes can fit within the MFT file record for that file, they are called resident attributes. Information such as file name and timestamp are always resident attributes. When the information for a file is too large to fit in its MFT file record, some of the file attributes are nonresident. Nonresident attributes are allocated one or more clusters of disk space and are stored as an alternate data stream in the volume. NTFS creates the Attribute List attribute to describe the location of all of the attribute records.

Table 17.8 lists the file attributes currently defined by NTFS.

Table 17.8   NTFS File Attribute Types

Attribute Type	Description
Standard Information	Includes information such as timestamp and link count.
Attribute List	Lists the location of all attribute records that do not fit in the MFT record.
File Name	A repeatable attribute for both long and short file names. The long name of the file can be up to 255 Unicode characters. The short name is the 8.3, case-insensitive name for the file. Additional names, or hard links, required by POSIX can be included as additional file name attributes.
Security Descriptor	Describes who owns the file and who can access it.
Data	Contains file data. NTFS allows multiple data attributes per file. Each file typically has one unnamed data attribute. A file can also have one or more named data attributes, each using a particular syntax.
Object ID	A volume-unique file identifier. Used by the distributed link tracking service. Not all files have object identifiers.
Logged Tool Stream	Similar to a data stream, but operations are logged to the NTFS log file just like NTFS metadata changes. This is used by EFS.

(continued)

Table 17.8   NTFS File Attribute Types *(continued)*

Attribute Type	Description
Reparse Point	Used for volume mount points. They are also used by Installable File System (IFS) filter drivers to mark certain files as special to that driver.
Index Root	Used to implement folders and other indexes.
Index Allocation	Used to implement folders and other indexes.
Bitmap	Used to implement folders and other indexes.
Volume Information	Used only in the $Volume system file. Contains the volume version.
Volume Name	Used only in the $Volume system file. Contains the volume label.

MS-DOS-Readable File Names on NTFS Volumes

By default, Windows 2000 generates MS-DOS-readable file names on all NTFS volumes for use by 16-bit programs that run under Windows 2000. To improve performance on volumes with many long, similar names, you can change the default value of the **NtfsDisable8dot3NameCreation** registry entry (in HKEY_LOCAL_MACHINE\System\CurrentControlSet\Control\FileSystem) to **1**.

> **Warning** Do not use a registry editor to edit the registry unless you have no alternative. The registry editors bypass the standard safeguards provided by administrative tools. These safeguards prevent you from entering conflicting settings or settings that are likely to degrade performance or damage your system. Editing the registry directly can have serious, unexpected consequences that can prevent the system from starting and require that you reinstall Windows 2000. To configure or customize Windows 2000, use the programs in Control Panel or Microsoft Management Console (MMC) whenever possible.

Windows 2000 does not generate short (8.3) file names for files created by POSIX-based applications on an NTFS volume, regardless of the value of the **NtfsDisable8dot3NameCreation** registry entry. This means that MS-DOS-based and 16-bit Windows-based applications cannot view these file names if they are not valid 8.3 file names. Use standard MS-DOS 8.3 naming conventions if you want to use files that are created by a POSIX application with MS-DOS-based or Windows-based applications.

NTFS Maintenance

It is recommended that the Disk Defragmenter tool be a part of a frequent and regular maintenance program to maintain the optimum performance of NTFS volumes. Unlike FAT volumes, which can be fully defragmented on an infrequent basis, NTFS volumes derive only limited benefit from occasional file defragmentation. Only with regular use of this tool does NTFS gain the full benefit of file defragmentation. For more information about the Disk Defragmenter tool, see "Troubleshooting Tools and Strategies" in this book.

Compact Disc File System

Windows 2000 provides support for the ISO 9660–compliant compact disc file system (CDFS), which supports LFNs as listed in the ISO 9660 Level 2 standards.

When creating a CD-ROM to be used on Windows 2000, you must adhere to the following standards:

- All folder and file names must have fewer than 32 characters.
- All folder and file names must be in capital letters.
- The folder tree cannot exceed eight levels from the root.
- File name extensions are not mandatory.

Universal Disk Format

The Universal Disk Format (UDF) is new for Windows 2000. UDF is a file system defined by the Optical Storage Technology Association (OSTA). UDF is compliant with the ISO 13346 standard and is the successor to the CD-ROM file system (CDFS or ISO 9660).

UDF is targeted for removable disk media like DVD, CD, and Magneto-Optical (MO) discs. Since UDF is based on open standards, it is intended to facilitate data interchange between operating systems, and between consumer devices. The standard supports a number of advanced features, including:

- Long and Unicode file names.
- Sparse files.
- Support for a wide range of media types including digital video disc (DVD), write once, read many (WORM) disk, and compact disc-recordable (CD-R).

Note   Windows 2000 reads both UDF versions 1.02 and 1.50. Windows 2000 does not support writing to UDF volumes.

Using Long File Names

File names on the Windows 2000 platform can be up to 255 characters, and can contain spaces, multiple periods, and special characters that are forbidden in MS-DOS file names. Windows 2000 makes it possible for other operating systems to access files with long names by automatically generating an MS-DOS-readable (8.3) name for each file. Files are accessible over a network by computers using MS-DOS and Windows 3.*x*, as well as by computers using Windows 95, Windows 98, Windows NT, and Windows 2000 operating systems.

By creating 8.3 file names, Windows 2000 also enables MS-DOS-based and Windows 3.*x*–based applications to recognize and load files that have LFNs. In addition, when an application saves a file on a computer running Windows 2000, both the 8.3 file name and LFN are retained.

If the long name of a file or folder contains spaces, surround the name with quotation marks. For example, if you have a program called Dump Disk Files that you want to run from the command line and you enter the name without quotation marks, it generates the error message "Cannot find the program Dump or one of its components."

You must also use quotation marks around each set of LFNs referenced when a path typed at the command line includes spaces, as in the following example:

move "c:\This month's reports*.*" "c:\Last month's reports"

Use wildcard characters such as the asterisk (*) and question mark (**?**) carefully in conjunction with the **del** and **copy** commands. Windows 2000 searches both long and short file names for matches to the wildcard character combination you specify, which can cause additional files to be deleted or copied. It is always a good idea to run the **dir** command first on the files specified to be sure you are only affecting the files you intend to use.

In Windows 2000, both FAT and NTFS use the Unicode character set for their names, which contain several forbidden characters that MS-DOS cannot read. To generate a short MS-DOS-readable file name, Windows 2000 deletes all of these characters from the LFN and removes any spaces. Because an MS-DOS-readable file name can have only one period, Windows 2000 also removes all extra periods from the file name. Next, Windows 2000 truncates the file name, if necessary, to six characters and appends a tilde (~) and a number. For example, each non-duplicate file name is appended with **~1**. Duplicate file names end with **~2**, then **~3**, and so on. After the file names are truncated, the file name extensions are truncated to three or fewer characters. Finally, when displaying file names at the command line, Windows 2000 translates all characters in the file name and extension to uppercase.

Note You can permit extended characters by setting the value of HKEY_LOCAL_MACHINE\SYSTEM\CurrentControlSet\Control\FileSystem \NtfsAllowExtendedCharacterIn8dot3Name to 1.

Warning Do not use a registry editor to edit the registry directly unless you have no alternative. The registry editors bypass the standard safeguards provided by administrative tools. These safeguards prevent you from entering conflicting settings or settings that are likely to degrade performance or damage your system. Editing the registry directly can have serious, unexpected consequences that can prevent the system from starting and require that you reinstall Windows 2000. To configure or customize Windows 2000, use the programs in Control Panel or Microsoft Management Console (MMC) whenever possible.

When there are five or more files that can result in duplicate short file names, Windows 2000 uses a slightly different method for creating short file names. For the fifth and subsequent files, Windows 2000:

- Uses only the first two letters of the LFN.
- Generates the next four letters of the short file name by mathematically manipulating the remaining letters of the LFN.
- Appends **~1** (or another number, if necessary, to avoid a duplicate file name) to the result.

This method substantially improves performance when Windows 2000 must create short file names for a large number of files with similar LFNs. Windows 2000 uses this method to create short names for files on both FAT and NTFS volumes.

Table 17.9 shows the short file names for files that were created by six tests.

Table 17.9   Short File Names Created by Windows 2000 – Example One

Long File Name	Short File Name
This is test 1.txt	THISIS~1.TXT
This is test 2.txt	THISIS~2.TXT
This is test 3.txt	THISIS~3.TXT
This is test 4.txt	THISIS~4.TXT
This is test 5.txt	TH0FF9~1.TXT
This is test 6.txt	THFEF5~1.TXT

If the LFNs in Table 17.9 are created in a different order, their short file names are different, as shown in Table 17.10.

Table 17.10   Short File Names Created by Windows 2000 – Example Two

Long File Name	Short File Name
This is test 2.txt	THISIS~1.TXT
This is test 3.txt	THISIS~2.TXT
This is test 1.txt	THISIS~3.TXT
This is test 4.txt	THISIS~4.TXT
This is test 5.txt	TH0FF9~1.TXT
This is test 6.txt	THFEF5~1.TXT

To see both the long and short file names for each file in the folder, at the command line, type:

dir /x

File System Tools

The tools described in this section are available from either the Windows 2000 operating system CD or the *Windows 2000 Resource Kit* companion CD. Table 17.11 shows where on your computer to find the tools.

Table 17.11   Location of File System Tools

Tool	Default Installed Location of Program
Cacls.exe	%SystemRoot%\System32
Cipher.exe	%SystemRoot%\System32
Compact.exe	%SystemRoot%\System32
Compress.exe	C:\Program Files\Resource Kit
Convert.exe	%SystemRoot%\System32
Diruse.exe	C:\Program Files\Resource Kit
Efsinfo.exe	C:\Program Files\Resource Kit
Expand.exe	%SystemRoot%\System32
Mountvol.exe	%SystemRoot%\System32

Cacls: Displays and Modifies NTFS Access Control Lists

You can use Cacls to display or modify access control lists (ACLs) of files or folders. The syntax of Cacls is:

```
cacls filename|folder [/t] [/e] [/c] [/g user:right] [/r user [...]]
    [/p user:right [...]] [/d user [...]]
```

Table 17.12 follows the command syntax and describes the command switches.

Table 17.12   Cacls Switches

Switch	Description
filename or *folder*	Displays ACLs.
/t	Changes ACLs of specified files in the current folder and all subfolders.
/e	Edits ACL instead of replacing it.
/c	Continues on access-denied errors.
/g *user:right*	Grants a specified user account access rights, such as: R (Read) C (Change [write]) F (Full Control)
/r *user*	Revokes a specified user account's access rights (only valid with **/e**).
/p *user:right*	Replaces a specified user account's access rights, such as: N (None) R (Read) C (Change [write]) F (Full Control)

(continued)

Table 17.12   Cacls Switches *(continued)*

Switch	Description
/d *user*	Denies access to a specified user account.
/?	Displays user help.

Wildcard characters can be used to specify more than one file in a command. You can also specify more than one user in a command, separating the user account listings with spaces.

If you already have permissions set for multiple users on a folder or file and do not use the **/e** switch, all existing user permissions are removed and replaced by the user and permissions specified at the command line. Use the following syntax when modifying user permissions to include read, change, and full control:

```
cacls filename|folder /e /r user
cacls filename|folder /e /g user:right
cacls filename|folder /e /p user:right
```

The Cacls tool does not provide a **/y** switch that answers automatically with **Y** to the **Are you sure? Y/N** prompt. However, you can use the **echo** command to pipe the character **Y** as input to the prompt when you are running Cacls in a batch file. Use the following syntax to automatically answer **Y**:

```
echo y|cacls filename|folder /e /g user:right
```

Important   Do not enter a space between the **Y** and the pipe symbol (|), or Cacls cannot make the permissions change.

Cipher: Displays or Alters Encryption of Files or Folders

Cipher is a command-line tool that is used to manage or display the Encrypting File System feature of NTFS. You can use it to encrypt or decrypt files and folders, and you can set switches to ignore errors and to force encryption on objects that might already be encrypted. You can also create a new encryption key. Cipher is especially useful when manipulating encryption attributes by using batch files.

The syntax of Cipher is:

```
cipher [/e|/d] [/s:folder] [/a] [/i] [/f] [/q] [/h] [/k] [pathname
[...]]
```

Table 17.13 describes the switches available with Cipher.

Table 17.13 Cipher Switches

Switch	Description
/e	Encrypts the specified folders. Folders are marked so that files added afterward are encrypted.
/d	Decrypts the specified folders. Folders are marked so that files added afterward are not encrypted.
/s:*folder*	Performs the specified operation on folders in the specified folder and all subfolders.
/a	Specifies that the operation is for files as well as folders. The encrypted file might become decrypted when it is modified if the parent folder is not encrypted. Make sure to encrypt the file and the parent folder.
/i	Continues performing the specified operation even after errors have occurred. By default, cipher stops when an error is encountered.
/f	Forces the encryption operation on all specified objects, even those that are already encrypted. Already-encrypted objects are skipped by default.
/q	Reports only the most essential information.
/h	Displays files with the hidden or system attributes. These files are omitted by default.
/k	Create a new file encryption key for the user running Cipher. If this switch is used, all the other switches are ignored.
pathname	Specifies a file or folder. Wildcards are acceptable.
/?	Displays user help.

Note Used without switches, Cipher displays the encryption state of the current folder and any files it contains. You can use multiple folder names and wildcards. Include spaces between multiple switches.

Compact: Compresses and Decompresses NTFS Files and Folders

Compact is the command-line version of the real-time NTFS compression functionality used in Windows Explorer. Compact displays and alters the compression of folders and files on NTFS volumes. It also displays the compression state of folders. The syntax of Compact is:

```
compact [/c|/u] [/s[:folder]] [/a] [/i] [/f] [/q] [filename [...]]
```

Table 17.14 describes the switches available with Compact.

Table 17.14   Compact Switches

Switch	Description
none	Displays the compression state of the current folder.
/c	Compresses the specified folder or file.
/u	Decompresses the specified folder or file.
/s[:*folder*]	Specifies that the requested action (compress or decompress) be applied to all subfolders of the specified folder, or to the current folder if none is specified.
/a	Displays files with the hidden or system attribute.
/i	Ignores errors.
/f	Forces a specified folder or file to compress or decompress.
/q	Reports only the most essential information.
filename	Specifies a file or folder. You can use multiple file names and wildcard characters.
/?	Displays user help.

The following are reasons to use this tool rather than the Windows Explorer equivalent:

- You can use Compact in a batch file. Using the **/i** switch enables you to skip files that cannot be opened when you are running in batch mode, such as files already in use by another program.

- If the system failed during compression or decompression when using Windows Explorer, the file or folder is marked as Compressed or Uncompressed, even if the operation did not complete. You can force the operation to complete by using Compact with the **/f** switch (with either the **/c** or **/u** switch).

Note Compact automatically compresses or decompresses all of the files and subfolders when you change the compression state of a folder. It does not ask whether you want to change the compression state of the files or subfolders in it.

For more information about real-time compression support in NTFS, see "Volume, Folder, and File Compression" earlier in this chapter.

When you attempt to compress a volume that is very low on free space, you might receive an error indicating that there was insufficient space to perform the action.

These errors indicate that the system needs additional free space to perform a compression. The system is not designed to manipulate the data in place on the disk. Additional space is needed to buffer the user data and to possibly hold additional file system metadata. The amount of additional free space required depends on the cluster size, file size, and available space.

Compress: Compresses Files or Folders

Compress is a command-line tool that can be used to create compressed copies of one or more files, similar to popular third-party file compression tools. If the destination listed on the command line does not include a new file name for the compressed file, the file's original name is used (a new name is required to save the compressed file in the same folder as the original).

You cannot work with a file that has been compressed by this tool until you have uncompressed it with the tool Expand. The compressed file appears to be corrupted if you attempt to use it. Typically, files compressed with this tool are named with the last letter of the file name extension replaced with an underscore character (_) to clearly identify the file as compressed. Many of the files on the Windows 2000 operating system CD are compressed and use this naming scheme to indicate to the user that they need to be uncompressed before they can be used. The syntax of Compress is:

```
compress [-r] [-d] [-z] source destination
```

Table 17.15 describes the switches available with Compress.

Table 17.15   Compress Switches

Switch	Description
–r	Renames compressed files.
–d	Updates compressed files only if out-of-date.

-z	Types of compression used:
	
	`-z - MS-ZIP compression`
	`-zx - LZX compression`
	`-zq[n] - Quantum compression and optional level,`
	`ranging from 1-7`
	                                    `(default is 4)`

source	Specifies the source file. The asterisk (*) and question mark (**?**) wildcard characters can be used.
destination	Specifies the destination file or path. The destination can be a folder. If *source* specifies multiple files and the **–r** switch is not specified, then *destination* must be a folder.
/?	Displays user help.

Note   Do not use Compress to compress files or folders on NTFS volumes. Instead, compress NTFS files and folders by using Compact or by setting or clearing the **Compressed** attribute in Windows Explorer.

Compress is a *Windows 2000 Resource Kit* tool. Install this tool from the *Windows 2000 Resource Kit* companion CD.

Convert: Converts a Volume from FAT to NTFS

Convert is a command-line tool that can be used to convert a volume formatted with FAT16 or FAT32 to NTFS. This tool performs the conversion within the existing volume without loss of data. You do not need to back up and restore the files when you use this program.

You cannot convert the Windows 2000 boot volume while you are running Windows 2000, so Convert allows you to convert the volume the next time you start Windows 2000. When you convert the volume this way, Windows 2000 restarts twice to complete the conversion process. The syntax of Convert is:

```
convert volume: /fs:ntfs [/v]
```

Table 17.16 describes the switches available with Convert.

Table 17.16   Convert Switches

Switch	Description
volume:	Specifies drive letter (followed by a colon), volume mount point, or volume name that you want to convert.
/fs:ntfs	Specifies that you want to convert to NTFS.
/v	Runs the tool in verbose mode.
/?	Displays user help.

Important   Volumes that are converted from FAT to NTFS (rather than being initially formatted with NTFS) lack some performance benefits. Fragmentation of the MFT might occur, and on boot volumes, NTFS permissions are not applied after the volume is converted.

DirUse: Scans a Folder and Reports On Disk Space Usage

DirUse is a command-line tool that can be used to determine the actual usage of space for compressed files and folders in NTFS volumes. The syntax of the command is:

```
diruse [/s | /v] [/m | /k | /b] [/c] [/,] [/l] [/*] [/q:#] [/a] [/d]
       [/o] [folders]
```

Table 17.17 describes the switches available with DirUse.

Table 17.17   DirUse Switches

Switch	Description
/s	Specifies whether subfolders are included in the output.
/v	Outputs progress reports while scanning subfolders. Ignored if /s is specified.
/m	Displays disk usage, in megabytes.
/k	Displays disk usage, in kilobytes.
/b	Displays disk usage, in bytes (default).
/c	Uses Compressed size instead of apparent size.
/,	Uses thousand separator when displaying sizes.
/l	Outputs overflow to log file Diruse.log.
/*	Uses the top-level folders residing in the specified *dirs*.
/q:#	Marks folders that exceed the specified size (#) with a "!". (If /m or /k is not specified, then bytes is assumed.)
/a	Specifies that an alert is generated when specified sizes are exceeded. (The Alerter service must be running.)
/d	Displays only folders that exceed specified sizes.
/o	Specifies that subfolders are not checked for specified size overflow.
folders	Specifies a list of the paths to check.
/?	Displays user help.

The important switch for compressed folders and files is /c, which causes DirUse to display the actual size of a compressed file or folder instead of apparent uncompressed size. For example, if your drive D is an NTFS volume, to get the disk space actually used (in megabytes) and the number of files in each of the folders, at the command prompt type:

diruse /s /m /c d:

To see compression information for an individual file, open Windows Explorer, right-click the file, and then click **Properties**.

For more information about DirUse, see the *Windows 2000 Resource Kit* Tools Help.

Note DirUse is a *Windows 2000 Resource Kit* tool. Install this tool from the *Windows 2000 Resource Kit* companion CD.

Efsinfo: Displays Information on Encrypted Files and Folders

Efsinfo is a command-line tool that can be used to display information about files and folders on NTFS volumes that are encrypted with Encrypting File System. Information about authorized users, recovery agents, and an enumeration of the encrypted files and folders on the local computer can be displayed. The syntax of the command is as follows:

```
efsinfo [/u] [/r] [/c] [/i] [/y] [/s:folder] [pathname [...]]
```

Table 17.18 describes the switches available with Efsinfo.

Table 17.18   Efsinfo Switches

Switch	Description
/u	Displays user information. This is the default.
/r	Displays recovery agent information.
/c	Displays certificate thumbnail information.
/i	Continues performing the specified operation even after errors have occurred. By default, Efsinfo stops when an error is encountered.
/y	Displays your current EFS certificate thumbnail on the local computer. The specified files might not be on this computer.
/s:_folder_	Performs the specified operation on folders in the specified folder and all subfolders.
pathname	Specifies a file or folder. Wildcards are acceptable.
/?	Displays user help.

Note Efsinfo is a *Windows 2000 Resource Kit* tool. Install this tool from the *Windows 2000 Resource Kit* companion CD.

Expand: Expands Compressed Files

Expand is a command-line tool that can be used to create uncompressed copies of compressed files from your *Windows 2000 Resource Kit* companion CD or any file compressed by the Compress tool.

The syntax of the command is:

```
expand [-r] source [destination]
```

Table 17.19 describes the switches available with Expand.

Table 17.19 **Expand Switches**

Switch	Description
–r	Renames expanded files.
source	Specifies the source file. The asterisk (*) and question mark (**?**) wildcard characters can be used.
destination	Specifies the destination file or path. The destination can be a folder. If *source* specifies multiple files and the **–r** switch is not specified, then *destination* must be a folder.
/?	Displays user help.

Mountvol: Displays, Creates, and Deletes Volume Mount Points

Mountvol is a command-line tool that can be used to create, list, or delete volume mount points in your system. The syntax of the command is:

```
mountvol [[drive:]path VolumeName|/d|/l]
```

Table 17.20 describes the switches available with Mountvol.

Table 17.20 **Mountvol Switches**

Switch	Description
[drive:]path	Specifies the existing NTFS folder where you want the mount point to reside.
VolumeName	Creates a new volume mount point. Specifies either a drive letter root folder or an existing empty NTFS folder as the source of the mount point and a volume name as the target.
/d	Removes the volume mount point from the specified folder.
/l	Lists the mounted volume name for the specified volume mount point.
/? or blank	Displays user help, the name, globally unique identifier (GUID), and location of the volume.

Important A volume can have only one drive letter. Using Mountvol to assign a drive letter fails if the volume already has a drive letter. To avoid this problem, delete the drive letter of the volume before assigning a drive letter using Mountvol.

C H A P T E R   1 8

Removable Storage and Backup

Managing data allows you to create storage hierarchies and provides ready access to information. Microsoft® Windows® 2000 Professional includes a feature called Removable Storage that can be used to manage the data that is stored in your system. Because backing up the data on your system is one of the most important aspects of data management, Windows 2000 Professional also includes Backup, a tool that uses Removable Storage technology to ensure that up-to-date copies of your data can be readily restored.

In This Chapter

Related Information in the Resource Kit

- For more information about the NTFS file system and the FAT file system, see "File Systems" in this book.

- For more information about disaster recovery, see "Troubleshooting Tools and Strategies" in this book.

Quick Guide to Removable Storage

Backing up and managing data are essential tasks in maintaining an efficient system, whether you are working on a stand-alone computer or you are working within a network. Use this guide to determine your storage management needs and to learn how to use the backup and storage management features that are included with Windows 2000 Professional.

Understand the basic concepts of data storage management in Windows 2000 Professional.

Removable Storage provides a single interface for managing the data that is stored in stand-alone drives and in storage libraries, and it allocates media to applications. Understand how this feature can help you manage your data and storage media.

- See "Overview of Removable Storage" in this chapter.

Use Removable Storage to manage your data.

Review the options provided by the Microsoft Management Console (MMC) Removable Storage snap-in, including those for installing new storage devices and applications and for preparing media. Understand this tool and how to use it to manage the Removable Storage service.

- See "Administering Removable Storage" in this chapter.

Troubleshoot problems in using Removable Storage.

Problems in using Removable Storage can be caused by either hardware or software. If Removable Storage cannot configure your devices or if operator requests are failing, review common troubleshooting procedures.

- See "Troubleshooting Removable Storage" in this chapter.

Back up your data to protect against disasters.

Regular backups are integral to planning a reliable configuration. Review the types of backup and media that you can use and their relative advantages and disadvantages. Also review the security considerations for backups.

- See "Overview of Backups" in this chapter.

Determine the most appropriate backup schedules and methods for your system.

The type of backup that you choose and the backup schedule that you implement depend on several factors, including whether you are working as part of a network or on a stand-alone computer and how often the data on your computer changes. Review some common backup scenarios, and determine which methods best fit your needs.

- See "Establishing a Backup Plan" in this chapter.

Back up important system data.

System State data includes protected system files and registry files. Review the methods and important considerations for backing up this type of data.

- See "Backing Up System State Data" in this chapter.

Use the Backup tool that is included with Windows 2000 Professional.

Backup allows you to schedule backup jobs on local and remote computers. Review the options for backing up data that this tool provides, and note some important differences between it and the backup tool that is included with Microsoft® Windows NT® 4.0.

- See "Using the Backup Tool" in this chapter.

Overview of Removable Storage

Removable Storage provides services to applications and system administrators that facilitate the use, sharing, and management of removable media devices, such as tape drives and robotic storage libraries. The availability of Removable Storage technology eliminates the need for independent software vendors (ISVs) to develop customized solutions and support for these devices on a per-device basis. More importantly, Removable Storage enables multiple applications to share expensive removable media storage devices. This allows the focus of storage applications to be directed to customer features rather than hardware issues.

As shown in Figure 18.1, Removable Storage provides a single set of application programming interfaces (APIs) that allow applications to catalog all removable media (except floppy disks and similar small-capacity media), such as disk, tape, and optical media, which are either stored on shelves (offline) or in libraries (online). Also, by disguising the complexities of underlying robotic library systems, Removable Storage both lowers the costs of developing and operating storage applications and provides consistency to customers who purchase these applications.

Before Removable Storage

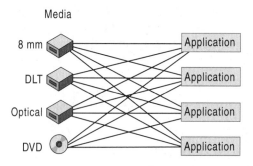

After Removable Storage

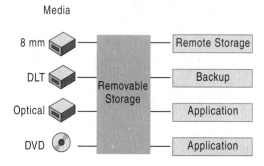

Figure 18.1   Removable Media with and Without Removable Storage

Removable Storage uses media pools to organize media. Media pools control access to media; group media by their use; allow media to be shared across applications; and allow such sharing to be tracked.

Basic Concepts

Removable Storage can be described in terms of five basic concepts: media, physical location, media pools, work queue items, and operator requests. The first item in this list, "media," is the most fundamental and affects all others. The remaining four items in the list are the top-level nodes in Removable Storage.

Media

Units of media store information. Each unit of media (or "medium," also referred to as a "cartridge") is of a certain type, such as 8mm tape, magnetic disk, optical disk, or CD-ROM.

Most types of cartridges have a single side, but some, such as magneto-optic (MO) disks, have two sides. Cartridges and the sides they contain are tracked in Removable Storage and can take on various states as they are entered into a library and used. For more information about cartridges and side states, see "Media Handling and Usage" later in this chapter.

Physical Location

Removable Storage manages two classes of physical locations: libraries and offline media physical locations. Libraries include both cartridges and the means to read and write them. The offline media physical location is a special holder for cartridges that are cataloged by Removable Storage but do not reside in a library.

Libraries

In its simplest form, a *library* consists of data storage cartridges and a means of reading and writing to the cartridges. A CD-ROM drive is a simple library with one drive, no slots, an insert/eject (IE) port, and no transport. A more complex example of a library is a robotic-based tape library, which can hold up to several thousand tapes, have one or more tape drives, and have a mechanical means of moving tapes into and out of the drives.

Specifically, libraries consist of the following:

Slots   *Slots* are storage locations in the library. For example, a tape library has one slot for each tape that the library can hold. A stand-alone drive library has no slots. However, most libraries have at least four slots. Sometimes slots are organized into collections of slots called *magazines*. Magazines are usually removable.

Drives   A *drive* is a device that can read or write to a cartridge. A tape drive, for example, can read and write to a tape that is inserted into it. All libraries have at least one drive.

Transports   A *transport* is the robotic device that moves a cartridge from its slot to a drive and back again. Robotic libraries usually have only one transport.

Bar Code Readers   A cartridge can have a bar code label attached, which is a label that can be read by both humans and computers. Libraries that hold cartridges with bar codes attached might have a bar code reader. The single reader is usually mounted on the transport.

Doors A *door* is a means for gaining unconstrained access to cartridges in a library. For larger libraries, a door might resemble an actual door. Some libraries have no doors, while others have several.

Insert/Eject Ports In contrast to doors, which allow unconstrained access to the cartridges in a library, IE ports, also called "mailslots," control access. When an administrator adds cartridges to a library through an IE port, the cartridges are placed in the IE port and then the library uses the transport to move the cartridges from the IE port to a slot. Some libraries have no IE ports; others have several. Some IE ports handle only one cartridge at a time; others can handle several at one time.

Types of Libraries

A robotic library can have any of the components described in the preceding list. The minimum that a robotic library contains is cartridges, slots to hold the cartridges, one or more drives, a transport, and either a door or an IE port. Robotic libraries are sometimes referred to as *changers* or *jukeboxes*. No human intervention is required to place a cartridge in a library in one of its drives.

A stand-alone drive library, or *stand-alone drive*, is a special kind of library. A cartridge must be placed in a drive manually. The CD-ROM drive on most desktop computers is a stand-alone-drive library. Removable Storage treats stand-alone drives as libraries with one drive and an IE port. An application does not need to know whether a cartridge is mounted by a transport or a human.

Offline Media Physical Location

The offline media physical location is where Removable Storage lists the cartridges that are not in a library. The physical location of cartridges in an online library is the library in which it resides. Cartridges that are not in any of these libraries, such as archived backup tapes on a shelf, are offline media and reside in the offline media physical location. When a user or administrator moves an offline medium into a library, Removable Storage changes its physical location to be the library into which it was placed. When a cartridge is taken out of an online library, Removable Storage designates its locations as the offline media physical location.

Media Pools

A *media pool* is a logical collection of cartridges that share some common attributes. A media pool contains media of only one type, but media in the media pool can reside in more than one library. Each cartridge is in a media pool. Both sides of a two-sided cartridge are always in the same pool.

Each media pool can control access to the media that belong to it. Although these permissions do not control access to the data that is contained on the cartridges, they do control the how the cartridges are manipulated, including an application's ability to move a cartridge from the pool or to allocate a cartridge for its own use.

Media pools can be used hierarchically. A media pool can be used to hold other media pools, or it can be used to hold cartridges. An application that needs to group media of several types into one collection can create one application media pool for the whole collection and then additional media pools within the original pool—one for each media type. The *free pool*, for example, contains a media pool for each media type. There are two classes of media pools: system and application. System media pools are created by Removable Storage for its own use and include the free pools, import pools, and unrecognized pools. Application media pools are created by applications to group media. Grouping media is especially important if several applications share the libraries that are attached to a system.

System Pools

The system pools are used to hold cartridges that are not currently in use. The free pool holds unused cartridges that are available to applications, and the unrecognized and import pools are temporary holding places for cartridges that have been newly placed in a library. For more information about how Removable Storage uses these pools, especially the unrecognized pools and import pools, see "Media Handling and Usage" later in this chapter.

Free Pools   The free pools support sharing cartridges among applications. They contain cartridges that are freely available to any application, and they hold no useful data. An application can draw cartridges from the free pools, and it can return cartridges to the free pools when the cartridges are no longer needed.

Unrecognized Pools   When a cartridge is placed in a library, Removable Storage tries to identify it. If it has not seen this particular cartridge before, has not identified the format of the cartridge, or has not identified the application that last wrote data to the cartridge, Removable Storage places the cartridge in the unrecognized pool for its media type. Blank cartridges are treated this way. Cartridges in the unrecognized pools might have data on them, but Removable Storage cannot read any data on these cartridges, and they are not cataloged.

Import Pools   If Removable Storage can identify the format or the application that is associated with a cartridge that has just been placed in a library but has not been seen before, it places the cartridge in the import pool. For example, if an administrator places a tape written by Backup on one system into a library that is attached to a second system, the instance of Removable Storage on the second system recognizes that the tape was written using Microsoft Tape Format (MTF) and places it in the proper media type import pool.

Application Pools

Each application that uses cartridges managed by Removable Storage uses one or more application pools. Applications can create these pools, or they can be created by using Removable Storage. Permissions for application pools can allow applications to share pools or to assign each application its own set of pools.

Work Queues

When applications make a library request, Removable Storage places the requests in a queue and processes them as resources become available. For example, a request to mount a tape in a library results in a mount work queue item, which might wait until a drive is available.

Table 18.1 describes the states that a work queue item can have while it is being handled by Removable Storage.

Table 18.1   Work Queue States

State	Description
Queued	A work item is queued from the time an application issues a request until the time Removable Storage examines the request.
In Process	A work item is in process when Removable Storage is actively working on completing it.
Waiting	If Removable Storage examines the request and finds that one or more of the resources that are needed to satisfy the request is busy (for example, the requested drive is being used by another application), the request enters the waiting state.
Completed	When Removable Storage completes the request, the work queue item for that request enters the completed state.
Failed	If Removable Storage is unable to complete the request, the work queue item for that request enters the failed state.

Operator Requests

Note "Operator" as used here, is synonymous with "administrator."

Sometimes, even with robotic libraries, manual assistance is needed to complete a request or perform maintenance or support. If an application requests that a cartridge in the offline media physical location be mounted, the cartridge has to be manually entered into an online library; this generates a request to the operator to enter the cartridge.

A Removable Storage *operator request* is a request for an administrator to perform a task. Operator requests can be issued by Removable Storage or by Removable Storage client applications, and they are displayed in the Removable Storage console. Removable Storage generates operator requests in the following situations:

- Cartridges must be moved online because an application has initiated a mount request for a cartridge that is offline.

- There are no available cartridges online. The administrator can supply either new cartridges or available offline cartridges to satisfy the request.

- A device failed and requires service.

- A drive needs to be cleaned, and there is no usable cleaner cartridge available.

Operator requests can be presented to an administrator through the Windows 2000 Messenger Service or through the system tray. An administrator can complete or refuse the request. The operator request states are described in Table 18.2.

Table 18.2   Operator Request States

State	Description
Submitted	The operator request is waiting for the operator to complete the requested operation.
Refused	An operator has indicated that the requested action is not going to be performed.
Completed	An administrator has indicated that the action was completed, or Removable Storage has detected that the action was completed.

Administrators can satisfy or cancel operator requests. After he or she satisfies an operator request, the administrator must acknowledge the request in the Removable Storage console. When an administrator cancels an operator request, Removable Storage notifies the application that generated the request. Removable Storage saves operator requests for less than one hour after they have been satisfied or canceled.

Removable Storage Service

Removable Storage can perform the following requests made by client applications:

- Mount and dismount cartridges
- Clean drives
- Add and remove cartridges
- Check the inventory of the library
- Enable and disable libraries, drives, or cartridges
- Provide access to media and library attributes

Removable Storage provides these services to client applications by means of an API that hides the details of the various drives and libraries. Removable Storage implements a generic changer model, which incorporates all essential aspects of libraries and drives. Removable Storage drivers map real drives and changers to this model.

Removable Storage can move cartridges within a robotic-based library. The cartridge-moving hardware (usually referred to as a "transport") on robotic libraries varies widely. Some robotic libraries have hands that grab cartridges and move them from a home storage location (usually referred to as a "slot") to a drive. Other types of robotic libraries move magazines that contain cartridges and then push individual cartridges into drives. A mount request from a Removable Storage application mounts cartridges of either description. Figure 18.2 shows the Removable Storage components.

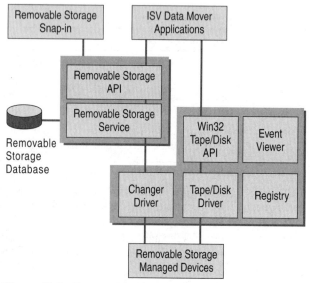

Figure 18.2   Removable Storage Components

Media Handling and Usage

The primary function of Removable Storage is to move cartridges within and between libraries and control access to those cartridges. While Removable Storage is handling the cartridges, they have states associated with them that determine which operations are permitted and which are prevented. While a cartridge is available, for example, any application can claim the cartridge for its own use; however, a cartridge that is in use by one application cannot be claimed by another application.

There are two sets of media-related states that govern most of the handling and usage by Removable Storage and its applications: media states and side states.

Media Naming

When new cartridges are placed in a library, Removable Storage assigns an initial display name to the cartridge. This name is derived from several sources, including the on-cartridge label and the bar code. The rules include the following:

- If the cartridge has a bar code label, its alphanumeric value is used as the display name.

- If the cartridge is single-sided and has a recognized label type, the name is taken from the label. If the format is Microsoft Tape Format (MTF), the label is taken from the MTF header. If the format is a file system, the name is taken from the volume name.

- The sequence number is used.

Media States

The states associated with cartridges reflect the fact that the operations performed on them mostly involve movement. Table 18.3 describes the Removable Storage media states.

Table 18.3   Media States in Removable Storage

Physical Media State	Description
Idle	The cartridge is in a slot in a library or on a shelf in the offline physical location.
In Use	Removable Storage is in the process of moving the cartridge.
Mounted	The cartridge is in a drive, but it might not be accessible yet.
Loaded	The cartridge is in a drive, and the contents of one of its sides are accessible.
Unloaded	The cartridge is still in a drive, but the contents of the side that was loaded are no longer accessible.

A side is accessible if an application can perform input/output (I/O) operations on it. This definition is important because inserting a tape into a drive does not necessarily make its contents accessible. For some tape drives, a portion of the tape must be pulled out of the cartridge and wrapped around the tape drive head, a process that is sometimes referred to as *loading*.

Side States

Because data is stored on a cartridge side, the states associated with the sides reflect usage rather than physical location. Table 18.4 lists and describes the Removable Storage side states.

Table 18.4   Side States in Removable Storage

Side State	Description
Allocated	A side that has been claimed for use by an application. The side is not available to any other application.
Available	A side that is available to be claimed and used by any application.
Completed	A side that is in use, but can no longer be used for write operations. The side is physically or logically full.
Decommissioned	A side that can no longer be used because it has crossed a usage threshold. It has reached its allocation maximum (specified by the administrator or an application) and cannot be used again.
Unrecognized	A side whose label types and label IDs are not recognized by Removable Storage.
Imported	A side whose label type is recognized by Removable Storage, but whose label ID is not recognized. It is a new side that Removable Storage has not seen before, but whose format is recognized by Removable Storage.
Inaccessible	An inaccessible side of a multisided cartridge that is in a drive.
Incompatible	A side that is not compatible with the pool in which its cartridge was identified. The cartridge that contains this side must be ejected immediately from the library.
Reserved	The second side of a two-sided cartridge. It is unavailable for allocation to all but the application which already has the first side allocated.
Unprepared	A side that is not claimed or used by any application but does not have a free label on it. This is a temporary state. Applications cannot allocate unprepared cartridges. See the following discussion about the interplay between media states and pools.

Free Media

Sides that are freely available for any application to use are in the available state in the free pool. Removable Storage writes a special label (called a "free label") on these cartridges to clearly identify that these cartridges hold no useful data. While Removable Storage is in the process of writing a free label, it marks the side as "unprepared." This is usually a transitory state, but it can persist if, for example, the cartridge with the side being labeled is in the offline physical media location. Such a side stays in this state until it is inserted into a library. Any transition into the available state causes a free label to be written and, therefore, passes through the unprepared state.

When an application needs to claim a side, it allocates an available side, which changes the state of the side from "available" or "imported" to "allocated." An application allocates a cartridge that is in the imported state when it needs data that is on the new side. When the application no longer needs any of the data on the side, it deallocates the side, which returns the state of the side to available.

When a cartridge is full—either the side can hold no more data, or the application can write no more data — an application can mark the cartridge as complete.

Removable Storage keeps track of the number of times that a side is allocated. When this count crosses a certain threshold, the side is decommissioned. This count is checked each time a side is deallocated. To set the threshold for the number of times that a side can be allocated, right-click the media pool that contains the cartridge, and select **Properties**.

Because the sides of a two-sided cartridge are allocated separately, it is possible for an application to try to allocate both sides or to have the second side claimed by a different application. This can be problematic, especially when cartridges are moved between systems. To eliminate this problem, Removable Storage places the second side of a two-sided cartridge in the reserved state when an application allocates the first side of the cartridge. Only the application that allocated the first side can allocate the reserved second side. If the application determines that it does not need the second side, it can change the state of the second side back to available.

When an application deallocates one side of a cartridge that contains reserved sides, Removable Storage changes the state of all reserved partitions to available.

Administering Removable Storage

Systems with a few stand-alone drives and a single Removable Storage-aware application usually require no Removable Storage administration. Systems with more complex configurations, such as those with tape or optical disk libraries or with multiple Removable Storage-aware applications, do require administration, however. There are also rare cases in which a Removable Storage-aware application requires some administration on a system with a simple configuration.

For information about drives and robotic libraries that are supported for use with Windows 2000, see the Hardware Compatibility List (HCL) link on the Web Resources page at http://windows.microsoft.com/windows2000/reskit/webresources. Each supported robotic library has its own configuration method and options. See the HCL for the proper configuration settings for all supported drives and robotic libraries.

Installing and Configuring Removable Storage-aware Applications

Removable Storage-aware applications usually can perform any Removable Storage configuration or setup that they need when they are installed. If such an application requires an application media pool, for example, the pool must be created and the permissions set at the time the application is installed.

Some applications use their own format or labeling scheme. For Removable Storage to correctly process on-media identifiers (OMIDs) on the sides that are written by these applications, it requires a special dynamic-link library (DLL) file that can read the label and determine the OMID. Such a DLL is called a media label library (MLL), and the client applications that use them must install them.

Preparing Media

Most applications draw available cartridges from the free pool. Placing cartridges in the free pool is also called "preparing" the media, and it must be done either by a Removable Storage-aware application or by an administrator. If your Removable Storage-aware applications do not prepare media automatically, you might have to use Removable Storage to do so manually. You can prepare media in the unrecognized pool, and if you are certain that the cartridges contain no useful data, you can prepare media in the import pool. You can also prepare available cartridges in application pools, but Removable Storage does not prepare allocated media.

To prepare a tape, in the Removable Storage console, right-click the media in the details pane, and then click **Prepare**.

Controlling the Service

Removable Storage is configured to start when you start your computer. Although you can change the service to be started manually, this is not recommended because starting the service manually creates problems with several applications that are included with Windows 2000, such as Backup. As with other Windows 2000 services, Removable Storage can be stopped, started, and restarted by means of the service control manager.

Device Configuration

Removable Storage relies on Plug and Play to tell it what devices are attached to a system, but it must match drives with robotic libraries. If Plug and Play indicates that a robotic library is attached to a system, Removable Storage reviews the list of drives that are also attached and detects which ones are inside the robotic library and which ones are stand-alone drive libraries. If the rules for autoconfiguration are followed, Removable Storage can do this mapping entirely on its own; if these rules cannot be followed, you must manually map drives to robotic libraries.

Auto-Configuration

Removable Storage auto-configures robotic libraries if the following are true:

- Robotic library hardware units support drive element address reporting with the small computer system interface (SCSI) command **ReadElementStatus**. Consult the manufacturer to find out whether your library hardware unit supports this feature.

- All drives inside a robotic library are on the same SCSI bus as the library.

Manual Configuration

Because not all library hardware units and system configurations support the auto-configuration feature, Removable Storage provides a method for manually configuring library hardware units. However, use this method only when it is necessary because Removable Storage cannot detect manually configured changes. In general, configure Removable Storage manually only when it detects a robotic library that it cannot configure. After you set it for manual configuration, a changer cannot be autoconfiguration even if its configuration is changed.

In most cases, Removable Storage starts autoconfiguration after you install, move, or remove hardware. This happens automatically when you restart after adding a device. For changers that cannot be auto-configured, Removable Storage adds incomplete registry entries and generates an operator request for manual configuration.

▶ **To manually configure Removable Storage**

You must complete all of the following steps to manually configure Removable Storage:

1. Stop Removable Storage.

2. Back up the Removable Storage database by copying the files in %SystemRoot%\System32\NtmsData to a secure temporary folder.

3. Restart Removable Storage. Removable Storage displays all drives that are not mapped to a changer as stand-alone drive libraries, including ones that are actually in the changer but are unmapped.

4. Empty all drives on your system.

5. Place a cartridge in a drive in the library that you are trying to configure, either by opening the library door or through a front panel and IE port. (See your changer's documentation for details about how to do this.) In the console, click **Refresh** for each stand-alone drive, and then find the drive that shows that it contains cartridges. On the **Device Info** property page, note the device name. Complete this step for each drive in the changer that you are trying to configure.

6. From the **Start** menu, click **Run**, and then type one of the following:

   regedt32.exe

   –Or–

   regedit.exe

7. Click **OK**.

Caution Do not use a registry editor to edit the registry directly unless you have no alternative. The registry editors bypass the standard safeguards provided by administrative tools. These safeguards prevent you from entering conflicting settings or settings that are likely to degrade performance or damage your system. Editing the registry directly can have serious, unexpected consequences that can prevent the system from starting and require that you reinstall Windows 2000. To configure or customize Windows 2000, use the programs in Control Panel or Microsoft Management Console (MMC) whenever possible.

---

8. In the Removable Storage configuration information in the registry subkey HKEY_LOCAL_MACHINE\System\CurrentControlSet\Services\NtmsSvc \Config, create a REG_DWORD entry called **AutoCfg** and set the value to **0**.

9. Stop Removable Storage.

10. The Config subkey contains a subkey for each changer (such as Changer0) and a subkey for each stand-alone drive. Each changer subkey contains an entry for each drive bay in the changer, such as **DriveBay0**.

11. For each drive bay entry that has the value "**???**", replace that value with the device name (without any initial "\" or "." characters—for example, "Tape3") of the drive in that bay.

12. Close the registry editor.

13. Restart Removable Storage. Removable Storage reads the new configuration information and initializes the devices. After Removable Storage is initialized, mount a cartridge in each drive in the library.

    If a configuration is incorrect, Removable Storage generates an error message either during initialization or when the cartridge is mounted.

    If Removable Storage does not generate any error messages, the manual configuration was successful.

14. If the manual configuration was unsuccessful, stop Removable Storage. Copy your backup version of the Removable Storage database files back to the %SystemRoot%\System32\NtmsData\ folder to restore the database, and restart the manual configuration process.

Using the Removable Storage Console

The snap-in can be started from the storage node in Computer Management or directly from the command line, by running **Ntmsmgr.msc**. It allows you to perform several tasks, including inserting and ejecting media, setting inventory methods, and cleaning drives.

Inserting and Ejecting Media

Removable Storage uses a library's IE port or door for inserting and ejecting cartridges. When you use a door access to enter or remove cartridges, consult the property page for the library and the documentation for the changer to determine the proper slot numbers. Most changers label each slot clearly, but some do not.

Caution If during a door access you exchange cartridges in libraries that do not have bar codes, run a full inventory after you complete the door access. The change is not detected by a fast inventory, and an identity mismatch occurs the next time a cartridge in the slot is mounted.

Table 18.5, Table 18.6, and Table 18.7 show the results of moving CD media, tape media, and optical/rewritable media among the media pools.

Note Because CDs are read-only, Removable Storage does not allow them to be placed in the free pool.

CDs appear in the unrecognized pool only if they are formatted with a file system that Windows 2000 does not recognize. For more information about Windows 2000 file systems, see "File Systems" in this book.

Table 18.5   Moving CD Media Among Media Pools

From/To	Import Pool	Unrecognized Pool	Application Pool
Import	N/A	Not Allowed	OK
Unrecognized	Not Allowed	N/A	Not Allowed
Application	OK	Not allowed	N/A

Table 18.6   Moving Tape Media Among Media Pools

From/To	Free Pool	Import Pool	Unrecognized Pool	Application Pool
Free	N/A	Not Allowed	Not Allowed	Retains Free Label until application writes new label.
Import	Write Free Label	N/A	Not Allowed	Not Allowed.
Unrecognized	Write Free Label	Not Allowed	N/A	Not Allowed.
Application	Write Free Label	Not Allowed	Not Allowed	Retains current label.

Table 18.7   Moving Optical/Rewritable Media Among Media Pools

From/To	Free Pool	Import Pool	Unrecognized Pool	Application Pool
Free	N/A	Not Allowed	Not Allowed	Retains Free Label until application writes new label.
Import	Write Free Label	N/A	Not Allowed	Retains label already on media.
Unrecognized	Write Free Label	Not Allowed	N/A	Not Allowed.
Application	Write Free Label	Not Allowed	Not Allowed	Retains current Label. Both sides are moved.

Inventories

There are two types of inventories, fast and full. You can set the default inventory method in the library's property page in the Removable Storage console.

Note   In the Removable Storage console, all nodes beneath **Physical Locations**, except **Off-line Media**, are considered libraries.

A fast inventory checks for slot state changes between full and empty. If the Removable Storage database indicates that a slot has a cartridge in it, but the fast inventory shows that it no longer has a cartridge, Removable Storage marks the cartridge that was in the slot as offline. If a slot was empty and is now full, Removable Storage identifies the cartridge in the slot. Slots that remain full are assumed to contain the same cartridge. Full inventory actually identifies each cartridge. This can take time, unless the cartridges have bar code labels. A full inventory of bar code–labeled cartridges reads only the bar codes. A full inventory of cartridges that are not bar coded reads the on-media identifier on each cartridge in the library.

Cleaning Drives

Some drives, especially tape drives, require periodic cleaning. A light on the front of the drive usually indicates whether a drive is dirty; a dirty drive can cause most I/O operations to fail. In most circumstances, a drive detects that it is dirty while a Removable Storage client application is running. How the client application handles this situation is usually described in the documentation for that application; for some changers, Removable Storage can clean the drive automatically after the application has finished using it.

In the Removable Storage model of device maintenance, each library unit can contain one cleaner cartridge. There is a wizard available through the console, which you can use to insert a cleaning cartridge into each library that supports automatic cleaning.

Removable Storage maintains a usage count for each cleaner cartridge. When a cleaner reaches its maximum usage count, Removable Storage generates an operator request. If the administrator ejects a cleaner cartridge before it has reached its maximum usage count, Removable Storage displays the usage count information. To see the remaining number of available cleanings without ejecting the cleaner cartridge, right-click the media pool that contains the cleaner cartridge and select **Properties**. Click the **Media** tab; the remaining number of cleanings available is displayed.

Caution Problems occur if Removable Storage attempts to identify a cleaning cartridge as a regular cartridge. These problems might appear if the database becomes inconsistent or is restored from an old backup. Most drives treat cleaning cartridges differently from regular cartridges, and this behavior can cause error messages that make it appear as if Removable Storage or the library is malfunctioning. Never start Removable Storage for the first time with a cleaning cartridge in the library or attach a new library that has a cleaning cartridge inside. In both cases, Removable Storage performs a full inventory of the library, which includes trying to identify each cartridge. In addition, never insert a cleaning cartridge by using the same mechanism that is used for ordinary cartridges. If there is any doubt about the consistency of the Removable Storage database, remove the cleaning cartridges from the attached libraries.

Work Queue Items

You can use the property page for the work queue item to control how long completed and failed work queue items are retained. You can set the work queue to retain failed items to investigate problems. The property page for each failed item shows the reason for the failure.

During startup you might see a number of canceled work queue items. If there are work queue items still queued when Removable Storage is shut down, they are canceled the next time Removable Storage starts.

Operator Requests

The two available methods for making an operator request are Windows 2000 Messenger Service and a system tray icon. When the messenger service is selected, an message appears whenever there is an operator request. Make sure that the Messenger Service is running if this option is selected, and then open Removable Storage to view the operator request queue.

If the system tray method is selected, a system tray icon appears whenever there is an outstanding operator request. Clicking the system tray icon displays the Removable Storage snap-in operator requests node that is used to refuse or complete requests. All operator requests must be completed or refused.

The property page of the operator request node in Removable Storage allows you to set how long to retain completed and failed (including canceled) operator requests. It also provides buttons that can be used to process deleted, completed, and failed operator requests immediately. The **Default** button deletes all requests that are specified by the controls on the properties sheet; the **Delete all now** button deletes all completed and failed requests.

Library and Drive States

A library is online while it is operating and connected to the computer that is running Removable Storage. A library is not present if it is not operating or if it is disconnected from the computer. Both robotic and stand-alone libraries can be either online or not present. If a library is removed, delete the library from Removable Storage manually. Removable Storage does not delete libraries automatically in case the library is disconnected inadvertently or temporarily.

Drives in offline libraries are offline, but cartridges in offline libraries are considered online because they reside in a library. Offline media physical locations, then, are different from offline libraries.

Troubleshooting Removable Storage

Problems with Removable Storage can be caused by either hardware or software. The information that is required for you to resolve either type of problem is contained in the following paragraphs.

Configuration

If you are having problems with Removable Storage configuring your devices, please consult the HCL to make sure your device is supported. If the device is supported, make sure you have configured it according to the guidelines that are listed in the HCL. Many changers support multiple operational configurations, but Removable Storage requires specific settings.

Make sure that the hardware is configured correctly. If the device is attached to the host by means of a SCSI bus, ensure that the bus is configured correctly, with no SCSI ID collisions, with proper termination, in accordance with all cable length and SCSI controller parameters, and so on. Advanced Technology Attachment (ATA) devices must be properly configured as master, slave, or stand-alone devices.

If the hardware is configured properly, make sure that Windows 2000 has found the devices and has loaded the drivers for them. Make sure you see your changer under **Media Changers** in Device Manager and that you see any drives under **Disk drives** or **Tape drives**. If a driver is loaded, check the system Event Log to see if the driver encountered an error when it initialized the device.

If all the devices are working properly but Removable Storage is still unable to configure them automatically, configure the devices manually.

Operation

If a work queue item is failing, check its property page for the reason for the failure.

If your library is configured correctly, but it begins malfunctioning, check the system log. Look for Removable Storage messages and for changer, drive, and controller error messages. If these devices are experiencing errors, take appropriate actions to clear the errors, such as power cycling or resetting the device.

Operations can begin failing when the system runs low on system resources, such as memory or disk space. Check the system Event Log to determine whether this is the case.

If the devices and the system appear to be operating normally, try stopping and restarting Removable Storage.

If known cartridges are always placed in the unrecognized pool when they are inserted, or if mount requests fail because of an OMID mismatch, the MLL might be missing or installed incorrectly. Information about MLLs is contained in the registry entry HKEY_LOCAL_MACHINE\SYSTEM\CurrentControlSet\Control\NTMS\OMID\Tape.

Caution   Do not use a registry editor to edit the registry directly unless you have no alternative. The registry editors bypass the standard safeguards provided by administrative tools. These safeguards prevent you from entering conflicting settings or settings that are likely to degrade performance or damage your system. Editing the registry directly can have serious, unexpected consequences that can prevent the system from starting and require that you reinstall Windows 2000. To configure or customize Windows 2000, use the programs in Control Panel or Microsoft Management Console (MMC) whenever possible.

The folder %SystemRoot%\System32 usually contains all media label library DLLs and is accessible only by administrators.

Overview of Backups

Regular backups of local hard disks prevents data loss from disk drive failures, disk controller errors, power outages, virus infection, and other possible problems. Backup operations that are based on careful planning and reliable equipment make file recovery easier and less time consuming.

Windows 2000 Professional provides a tool called "Backup" for use with your computer. It can back up data to tape or to a compressed file. You can even store your backup file on a network share.

Backup Types

Backup can perform several types of backups:

Normal   A normal backup copies all selected files and marks each as having been backed up. Normal backups are the easiest to use for restoring files because you need only the most recent backup file or tape to restore all of the backed up files. Normal backups take the most time because every file that is selected is backed up, regardless of whether it has changed since the last backup.

Incremental   An incremental backup backs up only those files that have been created or changed since the last normal or incremental backup, which can reduce the amount of time that is required to complete the backup process. It marks files as having been backed up. You should create a complete normal backup of your system before you run incremental backups. If you use a combination of normal and incremental backups, you must have the last normal backup set as well as every incremental backup set that has been made since the last normal backup—in chronological order—to restore your data.

Differential   A differential backup copies files that have been created or changed since the last normal or incremental backup, which can reduce the amount of time that is required to complete the backup process. It does not mark files as having been backed up. You should create a complete normal backup of your system before you run differential backups. If you are doing normal and differential backups, you must have the last normal backup set and the last differential backup sets to restore your data.

Copy   A copy backup copies all selected files, but it does not mark each file as having been backed up. Copying is useful to back up files between normal and incremental backups because it does not affect other backup operations.

Daily   A daily backup copies all selected files that have been modified on the day that the daily backup is performed. The backed up files are not marked as having been backed up.

Some backup types use a backup marker, also known as an "archive attribute," to track when a file has been backed up. When the file changes, Windows 2000 marks the file to be backed up again. Files or directories that have been moved to new locations are not marked for backup. Backup allows you to back up only files with this marker set and to choose whether or not to mark files when they are backed up.

Make sure that all applications are closed and that no one is using network shares on your computer when you perform backups. Any files that are open or in use when the backup process is run probably are not going to be backed up, which negates the value of the backup.

Caution   Backups protect against data loss that is caused by a virus. Because some viruses take weeks to appear, keep normal backup tapes for at least a month to make sure that you can restore a system to its uninfected status.

Storage Devices and Media

Windows 2000 can back up files to a variety of storage devices, including tape drives. Data can be backed up to disk volumes, removable disks, or network shares, or to a library of disks or tapes that are organized into a media pool and controlled by a robotic changer. If you do not have a separate storage device, you can back up to another local hard disk or to floppy disks.

Storage Devices

Storage technology changes rapidly, so it is important to research the merits of various media before you make a purchase. Take into account drive and media costs, as well as reliability and capacity, when you select a storage device. Ideally, a storage device should have more than enough capacity to back up all of the combined space of all local hard drives and be able to detect and correct errors during backup-and-restore operations. For information about supported storage devices, see the Hardware Compatibility List (HCL) link on the Web Resources page at http://windows.microsoft.com/windows2000/reskit/webresources.

Tip To make sure that your storage devices and cartridges are working correctly, verify your backups by performing test restores.

Media Types

The most common type of medium is magnetic tape. The tape drives that are commonly used for backup include a quarter-inch cartridge (QIC), digital audio tape (DAT), 8mm cassette, and digital linear tape (DLT). High-capacity, high-performance tape drives usually use SCSI controllers. Other types of media include magnetic disks, optical disks, and CD-ROMs (CD-R and CD-RW).

Security Considerations

There are several steps that you can take to enhance the security and operation of your backup-and-restore operations. You should also take steps to secure your backup cartridges.

When you develop a backup plan, consider the following methods:

- Secure both the storage device and the backup cartridges. Data can be retrieved from stolen cartridges and restored to another computer.
- Back up an entire volume by using the normal backup procedure. In case of a disk failure, it is more efficient to restore the entire volume in one operation.

- Always back up the System State data to prevent the loss of local user accounts and security information.

- Keep at least three current copies of backup cartridges. Store one copy at an off-site location in a properly controlled, secure environment.

Backup and Restore Rights

In many cases, the local administrator performs backup and restore operations on Windows 2000 Professional systems. However, when Windows 2000 Professional is used as a file server in a peer-to-peer, local area network (LAN), backup and restore rights can be given to a user without granting full administrative privileges.

Important You must be a member of the Administrators group to restore the System State, but members of the Backup Operators group can restore files.

If you are the system administrator of a networked computer with shared volumes or of a publicly-used computer, you should extend backup and restore rights only to those users who are responsible for backing up the computer. This is done by adding the user to the Backup Operators local group. In a high-security environment, only you should restore files, although it is a good idea to train personnel to perform all restore tasks in the even that you are unavailable.

Caution A person who does not have permission to write to a file might have permission to restore the file. During restoration, such permission conflicts are ignored and the existing file can be overwritten.

File Permissions

In Windows 2000, access to NTFS files is limited by NTFS file and folder permissions, share permissions, and file attributes. You cannot back up or restore NTFS files to which you do not have access rights unless you are a member of either the Administrators or Backup Operators local group.

Note Neither of the file allocation table (FAT) file systems (FAT16 and FAT32) provides file permissions.

Storing Backup Media

You should store some data off-site for long-term storage or to have available in the event of a disaster; however, other data needs to be readily available.

Caution   Backup cartridges lasts longer in cool, humidity-controlled locations. Your storage area should also be free of magnetic fields, such as those near the backs of computer terminals and telephone equipment.

Daily backups, whether full or incremental   Store cartridges in a fireproof safe or cabinet to protect against natural disaster, theft, and sabotage.

Copies of cartridges   If more than one copy of a software program is purchased, store one off-site if this is possible. If you have only one copy, back it up to a cartridge, label it as a backup, and store the original off-site. If you have to reinstall software, you can restore it from the backup to a computer that is running Windows 2000.

For highly confidential data that must be stored off-site, consider assistance from a company that specializes in secure data storage. If the cost or logistics of such protection is too great, use an alternative solution, such as a safe-deposit box or an off-site fireproof safe that is designed to protect magnetic media (assuming your backups are not stored on writable CD-R disks).

For maximum security, store the following items off-site:

- A full, normal backup of the entire system, performed weekly.
- Original software that is installed on computers. (Keep only copies on-site.)
- Documents that are required for processing an insurance claim, such as purchase orders or receipts.
- Information that is required to get network hardware reinstalled or reconfigured.
- Information that is required to reconfigure your storage subsystem.

Tip   Make sure that your off-site storage location is bonded.

Establishing a Backup Plan

When you develop your backup plan, keep the following in mind:

- Be sure you have spare hardware and cartridges on hand in case of a failure.
- Test backed-up data regularly to verify the reliability of your backup procedures and equipment.
- Include stress testing of backup hardware (storage drives, optical drives, and controllers) and software (backup program and device drivers).

There is a range of system configurations that can affect your backup strategies. At one end of the range is a simple, stand-alone computer with one user. At the other is a workgroup network with a computer that is hosting a network public file share.

Caution   Backup does not back up files on computers that are running MS-DOS. Consider reserving some space on a network share so that users of MS-DOS and Microsoft® Windows® version 3.1 can copy important files. After these files are on the network share, they can be backed up during regular file server backups.

You can work out a backup solution by following these four steps:

1. Research and select a device on which to record your backups. When considering new backup hardware, be sure to consider its reliability, speed, capacity, cost, and compatibility with Windows 2000. The cartridges should provide more than enough space to back up all of your data.
2. If necessary, install a controller card in the computer. If you choose to use a SCSI-based tape drive, put the tape drive on its own controller.
3. Connect your new backup drive to the computer so that you can back up the System State data. If you are using an external SCSI drive, start the drive before you start the computer so that the driver can be loaded properly.
4. Establish a backup cartridge rotation schedule. You need to continue making backups as long as data is created or changed.

Over a period of time, you should use several separate disks or tapes when you run your backup regimen. By using multiple disks or tapes instead of repeatedly using the same disk or tape, you gain additional benefits with your backup program:

- It preserves access to multiple versions of data files in case a user needs to restore an older copy of a data file.

- If the last backup fails as a result of a bad cartridge, you have a backup from the previous process.
- You extend the useful life span of each cartridge.

Tip Have several extra, new, blank, formatted media available in case of cartridge failure. Regularly scan the Backup log for errors that might indicate that a backup cartridge is beginning to fail.

Be sure to clean a tape drive's recording heads regularly. Failure to do so can lead to unusable backups and the premature failure of the tape drive. See the tape drive manufacturer's recommendations for the proper method and frequency of cleaning.

Stand-alone Computer

You need to choose a backup medium to use. If the quantity of data that you need to backup is small, a removable hard disk or writable CD might be all that you need. However, for more flexibility and capacity for growth, tape is still the backup medium of choice.

After your tape drive is installed, decide on a backup schedule and the types of backups. If the data that is created on a daily basis is irreplaceable, daily backups are recommended. If the data is less valuable, the frequency of backups can be less often. It should be recognized, however, that the longer the period between backups, the greater the potential for loss. Just as it is unwise to work on a document all day without saving the file, it is unwise to work on a document all week with backing it up. The value of the data should help you determine the appropriate frequency of backups.

The type of backups you make determines how easy or difficult it is to restore the data in an emergency. The compromise is between security and convenience. If you choose to run full, normal backups every day, you can restore lost data easily, but the backups can take a substantial amount of time (depending upon the quantity of data to be backed up and the data transfer speed of the recording device). If you choose to make incremental backups for a month after making a full backup, you save substantial time in the backup process. However, to fully restore a corrupted hard disk, it is likely to require that you restore the normal backup, then each incremental backup in successive order. Substituting a differential backup for the incremental backup shortens the restore process, but as each day's backup process takes more time than the previous day, the total accumulation of changed files continues to grow. In addition, you can lose the ability to retrieve earlier versions of document files, unless you use separate cartridges for each differential backup.

Method One

Computers that contain frequently changing data, that contain data that is hard to replace or reproduce, or that provide a public network share should be backed up daily. Run a full, normal backup every Friday. Every Monday through Thursday run a differential backup to a different tape or disk. After the second Friday, full backup has been successfully made, put the first full backup away as a temporary archive. Then after every following Friday's full backup, alternate the full backups as temporary archives. On every eighth Friday, save the full backup as a permanent archive, which should be stored in a secure, off-site location. Over the course of a year, this method uses at least 14 tapes or disks.

Note If the computer is used seven days a week, add a Saturday and Sunday differential backup to the schedule.

Use new tapes if you choose to make permanent archives on tape.

Method Two

If the computer is used less often or if the data is not as valuable, consider making one incremental backup each week for three weeks and one full, normal backup every fourth week, alternating the full backups between two cartridges to ensure that at least one always exists. This reduces the amount of time spent creating backups, but it also reduces protection against data corruption or erasure. Over the course of a year this method uses at least fives tapes or disks.

Workgroup LANs

The following scenario illustrates a possible approach for backing up a small network that consists of a computer that is running Windows 2000 Professional and that is hosting a public file share for 20 other client computers.

Connect a tape drive to the share host computer. From the share host computer, you can back up user files on remote computers that are running Microsoft® Windows for Workgroups, Microsoft® Windows 95, Microsoft® Windows 98, Microsoft® Windows NT®, and Microsoft® Windows 2000. (See the two suggested methods for doing this that follow.) Establish a tape rotation schedule. If conserving tapes is a requirement, back up clients less frequently than you back up the share host and encourage users to copy critical files to the network share at the end of the day.

In the descriptions of the following methods for backing up remote computers, the computer that contains the data to be backed up is called "Data." The computer that runs the backup process is called "Target."

Method One

Back up Data locally to disk. Use a networked backup or Xcopy to move the resulting backup file to Target. Make sure you run a backup verification pass that compares the data on Data and the data on Target on a regular basis. Ethernet or Token Ring transfer speeds usually are approximately 1 megabyte (MB) per second if the network is not busy. You can use this transfer rate and the total amount of data being transferred to estimate the transfer time. If the transfer time is too long, you might need to use a faster network connection or a different backup method.

Method Two

Copy the data that you want to back up to another disk or disks on Data. Bring Data online, and copy the data by using a backup device that is connected to Data. You can also back up Data over the network to Target. Whether to perform the backup from Data or from Target depends on the following factors:

- The availability of a target computer.

- Any backup policies that require that backups be performed on designated computers.

- The time and cost of performing the backup from Data versus transferring the files to Target.

Backup Schedule

Important Back up file servers often. If the data is critical, it must be mandatory for users to close their files at the end of the day.

After you have determined the best method for giving Target access to the data it needs to back up, you can begin your backup schedule plan. On Target, run a full, normal backup every Friday. Every Monday through Thursday, run a differential backup to a different tape. Run this program for four weeks before you reuse tapes in the backup program. On every fourth Friday, save the full backup as a permanent archive, which should be stored in a secure, off-site location. Over the course of a year, this method uses at least 31 tapes.

Note To allow users access to even more old versions of document files, you can lengthen the backup program to six weeks before tapes are reused. This increases the number of tapes used in a year to at least 41.

If the computer is used seven days a week, add a Saturday and Sunday differential backup to the schedule.

Documenting Backup-and-Restore Procedures

Keeping accurate backup records is essential for locating backed up data quickly, particularly if you have accumulated a large number of backup cartridges. Thorough records include cartridges labels, catalogs, and online log files and log books.

Cartridges labels   Labels for write-once cartridges should contain the backup date, the type of backup (normal, incremental, or differential), and a list of contents. If you are restoring from differential or incremental backups, you need to be able to locate the last normal backup and either the last differential backup or all incremental backups that have been created since the last normal backup. Label reusable media, such as tapes or removable disks, sequentially, and keep a log book in which you note the content of cartridges, the backup date, the type of backup, and the date the medium was placed in service. If you have to replace a defective cartridge, label it with the next unused sequential ID, and record it in the log book.

Catalogs   Most backup software includes a mechanism for cataloging backup files. Backup stores backup catalogs on the backup cartridge and temporarily loads them into memory. Catalogs are created for each backup set or for each collection of backed up files from one drive.

Log files   Log files include the names of all backed up and restored files and directories. A log file is useful when you are restoring data because you can print or read this file from any text editor. Keeping printed logs in a notebook makes it easier to locate specific files. For example, if the tape that contains the catalog of the backup set is corrupted, you can use the printed logs to locate a file.

Conducting Verify Operations

A verify operation compares the files on disk to the files on the backup cartridge. It occurs after all files are backed up or restored, and it takes about as long as the backup procedure. It is recommended that you perform a verify operation after every backup, especially if you back up to a set of cartridges for long-term storage. A verify operation is also recommended after file recovery.

Note   If a verify operation fails for a given file, check the date that the file was last modified. If the file changes between a backup operation and a verify operation, the verify operation fails. Other factors also might cause a verify to fail, such as a change in the size of a file or corruption of the data on the disk or backup cartridge.

Backing Up System State Data

System State data includes the following:

- Boot files, including the system files, and all files protected by Windows File Protection (WFP).
- The registry.
- Performance counter configuration information.
- Component Services Class registration database.

Restoration of the System State replaces boot files first and commits the system hive of the registry as a final step in the process.

System State backup and restore operations include all System State data. You cannot choose to backup or restore individual components because of dependencies among the System State components. However, you can restore System State data to an alternate location in which only the registry files and system boot files are restored. The Component Services Class Registration database is not restored to the alternate location.

Although you cannot change which components of the System State are backed up, you can back up all protected system files with the System State data by setting advanced backup options.

▶   **To back up System State data**

1. Click **Start**, **Programs**, **Accessories**, and **System Tools**, and then click **Backup**.
2. Click the **Backup** tab, and then select the **System State** check box.

   This backs up the system state data along with any other data that you have selected for the current backup operation.

Keep the following in mind when you are backing up System State data:

- You must be an administrator or a backup operator to back up files and folders.
- You can back up the System State data only on a local computer.
- You can use the Backup wizard to back up System State data.

Boot and System Files

Backup considers the functionality of WFP when backing up and restoring boot and system files. System files are backed up and restored as a single entity. The WFP service catalog file, which is located in the folder %SystemRoot%\System32 \catroot\{F750E6C3-38EE-11D1-85E5-00C04FC295EE}, is backed up with the system files.

In Windows NT 4.0 and earlier, backup programs could selectively backup and restore operating system files as they would data files, allowing for incremental backup and restore operations of most operating system files. Windows 2000, however, does not allow incremental restoration of operating system files.

The Advanced Backup option **Automatically back up system protected files with the System State** backs up all system files that are in your %SystemRoot% folder in addition to the startup files that are included with the System State data.

▶ **To set advanced backup options**

1. In the **Backup** dialog box, click the **Backup** tab, and then select the files and folders that you want to back up.

2. Click **Start Backup**.

3. In the **Backup Job Information** dialog box, click **Advanced**.

4. Set the advanced backup options that you want, and then click **OK**.

The advanced backup options are described in Table 18.8.

Table 18.8   Advanced Backup Options

Option	Description
Back up data that is in Remote Storage.	Backs up data that has been designated for Remote Storage. You can restore Remote Storage data only to an NTFS volume that is used with Windows 2000.
	Note that Remote Storage is available only on Windows 2000 Server–based networks.
Verifies data after backup.	Verifies that the backed up data is exactly the same as the original data. This can substantially increase the time it takes to perform a backup.
If possible, compresses the backup data to save space.	Compresses the data that you are backing up so you can save more data on a tape. If this option is disabled, you do not have a tape drive on your computer or your tape drive cannot compress data.
Automatically backs up system protected files with the system state.	Backs up all of the system files that are in your %SystemRoot% folder in addition to the boot files that are included with the System State data. This can substantially increase the size of your backup job.

Registry

The contents of the registry are backed up and restored when you back up and restore System State data. When you back up the System State data, a copy of your registry files is also saved in the folder %SystemRoot%\Repair\Regback. If your registry files become corrupted or are accidentally erased, you can use these files to repair the registry without performing a full restore of the System State data. This method of repairing the registry is recommended only for advanced users. For more information about restoring the registry from the backup stored in the Regback folder, see "Troubleshooting Tools and Strategies" in this book.

Important It is important that you have current, reliable backup copies of the registry. Back up the registry before you edit the registry and as part of your regular backup routine. If you select the **System State** check box on the **Backup** tab in Backup, the registry is backed up automatically.

Performance Counter Configuration

The performance counter configuration files are also backed up and restored as part of the System State data.

Component Services Class Registration Database

Component Object Model (COM) is a binary standard for writing component software in a distributed systems environment. The Component Services Class Registration Database is backed up and restored with the System State data.

Component Services have special backup and restore considerations. There are two Component Services elements on each system: the component binaries, including DLLs and executable files (EXEs), and the Component Services database. The components are backed up as a part of normal file enumeration. The Component Services database, however, is backed up and restored as a part of the System State data.

Using the Backup Tool

Backup is a graphical tool that is used with a variety of storage media to back up and restore files on volumes using any file system supported by Windows 2000. Backup also simplifies archiving and allows you to use the Windows 2000 Job Scheduler for automating backup jobs.

Tasks such as mounting and dismounting a tape or disk are done by Removable Storage. It tracks and controls backup cartridges, which are usually organized into pools, on storage devices and allows applications such as Backup to share robotic changers and cartridge libraries. After it is started, Removable Storage is transparent, so you only need access to it when you change cartridges, not when you perform a backup or restore operation.

Note Backing up to files on random access media, such as hard or removable disks, is not managed by Removable Storage.

Because of the use of Removable Storage technology, the target media of Backup is not drive-oriented in Windows 2000 as it is in versions of Backup that are included in Windows NT. In the past, backup data was written to drives (for example, tape or disk drives).

In Windows 2000, Backup uses cartridges in media pools to store backed up data. Backup still writes backup data to tapes or files on disks; however, the media is managed by Removable Storage, which references media instead of drives. Backup recognizes each cartridge to which it gains access as either a member of an existing media pool or as unallocated media. The significance of this change can be seen when a user sets up a regular backup schedule.

In the past, users scheduled Backup to run on specified days, and they could use any cartridge for that day's job. Removable Storage tracks the use of all cartridges, so it does not allow indiscriminate use of unrecognized cartridges in the applications it manages.

Each cartridge that is used by Backup must be added to Backup's application media pool and it requires its own scheduled job to be automated. If you choose to backup your data to a different cartridge each night over the course of a week, you have to create seven scheduled jobs, or one job for each tape. This is because the Job Scheduler feature included with Backup requires that you specify a particular cartridge name in the scheduled job. (Each cartridge has a unique name recorded in the header of the data area.) If you place the Tuesday cartridge in the recording drive on Friday, the scheduled job fails because not all of the required criteria for completing the job were met.

You can avoid this potential problem in one of two ways. You can run the backup job manually the first time the cartridge is used and assign the cartridge a unique name (such as "Monday") in the process. You can also use the Removable Storage console to assign a unique name to the cartridge and place that cartridge in Backup's application media pool. After the cartridge has a unique name assigned to it, you can create a set of scheduled backup jobs, one for the name of each cartridge that is to be used. As long as the specified cartridge is used with the correct scheduled job, all scheduled backups can run normally.

Note If you use a multicartridge library drive (such as a tape drive that contains a magazine of tapes) and set Backup to always draw cartridges from the free media pool, you only need to schedule one job. However, each previously used cartridge must be erased, which places it back into the free media pool, before it can be used again.

Selecting Backup Media

Backup displays a list of all available storage devices on the **Backup destination** list in the **Backup** tab. If no external devices are detected, you can back up to a file on disk. If you want to back up to media that is not managed by Removable Storage, make sure that the disk is loaded in an appropriate storage device.

Note If you are backing up to cartridges that are managed by Removable Storage, the Removable Storage system service must be running (you can confirm this in the Services console). To back up to new cartridges, first make the cartridges available in the media pool. If you want to back up to an existing media pool, the cartridges must be loaded in the library. For more information about using Removable Storage, see "Removable Storage " earlier in this chapter.

Files Skipped During Backup

Backup skips the following types of files during the backup and restore processes:

- Files that are skipped by default by Backup.
- Files that are held open by other applications.

Files Skipped by Default

Backup skips certain files by default, including the following:

- Files that you do not have permission to read. Only users with backup rights can copy files that they do not own.

- Files that are temporary in nature, such as Pagefile.sys, Hiberfil.sys, Win386.swp, 386spart.par, Backup.log, and Restore.log. These files are neither backed up nor restored by Backup. The list of skipped files is embedded in Backup and cannot be changed.

- Registry files on remote computers. Windows 2000 backs up only local registry files.

Locked Files

Windows 2000 lets you back up local files that are exclusively locked by the operating system, such as event logs and registry files. However, Backup skips those files that are held open by other processes. It is a good practice to avoid running applications while Backup is running to minimize the number of files that are not backed up.

Encrypted Files

If the files to be backed up are encrypted, they remain encrypted when they are backed up. Therefore, it is important to ensure that user keys, particularly the recovery agent keys, are also stored safely on backup cartridges. The Certificates console provides methods for exporting keys to floppy disks or to other removable media so that they can be secured in a trusted location.

For information about Encrypting File System (EFS), see "File Systems" in this book.

Backing Up Files on Your Local Computer

Backup lets you back up any file on your local disk system.

Most changes on a server occur as users add, modify, or delete files from their computers. It is recommended that you back up changes to users' folders daily.

Some users keep most of the files that they want backed up on network shares. Other users require that data on local computers be backed up. Your backup procedures need to take into account both situations.

Network users primarily use applications such as Microsoft® Word. You can reinstall the executable files from the original distribution media, but the time and productivity that is lost doing this make the approach less than ideal. In addition, if you have customized the applications to suit the needs of your organization, reproducing those settings can be more difficult than reloading the programs themselves. Because the applications rarely change, backing them up as part of your backup procedure ensures that the latest version is always available without using a lot of offline storage space.

Backing Up Files On Remote Computers

You can use Backup to back up files on any computers to which you can connect remotely. This allows a single media drive to be shared across an entire network and one backup policy to be in effect for the entire network.

You can only back up files and folders on a remote computer by using a shared folder. It is not possible to back up System State data from a remote computer directly by using Backup. If you want to back up the System State data of a remote computer, run Backup locally on the remote computer to save the System State data to a file on a shared volume; then back up the System State data file remotely on the shared volume. To restore the remote computer's System State data, restore the System State data file remotely to the shared volume, and then restore the System State data locally on the local computer.

Note Backup does not recognize computers that are running MS-DOS or Windows 3.1.

C H A P T E R   1 9

Device Management

Microsoft® Windows® 2000 Professional includes support for Plug and Play devices, and simplifies the process of installing and configuring new devices on your system. In addition, it includes enhancements that allow users to share devices between Windows 2000 Professional and Microsoft® Windows® 98 and that ensure that updated device drivers are available to users.

In This Chapter

Related Information in the Professional Resource Kit

- For information about how devices are detected during system startup, see "Setup and Startup" in this book.

- For information about Advanced Configuration and Power Interface (ACPI), see "Power Management" in this book.

- For more information about troubleshooting device problems, see "Troubleshooting Tools and Strategies" in this book.

Quick Guide to Device Management

Windows 2000 Professional is designed to simplify the process of installing and configuring devices. Understanding how to correctly configure devices can help you avoid many problems; understanding how to reconfigure or update your hardware devices and device drivers is also important when problems do occur.

Understand the new features for installing and updating devices and drivers.

Windows 2000 Professional offers several enhancements for installing, configuring, and updating devices attached to your computer. Some of these features were available in Windows 98 but are new to users coming from Microsoft® Windows NT®.

- See "What's New" later in this chapter.

View the devices installed in your computer.

Use the device tree to view the devices installed in your computer and to troubleshoot problems and update devices and drivers. You can also use the device tree to view devices that have been configured on your computer but are not currently attached.

- See "Device Tree" later in this chapter.

Understand how Windows 2000 Professional implements Plug and Play.

Plug and Play support allows users to install and configure Plug and Play devices and drivers. Review the enhancements to the Windows 2000 Professional implementation of Plug and Play and learn about the device types that are supported.

- See "Plug and Play" later in this chapter.

Install new hardware devices and update device drivers.

Install Plug and Play devices by plugging them in and turning them on. Use the wizards included with Windows 2000 Professional to install non–Plug and Play devices. Review update and installation options for device drivers.

- See "Device Installation" later in this chapter.

Configure and customize your devices.

Change or update device drivers, set up hardware profiles, or customize the behavior of devices installed on your computer. Configure your display or set up multiple monitors for use as a single desktop.

- See "Configuring Device Settings" later in this chapter.

Troubleshoot problems with hardware devices and device drivers.

Some problems are caused by outdated device drivers or by incorrectly configured device settings. Review some of the most commonly encountered problems to troubleshoot them on your own.

- See "Troubleshooting Device Management" later in this chapter.

What's New

Windows 2000 Professional includes a host of enhancements that make installing and managing devices more efficient. These include support for Plug and Play devices, the Microsoft® Win32® Driver Model (WDM), and more devices, including digital video disc (DVD) and other removable storage devices.

Support for Plug and Play   As with Windows 98, Windows 2000 Professional supports the use of Plug and Play devices. *Plug and Play* is an independent set of computer architecture specifications that hardware manufacturers use to produce computer devices that can be configured with no user intervention. When you install a device, you do not need to know its Plug and Play requirements, because they are set automatically.

Windows Update   Users can install or update device drivers from the Windows Update Web site. By using an ActiveX® control, Windows Update compares the available drivers with those on the user's system and offers to install new or updated versions.

Support for PC Cards   Windows 2000 Professional supports the new features of products designed for the PC Card standard, also known as the Personal Computer Memory Card International Association (PCMCIA) standard.

Support for Multiple Monitors   Windows 2000 Professional allows you to configure multiple monitors for use with a single CPU. This feature was introduced in Windows 98 but has been enhanced for Microsoft® Windows® 2000 to support switching between the primary and secondary display.

Device Tree

The Windows 2000 Professional device tree is a record of the devices currently loaded, based on the configuration information in the registry. The device tree is created in random access memory (RAM) each time the system is started or whenever a dynamic change occurs to the system configuration.

Each branch in the tree defines a *device node* with the following requirements for system configuration:

- Unique identification code, or device ID.
- List of required resources, such as interrupt request (IRQ) and memory range, including resource type.
- List of allocated resources.
- Indication that the device node is a bus, if applicable (each bus device has additional device nodes under it in the tree).

Viewing Devices in the Device Tree

Most information in the device tree can be accessed through Device Manager, shown in Figure 19.1. Device Manager contains a representation of the active device tree, listing the system device nodes. Under each node are listed the actual devices configured for your system; double-clicking a device node exposes its device list. You can use Device Manager to install or uninstall devices, troubleshoot problems with devices, update drivers, and change the resources that are assigned to devices.

For more information about using Device Manager to configure devices, see "Configuring Device Settings" later in this chapter.

Note You can also see the information in the device tree in the registry. For more information about the registry, see the Technical Reference to the Windows 2000 Registry (Regentry.chm) on the *Microsoft® Windows® 2000 Resource Kit* companion CD.

Figure 19.1   Device Manager

Viewing Hidden Devices

Device Manager does not display all devices by default. Non–Plug and Play devices and certain other devices are hidden. At times, you might need to view these hidden devices for troubleshooting problems with devices installed on your computer.

▶ **To view hidden devices**

- In Device Manager, click the **View** menu, and then select **Show hidden devices**.

In addition to hiding non–Plug and Play devices, Device Manager also hides phantom devices. These are devices which are not currently attached to the computer.

▶ **To view phantom devices**

1. At the command prompt, type:

   set DEVMGR_SHOW_NONPRESENT_DEVICES=1

2. Start Device Manager.

3. From the command prompt, type:

   start devmgmt.msc

You can now troubleshoot problems with hidden devices. For more information about troubleshooting device problems, see "Troubleshooting Device Management" later in this chapter and "Troubleshooting Tools and Strategies" in this book.

Note You can set Device Manager to always show phantom devices. In Control Panel, double-click **System**, click the **Advanced** tab, and then in the **Environment Variables** dialog box, create the variable **set DEVMGR_SHOW_NONPRESENT_DEVICES=1**.

Plug and Play

Plug and Play is a combination of the system BIOS, hardware devices, system resources, device drivers, and the operating system software. This combination provides for dynamic installation and configuration of new hardware components with little or no manual intervention.

You can install Plug and Play devices by plugging in the device. For other devices, such as Plug and Play Industry Standard Architecture (ISA) cards, turn off the computer to install the device, then restart the computer to initialize the device.

Plug and Play allows users to do the following:

- Insert and remove Plug and Play devices such as PC Cards without having to configure them.
- Connect to or disconnect from a docking station or network without restarting the computer or changing configuration parameters.
- Add a new monitor or USB keyboard by plugging it in and turning it on.

Plug and Play support depends on both the hardware device and the device driver. A legacy device can gain some benefit by using a Plug and Play driver. For example, an ISA sound card or an Extended Industry Standard Architecture (EISA) network adapter can be manually installed and gain some Plug and Play functionality by means of a Plug and Play driver.

If a driver does not support Plug and Play, its devices behave as non–Plug and Play devices, regardless of hardware Plug and Play support.

Table 19.1 shows how the level of Plug and Play for a device depends on hardware and software.

Table 19.1   Plug and Play Requirements in Windows 2000 Professional

Device Type	Plug and Play Driver	Non–Plug and Play Driver
Plug and Play device	Full Plug and Play	No Plug and Play
Non–Plug and Play device	Partial Plug and Play	No Plug and Play

Note Windows 2000 Professional supports Plug and Play for monitors only if the monitor, the display adapter, and the display driver are Plug and Play; otherwise, the monitor is detected as "Default Monitor." For more information about Plug and Play device detection, see "Setup and Startup" in this book.

Plug and Play in Windows 2000 Professional

In Windows 2000 Professional, Plug and Play support is optimized for computers that include Advanced Configuration and Power Interface (ACPI) system boards. In addition, Plug and Play support for many device classes is provided by the Win32 Driver Model (WDM), which includes support for power management and other new capabilities that are configured by the operating system.

The Plug and Play implementation in the Windows 2000 Professional operating system provides the following benefits:

- Dynamically loads, initializes, and unloads drivers.
- Enumerates devices.
- Automatically allocates resources during enumeration.
- Notifies other drivers and applications when a new device is available for use. Windows 2000 Professional also includes an automatic installation procedure to ensure that appropriate drivers are installed and loaded.
- Provides a consistent driver and bus interface for all devices.
- Works with power management to handle insertion and removal of devices.
- Supports a wide range of device types.

Windows 2000 Professional detects the presence of a Plug and Play device in a process called enumeration. After enumeration, the device driver can be configured and loaded dynamically, requiring little or no user input. Certain buses, such as the peripheral component interconnect (PCI) and Universal Serial Bus (USB), take full advantage of Plug and Play capability and are also automatically enumerated.

Important Although Plug and Play devices can be hot-plugged, or installed without restarting the computer, some devices, such as internal modems and network adapters, should not be unplugged while the computer is running. This is also true for removable storage devices.

Computers running Windows 2000 Professional that do not have an ACPI BIOS can gain Plug and Play functionality by adding Plug and Play devices. To be able to use *all* Plug and Play features, however, your system must include an ACPI BIOS and Plug and Play hardware devices. If you have an Advanced Power Management (APM) BIOS or a Plug and Play BIOS, you still have many advantages of Plug and Play, but it is not as robust. With a non-ACPI BIOS, Plug and Play is provided by the BIOS and not by the operating system.

This difference can become important during troubleshooting or if you manually change resource settings. On a non-ACPI system, if you manually change resource settings, they become fixed, and those resources cannot be reallocated by the operating system and you no longer have Plug and Play functionality.

For more information about how Plug and Play detects devices during startup on ACPI and non-ACPI computers, see "Setup and Startup" in this book. For more information about ACPI, see "Power Management" in this book.

Plug and Play Devices

A variety of devices are compliant with Plug and Play. The following sections describe the types of devices and provide details for Plug and Play.

USB Devices

Universal Serial Bus is a bus standard that brings Plug and Play capability to external hardware devices, such as keyboards, mouse devices, speakers, and cameras. USB devices are *hot pluggable*, meaning that they can be connected even when the computer is running. USB devices are automatically configured when they are attached—without the need to restart the computer or run Setup.

IEEE 1394 Devices

The IEEE 1394 bus is designed for high-bandwidth devices such as digital camcorders, cameras, and videodisc players. Windows 2000 Professional supports hot plugging of IEEE 1394 devices. To use an IEEE 1394 device, obtain the appropriate Win 32 Driver Model (WDM) driver.

For more information about USB and the IEEE 1394 bus, see "Hardware Support" in this book.

SCSI Devices

Small computer system interface (SCSI) is a multiple-device chained interface used for many devices such as hard disks and CD-ROM drives. Plug and Play SCSI devices support dynamic changes to the adapter and automatic configuration of device ID and termination, as long as the driver supports it.

Configuration of a SCSI device can be separated into two distinct processes:

- Configuring the SCSI bus itself, for example, by terminating both ends of the SCSI bus and setting device IDs.

- Configuring the SCSI host adapter, for example, by assigning an interrupt request (IRQ) channel, direct memory access (DMA) channel, and so on.

PC Card Devices and CardBus

Products designed for the PC Card standard include multifunction cards, 3.3-V cards, and 32-bit PC Cards (CardBus). These advances add the modularity and bus-independence of Plug and Play without affecting device drivers.

Windows 2000 Professional also supports CardBus, a 32-bit implementation of PC Card also known as PC Card 32. CardBus brings 32-bit performance and the benefits of the PCI bus to the PC Card format. CardBus allows portable computers to run high-bandwidth applications such as Video Capture. For more information about how Windows 2000 Professional supports Video Capture, see "Hardware Support" in this book.

VL Devices

The Video Electronics Standards Association (VESA) Local (VL) bus standard allows high-speed connections to peripheral devices. VL bus devices are not completely Plug and Play but work similarly to ISA devices.

PCI Devices

The peripheral component interconnect (PCI) local bus meets most Plug and Play requirements. It is considered the successor to the VL bus. The PCI bus and devices use agreed-upon mechanisms for identifying themselves and declaring their resource settings and requirements. Windows gathers PCI and ISA Plug and Play device resource information from the system BIOS, which provides the PCI IRQ Steering Table for PCI devices. With the information from the PCI IRQ Steering Table, Windows 2000 Professional can reassign PCI device resource requirements dynamically, if necessary. For example, when a PCI-based portable computer is hot-docked into a docking station, Windows 2000 Professional might dynamically reassign a PCI device's IRQ to accommodate the new hardware.

Note Windows 2000 Professional can manipulate only the physical IRQ that is mapped to a particular PCI INT#. It cannot alter the link value for the PCI device listed in the PCI IRQ Routing Table. (The *link value* is the combination of the device's INT# assignment and the specific PCI slot the device is installed in.)

ISA Devices

Industry Standard Architecture (ISA) bus design is the architecture specified for the IBM PC/AT. Plug and Play ISA devices can be used on existing computers, because the specification does not require any change to ISA buses. To configure Plug and Play ISA devices, the system performs the following actions:

- Isolates each card and retrieves a unique device ID and a unique serial number.

- Reads the resource requirements and capabilities stored on each card.

- Allocates resources to each card, reserving these resources so that they cannot be assigned to other Plug and Play cards in the computer.

- Activates the Plug and Play ISA cards.

For legacy devices, standard ISA cards can coexist with Plug and Play ISA cards in the same computer. Windows 2000 Professional determines the type of hardware and its configuration during Setup, by either polling the hardware or asking the user to supply values. This configuration information is stored as static values in the registry and cannot be changed dynamically, but it is used to determine resource assignments for Plug and Play devices.

EISA Devices

Extended Industry Standard Architecture (EISA) is a bus design specified by an industry consortium. EISA devices use cards that are upwardly compatible from ISA and standard software mechanisms for identification and configuration. Windows 2000 Professional includes a bus enumerator that makes configuration information from these devices accessible to the operating system. Windows 2000 Professional does not reconfigure EISA cards, but it uses the information that hardware detection derives from the EISA nonvolatile RAM storage to determine which resources are used.

Other Device Types

Other device types can take advantage of Plug and Play if they provide mechanisms for identification and configuration. These include integrated device electronics (IDE) controllers, Extended Capabilities Ports (ECPs), and communications ports.

Parallel ports can also take advantage of Plug and Play. The most common parallel port type is the Centronics interface. Plug and Play parallel ports meet Compatibility and Nibble mode protocols defined in IEEE P1284. Compatibility mode provides a byte-wide channel from the computer to the peripheral. Nibble mode provides a channel from the peripheral to the host through which data is sent as 4-bit nibbles using the port's status lines. These modes provide two-way communication between the host and the peripheral. Nibble mode is also used to read the device ID from the peripheral for device enumeration.

For totally Plug and Play–compliant computers, the BIOS must also meet Plug and Play specifications.

With Plug and Play, the operating system and the BIOS can communicate with each other to share information about system resources. This communication channel is not new, but with newer system BIOSs combined with either Windows 2000 Professional or Windows 98, this process is more effective than with previous Plug and Play implementations.

Device Installation

In Windows 2000 Professional, how you install a device depends on whether the device and the computer are Plug and Play–compliant. To take full advantage of Plug and Play technology, a computer needs the following:

- Plug and Play operating system (Windows 2000 Professional).
- Plug and Play BIOS or ACPI BIOS.
- Plug and Play hardware devices with drivers.

The Plug and Play components perform the following tasks:

- Identify the devices.
- Determine the device resource requirements.
- Create a nonconflicting system configuration.
- Program the devices.
- Load the device drivers.
- Notify the system of a configuration change.

Windows 2000 Professional uses a large number of subsystems to control various classes of devices that identify logical device types, such as the display, keyboard, and network. For many devices, use Device Manager to make manual changes. Some devices can be configured using Control Panel options.

Note   Drivers that support features specific to Windows NT 4.0 or Windows 2000 are not compatible with Windows 98. The Win32 Driver Model (WDM) is designed to provide a bridge between Windows 98 and Windows 2000.

How Windows 2000 Professional Installs a Device

Windows 2000 Professional Setup performs an inventory of all devices on the computer and records the information about those devices in the registry. Setup gets configuration information for system devices from the INF file associated with each device and, with Plug and Play devices, from the device itself.

When a new device is installed, Windows 2000 Professional uses the device ID to search Windows 2000 Professional INF files for an entry for that device. Windows 2000 Professional uses this information to create an entry for the device under the HKEY_LOCAL_MACHINE branch in the registry, and it copies the drivers needed. Then the registry entries are copied from the INF file to the driver's registry entry.

When you need to install a new device, rely first on Windows 2000 Professional to detect and configure it. How you do so depends on what type of device you have, as the following list explains:

- For Plug and Play–compliant devices, insert the device.
- For PCI and ISA Plug and Play cards, turn the computer off and then install the device. When you restart the computer, Windows 2000 Professional enumerates the device and starts the Plug and Play installation procedures automatically.
- For legacy devices, run the Add/Remove Hardware wizard and let Windows 2000 Professional detect the device. This requires administrator privileges.

Devices are installed after the user logs on to the computer. For more information about how Windows 2000 Professional detects devices, see "Setup and Startup" in this book.

Whenever possible, choose new Plug and Play devices, even for a computer that does not have an ACPI BIOS, to gain some Plug and Play functionality.

Important Most Plug and Play devices can be installed without requiring administrator privileges, which reduces security and damage risks and benefits mobile and remote users.

If Plug and Play cannot configure a device and you are prompted to provide installation instructions, such as the location of the device driver, you need administrator privileges to complete the installation.

Using the Add/Remove Hardware Wizard

Windows 2000 Professional automatically installs and configures most Plug and Play–compliant devices. For devices that are not automatically configured, the Add/Remove Hardware wizard, shown in Figure 19.2, installs and configures legacy and Plug and Play devices that require installation information, such as the driver location.

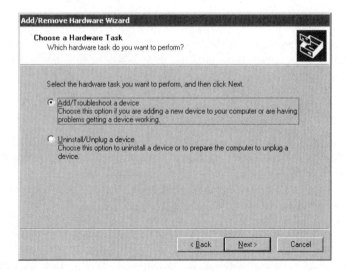

Figure 19.2   Add/Remove Hardware Wizard

The Add/Remove Hardware wizard provides an easy way to install and configure non–Plug and Play devices that have not been automatically recognized by Windows 2000 Professional.

▶ **To use the Add/Remove Hardware wizard to install hardware:**

1. In the Control Panel, double-click the **Add/Remove Hardware** icon, and then click **Next**.

2. Click **Add/Troubleshoot a device**, and then click **Next**.

3. The wizard now searches for new Plug and Play hardware.

If the wizard does not find a new device, it displays a list of the existing devices and gives you the option to troubleshoot any of them. You can select a device from the list to launch the Hardware Troubleshooter.

Installing Drivers

Many device drivers are installed with no user intervention. For example, with Point and Print, printer drivers can be automatically installed on a client computer by connecting to the print server's print queue.

Drivers are installed without any user interface if certain conditions exist:

- Installing the driver does not require showing a user interface.
- The driver package contains all of the files needed to complete the installation.
- The driver package has been digitally signed.
- No errors occur during the installation.

If any of these conditions are not met, the Plug and Play process is restarted and the user may need to respond to dialog boxes or messages. Manual installation of a driver requires administrator privileges.

Windows Update

Windows 2000 and Windows 98 users can install or update drivers from the Windows Update Web site. When a user accesses the Windows Update Web site, Microsoft® ActiveX® controls compare the drivers installed on the user's system with the latest updates available. If newer drivers are found, Windows Update downloads and installs them automatically.

Drivers, including third-party drivers, are included on Windows Update only if they are digitally signed, meet certain Web publishing standards, and have passed the testing requirements for the Windows Logo Program. This ensures that the drivers offered to users from Windows Update are of the highest quality.

You can access Windows Update directly through your browser, from the **Start** menu, from Device Manager, or from the Add Printer wizard. For more information about Windows Update, see the Windows Update link on the Web Resources page at http://windows.microsoft.com/windows2000/reskit/webresources.

Only drivers that have the exact hardware ID as the installed devices are offered for download and installation. If there is an an exact hardware ID match, Windows Update checks the driver version date to determine if the driver being offered is newer than the existing one.

If there is an updated driver on Windows Update, the CAB file is downloaded, and the Windows Update ActiveX control points the Windows Device Manager at the INF for installation.

Administrators can also restrict users' access to Windows Update. For more information about levels of restriction and how to restrict access, see "Troubleshooting Tools and Strategies" in this book.

Driver Signing

Driver Signing is included in Windows to help promote driver quality by allowing Windows 2000 and Windows 98 to notify users if a driver has passed all Windows Hardware Quality Labs (WHQL) tests.

WHQL tests drivers that run on Windows 98 or Windows 2000. The digital signature is associated with individual driver packages and is recognized by Windows 2000. This certification proves to users that a driver is identical to those Microsoft has tested and notifies users if a driver file has been changed since its inclusion on the Hardware Compatibility List.

Driver Signing allows for following three responses:

- **Warn** tells the user if the driver has not been signed and provides the option whether to install it.
- **Block** prevents all unsigned drivers from being installed.
- **Ignore** allows all drivers to be installed, even if they have not been signed.

The Warn mode is set by default.

▶ **To set signature verification options**

1. In Control Panel, double-click **System**.
2. Click the **Hardware** tab, and then click **Driver Signing**.

3. Under **File signature verification**, click the option for the level of signature verification that you want to set.

Note If you are logged on as a member of the Administrators group, you can click **Apply setting as system default** to apply the selected setting as the default for all users who log on to this computer.

Using PC Cards

To take advantage of Plug and Play, a PC Card must contain information that Windows 2000 Professional can use to create a unique device ID for the card. This is called the *card information structure (CIS)*. Device drivers can be implemented under three possible schemes:

- A standard Plug and Play device driver for PC Card (the preferred driver) can handle dynamic configuration and removal, and receive configuration information from the operating system without knowledge of the card in the PC Card bus. The recommended choices are NDIS version 5.*x* drivers for network adapters and mini-port drivers for SCSI cards.

- Generic Windows 2000 Professional device drivers are supported automatically for devices such as modems and disk drives. If the card contains complete configuration information, the operating system initializes the device and passes the information to the driver.

- Manufacturer-supplied drivers are required for device classes that Windows 2000 Professional does not natively support and devices that are not supported by the standard drivers provided.

Windows 2000 Professional supports many PC Cards, including modems, network adapters, SCSI cards, and others. If Windows 2000 Professional includes supporting drivers for the PC Card and for the socket, installation and configuration is automatic.

For more information, see Windows 2000 Professional Help and the PC Card Troubleshooter.

Important If you are using a network adapter, your PC Card socket driver and network driver both must be Plug and Play drivers.

▶ **To verify that Windows 2000 Professional has properly detected your PC Card socket**

1. In Control Panel, double-click **System**, click the **Device Manager** tab, and then click the **Device Manager** button.

2. Look for a **PC Card Socket** listing.

   If Windows 2000 Professional has not detected a PC Card socket, your socket controller might not be supported by Windows 2000 Professional.

▶ **To find out if a PC Card socket is supported**

1. In Control Panel, double-click **Add/Remove Hardware**.

2. On the first screen in the Add/Remove Hardware wizard, click **Next**.

3. When the Add/Remove Hardware wizard asks you to choose a hardware task, select **Add/Troubleshoot**, and then click **Next**.

4. From the list of devices that were detected, select **PC Card Socket**, and then click **Next**.

5. Select the manufacturer for your device, and examine the **Models** list.

If your socket does not appear in the list, you might want to find out if this type of socket is supported. Most likely, if it did not install automatically, the socket type is not supported. Contact your independent hardware vendor (IHV) for a new driver.

Configuring Device Settings

For Plug and Play devices, there are no true default settings. Instead, Windows 2000 Professional identifies devices and their resource requests and arbitrates requests among them. If no device requests the same resources as another device, their settings do not change. If another device requests the same resources, the settings might change to accommodate the request. Consequently, you must never change resource settings for a Plug and Play device unless absolutely necessary. Doing so fixes its settings, making it impossible for Windows 2000 Professional to grant another device's request to use that resource. Changed resource settings can be brought back to the original values by checking the **Use automatic settings** box under the **Resources** tab of the **Device Properties Page** in Device Manager. See the procedure "To change a device's resource settings using Device Manager" later in this section.

Note Windows 2000 Professional might allocate a single resource to more than one device.

Legacy devices that have fixed resource settings are discovered either during Windows Setup or through the Add/Remove Hardware wizard.

Certain circumstances might require users to change resource settings after Windows 2000 Professional has configured a device. For example, Windows 2000 Professional might not be able to configure one device without creating conflicts with another device. In such a case, a message usually appears to explain what is happening and what you can do about the problem—turn off a device to make room for the new device, disable the new device, or reconfigure a legacy device to make room for the new device.

For more information about troubleshooting problems with devices, see "Troubleshooting Device Management" later in this chapter and "Troubleshooting Tools and Strategies" in this book.

Use Device Manager instead of a registry editor to manually change a device's configuration. Before making any changes to your device configuration, back up your registry so that you can restore your original settings in the event of any problems.

Caution Do not use a registry editor to edit the registry directly unless you have no alternative. The registry editors bypass the standard safeguards provided by administrative tools. These safeguards prevent you from entering conflicting settings or settings that are likely to degrade performance or damage your system. Editing the registry directly can have serious, unexpected consequences that can prevent the system from starting and require that you reinstall Windows 2000. To configure or customize Windows 2000, use the programs in Control Panel or Microsoft Management Console (MMC) whenever possible.

If you need or want to resolve device conflicts manually, you can use Device Manager and try the following strategies:

- Identify a free resource, and assign the device to use that resource.
- Disable a conflicting Plug and Play device to free its resources.
- Disable a legacy device to free its resources, by removing the legacy device card and not loading the device drivers.
- Rearrange resources used by another device or devices to free resources needed by the device with a conflict.
- After turning off and unplugging your computer, change jumpers on your hardware to match the new settings.

Caution Changing default settings using either Device Manager or a registry editor can cause conflicts that make one or more devices unavailable on the system.

▶ **To use Device Manager**

1. In Control Panel, double-click **System**, click the **Hardware** tab, and then click the **Device Manager** button.

2. Double-click the device type in the list to display the devices of that type on your computer.

3. Double-click the device that you want to configure, or select the device, and then click **Properties** to view or change its settings.

You can use Device Manager to print reports about system settings, including the following:

- System summary
- Selected class or device
- All devices and system summary

▶ **To print a report about system settings**

1. In Device Manager, click **Print**.

2. In the **Print** dialog box, click the type of report you want.

The following procedure explains how to change a device's resource settings using Device Manager. Change resource settings only if absolutely necessary. Changing resource settings can cause conflicts and can cause you to lose Plug and Play functionality. Also, before changing resource settings, make sure that your problem is a resource conflict and not a missing driver.

▶ **To change a device's resource settings using Device Manager**

1. In Device Manager, expand the device class to show the available devices.

2. Click a device, and then click **Properties**. The **Device Properties** dialog box is displayed.

3. Click the **Resources** tab. Notice that the **Conflicting device list** shows any conflicting values for resources used by other devices.

4. In the **Resource type** list, select the setting you want to change. Make sure the **Use automatic settings** box is unchecked.

5. Click **Change Setting**. The dialog box for editing the particular setting is displayed.

   If there is a conflict with another device, a message is displayed in the **Conflict Information** field.

Note When you click **Change Setting**, you might see an error message saying, "This resource setting cannot be modified." In this case, you need to choose a different basic configuration until you find one that allows you to change resource settings.

---

6. Choose a setting that does not conflict with any other devices, and then click **OK**.

7. Restart Windows 2000 Professional. Then verify that the settings are correct for the device.

Note Many legacy devices have jumpers or switches that set the IRQ, DMA, and I/O addresses. If you change these settings in Device Manager, you must also change the settings on the device to match them.

Changing Device Drivers

If your device is not working properly and you suspect that you have either an outdated device driver or the wrong device driver for your device, you can change your device driver from within Device Manager.

▶ **To change the device driver using Device Manager**

1. In Device Manager, expand the device class. The tree expands to show the available devices.

2. Click the device whose driver you want to change, and then click **Properties**. The **Device Properties** dialog box is displayed.

3. Click the **Driver** tab.

4. Click **Update Driver** in the **Device Properties** dialog box. The Upgrade Device Driver wizard is displayed.

5. Click **Next**.

6. The wizard asks whether you want to search for a better driver. If you want Windows 2000 Professional to detect your driver automatically, click **Search for a suitable driver for my device**.

   –Or–

   If you want to choose a driver yourself, click **Display a list of the known drivers for this device so that I can choose a specific driver**.

7. Click **Next** and follow the instructions to upgrade the driver.

Using Hardware Profiles for Alternate Configurations

Windows 2000 Professional uses hardware profiles to determine which drivers to load when system hardware changes. Hardware profiles are an especially important feature for portable computers that can be docked. Windows 2000 Professional uses one hardware profile to load drivers when the portable is docked and another when it is undocked—for example, at a customer site that has a different monitor from the one at the office.

Configurations are created when Windows 2000 Professional queries the BIOS for a dock serial ID and then assigns a name for the docked and undocked configurations. Windows 2000 Professional then stores the hardware and software associated with these configurations. Applications access and store information for each of the different hardware configurations used by the mobile user. The registry support enables applications to adapt gracefully to different hardware configurations.

The only time Windows 2000 Professional prompts you for the name of a hardware profile is when two profiles are so similar that Windows 2000 Professional cannot differentiate between them. If this happens, Windows 2000 Professional displays a **Hardware Profile** menu from which you can choose the correct one.

▶ **To create a hardware profile**

1. In Control Panel, double-click **System**, and then click the **Hardware** tab. Click **Hardware Profiles** button.

2. Click the name of the hardware profile on which you want to base the new hardware profile, and then click **Copy**.

3. Type a name for the hardware profile you are creating.

4. Change the hardware which is enabled or disabled in this profile by using Device Manager, as described in the following procedure.

▶ **To enable or disable hardware in a hardware profile**

1. In Device Manager, expand the hardware type, and then double-click the hardware.

2. In the **Device Usage** box, clear or select **Disable in this hardware profile**.

3. Click **Yes** if you are prompted to restart your computer.

▶ **To delete or rename a hardware profile**

1. In Control Panel, double-click **System**, and then click the **Hardware** tab. Click **Hardware Profiles** button.

2. Click the name of the hardware profile that you want to change.

3. If you want to remove this profile, click **Delete**.

–Or–

If you want to change the name of the profile, click **Rename**, and then type a new name.

Configuring the Display

In Windows 2000 Professional, you can use the Display option in Control Panel to do the following:

- Change the display driver.

- Change screen resolution and color depth (without restarting the computer when using display drivers that support this functionality).

- Change color schemes and text styles in all screen elements, including fonts used in dialog boxes, menus, and title bars.

- View changes in colors, text, and other elements of display appearance before the changes are applied.

- Configure display settings for each hardware profile, for example, docked and undocked configurations.

- Configure multiple monitors. For information, see "Configuring Multiple Monitors" later in this chapter.

Windows 2000 Professional also includes mechanisms to ensure that incompatible display drivers cannot prevent a user from accessing the system. If a display driver fails to load or initialize when Windows 2000 Professional is started, Windows 2000 Professional automatically uses the generic VGA display driver. This ensures that you can start Windows 2000 Professional to fix a display-related problem.

For displays, colors are described in bits per pixel (BPP). Table 19.2 lists the BPP-to-color conversions.

Table 19.2   BPP-to-Color Conversions

Bits Per Pixel	Color Conversion
1 BPP	Monochrome
4 BPP	16 colors
8 BPP	256 colors
15 BPP	32,768 (32K) colors
16 BPP	65,536 (64K) colors
24 BPP	16.7 million colors [1]
32 BPP	16.7 million colors [1]

[1] This is another description of true color that includes an 8-bit alpha component in addition to the 24-bits used for 16.7 million colors. Alpha is a degree of transparency or translucency.

Resolutions are described in the horizontal number of pixels multiplied by the vertical number of pixels—for example, 640 x 480.

Changing the Display Driver

You can change or upgrade a display driver by using the **Display** option in Control Panel or by using Device Manager. For more information about adding or changing a device driver, see Windows 2000 Professional Help.

If you install a new Plug and Play monitor, the system detects the monitor and the Add/Remove Hardware wizard guides you through the installation process. After attaching the monitor, in Device Manager, in the **Monitors** node, right-click the previous monitor, and then select **Uninstall** to remove the old monitor. On the **Action** menu, click **Scan for hardware changes** to scan for the new hardware.

If the monitor is detected as **Default Monitor**, either the display adapter or the monitor is not Plug and Play. If the monitor is detected as **Plug and Play Monitor**, the monitor is not included in the monitor INF files. Contact your hardware manufacturer for an updated Windows 2000 INF file.

Warning   Some monitors can be physically damaged by incorrect display settings. Carefully check the manual for your monitor before choosing a new setting.

▶ **To change the monitor driver**

1. In Device Manager, expand the **Monitors** node.

2. Right-click the entry for the monitor, select **Properties**, and then click the **Drivers** tab.

3. Click the **Update Driver** button, **select Display a list of the known drivers for this device so that I can choose a specific driver**, and then click **Next**.

4. Under **Models**, choose a driver from the list of compatible drivers.

   If your model is not listed, select **Show all hardware of this device class**. In the Upgrade Device Driver wizard, choose the manufacturer and model for your device. If you do not see the correct make and model for your display device, you need to install the correct driver.

▶ **To install a monitor driver**

Note   If a driver was not included with your monitor (for example, on a floppy disk), check the manufacturer's Web site for the most recent driver.

1. In Device Manager, expand the **Monitors** node.

2. Right-click the entry for the monitor, select **Properties**, and then click the **Drivers** tab.

3. Click the **Update Driver** button, insert the floppy disk with the correct driver, and then click **Next**.

4. Select **Display a list of known drivers for this device so that I can choose a specific driver**.

5. Select **Have Disk**, and then click **Next**.

6. Windows 2000 scans the floppy disk and displays a list of supported drivers. Highlight the driver that you want to use, and then click **Next**.

7. When the needed files have been copied to your hard disk drive, click **Finish**.

Changing Hardware Acceleration Settings

Windows 2000 Professional uses hardware acceleration to improve display performance. In some cases, this might cause problems. If so, you can turn off part or all of your hardware acceleration.

Note If you are using multiple monitors, changing hardware acceleration settings affects all monitors.

▶ **To turn off hardware acceleration**

1. In Control Panel, double-click **Display**.

2. In the **Display Properties** dialog box, click the **Settings** tab, and then click the **Advanced** button.

3. Click the **Troubleshooting** tab, and choose the level of hardware acceleration you need.

Configuring Display Resolution and Colors

You can configure the display resolution and color choices for your display or customize the font size used by using Display in Control Panel.

New features in Windows 2000 Professional allow you to change resolution and color depth without restarting the computer, if the installed display adapter is using a video driver provided by Windows 2000 Professional. You must also restart the computer if you are not using a Plug and Play display adapter and driver.

Configuring Display Appearance

You can use Display in Control Panel to set the screen saver and the background pattern used on the desktop.

You can also use settings in Screen Saver properties to take advantage of power management support in Windows 2000 Professional if your hardware supports this feature. This is similar to the standby mode commonly used in portable computers to save power. Windows 2000 Professional can support screen saver power management if both of the following conditions are true for your computer:

- In the **Properties** dialog box for your display adapter with the **Monitor** tab active, the option **Monitor Is Energy Star Compliant** is checked.

  This option is checked automatically if, during Setup, hardware detection determined that the monitor supports the VESA Display Power Management System (DPMS) specification. You can also check this option manually.

- The device driver for this display uses either the Advanced Power Management (APM) version 1.1 or later BIOS interface with support for device "01FF" (which is not supported by every APM 1.1 or later BIOS), or the VESA BIOS Extensions for Power Management. For information about whether your display adapter supports these BIOS interfaces, see the documentation for your device driver.

The display monitor is typically one of the most "power-hungry" components of a computer. Manufacturers of newer display monitors have incorporated energy-saving features into their monitors based on the DPMS specification. Through signals from the display adapter, a software control can place the monitor in standby mode or even turn it off completely, thus reducing the power the monitor uses when inactive.

Enabling Mode Pruning

Mode Pruning is a Windows 2000 feature that can be used to remove display modes that the monitor cannot support. In Mode Pruning, the graphics modes of the monitor and of the display adapter are compared, and only the modes that are common to both are made available to the user.

Mode Pruning is only available if a Plug and Play monitor is detected or if a specific monitor driver is specified in Device Manager; it is not available if the monitor driver is loaded as "Default Monitor." On Plug and Play monitors, Mode Pruning is enabled by default.

▶ **To enable Mode Pruning**

1. In Control Panel, double-click **Display**.

2. Click the **Settings** tab, click **Advanced**, and then click the **Monitor** tab.

3. Select **Hide modes that this monitor cannot display**, and then click **Apply**.

Using Digital Flat Panel Monitors

Windows 2000 Professional supports using digital flat panel (DFP) monitors with display adapters that have the appropriate output connectors for this feature. (Most display adapters also have standard CRT connectors for use with more common monitors.)

▶ **To install a DFP**

1. Turn off the computer.

2. Disconnecting the existing monitor, and then connect the new monitor to the DFP connector on the display adapter.

3. Restart the computer.

Multiple Monitors

Multiple Monitors allows you to configure up to nine monitors so that the Windows 2000 Professional desktop can be spread out over their display areas. For each display, you can adjust the position, resolution, and color depth.

The monitor that is designated as the **Primary Display** in the **Display Properties** dialog box is the primary display. This is the default display that is used for prompts and pop-up windows and has full hardware Microsoft® Direct 3D® acceleration. It is also the only display that can run Microsoft® DirectX® applications in full-screen mode.

Note Some third-party display adapters have drivers that support multiple monitor configurations on computers running Windows NT 4.0. However, you must only use drivers and secondary monitors that are supported for Windows 2000 when configuring your computer with multiple monitors.

POST vs. Primary Display Device

In Windows 2000 Professional, any supported VGA monitor can be used as the power-on self test (POST) device. The adapter that displays the system BIOS and system memory count when the computer is turned on is the POST device. This device is the only one that can be used for MS-DOS® mode operations in full-screen. The POST device does not have to be the same as the Primary Display.

If an unsupported secondary monitor is used, it must be used as the VGA display. In most computers, PCI bus slots are numbered, with the priority given to slot 1. It might be necessary to place the secondary display in this slot.

When using an AGP architecture monitor, you need to determine whether the POST routine runs on the AGP or the PCI display adapters first. For more information about BIOS settings that can be set to determine which device starts first, refer to the documentation included with your hardware.

Newer system BIOSs usually have a setting called Primary Display that can be used to choose AGP or PCI. If this option is available, set the Primary Display to be the display adapter that does not support secondary monitors. If this option is not available, and you want to use an AGP secondary monitor, choose a secondary monitor with a hardware option to disable VGA. When VGA is disabled with hardware, it does not run the POST routine, regardless of the bus slot in which it is installed.

Configuring Multiple Monitors

To use a monitor as a secondary monitor, it must meet certain criteria. It must be a PCI or AGP device, and it must be able to run in graphical user interface (GUI) mode or without using VGA resources. It also must have a Windows 2000 Professional driver that enables it to be a secondary display. For more information about monitors that can be used for multiple monitors, see the Hardware Compatibility List link on the Web Resources page at http://windows.microsoft.com/windows2000/reskit/webresources.

Note You need to have a working monitor capable of VGA graphics connected to all installed display adapters.

If you have an onboard display device, it must be used as the VGA device. Some computers cannot activate the onboard display when a VGA-capable PCI display device is also present. In this case, disable the hardware VGA for the secondary devices so that the onboard device runs a POST routine.

If your onboard display device can function as a secondary device, contact the hardware manufacturer to make sure that you have the most updated system BIOS to avoid potential problems. You can also disable the hardware VGA for the secondary displays.

▶ **To add a second monitor to your computer**

1. Verify that your primary display adapter works properly. In Control Panel, double-click **Display**. In the **Display Properties** dialog box, click the **Settings** tab and verify that your display adapter is not listed as VGA.

2. Install the second video adapter. Windows 2000 Professional detects the new adapter.

Note To test which card will be primary, watch to see which card performs a power-on self test (POST). The one that performs a POST is the primary, and the one that seems inactive is the secondary. To change the order, reverse the order of the cards in the PCI slots.

3. Restart the computer when prompted and check that the display is initialized properly. When Windows 2000 Professional detects the new display adapter, the Add/Remove Hardware wizard appears and prompts you to confirm that the correct adapter has been detected.

4. Click **Search** when you are prompted for a driver, and then click **Next**.

5. Insert the Windows 2000 product CD when prompted, and then click **OK**. Click **Finish** twice.

6. In Control Panel, double-click **Display**.

7. In the **Display Properties** dialog box, click the **Settings** tab. Both monitors are displayed.

8. Click the icon for the new monitor. You can use the **Colors** drop-down list box to adjust the color depth and the **Screen area** slider to adjust the resolution. Make sure that the on-screen arrangement of the monitors matches the physical configuration of your monitors.

9. Select **Extend my Windows desktop to this monitor**, and then click **Restart** to restart the computer. After you log on to Windows 2000 Professional, both monitors are functional.

Multiple Monitors and DirectX

Only the primary monitor in a multiple monitor configuration can accelerate Direct 3D functions using the full capabilities of the monitor. Additionally, only the primary monitor can run DirectX applications in full-screen mode. For this reason, you need to make sure that the monitor with the best Direct 3D performance and features is the primary monitor.

▶ **To set the primary monitor in a multiple monitor configuration**

1. In Control Panel, double-click **Display**.

2. Click the **Settings** tab, and select **Use this monitor as the primary display**.

3. Click **OK**.

Note With each monitor that you add, system performance is compromised, due to increased use of system resources. For applications that require a lot of system resources, such as those that use DirectX, you might want to set up a hardware profile that uses only one monitor.

Using Multiple Monitors with Portable Computers

You can use docked portable computers in a multiple monitor configuration if the docking station allows the use of PCI display devices. The onboard display on the portable computer must be used as the VGA device.

Windows 2000 does not support hot undocking portable computers with an active multiple monitor configuration. To hot undock a portable computer, set up a non-multiple monitor hardware profile and log on again using that profile. You can also use Display in Control Panel to detach the secondary display before undocking.

Configuring the Mouse

Windows 2000 Professional makes mouse configuration and customization easier by providing a single Control Panel option for mouse settings.

Windows 2000 Professional Setup detects installed mouse devices, and installs the appropriate drivers.

Mouse and Pointing Device Driver Overview

Windows 2000 Professional provides the following improvements in mouse and pointing device support:

- Supports Plug and Play for easy installation of pointing devices. For example, the VMOUSE driver interface supports Plug and Play.
- Supports USB mouse devices.
- Supports multiple simultaneous devices, for example, when using PS/2 and serial devices at the same time.

In addition to better mouse services, Windows 2000 Professional allows the use of serial ports COM1 through COM4 for connecting a mouse or another pointing device.

For more information about devices designed to enhance accessibility, see "Accessibility for People with Disabilities" in this book.

Changing Mouse Drivers

You can use the **Mouse** option in Control Panel to update the driver for your mouse.

▶ **To update your mouse driver**

1. In Control Panel, double-click **Mouse**.

2. On the **Hardware** tab, click **Properties**.

3. On the **Driver** tab, click **Update Driver**, and then follow the prompts in the Update Driver wizard.

For more information, see Windows 2000 Professional Help.

For pointing device drivers that do not appear in the **Select Device** dialog box (those that are not provided with Windows 2000 Professional), check the Windows Update Web site. For information about Windows Update, see the Windows Update link on the Web Resources page at http://windows.microsoft.com/windows2000/reskit/webresources.

Configuring Mouse Behavior

You can use the Mouse option in Control Panel to configure buttons, customize mouse cursor appearance, set mouse speed, and make other changes. Different functions might be available, depending on the pointing device used with your computer.

▶ **To specify mouse behavior**

1. In Control Panel, double-click **Mouse**.

2. Click the tab for the behavior that you want to set.

3. After changing the settings to the ones you want, click **OK**.

   For more information about the configuration options, see Windows 2000 Professional Help.

Configuring Communications Resources

A communications resource is a physical or logical device that provides a single, asynchronous data stream. Communications ports, printer ports, and modems are examples of communications resources.

Two types of ports appear in Device Manager:

- Communications ports, also known as COM ports, serial ports, or RS-232 COM ports, are used to connect RS-232-compatible serial devices, such as modems and pointing devices, to the computer.

- Printer ports, also known as LPT ports or parallel ports, are used to connect parallel devices, such as printers, to the computer. For more information about configuring printer ports, see "Printing" in this book.

Several types of communications ports might be listed in Device Manager:

- Serial ports, also known as RS-232 COM ports. Serial ports are ports to which external serial devices can be attached. These usually require a 9-pin or 25-pin plug. Serial ports designed for Windows 2000 Professional use the 16550A buffered UART, which has a 16-byte FIFO that gives the CPU more time to serve other processes and that can serve multiple characters in a single interrupt routine.

- Internal modem adapters. Internal modems are modems that are constructed on an expansion card to be installed in an expansion slot inside a computer.

Note Windows 2000 cannot detect some internal modems. In this case, the internal modem needs to be installed and configured using the Modems option in Control Panel.

When you install a communications device, Windows 2000 Professional automatically assigns COM names to communication ports, internal modem adapters, and PC Card modem cards according to their base I/O port addresses as shown in the following list:

- COM1 at 3F8 (input/output range)

- COM2 at 2F8

- COM3 at 3E8

- COM4 at 2E8

If a device has a nonstandard base address, or if all four standard ports have been assigned to devices, Windows 2000 Professional automatically assigns the modem to COM5 or higher. Some 16-bit Microsoft® Windows® 3.1-based applications might not be able to access ports higher than COM4. Consequently, in the System option in Control Panel, you must adjust the base address in Device Manager or delete other devices to free up a lower COM port.

In addition, if some of the devices installed on a computer are not Plug and Play, you might have to change resource settings for their communications ports. You can change communications port settings by using Device Manager, as described in "Installing Devices" earlier in this chapter.

Tip For future reference, you might want to record the settings that appear on the Resources sheet for each communications port.

Troubleshooting Device Management

As a general troubleshooting step, always make sure that you are using updated drivers. You can get updated drivers from the Windows Update Web site. For information about Windows Update, see the Windows Update link on the Web Resources page at http://windows.microsoft.com/windows2000/reskit/webresources.

Make sure that your drivers have been digitally signed by Microsoft. If they have not been digitally signed, look on the Windows Update Web site. If you do not find drivers there, contact your hardware manufacturer and ask for drivers that bear the "Designed for Microsoft Windows 2000 Professional/Windows NT" logo.

For information about Windows 2000 Professional tools that can be used in troubleshooting, Windows Update, or driver signing, or what to do if you are having trouble starting your computer in safe mode, see "Troubleshooting Tools and Strategies" in this book.

Problems with Enabling PC Cards

If you have the correct drivers but your PC Card is still not available, your computer is probably using the wrong memory window for the device. Windows 2000 Professional selects a default set of commonly supported settings. Your socket might not support certain interrupt settings, so you might be able to get a PC Card socket to work by changing the IRQ. Similarly, your socket might not work on certain memory windows, and changing the memory window might solve your problem.

▶ **To change the memory window for a PC Card device**

1. In Device Manager, click the node for your PC Card socket, and then click **Properties**.

2. In the PC Card controller properties, click the **Global Settings** tab.

3. Make sure that the **Automatic Selection** check box is not checked.

4. Change the Start address according to information from your hardware manual.

   Typically, selecting a Start value higher than 100,000 works.

5. Restart Windows 2000 Professional.

▶ **To change the IRQ for a PC Card device**

1. In Device Manager, click the node for your PC Card socket, and then click **Properties**.

2. Change the IRQ from its default to a value that does not conflict with other IRQ settings used on your computer.

3. Restart Windows 2000 Professional.

Correcting Problems with the Display

If your computer has problems with the display, determine whether the problems persist when you use lower screen resolutions and different color depths with the display driver. If the display driver fails and changing resolutions does not resolve the problem, check or replace the current display driver. Also, make sure the installed display driver is the correct one for the installed display adapter.

Windows 2000 Professional includes safeguards that prevent unsupported settings from being implemented in most cases. However, problems result when Windows 2000 Professional has incorrect information about a monitor or display adapter supporting certain features.

If Windows 2000 Professional correctly identifies your display adapter and you attempt to set the adapter to a setting it does not support, in most cases you see an error message stating that the display adapter does not support the selected resolution or color depth. Less commonly, Windows 2000 Professional tries to set the selected resolution or color depth, and your system stops responding.

Windows 2000 Professional can identify Plug and Play monitors and automatically adjust the refresh rates available in the user interface to correspond to the settings provided in the monitor's INF file listing the monitor's capabilities. This results in reliable monitor operation and usually prevents users from setting incorrect or incompatible refresh rates.

With older monitors, however, it is possible to set refresh rates incorrectly. If you select a higher refresh rate than the monitor can support, you see a corrupted display with an image that looks like a maladjusted horizontal display with oscillating multiple images. If this happens, Windows 2000 Professional returns the monitor to its original refresh rate after a few moments.

Note If the video signal is set to an unsupported refresh rate, newer monitors might mute the video signal and return an error message such as "Invalid sync" or "Unsupported mode."

If Windows 2000 Professional does not recognize the display adapter, try using the basic VGA driver (by definition, a generic 640 x 480, 16-color driver). However, keep in mind that multiple monitor support is not available when you are using a basic VGA driver. If you have a vendor-supplied driver disk for the display adapter, you can install the drivers on that disk. If the drivers were not written for Windows 2000 Professional, some advanced display features might be disabled.

If an error occurs during display adapter initialization, the computer stops responding. To restart the computer, press CTRL+ALT+DEL. This problem might occur if you are using a video accelerator card and you change the display from the default setting (640 x 480, 16 colors) to 1024 x 768, 256 colors in the **Display Properties** dialog box for your display adapter. Although Windows 2000 Professional might accept the changes, the error still results. The Super VGA (SVGA) driver (1024 x 768) included with Windows 2000 Professional is designed only for nonaccelerated SVGA display adapters. To correct this problem, change the display driver back to the default VGA setting.

▶ **To see if the display error is corrected by changing the screen color setting**

1. In Control Panel, double-click **Display**, and then click the **Settings** tab.

2. Check the setting in **Colors**. If the selection is other than **16 Colors**, select **16 Colors**.

3. Click **OK**.

4. Retest the condition that was causing the display error. If the error does not recur, you might want to temporarily operate at a lower resolution until you can upgrade the display driver to a version that functions without error.

▶ **To check the display drivers**

1. In Device Manager, expand **Display adapters**.

2. Double-click the specific display adapter shown.

3. In the **Adapter Properties** dialog box, click the **Driver** tab, and then click **Driver Details**.

4. Click each file shown in the **Driver files** box. If available, the **Provider**, **File version**, and **Copyright** information appears below the file tree (some vendors' display drivers might not contain version information).

5. Check the displayed file versions for compatibility. Windows 2000 Professional display driver files have version numbers starting at 4.00.

6. If you have an incompatible driver, you can reinstall the original driver from the Windows 2000 Professional product CD or get new drivers from the Windows Update Web site. For information about Windows Update, see the Windows Update link on the Web Resources page at http://windows.microsoft.com/windows2000/reskit/webresources.

▶ **To find out if an incorrect display driver is installed**

- Restart the computer in safe mode. When the message "For troubleshooting and advanced startup options for Windows 2000, press F8" appears, press F8 to display the **Windows 2000 Advanced Options Menu**, and then select **Safe Mode**.

  If this resolves the display problem, the display driver is probably involved. Try replacing the driver with a newer version, or reinstall the driver from the original disks. For more information about troubleshooting problems in safe mode, see "Troubleshooting Tools and Strategies" in this book.

▶ **To see if the display error is corrected by changing screen resolution**

1. In Control Panel, double-click **Display**, and then click the **Settings** tab.
2. Check the setting in the **Screen area** menu. Select a setting with a lower resolution.
3. Click **OK**.
4. Retest the condition that was causing the display error.

▶ **To change your display driver back to VGA**

1. Restart the computer in safe mode.
2. In Control Panel, double-click **Display**, and then click the **Settings** tab.
3. Click **Advanced**, and then click the **Monitor** tab.
4. In **Monitor Type**, click **Properties**.
5. On the **Driver** tab, click **Update Driver**.
6. The **Upgrade Device Driver** wizard is displayed. Click **Next**, and then follow the instructions on the screen.

If you want to use a high-resolution display driver with Windows 2000 Professional, consult your display adapter manufacturer for the proper driver to use.

Correcting Problems with Multiple Monitors

This section describes problems that might occur when using multiple monitors. As a general troubleshooting step, make sure that your video card is included on the Hardware Compatibility List (HCL) and that you are using an updated driver.

The system does not detect the secondary adapters.

Make sure that you have the correct drivers for your monitors. Restart the computer, and start Device Manager. Expand the node for the monitor, and right-click to open the **Properties** dialog box. On the **Drivers** tab, click **Update Driver**, insert a disk containing the correct drivers, and then select **Display a list of known drivers for this device so that I can choose a specific driver**. Select **Have Disk**, and then click **Next**. When the files have been copied, click **Finish**.

If the problem is not corrected, you might have an unsupported display adapter. Choose an adapter that is supported and repeat the procedure for setting up multiple monitors. For more information about supported adapters, see the Hardware Compatibility List link on the Web Resources page at http://windows.microsoft.com/windows2000/reskit/webresources.

The primary monitor displays the startup screen and the secondary monitor is blank.

Check that the secondary monitor is plugged in and turned on. Check the power connections and cabling. Check that the monitor is capable of displaying the mode and refresh rates that are set up for it.

If you are still having a problem, switch the primary and secondary monitors.

The primary monitor displays the startup screen and the secondary monitor displays the desktop.

Shut down the computer and remove the secondary adapter. Check that you disabled VGA on the secondary adapter display. Disable VGA and reinstall the adapter.

If the VGA was disabled, restart the computer and open Device Manager. Under **Display Adapters** double-click the secondary adapter. On the **General** tab, check **Device Status** to see if there is a resource conflict. Change the resource and restart.

If neither of these procedures resolves the problem, you might have incompatible display adapters. Select a new primary or secondary display adapter and repeat the procedure "To add a secondary monitor to your computer" earlier in this chapter.

After installing the secondary monitor, the system does not complete the POST routine and there is no display on either monitor.

Turn off the computer and place the secondary display adapter in another PCI slot. Make sure that the primary display adapter is in PCI slot 1. Restart the computer and set up the primary display. Confirm that the drivers are correctly loaded. If this does not work, you might need to use a different PCI slot for your primary adapter. If the display adapters do not work in any of the PCI slots, you might have incompatible display adapters. Select a new primary or secondary display adapter and repeat the procedure "To add a secondary monitor to your computer" earlier in this chapter.

If one of the displays is AGP, check in the BIOS to make sure that the Primary Video option is set correctly for the VGA-enabled device. For example, if the VGA device is PCI, set the Primary Video to PCI.

The secondary monitor performs a POST, and only the secondary monitor is listed in the Display Properties.

The VGA-disabled device completed the POST routine instead of the primary display, preventing the multiple monitor configuration from working with the VGA device. Switch PCI slots between the two adapters (if they are both PCI) or set the BIOS option to run the POST routine the display port that corresponds to the VGA device.

After restarting, the secondary monitor has no display.

In Control Panel, double-click **Display**, and then click the **Settings** tab. Check that **Extend my Windows desktop into this monitor** is selected. If it is not, select this option and restart the computer.

If two monitor icons are not displayed in the **Display Properties** dialog box on the **Settings** tab, you might have incompatible display adapters. Select a new primary or secondary display adapter and repeat the procedure "To add a secondary monitor to your computer" earlier in this chapter.

Correcting Problems with SCSI Devices

This section includes problems that might occur with SCSI devices.

A SCSI device fails to work.

The SCSI and CD-ROM support built into Windows 2000 Professional requires that CD-ROM drives provide SCSI parity to function properly. For many drives, this is a configurable option or is active by default.

If you have trouble with a SCSI drive, make sure the SCSI bus is set up properly (refer to your hardware documentation for specific details).

In some cases, adding or removing a SCSI adapter might prevent your computer from starting correctly. Check the following:

- The ends of the SCSI bus must have terminating resistor packs (also called *terminators*) installed.

  If you have only internal or only external SCSI devices, the ends of the bus are probably the SCSI adapter and the last device on the cable. If you have both internal and external SCSI devices, the adapter is probably in the middle of the bus and must not have terminators installed. If you disconnect a device that has terminators installed (such as an external CD-ROM drive), be sure to install terminators on whatever device then becomes the last one on the bus. One of the devices on the SCSI bus (usually the adapter) needs to be configured to provide termination power to the bus.

  Windows 2000 Professional supports as many internal and external SCSI devices as the SCSI controller supports. In addition to the requirement that the last external and the last internal SCSI device be terminated, some hardware has additional requirements for where it must be placed in the SCSI chain.

- Removable media must be mounted on the drive before running Setup.

  If you have a SCSI removable media device, such as a cartridge drive, make sure the media is mounted on the drive before running Setup. If no media is mounted on the drive, errors might occur during Setup that prevent installation of Windows 2000 Professional.

Setup does not recognize the correct SCSI CD-ROM drive.

Windows 2000 Professional Setup can recognize multiple CD-ROM drives connected to the same SCSI host adapter. Therefore, if it does not recognize one of the CD-ROM drives, there is a hardware problem. For example, it might be caused by a legacy adapter with more than one device with the same SCSI ID.

Some drivers that are supported in Windows NT 4.0 do not work under Windows 2000. Also, devices that use microchannel architecture are not supported for use with Windows 2000.

Correcting Problems with Other Devices

This section describes problems that might occur with devices other than the display or SCSI devices.

The computer stops responding when you install a PCI device.

If Windows 2000 Professional stops responding or restarts when you are installing a PCI device, uninstall the device.

The system stalls when accessing the CD-ROM.

After you press CTRL+ALT+DEL to shut down and restart the computer, Windows 2000 Professional might be unable to find the CD-ROM or might stall when trying to access the drive; sometimes, pressing CTRL+ALT+DEL does not reset the computer. If this happens, turn off and then restart the computer. Use the Add/Remove Hardware option in Control Panel to install the drivers provided with Windows 2000 Professional for the specific CD-ROM device.

WAV files cannot be played.

If Windows 2000 Professional cannot recognize the sound card, you might not be able to play WAV files.

▶ **To verify sound card settings**

1. In Device Manager, double-click **Sound, video and game controllers**.

2. Double-click the specific sound card, and then in the card's properties, click the **Driver** tab so you can verify the drivers.

Note   Some of the entries displayed are subcomponents of the audio device, and do not have driver tabs. Search the tree for entries with numbers in their descriptions (for example, Super 23 Audio Device). This is the "root" device.

---

3. Click the **Resources** tab, and verify resource settings.

4. Check the **Conflicting device list**, and verify that no conflicts for the sound card settings appear in the list.

Ports for sound cards with multiple CD-ROM adapters are not detected.

If a sound card has multiple CD-ROM adapters, they often include a program that activates the port to be used. This program must run before Windows 2000 Professional starts. If it does not, Windows 2000 Professional does not detect the port.

An input device fails.

If an input device, such as the keyboard or the mouse, fails, do the following:

- Check the physical connection.

- In Device Manager, check the driver used for the device.

- Check for conflicts with the I/O and IRQ resources used.

- Check for conflicting drivers or applications.

The mouse moves erratically, or keyboard input fails.

For specific problems concerning mouse or keyboard operation, do the following:

- Check that there is no dust or debris caught in the mouse or on the surface where the mouse is gliding.

- In Device Manager, check the mouse and keyboard drivers, replacing them if necessary.

- In Control Panel, double-click **Mouse**, click the **Motion** tab, and then configure the pointer speed.

- Check the port used for the mouse.

- Check the physical connection of the mouse and keyboard.

- Restart the computer and hold down the left CTRL key until the Microsoft Windows 2000 Professional Startup Menu message appears, and then choose the **Logged** option. Check the Bootlog.txt file and verify that the mouse driver is loading.

Additional Resources

- For more information about updating device drivers, see the Windows Update Web site link on the Web Resources page at http://windows.microsoft.com/windows2000/reskit/webresources.

- For more information about driver signing and development, see the Device Driver Development Kit (DDK) link on the Web Resources page at http://windows.microsoft.com/windows2000/reskit/webresources.

- For more information about troubleshooting problems with devices, see the Knowledge Base link on the Web Resources page at http://windows.microsoft.com/windows2000/reskit/webresources.

C H A P T E R   2 0

Power Management

Windows 2000 Professional offers enhanced power management features that enable the operating system to control the use of power by computers and hardware. Power management in Windows 2000 Professional is based on the Advanced Configuration and Power Interface (ACPI) specification, which enables reliable power management through improved hardware and operating system coordination. Refer to this chapter for power management information, procedures to customize power settings, and techniques to troubleshoot power management problems.

In This Chapter

Related Information in the Professional Resource Kit

- For more information about power management on portable computers, see "Mobile Computing Configuration" in this book.

- For more information about troubleshooting power management, see "Troubleshooting Tools and Strategies" in this book.

Quick Guide to Power Management

How does Windows 2000 Professional incorporate power management into the operating system?

Windows 2000 Professional assumes the central role of coordinating power management activities for the system. Power management in Windows 2000 Professional is based on the OnNow power management design initiative. OnNow makes computers more convenient to access and more energy efficient by defining requirements for their various components to work together effectively to manage power use and conservation.

- See "Power Management Features" in this chapter.

What is the ACPI specification, and what does it enable?

Windows 2000 Professional supports the Advanced Configuration and Power (ACPI) specification, a power management open standard that allows the operating system to optimize how hardware and legacy devices use electrical power. On computers that are ACPI-compliant, you get the full benefit of the centrally-controlled and robust power management capabilities of Windows 2000 Professional.

- See "Understanding the Advanced Configuration and Power Interface" in this chapter.

Can I configure power management settings?

A feature of the operating system-directed power management system in Windows 2000 Professional is the ability to customize certain power settings using the user interface. There is a Power Options icon in Control Panel that exposes these settings and enables the creation of custom power schemes that you can implement in specific circumstances.

- See "Using the Power Management Interface" in this chapter.

How do I troubleshoot power management problems?

In order for Windows 2000 Professional to manage power, the devices and device drivers in the computer must be ACPI-compliant. When devices and device drivers are not ACPI-compliant, unexpected behavior can occur. Using troubleshooting information, you can often determine which devices and device drivers are causing problems.

- See "Troubleshooting Power Management" in this chapter.

Overview of Power Management

Power management in Windows 2000 Professional encompasses a number of features that enable the operating system to control the use and conservation of power by your computer and other hardware devices. Windows 2000 Professional takes a system-wide approach to power management with the OnNow power management design initiative. OnNow provides a fully integrated power management system that defines the requirements for the various components of the computer to work together to deliver consistent, intuitive, and effective power management.

What's New

Windows 2000 Professional provides enhanced support for power management by adhering to the OnNow power management design initiative, which includes support for the Advanced Configuration and Power Interface (ACPI).

Windows 2000 Professional takes a system-wide approach to configuration and power management, which is enabled by ACPI specification, a result of the OnNow design initiative. OnNow is a set of design specifications that enables a computer to deliver the same instant-on capability available in consumer devices, such as TVs and VCRs.

ACPI defines a hardware level interface that enables operating systems to implement power management in a consistent, platform-independent way. In Windows 2000 Professional, ACPI allows the operating system to have direct control over how power is consumed on the computer. This means that transitioning the CPU or individual devices to low-power states is at the direction of the operating system.

Power Management Features

Power management controls a computer's use and conservation of power. Windows 2000 Professional implements a system-wide, integrated approach to power management. In compliance with the OnNow design initiative, the operating system's power management features conserve energy while the computer is working and put the computer to sleep when it is not working. Power management features in Windows 2000 Professional include the following:

System Power Management   The ACPI defines mechanisms for controlling the computer's sleep and wake states, allowing any device to wake up the computer.

Device Power Management   Windows 2000 Professional can put a device into a low power state based on the level of usage of the device. The ACPI design separates the decision process from the actual implementation, so decisions regarding a device's power state are made by the component best able to do so.

Processor Power Management Windows 2000 Professional controls the processor's power state, enabling it to meet conservation, thermal, and audible noise goals.

System Events The ACPI defines a mechanism for handling thermal events, docking, device insertion and removal, and system events.

Battery Management On an ACPI-compliant computer running Windows 2000 Professional, battery management is provided by the operating system. For example, it is the operating system that determines battery-warning thresholds and calculates remaining battery capacity.

Power management provides for:

Minimal Startup and Shutdown Delays The system can sleep in a low power state from which it can "wake up" without rebooting.

Greater Overall Power Efficiency and Prolonged Battery Life Power is only applied to devices that are being used. When a device is not being used, it can be powered down and then powered up later, on demand.

Quieter Operation Powering down unused devices reduces noise.

Unlike previous approaches to power management, OnNow manages power for the entire system including all system devices and peripherals. To make this possible, the operating system must direct power to the computer.

With legacy power management architectures, the BIOS controls the power state of system devices. However, OnNow makes it possible for the operating system to coordinate power management activities at all levels and define the power-state transitions for the system.

Computer power management means there is control over how the computer consumes energy and integrates its components. For example, a program that is active or input from a device such as a mouse, keyboard, or joystick indicates to the power management system that the computer is in use. As a result, the power management system allocates full power to the computer. Otherwise, the power management system puts the computer into a sleep state. Another example is a fax modem, which does not need to use full power all the time. The fax modem can operate in a "standby" state, consuming less energy until it needs to receive an incoming fax, at which time it is given full power. This section describes how Windows 2000 Professional supports power management.

How Power Management Works

By using Windows 2000 Professional power management, a computer can do the following:

Turn On Instantly It can be ready for immediate use upon awakening from a sleep state when the user presses the power button.

Respond to Wake Up Events It appears to be shut down when not in use, but it can still respond to wakeup events. Wakeup events might be triggered by a device receiving some input (such as modem receiving a call) or by software requesting that the computer wake up at a predetermined time (for example, an e-mail client that automatically downloads your e-mail in the morning).

Adjust Software To Changing Power States Software adjusts its behavior when the power state of the computer changes. The operating system and applications work together to operate the computer, to deliver effective power management according to the user's current needs and expectations. For example, applications do not keep the computer busy unnecessarily; instead they proactively participate in shutting down the computer to conserve energy and reduce noise.

Incorporate New Devices Into Power Management All devices, whether originally installed in the computer or added later by the user, participate in the power management scheme. Any new device can have its power state changed as system use dictates.

Figure 20.1 shows the components of power management.

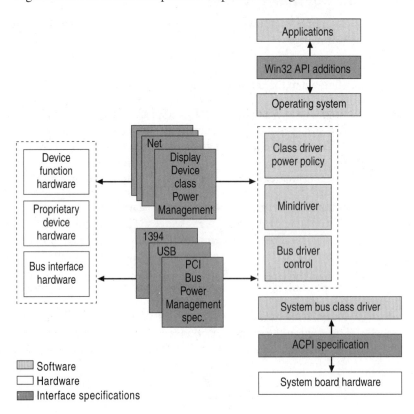

Figure 20.1   Power management components

Note Applications developed before the advent of OnNow power management assume that the computer is always fully powered while the application is running. Such applications can inadvertently cause the system to enter a lower power state. In addition, these applications might stop responding when the computer wakes up, either when enough time passes or when a device is removed. In such cases, you can disable power management in Control Panel, or you can shut down the applications before the system goes to sleep.

Though Windows 2000 Professional performs most of the work for power management, applications must be designed for OnNow power management to make progression through various power states a seamless activity.

Understanding Power Policy

The goal of power management is to conserve power while the computer is working and to put the computer to sleep when it is not working. The decisions that determine how to save energy and when to go to sleep are implemented by the *power policy*. The power policy of OnNow is based on the preferences of the end user, the requirements of applications, and the capabilities of the system hardware. The implementation of power policy is distributed throughout the system, with different system components acting as *policy owners* for different aspects. For example, the operating system is the policy owner that is responsible for determining when the computer should go to sleep, determining the level of sleep into which the computer should go, and knowing how to operate the processor to reduce power consumption, heat, and noise.

Each device in the computer has a policy owner. The policy owner is the component that knows how end users and applications use the device. Each policy owner must make appropriate decisions about power management for its device and work consistently with the operating system's policy for putting the computer to sleep.

Carrying out power policy—actually controlling devices so that power consumption or capabilities change—is the responsibility of the device drivers for the affected device and is shared among the drivers in the stack. Device-specific drivers, known as *minidrivers*, are responsible for saving and restoring the device's settings across transitions to and from low-power states. When a policy owner makes the decision to put a device into a low-power state and communicates that to the device driver through the system, the device driver saves the device's settings and sends the request to the bus driver. The bus driver gives the command to the device to enter the low-power state. When the device is turned on, the bus driver powers up the device, and the device-specific driver restores the saved context.

Understanding the Advanced Configuration and Power Interface

For the OnNow system to work correctly, Windows 2000 Professional must be aware of how power management features integrate throughout the computer. This is done through the Advanced Configuration and Power Interface (ACPI), a system interface that provides a standard method for managing power consumption by the computer hardware. ACPI allows the motherboard to describe its device configuration and the interface of its power control hardware to Windows 2000 Professional. This allows the operating system to automatically turn on and turn off standard devices, such as disk drives, network adapters, and printers, as well as other electronic devices that might be connected to the computer, such as VCRs, TVs, telephones, or stereos.

ACPI allows the operating system to have direct control over how the computer consumes power. It can control when the computer enters and leaves sleep states. It also allows the operating system to put individual devices, including the CPU, into low-power states based on usage. The parameters that determine the behavior of the power management system can be configured using *power schemes*. Power schemes determine battery management policy and also allow you to define the point at which the system, the monitor, and the disk drive enter a sleep state in different circumstances. For more information about power schemes, see "Configuring Power Schemes" in this chapter.

ACPI Overview

To use all the features of OnNow, the system BIOS must support ACPI. The BIOS plays an important role in the ACPI by working with Windows 2000 Professional to perform the necessary initialization and hand off during system start up and when resuming to the working (full power) state.

Windows 2000 Professional Setup contains checks that prevent ACPI from working on a computer with a BIOS that does not support ACPI or does so incorrectly. Before you upgrade a computer to Windows 2000 Professional, you should determine whether it has a BIOS that supports ACPI. To do so, you can use the Microsoft System Information (MSInfo) utility to get the computer's type and BIOS version. To check to see if your BIOS is up-to-date, see the Hardware Update link on the Web Resources page at http://windows.microsoft.com /windows2000/reskit/webresources.

Once you upgrade to Windows 2000 Professional, you can check whether support for ACPI is installed on a computer by checking the list of system devices in Device Manager. You must use the **Devices by connection** view to do this. Under the Computer node, you should see **Advanced Configuration and Power Interface (ACPI) PC** (or in the case of a computer with multiple processors, the **PC** is replaced with **MP**).

Figure 20.2 shows the relationship of the various components that constitute a computer system that uses ACPI.

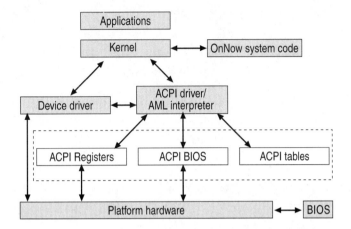

Figure 20.2   Relationship Between System and ACPI Components

---

Note Windows 2000 Professional provides very limited support for computers with a BIOS that does not support ACPI. With such systems, the power management features of Windows 2000 Professional function, but the BIOS must control power management.

The ACPI specification has two parts: configuration and power management. ACPI gives Windows 2000 Professional and the device drivers complete control of power management. The BIOS simply provides Windows 2000 Professional with access to the hardware controls for controlling power in the system. Windows 2000 Professional and the device drivers, which already know when the system is active, decide when to turn off devices that are not in use and when to put the entire system to sleep. For more information about the ACPI specification, see the ACPI link on the Web Resources page at http://windows.microsoft.com /windows2000/reskit/webresources.

Because power management is controlled by the operating system, there is a single user interface for managing power that works on all ACPI computers and simplifies the experience for the end user. ACPI provides more detailed information to the operating system about what the system can do and about the sources of events.

For example, a computer, operating system, and application that uses ACPI can do the following:

- Make sure the screen does not turn off in the middle of a presentation.
- Let the computer wake automatically in the middle of the night to perform some task, yet not turn on the monitor and drives needlessly.
- Let the user choose what the power and sleep buttons do to the system.

During Windows 2000 Professional Setup, ACPI is installed only on systems that have an ACPI-compatible BIOS. If you need to update your BIOS to support ACPI, you can do so using the following procedure.

▶ **To enable ACPI**

1. Update (flash) the BIOS to the latest version. (see the manufacturer's Web site for instructions about how to do this with your particular computer.)
2. Reinstall Windows 2000 Professional.

Note You do not need to reinstall Windows 2000 if you had an ACPI-compliant BIOS and then upgraded to a newer ACPI-compliant BIOS. You only need to reinstall Windows 2000 if you did not have an ACPI BIOS or an ACPI-compliant BIOS before you upgraded the BIOS.

Advanced Power Management Support

Advanced Power Management (APM) is the previous version power management solution that was introduced in Windows 95. ACPI supercedes APM. While Microsoft strongly recommends using systems with an ACPI-capable BIOS, Microsoft recognizes that many computers only support APM

Windows 2000 Professional has limited support for APM, and that support is intended only for older portable computers. It is not designed for use on desktop computers or other computers that do not use batteries for system power.

Microsoft places portable computers in one of three categories based on the support for APM offered by the systems. Windows 2000 Professional recognizes the following categories:

AutoEnable APM During installation of the operating system, Windows 2000 Professional Setup automatically installs and enables APM on systems in this category, and the **APM** tab is present when you open **Power Options** in Control Panel.

Disable APM   Microsoft has determined through testing that APM does not work properly on systems in this category. During installation of the operating system, Windows 2000 Professional Setup does not install APM. The **APM** tab is not present in Power Options.

Neutral Systems   The APM functionality of systems in this category has not been determined. During installation of the operating system, Windows 2000 Professional Setup installs APM, but does not enable it. You can manually enable APM support on the **APM** tab of **Power Options** in Control Panel.

For more information about APM, see "Mobile Computing" in this book. For more information about APM and ACPI BIOS detection, see the Microsoft Knowledge Base link on the Web Resources page at http://windows.microsoft.com/windows2000/reskit/webresources. Search for the articles "Windows 2000 and Advanced Power Management (APM) Support" and "How Windows 2000 Determines ACPI Compatibility."

Using the Power Management Interface

Windows 2000 Professional allows you to configure and monitor power management features and set power management options called *power schemes* by using **Power Options** in Control Panel. You can configure optional features, such as support for hibernation, and you can monitor the status of power components, such as the remaining power in your laptop's battery.

Windows 2000 Professional includes the following features for power management:

Simplified, Single-user Interface   This includes a power meter, low-battery alarms, Power Options in Control Panel, Hibernate, and Standby in the **Shutdown** dialog box.

Instant Access With Standby Mode   While on standby, your monitor and disk drives turn off, and your computer uses less power. When you want to use the computer again, it comes out of standby quickly. Standby is particularly useful for conserving battery power in portable computers. ACPI-enabled computers have a feature that toggles between power and sleep modes that you can access from a button on the front of the computer or from the operating system.

Note   When you plan to be away from your computer for a long period of time (more than a couple of hours), you should put it in hibernate rather than standby mode. If you use standby for an extended period of time, you run the risk of draining the battery.

Automatic Standby After Inactivity   You can tell your system to automatically go into standby mode when it detects that no activity has taken place for a specified interval of time. This conserves power because it does not require that you remember to manually put your computer in standby mode.

Wake Events   Windows 2000 Professional enables the system to automatically wake to handle events, such as backing up the system, downloading e-mail, and defragmenting the hard disk. This is done through Task Scheduler. For more information about Task Scheduler, see "Introduction to Configuration and Management" in this book.

Enhanced Application Messaging   This feature allows applications to adjust their behavior appropriately for changes in battery state.

Windows 2000 Professional provides power schemes that configure the system so that it turns off monitors and disk drives, and goes on standby, after predetermined periods of system inactivity. The following set of power schemes is built into Windows 2000 Professional:

Home/Office Desk   For desktop computers. This scheme is installed with Typical/Compact/Custom Setup options.

Portable/Laptop   Optimized for portable computers. This scheme includes aggressive settings for running on batteries (the AC settings are the same as desktop). This scheme is installed with Typical/Compact/Custom/Portable Setup options.

Presentation   This scheme prevents the computer from going into Standby mode. It is intended for use with computer presentations, when you need the computer display to stay on.

Always On   For use with personal servers. This scheme is similar to Home/Office, but has the standby timer disabled and disk drive timer increased. It is installed when you install a server.

Minimal Power Management   In this scheme, some power management features, such as timed hibernation or a timed event that can put the disk drive in a sleep mode, are disabled.

Max Battery   To conserve as much battery power as possible, this scheme allows a relatively short time of inactivity before it places the computer in a power saving state.

If none of the built-in schemes is appropriate, you can change the properties of a built-in scheme or create an entirely new scheme through the **Power Options Properties** dialog box.

Configuring Power Schemes

Using the power management features for the desktop, you can create a power scheme and display the Power Options icon on the taskbar. You can choose from the six preset configurations discussed earlier in this section: Home/Office Desk, Portable/Laptop, Presentation, Always On, Minimal Power Management, and Max Battery. Figure 20.3 shows the Power Options Properties page.

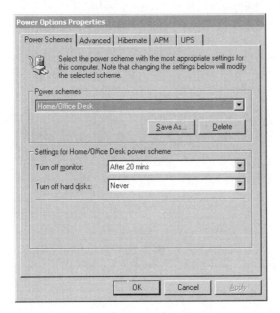

Figure 20.3   The Power Options Properties Page

▶ **To change the properties of an existing power scheme**

1. In Control Panel, click **Power Options**. The **Power Options Properties** page displays. Make sure that the **Power Schemes** tab is active.

2. Select a power scheme from the **Power schemes** list.

3. Select the time setting you want in the **Turn off monitor** list, and then click **OK**.

▶ **To create a new power scheme**

1. In Control Panel, click **Power Options**. The **Power Options Properties** page displays. Make sure the **Power Schemes** tab is active.

2. Select a power scheme from the **Power schemes** list.

3. Select the time setting you want in the **Turn off monitor** list**.**

4. Click **Save As** and then enter a name for the new power scheme. Click **OK**.

The **Advanced** tab lets you control whether the Power Options icon appears on the taskbar. Double-click the taskbar icon to open the **Power Options Properties** page, or click the icon to change the power scheme while you work.

▶ **To add the Power Options icon to the status area of the taskbar**

1. On the **Power Options Properties** page, click the **Advanced** tab.

2. Select the **Always show icon on the taskbar** check box.

3. Click **Apply**.

You can use the **Advanced** tab to make your computer go into standby or shutdown mode by pressing the power button or closing the lid, if your computer supports these options.

▶ **To use the Power Management power buttons**

1. On the **Power Options Properties** page, click the **Advanced** tab.

2. Click the **When I press the power button on my computer** list box, and then click **Standby, Shutdown,** or **Hibernate**.

3. Click **OK**.

▶ **To use the Hibernate feature**

1. On the **Power Options Properties** page, click the **Hibernate** tab, and then select the **Enable hibernate support** check box.

2. Click **Apply** and then click the **Advanced** tab.

3. If you want, check **Prompt for password** to clear it. If you do this, you can wake up your computer without needing to enter your password.

4. Click **OK**.

Using Power Management for Portable Computers

In addition to the tabs provided for the desktop, power management for portable computers includes the **Alarms** and **Power Meter** tabs. A major difference between power management for desktop and portable computers is that you can change settings based on battery use for a portable computer. Figure 20.4 shows the Portable/Laptop options of the Power Options Properties page

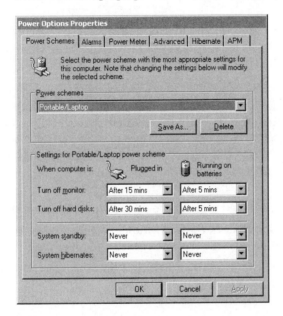

Figure 20.4   Portable/Laptop Options of the Power Options Properties Page

System standby can reduce the power consumption of your computer. Depending on whether your computer is plugged in or running on batteries, you can choose a different length of time for the computer to go into standby. The time specifies the length of time that your computer is inactive before going into standby mode.

You can change the properties of an existing power scheme or create a new power scheme using **Power schemes**. Select a power scheme that works best with the way you use your computer. You can choose from the six preset power management configurations discussed earlier in this section: Home/Office Desk, Portable/Laptop, Presentation, Always On, Minimal Power Management, and Max Battery.

▶ **To change the properties of an existing power scheme**

1. In Control Panel, click **Power Options**. The **Power Options Properties** page displays. Make sure the **Power Schemes** tab is active.

2. Select the power scheme from the **Power schemes** list.

3. Select the time settings you want on the **Turn off monitor, Turn off hard disks**, **System standby**, or **System hibernates** lists, and then click **Apply**.

▶ **To create a new power scheme**

1. In Control Panel, click **Power Options**. The **Power Options Properties** page displays. Make sure the **Power Schemes** tab is active.

2. Select the power scheme from the **Power schemes** list.

3. Select the time settings you want on the **Turn off monitor, Turn off hard disks**, **System standby**, or **System hibernates** lists. If you want, set other options.

4. Click **Save As**, enter a name for the new power scheme, click **OK**, and then click **Apply**.

▶ **To change the elapsed time before your disk drive automatically turns off**

1. In Control Panel, click **Power Options**. The **Power Options Properties** page displays. Make sure the **Power Schemes** tab is active.

2. In the **Turn off hard disks** lists, select the time intervals you want under **Plugged in** and **Running on batteries**.

3. Click **OK**.

▶ **To change the elapsed time before your monitor automatically turns off**

1. In Control Panel, click **Power Options**. The **Power Options Properties** page displays. Make sure the **Power Schemes** tab is active.

2. In the **Turn off monitor** lists, select the time intervals you want under **Plugged in** and **Running on batteries.**

3. Click **OK**.

The **Alarms** tab lets you set a low-battery alarm and a critical battery alarm. You can set the type of notification—an audible alarm or a displayed message—when your battery power drops to the levels you specify. You can also specify whether the computer goes on standby or shuts down when the battery alarms go off, or you can specify a program to run.

Note The critical battery alarm level must be less than the low battery alarm.

▶ **To set the battery alarms**

1. On the **Power Options Properties** page, click the **Alarms** tab.

2. Select the **Activate low battery alarm when power level reaches** check box or the **Activate critical battery alarm when power level reaches** check box.

3. Drag the slider to change the battery level at which a low battery alarm or message is activated.

4. Click **Alarm Action**, and then click either the **Sound alarm** or the **Display message** check box, or both.

5. If you want, click the **When the alarm goes off, the computer will** list and select **Standby**, **Hibernate**, or **Power Off**. This specifies whether your computer immediately goes into standby or shuts down when the alarm sounds or a message is displayed.

6. Click the **Force standby or shutdown even if a program stops responding** check box if you want the computer to go into standby or shut down even if a program is not responding.

7. Click the **When the alarm occurs, run this program** check box, and then click **Configure program**, if you want to have a special program run when the alarm goes off.

8. Click **OK**, and then click **OK** again.

The **Power Meter** tab shows the current source of power and displays the percentage of power level remaining for all of the batteries in your computer.

▶ **To check the power level of the batteries**

1. On the **Power Options Properties** page, click the **Power Meter** tab.

2. Click the **Show details for each battery** check box to display the power level for each battery.

3. Click a battery icon for more information about each battery.

4. Click **OK**.

You can configure display of the Power Options icon on the taskbar from the **Advanced** tab. When you enable this feature, you can right-click the Power Options icon in the status area of the taskbar to display the Power Meter and get the status, and other details, of each battery, or click the icon to change power schemes while you work.

▶ **To show the Power Options icon in the taskbar**

1. On the **Power Options Properties** page, click the **Advanced** tab.

2. Check the **Always show icon on the taskbar** check box.

3. Click **OK**.

You can choose to be prompted for a password when the computer goes off standby using the **Advanced** tab.

▶ **To be prompted for a password when the computer goes off standby**

1. On the **Power Options Properties** page, click the **Advanced** tab.

2. Click the **Prompt for password when computer goes off standby** check box The password you use is the same as the screen saver password.

3. Click **OK**.

If your computer supports these options, you can use the **Advanced** tab to make your computer go into standby or power off mode by pressing the power button, closing the lid, or pressing the sleep button.

▶ **To use the Power Management power buttons**

1. On the **Power Options Properties** page, click the **Advanced** tab.

2. In the **When I close the lid of my portable computer** list, select either **Standby** or **Power Off** or **None**.

3. In the **When I press the power button on my computer** list, select either **Standby, Hibernate** or **Power Off**.

4. In the **When I press the sleep button on my computer** list, select either **Standby** or **Power Off**.

5. Click **OK**.

▶ **To use the Hibernate feature**

1. On the **Power Options Properties** page, click the **Hibernate** tab, select the **Enable hibernate support** check box, click **Apply**, and then click the **Advanced** tab.

2. In the **When I press the power button on my computer** list, select **Hibernate**.

   – Or –

   In the **When I close the lid of my computer** list, select **Hibernate**.

   –Or–

   In the **When I press the sleep button on my computer** list, select **Hibernate**.

3. Click **OK**, and then either press the power button, close the lid of the computer, or press the sleep button, depending on which feature you selected.

For more information about power management for laptop computers, see "Mobile Computing" in this book.

Troubleshooting Power Management

This section contains troubleshooting information for the Windows 2000 Professional power management system.

For more information about troubleshooting problems with devices, see "Device Management" and "Troubleshooting Tools and Strategies in this book.

The following sections describe common problems, and ways to resolve them.

The system stops responding

In the past, when a system stopped responding, the cause was improperly configured hardware. With ACPI-compliant systems, it is more likely the result of a device driver that cannot support a certain power state, such as sleep. When Windows 2000 Professional attempts to switch the device to the unrecognized state, the system stops responding. One common cause for this is the use of older device drivers designed for Windows NT.

Try the following solutions:

- Disable power management to see if the system still stops responding.
- Obtain an updated driver for the device in question. If none is available, you cannot enable power management.

The computer appears to stop responding while in standby mode

To determine whether the problem is due to standby mode, hibernate mode, the shutdown of the monitor, or the shutdown of the disk drive, on the **Power Schemes** tab in the **Power Options Properties** page, set three of the four options to **Never** and the fourth to its original setting. Allow the time out to occur, and determine whether the system appears to stop responding. Isolate the failure by trying each of the four combinations, first test the monitor timer, then the disk drive timer, then the system standby timer, and then the system hibernate timer.

The system appears to stop responding after turning off the monitor

The system can stop responding for one of the following reasons:

- The system responds, but the display does not properly reinitialize.
- The display adapter does not fully support the commands made from Windows to turn off the display.

Try the following solutions:

- While the display is turned off, move the mouse or press a key on the keyboard to try turning it back on. If this fails, perform the following keystrokes:

CTRL+ESC

r

a:

ENTER

If the system is working, but the display is simply not properly initializing, this causes the system to look for a floppy disk in the A: drive. Check for disk activity in this drive.

- Contact your hardware vendor for more information.

The system appears to stop responding after shutting off the disk drives

Contact your hardware manufacturer for more information.

The disk drive does not support spin-down functionality or is malfunctioning

Contact your hardware manufacturer for more information.

The system appears to stop responding while in standby mode

The system could stop responding for one of the following reasons:

- The system responds, but the display does not properly reinitialize.
- An application or driver is allowing the system to go on standby but is causing the system to stop responding.
- The BIOS causes the system to stop responding.

Try the following solutions:

- While the display is turned off, move the mouse or press a key on the keyboard to try turning it back on. If this fails, perform the following keystrokes:

CTRL+ESC

r

a:

ENTER

If the system is working, but the display is simply not properly initializing, this causes the system to look for a floppy disk in the A: drive. Check for disk activity in this drive.

- Close all applications. Press CTRL+ALT+DEL, and end all tasks except Explorer and Systray. Uninstall third-party system management programs, such as crash protectors, memory managers, and performance enhancement utilities.

- Disable all devices in Device Manager except the display adapter(s), the mouse, anything under the **USB Devices** category (if you have either a USB keyboard or a USB mouse), and anything under the **System Devices** category. Restart the computer. If the system goes on standby successfully, re-enable one half of the currently disabled devices. Restart again. If the system continues to go on standby successfully, re-enable half of the remaining disabled devices. Otherwise, disable the devices you just re-enabled, and re-enable the devices that were disabled. Continue in this manner until the offending device is pinpointed.

- Contact your hardware vendor for more information.

The system cannot go into standby mode

You attempt to put your computer into Hibernate mode, and you receive the following error message:

```
The system cannot go to standby mode because the driver <drive>\<device
driver name> failed the request to standby.
```

The system might not go into standby mode for the following reason:

- The device driver does not support a sleep level sufficient for hibernation. This can be the result of out-of-date device drivers.

Try the following solutions:

- Verify that you are using a device driver written for Windows 2000.

- Verify that the device itself supports hibernation and that you are using the latest driver. To find current drivers, see the Windows update link on the Web Resources page at http://windows.microsoft.com/windows2000/reskit /webresources.

The computer cannot go into a Hibernate mode unless every device installed on the computer supports hibernation.

Additional Resources

- For more information about device support and hardware development, see the device support and hardware development link on the Web Resources page at http://windows.microsoft.com/windows2000/reskit/webresources.

- For more information about the OnNow power management initiative, see the Microsoft OnNow link on the Web Resources page at http://windows.microsoft.com/windows2000/reskit/webresources

- For more information about ACPI, see the Advanced Configuration and Power Interface link on the Web Resources page at http://windows.microsoft.com /windows2000/reskit/webresources

P A R T   4

Network Configuration and Management

In This Part

CHAPTER 21

Local and Remote Network Connections

The Microsoft® Windows® 2000 Professional Network and Dial-up Connections feature provides connectivity to local and remote networking resources, as well as Internet resources. Network and Dial-up Connections improves upon the dial-up networking functionality in Microsoft® Windows® 98 and Microsoft® Windows NT® version 4.0 by providing improved autoconfiguration of networking components and devices, and a single folder in which to configure all networking options. Tools, such as local Group Policy and Connection Manager, can assist you in managing connections in your enterprise. This chapter describes the Network and Dial-up Connections feature and includes a remote networking scenario.

In This Chapter

Related Information in the Windows 2000 Professional Resource Kit

- For more information about TCP/IP, see "TCP/IP in Windows 2000 Professional" in this book.

- For more information about troubleshooting network and dial-up connections with diagnostic tools, see "Troubleshooting Tools and Strategies" in this book.

Related Information in the Windows 2000 Server Resource Kit

- For more information about remote access server issues, see "Remote Access Server" in the *Microsoft® Windows® 2000 Server Resource Kit Internetworking Guide.*

Quick Guide to Local and Remote Network Connections

Use the quick guide to configure connections for local and remote network connectivity, and learn about the new features and functionality improvements upon previous versions of Windows. Also use the quick guide to learn how to configure security Group Policy settings and to use the Internet Connection Sharing feature.

Understand local and remote network connections.

Learn about the Network and Dial-up Connections folder, which combines features that were formerly configured in the Network Control Panel with functionality found in Windows 98 and Windows NT 4.0 Dial-up Networking. Learn what a connection is and what types of connections you can configure. Read an overview of the Connection Manager and Connection Point Services tools, which provide the opportunity for you to deploy preconfigured connections and customized dialers to your enterprise users.

- See "Overview to Local and Remote Network Connections" later in this chapter.

How do I create and configure connections?

Setup automatically creates a local area connection for each network adapter. This connection is preconfigured with the services needed for file and print sharing and the TCP/IP protocol. All other types of connections can be created by using **Make New Connection** in the Network and Dial-up Connections folder. Review the process of logging on and authentication for connections, and find out how to view the status of a local area connection. Determine which clients, services, and protocols are installed by default with a local area connection. Learn how to configure protocols, remote connections, and advanced settings.

- See "Creating, Configuring, and Monitoring Connections" later in this chapter.

Understand network security.

Connection security for dial-up, virtual private network (VPN), and direct connections is implemented through a combination of password authentication, data encryption, and callback options. Authentication options range from unencrypted passwords to the use of public key authentication methods, such as smart cards and certificates. Review the available authentication protocols and data encryption, and learn how authentication and encryption work. Review the process of callback.

- See "Remote Network Security" later in this chapter.

Review and use Group Policy settings.

You can use Group Policy to manage the configuration of connections in your enterprise. For example, a Group Policy can be set to prevent your users from deleting their connections. Review the Group Policy settings that affect the Network and Dial-up Connections folder.

- See "Local Group Policy Settings" later in this chapter.

Learn how to share an Internet connection.

If you are in an environment in which it is not cost-effective or feasible to provide direct Internet access for all computers, such as a small office or branch office network environment, you can use the Internet Connection Sharing (ICS) feature to share one Internet connection between all of your computers.

- See "Internet Connection Sharing" later in this chapter.

Review an Internet Connection Sharing scenario.

Learn how to establish a shared connection and review a scenario in which a fictitious organization establishes and uses a shared connection.

- See "Internet Connection Sharing Scenario: Connecting Your Branch Office's Intranet to the Internet" later in this chapter.

Use diagnostic tools to troubleshoot networking problems.

Diagnostic tools allow you to record modem or Point-to-Point Protocol (PPP) activity, or to diagnose networking problems. Learn which tools to use, and review solutions to common problems.

- See "Troubleshooting" later in this chapter.

Overview of Local and Remote Network Connections

Network and Dial-up Connections combines functionality found in Windows 98 and Windows NT 4.0 Dial-up Networking, with features that were formerly configured in the Network Control Panel, such as network protocol and service configuration. Each connection in the Network and Dial-up Connections folder contains a set of features that creates a link between your computer and another computer or network. System-wide configuration settings that were formerly configured in the Network Control Panel, such as network protocol configuration, are now established per-connection and are accessed by right-clicking a connection in the folder, and then selecting **Properties**. All of the connection's settings are configured in its properties. As a result, there is no longer a need for the Network Control Panel.

What Is a Connection?

All of the connections that appear in the Network and Dial-up Connections folder contain a set of features that you can use to create a link between your computer, and another computer or network. These features are used to establish end-to-end connectivity, and, for those connections configured for remote access, to define authentication negotiation and data encryption rules. For example, a dial-up connection might be configured with the following settings:

- A standard modem, capable of 56 kilobits per second (Kbps), for dialing.
- A phone number to dial.
- Any encrypted authentication protocol. Your computer will negotiate with the server to decide whether to use Challenge-Handshake Authentication Protocol (CHAP), Microsoft Challenge-Handshake Authentication Protocol (MS-CHAP), or Microsoft Challenge-Handshake Authentication Protocol version 2 (MS-CHAP v2).
- Data encryption required.
- TCP/IP protocol enabled, with the address obtained automatically.

When you double-click this connection, it dials the number by using the specified modem. The connection only allows the session to continue if the remote access server uses one of the specified encrypted authentication methods, and if the remote access server agrees to encrypt data. When connected, the remote access server assigns the connection a unique IP address. This ensures a unique and non-conflicting address for the connection, so that remote network resources, such as file shares, can be accessed. A dial-up connection's properties provide all of the parameters required to dial the connection, negotiate password and data handling rules, and provide remote network connectivity.

You can modify a local area connection at any time, but you cannot create one. A local area connection is created for each network adapter detected by the Plug and Play service.

Connection Types

Five types of connections can be created in the Network and Dial-up Connections folder. A permanent local area connection is automatically created for each network adapter that Plug and Play detects. You can also create dynamic connections, including dial-up, VPN connections, direct connections, and incoming connections. Except for local area connections, these other types of connections are created by double-clicking **Make New Connection** in the Network and Dial-up Connections folder. If you upgraded from Windows NT 4.0 or Windows 98, each Dial-up Networking phonebook entry is automatically converted into the appropriate connection type in the Network and Dial-up Connections folder.

Local area connections are created automatically. The network adapter is detected, the connection is created and placed in the Network and Dial-up Connections folder, and so on. By default, clients, protocols, and services are installed with a local area connection.

Note Certain conditions, such as a malfunctioning network adapter card, can keep your connection from appearing in the Network and Dial-up Connections folder.

Table 21.1 provides an example of each type of connection, and the possible communication methods you can use to establish connectivity.

Table 21.1   Connection Types

Connection Type	Communication Method	Example
Dial-up connections	Modem, Integrated Services Digital Network (ISDN), X.25	Connect to a corporate network or the Internet by using dial-up access.
Local area connections	Ethernet, Token Ring, cable modem, digital subscriber line (DSL), Fiber Distributed Data Interface (FDDI), IP over Asynchronous Transfer Mode (ATM), IrDA, wireless, wide area network (WAN) technologies (T1, Frame Relay)	Typical corporate user.
Virtual private network (VPN) connections	VPNs, over Point-to-Point Tunneling Protocol (PPTP) or Layer Two Transfer Protocol (L2TP), to corporate networks or the Internet	Connect securely to a corporate network over an existing connection to the Internet.
Direct connections	Serial cabling, infrared link, DirectParallel cable	Synchronize information between a handheld Windows CE computer and a desktop computer.
Incoming connections	Dial-up, VPN, or direct connections	Allow other computers to dial into this computer.

Deploying Managed Connections Using Connection Manager and the Connection Manager Administration Kit

Windows 2000 Server includes a set of tools that enables a network manager to deliver preconfigured connections to network users. These tools are the Connection Manager Administration Kit (CMAK) and Connection Point Services (CPS). A related feature, the Connection Manager dialer, is included in Windows 2000 Professional.

Connection Manager

Connection Manager is a client dialer with several advanced features over basic dial-up networking. A network manager can tailor the appearance and behavior of connection made with Connection Manager by using CMAK. By using it, an administrator can develop client dialer and connection software that allows users to connect to the network by using only the connection features that the administrator defines for them. In addition, CMAK allows the administrator to create a phone book that is available to each user when the user runs the Connection Manager. This phone book support allows the administrator to define local and remote connections to your network by using a network of dial-up access points, such as those available through Internet service providers worldwide. If the administrator requires secure connections over the Internet, users can also use Connection Manager to establish virtual private network (VPN) connections.

CMAK

Connection Manager is brandable, meaning that you can customize the installation package that you deliver to your customers, so that Connection Manager reflects the identity of your organization; you determine which functions and features you want to include and how Connection Manager appears to your customers. You can do this by using the Connection Manager Administration Kit (CMAK) wizard to build custom service profiles.

A service profile consists of all of the files required by Connection Manager to run the installation file, which then enables users to establish connections with your service. You can maximize or minimize the identification of your service or organization, depending on what you decide to include in a service profile. For example, you can include custom corporate logos or other graphics, custom icons, and your own online Help. You can also add autoapplications, specify actions to run before, during, and after a connection, and customize other features available in Connection Manager.

CPS

With Connection Point Services (CPS), you can automatically distribute and update custom phonebooks to your users. These phonebooks contain one or more Point of Presence (POP) entries, with each POP entry supplying a telephone number that provides dial-up access to an Internet access point. The phonebooks provide users with complete POP information, so they can connect to different Internet access points rather than being restricted to a single POP during travel.

Without the ability to update phonebooks (a task CPS handles automatically), users typically must contact technical support to be informed of changes in POP information, and to reconfigure their client dialer software.

Remote Security

To secure dial-up, VPN, and direct connections, various levels of password authentication and data encryption can be enforced. In addition, callback options can increase dial-up security. Advanced settings, such as Autodial and callback preferences, network identification, and binding order, are configured from the **Advanced** menu in the Network and Dial-up Connections folder. Optional networking components, such as SNMP Services, can also be installed from the **Advanced** menu.

Management

As an administrator, you can apply local Group Policy settings to your Network and Dial-up Connections users. These settings affect to what extent your users can or cannot manipulate their connections. Additionally, tools such as Connection Manager can be used to deploy customized versions of dial-up connections for your users.

Diagnostic tools such as Point-to-Point Protocol (PPP) logging, modem diagnostics, and the Netdiag tool can be used to troubleshoot connections. For more information about troubleshooting, see "Troubleshooting Tools" later in this chapter.

What's New

In addition to the improvements upon the features and functionality available in Windows NT 4.0 and Windows 98 Dial-up Networking, new networking component functionality in Network and Dial-up Connections automatically installs and configures networking components and devices, such as network adapters, modems, and protocols.

New features introduced with Network and Dial-up Connections enable the following tasks:

- Sharing a single Internet connection among your branch office network.
- Using the L2TP protocol in conjunction with IPSec to establish and use secure Windows 2000 virtual private network (VPN) connections.
- Enabling your computer to function as a dial-in server by creating an Incoming connection.
- Dynamic multilink connections for dialing multiple devices as you need them.

New Ways to do Familiar Tasks

Network and Dial-up Connections unifies local and remote networking into a single folder. Whether you are configuring connectivity to a corporate local area network (LAN), a dial-up Internet service provider (ISP), or granting rights so that others can connect to your computer, these tasks are completed by creating or modifying individual connections. For example, your corporate LAN connection and your dial-up ISP connection are defined with different TCP/IP addresses. In previous versions of Windows operating systems, these functions required modifying settings in Dial-up Networking and the Network Control Panel. In Network and Dial-up Connections, the TCP/IP addresses are assigned to each connection.

Table 21.2 compares how and where specific tasks are accomplished between Windows NT 4.0, Windows 98, and Windows 2000.

Table 21.2   New Ways to Do Familiar Tasks

Task	Windows 2000 Network and Dial-Up Connections	Windows NT 4.0	Windows 98
Configure connectivity to a corporate local area network.	Local area connection	Network Control Panel	Network Control Panel
Allow others to connect to my computer by modem, VPN, or direct cabling.	Incoming connections	Feature not available	Install Dial-up Server in Dial-up Networking
Configure TCP/IP.	Connection properties, **Networking** tab	Network Control Panel, **Protocols** tab	Network Control Panel

(continued)

Table 21.2   New Ways to Do Familiar Tasks *(continued)*

Task	Windows 2000 Network and Dial-Up Connections	Windows NT 4.0	Windows 98
Add a client, service, or protocol.	Connection properties, **Networking** tab	Network Control Panel	Network Control Panel
Add optional networking components, for example, Simple Network Management Protocol (SNMP) service or the TCP/IP Print Server.	**Advanced** menu, **Optional Networking Components**	Network Control Panel, **Services** tab	Feature not available
Monitor connections.	Right-click active connection, click **Status**.	Dial-up Monitor	Right-click active connection, click **Status**
Enable sharing of my files.	Connection properties, **Networking** tab, enable **File and Print Sharing for Microsoft Networks**	Server Service in Network Control Panel	Network Control Panel, File and Print Sharing
Configure bindings.	**Advanced** menu in Network and Dial-up Connections	Network Control Panel, **Bindings** tab	Network Control Panel, TCP/IP properties
Change computer name or domain.	**Advanced** menu, **Network Identification**	Network Control Panel	Network Control Panel
Configure an adapter.	Connection properties, **General** tab	Network Control Panel	Network Control Panel
Configure bindings.	**Advanced** menu, **Advanced Settings**	Network Control Panel, **Bindings** tab	Network Control Panel

New Networking Support

Windows 2000 has automated the configuration of many networking components and devices, with functionality unified into a single folder. Modems and COM ports are automatically detected and configured. In addition, TCP/IP includes enhancements that make it a better transport protocol for networking in high bandwidth LAN and WAN environments.

Autoconfiguration of Networking Components and Devices

The Network and Dial-up Connections folder is installed by default, so the feature is immediately available for your users. In Windows NT 4.0, the Remote Access Service (RAS) must be installed before remote connectivity can be established. In Windows 98, the Dial-up Server had to be installed separately to enable incoming connectivity. Where devices previously might have been manually installed and configured, the Plug and Play service now automatically detects and enumerates devices, such as modems and COM ports.

Tip In Windows NT 4.0, some modems had to be set to legacy mode to work. For the same modem to automatically be detected by Windows 2000, set the modem to Plug and Play mode.

Table 21.3 demonstrates how networking support in Windows 2000 Professional has improved upon Windows NT 4.0 and Windows 98.

Table 21.3   Comparing Networking Support

Windows 2000 Professional	Windows NT 4.0	Windows 98
Network and Dial-up Connections installed by default.	Must install Remote Access Service (RAS).	Dial-up Networking installed by default, but must install Dial-up Server to create incoming connectivity.
Modem detected and configured by Plug and Play.	Must install modem in Modems in Control Panel.	Modem detected and configured by Plug and Play.
COM port detected and enumerated by Plug and Play.	Must configure COM port.	COM port detected and enumerated by Plug and Play.
Protocol change does not require restart.	Restart when RAS is installed or protocol changes.	Protocol change requires restart.
VPN connections can be configured to automatically dial a connection to the ISP before establishing the VPN connection.	VPN connections may require activating two connections.	VPN connections may require activating two connections.

Unified Networking Configuration

The functionality of the Network Control Panel and Dial-up Networking has been combined into the single Network and Dial-up Connections folder.

Because all services and communication methods are configured within each connection, you do not need to use external components to configure connection settings. For example, the settings for a dial-up connection include features to be used before, during, and after connecting. These include the modem used to dial, the type of password encryption to be used upon connecting, and the network protocols to use on the remote network after you connect. Connection status, which includes the duration and speed of a connection, is viewed from the connection itself; you do not need to use an external status tool. For more information about configuring a connection, see "Creating, Configuring, and Monitoring Connections" later in this chapter.

In addition, you do not have to restart your computer, as you did when you installed RAS in Windows NT 4.0 or added or changed a protocol.

TCP/IP Improvements

Windows 2000 Professional's TCP/IP is the default protocol installed by Setup. It includes several performance enhancements, new features, and services that make it a better transport protocol for networking in high-bandwidth LAN and WAN environments and makes Windows 2000 Professional Internet-ready. Some of these features are self-adjusting, such as TCP window size, and others require configuration, such as Quality of Service (QoS).

Internet Connection Sharing

Using the Internet Connection Sharing (ICS) feature, all of the clients on your branch office network can use the same connection to access the Internet. For more information, see "Internet Connection Sharing" and "Internet Connection Sharing Scenario: Connecting Your Branch Office's Intranet to the Internet" later in this chapter.

L2TP

Windows NT 4.0 and Windows 98 enabled you to use the Point-to-Point Tunneling Protocol to access a private network through the Internet or other public network by using a VPN connection. Windows 2000 also enables you to use the Layer Two Tunneling Protocol (L2TP) for the same purpose. L2TP is an industry-standard Internet tunneling protocol with roughly the same functionality as PPTP. The Windows 2000 implementation of L2TP is designed to run natively over IP networks. The Microsoft implementation of L2TP does not support native tunneling over X.25, Frame Relay, or ATM networks.

Based on the Layer Two Forwarding (L2F) and PPTP specifications, L2TP can be used to set up tunnels through intervening networks. Like PPTP, L2TP encapsulates Point-to-Point Protocol (PPP) frames, which in turn encapsulate IP, AppleTalk, Internetwork Packet Exchange (IPX), or NetBIOS Extended User Interface (NetBEUI) protocols, thereby allowing users to remotely run applications that are dependent upon specific network protocols. Figure 21.1 shows an L2TP tunnel through an intervening network.

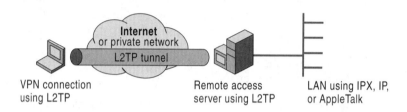

Figure 21.1   L2TP Tunneling

With L2TP, the computer running Windows 2000 Server that you are logging on to performs all security checks and validations. Data encryption is enabled using IPSec, a strong encryption mechanism, which makes it much safer to send information over non-secure networks. For more information about IPSec, see "IPSec" later in the chapter.

Note VPNs use encryption depending on the type of server to which they are connecting. If the VPN connection is configured to connect to a PPTP server, then Microsoft Point-to-Point Encryption (MPPE) is used. If the VPN is configured to connect to an L2TP server, then IPSec encryption methods are used. If the VPN is configured for an Automatic server type, which is the default selection, L2TP and its associated IPSec encryption, are attempted first, then PPTP and its associated MPPE encryption are attempted.

For more information about VPNs, see Windows 2000 Help.

IPSec

Internet Protocol security (IPSec) provides machine-level authentication, as well as data encryption, for VPN connections that use L2TP. IPSec negotiates a secure channel of communication between your computer and its remote tunnel server before an L2TP connection is established, which secures both the user authentication phase — including user name and passwords — and the data phase. For more information about IPSec, see "Data Encryption" later in this chapter.

Dynamic Multiple Device Dialing

Network and Dial-up Connections can dynamically control the use of multilinked lines. The Network and Dial-up Connections feature uses PPP Multilink dialing over multiple ISDN, X.25, or modem lines and the use of Bandwidth Allocation Protocol (BAP). Multilink combines multiple physical links into a logical bundle and the resulting aggregate link increases your connection bandwidth. To dial multiple devices, both your connection and your remote access server must have Multilink enabled. BAP enables the dynamic use of multiple-device dialing by allocating lines only as they are required, thereby limiting communications costs to the bandwidth requirements. You can realize a significant efficiency advantage by doing this. The conditions under which extra lines are dialed, and underused lines are disconnected, are configured through the **Options** property page of a dial-up connection. For more information, see Windows 2000 Help.

Incoming Connections

By creating an incoming connection, a computer running Windows 2000 Professional can act as a remote access server. You can configure an incoming connection to accept the following connection types: dial-up (modem, ISDN, X.25), virtual private network (VPN) (PPTP, L2TP), or direct (serial, infrared). On a computer running Windows 2000 Professional, an incoming connection can accept up to three incoming calls, up to one of each of these types. This can be an effective, low-cost option in a small environment, such as a remote sales office to which the corporate network occasionally needs to dial in to upload sales data.

Creating, Configuring, and Monitoring Connections

Each connection in the Network and Dial-up Connections folder contains a set of features that you can use to create a link between your computer and another computer or network. Outgoing connections contact a remote access or VPN server by using a configured access method (LAN, dial-up modem, ISDN line, and so on) to establish a connection with the network. Conversely, an incoming connection enables a computer running Windows 2000 Professional to be contacted by other computers, effectively turning your computer into a dial-in server. Whether you are connected locally (by a LAN), remotely (by dial-up, ISDN, and so on), or both, you can configure a connection so that it performs any network function that you want. For example, you can print to network printers, access network drives and files, browse other networks, and access the Internet. If you have upgraded to Windows 2000 Professional, **Network and Dial-up Connections**, shown in Figure 21.2, detects Windows 98 and Windows NT 4.0 Dial-up Networking phonebooks and creates a connection for each phonebook entry.

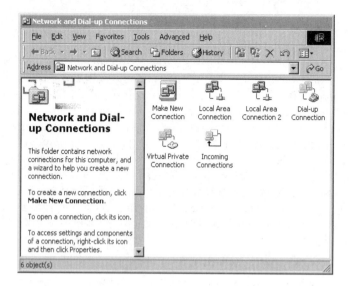

Figure 21.2   Network and Dial-up Connections

The **Make New Connection** wizard always appears in the Network and Dial-up Connections folder. It launches the Network Connection Wizard, which guides you through the process of creating all connection types, except for local area connections. Figure 21.3 shows the **Network Connection Wizard**.

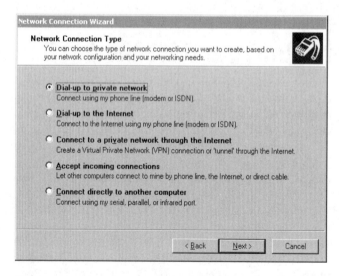

Figure 21.3   Network Connection Wizard

The steps in the wizard guide you through the selection of the configuration options that are required for each type of connection. The wizard enables you to select among five common tasks to create a connection type. Each connection type is then automatically configured with the most appropriate defaults for most cases. The following types of connections are available:

Dial-up to private network

This type of connection enables you to connect to a corporate network, rather than the Internet. File and Printer Sharing is enabled.

Dial-up to the Internet

This type of connection enables you to connect to the Internet. It launches the Internet Connection Wizard. File and Printer Sharing for Microsoft Networks is disabled. This protects your computer's file and print share from computers on the Internet.

The Internet Connection Wizard automatically connects you to the Microsoft Referral Service to help you select an ISP if you choose **Dial-up to the Internet** and either:

- **I want to sign up for a new Internet account. (My telephone line is connected to my modem.)**
- **I want to transfer my existing Internet account to this computer. (My telephone line is connected to my modem.)**

The Microsoft Referral Service automates the process and provides the phone numbers to you.

Note   Before you create an Internet connection, check with your Internet service provider (ISP) to verify the required connection settings. A connection to your ISP might require one or more of the following settings:

- A specific IP address.
- An IP header compression (for PPP).
- A DNS addresses and domain names.
- Other optional settings, such as Internet Protocol security (IPSec).

Connect to a private network through the Internet

This type of connection enables you to create a VPN. By default, it is set to automatically detect whether to create a VPN using L2TP or PPTP.

Accept incoming connections

This type of connection enables other users to dial into your computer.

Connect directly to another computer

This type of connection enables you to connect through a serial port, parallel port, or infrared.

Note Local area connections cannot be created, because they are automatically created when the Plug and Play service detects network adapters. However, local area connections can be configured at any time.

Accessing Network Resources

Network and Dial-up Connections provides data communications-level access to your network, based on the user name and password credentials that you supply. This access does not imply privilege to use resources on the network. The network authorization process confirms your access rights to any network resource each time that you attempt to access it. For more information about authentication and authorization methods, see "Authentication" later in this chapter.

After you have connected to your network, access to resources is further controlled by various administrative controls on both your own computer and on the servers you are trying to access. These include File and Printer Sharing, Local Group Policy, and Group Policy through the Active Directory™ directory service.

The way network authentication credentials are processed depends on whether you use the **Log on using dial-up connection** option when you log on. The authentication process can be streamlined and made more complete by using this option.

Note If your computer is connecting to a domain-protected network, you must have a user account on that network before you can be granted access to network resources.

Log On Using Dial-Up Connection

You can connect to your network using a dial-up or VPN connection, and log on to the network simultaneously by using the **Log on using dial-up connection** option. If your remote access server user name and password are the same as your domain user name and password, which they usually are, then you can provide a single set of credentials, and simultaneously log on to your network and provide information needed to access network resources. This provides maximum network access. Your computer and user accounts are authenticated, applicable computer and user account policies are invoked, and logon scripts are run.

If you do not choose the **Log on using dial-up connection** option, but log on to the computer and then invoke a connection after logon, you can be connected to the remote network if your credentials are acceptable to the remote access (dial-in) server, but your access to network resources may be limited. Consider the following cases:

In one case, if you logged onto your computer using domain credentials, then these credentials enable access to most network resources. However, your functionality might not be complete because your domain policy settings (such as IPSec policies) were not applied, and domain logon scripts were not run.

In another case, if you logged onto your computer using the account of a local user on the computer, then your logon credentials will not be appropriate for network access, so you will be challenged to provide domain credentials each time you attempt to access a network resource. As before, your access may be further limited by the fact that domain policy settings were not applied and that domain logon scripts were not run.

Note If you are in a local area network environment, you can also simultaneously log on to your local computer and your network domain by logging on with domain credentials. For more information, see "Interactive Logon Process" later in this chapter.

Administrative Controls That Affect Network Access

After you have connected to your network, access to network resources such as files and printers might be affected by one or more administrative controls.

File and Printer Sharing is established by each resource, and permissions depend on user name or group membership.

Group Policy enforces specified requirements for your users' environments. For example, by using Group Policy, you can enforce local and domain security options, specify logon and logoff scripts, and redirect user folder storage to a network location. Local Group Policy can be applied at the local computer or workgroup level. In the domain environment, Local Group Policy, and Group Policy can be applied by means of Active Directory.

For more information about Group Policy in Windows 2000, see "Security" in this book.

What Can I Configure?

Your ability to configure connections depends on several factors, including your administrative rights, whether a connection was created by using **Only for myself** or **For all users**, and depending on what Group Policy settings are applied to you. If you have rights to configure your connections, you can modify settings on the **General**, **Options**, **Security**, **Networking,** and **Sharing** properties pages.

Configuration Privileges

If you are logged on with administrator-level rights, the Network Connection Wizard prompts you to choose whether a connection that you are creating is to be made available **For all users**, or **Only for myself**. If a connection is **For all users**, then this connection is available to any user who logs on to that computer, and only an administrator-level user who is logged on to that computer can modify the connection. If a user creates a connection **Only for myself**, then only the creator of that connection can modify or use it.

Note If you choose **Log on using dial-up connection** when you start your Windows 2000 session, you only see the connections that are made available **For all users**. This is because before you log on, you are not authenticated to the network and your identity has not been verified. After you have logged on and proven your identity, you see the connections available as **Only for myself**.

Group policy settings, which are designed to help manage large numbers of users in enterprise environments, can be used to control access to the Network and Dial-up Connections folder, and the connections in it. Settings can be used that enable or disable the ability to create connections, delete connections, or modify connection properties. For more information about these Group Policy settings, see "Local Group Policy Settings" later in this chapter.

Property Pages

When a connection is created, its default properties are appropriate for most uses; however, property pages are available for any connection-specific settings you need to make. All of the following property pages apply to dial-up, VPN, and direct connections. A local area connection has **General** and **Sharing** property pages only.

To configure dialing devices, phone numbers, host address, country/region codes, or dialing rules, click the **General** tab, shown in Figure 21.4.

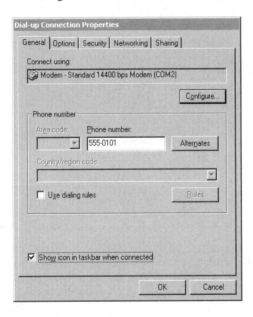

Figure 21.4   General Tab of the Dial-up Connection Properties Page

To configure dialing and redialing options, multilink configuration, or X.25 parameters, click the **Options** tab, shown in Figure 21.5. If you are connecting to a network that is protected by a domain controller, check the **Include Windows logon domain** box so you are prompted for the domain name.

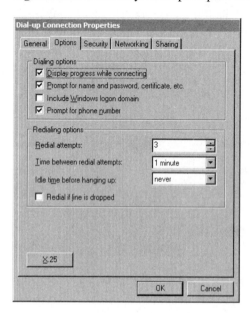

Figure 21.5   Options Tab of the Dial-up Connection Properties Page

To configure identity authentication, data encryption, or terminal window and scripting options, click the **Security** tab, shown in Figure 21.6. The **Typical** option is appropriate for most connections. Using that option, you can determine how your credentials are passed by selecting **Validate my identity as follows**. You can also use your logon credentials as credentials for this connection by selecting **Automatically use my Windows logon name and password**.

You only need to use the **Advanced** settings if you need more precise encryption and authentication settings. It is used for Extensible Authentication Protocol (EAP), discussed in "Remote Security" later in this chapter.

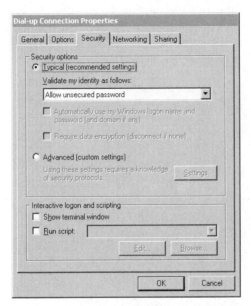

Figure 21.6   Security Tab of the Dial-up Connection Properties Page

To configure the dial-up server and protocols used for this connection, click the **Networking** tab, shown in Figure 21.7. This tab provides access to more advanced configuration, allowing you to install, uninstall, and configure protocols. For a VPN connection, you would use this tab to manually select PPTP or L2TP rather than allowing these VPN protocols to be selected automatically.

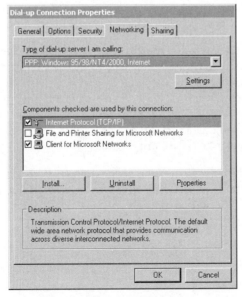

Figure 21.7   Networking Tab of the Dial-up Connection Properties Page

To enable or disable Internet Connection Sharing and on-demand dialing, click the **Sharing** tab, shown in Figure 21.8. By selecting **Enable Internet Connection Sharing**, you enable sharing and enable this computer to become your default gateway and name server for your network.

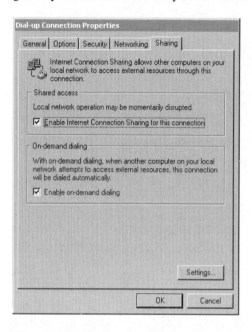

Figure 21.8   Sharing Tab of the Dial-up Connection Properties Page

Local Area Connections

A local area connection is automatically created for each network adapter in your computer that is detected by the Plug and Play service. After a card is physically installed, it is detected by the Plug and Play service. Network and Dial-up Connections enumerates the adapter and populates the Network and Dial-up Connections folder with a local area connection. Because local area connections are dependent upon a network card being recognized in the computer, they cannot be created by using **Make New Connection**.

For the adapter to be detected and the connection created, the Plug and Play service, Network and Dial-up Connections service, and Remote Procedure Call (RPC) services must be started. All of these services start automatically, no user interaction is required.

If a local area connection does not appear in the Network and Dial-up Connections, there might be several reasons:

- The network adapter was removed. (A local area connection only appears if an adapter is detected.)

- The installed network adapter is malfunctioning.

- If your network adapter is a legacy adapter that is not detected by the Add New Hardware wizard or the Plug and Play service, then you might need to set up the adapter manually in Device Manager before you see a local area connection in the Network and Dial-up Connections folder.

- If the driver is not recognized, the adapter appears in Device Manager but you cannot see a local area connection.

If your network adapter driver needs to be updated, use the **Update Driver** feature in the adapter's properties.

If your computer has one network adapter, but you need to connect to multiple LANs (for example, when traveling to a regional office), your local area connection network components need to be reconfigured each time you connect to a different LAN. However, you do not need to restart when you change TCP/IP or other connection settings.

Tip Use the network adapters that are listed in the Hardware Compatibility List link on the Web Resources page at http://windows.microsoft.com/windows2000/reskit/webresources.

Also, use network adapter drivers that are supported by Windows 2000 Professional.

Clients, Services, and Protocols

By default, the following clients, services, and protocols are installed by default with a local area connection:

- Clients: Client for Microsoft Networks (allows you to access file and print shares of other Windows computers).

- Services: File and Print Sharing for Microsoft Networks (allows you to share your own computer resources).

- Protocols: TCP/IP, with automatic addressing enabled.

Any other clients, services, and protocols, including Internetwork Packet Exchange/Sequenced Packet Exchange (IPX/SPX), must be installed separately.

▶ **To configure TCP/IP for a local area connection**

1. In **Network and Dial-up Connections**, shown in Figure 21.9, right-click the local area connection, and then click **Properties**.

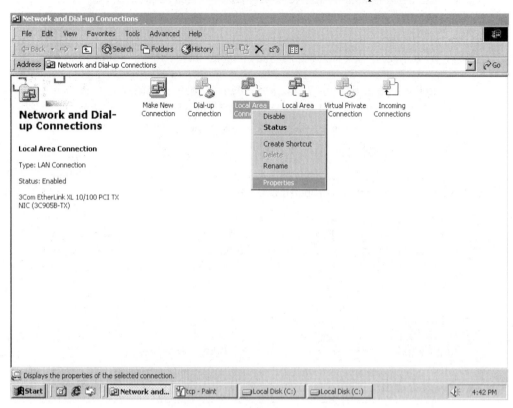

Figure 21.9   Network and Dial-up Connections

2. In **Local Area Connection Properties**, shown in Figure 21.10, select **Internet Protocol (TCP/IP)**, and then click **Properties**.

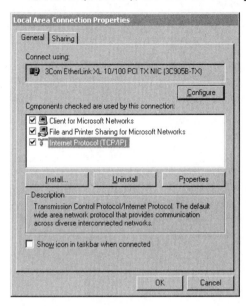

Figure 21.10   Local Area Connection Properties

3. Do one of the following:

- If you want IP settings to be assigned automatically, click **Obtain an IP address automatically**, and then click **OK**.

- If you want to specify an IP address or a DNS server address, do the following in the **Internet Protocol (TCP/IP) Properties** dialog box, shown in Figure 21.11:

  - Click **Use the following IP address**, and in the **IP address** field, type the IP address.

  - Click **Use the following DNS server addresses**, and in **Preferred DNS server** and **Alternate DNS server**, type the IP addresses of the preferred and alternate DNS servers.

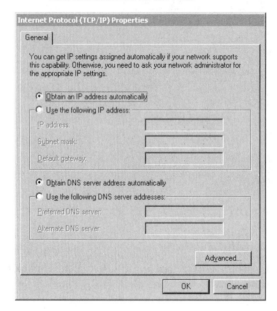

Figure 21.11   Internet Protocol (TCP/IP) Properties

4. To configure advanced TCP/IP options, such as multiple DNS server addresses, WINS addresses, and other options, click **Advanced**.

Whenever possible, use automated TCP/IP settings, such as automatic addressing, for the following reasons:

- Automatic addressing is enabled by default.

- If your location changes, you do not have to modify your IP settings.

- Automated IP settings are used for all connections, and they eliminate the need to configure settings such as DNS, WINS, and so on.

Limiting Protocols to Enhance Network Performance

Limiting the number of protocols on your computer enhances network performance and reduces network traffic. Windows 2000 attempts to establish connectivity by using every network protocol that is installed. By only installing and enabling the protocols that your system can use, Windows 2000 does not attempt to connect with additional protocols and creates connections more efficiently.

Local Area Connection Status

Like other connections, the appearance of the local area connection icon changes according to the status of the connection. The icon appears in the Network and Dial-up Connections folder, or if the network cable is disconnected, an additional icon appears in the taskbar. By design, if a network adapter is not detected by your computer, a local area connection icon does not appear in the Network and Dial-up Connections folder. Table 21.4 describes the different local area connection icons.

Table 21.4   Local Area Connection icons

Icon	Description	Location
Local Area Connection	The local area connection is active.	Network and Dial-up Connections folder
Local Area Connection	The cable is unplugged from your computer, or from the wall or hub.	Network and Dial-up Connections folder
	The cable is unplugged from your computer, or from the wall or hub.	Taskbar
Local Area Connection	The driver is disabled.	Network and Dial-up Connections folder
None	The network adapter was not detected.	No icon appears in the Network and Dial-up Connections folder

▶ **To view the status of a local area connection**

1. Right-click the local area connection, and then click **Status**.

2. To automatically enable the Status monitor each time the connection is active, right-click the local area connection, click **Properties**, and then select the **Show icon in taskbar when connected** check box. By default, the Status monitor is disabled for local area connections, but enabled for all other types of connections.

WAN Adapters

Permanent connection WAN adapters such as T1, Frame Relay, and ATM, also appear in the Network and Dial-up Connections folder as local area connections. For these adapters, some settings are autodetected, and some need to be configured. For example, for a Frame Relay adapter, the appropriate management protocol, Committed Information Rates (CIR), Data Link Connection Identifiers (DLCIs), and line signaling, must be configured. For these settings, refer to the product documentation included with the adapter or contact the manufacturer. Defaults might vary according to the adapter.

Configuring Remote Connections

Because all services and communication methods are configured within the connection, you do not need to use external management tools to configure dial-up, VPN, or direct connections. For example, the settings for a dial-up connection include the features to be used before, during, and after connecting. These include the modem you use to dial, the type of password authentication and data encryption you use upon connecting, and the remote network protocols you use after you connect.

Because settings are established per connection, you can create different connections that apply to different connection scenarios and their specific needs. For example, if you use a reserved TCP/IP address when you dial into your corporate office, you can configure a connection with a static TCP/IP address. You might also have a connection configured for an ISP. If your ISP allocates TCP/IP addresses using PPP, that connection's TCP/IP settings are set to **Obtain an IP address automatically**.

Connection status, which includes the duration and speed of a connection, is viewed from the connection itself; you do not need to use an external status tool. For more information about configuring connections, see Windows 2000 Help.

All connections are configured by right-clicking the connection, and then clicking **Properties**.

Configuring Advanced Settings

The settings in **Advanced** apply to all Network and Dial-up Connections. You can specify manual dialing preferences, network identification options such as your computer name or the domain to which your computer belongs, and you can install optional networking components such as the Simple Network Management Protocol (SNMP) service or the TCP/IP Print Server. You can also modify the order in which connections are accessed by network services, or the order in which your computer accesses network information.

Operator-Assisted Dialing

If you choose this setting, automatic dial-up settings are overridden where intervention is required. For example, if you are using a dial-up connection where you have to call through a manually operated switchboard.

Dial-Up Preferences

The settings in **Dial-up Preferences** affect connection creation privileges, Autodial options, and callback options.

You can enable or disable the **Dial-up Preferences** menu on your users' desktops by using the **Enable the Dial-up Preferences item on the Advanced menu** Group Policy setting. For more information, see "Local Group Policy Settings" later in this chapter.

Autodial

This preferences lists the available locations where you can enable Autodial. Autodial maps and maintains network addresses to connection destinations, which allows the destinations to be automatically dialed when referenced, whether from an application or from a command prompt. To enable Autodial for a location, select the check box next to the location. To disable Autodial for a connection, clear the check box next to the location.

The following is an example of how Autodial works:

- You are not connected to your ISP, and you click on an Internet address which is embedded in a word processing document.

- You are asked to choose which connection is used to reach your ISP, that connection is dialed, and then you access the Internet address.

- The next time you are not connected to your ISP and you click on the Internet address in the word processing document, the connection that you selected the first time is automatically dialed.

The Autodial feature works only when the Remote Access Auto Connection Manager service is started.

▶ **To start the Remote Access Auto Connection Manager service**

1. Right-click **My Computer**, and then click **Manage**.

2. In the console tree, double-click **Services and Applications**, and then click **Services**.

3. In the details pane, right-click **Remote Access Auto Connection Manager**, and then click **Start**.

4. **Started** displays in the **Status** column.

Callback

The settings in **Callback** indicate the conditions under which you want to use the feature. For example, you can configure callback to prompt you for a phone number during the dialing process, or you can specify that callback always call you back at a specific number.

Callback options are also configured by your remote access server system administrator on a per-user basis. The **Always Callback to** server setting overrides Network and Dial-up Connections settings. Therefore, if you have specified **Ask me during dialing when the server offers** in Network and Dial-up Connections, but your account on the remote access server designates **Always Callback to** (with a corresponding phone number), callback does not prompt you for a number when you dial in; it always calls you back at the number specified on the server.

Note If you have specified **No callback**, but the remote access server is set to **Always Callback to**, you cannot connect. With this combination of settings, the remote access server requests callback, your computer refuses, and then the remote access server disconnects your connection.

How Callback Works

Callback behavior is determined by a combination of the settings that you specify in Network and Dial-up Connections, and by the remote access server settings designated by your system administrator.

After your call reaches the remote access server, the server determines whether your user name and password are correct. If they are, what happens next depends upon the settings that you have specified in Network and Dial-up Connections, and your remote access server callback settings. Table 21.5 illustrates callback behavior based on these settings.

Table 21.5   Callback Behavior

Your Computer's Callback Setting	Remote Access Server Callback Setting	Behavior
No callback	No callback	The connection stays up.
No callback	Set by caller	The remote access server offers callback, the client declines, the connection stays up.

(continued)

Table 21.5   Callback Behavior *(continued)*

Your Computer's Callback Setting	Remote Access Server Callback Setting	Behavior
No callback	Always callback to	The remote access server offers callback, the client declines, the remote access server disconnects the connection.
Ask me during dialing when the server offers	No callback	The connection stays up.
Ask me during dialing when the server offers	Set by caller	The **Callback** dialog box appears on your computer. You then type the current calback number in the dialog box and wait for the server to disconnect and return the call. Optionally, you can press **Esc** at this point to cancel the callback process and remain connected.
Ask me during dialing when the server offers	Always callback to	The remote access server disconnects and then returns the call, using the number specified on the remote access server.
Always call me back at the number(s) below	No callback	The connection stays up.
Always call me back at the number(s) below	Set by caller	The remote access server disconnects and then returns the call, using the number specified in Network and Dial-up Connections.
Always call me back at the number(s) below	Always callback to	The remote access server disconnects and then returns the call, using the number specified on the remote access server.

For more information about how to configure your callback options, see Windows 2000 Help.

Note   If your computer is configured to accept incoming connections, you can enforce callback options on that computer.

Network Identification

Network Identification displays your computer name, and the workgroup or domain to which the computer belongs. You can change the name of your computer, or join a domain by clicking **Properties**.

Advanced Settings

Windows 2000 uses network providers and bindings in the order specified in **Advanced Settings**. By changing your provider order, and by changing the order of protocols bound to those providers, you can improve performance. For example, if your LAN connection is enabled to access NetWare and Microsoft Windows networks, which use IPX and TCP/IP, but your primary connection is to a Microsoft Windows network that uses TCP/IP, you can move **Microsoft Windows Network** to the top of the **Network providers** list on the **Provider Order** tab, and move **Internet Protocol (TCP/IP)** to the top of the **File and Printer Sharing for Microsoft Networks** binding on the **Adapters and Bindings** tab.

You can enable or disable the **Advanced Settings** option on the **Advanced** menu by using the **Enable the Advanced Settings item on the Advanced menu** setting in Group Policy. For more information, see "Local Group Policy Settings" later in this chapter.

Optional Networking Components

Optional networking components support network operations performed by Windows 2000 that are not automatically installed with Windows 2000. Some of these components include the Route Listening Service, Simple TCP/IP Services, SNMP Services, and Print Services for UNIX.

Remote Network Security

You can configure your dial-up, virtual private network (VPN), and direct connections to enforce various levels of password authentication and data encryption. Authentication methods range from unencrypted to custom, such as the Extensible Authentication Protocol (EAP). EAP provides flexible support for a wide range of authentication methods, including smart cards, certificates, one-time passwords, and public keys. You can also specify the type of data encryption, depending on the type of authentication protocol (MS-CHAP or EAP-TLS) that you choose. Finally, if allowed by your system administrator, you can configure callback options to save telephone charges, and to increase dial-up security.

On the server to which you are connecting, remote access permissions on a Windows 2000 remote access server are granted based on the dial-in settings of your user account and *remote access policies*. Remote access policies are a set of conditions and connection settings that give network administrators more flexibility in granting remote access permissions and usage. If the settings of your connection do not match at least one of the remote access policies that apply to your connection, the connection attempt is rejected, regardless of your dial-in settings.

The network administrator can configure Windows 2000 user accounts and domains to provide security by forcing encrypted authentication and encrypted data for remote communications. For more information about Windows 2000 security, see Windows 2000 Server Help.

How Security Works at Connection

The following steps describe what happens during a call to a remote access server:

1. Your computer dials a remote access server.

2. Depending on the authentication methods you have chosen, one of the following happens:

If You Are Using PAP or SPAP

1. Your computer sends its password to the server.

2. The server checks the account credentials against the user database.

If You Are Using CHAP or MS-CHAP

1. The server sends a challenge to your computer.

2. Your computer sends an encrypted response to the server.

3. The server checks the response against the user database.

If You Are Using MS-CHAP v2

1. The server sends a challenge to your computer.

2. Your computer sends an encrypted response to the server.

3. The server checks the response against the user database, and sends back an authentication response.

4. Your computer verifies the authentication response.

If You Are Using Certificate-based Authentication

1. The server requests credentials from your computer, and sends its own certificate.

2. If you configured your connection to **Validate server certificate**, it is validated. If not, this step is skipped.

3. Your computer presents its certificate to the server.

4. The server verifies that the certificate is valid, and that it has not been revoked.

3. If the account is valid, the server checks for remote access permission.

4. If remote access permissions have been granted, the server accepts your connection. For a Windows 2000 server, permission is granted based on the remote access permission of the user account and the remote access policies.

   If callback is enabled, the server calls your computer back and repeats steps 2 through 4.

Note If you are using an L2TP-enabled VPN, IP Security (IPSec) authenticates your computer account and provides encryption before any of these steps take place. For more information about IPSec, see "Data Encryption" later in this chapter.

Authentication

For dial-up, virtual private network (VPN), and direct connections, Windows 2000 authentication is implemented in two processes: interactive logon and network authorization. Successful user authentication depends on both of these processes.

Interactive Logon Process

The interactive logon process confirms the user's identity to either a domain account or a local computer. Depending on the type of user account and whether the computer is connected to a network protected by a domain controller, the process can vary as follows:

- A domain account

  A user logs on to the network with a password or smart card, using credentials that match those stored in Active Directory. By logging on with a domain account, an authorized user can access resources in the domain and any trusting domains. If a password is used to log on to a domain account, Windows 2000 uses Kerberos v5 for authentication. If a smart card is used instead, Windows 2000 uses Kerberos v5 authentication with certificates.

- A local computer account

    A user logs on to a local computer, using credentials stored in Security
    Account Manager (SAM), which is the local security account database. Any
    workstation can maintain local user accounts, but those accounts can only be
    used for access to that local computer.

Network Authorization

Network authorization confirms the user's identification to any network service or
resource that the user is attempting to access. To provide this type of
authorization, the Windows 2000 security system supports many different
mechanisms, including Kerberos v5, Secure Socket Layer/Transport Layer
Security (SSL/TLS), and, for compatibility with Windows NT 4.0 and
Windows NTLM.

Users who have logged onto a domain account do not see network authorization
challenges during their logon session. Users who have logged onto a local
computer account must provide credentials (such as a user name and password)
every time they access a network resource.

Logging On Using Domain Credentials

The credentials that you use to initially log on to your computer are also the
credentials that are presented to a domain when attempting to access a network
resource. Therefore, if your local logon and network authorization credentials
differ, you are prompted to provide Windows 2000 domain credentials each time
you access a network resource. You can avoid this by logging on to your
computer by using your Windows 2000 domain name, your Windows 2000
domain user name, and your Windows 2000 domain password before you try to
connect to a network resource. If you log on without being connected to the
network, Windows 2000 recognizes that your credentials match a previous
successful logon, and you receive the following message: "Windows cannot
connect to a server to confirm your logon settings. You have been logged on
using previously stored account information." When you connect to your network,
the cached credentials are sent to your Windows 2000 domain and you are able to
access network resources without having to provide a password again.

Authentication Protocols

With Network and Dial-up Connections, you can use the following authentication
methods and protocols.

PAP

Password Authentication Protocol (PAP) uses plaintext (unencrypted) passwords and is the least sophisticated authentication protocol. PAP is typically used when your connection and the server cannot negotiate a more secure form of validation. You might need to use this protocol when you are calling a non-Windows-based server.

SPAP

With Shiva Password Authentication Protocol (SPAP), Shiva clients can dial in to computers running Windows 2000 Server, and Windows 2000 clients can dial into Shiva servers.

CHAP

The Challenge Handshake Authentication Protocol (CHAP) negotiates a secure form of encrypted authentication, by using Message Digest 5 (MD5), an industry-standard hashing scheme. A *hashing scheme* is a method for transforming data (for example, a password) in such a way that the result is unique and cannot be changed back to its original form. CHAP uses challenge-response with one-way MD5 hashing on the response. In this way, you can prove to the server that you know your password without actually sending the password over the network. By supporting CHAP and MD5, Network and Dial-up Connections is able to securely connect to almost all third-party PPP servers.

Note If your server requires you to use PAP, SPAP, or CHAP, you cannot require data encryption for dial-up or PPTP connections.

If the connection is configured to require encrypted authentication, and connects to a server that is only configured for cleartext authentication, the connection hangs up.

MS-CHAP

Microsoft created Microsoft Challenge Handshake Authentication Protocol (MS-CHAP), an extension of CHAP, to authenticate remote Windows workstations, providing the functionality to which LAN-based users are accustomed while integrating the encryption and hashing algorithms used on Windows networks. Like CHAP, MS-CHAP uses a challenge-response mechanism with one-way encryption on the response.

Where possible, MS-CHAP is consistent with standard CHAP. Its response packet is in a format specifically designed for networking with computers running Microsoft® Windows NT and Windows 2000, and Microsoft® Windows 95 and Microsoft® Windows 98.

Your system administrator can define authentication retry and password changing rules for the users connecting to your server.

A version of MS-CHAP is available specifically for connecting to a Windows 95 server. This is required only if your connection is being made to a Windows 95 server.

MS-CHAP v2

A new version of the Microsoft Challenge Handshake Authentication Protocol (MS-CHAP v2) is available. This new protocol provides mutual authentication, stronger initial data encryption keys, and different encryption keys for sending and receiving. To minimize the risk of password compromise during MS-CHAP exchanges, MS-CHAP v2 supports only a newer, more secure, version of the MS-CHAP password change.

For VPN connections, Windows 2000 Server offers MS-CHAP v2 before offering MS-CHAP. Updated Windows clients accept MS-CHAP v2 when it is offered. Dial-up connections are not affected.

In Windows 2000, both dial-up and VPN connections can use MS-CHAP v2. Windows NT 4.0 and Windows 98-based computers can use only MS-CHAP v2 authentication for VPN connections.

EAP

The Extensible Authentication Protocol (EAP) is an extension to the Point-to-Point Protocol (PPP). EAP was developed in response to an increasing demand for remote access user authentication that uses third-party security devices. EAP provides a standard mechanism for support of additional authentication methods within PPP. By using EAP, support for a number of authentication schemes might be added, including token cards, one-time passwords, public key authentication using smart cards, certificates, and others. EAP is a critical technology component for secure virtual private network (VPN) connections, because it can offer stronger authentication methods (such as public key certificates) that are more secure against brute-force attacks, dictionary attacks, and password guessing than older password-based authentication methods.

To find out if you can use EAP, see your system administrator.

Smart Card and Other Certificate Authentication

If a user certificate is installed either in the certificate store on your computer or on a smart card, and the Extensible Authentication Protocol Transport Level Security (EAP-TLS) is enabled, you can use certificate-based authentication in a single network logon process, which provides tamper-resistant storage of authentication information.

A certificate is an encrypted set of authentication credentials. A certificate includes a digital "signature" from the certificate authority that issued the certificate. In the certificate authentication process, your computer presents its certificate to the server, and the server presents its certificate to your computer, enabling mutual authentication. Certificates are authenticated by verifying the digital signature by means of a public key, which is contained in a trusted authority root certificate that is already stored on your computer. These root certificates are the basis for certificate verification, and are supplied only by a system administrator. Windows 2000 provides a number of trusted root certificates. Add or remove trusted root certificates only if your system administrator advises.

Certificates can reside either in the certificate store on your computer or on a smart card. A smart card is a credit card–sized device that is inserted into a smart card reader, which is either installed internally in your computer or connected externally to your computer.

By setting the security options of a connection, you can choose to use a smart card or other certificate, and you can specify particular certificate requirements. For example, you can specify that the server's certificate must be validated, and you can also specify the server's certificate root authority, which is trusted.

When you double-click **Make New Connection** in the Network and Dial-up Connections folder, if a smart card reader is installed, Windows 2000 detects it and prompts you to use it as the authentication method for the connection. If you decide not to use the smart card at the time you create a connection, you can modify the connection to use the smart card or other certificate at a later time.

Data Encryption

You can think of encryption as locking something valuable into a strong box with a key. Sensitive data is encrypted by using a key algorithm, which renders it unreadable without the knowledge of the key. Data encryption keys are determined at connect time between a connection and the computer on the other end. The use of data encryption can be initiated by your computer or by the server to which you are connecting.

For dial-up, virtual private network (VPN) and direct connections, Network and Dial-up Connections supports two types of encryption: Microsoft Point-to-Point Encryption (MPPE), which uses Rivest-Shamir-Adlemen (RSA) RC4 encryption, and an implementation of Internet Protocol security (IPSec) that uses Data Encryption Standard (DES) encryption. Both MPPE and IPSec support multiple levels of encryption.

Server controls are flexible and can be set to deny the use of encryption, require a specific encryption method, or allow your computer to select an encryption method. By default, most servers allow encryption and allow clients to select their encryption methods. This works for most computers. For a Windows 2000-based remote access or VPN server, the system administrator sets encryption requirements through settings on remote access policies. To determine your encryption settings, contact your system administrator.

To enable MPPE-based data encryption for dial-up or VPN connections, you must select the MS-CHAP, MS-CHAP v2, or Extensible Authentication Protocol-Transport Level Security (EAP-TLS) authentication methods. These authentication methods generate the keys used in the encryption process.

Virtual private networks (VPNs) use encryption depending on the type of server to which they are connecting. If the VPN connection is configured to connect to a PPTP server, MPPE is used. If the VPN is configured to connect to an L2TP server, IPSec encryption methods are used. If the VPN is configured for an automatic server type (which is the default selection), then L2TP is attempted first, followed by PPTP.

MPPE

Microsoft Point-to-Point Encryption (MPPE) encrypts data in PPP-based dial-up connections or PPTP VPN connections. Strong (128-bit key) and standard (56-bit key or 40-bit key) MPPE encryption schemes are supported. MPPE provides data security between your computer and your dial-up server (for dial-up PPP connections) and between your computer and your PPTP-based VPN server (for VPN connection).

Note MPPE requires common client and server keys as generated by MS-CHAP, MS-CHAP v2, or EAP-TLS authentication.

IPSec

IP security (IPSec) is a suite of cryptography-based protection services and security protocols. Because it requires no changes to applications or protocols, you can easily deploy IPSec for existing networks.

IPSec provides machine-level authentication, as well as data encryption, for L2TP-based VPN connections. IPSec negotiates a secure connection between your computer and its remote tunnel server before an L2TP connection is established, which secures user names, passwords, and data.

IPSec encryption does not rely on the authentication method to provide initial encryption keys. Therefore, L2TP connections use all standard PPP-based authentication protocols, such as EAP-TLS, MS-CHAP, CHAP, SPAP, and PAP, to authenticate the user after the secure IPSec communication is established.

Encryption is determined by the IPSec Security Association, or SA. A security association is a combination of a destination address, a security protocol, and a unique identification value, called a Security Parameters Index (SPI). The available encryptions include:

- Data Encryption Standard (DES) with a 56-bit key.
- Triple DES (3DES), which uses three 56-bit keys and is designed for high-security environments.

Note The IP security settings that are associated with TCP/IP properties apply to all connections for which TCP/IP is enabled.

Callback

The callback feature provides cost advantages to you. Callback instructs your dial-in server to disconnect, and then to call you back after you dial in. By immediately hanging up and then calling you back, your phone charges are reduced.

If the feature is required by your system administrator, it also provides security advantages to your network. Requiring callback to a particular number enhances network security by ensuring that only users from specific locations can gain access to the server. Dropping the call and then immediately calling back to the preassigned callback number makes impersonation more difficult.

For more information about callback, see "Configuring Advanced Settings" earlier in this chapter.

Group Policies for Network and Dial-up Connections

You can use Group Policy settings or a combination of policies to control access to the Network and Dial-up Connections folder, and how it can be used. For example, a Group Policy setting can be applied which makes the **Advanced Settings** menu unavailable in the Network and Dial-up Connections folder. For more information about using Group Policy with Windows 2000 Server, see Windows 2000 Server Help.

The following sections describe the local Group Policy settings that can be applied in Windows 2000 Professional, including a description of each setting and registry information.

Computer Configuration Group Policy Settings

The location in the Group Policy that the setting modifies is shown in Figure 21.12.

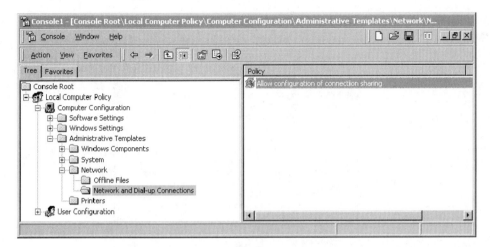

Figure 21.12   Computer Configuration in Group Policy

Allow configuration of connection sharing

This setting determines whether administrators can enable, disable, and configure the Internet Connection Sharing feature of a dial-up connection.

If you enable this setting or do not configure it, the system displays the **Sharing** tab in the **Properties** for a dial-up connection. On Windows 2000 Server, it also displays the Internet Connection Sharing (ICS) page in the Network Connection Wizard. (This page is available only in Windows 2000 Server.) If you disable this setting, the **Sharing** tab and Internet Connection Sharing wizard page are removed.

Caution   Allowing users in your organization to enable ICS means that they could create an unauthorized DHCP server on the subnet on which the computer is located. The ICS-enabled computer will allocate incorrect IP address configurations to all other DHCP clients on the same subnet and prevent them from communicating with other computers located on different subnets.

Note   This setting appears in the **Computer Configuration** and **User Configuration** folders. If both settings are configured, the setting in **Computer Configuration** takes precedence over the setting in **User Configuration**. Also, this setting applies only to users in the Administrators group.

User Configuration Group Policy Settings

The location in the Group Policy that these policies modify is shown in Figure 21.13.

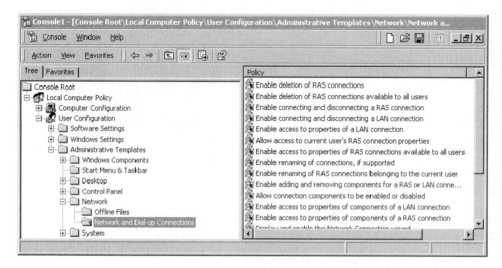

Figure 21.13   User Configuration in Group Policy

Enable deletion of RAS connections

This setting determines whether users can delete their private dial-up network connections. If you enable this setting or do not configure it, users can delete their private dial-up connections. Private connections are those that are available only to one user. (By default, only administrators can delete connections available to all users, but you can change the default by using the **Enable deletion of RAS connections available to all users** setting.) If you disable this Group Policy setting, users (including administrators) cannot delete any dial-up connections. This setting also disables the **Delete** option on the context menu for a dial-up connection and on the **File** menu in Network and Dial-up Connections.

Note When disabled, this setting takes precedence over the **Enable deletion of RAS connections available to all users** setting. Users cannot delete any dial-up connections, and the **Enable deletion of RAS connections available to all users** setting is ignored.

Enable deletion of RAS connections available to all users

This setting allows users to delete shared dial-up (RAS) connections. Shared connections are available to all users of the computer.

If you enable this setting, users can delete shared dial-up connections. If you do not configure this setting, only administrators can delete shared dial-up connections. If you disable this setting, no one can delete shared dial-up connections. (By default, users can still delete their private connections, but you can change the default by using the **Enable deletion of RAS connections** setting.)

Note   When disabled, the **Enable deletion of RAS connections** setting takes precedence over this setting. Users (including administrators) cannot delete any dial-up connections and this setting is ignored.

Enable connecting and disconnecting a RAS connection

This setting determines whether users can connect and disconnect dial-up connections.

If you enable this setting, the **Connect** and **Disconnect** options for dial-up connections are available to users in the group. Users can connect or disconnect a dial-up connection by double-clicking the icon representing the connection, by right-clicking it, or by using the **File** menu. If you disable this setting, then double-clicking the icon has no effect, and the **Connect** and **Disconnect** menu items are disabled.

Enable connecting and disconnecting a LAN connection

This setting determines whether users can connect and disconnect local area connections.

If you enable this setting, the **Connect** and **Disconnect** options for local area connections are available to users in the group. Users can connect or disconnect a local area connection by double-clicking the icon representing the connection, by right-clicking it, or by using the **File** menu. If you disable this setting, then double-clicking the icon has no effect, and the **Connect** and **Disconnect** menu items are disabled.

Enable access to properties of a LAN connection

This setting determines whether users can view and change the properties of a local area connection. It also determines whether the **Local Area Connection Properties** dialog box is available to users.

If you enable this setting, the **Local Area Connection Properties** dialog box appears when users right-click the icon representing a local area connection, and then click **Properties**. Also, when users select the connection, **Properties** is available on the **File** menu. If you disable this setting, users cannot open the **Local Area Connection Properties** dialog box.

Important   This setting supersedes settings that remove or disable parts of the **Local Area Connection Properties** dialog box, such as those that hide tabs, remove the check boxes for enabling or disabling components, or that disable the **Properties** button for components that a connection uses. If you disable this policy, then the settings that disable parts of the **Local Area Connection Properties** dialog box are ignored.

Allow access to current user's RAS connection properties

This setting determines whether users can view and change the properties of their private dial-up connections.

Private connections are those that are available only to one user. To create a private connection, on the **Connection Availability** page in the Network Connection Wizard, click **Only for myself**. This setting determines whether the **Dial-up Connection Properties** dialog box is available to users.

If you enable this setting, the **Local Area Connection Properties** dialog box appears when users right-click the icon representing a local area connection, and then click **Properties** Also, when users select the connection, **Properties** is available on the **File** menu. If you disable this setting, users cannot open the **Local Area Connection Properties** dialog box.

Important   This setting supersedes settings that remove or disable parts of the **Dial-up Connection Properties** dialog box, such as those that hide tabs, remove the check boxes for enabling or disabling components, or that disable the **Properties** button for components that a connection uses. If you disable this setting, it overrides these subsidiary policies.

Enable access to properties of RAS connections available to all users

This setting determines whether a user can view and change the properties of dial-up connections that are available to all users of the computer. This setting also determines whether the **Dial-up Connection Properties** dialog box is available to users.

If you enable this setting, the **Local Area Connection Properties** dialog box appears when users right-click the icon representing a local area connection, and then click **Properties**. Also, when users select the connection, **Properties** is available on the **File** menu. If you disable this setting, users cannot open the **Local Area Connection Properties** dialog box.

To create a dial-up connection that is available to all users, on the **Connection Availability** page in the Network Connection Wizard, click the **For all users** option. To find connections available to all users, see the Connections folder on your system drive (Documents and Settings\All Users\Application Data\Microsoft\Network\Connections).

Important This setting supersedes settings that remove or disable parts of **the Dial-up Connection Properties** dialog box, such as those that hide tabs, remove the check boxes for enabling or disabling components, or that disable the **Properties** button for components that a connection uses. If you disable this setting, it overrides these subsidiary policies.

Enable renaming of connections, if supported

This setting determines whether users can rename the dial-up and local area connections available to all users.

If you enable this setting, the **Rename** option is enabled. Users can rename connections by clicking the icon representing a connection or by using the **File** menu. If you disable this setting, the **Rename** option is disabled.

Enable renaming of RAS connections belonging to the current user

This setting determines whether users can rename their private dial-up connections.

Private connections are those that are available only to one user. To create a private connection, on the **Connection Availability** page in the Network Connection Wizard, click **Only for myself**.

If you enable this setting, the **Rename** option is enabled for users' private dial-up connections. If you disable this setting, the **Rename** option is disabled on the user's private connections.

Enable adding or removing components of a RAS or LAN connection

This setting determines whether administrators can add and remove network components.

If you enable this setting, the **Install** and **Uninstall** buttons for components of connections in Network and Dial-up Connections are enabled. Also, administrators can gain access to network components in the Windows Components Wizard. If you disable this setting, the **Install** and **Uninstall** buttons for components of connections are disabled, and administrators are not permitted access to network components in the Windows Components Wizard.

The **Install** button opens the dialog boxes used to add network components. Clicking the **Uninstall** button removes the selected component in the components list (above the button). The **Install** and **Uninstall** buttons appear when administrators right-click a connection, and then click **Properties**. These buttons are on the **General** tab for local area connections and on the **Networking** tab for dial-up connections.

Tip The Windows Components wizard permits administrators to add and remove components. To use the wizard, double-click **Add/Remove Programs** in Control Panel. To go directly to the network components in the Windows Components wizard, click the **Advanced** menu in Network and Dial-up Connections, and then click **Optional Networking Components**.

Allow connection components to be enabled or disabled

This setting determines whether administrators can enable and disable the components used by dial-up and local area connections.

If you enable this setting, the Properties dialog box for a connection includes a check box beside the name of each component that the connection uses. Selecting the check box enables the component, and clearing the check box disables the component. Disabling this setting dims the check boxes for enabling and disabling components. As a result, administrators cannot enable or disable the components that a connection uses.

Enable access to properties of components of a LAN connection

This setting determines whether administrators can change the properties of components used by a local area connection.

This setting determines whether the **Properties** button for components of a local area connection is enabled. If you enable this setting or do not configure it, the **Properties** button is enabled. If you disable this setting, the **Properties** button is disabled.

To find the **Properties** button, right-click the connection, and then click **Properties**. You will see a list of the network components that the connection uses. To view or change the properties of a component, click the name of the component, and then click **Properties**.

Note Not all network components have configurable properties. For components that are not configurable, the **Properties** button is always disabled.

Enable access to properties of components of a RAS connection

This setting determines whether users can view and change the properties of components used by a dial-up connection.

This setting determines whether the **Properties** button for components used by a dial-up connection is enabled. If you enable this setting or do not configure it, the **Properties** button is enabled. If you disable this setting, the **Properties** button is disabled.

To find the **Properties** button, right-click the connection and then click **Properties**, and then click the **Networking** tab. You will see a list of the network components that the connection uses. To view or change the properties of a component, click the name of the component, and then click **Properties**.

Not all network components have configurable properties. For components that are not configurable, the **Properties** button is always disabled.

Display and enable the Network Connection Wizard

This setting determines whether users can use the Network Connection Wizard, which creates new network connections.

If you enable this setting, **Make New Connection** appears in the Network and Dial-up Connections folder. Clicking **Make New Connection** starts the Network Connection Wizard. If you disable this setting, **Make New Connection** does not appear. As a result, users cannot start the Network Connection Wizard.

Enable status statistics for an active connection

This setting determines whether users can view the Status page for an active connection.

Status displays information about the connection and its activity. It also provides buttons to disconnect and to configure the properties of the connection.

If you enable this setting, **Status** appears when users double-click an active connection. Also, an option to display **Status** appears on a menu when users right-click the icon for an active connection, and the option appears on the **File** menu when users select an active connection. If you disable this setting, **Status** is disabled, and **Status** doesn't appear.

Enable the Dial-up Preferences item on the Advanced menu

This setting determines whether **Dial-up Preferences** on the **Advanced** menu in Network and Dial-up Connections is enabled.

If you enable this setting, **Dial-up Preferences** is enabled. If you disable this setting, it is disabled. By default, **Dial-up Preferences** is enabled.

Dial-up Preferences allows users to configure Autodial and callback features.

Enable the Advanced Settings item on the Advanced menu

This setting determines whether **Advanced Settings** on the **Advanced** menu in Network and Dial-up Connections is enabled.

If you enable this setting, **Advanced Settings** is enabled. If you disable this setting, it is disabled. By default, **Advanced Settings** is enabled.

Advanced Settings allows administrators to view and change bindings and view and change the order in which the computer accesses connections, network providers, and print providers.

Allow configuration of connection sharing

This setting determines whether administrators and can enable, disable, and configure the ICS feature of a dial-up connection.

If you enable this setting or do not configure it, the system displays the **Sharing** tab in the properties for a dial-up connection. On a computer running Windows 2000 Server, it also displays the **Internet Connection Sharing** page in the Network Connection Wizard. (This page is available only in Windows 2000 Server.) If you disable this setting, the **Sharing** tab and the **Internet Connection Sharing** Wizard page are removed.

This setting appears in the Computer Configuration and User Configuration folders. If both settings are configured, the setting in Computer Configuration takes precedence over the setting in User Configuration.

Important This setting applies only to users in the Administrators and group.

For more information about disabling the configuration of ICS at the computer level, see "Computer Configuration Group Policy Settings" earlier in this chapter.

Allow TCP/IP advanced configuration

This setting determines whether users can use Network and Dial-up Connections to configure TCP/IP, DNS, and WINS settings.

If you enable this setting, the **Advanced** button on **Internet Protocol (TCP/IP) Properties** is enabled. As a result, users can open **Advanced TCP/IP Settings** and modify IP settings, such as DNS and WINS server information. If you disable this setting, the **Advanced** button is disabled and the users cannot open **Advanced TCP/IP Settings**.

Important If the **Enable access to properties of a LAN connection** setting or the **Enable access to properties of components of a LAN connection** setting are disabled, users cannot gain access to the **Advanced** button. As a result, this setting is ignored.

Internet Connection Sharing

With the Windows 2000 Internet Connection Sharing (ICS) feature of Network and Dial-up Connections, you can use Windows 2000 to connect your branch office network to the Internet. For example, you might have a home network, with only one of the home network computers connected to the Internet by using a dial-up connection. By enabling Internet Connection Sharing on the computer that uses the dial-up connection, you are providing Internet access to all of the computers on your home network, with only one computer physically connected to the Internet. ICS provides network address translation, IP address allocation, and name resolution services for all computers on your small office or branch office network that are configured for automatic addressing. For a detailed scenario that discusses setting up ICS in a branch office network, see "Internet Connection Sharing Scenario: Connecting Your Branch Office's Intranet to the Internet" later in this chapter.

After ICS is enabled and users verify their networking and Internet options, branch office network users can use applications, such as Internet Explorer and Outlook Express, as if they were already connected to the ISP. If the ICS computer is not already connected to the ISP, it dials the ISP and creates the connection so that the user can reach the specified Web address or resource.

The computer enabled with ICS needs two connections: One connection is for a network adapter, and connects to the computers on the home network. The other connection connects the home network to the Internet. You need to ensure that ICS is enabled on the connection that connects your home network to the Internet. As a result, the home network connection appropriately allocates TCP/IP addresses to its own users, the shared connection connects your home network to the Internet, and users outside your home network are not at risk of receiving inappropriate addresses from your home network. By enabling ICS on a connection, the ICS computer becomes a Dynamic Host Configuration Protocol (DHCP) allocator for the home network. DHCP distributes TCP/IP addresses to users as they start up. If Internet Connection Sharing is enabled on the wrong network adapter, users outside your home network might be granted TCP/IP addresses by the home network DHCP allocator, causing problems on their own networks.

The ICS feature is intended for use in a small office or branch office networking environment, where network configuration and the Internet connection are managed by the computer running Windows 2000 (where the shared connection resides). It is assumed that on its network, this computer is the only connection and gateway to the Internet, and that it sets up all internal network addresses. The Internet Connection Sharing feature does not work if the network contains DHCP or DNS servers.

The following protocols, services, interfaces, and routes shown in Table 21.6 are configured when you enable Internet Connection Sharing.

Table 21.6   Internet Connection Sharing Settings

Item	Configuration
IP address 192.168.0.1	Configured with a subnet mask of 255.255.255.0 on the network adapter that is connected to the small office or branch office network.
Autodial feature	Enabled.
Static default IP route	Created when the dial-up connection is established.
Internet Connection Sharing service	Started automatically.
DHCP allocator	Enabled with the default range of 192.168.0.2 to 192.168.0.254 and a subnet mask of 255.255.255.0.
DNS proxy	Enabled.

To use the Internet Connection Sharing feature, users on your branch office network must configure TCP/IP on their local area connection to obtain an IP address automatically. For more information about configuring Internet Connection Sharing, see Windows 2000 Help.

Note   For branch office clients to access the Internet, the computer with Internet Connection Sharing (ICS) enabled on it must either have an active connection, or the shared connection must have on-demand dialing enabled.

Internet Connection Sharing Scenario: Connecting Your Branch Office's Intranet to the Internet

This scenario describes how to connect a branch office of a corporation to the Internet. It also explains the differences between setting up an analog modem or ISDN connection, and setting up a cable modem or DSL connection. It also discusses how to configure a computer on the branch office's intranet to connect to the corporate network using a virtual private networking (VPN) connection.

Overview

This section describes the basics of this scenario: the branch office's current configuration, and the proposed solution using Windows 2000 Internet Connection Sharing (ICS). Figure 21.14 shows the current configuration for a branch office.

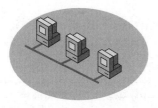

Figure 21.14   Current Configuration of a Branch Office

Using Internet Connection Sharing

The Internet Connection Sharing (ICS) feature in Windows 2000 provides a simple solution to allow all of the computers on a local intranet to share the same external connection to the Internet.

Using ICS, you designate one branch office computer as the ICS computer. Typically, this is the computer with the fastest external connection, such as a DSL or cable modem. You use the ICS computer to establish the connection to the Internet. All of the other computers on your branch's intranet—referred to from this point as "clients" to distinguish them from the ICS computer — use the shared connection on the ICS computer to access the Internet. In general, this is a three step process:

1. Configure the ICS computer for Internet access. How you set up the ICS computer depends on whether it uses an analog modem or ISDN connection, or a DSL or cable modem connection to the outside world.

2. Enable Internet Connection Sharing on the ICS computer to provide Internet access to everyone on the branch intranet.

3. Configure your client computers for automatic IP addressing.

Note Never turn off the ICS computer while any of the clients are running, as the ICS computer provides IP address configuration, name resolution services, and a gateway to the Internet. If you do lose power to the ICS computer, the other branch office clients cannot access the Internet because the shared connection on the ICS computer is not available.

Configuring the ICS Computer

How you configure the ICS computer depends on whether it connects to the Internet using an analog modem or ISDN connection, or a high-speed device such as a DSL or cable modem.

Note The ICS computer automatically assigns IP addresses, forwards DNS names to the Internet for resolution, and assigns itself as the default gateway for connecting to the Internet. If any of the clients on the branch office's intranet are providing these functions, Internet Connection Sharing might not work.

Configuring an ICS Computer with an Analog Modem or ISDN Connection

In this configuration, the ICS computer connects to the Internet using an analog modem or ISDN connection. The ICS computer and all of the other computers in the Seattle branch office, are connected to the branch office's intranet using network adapters. Figure 21.15 shows how an Internet connection is shared using an analog modem or an ISDN connection.

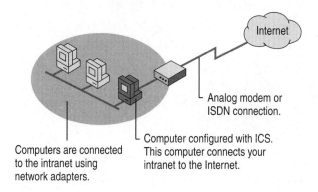

Figure 21.15   Internet Connection Sharing Using an Analog Modem or ISDN Connection

Install the analog modem (or make sure you have a modem installed) on the ICS computer you want to use to access the Internet. If you are installing an analog modem in the ICS computer for the first time, Windows 2000 Plug and Play automatically detects and configures it.

Open the Network and Dial-Up Connections folder, and then double-click **Make New Connection**. This starts the Windows 2000 Network Connection Wizard to set up the connection to your Internet service provider (ISP). Configure the connection by using the settings provided by your ISP.

After the wizard has created the new connection to your ISP, Windows 2000 adds a new icon for the connection in the Network and Dial-Up Connections folder. Test the new Internet connection by connecting to your ISP and verifying that you can browse the World Wide Web.

Next, open the **Properties** of the new connection, click the **Sharing** tab, and then select the **Enable Internet Connection Sharing for this connection** check box.

Next, check the configuration of the clients, as described in "Configuring the Branch Office Client Computers" later in this section. Finally, verify the shared ICS connection by browsing the World Wide Web from one of the clients on the branch office intranet.

Configuring an ICS Computer with a DSL or Cable Modem Connection

In this configuration, the ICS computer connects to the Internet using a second network adapter connected to a high-speed DSL or cable modem. The ICS computer connects to the other computers in the Seattle branch office's intranet using the first network adapter. The rest of the computers in the branch office connect to the local intranet using other network adapters. Figure 21.16 shows how an Internet connection is shared by using a DSL or cable modem connection.

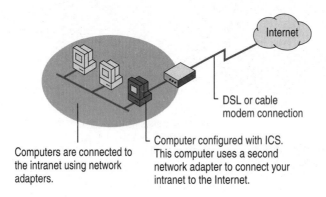

Figure 21.16   Internet Connection Sharing Using a DSL or Cable Modem Connection

Rename the local area connection for the branch intranet ("Office Intranet," for example) on the ICS computer that you want to use to access the Internet, and then install the second network adapter (or make sure you have a second network adapter installed) to connect to the DSL or cable modem connection. If you are installing the second network adapter for the first time, Windows 2000 Plug and Play automatically detects and configures it.

Next, open the **Properties** of the new connection, and configure the connection by using the settings provided by your ISP. Next, click the **Sharing** tab, and then select the **Enable Internet Connection Sharing for this connection** check box.

Note   Rename the new external connection to the Internet to differentiate it from the branch office's intranet.

Test the new Internet connection by connecting to your ISP and verifying that you can browse the World Wide Web.

Finally, check the configuration of the clients (as described in the following section) and then verify the shared ICS connection by browsing the World Wide Web from one of the clients.

Configuring the Branch Office Client Computers

To verify that the network settings on each client in the branch office are configured properly to use the new ICS computer to connect to the Internet, do the following:

- Verify that the local area connection to the branch office intranet uses the Client for Microsoft Networks, File and Printer Sharing, and Internet Protocol (TCP/IP) components. (These are the default settings in Windows 2000.)

- Verify that the TCP/IP properties for the connection are configured to obtain an IP address and a DNS server address automatically. (These are the default settings in Windows 2000.)

- After the ICS computer has been initially configured and tested, restart all of the clients. Do not restart the ICS computer.

Tip If you have trouble accessing the Internet from a client, verify that the client's Internet browser is configured to connect using the LAN. If this is not the problem, ping the ICS computer by typing **ping 192.168.0.1** at a command prompt. If this also fails, verify the client's physical connection to the office intranet. Finally, you can use IPConfig, a diagnostic tool included with Windows 2000 Professional, to view details of the client's IP configuration. Open a command window, and then type **ipconfig**. If you want help with using the tool, type **ipconfig /?**.

The only necessary modification for client applications is to configure Internet Explorer to use the branch office LAN connection to the Internet.

▶ **To configure Internet Explorer to use a shared ICS connection**

1. On the **Tools** menu, click **Internet Options,** and then click the **Connections** tab.

2. In **Dial-Up Settings**, click **Never dial a connection**, and then click **LAN Settings**.

3. In **Automatic Configuration**, check the **Automatically detect settings** check box and clear the **Use automatic configuration script** check box.

4. In **Proxy Server**, clear the **Use a proxy server check box**.

Configurations to Avoid

ICS is designed to enable a computer to be a translating gateway to the Internet. In some configurations involving cable modems or DSL, the equipment provided and the setup is contrary to this purpose. To properly use ICS, do not connect a cable or DSL modem, the ICS computer, and all of the other clients on the branch office intranet directly into a network hub, as shown in Figure 21.17.

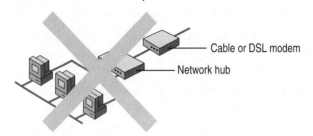

Figure 21.17   Do Not Connect a Cable or DSL Modem Directly into a Network Hub

---

Note You can use this type of configuration when your ISP has assigned a static IP address to each client on your intranet. In this scenario, ICS is not needed for Internet access. However, in this configuration, you must disable **File and Printer Sharing** on all computers to prevent access to your computers from Internet users. Most branch offices avoid this configuration because it disables file and printer sharing between the clients on the branch's intranet.

Some cable or DSL modems provide a built-in network hub. In this scenario, do not connect the network adapters of all the computers on your intranet directly into the cable modem, as shown in Figure 21.18.

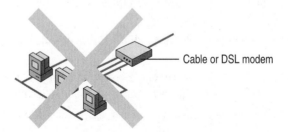

Figure 21.18   Do Not Connect Multiple Computers Directly into a Cable Modem

Creating a VPN Connection to the Corporate Network

As network administrator of the branch office, you want to configure a few individual clients for access to the corporate network to send and receive e-mail, install software updates, transfer files, and otherwise access network servers and company-wide resources.

You can create a virtual private network (VPN) connection from one of the branch office's clients that tunnels through the Internet (using PPTP) to the corporate network by using a VPN connection. It is a safe, secure way of connecting directly to the corporate network from a computer on the branch office network. Figure 21.19 shows how one client on the office intranet is connected to a corporate network by means of a PPTP tunnel.

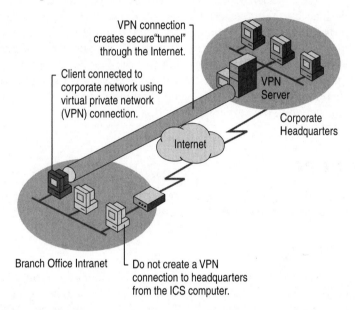

Figure 21.19   Connect a Branch Office Client to the Corporate Network Using a VPN Connection

Note Do not create a VPN connection to the corporate network from the ICS computer. If you do, then by default all traffic from the ICS computer including traffic from intranet clients will forwarded over the VPN connection to the corporate network. This means that Internet resources will no longer be reachable and all the branch office computers will be sending data over a logical connection created with the credentials of the ICS computer user, a questionable security practice.

The first time you launch a new VPN connection, it takes a few moments to connect using L2TP and IPSec, and then tries to connect using PPTP. Subsequent connections do not take as long because the VPN connection memorizes which VPN protocol was successful for the initial connection.

After the VPN connection is made, the client on the branch office's intranet has access to the shared resources (such as file servers and printers) on the corporate network.

Note   While the client computer is connected to the corporate network using VPN, the client is logically disconnected from the Internet unless the corporate network provides its own Web access. To access the Web through the corporate network, a branch office client must be configured to use the rules established for Web access from the corporate network. For example, many corporations use a proxy server. In this scenario, you need to configure the client's browser to use the corporate proxy server to access the Web. You can configure Internet Explorer to use specific proxy settings with specific Internet connections. After doing so, the client computer can easily shift between accessing the Internet by using the shared connection on the ICS computer, or accessing the Internet through a VPN connection to the corporate network.

Troubleshooting

The following sections describe the common problems with Network and Dial-up Connections and the troubleshooting tools provided with Windows 2000.

Troubleshooting Tools

There are many tools within Windows 2000 that allow you to monitor and diagnose network and dial-up connections. PPP logging records the series of programming functions and PPP control messages during a PPP connection. You can verify whether your modem is working properly by using modem diagnostics and logging. The Netdiag tool can be used to test many networking components. It can be configured to run and report on tools such as Ping, IPConfig, and so on.

PPP Logging

You can troubleshoot Windows 2000 Professional PPP client connections by using PPP logging on Windows 2000. PPP logging records the series of programming functions and PPP control messages during a PPP connection and is a valuable source of troubleshooting information when you are troubleshooting the failure of a PPP connection. To enable PPP logging on your Windows 2000 remote access server, select the **Enable Point-to-Point Protocol (PPP) logging** option on the **Event Logging** tab from the properties of a remote access server using the Routing and Remote Access administrative tool.

To enable PPP logging on the client that is initiating the connection, use the Netsh command. The syntax for the command is:

```
Netsh ras set tracing ppp enabled
```

Conversely, if you want to stop PPP logging, the command syntax is:

```
Netsh ras set tracing ppp disabled
```

Modem Logging

By using **Phone and Modem Options** in Control Panel, you can record a log of commands as they are sent to your modem by communication programs or the operating system. On Windows 2000 Professional, logging is always turned on and the log is overwritten at the beginning of every session unless you select the **Append to Log** check box.

Note Commands sent to the modem are captured in the file *%SystemRoot%*\ModemLog_*Model*.txt. *%SystemRoot%* is usually C:\Winnt\System32\. *Model* is the name of the modem as it appears in the list of installed modems on the **Modems** tab of **Phone and Modem Options**.

Modem Diagnostics

You can verify whether your modem is working properly by using the diagnostics that are available by means of **Phone and Modem Options** in Control Panel.

When you query a modem, Windows 2000 runs the commands and displays the results, as shown in Table 21.7.

Table 21.7   Modem Query Commands and Responses

Command	Response
ATQ0V1E0	Initializes the query.
AT+GMM	Model identification (ITU V.250 recommendation is not supported by all modems).
AT+FCLASS=?	Fax classes supported by the modem, if any.
AT#CLS=?	Shows whether the modem supports the Rockwell voice command set.
ATI*n*	Displays manufacturer's information for $n = 1$ through 7. This provides information such as the port speed, the result of a checksum test, and the model information. Check the manufacturer's documentation for the expected results.

NetDiag

The Netdiag tool is available in the \support tools directory of your Windows 2000 Professional operating system CD. Netdiag isolates networking and connectivity problems by performing a series of tests to determine the state of your network client and its functionality. Optionally, it can generate a report of the results. For example, it can report on the network adapter configuration details, including the adapter name, configuration, media, globally unique identifier (GUID), and statistics. Using it, you can run a comprehensive sequence of networking tools such as Ping, IPConfig, and so on. For more information about Netdiag, see "Troubleshooting Tools and Strategies" in this book.

Device Manager

Device Manager provides you with information about how the hardware on your computer is installed and configured. It can help you determine the source of resource conflicts, and the status of COM ports. You can also use Device Manager to check the status of your hardware and update device drivers, such as modem drivers, on your computer.

Troubleshooting Configuration Problems

The following sections describe common problems that you might encounter, and possible causes and solutions for them.

The modem does not work.

- The modem is incompatible. If you have access to another computer with an Internet connection, check the list of compatible modems in the Hardware Compatibility List link on the Web Resources page at http://windows.microsoft.com/windows2000/reskit/webresources.

- The modem is not connected properly or is turned off. Verify that the modem is connected properly to the correct port on your computer. If the modem is external, verify that the power is on.

- The remote access server is not running. Ask your system administrator to verify that the remote access server is running. If the server is down, the administrator needs to check the error and audit logs to see why the service stopped. After the problem is fixed, restart the service. If the service is running, the administrator needs to check whether other remote access clients can connect properly. If other clients can connect, the problem might be specific to your workstation.

- You do not have a valid user account, or you do not have remote access permission. Verify with your system administrator whether your user account has been established, and that you have remote access permission.

- You dialed the wrong number, or you dialed the correct number but forgot to dial an external line-access number, such as 9. Verify that the number is correct as dialed.

- Your modem cannot negotiate with the modem of the server. Try using the same type of modem as the server.

- The modem cabling is faulty. Do not use the 9-to-25-pin converters that are included with most mouse hardware because some of them do not carry modem signals. To be safe, use a converter made especially for this purpose.

- The telephone line (for example, in your hotel room) does not accommodate your modem speed. Select a lower bits-per-second (bps) rate (or call the hotel manager to request a direct line).

- The line you are trying to use is digital. Most modems work only with analog phone lines. Verify that you have analog phone lines installed or, if you have digital phone lines installed, verify that the servers and clients have digital modems.

When trying to connect, a message is received that says the remote access server is not responding.

- At higher bits-per-second (bps) rates, your modem is incompatible with the modem of the server.

- There is a lot of static on the phone line, which prevents a modem from connecting at a higher bps rate.

- There is some kind of switching equipment between the client and server that prevents the two modems from negotiating at a higher bps rate. Adjust the speed of your modem to a lower bits-per-second (bps) rate.

- The remote access server is not running. Ask your system administrator to verify that the server is running. The modem always connect at a lower bit-per-second (bps) rate than specified.

- The modem and telephone line are not operating correctly. Excessive static on the telephone line causes sessions to be dropped. You can use modem diagnostics to confirm correct modem operation.

- The destination server is not running properly. Ask your system administrator to verify that the destination server is running properly. Try connecting to the same server from another workstation. If other workstations are having the same problem, there might be problems with server applications or hardware. If not, the problem is specific to your workstation.

- The quality of your line is insufficient. Contact your telephone company to verify the quality of your line.

- The line you are dialing is affecting the speed. If you can connect to your remote access server by using more than one number, try another number and see if the speed improves.

- Your modem software needs to be updated. Check with your modem manufacturer for modem software updates.

The sessions with a remote access server on the network keep getting dropped.

- Call waiting is disrupting your connection. Verify that the phone has call waiting. If so, disable call waiting and try calling again.

- The remote access server disconnected you because of inactivity. Try calling again.

- Someone picked up the phone. Picking up the phone automatically disconnects you. Try calling again.

- Your modem cable is disconnected. Verify that the modem cable is connected properly.

- Your modem software needs to be updated. Check with your modem manufacturer for modem software updates.

- Your modem settings need to be changed because of a remote access server change. Verify the modem settings with your system administrator.

Connections are disconnecting abnormally.

- The remote access server is not running. Ask your system administrator to verify that the server is running.

- Your modem is unable to negotiate correctly with the modem of the remote access server. The serial port of the computer cannot keep up with the speed you have selected. Try to connect at a lower initial port speed.

- Your modem software needs to be updated. Check with your modem manufacturer for modem software updates.

When trying to connect, a hardware error is received.

- The modem is turned off. Verify that the modem is turned on. If the modem is turned off, turn it on and redial.

- Your modem is not functioning properly. Enable modem logging to test the connection.

- Your cable is incompatible. If your modem communicates through Terminal, but not through Network and Dial-up Connections, the cable that attaches your modem to the computer is probably incompatible. You need to install a compatible cable.

Connections do not appear in the Network and Dial-up Connections folder.

- The folder might need to be refreshed. Press F5 to refresh the folder.

Conflicts between serial ports are causing connection problems.

- The serial ports are conflicting. COM1 and COM3 share interrupt request (IRQ) 4. COM2 and COM4 share IRQ 3. As a result, for serial communications, you cannot use COM1 and COM3 simultaneously, or COM2 and COM4 simultaneously. For example, you cannot use Network and Dial-up Connections on COM1 and Terminal on COM3.

  This rule applies if you are using the mouse in addition to other serial communications programs such as Network and Dial-up Connections or the Windows 2000 Terminal program. The rule does not apply if you are using an intelligent serial adapter such as a DigiBoard serial card.

When trying to connect by using ISDN, a "No Answer" message is received.

- The remote access server did not answer because it is turned off or the modem is not connected. Contact your system administrator.

- The line is busy. Try calling later, or contact your system administrator.

- There is a problem with the hardware. Verify that the ISDN adapters are installed and configured correctly.

- Your phone number is not configured correctly. In some cases, each B channel on an ISDN line has its own number, while in other cases both B channels share a single number. Your telephone company can tell you how many numbers your ISDN line has.

- If you are located in the United States or Canada, your Service Profile Identifier (SPID) is configured incorrectly. The SPID normally consists of the phone number with additional digits added to the beginning, the end, or both. The SPID helps the switch understand what type of equipment is attached to the line and routes calls to appropriate devices on the line. If an ISDN channel requires a SPID, but it is not entered correctly, then the device cannot place or accept calls. Verify that the SPID is entered correctly.

- A poor line condition (for example, too much static) interrupted your connection. Wait a few minutes and try dialing again.

- You did not enable line-type negotiation, or a connection cannot be made with the line type you selected. Enable line-type negotiation.

- Your ISDN switching facility is busy. Try again later.

- Your DigiBoard card is too old. If you do not have the latest PCIMAC-ISA DigiBoard card, serial number A14308 or greater, contact DigiBoard for a replacement.

Connections made by using X.25 fail.

- The dial-up PAD is configured with the wrong X.3 parameters or serial settings. If the remote access server is running and you cannot connect to it directly through an X.25 smart card or an external PAD, modify the dial-up PAD X.3 parameters or serial settings. Ask your system administrator for the correct settings.

- New Pad.inf entries are incorrect. You can check other Pad.inf entries for direct connections and external PADs, and view the comments that go with them. You might need a line analyzer or a terminal program to see the response for the PAD. For dial-up PAD entries, you can use an entry in Pad.inf as an example, paying attention to the comments that go with the example.

- Your modem is incompatible. If the modem that connects to a dial-up PAD connects at a lower speed than it should, replace the modem with a compatible one.

- The line for the remote access server is congested. If a connection has been established, but the network drives are disconnecting, and you are dropping sessions or getting network errors, the cause might be congestion on the leased line for the remote access server.

  For example, four clients connecting at 9,600 bps (through dial-up PADs) require a 38,400-bps (four times 9,600) leased line on the server end. If the leased line does not have adequate bandwidth, it can cause time-outs and degrade performance for connected clients. This example assumes that Routing and Remote Access is using all the bandwidth. If Routing and Remote Access is sharing the bandwidth, fewer connections can be made.

  Your system administrator needs to verify that the speed of the leased line can support all the COM ports at all speeds clients use to dial in.

Connections through PPTP fail.

- TCP/IP connectivity problems are keeping you from connecting to the PPTP server. You or your system administrator can use the **ipconfig** and **ping** commands to verify a connection to your server.

- A Winsock Proxy client is active. A VPN connection cannot operate with an active Winsock Proxy client. Winsock Proxy immediately redirects packets to the proxy server before they can be processed by a virtual private network connection for encapsulation. Ask your system administrator to disable the Winsock Proxy client.

- You do not have the appropriate connection and domain permissions on the remote access server. Contact your system administrator.

- If you are using the TCP/IP protocol, you do not have a unique TCP/IP address. Contact your system administrator.

- Name resolution problems are keeping you from resolving names to IP addresses. Specify fully qualified domain names and IP addresses in your connection.

Connections made by using PPP or TCP/IP utilities are failing.

- The server does not support LCP extensions. If you cannot connect to a server by using PPP, or the remote computer terminates your connection, the server might not support LCP extensions. In **Network and Dial-up Connections**, clear the **Enable LCP extensions** check box.

- IP header compression is keeping TCP/IP tools from running. If you successfully connect to a remote server by using PPP, but TCP/IP tools do not work, the problem might be IP header compression. Try to reconnect after turning off IP header compression.

Connections made by using Internet Connection Sharing are failing.

- The wrong LAN network adapter is shared. A computer with Internet Connection Sharing needs two connections. One connection, typically a LAN adapter, connects to the computers on the home network and the other connection connects the home network to the Internet. You need to ensure that Internet Connection Sharing is enabled on the connection that connects your home network to the Internet.

- TCP/IP is not installed on home network computers. By default, the TCP/IP protocol is installed on computers running Windows 2000, Windows 98, and Windows NT 4.0. If users on your home network are running operating systems other than these, verify that TCP/IP is installed on their computers.

- If users on your home network cannot reach the Internet, TCP/IP is incorrectly configured on their home network computers. Verify that the following TCP/IP settings are established on home network local area connections:

  - IP address: Obtain an IP address automatically (through DHCP).

  - DNS server: Obtain DNS server address automatically.

  - Default gateways: None specified.

  For computers running Windows 95, Windows 98, or Windows NT 4.0, you can find the TCP/IP settings in Network Control Panel.

- If users on your home network cannot reach the Internet, their Internet options need to be modified. Home network user Internet options must be modified for use on the local area network. For more information, see Windows 2000 Help.

- The Internet Connection Sharing service is not started. Use Event Viewer to verify that the Internet Connection Sharing service is started.

- The Internet Connection Sharing computer is not properly configured for name resolution. You might need to configure the DNS name resolution services on the computer. If computers on the branch office network cannot resolve names to IP addresses, you can check the name resolution configuration of the Internet Connection Sharing computer by using the **ipconfig** command.

There are two ways that your ISP can configure name resolution:

- Statically assigned name servers

  You must manually configure the TCP/IP protocol with the IP address (or addresses) of the name servers provided by the ISP. If you have statically assigned name servers, you can use the **ipconfig** command at any time to get the IP addresses of your configured name servers.

- Dynamically assigned name servers

  Manual configuration is not required. The IP addresses of the name servers provided by the ISP are dynamically assigned whenever you dial the ISP. If you have dynamically assigned name servers, you must run the **ipconfig** command after a connection to the ISP has been made.

- If you cannot play a game across the Internet, the protocol used by the application is not translatable. Try running the application from the ICS computer. If the application works from the ICS computer but not from a computer on the home network, then the application might not be translatable.

- If you cannot play a game across the Internet, the application is not configured on the computer running Internet Connection Sharing. Verify that the application, including port numbers, is configured correctly.

  For more information, see Windows 2000 Help.

- If Internet users cannot see services on your home network, such as a Web server, the service is not configured correctly. Verify that the service, including port numbers and TCP/IP addresses, is configured correctly.

- If users on your home network cannot reach the Internet sites by using friendly names, there is a DNS resolution problem. Users on your home network must use fully qualified domain names or IP addresses when accessing Internet resources.

When using a local area network connection, there is no response.

- There might be problems with your network adapter. Check the appearance of the local area connection icon. Depending on the status of the local area connection, the icon appears in different ways in the Network and Dial-up Connections folder. Also, if the local area connection media is disconnected (for example, the cable is unplugged), a status icon is displayed in the taskbar. Also, use Device Manager to verify that your network adapter is working correctly.

- The LAN cable might not be plugged into the network adapter. Check to make sure the LAN cable is inserted into the network adapter. When using a laptop to connect to an ISP, some or all of the applications do not run properly.

- The Winsock Proxy client might be preventing your applications from running properly when you use the ISP connection. If you are a mobile user and use your portable computer in your corporate environment, you might need to disable the Microsoft Winsock Proxy client (WSP Client in Control Panel) when you use the same computer to dial to an ISP or other network. For example, if you use a portable computer in your office and use the same computer to connect to an ISP or other network from your home, you might have problems running all of your applications when you use the ISP connection. (For example, your applications might not be able to find the resources or servers they need.) If this is the case, disable the Microsoft Winsock Proxy client (WSP Client in Control Panel) to run the applications that you typically run when you use your portable computer in the corporate office.

I can connect to my ISP, but I cannot browse the Internet.

- DNS options might need to be configured. Check with your ISP or your system administrator to see if you need to configure DNS settings in the TCP/IP settings for their connection. For example, you might need to specify a preferred or alternate DNS server address, rather than letting the DNS server address be obtained automatically.

Incoming connection clients cannot see resources beyond the incoming connection computer.

- If the addresses that are being allocated to incoming clients are not a subset of the network to which the incoming connection computer is attached, you must create a route to the incoming clients on the intranet computers.

  Reconfigure your range of IP addresses that are being allocated to incoming clients so that it is a subset of the network to which the incoming connections computer is attached. If you cannot do this, then configure your intranet hosts with the IP address of the incoming connection computer as a default gateway.

- If your intranet hosts are configured to obtain an IP address automatically and a DHCP server is present, you can configure your DHCP server to assign the default gateway.

- If your intranet hosts are configured to obtain an IP address automatically and a DHCP server is not present (you are using the Automatic Private IP Addressing feature of Windows 2000 and Windows 98), then you must manually configure all of your intranet hosts with an IP address, subnet mask, and default gateway.

- The calculated range of addresses allocated to connecting clients is larger than the range that you configured. Most TCP/IP networks use subnets to effectively manage routed IP addresses. For the range that you specified in **From** and **To**, Windows 2000 calculates the closest matching subnet. The range of addresses in the closest matching subnet might exceed the range that you specified. Unless the addresses specified in **From** and **To** are subnet boundaries, the range based on the calculated subnet is larger than the range that you specified. To avoid this, specify a range that falls on subnet boundaries. For example, if you are using the 10.0.0.0 private network ID for your intranet, a range that falls on subnet boundaries is 10.0.1.168 to 10.0.1.175. Or, if you are using the 192.168.0.0 private network ID for your intranet, a range that falls on subnet boundaries is 192.168.1.0 to 192.168.1.255.

C H A P T E R   2 2

TCP/IP in Windows 2000 Professional

Microsoft has adopted TCP/IP as the strategic enterprise network transport for its platforms. TCP/IP for Microsoft® Windows® 2000 is a high-performance, scaleable implementation of the industry-standard TCP/IP protocol. This chapter provides technical and configuration details about the Microsoft TCP/IP protocol as implemented in Microsoft® Windows® 2000 Professional.

In This Chapter

Related Information in the Windows 2000 Resource Kit

- For more information about installing and configuring a DHCP server, see "Dynamic Host Configuration Protocol" in the *Microsoft® Windows® 2000 Server Resource Kit TCP/IP Core Networking Guide.*

- For more information about IP routing, address translation and IP packet handling, see "Unicast IP Routing" in the *Microsoft® Windows® 2000 Server Resource Kit Internetworking Guide.*

TCP/IP Configuration Quick Guide

This chapter provides information about installing, configuring and troubleshooting the TCP/IP protocol in Windows 2000 Professional. Additionally, there is information to assist you in planning and deploying TCP/IP installation on a Windows 2000–based computer. Use the following Quick Guide to determine where to find the information you need to configure TCP/IP to meet your networking requirements.

Understand your network requirements for TCP/IP.

An understanding of the features found in the Windows 2000 Professional implementation of TCP/IP will assist in your implementation of the protocol on a client, as well as illustrate how it compares to other Microsoft operating systems, such as Microsoft® Windows NT®.

- See "Overview of Windows 2000 TCP/IP" later in this chapter.

Verify that TCP/IP is properly installed.

TCP/IP is installed as the default protocol in a clean install of Windows 2000 Professional. If you have installed Windows 2000 Professional over an existing client, or performed a custom installation, make sure to confirm TCP/IP installation.

- See "Install TCP/IP" later in this chapter.

Choose and configure an IP addressing method.

Depending on your home, small business, or enterprise network configuration, two methods of IP address assignment are available for a Windows 2000 Professional–based client: automatically obtain an IP address or manually specify an IP address. When you configure TCP/IP to automatically obtain an IP address, either Dynamic Host Configuration Protocol (DHCP) or Automatic Private IP Assignment (APIPA) is used to provide an IP address (default setting). Select and configure the addressing method that best meets your needs.

- See "Configure IP Address Assignment" later in this chapter.

Choose and configure a name resolution method.

Depending on the type of network access needed by your Windows 2000 Professional–based client, one or more of the following methods can be used to identify your computer by name, rather than IP address: Domain Name System (DNS), Windows Internet Name Service (WINS), Lmhosts/Hosts file, or B-node (broadcast) name resolution.

- See "Configure TCP/IP Name Resolution" later in this chapter.

Configure multihoming, if needed.

If your Windows 2000 Professional configuration requires multiple network adapters, is connected logically to multiple networks, or uses different network connection types, configure TCP/IP addressing for each logical connection.

- See "Configure Multihoming" later in this chapter.

Configure local routing table.

The local IP routing table on your Windows 2000 Professional computer must be configured to enable communication with other computers outside the local subnet. Depending on the enterprise configuration, the local route table can be automatically configured by using routers meeting specifications for ICMP Router Discovery or Routing Information Protocol (RIP). Otherwise, default gateways and the routing table might be necessary.

- See "Configure Local Routing Table" later in this chapter.

Install and configure Internet Connection Sharing, if needed.

For small business and home office configurations, Internet Connection Sharing (ICS) can be installed and configured to allow computers in a private network to share a single public IP address and Internet connection to access the Internet.

- See "Configure Internet Connection Sharing" later in this chapter.

Configure IP security methods, if needed.

To secure information within the network, IP filtering can be enabled on the Windows 2000 Professional–based client to limit the type of IP packets received. On a stand-alone computer or a member of a Windows 2000 domain, IP security can be enabled to provide data validation and encryption at the packet layer.

- See "Configure IP Security and Filtering" later in this chapter.

Configure Quality of Service, if needed.

In a Windows 2000–based enterprise with QoS-aware devices, enabling QoS at the Windows 2000–based client can assist in the management of network bandwidth and allow prioritization of data within the network.

- See "Configure Quality of Service" later in this chapter.

Diagnose network failures by troubleshooting your configuration.

Follow the troubleshooting guidelines to recover from an installation or configuration failure or to perform other diagnostic functions related to TCP/IP.

- See "Perform TCP/IP Troubleshooting" later in this chapter.

Overview of Windows 2000 TCP/IP

Transmission Control Protocol/Internet Protocol (TCP/IP) provides communication across interconnected networks that use diverse hardware architectures and various operating systems. TCP/IP can be used to communicate with computers running Windows 2000, with devices using other Microsoft networking products, or with non-Microsoft systems such as UNIX.

TCP/IP in Windows 2000 Professional improves upon the functionality that TCP/IP provided in Microsoft® Windows NT® Workstation version 4.0. Table 22.1 shows Windows 2000 TCP/IP features:

Table 22.1   Features of TCP/IP in Windows 2000

Feature	Benefit
Logical and physical multihoming	Allows association of multiple IP addresses to a single or multiple network adapters for internetwork connectivity.
Internal IP routing capability	Allows a Windows 2000 Professional workstation to route packets between multiple network adapters.
Multiple configurable default gateways	Allows configuring multiple default gateways to improve network reliability and uptime.
Dynamic Host Configuration Protocol (DHCP)	Simplifies host configuration through automatic configuration of IP address and other parameters.
Virtual private networking	Permits secured transmission of data across public networks through encapsulated and encrypted packets.
Windows Sockets Version 2 (Winsock2) interface	Standard application programming interface (API) permits access to networking features.
Domain Name System (DNS)	A server-based mapping of friendly names to IP addresses.
NetBIOS interface	The use of NetBIOS sessions, datagrams, and name management over TCP/IP.
Windows Internet Name Service (WINS)	A server-based mapping of NetBIOS names to IP addresses.
Microsoft browsing support	Browser-enabled services can view resources on a TCP/IP internetwork.
Simple Network Management Protocol (SNMP) agent	Permits performance and resource monitoring of a TCP/IP-based client.
TCP/IP connectivity tools	Finger, Ftp, Rcp, Rexec, Rsh, Telnet and Tftp commands allow access to heterogeneous hosts across a TCP/IP-based network.

(continued)

Table 22.1   Features of TCP/IP in Windows 2000 *(continued)*

Feature	Benefit
TCP/IP simple services	Chargen, daytime, discard, echo, and Quote of the Day client and server utilities.
TCP/IP management and diagnostic tools	Arp, Ipconfig, Nbtstat, Ping, Route, Nslookup, Tracert, and Pathping provide maintenance and diagnostic features.
TCP/IP network printing	Permits printing on non-Windows connected devices, such as UNIX-connected devices.

What's New in Windows 2000 TCP/IP

TCP/IP in Windows 2000 builds upon the networking strengths found in Windows NT Workstation 4.0 and Microsoft® Windows® 98. These improvements result in a scalable networking platform that can be implemented in a variety of environments, from a small office/home office configuration, to a powerful workstation within a multidomain enterprise.

The improvements made in Windows 2000 Professional can be categorized into five areas, each presented in this chapter:

- Address assignment and IP packet handling
- Name resolution
- IP security
- Quality of Service (QoS)
- TCP Performance

Address Assignment and IP Packet Handling

Windows 2000 makes setting up small office/home office (SOHO) configurations easier through two new features. *Automatic Private IP Addressing* (APIPA) assigns an IP address and subnet mask to a Windows 2000 Professional computer if a DHCP server is not available. Access to outside networks is also facilitated through *Internet Connection Sharing (ICS)*, which translates private IP addresses to a single public IP address, which can access other intranets or the Internet.

Configuration of large enterprise networks is facilitated through the addition of several new features. *ICMP Router Discovery* automatically configures a default gateway for a Windows 2000 Professional host. ICMP *Router Discovery* allows clients to discover gateways dynamically. *TCP/IP over ATM* permits the use of Asynchronous Transfer Mode (ATM) adapters connected to ATM-based, packet-switched networks.

Name Resolution

Windows 2000 Professional includes several modifications to its IP address/name resolution process to make it an Internet-ready client. DNS is the default name resolution method for the Windows 2000 environment, replacing NetBIOS as the default name management method for Windows-based domains.

To facilitate maintenance of DNS record databases, Microsoft® Windows® 2000 Server supports *dynamic update*, as specified in Request for Comments (RFC) 2136. Windows 2000 Professional provides dynamic update of DNS servers that are compliant with RFC 2136, providing address and domain name updates directly or through a DHCP server.

A number of additional improvements have been made in DNS, including support for an extended character set (RFC 2181), client-side caching, connection-specific domain names, and improved performance through subnet prioritization.

IP Security

Windows 2000 provides network security through the implementation of *IP security* (IPSec). IPSec is a set of rules and protocols defined by the Internet Engineering Task Force (IETF) that provide encryption, data authentication, and data integrity at the packet level. These features are enabled below the network layer, requiring no change to the existing network and application infrastructure to deploy IP security. Local and domain-based IPSec policies can be created to implement IP security.

Quality of Service

As multimedia-rich applications such as video conferencing and video-on-demand become more pervasive within a network, the issues of network bandwidth and the quality of data transmission become more critical. Windows 2000 Professional addresses this through its implementation of *Quality of Service (QoS)*, a set of specifications that determine the network requirements needed by a multimedia or qualitative application. Windows 2000 Professional also implements the *Resource Reservation Protocol (RSVP)*, which allows an application or service to reserve a specific amount of bandwidth needed for data transmission.

TCP Performance

Windows 2000 Professional includes enhancements to TCP that improve the performance of TCP/IP-based networks. *Larger default TCP receive window size* increases performance on high-speed network*s. Window scaling*, as documented in RFC 1323, allows the use of a very large TCP receive window in high bandwidth, high delay environments. To improve performance in high-loss environments such as the Internet, *selective acknowledgments (SACKs)* enables a receiving host to selectively acknowledge only the data it has received.

Comparison of Windows 2000 Features

Table 22.2 displays the new features implemented in Windows 2000, compared to Windows 98 and Microsoft® Windows NT® version 4.0.

Table 22.2   Comparison of Windows 2000 TCP/IP Features

Windows 2000 TCP/IP Feature	Windows 98	Windows NT 4.0
Address Assignment/Packet Handling		
Automatic Private IP Addressing (APIPA)	yes	no
Shared Internet connection	yes (SE)	no
ICMP Router Discovery	yes	no
IP multicasting (IGMP version 2)	yes	yes (IGMP version 1)
TCP/IP over ATM	no	no
Name Resolution		
Dynamic update of DNS	no	no
Support for extended character set (RFC 2181)	yes	no
Connection-specific domain names	yes	no
DNS integration with Active Directory	no	no
Security Features		
IP packet-level security	no	no
Rules-based security policies	no	no
Data encryption	no	no
Kerberos authentication method	no	no
Public and private key authentication	yes	yes
Data authentication	no	no
PPTP	yes	yes
L2TP	no	no
Quality of Service		
QoS packet scheduling	no	no
RSVP support	no	no
TCP/IP Performance		
Larger default window sizes	no	no
Scalable window sizes	no	no
Selective acknowledgment	yes	no

Install TCP/IP

Setup installs TCP/IP by default if you have accepted the default Windows 2000 Professional installation options. If you are upgrading to Windows 2000 Professional, however, Setup replaces your existing network configuration.

If your original Windows installation included a third-party TCP/IP protocol stack, Setup replaces the existing TCP/IP protocol. If there are features that are required by your third-party stack you must determine whether they are supported by Windows 2000 TCP/IP. If these features are required, you must install the third-party stack by using the installation tool provided by your network vendor.

▶ **To install Windows 2000 TCP/IP after Windows 2000 Professional Setup**

1. In Control Panel, double-click **Network and Dial-up Connections**.

2. Right-click the connection you want to modify.

3. Select **Properties**.

4. On the **General** tab, click **Install**.

5. Select **Protocol**.

6. Click **Add**.

7. In **Network Protocol**, select **TCP/IP** and click **OK**

8. When prompted, click **Yes** to restart the computer.

Configure IP Address Assignment

This section provides an overview of the methods available for assigning IP addresses to individual Windows 2000 Professional–based clients in a TCP/IP network. It presents an explanation of each configuration method, including issues you might want to consider when implementing each method.

Choose an IP address assignment method. Windows 2000 Professional provides three methods for assignment of IP addresses to TCP/IP clients: Dynamic Host Configuration Protocol (DHCP), which automatically configures clients in an enterprise with a DHCP server; Automatic Private IP Addressing (APIPA), which automatically assigns an IP address to clients in a single-subnet environment; and manual configuration of IP addresses. Choose the method that meets your environment and client requirements. See "Overview of IP Address Assignment" later in this chapter.

If automatic host configuration is desired, and a DHCP server is available, enable DHCP.

DHCP provides automatic configuration of IP addresses and other configuration options for clients in a network with one or more DHCP servers. It is the default addressing method in Windows 2000 Professional. See "Configure DHCP" later in this chapter.

If automatic IP address assignment is desired, but no DHCP server is available, enable DHCP to use Automatic Private IP Addressing (APIPA).

APIPA provides automatic IP address assignment for computers on networks without a DHCP server. A Windows 2000 Professional–based client assigns itself an IP address from a reserved class B network (169.254.0.0 with the subnet mask of 255.255.0.0), which cannot directly communicate with hosts outside this subnet, including Internet hosts. This option is most suitable for small, single-subnet networks, such as a home or small office. APIPA is configured by default if no DHCP servers are available on the network. See "Configure Automatic Private IP Addressing" in this chapter.

If DHCP or APIPA cannot be used, configure IP address manually.

If your network does not include a DHCP server, and APIPA cannot be used, use manual IP addressing. You must configure the IP address and subnet mask to meet your client's connectivity requirements. See "Configure IP Address Manually" in this chapter.

Overview of IP Address Assignment

Each computer on a TCP/IP network must be identified by a unique 32-bit IP address to be able to communicate on a private network or the Internet. IP addresses can be grouped into two classes of IP addresses, *public* IP addresses and *private* IP addresses. These address classes are assigned by the Internet Assigned Numbers Authority (IANA), which is responsible for the management and assignment of IP addresses on the Internet and to private organizations.

Public IP addresses

On the Internet, the IANA assigns groups of IP addresses to organizations. The organizations can then assign IP addresses within those groups to individual computers. This prevents multiple computers from having the same IP address. For a computer to be visible on the Internet, it must be reachable through a public IP address.

The public IP address for your Windows 2000 Professional–based computer can be assigned through a Dynamic Host Configuration Protocol (DHCP) server available in your enterprise network, configured manually, or provided by an Internet service provider (ISP) through a dial-up connection.

Private IP addresses

The IANA has reserved a certain number of IP addresses that are never used on the global Internet. These *private IP addresses* are used for networks that do not want to directly connect to the Internet, but require IP connectivity. For example, a user wanting to connect multiple Windows 2000 Professional–based computers in a home network can use the Automatic Private IP Addressing (APIPA) feature to allow each computer to automatically assign itself a private IP address. The user does not need to configure an IP address for each computer, nor is a DHCP server needed.

Internet connectivity can be obtained in a network by using private IP addressing through the use of a computer with proxy or network address translator (NAT) capabilities. Windows 2000 Professional includes the Internet Connection Sharing (ICS) feature that provides NAT services to clients in a private network. For more information about Internet Connection Sharing, see "Configure Internet Connection Sharing" later in this chapter.

Dynamic Host Configuration Protocol

A configured DHCP server provides a database of available IP addresses. The server can also be set up to provide configuration options for DHCP clients, including addresses of DNS and WINS servers, gateway addresses, and other information.

At startup, each DHCP client requests configuration data from the server, permitting automatic configuration of the IP address, subnet mask and other options. The IP address is assigned to each client for an amount of time determined at the server, called a *lease,* which can be periodically renewed. At conclusion of the lease, the client attempts to renew the lease, or the IP address is returned to the database and is made available to other DHCP clients. DHCP provides an efficient IP configuration option for larger networks, providing simplified client configuration, and reuse of IP addresses.

Automatic Private IP Addressing

Automatic Private IP Addressing (APIPA) is appropriate for simple networks that have only one subnet. With APIPA, if no DHCP server is available, the computer automatically assigns itself a private IP address. If a DHCP server later becomes available, the computer changes its IP address to one obtained from a DHCP server. Computers using APIPA addresses can communicate only with other computers using APIPA addresses, on the same subnet. They are not directly reachable from the Internet.

Static IP Addressing

With static IP addressing, you must manually configure the IP address. This method can be time-consuming and prone to error, especially on medium to large networks. It is recommended if DHCP and APIPA are not available or feasible.

Configure DHCP

In an effort to make implementing the TCP/IP protocol more manageable, Microsoft worked with other industry leaders to create an Internet standard called Dynamic Host Configuration Protocol (DHCP) for the automatic allocation of TCP/IP configuration. DHCP is not a Microsoft standard, but a public Request for Comments (RFC) 2131 that Microsoft has implemented.

Implementing a DHCP server within an enterprise allows a network administrator to establish a range of valid IP addresses to be used per subnet and a series of options providing configuration beyond the IP address such as the subnet mask, the default gateway, and DNS and WINS server addresses. An individual IP address from the range and its associated options are assigned dynamically to any DHCP client requesting an address. If DHCP is available company-wide, users can move from subnet to subnet and always have a valid IP address. DHCP also allows the establishment of a lease time that defines how long an IP address configuration is to remain valid. A Microsoft® Windows NT® Server version 3.5 or later computer running the DHCP service can act as a DHCP server.

Note For more information about installation and configuration of the DHCP service on Windows 2000 Server, see "Dynamic Host Configuration Protocol" in the *TCP/IP Core Networking Guide*.

DHCP Lease Process

The first time a Windows 2000 Professional–based client with DHCP enabled starts and attempts to join a network, it automatically follows an initialization process to obtain a lease from a DHCP server. Figure 22.1 shows the lease process.

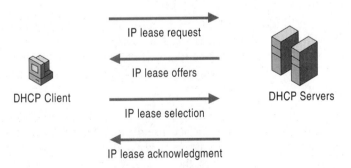

Figure 22.1   The DHCP Lease Process

1. The Windows 2000 Professional DHCP client requests an IP address by broadcasting a message (known as a DHCPDiscover message) to the local subnet.

2. The client is offered an address when a DHCP server responds with a message containing an IP address and configuration information for lease to the client (DHCPOffer). If no DHCP server responds to the client request, the Windows 2000 Professional–based client can proceed in two ways:

   - If the Automatic Private IP Addressing (APIPA) feature has not been disabled, the client self-configures a unique IP address from the range 169.254.0.1 to 169.254.255.254. For more details, see "Configure Automatic Private IP Addressing" in this chapter.

   - If APIPA has been disabled, the client network initialization fails. The client continues to resend DHCPDiscover messages in the background until it receives a valid lease from a DHCP server. The client makes four attempts to obtain a lease, one every five minutes.

3. The client indicates acceptance of the offer by selecting the offered address and replying to the server with a DHCPRequest message.

4. The client is assigned the address and the DHCP server sends an acknowledgment message (DHCPAck), approving the lease. Other DHCP option information, such as default gateway and DNS server addresses might be included in the message.

5. After the client receives acknowledgment, it configures its TCP/IP properties using any DHCP option information in the DHCPAck message, and completes the initialization of TCP/IP.

In rare cases, a DHCP server might return a negative acknowledgment to the client. This can happen if a client requests an invalid or duplicate address. If a client receives a negative acknowledgment (DHCPNak), the client must begin the entire lease process again.

Restarting a DHCP Client

When a Windows 2000 Professional–based client that previously leased an IP address restarts, it broadcasts a DHCPRequest message, containing a request for the previously assigned IP address. If the requested IP address is available, the DHCP server responds with an acknowledgment message, and the client joins the network.

If the IP address cannot be used by the client because it is no longer valid, in use by another client, or invalid because the client has been physically moved to a different subnet, the DHCP server responds with a negative acknowledgment (DHCPNak). If this occurs, the client must restart the lease process.

DHCP Lease Renewals

To ensure that addresses are not left in an assigned state when they are no longer needed, the DHCP server places an administrator-defined time limit, known as a *lease duration*, on the address assignment.

Halfway through the lease period, the DHCP client requests a lease renewal, and the DHCP server extends the lease. If a computer stops using its assigned IP address (for example, if a computer is moved to another network segment or is removed), the lease expires and the address becomes available for reassignment.

Configuring the Windows 2000 Professional DHCP Client

When TCP/IP is first installed, Windows 2000 Professional automatically enables the option to obtain an IP address from a DHCP server. You can disable this option if you want to manually enter IP addresses. For more information about disabling DHCP, see "Configure IP Address Manually" late in this chapter.

The IP configuration tool (Ipconfig) allows users or administrators to examine the current IP address configuration assigned to the computer, the IP address lease time, and other useful data about the TCP/IP configuration.

Configure Automatic Private IP Addressing

The new IP address autoconfiguration feature of TCP/IP in Windows 2000, known as *Automatic Private IP Addressing (APIPA),* allows home users and small business users to create a functioning, single subnet TCP/IP network without having to manually configure the TCP/IP protocol or set up a DHCP server.

APIPA allows a Windows 2000 Professional DHCP client to assign itself an IP address in the following circumstances:

- The client is configured to obtain a lease DHCP, but a DHCP server cannot be found, is unavailable, or is not used (for example, in a small office/home office network).

- The client used DHCP to obtain a lease, but attempts to renew the lease through a DHCP server have failed.

For more information about the DHCP lease and renewal process, see the previous discussion in "Configure DHCP" earlier in this chapter.

In these circumstances, a Windows 2000 Professional DHCP client autoconfigures the TCP/IP protocol with a selected IP address from the Internet Assigned Numbers Authority (IANA)-reserved class B network 169.254.0.0 with the subnet mask 255.255.0.0. The DHCP client performs duplicate address detection to ensure that the IP address it has chosen is not already in use. If the address is in use, it selects another IP address and reselects addresses up to 10 times. After the DHCP client has selected an address that is verifiably not in use, it configures the interface with this address. The client continues to check for a DHCP server in the background every five minutes, and if a DHCP server is found, the autoconfiguration information is abandoned and the configuration offered by the DHCP server is used instead.

▶ **To determine whether Automatic Private IP Addressing is currently enabled**

- At the command prompt, type **ipconfig /all**. The resulting text identifies your IP address and other information. Check the line that reads "Autoconfiguration Enabled." If the text reads "YES" and the IP address lies in the 169.254.*x.x* range, Automatic Private IP Addressing is enabled.

You can disable automatic private IP addressing in one of two ways:

- You can manually configure TCP/IP by following the procedure outlined in the section "Configure IP Address Manually" later in this chapter. This method also disables DHCP.

- You can also disable automatic private IP addressing for a given adapter (but not DHCP) by editing the registry.

You do this by adding the registry entry **IPAutoconfigurationEnabled** with a value of 0x0 (REG_DWORD data type) in the following subkey:

HKEY_LOCAL_MACHINE\SYSTEM\CurrentControlSet\Services \Tcpip\Parameters\Interfaces\<*adapter*>

Use a registry editor to add this entry, then shut down and restart the computer.

This registry entry is specific to each adapter. If multiple adapters are installed, you can disable APIPA for all installed adapters by setting the value of the **IPAutoconfigurationEnabled** entry to 0 (REG_DWORD data type) in the following registry subkey:

HKEY_LOCAL_MACHINE\SYSTEM\CurrentControlSet\Services \Tcpip\Parameters

Caution Do not use a registry editor to edit the registry directly unless you have no alternative. The registry editors bypass the standard safeguards provided by administrative tools. These safeguards prevent you from entering conflicting settings or settings that are likely to degrade performance or damage your system. Editing the registry directly can have serious, unexpected consequences that can prevent the system from starting and require that you reinstall Windows 2000. To configure or customize Windows 2000, use the programs in Control Panel or Microsoft Management Console (MMC) whenever possible.

Note APIPA only assigns an IP address and subnet mask. APIPA does not assign a default gateway, the IP addresses of DNS server, or the IP addresses of WINS servers. Use APIPA only on a single subnet network that contains no routers. If your small office or home office network is connected to the Internet or an organization intranet, then do not use APIPA.

Configure IP Address Manually

If you cannot use DHCP or APIPA for IP address and subnet assignment, the IP address for the Windows 2000 Professional–based client must be manually configured. The required values include the following:

- The IP address for each network adapter installed on the computer.

- The subnet mask corresponding to each network adapter's local network.

▶ **To configure TCP/IP manually**

1. In Control Panel, open **Network and Dial-up Connections**.

2. Right-click the local area connection you want to modify.

3. Select **Properties**.

4. In the **General** dialog box, select **Internet Protocol (TCP/IP)**.

5. Click **Properties**.

6. In the **General** dialog box, select the **Use the following IP address** option.

7. Type the IP address, subnet mask, and default gateway in the respective boxes.

   The network administrator must provide these values for individual users, based on the IP addressing plan for your site.

   - The value in the **IP Address** box identifies the IP address for the interface.

   - The value in the **Subnet Mask** box is used to identify the network ID for the selected network adapter.

8. Click **OK** to save the IP addressing information.

9. Click **OK** to save the connection properties.

Configure TCP/IP Name Resolution

This section provides an overview of the methods available for configuring TCP/IP name resolution on a Windows 2000 Professional–based client. It presents an explanation of each configuration method, including issues you might want to consider when implementing each method.

Choose name resolution method. Windows 2000 Professional provides four methods for resolving names to IP addresses:

- Domain Name System (DNS) for applications and services that require host-to-IP name resolution, such as Active Directory

- Windows Internet Name Service (WINS), for compatibility with applications and services that require NetBIOS-to-IP name resolution, such as browsing functions of previous versions of Windows

- Hosts and Lmhosts files, which provide host-to-IP and NetBIOS-to-IP name resolution via manually-maintained local files; and b-node broadcasts, which can be used for NetBIOS name resolution within the local subnet.

Choose the methods that meet your environment and client requirements. See "Overview of TCP/IP Name Resolution" later in this chapter.

If DNS is used, configure settings. DNS is the default name resolution method for Windows 2000–based clients, and is required for integration in a Windows 2000 Active Directory domain. To use this name resolution method, it must be properly configured. Use Table 22.3 to find information on the area of DNS you are configuring.

Table 22.3 DNS Configuration Topics

To configure this DNS setting...	...refer to this section
Configure client name	"Configuring Host and DNS Domain Names"
Configure primary DNS suffix	"Configuring Host and DNS Domain Names"
Configure connection-specific DNS suffix	"Configuring Host and DNS Domain Names"
Specify the addresses of available DNS servers	"Specifying DNS Servers"
Configure the way the DNS client resolves host names	"Configuring DNS Query Settings"
Optimize the local DNS cache	"DNS Performance and Security"
Prevent DNS client from accepting non-queried servers	"DNS Performance and Security"
Configure dynamic update, if used	"Configure Dynamic Update"

If Hosts file is used for host name resolution, edit file. For networks without access to a DNS name server, creation of a Hosts file can provide host name resolution for applications and services. This file can also be used in an environment where name servers are available, but not all hosts are registered; for example, a server that is not available for general use, but is only to be accessed by a limited number of clients. This file must be manually created and updated as host names and addresses change. See "Configure Hosts File" later in this chapter.

If WINS is used, configure settings. WINS provides name-to-IP resolution for applications and services using the NetBIOS command set for networks with a WINS server. If your network environment meets these requirements, the IP addresses of WINS servers needs to be configured on your Windows 2000 Professional–based client to provide NetBIOS name resolution. In a network where dynamic update is not available, a WINS server can provide a DNS server configured for WINS lookup with dynamic updates of host names, provided that WINS is enabled at each client. See "Configure NetBIOS Name Resolution" later in this chapter.

If Lmhosts file is used, modify file and configure settings. For networks without access to a WINS name server, creation of an Lmhosts file can provide NetBIOS name resolution for application and services. This file can also be used in an environment where name servers are available, but not all hosts are registered; for example, a server that is not available for general use, but is only to be accessed by a limited number of clients. This file must be manually created and updated as computer names and addresses change. See "Configure NetBIOS Name Resolution" later in this chapter.

If none of the above name resolution methods are enabled or successful in name resolution, local broadcasts are used.

To resolve NetBIOS names within the local subnet, *b-node*, or broadcast name resolution, can be used to determine the IP address for a NetBIOS name. See "Configure NetBIOS Name Resolution" later in this chapter.

Overview of TCP/IP Name Resolution

TCP/IP-based services use IP addresses to identify each other, but users and applications frequently require computer names for host identification. A name resolution mechanism must be available on a TCP/IP network to resolve names to IP addresses.

When a request for name-to-IP address resolution is made, the Windows 2000 resolver first submits the name query to DNS. If DNS name resolution fails, the resolver checks to see whether the name is longer than 15 bytes. If it is longer, resolution fails. If not, the resolver then checks to see if NetBIOS is running. If it is not running, resolution fails. If it is running, the resolver then tries NetBIOS name resolution.

Figure 22.2 and Figures 22.6 and 22.7 show an overview of the process.

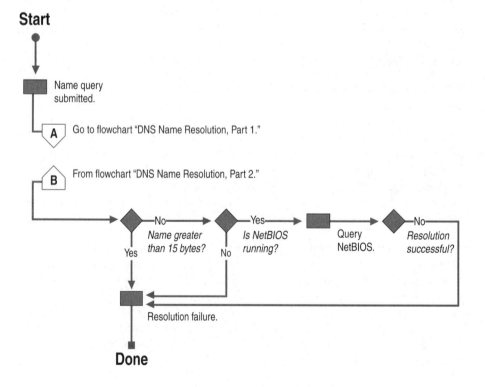

Figure 22.2   Overview of Name Resolution

Windows 2000 Professional provides several different types of name resolution, including DNS, WINS, name resolution using Hosts or Lmhosts files, and broadcast name resolution. Generally, a Windows 2000 Professional–based computer uses a combination of these name resolution types, summarized in this section.

Domain Name System Name Resolution

The Domain Name System (DNS) is a global, distributed database based on a hierarchical naming system. DNS name resolution is used on the Internet to map friendly names to IP addresses, and vice versa. DNS replaces the functionality of the Hosts file, which requires manual maintenance at each workstation.

In previous versions of Windows, NetBIOS was used as the primary method of name-to-IP resolution. In Windows 2000, DNS is the default name resolution method. The hierarchical naming structure of DNS compliments the hierarchical planning structure implemented in the Active Directory™ directory service, and is used as its naming service. Active Directory is integrated into DNS in other ways as well, for example, system administrators can integrate DNS zones into Active Directory, which provides greater fault tolerance.

Windows 2000 Professional supports DNS dynamic update. *Dynamic update* is a new standard, specified in RFC 2136, that provides a means of dynamically updating host data in a DNS database. Updates can come from DNS clients and servers, DHCP servers, or Active Directory domain controllers. For more information about dynamic update, see "Configure Dynamic Update" later in this chapter.

Windows Internet Name Service

Windows Internet Name Service (WINS) name resolution provides mapping of static and dynamic NetBIOS names to IP addresses. Computers running Windows 2000 TCP/IP can use WINS if one or more Microsoft® Windows NT® Server–based computers configured as WINS servers are available. WINS is a dynamic replacement for the Lmhosts file.

WINS client support is configured with Windows 2000 Professional to maintain compatibility with non-Windows 2000–based hosts, including clients and servers running previous versions of Windows.

Hosts and Lmhosts Files

Hosts and Lmhosts files, also called *host tables*, are files that Windows 2000 Professional can use for local name resolution when other methods are not available. An Lmhosts file is a list of NetBIOS name and IP address mappings. When WINS is not available, it is used as a WINS equivalent to resolve remote NetBIOS names to IP addresses. Likewise, a Hosts file is a list of host name to IP address mappings. It is used as a local name resolution resource to resolve host names to IP addresses. You must manually enter the name-to-IP address mappings in Hosts and Lmhosts files.

Broadcast Name Resolution

Computers running Windows 2000 TCP/IP can use local broadcast name resolution, which is a NetBIOS-over-TCP/IP mode of operation defined in RFC 1001/1002 as *b-node*. It is restricted to the local subnet. This method relies on IP subnet and media access control (MAC)-level broadcasts by a host for name registration and announcement on the network. Each computer in the broadcast area is responsible for challenging attempts to register a duplicate unique name and for responding to name queries for its registered unique name.

Determining Which Name Resolution Method to Use

You need to determine whether Windows 2000 Professional–based clients must be configured to use DNS, WINS, or a combination of the two. In general, DNS is recommended under the following circumstances:

- The client is a member of a Windows 2000 domain that uses Active Directory.

  If the Windows 2000 Professional–based computer is to be made a member of a Windows 2000 domain, DNS must be configured. Active Directory is tightly integrated with DNS, and DNS is used by Active Directory as its locator service. A locator service assists clients in a Windows 2000 domain to find other hosts and services by knowing only the domain name.

- Internet or intranet access using DNS is required.

  You must use DNS if you are using TCP/IP to communicate over the Internet or if your private internetwork uses DNS to resolve host names. If the DNS server is not dynamic update-compliant, DNS can be used in conjunction with WINS to automatically resolve host names.

NetBIOS over TCP/IP (NetBT) support is provided as part of Windows 2000 Professional configuration to provide name resolution and connection services for clients using earlier versions of the Windows operating system, applications and services. If a WINS server is available within your network, configure your Windows 2000 Professional–based computer to use WINS under the following circumstances:

- The client is a member of a non-Windows 2000 domain or workgroup.

- The client is a member of a Windows 2000 workgroup where a DNS server is not available.

- The client is part of a network where the DNS server uses WINS lookup for dynamic name resolution.

- The client uses applications or services that require NetBIOS name resolution.

If a WINS server is not available, configure the Windows 2000 Professional–based client to use a Hosts file for DNS host name resolution, or Lmhosts for NetBIOS name resolution. Otherwise, broadcasts are used to provide NetBIOS name resolution, which cannot resolve host names outside the local subnet.

You also need to determine if automatic configuration is available at the DHCP server. If you use DHCP for automatic configuration, a DHCP server can provide client configuration details (DNS and WINS server addresses, host name). If you do not use DHCP, you must manually configure these parameters.

Configure DNS Name Resolution

The Domain Name System (DNS) provides name-to-IP mapping by a distributed database. A Windows 2000 Professional–based client configured for DNS name resolution can query one or more DNS servers for name resolution services. This section describes the procedures for performing the following tasks:

- Configuring DNS Host and Domain Names
- Configuring DNS Query Settings
- Specifying DNS Servers
- DNS Performance and Security

Configure DNS Host and Domain Names

Table 22.4 summarizes the differences between each kind of name used in TCP/IP under Windows 2000, using the example fully qualified domain name (FQDN) client1.reskit.com.

Table 22.4   DNS and NetBIOS Names

Name Type	Description
NetBIOS name	A NetBIOS name is used to uniquely identify a NetBIOS service listening on the first IP address that is bound to an adapter. This unique NetBIOS name is resolved to the IP address of the server through broadcast, WINS, or the Lmhosts file. By default, it is the same as the host name up to 15 characters, plus any spaces necessary to make the name 15 characters long, plus the service identifier.
	The NetBIOS name is also known as a *NetBIOS computer name*.
	For example, a NetBIOS name might be Client1.
Host name	The term *host name* can mean either the FQDN or the first label of an FQDN. In this chapter, host name refers to the first label of an FQDN.
	For example, the first label of the FQDN client1.reskit.com is client1.

(continued)

Table 22.4   DNS and NetBIOS Names *(continued)*

Name Type	Description
Primary DNS suffix	Every Windows 2000–based computer can be assigned a primary DNS suffix to be used in name resolution and name registration. The primary DNS suffix is specified on the **Network Identification** tab of the properties page for **My Computer**.
	The primary DNS suffix is also known as the *primary domain name* and the *domain name*.
	For example, the FQDN client1.reskit.com has the primary DNS suffix reskit.com.
Connection-specific DNS suffix	The connection-specific DNS suffix is a DNS suffix that is assigned to an adapter.
	The connection-specific DNS suffix is also known as an *adapter DNS suffix*.
	For example, a connection-specific DNS suffix might be *reskit.com*.
Fully qualified domain name (FQDN)	The FQDN is a DNS name that uniquely identifies the computer on the network. By default, it is a concatenation of the host name, the primary DNS suffix, and a period.
	The fully qualified domain name is also known as the *full computer name*.
	For example, an FQDN might be client1.reskit.com.

Computer and NetBIOS Names   The DNS host name is taken from the computer name assigned to it during Windows 2000 Professional installation. The host name can be 63 characters long, and uses the character set specified in RFC 2181, as shown in Table 22.5. The host name is used in combination with the primary domain name to form the fully qualified domain name (FQDN).

The NetBIOS computer name is used to identify the local computer for authentication by hosts and tools that use NetBIOS over TCP/IP (NetBT) for name resolution. NetBIOS names contain 15 characters, with an additional character used as the service descriptor. In a new Windows 2000 Professional installation, the NetBIOS name is initially taken from the assigned DNS host name. If the DNS host name exceeds 15 characters, the host name is truncated to form the NetBIOS computer name.

Figure 22.3 shows an example of a computer that has a DNS host name of **serverislongerthan15bytes**. Note that the NetBIOS name is truncated to 15 characters.

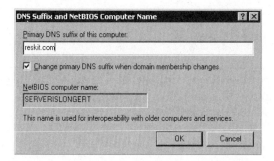

Figure 22.3   NetBIOS and DNS Domain Names

The DNS host name can be changed after installation by means of the **Network Identification** tab in the **System** control panel. The NetBIOS computer name changes also, based on the restrictions of NetBIOS.

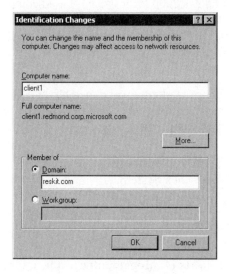

▶   **To change the host name for DNS**

1. In Control Panel, double-click **System**.

2. Select **the Network Identification** tab.

3. Click **Properties**.

4. Type the new host name in the **Computer name** text box and click **OK**.

5. When prompted, click **OK**.

6. Click **OK**.

7. When prompted, click **Yes** to restart the computer.

Note If you enter a DNS name that includes characters not listed in RFC 1123 during the setup for Windows 2000 DNS, a warning message appears suggesting that you use characters specified by RFC 1123.

Computer names in previous versions of Windows are based on NetBIOS names. If a Windows 2000 Professional–based computer has been migrated from a previous version of Windows, its DNS host name is taken from the previous NetBIOS-based computer name. In a network that contains non-Windows 2000–based hosts, this might present problems.

Primary DNS Suffix The primary DNS suffix is the name of the domain in which the host resides. If a Windows 2000 Professional–based computer is a member of a Windows 2000 domain, its primary DNS domain name is identical to its Windows 2000 domain. This information is provided during Windows 2000 Professional installation, migration, or when the computer joins a Windows 2000 domain.

If a computer is a member of workgroup, or a member of a Windows NT domain, the primary domain name is manually specified by using the **Network Identification** tab in the **System** control panel.

▶ **To set or change the primary DNS suffix**

1. In Control Panel, double-click **System**.

2. Select the **Network Identification** tab.

3. Click **Properties**.

4. Click **More**.

5. In the **Primary DNS suffix of this computer** text box, type the primary DNS suffix, and then click **OK**.

When a Windows 2000 Professional–based computer changes Windows 2000 domains, its DNS domain membership can be changed as well. To allow Windows 2000 to automatically change the primary DNS domain name when its Windows 2000 domain membership changes, select **Change DNS domain name when domain membership changes**.

Connection-Specific DNS Suffix   Windows 2000 also permits each adapter to have a unique domain name, known as the *connection-specific domain name.*

For example, suppose the computer Client1 has the primary DNS domain name reskit.com, and it is connected to both the Internet and the corporate intranet. For each connection, you can specify a connection-specific domain name. For the connection to the corporate intranet, you specify the name reskit.com, and the FQDN is then Client1.reskit.com. For the connection to the Internet, you specify the name isp01.com, and the FQDN is then Client1.isp01.com.

Figure 22.4 shows this configuration.

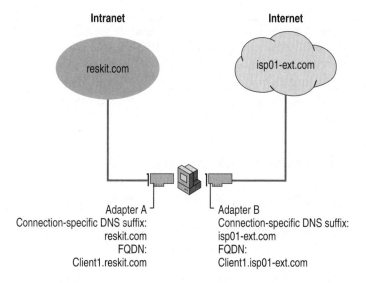

Figure 22.4   Connection-Specific Domain Names

Connection-specific domain names for each adapter are specified on the **DNS** tab of the **Advanced TCP/IP Settings** page. From that page, you can also specify whether a dynamic update client registers the computer's fully qualified domain name or the adapter-specific name. For more information, see "Configure Dynamic Update" later in this chapter.

▶   **To set or change the connection-specific DNS suffix**

1. In Control Panel, double-click **Network and Dial-up Connections**.

2. Right-click the local area connection you want to modify, and then select **Properties**.

3. Select **Internet Protocol (TCP/IP)**, and then click **Properties**.

4. Click **Advanced**.

5. Select the **DNS** tab.

6. In the **DNS suffix for this connection** text box, type the domain name for the connection.

Fully Qualified Domain Name   By default, the DNS domain name is used with the primary host name to create a fully qualified domain name (FQDN) for the computer. During DNS queries, the local domain name is appended to short names. A short name consists of only a host name, such as **client1**. When querying the DNS server for the IP address of **client1**, the domain name is appended to the short name, and the DNS server is actually asked to resolve the FQDN of **client1.reskit.com**.

Note   If an entry is specified in the **Search these DNS domains (in order)** box in the **DNS** section of **Advanced TCP/IP settings** dialog box, that entry is used instead of the domain and host name to create an FQDN.

For detailed information about how the FQDN is used to perform name-to-IP address resolution, refer to "Configure DNS Name Resolution" earlier in this chapter.

DNS Naming Restrictions

Different DNS implementations impose different character and length restrictions. Table 22.5 shows the restrictions for each implementation.

Table 22.5   Naming Restrictions

Restriction	Standard DNS (including Windows NT 4.0)	DNS in Windows 2000	NetBIOS
Characters	Supports RFC 1123, which permits A- Z, a-z, 0-9, and the hyphen (-).	Supports RFC 2044, which permits more characters than RFC 1123, but it is best to use only the characters permitted by RFC 1123.	*Unicode* characters, numbers, white space, symbols: ! @ # $ % ^ & ') (. - _ { } ~
Computer/host name length	63 bytes per label and 255 bytes for FQDN	63 bytes per label and 255 bytes for FQDN; domain controllers are limited to 155 bytes for FQDN.	15 characters

According to RFC 1123, the only characters that can be used in DNS labels are A-Z, a-z, 0-9, and the hyphen (-). (The "." character is also used in DNS names, but only between DNS labels and at the end of a FQDN.) Many DNS servers, including Windows NT 4.0 DNS servers, follow RFC 1123.

However, adherence to RFC 1123 can present a problem on Windows 2000 networks that still use NetBIOS names. NetBIOS names can use additional characters, and it can be time-consuming to convert all the NetBIOS names to standard DNS names.

To simplify the migration process from Windows NT 4.0, Windows 2000 supports a wider character set. RFC 2181, "Clarifications to the DNS Specification," extends the character set allowed in DNS names. Based on this definition, the Windows 2000 DNS service has been adjusted to accommodate a larger character set: UTF-8 character encoding, as described in RFC 2044. UTF-8 character encoding is a superset of ASCII and a translation of the UCS-2 (also known as *Unicode*) character encoding. The UTF-8 character set includes characters from most of the world's written languages, allowing a far greater range of possible names.

However, before using the extended character set, consider the following issues:

- If a client name containing UTF-8 characters is to be used, all DNS servers to which the client is to be registered must support RFC 2181. Avoid using UTF-8-compliant host names if your network includes servers that do not comply with this standard.

- Some third-party resolver software supports only the characters listed in RFC 1123. If there are any computers in your network that use third-party resolver software, that software probably cannot look up Windows 2000–based clients with names that have nonstandard characters.

Configuring DNS Query Settings

The DNS resolver adds a domain name suffix to a name specified in a query that meets either of the following conditions:

- The name is a single-label unqualified name.

- The name is a multiple-label unqualified name and the resolver cannot resolve it as a fully qualified domain name.

The query process is shown in Figures 22.5 and 22.6.

Note   The flowcharts in Figures 22.5 and 22.6 direct you to other flowcharts in other figures. To locate the correct flow chart, see the figure captions.

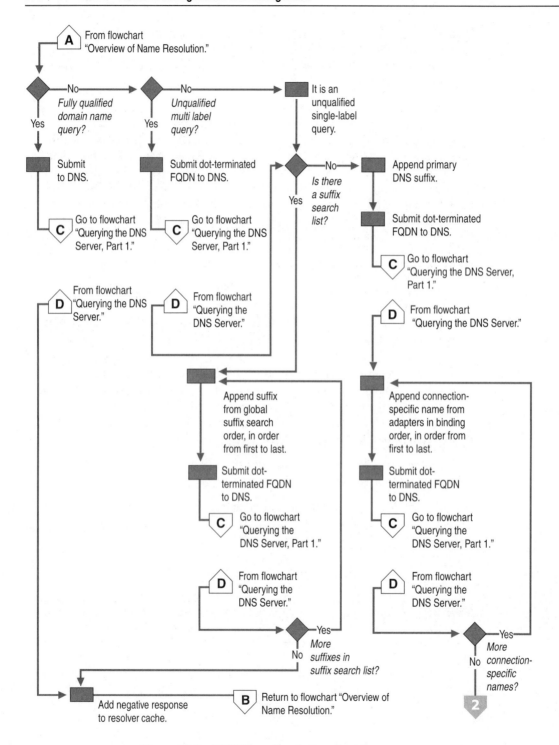

Figure 22.5   DNS Name Resolution, Part 1

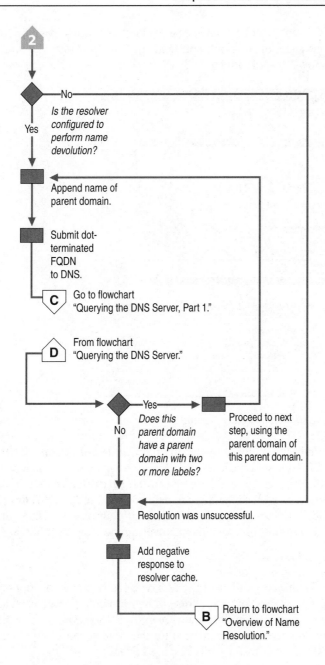

Figure 22.6   DNS Name Resolution, Part 2

You can configure how suffixes are added to queries from the **Advanced TCP/IP Settings** page, in **Network and Dial-up Connections** in Control Panel. Figure 22.7 shows the **Advanced TCP/IP Settings**:

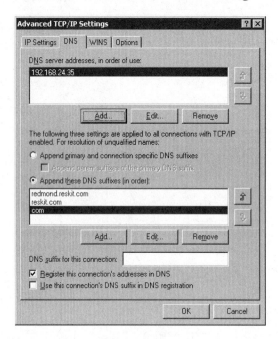

Figure 22.7   DNS Query Settings

By default, the option **Append primary and connection specific DNS suffixes** is selected. This option causes the resolver to append the client name to the primary domain name, as defined in the **Network Identification** tab of the system properties, as well as the domain name defined in the **DNS domain name** field of each network connection. For example, if your primary DNS suffix is *dom1.acquired01-int.com*, the resolver queries for the following FQDN:

```
client1.dom1.acquired01-int.com
```

Next, if that query fails and if you have specified a connection-specific DNS suffix in the **DNS suffix for this connection** box, it appends that name. For example, if you entered the name *acquired01-ext.com* in the **DNS suffix for this connection** box and then queried for the unqualified, single-label name *client1*, the resolver queries for the following FQDN:

```
client1.acquired01-ext.com.
```

Next, if you select the check box **Append parent suffixes of the primary DNS suffix**, the resolver performs *name devolution* on the primary DNS suffix, stripping off the leftmost label, and attempting the resulting domain name until only two labels remain. For example, if your primary DNS suffix is *dom1.acquired01-int.com*, and you selected the check box **Append parent suffixes of the primary DNS suffix** and then queried for the unqualified, single-label name *client1* the resolver queries in order the following FQDNs:

```
client1.dom1.acquired01-int.com.
client1.acquired01-int.com.
```

▶   **To disable name devolution**

1. In Control Panel, double-click **Network and Dial-up Connections**.

2. Right-click the local area connection you want to change, and then select **Properties**.

3. Select **Internet Protocol (TCP/IP)**, and then click **Properties**.

4. Click **Advanced**.

5. Click the **DNS** tab.

6. Clear the check box **Append parent suffixes of the primary DNS suffix**, and then click **OK**.

The box labeled **Append these DNS suffixes (in order)** allows you to specify a list of domains to try, called a *domain suffix search list*. If you enter a domain suffix search list, the resolver adds those domain name suffixes in order and does not try any other domain names. For example, if the **Append these DNS suffixes (in order)** box includes the names listed in Figure 22.7 and you enter the unqualified, single-label query "coffee", the resolver queries in order for the following fully qualified domain names:

```
coffee.redmond.reskit.com.
coffee.reskit.com.
coffee.com.
```

▶   **To add entries to the domain suffix search list**

1. In Control Panel, double-click **Network and Dial-up Connections**.

2. Right-click the local area connection you want to change, and then select **Properties**.

3. Select **Internet Protocol (TCP/IP)**, and then click **Properties**.

4. Click **Advanced**.

5. Click the **DNS** tab.

6. Select **Append these DNS suffixes (in order)**.

7. Click **Add**, and then type the domain suffix you want to include.

8. Click **Add**.

- To remove a domain suffix from the list, select it, and then click **Remove**.

- To change the domain suffix search order, select it, then click the up or down arrows.

Specifying DNS Servers

When a name is submitted to DNS, if the resolver is caching names, the resolver first checks the cache. If the name is in the cache, the data is returned to the user. If the name is not in the cache, the resolver queries the DNS servers that are listed in the TCP/IP properties for each adapter.

The resolver can query through all adapters in the computer, including remote access adapters. In Windows NT 4.0, the resolver queried all servers through all adapters. In Windows 2000, however, you can specify a list of DNS servers to query for each adapter.

Figures 22.8, 22.9, and 22.10 illustrate the process by which the resolver queries the servers on each adapter.

Note The flowcharts in Figures 22.8, 22.9, and 22.10 direct you to other flowcharts in other figures. To locate the correct flow chart, see the figure captions.

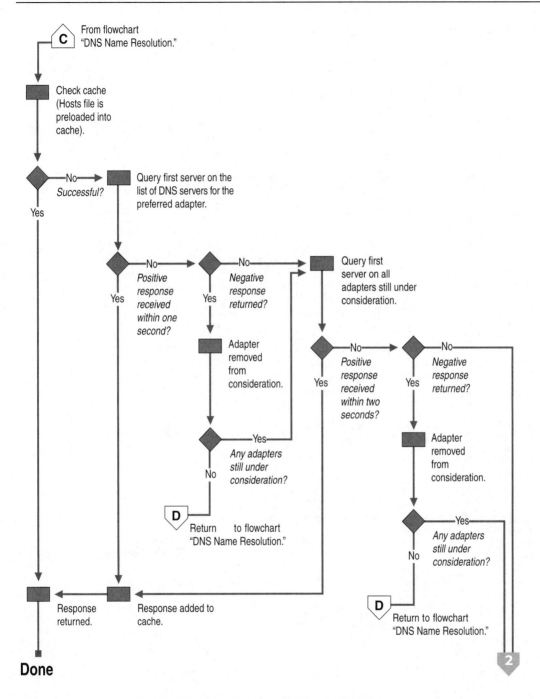

Figure 22.8   Querying the DNS Server, Part 1

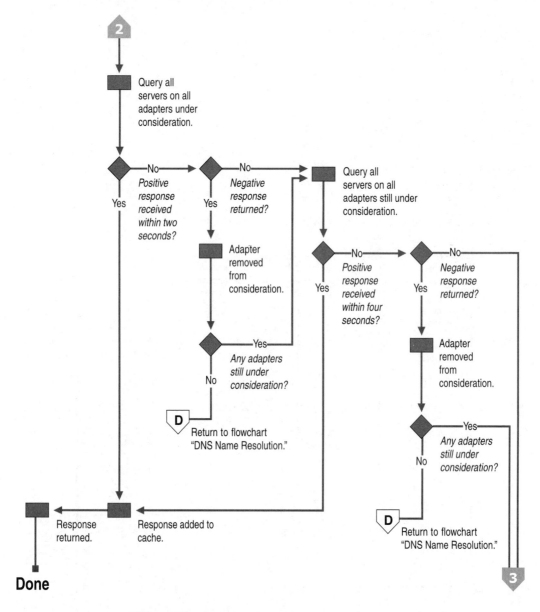

Figure 22.9   Querying the DNS Server, Part 2

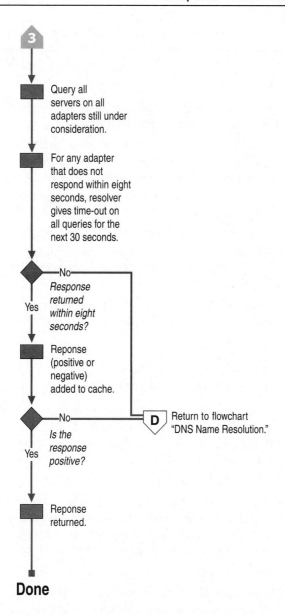

Figure 22.10   Querying the DNS Server, Part 3

Windows 2000 Professional allows multiple DNS servers to be specified. The first DNS server, known as the *preferred* DNS server, can be followed by an unlimited number of *alternate* DNS servers. The resolver queries the DNS servers in the following order:

1. The resolver sends the query to the first server on the preferred adapter's search list and waits for one second for a response.

2. If the resolver does not receive a response from the first server within one second, it sends the query to the first DNS servers on all adapters still under consideration and waits two seconds for a response.

3. If the resolver does not receive a response from any server within two seconds, the resolver sends the query to all DNS servers on all adapters still under consideration and waits another two seconds for a response.

4. If the resolver still does not receive a response from any server, it sends the query to all DNS servers on all adapters still under consideration and waits four seconds for a response.

5. If it still does not receive a response from any server, the resolver sends the query to all DNS servers on all adapters still under consideration and waits eight seconds for a response.

If the resolver receives a positive response, it stops querying for the name, adds the response to the cache and returns the response to the client.

If it has not received a response from any server by the end of the eight-second time period, the resolver responds with a time-out. Also, if it has not received a response from any server on a specified adapter, then for the next 30 seconds, the resolver responds to all queries destined for servers on that adapter with a time-out and does not query those servers.

If at any point the resolver receives a negative response from a server, it removes every server on that adapter from consideration during this search. For example, if in step 2, the first server on Alternate Adapter A gave a negative response, the resolver would not send the query to any other server on the list for Alternate Adapter A.

The resolver keeps track of which servers answer queries more quickly, and might move servers up or down on the list based on how quickly they reply to queries.

Figure 22.11 shows how the resolver queries each server on each adapter.

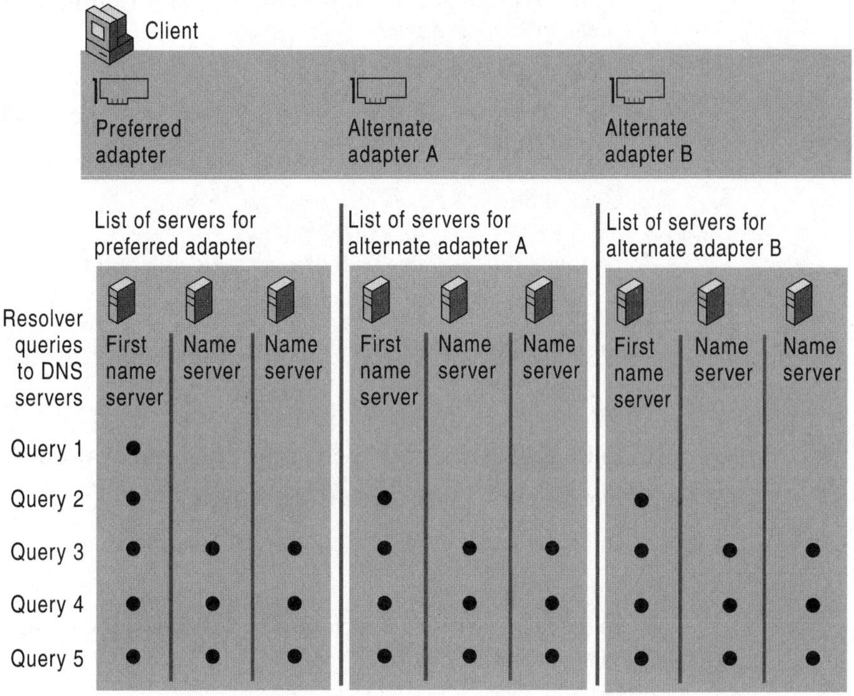

Client

Preferred
adapter

Alternate
adapter A

Alternate
adapter B

List of servers for
preferred adapter

List of servers for
alternate adapter A

List of servers for
alternate adapter B

Resolver queries to DNS servers	First name server	Name server	Name server	First name server	Name server	Name server	First name server	Name server	Name server
Query 1	●								
Query 2	●			●			●		
Query 3	●	●	●	●	●	●	●	●	●
Query 4	●	●	●	●	●	●	●	●	●
Query 5	●	●	●	●	●	●	●	●	●

Figure 22.11   Multihomed Name Resolution

▶ **To specify a preferred and alternate DNS server**

1. In Control Panel, double-click **Network and Dial-up Connections**.

2. Right-click the local area network connection you want to change, and then click **Properties**.

3. Select **Internet Protocol (TCP/IP)**, and then click **Properties**.

4. In the **General** page, select the method to be used to access the DNS servers for your network:

   ▪ If a DHCP server is available for automatic IP addressing and is configured to provide parameters for automatic DNS server configuration, select **Obtain DNS server address automatically**.

   ▪ If the IP addresses for the DNS servers are to be manually configured, select **Use the following DNS server addresses** option button. Type the IP addresses of the preferred and alternate DNS servers in the appropriate boxes.

▶ **To specify additional alternate DNS servers**

1. In the **General** section of the **Network and Dial-up connections** properties sheet, click **Advanced**.

2. Click the **DNS** tab.

3. Under **DNS server addresses**, in order of use, click **Add**.

4. Type the IP address of the DNS server you want to add.

5. Click **Add**.

To remove an IP address from the list, select it, and then click **Remove**.

The order of the IP addresses can be rearranged as needed to reflect changes in name server availability, performance, or to implement load balancing.

▶ **To set the DNS server search order**

1. In Control Panel, double-click **Network and Dial-up Connections**.

2. Double-click **Local Area Connections**.

3. In the **General** dialog box, click **Advanced**.

4. Click the **DNS** tab.

5. In the **DNS Server Search Order** box, select the IP address of the DNS server you want to reposition.

6. Click the up or down buttons to reposition the selected IP address within the list of DNS servers.

DNS Performance and Security

The default settings of DNS might need to be changed in order to optimize the performance and security of the Windows 2000 Professional DNS client. The following sections describe the configuration changes that can be made to:

- Configure caching and negative caching
- Configure subnet prioritization
- Prevent the resolver from receiving responses from nonqueried servers

Configuring Caching and Negative Caching

When the Windows 2000 resolver receives a positive or negative response to a query, it adds that positive or negative response to its cache. The resolver always checks the cache before querying any DNS servers, so if a name is in the cache, the resolver uses the name from the cache rather than querying a server. This expedites queries and decreases network traffic for DNS queries.

You can use the Ipconfig tool to view and flush the cache.

▶ **To view the resolver cache**

- At the command prompt, type:

  ipconfig /displaydns

Ipconfig displays the contents of the DNS resolver cache, including names preloaded from the Hosts file and any recently queried names resolved by the system.

After a certain amount of time, specified in the Time to Live (TTL) associated with the name, the resolver discards the name from the cache. You can also flush the cache manually. After you flush the cache, the computer must query DNS servers again for any names previously resolved by the computer.

▶ **To flush the cache manually by using Ipconfig**

- At the command prompt, type:

  ipconfig /flushdns

The local Hosts file is preloaded into the resolver's cache and reloaded into the cache whenever Hosts is updated.

The length of time for which a positive or negative response is cached depends on the values of entries in the following registry subkey:

HKEY_LOCAL_MACHINE\SYSTEM\CurrentControlSet\Services
\DNSCache\Parameters

Positive responses are cached for the number of seconds specified in the query response the resolver received, but never for longer than the value of the entry **MaxCacheEntryTtlLimit** (REG_DWORD data type). The default value is 86,400 seconds (1 Day).

Negative responses are cached for the number of seconds specified in the **NegativeCacheTime** entry (DWORD data type). The default value is 300 seconds. If you do not want negative responses to be cached at all, set the value of this entry to 0.

If all DNS servers on an adapter are queried and none reply, either positively or negatively, all subsequent name queries to any server listed on that adapter fail instantly and continue to fail for a default of 30 seconds. This feature decreases network traffic.

Configuring Subnet Prioritization

If the resolver receives multiple IP address mappings (A resource records) from a DNS server, and some have IP addresses from networks to which the computer is directly connected, the resolver orders those resource records first. This reduces network traffic across subnets by forcing computers to connect to network resources that are closer to them.

For example, suppose there are three Web servers that all host the Web page for www.reskit.com, and they are all located on different subnets. The DNS name server for the network contains the following resource records:

```
www.reskit.com.      IN   A      172.16.64.11
www.reskit.com.      IN   A      172.17.64.22
www.reskit.com.      IN   A      172.18.64.33
```

When a Windows 2000 Professional–based computer queries www.reskit.com, its resolver puts IP addresses from subnets to which the computer is directly connected first in the list. For example, if a computer with the IP address 172.17.64.93 queried for www.reskit.com, the resolver returns the resource records in the following order:

```
www.reskit.com.      IN   A      172.17.64.22
www.reskit.com.      IN   A      172.16.64.11
www.reskit.com.      IN   A      172.18.64.33
```

Subnet prioritization prevents the resolver from choosing the first IP address returned in the DNS query and using the DNS server round robin feature defined in RFC 1794. With round robin, the server rotates the order of resource record data returned in a query answer in which multiple resource records of the same type exist for a queried DNS domain name. Thus, in the example described earlier, if a user queried for www.reskit.com, the name server replies to the first client request by ordering the addresses as the following:

```
172.16.64.11
172.17.64.22
172.18.64.33
```

It replies to the second client response by ordering the addresses as the following:

```
172.17.64.22
172.18.64.33
172.16.64.11
```

If clients are configured to use the first IP address in the list they receive, then different clients use different IP addresses, balancing the load among multiple network resources with the same name. However, if the resolvers are configured for subnet prioritization, the resolvers reorder the list to favor IP addresses from networks to which they are directly connected, reducing the effectiveness of the round robin feature.

Although subnet prioritization does reduce network traffic across subnets, in some cases you might prefer to have the round robin feature work as described in RFC 1794. If so, you can disable the subnet prioritization feature on your clients by adding the **PrioritizeRecordData** entry with a value of 0 (REG_DWORD data type) in the following registry subkey:

HKEY_LOCAL_MACHINE\SYSTEM\CurrentControlSet\Services \DnsCache\Parameters

Preventing the Resolver from Accepting Responses from Nonqueried Servers

By default, the resolver accepts responses from servers it did not query. This presents a possible security liability, as unauthorized DNS servers might pass along invalid A resource records to misdirect DNS queries. If you want to disable this feature, add the registry entry **QueryIpMatching** with a value of 1 (REG_DWORD data type) to the following registry subkey:

HKEY_LOCAL_MACHINE\SYSTEM\CurrentControlSet\Services \DnsCache\Parameters

Configure Dynamic Update

Windows 2000 contains an implementation of dynamic update that follows RFC 2136. Dynamic update allows clients and servers to register DNS domain names (PTR resource records) and IP address mappings (A resource records) to an RFC 2136–compliant DNS server. This frees administrators from the time-consuming process of manually updating DNS entries.

Note A Windows 2000 Professional–based computer can be a member of a Windows 2000 domain without dynamic update, but the network administrator's workload increases significantly because of the work involved in manually updating DNS information.

In Windows 2000, clients can send dynamic updates for three different types of network adapters: DHCP adapters, statically configured adapters, and remote access adapters. Regardless of which adapter is used, the DHCP client service sends dynamic updates to the authoritative DNS server. The DHCP client service runs on all computers regardless of whether they are configured as DHCP clients.

Configuring Dynamic Update for DHCP Clients

By default, Windows 2000–based DHCP clients are configured to request that the client register the A resource record and the server register the PTR resource record. By default, the name used in the DNS registration is a concatenation of the computer name and the primary DNS suffix. You can change this default from within the TCP/IP properties of your network connection.

▶   **To change the dynamic update defaults on the dynamic update client**

1. Right-click **My Network Places**, and then click **Properties**.

2. Right-click the connection you want to configure, and then click **Properties**.

3. Select **Internet Protocol (TCP/IP)**, click **Properties**, click **Advanced**, and then select the **DNS** tab.

4. By default, **Register this connection's address in DNS** is selected and **Use this connection's DNS suffix in DNS registration** is not selected, causing the client to request that the client register the A resource record and the server register the PTR resource record. In this case, the name to be used in DNS registration is a concatenation of the computer name and primary DNS suffix of the computer.

You can also select the check box **Use this connection's DNS suffix** in DNS registration. If you choose this option, the client requests that the server update the PTR record, using the name that is a concatenation of the computer name and the connection-specific DNS suffix. If the DHCP server is configured to register DNS records according to the client's request, the client will then register the following records:

- The PTR record, using the name that is a concatenation of the computer name and the primary DNS suffix.

- The A record, using the name that is a concatenation of the computer name and the primary DNS suffix.

- The A record, using the name that is a concatenation of the computer name and the connection-specific DNS suffix.

To configure the client to make no requests for DNS registration, deselect **Register this connection's address in DNS**. If this configuration is chosen, the client will not attempt to register any A or PTR DNS records corresponding to this connection.

Statically Configured and Remote Access Clients

Statically configured clients and remote access clients do not communicate with the DHCP server. Statically configured Windows 2000–based clients dynamically update their A and PTR resource records every time they start, in case the records become corrupted in the DNS database. Remote access clients dynamically update A and PTR resource records when a dial-up connection is made. They also attempt to deregister the A and PTR resource records when the user closes down the connection. However, if a remote access client fails to deregister a resource record within four seconds, it closes the connection, and the DNS database will contain a stale record. If the remote access client fails to de-register a resource record, it adds a message to the event log, which you can view by using the Event Viewer. The remote access client never deletes stale records.

Multihomed Clients

If a dynamic update client is multihomed (has more than one adapter and associated IP address), by default it registers all its IP addresses with DNS. If you do not want it to register all of its IP addresses, you can configure it to not register one or more IP addresses from the properties page for the network connection.

▶ **To prevent the computer from registering all its IP addresses**

1. Right-click My Network Places, and then click **Properties**.

2. Select the connection you wish to configure, and then click **Properties**.

3. Select **Internet Protocol (TCP/IP)**, click **Properties**, click **Advanced**, and then select the **DNS** tab.

4. Clear the **Register this connection's address in DNS** check box.

The dynamic update client does not register all IP addresses with all DNS servers. For example, Figure 22.12 shows a multihomed computer, client1.noam.reskit.com, that is connected to both the Internet and the corporate intranet. Client1 is connected to the intranet by adapter A, a DHCP adapter with the IP address 172.16.8.7. Client1 is also connected to the Internet by adapter B, a remote access adapter with the IP address 131.107.99.1. Client1 resolves intranet names by using a name server on the intranet, NoamDC1, and resolves Internet names by using a name server on the Internet, ISPNameServer.

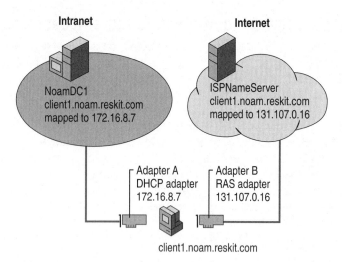

Figure 22.12   Dynamic Update for Multihomed Clients

Notice that although Client1 is connected to both networks, the IP address 172.16.8.7 is reachable only through adapter A, and the IP address 131.107.99.1 is reachable only through adapter B. Therefore, when the dynamic update client registers the IP addresses for Client1, it does not register both IP addresses with both name servers. Instead, it registers the name-to-IP address mapping for adapter A with NoamDC1 and the name-to-IP address mapping for adapter B with ISPNameServer.

You can also configure the computer to register its domain name in DNS. For example, if you have a client that is connected to two different networks, and you want it to have a different domain name on each network, you can configure it to do so.

Disabling Dynamic Update

Dynamic update is configured on Windows 2000 Professional–based clients by default. Dynamic update can be disabled by adding the **DisableDynamicUpdate** registry entry with a value of 0x1 (REG_DWORD data type) to the following registry subkey:

HKEY_LOCAL_MACHINE\SYSTEM\CurrentControlSet\Services\ Tcpip\Parameters

to disable dynamic update for all network interfaces on the computer, or

HKEY_LOCAL_MACHINE\SYSTEM\CurrentControlSet\Services\ Tcpip\Parameters\Interfaces\<*interface*>

to disable dynamic update for the network interface card with the device ID of <*interface*>.

Configure Hosts File

TCP/IP in Windows 2000 can be configured to search Hosts (the local host table file) for mappings of remote host names to IP addresses. The Hosts file format is the same as the format for host tables in the 4.3 Berkeley Software Distribution (BSD) UNIX */etc/hosts* file. For example, the entry for a computer with an address of 192.176.73.6 and a host name of client1.reskit.com looks like this:

```
192.176.73.6     client1.reskit.com
```

By using a text editor, you can create and change the Hosts file because it is a simple text file. An example of the Hosts format is provided in the file named Hosts in the Windows 2000 *%SystemRoot%*\System32\Drivers\Etc directory. Edit the Hosts file (created when you install TCP/IP) to include remote host names and IP addresses for each computer with which you communicate.

Configure NetBIOS Name Resolution

Microsoft TCP/IP uses NetBIOS over TCP/IP (NetBT) as specified in RFCs 1001 and 1002, which define a software interface that supports name resolution for NetBIOS client and server programs in the LAN and WAN environments. Although DNS is the default name resolution method for Windows 2000, NetBT is still provided as a method of providing name resolution for older clients, and for Windows 2000 domains and workgroups that do not implement Active Directory.

The following section describes the type of name resolution methods that are available through NetBIOS over TCP/IP, including WINS. Procedures for configuring the different resolution methods are provided throughout this discussion.

NetBIOS Name Resolution Basics

RFCs 1001 and 1002 define the following four node types:

- B-node. Uses broadcasts to resolve names.
- P-node. Uses point-to-point communications with a NetBIOS server (such as a WINS server) to resolve names.
- M-node. Uses broadcasts first (b-node), then directed name queries (p-node) if broadcasts are not successful.
- H-node. Uses name queries first (p-node), and then uses broadcasts (b-node) if the name server is unavailable or if the name is not registered in the WINS database.
- Microsoft-enhanced. Uses the local Lmhosts file plus Windows Sockets **gethostbyname( )** calls (using standard DNS and/or local Hosts files) in addition to standard node types.

Microsoft includes a NetBIOS name server known as the Windows Internet Name Service (WINS). If WINS is enabled on a Windows 2000 Professional–based computer, the system uses h-node by default. Without WINS, the system uses b-node by default. Non-WINS clients can access WINS through a WINS proxy, which is a WINS-enabled computer that listens to name query broadcasts and then query the WINS server on behalf of the requesting client.

▶ **To see which node type is configured on a Windows 2000 Professional–based computer**

1. At the command prompt, type:

   ipconfig /all

2. The node type is indicated to the right of the heading **Node type**.

Using a name server to locate resources is generally preferable to broadcasting for two reasons:

- Broadcasts are not usually forwarded by routers. Therefore, only local subnet NetBIOS names can be resolved.

- Broadcast frames are processed by all computers on a subnet.

Figures 22.13 and 22.14 illustrate the NetBIOS name resolution methods used by Windows 2000.

Start

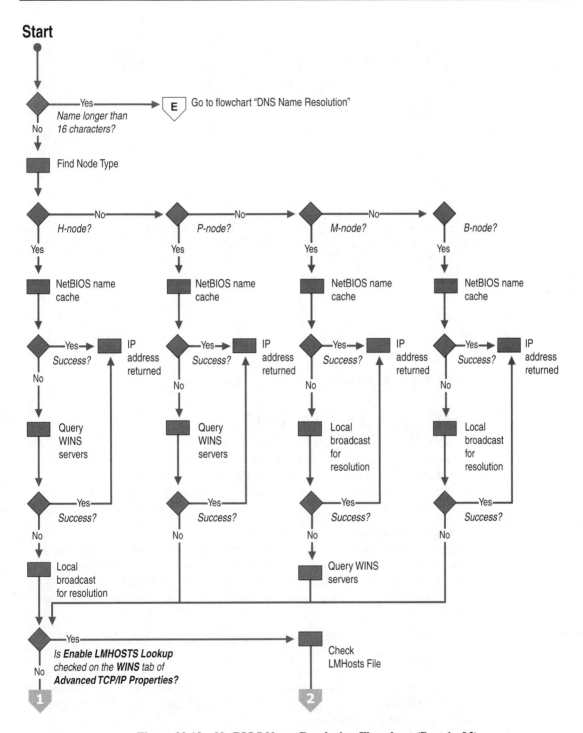

Figure 22.13   NetBIOS Name Resolution Flowchart (Part 1 of 2)

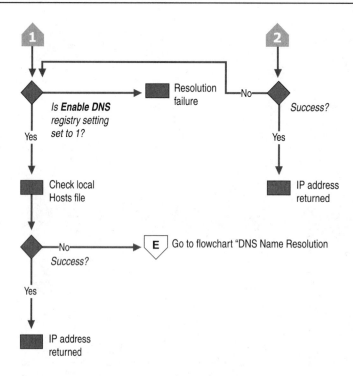

Figure 22.14   NetBIOS Name Resolution Flowchart (Part 2 of 2)

Name Resolution Using WINS

Windows Internet Name Service (WINS) is a service that runs on Windows 2000 Server to provide NetBIOS name resolution. It provides a database for registering and querying dynamic NetBIOS name-to-IP address mappings in a routed network environment. You can use WINS either alone or in conjunction with DNS.

WINS reduces the use of local broadcasts for name resolution and allows users to locate computers on remote networks. Furthermore, when dynamic addressing through DHCP results in new IP addresses for computers that move between subnets, the changes are updated automatically in the WINS database. Neither the user nor the network administrator needs to make manual accommodations for name resolution.

WINS consists of two components: the WINS server, which handles name queries and registrations, and the client software (NetBIOS over TCP/IP), which queries for computer name resolution. A WINS server is a Microsoft® Windows NT® Server version 3.5 or later computer running the WINS server service. When Microsoft TCP/IP is installed under Windows 2000 Professional, WINS client software is installed automatically.

If there are WINS servers installed on your network, you can use WINS in combination with broadcast name queries to resolve NetBIOS computer names to IP addresses. If you do not use this option, Windows 2000 Professional can use name query broadcasts (b-node mode of NetBIOS over TCP/IP), and the local Lmhosts file to resolve computer names to IP addresses. However, broadcast resolution is limited to the local network.

Additionally, a WINS server can be used in conjunction with a DNS server to provide dynamic registration of hosts in an environment without DNS update. When configured to use WINS lookup, a DNS server can forward queries to a WINS server for resolution of unknown A resource records for all WINS clients.

If DHCP is used for automatic configuration, WINS server parameters can be provided by the DHCP server. Otherwise, you must configure information about WINS servers manually. WINS configuration is global for all network adapters on a computer.

Configuring WINS

The following procedure describes how to configure WINS and how to enable DHCP.

▶ **To configure a computer to use WINS for name resolution**

1. In Control Panel, double-click **Network and Dial-up Connections**.

2. Right-click **Local Area Connections**.

3. Select **Internet Protocol (TCP/IP)**, and then click **Properties**.

4. If a DHCP server is available that is configured to provide information on available WINS servers, select **Obtain an IP address automatically**.

   The addresses of available WINS servers are provided as part of the configuration parameters for the client.

5. If DHCP is not used, or the WINS address is to be manually configured, click **Advanced**.

6. Select the **WINS** tab.

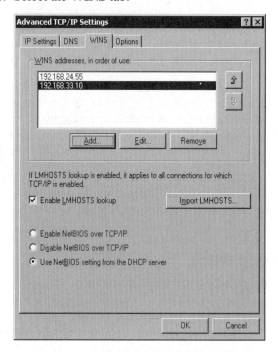

7. Click **Add**.

8. Enter the address of the WINS server, and click **Add**.

The order of the IP addresses can be rearranged as needed to reflect changes in name server availability, performance, or to implement load balancing.

▶ **To set the WINS server search order**

1. On the **WINS** tab, under the **WINS addresses, in order of use** box, select the IP address of the WINS server you want to reposition.

2. Click the up or down buttons to reposition the selected IP address within the list of WINS servers.

B-Node Broadcasts and Lmhosts

By installation default, a Windows 2000–based computer not configured as a WINS client or WINS server, is a *b-node* computer. A b-node computer is one that uses IP broadcasts for NetBIOS name resolution.

IP broadcast name resolution can provide dynamic name resolution. However, the disadvantages of broadcast name queries include increased network traffic and ineffectiveness in routed networks. Resources located outside the local subnet do not receive IP broadcast name query requests because IP-level broadcasts are not passed to remote subnets by the router (default gateway) on the local subnet.

As an alternate method to IP broadcasts, Windows 2000 enables you to manually provide NetBIOS name and IP address mappings for remote computers by using the Lmhosts file. Selected mappings from the Lmhosts file are maintained in a limited cache of NetBIOS computer names and IP address mappings. This memory cache is initialized when a computer is started. When the computer needs to resolve a name, the cache is examined first and, if there is no match in the cache, Windows 2000 uses b-node IP broadcasts to try to find the NetBIOS computer. If the IP broadcast name query fails, the complete Lmhosts file is parsed to find the NetBIOS name and the corresponding IP address. This strategy enables the Lmhosts file to contain a large number of mappings, without requiring a large amount of static memory to maintain an infrequently-used cache.

The Lmhosts file can be used to map computer names and IP addresses for computers outside the local subnet, an advantage over the b-node broadcast method. You can use the Lmhosts file to find remote computers for network file, print, and remote procedure services. The Lmhosts file is typically used for smaller networks that do not have name servers.

The Lmhosts file is a local text file that maps IP addresses to NetBIOS names. It contains entries for Windows-networking computers located outside the local subnet. The Lmhosts file is read when WINS or broadcast name resolution fails; resolved entries are stored in a local cache for later access.

You can create an Lmhosts file by using a text editor. Lmhosts is a simple text file. An example of the Lmhosts format is provided in the file named Lmhosts.sam in the Windows 2000 *%SystemRoot%*\System32\Drivers\Etc directory. This is only an example file. To active the Lmhosts file, rename Lmhosts.sam to Lmhosts. Edit the Lmhosts file to include remote NetBIOS names and IP addresses for each computer with which you communicate.

The keywords listed in Table 22.6 can be used in the Lmhosts file in Windows 2000 Professional.

Table 22.6   Lmhosts Keywords

Keyword	Description
\0x*nn*	Support for nonprinting characters in NetBIOS names. Enclose the NetBIOS name in double quotation marks and use \0x*nn* notation to specify a hexadecimal value for the character. This enables custom applications that use special names to function properly in routed topologies. However, Microsoft® LAN Manager TCP/IP does not recognize the hexadecimal format.
	Note that the hexadecimal notation applies only to one character in the name. Pad the name with blanks so that the special character is last in the string (character 16).
#BEGIN_ALTERNATE	Used to group multiple #INCLUDE statements. Any single successful #INCLUDE statement causes the group to succeed.
#END_ALTERNATE	Used to mark the end of an #INCLUDE statement grouping.
#DOM:<*domain*>	Part of the computer name-to-IP address mapping entry that indicates that the IP address is a domain controller in the domain specified by <*domain*>. This keyword affects how the Browser and Logon services behave in routed TCP/IP environments. To preload a #DOM entry, you must *first* add the #PRE keyword to the line. #DOM groups are limited to 25 members.
#INCLUDE <*file name*>	Forces the system to seek the specified <*file name*> and parse it as if it were local. Specifying a Uniform Naming Convention (UNC) <*file name*> allows you to use a centralized Lmhosts file on a server. If the server on which the specified <*file name*> exists is outside of the local broadcast subnet, you must add a preloaded entry for the server.
#MH	Part of the computer name-to-IP address mapping entry that defines the entry as a unique name that can have more than one address. The maximum number of addresses that can be assigned to a unique name is 25. The number of entries is equal to the number of network adapters in a multihomed computer.

(continued)

Table 22.6   Lmhosts Keywords *(continued)*

Keyword	Description
#PRE	Part of the computer name-to-IP address mapping entry that causes that entry to be preloaded into the name cache. (By default, entries are not preloaded into the name cache but are parsed only after WINS and name query broadcasts fail to resolve a name.) The #PRE keyword must be appended for entries that also appear in #INCLUDE statements; otherwise, the entry in the #INCLUDE statement is ignored.
#SG *<name>*	Part of the computer name-to-IP address mapping entry that associates that entry with a user-defined special (Internet) group specified by *<name>*. The #SG keyword defines Internet groups by using a NetBIOS name that has 0x20 in the 16th byte. A special group is limited to 25 members.

The following example shows how all of these keywords are used:

```
192.176.94.102   "appname        \0x14"                 #special app server
192.176.94.123   printsrv        #PRE                   #source server
192.176.94.98    localsrv        #PRE
192.176.94.97    primary         #PRE #DOM:mydomain   #PDC for
mydomain

#BEGIN_ALTERNATE
#INCLUDE \\localsrv\public\lmhosts      #adds Lmhosts from this server
#INCLUDE \\primary\public\lmhosts       #adds Lmhosts from this server
#END_ALTERNATE
```

In the preceding example:

- The servers named printsrv, localsrv, and primary are defined by using the #PRE keyword as entries to be preloaded into the NetBIOS cache at system startup.

- The servers named localsrv and primary are defined as preloaded and also identified in the #INCLUDE statements as the location of the centrally maintained Lmhosts file.

- Note that the server named "appname   \0x14" contains a special character after the first 15 characters in its name (including the blanks), and so its name is enclosed in double quotation marks.

- The number sign (#), when not used with a keyword, designates the start of a comment.

Disabling NetBT

Windows 2000 file and print sharing components uses NetBIOS over TCP/IP to communicate with prior versions of Windows and other non-Microsoft clients. However, the Windows 2000 file and print sharing components (the redirector and server) now support *direct hosting* for communicating with other computers running Windows 2000. With direct hosting, DNS is used for name resolution. No NetBIOS name resolution (WINS or broadcast) is used and no NetBIOS sessions are established.

By default, both NetBIOS and direct hosting are enabled, and both are tried in parallel when a new connection is established. The first to succeed in connecting is used for any attempt. NetBIOS support can be disabled to force all traffic to use direct hosting.

▶ **To disable NetBIOS support**

1. From **Network and Dial-up Connections**, select the connection you want to modify, and then right-click **Properties**.

2. Select **Internet Protocol (TCP/IP)**, and then click **Properties**.

3. Click **Advanced**.

4. Select the **WINS Address** tab.

5. Select **Disable NetBIOS over TCP/IP**.

Note Applications and services that depend on NetBIOS over TCP/IP no longer function after this is done, so it is important that you verify that clients and applications no longer need NetBIOS over TCP/IP support before you disable it. Disabling NetBIOS over TCP/IP can prevent the creation of file and print sharing connections with non-Windows 2000 clients and servers.

Configure Multihoming

When a computer is configured with more than one IP address, it is referred to as a multihomed system. Multihoming is supported in two different ways:

- Multiple network adapters or media types per physical network.

  The network adapters can be for similar or dissimilar networks. For example, a host with one Ethernet and one Token Ring adapter installed, each linked to a separate network, requires IP addresses to be bound to both adapters. There are no restrictions other than hardware.

- Multiple IP addresses per network adapter.

  A computer can access multiple subnets that are logically separated, but bound to a single network adapter. Such a configuration might be used in an environment where a host requires access to different divisions of a corporation network that are separated by different subnets.

  Windows 2000 Professional allows an unlimited number of IP address/subnet mask pairs.

  Figure 22.15 shows an example of a Windows 2000 Professional computer using multihoming to connect to two subnets. These subnets can be physically separated by disparate or disconnected cabling, or logically separated through subnetting.

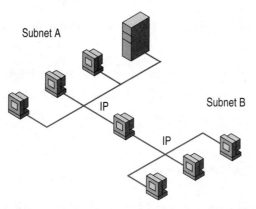

Figure 22.15   Multihomed Windows 2000 Professional Computer Connected to Two Separate Networks

Configure Multiple Network Adapters or Media Types

Windows 2000 Professional places no restrictions on physically multihomed computers, so you can add as many network adapters as the computer hardware can accommodate, and assign each a separate address.

As each new network adapter is installed, Windows 2000 Plug and Play autodetects the adapter. The device drivers for each adapter are installed, and any internal resources are automatically configured. The network adapter is bound to the TCP/IP protocol. If the network adapter is not Plug and Play–compliant, the adapter software must be installed and configured manually, using the manufacturer's instructions.

For a multihomed computer that uses multiple network adapters for physical connections to the LAN, each adapter appears as a separate adapter in the Network and Dial-up Connections folder.

For a system configured to support multiple network or media types, there are no restrictions for this type of configuration other than hardware and media support. Microsoft Windows 2000 TCP/IP supports the following:

- Ethernet (Ethernet II and IEEE 802.3 SNAP encapsulation).
- Token Ring (IEEE 802.5 encapsulation).
- Asynchronous Transfer Mode (ATM).
- Fiber Distributed Data Interface (FDDI).
- WAN, using circuit-switched media such as ISDN and dial-up or dedicated asynchronous lines and virtual-circuit wide-area media such as X.25 and Frame Relay.

By default, each new network adapter is configured to use DHCP to assign an IP address to it.

▶   **To manually configure IP addresses on a multihomed system**

1. In Control Panel, double-click **Network and Dial-up Connections**.
2. Right-click the local area network connection you want to modify, and then select **Properties**.
3. Add TCP/IP configuration information for the network adapter, as described in "Configure IP Address Manually."

Configure Multiple IP Addresses on a Network Adapter

Windows 2000 Professional supports multihoming through multiple addresses on a single network adapter. This configuration is useful in an environment where a single physical network is logically divided into subnets.

▶   **To configure a multihomed system using a single network adapter**

1. In Control Panel, double-click **Network and Dial-up Connections**.
2. Right-click the local area connection you want to modify, and then select **Properties**.
3. Add TCP/IP configuration information for the first IP address, as described in "Configure IP Address Manually."
4. Click Advanced.

5. Click **Add** to enter the IP address and subnet mask for each additional subnet.

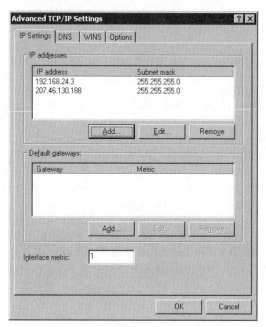

Each IP address and subnet mask pair is stored in the registry entries **IPAddress** and **SubnetMask**, in the subkey HKEY_LOCAL_MACHINE\SYSTEM\CurrentControlSet\Services\Tcpip \Parameters\Interfaces\<*adapter*>.

Windows 2000 Professional allows an unlimited number of IP address/subnet mask pairs.

Multihoming Considerations

If TCP/IP is configured for multiple network adapters, or for a single network adapter with multiple IP addresses, you must consider the following issues:

NetBIOS over TCP/IP (NetBT) binds to the first IP address for each network adapter only.

When a NetBIOS name registration is sent out, only one IP address is registered per adapter. This registration occurs over the IP address that is listed first in the properties of the TCP/IP protocol for the adapter.

A unique IP address and subnet mask are defined for each adapter.

For each network adapter, an instance of TCP/IP is bound to the adapter. You can choose to have IP addresses dynamically assigned by DHCP (or APIPA if a DHCP server is not present) or defined manually as static addresses.

Domain Name System (DNS) configuration settings are global.

The settings on the **DNS** tab in **Advanced TCP/IP Properties** are used for all adapters on the computer. Therefore, for a multihomed computer, you must carefully define options for DNS that are applicable for all adapters using TCP/IP. Usually, this means that if you want to use DNS for name resolution with any TCP/IP connection, make sure DNS is configured.

Windows Internet Name Service (WINS) configuration settings are defined for each adapter.

The settings on the **WINS** configuration tab are used only for the adapter you are configuring. For example, NetBIOS over TCP/IP (NetBT) can be enabled or disabled for each network adapter. If you enable the option **Disable NetBIOS over TCP/IP** for a LAN adapter, this option is enabled only for that adapter, not for other LAN adapters on the computer.

The default gateway can be different for each adapter.

While it is possible to configure a default gateway IP address for each network interface, there is only a single active default route in the IP route table. If there are multiple default routes in the IP route table (assuming a metric of 1), then the specific default route is chosen randomly when TCP/IP is initialized. This behavior can lead to confusion and loss of connectivity.

It is recommended that when you are configuring a computer to be multihomed on two disjoint networks, configure a default gateway IP on the interface that is attached to the portion of the IP internetwork that contains the most network segments. Then, either add static routes or use a routing protocol to provide connectivity to remote networks reachable through the other interfaces.

Only one default gateway is used at a time.

Although you can have a different default gateway for each adapter, Windows 2000 Professional uses only one default gateway at a time. This means that only certain hosts are reachable:

- Hosts on the local subnet
- Hosts that are reachable by the default gateway

As a result, in some cases you might lose network connectivity. For example, suppose your computer is first connected to the corporate TCP/IP network and you make a PPP dial-up connection to the Internet. Your computer stops using the default gateway that connects your computer to the corporate network and instead uses the default gateway that connects your computer to the Internet. Therefore, you can reach hosts on your local subnet, but you cannot reach other hosts on your network.

To discover methods to access multiple gateways, see "Configure Local Route Table" later in this chapter.

Configure Local IP Routing Table

A Windows 2000 Professional computer uses its local IP routing table to determine how to forward an IP packet to reach a designated host. The local routing table can be configured in the following ways:

- The routing table is manually maintained at the Windows 2000 Professional–based computer.

- The routing table that is automatically maintained at the Windows 2000 Professional–based computer by means of Routing Information Protocol (RIP) broadcasts from routers on the subnet.

- The default gateway is manually configured, or specified through the Dynamic Host Configuration Protocol (DHCP).

- The default gateway is automatically configured and maintained through Internet Control Message Protocol (ICMP) Router Discovery.

Determine the methods needed to identify gateways and manage routing paths.
In an enterprise with multiple subnets, a route to non-local destinations must exist to communicate with hosts in other networks. Windows 2000 Professional supports manual entry of the default gateways and the use of ICMP Router Discovery to find and specify default gateways. Routing is supported by means of manual configuration of the routing table and a Routing Information Protocol (RIP) Listener to permit manual and automated maintenance of the local routing table. Select the methods that reflect your network configuration. See "Overview of IP Routing" later in this chapter.

Configure default gateways. Specify the default gateways to be used to direct IP packets if ICMP Router Discovery-enabled routers or RIP-enabled routers are not available in your network. For multihomed computers, the default gateways are used for all adapters, and you might need to manually configure the local route table for separate default gateways. See "Configure Default Gateways" later in this chapter.

Configure ICMP Router Discovery, if ICMP-enabled routers are available.
ICMP Router Discovery automates the discovery and configuration of the default gateways for a Windows 2000 Professional–based client. If ICMP-enabled routers are used within the network, use this method of specifying default gateways. See "Configure ICMP Router Discovery" later in this chapter.

Manually edit the routing table, if necessary. If you want to manually specify the optimal route for IP packets, or have a multihomed computer and need to maintain separate default gateways, use the **route** command to display, add, and edit the local route tables for your Windows 2000 Professional–based computer. See "Manually Edit the Route Table" later in this chapter.

Install RIP listening support, if RIP-enabled routers are available. RIP-enabled routers simplify administration of the routing tables of Windows 2000 Professional–based clients by automatically updating the routing table as necessary. Enable RIP listening support on the client when RIP is supported in your network. See "Configure RIP Listening Support" later in this chapter.

Overview of IP Routing

Multiple TCP/IP networks are interconnected by routers, devices that forward IP packets from one subnet to another.

When IP prepares to send a packet, it inserts the local (source) IP address and the destination address of the packet in the IP header. It then examines the destination address, compares it to a locally maintained route table, and takes appropriate action based on what it finds. There are three possible actions:

- IP can pass the packet up to a protocol layer above IP on the local host.
- The packet can be forwarded through one of the locally attached network adapters.
- The packet can be discarded.

IP finds a match of the destination address in the routing table from the specific to the general in the following order:

- An exact match (host route).
- A match for the locally attached subnet (subnet route).
- A match for the default gateway (default route)
- If a default gateway has not been specified, the packet is discarded.

Because the default gateway contains information about the network IDs of the other networks in the internetwork, it can forward the packet to other routers until the packet is eventually delivered to a router connected to the subnet of the destination. This process is known as *routing* and is illustrated in Figure 22.16.

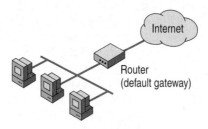

Figure 22.16   Routing

For each Windows 2000 Professional–based computer on a TCP/IP network, you can maintain a table with an entry for every other computer or network with which the local computer communicates. For a limited number of IP hosts, this method can be used for network interconnectivity. But for most networks this is not a practical solution, due to the large number of IP hosts and networks that must be listed and maintained in the route table. Instead, you can configure other methods to direct IP packets:

- IP packets are forwarded to an IP address by using a route table maintained by Router Information Protocol (RIP)-enabled routers.

  If your network contains RIP-enabled routers, you can install RIP listening support on the Windows 2000 Professional–based client to permit automatic configuration and maintenance of the local route table.

- IP packets are forwarded to a user-specified default gateway, which provides the routing information for the packet.

  The gateway address can also be automatically configured by DHCP. Multiple routers can be specified as default gateways.

- IP packets are forwarded to a default gateway identified by ICMP Router Discovery.

  If your network contains routers that meet the ICMP Router Discovery specifications, defined in RFC 1256, you can configure your Windows 2000 Professional–based computer to "listen" for available gateways.

Configure Default Gateways

If the local route table cannot provide a path for handling an IP packet, it is directed to the default gateway. Windows 2000 Professional allows you to specify multiple default gateways. You can list them in order, based on availability, load balancing, or other criteria. You can also assign a value to each gateway, the cost *metric*, which determines the cost of forwarding an IP packet to the specific router. The lowest metric is the most preferred entry in the routing table.

▶ **To specify default gateways**

1. In Control Panel, open **Network and Dial-up Connections**.

2. Select the local area connection you want to modify, and then click **Properties**.

3. Select **Internet Protocol (TCP/IP)**, click **Properties**, and then click **Advanced**.

4. Under the **Default gateways** box, click **Add**.

5. Type the IP address and metric for the default gateway.

   The *metric* is the cost of using a specified route. The gateway with the lowest metric is used first. The default metric value for each gateway is 1.

6. Click **OK**.

7. Click **OK** when you have specified all the default gateways for the connection.

Gateway addresses and metrics can also be provided by means of a DHCP server. Gateway configuration information specified in the connection properties override addresses provided through DHCP. For information about configuring DHCP, see "Configure DHCP" in this chapter.

Configure ICMP Router Discovery

As specified in RFC 1256, Windows 2000 provides host support for ICMP Router Discovery. Router discovery provides an improved method of detecting and configuring default gateways. Instead of configuring a default gateway manually or through DHCP, Windows 2000–based computers can dynamically discover the best default gateway to use on their subnet and can automatically switch to another default gateway if the current default gateway fails or the network administrator changes router preferences.

When a Windows 2000 Professional–based computer configured for ICMP Router Discovery initializes, it joins the all-hosts IP multicast group (224.0.0.1) and listens for ICMP Router Advertisement messages. RFC 1256–compliant routers periodically send ICMP Router Advertisements containing their IP address, a preference level, and a time after which they can be considered down. Hosts receive the ICMP Router Advertisements and select the router with the highest preference level as their default gateway.

A Windows 2000 Professional–based computer can also send ICMP Router Solicitation messages to the all-routers IP multicast address (224.0.0.2) at initialization or when it has not received a router advertisement from the router for the current default gateway within the router's advertised lifetime. Windows 2000 –based hosts send a maximum of three solicitations at intervals of approximately 600 milliseconds.

ICMP Router Discovery is determined by the values of two registry entries **PerformRouterDiscovery** in the subkey HKEY_LOCAL_MACHINE\SYSTEM\CurrentControlSet\Services\Tcpip\Param eters and **SolicitationAddressBcast** in the subkey HKEY_LOCAL_MACHINE\SYSTEM\CurrentControlSet\Services\adaptername\ Parameters\Tcpip. To enable ICMP Router Discovery, add the two entries to the registry, each with a value of 0x1 (REG_DWORD).

The Router Advertisement parameters are controlled from a RFC 1256–compliant router. Windows 2000 Server and the Routing and Remote Access service support router discovery. For more information, see "Unicast IP Routing" in the *Internetworking Guide*.

Manually Edit the Route Table

There are several instances where you might need to manually edit the local route table for your Windows 2000 Professional–based computer:

- The computer has multiple network adapters (multihomed), and must access different default gateways for each adapter.

  If your computer is multihomed and has connections to two separate IP networks, such as the corporate network and the Internet, the default gateway for only one network is used. For the computer to be able to communicate with the other network, routes must be manually added to the route table.

- The computer is multihomed, and has no access to a default gateway.

  The computer in this case must provide the routing information to send IP packets from one network to the next, because no router is provided to perform this task.

- The required routing information is not provided by any default gateway, or a different route is wanted.

You can display the current route table to determine whether any changes are required. To see the route table for your computer, at the command prompt type **route print**.

The following example is a sample route table from a single-homed Windows 2000 Professional–based computer.

```
route print
===========================================================================
Interface List
0x1 ......................... MS TCP Loopback interface
0x2000002 ...00 c0 4f 49 f3 b2 ...... 3Com EtherLink PCI (QoS Packet
Scheduler)
===========================================================================
===========================================================================
Active Routes:
Network Destination        Netmask          Gateway       Interface  Metric
        0.0.0.0          0.0.0.0      157.59.0.1   157.59.4.120       1
      127.0.0.0        255.0.0.0      127.0.0.1      127.0.0.1        1
     157.59.0.0    255.255.248.0   157.59.4.120   157.59.4.120       1
   157.59.4.120   255.255.255.255    127.0.0.1      127.0.0.1        1
 157.59.255.255  255.255.255.255  157.59.4.120   157.59.4.120       1
      224.0.0.0        224.0.0.0   157.59.4.120   157.59.4.120       1
255.255.255.255  255.255.255.255    127.0.0.1      127.0.0.1        1
Default Gateway:      157.59.0.1
===========================================================================
Persistent Routes:
  None
```

This example shows a computer with the IP address 157.59.4.120, subnet mask of 255.255.248.0, and a default gateway of 157.59.0.1. The table contains the following seven entries:

1. The first entry is the default route. This is the route to which the computer sends IP packets when the other route entries do not specify where to send them.

2. The second entry is the loopback route. This is the route a host uses when sending packets to itself.

3. The third entry is a subnet route for the locally attached subnet.

4. The fourth entry is a host route for the local host (the route for this host computer).

5. The fifth entry is a host route for a special type of IP broadcast address called the all-subnets directed broadcast.

6. The sixth entry is the IP multicast route. This is the route used when the computer sends packets to reach an IP multicast group.

7. The seventh entry is a host route for the limited broadcast address.

The following sections describe the columns shown in the "Active Routes" section of the **net print** command.

Network Address

The network address in the route table is the destination address. The network address column can have three different types of entries, listed here in the order in most to least specific.

1. Host address (a route to a single, specific destination IP address).

2. Subnet address (a route to a subnet).

3. Default route (a route used when there is no other match).

If no match is found, the packets are discarded.

Netmask

The *netmask* defines which portion of the network address must match in order for that route to be used. When the mask is written in binary, a 1 indicates a bit that must match and a 0 indicates a bit that does not have to match.

For example, the mask of all 255s (all 1s) means that the destination address of the packet to be routed must exactly match the network address in order for this route to be used. For another example, if the network address 172.20.232.0 has a netmask of 255.255.255.0, then the first three octets must match exactly, but the last octet need not match.

Gateway Address

The gateway address is the forwarding IP address of where the packet must be sent. This can be the IP address of the host or the address of a gateway (router) on the local subnet. If the gateway address of the route is the host IP address, then the forwarding IP address is set to the destination IP address in the IP datagram.

Interface

The interface is the address of the network adapter over which the packet must be sent. 127.0.0.1 is the software loopback address.

Metric

The metric indicates the cost of the route and is commonly the number of hops to the destination. Anything on the local subnet is one hop, and each router crossed after that is an additional hop. The metric is used to determine the best route among multiple routes that most closely match the destination.

To add static routes, use the following format:

```
Route add <subnet> mask <netmask> <gateway> metric <metric> if
<interface>
```

The following is an example route:

```
Route add 172.20.255.0 mask 255.255.255.0 172.20.234.232 metric 2 if 3
```

The route in this example means that to get to the subnet 172.20.255.0 with a mask of 255.255.255.0, use gateway 172.20.234.232, and that the route has a cost metric of 2 (for example, the subnet is 2 hops away), using interface 3.

Manual maintenance of route tables is error-prone. An error in one of the routes can prevent accessibility to a network location. Additionally, the status of many routes is dynamic—routers can go down or online, new routers might be added, or the metric of a route might change. Each change in the status of a route necessitates an equivalent alteration in the route table. Finally, the challenges of manually maintaining local route tables is multiplied when supporting a large number of computers in a department or enterprise.

Configure RIP Listening Support

To address the challenges of supporting routing in an enterprise environment, Routing Information Protocol, or RIP, can be used. If one or more of the routers on the subnet uses RIP to send routing information, the computer can be configured to "listen in" to RIP messages. Your computer can learn other routes on the network by listening to RIP messages and then add the appropriate routes to the IP routing table. This process is called *RIP listening* or *silent RIP*.

Network administrators can use RIP listening on multihomed hosts to solve the multiple default gateway problem without manually adding routes to the route table. Figure 22.17 shows an example of a multihomed host that uses RIP listening.

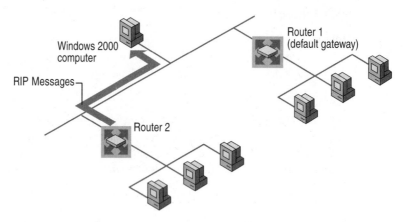

Figure 22.17   Multihomed Host Using RIP Listening

Router 2 sends RIP messages, and the Windows 2000 Professional–based computer listens in on those messages. Router 1 does not send RIP messages, so the Windows 2000 Professional–based computer is configured to use Router 1 as the default gateway. Thus, the Windows 2000 Professional–based computer can communicate with hosts on both networks without the use of ICMP Redirect messages from Router 1.

The route table chosen by the Windows 2000 Professional–based host computer is based on the *hop count* of the sending RIP server. The hop count is the number of routers that must be crossed in order to reach the wanted destination. The hop count is used as the metric, or the measurement by which routes are selected. Routes with the lowest metric are selected first.

Windows 2000 Professional supports routers using either RIP version 1 or RIP version 2 as long as the RIP messages are sent as subnet-level broadcasts. RIP v2 messages sent as multicasts are not received by the RIP listener.

RIP listening support is installed as an optional service to Windows 2000 Professional.

▶ **To install RIP listening support**

1. In Control Panel, double-click **Add and Remove Programs**.

2. Select Add/Remove Windows Components.

3. In the Windows Component wizard, click **Next**.

4. Select Networking Services.

5. Click **Details**.

6. Select the **RIP Listener** check box.

7. Click **OK**.

8. Click **Next**.

Configure Internet Connection Sharing

Internet Connection Sharing (ICS) allows multiple computers in a small office or home office to access an Internet connection using a single public IP address. For example, you may have a computer in an intranet that connects to the Internet by using a dial-up connection. By enabling ICS on the computer that uses the dial-up connection, you can provide Internet access to all computers in the network. ICS provides network address translation, address allocation, and name resolution services for all computers on your network. ICS can also be enabled for high-speed networks, such as Integrated Services Digital Network (ISDN), Digital Subscriber Line (DSL), and cable-based Internet connections.

ICS is a version of a network address translator (NAT). A network address translator is an IP router defined in RFC 1631 that can translate IP addresses and TCP/UDP port numbers of packets as they are being forwarded. Consider a small business network with multiple computers connecting to the Internet. A small business normally has to obtain an Internet Service Provider (ISP)–allocated public IP address for each computer on its network. With a NAT, however, the small business can use private addressing (as described in RFC 1918) and have the NAT map its private addresses to a single or to multiple public IP addresses as allocated by its ISP. ICS uses the private network 192.168.0.0 with a subnet mask of 255.255.255.0 for all computers in an ICS-enabled network, permitting a maximum of 254 hosts.

Figure 22.18 shows an example of a small business intranet using ICS. The small business has obtained a public IP address of 207.46.140.35 by its ISP. ICS assigns IP addresses from the private network address 192.168.0.0 for all computers in the business intranet.

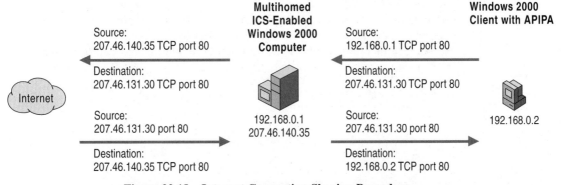

Figure 22.18   Internet Connection Sharing Procedure

1. When a user on the small business intranet connects to an Internet resource, the user's TCP/IP protocol creates an IP packet with the following values set in the IP and TCP or UDP headers (bold text indicates the fields changed by ICS):

   - Destination IP Address: Internet resource IP address
   - Source IP Address: **Private IP address**
   - Destination Port: Internet resource TCP or UDP port
   - Source Port: **Source application TCP or UDP port**

2. The computer forwards this IP packet to ICS, which translates the addresses of the outgoing packet as follows:

   - Destination IP Address: Internet resource IP address
   - Source IP Address: **ISP-allocated public address**
   - Destination Port: Internet resource TCP or UDP port
   - Source Port: **Remapped source application TCP or UDP port**

3. ICS sends the remapped IP packet over the Internet. The responding computer sends back the response to ICS. When received by ICS, the packet contains the following addressing information:

   - Destination IP Address: **ISP-allocated public address**
   - Source IP Address: Internet resource IP address
   - Destination Port: **Remapped source application TCP or UDP port**
   - Source Port: Internet resource TCP or UDP port

4. When ICS maps and translates the addresses and forwards the packet to the intranet client, it contains the following addressing information:

   - Destination IP Address: **Private IP address**
   - Source IP Address: Internet resource IP address
   - Destination Port: **Source application TCP or UDP port**
   - Source Port: Internet resource TCP or UDP port

For outgoing packets, the source IP address and TCP/UDP port numbers are mapped to a public source IP address and a possibly changed TCP/UDP port number. For incoming packets, the destination IP address and TCP/UDP port numbers are mapped to the private IP address and original TCP/UDP port number.

ICS includes a DHCP allocator service to assign private IP addresses, and a proxy DNS server to perform name resolution services on behalf of all computers in the intranet.

Note Do not enable ICS in an existing network that has DNS servers, gateways, DHCP servers, or computers configured with static IP addresses. If your Windows 2000 Professional–based computer is in a network where one or more of these conditions exist, you must use Windows 2000 Server network address translation. For more information, see "Unicast IP Routing" in the *Internetworking Guide*.

Enable Internet Connection Sharing

To enable ICS, you must be logged on to an account that has administrative rights.

▶   **To enable Internet Connection Sharing**

1. In Control Panel, open **Network and Dial-Up Connections**.

2. Right-click the connection you want to share (the connection that connects to the Internet), and then click **Properties**.

3. On the **Sharing** tab, select **the Enable Internet Connection Sharing for this connection** check box.

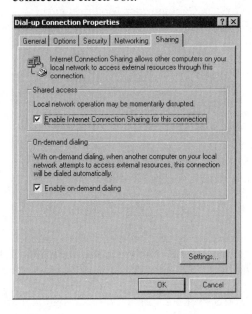

If the shared connection is a dial-up connection and you want the connection to dial automatically when another computer on your network attempts to use external resources, select the **Enable on-demand dialing** check box.

4. Click **OK**.

A dialog box is displayed, indicating that the intranet's connection's IP address is set to 192.168.0.1, and warns that connectivity with other computers on the network might be lost.

5. Click **Yes**.

Note If your office users need to gain access to a corporate network via a VPN server that is connected to the Internet, they need to create a PPTP-based virtual private network (VPN) connection to tunnel from the computer on the intranet to the corporate VPN server on the Internet. The VPN connection is authenticated and secure, and creating the tunneled connection allocates proper IP addresses, DNS server addresses, and WINS server addresses for the corporate network. For more information about configuring a VPN connection, see "Local and Remote Networking" in this book.

When ICS is enabled, the TCP/IP configuration is modified on the computer with the shared connection, and services related to network translation are started. Table 22.7 shows the modified system configuration on the sharing computer:

Table 22.7   ICS System Configuration Modifications

Modified Configuration	ICS Setting
IP address	Configured for the reserved private IP address 192.186.0.1, subnet 255.255.255.0.
IP routing	Created when the shared connection is established.
DHCP allocator	Enabled with the default range of 192.168.0.0, subnet 255.255.255.0.
DNS proxy	Enabled through ICS
Internet Connection Sharing service	Started
Autodial feature	Enabled

Note You cannot modify the default configuration of ICS. This includes items such as disabling the DHCP allocator or modifying the range of private IP addresses that are handed out. If you want to modify any of these items, you must use Windows 2000 Server network address translation. For more information about network address translation as implemented in Windows 2000 Server, see "Unicast IP Routing" in the *Internetworking Guide*.

All computers on your network that access the Internet by means of Internet Connection Sharing must reconfigure their TCP/IP configurations to use DHCP. Each computer in the network is reassigned an IP address from the reserved IP address range 192.168.0.2 to 192.168.0.254, with a subnet mask of 255.255.255.0. As with the ICS-enabled computer, the change in IP address might cause you to lose connectivity with other computers in the network that use static addressing.

Configure Applications and Services

You might need to configure Internet Connection Sharing to provide access to remote programs and services to users in your network. For example, if users on your intranet want to use a videoconferencing application such as NetMeeting, ICS must be configured to support the application on the connection in which shared access is enabled.

Conversely, you might want to provide services to applications and services on remote computers. Services that you provide must be configured so that Internet users can gain access to them. For example, if you are hosting a Web server on your home network and you want Internet users to be able to connect to it, you must configure ICS to provide the Web Server service.

ICS provides support for remote services and applications via ports. *Ports* are used by TCP and UDP to identify the ends of logical connections to deliver data to applications. For the purpose of providing services to unknown callers, a service contact port is defined. The contact port is sometimes called the *well-known port*. For a list of standard UDP and TCP ports, see "Well Known Port Numbers" in RFC 1700, "Assigned Numbers."

▶ **To configure applications to access remote services**

1. From **Network and Dial-up Connections**, right-click the shared connection, and then select **Properties**.

2. On the **Sharing** tab, verify that the **Enable Internet connection sharing for this connection** check box is selected, and then click **Settings**.

3. To configure a network application for the computers sharing the connection, on the **Applications** tab, click **Add**, and then do the following:

   • In **Name of application**, type an easily recognized name for the application.

   • In **Remote server port number**, type the port number of the remote server where the application resides, and then click either **TCP** or **UDP**.

   • In **TCP** or **UDP** or both, type the port number for the port on your home network to which the application connects. Some applications require TCP and UDP port numbers.

▶ **To configure services for remote applications**

1. From **Network and Dial-up Connections**, right-click the shared connection, and then select **Properties**.

2. On the **Sharing** tab, verify the **Enable Internet connection sharing for this connection** check box is selected, and then click **Settings**.

3. Click the **Services** tab, and then select the standard services in the **Services** box.

   –Or–

   To add a service that is not in the list, click **Add**, and then do the following:

   ▪ In **Name of Service**, type an easily recognized name for the service.

   ▪ In **Service port number**, type the port number of the computer where the service resides, and then click either **TCP** or **UDP**.

   ▪ In **Name or address of server computer on private network**, type the name or TCP/IP address of the computer on your network where the service is located.

Configure IP Security and Filtering

Windows 2000 Professional incorporates two primary methods for securing IP packets: IP security and TCP/IP filtering. IP security is a new feature of Windows 2000 Professional. IP security protects data by securing and optionally encrypting IP packets prior to transmission on the network. The following section discusses the features of IP security, and describes the methods for installing and configuring this feature. TCP/IP filtering, known as *TCP/IP Security* in Windows NT 4.0, is also discussed as a method of controlling the IP traffic received by the network interface.

Determine IP security method to be implemented. Windows 2000 Professional supports two methods to secure and control the transmission of IP packets: *IP security,* an industry-defined set of standards that verifies, authenticates, and optionally encrypts data at the IP packet level; and *TCP/IP filtering*, which controls the ports and packet types for incoming local host data. Either or both of these methods can be implemented within the same Windows 2000 Professional–based client. For more information about IP security, see "Overview of IPSec," "Considerations for IPSec," and "Configure IP Filtering" in this chapter.

Enable and configure IP Security, if required. IP Security may be enabled in the registry of the Windows 2000 Professional computer through local policies, or implemented via Active Directory group policies in an enterprise environment. If implemented locally, built-in or custom policies created via the Policy Manager snap-in can determine the rules required for negotiating and starting communications with other hosts. See "Configuring IPSec Policies" later in this chapter.

Enable IP filtering, if required. You may wish to restrict the type of IP traffic that can be received by a Windows 2000 Professional–based client. IP filtering allows the creation of rules that limit packet reception by TCP and UDP port, or by IP protocol type. See "TCP/IP Filtering" later in this chapter.

Overview of IPSec

The need for Internet Protocol (IP)-based network security is already evident. In today's massively interconnected business world of the Internet, intranets, branch offices, and remote access, sensitive information constantly crosses the networks. The challenge for network administrators and other information service professionals is to ensure that this traffic is:

- Safe from data modification while en route.
- Safe from interception, viewing, or copying.
- Safe from being accessed by unauthenticated parties.

These issues are known as *data integrity*, *confidentiality*, and *authentication*. In addition, replay protection prevents acceptance of a packet that has been captured and later resent.

For these reasons, Internet Protocol security, or IPSec, was designed by the Internet Engineering Task Force (IETF). IPSec supports network-level authentication, data integrity and encryption. IPSec integrates with the inherent security of the Windows 2000 operating system to provide the ideal platform for safeguarding intranet and Internet communications.

IP security uses industry-standard encryption algorithms and a comprehensive security management approach to provide security for all TCP/IP communications on both sides of an organization's firewall. The result is a Windows 2000, end-to-end security strategy that defends against both external and internal attacks.

IP security is deployed below the transport layer, sparing network managers (and software vendors) the difficulty and expense of trying to deploy and coordinate security one application at a time. By simply deploying Windows 2000 IP security, network managers provide a strong layer of protection for the entire network, with applications automatically inheriting from IPSec-enabled servers and clients.

How IP Security Prevents Network Attacks

Without security measures and controls in place, data might be subjected to an attack. Some attacks are passive, meaning information is simply monitored; others are active, meaning the information is altered with intent to corrupt or destroy the data or the network itself. Table 22.8 presents some common security risks found in today's networks.

Table 22.8   Types of Network Attacks

Attack type	Description	How IPSec prevents
Eavesdropping (also called *sniffing*, *snooping*)	Monitoring of *cleartext* or unencrypted packets. Encapsulated packets can also be monitored if attacker has access to key and packets are unencrypted.	Data is encrypted before transmission, preventing access even if the packet is monitored or intercepted. Only the intended receiving party can decrypt the data.
Data modification	Alteration and transmission of modified packets.	Data hashing attaches a digital "signature" to each packet, which is checked by the receiving computer to detect modification.
Identity spoofing	Use of constructed or captured packets to falsely assume the identity of a valid address.	Kerberos v5, MS-CHAP, and other authentication methods secure Windows 2000 –based computers.
Denial-of-service	Preventing access of network by valid users. An example is to flood the network with packet traffic.	Authentication methods limit access from unauthorized users.
Man-in-the-middle	Diversion of IP packets to an unintended third party, to be monitored and possibly altered.	Anti-replay mechanisms, data hashing.
Known-key	Access or construction of a security key, used to decrypt or modify data. A compromised key might be used to create additional keys.	Under Windows 2000, public keys are periodically refreshed, reducing the possibility that a captured key can be used to gain access to secure information.
Application layer attack	Mainly directed at application servers, this attack is used to cause a fault in a network's operating system or applications or to introduce viruses into the network.	Since IPSec is implemented at the network layer, packets that do not meet the security filters at this level are never filtered upwards, protecting applications and operating systems.

IPSec prevents the previous type of attacks by using cryptography-based mechanisms. Cryptography allows information to be transmitted securely by *hashing* (digitally signing data) and *encrypting* (encoding) the information.

A combination of an algorithm and a key is used to secure information:

- The *algorithm* is the mathematical process by which the information is secured.

- A *key* is the secret code or number required to read, modify, or verify secured data.

IPSec uses a policy-based mechanism to determine the level of security required during a communications session. Policies can be distributed throughout a network by means of Windows 2000 domain controllers, or created and stored locally within the registry of a Windows 2000 Professional–based computer.

Before the transmission of any data, an IPSec-enabled computer negotiates the level of security to be maintained during the communications session. During the negotiation process, the authentication method is determined, a hashing method is determined, a tunneling method is chosen (optional), and an encryption method is determined (optional). The secret authentication keys are determined locally at each computer by using information exchanged at this time; no actual keys are ever transmitted. After the key is generated, it is used to authenticate the session, and secured data exchange can begin.

The resulting level of security can be low or high, based on the IP security policy of the sending or receiving computer. For example, a communications session between a Windows 2000 Professional–based computer and a non-IPSec host might not require a secure transmission channel. Conversely, a communications session between a Windows 2000 server containing sensitive information and a dial-in host might be high, using data encryption by means of a securing transmission.

An Example of IPSec

Figure 22.19 provides an overview of the procedure of establishing an IP security session:

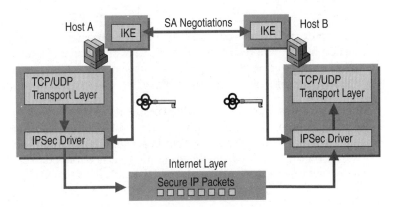

Figure 22.19   Overview: the IPSec Process

1. An application on Computer A generates outbound packets to send to Computer B across the network.

2. IPSec checks IP Security Group Policy settings on Computer A to determine the computer's active IP Security policy. The default policies allow a computer to demand secure communication, to request secure communication but proceed unsecurely if necessary, or to never request IP security.

3. Computer A begins security negotiations with Computer B. The two computers exchange public keys and establish a shared, secret key that is created independently at both ends without being transmitted across the network.

4. The IPSec driver on Computer A signs the outgoing packets for integrity, and optionally encrypts them for confidentially. It transmits the packets to Computer B.

5. Routers and servers along the network path from Computer A to Computer B do not require IPSec. They simply pass along the packets in the usual manner.

6. The IPSec driver on Computer B checks the packets for integrity and decrypts their content if necessary. It then transfers the packets to the receiving application.

Although routers and switches can freely forward encrypted IP packets, firewalls, security routers, and proxy servers must enable IP forwarding to ensure packet delivery. For more information about IP forwarding, see "Unicast Routing Overview," in the *Internetworking Guide*.

Considerations for IPSec

IP security provides encryption of outgoing IP packets, but at the cost of local computer performance. On a computer with IP encryption enabled, packets are encrypted before being passed to the network, which is a processor-intensive procedure. Although IPSec implements symmetric encryption of network data, encryption of a large amount of IP packets can tax all but the fastest workstations.

IPSec supports processing offload by the network adapter. Many network adapters include onboard processors that perform many of the tasks that are normally performed by the computer's central processor, including packet encryption. Consult the product documentation for your network adapter to see if it supports encryption processing offload.

Configuring IPSec Policies

IPSec policies, rather than applications or operations systems, are used to configure IPSec services. The policies provide variable levels of protection for most traffic types in most existing networks.

There are two storage locations for IPSec policies:

1. Active Directory in a Windows 2000 domain controller.

2. Locally defined in the registry for computers that are not part of a Windows 2000 domain.

Your network security administrator can configure IPSec policies to meet the security requirements of a user, group, application, domain, site, or global enterprise from a Windows 2000 domain controller. IPSec policy can also be implemented in a non-Windows 2000–based domain environment through local IPSec policies.

The IPSec policies are based on your organization's guidelines for secure operations. Through the use of security actions, called *rules*, one policy can be applied to heterogeneous security groups of computers or organizational units. Windows 2000 Professional provides an MMC console called **Local Security Policy** to create and manage IPSec policies.

This section describes the procedure for configuring domain-based and local IPSec policies on a Windows 2000 Professional–based computer. For detailed information on planning, creating and implementing IPSec policies on a Windows 2000 domain controller, see "Internet Protocol Security" in the *TCP/IP Core Networking Guide*.

Configuring Domain-based IPSec Policies

For an organization that wishes to implement IP security, creating IP security policies at the domain controller provides the most efficient method of controlling enterprise security policy. Windows 2000 provides an administrative interface, the **Local Security Policy** snap-in, to create and administer security policies. An IP security administrator can create security policies at varying levels or granularity, from the site, domain, organizational unit, user or computer levels. Different security policies can be applied for different groups, based on identified needs for security.

After an IPSec policy has been created at the domain controller, security policy can be applied to members of a specific container. For example, if Sally is a member of an organizational unit (OU) that has a security policy applied to it, the OU's security policy is automatically applied at startup. No user intervention is required. Using domain-based policies ensure that the proper security is always implemented at users' machines, regardless of the existence of local security policies.

When a computer that is normally a member of a Windows 2000 domain is temporarily disconnected, the security policy information is cached in the local registry.

IPSec Precedence Rules

IP security policy precedence is identical to that of other Group Policy settings. In a domain, Group Policy is applied hierarchically from the least restrictive object (site) to the most restrictive object (organizational unit).

For more information about Active Directory and Group Policy, see chapters under "Active Directory" and "Desktop Configuration Management" in the *Distributed Systems Guide*.

Configuring Local IPSec Policies

Local IPSec policies can be selected and stored locally at a Windows 2000 Professional–based computer. This can be done to implement local IP security in the following situations:

- The computer is a member of a Windows 2000 domain that does not implement IPSec policies.

- The computer is a member of a Windows NT domain.

- The computer is part of a workgroup.

- The computer is not a member of any domain or workgroup, but is connected to other hosts by means of an enterprise intranet or the Internet.

By implementing local IP security, the Windows 2000 Professional–based computer can transfer IP packets based on the security policy stored in its registry. Three preconfigured local IPSec policies are provided at system installation: **Client**, **Server**, and **Secure Server**. Table 22.9 summarizes the attributes of the default security policies.

Table 22.9 Default Local IP Security Policies

Policy Name	Security Requirements	Attributes
Client (Respond Only)	Low	For computers that do not require secure communications, this policy enables a Windows 2000 Professional–based computer to respond to requests for secured communications. Unsecured communications are available with non-IPSec hosts.

(continued)

Table 22.9 Default Local IP Security Policies *(continued)*

Policy Name	Security Requirements	Attributes
Server (Request Security)	Moderate	Enables a Windows 2000 Professional–based computer to accept unsecured communications, but attempt to establish a secure channel by requesting security from the sending host. Communications are unsecured if the requesting host is not IPSec-enabled.
Secure Server (Require Security)	High	Requires that all communications with a Windows 2000 Professional–based computers be secured. All unsecured incoming communications are rejected, and all outgoing communications are secured.

The default security policies can be used as-is, eliminating the need to create custom policies unless you have special requirements. You must have administrative privileges in order to select or change IP security policies.

By default, no local IPSec policies are active. To select one of the default local IPSec policies, use the following procedure.

▶ **To activate a local IPSec policy**

1. In Control Panel, double-click **Network and Dial-up Connections**.

2. Right-click **Local Area Connection**, and then select **Properties**.

3. Select **Internet Protocol (TCP/IP)**, and then click **Properties**.

4. Click **Advanced**, and then click the **Options** tab.

5. Select **IP security**, and then click **Properties**.

6. Select **Use this IP security policy**, and then select the IPSec policy you want from the list.

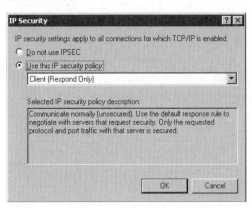

For any Windows 2000 Professional–based computer that is a member of a domain, IPSec policies assigned at the domain override any local IPSec policy when that computer account is connected to the domain.

IPSec Policy Management Snap-in

The Microsoft Management Console (MMC) IP Security Policy Management snap-in allows you to perform the following tasks:

- Create and manage local and domain-based IPSec policies
- Manage IP filter lists and filter actions
- Check IPSec policies
- Restore default IPSec policies
- Import and export IPSec policies

The IP Security Policy Management snap-in is not loaded in Windows 2000 Professional by default. To install the IP Security Policy Management snap-in, perform the following steps while logged on to an account with administrative rights.

▶ **To install the IP Security Policy Management snap-in**

1. In an empty or existing MMC console, select **Console/Add/Remove Snap-in**.
2. In the **Standalone** dialog box, click **Add**.
3. In the **Available Standalone Snap-ins** box, select **IP Security Policy Management**, and then click **Add**.
4. In the **Select which computer this Snap-in will manage** dialog box, select the option that matches the security policy environment to be managed by the target computer.
5. From the target computer, you can manage the security policy of the target computer (stored in its registry), the IP security policy of the local or another domain (if appropriate permissions have been granted) or manage the local security policy of another computer, stored in its registry.
6. Click **Finish**.

Creating Local IPSec Policies

New IPSec policies can be created by selecting **Create IP Security Policy** from the **Actions** menu of the IP Security Policy Management console, or by right-clicking the details panel of the console, and then selecting **Create IP Security Policy**. This action starts the IP Security Policy wizard.

The IP Security Policy wizard prompts you for the information needed to configure the initial response rule for the new policy. The following information is required:

- Policy name and description
- Application of default rule

    A security rule determines how IPSec policy secures communication. Selection of this option specifies that a default rule is created for use as the response rule if no other rule exists or applies.

    Additional rules can be created after the default rule by editing the IP security policy.

- Authentication method for default rule

    An authentication method for the two computers must be determined before secure communications can begin. Use this option to select the method of authentication for the default rule, if chosen:

    - Kerberos v5
    - Certificate-based
    - Preshared key

A detailed discussion of the creation of IP security policies is beyond the level of this section. For more information on IP policy and rule creation, refer to Windows 2000 Help and "Internet Protocol Security" in the *TCP/IP Core Networking Guide*.

TCP/IP Filtering

Windows 2000 Professional includes support for *TCP/IP filtering* (known as *TCP/IP Security* in Windows NT 4.0). TCP/IP filtering allows you to specify exactly which types of incoming IP traffic are processed for each IP interface. This feature is designed to isolate the traffic being processed by Internet and intranet clients in the absence of other TCP/IP filtering provided by the Routing and Remote Access service or other TCP/IP applications or services. TCP/IP filtering is disabled by default.

TCP/IP filtering is a set of input filters for nontransit TCP/IP traffic. Nontransit traffic is traffic that is processed by the host because the destination IP address of inbound IP datagrams are addressed to an assigned interface address, appropriate subnet broadcast address, or multicast address. TCP/IP filtering does not apply to transit or routed traffic that is forwarded between interfaces.

TCP/IP filtering allows you confine nontransit inbound TCP/IP traffic based on the:

- Destination TCP port
- Destination UDP port
- IP protocol

▶   **To configure TCP/IP filtering**

1. In Control Panel, double-click **Network and Dial-up Connections** select **Local Area Connection**, and then right-click **Properties**.

2. On the **General** tab, click **Internet Protocol (TCP/IP)** in the list of components, and then click **Properties**.

3. Click **Advanced**.

4. Click the **Options** tab, **TCP/IP filtering**, and then **Properties**.

TCP/IP filtering can be enabled and disabled for all adapters by means of a single check box. This can help troubleshoot connectivity problems that might be related to filtering. Filters that are too restrictive do not allow expected kinds of connectivity. For example, if you do not include the RIP protocol, then the RIP Listener service will not function.

Configure Quality of Service

Quality of Service (QoS) facilitates the deployment of media-rich applications, such as video conferencing and Internet Protocol (IP) telephony. QoS also improves the performance of traditional mission-critical (qualitative) software such as Enterprise Resource Planning (ERP) applications. Through the full implementation of QoS in a Windows 2000 domain, QoS-aware applications running on Windows 2000–based clients can be provided a guaranteed or prioritized level of delivery service, while allowing centralized management of network resources.

Understand the purpose and function of Quality of Service and how it is implemented in your network.

Although largely implemented through a collection of servers, switches, and routers, an understanding of QoS in Windows 2000 is critical to the successful implementation of QoS at a Windows 2000 Professional–based client. This section explains the architecture of QoS, the protocols used, and provides a scenario to demonstrate these concepts. See "Overview of Quality of Service" and "Windows 2000 QoS Components" in this chapter.

Verify that the client meets requirements to implement QoS, and install the QoS Packet Scheduler.

In order to successfully implement QoS on a Windows 2000 Professional–based client, the client must meet hardware and software requirements. In addition, the QoS Packet Scheduler must be installed for each Windows 2000 Professional–based client that requests QoS. See "QoS Configuration Requirements" in this chapter.

Overview of Quality of Service

Multimedia streams, such as those used in IP telephony or videoconferencing, can be extremely bandwidth- and delay-sensitive, imposing unique demands on the underlying networks that carry them. Conversely, enterprise network administrators might be primarily concerned with the quality of network transmissions for mission-critical applications, such as Enterprise Resource Planning (ERP) applications, and secondarily concerned with providing sufficient bandwidth for multimedia applications.

To deploy real-time applications over IP networks with an acceptable level of quality, specific network requirements must be met. These requirements are *bandwidth*, *latency*, and *jitter*. In addition, the traffic must *coexist* with traditional data traffic on the same network. Table 22.10 summarizes these requirements.

Table 22.10   Network Requirements for Real-Time Applications

Network Requirement	Effect
Bandwidth	Multimedia data, especially video, requires larger amounts of bandwidth than traditional networks can handle. Even compressed, a handful of multimedia streams can completely overwhelm any other traffic on the network.
Latency	The amount of time that a multimedia packet takes to get from the source to the destination has a major impact on the perceived quality of the call. Latency must be minimized to maintain a certain level of interactivity and to avoid pauses in conversation.
Jitter	Variations in packet arrival time must be below a certain threshold to avoid dropped packets, resulting in gaps in audio and video transmission. Jitter, by determining receive buffer sizes, also affects latency.
Coexistence	In comparison with multimedia traffic, data traffic arrives in unpredictable chunks. Aggregations of such bursts cause gaps in teleconferencing applications. Multimedia bandwidth must be protected from data traffic, and vice versa.

QoS is a combination of mechanisms that cooperatively provide a specific quality level to application traffic crossing a network or multiple, disparate networks. Implementing QoS means combining a set of technologies defined by the Internet Engineering Task Force (IETF), designed to reduce the problems caused by shared network resources and finite bandwidth.

QoS provides two distinct benefits:

- A mechanism for applications to request service quality parameters, such as low latency and jitter.
- Higher levels of administrative control over congested subnet bandwidth resources.

Implementing QoS enables network administrators to make the most efficient use of subnet bandwidth when deploying resource-intensive applications. A QoS-enabled network can provide guarantees of sufficient network resources for some traffic, and the ability to prioritize other important traffic, giving a congested, shared network segment a level of service approaching that of a private network. Different classes of applications have varying degrees of tolerance for delay in network throughput. An accepted QoS request can ensure that an application can transmit data in an acceptable way, in an acceptable time frame so that the transmission is not delayed, distorted, or lost.

To enable end-to-end QoS requires cooperation from the sending host, the receiving hosts and routers and switches between the two end nodes. Without QoS, each of these network devices treat all data equally and provide service on a first-come, first-served basis, known as *best-effort delivery*. In addition, for an application to make use of QoS, it must have some level of QoS awareness so that it can request bandwidth and other resources from the network.

The efficient use and allocation of bandwidth is critical for productivity. Real-time applications, media-rich applications, and Enterprise Resource Planning applications require a large amount of uninterrupted bandwidth for transmission to be successful, and therefore can strain existing network resources. When traffic is heavy, overall performance degrades, which results in traffic and packet loss. This degradation causes problems with video conferencing, real-time audio, and interactive communication, causing distortion of voices and images. Because media-rich applications use large quantities of bandwidth, traditional mission-critical applications suffer from the lack of available resources. QoS provides a delivery system for network traffic that can guarantee limited delays and data loss, or allow certain types of traffic to receive priority queuing over other types of traffic.

It is important to realize that QoS cannot create bandwidth; it can only efficiently partition bandwidth based on differing parameters.

Windows 2000 QoS Components

The Windows 2000 QoS architecture is built upon a tightly-integrated set of industry standard protocols, services, and mechanisms that control access to network resources, classify and schedule network traffic, and protocols that signal network devices to apply QoS by handling specific traffic flows with greater priority. Figure 22.20 illustrates the Windows 2000 QoS architecture.

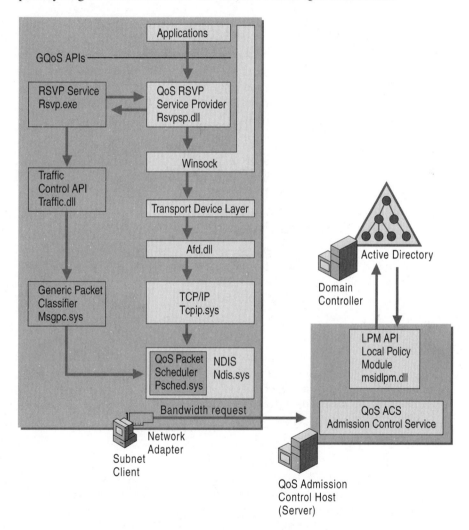

Figure 22.20   Windows 2000 QoS Components

All of these components work together seamlessly to provide QoS on a network. Appearing as shaded boxes in this figure are the Windows 2000 QoS components. Not pictured in Figure 22.20 are the elements in the network infrastructure required to fully ensure QoS end-to-end. All routers and switches between the sender and receiver must also support one of several possible QoS mechanisms, such as RSVP, 802.1p, or DiffServ, otherwise traffic receives best-effort delivery on that segment.

Generic QoS API (GQoS API)

Applications can use the Generic QoS application programming interface (GQoS API) to specify or request bandwidth requirements, such as preventing latency when streaming audio. They can also use the GQoS API to prioritize traffic generated by mission-critical applications.

GQoS is part of the Windows Sockets 2.0 (Winsock2) API. The abstraction of the QoS API enables applications to invoke QoS without a full knowledge of the QoS mechanisms available or the specific underlying network media. As such, QoS can be implemented in a variety of diverse media, such as Ethernet or IP over Asynchronous Transfer Mode (ATM).

Resource Reservation Protocol

When QoS is requested, GQoS calls upon the services of the underlying QoS service provider, *Resource Reservation Protocol Service Provider* (Rsvpsp.dll). The RSVP SP issues RSVP signaling to participating network devices along the data path of the bandwidth requirements, traffic control, and Admission Control support.

Resource Reservation Protocol (RSVP) is an IETF-defined signaling protocol that carries QoS requests for priority bandwidth through the network. RSVP (Rsvp.exe) bridges the gap between the application, the operating system, and the media-specific QoS mechanisms. RSVP sends messages in a format that is media-independent, so that end-to-end QoS is possible over networks that combine different types of low-layer network devices.

Traffic Control

Traffic control creates and regulates data flows by using defined QoS parameters, such as transmission latency and delay variation. It also facilitates the creation of filters to direct selected packets through a data flow. The capabilities of traffic control are accessed via the *Traffic Control API*, implemented through the dynamic link library Traffic.dll. Traffic control is called upon by the GQoS API.

The *Generic Packet Classifier* (Msgpc.sys) determines the service class to which an individual packet belongs. Table 22.11 shows the possible service classes for a packet.

Table 22.11   Windows 2000 Service Classes

Service Class	Definition
Best Effort	Network devices make reasonable effort to deliver packets (standard service level).
Controlled Load	Approximates the standard packet error loss of the transmission medium. Approximates the behavior of best-effort service in lightly loaded (not heavily loaded or congested) network conditions.
Guaranteed	Guarantees the ability to transmit data at a determined rate for the duration of the connection.
Qualitative	Although not implemented, the qualitative service class is designed for applications that require prioritized traffic but cannot to quantify their resource needs. The level of service is determined by an entry in a policy server by a network administrator.

Packets are then queued by service class, managed by the QoS Packet Scheduler. The *QoS Packet Scheduler* (Psched.sys) enforces QoS parameters for a particular data flow. Traffic is marked with a particular priority by the QoS Packet Scheduler, differentiated by priority and by device type. *802.1p* provides prioritization of packets for devices that correspond to Layer 2 of the OSI model, such as switches. For Layer 3 devices such as routers, the *Differentiated Class of Service* enables packets that pass through network devices to have their relative priority differentiated from one another.

The QoS Packet Scheduler then determines the delivery schedule of each packet queue and handles competition between queued packets that need simultaneous access to the network.

QoS Admission Control Service

To deploy real-time multimedia or qualitative applications with an acceptable traffic rate, a network must commit to some level of guaranteed resource availability. In addition, the subnet management service must find some way for this priority traffic to coexist with traditional data traffic.

The *QoS Admission Control Service* (QoS ACS), located in a designated ACS server, solves this problem by allowing the network administrator to centrally designate how, by whom, and when shared network resources are used. A QoS ACS server performs logical allocation of network resources based on policies located in Active Directory on the domain controller. Note that the ACS server does not allocate the physical network resources, but performs the policy and Admission Control function of accepting or rejecting requests. After a request has been accepted, the sending host can mark the packets accordingly. Figure 22.21 illustrates this procedure.

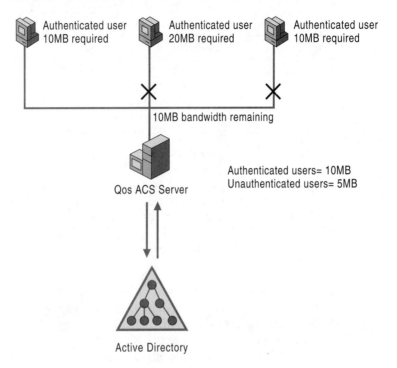

Figure 22.21 How QoS ACS Works

As each request for network resources is received by the QoS ACS server:

- The QoS ACS verifies whether network resource levels are adequate. The ACS can verify for the sender, receiver, or both.

- The requesting user identity is verified by using the Kerberos protocol, the default Windows 2000 authentication service.

- The QoS ACS policy for that user is retrieved from Active Directory or from the local ACS policy cache.

- The QoS ACS server checks the policy to see whether the user has adequate rights for the request.

- The QoS ACS approves or rejects the request.

A single QoS ACS server can be configured to manage multiple subnets. Typically, QoS ACS servers are implemented on an enterprise's most congested segments, often at the ingress to an expensive WAN link.

QoS ACS policies are defined in Active Directory by the network administrator by using the ACS MMC snap-in. Policies can be defined at varying levels of granularity, from specific (a particular user policy in a domain) to general (any authenticated user in the enterprise). QoS ACS policies are processed hierarchically, from most specific to least specific. Additionally, enterprise-level policies can be differentiated between authenticated users (users with valid domain accounts) and unauthenticated users (users who have access to the network, but are not authenticated by a Windows 2000 domain controller).

Note For more information about planning and implementing a QoS ACS server in an Active Directory domain, see "Quality of Service" in the *TCP/IP Core Networking Guide*, and "Group Policy" in the *Distributed Systems Guide*.

The *Local Policy Module* (LPM) is a component of the QoS ACS that provides a means of retrieving policy information from Active Directory. When a Windows 2000 Kerberos ticket is received by the ACS server, the QoS ACS invokes the LPM dynamic-link library Msidlpm.dll. The LPM extracts the user name from the RSVP message and looks up the user's Admission Control policy in Active Directory.

Putting It All Together: A QoS Scenario

IP telephony provides an excellent example of the need for Quality of Service controls. When a user initiates a teleconference call to another user, the success of the communication relies on available priority bandwidth. Any new IP telephony sessions have the potential to degrade the quality of the first call that is still in progress, because these calls must share the same bandwidth. To guarantee QoS and successful throughput of the original call, the various components of QoS are put to use:

- A QoS-enabled sending application initiates a session with a receiving client, signaling a request for desired resource requirements.

- The Admission Control Service verifies the user's right to request a bandwidth reservation.

- A receiving client accepts or rejects the request, and if accepted, sends a Reservation Confirmation (RESV) message back to the sending client.

   This RESV message from the receiver traverses back along the same path as the sending message, and routers along the way that understand RSVP also have the opportunity to accept or reject the request. If the request is accepted by a network entity, then the requested bandwidth is allocated on that device. Admission Control can also be applied on the receiver.

- Traffic Control prioritizes and schedules IP packets between the two clients when the RESV message reaches the sender's system.

This section describes how these components work together in a common QoS scenario. Figure 22.22 illustrates a common QoS deployment.

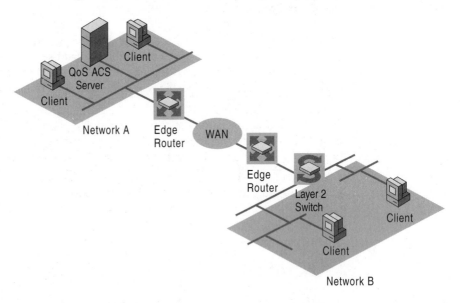

Figure 22.22   How QoS Works

1. A user on a client in Network A starts a videoconferencing session with a user in Network B. The application used to transmit data is QoS-enabled. The application requests QoS from the RSVP SP.

2. The RSVP SP requests the RSVP service to signal the necessary bandwidth requirements, and notifies traffic control that QoS has been requested for this flow. Traffic is currently sent at a best-effort delivery level.

3. An RSVP message is sent to the QoS ACS server, requesting a reservation. Note that it is RSVP messages that are passed to the QoS ACS, not the data packets that are ultimately transmitted from sender to receiver.

4. The QoS ACS server verifies that enough network resources are available to meet the QoS level requested, and that the user has the policy rights to request that amount of bandwidth. The Local Policy Module uses the Kerberos ticket in the RSVP request to authenticate the user identity and look up the user policy in Active Directory. Note that the QoS ACS can verify resources for the sender, receiver, or both.

5. After verification is complete, the QoS ACS server approves the request and logically allocates bandwidth. The QoS ACS server forwards the request to the receiver of the videoconferencing session on the client in Network B.

6. When the RSVP request passes the edge router for Network A, the router keeps track of the resources (bandwidth) that are requested, although the bandwidth is not yet physically allocated. RSVP is a receiver-initiated protocol and bandwidth can only be reserved by the receiver. The same process is repeated on the edge router for Network B.

7. The request is passed through each network device in the data path before it arrives at the receiver. The receiving client indicates that it wants to receive the data and returns an RSVP message requesting a reservation.

8. When the receiver's request for bandwidth passes through the edge router for Network B, it already has cached the information about the requested bandwidth (from the sender's request). The router matches the receiver request with the sender's request, and installs the reservation by physically granting the bandwidth. The same process is repeated on the edge router for Network A.

9. The reservation is sent back to the sender. The Layer 3 network devices (the edge routers) are capable of approving and allocating the physical bandwidth. The reservation simply passes through the Layer 2 switch.

10. During this process, the traffic is sent by traffic control on the sender as best-effort. Upon receiving the reservation message, the traffic control on the sending host begins the process of classifying, marking, and scheduling the packets to accommodate the QoS level requested. The QoS Packet Scheduler performs the priority marking for RSVP, 802.1p for prioritization on Layer 2 devices (shown as the switch in Figure 22.22), and for Differentiated Class of Service for Layer 3 devices (shown as the edge routers).

11. The QoS Packet Scheduler begins sending the prioritized traffic. The data is handled as priority by all devices along the data path, providing greater speed of throughput and a more successful videoconference session between the clients on networks A and B.

Note that this example is a general description. Variations are possible depending on network topology as well as the presence of different network devices.

QoS Configuration Requirements

To maintain the integrity of RSVP reservations on a shared subnet, it is important that any client that can issue RSVP messages is a QoS Subnet Bandwidth Manager client. On Windows 2000 Professional, the required QoS client software must be configured and enabled to request bandwidth. The requesting applications installed on the Windows 2000 Professional–based client must also be QoS-enabled. Applications that are not QoS-aware do not interact with the QoS ACS server, and receive best-effort service traffic levels from the network.

To fully implement QoS, there are several considerations that must be met by the Windows 2000 Professional–based client.

Hardware   Network adapters must be compatible with the IEEE 802.1p standard, and must support 802.1p to allow prioritization over a shared subnet. This standard provides the mechanism necessary for traffic control.

Admission Control Policies   Verify with your network administrator that a valid Admission Control policy exists for your user or group in the domain. The ACS policy determines the level or service to be provided to each user or group account, and directly affects the level of service provided. Also, check to see what the enterprise policy for nonauthenticated users is – for example, a member of a workgroup within the enterprise. Depending on enterprise policy, unauthenticated users are allowed access to network services at a lower policy-defined level, at best-effort levels, or no access at all.

QoS Packet Scheduler   The QoS Packet Scheduler service must be installed on every Windows 2000 Professional–based client on which you want to have traffic control services. The QoS Packet Scheduler must be installed on all end-systems that make reservations on subnets where you are running a QoS Admission Control Service.

▶   **To install the QoS Packet Scheduler**

1. From Control Panel, double-click **Network and Dial-up Connections**.

2. Right-click the local area connection you want to modify, and then select **Properties**.

3. Click **Install**.

4. Click **Service**.

5. Select **QoS Packet Scheduler**, and then click **OK**.

6. Click **Close**.

Perform TCP/IP Troubleshooting

Many network troubleshooting tools are available to assist in diagnosing TCP/IP problems for Windows 2000 Professional. This section summarizes the most common and most helpful tools included with the operating system, and provides an organized approach for deploying them.

Assess the situation.   After assessing the TCP/IP problem, create a plan to determine the true nature of the problem: IP addressing and routing, host name resolution, NetBIOS name resolution, or IP security. A flowchart is provided to assist you in this task in Figures 22.24 through 22.26. See "TCP/IP Troubleshooting Overview" in this chapter.

Determine and obtain required troubleshooting tools.   After you have determined the possible source of the problem, obtain the tools that you need to prove your hypothesis and resolve the problem. See "TCP/IP Troubleshooting Tools" in this chapter.

Determine and resolve name resolution problems. First, determine whether the error condition was caused by a failure in host (for example, www.reskit.com) or NetBIOS (for example, \\computername) name resolution. Use the tools to determine the nature of the IP-to-name resolution problem. See "Troubleshooting Name Resolution" in this chapter.

Determine and resolve IP addressing problems. If name resolution is not the nature of the TCP/IP problem, verify that IP addressing, routing, IP security and filtering have been correctly configured on the Windows 2000 Professional–based client. Additionally, confirm that the route to the remote computer is properly configured and available. See "Troubleshooting IP Addressing" in this chapter.

Determine and resolve IP routing problems. If the nature of the TCP/IP problem occurs outside the current subnet, or is related to access of a remote host or router, verify the configuration of the routing table gateways, and check the status of routers along the route path. See "Troubleshooting Routing" in this chapter.

TCP/IP Troubleshooting Overview

When troubleshooting any problem, ask yourself the following questions:

- What application is failing? What works? What doesn't work?
- Is the problem basic IP connectivity or is it name resolution? If the problem is name resolution, does the failing application use NetBIOS names or DNS names and host names?
- How are the things that do and don't work related?
- Have the things that don't work ever worked on this computer or network?
- If so, what has changed since they last worked?

Ideally, a review of the location and timing of the problem helps narrow the problem's scope. In addition, you can examine TCP/IP failures systematically by referring to the steps needed for successful computer communications.

TCP/IP for Windows 2000 allows an application to communicate over a network with another computer by using three basic types of destination designations:

- IP address (for example, 172.10.1.32)
- Host name (for example, client1.reskit.com)
- NetBIOS name (for example, client1)

This section describes how to troubleshoot either host name or NetBIOS name resolution problems. Both of these issues are outlined in Figures 22.23 through 22.25, which provide a simplified flowchart to guide troubleshooting.

Start

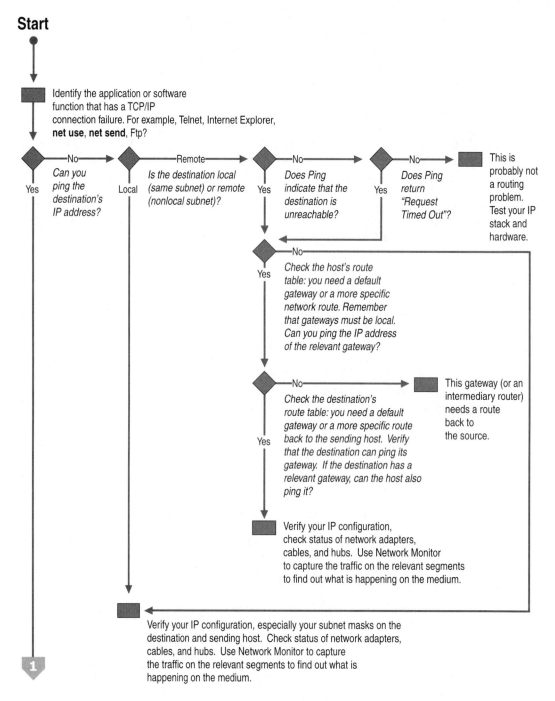

Identify the application or software function that has a TCP/IP connection failure. For example, Telnet, Internet Explorer, **net use**, **net send**, Ftp?

—No—
Can you ping the destination's IP address?

Yes

Local

—Remote—
Is the destination local (same subnet) or remote (nonlocal subnet)?

Yes

—No—
Does Ping indicate that the destination is unreachable?

Yes

—No—
Does Ping return "Request Timed Out"?

Yes

This is probably not a routing problem. Test your IP stack and hardware.

—No—
Yes
Check the host's route table: you need a default gateway or a more specific network route. Remember that gateways must be local. Can you ping the IP address of the relevant gateway?

—No—
Check the destination's route table: you need a default gateway or a more specific route back to the sending host. Verify that the destination can ping its gateway. If the destination has a relevant gateway, can the host also ping it?

Yes

This gateway (or an intermediary router) needs a route back to the source.

Verify your IP configuration, check status of network adapters, cables, and hubs. Use Network Monitor to capture the traffic on the relevant segments to find out what is happening on the medium.

1

Verify your IP configuration, especially your subnet masks on the destination and sending host. Check status of network adapters, cables, and hubs. Use Network Monitor to capture the traffic on the relevant segments to find out what is happening on the medium.

Figure 22.23   TCP/IP Troubleshooting Flowchart (Part 1 of 3)

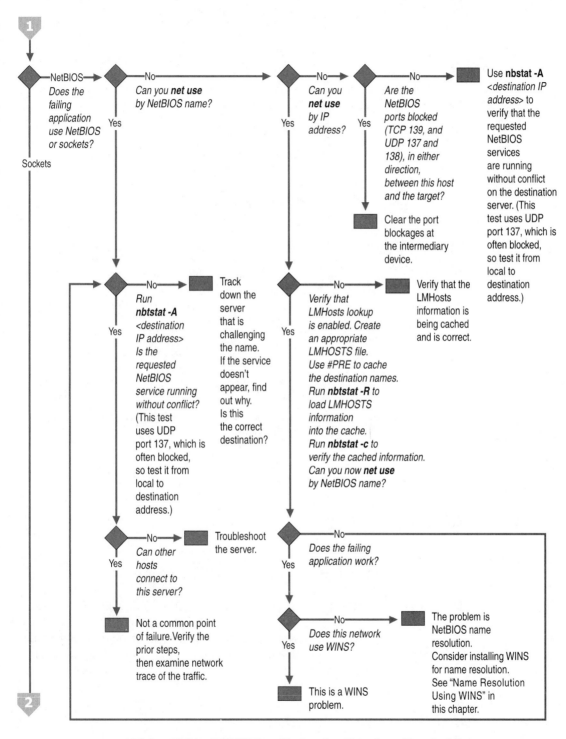

Figure 22.24   TCP/IP Troubleshooting Flowchart (Part 2 of 3)

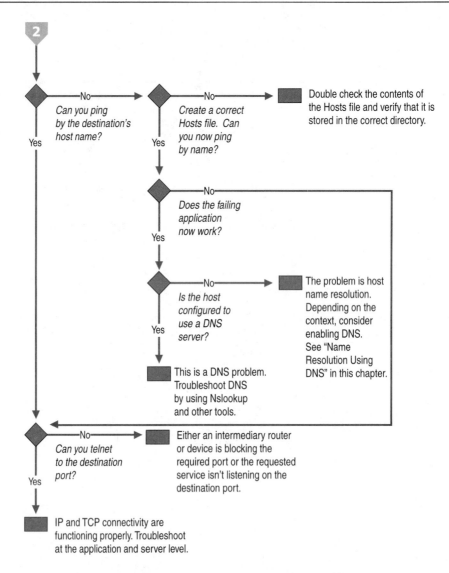

Figure 22.25   TCP/IP Troubleshooting Flowchart (Part 3 of 3)

The first step is to determine which application is failing. Typically, this is Telnet, Internet Explorer, **net use**, or another application that uses NetBIOS or Sockets to find network resources. Making this determination helps with the next step, which is to determine whether the problem is a host name or NetBIOS name resolution problem.

The easiest way to distinguish host name problems from NetBIOS name resolution problems is to find out whether the failing application uses NetBIOS or Sockets. If it uses Sockets, the problem lies with a DNS/host name resolution. If the application uses NetBIOS, the problem is with NetBIOS name resolution (broadcast, Lmhosts or WINS). Among the most common applications, the NetBIOS family includes the various **net** commands or the Windows NT 4.0 administrator tools. Most Internet- or intranet-based applications such as Internet Explorer and other web browsers, ftp clients and telnet use Windows Sockets.

TCP/IP Troubleshooting Tools

Table 22.12 lists the diagnostic tools discussed in this section. There are other troubleshooting tools available for TCP/IP; they are described in more detail in "Troubleshooting Tools and Strategies" in this book.

Table 22.12   TCP/IP Diagnostic Tools

Tool	Used to
Hostname	Display the host name of the computer.
Ipconfig	Display current TCP/IP network configuration values, and update or release Dynamic Host Configuration Protocol (DHCP) allocated leases, and display, register, or flush Domain Name System (DNS) names.
Nbtstat	Check the state of current NetBIOS over TCP/IP connections, update the NetBIOS name cache, and determine the registered names and scope ID.
Pathping	Trace a path to a remote system and report packet losses at each router along the way.
Ping	Send ICMP Echo Requests to verify that TCP/IP is configured correctly and that a remote TCP/IP system is available.
Route	Display the IP routing table, and add or delete IP routes.
Tracert	Trace a path to a remote system.

To view the proper syntax for each command, type **/?** after each command.

In addition to the TCP/IP-specific tools, the following Microsoft Windows 2000 tools and utilities might be needed in problem determination and resolution:

- Event Viewer—Tracks system errors and events.
- Control Panel—Allows changes to networking and other system components.
- Registry editors— Both Regedit.exe and Regedt32.exe allow viewing and editing of registry parameters.

Troubleshooting Name Resolution

The following section details the procedures for detecting and resolving a variety of host and NetBIOS name resolution problems.

NetBIOS Name Resolution

The following section describes the methods for detecting and resolving the most common types of NetBIOS name resolution problems.

Resolving NetBIOS Error 53

The most common symptom of a problem in NetBIOS name resolution is when the Ping tool returns an Error 53 message. The Error 53 message is generally returned when name resolution fails for a particular computer name. Error 53 can also occur when there is a problem establishing a NetBIOS session. To distinguish between these two cases, use the following procedure:

▶ **To determine the cause of an Error 53 message**

1. From the **Start** menu, open a command prompt.
2. At the command prompt, type:

   net view * \\\<*hostname*>

   where **<*hostname*>** is a network resource you know is active.

   If this works, your name resolution is probably not the source of the problem. To confirm this, ping the host name, as name resolution can sometimes function properly, yet **net use** returns Error 53 (such as when a DNS or WINS server has a bad entry). If Ping also shows that name resolution fails (by returning the "Unknown host" message), check the status of your NetBIOS session.

▶ **To check the status of your NetBIOS session**

1. From the **Start** menu, open a command prompt.
2. At the command prompt, type:

   net view \\\<*ip address*>

   where **<*ip address*>** is the same network resource you used in the earlier procedure. If this also fails, the problem is in establishing a session.

If the computer is on the local subnet, confirm that the name is spelled correctly and that the target computer is running TCP/IP as well. If the computer is not on the local subnet, be sure that its name and IP address mapping are available in the DNS database, the Hosts or Lmhosts file, or the WINS database.

If all TCP/IP elements appear to be installed properly, use Ping with the remote computer to be sure its TCP/IP protocol is working.

Check the Lmhosts File

The name resolution problem might be in your Lmhosts file, which looks for addresses sequentially from the top down. If more than one address is listed for the same host name, TCP/IP returns the first value it encounters, whether that value is accurate or not.

You can find the Lmhosts file in \%SystemRoot%\System32\Drivers\Etc. Note that this file does not exist by default; a sample file named Lmhosts.sam exists. This file must be renamed to Lmhosts before it is used.

Note   While \%SystemRoot%\System32\Drivers\Etc is the default directory for this file, exactly which Lmhosts file is consulted depends on the value of the **databasepath** registry entry located in:
HKEY_LOCAL_MACHINE\SYSTEM\CurrentControlSet\Services \Tcpip\Parameters\
The database path tells the local computer where to look for the Lmhosts file.

Check the WINS Configuration

Make sure your computer's WINS configuration is correct. In particular, check the address for the WINS server.

▶   **To examine your WINS configuration**

1. In **Control Panel**, double-click **Network and Dial-Up Connections**.
2. Right-click **Local Area Connection**, and then click **Properties**.
3. In the **Local Area Connection Properties** dialog box, select **Internet Protocol (TCP/IP)**, and then click **Properties**.
4. In the **Internet Protocol (TCP/IP) Properties** dialog box, click **Advanced**.
5. In the **Advanced TCP/IP Settings** dialog box, click the **WINS** tab.

In the **WINS configuration** dialog box, add the server's IP address (if none is listed) and check to see whether Lmhosts lookup is enabled. Also check to see whether NetBIOS over TCP/IP is taken from the DHCP server, enabled, or disabled. If you are using DHCP for this host computer, take the value from the DHCP server. Otherwise, enable NetBIOS over TCP/IP.

Host and DNS Name Resolution

If the problem is not NetBIOS but Sockets, the problem is related to either a Hosts file or a DNS configuration error. To determine why only IP addresses, but not host names, work for connections to remote computers, make sure that the appropriate Hosts file and DNS setup have been configured for the computer.

▶   **To check host name resolution configuration**

1. In Control Panel, double-click **Network and Dialup Connection**.

2. Right-click **Local Area Connections**, and then select **Properties**.

3. Click on **Internet Protocol (TCP/IP)**, and then click **Properties**.

4. In the **Microsoft TCP/IP Properties** dialog box, click the **Advanced** tab.

5. Click the **DNS** tab.

6. Confirm that DNS is configured properly. If the DNS server IP address is missing, add it to the list of DNS server addresses.

Note that this procedure does not take DHCP clients into account; these clients do not have DNS servers in the list.

Check the Hosts File

If you are having trouble connecting to a remote system using a host name and are using a Hosts file for name resolution, the problem might be with the contents of that file. Make sure the name of the remote computer is spelled correctly in the Hosts file and by the application using it.

The Hosts file or a DNS server is used to resolve host names to IP addresses whenever you use TCP/IP tools such as Ping. You can find the Hosts file in *\%SystemRoot%*\System32\Drivers\Etc.

This file is not dynamic; all entries are made manually. The file format is the following:

```
172.16.48.10            testpc1  # Remarks are denoted with a #.
```

The IP address and friendly host name are always separated by one or more space or tab characters.

The following Hosts file problems can cause networking errors:

- The Hosts file does not contain the particular host name.

- The host name in the Hosts file or in the command is misspelled.

- The IP address for the host name in the Hosts file is invalid or incorrect.

- The Hosts file contains multiple entries for the same host on separate lines. Because the Hosts file is parsed from the top, the first entry found is used.

Check Your DNS Configuration

If you are using DNS, be sure that the IP addresses of the DNS servers are correct and in the proper order. Use Ping with the remote computer's host name, and then use its IP address to determine whether the host address is being resolved properly. If the host name ping fails and the IP address ping succeeds, the problem is with name resolution. You can test whether the DNS servers are running by pinging their IP addresses or by opening a Telnet session to port 53 on the DNS server. If the connection is established successfully, the DNS service is working on the DNS server. After you've verified that the DNS service is running, you can perform Nslookup queries to the DNS server to further verify the status of the records for which you are looking.

If ping by IP address and by name fail, the problem is with network connectivity, such as basic connectivity or routing. For more information about troubleshooting network connectivity, see "Troubleshooting Routing" later in this chapter.

For a brief summary about how DNS resolves host names, see "Name Resolution Using DNS" earlier in this chapter.

DNS Error Messages

Errors in name resolution can occur when the entries in a DNS server or client are not configured correctly, when the DNS server is not running, or when there is a problem with network connectivity. To determine the cause of any name resolution problem, you can use the Nslookup tool.

Failed queries return a variety of messages, depending on whether the name cannot be resolved, whether the server does not provide a response, or the request times out. The server might be offline, the host computer might not have the DNS service enabled, or there might be a hardware or routing problem.

Troubleshooting IP Addressing

If host name resolution occurs successfully, the problem might lie elsewhere. In this case, the problem might be simply a matter of correcting the IP configuration rather than examining the name resolution process.

TCP/IP troubleshooting generally follows a set pattern. In general, first verify that the problem computer's TCP/IP configuration is correct, and then verify that a connection and a route exist between the computer and destination host by using Ping.

Compile a list of what works and what doesn't work, and then study the list to help isolate the failure. If link reliability is in question, try a large number of pings of various sizes at different times of the day, and plot the success rate or use the PathPing tool.

Check Configuration with Ipconfig

When troubleshooting a TCP/IP networking problem, begin by checking the TCP/IP configuration on the computer experiencing the problem. Use the **ipconfig** command to get the host computer configuration information, including the IP address, subnet mask, and default gateway.

When Ipconfig is used with the **/all** switch, it produces a detailed configuration report for all interfaces, including any configured remote access adapters. Ipconfig output can be redirected to a file and pasted into other documents. To do so, type **ipconfig** >*directory\file name*. The output is placed in the directory you specified with the file name you specified.

The output of Ipconfig can be reviewed to find any problems in the computer network configuration. For example, if a computer has been configured with an IP address that is a duplicate of an existing IP address that has already been detected, the subnet mask appears as 0.0.0.0.

If no problems appear in the TCP/IP configuration, the next step is to test the ability to connect to other host computers on the TCP/IP network.

Test Network Connection with Ping and PathPing

Ping is a tool that helps to verify IP-level connectivity; PathPing is a tool that detects packet loss over multiple-hop trips. When troubleshooting, the **ping** command is used to send an ICMP Echo Request to a target host name or IP address. Use Ping whenever you want to verify that a host computer can send IP packets to a destination host. You can also use the Ping tool to isolate network hardware problems and incompatible configurations.

Note If you call **ipconfig /all** and receive a response, there is no need to ping the loopback address and your own IP address—Ipconfig has already done so to generate the report.

It is best to verify that a route exists between the local computer and a network host by first using Ping and the IP address of the network host to which you want to connect. The command syntax is:

ping <*IP address*>

Perform the following steps when using Ping:

1. Ping the loopback address to verify that TCP/IP is installed and configured correctly on the local computer.

   ping 127.0.0.1

   If the loopback step fails, the IP stack is not responding. This might be because the TCP drivers are corrupted, the network adapter might not be working, or another service is interfering with IP.

2. Ping the IP address of the local computer to verify that it was added to the network correctly. Note that if the routing table is correct, this simply forwards the packet to the loopback address of 127.0.0.1.

   ping *<IP address of local host>*

3. Ping the IP address of the default gateway to verify that the default gateway is functioning and that you can communicate with a local host on the local network.

   ping *<IP address of default gateway>*

4. Ping the IP address of a remote host to verify that you can communicate through a router.

   ping *<IP address of remote host>*

5. Ping the host name of a remote host to verify that you can resolve a remote host name.

   ping *<Host name of remote host>*

6. Run a PathPing analysis to a remote host to verify that the routers on the way to the destination are operating correctly.

   pathping *<IP address of remote host>*

Note If your local address is returned as 169.254.*y.z*, you have been assigned an IP address by the Automatic Private IP Addressing (APIPA) feature of Windows 2000. This means that the local DHCP server is not configured properly or cannot be reached from your computer, and an IP address has been assigned automatically with a subnet mask of 255.255.0.0. Restart the Windows 2000 Professional–based computer, and see if the networking problem persists.

If your local address is returned as 0.0.0.0, the Microsoft MediaSense software override started because the network adapter detects that it is not connected to a network. To correct this problem, turn off MediaSense by making sure that the network adapter and network cable are connected to a hub. If the connection is solid, reinstall the network adapter's drivers or a new network adapter.

Ping uses host name resolution to resolve a computer name to an IP address, so if pinging by IP address succeeds, but fails by name, then the problem lies in host name resolution, not network connectivity. For more information about troubleshooting host name resolution, see "Troubleshooting Name Resolution" earlier in this chapter.

If you cannot use Ping successfully at any point, check the following:

- The local computer's IP address is valid and appears correctly in the **IP Address** tab of the **Internet Protocol (TCP/IP) Properties** dialog box or when using the Ipconfig tool.

- A default gateway is configured and the link between the host and the default gateway is operational. For troubleshooting purposes, make sure that only one default gateway is configured. While it is possible to configure more than one default gateway, gateways beyond the first are only used when the IP stack determines that the original gateway is not functioning. Because the point of troubleshooting is to determine the status of the first configured gateway, delete all others to simplify your troubleshooting.

- IP Security is not currently enabled. In some cases, IPSec functions interfere with ping packets being sent to or from a remote host. For more information about IPSec, see "Configuring IPSec Policies" earlier in this chapter.

Important If the remote system being pinged is across a high-delay link such as a satellite link, responses might take longer to be returned. The **-w** (wait) switch can be used to specify a longer time-out.

Clear ARP Cache

If you can ping both the loopback address and your own IP address, the next step is to clear out the ARP cache and reload it. This can be done by using the Arp tool. Use commands **arp -a** or **arp -g** to display the cache contents. Delete the entries with **arp -d** *<IP address>*.

Verify Default Gateway

Next, look at the default gateway. The gateway address must be on the same network as the local host; if not, no messages from the host computer can be forwarded to any location outside the local network. Next, check to make sure that the default gateway address is correct as entered. Finally, check to see that the default gateway is a router, not just a host, and that it is enabled to forward IP datagrams.

Ping Remote Host

If the default gateway responds correctly, ping a remote host to ensure that network-to-network communications are operating as expected. If this fails, use Tracert to examine the path to the destination. For IP routers that are Windows NT or Windows 2000–based computers, use the Route tool or the Routing and Remote Access administrative tool on those computers to examine the IP route table. For IP routers that are not Windows NT or Windows 2000–based computers, use the appropriate tool or facility to examine the IP route table.

Four error messages are commonly returned by Ping during troubleshooting as shown in Table 22.13.

Table 22.13   Ping Error Messages

Error Message	Meaning and Action
TTL Expired in Transit	Number of required hops exceeds TTL. Increase TTL by using the **ping -i** switch.
Destination Host Unreachable	A local or remote route does not exist for destination host. Modify the local route table or notify the router administrator.
Request Timed Out	No Echo Reply messages were received due to network traffic, failure of the ARP request packet filtering, or router error. Increase wait time using the **ping -w** switch.
Unknown Host	Destination host name cannot be resolved. Verify name and availability of DNS servers.

Check IP Security

IPSec can increase the defenses of a network, but it can also make changing network configurations or troubleshooting problems more difficult. In some cases, IPSec running on a Windows 2000 Professional–based computer can create difficulties in connecting to a remote host. If IPSec is implemented locally, turn off IPSec and attempt to run the requested network service or function.

▶ **To disable local IPSec policies**

1. In Control Panel, double-click **Network and Dial-up Connections**.

2. Right-click the local area connection you want to change, and then select **Properties**.

3. Select **Internet Protocol (TCP/IP)**, and then click **Properties**.

4. Click **Advanced**.

5. Click the **Options** tab.

6. Select **IP Security**, and then click **Properties**.

7. Click **Do not use IPSEC**, and then click **OK**.

If IPSec is implemented through IPSec policies at a Windows 2000 domain controller, contact the security administrator to disable the security policy for that computer.

If the problem disappears when IPSec policies are turned off, you know that the additional IPSec processing burden or its packet filtering are responsible for the problem. Contact the security administrator to permanently modify the IPSec policy for the computer.

For more information about IPSec issues, see "Configuring IPSec Policies" earlier in this chapter.

Check Packet Filtering

Any mistakes in packet filtering can make address resolution or connectivity fail. To determine if packet filtering is the source of a network problem, you must disable the TCP/IP packet filtering.

▶ **To disable TCP/IP packet filtering**

1. In Control Panel, double-click the **Network and Dial-Up Connections**.
2. Right-click the **Local Area Connection**, and then click **Properties**.
3. Select **Internet Protocol (TCP/IP)**, and then click the **Properties** tab.
4. Click **Advanced**, and then click **Options**.
5. In the **Optional Settings** window, click **TCP/IP Filtering,** and then click the **Properties** tab.
6. Clear the **Enable TCP/IP Filtering (All Adapters)** check box, and then click **OK**.

Try pinging an address by using its DNS name, its NetBIOS name, or its IP address. If the attempt succeeds, the packet filtering options might be misconfigured or might be too restrictive. For instance, the filtering might permit the computer to act as a Web server, but might in the process disable tools like Ping or remote administration. Restore a wider range of permissible filtering options by changing the permitted TCP, UDP, and IP port values.

If the attempt still fails, another form of packet filtering might still be interfering with your networking. For more information about Routing and Remote Access service filtering functions, see "Unicast IP Routing" in the *Internetworking Guide*. For more information about IPSec packet filtering, see "Internet Protocol Security" earlier in this chapter.

Troubleshooting Routing

Windows 2000 supports routing on both single- and multi-homed computers with or without the Routing and Remote Access service. The Routing and Remote Access service includes the Routing Information Protocol (RIP) and the Open Shortest Path First (OSPF) routing protocols. Routers can use RIP or OSPF to dynamically exchange routing information.

For more information about TCP/IP routing, see "Unicast IP Routing" in the *Internetworking Guide*. For information about troubleshooting IP multicast routing, see "IP Multicast Support" in the *Internetworking Guide*.

Cannot Connect to a Specific Server

To determine the cause of connection problems when trying to connect to a specific server using NetBIOS-based connections, use the **nbtstat -n** command to determine what name the server used to register on the network.

Nbtstat -n output lists several names that the computer has registered. A name resembling the computer's name as shown on the desktop must be present. If not, try one of the other unique names displayed by Nbtstat.

The Nbtstat tool can also display the cached entries for remote computers from either #PRE entries in the Lmhosts file or from recently resolved names. If the name the remote computers are using for the server is the same, and the other computers are on a remote subnet, be sure that they have the computer's mapping in their Lmhosts files or WINS servers.

Connection to Remote Host Hangs

To determine why a TCP/IP connection to a remote computer is not working properly, use the **netstat -a** command to show the status of all activity on TCP and UDP ports on the local computer.

A good TCP connection usually shows 0 bytes in the Sent and Received queues. If data is blocked in either queue or if the state is irregular, the connection is probably faulty. If not, you are probably experiencing network or application delay.

Examining the Routing Table with Route

For two hosts to exchange IP datagrams, they must both have a route to each other, or use default gateways that know of a route. Normally, routers exchange information with each other by using a routing protocol such as RIP. For information about how to examine and configure the local route table, see "Configuring Local Route Table" earlier in this chapter.

Examine Paths with Tracert

Tracert is a route tracing tool that uses incrementally higher values in the TTL field in the IP header to determine the route from one host to another through a network. It does this by sending ICMP Echo Request messages and analyzing ICMP error messages that return. Tracert allows you to track the path of a forwarded packet from router to router for up to 30 hops. If a router has failed or if the packet is routed into a loop, Tracert reveals the problem. After the problem router is found, its administrator can be contacted if it is an offsite router, or the router can be restored to fully functional status if it is under your control.

Troubleshooting Gateways

If you see the message "Your default gateway does not belong to one of the configured interfaces..." during setup, find out whether the default gateway is located on the same logical network as the computer's network adapter. The easiest way to do this is to compare the network ID portion of the default gateway's IP address with the network IDs of the computer's network adapters. In other words, check that the bitwise logical AND of the IP address and the subnet mask equals the bitwise logical AND of the default gateway and the subnet mask.

For example, a computer with a single network adapter configured with an IP address of 172.16.27.139 and a subnet mask of 255.255.0.0 requires a default gateway of the form 172.16.*y.z*. The network ID of the IP interface is 172.16.0.0. Using the subnet mask, TCP/IP can determine that all traffic on this network is local; everything else must be sent to the gateway.

Additional Resources

- For more information about creating IP security policies, see "Internet Protocol Security" in the *TCP/IP Core Networking Guide.*

- For more information about the design and structure of the Active Directory, see chapters under "Active Directory" in the *Microsoft® Windows® 2000 Server Resource Kit Distributed Systems Guide.*

- For more information about Group Policy, see chapters under "Desktop Configuration Management" in the *Microsoft® Windows® 2000 Server Distributed Systems Guide.*

- For more information about Quality of Service, see "Quality of Service" in the *TCP/IP Core Networking Guide.*

- For more information about IP multicast support, see "IP Multicast Support" in the *Internetworking Guide.*

- For more information about configuring virtual private networks, see "Local and Remote Networking" in this book.

C H A P T E R   2 3

Windows 2000 Professional on Microsoft Networks

Microsoft® Windows® 2000 Professional can be a member of a variety of network configurations, from a small home network consisting of two computers, to a large enterprise network comprising thousands of computers worldwide. This chapter describes the network environments where you can use Windows 2000 Professional.

In This Chapter

Related Information in the Resource Kit

- For more information about configuring TCP/IP in Windows 2000 Professional, see "TCP/IP in Windows 2000 Professional" in this book.

- For more information about account authentication in Windows 2000 domains, see "Security" in this book.

- For more information about implementing Windows 2000 Group Policy on a Windows 2000 Professional client, see "Defining Client Administration and Configuration Standards" in the *Microsoft® Windows® 2000 Server Resource Kit Deployment Planning Guide.*

Quick Guide to Windows 2000 Professional on Microsoft Networks

This section provides a quick glance at the topics and tasks related to adding a Windows 2000 Professional client to a Windows domain or workgroup. Use the quick guide to find the information or task you are seeking.

 Assess the current networking environment.

To add a Windows 2000 Professional–based computer to a network, you must determine if the computer is to be added to a Windows 2000 domain, a Microsoft® Windows NT® domain, or a workgroup consisting of computers running Microsoft network-compatible software, including Microsoft® Windows® 95 and Microsoft® Windows® 98. The network environment determines the authentication methods you choose to access the network, the means you choose to enforce desktop and security rules (group and system policies), and the method you use to handle logon scripts.

- See "Overview of Microsoft Networking" later in this chapter.

 Ensure that the network protocol (NetBEUI or TCP/IP) is installed and properly configured.

Before you can add a Windows 2000 Professional computer to the existing network environment, you must first establish client connectivity. Two common protocols used for network connectivity are NetBIOS Enhanced User Interface (NetBEUI) and Transmission Control Protocol/Internet Protocol (TCP/IP). Although NetBEUI is commonly used in small-sized to medium-sized networks, TCP/IP is a more scalable network protocol and the standard protocol for access to the Internet. Install and configure the protocol to meet the connectivity needs of the Windows 2000 Professional client.

- See "Configure Transport Protocols" later in this chapter.

Join the network environment that meets your specifications.

A user with appropriate permissions can join a domain or workgroup by using a number of different methods. You can create the computer account during Windows 2000 Professional installation. Use the Network Identification wizard to join the Windows 2000 Professional–based computer to a specified domain or workgroup. You can manually add a computer to a network by using the **Network Identification** tab of the My Computer properties sheet. Specify the name of the domain or workgroup to be joined.

- See "Join Network Environment" later in this chapter.

Verify that a Windows 2000 Professional–based computer has successfully joined the network environment.

To verify that a Windows 2000 Professional–based client has been added to the network, attempt to log on to the domain where you added the computer, or log on locally if you added the computer to a workgroup. In a domain environment, verify that logon scripts function as designed and that no conflicts occur between local Group Policy and Windows NT system policy or Windows 2000 domain Group Policy settings

See "Confirm Group Membership" later in this chapter.

 Perform troubleshooting tasks for Windows networks.

If a user is unable to log on to a workgroup by using a local account or to a domain by using an account residing at a domain controller, perform troubleshooting tasks to determine the nature of the problem and to resolve the problem.

- See "Troubleshooting Microsoft Networking" later in this chapter.

Overview of Microsoft Networking

This section describes the features and technical aspects of Microsoft networking including new networking features implemented in Windows 2000 Professional. The authentication methods, logon procedures, policy procedures, protocols, and resource allocation used in each environment are also explored.

What's New

The networking capabilities of Windows 2000 are built upon the foundation of features found in Windows NT. The improvements made in Windows 2000 result in a scalable networking platform that you can implement in a variety of environments, from a small office/home office configuration, to a powerful workstation within a multidomain enterprise.

The improvements made in Windows 2000 Professional can be categorized into three areas, each of which is presented in this chapter:

- Directory services
- Account authentication
- Policy handling

Directory Services

A directory service provides information about objects in a network environment, including user and computer accounts, and shared resources such as printers and directories. Active Directory™, the directory service included with Windows 2000, is the Microsoft domain-based directory service found in Windows 2000 domains, which presents domain information in a hierarchical, object-oriented fashion. Active Directory provides several advantages not found in the Security Access Manager (SAM) account database used in the Windows NT 4.0 domain environment:

- Active Directory can be accessed by a variety of domain clients, by Active Directory–aware applications and by non–Active Directory applications that use industry protocols, such as Lightweight Directory Access Protocol (LDAP).

- The Active Directory hierarchy is flexible and configurable, so organizations can organize resources in a way that optimizes data usability and manageability.

- Active Directory stores network-related information as objects. These objects can be assigned attributes, which describe specific characteristics about the object. This allows administrators to assign a wide range of information in the directory and tightly control access to it.

- Active Directory can be scaled to meet the requirements of many enterprises, having been tested with up to one million objects per directory.

- Active Directory uses multiple-master replication, where changes made to any of the copies of the directory are automatically replicated throughout the enterprise. This is an advantage over the replication process in Windows NT, where all changes must be made through a master directory replica.

Active Directory is available only on Windows 2000 domain controllers, although an Active Directory domain can consist of heterogeneous clients, including Microsoft Windows NT version 4.0, Windows 95 and Windows 98, and UNIX workstations. For more information about Active Directory, see "Windows NT Domain Environments" later in this chapter.

Account Authentication

Windows 2000 uses Kerberos security as the default authentication method for domain and local access. The Kerberos v5 authentication protocol is an industry-supported distributed security protocol based on Internet standard security.

Windows 2000 also supports NTLM security as a method for account authentication. NTLM is used as the account authentication method in Windows NT domains. For more information about Kerberos security, see "Account Authentication" in this chapter.

Policy Handling

In a Windows NT domain, administrators use system policy to control the user work environment and to enforce system configuration settings. In a Windows 2000 domain, Group Policy settings are the administrator's primary method for enabling centralized change and configuration management. A domain administrator can create Group Policy settings at a Windows 2000 domain controller to create a specific system configuration for a particular group of users and computers. Group policy can be used to:

- Enable IntelliMirror™ management technologies to automatically install assigned applications and provide location independence for roaming users.
- Permit desktop customization and lockdown.
- Configure security policies.

Group Policy settings can also be created locally for individual workstation, and for customized environments that differ from the domain's.

For more information about Group Policy, see "Group and System Policies" in this chapter.

Comparison of Windows 2000 Features

Table 23.1 compares the features implemented in Windows 2000 to those in Windows 98 and Windows NT 4.0.

Table 23.1   Comparison of Windows 2000 Networking Features

Windows 2000 Networking Feature	Windows 98	Windows NT 4.0
Directory Services		
Can be a member of a Windows 2000 domain.	Yes	Yes
Can be a member of a Windows NT domain.	Yes	Yes
Can access Active Directory.	Yes[1]	No
Account Authentication		
Uses Kerberos default account authentication.	No	No
Uses NTLM default account authentication.	Yes	Yes
Policy Handling		
Can use Windows 2000 Group Policy settings.	No	No
Can use Windows NT system policies.	Yes	Yes

[1]You must install Active Directory client software before a Windows 98–based client can access Active Directory.

Peer-to-peer Network Environments

A *peer-to-peer network* (also known as a *workgroup*) is a single-subnet network that is used as a convenient way to connect a small number of users to share resources. Peer-to-peer clients have the identical level of authority on a network, which eliminates the need for domain controllers. User authentication is decentralized, with the local account database located on each client. A user must have a user account on each computer in order to gain access. Figure 23.1 shows an example of a peer-to-peer network.

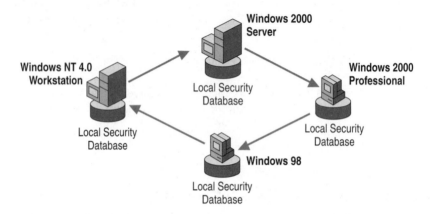

Figure 23.1   Peer-to-Peer Network

Peer-to-peer networks are ideal for small office/home office (SOHO) configurations consisting of two to ten users, where a user needs to use more than one computer and also needs to be able to share resources from one computer to another, such as files, applications, or printers.

Windows 2000 Professional is compatible with all Microsoft products that use the server message block (SMB) protocol. This includes support for peer-to-peer networking with other Microsoft networking products, including Microsoft® LAN Manager, Microsoft® Windows® 3.*x*, Microsoft® Windows® for Workgroups, Windows 95, Windows 98, Microsoft® Windows NT® Workstation, and Microsoft® Workgroup Add-on for MS-DOS® networking software for computers running MS-DOS.

Windows 2000 Professional in a peer-to-peer environment performs account authentication locally. Windows 2000 Professional attempts Kerberos authentication first, searching for the local Kerberos Key Distribution Center (KDC). If the KDC service is not found for Kerberos authentication, Windows 2000 Professional uses NTLM security to authenticate users in the local account database. For more information about account authentication, see "Account Authentication" later in this chapter.

Peer-to-peer networks communicate with clients and servers that share a common protocol. Although they are independent of any networking protocol, the NetBEUI protocol was historically chosen because of its small size, speed, and minimal setup requirements. However, a peer-to-peer network with NetBEUI as its only transport protocol is unable to access the Internet or communicate with any workgroups or domains outside its subnet. Therefore, TCP/IP is now seen as the preferred protocol choice. For more information about configuring these protocols, see "TCP/IP In Windows 2000 Professional" in this book and also see "Configuring Transport Protocols" later in this chapter.

Windows NT Domain Environments

A *domain* is a logical grouping of networked computers that share a central directory database that contains user account and security information for resources within the domain.

In a domain, the directory database resides on computers that are configured as domain controllers. A domain controller manages all security-related aspects of user/domain interactions. Security and administration are centralized. Figure 23.2 shows an example of a domain configuration.

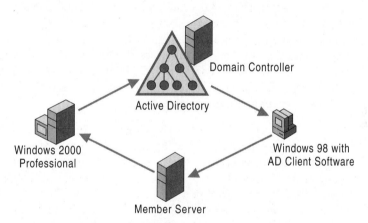

Figure 23.2   Example of a Domain-based Network

In a domain with more than one domain controller, the domain accounts database is replicated between domain controllers within the domain for better scalability and fault tolerance.

The primary difference between domains implemented in Windows NT and those implemented in Windows 2000 is the centralized security database. In Windows 2000, Active Directory is the database used to validate user objects. Additionally, differences in authentication methods, network naming methods, and handling of system policies differentiate the two network operating systems.

Windows 2000 Professional provides full compatibility with Windows NT and Windows 2000 domains.

Note For a complete discussion of whether to migrate an existing Windows NT domain to Windows 2000, see "Determining Domain Migration Strategies" in the *Microsoft® Windows® 2000 Server Resource Kit Deployment Planning Guide.*

Windows 2000 Active Directory

A *directory service* provides a place to store information about network-based entities, such as applications, files, printers, and users. It provides a consistent way to name, describe, locate, access, manage, and secure information about these individual resources.

Active Directory is the Microsoft implementation of a domain-based directory service found in Windows 2000 domains. Active Directory presents domain information in a hierarchical, object-oriented fashion. Active Directory also protects network data from unauthorized access and replicates directory data across a network so that data is not lost if one domain controller fails.

Active Directory is available only on Windows 2000 domain controllers. An Active Directory domain can consist of heterogeneous clients, including Windows NT 4.0, Windows 95 and Windows 98, and UNIX workstations. Clients have full access to shared resources within the domain. However, only Windows 2000 Professional–based, Windows 95–based, or Windows 98–based clients with the Active Directory client software can use Active Directory to query information about these shared resources.

Active Directory uses objects to represent network resources such as users, groups, and computers. Active Directory *objects* are the entities that make up a network. An object is a distinct, named set of attributes that represents something concrete, such as a user, a printer, or an application. Each object is defined by a set of rules, or *schema*. When you create an Active Directory object, Active Directory generates values for some of the object's attributes, and you provide other values. For example, when you create a user object, Active Directory assigns the globally unique identifier (GUID), and you provide values for such attributes as the user's given name, surname, and the logon identifier.

You can place Active Directory objects in *containers* so that you can organize them according to their use or to your enterprise's organizational structure. Active Directory containers can represent organizations, such as the marketing department, or collections of related objects, such as printers. Active Directory organizes information into a tree structure made up of these objects and containers, similar to the way the Windows operating system uses folders and files to organize information on a computer. Figure 23.3 shows an example of an Active Directory domain.

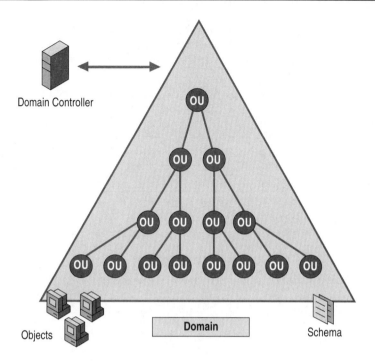

Figure 23.3   Active Directory Domain

Active Directory objects and containers can be created at the Windows 2000 domain controller by the domain administrator. You can create Active Directory objects from the Windows 2000 Professional client if you have sufficient permissions.

Note   For more information about Active Directory objects, see "Active Directory Logical Structure" in the *Microsoft® Windows® 2000 Server Resource Kit Distributed Systems Guide.*

Active Directory Security

A *security identifier* (SID) is a unique number created by the security subsystem of the Windows 2000 and Windows NT operating systems and assigned to security principal objects such as user, group, and computer accounts. Every account on a network is issued a unique SID when that account is first created. For example, when an administrator joins a computer to a Windows 2000 domain, a SID is created for that computer account. Internal processes in the Windows 2000 operating system refer to an account's SID rather than to the account's user or group name.

Each directory object is protected by *access control entries* (ACEs) that identify which users or groups can access that object. An ACE is created for an object by assigning permissions to a shared resource. Each ACE contains the SID of each user or group who has permission to access that object and defines what level of access is allowed. For example, a user might have read-only access to certain files, read-and-write access to others, and no access to others.

If you create an account, delete it, and then create an account with the same user name, the new account does not have the rights or permissions previously granted to the old account because the accounts have different SID numbers.

Note For more information about planning and implementing access permissions, see "Security" in this book.

DNS and Active Directory Domains

The integration of the Domain Name System (DNS) and Active Directory is a central feature of the Windows 2000 Server operating system. Active Directory is integrated with DNS for the following reasons:

- The hierarchical structure of DNS reflects the structure of Active Directory domains.

- DNS zone information can be copied to Active Directory domain controllers to speed name resolution and provide security within the domain.

- DNS is the standard for name resolution, making Windows 2000 clients accessible to non–Windows 2000 clients.

- DNS is the name resolution method of the Internet, making Windows 2000 clients available universally.

To implement Active Directory, one or more DNS servers must be available to the Windows 2000 domain, and DNS client software must be configured at each member computer.

Domain names for Windows 2000 domains are based on the DNS hierarchical naming structure, which is an inverted tree structure: a single root domain, underneath which can be parent and child domains (branches and leaves). For example, a Windows 2000 domain name such as *child.parent.reskit.com* identifies a domain named *child,* which is a child domain of the domain named *parent,* itself a child of the domain reskit.com.

Each computer in a DNS domain is uniquely identified by its fully qualified domain name (FQDN). The FQDN of a computer located in the domain child.parent.reskit.com is *computername.child.parent.reskit.com.* Figure 23.4 shows an example of a Windows 2000 domain that uses the DNS hierarchical naming structure.

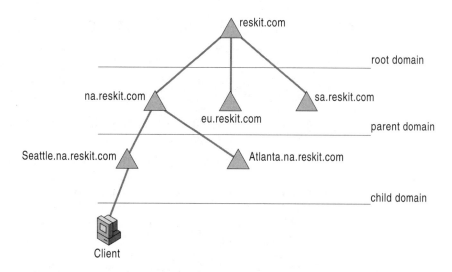

Figure 23.4   Windows 2000 Domain Hierarchy

Every Windows 2000 domain has a DNS name (for example, *supplier01-int.com*), and every Windows 2000-based computer has a DNS name (for example, *AcctServer.supplier01-int.com*). Thus, domains and computers are represented both as Active Directory objects and as DNS nodes (a node in the DNS hierarchy represents a domain or a computer). When a computer is added to a Windows 2000 domain, the FQDN name, consisting of the computer name and domain name, must be specified. This information is provided when the computer account is added to the domain during initial Windows 2000 Setup or after installation, by using the Network Identification wizard or the **Identification Changes** dialog box. For more information about adding Windows 2000 Professional–based clients to a Windows 2000 domain, see "Join Network Environment" later in this chapter.

Although the two namespaces share an identical domain structure, it is important to understand that they are not the same namespace. Each stores different data and therefore manages different objects. DNS stores zones and resource records; Active Directory stores domains and domain objects.

For more information about DNS, see "TCP/IP in Windows 2000 Professional" in this book.

Windows NT 4.0 Account Database

In addition to using the Active Directory account database, Windows 2000 Professional can access the account database used in Windows NT 4.0 domains. As with Active Directory, the Windows NT 4.0 account database includes two types of accounts in its domain environment:

- *Computer accounts*. Determines which Windows NT–based and Windows 2000–based computers can access the domain.

- *User accounts*. Lists the users who can access the domain.

Shared resources defined within the domain are associated with accounts through ACEs, which determine the permissions to domain resources such as shared files and printers. A Windows 2000 Professional–based computer can access objects stored in a Windows NT account database without modification.

In a Windows NT 4.0 domain, an administrator creates and manages user and computer accounts at a Windows NT domain controller. Additionally, you can create user and computer accounts if the account performing the installation has the administrative rights to do so. After you perform the initial Windows 2000 Professional Setup, you can change domain membership at the client by using the Network Identification wizard or the **Identification Changes** dialog box. For more information about adding Windows 2000 Professional–based clients to a Windows NT domain, see "Join Network Environment" in this chapter.

Note For more information about Windows 2000 Professional Setup, see "Windows 2000 Professional Setup" in this book.

A Windows 2000 Professional–based computer attempts to find a Windows 2000 domain controller by using Kerberos authentication. If a domain controller running the Kerberos Key Distribution Center (KDC) service is not found, Windows 2000 Professional looks for a Windows NT 4.0 domain controller and uses NTLM security to authenticate users in the domain's account database.

Account Authentication

A computer and its information should be protected from unauthorized access. Windows 2000 secures the computer through *account authentication,* which restricts the ability of a user to access a computer or domain. Account authentication is the process of confirming the identity of a user—either by typing in a user name and password or by inserting a smart card into a card reader —and comparing it with an entry in the account database. After authentication identifies the user, the user is granted access to a specific set of network resources based on permissions. Authorization takes place through the mechanism of *access control*, using access control lists (ACLs) that define permissions on file systems, network file and print shares, and entries in the account database.

Account authentication is performed in two methods:

- Authentication by the local account database for computers in workgroups and stand-alone computers

- Authentication by a domain account database located on a domain controller for computers in a domain.

Note Creation of a user account in a Windows NT 4.0 domain does not automatically grant local logon rights to a Windows 2000 Professional–based computer. To grant local logon rights to a computer, a local user account must be explicitly created. For more information about creating local user accounts, see "Security" in this book.

Windows 2000 uses Kerberos security as the default authentication method for domain and local access. The Kerberos v5 authentication protocol is an industry-supported distributed security protocol based on Internet standard security.

Windows 2000 Professional also supports NTLM security as a method for account authentication. NTLM is used as the account authentication method when users log on to Windows NT, either locally or through a domain.

When you log on to a Windows domain, Windows 2000 Professional uses both authentication procedures. Windows 2000 Professional attempts to use Kerberos as the primary source of user authentication, searching for the Kerberos *Key Distribution Center* (KDC) service at the domain controller. KDC is the account authentication service that runs on all Windows 2000 domain controllers.

If the KDC service is not found at the domain controller for Kerberos authentication, Windows 2000 uses NTLM security to authenticate users in the domain's Windows NT account database by using the Security Account Manager (SAM) service at the Windows NT domain controller.

When users log on locally, the procedure is similar, but all authentication takes place locally. If the KDC service is not available when a user logs on to a computer, Kerberos cannot authenticate the user. Windows 2000 Professional then attempts authentication by using the NTLM security system for compatibility with Windows NT domain controllers.

Logon authentication to a Windows NT domain uses the following steps:

1. The user types a user name and password. The Graphical Identification and Authentication (GINA) component collects the user name and password.

2. GINA passes the secure information to the Local Security Authority (LSA) for authentication.

3. The LSA passes the information to the Security Support Provider Interface (SSPI). SSPI is an interface that communicates to both Kerberos and NTLM services.

4. SSPI passes the user name and password to the Kerberos security support provider.

5. The user name and password is passed to a nonexistent Kerberos server, which generates an error message.

6. The internal error message triggers SSPI to start the process over again with GINA. GINA passes the information to LSA again, and then LSA passes the information to SSPI again.

7. SSPI passes the user name and password to the NTLM driver. The NTLM driver uses the Net Logon service to validate the user against the local Security Access Manager (SAM) database.

8. The local Net Logon service sends the request to the Net Logon service on the domain controller.

9. The domain controller's Net Logon service passes the request to the domain controller's SAM.

10. The SAM queries the directory database for user name and password approval.

11. The SAM of the domain controller passes the result of the logon attempt to the domain controller's Net Logon service.

12. The Net Logon service of the domain controller passes the result to the Net Logon service of the client.

13. The Net Logon service passes the result to the Local Security Authority of the client, which generates an access token with the granted access rights.

The user will receive the following error message only if both Kerberos and NTLM fail to authenticate your user account:

```
The system could not log you on. Make sure your User name and domain are
correct, then type your password again. Letters in passwords must be
typed using the correct case. Make sure that Caps Lock is not
accidentally on.
```

Note This error message is the same whether the password is typed incorrectly or the user name is not in the local SAM database. This is done to increase security.

Logon Names

A unique logon name is required for users to gain access to a domain and its resources. In a domain environment, a user is a type of security principal. A *security principal* is an object to which Windows security is applied in the form of authentication and authorization. Users are authenticated (their identity is verified) at the time they log on to the domain or local computer. They are authorized (allowed or denied access) when they use resources.

A user security principal can have two types of logon names, depending on the user's domain or workgroup membership: a *SAM account name* and/or a *user principal name*:

- *SAM Account Name.* A SAM account name is a name that is required for compatibility with Windows NT 4.0 domains and workgroups. In a Windows NT domain or workgroup, every account name must be unique.

- *User Principal Name.* In a Windows 2000 domain, an account can have a user principal name in addition to its SAM account name. The user principal name consists of the user name, the "at" sign (@), and a user principal name suffix. For example, the user James Smith, who has a user account in the reskit.com domain, might have the user principal name JSmith@reskit.com. The user principal name usually reflects the hierarchical structure of the domain; however, an account administrator might choose an alternative naming convention if the domain structure is complex or is difficult to remember.

  The user principal name is independent of the *distinguished name* of the user object, which is the name that identifies the object and its location within Active Directory. As it is the distinguished name that differentiates the object, not the SAM or user principal names, two accounts can have the same SAM account name. Additionally, a user object can be moved or renamed without affecting the user principal name and can have multiple user principal names.

Group and System Policies

In Windows NT 4.0, Microsoft introduced System Policy Editor, which is used to specify user and computer configurations that are stored in the Windows NT registry. With the System Policy Editor, administrators can create a system policy to control the user work environment and to enforce system configuration settings for all computers running either Windows NT 4.0 Workstation or Windows NT 4.0 Server.

There are 72 policy settings in Windows NT 4.0. These settings:

- Are limited to assigning the values of registry entries based on .adm files.

- Can only be applied to users on Windows NT–based computers, or Windows 95–based and Windows 98–based computers within a domain.

- Are controlled by user name and membership in security groups.

- Are not secure.

- Remain in users' profiles until the specified policy is reversed or until the user edits the registry.

- Are primarily used to customize desktop environments.

In Windows 2000, Group Policy settings are the administrator's primary method for enabling centralized change and configuration management. A domain administrator can use Group Policy at a Windows 2000 domain controller to create a specific desktop configuration for a particular group of users and computers. You can also create local Group Policy settings for individual workstations to customize environments that differ from the domain's. The Microsoft® Management Console (MMC) Group Policy snap-in replaces the Windows NT 4.0 System Policy Editor and gives the administrator greater control over configuration settings for groups of computers and users.

With more than 100 security-related settings and more than 450 registry-based settings, Windows 2000 Group Policy provides a broad range of options for managing the user's environment. Windows 2000 Group Policy has the following attributes:

- Defined in a Windows 2000 domain or defined locally.

- Extended using Microsoft Management Console (MMC) or .adm files.

- Is secure.

- Does not leave settings in the users' profiles when the effective policy is changed or removed.

- Applied to users or computers in a specified Active Directory container (sites, domains, and organizational units).

- Further controlled by user or computer membership in security groups.

- Used to configure many types of security settings.

- Used to apply logon, logoff, startup, and shutdown scripts.

- Used to install and maintain software (Windows 2000 domain-based policies only).

- Used to redirect folders (such as My Documents and Application Data).

- Used to perform maintenance on Microsoft® Internet Explorer (Windows 2000 domain-based policies only).

You can use the Group Policy MMC snap-in to edit local Group Policy objects to make the following changes at the local computer:

- Define security settings for a local computer only, not for a domain or network.

- Use administrative templates to set more than 450 operating system behaviors.

- Use scripts to automate computer startup and shutdown as well as automate how a user logs on and off.

On a stand-alone computer running Windows 2000 Professional, local Group Policy objects are located at \%SystemRoot%\System32\GroupPolicy.

For more information about implementing Group Policy within a Windows 2000 domain, see "Group Policy" in the *Microsoft® Windows® 2000 Server Resource Kit Distributed Systems Guide*.

System Policy and Group Policy Coexistence

You might have instances where Windows NT system policy must coexist with Windows 2000 Group Policy. Two possible scenarios are:

- A Windows 2000 Professional–based computer uses local Group Policy with Windows NT 4.0 system policy to enable Windows 2000 security settings.

- A Windows 2000 Professional–based computer is in a Windows NT 4.0 domain that you are in the process of migrating to Windows 2000; user and computer accounts are split between the two domains.

In an environment where Windows NT system policy exists with Windows 2000 Group Policy, the resulting computer and user configuration is dependent on the following factors:

- The location of the user account (Windows NT or Windows 2000 domain controller).

- The location of the computer account (Windows NT or Windows 2000 domain controller).

- The activity taking place (a computer starting up, a user logging on, or a refresh of the user or system accounts).

Table 23.2 summarizes the expected behavior of computer and user accounts in an environment where Windows NT system policy coexists with Windows 2000 Group Policy.

Table 23.2   Expected Behaviors of System Policies/Group Policy Settings

Environment	Account Object Location	Result at Windows 2000 Professional Client
Pure Windows NT 4.0	Computer: Windows NT 4.0	**At computer startup**: Computer local Group Policy (only if changed). **Every time the user logs on**: Computer system policy.
	Computer refresh	**Before Control-Alt-Delete**: Computer local Group Policy only. **After the user logs on**: Computer local Group Policy and computer system policy.
	User: Windows NT 4.0	**When the user logs on**: User system policy. **If local Group Policy changes**: User local Group Policy and user system policy.
	User refresh	User local Group Policy and user system policy.
Mixed (migration)	Computer: Windows NT 4.0	**At computer startup**: Computer local Group Policy (only if changed). **Every time the user logs on**: Computer system policy.
	Computer refresh	**Before Control-Alt-Delete**: Computer local Group Policy only. **After the user logs on**: Computer local Group Policy and computer system policy.
	User: Windows 2000	**When the user logs on**: Group Policy is processed after computer system policy.
	User refresh	User Group Policy.
Mixed (migration)	Computer: Windows 2000	**During system startup**: Group Policy.
	Computer refresh	Computer Group Policy.
	User: Windows NT 4.0	**When the user logs on**: User system policy. **If local Group Policy changes**: User local Group Policy and user system policy.
	User refresh	User local Group Policy and user system policy.
Windows 2000	Computer: Windows 2000	**During computer startup and when the user logs on**: Group Policy.
	User: Windows 2000	
Workgroup	Local	Local Group Policy only.

Note In a system environment where local Group Policy on a Windows 2000 Professional–based computer exists with a Windows NT 4.0 domain policy, you must check that the policies do not conflict or override each other. For example, in a Windows NT 4.0 domain with computer system policies enabled, a Windows 2000 Professional–based computer with local Group Policy processes both policies at computer refresh and after the user logs on.

For more information about implementing Windows 2000 Group Policy on a Windows 2000 migration client, see "Defining Client Administration and Configuration Standards" in the *Microsoft® Windows® 2000 Server Resource Kit Deployment Planning Guide*.

Logon Scripts

A logon script is a batch file (*.bat or *.cmd), executable, or procedure (including VBScript, JavaScript or Windows Script Host) that you can use to configure the user environment after the system or Group Policy is enabled. Logon scripts are often used to set up network directory and printer shares or start maintenance applications, such as an antivirus application.

The functionality of logon scripts that were designed for a Windows NT domain does not change in the Windows 2000 Professional–based client; however, you need to test logon scripts after you perform migration to verify that your applications and procedures are compatible with Windows 2000 Professional.

Transport Protocols

You need to configure the Windows 2000 Professional–based client to use the same transport protocol used by other clients within its domain or workgroup in order to communicate with the other clients. If other clients already exist within the network, simply install the same protocol on the workstation that you are configuring and specify the appropriate settings. However, if this is the first Windows 2000 Professional–based computer in a workgroup environment, the administrator must decide which protocol to use. This section describes the most widely used networking protocols in a workgroup environment: TCP/IP and NetBEUI.

Note For more information about installing and configuring the Internetwork Packet Exchange/Sequenced Packet Exchange (IPX/SPX) protocol on a Windows 2000 Professional–based client, see "Interoperability with NetWare" in this book.

TCP/IP

Transmission Control Protocol/Internet Protocol (TCP/IP) is the most widely used network protocol. Windows 2000 includes a complete implementation of the standard, routable TCP/IP protocol suite, which is often the protocol of choice for medium-sized to enterprise-sized networks. TCP/IP provides the following benefits:

- Support for Internet connectivity.

- Ability to route packets, which allows you to divide networks into subnets to optimize networking performance or to facilitate network management.

- Connectivity across interconnected networks that use different operating systems and hardware platforms, including communication with many non-Microsoft systems, such as Internet hosts, Apple Macintosh systems, IBM mainframes, UNIX systems, and Open Virtual Memory System (VMS) systems.

- Support for automatic TCP/IP configuration by using Dynamic Host Configuration Protocol (DHCP).

- Support for Automatic Private IP Addressing (APIPA), allowing computers in small networks without a DHCP server to automatically assign themselves IP addresses.

- Support for automatic mapping of IP addresses to NetBIOS names by using Windows Internet Name Service (WINS) servers.

- Support for the network basic input/output system (NetBIOS) interface, commonly known as NetBIOS over TCP/IP.

- Performance enhancements, including a larger default TCP receive window size and selective acknowledgments.

- TCP/IP is used for Internet access, including HTTP, FTP and other communications protocols.

TCP/IP is installed in the default installation of Windows 2000 Professional and can be configured during Setup or after system installation.

For more information about features of TCP/IP in Windows 2000 Professional, see "TCP/IP in Windows 2000 Professional" in this book.

NetBEUI

Windows 2000 Professional includes an implementation of the NetBIOS Enhanced User Interface (NetBEUI). This protocol is fully compatible with previous versions of Microsoft networking products, including Windows NT, Windows for Workgroups, LAN Manager, and Windows 98. In Windows 2000, NetBEUI includes support for the NetBIOS programming interface.

NetBEUI is often selected as the transport protocol for single-subnet Windows NT domains and workgroups consisting of 2 to 200 computers where Internet access is not required. As such, NetBEUI is optimized for high performance when you use it in departmental local area networks (LANs) or LAN segments. In Windows 2000, NetBEUI is completely self-tuning and is a simple protocol to implement, requiring no configuration of subnets or addresses for operability.

NetBEUI is a nonroutable protocol that cannot cross routers although it can cross bridges and source routing bridges. This feature makes NetBEUI vulnerable to broadcast storms and restricts network design because subnets cannot be created.

You can install NetBEUI with other protocols to enhance client flexibility. For example, on a computer that requires Internet connectivity or access to computers across a router, you can install NetBEUI with TCP/IP. If you set NetBEUI as the default protocol, Windows 2000 Professional uses NetBEUI for communication within the LAN and uses TCP/IP for communication across routers to other parts of the network.

For more information about installing and configuring NetBEUI in Windows 2000 Professional, see "Configure Transport Protocols" later in this chapter.

Locating Resources in Microsoft Networks

After users log on to the network, they need to locate shared resources. Windows 2000 provides shared resources by *publishing objects* in domains and by using the *browse* function in server message block (SMB)–based networks, such as Windows NT.

Publishing Objects in Active Directory

Publishing is the act of creating Active Directory objects that directly contain the information you want to make available or that provide a reference to it. For example, a user object contains useful information about users, such as their telephone numbers and e-mail addresses, and a volume object contains a reference to a shared file system volume. Published objects are available to Windows 2000–based, Windows 95–based, and Windows 98–based clients that have Active Directory client software installed. Publishing can only be implemented in an Active Directory domain where TCP/IP is the transport protocol.

The following provides two examples of publishing file and print objects in Active Directory:

Share publishing. Network administrators and authenticated users can publish a shared folder as a volume object (also called a shared folder object) in Active Directory by using the Active Directory Users and Groups snap-in. This means that users can now easily and quickly query Active Directory for a shared folder.

Printer publishing. In a Windows 2000 domain, the easiest way to manage, locate, and connect to printers is through Active Directory. When you add a printer by using the Add Printer wizard and you elect to share the printer, Windows 2000 Server publishes it in the domain as an object in Active Directory. Publishing (listing) printers in Active Directory lets users locate the most convenient printer. Users can now easily query Active Directory for any of these printers, searching by printer attributes, such as type (PostScript, color, legal-sized paper, and so on) and location. When you remove a printer from the server, it is unpublished by the server.

The Windows 2000 operating system introduces the *global catalog*, a database that resides on one or more domain controllers. The global catalog plays major roles in logging on users and querying.

In an enterprise that contains many domains, the global catalog allows clients to quickly and easily perform searches across all domains without having to search each domain individually. The global catalog makes directory structures within an enterprise transparent to end users seeking information.

Computer Browser and Browsing Roles

The Computer Browser service provides a method of locating shared resources within a domain or workgroup environment. Computers running the Server service (which includes both workstations and servers) announce their availability by means of broadcast messages, which are captured by computers designated as *browsers*. The function of the browser is to create, maintain, and distribute a *browse list*, which is a directory of all shared resources used on the network.

Browsing is required by network applications that use SMB block messaging in Windows 2000 and previous versions of Windows, such as My Network Places, the **net view** command, and Windows NT Explorer.

Domains that allow browsing are likely to be controlled by computers running earlier versions of Windows operating systems, such as Windows 98 or Windows NT. For purposes of compatibility, Windows 2000 domains support browsing with clients that use these operating systems; however, you can enhance the functionality of browsing by publishing shared resources in Active Directory and in global catalogs.

In an environment that supports browsing, computers can perform the following roles:

- Domain master browser
- Master browser
- Backup browser
- Potential browser
- Nonbrowser

Table 23.3 describes the browser roles and functions that computers operating this service can perform.

Table 23.3   Browser Roles and Functions

Browser Role	Function
Domain master browser	Used only in domain environments. By default, the primary domain controller (PDC) for a domain operates in this role. Collects and maintains the master browse list of available servers for its domain, as well as any names for other domains and workgroups used in the network. Distributes and synchronizes the master browse list for master browsers on other subnets that have computers belonging to the same domain. A Windows 2000 Professional–based computer cannot become a domain master browser.
Master browser	Collects and maintains the list of available network servers in its subnet. Fully replicates its listed information with the domain master browser to obtain a complete browse list for the network. Distributes its completed list to backup browsers located on the same subnet.
Backup browser	Receives a copy of the browse list from the master browser for its subnet. Distributes the browse list to other computers upon request.
Potential browser	Under normal conditions, operates similarly to a nonbrowser. Capable of becoming a backup browser if instructed to by the master browser for the subnet. This is the default configuration for a Windows 2000 Professional–based computer.
Nonbrowser	Does not maintain a browse list. Can operate as a browse client, requesting browse lists from other computers operating as browsers on the same subnet. Configured so it cannot become a browser.

Under some conditions, such as failure or shutdown of a computer that is designated for a specified browser role, browsers (or potential browsers) might change to a different role of operation. This is typically performed through a process known as *browser election*.

When a Windows 2000 Professional–based computer starts up, it first checks the registry entry **MaintainServerList** to determine whether a computer can become a browser. This entry is found in:

HKEY_LOCAL_MACHINE\SYSTEM\CurrentControlSet\Services\Browser\Parameters

Table 23.4 describes the values that you can assign to the **MaintainServerList** entry to specify how a computer participates in browser services.

Table 23.4   Allowable Values for the MaintainServerList Registry Entry

Value	Description
No	Prevents the computer from participating as a browser.
Yes	Makes the computer a browser. Upon startup, the computer attempts to contact the master browser to get a current browse list. If the master browser cannot be found, the computer forces a browser election. The computer becomes either an elected master browser or a backup browser.
Auto	Makes the computer a *potential browser*. It might become a browser, depending on the number of currently active browsers. The master browser notifies the computer whether it is to become a backup browser. This value is the default for computers running Windows 2000 Professional and Windows NT Workstation 4.0.

Tip It is a good idea to set the **MaintainServerList** entry to **No** on computers that are frequently powered off or removed from the network, such as portable computers. This ensures that a browse server is always available and helps to reduce browser elections. Disabling browsing on client computers also reduces the network overhead that results from browser announcements.

Another entry in this registry location, **IsDomainMaster**, determines if a Windows 2000 Professional computer can become a preferred master browser. A *preferred master browser* has priority over other computers in master browser elections. Whenever a preferred master browser starts, it forces an election. The default setting for a Windows 2000 Professional–based computer is **False**.

Browser Elections

After the browsing role for a Windows 2000 Professional–based computer is determined, the computer checks to see if a master browser is already on the domain. If a master browse server does not exist, a *browser election* determines which computer becomes a master browse server for the workgroup. Browser elections occur under the following circumstances:

- When a computer cannot locate a master browser.
- When a preferred master browser comes online.
- When a Windows NT domain controller starts.

If a master browse server already exists, Windows 2000 checks the number of computers in the workgroup and the number of browse servers present. If the number of computers in the workgroup exceeds the defined ratio of browse servers to computers (usually one browse server for every 32 computers) and the **MaintainServerList** registry entry is set to **Auto**, the master browser can select a Windows 2000 Professional–based computer to act as a backup browser.

For more information about the selection criteria used in browser elections, see "Browser Service" in the *Microsoft® Windows® 2000 Server Resource Kit TCP/IP Core Networking Guide*.

Building the Browse List for Microsoft Networks

In Windows 2000 Professional, the browse service maintains an up-to-date list of domains, workgroups, and computers and provides this list to applications when requested. The user sees the list in the following circumstances:

- If a user requests a list of computers in a workgroup, the browse service on the local computer randomly chooses a browse server and sends the request.
- If a user selects a workgroup in which the user's computer does not belong:
  - Windows 2000 Professional requests a list of the computers that belong in the selected workgroup, obtaining the list from a browse server in the selected workgroup.
  - The selected browse server also sends a list of the workgroups that are on the network and a list of computers in the user's workgroup.

The browse list is displayed anywhere that Windows 2000 Professional presents lists of browsable resources. The browse list can also be displayed by using the **net view** command. The list can contain the names of domains, workgroups, and computers that run the file and printer sharing service, including the following:

- Computers running Windows 98, Windows 95, Windows for Workgroups, and Windows NT Workstation.
- Windows NT domains and servers.
- Workgroups defined in Windows 98, Windows 95, Windows for Workgroups, Windows NT Server, and Windows NT Workstation.
- Workgroup Add-on for MS-DOS peer servers.
- LAN Manager 2.*x* domains and servers.

Adding New Computers to the Browse List

When a computer running Windows 2000 Professional is started on the network, it announces itself to the master browse server for its workgroup, and the master browse server adds that computer to the list of available computers in the workgroup. The master browse server then notifies backup browse servers that a change to the browse list is available. The backup browse servers then request the new information to update their local browse lists. It might take as long as 15 minutes before a backup browse server receives an updated browse list, and new computers on the network do not show up in a user's request for a browse list until after this time period.

Removing Computers from the Browse List

When a user shuts down a computer properly, the operating system informs the master browse server that it is shutting down. The master browse server then notifies backup browse servers that a change to the browse list is available. The backup browse servers then request the changes to the browse list.

If a user turns off the computer without shutting down, the computer does not get a chance to send the message to the master browse server. In such cases, the computer name continues to appear in the browse list until the name entry times out, which can take up to an hour.

Configure Transport Protocols

This section discusses the configuration requirements that enable TCP/IP or NetBEUI to be used as the transport protocol for network connectivity.

Configure TCP/IP

Setup installs TCP/IP in a default configuration. Perform the following steps if you need to install TCP/IP on a Windows 2000 Professional–based computer.

▶ **To install Windows 2000 TCP/IP after you have installed Windows 2000 Professional**

1. In Control Panel, double-click the **Network and Dial-up Connections** icon.

2. Right-click the connection you want to modify, and then click **Properties**.

3. On the **General** tab, click **Install**.

4. In the **Select Network Component Type** dialog box, select **Protocol**, and then click **Add**.

5. In the **Select Network Protocol** dialog box, select **TCP/IP**, and then click **OK**.

To connect to other TCP/IP clients within your local subnet, you must configure the IP address and subnet mask at a minimum. If your network crosses multiple subnets, you must configure these additional options:

- Name resolution method (WINS, DNS, Lmhosts or Hosts files)
- Default gateway

Other configuration options, such as IP security and IP filtering, might be required in advanced configurations. Ask your network administrator what options are required for full Windows 2000 Professional client functionality. The tasks necessary for configuring TCP/IP can be found in the chapter "TCP/IP in Windows 2000 Professional" in this book.

If a DHCP server is available, configure Windows 2000 Professional to use DHCP. The benefits of using DHCP are:

- You do not have to manually change the IP settings when a client, such as a roaming user, travels throughout the network. The client is automatically given a new IP address no matter which subnet it reconnects to, as long as a DHCP server is accessible from each of those subnets.

- You do not need to manually configure the settings for DNS or WINS servers or for other options. The DHCP server can give these settings to the client if the DHCP server is configured to issue such information to DHCP clients. For more information about DNS and WINS, see "TCP/IP in Windows 2000 Professional" in this book.

- You do not have conflicts caused by duplicate IP addresses.

Install NetBEUI

Windows 2000 Professional Setup does not install a default configuration of the NetBEUI protocol. To install NetBEUI on a Windows 2000 Professional–based computer, follow these steps:

▶ **To install NetBEUI after you have run Windows 2000 Professional Setup**

1. In Control Panel, double-click the **Network and Dial-up Connections** icon.

2. Right-click the connection you want to modify, and then click **Properties**.

3. On the **General** tab, click **Install**.

4. In the **Select Network Component Type** dialog box, select **Protocol**, and then click **Add.**

5. In the **Select Network Protocol** dialog box, select **NetBEUI Protocol** and then click **OK**.

NetBEUI functionality requires no additional protocol configuration.

Configure Protocol Binding Order

If multiple network protocols are installed on your Windows 2000 Professional computer, you can determine the *binding order* of each protocol with each service that uses the protocol. The binding order determines which protocol a service uses to connect to another client or service. Place the most-used protocol first, because this reduces the amount of time needed to find required clients and services.

Multiple services can bind with each protocol, but the service that controls access to the network is the **Client for Microsoft Networks**. The binding order is displayed in the **Adapters and Bindings** page of the **Advanced Settings** property sheet of a selected network adapter. Bindings are shown in the area labeled **Bindings for <*connection name*>**. Figure 23.5 shows the binding order for a selected network adapter.

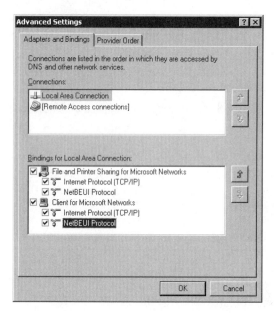

Figure 23.5   Configure Protocol Binding Order

▶ **To change the binding order of network protocols**

1. In Control Panel, double-click the **Network and Dial-up Connections** icon.

2. Select the connection you want to modify.

3. On the **Advanced** menu, click **Advanced Settings**.

4. On the **Adapters and Bindings** tab and in **Bindings for <*connection name*>**, click the protocol that you want to move up or down in the list, and then click the **Up** or **Down** button.

Join Network Environment

The act of adding a Windows 2000 Professional computer to a logical grouping of computers, such as a domain or workgroup, is called *joining the domain or workgroup*. The following section discusses the procedures for joining a Windows 2000 Professional computer to an existing domain or workgroup.

Network Identification Wizard

The Network Identification wizard, which is illustrated in Figure 23.6, provides a simple interface for joining a Windows 2000 Professional–based computer to a Windows NT or Windows 2000 domain or workgroup.

To add a computer to the domain, you must be logged on to the computer with an account that is a member of the Administrators group. Additionally, the account must have administrative rights at the domain controller, or another administrative account must be used.

Note In a Windows 2000 domain, permission to add computers to a domain can be delegated to nonadministrative user accounts. Contact your domain administrator to determine the delegation strategy used in your enterprise. For more information on delegation, see "Security" in this book.

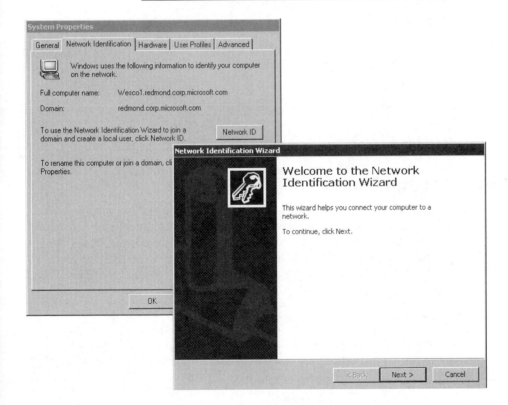

Figure 23.6   Network Identification Wizard

▶ **To start the Network Identification wizard**

1. Right-click **My Computer,** and then click **Properties.**

2. Click the **Network Identification** tab.

3. Click **Network ID,** and then click **Next.**

4. Select **This computer is part of a business network, and I use it to connect to other computers at work**, and then click **Next.**

5. If you are joining a domain, select **My company uses a network with a domain,** and then click **Next** twice.

   – Or –

   If you are joining a workgroup, select **My company uses a network without a domain,** and then click **Next.**

6. If you are joining a domain, enter the following information and then click **Next:**

   - User name

   - Password

   - Name of the domain that contains the user account

   – Or –

   If you are joining a workgroup, type the name of the workgroup and then click **Next.**

7. Click **Finish** to complete the wizard and restart the computer.

Manually Join a Windows Domain

To add a computer to the domain, you must be logged on to the computer with an account that is a member of the Administrators group. Additionally, the account must also be a member of the Domain Admins group in the domain, or another account that is a member of the Domain Admins group must be available. Figure 23.7 shows the Network Identification dialog box that is used to perform this task.

Note In a Windows 2000 domain, permission to add computers to a domain can be delegated to nonadministrative user accounts. Contact your domain administrator to determine the delegation strategy used in your enterprise. For more information about delegation, see "Security" in this book.

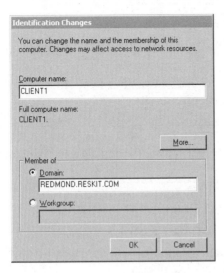

Figure 23.7   Network Identification Dialog Box

▶ **To join a Windows domain**

1. In Control Panel, double-click the **System** icon.

2. On the **Network Identification** tab, click **Properties**.

3. Under **Member of**, click **Domain,** and then type the name of the domain you want to join. Click **OK**.

4. If the computer account has already been created at the domain controller, enter the user name, password, and domain, and then click **Next**.

    – Or –

    If the computer account has not been created at the domain controller, enter the user name, password, and domain name, and then click **Next**. A dialog box appears and prompts you for the user name and password of an Administrator account. Enter the information and click **OK**. The new computer account is created at the domain controller.

5. Click **OK** twice to return to the **System Properties** dialog box.

6. Click **OK**.

7. Click **Yes** to restart the computer.

Manually Join Windows Workgroup

In the default Setup configuration, a Windows 2000 Professional–based computer is a member of a workgroup called WORKGROUP. To change workgroup membership or to move from a domain to a workgroup, you must log on to an account that has administrative privileges.

Important If your computer was a member of a domain before you joined the workgroup, it will be disjoined from the domain and your computer account will be disabled.

▶ **To join a Windows workgroup**

1. In Control Panel, double-click the **System** icon.

2. On the **Network Identification** tab, click **Properties**.

3. Under **Member of**, click **Workgroup**.

4. Type the name of the workgroup that you want to join, and then click **OK**.

5. Click **OK** twice to return to the **System Properties** dialog box.

6. Click **OK**.

7. Click **Yes** to restart the computer.

Confirm Group Membership

After you have added the Windows 2000 Professional–based computer to the domain or workgroup, you need to verify that the move was successful. To do so, restart the computer. After you perform the **Ctrl+Alt+Del** key combination, check the **Log on to** list. If you have joined a domain, the list should include the logon domain and any of its trusted domains. This is the first step to verify that you have successfully added the computer account to the logon domain.

To test a valid user account, log on to the logon or trusted domain. If you can log on to the domain by using the logon credentials located at the domain controller, then access to user accounts at the selected domain has been successfully granted. If a message is displayed indicating that you are connected by using cached credentials, it is an indication that the domain controller could not be contacted during the account authentication process. Verify that the physical connection (network adapter and cables) and logical connection (transport protocol configuration) permits access to the domain controller.

The Nltest.exe utility included with the *Windows 2000 Professional Resource Kit CD* is a command-line utility that can be used to test the logical connection between a Windows 2000 Professional computer and a Windows 2000 or Windows NT domain controller. Nltest.exe can also be used to determine if a user account can be successfully authenticated by a domain controller, to determine which domain controller will perform the authentication, and provide a list of trusted domains.

The "logical connection" between the Windows 2000 Professional computer and the domain controller is known as a *secure channel.* Secure channels are used to authenticate Windows 2000 and Windows NT computer accounts and to authenticate user accounts when a remote user connects to a network resource and the user account exists in a trusted domain (pass-through authentication). A secure channel must exist in order for account authentication to be performed. Nltest.exe can test secure channels and reset them if necessary.

The syntax of Nltest.exe is:

```
nltest [/OPTIONS]
```

Table 23.5 contains a list of options that are useful in determining authentication and secure channel status.

Table 23.5   Nltest.exe Options and Functions

Nltest Option	Function
/SERVER:*<ServerName>*	Specifies *<ServerName>*.
/SC_QUERY:*<DomainName>*	Queries secure channel for *<Domain>* on *<ServerName>*.
/DCLIST:*<DomainName>*	Obtains list of domain controllers for *<DomainName>*.
/DCNAME:*<DomainName>*	Obtains the PDC name for *<DomainName>*.
/DCTRUST:*<DomainName>*	Obtains name of DC is used for trust of *<DomainName>*.
/WHOWILL:*<DomainName>** *<User>* [*<Iteration>*]	Displays which *<DomainName>* will log on *<User>*.
/FINDUSER:*<User>*	Displays which trusted *<Domain>* will log on *<User>*.
/USER:*<UserName>*	Queries User info on *<ServerName>*.
/TRUSTED_DOMAINS	Queries names of domains trusted by workstation.

The following examples show a Windows 2000 Professional computer, Client1, that is a member of the Windows NT 4.0 domain Main_dom. The account User1 has been created within the domain.

To determine the domain controllers in the Main_dom domain:

```
C:\>nltest /dclist:Main_dom
List of DCs in Domain Main_dom
    \\NET1 (PDC)
The command completed successfully
```

To determine if the domain controller Net1 can authenticate the user account User1:

```
C:\>nltest /whowill:Main_dom User1
[20:58:55] Mail message 0 sent successfully (\MAILSLOT\NET\GETDC939)
[20:58:55] Response 0: S:\\NET1 D:Main_dom A:User1 (Act found)
The command completed successfully
```

S: indicates the domain controller that will authenticate the account, **D:** indicates the domain the account is a member of, and **A:** indicates the account name.

To determine if the workstation Client1 has a secure connection with a domain controller within the Main_Dom domain:

```
C:\>nltest /server:Client1 /sc_query:Main_Dom
Flags: 0
Connection Status = 0 0x0 NERR_Success
Trusted DC Name \\NET1
Trusted DC Connection Status Status = 0 0x0 NERR_Success
The command completed successfully
```

For more information about the Nltest.exe utility, including all option parameters, see the *Windows 2000 Professional Resource Kit CD*.

After computer and user account authentication has been verified, make sure all logon scripts perform as expected. Check to see that network shares, batch files, and utilities have been configured as indicated by the logon script.

Check to see if existing local Group Policy causes unexpected results when it is configured with a Windows NT system policy or Windows 2000 domain Group Policy. For example, if local Group Policy is configured to remove entries from the Start menu, they will be overridden by the Windows 2000 domain Group Policy when the user logs on to the domain. For more information about local Group Policy coexistence with Windows 2000 domain Group Policy settings or Windows NT system policy, see "Group and System Policies" in this chapter.

To test workgroup membership, log on to the local computer by using a valid user name and password. You should be able to access all local computer resources as well as see other workgroup computers in **My Network Places**.

Troubleshooting Microsoft Networking

This section lists tools and techniques that you can use to determine and resolve networking problems. Although this section is not meant to be all-inclusive, it includes many of the problems that you might encounter within a networking environment.

Always perform the following steps when you encounter a problem with a network connection in Windows 2000 Professional:

- Make sure that the cable connection between the network adapter and the port is secure. If it is, restart the computer in case you have temporarily lost connection.

- Make sure the network adapter is correctly installed. Use Device Manager to verify that it is functioning correctly.

- Check Event Viewer for the system and the application events that might explain the problem. For more information about using Event Viewer and the event logs, see "Troubleshooting Tools" later in this chapter.

- Verify that the domain controller(s) are available and functioning. Contact your network administrator if they are not.

For more information about troubleshooting techniques and tools, see "Troubleshooting Tools and Strategies" in this book.

Troubleshooting Tools

For detailed usage and syntax information about each of the troubleshooting tools, see "Troubleshooting Tools and Strategies" in this book.

Event Viewer

Event Viewer allows you to monitor events in your system. It maintains logs about program, security, and system events on your computer. You can use Event Viewer to view and manage the event logs, gather information about hardware and software problems, and monitor Windows 2000 security events. The Event Log service starts automatically when you start Windows 2000. All users can view application and system logs.

To access Device Manager, click the **Start** button, and then point to **Programs**. Point to **Administrative Tools**, and then click **Event Viewer**.

Event logs consist of a header, a description of the event (based on the event type), and optionally, additional data. Most Security log entries consist of the header and a description. Figure 23.8 shows a typical entry in the event log.

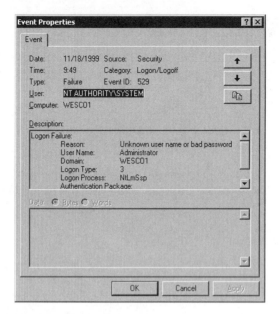

Figure 23.8   Event Log Entry

Event Viewer categorizes the events by log type (for example, security or system), and displays a separate log of every event. Each line of the log shows information about a single event, including date, time, source, event type, category, event ID, user account, and computer name.

The log types that directly relate to a user logging on are the security and system logs. Table 23.6 provides a description of the log types and how they can be used in troubleshooting:

Table 23.6   Log Contents

Log Type	Description
Security	The Security Log records security events, such as valid and invalid logon attempts, and events related to resource use, such as creating, opening, or deleting files or other objects. For example, the Security log records a user's inability to log on to a domain account due to an incorrect or invalid user ID/password combination.
System	The System Log records events logged by the Windows 2000 system components. For example, if a driver or other system component fails to load during startup, it is recorded in the System Log. Also, the System Log records a duplicate computer name on the domain as an error message sent by NetBT (NetBIOS over TCP/IP).

For more information about Event Viewer, see Windows 2000 Professional Help.

Network Connectivity Tester (Netdiag.exe)

This command-line diagnostic tool helps isolate networking and connectivity problems by performing a series of tests to determine the state of your network client and whether it is functional. These tests and the key network status information they expose give network administrators a more direct means of identifying and isolating network problems. Netdiag.exe performs LAN connectivity and domain membership tests, including network adapter status, IP configuration, domain membership and Kerberos security tests. The tests can be performed consecutively as a group or individually.

For more information about the function and syntax of Netdiag.exe, see "Troubleshooting Tools and Strategies" in this book.

Troubleshooting Joining Networks

This section describes the techniques and procedures that you can use to determine and resolve problems in joining a Windows 2000 Professional–based computer to a Windows NT or Windows 2000 domain, or to a workgroup consisting of other Microsoft networking clients.

Can't join a domain

The following message is displayed when you attempt to add a computer running Windows 2000 Professional to a Windows NT or Windows 2000 domain:

```
Unable to connect to the domain controller for this domain. Either the
user name or password entered is incorrect.
```

To join a domain, you must provide an account name that is a member of the Domain Admins group (Windows NT and Windows 2000 domains) or that is a member of a group that has been delegated the permission to add computers to a Windows 2000 domain. Contact your domain administrator if you receive the preceding message.

Can't find a domain controller

When you attempt to add a computer to a Windows NT or Windows 2000 domain or workgroup by using the Network Identification wizard or by manually adding the computer, the following message is displayed:

```
The specified domain does not exist or could not be contacted.
```

Perform the following steps to resolve the problem:

- Verify that the correct domain or workgroup name is specified. Check the Workgroup and Domain fields for incorrectly entered names.

- If TCP/IP is the transport protocol used, the problem might be caused by the configuration of TCP/IP options at the client. Log on to a local administrative account and use the following procedure to correct the problem:

  - Attempt to ping the domain controller by name, using the NetBIOS (that is, *DomainController1*) or fully qualified DNS name (that is, *DomainController1.domain1.reskit.com*). If unsuccessful, attempt to ping the domain controller by IP address.

  - If the attempt to ping the domain controller by name was not successful and DNS and/or WINS is used for name resolution, verify the IP addresses of the name servers. Attempt to ping the domain controller by name again.

  - If the attempt to ping the domain controller by name is unsuccessful and the Windows 2000 Professional–based client is in the same subnet as the domain controller, check the client's IP address.

  - If the Windows 2000 Professional–based computer is in a different subnet than the domain controller, confirm that the you have specified the correct default gateway(s).

  - If Internet Control Message Protocol (ICMP) Router Discovery is used to configure default gateways, configure ICMP Router Discovery. For more information, see "TCP/IP in Windows 2000 Professional" in this book.

  - If Routing Information Protocol (RIP)–enabled routers are used in the network, install RIP support.

  - A domain controller with an Internet Protocol security (IPSec) policy set at **Secure Server** denies transfer of IP packets with clients that do not have IPSec enabled through local or domain-based security policies. Contact your network administrator to determine the domain controller's IPSec policy. For more information about IPSec, see "TCP/IP in Windows 2000 Professional" in this book.

Can't rename a computer

When you attempt to name or rename a computer with a name that is identical or similar to the domain or workgroup name, the following message is displayed:

```
The new computer name may not be the same as the Workgroup (Domain)
name.
```

In a Windows NT workgroup or domain, or in a Windows 2000 domain where NetBIOS has not been disabled on all clients and servers, the first 15 characters of the Windows 2000 Professional computer cannot be the same as the names of existing clients, workgroups, or domains. For example, if the domain name is *Reskit1domainSEA*, you cannot use that same name as a computer name in the domain. Select a different computer name.

Troubleshooting Logon Problems

After joining a Windows 2000 Professional–based computer to a workgroup or domain, the computer running Windows 2000 Professional should be able to communicate with other clients in the network environment. This section describes the techniques and procedures that you can use to determine and resolve problems encountered when attempting to log on to a Windows NT or Windows 2000 domain, or to a workgroup consisting of other Microsoft networking clients.

Can't log on at a local workstation

After creating a computer account at the domain, you attempt to log on locally by using a nonadministrative account. The following message is displayed:

```
The system could not log you on. Make sure your user name and Domain are
correct, then type your password again.
```

Creation of a domain computer account does not migrate domain user accounts to the local computer. The local accounts must be created manually (by hand or through scripting).

Can't log on to a domain

After joining a Windows 2000 domain, you attempt to log on to the domain. The following message is displayed:

```
The system cannot log you on due to the following error: There is a time
difference between the Client and Server. Please try again or consult
your system administrator.
```

Kerberos security inspects the time stamp of the authentication request sent by the client that is logged on. The time stamp is compared to the current time of the domain controller. If there is a significant difference between the two times (the default is five minutes), authentication fails. Log on locally to an administrative account, and synchronize the time between the Windows 2000 Professional client and the domain controller.

You attempt to log on to a Windows 2000 domain and the following message is displayed:

```
Your account has been disabled. Please see your system administrator.
```

The user account has been configured for logging on by using a smart card. Each user account object in Active Directory contains a **User must log on using a smart card** option. If this option is selected and you attempt to log on without using a smart card, you receive the preceding message even though your account is not actually disabled. Contact your network administrator to disable the **User must log on using smart card** option.

Look for these common causes of logon failure:

- Incorrectly typed passwords or user names.
- Caps Lock is inadvertently turned on when you enter a password.
- Lack of a common protocol between a Windows 2000 Professional–based client and a domain controller.

If TCP/IP is the protocol that you used in the network, the client configuration might have changed since initial installation. Look for these causes:

- Incorrect static addresses or subnet masks.
- DHCP enabled in an environment where no DHCP server is available.
- Improperly configured default gateways.
- Incorrect addresses for DNS and/or WINS servers.
- Incorrectly configured Hosts/Lmhosts files.

Can't log on to a domain after renaming the computer

To rename a Windows 2000 Professional computer that is a member of a Windows NT domain, perform the following steps:

1. Create a new computer account (or have one created for you) by using the new computer name.
2. Leave the domain by temporarily joining a workgroup.
3. Restart the computer when prompted.
4. Join the domain by using the new computer name.
5. Restart the computer when prompted.

Troubleshooting Group and System Policies

Configuration conflicts can occur between local Windows 2000 Group Policy settings and Windows NT system policy, which can impede user access to system features and functions. For example, if a Windows 2000 Professional–based computer that was originally a stand-alone computer or a member of a workgroup, is added to a Windows NT domain that uses system policy, both the local Group Policy and Windows NT system policy may be processed at various points in the logon process. To determine the behavior of a Windows 2000 Professional–based computer with local Group Policy in a Windows NT domain with system policies, see "System Policy and Group Policy Coexistence" in this chapter.

For more information about troubleshooting Group Policy settings in a migration environment, see "Troubleshooting Change and Configuration Management" in the *Microsoft® Windows® 2000 Server Resource Kit Distributed Systems Guide.*

Troubleshooting Browsing and Publishing

This section discusses how you resolve problems that you have with the browser service in a Windows NT or Windows 2000 domain, or with published objects in a Windows 2000 domain.

Can't see member computers in a workgroup or domain

After successfully logging on to a workgroup or domain, you attempt to view shared resources in **My Network Places** or by entering **net view** from the command prompt. The resulting window shows no computers or does not show all members of the workgroup or domain.

Look for these possible causes for this situation:

- If you are in a workgroup, verify that you have specified the correct workgroup name (or have changed the default from **WORKGROUP**).
- A browser election has taken place, and the browse list is being updated on the domain master browser, on master browsers in the domain/workgroup, and on backup browsers. You can attempt to force an update of the browse list by refreshing the **My Network Places** window. Otherwise, it might take up to 15 minutes for all browsers to receive an updated browse list.

PART 5

Network Interoperability

C H A P T E R   2 4

Interoperability with NetWare

Microsoft® Windows® 2000 Professional provides services and protocols that allow you to integrate them with Novell Directory Services (NDS) or NetWare bindery-based servers. This chapter addresses the services and protocols used with Windows 2000 Professional and how to implement them for interoperability with NetWare servers.

In This Chapter

Related Information in the Windows 2000 Professional Resource Kit

- For more information about networking with Windows 2000 Professional, see "Local and Remote Networking" in this book.

- For more information about troubleshooting networking problems, see "Troubleshooting Tools and Strategies" in this book.

Quick Guide to NetWare Interoperability

You can use computers running Windows 2000 Professional in a Novell NetWare environment. Use this guide to make planning decisions, such as which client to use, and to determine how to set up and troubleshoot client configurations.

Review new features and basic concepts in NetWare connectivity.

Understand the basic concepts in connecting Windows 2000 Professional in a NetWare environment. Review the new features included with Windows 2000 Professional.

- See "Overview of Windows 2000 Professional and NetWare Connectivity" in this chapter.

Choose the appropriate redirector: Client Service or Gateway Service.

Select one depending on whether your organization plans to migrate from NetWare to Windows 2000 or maintain a mixed-mode environment.

- See "Client Service and Gateway Service" in this chapter.

Configure Client Server for NetWare.

You must configure Client Service for NetWare if you have chosen it as your redirector for Windows 2000 Professional.

- See "Configuring Client Service for NetWare" in this chapter.

Access NetWare resources.

After installing Client Service for NetWare you can access NetWare resources and bindery-based utilities directly from computers running Windows 2000 Professional.

- See "Accessing NetWare Resources" in this chapter.

Administer NetWare server functions and resources.

Windows 2000 Professional can be used as the system console to administer NetWare servers.

- See "NetWare Administration through Windows 2000 Professional" in this chapter.

Maintain security structure between Windows 2000 Professional and NetWare.

Because the security structures are different between Windows 2000 Professional and NetWare, it is necessary to understand the differences to ensure security when transmitting data from one security structure to the other.

- See "Windows 2000 Professional and NetWare Security" in this chapter.

Understand NWLink architecture.

The NWLink IPX/SPX/NetBIOS-compatible transport protocol is primarily used when connecting to NetWare servers.

- See "NWLink" in this chapter.

 Recover from common NetWare connectivity-related problems.

Follow the troubleshooting guidelines to recover from NetWare installation, configuration, and connecivity-related problems.

- See "Troubleshooting Windows 2000 Professional and NetWare Connectivity" in this chapter.

Overview of Windows 2000 Professional and NetWare Connectivity

Windows 2000 Professional uses Client Service for NetWare and the NWLink protocol to provide connectivity between Windows 2000 Professional and servers running Novell Directory Services (NDS) or Netware bindery-based servers. NWLink is the Microsoft equivalent to the IPX/SPX protocol.

What's New for Windows 2000 Professional and NetWare Connectivity

On computers running Microsoft® Windows® 95, Microsoft® Windows® 98, or Microsoft® Windows NT® version 4.0 Workstation, it is necessary to remove Novell Client 32 before upgrading the operating system, and then reinstall and reconfigure the computer after the upgrade.

When using Windows 2000 Professional, you can leave Novell Client 32 on the operating system while upgrading from Windows 95, Windows 98, or Windows NT 4.0 Workstation. Windows 2000 Professional upgrades computers running versions of Novell Client 32 earlier than 4.7. During the upgrade to Windows 2000 Professional, Novell Client 32 version 4.51 is installed. This process allows for a seamless upgrade of Novell Client 32 with no loss in functionality.

For a full version of Novell Client 32 for Windows 2000, contact Novell directly.

Introduction to Windows 2000 Professional and NetWare Connectivity

To connect a computer running Windows 2000 Professional to Novell NetWare servers, you need protocols and services that allow the two networking systems to communicate with each other. Windows 2000 Professional uses the Common Internet File System (CIFS) protocol for file and print services. CIFS is an enhanced version of the Microsoft Server Message Block (SMB) protocol. NetWare servers, however, use the NetWare Core Protocol (NCP) for file and print services.

For the two types of file and print services to communicate with each other, a client service or redirector and a network protocol are needed. A redirector or client makes remote files and printers available to the local computer. Installing a redirector on Windows 2000 Professional allows you to send and receive NCP packets by using NetWare servers.

A network protocol (NWLink IPX/SPX/NetBIOS Compatible Transport Protocol) and a redirector or client service (Client Service for NetWare) are provided with Windows 2000 Professional:

NWLink IPX/SPX/NetBIOS-Compatible Transport Protocol NWLink is the Windows 2000 Professional 32-bit implementation of the Internetwork Packet Exchange/Sequenced Packet Exchange (IPX/SPX) protocol, which can be used to connect computers running Microsoft® Windows® 2000 to NetWare servers running IPX/SPX. NWLink also provides NetBIOS functionality.

NWLink can also be used to connect computers running Windows 2000, Microsoft® Windows NT®, Microsoft® Windows® for Workgroups, Windows 95, Windows 98, and Microsoft® MS-DOS®, as well as function as an alternative transport protocol for servers running Microsoft® Exchange Server, Microsoft® SQL Server™, and Microsoft® SNA Server.

Client Service requires the NWLink protocol, which is installed with Client Service.

Client Service Client Service for NetWare works with NWLink to provide access to NetWare file, print, and directory services on NetWare servers running IPX/SPX. Client Service is installed on individual Windows 2000 Professional clients and provides direct access for each client to NetWare file, print, and directory services.

Figure 24.1 provides an illustrated example of Windows 2000 Professional communicating to a NetWare server through an NCP-based redirector. The computer running Windows 2000 Professional that is running a client service creates NCP protocol packets and passes them directly to the network. The packet is then picked up by the NetWare server.

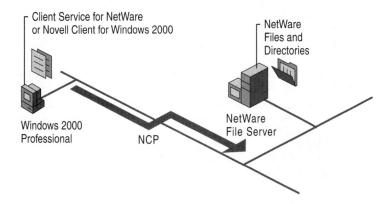

Figure 24.1   Client Redirectors for NetWare Access

Client Redirectors

You can install either Client Service for NetWare, or obtain and install the redirector from Novell, Novell Client for Windows 2000. Table 24.1 shows a comparison of both client redirectors.

Table 24.1   Comparison of Client Redirectors

Feature	Microsoft Client Service for NetWare	Novell Client for Windows 2000
Single logon and password for Windows 2000 and NetWare	Yes	Yes
File and print services access on NetWare servers	Yes	Yes
Protocols supported	Requires IPX/SPX protocol on Windows 2000 Professional	TCP/IP and IPX/SPX protocols
NDS aware/compatible	Authenticates user on nonbindery mode NDS servers	Fully integrates with NDS applications, for example, Z.E.N. Works, Novell Distributed Print Services, and Novell Storage Management Services

(continued)

Table 24.1   Comparison of Client Redirectors *(continued)*

Feature	Microsoft Client Service for NetWare	Novell Client for Windows 2000
Supports NetWare/IP	No	No
Supports NetWare administration utilities such as NWAdmin	No	Yes

Caution Do not install both Client Service for NetWare and Novell Client for Windows 2000 on the same computer running Windows 2000 Professional.

Novell Client for Windows 2000 does not allow connectivity to a Windows 2000-based computer. Client for Microsoft Networks must also be installed for connectivity to a Windows 2000-based computer.

Gateway Redirectors

A third option is to install the redirector, Gateway Service for NetWare on a computer running Microsoft® Windows® 2000 Server. This allows Windows 2000 Server to act as a gateway or translator: Windows 2000 Server receives CIFS packets from Windows 2000 Professional and then translates them to NCP packets before sending them to the NetWare servers.

Through the gateway, multiple clients running Windows 2000 Professional, Microsoft® Windows NT® Workstation, Windows 98, Windows 95, and Microsoft® Windows® 3.*x* can access NetWare file and print services. Because the gateway provides a single access point to NetWare services, you do not need to install NetWare client software (such as Client Service) on each workstation. Gateway Service also supports direct access to NetWare services from the computer running Windows 2000 Server, just as Client Service supports direct access from the client computer.

Figure 24.2 illustrates a computer running Windows 2000 Professional that is communicating to a NetWare server through a computer running Windows 2000 Server with Gateway Service installed. The CIFS-based protocol traffic is translated to NCP protocol, which is then passed to the NetWare server.

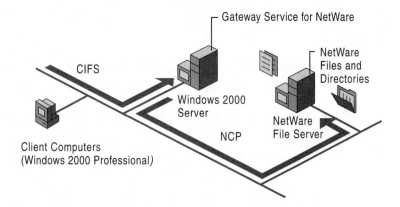

Figure 24.2   Server Redirector for NetWare Access

The capabilities of the Gateway Service redirector include the following:

- Single login and password for Windows 2000 and NetWare.
- File and print services access on NetWare servers.
- Enables Windows 2000 Server to understand the NCP protocol. Acts as a gateway to allow CIFS-capable Windows clients to access NetWare servers.
- Requires IPX/SPX protocol on Windows 2000 Server.
- NDS awareness.

Caution   Do not install both Gateway Service for NetWare and Novell Client 32 on the same computer running Windows 2000 Server.

Client Service and Gateway Service

Client Service for NetWare provides client-based NetWare connectivity, and Gateway Service for NetWare acts as a gateway through which multiple clients can access NetWare resources. Both depend on and work with the NWLink protocol, which is automatically installed with either redirector. For more information about NWLink, see "NWLink" later in this chapter.

Client Service uses a subset of Gateway Service code.

Choosing Between Client Service and Gateway Service

If you intend to create or indefinitely maintain a mixed-mode environment composed of both Windows 2000 and NetWare servers, consider using Client Service for NetWare. If you intend to migrate gradually from NetWare to Windows 2000 or if you want to reduce administration, consider using Gateway Service for NetWare.

Advantages of Client Service for NetWare

Client Service provides the following advantages over Gateway Service:

Client Service allows for user-level security rather than share-level security.
By using Client Service for NetWare, you can allow users access to individual *user home directories* (directories where individual user data resides) that are stored on NetWare volumes. Users can then map to their home directories and any additional volumes to which they have been granted user-level security. To allow users access to individual home directories by using Gateway Service you need to give each user a separate drive letter.

Client Service might perform better than Gateway Service. Client Service communicates directly with NetWare servers, avoiding potential bottlenecks caused by excessive traffic moving through a single network connection.

Disadvantages of Client Service for NetWare

Client Service has the following disadvantages:

Client Service requires you to manage multiple user accounts for each user.
For each user, you must create and manage separate user accounts for both Windows 2000 and NetWare.

Client Service requires more installation and management overhead.
With Client Service, you must install and maintain additional Client Service software on each computer running Windows 2000 Professional.

Client Service requires you to add IPX to your entire network. Servers running Windows 2000 and servers running NetWare 5.0 use TCP/IP as the native protocol. However, Client Service requires you to use IPX (through NWLink), and does not enable you to restrict IPX to a certain portion of your network. Even if clients on only one subnet use IPX, it might be routed through the entire network.

Note For detailed information about IPX routing and Windows 2000, see "IPX Routing" in the *Microsoft® Windows® 2000 Server Resource Kit Internetworking Guide*.

Advantages of Gateway Service for NetWare

Gateway Service provides the following advantages over Client Service:

Gateway Service allows you to manage a single user account for each user.
Gateway Service becomes the central interface for user access to NetWare resources and you can perform all Windows 2000 user account management within the Gateway Service user interface. You can secure regular share-level permissions and assign users or groups to the access control list (ACL) of each share.

Gateway Service reduces installation overhead. With Gateway Service, you can give clients access to NetWare resources without installing NetWare client software. Thus, you do not need to deploy and maintain network client software on multiple client computers.

Gateway Service provides protocol isolation for IPX. With Gateway Service, you can isolate the IPX protocol to your local area network (LAN), preventing IPX traffic from passing over wide area links.

Disadvantages of Gateway Service for NetWare

Gateway Service has the following disadvantages:

Gateway Service allows limited user-level security. With Gateway Service, all Windows 2000 users access NetWare resources as if they were the same NetWare user. Gateway Service assigns drive letters to separate NetWare files or directories, and then Windows 2000 share-level access is applied to the entire share. Therefore, the only way to provide user-level security while using Gateway Service is to assign separate drive letters for each user. Because servers need to reserve some drive letters for local drives, mapped drives, and other applications, user-level security is impractical if you have a large number of users.

Gateway Service might not perform as well as Client Service. Using Gateway Service, the Windows 2000 Server–based computer must act as a gateway between clients and NetWare servers. All requests for NetWare services are processed through a single gateway connection, creating potential bottlenecks. However, in some cases, Gateway Service performs better than Client Service (for example, if most of your traffic is NCP rather than CIFS).

When Client Service or Gateway Service is installed on a computer running Windows 2000, NWLink is installed automatically.

Using Client Service for NetWare

Client Service for NetWare is installed on Windows 2000 Professional computers to access NetWare services directly. The computer running Client Service creates NCP protocol packets and passes them directly to the network. The packet is then picked up by the NetWare server.

One example of accessing NetWare resources is to map a drive to a NetWare volume. When a drive is mapped to a NetWare volume, the computer running Windows Professional uses a NetWare account to create a validated connection to the NetWare server.

For example, to create a connection from computer A (running Client Service) to the NetWare NDS volume \\B\Volname.Orgunit.Org\Folder, where B is the name of the NDS tree, Volname.Orgunit.Org is the path to the volume name in the NDS tree, and Folder is a subfolder on the Volname volume. In Windows Explorer, select **Tools**, and then click **Map Network Drive**. You can also use the **net use** command-line utility and specify the path \\B\Volname.Orgunit.Org\Folder for the NetWare resource. For more information about mapping drives, see Windows 2000 Professional Help.

When using **Map Network Drive** the mapped connection is always persistent if you select the **Reconnect at logon** check box.

When using the **net use** command, after the mapped connection is established, it is disconnected only if the computer running Windows 2000 Professional is shut down, if the drive is manually disconnected, or if a network problem prevents access to the NetWare server. The mapped drive is then reestablished when the user logs on to the network.

Using Gateway Service for NetWare

Gateway Service for NetWare is installed on Windows 2000 Server–based computers for Windows 2000 Professional-based computers without a client for NetWare access installed to directly access NetWare services. The Windows 2000 Server–based computers with Gateway Service translate the CIFS packet received from computers running Windows 2000 Professional into NCP packets and sends the request to the NetWare server.

One example of accessing NetWare resources is to map a drive to a NetWare volume. To give Windows-based clients access to a NetWare volume, the Windows 2000 Server–based computer running Gateway Service redirects one of its drives to the NetWare volume and then shares that drive to the Windows-based clients. The gateway uses a NetWare account to create a validated connection to the NetWare server. This connection appears on the computer running Windows 2000 Server as a redirected drive. When you share the redirected drive, it appears to users as a Windows 2000 Server resource, although it is actually a resource on a NetWare server.

For example, to create a gateway from computer A (running Gateway Service) to the bindery-based NetWare volume \\Server1\Volname\Folder, where Server1 is the server name, Volname is the volume on that server, and Folder is a sub-folder on the Volname volume. In the **Configure Gateway** dialog box, specify \\Server1\Volname\Folder as the NetWare resource, and then specify a share name for Windows 2000–based clients, such as Nw_Folder. Windows clients then refer to this resource as \\A\Nw_Folder.

After the gateway connection is established, it is disconnected only if the computer running Windows 2000 Server is shut down, if the administrator disconnects the shared resource or disables the gateway, or if a network problem prevents access to the NetWare server. Logging off the computer running Windows 2000 Server does not disconnect the gateway.

Configuring Client Service for NetWare

When you install Client Service for NetWare on Windows 2000 Professional, the NWLink IPX/SPX/NetBIOS Compatible Transport Protocol is automatically installed.

Note To install Client Service you need Administrator rights to the computer running Windows 2000 Professional.

Microsoft Unattended Setup Mode can be used for large deployments of Windows 2000 Professional and Client Service for NetWare. For more information about Unattended Setup Mode, see "Custom and Automated Installations" in this book.

▶ **To install Client Service for NetWare**

1. Open **Network and Dial-Up Connections** in Control Panel.

2. Right-click the local area connection for which you want to install Client Service for NetWare, and then click **Properties**.

3. On the **General** tab, click **Install**.

4. In the **Select Network Component Type** dialog box, click **Client**, and then click **Add**.

5. In the **Select Network Client** dialog box, click **Client Service for NetWare**, and then click **OK**.

Table 24.2 lists the files that are installed with Client Service.

Table 24.2   Client Service Files

File Name	Description	Location
Nwlnkipx.sys, Nwlnknb.sys, Nwlnkspx.sys	Basic drivers that provide NWLink support	%windir%\system32\drivers
Ipxroute.exe	Diagnostic tool	%windir%\system32
Nwlnkflt.sys, Nwlnkfwd.sys	Routing and Remote Access service filter driver and forwarder table manager (installed if the Routing and Remote Access service feature is installed)	%windir%\system32\drivers
Nwrdr.sys	Redirector	%windir%\system32\drivers
Nwnks.dll, Nwapi32.dll, Nwapi16.dll	Client and service	%windir%\system32
NetWare.drv, Nw16.exe, Vwipxspx	Provide support for older 16-bit applications	%windir%\system32
Nwscript.exe	Login script processor	%windir%\system32
Nwc.cpl	Control panel program	%windir%\system32
Nwdoc.hlp, Nwdocgw.hlp	Help files	%windir%\system32\help
Nwcfg.dll	Client install and uninstall utility	%windir%\system32
Perfnw.dll	Performance counter	%windir%\system32
Nwevent.dll	Event log string	%windir%\system32

Note If you are unable to install clients, services, or protocols under Network and Dial-up Connections, then it is possible that policies have been implemented for your computer. For more information about policies, see "Group Policy" in the *Microsoft® Windows® 2000 Server Resource Kit Distributed Systems Guide* and the *Microsoft® Windows® 2000 Resource Kit* Group Policy Reference (Gp.chm) on the *Microsoft® Windows® 2000 Resource Kit* companion CD.

Figure 24.3 shows the dialog box that is displayed during the installation process.

Figure 24.3   Select NetWare Logon Dialog Box

Preferred Server or Default Tree and Context

To be authenticated by NetWare servers through Client Service, you must specify either the correct default tree and context for the user or the correct preferred server.

If you do not want to set a preferred server in the **Select NetWare Logon** dialog box, select **None** from the **Preferred Server** list box. You are then connected to the first NetWare server to respond to the **Get Nearest Server** request. You are not logged on to this server, but you can use it to browse (viewing other servers on the network), the same as when you enter the NetWare **slist** command.

The NetWare bindery-based environment is server-centric. For example, when logging-on to a bindery-based server, the user needs to have a login account and security access to a specific NetWare server. However, NDS uses an object-oriented distributed hierarchical database model. For example, when logging on in an NDS environment, the user is treated as an object and can access assigned resources within the NDS environment. The user accesses resources from one or more distributed NetWare servers.

To determine whether to select **Preferred Server** or **Default Tree and Context**, determine whether the NetWare server you are authenticating from is configured as bindery-based or NDS-based. Knowing the version of the NetWare server will assist in finding out whether it is bindery-based or NDS-based. For example, Table 24.3 lists the current supported versions of NetWare in a Windows 2000 network and whether or not they support bindery or NDS.

Table 24.3   NetWare Bindery and NDS

Netware Version	Bindery	NDS
NetWare 3.*x*	X	
NetWare 4.*x*	X	X
NetWare 5.*x*	X	X

If users need to connect to bindery-based resources, specify a preferred server. If users need to connect to NDS resources, specify the tree and context.

Setting a Preferred Server in a Bindery-Based Server Environment

In a NetWare bindery-based server environment, you must direct the computer running Client Service to the NetWare server where the Windows 2000 user and group accounts with the appropriate rights are located. Select the appropriate NetWare server as the preferred server. Your computer can then log on to the NetWare server, and then you can attach to another server.

Specifying the Tree and Context in an NDS Environment

In NDS, *tree* refers the NDS hierarchical directory structure, and *context* refers to the location of an object in the directory tree. If there is only one tree in an organization, it is easy to select and specify. The context, on the other hand, is not so obvious. To locate the necessary network resources for the particular user object, you must define the context correctly when accessing NDS servers through Client Service or Gateway Service.

For example, in Figure 24.4, **Reskit**, at the top of the NDS directory tree, is the actual name of the root object.

Specify the context in the **Client Service for NetWare** dialog box. You can type it in either the typefull name or typeless name formats.

Within the tree, the context in typefull name format for the user JDOE is
ou=sales.ou=milan.ou=eu.o=reskit, and the context in the typeless name format is
sales.milan.eu.reskit. Both the typefull name and the typeless name formats are
valid entries in the **Context** field of the **Client Service for NetWare** dialog box.

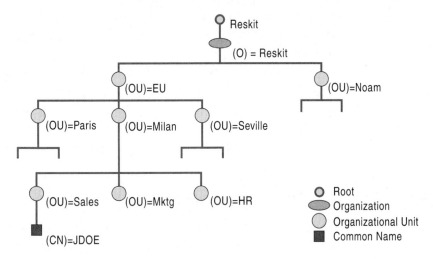

Figure 24.4   NDS Directory Tree

Run Login Script

A NetWare login script is a list of commands that are carried out each time the
user logs on to the NetWare network. Login scripts can be used to set user
defaults such as drive mappings, search drive mappings, printer configurations,
and other variable settings which define the user's environment configuration on
the NetWare network. They enable you to create a consistent user environment.

Login scripts reside on NetWare servers and can be run when you access NetWare
networks through Client Service. To use a NetWare login script to set up variables
on the NetWare network each time a user connects, enable the **Login Script**
option in the **Client Service for NetWare** dialog box. Enabling this option causes
the NetWare login script to run when the user is authenticated to the NetWare
network. The NetWare login script variables only apply to the individual user.

Bindery-based and NDS versions of NetWare enable you to use different login
scripts. The bindery-based server version provides system and user login scripts
that are run at the system-wide level and at the user level, respectively. The
system login script sets variables for all users on a server.

NDS, on the other hand, enables you to use four types of login scripts that work in sequence to set users rights at the container, profile, and user level. NDS enables you to use the following login scripts:

- The NDS container login script is similar to the system login script in the NetWare bindery-based server version, but it sets global variables at the container level so that you can set variables for different organizations.

- The NDS profile login script allows you to set variables for users who need common access to specific applications or to members of workgroups.

- The user login script allows you to set variables for individual users.

- The default login script is run when a user login script is not available.

For more information about setting up a NetWare login script, see your NetWare documentation.

NWLink IPX/SPX/NetBIOS Compatible Transport Protocol

When you install Client Service on a computer running Windows 2000 Professional, the NWLink IPX/SPX/NetBIOS Compatible Transport Protocol is automatically installed.

Figure 24.5 shows the **NWLink IPX/SPX/NetBIOS Compatible Transport Protocol** dialog box.

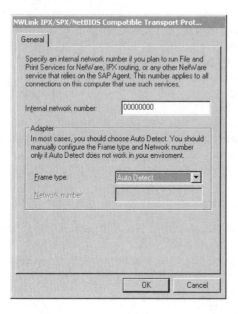

Figure 24.5   NWLink IPX/SPX/NetBIOS Compatible Transport Protocol Dialog Box

Internal Network Number

The internal network number is used for internal routing purposes when the computer running Windows 2000 is also hosting IPX services. When calculating the best possible route for transmitting packets to a specified computer, multiple routes with the same route metrics can present ambiguity to computer hosts. When you specify a unique internal network number, you create a virtual network inside the computer. This allows for a singular optimum path from the network to the services running on the computer.

Generally, you do not need to change the internal network number. For more information about the internal network number, see "IPX Routing" in the *Internetworking Guide*.

▶ **To change the internal network number**

1. In Control Panel, double-click **Network and Dial-up Connections**.

2. Right-click a local area connection, and then click **Properties**.

3. On the **General** tab, click **NWLink IPX/SPX/NetBIOS Compatible Transport Protocol**, and then click **Properties**.

4. Type a value in the **Internal Network Number** box, and then click **OK**.

Frame Type and Network Number

NWLink IPX/SPX/NetBIOS-Compatible Transport Protocol supports the frame types shown in Table 24.4.

Table 24.4   Supported Frame Types

Network Type	Supported Frame Types
Ethernet	Ethernet II, 802.2, 802.3, 802.2 SNAP
Token Ring	802.5 and 802.5 Subnet Access Protocol (SNAP)
FDDI	802.2 and SNAP

Frame types define packet formats used by the different network types.

During the Auto Detect process, NWLink tries each available frame type in the list for the associated medium access type. For example, on an Ethernet network, Ethernet 802.2, Ethernet 802.3, Ethernet II, and Ethernet SNAP are tested to see which frame types NWLink can communicate with. When NWLink receives a response from a NetWare server with one of the frame types, it also receives the network number associated with the frame type for the network segment where the client resides. NWLink then rebinds using the frame types from which it received responses.

The *external network number* is a unique number which represents a specific network segment and associated frame type. All computers on the same network segment that use a particular frame type must have the same external network number, which must be unique for each network segment.

The IPX frame type and network number are set during the initial NetWare server configuration. The Windows 2000 Professional NWLink Auto Detect feature then detects the frame type and network number that was configured on the NetWare servers. NWLink Auto Detect is the recommended option for configuring both the network number and the frame type.

Occasionally, Auto Detect selects an inappropriate network number and frame type combination for the adapter. Because Auto Detect uses the responses it receives from computers on the same network segment, Auto Detect might select an incorrect frame type and network number if computers responded with incorrect values. This is usually caused by an incorrect manual setting on one or more computers on the network.

If the Auto Detect feature selects an inappropriate frame type and network number for a particular adapter, you can manually reset an NWLink frame type or network number for that particular adapter. The frame type and network number on Windows 2000 Professional need to match the frame type and network number configured on the NetWare server. You can specify a frame type and network number of 00000000, so that the network number of the network segment is automatically detected. To manually determine the frame type and network number set on the server, inspect the Autoexec.ncf file, or at the command prompt, type:

config

In the following excerpt from an Autoexec.ncf file, the frame type is Ethernet 802.2 and the network number is set to 17216720.

```
load c:\EPRO port=300 int=5 FRAME=ETHERNET_802.2
bind IPX to EPRO net=17216720
```

To manually determine the frame type and network number set on a computer running Windows 2000, carry out the **ipxroute config** command at the command prompt. Figure 24.6 illustrates the resulting screen.

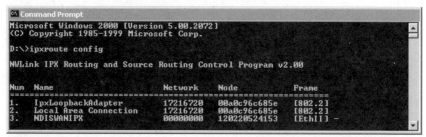

Figure 24.6   Frame Type Displayed in the Command-Line Interface

The network number, 17216720, and the frame type, Ethernet 802.2, in the IPXROUTE CONFIG display screen correspond to the settings in the Autoexec.ncf file.

To change the frame type and network number on your Windows 2000–based computer, you must be a member of the Administrator group.

Caution   In most cases, you do not need to change the network number and frame type, because Auto Detect usually detects the frame type and network number. If you choose an incorrect setting, the client cannot connect to NetWare servers.

▶ **To change the network number and frame type**

1. In Control Panel, double-click **Network and Dial-up Connections**.

2. Right-click a local area connection, and then click **Properties**.

3. On the **General** tab, click **NWLink IPX/SPX/NetBIOS Compatible Transport Protocol**, and then click **Properties**.

4. In the **Frame type** list box, select a frame type.

5. In the **Network number** text box, type a network number, and then click **OK**.

Accessing NetWare Resources

You can use Client Service for NetWare to access resources on a NetWare server. You can also access bindery-based NetWare utilities, such as System Console (Syscon), Remote Console (Rconsole), and Printer Console (Pconsole). In a NetWare bindery-based server environment, use Syscon, the primary administration tool, to set up user accounts, define policies, and grant user access permissions to the NetWare network.

Note   Although Client Service supports connections to NDS servers, you cannot use Virtual Loadable Module (VLM) utilities or other utilities specific to NDS. To access these utilities you need to install Novell Client for Windows 2000.

Many Windows 2000 commands can be used to perform functions on a NetWare server by using Windows 2000. Table 24.5 lists some commonly used NetWare utilities and their Windows 2000 equivalents.

Table 24.5 NetWare Utilities and Their Windows 2000 Equivalents

NetWare Utility	Windows 2000 Equivalent
Slist	Net view /network:nw or /n:nw
Attach, Login, and Logout	Net use
Map	Net use
Map root	Net use \\server\share\
Capture (to make MS-DOS and Windows applications print to a specific port)	Net use

Additionally, you can use the Printers folder to connect to and manipulate a NetWare printer.

Caution The NetWare **Attach**, **Capture**, **Login**, and **Logout** utilities are not supported in Windows 2000 and can cause errors when run on a computer running Windows 2000.

For more information about NetWare utility support in Windows 2000, see Windows 2000 Professional Help.

For information about NetWare administration utilities, see your NetWare documentation.

Accessing NetWare Volumes

You can access NetWare volumes either through the Windows 2000 user interface or through the Windows 2000 command-line interface.

▶ **To connect to a NetWare volume using the graphical user interface**

1. On the desktop, double-click **My Network Places**.

2. If only Windows 2000 or Windows NT–based network resources are shown, double-click **Entire Network**, and then double-click **NetWare or Compatible Network**. Tree icons for NDS directory trees and computer icons for individual NetWare computers appear.

3. Double-click a tree or volume to see its contents; you can double-click these to see other computers or volumes.

4. When you find the volume or folder you want to access, double-click it to expand it.

–Or–

To map a local drive to the volume or folder, right-click the volume or folder, and then click **Map Network Drive**.

Note When you map a network drive, by default you are connected under the user name and password you used to log on. To connect under a different user name, type the user name in the **Connect As** text box.

You can also connect to a NetWare volume from the command prompt.

▶ **To connect to an NDS tree**

At the command prompt, type:

net use drive: *treename**volume.OrgName.OrgName* **[/u:*UserName.OrgName.OrgName[password]]***

where:

- *treename* is the name of the tree *volume*.

- *OrgName* is the tree location to which you want to connect.

- *UserName.OrgName.OrgName* is the user name and context for this tree (unless it is your default tree).

▶ **To connect to an individual NetWare volume**

At the command prompt, type:

net use *drive: UNCname\\NetWarename*

For example, to use UNC naming syntax to redirect drive G to the folder \Data\Mydata of the Thor volume on a server called Nw4, type:

net use G: \\nw4\thor\data\mydata

The message "The password is invalid for \\server name\volume name[\directory name…]" indicates that your user name and password are not authenticated.

▶ **To connect with a valid user name and password**

At the command prompt, add your user name and password to the command line by typing:

/user: *username password*

For example, to use drive G to connect a user named User1 with the password Password1 to the \Data\Mydata directory within the volume Volume1 on a server called Nw4, type:

net use G: \\nw4\volume1\data\mydata /user:user1 password1

Note When you connect to NetWare file resources from the command prompt, you can use the next available drive letter by replacing the drive letter with an asterisk (*) in the syntax. For example:

net use * UNCname or NetWarename

If you prefer to be prompted for a password, you can replace the password in the command line with an asterisk (*). When you type your password at the comand prompt, it does not appear on the screen.

Accessing NetWare Printers

You can access NetWare printers either through the Windows 2000 user interface or through the Windows 2000 command-line interface.

▶ **To connect to a NetWare printer using the graphical user interface**

1. Open **Printers** to start the Add Printer Wizard.

2. Double-click **Add Printer**, and then click **Next**.

3. Click **Network printer**, and then click **Next**.

4. In **Name**, type the name of a printer in the following format:

   \\servername\sharename

   –Or–

   To find the NetWare printer, click **Next**. Follow the remaining instructions in the Add Printer Wizard.

   The icon for the printer appears in your Printers folder.

You can also connect to a NetWare printer from the command prompt.

Note When you run any application that writes directly to a predefined port, the **net use** command works like the NetWare **capture** utility, associating the NetWare print queue with the port.

▶ **To redirect output from a port to a print queue**

- At the command prompt, type:

  net use lpt1 \\nw4\memos

  This redirects output from LPT1 to the NetWare print queue called Memos on the server Nw4. This is equivalent to the NetWare **capture q=memos s=nw4 l=1** command line.

▶ **To send files that do not require formatting to LPT1**

- After you redirect output with **net use**, type:

  copy *<filename> <servername\printqueue>*

▶ **To connect to a printer in an NDS tree**

- At the command prompt, type:

  net use *drive***: ***<treename>******<printer.OrgName.OrgName>* **[/u:**<*UserName.OrgName.OrgName*> **[**<*password*>**]]**

  where *treename* is the name of the tree printer, *OrgName* is the tree location to which you want to connect, and *UserName.OrgName.OrgName* is the user name and context for this tree (unless it is your default tree).

Note   For more information about NetWare printing, see "Printing" in this book.

NetWare Administration Through Windows 2000 Professional

You can use a computer running Windows 2000 Professional that is configured with Client Service for NetWare to administer most NetWare server functions and resources.

Administering NetWare Servers

You cannot administer NetWare servers directly from NetWare 3.*x* or 4.*x* server consoles. Although you can perform some administrative tasks, you cannot set up users, user rights, and so on. Instead, you can use a networked computer running Windows 2000 Professional as the system console to administer NetWare servers.

When you configure Windows 2000 Professional with Client Service, you can use it to access bindery-based NetWare utilities, such as System Console (Syscon), Remote Console (Rconsole), and Printer Console (Pconsole). In a NetWare bindery-based server environment, use Syscon, the primary administration tool, to set up user accounts, define policies, and grant user access permissions to the NetWare network.

Note Although Client Service supports connections to NDS servers, you cannot use Virtual Loadable Modules (VLM) utilities or other utilities specific to NDS. To access these utilities you need to install Novell Client for Windows 2000.

Table 24.6 lists the supported 16-bit NetWare administrative utilities that you can run from a Windows 2000 Professional–based computer.

Table 24.6   16-Bit NetWare Utilities

Utility	Functions	Notes
Chkvol	Provides information about any volume on the NetWare server.	NetWare 4.x and later do not support this utility. Use the **ndir [path] /vol** command.
Colorpal	Provides the ability to modify NetWare's default color scheme.	
Dspace	Limits the disk space that a user can use on a volume.	NetWare 4.x and later do not support this utility. Use the **filer** command.
Fconsole	Broadcasts messages, views current user connections, and alters the status of file server.	Windows 2000 does not support all menus. **Down File Server** does not function properly.
Filer	Modifies a directory's owner, creation date, and timestamps.	
Flag	Displays and changes attributes of files in a specified directory.	You might have problems with NetWare 5.0.
Flagdir	Displays and changes attributes of subdirectories in a specified directory.	NetWare 4.x and later do not support this utility. Use the **flag path attributes /do** command.

(continued)

Table 24.6   16-Bit NetWare Utilities *(continued)*

Utility	Functions	Notes
Grant	Grants trustee rights to users or groups in a specified file or directory.	NetWare 4.*x* and later do not support this utility. Use the **rights path attributes /name= l/group=usernames** command.
Help	Provides online information about NetWare utilities, system messages, and concepts.	The normal syntax is *<utility name>* **/help**
Listdir	Displays directories, subdirectories, and their inherited rights mask, effective rights, and creation dates.	NetWare 4.*x* and later do not support this utility. Use **ndir [path] /do** command.
Ncopy	Provides the ability to copy one or more files from one network directory to another.	You might have problems with NetWare 4.*x* and NetWare 5.0.
Ndir	Displays information about file names, sizes, and their modification, access, creation, and archive dates.	You might have problems using Windows 2000 with NetWare 5.0.
Pconsole	Provides tools to manage print servers.	**Change Current Server** does not work
Psc	Displays status about and controls print servers and network printers.	NetWare 5.0 does not support this utility.
Rconsole	Provides a remote view of the NetWare system console. The console functions can be performed on the remote console.	
Remove	Provides the ability to delete a user or group from the trustee list of a file or directory.	NetWare 4.*x* and later do not support this utility. Use the **rights** command.
Revoke	Provides the ability to revoke trustee rights from a user or group in a file or directory.	NetWare 4.*x* and later do not support this utility. Use the **rights** command.
Rights	Displays the effective rights in a file or directory.	You might have problems with NetWare 5.0.

(continued)

Table 24.6   16-Bit NetWare Utilities *(continued)*

Utility	Functions	Notes
Send	Sends a brief message between workstations.	Send is not supported when connected to an NDS server.
		You might have problems using this command with Windows 2000 and NetWare 4.*x* or NetWare 5.0.
Session	Performs temporary drive mappings, creates, changes, and deletes search drives, displays groups on network, or sends messages.	Search mapping option not supported because it always maps as root.
		NetWare 4.*x* does not support this utility. Use the **netuser** command in NetWare 4.*x*.
Setpass	Sets or changes passwords on one or more file servers.	Use this command only for bindery servers. Use CTRL+ALT+DEL to change NDS passwords.
Settts	Provides ability to verify that the Transaction Tracking System (TTS) is tracking transactions.	NetWare 5.0 does not support this utility.
Slist	Provides a list of file servers on the internetwork.	NetWare 4.*x* and later do not support this utility. Use the **nlist server** command.
Syscon	Used to set up user accounts, define policies, and grant user access permissions to the NetWare network.	NetWare 4.*x* and later do not support this utility.
Tlist	Provides ability to view the trustee list of a directory or file.	NetWare 4.*x* and later do not support this utility. Use the **rights** command.
Userlist	Displays a list of current users for a file server, each user's connection number, the time at which the user logged in, and the network address.	NetWare 4.*x* and later do not support this utility. Use the **nlist /A /B** command.

(continued)

Table 24.6   16-Bit NetWare Utilities *(continued)*

Utility	Functions	Notes
Volinfo	Displays information about each volume on NetWare file servers.	If update interval equals 5, command carries out very slowly.
		NetWare 4.*x* and later do not support this utility. Use the **filer** command.
Whoami	Displays information about logged-on users, including user names on each server, file servers to which users are attached, groups to which users belong, and rights.	Whoami is not supported when connected to an NDS server.

Note For information about NetWare administration utilities, see your NetWare documentation.

To simplify network management, you can run multiple sessions of the administration tools on a single computer running Windows 2000 Professional. You can open separate windows on one computer to monitor multiple NetWare servers at once.

▶ **To connect to additional NetWare servers**

1. From the **Start** menu, point to **Programs**, click **Accessories**, and then click **Windows Explorer**.

2. On the **Tools** menu, click **Map Network Drive**.

3. In the **Drive** text box, enter a drive letter, if necessary.

4. In the **Folder** text box, type the path to the NetWare server.

5. Click **Finish**.

Windows 2000 Professional and NetWare Security

Although Windows 2000 Professional and NetWare security structures are not directly equivalent, you can maintain security when transmitting data from one security structure to the other.

The following sections describe how Microsoft permissions are translated to NetWare rights in a heterogeneous environment using Windows 2000 servers and workstations and NetWare servers.

Note For more information about Windows 2000 Professional security, see "Security" in this book.

Windows 2000 Professional Permissions

You can protect Windows 2000 Professional file allocation table (FAT) partitions and partitions using the version of NTFS included with Windows 2000 Professional against network access using share-level security. However, you can protect only NTFS file system partitions with user-level security.

NetWare Trustee Rights

NetWare file security is similar to NTFS security because you can control group and user rights to access files, called *rights* in NetWare. A NetWare trustee right, which is equivalent to a Windows 2000 permission, is a rule associated with an object (usually a folder, file, or printer) that regulates which users can gain access to the object and in what manner. Typically, the creator or owner of the object sets the permissions for the object.

The primary design difference between Windows 2000 permissions and NetWare trustee rights are that Windows 2000 permissions are subtractive and NetWare trustee rights are additive. When you create folders and files in Windows 2000, full access is granted and then access rights can be subtracted or restricted; in NetWare when you create a directory or file, access is denied and then access rights are added.

NetWare uses a combination of trustee assignments and inherited rights masks, or filters, to establish security settings. The intersection of these two access control mechanisms determines the actual access rights, known as NetWare effective rights, that a user or group has for a particular directory or file. There are eight NetWare directory rights settings: Read, Write, Create, Erase, Modify, File Scan, Access Control, and Supervisor.

The NetWare directory rights, are descibed in Table 24.7.

Table 24.7   NetWare Directory Rights

Directory Rights	Description
Read (R)	Read data from an existing file.
Write (W)	Write data to an existing file.
Create (C)	Create a new file or subdirectory.
Erase (E)	Delete an existing file or directory.
Modify (M)	Rename and change attributes of a file.
File Scan (F)	List the contents of a directory.
Access Control (A)	Control the rights of other users to access files or directories.
Supervisor (S)	Automatically allowed all rights.

Windows 2000 Professional Folder Permissions and NetWare Directory Rights

Table 24.8 shows how Windows 2000 Professional folder permissions correspond to NetWare directory rights.

Table 24.8   Windows 2000 Professional Folder Permission to NetWare Directory Rights

Windows 2000 Folder Permissions	NetWare Directory Rights
List Folder Contents	File Scan (F)
Read	Read, File Scan (RF)
Write	Write, Create, Modify (WCM)
Modify	Read, Write, Create, Erase, Modify, File Scan (RWCEMF)
Full control	Supervisor (S)

Windows 2000 Professional File Permissions and NetWare File Rights

Table 24.9 shows how Windows 2000 Professional file permissions correspond to NetWare file rights.

Table 24.9   Windows 2000 Professional File Permissions to NetWare File Rights

Windows 2000 File Permissions	Corresponding NetWare File Rights
Read	Read, File Scan (RF)
Modify	Read, Write, Erase, Modify (RWEM)
Full Control	Supervisor (S)

Windows 2000 Professional and NetWare File Attributes

NetWare file attributes, also known as flags, are not exactly the same as Windows 2000 Professional file attributes. Table 24.10 shows how Windows 2000 Professional file attributes correspond to NetWare file attributes when you open a NetWare file through Client Service for NetWare. The four attributes shown are a subset of many attributes supported by NetWare. Windows 2000 Professional does not support any additional NetWare file and directory attributes.

Table 24.10   Windows 2000 Professional and NetWare File Attributes

Windows 2000 File Attributes	NetWare File Attributes
Archive (A)	A (Archive needed)
System (S)	Sy (System file)
Hidden (H)	H (Hidden)
Read-only (R)	Ro (Read only), Di (Delete inhibit), Ri (Rename inhibit)

When you copy a file from a Windows–based network client to the NetWare file server by means of Client Service, the A, S, H, and R attributes are assigned the corresponding NetWare A, Sy, H, and Ro attributes.

When you use a computer running Client Service to access NetWare servers and you need to set attributes that are not supported by Client Service, you can use NetWare utilities, such as the **filer**, **rights**, or **flag** command, from the command prompt to set those attributes.

NDS Object and Property Rights

The NetWare NDS security structure adds NDS object and property rights to the directory and file rights in the NetWare bindery-based server security structure. In NDS, a network structure is organized by using NDS objects. Objects are components of the NDS hierarchical tree structure. The tree structure includes the following:

- Root objects at the top of the tree.
- Container objects, which are composed of various organizational units.
- Leaf objects, such as users, groups, servers, and volumes.

The following NDS object settings exist: Supervisor, Browse, Create, Delete, and Rename.

Properties are contained within an object that represent that object. A user object can contain properties such as a user telephone number, office location, and title. Property rights are implemented as a separate security structure than object rights in the NetWare NDS security structure. Therefore, you can configure security separately for objects and object properties. The following five object properties exist: Supervisor, Compare, Read, Write, and Add/Delete Self.

Note   NDS object and property rights apply only to NetWare NDS volumes, and you can change them only by using the NetWare network operating system software.

NWLink

NWLink IPX/SPX/NetBIOS-compatible transport protocol is the Microsoft 32-bit implementation of the Internetwork Packet Exchange/Sequenced Packet Exchange (IPX/SPX) protocol suite. Use this protocol to connect to NetWare servers by using Client Service for NetWare or Gateway Service for NetWare.

NWLink provides only the transport protocol to support communications with NetWare file servers. To log on to a NetWare network from a Windows 2000 Professional–based computer, you must use Client Service, or a NetWare client such as Novell Client for Windows 2000.

Because NWLink supports the Network Driver Interface Specification (NDIS) or is NDIS-compliant, the Windows 2000–based computer can simultaneously run other protocol stacks such as TCP/IP to communicate with TCP/IP–based computers. NWLink can be bound to multiple network adapters.

Note   NetWare 5.0 uses TCP/IP as the native protocol, and IPX is not installed by default. Therefore, to use NWLink to connect to NetWare 5.0 servers, enable IPX on the NetWare 5.0 servers. To use TCP/IP to connect to NetWare 5.0 servers, use Novell Client for Windows 2000.

NWLink supports the networking application programming interfaces (APIs) NetBIOS and Windows Sockets. These APIs allow communication among computers running Windows 2000 and between computers running Windows 2000 and NetWare servers.

In addition to using NWLink to connect computers running Windows 2000 and computers running NetWare, you can use NWLink whenever you need IPX/SPX. For example, you can use NWLink to connect proxy servers or servers running Microsoft® Systems Management Server (SMS), SNA Server, SQL Server, or Exchange Server, when an IPX/SPX-based protocol is used.

Note NWLink requires little or no initial client configuration on small nonrouted networks.

NWLink Architecture

NWLink provides a comprehensive set of transport and network layer protocols that allow for integration with the NetWare environment. Table 24.11 lists the subprotocols and components and shows their function and associated drivers.

Table 24.11   NWLink Protocols

Protocol	Description	File Name
IPX	Provides routable, connectionless datagram transfer services.	Nwlnkipx.sys
SPX and SPXII	Provide connection-oriented transfer services.	Nwlnkspx.sys
Routing Information Protocol (RIP)	Provides route and router discovery services.	Nwlnkipx.sys
Service Advertising Protocol (SAP)	Collects and distributes service names and addresses.	Nwlnkipx.sys
NetBIOS	Provides compatible support with NetBIOS for IPX/SPX on NetWare servers.	Nwlnknb.sys
Forwarder	Provides IPX router support.	Nwlnkfwd.sys

Figure 24.7 illustrates NWLink in the Windows 2000 Professional architecture and the files in which each protocol is implemented.

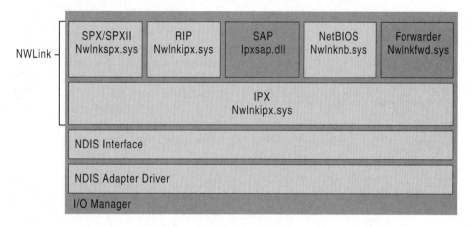

Figure 24.7   NWLink in the Windows 2000 Professional Architecture

IPX

IPX is a protocol that provides connectionless datagram transfer services and controls addressing and routing packets of data within and between network segments. With connectionless transmission, a session does not need to be set up each time packets are transmitted; packets are simply sent out on the wire. This requires less overhead than connection-oriented transmission in which a session must be established each time packets are transmitted. Therefore, connectionless transmission is best when data is generated in intermittent short bursts.

Because IPX is a connectionless protocol, it does not provide for flow control or acknowledgment that the receiving station has received the datagram packet. Instead, individual datagram packets travel independently to their destination. There is no guarantee that packets arrive at their destination or that they arrive in sequence. However, because transmission on LANs is relatively error-free, IPX is efficient in delivering data on LANs.

NWLink enables application programming for Windows Sockets and remote procedure calls (RPC) over Sockets. IPX supports Socket IDs for use by Sockets applications. IPX enables NetBIOS, Named Pipes, Mailslot, Network Dynamic Data Exchange (NetDDE), RPC over NetBIOS, and RPC over Named Pipes programming over NBIPX. NWLink also supports other applications that use IPX, through direct hosting. *Direct hosting* is a feature that allows CIFS-capable computers to communicate over IPX, bypassing the NetBIOS layer. Direct hosting can lower overhead and increase throughput.

SPX

SPX is a transport protocol that offers connection-oriented services over IPX. Although connection-oriented service requires overhead for session setup, after a session is established, connection-oriented service requires less overhead for data transmission than connectionless service. Therefore, it works best for applications that require a continuous connection. SPX provides reliable delivery through sequencing and acknowledgments and verifies successful packet delivery to any network destination by requesting a verification from the destination upon receipt. SPX can track data transmissions consisting of a series of separate packets. If an acknowledgment request brings no response within a specified time, SPX retransmits the request up to eight times. If no response is received, SPX assumes the connection has failed.

SPX also provides a packet burst mechanism. *Packet burst*, also known as *burst mode*, allows the transfer of multiple data packets without requiring that each packet be sequenced and acknowledged individually. By allowing multiple packets to be acknowledged once, burst mode can reduce network traffic on most IPX networks. Additionally, the packet burst mechanism monitors for dropped packets and retransmits only the missing packets. In Windows 2000 Professional, burst mode is enabled by default.

SPXII

SPXII improves over SPX in the following ways.

SPXII allows for more outstanding unacknowledged packets than SPX

In SPX there can be only one outstanding unacknowledged packet at any time, but in SPXII there can be as many outstanding packets as negotiated by the networked peers at connection setup time.

SPXII allows for larger packets   SPX has a maximum packet size of 576 bytes, while SPXII can use the maximum packet size of the underlying LAN. For example, on an Ethernet network SPXII can use 1,518 bytes.

RIP

NWLink uses RIP over IPX (RIPX) to implement route and router discovery services used by SPX and NBIPX. RIP determines the forwarding media access control (MAC) address for outbound traffic.

NWLink includes the RIP protocol for Windows-based clients and for computers running Windows 2000 Server that do not have the Routing and Remote Access service installed. These computers do not forward packets the way that routers do, but they use RIP to determine where to send packets. RIP clients, such as workstations, can locate the optimal route to an IPX network number by broadcasting a RIP GetLocalTarget request. Each router that can reach the destination responds to the GetLocalTarget route request. Based on the RIP responses from the local routers, the sending station chooses the best router to use to forward the IPX packet.

SAP

SAP is the protocol used to distribute the names and addresses of services running on IPX nodes.

SAP clients use SAP broadcasts only when bindery-based or NDS queries fail and send the following types of messages:

- SAP GetNearestServer request for the name and address of the nearest server of a specific type.

- SAP general service request for the names and addresses of all services, or of all services of a specific type.

NetBIOS

The NWLink NetBIOS protocol is automatically installed with Client Service. To facilitate the operation of NetBIOS-based applications on an IPX internetwork, NetBIOS over IPX provides standard NetBIOS services such as the following:

- Datagrams. Single packets sent without acknowledgment, for example, broadcasts.

- Sessions. Multiple packets sent with acknowledgments between two endpoints.

- Name management. Registering, querying, and releasing NetBIOS names.

An additional module, NWLnkNB, formats NetBIOS-level requests and passes them to NWLink for transmission. NWLnkNB includes the following performance enhancements:

- PiggyBackAck. An acknowledgment of previous frames within the response frames.
- A sliding window acknowledgment mechanism. A dynamic window–sizing algorithm that allows burst mode to adjust the number of frames that it can send.

Alternately, computers can communicate directly over IPX, through direct hosting. For more information about direct hosting, see "Client Service and Gateway Service" earlier in this chapter.

Forwarder

The forwarder component is installed with NWLink but is used only when the Windows 2000–based server is used as an IPX router running the Routing and Remote Access service. It operates in kernel mode.

When the IPX router software is activated, the forwarder component works with the IPX Router Manager component of Routing and Remote Access and the filtering component to forward packets. The forwarder component obtains configuration information from the IPX Router Manager and stores a table of the best routes. When it receives an incoming packet, it passes it to the filtering driver to check for input filters. When it receives an outgoing packet, it first passes it to the filtering driver. Assuming that no outgoing filters prevent the packet from being transmitted, the packet is passed back, and the forwarder component forwards the packet over the appropriate interface.

Troubleshooting Windows 2000 Professional and NetWare Connectivity

The following sections describe the tools that you can use to troubleshoot connectivity problems and monitor network traffic. Troubleshooting common problems is also discussed; for example, connectivity-related problems, login scripts, client server installation and configuration, and password synchronization are some of the common problems discussed.

Windows 2000 Professional Troubleshooting Tools

Windows 2000 Professional includes several tools that allow you to determine computer settings and perform diagnostic tests to resolve communication problems in an IPX/SPX networking environment.

ipxroute config   This command-line tool allows you to troubleshoot IPX connectivity problems and provides information about the current state of the stack. It displays the current IPX status, including the network number, MAC address, interface name, and frame type. At the command prompt, type:

ipxroute config

ipxroute ripout   This command uses RIP to determine if there is connectivity to a specific network. At the command prompt, type:

ipxroute ripout ####

where #### is the network number (an 8-digit hexadecimal number).

Network Monitor   Network Monitor, or Netmon, allows you to detect and troubleshoot problems on LANs and on WANs, including Routing and Remote Access links. By using Network Monitor you can identify network traffic patterns and network problems. For example, you can locate client-to-server connection problems, find a computer that makes a disproportionate number of work requests, capture frames (packets) directly from the network, display and filter the captured frames, and identify unauthorized users on your network.

Windows 2000 Server includes a version of Network Monitor that allows you to capture traffic coming to or going from the local computer. This version of Netmon is not available with Windows 2000 Professional.

Troubleshooting Common Problems

The majority of connectivity problems between Windows 2000 Professional and NetWare are caused by an incorrect setup.

Because connectivity involves resources on both Windows 2000 Professional and NetWare computers, resources must be set up correctly on computers running both Windows 2000 Professional and NetWare.

The following symptoms when connecting to the NetWare network are likely caused by an incorrect setup:

- Access is denied to applications on NetWare servers.
- Programs fail to run and display error messages.
- Data throughput is slow.
- Users see the error message "Server not found."
- Users are denied access to network resources on NetWare servers.
- Access to NetWare resources is limited.

- Clients have varying access to NetWare services.

- Users can connect to servers running Windows 2000 and Windows NT, but not to NetWare servers.

- Users can connect to some NetWare servers but not to others.

First, verify that access to NetWare resources is correctly configured on the NetWare file servers. You need to check a variety of parameters depending on the problem and its severity. Consider the following questions when resolving connectivity problems:

- Are user accounts set up correctly on the NetWare file server?

- Are the appropriate groups set up?

- Is group membership set up correctly?

- Are the correct rights set for the required resources?

Note Contact your NetWare administrator or consult your NetWare documentation for information on proper NetWare configuration procedures.

When you have verified that the necessary configurations and rights are set up on the NetWare file servers and the problem has still not been resolved, test the configuration on the Windows 2000 Professional computer, by using the steps in Figure 24.8.

Start

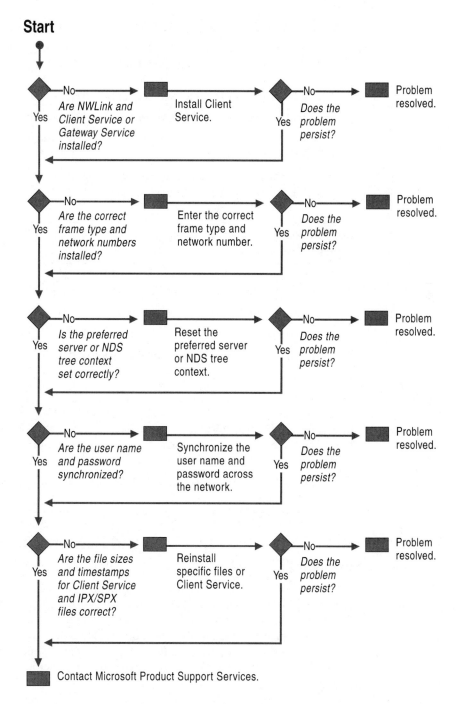

Figure 24.8   Troubleshooting NetWare Connectivity Problems

Are NWLink and Client Service for NetWare Installed?

For a client running Windows 2000 Professional to access NetWare servers, NWLink and Client Service must be installed.

▶ **To verify NWLink and Client Service installation**

1. Double-click **Network and Dial-up Connections** in Control Panel.

2. In **Network and Dial-up Connections**, right-click **Local Area Connection**, and then click **Properties**.

3. In the **Local Area Connection Properties** dialog box, verify that **NWLink** and **Client Service for NetWare** are listed.

Note   For installation instructions, see "Configuring Client Service for NetWare" earlier in this chapter.

▶ **To verify that Client Service for NetWare is running**

1. In **Control Panel**, double-click **Administrative Tools.**

2. Double-click **Services.**

3. Verify that **Client Service for NetWare** is listed as started under the **Status** column.

Note   Although Client Service provides access to NetWare file, print, and directory services from Windows 2000, the correct user accounts, necessary rights for resources, appropriate group rights, and associated login scripts need to be configured on the NetWare servers.

Contact your NetWare administrator or see your NetWare documentation for more information.

Are the Correct Frame Type and Network Number Installed?

When you install Client Service and NWLink, the Auto Detect feature is enabled. For more information about Auto Detect, see "NWLink IPX/SPX/NetBIOS Compatible Transport Protocol" earlier in this chapter. In most cases, Auto Detect detects the correct frame type and network number. However, problems can occur when a network is using multiple frame types or when an incorrect frame type is set manually. If NWLink detects no network traffic, NWLink sets the frame type to 802.2.

▶ **To verify that the frame type is set to Auto Detect**

1. In the **Local Area Connection Properties** dialog box, double-click **NWLink IPX/SPX/NetBIOS Compatible Transport Protocol**.

2. On the **General** tab, verify that **Auto Detect** is selected in the **Frame type** field.

▶ **To determine the frame type set on the NetWare server**

- At the NetWare server system console, type:

   Config

   –Or–

   Remotely, using the NetWare Rconsole utility, type:

   Config

   In either case, the frame type is displayed.

▶ **To determine the installed network number and frame type on the Windows 2000 Professional–based computer**

- At the command prompt, type:

   ipxroute config

   Verify that the network number and frame in the **Network** and **Frame** columns are correct for your installation.

   If you have multiple network adapters, examine the **Node** MAC address column to determine the network number that is associated with the specified card.

▶ **To manually set the correct frame type and network number**

1. In the **Local Area Connection Properties** dialog box, double-click **NWLink IPX/SPX/NetBIOS Compatible Transport Protocol**.

2. On the **General** tab, select the **Frame type** field.

3. Select the appropriate frame type for your network from the list box.

4. Type the correct network number for your network in the **Network number** dialog box, and then click **OK**.

Is the Computer Set to the Correct Bindery Server or NDS Tree and Context?

When Client Service is configured with an incorrect bindery server or an incorrect context within the NDS tree, users have problems accessing network resources.

▶ **To reset the current preferred server or default tree and context**

1. In **Control Panel**, double-click **CSNW**.

2. The preferred bindery server or default tree and context is displayed.

3. If the default tree and context or preferred server is incorrect, select the correct default tree and context or preferred server, and then click **OK**.

Note If you do not want to set a preferred server, click **None**. You then connect to NetWare through the nearest available NetWare bindery-based server, but you are not logged on to this server; you can use it only for browsing.

Are the User Name and Password the Same Across the LAN Servers?

To access NetWare resources by using Client Service for NetWare, a valid set of NetWare credentials (user account and password) must be created, and appropriate NetWare permissions must be granted to the account.

Once valid NetWare credentials and permissions are created, you can synchronize Windows 2000 and NetWare user credentials. Having identical credentials in both environments allows Windows 2000 with Client Service to "pass through" authentication, at Windows 2000 logon, to NetWare Bindery or NDS Tree. Users are not prompted to specify a separate set of credentials for NetWare at logon. Users can access all available NetWare resources for which those credentials have privileges without being further prompted.

To synchronize credentials, create a user account in NetWare with the identical name and password as Windows 2000 user account.

If a user's Netware password becomes "out of sync" with the Windows 2000 password, you can reset the NetWare password to the same password used in Windows 2000.

▶ **To reset the password on a NetWare NDS tree**

1. Press **Ctrl+Alt+Del**.

2. Click **Change Password**.

3. In the **Log on to** dialog box select **NetWare or Compatible Network**.

4. In the **Old Password** text box, type your current NetWare password.

5. In the **New Password** text box, type your new password (in this case, your password for Windows 2000 Professional).

6. In the **Confirm New Password** text box type your new password again.

▶ **To reset the password on a NetWare bindery server**

1. At the Command Prompt, enter the logical drive letter of the NetWare server, and then type:

   cd \public

   Note To change your password on more than one server, connect to all the servers before proceeding to the next step.

   ---

2. Type **setpass**, followed by the name of the NetWare server for which you want to change your password. When prompted for each password, type your old password and then your new password (in this case, your password for Windows 2000 Professional) twice. A message confirms that you have successfully changed your password.

3. If prompted, type **y**, and then press Enter to change your password on other NetWare servers.

Note If you are using Client Service and working from a command prompt, use the 32-bit version of the command prompt program, Cmd.exe, which is available on the **Programs** menu, not the 16-bit version, Command.com.

Are the File Sizes and Timestamps for Client Service and IPX/SPX Files Correct?

In some instances files do not copy correctly, or they become corrupted during the file copy process.

▶ **To determine if the file sizes and timestamps are correct**

1. Examine the file sizes and timestamps for the files created when Client Service and NWLink are installed on the client that is having a problem.

   For a list of files that are installed with Client Service see Table 24.2 earlier in this chapter.

2. Make sure that these files are identical to the files on a working Windows 2000 Professional–based client.

   If the file sizes and timestamps are not identical, your files might be corrupted.

▶ **To correct a problem with file corruption**

1. In the **Local Area Connection Properties** dialog box, select **Client Service for NetWare**, click **Uninstall**, and then click **OK**.

2. Check that all Client Service and NWLink files have been deleted. If any files remain, rename them in case you need them later. To rename the files, replace each file extension with .bak (for example, rename file Nwlnknb.sys to Nwlnknb.bak.)

3. Reinstall Client Service.

Troubleshooting NetWare Login Scripts

Login scripts set the user environment on NetWare servers and are used to access servers. You might experience the following problems when login scripts are activated through Client Service:

CX command   The user receives the following error message when the NetWare login script attempts to change context using a relative path: "The context you want to change to does not exist."

Nwscript.exe parses the NetWare login script. The CX command changes the context to move the user's context one level up within the NDS hierarchy. Instead, the user receives an error message.

To correct this problem, use absolute paths in login scripts. For example, type:

cx .somecontainer

Capture command

Error 255 is reported in line 668 of Spool.c when the login script containing the following line is run:

#COMMAND /c CAPTURE /S=*<servername>* /Q=*<queuename>*

To correct this problem, replace this line with the following:

#CAPTURE /S=<servername> /Q=<queuename>

Warning   Capture.exe is not a supported application and often fails when run from the command line. The login script processor does not actually run Capture.exe. Instead, it parses the #CAPTURE command and works in the background. Therefore, when you use the #CAPTURE command, you are running the actual Capture.exe application.

Troubleshooting Other Problems

In addition to NetWare and Windows 2000 Professional connectivity problems related to setup and login scripts, you might experience the following problems.

Extra page printing at beginning or end of print job

When installing Client Service you can select and enable **Add Form Feed** and **Print Banner**. **Add Form Feed** instructs the printer to eject a page at the end of each document that you print. **Print Banner** prints a banner page before each document. To disable **Add Form Feed** or **Print Banner**, in Control Panel, open **Client Service for Netware**, and then deselect the corresponding check box.

Client Service creates multiple licensed connections to NDS servers

If you have a NetWare NDS tree that includes more than one NetWare server, you might be using multiple licensed connections by connecting to one server for authentication and login, and then mapping connections through a login script to another server. This can cause you to use twice the number of Novell licensed connections as necessary.

For more information about how to correct this problem, see the Knowledge Base link on the Web Resources page at http://windows.microsoft.com/windows2000/reslink/webresources Use the keywords "connect to multiple servers," "CSNW," and "NDS."

NetBIOS over IPX packets do not propagate across routers

If an incomplete browse list is displayed for a NetWare directory, or you cannot browse a server across a WAN link, you might have a problem with propagating NetBIOS over IPX packets.

To facilitate the communication of a LAN-based protocol, such as NetBIOS, across an IPX internetwork, IPX routers must propagate NetBIOS over IPX broadcast packets (type 20 packets), also known as IPX WAN broadcast packets. However, many router manufacturers set router parameters not to pass type 20 packets by default. If your router is configured not to pass type 20 packets, contact your router manufacturer.

Windows 2000 Professional–based computers cannot connect to other Windows clients

By default, Windows for Workgroups, Windows 95, and Windows 98–based computers use client and server-side direct hosting for the IPX/SPX protocol. Direct hosting allows computers to communicate over IPX, bypassing the NetBIOS layer.

Windows 2000 supports server-side direct hosting but does not support client-side direct hosting. Therefore, although a Windows for Workgroups, Windows 95, and Windows 98–based client running only the IPX/SPX protocol can connect to a Windows 2000–based server, a Windows 2000 Professional–based client cannot connect to a Windows 2000–based server running only the IPX/SPX protocol. To resolve this problem, enable NetBIOS on computers running Windows 2000 Professional and Windows 2000 Server.

For instructions about how to enable NetBIOS on the Windows 2000–based client running on your computer, see the documentation provided with the operating system.

CHAPTER 25

Interoperability with UNIX

Microsoft® Windows® 2000 Professional and Microsoft® Windows® Services for UNIX 2.0 allow for complete interoperability with UNIX platforms. Services for UNIX 2.0 is the easiest way to integrate Microsoft® Windows NT® and Windows 2000 into existing UNIX-based network environments. This is accomplished by providing interoperability components that use existing UNIX network resources and knowledge in your organization, and manageability components that simplify network administration and account management.

In This Chapter

Quick Guide to UNIX Interoperability

This guide can help you determine if a particular section in this chapter contains the information you need to accomplish a specific task.

Review key features of interoperability with UNIX platforms.

Windows 2000 Professional and Services for UNIX 2.0 provide a comprehensive solution for interoperability between Windows 2000 networks and UNIX.

- See "Overview of Windows 2000 Professional and UNIX Connectivity" in this chapter.

Plan and install Services for UNIX on Windows 2000 Professional.

Determine which Services for UNIX components should be used for your specific networking environment and understand how to install the components for Windows 2000 Professional.

- See "Planning and Installing Services for UNIX on Windows 2000 Professional" in this chapter.

Configure Services for UNIX on Windows 2000 Professional.

Understand how to configure the Services for UNIX components for Windows 2000 Professional.

- See "Configuring Services for UNIX on Windows 2000 Professional" in this chapter.

Understand the included UNIX utilities, shell, and commands.

Understand how to use the Korn shell, utilities, and manage your network through Microsoft® Management Console (MMC) snap-ins.

- See "Tools" in this chapter.

Recover from common UNIX connectivity-related problems.

Follow the troubleshooting guidelines to recover from problems with connectivity.

- See "Troubleshooting" in this chapter.

Overview of Windows 2000 Professional and UNIX Connectivity

Services for UNIX 2.0 provides a set of additional features to Windows NT and Windows 2000 that allows for greater interoperability with existing UNIX servers in the enterprise. Services for UNIX 2.0 provides fully supported and fully integrated interoperability components that allow customers to integrate Windows NT 4.0 and Windows 2000 operating systems into their existing UNIX environments. It also provides manageability components that enable customer organizations to simplify network administration and account management across both platforms.

What's New for Windows 2000 Professional and UNIX Connectivity

The add-on pack Services for UNIX version 2.0 adds to Services for UNIX version 1.0 the following new capabilities:

- Two-way password synchronization between Windows NT and UNIX.
- Administration of Services for UNIX through Microsoft Management Console (MMC).
- Gateway for NFS allows client computers running Microsoft® Windows® 95 or Microsoft® Windows® 98, Windows NT, and Windows 2000 to access NFS shared files.
- Network File System (NFS) version 3.0 support.
- Network Information Service (NIS) support.
- Additional UNIX Utilities support.
- Migration wizard to migrate NIS source files to Active Directory™ directory service on a Microsoft® Windows® 2000 Server configured as a domain controller.
- Username Mapping Server
- ActiveState Perl engine.

Introduction to Windows 2000 Professional and UNIX Connectivity

With the growing adoption of the Windows NT and Windows 2000 operating systems in established UNIX environments, the need for the two platforms to interoperate has increased.

To connect a computer running Windows 2000 Professional to UNIX computers, you need protocols and services that allow the two networking systems to communicate with each other. Windows 2000 Professional uses the Common Internet File System (CIFS) protocol for file and print services. CIFS is an enhanced version of the Microsoft Server Message Block (SMB) protocol. UNIX, however, uses the Network File System (NFS) protocol for file services and, for print services, uses Line Printer (LPR)/Line Printer Daemon (LPD) or personal computer network file system daemon (PCNFSD).

Services for UNIX 2.0 implements a subset of Transmission Control Protocol/Internet Protocol (TCP/IP) network protocols that enables interoperability of Windows 2000 Professional and UNIX.

Services for UNIX 2.0 provides a set of additional features to Windows NT and Windows 2000 that allow for greater interoperability with existing UNIX servers in the enterprise.

Services for UNIX 2.0 is made up of multiple components that allow you to interoperate Windows 2000 Professional and UNIX in the way that best fits your environment. Table 25.1 lists the components that are included with Services for UNIX 2.0 and provides a description of their capabilities.

Table 25.1   Components in Services for UNIX 2.0

Components	Description
Client for NFS	Enables a computer running Windows NT 4.0 or Windows 2000 to act as a client and access files and directories located on an NFS server.
Server for NFS	Enables a computer running Windows NT 4.0 or Windows 2000 to act as an NFS server so that NFS-enabled client computers can access files and directories on the Windows-based NFS server.
Gateway for NFS	Enables a computer running Windows NT 4.0 Server or Windows 2000 Server to act as an NFS gateway. This enables clients running Windows 95 or Window 98, Windows NT, and Windows 2000 to access exported (shared) NFS files and directories.
Server for NIS	Enables a computer running Windows 2000 Server and configured as a domain controller to function as an NIS server, which maintains databases of administrative information (for example, password and group databases) for UNIX-based computers.

(continued)

Table 25.1   Components in Services for UNIX 2.0 *(continued)*

Components	Description
Server for PCNFS	Enables a computer running Windows NT 4.0 or Windows 2000 to act as a PCNFSD server, which provides user authentication services for file access on NFS servers.
Two-way Password Synchronization	Enables the two-way automatic synchronization of passwords between computers running Windows 2000 and UNIX when the user password is changed either on Windows 2000 computer or on UNIX.
Telnet Client	Enables a computer running Windows NT 4.0 or Windows 2000 to access Telnet servers for remote administration.
Telnet Server	Enables a computer running Windows NT 4.0 or Windows 2000 to act as a Telnet server.
UNIX Shell and Utilities	Provides a Korn shell with over 60 popular UNIX utilities and support for PERL scripting.
Username Mapping Server	Parses files from either a PCNFSD server or NIS server from which it provides authentication or mapping to users of Client for NFS.

Planning and Installing Services for UNIX on Windows 2000 Professional

To best integrate Windows 2000 Professional and Services for UNIX 2.0 into your networking environment, you need to understand the capabilities and limitations of the components you install and configure. This section discusses the Services for UNIX components that you can implement when working in the following areas:

- File access
- Authentication
- Account management
- UNIX printing

File Access

Client for NFS, Server for NFS, and Gateway for NFS are solutions for file access between computers running Windows 2000 Professional and UNIX. Before installing Services for UNIX 2.0, you need to select the NFS component that best suits your needs.

Client for NFS Client for NFS installed on Windows 2000 Professional allows for file access on an NFS server, generally a UNIX-based computer. Figure 25.1 shows an example of this scenario.

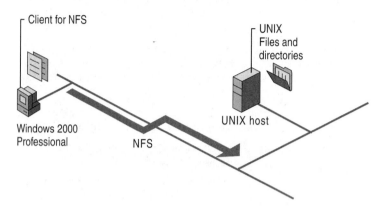

Figure 25.1   UNIX File Access Using Client for NFS

Server for NFS Server for NFS can be installed on either Windows 2000 Professional, Windows 2000 Server, or Windows NT. Server for NFS allows NFS-enabled client computers, generally those running UNIX, to access files, as Figure 25.2 illustrates.

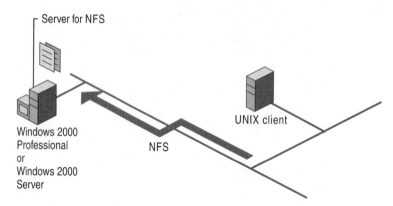

Figure 25.2   Server for NFS: UNIX File Access

Gateway for NFS Gateway for NFS must be installed on Windows 2000 Server. Gateway for NFS allows clients running Windows 95, Windows 98, Windows NT, and Windows 2000 to access UNIX files without having to install an NFS Client. Figure 25.3 illustrates how Gateway for NFS enables Windows 2000 Server to act as a translator between the CIFS protocol that Windows 2000 Professional uses and the NFS protocol that UNIX uses.

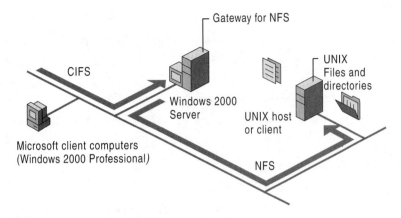

Figure 25.3   Gateway for NFS Acts As a Translator

Choosing Among Client for NFS, Server for NFS, or Gateway for NFS

Client for NFS provides clients that are running Windows 2000 Professional access to UNIX files on an NFS server. Server for NFS allows Windows NT, Windows 2000 Professional, or Windows 2000 Server to act as an NFS Server. Gateway for NFS allows Windows 2000 Server to act as a bridge between the CIFS protocol used by Windows 2000 Professional–based computers and the NFS protocol used by the UNIX NFS network. To help you decide which component is best suited to your networking environment, read the following lists of details and capabilities for each of the three different NFS components.

Client for NFS

- Installs on each Windows 2000 Professional–based computer that needs NFS file access.

- Provides access to NFS files on a UNIX NFS network.

- Resolves all UNIX path names to follow the Universal Naming Convention (UNC).

- Integrates with Server for PCNFS or Server for NIS to provide user authentication.

Server for NFS

- Installs on either Windows 2000 Professional or Windows 2000 Server.

- Enables Windows 2000 (Professional or Server) to act as an NFS server.

- Allows users on computers running NFS client software, generally those running UNIX, to access files on Windows 2000.

- Integrates with Server for PCNFS or Server for NIS to provide user authentication.

Gateway for NFS

- Installs on Windows 2000 Server.

- Provides access to NFS files for computers running Windows 95 or Windows 98, Windows NT, and Windows 2000 Professional without Client for NFS installed.

- Acts as a gateway or translator between the CIFS protocol that Windows 2000 Professional uses and the NFS protocol that UNIX uses.

Installing Client for NFS

If you select Client for NFS for file access from an NFS Server, you need to install Client for NFS on each Windows 2000 Professional–based computer that needs access to NFS files.

Note To install Client for NFS, you need administrator rights to the computer running Windows 2000 Professional.

▶ **To install Client for NFS from Windows**

1. Run **Services for UNIX** Setup.

2. Click **typical installation**.

3. Select **Client for NFS,** and then select **run it from my computer**.

▶ **To install Client for NFS from the command prompt**

- At the command prompt type:

   msiexec /I sfusetup.msi /qb ADDLOCAL="NFSClient"

Note The preceding command assumes Sfusetup.msi exists in the same directory from which you execute the command. If Sfusetup.msi is in a different directory, include the full path. You can find Sfusetup.msi on the Services for UNIX installation CD.

Whenever you install any of the components from Services for UNIX, the files listed in Table 25.2 are also installed.

Table 25.2   Common Services for UNIX Files

File Name	Description	Location
Cligrps.dll	Object for enumerating Client Groups of NFS Server	\<SFU directory>\admin
Clilocks.dll	Object for enumerating locks of NFS Server	\<SFU directory>\admin
Listview.lpk	Licensed Package for listview	\<SFU directory>\admin
Pcctrl.dll	Object for PCNFSD Administrator	\<SFU directory>\admin
Sfuadmin.dll	Services for UNIX snap-in	\<SFU directory>\admin
Client.htm, Gateway.htm, Mmain.htm, Nisdmain.htm, Nissmain.htm, Pcmain.htm, Psmain.htm, Server.htm, Tnmain.htm	All .htm files are HTML for administrative UI	\<SFU directory>\admin
Agroup.js, Auser.js, Clifiles.js, Cliperf.js, Clisec.js, Gtwmapng.js, Gtwshrng.js, Maintain.js, Maps.js, Nispush.js, Pcgroups.js, Pcusers.js, Psaudit.js, Pshosts.js, Psport.js, Pssec.js, Slaves.js, Srvaudit.js, Srvclgrp.js, Srvfiles.js, Srvsecur.js, Suser.js, Tnaudit.js, Tnauth.js, Tnsess.js, Tnsvset.js, View.js	All .js files are scripts for administrative UI	\<SFU directory>\admin

Table 25.3 lists the files that are installed during the installation of Client for NFS.

Table 25.3   Client for NFS Files

File Name	Description	Location
Gwdll.dll	Gateway network provider	%windir%\system32
Nfsccfg.dll	Client network provider helper	%windir%\system32
Nfsclnt.exe	NFS client	%windir%\system32
Nfscprop.dll	NFS shell	%windir%\system32

(continued)

Table 25.3   Client for NFS Files *(continued)*

File Name	Description	Location
Nfsnp.dll	Client network provider	%windir%\system32
Nfsrdr.sys	Client redirector	%windir%\system32\drivers
Clinotfy.mof, Cliauth.mof, Clifiles.mof, Cliperf.mof, Clisec.mof	All .mof files are Windows Management Instrumentation (WMI) classes for Services for UNIX administrator	%windir%\system32\wbem
Clinfs.chm, Clinfs_.chm, Gatenfs.chm, Gatenfs_.chm, Mapserv.chm, Mapserv_.chm, Nisserv.chm, Nisserv_.chm, Passynch_.chm, Pcnfsd.chm, Servnfs.chm, Servnfs_.chm, Stuart.chm, Sfushare.chm, Sfuwipro.chm, Svcsunix.chm, Telclin_.chm, Telclint.chm, Telserv.chm, Telserv_.chm, Unixutil.chm, Readme.txt	Help files	\<SFU directory>\help

Installing Server for NFS

If you select Server for NFS to enable Windows 2000 Professional or Windows 2000 Server to act as an NFS server, you need to install a copy of Server for NFS on each Windows 2000 Professional or Windows 2000 Server that acts as an NFS server.

Note To install Server for NFS, you need administrator rights to the computer that is running Windows 2000.

▶ **To install Server for NFS from Windows**

1. Run **Services for UNIX** Setup.

2. Click **typical installation**.

3. Select **Server for NFS,** and then select **run it from my computer**.

▶ **To install Server for NFS from the command prompt**

- At the command prompt type:

msiexec /I sfusetup.msi /qb ADDLOCAL="NFSServer, NFSServerAuth"

Note To use the preceding command, Sfusetup.msi must exist in the same directory from which you execute the command. If Sfusetup.msi is in a different directory, include the full path. You can find Sfusetup.msi in the i386 directory on the installation CD.

Table 25.4 lists the files that are installed during the installation of Server for NFS.

Table 25.4   Server for NFS Files

File Name	Description	Location
Dsctrnm.h	Performance counter data	<SFU directory>\nfs
Dsctrs.dll	Performance counter	<SFU directory>\nfs
Dsctrs.ini	Performance counter	<SFU directory>\nfs
Monitor.lst	Status monitor data	<SFU directory>\nfs
Nlm.lck, Pend.lck, Share.lck	NLM data	<SFU directory>\nfs
Rpcinfo.exe	Remote procedure call (RPC) information	<SFU directory>\common
Sfueula.txt	End-User License Agreement for Services for UNIX	<SFU directory>\common
Sfumgmt.msc	MMC Console for Services for UNIX Admin Snap-in	<SFU directory>\common
SfuWbem.dll	Wrapper for Microsoft® ActiveX® Objects	<SFU directory>\common
Showmnt.exe	Showmount utility	<SFU directory>\common
Style.css	Cascading style sheet for admin HTML pages	<SFU directory>\common
Tnadmin.exe	Command Line Administration for Telnet	<SFU directory>\common
Sfuhelp.gif, Sfurefr.gif, Sfusave.gif	Images in Services for UNIX Admin	<SFU directory>\common
Gwdll.dll	Gateway network provider	%windir%\system32
Nfsext.dll	Shell extension	%windir%\system32
Nfssa.dll	Server for NFS authentication	%windir%\system32

(continued)

Table 25.4   Server for NFS Files *(continued)*

File Name	Description	Location
Nfssvc.exe	Server for NFS service	%windir%\system32
Nfssvr.sys	Server for NFS driver	%windir%\system32\drivers
Portmap.sys	Portmapper driver	%windir%\system32\drivers
Rpcxdr.sys	RPC driver	%windir%\system32\drivers
Srvaudit.mof, Srvauth.mof, Srvfiles.mof, Srvsec.mof, Srvnotfy.mof	All .mof files are WMI classes for Services for UNIX administrator	%windir%\system32\wbem
Clinfs.chm, Clinfs_.chm, Gatenfs.chm, Gatenfs_.chm, Mapserv.chm, Mapserv_.chm, Nisserv.chm, Nisserv_.chm, Passync.chm, Passync_.chm, Pcnfsd.chm, Servnfs.chm, Servnfs_.chm, Sfuart.chm, Sfushare.chm, Sfuwipro.chm, Svcsunix.chm, Telclin_.chm, Telclint.chm, Telserv.chm, Telserv_.chm, Unixutil.chm	Help files	<SFU directory>\help

User Authentication

When an attempt is made to access NFS resources located on Server for NFS, user name mapping and authentication are performed. During an NFS call, Server for NFS receives a UNIX user identifier (UID) from an NFS client. Server for NFS then uses the mapping server to map this UID to a Windows user name. Server for NFS uses its authentication feature to authenticate the mapped Windows user name. It uses the credentials of the mapped user to access the files and provide them to the NFS client. Thus, only valid UNIX users get access to files stored on Windows-based computers when their access privileges are the same as the corresponding Windows user. Authentication is provided by Server for NFS Authentication, which you must install either on all domain controllers, for validation of domain users, or on the computer running Server for NFS, for validation of local users.

Services for UNIX 2.0 provides the following components, which you can use for authentication of file access on an NFS server.

Server for PCNFS   You can install Server for PCNFS on either Windows 2000 Professional or Windows 2000 Server. Server for PCNFS is one option for providing user authentication services when NFS-based clients (Client for NFS or third-party NFS clients) need to access NFS files. Server for PCNFS works with the mapping server. The mapping server can parse files from any PCNFSD server and then provide authentication and mapping to client computers running Client for NFS.

Server for NIS   Server for NIS must be installed on a Windows 2000 Server that is configured as a domain controller. Server for NIS allows a Windows 2000 Server that is configured as a domain controller to act as the NIS master for a particular UNIX domain. One service that Server for NIS provides is the capability to authenticate requests for NFS shares.

Note   You can also configure a UNIX NIS server to provide authentication for computers that have Client for NFS installed.

Installing Server for PCNFS

If you select Server for PCNFS for authentication, you need to install it on any computer that is running either Windows NT or Windows 2000, which you want to act as a PCNFSD server.

▶ **To install Server for PCNFS from Windows**

1. Run **Services for UNIX** Setup.

2. Click **typical installation**.

3. Select **Server for PCNFS**, and then select **run it from my computer**.

▶ **To install Server for PCNFS from the command prompt**

▪ At the command prompt type:

   msiexec /I sfusetup.msi /qb ADDLOCAL="PCNFSDServer"

Note To use the preceding command, Sfusetup.msi must exist in the same directory from which you execute the command. If Sfusetup.msi is in a different directory, include the full path. You can find Sfusetup.msi in the i386 directory on the installation CD.

Table 25.5 lists the files that are installed during the installation of Client for NFS.

Table 25.5   Server for PCNFS Files

File Name	Description	Location
Pcnfsd.exe	PCNFSD service	%windir%\system32
Kepcnfsd.sys	Kernel-mode component	%windir%\system32\drivers
Portmap.sys	Portmapper	%windir%\system32\drivers
Rpcxdr.sys	RPC/XDR	%windir%\system32\drivers
Pcnotify.mof	WMI class for Services for UNIX admin	%windir%\system32\wbem
Clinfs.chm, Clinfs_.chm, Gatenfs.chm, Gatenfs_.chm, Mapserv.chm, Mapserv_.chm, Nisserv.chm, Nisserv_.chm, Passync.chm, Passync_.chm, Pcnfsd.chm, Servnfs.chm, Servnfs_.chm, Sfuart.chm, Sfushare.chm, Sfuwipro.chm, Telclin_.chm, Telclint.chm, Telserv.chm, Telserv_.chm, Unixutil.chm, Readme.txt	Help files	<SFU directory>\help

Username Mapping Server

The computer on which you install Username Mapping Server can be running either Windows 2000 Professional or Windows 2000 Server. Username Mapping Server depends on either an NIS server or a PCNFSD server to provide the UNIX user information. This UNIX user information is used by Username Mapping Server to map and authenticate users. As Figure 25.4 illustrates, all the NFS components (Client for NFS, Server for NFS, and Gateway for NFS) must first go through Username Mapping Server during the mapping and authentication process.

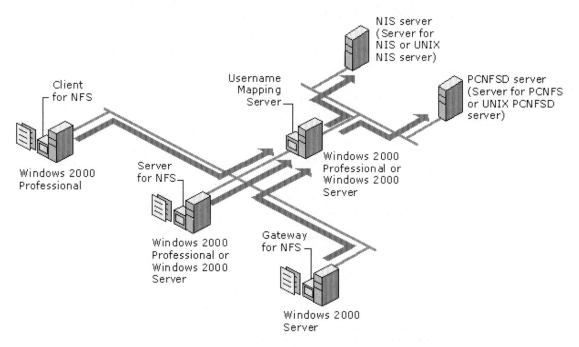

Figure 25.4   Username Mapping Server

Username Mapping Server provides two kinds of mappings. The easiest is simple mapping: a UNIX user is mapped to a user with the same user name in the Windows domain and vice versa. Administrators can also configure advanced mapping: a UNIX user is mapped to a user with a completely different user name in a Windows domain and vice versa.

When Username Mapping Server receives a request, it first checks if there is an advanced mapping for the given user and returns the mapping if it finds one. If it does not find such a mapping, it looks for a simple mapping. If it finds such a user, it provides the mapped user.

Note When using Username Mapping Server, you can use Server for PCNFS or Server for NIS from Services for UNIX, or you can use a PCNFSD server or NIS server on a UNIX computer.

Installing Username Mapping Server

If you select Username Mapping Server to map and authenticate your users, you need to install it on any computer that is running Windows NT or Windows 2000 and acting as a mapping server.

▶ **To install Username Mapping Server from Windows**

1. Run Services for UNIX Setup.

2. Click custom installation.

3. Select Username Mapping Server, and then select run it from my computer.

▶ **To install Username Mapping Server from the command prompt**

- At the command prompt type:

  msiexec /I sfusetup.msi /qb ADDLOCAL="Username Mapping Server"

Note To use the preceding command, Sfusetup.msi must exist in the same directory from which you execute the command. If Sfusetup.msi is in a different directory, include the full path. You can find Sfusetup.msi in the i386 directory on the installation CD.

Table 25.6 lists the files that are installed when you install Username Mapping Server.

Table 25.6   **Username Mapping Server Files**

File Name	Description	Location
Mapadmin.exe	Mapping utility	\<SFU directory>\common
Mapsvc.exe	Mapping server	\<SFU directory>\mapper
Clinfs.chm, Clinfs_.chm, Gatenfs.chm, Gatenfs_.chm, Mapserv.chm, Mapserv_.chm, Nisserv.chm, Nisserv_.chm, Passync.chm, Passync_.chm, Pcnfsd.chm, Servnfs.chm, Servnfs_.chm, Sfuart.chm, Sfushare.chm, Sfuwipro.chm, Telclin_.chm, Telclint.chm, Telserv.chm, Telserv_.chm, Unixutil.chm, Readme.txt	Help files	\<SFU directory>\help

Password Synchronization

The computer on which you install Password Synchronization can be running either Windows 2000 Professional or Windows 2000 Server. Password Synchronization eliminates the need to enter two different passwords when you log on and access resources from either UNIX or Windows 2000.

Services for UNIX 2.0 allows for two-way password synchronization. For example, if you change the password for a user on Windows 2000 Professional, the password for the UNIX account of that user is automatically synchronized to the same password, and a password change under UNIX causes synchronization of the Windows 2000 password.

Password Synchronization can be used in an environment with or without Windows 2000 Server configured as a domain controller. If you have Windows 2000 Professional–based computers in an environment without a domain controller, then install the Services for UNIX Password Synchronization component on the individual Windows 2000 Professional–based computers. In a Windows 2000 environment with multiple domain controllers, you must install Password Synchronization on each domain controller.

Password Synchronization can synchronize passwords with multiple UNIX-based computers at the same time, instantaneously, and securely. It also provides administrative control over the computers and users who participate in password synchronization. In addition, Password Synchronization interoperates with the Services for UNIX 1.0 single sign-on daemon installed on UNIX-based computers.

Installing Password Synchronization

If you select Password Synchronization, you need to install a copy of Password Synchronization on each Windows 2000 Professional–based computer that needs access to NFS files or on each domain controller in the domain.

You also need to install the single sign-on daemon (SSOD) on the UNIX-based computer with which you synchronize passwords. If you are using NIS, verify that SSOD is installed on the NIS master and that the Ssod.config file is configured with the full path to the Makefile located on the NIS master .

In addition, if you are using shadow passwords, edit the Ssod.config file and set USE_SHADOW equal to 1 (default is 0).

For propagating password changes from UNIX to Windows NT or Windows 2000, you need to install the supplied Windows NT Password Authentication Module (PAM) on UNIX.

▶ **To install Password Synchronization**

1. Run **Services for UNIX** Setup.

2. Click **typical installation**.

3. Select **Password Synchronization**, and then select **run it from my computer**.

▶ **To install Password Synchronization from the command prompt**

- At the command prompt type:

   msiexec /I sfusetup.msi /qb ADDLOCAL="Password Synchronization"

Note To use the preceding command, Sfusetup.msi must exist in the same directory from which you execute the command. If Sfusetup.msi is in a different directory, include the full path. You can find Sfusetup.msi in the i386 directory on the installation CD.

Table 25.7 lists the files that are installed when you install Password Synchronization.

Table 25.7   Password Synchronization Files

File Name	Description	Location
Psadmin.exe	No longer required; HTML UI takes over	\<SFU directory>\pswdsync
Pswdsync.dll	Ssynchronizes passwords from Windows to UNIX	%windir%\system32
Psync.mof	All .mof files are WMI classes for Services for UNIX administrator	%windir%\system32\wbem
Clinfs.chm, Clinfs_.chm, Gatenfs.chm, Gatenfs_.chm, Mapserv.chm, Mapserv_.chm, Nisserv.chm, Nisserv_.chm, Passynch.chm, Passynch_.chm, Pcnfsd.chm, Servnfs.chm, Servnfs_.chm, Sfuart.chm, Sfushare.chm, Sfuwipro.chm, Svcsunix.chm, Telclin_.chm, Telclint.chm, Telserv.chm, Telserv_.chm	Help files	\<SFU directory>\help

Account Management

In an NIS environment, clients and servers are logically grouped together to form a domain. Each NIS domain can have specific parameters for the NIS maps that you configure. The NIS maps are databases that contain the parameters or system information. For example, host names, user names, and passwords are some of the NIS maps.

Server for NIS enables a Windows 2000 Server that is configured as a domain controller to act as the NIS master for a particular UNIX NIS domain. This provides you with the capability to migrate NIS maps and then centrally manage UNIX NIS domains from Windows 2000 Server. The NIS maps that you select to migrate are then migrated into Active Directory. A Windows 2000 Server that is Active Directory–enabled can then act as the NIS master for the specified UNIX domains. For more information about Server for NIS, see Services for UNIX Help.

UNIX Printing

Windows 2000 Professional provides services for printing to and from UNIX resources. There are multiple ways to implement these services; one option, as illustrated in Figure 25.5, is to configure Windows 2000 Professional with Line Printer (LPR), which sends print requests to a print queue on a UNIX host that is configured with Line Printer Daemon (LPD). LPD manages the print queue and sends the print job to the correct UNIX printer.

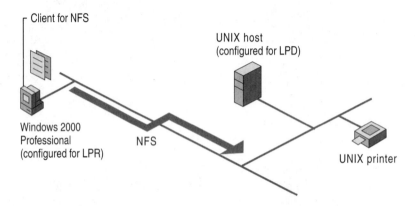

Figure 25.5   Printing to a UNIX Printer from Windows 2000 Professional

Another option is for Windows 2000 Server to act as an LPR/LPD gateway so that Windows computers without LPR/LPD services can print to a UNIX printer, as shown in Figure 25.6.

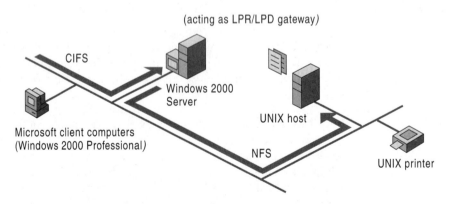

Figure 25.6   Printing Through an LPR/LPD Printer Gateway to a UNIX Printer

Another option, as illustrated in Figure 25.7, is to configure a UNIX computer with Line Printer (LPR), which sends print requests to a print queue on a Windows 2000–based computer configured with Line Printer Daemon (LPD). LPD manages the print queue and sends the print job to the correct Windows 2000 printer.

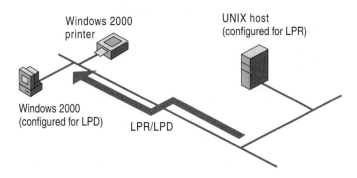

Figure 25.7   Printing to a Windows 2000 Printer from UNIX

Configuring Services for UNIX on Windows 2000 Professional

There are different ways to implement the components included with Services for UNIX on Windows 2000 Professional. One scenario is to implement Services for UNIX on Windows 2000 Professional–based computers in an environment without Windows 2000 Server. To do this, install and configure the following Services for UNIX components: Username Mapping Server, Client for NFS, and Password Synchronization. Then, install and configure LPR printing on each of the Windows 2000 Professional–based computers. With these components installed on Windows 2000 Professional, you can now be authenticated and access NFS files on UNIX computers, synchronize passwords, and print to a UNIX printer from Windows 2000 Professional. In this scenario, Username Mapping Server depends upon a UNIX NIS server or a UNIX PCNFSD server. Figure 25.8 illustrates this scenario.

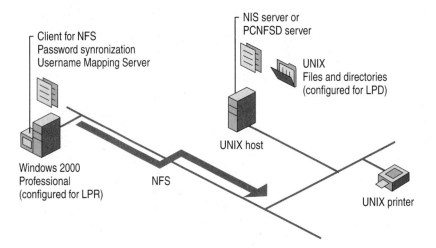

Figure 25.8   Scenario I

Another scenario for implementing Services for UNIX on Windows 2000
Professional–based computers is to install and configure Client for NFS,
Password Synchronization, and LPR printing on each of the Windows 2000
Professional–based computers. Then, for the ability to migrate UNIX NIS maps
into Active Directory, install Server for NIS on Windows 2000 Server (configured
as a domain controller). With these components installed on Windows 2000
Professional and Windows 2000 Server, you can authenticate users on your
network, grant access to NFS files on UNIX computers, synchronize passwords,
and print to a UNIX printer from Windows 2000 Professional. Figure 25.9
illustrates this scenario.

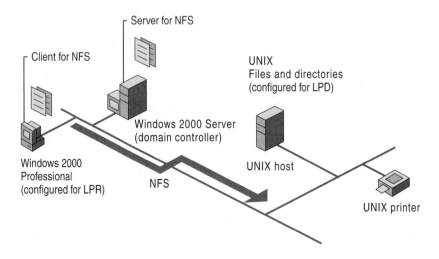

Figure 25.9   Scenario II

For user authentication and mapping in both of the preceding scenarios, you can use either Server for PCNFS or Server for NIS components from Services for UNIX, or PCNFSD server or NIS server on a UNIX computer.

The Services for UNIX components that are used in the preceding scenarios and that you can install on Windows 2000 Professional (Server for PCNFS, Client for NFS, Password Synchronization, and Username Mapping Server) are described in greater detail in the following sections.

Configuring Server for PCNFS

When configuring Server for PCNFS on Windows 2000 Professional, you have the ability to define both users and groups. The users and groups that you define when you configure the Server for PCNFS, must already be defined on the UNIX hosts from which you access files. If you do not know the user name, user identifier (UID), or group identifier (GID), you can acquire this information from the UNIX host. For more information about how to determine the user name, UID, and GID, see your UNIX software documentation.

▶ **To access Server for PCNFS**

1. Click the **Start** button, point to **Programs,** and then click **Windows Services for UNIX**.

2. Click **Services for UNIX Administration**.

3. Double-click **Server for PCNFS**.

   You can configure Server for PCNFS from this screen.

Configuring Client for NFS

When configuring Client for NFS on Windows 2000 Professional, you only need to know the name of the mapping server that you use for authenticating and mapping users.

You can use Nfsadmin.exe, a command-line utility, for configuration and administration of Client for NFS. Nfsadmin uses the following syntax:

   nfsadmin *client computer-name option=value*

where *client* indicates that you want to configure the NFS Client and *computer-name* is the name of the computer which is running the NFS Client.

Table 25.8 lists the command-line options that you can use with Nfsadmin to configure Client for NFS.

Table 25.8   Nfsadmin Command-Line Options

Option	Value
mapsvr	Computer name of the mapping server.
preferTCP	YES or NO, to indicate whether to use TCP.
mtype	HARD or SOFT, to indicate the type of mount.
retry	Number of retries for a soft mount. The default value is 5.
timeout	Time-out, in seconds, for an RPC call.
perf	MANUAL or DEFAULT, to indicate the method of determining performance parameters.
rsize	Size of the read buffer, in kilobytes.
wsize	Size of the write buffer, in kilobytes.
fileaccess	UNIX file permissions for reading, writing, and executing. For more information about UNIX file permissions, see Services for UNIX Help.

▶ **To access Client for NFS**

1. Click the **Start** button, point to **Programs,** and then click **Windows Services for UNIX**.

2. Click **Services for UNIX Administration**.

3. Double-click **Client for NFS**.

   You can configure Client for NFS from this screen.

After you configure Client for NFS, you can mount files directly from UNIX hosts in Windows 2000 Professional by using either Windows Explorer or the command prompt.

▶ **To access NFS Files and Directories with Windows Explorer**

1. In Windows Explorer, double-click **My Network Places.**

2. Double-click **Entire Network.**

3. Double-click **NFS Network.**

4. Double-click the appropriate NFS LAN, for example, **Default LAN.**

   A list of available NFS servers appears.

5. Double-click the appropriate NFS server.

   A list of exported NFS shares appears.

6. Select the file and/or folders you want to open.

Note When you attempt to access NFS files and directories from Windows 2000 Professional and do not see any NFS volumes available, it is likely that the NFS directories and files have not been configured to be exported on your UNIX host. Refer to your UNIX documentation for more information about exporting NFS directories and files.

Note If your user name exists in the authentication domain (PCNFSD/NIS), you are able to access the NFS resources with proper credentials. If your user name does not exist in the NIS/PCNFSD domain, you must access the resources as an anonymous user. However, you can change logon credentials by selecting **Connect using a different user name**. You can then provide the NIS/PCNFSD credentials you want to use to access Server for NFS.

▶ **To access NFS Files and Directories from the Command Prompt**

- At the command prompt, type the following command:

   mount *[switches] [network path] [drive | *]*

   where *switches* is one or more of the switches listed in Table 25.9, *network path* is the network path to the NFS volume you want to mount, and *drive* is the drive letter to assign to the mounted volume (asterisk indicates the next available letter).

Table 25.9   Mount Parameters and Descriptions

Switches	Description
-u:[*user name*] [*password*	*]	*User name* and *password* are the user name and password to use for mounting the NFS volume. If you use an asterisk for *password*, you are prompted for the password.
-o rsize=n	Size of the read buffer, in kilobytes.
-o wsize=n	Size of the write buffer, in kilobytes.
-o timeout=n	Time-out for NFS connections, in tenths of a second.
-o retry=n	Number of times to attempt a soft mount. Default value is 5.
-o mtype=[*soft*	*hard*]	Specify soft or hard mount.
-o anon	Mount as anonymous user.
-o nolock	Disable locking. This option improves performance if you only need to read files.
-o EUC	Enable extended UNIX code set (EUC).

Configuring Password Synchronization

When configuring Password Synchronization on Windows 2000 Professional, you need to specify the name of the Windows 2000 computer that is running the Password Synchronization service. You also need to know the name of the UNIX host with which you synchronize passwords.

▶ **To access Password Synchronization**

1. Click the **Start** button, point to **Programs,** and then click **Windows Services for UNIX**.

2. Click **Services for UNIX Administration**.

3. Double-click **Password Synchronization**.

   You can configure Password Synchronization from the **Password Synchronization** dialog box.

Note It is also necessary to verify that the single sign-on daemon (SSOD), which is on the UNIX host where you synchronize passwords, is installed and configured correctly. For more information about SSOD, see "Installing Password Synchronization" earlier in this chapter.

Configuring Username Mapping Server

When configuring Username Mapping Server on Windows 2000 Professional, there are two ways to specify how mappings can occur. Username Mapping Server allows either simple user maps or advanced user maps.

With simple user maps, the accounts with the same user name in the Windows domains and the UNIX domains are mapped. You can use either a PCNFSD server, where password and group files reside, or an NIS server for authentication. This is true for both simple and advanced user maps; you only need to know the name of the authentication server.

Advanced user maps do not require that the user names match. When using advanced user maps, you only need to know the name of the Windows domain and the UNIX domain for the users that need service from Username Mapping Server. After you enter the correct names, a listing of defined users in each domain is displayed from which you can map users between both domains.

Configuring LPR Printing

To print to a remote UNIX printer configured with Line Printer Daemon (LPD), you must first configure Windows 2000 Professional to print with Line Printer (LPR). Do this by installing Print Services for UNIX and installing and configuring a print driver to print with LPR as the printer port.

▶ **To install Print Services for UNIX**

1. In Control Panel, double-click the **Network and Dial-up Connections** icon.

2. On the **Advanced** menu, click **Optional Networking Components**.

3. In the **Components** list, click **Other Network File and Print Services,** and then click **Details**.

4. Click **Print Services for UNIX,** and then click **OK**.

▶ **To add an LPR port**

1. In Control Panel, double-click the **Printers** icon.

2. Double-click **Add Printer**, and then click **Next**.

3. Click **Local printer**, clear the **Automatically detect my printer** check box, and then click **Next**.

4. Click **Create a new port**, and then click **Standard TCP/IP Port**.

5. Click **Next**, and follow the instructions on the screen to finish installing the TCP/IP printer.

Tools

Services for UNIX allows for central management of all included components. Services for UNIX also provides UNIX utilities and a Korn shell to automate common processes across Windows NT, Windows 2000, and UNIX platforms using scripts.

Network Management

Because all the Services for UNIX components are integrated into Microsoft Management Console (MMC) as snap-ins, you can centrally manage them from a computer running Windows 2000 Professional.

▶ **To access Services for UNIX Components**

1. Click the **Start** button, point to **Programs,** and then click **Windows Services for UNIX**.

2. Click **Services for UNIX Administration**.

   You can configure all the Services for UNIX components from this window.

UNIX Shell

Services for UNIX 2.0 includes an implementation of the Korn shell. The shell is a command language interpreter that acts as the interface to the UNIX operating system. The shell interprets commands, calls the appropriate program, and returns standard output. Many shells also provide a high-level programming language that you can use to accomplish complex tasks by combining basic utilities and functions provided by the operating system.

The Korn shell, developed by David Korn at AT&T, combines many of the desirable features of the C and Bourne shells. The Bourne shell, developed at AT&T by Steven Bourne, was the first UNIX shell. The Bourne shell provides a powerful programming language. The C shell, another UNIX shell, provides a number of features not available with the Bourne shell, such as command aliases, a command history mechanism, and job control of command processing. Table 25.10 provides a feature summary of these three common shells.

Table 25.10   Shell Feature Summary

Features	Bourne	C	Korn
Command alias		X	X
Command history		X	X
Command-line editing			X
Job control		X	X
Shell scripting	X	X	X

Other shells are available for the UNIX operating system. Bash (Bourne Again shell) is an extension of the Bourne shell that incorporates features of both the Korn and C shells and is common on Linux systems. Tcsh is an extended version of the C shell that includes command completion, a command-line editor, and enhanced history manipulation.

Using the Korn Shell

The implementation of the Korn shell included with Services for UNIX differs from the standard UNIX Korn shell in the following ways:

- Semicolons are used instead of colons to separate entries in the PATH variable.
- Current directory in PATH is referred to as ;; or ;.; instead of period (.).
- Startup file is called Profile.ksh instead of .profile.
- Startup file for systemwide environment variables is called /etc/profile.ksh instead of /etc/profile.

- History file, which stores the command history of a user, is called Sh_histo file instead of Sh_history.

- Partial job control enables running of jobs in the background by using the ampersand (&) on the command line.

If your system administrator sets up the Korn shell as your default shell in Telnet Server, it is the shell you log in to when accessing a Services for UNIX server by means of Telnet. If you want to use the Korn shell without logging on to it, you can access it by using the **sh** command (**ksh** in standard UNIX).

Environment Variables

A variable consists of a name and its assigned value. You can define variables and use them in shell scripts. Other variables, called *shell variables*, are set by the shell. A variable name can contain letters, numbers (but not as the first character), and the underscore. The equal sign with no spaces on either side is used to assign a value to the variable. Once a variable is defined, you must use the **export** command to make the value of the variable available to other processes running under the shell.

The Korn shell runs the Profile.ksh file when you log on. The Profile.ksh file is used to set user-specific environment variables and terminal modes. (The system administrator can also use /etc/profile.ksh to set variables systemwide for all user accounts on the system.) Some of the variables that you can use in Profile.ksh include PATH, HOME, VISUAL, EDITOR, SHELL, HISTSIZE, HISTFILE, PS1, PS2, CDPATH.

Table 25.11 lists many of the environment variables used by the Services for UNIX Korn shell. For a complete list of the shell variables supported by the Services for UNIX Korn shell, see Services for UNIX Help under the topic **sh**.

Table 25.11   Korn Shell Environment Variables

Variable Name	Description
_	Expands to the argument of the previously executed command.
CDPATH	Defines the search path used by the **cd** command.
COLUMNS	Defines the width of the output display for programs that read the value; for example, the text editor **vi**.
EDITOR	Specifies a default editor for the system to call when no editor is specified.
ENV	Performs parameter substitution on the value if ENV is set. When the shell is invoked, the named file runs first.
ERRNO	Displays the value set by the most recently failed subroutine.
FIGNORE	Contains a pattern that defines which files are ignored during file expansion.

(continued)

Table 25.11   Korn Shell Environment Variables *(continued)*

Variable Name	Description
FCEDIT	Displays the editor for the **fc** command.
HISTFILE	Displays the absolute path of the file (default.sh_histo) that contains the command history.
HISTSIZE	Displays the number of commands in the history file.
HOME	Contains the absolute path of your home directory, which becomes your current directory when you log on.
IFS	Contains the characters used as internal field separators.
LINENO	Displays the number of the line from standard input that the shell script is currently executing.
LINES	Defines the number of output lines used by the **select** statement when printing its menu. Select writes specific words to standard error.
MAIL	Contains the absolute path of the file where your mail is stored.
MAILCHECK	Defines the number of seconds the shell waits before checking for new mail.
MAILPATH	Contains the mailbox files where new mail notification is sent.
OLDPWD	Displays the path of the previous working directory.
PATH	Defines the absolute paths of the directories where the shell searches for executable files.
PPID	Displays the process ID of the parent of the shell.
PS1	Contains the prompt displayed by the shell. The default Korn shell prompt is $. Other options exist.
PS2	Contains the secondary shell prompt.
PWD	Contains the path of the current working directory.
RANDOM	Generates a random number.
REPLY	Contains user input from the select statement.
SHELL	Defines the absolute path of the current shell. Is used by commands to invoke the shell.
TMOUT	Defines the number of seconds the shell remains inactive before it terminates.
VISUAL	Specifies a default editor that overrides the EDITOR variable.

Metacharacters

The Korn shell recognizes a special meaning for certain characters. When a regular expression contains a metacharacter, the Korn shell interprets the character as shown in Table 25.12.

Table 25.13   Shell Programming Services for UNIX Korn Shell

Command	Use
case	Runs commands based on a particular setting of another variable.
for	Runs a specific list of commands.
if	Specifies conditions in a script.
select	Writes specified words to standard error.
until	Runs a list of commands until a zero value is returned.
while	Runs a list of commands while a certain condition is true.

The Services for UNIX Korn shell has *built-in commands*. Built-in commands are run by the shell's own process. Table 25.14 lists the built-in commands that are available with the Services for UNIX Korn shell. For details about each command, see Services for UNIX Help.

Table 25.14   Services for UNIX Korn Shell Built-in Commands

Command	Description
.	Runs a shell file in the current environment.
:	Expands arguments. Returns an exit status of 0 (success).
alias	Assigns a new name to a command.
break	Exits from a for, while, or until loop.
cd	Changes the current working directory.
continue	Resumes with the next iteration of a for, while, or until loop.
echo	Displays its arguments to standard output.
environ	Standard environmental variables.
eval	Scans and runs the specified command.
exec	Runs the specified command without creating a new process.
exit	Exits the shell.
export	Makes the value of the variable available to child processes.
false	Returns an exit status of 1 (failure).
fc	Selects specified commands from command history.
getopts	Parses command line options.
jobs	Displays current jobs.
kill	Ends the specified job.
let	Evaluates the expression.
print	Displays arguments from the shell.
pwd	Displays the current working directory.

(continued)

Table 25.14   Services for UNIX Korn Shell Built-in Commands *(continued)*

Command	Description
read	Reads one line from standard output.
readonly	Makes the value of the variable read-only so it cannot be changed.
return	Exits a function.
set	Sets shell flags or command line argument variables.
shedit	Interactive command and history editing in the shell.
shift	Promotes each command line argument (for example, $3 to $2).
shpc	Features of Korn shell specific to Windows NT.
test	Checks for the properties of files, strings, and integers, and returns the results of the test as an exit value.
time	Displays run time and CPU time.
times	Displays the user program and system times accumulated by the shell.
trap	Specifies commands to run at a signal.
true	Returns exit status of 0 (success).
type	Identifies a name as interpreted by the shell.
typeset	Sets attributes and values for shell parameters.
umask	Changes access permissions.
unalias	Removes an alias.
unset	Removes a variable definition from the environment.
wait	Waits for a child process to terminate.
whence	Describes how the shell interprets a command name (as a function, shell keyword, command, alias, or executable file).

Command Aliases

For commands and command-line options, you can assign an *alias* or name that the shell translates to another name or string. (Be sure to choose an alias that is easy to remember.) The shell substitutes the command and options for the alias you enter. Creating an alias at the command line makes the alias available in the current shell environment. To make the alias a part of the work environment, add the following line to the shell start-up file (.kshrc) that defines the alias and exports it:

alias *newname=´command -option´*; **export** *newname*

The command **alias -x** exports the alias to the child process only.

To remove an alias, use **unalias** followed by the alias name:

unalias *newname*

The Services for UNIX Korn shell provides a set of predefined aliases. For more information about the alias command, see Services for UNIX Help.

Command History

The Services for UNIX Korn shell features a history file, which contains a list of a defined number of executed commands. These commands can be accessed for editing and persist in the file between logon sessions.

You can set the maximum number of commands to be saved in the history file by using the HISTSIZE variable:

HISTSIZE=*number*; **export HISTSIZE**

If you do not define this variable, UNIX saves a system-defined number of commands.

You can define the name and location of the history file by using the HISTFILE variable:

HISTFILE=*file-name*; **export HISTFILE**

If you do not define this variable, your history file is named **.sh_histo** and stored in your home directory.

Command Line Editing

You can edit the commands in the history file by using built-in Korn shell editors, such as vi, or the built-in **fc** command. You can use this feature to correct mistakes or to reuse work you have completed.

To define vi as your default editor:

set -o vi

–Or–

VISUAL=/sfu/shell/vi; export VISUAL

The built-in editor that is provided with the Korn shell offers a subset of the full functionality available with vi. You can access vi to edit a command by entering the command, pressing ENTER, and then typing **vi**. This allows you to edit a multiline command.

Arithmetic Evaluation

The Services for UNIX Korn shell has a built-in arithmetic expression feature. It supports logical and arithmetic operators. The syntax for arithmetic operators is **$((**<*arithmetic expression*>**))** or **$(**<*arithmetic expression*>**)**. The Korn shell replaces the arithmetic expression with its value, beginning with the innermost nested expression. Table 25.15 lists the operators.

Table 25.15   Arithmetic and Logical Operators

Operator	Description
+	Plus
-	Minus
*	Multiply
/	Divide (with truncation)
%	Remainder
<<	Bit-shift left
>>	Bit-shift right
&	Bitwise and
&&	Logical and
|	Bitwise or
||	Logical or
^	Bitwise exclusive or
!	Logical not
~	Bitwise not
<	Less than
>	Greater than
<=	Less than or equal to
>=	Greater than or equal to
!=	Not equal to
=	Equal to

Shell Scripts

A shell script is a file containing a series of commands that together perform a function. You can access a Korn shell script from the command prompt if you are running the Korn shell and have permission to execute the script by typing the file name. You can also run the shell script if the Korn shell is not running by entering the following command:

sh *file-name*

Note   Windows NT does not execute a script when you invoke it from the command prompt with only a file name; UNIX, however, does execute scripts if you specify the path and file name of the shell on the first line of the script, such as in the following:

#!/bin/sh

You must link each file or file name extension to a program. In particular, **.sh** or **.ksh** can be associated with the Korn shell.

Job Control

You can use job control to run a command in the foreground or the background, or to temporarily suspend it. In addition, you can see a list of the commands currently running.

When you enter a command, if it is not a built-in command, the shell forks a new process in which to run the command. The kernel schedules the process and gives it a process ID (PID). The shell keeps track of the process and gives it a job number.

Some processes are run in the foreground: they might be interactive or take only a short time to run. Other processes are better run in the background, especially commands that take a long time to run, such as a large sort. You can move a process to the foreground or the background and get a list of the current jobs. You can also temporarily suspend a process or terminate it.

Table 25.16 lists the job control commands that Services for UNIX supports.

Table 25.16   Job Control Commands

Command	Description
jobs –l	Lists the current jobs. Each job is numbered. The -l option displays the PID.
Command **&**	Runs the command in the background. For example, **sort** *file-name newfile* **&**
kill *job-number*	Terminates the job specified by *job-number*. The job number is displayed when a job is started by using **&** or the **jobs** command.

UNIX Utilities

The following UNIX utilities are available in Services for UNIX 2.0.

- Table 25.17 lists the new utilities that are available in Services for UNIX 2.0.
- Table 25.18 lists the utilities that were previously available in Services for UNIX 1.0 and that are included in Services for UNIX 2.0.

For more information about these commands, see Services for UNIX Help.

Table 25.17   New Utilities in Services for UNIX 2.0

UNIX Command	Description
cron	Schedules tasks.
crontab	Lists scheduled tasks and edits them.
cut	Cuts out bytes, character, or character-delimited fields from each line in one or more files, concatenates them and writes them to standard output..
date	Writes the date and time.
diff	Compares two files and displays line-by-line differences.
du	Prints the disk usage of a file or directory.
kill	Terminates or signals processes.
nice	Invokes a command with a specified scheduling priority.
od	Displays files in specified formats.
paste	Merges corresponding or subsequent lines of files.
perl	Runs Perl programs.
printenv	Prints environment variables that are set.
printf	Writes formatted output.
ps	Lists processes and their status.
pwd	Prints the current working directory.
renice	Reprioritizes a running process.
sdiff	Prints differences side-by-side.
sleep	Suspends execution for a specified interval.
split	Splits a file into pieces.
strings	Finds printable strings in an object or binary file.
su	Becomes another user (or administrator).
tar	Creates tape archives, and adds or extracts files from an archive.
top	Shows top processes sorted by CPU usage.
tr	Translates characters in input stream.
uname	Prints names of the current system.

(continued)

Table 25.17   New Utilities in Services for UNIX 2.0 *(continued)*

UNIX Command	Description
uudecode	Decodes a text file into a binary file.
uuencode	Encodes a binary file.
wait	Waits for process completion.
which	Locates command and print pathname/alias.
xargs	Constructs argument lists and invoke a utility.

Table 25.18   Utilities in Services for UNIX 1.0

UNIX Command	Description
sh	Invokes the Korn shell.
basename	Removes the path, leaving only the file name. Deletes any prefix ending in / and any suffix from *string* and prints the result to standard output.
cat	Concatenates and displays a file.
chmod	Changes or assigns the permissions mode of a file.
chown	Changes the owner of a file.
cp	Copies files.
dirname	Delivers all but the last level of the path in a string. See *basename*.
find	Recursively searches a directory hierarchy, looking for files that match a specified Boolean expression.
grep	Searches files for a pattern and prints all lines containing that pattern.
head	Copies first *n* lines of specified file names to standard output.
ln	Creates a hard link to a file. Links a file name to a target by creating a directory entry that refers to the target.
ls	Lists the contents of a directory.
mkdir	Creates a named directory with read, write, and execute permission for every type of user.
more	Filters and displays the contents of a text file on the terminal, one screen at a time.
mv	Moves a file name to a target.
rm	Removes an entry for a file from a directory.
rmdir	Removes a directory.
sed	Copies named file names to a standard output; edits according to a script of commands (a stream editor).

(continued)

Table 25.18 Utilities in Services for UNIX 1.0 *(continued)*

UNIX Command	Description
sort	Sorts the lines of all named files, groups them, and writes the result to standard output.
tail	Copies a named file to standard output, beginning at a designated place.
tee	Transcribes standard input to standard output and makes copies in a file name.
touch	Updates the access time or the modification time of a file.
uniq	Reports on repeated lines in a file.
wc	Displays a count of lines, words, or characters in a file.
vi	Edits text in a screen-based environment.
perl	An interpreted language that scans text files, extracts information from those files, and prints reports based on that information.

Using vi

The vi editor is an interactive text editor for creating and editing ASCII files. The vi editor requires you to enter a command to perform an action, such as entering text, deleting text, or moving the cursor. You can be in one of two modes when using vi: command mode or input mode. In command mode, you can enter commands to perform such actions as deleting text or moving the cursor in the file. In input mode, you can enter and change text. You enter input mode by entering a specific vi command. You leave input mode by pressing ESC.

This section provides basic information to get you started using vi. After you understand the mechanics of using vi, you can explore its functionality. (The mechanics are simple; the details can seem obscure at first.) For more information about the complete functionality of vi, see any of the available print or online sources, including Services for UNIX Help.

To edit a file by using vi, at the command prompt type:

vi *file-name*

and press ENTER.

If the file already exists, it appears on the screen. If the file does not exist, vi creates it.

Note You can take advantage of a file recovery feature that is provided with vi. If the system saves a copy of the last saved version of your file in a buffer, you can access that copy of the file by typing **vi -r** *file-name* and pressing ENTER.

What you see on the screen is the text of the file (if it exists), a blinking cursor in the left corner of the screen, a column of tildes along the left margin of the file that represent blank lines (if any are in view), and the name of the file in the last line of the screen. (The bottom of the screen is also used to display messages, to show commands you enter that begin with /, ?, !, and :, and to indicate input mode if the showmode option is set.)

To begin entering text, press **i** (to insert text). You can then begin typing. The text you enter appears, beginning at the position of the cursor. When you are done entering text, press ESC.

To save the file and exit vi, type

> **:wq**

and press ENTER.

Use the *colon* to escape to the shell so that you can enter a command at the bottom of the screen. Press **w** to write the file to disk. Press **q** to quit the vi editor. Table 25.19 provides a summary of the of the commands used for starting and quitting vi.

Table 25.19   Starting and Quitting vi

Command	Description
vi *file-name*	Edits *file-name* (this creates a new file or edits an existing one).
vi -r *file-name*	Recovers a file after a system failure and edits it.
:q	Quits vi if no changes have been made.
:q!	Quits vi without saving changes.
:wq	Writes (saves changes) and quits vi.

As the size of the file increases, you can more easily move throughout the file by using the following commands in command mode, as shown in Table 25.20.

Table 25.20   Moving the Cursor in Command Mode

Command	Description
Spacebar	Moves the cursor forward one character.
Backspace	Moves the cursor back one character.
l	Moves the cursor one character to the right.
h	Moves the cursor one character to the left.
j	Moves the cursor down one line.
k	Moves the cursor up one line.
Ctrl-d	Scrolls down half a screen.

(continued)

Table 25.20   Moving the Cursor in Command Mode *(continued)*

Command	Description
Ctrl-u	Scrolls up half a screen.
Ctrl-f	Scrolls down one screen.
Ctrl-b	Scrolls up one screen.
*n***G**	Moves the cursor to line *n*.
G	Moves the cursor to the end of the file.

Tables 25.21 and 25.22 list many ways for inserting and changing text that allow for detailed control.

Table 25.21   Input Mode

Command	Description
a	Inserts text after the cursor.
A	Inserts text at the end of the current line.
I	Inserts text before the cursor.
I	Inserts text before the current line.
o	Opens a line in the text below the cursor.
O	Opens a line in the text above the cursor.

Table 25.22   Changing Text

Command	Description
r	Replaces the current character with the next character typed; returns to Command mode.
R	Replaces text beginning with the current character until you pressESC.
Cc	Changes the entire current line to the new text entered.
Cw	Changes the current word, beginning at the cursor position, to the new text entered.
S	Substitutes the character at the cursor position with the new text entered.
S	Substitutes the entire current line with the new text entered.

Table 25.23 lists ways to delete text in vi.

Table 25.23   Deleting Text in vi

Command	Description
D	Deletes from the cursor to the end of the line.
x	Deletes the current character.
dd	Deletes the current line.

You can *yank* and *put*—that is, copy and paste—text within a file and between files. The yank command, as shown in Table 25.24, copies selected text and places it in a buffer. The put commands copy the text from the buffer to a specified place in the file. Named buffers and numbered buffers are available but are beyond the scope of this discussion.

Table 25.24   Yank and Put Commands

Command	Description
yy or Y	Yanks (copies) the current line and places it in a buffer.
5yy	Yanks (copies) five lines and places them in a buffer.
P	Puts (pastes) the text that is in the buffer into the line after the current one.
P	Puts (pastes) the text that is in the buffer into the line before the current one.

You can search for a character string within the file. The search tools are case-sensitive. If the pattern is not found, vi displays a message at the bottom of the screen telling you that it is unable to find the pattern. Table 25.25 lists the available search commands and their descriptions.

Table 25.25   Search Commands

Command	Description
/pattern	Moves forward to the first character in the next occurrence of the character string *pattern*.
/	Repeats the previous forward search.
?pattern	Moves backward to the first character in the next occurrence of the character string *pattern*.
?	Repeats the previous backward search.

You can access global pattern substitution from the command prompt.

The command takes the following form:

:s/*string*/*replacement*/**g**

In this command, *string* represents any regular expression that you want to search for, *replacement* represents the text that replaces *string*, and **g** specifies global replacement of all occurrences of *string*. If the trailing **g** is omitted, only the first occurrence of the string in each line is replaced. If you want to be prompted to confirm each substitution, type a **c** after the **g** in the command, as follows:

:s/*string*/*replacement*/**gc**

Table 25.26 lists a few of the many other commands available in vi.

Table 25.26   Other Useful Commands

Command	Description
:sh	Escapes to the shell to run a command.
:!*command*	Runs one command.
u	Undoes the last change.
U	Restores the last deleted line.
~	Toggles the case of the current character.
xp	Transposes the character in the current cursor position with the next character.
.	Repeats the last change.

Scripting

Services for UNIX includes two tools that you can use for scripting: Perl and sh.

Perl is a scripting language that is useful for automated tasks, such as processing text files by using pattern matching techniques. Perl is "open source" software. Not all Perl functions are implemented in Services for UNIX. For more information about Perl, see Services for UNIX Help.

The Korn shell provided with Services for UNIX can be used as a shell script processor. For more information about using the Korn shell for scripting, see Services for UNIX Help under the topic **sh**.

Troubleshooting

Connectivity between Windows 2000 Professional and UNIX hosts requires correct configuration on both computers. This section lists the common UNIX connectivity errors that occur when you configure both Windows 2000 Professional and Services for UNIX.

Commonly Encountered Errors

Following are some common error messages and troubleshooting suggestions.

"An error ocurred while attempting to communicate with the Client for NFS service."

Check if Client for NFS is started. Do this by typing **net start** at the DOS prompt and see if the Client for NFS service is running.

"NFS will use anonymous UID (-2), GID (-1), and factory default mount options."

If UID is -2 and GID is -1, the user is probably authenticated as an anonymous user. Verify that your mapping server is configured correctly and set to connect correctly to the NIS server or PCNFSD server. Also check if your NIS server or PCNFSD server is configured correctly and functioning.

"Owner is nobody or group is nogroup"

This error message can occur when accessing files and the file permissions are incorrectly reported. Use the following steps to troubleshoot the problem.

1. Ensure that local or domain users are correctly mapped by means of the Username Mapping Server and that Services for UNIX is configured to use the correct mapping server.

2. Check the /etc/exports file on the UNIX server and make sure it isn't configured to only allow anonymous connections.

3. If using PCNFSD, make sure that the UIDs and GIDs match on the mapping server and the UNIX server.

4. If the problem is with an NFS server running Services for UNIX, make sure that the Server for NFS Authentication component is installed on Windows 2000 Professional. If you have a domain environment and are using domain accounts for mapping, the Server for NFS Authentication component must be installed on all domain controllers in the domain.

Cannot Mount a UNIX NFS Volume

If you are unable to access an NFS volume with Windows 2000 Professional that is running Services for UNIX, use the following steps to troubleshoot the problem.

1. Check the /etc/exports file to ensure that there aren't any host restrictions that are preventing you from mounting the NFS volume.

2. Make sure the file system is properly exported by running the following command:

   showmount -e *<IP address of UNIX host>*

3. Make sure that the daemons mountd, nfsd, and rpcbind are running by running the following command:

   rpcinfo -p *<IP address of UNIX host>*

4. Some versions of UNIX might incorrectly report that they support NFS version 3. You might need to force the Services for UNIX client to use NFS version 2. To force the client to use NFS version 2, add the registry entry **DisableV3** to the following registry subkey:

   HKEY_LOCAL_MACHINE\SOFTWARE\Microsoft\Client for NFS \CurrentVersion\Default

   Set **DisableV3** to data type REG_DWORD with a value of 0x1.

Caution Do not use a registry editor to edit the registry directly unless you have no alternative. The registry editors bypass the standard safeguards provided by administrative tools. These safeguards prevent you from entering conflicting settings or settings that are likely to degrade performance or damage your system. Editing the registry directly can have serious, unexpected consequences that can prevent the system from starting and require that you reinstall Windows 2000. To configure or customize Windows 2000, use the programs in Control Panel or Microsoft Management Console (MMC) whenever possible.

Cannot Telnet into my UNIX server as root

If you are unable to log into a UNIX server as root by using telnet, verify that your version of UNIX is configured to allow a root user to log in remotely. For example, Sun Solaris requires editing the /etc/default/login file.

Cannot map a drive after using Telnet to access a Services for UNIX Telnet Server

If you cannot map a drive by using **net use** after using Telnet to connect to a Services for UNIX Telnet Server and using NTLM authentication, read the following to troubleshoot the problem.

When you are within the Telnet session, you cannot connect to network resources by using your implied user credentials. You must explicitly specify your credentials when making network connections from within the Telnet session. There is no mechanism in Windows NT to perform delegation of security, known as passthrough, for network logon attempts. As a workaround, explicitly specify credentials when mapping drives, that is, do as follows:

net use *<server>**<share name>* **/user:***<domainname>**<username>* **password**

Password synchronization isn't working properly

If the Services for UNIX Password Synchronization component is not working properly, follow the proceeding steps to troubleshoot the problem.

1. Ensure that SSOD is running on the UNIX server and that the Password Synchronization component has been installed on a computer running Windows 2000 (or on all domain controllers within a domain).

2. Ensure that the port number and passwords match on both the Windows 2000 computer and the UNIX server.

3. If you are using shadow passwords, edit the Ssod.config file and change the line USE_SHADOW=0 to USE_SHADOW=1

4. If you are using NIS, be sure that the SSOD is installed on the NIS master and that the Ssod.config file is configured with the correct path for the Makefile for password push.

CHAPTER 26

Interoperability with IBM Host Systems

Microsoft® Windows® 2000 Professional and Microsoft® SNA Server allow users to gain direct access to IBM Corporation host systems. SNA Server is the solution that has been developed by Microsoft for connecting personal computer–based clients and servers to IBM host systems. It is also possible for users to connect to an IBM host system directly without using a gateway like SNA Server—through TCP/IP. This requires the IBM host to support and be configured for SNA Telnet access, either as TN3270 or TN5250, and then to use host emulation software that supports SNA Telnet. This chapter describes the components that are required for integrating, managing, and troubleshooting Windows 2000 Professional with IBM host systems.

In This Chapter

Quick Guide to Interoperability with IBM Host Systems

You can use computers running Windows 2000 Professional in an IBM host environment. Use this quick guide to make planning decisions, such as whether to use SNA Server to communicate with an IBM host, how to secure your system, and how to set up and troubleshoot your configurations.

Review key features of interoperability with IBM host systems.

Windows 2000 Professional can interoperate with IBM hosts by communicating through SNA Server or by communicating directly with a common networking protocol. IBM hosts are part of Systems Network Architecture (SNA).

- See "Overview to Interoperability with IBM Host Systems" in this chapter.

Connect to an IBM Host by using the Microsoft DLC Protocol.

If you have a third-party host emulation application, you can use the Microsoft Data Link Control (DLC) protocol that is included with Windows 2000 Professional as a way to connect to IBM hosts.

- See "DLC Protocol" in this chapter.

Configure Microsoft® SNA Server Client, and choose the appropriate component.

If you decide to use SNA Server to connect to the IBM host, you must configure SNA Server Client on Windows 2000 Professional. You can also use either the 3270 Applet or the 5250 Applet as your host emulation product.

- See "SNA Server Client and Components" in this chapter.

Remotely configure and manage computers that are running SNA Server from Windows 2000 Professional.

If you decide to remotely manage SNA Server from Windows 2000 Professional, there are various resources and services that can be controlled from SNA Server Manager, a Microsoft Management Console (MMC) snap-in.

- See "Network Management Integration" in this chapter.

Familiarize yourself with Windows 2000 Professional and IBM Host Security.

In both Windows 2000 Professional and SNA Server, you can implement authentication, resource allocation, and data encryption services for IBM host access.

- See "Windows 2000 Professional and IBM Host Security" in this chapter.

Troubleshoot SNA Server Client problems and other errors.

Follow the troubleshooting guidelines to recover from SNA Server Client errors and other common problems.

- See "Troubleshooting" in this chapter.

Overview of Interoperability with IBM Host Systems

IBM host systems use a different network architecture, Systems Network Architecture (SNA), than does Windows 2000 Professional. Therefore, in order for Windows 2000 Professional–based computers to communicate with IBM host systems, either a gateway device to interpret the two different network protocols or a common network protocol is required.

Note For a general description of SNA, see "IBM Systems Network Architecture" later in this chapter.

To connect to IBM hosts by using a gateway device, you must have a local area network (LAN) protocol on Windows 2000 Professional and a gateway that provides the translation between the LAN protocol and the IBM host protocol or data stream. SNA Server is a gateway that provides this translation service. Figure 26.1 illustrates how SNA Server acts as the gateway between IBM hosts and Windows 2000 Professional.

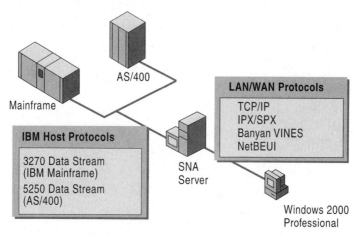

Figure 26.1   Host Connectivity Through SNA Server

Table 26.1 lists the LAN protocols that are supported for access to an IBM host system through an SNA Server.

Table 26.1   SNA Server LAN-to-Host Protocols

Protocol	Description	Client Requirements
Microsoft Networking (Named Pipes)	Microsoft application programming interface (API) that is used for communication between Microsoft Networking–based computers.	SNA Server components or third-party host emulation software. Any Windows 2000 Professional LAN protocol.
Novell NetWare (IPX/SPX)	Internetwork Packet Exchange/Sequenced Packet Exchange (IPX/SPX) protocol. Primarily used for access to NetWare resources.	SNA Server components or third-party host emulation software. IPX/SPX protocol.
TCP/IP	Transmission Control Protocol/Internet Protocol. Protocol that is designed for the Internet and wide area networks (WANs).	SNA Server components or third-party host emulation software. TCP/IP protocol.
Banyan Vines	Banyan Virtual Integrated Network Service (VINES). Proprietary protocol that is used to connect to Banyan networks.	SNA Server components or third-party host emulation software. Banyan IP protocol.

To connect to an IBM host without SNA Server providing the gateway services, you must ensure that both Windows 2000 Professional and the IBM host have the same protocol installed and configured. Figure 26.2 presents an example of direct connectivity between Windows 2000 Professional and the IBM host.

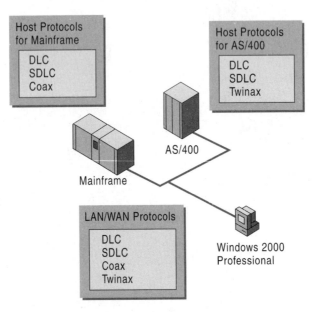

Figure 26.2   Direct Connectivity to an IBM Host

Common network protocols that can be implemented on IBM host systems and Windows 2000 Professional–based computers for direct communication, without using a gateway, are listed in Table 26.2.

Table 26.2   Common Network Protocols

Protocol	Description	Client Requirements
TCP/IP	Transmission Control Protocol/Internet Protocol. A protocol that is designed for the Internet and WANs.	Third-party host emulation software that supports direct TN3270 or TN5250 connectivity. TCP/IP protocol.
DLC	Data Link Control or 802.2. A non-routable LAN protocol that is used primarily for host connectivity.	Third-party host emulation software that supports DLC connectivity. DLC protocol.
SDLC	Synchronous Data Link Control. A WAN protocol that is used for point-to-point or point-to-multipoint connections.	Third-party host emulation software that supports SDLC connectivity. SDLC adapter. Synchronous modem. SDLC protocol.
Coax	A direct cabling point-to-point connection for IBM mainframe access.	Third-party host emulation software that supports Coax connectivity. Coax adapter.
Twinax	A direct cabling, point-to-point connection for AS/400 access.	Third-party host emulation software that supports Twinax connectivity. Twinax adapter.

SNA Server

SNA Server provides administrators with a range of solutions for integrating heterogeneous networks and intranets with IBM mainframe, midrange, and AS/400 host systems. (See Figure 26.3.) SNA Server is a Microsoft® BackOffice® application that runs on the Microsoft® Windows® 2000 Server operating system and which provides advanced network-to-host and Web-to-host integration services.

SNA Server provides interoperability between host systems that run SNA or TCP/IP protocols. If your IBM host system runs SNA protocols, SNA Server provides network connectivity by acting as a secure, high-performance gateway between heterogeneous clients and IBM host systems. Because SNA Server runs on Windows 2000, heterogeneous clients can connect to SNA Server by using standard networking protocols such as TCP/IP, IPX/SPX, NetBIOS Enhanced User Interface (NetBEUI), Banyan VINES IP, AppleTalk, and Windows 2000 routing and remote access services. SNA Server then completes the network connection to the mainframe or AS/400 system using standard IBM SNA protocols.

After SNA or TCP/IP-based network connectivity is established, clients can use the advanced host integration features of SNA Server to gain secure access to IBM host data, applications, and network services without leaving their familiar desktop or Web browser interface.

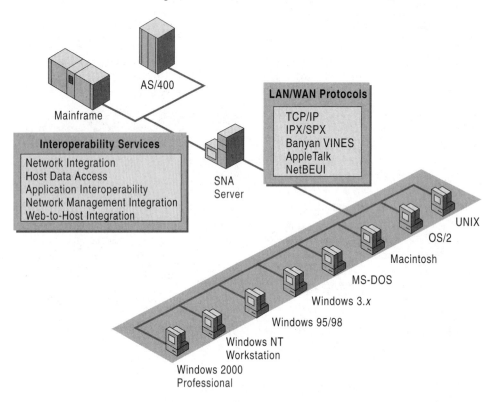

Figure 26.3   Heterogeneous Networks Integrated with IBM Host Systems Through SNA Server

SNA Server's power lies in its ability to provide a wide range of host integration services. These host integration services and how they apply to each layer of the Windows 2000 interoperability model are described in the following list.

Network Integration   Network integration provides cross-platform network connectivity and protocols, security integration, and single sign-on. (Single sign-on allows users to log on once for access to multiple servers, systems, or applications.)

Data Access   Data access provides transparent file transfer services, universal data access technologies such as OLE DB and open database connectivity (ODBC), and host data replication.

Application Interoperability   Application interoperability provides terminal access, integrated transaction services, and Web-to-host integration.

Network Management Integration   Network management integration provides integration between Windows 2000 network management services and IBM NetView–based management services.

Note   For detailed information about SNA Server interoperability at each layer of the Windows 2000 interoperability model, see the *Microsoft® Windows® 2000 Server Resource Kit Internetworking Guide.*

IBM Systems Network Architecture

SNA is a computer networking architecture that was developed by IBM to provide a network structure for IBM mainframe, midrange, and personal computer systems. SNA defines a set of proprietary communication protocols and message formats for the exchange and management of data on IBM host networks.

SNA can be used for the following types of tasks:

- Terminal access to mainframe and midrange computer applications.
- File transfer of data between computer systems.
- Printing of mainframe and midrange data on SNA printers.
- Program-to-program communications that allow applications to exchange data over the network.

SNA can be implemented in a networking infrastructure that uses either a hierarchical or peer-to-peer model.

Hierarchical Networking

In the hierarchical SNA networking model, also called *subarea networking*, geographically disparate users have access to centralized mainframe systems. In a hierarchical network, centralized host-based communication systems (mainframes) must provide the networking services for all users on the network, as illustrated in Figure 26.4.

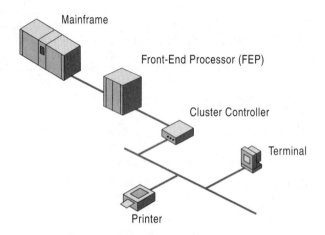

Figure 26.4   Hierarchical SNA Network

This model uses the SNA protocol for IBM mainframe computers known as 3270. This protocol facilitates conversations between the mainframe and devices such as terminals, printers, and controllers.

Peer-to-Peer Networking

The more recently developed Advanced Peer-to-Peer Networking (APPN) model makes use of LAN and WAN resources and client/server computing. APPN networking enables a form of distributed processing by allowing any computer on the network to use SNA protocols to gain access to resources on any other computer on the network. Computers on an APPN network do not have to depend on mainframe-based communication services.

Advanced Program-to-Program Communication (APPC) is generally used in an AS/400 environment; however, mainframe systems also can use APPC-based networking. APPC is used for a variety of applications, including 5250 access and file transfers. IBM SNA uses the 5250 protocol to facilitate conversations between an AS/400 and devices such as terminals and printers.

A typical APPN network is composed of several different devices, such as IBM host computers or personal computers connected to one or more LANs, as illustrated in Figure 26.5.

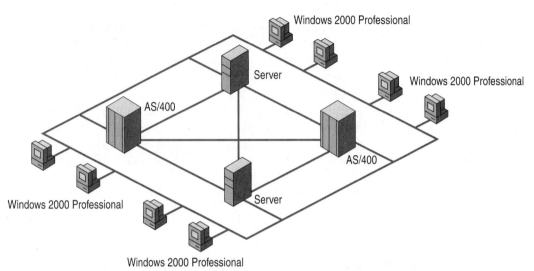

Figure 26.5   APPN Network Components

The peer-oriented model can be employed in many different environments. The AS/400 midrange computer, because of its popularity and primary use of APPN, is the host that is most often associated with APPN and the peer-oriented networking model. Mainframe systems are beginning to support APPN as well.

Because of the large installed base of legacy applications that run on IBM mainframe and midrange systems, both of these SNA networking models continue to be widely used in enterprise networks.

Note   SNA is gradually evolving into more of a peer-to-peer networking structure, where APPN networking is often combined with hierarchical SNA networking. For more detailed information about APPN see the appendix "IBM SNA Interoperability Concepts" in the *Windows 2000 Server Resource Kit Internetworking Guide*.

Both hierarchical and peer-to-peer SNA networking include several classes of components that support communication between different systems—mainframe, midrange, and personal computer systems. These components, as shown in Table 26.3, are the core components of IBM SNA.

Table 26.3   SNA Core Components

Components	Description
Hardware Components or Nodes	Hardware that provides the computing platforms and network devices that implement specific SNA communication and management functions.
Connection Types	Hardware and communication standards that provide the data communication paths between components in an SNA network.
Physical Units (PUs)	A combination of hardware and software that provides the configuration support and control of SNA network devices, connections, and protocols.
Logical Units (LUs)	Protocols that provide a standardized format for delivery of data for specific applications, such as terminal access and printing.
SNA Sessions	SNA communications that are based on the establishment and termination of logical sessions between network addressable units (NAUs).

DLC Protocol

Windows 2000 Professional includes a protected-mode, 32-bit, Data Link Control (DLC) protocol driver. You can use the DLC protocol to connect directly to an IBM host. However, you need third-party host emulation software to do so; DLC functions at the data-link layer of the Open Systems Interconnection (OSI) model. Because DLC functions at the data-link layer, it does not depend on other LAN protocols (for example, TCP/IP) for host connectivity; it is possible to have only the DLC protocol installed and bound to your network adapter.

▶ **To install the DLC Protocol**

1. Open **Network and Dial-Up Connections** in Control Panel.

2. Right-click the local area connection for which you want to install the DLC protocol, and then click **Properties**.

3. On the **General** tab, click **Install**.

4. In the **Select Network Component Type** dialog box, click **Protocol**, and then click **Add**.

5. In the **Select Network Protocol** dialog box, click **DLC Protocol**, and then click **OK**.

In most cases, it is not necessary to change the default values for the DLC protocol. Generally, the only reason to change any of these parameters is if you are told to do so by the customer support department of the company from which you have obtained your third-party host emulation software. If you do have to change the default values, you might be able to change some of them by using the third-party host emulation software, for example by specifying a service access point (SAP). There are also some parameters that you can modify in the registry of Windows 2000 Professional, as Table 26.4 illustrates.

Caution Do not use a registry editor to edit the registry directly unless you have no alternative. The registry editors bypass the standard safeguards provided by administrative tools. These safeguards prevent you from entering conflicting settings or settings that are likely to degrade performance or damage your system. Editing the registry directly can have serious, unexpected consequences that can prevent the system from starting and require that you reinstall Windows 2000. To configure or customize Windows 2000, use the programs in Microsoft Management Console (MMC) or Control Panel whenever possible.

To change any of these DLC parameters, go to the following path in a registry editor:

`HKEY_LOCAL_MACHINE\SYSTEM\CurrentControlSet\Services\DLC\Parameters`

Table 26.4   DLC Registry Parameters

DLC Parameter	Description	Default	Range
Swap	When DLC is bound to an Ethernet or token-ring driver, set this parameter to 1 (enable) to turn on address bit-swapping.	1	0-1(Boolean)
T1TickOne	Sets the retransmission-timer "short tick" value. This timer determines the delay (in units of 40 milliseconds) before retransmitting a link-level frame when no acknowledgment is received.	5	1-255
T1TickTwo	Sets the retransmission-timer "long tick" value. This timer determines the delay (in units of 40 milliseconds) before retransmitting a link-level frame when no acknowledgment is received.	25	1-255

(continued)

Table 26.4   DLC Registry Parameters *(continued)*

DLC Parameter	Description	Default	Range
T2TickOne	Sets the delayed-acknowledgment timer "short tick" value. This timer determines the delay (in units of 40 milliseconds) before acknowledging a received frame when the receive window has not been reached.	1	1-255
T2TickTwo	Sets the delayed-acknowledgment timer "long tick" value. This timer determines the delay (in units of 40 milliseconds) before acknowledging a received frame when the receive window has not been reached.	10	1-255
TiTickOne	Sets the inactivity-timer "short tick" value (in units of 40 milliseconds). This timer determines how often DLC checks an inactive link to see whether it is still operational.	25	1-255
TiTickTwo	Sets the inactivity-timer "long tick" value (in units of 40 milliseconds). This timer determines how often DLC checks an inactive link to see whether it is still operational.	125	1-255
UseDixOverEthernet	This parameter is used when transmitting DLC packets over an Ethernet network. When this parameter is set to 1, the DLC packets are transmitted using Ethernet DIX (Ethernet II) frames. For all other types of Ethernet frame, this parameter should be left at the default value of 0.	0	0-1(Boolean)

SNA Server Client and Components

Windows 2000 Professional uses SNA Server Client to establish connectivity to an IBM host when an SNA Server is implemented as the gateway. Included with SNA Server Client are two host emulation applications, 3270 Applet and 5250 Applet. The 3270 Applet is used for communicating with an IBM mainframe. The 5250 Applet is used for communicating with an AS/400. The SNA Server components communicate through SNA Server Client, which communicates with SNA Server. SNA Server communicates with the IBM host, as illustrated in Figure 26.6.

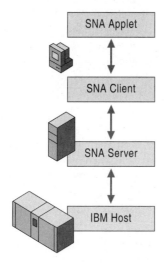

Figure 26.6   SNA Server Client Communication Path

Note All host emulation applications that have access to an IBM host through SNA Server communicate through SNA Server Client.

Installing SNA Server Client and Components

SNA Server Client is installed on Windows 2000 Professional. During the installation of SNA Server Client, you can choose which of the included components you want to install. For basic connectivity to an IBM mainframe and an AS/400, select the 3270 Applet and the 5250 Applet, respectively. SNA Server Client is located on the SNA Server installation CD in the path Clients\Winnt\I386\Setup.exe. Table 26.5 lists all of the components you can select during the installation of SNA Server Client.

Table 26.5   SNA Server Client Components

Components	Description
SNA Server Manager	SNA Server Manager allows you to manage SNA Server from Windows 2000 Professional. Users who have network administration privileges can use this tool to configure an SNA Server computer, LUs, LU pools, users, Host Print Service, Shared Folders Gateway Service, APPC modes, CPI-C symbolic names, and host security domains.
3270 Applet	The program 3270 Applet allows you access to an IBM host on an SNA network.
5250 Applet	The program 5250 Applet allows you access to AS/400 systems.
COM Transaction Integrator for CICS and IMS (COMTI)	COMTI provides computers running SNA Server Client with access to the IBM Customer Information Control System (CICS) and Information Management System (IMS) programs that are running on MVS mainframes.
OLE DB Provider for AS/400 and VSAM	Microsoft OLE DB Provider for AS/400 and VSAM allows record-level access to mainframe and AS/400 files.
OLE DB Provider/ODBC Driver for DB2	Microsoft OLE DB is the component database architecture that provides universal data integration over an enterprise network—from mainframe to desktop—regardless of the data type.
APPC File Transfer Protocol (AFTP) Client	AFTP Client allows your computer to connect to AFTP Service to share files among different platforms.
Host Account Manager	Host Account Manager connects users to all servers and domains to which they have access with a single password.
SNA Server Remote Access Service	SNA Server Remote Access Service enables a system administrator to create a virtual LAN connection between Windows NT systems across an existing SNA network without having redundant LAN-to-LAN networks or having to install dial-up modems at each site.
Host Connectivity SDK	Access to the Software Development Kit (SDK) makes it possible for software developers to create specialized SNA Server applications.
SNA NetView Alerter	This tool allows the NetView reporting system to send alerts and other messages between the host and the computers that connect to it.

Note For detailed information about SNA Server Client components, refer to SNA Server Help.

SNA Server Client is always installed, no matter what other component you choose to use from the list. During the installation and setup of SNA Server Client, you must select one of the following networking protocols for client-to-server communications. The protocol you select is used for communication between SNA Server Client and SNA Server. The available protocols are the following:

- Microsoft Networking (Named Pipes)
- Novell NetWare (IPX/SPX)
- TCP/IP
- Banyan VINES

You also must select one of the following methods for the client to use in locating computers that are running SNA Server:

- Client locates servers in an SNA Server subdomain.
- Client locates servers by name.

To select **Client locates servers in an SNA Server subdomain**, you must know the name of the subdomain in which SNA Server resides. Every server that runs SNA Server is a member of a Windows NT domain. Within the Windows NT domain is an SNA Server subdomain. SNA Server subdomains form a logical grouping of computers that run SNA Server and through which SNA Server clients can connect.

To select **Client locates server by name**, you must know the name of a specific server on which SNA Server resides in the SNA Server subdomain.

For more information about installing and configuring client software, see *Microsoft® SNA Server Getting Started* and SNA Server Help.

Network Management Integration

With Windows 2000 Professional, you can remotely configure and manage computers that are running SNA Server by using SNA Server Manager. SNA Server Manager is a graphical MMC snap-in that supports simultaneous monitoring, diagnosis, and management of SNA Server resources and services, including the following:

- SNA Server subdomains
- Computers
- Configurations
- Link services
- Connections

- LUs
- Sessions
- Services
- Users

SNA Server Manager integrates the administration of all services that are provided by SNA Server, including TN3270 Service, TN5250 Service, Host Print Service, Shared Folders Gateway Service, and Host Security Integration.

With SNA Server Manager, you can view all computers that are running SNA Server in an SNA Server subdomain and also manage multiple subdomains at the same time. This allows for central configuration and administration of all SNA Server resources throughout an enterprise network.

SNA Server Manager can run on any computer that is running Windows 2000 Professional and that is configured with SNA Server Client.

Note SNA Server also provides a command-line management interface that allows you to store and use configuration commands in command files. For more information about command-line management functions, see SNA Server version 4.0 Help and the *Microsoft® BackOffice® Resource Kit.*

Using Windows 2000 Professional MMC Snap-Ins with SNA Server Manager

SNA Server includes SNA Server Manager, which is tightly integrated with the Windows 2000 Professional MMC snap-ins that include the following:

- Local Users and Groups
- System Monitor
- Event Viewer

Integration with Local Users and Groups provides a common user account database and security system for Windows 2000 users, SNA Server Client–based computers, and users of other BackOffice applications. Integration with System Monitor allows you to configure performance counters that monitor the SNA traffic volumes of their SNA Server–based computers. With Event Viewer, you can quickly identify the type and sequence of the events leading up to problems on any SNA Server subdomain.

For more information about managing SNA Server resources and services from the Windows 2000 Professional MMC, see the SNA Server version 4.0 documentation and the *Microsoft® BackOffice® Resource Kit.*

Windows 2000 Professional and IBM Host Security

Windows 2000 Professional and SNA Server provide authentication, resource allocation, and data encryption services for maintaining a secure networking environment when you are integrating Windows 2000 Professional and IBM host systems.

Authentication

When you connect to an IBM host with Windows 2000 Professional and SNA Server, you can have single sign-on and password synchronization for authentication of access to resources on both your LAN host and on the IBM host. These services, which are provided with SNA Server, are integrated into the security features supported by Windows 2000 Professional and SNA Server. (For more information about security and Windows 2000 Professional, see the chapter "Security," in this book.)

Host Security Integration is the SNA Server feature that provides the single sign-on and password synchronization. Host Security Integration comprises the following three components:

- Host Account Synchronization Service
- Windows 2000 Account Synchronization Service
- Host Account Cache

Host Account Synchronization Service

This service can be installed on primary, backup, or member computers that are running SNA Server within the SNA Server subdomain. You can also install the service on non-SNA Server-based computers. Host Account Synchronization Service supports third-party interfaces to various host security databases, which allows you to coordinate password changes between the Windows 2000 security domain and the host security domain.

You do not need to use Host Account Synchronization Service if you use the single-sign-on feature with manual password updates in which the administrator or users store host account information in the Host Account Cache through the Host Account Manager application (UDConfig). For more information about using the UDConfig tool, see the SNA Server version 4.0 Help and the *Microsoft® BackOffice® Resource Kit*.

Windows 2000 Account Synchronization Service

Windows 2000 Account Synchronization Service can automatically synchronize the passwords for your host accounts and Windows 2000 domain accounts. It must be installed even if automatic password synchronization is not going to be used because it also coordinates the internal operation of other services.

Windows 2000 Account Synchronization Service is installed on a Windows 2000–based domain controller. Only one instance of Windows 2000 Account Synchronization Service can be designated as primary; all other domain controllers on which the service is installed must be backup servers for this feature.

The capability of synchronizing passwords from the Windows 2000 domain to an AS/400 security domain is built into SNA Server. Third-party products also can provide enhanced synchronization services, such as two-way and automatic synchronization, to other host systems.

Host Account Cache

Host Account Cache maintains an encrypted database that maps host user accounts to Windows 2000 domain user accounts. Host Account Cache is a Windows 2000 service that is installed on Windows 2000 domain controllers. For smaller networks, SNA Server itself might be installed on a Windows 2000 domain controller and, therefore, could be used to store the Host Account Cache.

Optionally, a backup of Host Account Cache can be installed on another or the same Windows 2000 domain controller. The backup cache maintains a local copy of the user database that can be used for recovery if it's installed on another computer, or, if it's installed on the same computer as SNA Server, for eliminating network traffic for single-sign-on lookups.

Note For detailed information about the Host Security Integration feature of SNA Server, see SNA Server Help.

Host Resource Allocation

In most cases, you probably have to control who can have access to SNA Server resources in your environment. The method you use to secure these resources depends on your host environment and the types of services you want to offer your users. Some of the SNA Server resources you can control access to are listed in the following sections.

3270 Terminal Access

Users or groups who require access to 3270 sessions from workstations using SNA Server Client applications must be members of the SNA Server subdomain. By virtue of their subdomain membership, users and groups are also members of the Windows 2000 domain of which the subdomain is a part. After you are enrolled in the SNA Server subdomain, you can assign specific 3270 (LU type 2) resources to the appropriate accounts. Users can have access only to the specific resources you allocate to them.

To maintain security in your environment, it is recommended that you use domain security to authenticate users and then limit their access by only assigning them specified resources.

5250 Terminal Access and APPC Access

Users who want APPC access do not have to be defined in the SNA Server subdomain, but they must be members of the Windows 2000 domain. For 5250 terminal access from a computer that is running SNA Server Client within the network, the AS/400 supplies the required logon security for access to the AS/400. For APPC access that is programmed into specific applications, security is maintained through the actual programmatic conversation.

TN3270 Service and TN5250 Service

TN3270 service and TN5250 service are secured by specifying client workstation IP addresses that have permission to use the specified resources. In the case of TN3270E clients, a workstation name can be specified in place of the client IP address. The method that is used to verify workstations can also be used to allow only specified IP addresses to request resources that are allocated to them.

Shared Folder Services

Access to AS/400 shared folders that are made available to Windows 2000 domain users through the Shared Folders Gateway Service can be controlled by specifying permissions for the resulting shared volumes and files. Permissions are set by using the standard Windows 2000 method for local shares.

Note For detailed information about controlling resources on a server that is running SNA Server, see SNA Server Help.

Data Encryption

SNA Server allows you to encrypt data for client-to-server and server-to-server communication, as shown in Figure 26.7.

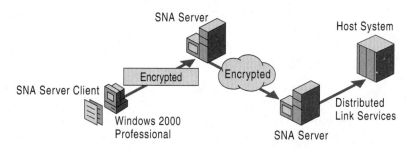

Figure 26.7   Model of Client-to-Server and Server-to-Server Data Encryption

Client-to-server encryption prevents information from being sent in plaintext between computers that are running SNA Server Client and computers that are running SNA Server. Data encryption enhances network security on the client-to-server communications path for all applications that are using SNA Server Client connections, including 3270/5250 emulators and APPC logon IDs and passwords. Data encryption can be enabled on a user-by-user basis with SNA Server Manager.

Server-to-server encryption can be used to provide secure communication across your network, the Internet, or any other WAN. If a user enables data encryption, information transferred through the Distributed Link Services is secure.

Troubleshooting

If you do not enter the correct information when you are configuring SNA Server Client on the computer that is running Windows 2000 Professional, you cannot connect to an IBM host. This section describes how to resolve commonly encountered connectivity-related problems when you are attempting to gain access to an IBM host.

Troubleshooting Commonly Encountered Problems

When SNA Server Client is installed on Windows 2000 Professional, it must be configured correctly in order to connect to an IBM host. Because connectivity involves resources on the IBM host, the computer that is running SNA Server, and the computer that is running SNA Server Client, resources must be set up correctly for all three for successful host connectivity.

If you are unable to connect to an IBM host, the first troubleshooting step is to verify with the SNA Server administrator that SNA Server is successfully connected to and communicating with the IBM host. When this has been confirmed, verify that your Windows 2000 Professional–based computer can connect to other network resources on the Windows 2000–based server on which SNA Server is installed. For example, determine whether you can map a network drive from the computer that is running Windows 2000 Professional to a drive on the server that is running Windows 2000 Server. If you are unable to do this, you must troubleshoot the problem as a network connectivity issue between the Windows 2000 Professional–based computer and the Windows 2000 Server–based computer. After you are able to gain access resources on the server that is running Windows 2000, you can proceed to troubleshoot the issue as an IBM host connectivity problem.

Figure 26.8 lists the troubleshooting steps to take when you are using SNA Server Client with Windows 2000 Professional. Each step that is listed in Figure 26.8 is discussed later in this section.

Start

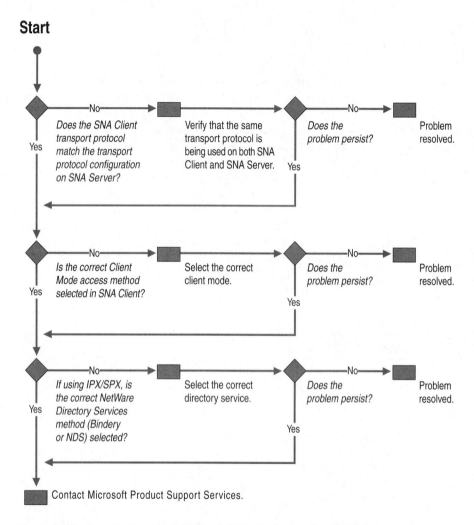

Figure 26.8   Troubleshooting Windows 2000 Professional and IBM Host Connectivity Problems

Is the Correct Transport Protocol Selected?

When you install SNA Server Client on Windows 2000 Professional, you are prompted to select a transport protocol. The transport protocol you select must match the transport protocol that is configured for SNA Server.

▶ **To verify the configuration of the transport protocol(s) on the computer that is running SNA Server**

1. In either SNA Server Manager or the SNA Management console, right-click the name of the server you want to modify.

2. In the **Server Properties** page, click the **Server Configuration** tab.

3. Under **Network Transports**, verify which protocol (or protocols) is configured to be used on the computer that is running SNA Server.

▶ **To change the transport protocol on the computer that is running SNA Server Client**

1. In SNA Server Client, select **Client Configuration**.

2. Select the **Client Protocol** tab, and then click the client/server transport protocol that matches the protocol that is configured for SNA Server.

3. Click **OK**.

Is the Correct Client Mode Selected?

When you install SNA Server Client, you have the option of selecting how SNA Server Client attempts to locate SNA Server. You can select either **Client locates servers in an SNA Server subdomain** or **Client locates servers by name**. When you are locating servers in an SNA Server subdomain, it is necessary that SNA Server Client be configured to use the same SNA Server subdomain that SNA Server is configured to use. When you are locating servers by name, you can type in either the IP address or the name of the server on which SNA Server is running.

▶ **To verify what the subdomain is configured on the SNA Server**

1. In either SNA Server Manager or the SNA Management console, right-click the name of the server you want to modify.

2. In the **Server Properties** page, click the **Server Configuration** tab.

3. Under **Subdomain**, verify which subdomain is configured to be used for the computer that is running SNA Server.

▶ **To change the subdomain on the computer that is running SNA Server Client**

1. In SNA Server Client, select **Client Configuration**.

2. Click the **Client Mode** tab, and then enter the name of the subdomain that is configured for SNA Server in the **Subdomain** text box.

3. Click **OK**.

If you select **Client locates servers by name** and are unable to connect to SNA Server after you enter the name of the computer that is running SNA Server, the problem might be the configuration of NetBIOS name resolution on your network. To test whether or not the issue is NetBIOS name resolution, type in the IP address of the computer that is running SNA Server. If you're able to connect to this server, the problem is that the NetBIOS name of the server is not being resolved to an IP address.

Note For detailed information about NetBIOS name resolution methods, see "Windows Internet Name Service" in the *Microsoft® Windows® 2000 Server Resource Kit TCP/IP Core Networking Guide.*

Is the Correct Directory Service Selected?

When you use IPX/SPX as the transport protocol to connect through SNA Server, the correct directory service (Novell Directory Services [NDS] or Bindery Services) must be selected in SNA Server Client. The directory service is configured when the NetWare server is installed. If your NetWare server is configured as NDS-based, you must also provide a default tree and context for the configuration of SNA Server Client.

Note For more information about NDS, Bindery Services, and the default tree and context, see the chapter "Interoperability with NetWare," in this book.

If you are unable to determine whether the server that is running NetWare is configured as NDS-based or Bindery Services–based, contact your NetWare administrator or consult your NetWare documentation.

▶ **To change the directory service on the computer that is running SNA Client**

1. In SNA Server Client, select **Client Configuration**.

2. Click the **NetWare** tab.

3. Select the directory service (**Bindery** or **Novell Directory Services**) that corresponds to the directory service configuration on the NetWare server.

4. Click **OK**.

Changing the Locally Administered Address

When you connect to an IBM host, it is possible that a locally administered address (LAA) has been associated with the IBM host resources for connection to a Windows 2000 Professional–based computer. On the IBM host side of the connection, LAAs usually are configured on either a Cluster Controlleror on the computer that is running SNA Server. Then an LAA also has to be configured on Windows 2000 Professional. When a specific Windows 2000 Professional–based computer, with its associated LAA, requests a resource on the IBM host, only the resources that are assigned to that LAA would be available. An LAA rather than a burned-in Universally Administered Address (UAA) on the network adapter is used so that neither the Cluster Controller nor the computer that is running SNA Server has to be reconfigured every time a network interface card card must be replaced on a workstation that is running Windows 2000 Professional.

The LAA is configured for Windows 2000 Professional through the **Advanced** tab of the network adapter.

▶ **To configure the LAA for the network adapter**

1. Open **Network and Dial-Up Connections** in Control Panel.

2. Right-click the local area connection for the network adapter you want to configure with an LAA.

3. Click **Properties**.

4. Click **Configure**.

5. Click the **Advanced** tab.

6. Highlight Network Address in the **Property** box.

7. Select **Value**, and then enter the LAA in the Value text box.

8. Click OK.

PART 6

Performance Monitoring

In This Part

C H A P T E R   2 7

Overview of Performance Monitoring

Monitoring performance is a necessary part of preventive maintenance for your computer system. Through monitoring, you obtain performance data that is useful in diagnosing system problems and in planning for the growth in demand for system resources.

In This Chapter

Related Information in the Windows 2000 Resource Kit

- For more information about diagnosing system problems, see "Troubleshooting Tools and Strategies"in this book.

- For more information about tools for monitoring performance, see *Microsoft® Windows® 2000 Resource Kit* Tools Help.

Quick Guide to Monitoring Performance

Use this quick guide to view the topics and tasks related to monitoring tools and processes in Microsoft® Windows® 2000 Professional covered in this chapter.

Learn about the operation of performance monitoring tools in Windows 2000 Professional for the purpose of preventive maintenance and diagnosis of performance problems.

By using the performance monitoring tools provided in Windows 2000 Professional for real-time observation and periodic logging, you can acquire important information about the health of your system. To use the tools efficiently, it is important to know how data is collected, what types of data are collected, and how to use the data to keep your system at its best.

- See "Performance Monitoring Concepts" and "Monitoring Tools" later in the chapter.

Set up a basic monitoring configuration.

Routine performance monitoring starts with establishing a default set of counters to track. This can be the set used for establishing a performance baseline. A performance baseline is the level of performance you can reliably expect during typical usage and workloads.

- See "Starting Your Monitoring Routine" later in this chapter.

Interpret data you collect.

The data you collect about system performance provides important indicators as to the efficiency of your system. However, data can sometimes be misleading and needs to be analyzed carefully if you are to have an accurate picture of the health of your system and to correctly diagnose problems.

- See "Analyzing Monitoring Results" later in this chapter.

Research the cause of bottlenecks prior to attempting corrective actions.

A bottleneck in one resource can come in combination with one in another resource. An analytical approach to investigating bottlenecks is important to determining the correct solution.

- See "Investigating Bottlenecks" later in this chapter.

Be aware of issues with the performance tools.

Occasionally you might have trouble collecting data or the data might seem inappropriate. If this occurs, make sure you understand some of the issues that can arise with the performance tools and how to respond to them.

- See "Troubleshooting Problems with Performance Tools" later in this chapter.

Learn about monitoring remote computers.

There are security and performance considerations associated with monitoring remote computers. If you intend to track data from counters on other computers on a network, make sure you are aware of these considerations.

- See "Monitoring Remote Computers" later in this chapter.

Experiment with using the System Monitor control in Office applications.

One of the benefits of the new design of the System Monitor control that provides the functionality of System Monitor in the Performance console is its ability to be used within Microsoft® Word or other Microsoft® Office applications. By learning about this capability, you can more fully integrate monitoring data into your management reporting.

- See "Integrating the System Monitor Control into Office and Other Applications" later in this chapter.

What's New

Users of Microsoft® Windows® 98 and Microsoft® Windows NT® Workstation version 4.0 will notice a few changes in Microsoft® Windows® 2000 with respect to performance monitoring tools. The following list provides a brief summary of the changes in features for these operating systems:

- Windows 98 users will notice that the tool named System Monitor differs significantly from the one provided in Windows 98 and from its predecessor, Performance Monitor, in Windows NT Workstation. The new tool supports printing and HTML output, as well as flexible configuration using colors, fonts, and highlighting. In addition, System Monitor in Windows 2000 can read data as it is being logged using the new Performance Logs and Alerts service. This service, new to users of Performance Monitor in Windows NT Workstation 4.0, can log data or generate alerts automatically on a user-defined schedule, even on unattended systems. The service also supports the new trace logging capability, whereby performance data is traced rather than sampled for greater accuracy.

- The new System Monitor exposes a much greater variety and level of detail in terms of the data that can be configured to be collected over what was available in Windows 98. System Monitor also uses different terminology to describe the performance data it collects: *objects*, *counters*, and *instances* rather than *items*. Users of Windows NT Workstation will also find that there are several new default objects and many new optional objects that can be installed by Windows 2000 services and features. In addition, counters can collect data from the registry, as in Windows NT Workstation, or from the Windows Management Interface, new to Windows 2000.

- System Monitor in Windows 2000 is instrumented as an ActiveX® control and is therefore portable for use in Microsoft Office applications and Web pages, providing more flexibility and extensibility over Performance Monitor in Windows NT Workstation 4.0. The Performance console that contains System Monitor is a Microsoft Management Console (MMC) snap-in that can be configured and loaded on other computers for monitoring purposes.

- Unlike System Monitor in Windows 98, System Monitor in Windows 2000 is installed by default. Unlike Windows NT Workstation 4.0, in Windows 2000 Professional, the **Administrative Tools** menu, in which the Performance console resides, is not available by default. Instead you need to add the **Administrative Tools** menu to the **Start** menu. The Administrative Tools also appears as an icon in Control Panel.

- Although, in general, Windows 2000 Task Manager offers access to a larger selection of data than Resource Meter in Windows 98, the two tools share some similarities in purpose and operation. For example, both tools provide general data on system resource utilization. In addition, with both tools you can view data in a window or as an icon in the taskbar. Updated from Windows NT Workstation 4.0, Task Manager can be configured to display the number of I/O operations as well as the number of GDI Objects and USER Objects information, thus expanding the usage data shown by the User Resources and GDI Resources progress indicators in Resource Meter.

Performance Monitoring Concepts

Regular performance monitoring ensures that you always have up-to-date information about how your computer is operating. When you have performance data for your system over a range of activities and loads, you can define a baseline —a range of measurements that represent acceptable performance under typical operating conditions. This baseline provides a reference point that makes it easier to spot problems when they occur. In addition, when you are troubleshooting system problems, performance data gives you information about the behavior of system resources at the time the problem occurs, which is useful in pinpointing the cause. Finally, monitoring system performance provides you with data to project future growth and to plan for how changes in your system configurations might affect future operation. Figure 27.1 shows the sequence for monitoring different system resources.

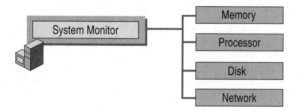

Figure 27.1   Overall Monitoring Sequence

The following sections describe the scope and type of performance data collected, the design of the performance data architecture, and the methods of data collection used by the performance tools.

Scope of Performance Data

In general, performance monitoring concentrates on how the operating system and any applications or services that are capable of performance-data collection use the resources of the system, such as the disks, memory, processors, and network components. *Throughput*, *queue*, and *response time* are terms that describe resource usage.

Throughput Defined

Throughput is a measure of the work done in a unit of time, typically evaluated from the server side in a client/server environment. Throughput tends to increase as the load increases up to a peak level. It then begins to fall, and a queue might develop. Throughput in an end-to-end system, such as client/server, depends on how each component performs. The slowest point in the system sets the throughput rate for the system as a whole. Often this slow point is referred to as a bottleneck. Performance monitoring tells you where bottlenecks occur in your system. The resource that shows the highest use is often the bottleneck, but not always—it can also mean a resource is successfully handling a lot of activity. As long as no queues develop, there is no bottleneck. Microsoft Windows 2000 Professional reports throughput data on resources such as disks and network components.

Queue Defined

A queue can form under a few different circumstances. For example, a queue can develop when requests come in for service by the resource at a faster rate than the resource's throughput, or if requests demand differing, particularly longer, amounts of time from the resource. A queue can also form if requests occur at random intervals—for example, in large batches for a time and then none at all. When a queue becomes long, work is not being handled efficiently, and you might experience delays in response time. Windows 2000 Professional reports queue development on disks and processors.

Response Time Defined

Response time is the measure of time required to do work from start to finish. In a client/server environment, you typically measure response time on the client side. Response time generally increases as the load increases. You can measure response time by dividing the queue length by the resource throughput. As an alternative, the new trace log feature in the Windows 2000 performance tools allows you to track units of work from start to finish in order to determine response times.

The following sections describe how performance monitoring tools enable users to collect data about the throughput, queue formation, and response time of different system resources.

Data Collection Architecture

Windows 2000 collects data about system resources, such as disks, memory, processors, and network components. In addition, applications and services that you might be running on your system can also perform data collection. By default, the performance counters obtain data for system resources using the registry.

When you use performance tools to access registry functions for performance data, the system collects the data from the appropriate system object managers, such as the Memory Manager, the input/output (I/O) subsystem, and so forth.

As an option, Windows 2000 supports collecting counter data using the Windows Management Instrumentation (WMI) interface by means of the following command syntax typed at the Windows command prompt:

perfmon / WMI

In addition to several of the system performance counter DLLs, the operating system installs managed object files for data collection using WMI instead of the registry. These files reside in System32\Wbem\Mof. The Windows Management service must be running on the monitoring and monitored computer (if different) in order to obtain data using WMI.

Windows 2000 defines the performance data it collects in terms of objects, counters, and instances. Think of a performance object as any resource, application, or service that you can measure. The following sections describe these entities in more detail.

Performance Objects

By default, Windows 2000 installs numerous performance objects corresponding to hardware or other resources in the system. Table 27.1 shows the default performance objects installed by the operating system on a Microsoft® Windows® 2000 Professional installation.

Table 27.1   Windows 2000 Performance Objects

Object Name	Description
ACS/RSVP Service	Reports activity of the Quality of Service (QoS) Admission Control Service used to manage the priority use of network resources (bandwidth) at the subnet level.
Browser	Reports activity of the browser service in Microsoft® Windows® 2000 Server that lists computers sharing resources in a domain and other domain and workgroup names across the wide area network (WAN). Windows 2000 provides the browser service for backward compatibility with clients that are running Microsoft® Windows® 95, Microsoft Windows 98, Microsoft® Windows® 3.*x*, and Microsoft Windows NT.
Cache	Reports activity for the file system cache, an area of physical memory that holds recently used data.
Distributed Transaction Coordinator	Reports statistics about activity of the Microsoft Distributed Transaction Coordinator, a part of Component Services (formerly known as Transaction Server) used to coordinate two-phase transactions by Message Queuing.
HTTP Indexing Service	Reports statistics regarding queries run by Indexing Service, a service that builds and maintains catalogs of the contents of local and remote disk drives to support powerful document-search capabilities.
IAS Accounting Clients	Reports activity of the Internet Authentication Service (IAS) as it centrally manages remote client accounting (usage).
IAS Accounting Servers	Reports activity of the Internet Authentication Service (IAS) as it centrally manages remote server accounting (usage). These counters report zero values if the service is not installed.
IAS Authentication Clients	Reports activity of the Internet Authentication Service (IAS) as it centrally manages remote client authentication.
IAS Authentication Servers	Reports activity of the Internet Authentication Service (IAS) as it centrally manages remote server authentication. These counters report zero values if the service is not installed.
ICMP	Reports the rates at which Internet Control Message Protocol (ICMP) messages are sent and received by using the ICMP protocol, which provides error correction and other packet information.

(continued)

Table 27.1   Windows 2000 Performance Objects *(continued)*

Object Name	Description
Indexing Service	Reports statistics pertaining to the creation of indexes and the merging of indexes by Indexing Service. Indexing Service indexes documents and document properties on your disks and stores the information in a catalog. You can use Indexing Service to search for documents, either with the **Search** command on the **Start** menu or with a Web browser.
Indexing Service Filter	Reports filtering activity of Indexing Service. Indexing Service indexes documents and document properties on your disks and stores the information in a catalog. You can use Indexing Service to search for documents, either with the **Search** command on the **Start** menu or with a Web browser.
IP	Reports activity at the Internet Protocol (IP) layer of Transmission Control Protocol/Internet Protocol (TCP/IP).
Job Object	Reports the accounting and processor usage data collected by each active, named job object.
Job Object Details	Reports detailed performance information about the active processes that make up a job object.
Logical Disk	Reports activity and usage of disk partitions and volumes.
	Use **diskperf -y** to enable disk counters and **diskperf -n** to disable them. To specify the type of counters you want to activate, include **d** for physical disk drives and **v** for logical disk drives or storage volumes. When the operating system starts up, it automatically sets the **diskperf** command with the **-yd** switch to activate physical disk counters. Type **diskperf -yv** to activate logical disk counters. For more information about using the **diskperf** command, type **diskperf -?** at the command prompt.
Memory	Reports usage of random access memory (RAM) used to store code and data.
NBT Connection	Reports the rate at which bytes are sent and received over connections that use the NetBT protocol, which provides NetBIOS support for the TCP/IP protocol between the local computer and a remote computer.
Network Interface	Reports rates at which bytes and packets are sent and received over a TCP/IP connection by means of the network adapters. Typically the first instance of the Network Interface object (Instance 1) that you see in System Monitor represents the loopback address; however, sometimes the loopback address does not appear. The loopback address is a local path through the protocol driver and the network adapter. All other instances represent installed network adapters (WAN interfaces, remote access modems, and so forth).

(continued)

Table 27.1   Windows 2000 Performance Objects *(continued)*

Object Name	Description
Objects	Reports data about system software objects, such as events.
Paging File	Reports usage of the paging file, used to back up virtual memory allocations.
Physical Disk	Reports usage of hard disks and redundant array of independent disks (RAID) devices.
Print Queue	Reports statistics for print jobs in the queue of the print server. New for Windows 2000.
Process	Reports activity of the process, which is a software object that represents a running program.
Processor	Reports activity of the processor (also called the CPU), the part of your computer hardware that carries out program instructions.
Redirector	Reports activity for the Redirector file system, which diverts file requests to network servers.
Server	Reports activity for the Server file system, which responds to file requests from network clients.
Server Work Queues	Reports the length of queues and objects in the queues for the Server service.
System	Reports statistics for systemwide counters that track file operations, processor time, and so on.
TCP	Reports the rates at which TCP segments are sent and received using the Transmission Control Protocol (TCP).
Telephony	Reports activity for telephony devices and connections.
Thread	Reports activity for a thread (the part of a process that uses the processor).
UDP	Reports the rates at which User Datagram Protocol (UDP) datagrams are sent and received using UDP.

For information about writing applications that install performance objects that can be integrated with the performance tools, see the Software Development Kit (SDK) documentation in the MSDN™ Library at http://windows.microsoft.com/windows2000/reskit/webresources.

Performance Counters and Instances

Each object has counters that are used to measure various aspects of performance, such as transfer rates for disks or the amount of processor time consumed for processors. Each object has at least one instance, which is a unique copy of a particular object type, though not all object types support multiple instances. This chapter and the following chapters describe objects, counters, and instances using the following syntax:

*Computer_name**Object*(*ParentInstance*/*ObjectInstance*#*InstanceIndex*)*Counter*

The *Computer_name* portion is optional; if you do not include a computer name, the default is the local computer.

Note that the syntax includes a parent instance, object instance, and an instance index. This applies, for example, if the object has multiple instances and these instances might be identifiable by name or number, as defined by the counter developer. (Typically, internal system counters use numeric instance indexes.)

For example, if you are monitoring threads of the Microsoft Windows Explorer process, track the Windows Explorer instance of the Thread object (Windows Explorer would be the parent instance), and then each thread running Windows Explorer (these threads are child instances). The instance index allows you to track these child instances. The instance index for the thread you want might be 0, 1, and so on, for each thread, preceded by the number sign (#). The operating system configures System Monitor properties to display duplicate instances by default. Instance index 0 is hidden; numbering of additional instances starts with 1. You cannot monitor multiple instances of the same process unless you display instance indexes.

An instance called _Total is available on most objects and represents a sum of the values for all instances of the object for a specific counter.

Data Collection and Reporting

Depending on the tools used, you can configure data collection to occur almost immediately or according to a predefined schedule. Performance data reported is sampled, meaning that data is collected periodically rather than traced, whereby data is obtained as events occur. This collection method has the advantage of keeping overhead low, but it might occasionally overestimate or underestimate values when activity falls outside the sampling interval.

If you want more precise performance data, use event tracing, a new capability in Windows 2000. Event tracing can measure activity as it happens, eliminating the inaccuracies of sampling and making it possible to correlate resource usage such as page faults, disk input/output (I/O), and processor time with workload that can include threads, processes, or transactions. This capability supplements counter-based monitoring methods. You can configure trace logs for providers you have or for the built-in system provider that runs traces for the Windows kernel provider using trace logs in **Performance Logs and Alerts**. Because running trace logs of page faults and file I/O data incurs some performance overhead, log this data only for brief periods. Note that an additional program is required to parse the log output into readable form. You can use Tracedmp.exe on the *Windows 2000 Resource Kit* companion CD for this purpose. For more information about tools for working with trace logs, see *Microsoft® Windows® 2000 Resource Kit* Tools Help. In addition, developers can create such a tool using APIs provided in the Platform Software Development Kit.

For information about writing a trace provider, see the Platform Software Development Kit (SDK) documentation in the MSDN Library at http://windows.microsoft.com/windows2000/reskit/webresources.

Depending on how a counter is defined, its values might be reported in one of the following ways:

- Instantaneous counters, which might have names containing the word "current," display the most recent measurement. Be aware that instantaneous counters might not provide meaningful data unless you have a steady workload.

- Averaging counters, which typically have names that include "per second" or "percent," measure a value over time and display the average of the last two measurements over the period between samples. (Because counters are never cleared, this is actually an average of the difference between the measurements.) When you start these counters, you must wait for the second measurement to be taken before any values are displayed. For example, Memory\Pages/sec shows the number of pages read over the sample interval, divided by the number of seconds in the interval.

  For averaging counters, the sampling method can result in a slight delay in displaying values as data is collected and computed. In addition, after a single large value is reported, causing spikes in a performance graph, averaging counter values can be artificially high for a while until the average starts to reflect more recent steady-state activity.

Windows 2000 supports other types of counters, such as percentage, difference, and text. Difference counters display the change in value between the last two measurements. By default, counters that display their values as percentages cannot exceed 100 percent.

For information about the preceding generic counter types and their specific subtypes, see the Windows 2000 Performance Counter Reference (Counters.chm) on the *Windows 2000 Resource Kit* companion CD.

Monitoring Tools

The primary monitoring tools in Windows 2000 are the Performance console and Task Manager. Task Manager offers an immediate overview of system activity and performance, and the Performance console provides detailed information that can be used for troubleshooting and bottleneck analysis. The Performance console hosts two tools: System Monitor, and Performance Logs and Alerts. The chapters in the Performance Monitoring section of the *Windows 2000 Resource Kit* concentrate on using the Performance console. The following sections describe the tools that are installed with the operating system.

You can start the Performance console from the **Administrative Tools** menu. To use the **Administrative Tools** menu in Windows 2000 Professional:

Add the Administrative Tools menu to the Programs menu.

–Or–

Use the **Administrative Tools** menu in Control Panel.

▶ **To add the Administrative Tools menu to the Programs menu on a computer running Windows 2000 Professional**

1. On the **Start** menu, point to **Settings**, and then click **Taskbar & Start Menu**.

2. Click the **Start Menu Options** tab. Under **Start Menu Settings**, select the **Display Administrative Tools** check box, and then click **OK**.

3. Click the **Start** button again, point to **Programs**, and then click **Administrative Tools**.

▶ **To use the Administrative Tools menu in Control Panel**

1. Double-click **My Computer** on the Windows 2000 desktop.

2. Under **My Computer**, double-click **Control Panel**.

3. In Control Panel, double-click **Administrative Tools**.

System Monitor

System Monitor in Windows 2000 extends the functionality provided by Performance Monitor, which shipped in Microsoft Windows NT 4.0 and Windows NT 3.51. Features of System Monitor include the following:

- The graph display is much more flexible and configurable. You can modify many attributes of the display, including changing font and color, adding borders, and so on.

- Counter configuration is simplified. You can now copy counter paths and settings from the System Monitor display to the Clipboard and paste counter paths from Web pages or other sources into the System Monitor display.

- Graphs can be printed when performance displays are saved as HTML files using the **Save As** command on the shortcut menu. In addition, you can save reports as tab-separated files (for use with Microsoft® Excel) by means of the **Save As** command. To use the shortcut menu, right-click the details pane of System Monitor.

- System Monitor is portable. Because System Monitor is hosted in Microsoft Management Console (MMC), you can save a console file containing a group of counters that you want to monitor—you can install it on any other computer and be able to monitor the same types of data on that computer. This is useful in monitoring other systems that you administer.

- The functionality of System Monitor chart, histogram, and report views is provided by an ActiveX control (Sysmon.ocx). This design gives a user the flexibility of including the control in an HTML page or of programming the control into a Microsoft Office or Microsoft® Visual Basic® application, as described in "Integrating the System Monitor Control into Office and Other Applications" later in this chapter. In most cases, you work with the control's functionality in the form it is presented in Perfmon.msc, the Microsoft Management Console component that hosts the performance tools.

For information about logging and alert capabilities of the Performance console, see "Performance Logs and Alerts" later in this chapter. Windows NT 4.0 Performance Monitor is provided under the name Perfmon4.exe on the *Windows 2000 Resource Kit* companion CD. Typing **perfmon.exe** at the command prompt causes the system to start System Monitor, not Performance Monitor.

Starting System Monitor

If you are running Windows 2000 Professional, you can start the Performance console as follows:

On the Administrative Tools menu, click Performance.

–Or–

On the **Start** menu, click **Run**, type **perfmon.msc**, and then click **OK**.

–Or–

Type **perfmon.msc** at the Windows command prompt.

When you start the Performance console, a blank System Monitor graph appears. **Performance Logs and Alerts** appears beneath System Monitor in the console tree, as shown in Figure 27.2.

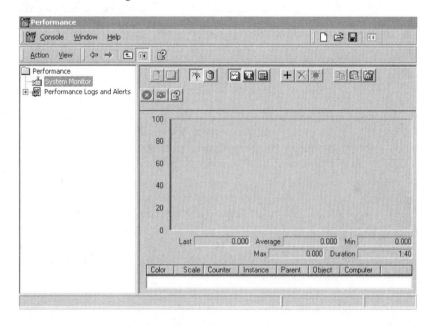

Figure 27.2   Performance Console

The following section describes the user interface for System Monitor and provides tips on how to use it.

Working with System Monitor

With System Monitor you can create graphs, bar charts (histograms), and text reports of performance counter data. System Monitor is designed for short-term viewing of data, troubleshooting, and diagnosis.

The System Monitor display consists of the following elements:

- An optional toolbar with capabilities such as copying and pasting counters, clearing counters, adding counters, and so on. The toolbar buttons provide the quickest way of configuring the monitoring display, but you can also use a shortcut menu to add counters and configure properties.

- The area where counter values are displayed. You can vary the line style, width, and color of these lines. You can also change the color of the window and of the chart within the window.

- A legend showing the selected counters and associated data such as the computer name, parent object, and instances.

- A value bar, where you see the last, minimum, maximum, and average values for the counter that is currently selected. The value bar also shows a **Duration** value that indicates the total elapsed time displayed in the graph (based on the update interval).

- A timer bar that moves across the graph indicates the passing of each update interval. Regardless of the update interval, the view shows up to 100 samples. System Monitor compresses log data as necessary to fit it in the display. For example, if there are 1,000 samples, the display might show every tenth sample.

You can configure System Monitor using either the toolbar or a shortcut menu. Using the shortcut menu offers more control and flexibility in configuring the display. The following sections describe these different configuration methods. To see procedures and a brief overview of System Monitor, click **Help** on the System Monitor toolbar.

Using the Toolbar

The toolbar is displayed by default. Using the toolbar, you can configure the following options:

- **Type of display.** Use the **View Chart**, **View Histogram**, or **View Report** button.

Figure 27.3 shows the different display options.

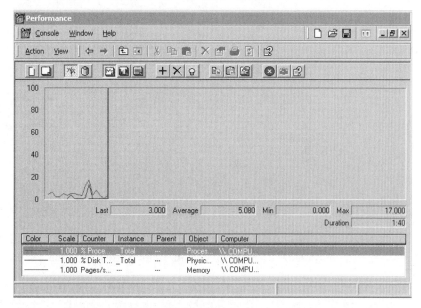

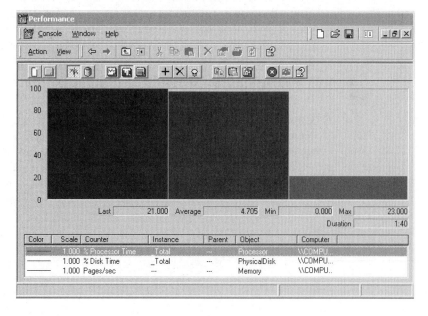

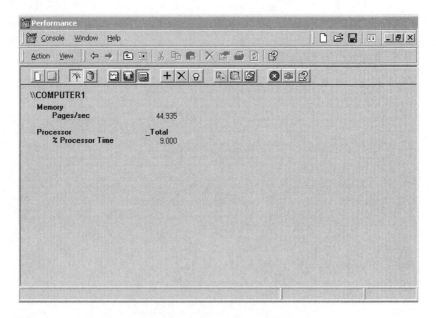

Figure 27.3   Display Options for System Monitor

Histograms and reports are useful for simplifying graphs with multiple counters. However, they display only a single value, so they are recommended only when you are charting current activity and watching the graphs as they change. When you are reviewing data logged over time, line graphs are much more informative so that trends can be identified.

- **Data source.** Click the **View Current Activity** button for real-time data or the **View Log File Data** button for data from either a completed or a currently running log.

- **Counters.** Use the **Add** or **Delete** buttons as needed. You can also use the **New Counter Set** button to reset the display and select new counters. Clicking the **Add** button displays the **Add Counters** dialog box, as shown in Figure 27.4. You can also press the DEL key to delete a counter that is selected in the legend.

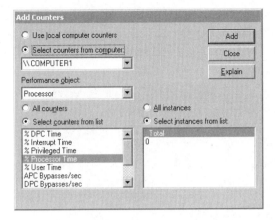

Figure 27.4   Add Counters Dialog Box

- **Data updates.** Click **Clear Display** to clear the displayed data and obtain a fresh data sample for existing counters. To suspend data collection, click **Freeze Display**. Use the **Update Data** button to resume collection.

- **Highlighting chart or histogram data.** To accentuate the line or bar for a selected counter with white (default) or black (for light backgrounds), click **Highlight** on the toolbar.

- **Importing or exporting counter settings.** To save the displayed configuration to the Clipboard for insertion into a Web page, click **Copy Properties**. To import counter settings from the Clipboard into the current System Monitor display, click **Paste Counter List**.

- **Configuring other System Monitor properties.** To access colors, fonts, or other settings that have no corresponding button on the toolbar, click **Properties**.

Using the Shortcut Menu

When you right-click the System Monitor display, a shortcut menu appears with the following options:

- **Add Counters.** Use this option in the same way you use the **Add** button in the toolbar.

- **Save As.** Use this if you want to save the current display configuration under a new name. If you click **Save** on the **Console** menu, the current settings are stored, overwriting the blank version of Perfmon.msc installed by Windows 2000 Setup and altering the default appearance of the tool.

- **Properties.** Click this button to access the five properties tabs that provide options for controlling all aspects of System Monitor data collection and display. The **General** properties tab appears by default, as shown in Figure 27.5.

Figure 27.5   General Tab in the System Monitor Properties Dialog Box

Many properties can be configured from the toolbar, but some are only configurable using **System Monitor Properties**. Table 27.2 lists property tabs alphabetically by name, along with the attributes they control.

Table 27.2   System Monitor Properties

Use this tab	To add or change this
Colors	Background color of results pane surrounding the chart area, color of chart data-display area.
	You can choose each color from a palette (in the **Property Name** list box) or you can base the colors on system colors (screen elements) defined using the Display icon in Control Panel. When using the palette, note the following:
	■ **BackColorCtl** refers to the area surrounding the chart.
	■ **BackColor** refers to the chart data-display area.
	■ **ForeColor** refers to the color of the text in the display and legend.
	Grid color, timer bar color.
Data	Color, width, style, or chart line.
	Notice that defining a nondefault line width limits the line styles that are available. Styles can be selected only when you are using the default line width.
	Scale of counter data values.
	Counter values can be scaled exponentially from .0000001 to 1000000. You might want to adjust the counter scale settings to enhance the visibility of counter data in the chart. Changing the scale does not affect the statistics displayed in the value bar.
	Objects, counters, and instances.
Fonts	Font type, size, and style.
General	View type: chart, histogram, or report.
	Update frequency and manual or periodic sampling.
	Histogram or report value type (choose between minimum, maximum, average values for the one displayed in a report view).
	Using report value types other than **Current** when monitoring real-time data incurs substantial overhead because of the need to make calculations across all samples for each value displayed.
	Display of counter legend.
	Display of last, minimum, and maximum values for a selected counter (the value bar).
	Border style, appearance of the entire control. You can include or omit a border, or configure three-dimensional or flat effects for the window.

(continued)

Table 27.2   System Monitor Properties *(continued)*

Use this tab	To add or change this
	Display of toolbar.
	Display of instance indexes (for monitoring multiple instances of a counter).
	The first instance (instance number 0) displays no index; System Monitor numbers subsequent instances starting with 1.
	Note: You need to select duplicate instances individually in the **Add Counters** dialog box in order to collect data from those instances. If you select All instances while adding counters to a counter log or a System Monitor view, duplicate instances are not added to the log settings or to the view legend. This is true even if the **Allow duplicate counter instances** option is selected in **General** properties for System Monitor.
Graph	Title of graph.
	Label on value axis, vertical or horizontal grid lines, and upper and lower limits of graph axes.
Source	Source of data displayed: current data input to the graph, current or archived data input from a log.
	Time range for a log and view time range.

Getting the Most from System Monitor

Windows 2000 Professional online Help for System Monitor explains how to perform common tasks. The following list supplements the information provided in online Help to enable you to use System Monitor more effectively.

- **Print data.** You can print performance data in several ways:
    - Copy the current view to the Clipboard (by pressing ALT+PRINT SCREEN), start a paint program, paste in the image from the Clipboard, and then print it.
    - Add the System Monitor control to a Microsoft Office application such as Microsoft Word or Microsoft Excel, configure it to display data, and then print from that program. For information about this process, see "Integrating the System Monitor Control into Office and Other Applications" later in this chapter.
    - Save the System Monitor control as an HTML file by right-clicking the details pane of System Monitor and typing a file name for the HTML file to be created. You can then open the HTML file and print it from Microsoft® Internet Explorer or another program.
    - Import a log file in comma-separated (.csv) or tab-separated (.tsv) format into an Excel spreadsheet and print from that application.

- **Learn about individual counters.** When adding counters, if you click **Explain** in the **Add Counters** dialog box for System Monitor or **Performance Logs and Alerts**, you can view counter descriptions.

- **Vary the data displayed in a report.** By default, reports display only one value for each counter. This is current data if the data source is real-time activity, or averaged data if the source is a log. However, using the **General** properties tab, you can configure the report display to show different values, such as the maximum, minimum, and so on. Notice that monitoring the nondefault value for a report can increase performance-monitoring overhead.

- **Arrange items in the legend.** To sort entries in ascending or descending order for that category, click **Object**, **Counter**, **Instance**, or **Computer** in the counter legend. For example, to sort all counters by name, click **Counter**.

- **Select a group of counters or counter instances to monitor.**

  - To select all counters or instances, click **All counters** or **All instances**.

  - To select specific counters or instances, click **Select counters from the list** or **Select instances from the list**.

  - To monitor a group of consecutive counters or instances in a list box, hold down the SHIFT key and scroll down through the items in the list box.

  - To select multiple, nonconsecutive counters or instances, select the item and press CTRL.

Important Monitoring large numbers of counters can incur a high amount of overhead, even to the point of making the system unresponsive to keyboard or mouse input. To reduce this burden, display data in report view when collecting from large numbers of counters or direct data to a binary log, and view the data in System Monitor as it is being written to the log.

- **Simplify detailed graphs.** You can maintain two separate instances of System Monitor if you want to monitor a large number of counters while keeping each graph relatively simple and uncluttered. It is also a good way to compare data from different sources.

- **Track totals for all instances of a counter.** Instead of monitoring individual instances for a selected counter, you can instead use the Total instance, which sums all instances' values and reports them in System Monitor.

- **Pinpoint a specific counter from lines in a graph.** To match a line in a graph with the counter for which it is charting values, double-click a position in the line. If chart lines are close together, try to find a point in the graph where they diverge.

- **Accentuate a specific counter's data.** To draw attention to a particular counter's data, use the highlighting feature. To do so, press CTRL+H or click **Highlight** on the toolbar. For the counter selected, a thick line replaces the colored chart line. For white or light-colored backgrounds (defined by the BackColor property), this line is black; for other backgrounds, this line is white.

- **View data from a running log.** If you are working with a log file that is currently collecting data, you need to click the **Select Time Range** button and keep moving the **Time Range** bar to the right to update the display with new samples.

- **Use Windows NT 4.0 settings files.** You can display legacy alert, report, chart, and log settings files in System Monitor by using the following command at the command prompt:

  perfmon.exe *settings_file_name*

  When you open one of these settings files, the system temporarily converts the file for use with System Monitor but discards the converted version after the console starts. If you want to save the settings file for permanent use with System Monitor, type the following command:

  perfmon.exe /HTMLFILE:*new_file_name settings_file_name*

Performance Logs and Alerts

Performance Logs and Alerts, a service in Windows 2000, improves the logging and alert capabilities that were provided in Windows NT 4.0. Logging is used for detailed analysis and record-keeping purposes. Retaining and analyzing log data collected over a period of several months can be helpful for capacity and upgrade planning.

Windows 2000 provides two types of performance-related logs—counter logs and trace logs—and an alerting function. The following list describes these new or enhanced tools:

- Performance Logs and Alerts replaces Performance Data Log in the *Microsoft® Windows NT® Server 4.0 Resource Kit*. As a result, data collection occurs regardless of whether any user is logged on to the computer.

- In Windows 2000, counter logs record sampled data about hardware resources and system services based on performance objects and counters in the same manner as System Monitor. When a counter log has been started, the Performance Logs and Alerts service obtains data from the system when the update interval has elapsed.

- Trace logs collect event traces that measure performance statistics associated with events such as disk and file I/O, page faults, or thread activity. When the event occurs, a data provider designed to track these events sends the data to the Performance Logs and Alerts service. The data is measured from start to finish, rather than sampled in the manner of System Monitor. The built-in Windows 2000 kernel trace data provider supports tracing system data; if other data providers are available, developers can configure logs with those providers as appropriate. A parsing tool is required to interpret the trace log output. Developers can create such a tool using APIs provided in the Platform Software Development Kit.

- With the alerting function, you can define a counter value that will trigger actions such as sending a network message, running a program, or starting a log. Alerts are useful if you are not actively monitoring a particular counter threshold value but want to be notified when it exceeds or falls below a specified value so that you can investigate and determine the cause of the change. You might want to set alerts based on established performance baseline values for your system. For information about establishing a baseline, see "Starting Your Monitoring Routine" later in this chapter.

- Viewing logged data is easier and more convenient. Counter logs can be viewed in System Monitor as they are collecting data as well as after data collection has stopped. Data in counter logs can be saved as comma-separated or tab-separated files that are easily viewed with Excel.

- Logs can be circular—that is, recording data until they achieve a user-defined size limit and then starting over. Alternatively, linear logs collect data according to user-defined parameters such as: run for a specified length of time, stop when that parameter is met, and start a new log. A binary file format can also be defined for logging intermittent data (such as for a process that is not running when you start the log but that begins and ends during the logged interval).

- You can save log settings to an HTML file or you can import settings from an HTML page to create new logs. When exported, the resulting HTML page hosts the System Monitor control, an ActiveX control that provides the performance monitoring user interface. If you open this page, you can dynamically observe, from a System Monitor view, the same counters you configured in the log. When imported, a new log or alert is created, based on the settings in the HTML page. This is a convenient way to insert the same settings into both a log and an alert, if appropriate.

- Configuring logs and alerts is flexible and easy to manage. Users can manage multiple logging sessions from a single console window. For each log, users can start and stop logging either manually, on demand, or automatically, at scheduled times or based on the elapsed time or the current file size. Users can also specify automatic naming schemes and stipulate that a program be run when a log is stopped.

Starting Performance Logs and Alerts

In Windows 2000 Professional, the Performance Logs and Alerts component is available in the Performance console and in the Computer Management console. The following procedure describes how to open the component from these locations.

Note This procedure assumes that you have added the **Administrative Tools** option to your **Programs** menu as described in "System Monitor" earlier in this chapter.

▶ **To start Performance Logs and Alerts from the Performance console**

1. Click **Start**, point to **Programs**, and then click **Administrative Tools**.

2. Click **Performance**.

3. Double-click **Performance Logs and Alerts** to display the available tools.

Figure 27.6 shows the Performance Logs and Alerts console tree.

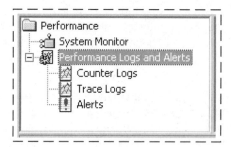

Figure 27.6   Performance Logs and Alerts Console Tree

Working with Logs and Alerts

To begin configuring logs and alerts, click the name of the tool to select it. If any logs or alerts have previously been defined, they will appear in the appropriate node of the details pane. A sample settings file for a counter log named System Overview is included with Windows 2000. You can use this file to see some basic system data such as memory, disk, and processor activity. For information about the types of data to monitor in your own configuration, see "Starting Your Monitoring Routine" later in this chapter.

Right-click in the details pane to create a new log or alert. You can do this in a new file or you can use settings from an existing HTML file as a template.

Note You must have Full Control access to a subkey in the registry in order to create or modify a log configuration. (The subkey is HKEY_CURRENT_MACHINE\SYSTEM \CurrentControlSet\Services\SysmonLog\Log_Queries.) In general, administrators have this access by default. Administrators can grant access to users by using the **Security** menu in Regedt32.exe. To run the Performance Logs and Alerts service, you must have the right to start or otherwise configure services on the system. Administrators have this right by default and can grant it to users by using Group Policy. For information about starting and using Group Policy, see Windows 2000 Help.

You are prompted to name your log or alert and then to define properties. Figure 27.7 is an illustration of the **General** properties tab for a counter log.

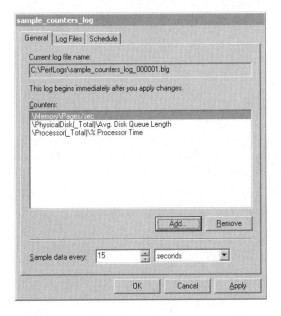

Figure 27.7 General Properties Tab for a Counter Log

If you are configuring a counter log or an alert, use the **Add Counters** dialog box to specify objects, counters, instances, and updating. If you are configuring a trace log, use the **General** properties tab shown in Figure 27.8.

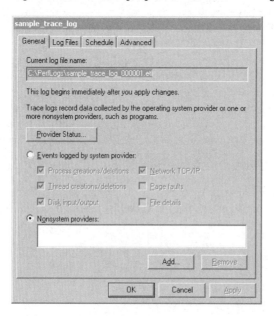

Figure 27.8   General Properties Tab for a Trace Log

Each tool offers some unique properties. The ability to configure scheduling is common to logs and alerts, but some options might not be available for all tools. Table 27.3 describes the options available in each tool and the property tab to use to configure it.

Table 27.3   Summary of Log and Alert Properties

For this feature	Use this tab	To configure these settings	Notes
Alerts	General	Counters, sample interval, alert threshold, and alert comment	
	Action	Actions to take when an event occurs	Examples of actions for an alert include running a program, sending a message, starting a counter log, and updating the event log.
	Schedule	Start and stop parameters for alerts	Automated restart is not available if you configure the alert to stop manually.
			You might need to update the Performance Logs and Alerts service properties if you opt to run a program that displays on the screen after the system triggers an alert. Use **Services** under **Services and Applications** in **Computer Management** for this purpose.
Counter Logs	General	Counter log counters and sample interval	
	Log Files	File type, file size limits, path and name, and automatic naming parameters	Counter logs can be defined as comma-separated or tab-separated text files, or as binary linear or circular files.
	Schedule	Manual or automated start and stop methods and schedule	Counter logs can be defined as comma-separated or tab-separated text files, or as binary linear or circular files.
			You can specify that the log stop when the log file is full.
			You cannot configure the service to automatically restart or to run a program if a log is configured to stop manually.
			You cannot configure a log to stop when full if the file is configured on the **Log Files** tab to grow to a maximum size limit.

(continued)

Table 27.3   Summary of Log and Alert Properties *(continued)*

For this feature	Use this tab	To configure these settings	Notes
Trace Logs	General	Trace log providers and events to log	You cannot configure the service to automatically restart if a log is configured to stop manually.
			You can have only one system trace log running at a time. You cannot enable multiple providers simultaneously.
			To obtain disk input/output data from the system provider, you must also select **File details**.
	Log Files	Trace log comment, file type, path and name, and automatic naming parameters	Only two types of trace logs are available: circular and sequential.
	Schedule	Start and stop parameters for a trace log	You cannot configure the service to automatically restart or to run a program if a log is configured to stop manually.
	Advanced	Trace log buffer size, limits, and transfer interval (periodic flushing)	

To start or stop a log or alert, right-click the name in the Performance Logs and Alerts window, point to **All Tasks**, and then click **Start** or **Stop**.

Getting the Most from Performance Logs and Alerts

Windows 2000 Professional online Help for Performance Logs and Alerts describes performing the most common tasks with logs and alerts. The following list provides some additional hints about using the tools effectively:

- Export log data to a spreadsheet for reporting purposes. Importing log data into a spreadsheet program such as Excel offers benefits, such as easy sorting and filtering of data. To format the data for easy export, configure the log file type as Text File-CSV or Text File-TSV on the **Log Files** properties tab.

- Record transient data in a log. Not all counter log file formats can accommodate data that is not persistent throughout the duration of the log. If you want to record intermittent data such as a process that starts after you start the log, select the binary linear or circular file format on the **Log Files** tab.

- Limit log file size to avoid disk-space problems. If you choose automated counter logging with no scheduled stop time, the file will grow to the maximum size allowed based on available space on your disk up to 1 gigabyte (the largest log file that System Monitor can read). Trace logs have no file-size limit. When setting this option, take into consideration your available disk space and any disk quotas that are in place. Change the file path from the default (the Perflogs folder on the local computer) to a location with adequate space if appropriate. An error might occur if your disk runs out of disk space due to logging.

- Name files for easy identification. Use **File name** and **End file names with** on the **Files** properties tab to make it easy to find specific log files. For example, if you set up periodic logging, such as a log for every day of the week, you can develop different naming schemes with the base name being the computer where the log was run, or the type of data being logged, followed by the date as the suffix. For example, you could have a scheme that generates a file named Workstation1_050212.blg, meaning it was created on a computer named Workstation1 at noon, assuming the **End file name with** entry was set at **mmddhh**.

- Determine what trace data providers are available for trace logging. On the **General** properties tab, click **Provider Status** to see all data providers that have been installed. To see only enabled (running) data providers, click the **Show only enabled providers** check box in the **Provider Status** dialog box. For more information about WMI data providers, see the WMI SDK documentation in the MSDN Library at http://windows.microsoft.com/windows2000/reskit/webresources. You can have only one instance of each provider running at the same time.

Task Manager

Task Manager provides information about applications currently running on your system, the processes and memory usage or other data about those processes, and statistics about memory and processor performance.

Comparison with System Monitor

Although useful as a quick reference to system operation and performance, Task Manager lacks the logging and alert capabilities of the Performance console. In addition, although the data displayed by Task Manager comes from the same source as some performance counters, Task Manager does not have access to the breadth of information available from all installed counters. However, Task Manager provides capabilities not available with the Performance console, as described in Table 27.4. For information about these capabilities, see online Help for Task Manager and the chapters identified in Table 27.4.

Table 27.4   Other Chapters on Task Manager

Capability	Chapter
Stop running processes.	"Analyzing Processor Activity" in this *Resource Kit*
Change the base priority of a process.	"Analyzing Processor Activity" in this *Resource Kit*
Set affinity for a process to a particular processor (on multiprocessor systems).	"Measuring Multiprocessor System Activity" in the *Server Operations Guide*

Starting Task Manager

To start Task Manager, use any of these methods:

- Press CTRL+SHIFT+ESC.
- Right-click the taskbar, and then click **Task Manager**.
- Press CTRL+ALT+DEL, and then click **Task Manager**.

You can also start Task Manager at the command prompt or the **Run** dialog box.

Working with Task Manager

Task Manager has three tabs: **Applications**, **Processes**, and **Performance**. While Task Manager is running, the status bar always displays the total number of processes, CPU use, and virtual memory use for the system. Note the following display possibilities:

- All Task Manager columns can be resized.
- Clicking a column sorts its entries in ascending or descending order.
- Select **Always on Top** from the **Options** menu to keep the window in view as you switch between applications.
- Press CTRL+TAB to toggle between tabs, or click the tab.

When Task Manager is running, an accurate miniature CPU usage gauge appears on the taskbar on the end opposite the **Start** button. When you place the mouse pointer over this icon, it displays the percentage of processor use in text format. The miniature gauge always matches the CPU Usage History chart on the **Performance** tab, as shown in Figure 27.9.

Figure 27.9   Task Manager CPU Gauge Shown on the Taskbar

To make Task Manager the top window, double-click the gauge, or right-click the gauge and then select **Task Manager** from the menu that appears.

If you run Task Manager frequently and do not want to see its button on the taskbar, click **Hide When Minimized** on the **Options** menu. To open an instance of Task Manager when it is hidden, click the Task Manager CPU gauge on the taskbar.

You can control the rate at which Task Manager updates its counts by setting the **Update Speed** option on the **View** menu.

- **High.** Updates every half-second.
- **Normal.** Updates once per second.
- **Low.** Updates every four seconds.
- **Paused.** Does not update automatically. Press F5 to update.

This will reduce Task Manager overhead, but might cause you to miss some data. You can force an update at any time by clicking **Refresh Now** on the **View** menu or by pressing F5.

Monitoring Processes

In **Task Manager**, click the **Processes** tab to see a list of running processes and measures of their performance. The Task Manager process table includes all processes that run in their own address space, including all applications and system services.

To include those in the display, on the **Options** menu, click **Show 16-bit Tasks**. Figure 27.10 shows an example of how Task Manager displays process information.

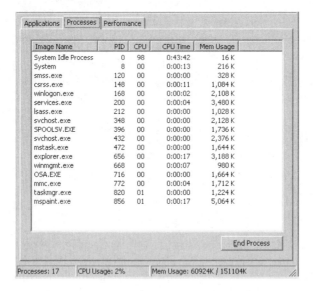

Figure 27.10   Processes Tab in Task Manager

Note System Monitor displays its values in bytes, whereas Task Manager displays its values in kilobytes, which are units of 1,024 bytes. When you compare System Monitor and Task Manager values, multiply Task Manager values by 1,024.

To add to or remove performance measures from the display for the processes listed, on the **View** menu, click **Select Columns**. Table 27.5 briefly describes the measures and their System Monitor counterparts, if any.

Table 27.5   Comparison of Process Data Supplied by Task Manager and System Monitor

Task Manager Process Measure	Description	System Monitor Process Object Counters
Base Priority	The base priority of the process, which determines the order in which its threads are scheduled for the processor.	Priority Base
	The base priority is set by the process code, not the operating system. The operating system sets and changes the dynamic priorities of threads in the process within the range of the base.	
	Use Task Manager to change the base priority of processes. For more information about changing priority to improve processor performance, see "Analyzing Processor Activity" in this book.	

(continued)

Table 27.5   Comparison of Process Data Supplied by Task Manager and System Monitor *(continued)*

Task Manager Process Measure	Description	System Monitor Process Object Counters
CPU Time	The total processor time, in seconds, used by the process since it was started.	None
CPU Usage	The percentage of time the threads of the process used the processor since the last update.	% Processor Time
GDI Objects	The number of Graphics Device Interface (GDI) objects currently used by a process. A GDI object is an object from the GDI library of application programming interfaces (APIs) for graphics output devices.	None
Handle Count	The number of object handles in the process's object table.	Handle Count
I/O Other	The number of input/output operations generated by a process that are neither reads nor writes, including file, network, and device I/Os. An example of this type of operation would be a control function. I/O Others directed to CONSOLE (console input object) handles are not counted.	I/O Other Operations/sec For more information about monitoring I/O, see the following chapters in this book: "Examining and Tuning Disk Performance" in this *Resource Kit* "Monitoring Network Performance" in the *Server Operations Guide*
I/O Other Bytes	The number of bytes transferred in input/output operations generated by a process that are neither reads nor writes, including file, network, and device I/Os. An example of this type of operation would be a control function. I/O Other Bytes directed to CONSOLE (console input object) handles are not counted.	I/O Other Bytes/sec
I/O Read Bytes	The number of bytes read in input/output operations generated by a process, including file, network, and device I/Os. I/O Read Bytes directed to CONSOLE (console input object) handles are not counted.	I/O Read Bytes/sec
I/O Reads	The number of read input/output operations generated by a process, including file, network, and device I/Os. I/O Reads directed to CONSOLE (console input object) handles are not counted.	I/O Read Operations/sec
I/O Write Bytes	The number of bytes written in input/output operations generated by a process, including file, network, and device I/Os. I/O Write Bytes directed to CONSOLE (console input object) handles are not counted.	I/O Write Bytes/sec

(continued)

Table 27.5   Comparison of Process Data Supplied by Task Manager and System Monitor *(continued)*

Task Manager Process Measure	Description	System Monitor Process Object Counters
I/O Writes	The number of write input/output operations generated by a process, including file, network, and device I/Os. I/O Writes directed to CONSOLE (console input object) handles are not counted.	I/O Write Operations/sec
Image Name	Name of the process.	The process name in the **Instances** box
Memory Usage	The amount of main memory, in kilobytes, used by the process.	Working Set
Memory Usage Delta	The change in memory use, in kilobytes, since the last update. Unlike System Monitor, Task Manager displays negative values.	None
Nonpaged Pool	The amount of memory, in kilobytes, used by a process. Operating system memory that is never paged to disk. Paging is the moving of infrequently used parts of a program's working memory from RAM to another storage medium, usually the hard disk.	Pool Nonpaged Bytes
Page Faults	The number of times that data had to be retrieved from disk for this process because it was not found in memory. This value is accumulated from the time the process is started.	None Page faults/sec is the rate of page faults over time.
Page Faults Delta	The change in the number of page faults since the last update.	None
Paged Pool	The amount of system-allocated virtual memory, in kilobytes, used by a process. The paged pool is virtual memory available to be paged to disk. Paging is the moving of infrequently used parts of a program's working memory from RAM to another storage medium, usually the hard disk. The paged pool includes all of user memory and a portion of system memory.	Pool Paged Bytes
Peak Memory Usage	The peak amount of physical memory resident in a process since it started.	None
PID (Process Identifier)	Numerical ID assigned to the process while it runs.	ID Process
Thread Count	The number of threads running in the process.	Thread Count

(continued)

Table 27.5   Comparison of Process Data Supplied by Task Manager and System Monitor   *(continued)*

Task Manager Process Measure	Description	System Monitor Process Object Counters
USER Objects	The number of USER objects currently being used by a process. A USER object is an object from Window Manager, which includes windows, menus, cursors, icons, hooks, accelerators, monitors, keyboard layouts, and other internal objects.	None
Virtual Memory Size	The amount of virtual memory, or address space, committed to a process.	Private Bytes

For more information about Task Manager and its use in monitoring processor and memory performance, see the following chapters in this book:

- "Evaluating Memory and Cache Usage" in this *Resource Kit*
- "Analyzing Processor Activity"in this *Resource Kit*

For multiprocessor systems, also see "Measuring Multiprocessor System Activity" in the *Server Operations Guide*.

Monitoring the System

To see a dynamic overview of system performance, including a graph and numeric display of processor and memory usage, click the Task Manager **Performance** tab, as shown in Figure 27.11.

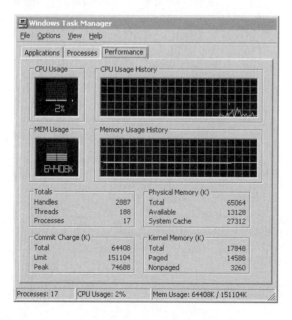

Figure 27.11   Task Manager Performance Tab

To graph the percentage of processor time in privileged or kernel mode, click **Show Kernel Times** on the **View** menu. This is a measure of the time that applications are using operating system services. The remaining time, known as user mode, is spent running threads within the application code.

Users of multiple-processor computers can click **CPU History** on the **View** menu and then graph the non-idle time of each processor in a single graph or in separate graphs.

The following table briefly describes the counts on the Performance tab and their System Monitor counterparts, if any.

Table 27.6   Comparison of System Data Provided by Task Manager and System Monitor

Task Manager Counts	Description	System Monitor Counters
CPU Usage	The percentage of time the processor is running a thread other than the Idle thread.	Processor\% Processor Time
MEM Usage	The amount of virtual memory used, in kilobytes.	Memory\Committed Bytes
Total Handles	The number of object handles in the tables of all processes.	Process(_Total)\Handle Count
Total Threads	The number of running threads, including one Idle thread per processor.	Process(_Total)\Thread Count
Total Processes	The number of active processes, including the Idle process.	Object\Processes is the same, but excludes the Idle process.
Physical Memory: Total	Amount of physical, random access memory, in kilobytes, installed in the computer.	None
Physical Memory: Available	Amount of physical memory available to processes, in kilobytes. It includes zeroed, free, and standby memory.	Memory\Available Bytes
Physical Memory: File Cache	Amount of physical memory, in kilobytes, released to the file cache on demand.	Memory\Cache Bytes

(continued)

Table 27.6   Comparison of System Data Provided by Task Manager and System Monitor *(continued)*

Task Manager Counts	Description	System Monitor Counters
Commit Charge: Total	Size of virtual memory in use by all processes, in kilobytes.	Memory\Committed Bytes
Commit Charge: Limit	Amount of virtual memory, in kilobytes, that can be committed to all processes without enlarging the paging file.	Memory\Commit Limit
Commit Charge: Peak	The maximum amount of virtual memory, in kilobytes, used in the session. The commit peak can exceed the commit limit if virtual memory is expanded.	None
Kernel Memory: Total	Sum of paged and nonpaged memory, in kilobytes.	None (Sum of Pool Paged Bytes and Pool Nonpaged Bytes)
Kernel Memory: Paged	Size of the paged pool, in kilobytes, allocated to the operating system.	Memory\Pool Paged Bytes
Kernel Memory: Nonpaged	Size of the nonpaged pool, in kilobytes, allocated to the operating system.	Memory\Pool Nonpaged Bytes

Resource Kit Performance Tools

The *Windows 2000 Resource Kit* companion CD contains other performance-related tools, such as the following:

- **Ctrlist.exe.** This prints counter descriptions to a file or to the screen.

- **Extctrlst.exe.** This lists all counter DLLs that are running and provides the capability of disabling them. For more information about disabling counters, see "Troubleshooting Problems with Performance Tools" later in this chapter.

- **Perfmtr.exe.** This command-line tool is useful for dynamically monitoring performance statistics relating to memory, processor, and I/O activity.

- **Showperf.exe.** This program is useful for developers who want to see the counter type, index, and the contents of the Performance Data block so they can view and debug the counter's raw data structure.

- **Typeperf.exe.** This is a command-line tool for displaying performance information from individual performance counters.

For information about the tools listed, see the *Windows 2000 Resource Kit* Tools Help. Programs used in specific bottleneck analysis contexts are described in the chapters to which they apply.

Starting Your Monitoring Routine

Setting up a monitoring routine consists of several steps, including setting up a basic monitoring configuration (sometimes called "overview" settings), testing the limits of acceptable performance under various conditions, and establishing a baseline. The following sections describe how to undertake these steps.

Your Minimum Monitoring Configuration

The minimum performance objects to monitor are those corresponding to the main hardware resources of your system: memory, processors, disks, and network components. Table 27.7 lists the appropriate counters and the categories of information they provide.

Table 27.7   Monitoring the Minimum Objects

Component	Performance Aspect Being Monitored	Counters to Monitor
Disk	Usage	LogicalDisk\% Free Space
		LogicalDisk\% Disk Time
		PhysicalDisk\Disk Reads/sec
		PhysicalDisk\Disk Writes/sec
		Use **diskperf -y** to enable disk counters and **diskperf -n** to disable them. To specify the type of counters you want to activate, include **d** for physical disk drives and **v** for logical disk drives or storage volumes. When the operating system starts up, it automatically sets the **diskperf** command with the **-yd** switch to activate physical disk counters. Type **diskperf -yv** to activate logical disk counters. For more information about using the **diskperf** command, type **diskperf - ?** at the command prompt.
		The % Disk Time counter must be interpreted carefully. Because the _Total instance of this counter might not accurately reflect utilization on multiple-disk systems, it is important to use the % Idle Time counter as well. Note that these counters cannot display a value exceeding 100 percent.
		For more information about disk performance counters, see "Examining and Tuning Disk Performance"in this book.
Disk	Bottlenecks	LogicalDisk\Avg. Disk Queue Length
		PhysicalDisk\Avg. Disk Queue Length (all instances)
Memory	Usage	Memory\Available Bytes
		Memory\Cache Bytes
		You can also use Memory\Committed Bytes and Memory\Commit Limit to detect problems with virtual memory.

(continued)

Table 27.7   Monitoring the Minimum Objects *(continued)*

Component	Performance Aspect Being Monitored	Counters to Monitor
Memory	Bottlenecks or leaks	Memory\Pages/sec
		Memory\Page Faults/sec
		Memory\Pages Input/sec
		Memory\Page Reads/sec
		Memory\Transition Faults/sec
		Memory\Pool Paged Bytes
		Memory\Pool Nonpaged Bytes
		Although not specifically Memory object counters, the following are also useful for memory analysis:
		Paging File\% Usage Object (all instances)
		Cache\Data Map Hits %
		Server\Pool Paged Bytes and Server\Pool Nonpaged Bytes
Network	Usage	Network Segment: % Net Utilization
		Note that you need to install the Network Packet Protocol driver for Network Monitor in order to use this counter.
Network	Throughput	Protocol transmission counters (varies with networking protocol); for TCP/IP:
		Network Interface\Bytes total/sec
		Network Interface\Packets/sec
		Server\Bytes Total/sec or Server\Bytes Sent/sec and Server\Bytes Received/sec
		You might want to monitor other objects for network and server throughput, as described in "Monitoring Network Performance" in the *Server Operations Guide*.
Processor	Usage	Processor\% Processor Time (all instances)
	Bottlenecks	System\Processor Queue Length (all instances)
		Processor\Interrupts/sec
		System\Context switches/sec

If you want to test the limits of your system as part of establishing a baseline, monitor the recommended counters during the following activities:

- Adding base services
- Adding connections
- Running network applications
- Opening a file

- Printing a file
- Copying or writing to a file
- Accessing a database
- Sending a message

Establishing the Baseline

After becoming familiar with System Monitor and the process of configuring graphs and logs, you are ready to incorporate monitoring into your daily routine of system administration. Routine monitoring over periods ranging from days to weeks to months allows you to establish a baseline for system performance.

A baseline is a measurement that is derived from the collection of data over an extended period during varying but typical types of workloads and user connections. The baseline is an indicator of how individual system resources or a group of resources are used during periods of normal activity.

When determining your baseline, it is important to know the types of work being done and the days and times when the work is being done. That will help you to associate work with resource usage and to determine the reasonableness of performance during those intervals.

For example, if you find that performance diminishes somewhat for a brief period at a given time of day, and you find that at that time many users are logging on or off, it might be an acceptable slowdown. Similarly, if you find that performance is poor every evening at a certain time and you can tell that time coincides with nightly backups when no users are logged on to the system, again that performance loss might be acceptable. But you can make that determination only when you know the degree of performance loss and its cause.

When you have built up data on performance over a period, with data reflecting periods of low, average, and peak usage, you can make a subjective determination of what constitutes acceptable performance for your system. That determination is your baseline. Use your baseline to detect when bottlenecks are developing or to watch for long-term changes in usage patterns that require you to increase capacity.

Analyzing Monitoring Results

The baseline you develop establishes the typical counter values you should expect to see when your system is performing satisfactorily. The following section provides guidelines to help you interpret the counter values and eliminate false or misleading data that might cause you to set your own target values inappropriately.

When you are collecting and evaluating data to establish a valid performance baseline, consider the following guidelines:

- When monitoring processes of the same name, watch for unusually large values for one instance and not the other. This can occur because System Monitor sometimes misrepresents data for separate instances of processes of the same name by reporting the combined values of the instances as the value of a single instance. Tracking processes by process identifier can help you get around this problem. For information about monitoring processes, see "Analyzing Processor Activity" later in this book.

- When you are monitoring several threads and one of them stops, the data for one thread might appear to be reported for another. This is because of the way threads are numbered. For example, you begin monitoring and have three threads, numbered 0, 1, and 2. If one of them stops, all remaining threads are resequenced. That means that the original thread 0 is now gone and the original thread 1 is renamed to 0. As a result, data for the stopped thread 0 could be reported along with data for the running thread 1 because old thread 1 is now old thread 0. To get around this problem, you can include the thread identifiers of the process's threads in your log or display. Use the Thread\Thread ID counter for this purpose.

- Do not give too much weight to occasional spikes in data. These might be due to startup of a process and are not an accurate reflection of counter values for that process over time. The effect of spikes can linger over time when using counters that average.

- For monitoring over an extended period of time, use graphs instead of reports or histograms because these views only show last values and averages. As a result, they might not give an accurate picture of values if you are looking for spikes.

- Unless you specifically want to include startup events in your baseline, exclude these events because the temporary high values tend to skew overall performance results.

- Investigate zero values or missing data. These can impede your ability to establish a meaningful baseline. There are several possible explanations for this. For more information, see "Troubleshooting Problems with Performance Tools" later in this chapter.

Identifying Potential Bottlenecks

Deviations from your baseline provide the best indicator of performance problems. However, as a secondary reference, Table 27.8 describes recommended thresholds for object counters. Use this table to help you identify when a performance problem is developing on your system. If the values listed are consistently reported on your system, consult additional chapters in the Performance Monitoring section of this book for how to investigate and correct the problems causing these values.

Table 27.8   Recommended Thresholds for the Minimum Set of System Counters

Resource	Object\Counter	Suggested Threshold	Comments
Disk	LogicalDisk\% Free Space	15 percent	None
Disk	LogicalDisk\% Disk Time	90 percent	None
Disk	PhysicalDisk\ Disk Reads/sec, PhysicalDisk\ Disk Writes/sec	Depends on manufacturer's specifications	Check the specified transfer rate for your disks to verify that this rate does not exceed the specifications. In general, Ultra Wide SCSI disks can handle 50 to 70 I/O operations per second.
Disk	PhysicalDisk\ Current Disk Queue Length	Number of spindles plus 2	This is an instantaneous counter; observe its value over several intervals. For an average over time, use PhysicalDisk\Avg. Disk Queue Length.
Memory	Memory\ Available Bytes	Less than 4 MB	Research memory usage and add memory if needed.
Memory	Memory\ Pages/sec	20	Research paging activity.
Network	Network Segment\% Net Utilization	Depends on type of network	You must determine the threshold based on the type of network you are running. For Ethernet networks, for example, 30 percent is the recommended threshold.
Paging File	Paging File\% Usage	Above 70 percent	Review this value in conjunction with Available Bytes and Pages/sec to understand paging activity on your computer.
Processor	Processor\% Processor Time	85 percent	Find the process that is using a high percentage of processor time. Upgrade to a faster processor or install an additional processor.
Processor	Processor\ Interrupts/sec	Depends on processor; for current CPUs, use a threshold of 1500 interrupts per second	A dramatic increase in this counter value without a corresponding increase in system activity indicates a hardware problem. Identify the network adapter or disk controller card causing the interrupts. You might need to install an additional adapter or controller card.

(continued)

Table 27.8   Recommended Thresholds for the Minimum Set of System Counters *(continued)*

Resource	Object\Counter	Suggested Threshold	Comments
Server	Server\Bytes Total/sec		If the sum of Bytes Total/sec for all servers is roughly equal to the maximum transfer rates of your network, you might need to segment the network.
Server	Server\Work Item Shortages	3	If the value reaches this threshold, consider tuning the InitWorkItems or MaxWorkItems entries in the registry (in HKEY_LOCAL_MACHINE \SYSTEM\CurrentControlSet \Services\lanmanserver\Parameters). For more information about MaxWorkItems, see the Microsoft Knowledge Base link on the Web Resources page at http://windows.microsoft.com /windows2000/reskit/webresources
			Caution: Do not use a registry editor to edit the registry directly unless you have no alternative. The registry editors bypass the standard safeguards provided by administrative tools. These safeguards prevent you from entering conflicting settings or settings that are likely to degrade performance or damage your system. Editing the registry directly can have serious, unexpected consequences that can prevent the system from starting and require that you reinstall Windows 2000. To configure or customize Windows 2000, use the programs in Control Panel or Microsoft Management Console whenever possible.
Server	Server Work Queues\Queue Length	4	If the value reaches this threshold, there might be a processor bottleneck. This is an instantaneous counter; observe its value over several intervals.
Multiple Processors	System\Processor Queue Length	2	This is an instantaneous counter; observe its value over several intervals.

Investigating Bottlenecks

Investigating performance problems should always start with monitoring the whole system before looking at individual components. In precise terms, a bottleneck exists if a particular component's limitation is keeping the entire system from performing more quickly. Therefore, even if one component in your system is heavily used, if other components or the system as a whole show no adverse effects, then there is no bottleneck.

For example, suppose that a process had 10 threads, each of which used exactly 0.999 seconds of processor time once every 10 seconds. If each thread made a request exactly 1 second after the previous one in perfect sequence, the processor would be 99.9 percent busy, but there would be no queue, no interference between the threads, and, technically, no bottleneck, although the system probably could not support any increased load or variation in its request scheduling without creating one.

Factors involved in the development of a bottleneck are the number of requests for service, the frequency with which requests occur, and the duration of each request. As long as these are perfectly synchronized, no queue will develop and no bottleneck will arise. The device with the smallest throughput ratio is probably the primary source of the bottleneck.

It is difficult to detect multiple bottlenecks in a system. You might spend several days testing and retesting to identify and eliminate a bottleneck, only to find that another appears in its place. Only thorough and patient testing of all elements can ensure that you have found all of the problems.

It is not unusual to trace a performance problem to multiple sources. Poor response time on a workstation is most likely to result from memory and processor problems. Servers are more susceptible to disk and network problems.

Also, problems in one component might be the *result* of problems in another component, not the cause. For example, when memory is scarce, the system begins moving pages of code and data between disks and physical memory. The memory shortage becomes evident from increased disk and processor use, but the problem is memory, not the processor or disk.

If you identify a resource that is out of range for your baseline or based on the recommended thresholds discussed in the preceding section, you need to investigate the activity of that resource in greater detail. This includes the following steps:

- Analyze your hardware and software configurations. Does your configuration match Microsoft recommendations for the operating system and the services you are supporting?

- Review entries in the event log for the time period when you begin seeing out-of-range counter values; these entries might provide information about problems that might result in poor system performance.

- Examine the kinds of applications you are running and what resources they demand, to determine their adequacy.

- Consider variables in your workload, such as processing different jobs at different times. For more efficient analysis, when you are looking for a specific problem, limit your charts and reports to specific events occurring at known times.

- For immediate diagnosis and problem solving of situations such as shutdowns and logon failures, log or monitor for a shorter time. Sampling should be frequent when monitoring over a short period. Similarly, for long-term planning and analysis, log for a longer period and set the update interval accordingly.

- Consider network or disk utilization or other activities occurring at the times that you see increasing resource utilization. Try to understand the usage patterns. Are they associated with specific protocols or computers?

- Approach bottleneck correction in a scientific manner. For example, never make more than one change at a time, always repeat monitoring after a change to validate the results, eliminate results that are suspect, and keep good records of what you have done and what you have learned.

When investigating bottlenecks in specific resources, focus on the performance objects and counters that pertain to the specific resource that appears to be your bottleneck. For more information about these resources, refer to the appropriate chapter in the *Windows 2000 Resource Kit*. These chapters also discuss how to use other Windows 2000 tools and tools on the *Windows 2000 Resource Kit* companion CD for bottleneck detection and tuning. Relevant chapters in the *Windows 2000 Resource Kit* include the following:

- "Evaluating Memory and Cache Usage"
- "Analyzing Processor Activity"
- "Examining and Tuning Disk Performance"

For information about monitoring servers, also see "Monitoring Network Performance" and "Measuring Multiprocessor System Activity" in the *Server Operations Guide*.

Troubleshooting Problems with Performance Tools

Occasionally you might have problems obtaining performance data, or you might find that monitoring a process is adding an unnecessary load to a computer you are monitoring. The following sections discuss how to handle some of these problems:

- Investigating Zero Values
- Investigating Other Problems with Performance Tools
- Controlling Performance Monitoring Overhead

Investigating Zero Values

If data for selected counters is consistently reported as zeroes, this might indicate a problem with the counters or the way you are using the performance tools, rather than only the absence of nonzero data. The following are descriptions of the possible causes and solutions to problems that result in missing or zero counter values.

- The process being monitored has stopped and, as a result, there is no data for the process in the performance tools. If you stopped the process manually, restart it to see the process in System Monitor. Otherwise, check Event Viewer for concurrent entries. You might find an error associated with this process.

- The counter DLL was disabled after you selected the corresponding counters in a log or display. The performance tools will not detect that the counter was removed or disabled, but will report the counter data as zeroes.

- You are attempting to monitor a computer that you don't have permission to access. This might occur if you are using a saved console that specifies a particular computer name. This causes System Monitor to report data as zeroes. It also causes System Monitor to start up slowly. For more information see "Security Issues" later in this chapter.

Investigating Other Problems with Performance Tools

You might occasionally believe that data reported by the performance tools is invalid, that data is incomplete, or that the tools are not operating properly. This section addresses some problems you might encounter with the tools and how to correct them.

Data seems to be missing.

- System Monitor might show gaps in its line graphs because data collection was subordinated to higher-priority processing activity on a system with a heavy load. When the system has adequate resources to continue with data collection, the graphing will resume as usual. A message appears describing this. Note also that you might see delays in display of data for some counters. Counters that display an average must wait for two samples to elapse before displaying a value. For ways to reduce the performance overhead of system monitoring, see "Controlling Performance Monitoring Overhead" later in this chapter.

- Values recorded in a log do not appear in the graph view. This is because the graph is limited to 100 samples. Reducing the size of the Time Window on the **Data** properties tab can allow you to see a more complete range of data.

Objects, counters, or instances seem to be missing or invalid.

In some cases you might not be able to find an object you want to monitor. The following conditions might cause this to occur:

- You have not started or installed the process that starts the object counters. Use Task Manager to verify that the process is running. If so, use Exctrlst.exe on the *Windows 2000 Resource Kit* companion CD to verify that the counter DLL is running.

- You have not enabled the counters (such as with the Network Segment object counters). If you do not see a counter that you want to monitor, make sure that the service or feature that provides the counter has been installed or configured. For information about how to install or configure the service or feature, see online Help for the service or feature.

- If counters have been disabled, then they will not appear in the **Add Counters** dialog box. There are several reasons that a counter DLL might be disabled:

  - A user disables counter DLLs using Exctrlst.exe on the *Windows 2000 Resource Kit* companion CD.

  - The Performance Library's built-in testing routines have found problems with the counter DLLs and have disabled them to prevent them from interfering with operation of the Performance console. If this has occurred, the Application Log in Event Viewer contains a message to this effect.

  To re-enable the counters for debugging purposes, locate the Performance subkey under the subkey for the service (typically, HKEY_LOCAL_MACHINE\SYSTEM\CurrentControlSet\Services *service_name*\Performance\\) and change the value for the Disable Performance Counters entry from 1 (disabled) to 0 (enabled). Notice that a counter DLL that the system has automatically disabled is likely to contain errors and can cause the system to slow.

- You lack permissions on the computer being monitored. If you do not have appropriate permissions to monitor the computer, an error message will be displayed when you attempt to select the computer. An administrator must ensure that your user account has permissions to use the performance tools. If you are trying to monitor a remote system, for information about security issues, see "Monitoring Remote Computers" later in this chapter.

- The DLL that installs the counters is generating errors. An example is if the counter does not handle localization functions correctly. Check Event Viewer to see if the counter DLL or the Performance Data Helper (PDH) library reported any errors. If necessary, you can disable counter DLLs that are causing errors by using Exctrlst.exe on the *Windows 2000 Resource Kit* companion CD.

- You are trying to monitor a 16-bit or MS-DOS application. Only 32-bit processes appear in the **Instances** box. Active 16-bit processes appear as threads running in a Windows NT Virtual DOS Machine (NTVDM) process. (Virtual DOS Machine is an environment system for MS-DOS and 16-bit Windows emulation.) If you want to monitor a 16-bit application, see "Monitoring 16-bit Windows Applications" later in this chapter.

> **Note**   When trying to monitor administrative tools hosted in MMC, note that they appear as instances of MMC in the **Add Counters** dialog box.

- The instance you want to monitor is not currently active. If you are configuring System Monitor to collect real-time data, you can only select active instances for data collection. (If you are viewing logged data, you can select inactive instances for which the log contains data.) If you select the process and it stops after you have selected it, it will continue to appear in the list box but the reported data will be zeroes.

- You might see situations where an instance seems inappropriate for the counter—such as the _Total instance for the Process\ID Process counter. All counters for an object have the same instances.

Data seems invalid.

There are several reasons that counters might report unlikely values:

- You sometimes see an extremely high value for one instance and not the other when you are monitoring processes of the same name. This is because the performance tools sometimes misrepresent data for separate instances of processes with the same name by reporting the combined values of the instances as the value of a single instance. Using the instance index and tracking the Process\ID Process and Process\Creating Process ID counters can help you get around this problem.

- Also, when monitoring several threads and one of them stops, the data for one thread might appear to be reported for another. This is because of the way threads are numbered. For example, you begin monitoring and have three threads, numbered 0, 1, and 2. If one of them stops, all remaining threads are resequenced. That means that the original thread 0 is now gone and the original thread 1 is renamed to 0. As a result, data for the stopped thread 0 could be reported along with data for the running thread 1 because old thread 1 is now old thread 0. Again, using the instance index can help you to track these threads.

Problems with System Monitor and MMC

- If you are trying to create a custom console with System Monitor and another tool, you might have a problem because System Monitor is not listed in the **Add Standalone Snap-in** dialog box. This is because System Monitor is not designed as an extension snap-in but as an ActiveX control. To create a custom console containing System Monitor, you select **ActiveX Control** in the **Add Standalone Snap-in** dialog box and select **System Monitor Control** in the **Insert ActiveX Control** dialog box. System Monitor Control will appear as the name of the tool in your custom console; you can change it as needed.

- Help for System Monitor does not appear in MMC; only Performance Logs and Alerts is shown in MMC Help. Because System Monitor is designed as an ActiveX control, it is unlike other MMC snap-ins. For example, System Monitor Help is not available by clicking **Help Topics** on the **Help** menu or by right-clicking **System Monitor** and selecting **Help** in the shortcut menu. Instead, click **Help** on the System Monitor display toolbar.

Problems with logs

- Trace log data is not output as readable text. You must use a parsing tool to interpret the trace log output such as Tracedmp.exe on the *Windows 2000 Resource Kit* companion CD. Developers can create such a tool with the APIs provided in the Platform Software Development Kit.

- An error message appears if you try to export log data to Microsoft Excel while the Performance Logs and Alerts service is actively collecting data to that log. The service must be stopped because Excel requires exclusive access to the log file. Other programs are not known to require this exclusive access; therefore, in general, you can work with data from a log file while the service is collecting data to that file.

- Data from a running log does not seem to be updating. If you are working in System Monitor with a log file that is currently collecting data, you will need to click **Select Time Range** and keep moving the **Time Range** bar to the right to update the display with new samples.

- Processes that started while a log was running do not appear in my exported log. Logged data can be saved as comma-separated or tab-separated files that are easily viewed with Microsoft Excel. However, some limitations apply when you use this format. Instances that start after the log is started will not be reflected. You need to use the binary log format to see data for these instances.

- Errors occur regarding counter log size. This could be because your counter log has consumed the available space on the hard disk drive that you specified in the log file path. Notice that large logs are unwieldy and slow to work with.

- An exported monitoring configuration is collecting data from the wrong computer. This is probably because you selected the **Select counters from computer** option when you saved the console and installed it on another system. Instead, select **Use local computer counters**.

- The Performance Logs and Alerts service stops and does not restart. If a network connection is lost during remote monitoring, or if there is a problem with a counter DLL, this could cause the Performance Logs and Alerts service to shut down. The service is configured to restart only once after the first failure. Thereafter, you need to start the service manually. To avoid recurrence of this problem, modify the startup properties of the services in **Services** under **Administrative Tools**. Also make sure to investigate the cause of the shutdown by reviewing the event log and disabling problem DLLs. To do this, use Exctrlst, a tool included on the *Windows 2000 Resource Kit* companion CD.

- Workspace (.pmw) files that were created with Windows NT 4.0 Performance Monitor are not fully compatible with Windows 2000 System Monitor. Only one of the views saved in the workspace is available in System Monitor. System Monitor can read log files created with earlier versions of Performance Monitor when you use the following syntax at the Windows 2000 command prompt:

   perfmon.exe *log_file_name*

   This command does not invoke Windows NT 4.0 Performance Monitor, but instead a shell program that starts System Monitor. Windows NT 4.0 Performance Monitor is available as Perfmon4.exe on the *Windows 2000 Resource Kit* companion CD.

Controlling Performance Monitoring Overhead

When you select a counter in any view, the performance tools collect data for all counters of that object, but display only the one you select. This causes only minimal overhead, because most of the tools' overhead results from the display. You can control monitoring overhead in the following ways:

- Use logs instead of displaying a graph. The user interface is more costly in terms of performance.

- Limit the use of costly counters; this increases monitoring overhead. For information about costly counters, see the Performance Counter Reference on the *Windows 2000 Resource Kit* companion CD.

- Lengthen collection intervals if possible. In general, 600-second (10-minute) intervals are sufficient for ordinary monitoring.

- Collect data during peak activity rather than over an extended interval.

- Reduce the number of objects monitored unless these are critical to your analysis.

- Put the log file on a disk that you are not monitoring.

- Check the log file size when logging multiple servers to a single computer to see how much space the data is taking up.

- Limit to brief periods the trace logs that are monitoring page faults or file I/O. Prolonged trace logging strains system performance.
- Avoid configuring System Monitor reports to display nondefault data. If you choose nondefault data (the defaults are Average value for logs; Last value for graphs) in the Report view, the statistic is calculated at each sample interval. This incurs some additional performance overhead.

Monitoring Remote Computers

In general, monitoring remote computers differs little from monitoring local computers. This section discusses some facts to consider when evaluating whether to monitor remotely or locally.

Methods of Monitoring

When monitoring activity on remote computers, you have some options with regard to how to collect data. For example, you could run a counter log on the administrator's computer, drawing data continuously from each remote computer. In another case, you could have each computer that is running the service collect data and, at regular intervals, run a batch program to transfer the data to the administrator's computer for analysis and archiving. Figure 27.12 illustrates these options.

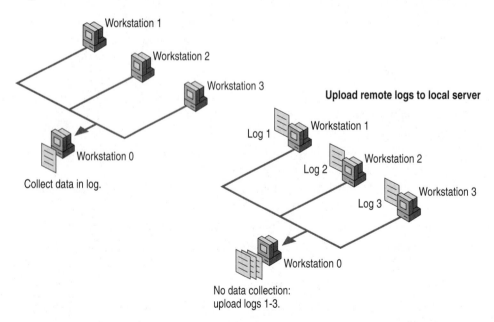

Figure 27.12   Comparison of Performance Data Logging Options

Choose a monitoring method based on your needs from the ones described in the following list:

- Centralized data collection (that is, collection on a local computer from remote computers that you are monitoring) is simple to implement because only one logging service is running. You can collect data from multiple systems into a single log file. However, it causes additional network traffic and might be constrained by available memory on the administrator's computer. Frequent updating also adds to network activity. Centralized monitoring is useful for a small number of servers (25 or fewer). For centralized monitoring, use the **Add Counters** dialog box to select a remote computer while running System Monitor on your local computer.

- Distributed data collection (that is, data collection that occurs on the remote computers you are monitoring) does not incur the memory and network traffic problems of local collection. However, it does result in delayed availability of the data, requiring that the collected data be transferred to the administrator's computer for review. This kind of monitoring might be useful if you suspect the server is part of the problem. It is also useful if you suspect that the network is the cause of performance problems and you are concerned that data packets you want to monitor are being lost, because it isolates the computers from the network during data collection. In general, local monitoring creates more disk traffic on each monitored computer. For distributed monitoring, use **Performance Logs and Alerts** under **Computer Management** to select the computer you want to monitor.

Security Issues

If you are collecting data using the registry, monitoring a remote computer requires the use of the Remote Registry Service. If the service stops due to failure, the system restarts it automatically only once. Therefore, if the service stops more than once, you must restart the service manually on the second and any subsequent failures. To change this default behavior, modify the properties for Remote Registry Service. You can access service properties using **Services** under **Services and Applications** in **Computer Management** or under **Administrative Tools**. Also check the application and system logs in Event Viewer for events that might explain why the service stopped.

In addition, remote data collection requires access to certain registry subkeys and system files. Users need a minimum of Read access to the Winreg subkey in HKEY_LOCAL_MACHINE\SYSTEM\CurrentControlSet\Control \SecurePipeServers to provide remote access to the registry for the purpose of collecting data on remote systems. By default, members of the Administrators group have Full Control access and members of the Backup Operators group have Read access. Users also need Read access to the registry subkey that stores counter names and descriptions used by System Monitor. This subkey is HKEY_LOCAL_MACHINE\SOFTWARE\Microsoft \Windows NT\CurrentVersion\Perflib*LanguageID*, where *LanguageID* is the numeric code for the spoken language for the operating system installation. (For the English language, the subkey is Perflib\009.) By default, members of the Administrators and Creator Owners groups, and the System account, have Full Control access. Therefore, a local user on a server who isn't logged on as an administrator will not be able to see performance counters.

Users might also require Read access to the files that supply counter names and descriptions to the registry, Perfc*.dat and Perfh*.dat. (The asterisk is a wildcard character representing the specific language code; for English, these are Perfc009.dat and Perfh009.dat.) If these files reside on an NTFS file system volume, then, in order to have access to them, the access control lists (ACLs) on these files must specify that the user has such access. By default, members of the Administrators and Interactive groups have sufficient access.

The remote computer allows access only to user accounts that have permission to access it. In order to monitor remote computers, the Performance Logs and Alerts service must be started in an account that has permission to access the remote computers you are attempting to monitor. By default, the service is started under the local computer's system account, which generally has permission to access only services and resources on the local computer. To start this under a different account, start Computer Management, double-click **Services and Applications**, and then click **Services**. Click **Performance Logs and Alerts**, and update the properties under the **Log On** tab. To monitor using counter logs or alerts, you must also have permission to read the HKEY_CURRENT_MACHINE\SYSTEM \CurrentControlSet\Services\SysmonLog\LogQueries registry subkey.) In general, administrators have this access by default. In each case, attempting to use the tools without appropriate permissions will generate an error message.

If you are collecting data remotely by means of WMI, the user must be a member of the Administrators group.

Monitoring Legacy Applications

For optimal performance, it is recommended that all applications you run under Windows 2000 be 32-bit. However, if you need to continue using 16-bit Windows or MS-DOS-based applications, this section describes how you can monitor their activity.

Monitoring 16-bit Windows Applications

In Windows 2000, by default, all active 16-bit Windows applications run as separate threads in a single multithreaded process called NT Virtual DOS Machine (NTVDM). The NTVDM process simulates a 16-bit Windows environment complete with all of the DLLs called by 16-bit Windows applications.

This configuration poses two challenges for running 16-bit applications:

- It prevents 16-bit applications from running simultaneously, which might impede their performance.

- It makes monitoring a bit trickier because 16-bit applications do not appear by name in the **Add Counters** dialog box for the performance tools; instead, they appear as undistinguishable NTVDM processes.

As a result, Windows 2000 includes an option to run a 16-bit application in its own separate NTVDM process with its own address space. You can monitor 16-bit Windows applications by identifying them by their thread identifier (ID) while they are running, or by running each application in a separate address space.

In addition to the 16-bit applications, each NTVDM process includes a heartbeat thread that interrupts every 55 milliseconds to simulate a timer interrupt, and the Wowexec.exe thread, which helps to create 16-bit tasks and to handle the delivery of the 16-bit interrupt. This thread supports 16-bit Windows applications in a 32-bit Windows environment. The WOW subsystem provides an NTVDM where all Win16 applications run. You will see the heartbeat and Wowexec threads when monitoring 16-bit applications.

Only one 16-bit Windows application thread in an NTVDM can run at one time and, if an application thread is preempted, the NTVDM always resumes with the same thread. This limits the performance of multiple 16-bit applications running in the same NTVDM process, although this limitation becomes an issue only when the processor is busy.

Because 16-bit applications run in the same process, monitoring more than one 16-bit application can be tricky. You need to distinguish among the threads of the NTVDM process.

To monitor one 16-bit application, select the NTVDM process in System Monitor. (Other performance tools used to monitor processes can be used for monitoring the NTVDM process. For more information, see "Analyzing Processor Activity" in this book.) If you have multiple 16-bit processes running in NTVDM, you can distinguish them by their thread identifiers (IDs). You might have to start and stop the 16-bit process to determine which ID is associated with which 16-bit process.

Figure 27.13 shows a System Monitor report on a single NTVDM process. The ID Process and ID Thread counters are included to help you distinguish among the threads. One of the threads is the heartbeat thread, one is the Wowexec thread, and one is a 16-bit application.

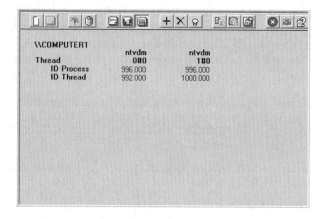

Figure 27.13   NTVDM Threads in System Monitor

System Monitor identifies threads by the process name and a thread number. The thread numbers are ordinal numbers (beginning with 0) that represent the order in which the threads started. The thread number of a running thread changes when a thread with a lower number stops, and all threads with higher numbers move up in order to close the gap. For example, if thread 1 stops, thread 2 becomes thread 1. Therefore, thread numbers are not reliable indicators of thread identity.

Instead, with System Monitor you can track processes and threads using the process IDs and thread IDs. The process ID identifies the process in which the thread runs. The thread ID identifies the thread. Unlike the thread number, which can change over the time the thread runs, the system assigns the thread ID when the thread starts and retains it until the thread stops.

As shown in Figure 27.14, Task Manager makes it easy to identify 16-bit applications because it displays the names of the executable files indented below the NTVDM process name. To monitor 16-bit processes in Task Manager, click the **Processes** tab, and on the **Options** menu, click **Show 16-bit Tasks**.

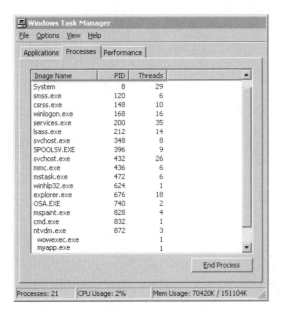

Figure 27.14   MyApp, Wowexec, and Ntvdm on the Task Manager Process Tab

In this example, you can see the Wowexec (Windows on Windows) and the MyApp threads. The heartbeat thread is not an executable and does not appear as a process in Task Manager. However, the **Thread Count** column on the far right shows that all threads are running in the NTVDM process.

Running 16-bit Windows Applications in a Separate Process

Windows 2000 lets you opt to run a 16-bit Windows application in a separate, unshared NTVDM process with its own memory space. This eliminates competition between NTVDM threads in a single process, making the 16-bit application thread fully multitasking and preemptive. It also simplifies monitoring.

▶ **To run a 16-bit application in its own address space**

- At the command prompt, type:

   start /separate *processname*

In Task Manager and System Monitor, two instances of the NTVDM process appear. You can use their process identifiers to distinguish between them. Figure 27.15 shows NTVDM threads with process identifiers.

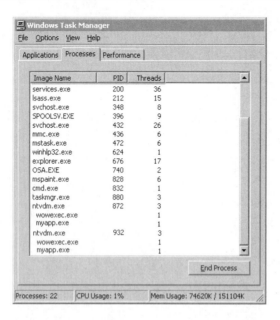

Figure 27.15   NTVDM Instances in Task Manager with Process Identifiers

Figure 27.15 shows Task Manager monitoring two copies of a 16-bit application, each in its own NTVDM process.

Monitoring MS-DOS Applications

In Windows 2000, each MS-DOS application runs in its own NTVDM process, eliminating some of the problems encountered in 16-bit Windows applications. All of the NTVDM processes are called Ntvdm.exe by default, but you can use the following procedure to change the name for easier tracking.

▶ **To create a new process name for an NTVDM process**

1. Copy Ntvdm.exe to a file with a different name.

2. Change the value of the **cmdline** entry in HKEY_LOCAL_MACHINE\SYSTEM\CurrentControlSet\Control\WOW to the name of your copy of Ntvdm.exe. The default value is *systemroot*\System32\Ntvdm.exe.

3. When you start an MS-DOS application, it will run in a process with that name. Figure 27.16 shows how your edited process name appears in Regedt32.

Figure 27.16   New Process Name in Regedt32

Tip   You do not have to restart the computer for the registry change to take effect. Thus, you can change the registry between starting different MS-DOS applications and have each start in a uniquely named process. It is also prudent to set the process name back to Ntvdm.exe when you are finished.

If you are not satisfied with the performance of your MS-DOS-based applications in Windows 2000, try changing the following settings, accessed by right-clicking the file in Windows Explorer:

- Under **Usage** in **Screen** properties for the .pif file, select **Full-Screen** to speed up video display performance. Press ALT+ENTER to get in and out of full-screen mode.

- Disable the Compatible Timer Hardware Emulation feature in the _Default.pif or the application's program information file (PIF). To disable it, clear the check box displayed when you click the **Windows NT** button under **Program** properties for the file. Because this feature causes a decrease in performance, use it only if it is required to allow an application to run under Windows 2000.

- If the application is in a window and seems to pause periodically, try reducing idle sensitivity by moving the **Idle Sensitivity** slider to the left in **Misc** properties for the application's .pif.

- If the MS-DOS-based application can be configured for printing, choose LPT1 or LPT2 rather than parallel port. Most of the applications use Int17 to print when configured for LPT. If you select parallel port mode, these applications print directly to printer ports. Parallel mode is significantly slower in Windows 2000 compared to Windows 3.x.

Integrating the System Monitor Control into Office and Other Applications

You can host the System Monitor ActiveX control in applications of the Microsoft Office 97 suite or later and in HTML pages. The following sections describe how to integrate and use these controls, including the following:

- Placing the Control in an Office Document or on a Web Page
- Formatting the Control in a Document

Placing the Control in an Office Document or on a Web Page

Integration of the Microsoft Office applications with Visual Basic for Applications makes the process of adding the System Monitor control almost identical across these applications. The following procedures describe how to insert the control in applications such as Microsoft Word, Microsoft Excel, and Microsoft® PowerPoint®. For purposes of this section, the word "document" is used to refer to PowerPoint slides, Word documents, or Excel spreadsheets.

- Default key settings in Microsoft Word might conflict with the CTRL+H combination used for System Monitor highlighting. You might need to change these to support highlighting when the System Monitor control (Sysmon.ocx in the *systemroot*\System32 folder) is used in Microsoft Word.

In addition, you can add the control to a Web page using an HTML editor that supports insertion of ActiveX controls or using a text editor as described in the procedure "To insert the control in an HTML Page" later in the chapter.

▶ **To insert the System Monitor control in a Microsoft Office application**

1. Start the application and select **Toolbars** under the **View** menu.
2. Under **Toolbars**, select **Control Toolbox**.
3. With the Control Toolbox displayed, click the **More Controls** icon, and then select the **System Monitor Control**.

   Figure 27.17 shows the System Monitor control selected in the Control Toolbox.

Figure 27.17   System Monitor Control in the Control Toolbox

4. Place the control on the page according to the requirements of the application. See the following differences among applications:

- In a Microsoft Word document, select the insertion point (where the I-beam is flashing) before selecting the control. The control will appear at the position you selected. Design mode is active and you need to exit Design mode before setting control properties or adding counters. Click the **Design Mode** icon to exit.

- In a Microsoft Excel spreadsheet, select the control and then select the insertion point. When the crosshair appears, note that you can create a placeholder for the control by holding down the left mouse button and dragging the mouse pointer across the columns and rows that you want the control to occupy. Releasing the mouse button causes the control to appear in the space you selected.

  If you do not create a placeholder, you can click any location on the spreadsheet and the control will be inserted in the location with a default size. Design mode is active and you need to exit Design mode before setting control properties or adding counters. Click the **Design Mode** icon to exit.

- In a Microsoft PowerPoint slide, select the control and then select the insertion point. With the crosshair visible on the screen, note that you can hold down and drag the mouse button to the size you want and the control will be inserted in the placeholder. Otherwise, you can click anywhere on the slide to place the control in that location with a default size and you can modify the size coordinates later (as described in the procedure "To format the control in a document" later in this chapter).

  The Design mode icon is not displayed after you insert the control although Design mode *is* in effect. To exit Design mode, on the **View** menu, click **Slide Show**.

Note   The System Monitor control is not displayed correctly until you exit Design mode.

With the control sited in the document, you can add counters or modify control properties, as described in the System Monitor Help file (Sysmon.chm).

If you select **Graph** for the Display Type and the size you define for the control is insufficient to show the graph data, only a portion of the graph will be displayed (such as the vertical minimum and maximum scale values, and the counter-data graph lines).

If you select **Report** for the Display Type and the size is insufficient to show all the report data, the control includes vertical and horizontal scroll bars so that you can scroll to view the data that does not fit in the display.

If you want to format the control in the application, resume Design mode by clicking the Design mode icon in the Control Toolbox and see the procedure "To format the control in a document" later in this chapter.

▶ **To insert the control in a Microsoft Visual Basic program**

1. On the **File** menu, choose **New** to open a new project (such as a Standard EXE or an ActiveX Document EXE).

2. On the **Project** menu, click **Components** to show the **Components** dialog box.

   You can also view the **Components** dialog box by right-clicking the Toolbox. If the Toolbox is not displayed, in the **View** menu, select the **Toolbox** command.

3. Under **Controls** in the **Components** dialog box, select the **System Monitor Control Library** check box, and then click **OK**.

   An icon for the System Monitor control now appears in the Toolbox.

4. With the form or the document displayed, double-click the **System Monitor Control** icon to add it to the form or document for your program.

   This places the control in the document, occupying the entire size of the form. If you want to select a size for the control, click the **System Monitor Control** icon *once* and then, when the crosshair appears, hold down and drag the mouse to the size you want the control to occupy on the form.

Immediately after inserting the control, the application is in Design mode, so you can format the control within a document. For more information, see the procedure "To format the control in a document" later in this chapter.

▶ **To insert the control in an HTML page**

- Using a text editor, create a page to include the control. To place the control on the page, insert the <OBJECT> tag and specify the class ID as follows:

```
<OBJECT classid="clsid:C4D2D8E0-D1DD-11CE-940F-008029004347">
</OBJECT>
```

This places the control in the document and, when you view the page in a Web browser, you can add counters or modify control properties as described in the procedures that appear later in this chapter.

To include functions in your page that automate the setting of properties or addition of counters, use scripts written in Visual Basic Scripting Edition (VBScript), or use Microsoft® FrontPage®, as described in the following procedure.

▶ **To insert the System Monitor control in a Web page created with Microsoft FrontPage**

1. In a new or existing FrontPage Web page, on the **Insert** menu, select **Other Components**, and then select **ActiveX Control**.

2. In the **ActiveX Control Properties** dialog box, select **Sysmon Graph Control** in the **Pick A Control** list box.

3. To add VBScript, click **Extended**, and complete the **Extended Attributes** dialog box as needed.

   For more information about VBScript, see the VBScript link on the Web Resources page at http://windows.microsoft.com/windows2000/reskit/webresources.

Formatting the Control in a Document

The default appearance of the control can vary based on the document in which it resides. This is because the control takes the ambient properties of the document in which it is running. For example, when placed in Microsoft Word or FrontPage, the graph background, font, and chart background color might be reset to the default color and font used by those documents. Therefore, after you insert the control in a Microsoft Office application, you might want to change its appearance with respect to the document itself.

Using Design mode in Visual Basic or Office documents, you can easily manipulate the control's attributes, such as size or position, as you can with any linked or embedded object. In addition, you have access to the control's properties, methods, and events from the Visual Basic editor for programming the control's behavior within the document. (The control's user interface is inactive when the document is in Design mode.) Note that there are slight differences in how some of the Office applications handle formatting the inserted control.

Note   When changing the properties of the control, it is possible to set colors for **BackColor**, **ForeColor**, or **GraphBackground**, or to set graph line colors that are not visible. Therefore, make sure to check the appearance of your control display after you make changes to its properties.

In addition, you cannot programmatically format the properties and methods of the control using the Visual Basic editor. Use VBScript or Microsoft® Jscript® in your HTML editor for this purpose.

▶ **To format the control in a document**

1. Resume Design mode and make the changes you want. To resume Design mode in PowerPoint, exit the Slide Show view.

   - To change the position of the control in the document, drag the control to another position in the container.

   - To change the height or width of the control in the document, drag one of the selection handles of the control in the appropriate direction.

2. To access the control properties or the Visual Basic code editor, right-click the control and select **Properties** or **View Code**, as appropriate. In the Visual Basic code editor window, you can view the Object Browser if needed.

   Notice that some commands on this shortcut menu (such as Cut, Copy, or Paste) are designed for other embedded or linked objects in that document; they are not relevant to the control and might be unavailable (dimmed).

   Note When you use Microsoft Office applications, it is possible to modify the control in the document so that the control's properties become inaccessible. This occurs because the control is being converted into an embedded object. For example, if you click the **System Monitor Control Object** command in Microsoft Word (by right-clicking the control) and select the **Convert** command, the **Convert** dialog box appears. If you click **OK** in this box, the control's properties and view-code option become unavailable. You will not be able to change the position or the size of the object in Word.

   ---

3. Exit Design mode before trying to add counters or to edit the control's default properties.

Notice that the appearance of the control might not update properly until you exit Design mode.

For information about the control's objects, properties, and so on, see the Software Development Kit (SDK) documentation in the MSDN Library at http://windows.microsoft.com/windows2000/reskit/webresources.

C H A P T E R 2 8

Evaluating Memory and Cache Usage

Use the Performance console and other Microsoft® Windows® 2000 tools to assess available memory and to observe the effects of a memory shortage, a common cause of poor computer performance. Examine the effectiveness of the file system cache—an area of physical memory where recently used data read from or written to the disk is mapped for quick access. In addition, use Windows 2000 tools to investigate memory problems caused by applications that have not been optimized.

In This Chapter

Related Information in the Resource Kit

- For general information about performance monitoring, see "Overview of Performance Monitoring" in this book.

- For more information about developer tools see the *Microsoft® Windows® 2000 Resource Kit* companion CD, or see the MSDN link on the Web Resources page at http://windows.microsoft.com/windows2000 /reskit/webresources.

Quick Guide to Monitoring Memory

Use this quick guide to view the topics and tasks related to monitoring memory usage in Microsoft® Windows® 2000 Professional.

Learn about memory requirements.

Memory has such an important influence on system performance that monitoring and analyzing memory usage is one of the first steps you take when assessing your system's performance.

- See "Overview of Memory Monitoring" later in this chapter.

Verify that you have the appropriate amount of installed memory.

A memory shortage is a significant cause of performance problems. Therefore, one of the first steps in examining memory usage is to rule out the existence of a shortage by learning both how much memory is required for the operating system and your workload and how much is available on your system.

- and "Determining the Amount of Installed Memory" later in this chapter.

Establish a baseline for memory usage.

A performance baseline is the level of performance you can reliably expect during typical usage and workloads. When you have a baseline established, it becomes easier to identify when your system is experiencing performance problems, because counter levels are out of the baseline range.

- See "Establishing a Baseline for Memory" later in this chapter.

Use memory counters to identify excessive paging, memory shortages, and memory leaks that slow system performance.

Changes in memory counter values can be used to detect the presence of various performance problems. Tracking counter values both on a system-wide and a per-process basis helps you to pinpoint the cause.

- See "Investigating Memory Problems" later in this chapter.

Monitor how your applications use the file system cache,and learn to use the cache and memory counters to evaluate application efficiency.

The cache and memory counters provide information about how applications running on your system make use of the file system cache. To accurately assess cache efficiency, you need to understand which counters to use and how to interpret their values.

- See "Resolving Memory and Cache Bottlenecks" later in this chapter.

Tune or upgrade memory resources as needed to improve performance.

When you have determined the cause of a memory bottleneck, you can undertake steps to correct the problem by adding memory, removing unnecessary services, tuning inefficient applications, or other tuning methods.

- See "Resolving Memory and Cache Bottlenecks" later in this chapter.

What's New

Users of Microsoft® Windows® 98 and Microsoft® Windows NT® version 4.0 Workstation will notice a few changes in Windows 2000 with respect to memory resources and utilization. The following list provides a brief summary of the changes in features for these operating systems.

- Changed from Windows NT 4.0, Windows 2000 Professional enlarges the default size of the paging file to 1.5 times the amount of installed random access memory (RAM).

- Users of Microsoft® Windows NT® Workstation version 4.0 will notice the new counters under the Memory performance object in System Monitor: Available KBytes and Available MBytes, reporting the amount of available memory in kilobytes and megabytes, respectively, rather than only in bytes as reported by Memory\Available Bytes. The Memory performance object counters are similar to the Memory Manager items. The Cache object counters are similar to the Disk Cache items available in Windows 98 System Monitor, but are named differently in Windows 2000.

- Task Manager's display of file-system cache size has been modified from Windows NT Workstation 4.0 for greater accuracy. The value reported by System Cache in Task Manager represents the currently mapped file system cache plus pages in transition to disk. These were not included in values reported under Windows NT 4.0.

Overview of Memory Monitoring

Low memory conditions can slow the operation of applications and services on your computer and impact the performance of other resources in your system. For example, when your computer is low on memory, *paging*—that is, the process of moving virtual memory back and forth between physical memory and the disk—can be prolonged, resulting in more work for your disks. Because it involves reading and writing to disk, this paging activity might have to compete with whatever other disk transactions are being performed, intensifying a *disk bottleneck*. (A disk bottleneck occurs when disk performance decreases to the extent that it affects overall system performance.) In turn, all this work by the disk can mean the processor is used less or is doing unnecessary work, processing numerous interrupts due to repeated *page faults*. (Page faults occur when the system cannot locate requested code or data in the physical memory available to the requesting process.) In the end, applications and services become less responsive.

Figure 28.1 illustrates the sequence in which you conduct the monitoring process. Memory has such an important influence on system performance that monitoring and analyzing memory usage is one of the first steps you take when assessing your system's performance.

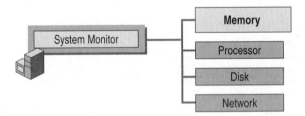

Figure 28.1   Role of Memory Monitoring in Overall Monitoring Sequence

In the first phase of analyzing memory usage, you need to understand your current memory configuration and workload. To help you do this, use the steps in the following list:

- Determine the amount of physical memory that is currently installed, and compare it against minimum operating system requirements.

- Read "Understanding Memory and the File System Cache" later in this chapter for information about the relationship between system memory and the file system cache.

- Establish a baseline for memory usage on your computer by determining performance ranges for low or idle, average, and peak usage periods.

- Optimize the system memory configuration to the system workload, including verifying cache and paging file sizes.

Focus subsequent monitoring on how your system uses memory, and on identifying memory shortages or other problems, by taking the following steps:

- Look at memory characteristics of processes using the Process\Working Set and Process\Private Bytes counters. The Working Set counter reports the amount of committed memory allocated to the process. This might include shared and private bytes currently residing in physical memory. The Private Bytes counter reports memory allocated exclusively to the process. Working set monitoring is important because, when memory is in short supply, the operating system trims the *working sets* of processes and paging occurs. (The working set of a process is the amount of physical memory assigned to that process by the operating system.)

- Monitor the counters listed in "Investigating Disk Paging" later in this chapter to understand the relationship between the amount of paging and the amount of disk activity and their effect on overall performance. Excessive paging can burden the disk.

- Determine the effectiveness of the file system cache. Your system performs better when it can find requested data in the cache, rather than when it must read from the disk.

- Learn how to tune the working sets of applications, if you have access to source code. Efficient applications maintain a small working set without generating page faults.

Determining the Amount of Installed Memory

Start your monitoring efforts by knowing that you have at least the minimum amount of memory required to run Windows 2000. Windows 2000 Professional requires at least 32 megabytes (MB) of memory.

The memory recommendation for Windows 2000 Professional is based on a typical desktop configuration including a business productivity application, such as a word processor or a spreadsheet program, an e-mail application, and a Web browser.

There are a few different ways to determine the amount of memory on your computer. You can find the amount of physical memory installed on your system by clicking the **Performance** tab in Task Manager. Or you can find the amount of available RAM by double-clicking **System** in **Control Panel**, and then clicking the **General** tab.

Note You can see the memory configuration on local or remote systems by using System Information. For more information about System Information, see Windows 2000 Professional Help.

The operating system distinguishes memory usage by applications and services depending on whether the usage involves the paged or the nonpaged pool. The paged pool contains memory for objects used by applications and services that can be paged to disk; objects in the nonpaged pool cannot be paged to disk. The operating system determines the size of each pool based on the amount of physical memory present. Memory pool usage can be an important factor in evaluating memory usage by your applications. For more information about memory pools, see "Investigating User-Mode Memory Leaks" and "Investigating Kernel-Mode Memory Leaks" later in this chapter.

The file system cache, which is a subset of physical memory used for fast access to data, and the *disk paging file*, which supports *virtual memory*, influence the amount of memory used by the operating system and applications. (The disk paging file, also called a swap file, is a file on the hard disk that serves as temporary, virtual memory storage for code and data.) Virtual memory is the space on the hard disk that Windows 2000 uses as memory. For purposes of monitoring, the most important types of virtual memory are committed memory (shown under Memory\Committed Bytes) that the system sets aside for a process in the paging file and available memory (shown under Memory\Available Bytes) that is not in use by a process. (Another type of memory managed by Windows 2000 is reserved memory, which the system sets aside for a process, but which might not be entirely used.) The following sections describe the influence of the cache and the paging file on performance and explain how best to adjust these for optimal memory usage.

Understanding Memory and the File System Cache

Windows 2000 allocates a portion of the virtual memory in your system to the *file system cache*. The file system cache is a subset of the memory system that retains recently used information for quick access. The size of the cache depends on the amount of physical memory installed and the memory required for applications. The operating system dynamically adjusts the size of the cache as needed, sharing memory optimally between process working sets and the system cache.

Microsoft® Windows® 2000 Server provides a user interface for adjusting the size of the file system cache, but this user interface is not available in Windows 2000 Professional. For information about adjusting the file-system cache size on systems running Windows 2000 Server, see "Evaluating Memory and Cache Usage" in the *Microsoft® Windows® 2000 Server Resource Kit Server Operations Guide*.

Adjusting Paging File Size

For virtual-memory support, Windows 2000 creates one paging file called Pagefile.sys on the disk or volume on which the operating system is installed. The default size is equal to 1.5 times the amount of physical memory. A small paging file limits what can be stored and might exhaust your virtual memory for applications. If you are short on RAM, more paging occurs, which generates extra activity for your disks and slows response times for the system.

Because the size and location of paging files can affect your system's performance, you might want to modify them. Also, because maintaining multiple files on multiple physical drives can improve performance, you might want to add a paging file. Figure 28.2 shows the **Virtual Memory** dialog box, which you use to change your paging file settings. See Windows 2000 Professional Help for specific instructions.

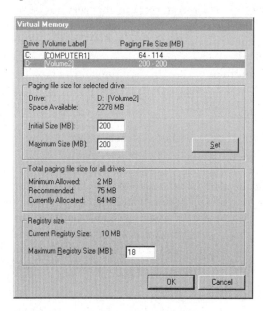

Figure 28.2   Virtual Memory Dialog Box

The following guidelines describe how to optimize the paging file.

Set the Same Initial and Maximum Size

Setting the paging file's initial size and maximum size to the same value increases efficiency because the operating system does not need to expand the file during processing. Setting different values for initial and maximum size can contribute to disk fragmentation.

Expand the Default Size

Expanding the default size of the paging file can increase performance if applications are consuming virtual memory and the full capacity of the existing file is being used. To determine how large your paging file needs to be based on your system workload, monitor the Process (_Total)\Page File Bytes counter. This indicates, in bytes, how much of the paging file is being used.

You can also determine the appropriate size of a paging file by multiplying the Paging File\% Usage Peak counter value by the size of Pagefile.sys. The % Usage Peak counter indicates how much of the paging file is being used. Consider expanding the page file whenever either this counter reaches 70 percent of the total size in bytes of all paging files or the Memory\% Committed Bytes In Use counter reaches 85 percent, whichever occurs first.

A large paging file uses disk storage space, so do not create a large paging file on a disk that is very active (for example, one that services heavy application or network activity) or one that has limited space. Change the file size gradually and test performance until you find the optimal balance between paging file and disk space usage. The operating system requires a minimum of 5 MB of free space on a disk. For more information, see "Examining and Tuning Disk Usage" in this book.

Move the Paging File

If disk space on your boot volume is limited, you can achieve better performance by moving the paging file to another volume. However, you might want to leave a smaller paging file on the boot volume and maintain a larger file on different volume with more capacity for the sake of recoverability. Depending on how you have configured your system's startup and recovery options, the configuration might require that you maintain a paging file of a certain size on the boot volume. Therefore, make sure to consider your startup and recovery settings when planning to move the paging file. For more information about startup and recovery options such as writing debugging information, see Windows 2000 Help.

Use Multiple Disks

Although Windows 2000 supports a limit of 4,095 MB for each paging file, you can supply large amounts of virtual memory to applications by maintaining multiple paging files. Spreading paging files across multiple disk drives and controllers improves performance on most modern disk systems because multiple disks can process input/output (I/O) requests concurrently in a round-robin fashion.

A mirrored or striped volume is a good candidate for the placement of a paging file. Placing the paging file on its own logical partition can prevent file fragmentation. Creating multiple paging files on a single logical volume or partition does not improve performance.

If you find that page writing and disk writing or page reading and disk reading are equivalent on a logical disk, splitting the paging file onto separate volumes is helpful.

Note   To see how the paging file is used during memory shortages, start the LeakyApp tool on the *Windows 2000 Resource Kit* companion CD, which simulates memory leaks for monitoring purposes. While running LeakyApp, monitor Paging File\% Usage Peak and Process(_Total)\Page File Bytes. Log these counters to get an idea of the rate of growth of the paging file.

Establishing a Baseline for Memory

After determining that you have an adequate amount of physical memory and that your configuration is appropriate, examine your physical memory usage under a normal workload to establish a baseline or reference point for physical memory usage. The baseline is generally not a single value but a range within which physical memory usage can fluctuate and still provide acceptable performance. You can use the baseline to identify trends, such as increasing physical memory demands over time, or to recognize problems that arise from a sudden change.

To determine a baseline for your system, use the following counters to create logs of memory usage over an extended period (from several weeks to a month).

- \Memory\Pages/sec
- \Memory\Available Bytes
- \Paging File(_Total)\% Usage

As you monitor the values of these counters, you might see occasional spikes. Typically, you can exclude these from your baseline because it is the consistent, repetitive values with which you are most concerned; the range of values that seem to appear consistently constitutes your baseline. When values fall outside of these ranges for extended periods, follow the instructions provided in this chapter to investigate the variations.

Virtual Memory Usage

Even if your system exceeds the minimum physical memory requirements for the operating system, you might face situations in which you do not have enough physical memory. For example, if you run several memory-intensive applications or if several users share your computer, the available physical memory of your system might be consumed, affecting your system's performance.

To see how much virtual memory your Windows 2000 Professional–based computer uses, start all applications and use Task Manager to see the Peak Commit Charge value. This value appears in the **Commit Charge** box on the **Performance** tab. Commit charge is the number of pages reserved for virtual memory that are backed by the paging file.

Peak committed memory is the highest amount of virtual memory (in bytes) that has been committed over this sample. To be committed, these bytes must either have a corresponding amount of storage available on disk or in main memory. Compare this value against the size of the paging file to determine whether the paging file is sized appropriately.

Under **Computer Management**, use **Shared Folders** under **System Tools** to view this information.

Default Services Memory Consumption

In general, Windows 2000 has been optimized so that only the most commonly used services run by default, and you do not have to turn off any services. However, you can reduce the memory requirements of your system by turning off some of the default services provided by the operating system. Administrators have access to Services in the Administrative Tools menu by default.

▶ **To stop a service**

1. From the **Start** menu, point to **Programs** and **Administrative Tools**, and then click **Services**.

2. Right-click the name of the appropriate service, and then click **Stop**.

This procedure stops the service for the current session. To disable the service permanently, you need to change the value for service startup in the properties dialog box for the service. To use this dialog box, click **Services** in the **Administrative Tools** menu or in the Computer Management console. Right-click the service you want to change, select **Properties** in the shortcut menu, and then change the value to Disabled in the **Startup type** box.

Investigating Memory Problems

After you have observed memory usage under normal conditions and established your memory baseline, you might notice that the memory counters sometimes stray from the typical range. The following sections describe how to investigate conditions that cause memory values to deviate from the baseline.

The following activities help you to learn about and analyze memory usage and memory bottlenecks by using System Monitor counters and other tools:

- Investigating memory shortages
- Investigating disk paging
- Investigating user-mode memory leaks
- Investigating kernel-mode memory leaks
- Monitoring the cache
- Resolving memory and cache bottlenecks

Table 28.1 summarizes the most important counters to monitor for analyzing memory usage.

Table 28.1   Counters for Analyzing Memory Usage

To monitor for	Use this *Object\Counter*
Memory shortages	Memory\Available Bytes Process (*All_processes*)\Working Set Memory\Pages/sec Memory\Cache Bytes
Frequent hard page faults	Memory\Pages/sec Process (*All_processes*)\Working Set Memory\Pages Input/sec Memory\Pages Output/sec
Excess paging with a disk bottleneck	Memory\Page Reads/sec Physical Disk\Avg. Disk Bytes/Read
Paging file fragmentation	PhysicalDisk\Split IOs\sec PhysicalDisk\% Disk Read Time PhysicalDisk\Current Disk Queue Length Process\Handle Count

(continued)

Table 28.1   Counters for Analyzing Memory Usage *(continued)*

To monitor for	Use this *Object\Counter*
Memory leaks; memory-intensive applications	Memory\Pool Nonpaged Allocations Memory\Pool Nonpaged Bytes Memory\Pool Paged Bytes Process(*process_name*)\Pool Nonpaged Bytes Process(*process_name*)\Handle Count Process(*process_name*)\Pool Paged Bytes Process(*process_name*)\Virtual Bytes Process(*process_name*)\Private Bytes
Cache Manager efficiency	Cache\Copy Read Hits % Cache\Copy Reads/sec Cache\Data Map Hits % Cache\Data Maps/sec Cache\MDL Read Hits % Cache\MDL Reads/sec Cache\Pin Read Hits % Cache\Pin Reads/sec To identify cache bottlenecks, also use Memory\Pages Input/sec with these counters.

Important The LogicalDisk object counters are not available by default. If you want to monitor the values for these counters, you must first activate the counters by typing **diskperf –yv** at the Windows command prompt.

Investigating Memory Shortages

Your system can develop a memory shortage if multiple processes are demanding much more memory than is available or you are running applications that leak memory. Monitor the following counters to track memory shortages and to begin to identify their causes.

- **Memory\Available Bytes** indicates how much physical memory is remaining after the working sets of running processes and the cache have been served.

- **Process (*All_processes*)\Working Set** indicates the number of pages that are currently assigned to processes. When there is ample memory, the working set structures can fill with pages that are not currently needed to do work but that were needed in the past and might be needed in the future. Because there is no memory shortage, the working set structures are not trimmed. As a result the working set approximates pages that have been referenced in a longer period of time. However, when memory is in short supply, the working set might be trimmed. As a result, the working set in that case approximates the number of pages referenced in a much shorter period of time.

- **Memory\Pages/sec** indicates the number of requested pages that were not immediately available in RAM and had to be read from the disk or had to be written to the disk to make room in RAM for other pages. If your system experiences a high rate of hard page faults, the value for Memory\Pages/sec can be high.

To maintain a minimum number of available bytes for the operating system and processes, the Virtual Memory Manager continually adjusts the space used in physical memory and on disk. In general, if memory is ample, working set sizes can increase as needed. If the memory supply is barely adequate or very close to the amount required, you might see the operating system trim some working-set sizes when another process needs more memory—at startup, for example. Figure 28.3 illustrates this situation.

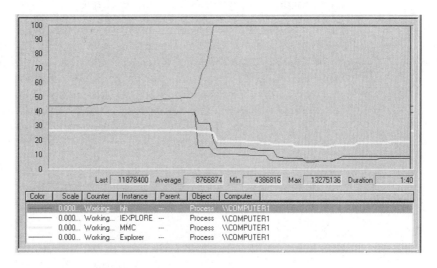

Figure 28.3   Working Set Values of Processes as One Process Starts Up

If the value for Memory\Available Bytes is consistently below the system-defined threshold and the value for Memory\Pages/sec spikes continuously, it is likely that your memory configuration is insufficient for your needs. To confirm that a high rate of paging is related to low memory, see "Investigating Disk Paging" later in this chapter.

Note You might see a low value for Memory\Available Bytes, which is not caused by a memory shortage, in the following situations:

- During large file-copy operations such as a system backup. In this case, you can verify that the copy operation is the cause by also monitoring Memory\Cache Bytes. You typically see Memory\Cache Bytes rise as Memory\Available Bytes falls. Otherwise, you need to investigate the cause as described in this chapter.

- The working sets of processes have become smaller and there is no demand for pages for other purposes. In this case the number of available bytes might be low but there is no need to trim working sets and there are few if any page faults.

To identify processes associated with low-memory conditions, examine memory usage by specific processes, and determine whether a process is leaking memory as described in "Investigating User-Mode Memory Leaks" and "Investigating Kernel-Mode Memory Leaks" later in this chapter.

If available memory is consistently low (2 MB or less), the computer becomes unresponsive because it is occupied exclusively with disk I/O operations. During paging due to low memory, the processor is idle while waiting for the disk to finish. Therefore, it is important to investigate and correct the cause of a low-memory condition. Notice which processes are running as well as the sizes of their working sets as you monitor memory counters. The processes might need to be updated or replaced if they are contributing to memory shortages and you do not want to acquire additional memory.

For information about how to address a memory shortage, see "Resolving Memory and Cache Bottlenecks" later in this chapter.

Investigating Disk Paging

Use memory counters that report paging activity to identify memory shortages resulting in disk bottlenecks. Start by monitoring the memory counters and working set values as you did when checking for a memory shortage in the preceding section. Confirm that hard page faults are occurring by using the Memory\Pages/sec counter.

If hard page faults are occurring, monitor disk counters to assess how the disk is behaving during paging: whether it is busy with other work or with handling page faults. Monitor disk paging by using the following steps and associated counters:

1. To confirm hard page faulting, use the following Memory and Process counters:

   - Memory\Pages/sec
   - Process (*All_processes*)\Working Set
   - Memory\Pages Input/sec
   - Memory\Pages Output/sec

2. To understand the impact of page faulting on the disk, compare the number of reads and read bytes measured by the following counters:

   - Memory\Page Reads/sec
   - PhysicalDisk\Disk Reads/sec
   - PhysicalDisk\Avg. Disk Read Bytes/sec

Confirming Hard Page Faults

To confirm hard page faults, examine boththe hard page fault rate by using Memory\Pages/sec and the working sets of active processes by using Process(*process_name*)\Working Set, as described in "Investigating Memory Shortages" earlier in the chapter. Memory\Pages/sec is the sum of Pages Input/sec and Pages Output/sec and reports the number of requested pages that were not immediately available in RAM and had to be read from the disk (resulting in hard page faults) or that had to be written to the disk to make room in RAM for other pages. Monitoring the working sets of processes enables you to correlate a particular application's memory usage with page faulting. When memory is in short supply, working sets are continuously trimmed and page faults are frequent.

Acceptable rates for Memory\Pages/sec range from 40 per second on older portable computers to 150 per second for the newest disk systems. Use a shorter monitoring period on client computers than on server computers (updating once per second is appropriate) because paging activity can occur in bursts on clients. Paging activity tends to reach a steady state on server computers; therefore, longer-term monitoring is appropriate.

Note Page Fault Monitor (Pfmon.exe), a tool on the *Windows 2000 Resource Kit* companion CD, lists hard and soft page faults generated by each function call in a running process. You can display the data, write it to a log file, or both. For more information, see Windows 2000 Resource Kit Tools Help (W2rktools.chm) on the *Windows 2000 Resource Kit* companion CD.

You can also monitor page faults and memory management data by using Trace Logs in the Performance snap-in. For more information, see "Overview of Performance Monitoring" in this book.

When values exceed the acceptable range for your type of disk, investigate disk activity to determine whether the faulting is causing a disk bottleneck. Memory\Pages Input/sec reflects the rate at which pages were read from the disk and thus gives you data on hard page faults. Depending on the capabilities of your disk, high values can indicate a lack of memory that is sufficient to hurt system performance. See Figure 28.4 for an example of page faulting.

Note You might see high levels of paging with Memory\Pages/sec when pages are read to and from noncached, memory-mapped files. When these files are used in this way, Memory\Pages/sec or Memory\Available Bytes is high but Memory\Paging File\%Usage and Memory\Cache Faults/sec are normal to low.

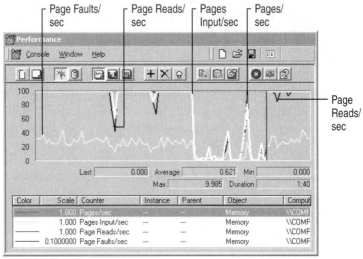

Figure 28.4   Paging Activity on a System with Low Memory

The other component of Memory\Pages/sec, Memory\Pages Output/sec, indicates the rate at which pages were written to the disk. Although this activity does not generate hard page faults, disk-write activity can indirectly reflect a memory shortage and indicates additional disk activity. This is because, as the Virtual Memory Manager needs to trim pages from a working set, it might find that some pages contain changed data. In this case, the changed data must be written to disk to free the pages. When memory is in ample supply, Memory\Pages Output/sec is likely to be low because there is less need to free changed pages and write that data to disk. For more information about investigating applications that generate disk-write activity, see "Examining and Tuning Disk Usage" in this book.

Assessing the Effect of Page Faults on the Disk

To understand the impact of page faulting on the disk, examine the number of disk operations that occur as a result of paging. If paging activity dominates your disk's workload, a memory shortage is causing a disk bottleneck. Start by looking at Memory\Page Reads/sec. This counter indicates the number of read operations by the disk that were required to retrieve faulted pages. Compare the number of reads performed against the number of pages faulted to determine how many pages are retrieved per read. A high ratio of reads to faults means a large number of pages are not found in physical memory and are being demanded from the disk, creating a disk bottleneck.

Next, determine what proportion of your disk's overall work is occupied with reading pages from memory. To do this, compare page reads against disk reads. If there is a correlation between the values of Memory\Page Reads/sec and PhysicalDisk\Disk Reads/sec, it is likely that paging activity makes up the majority of your disk activity and might be causing a disk bottleneck.

To see the relationship between paging and disk read operations from a different perspective, monitor the value of PhysicalDisk\Avg Disk Read Bytes/sec while you are monitoring Page Reads/sec. The Avg Disk Read Bytes/sec counter indicates the rate at which the disk is transferring data during reads. Because this is a measurement of bytes rather than of pages or of the number of reads, you need to convert to identical units. Use the following formula for this purpose: value of PhysicalDisk\Disk Read Bytes/sec ÷ 4096 (number of bytes in a page).

If the result is approximately equal to the value of Page Reads/sec, paging activity is the bulk of your disk read activity, and the memory shortage represented by heavy paging activity might in turn be causing a disk bottleneck. To see whether this activity is reaching a rate high enough to cause poor disk performance, see your disk manufacturer's documentation for the number of I/O transactions per second you can expect from your disk. Disks currently available can sustain a transfer rate of 70 I/O operations per second. For more information about locating disk bottlenecks, see "Examining and Tuning Disk Usage" in this book.

Figure 28.5 illustrates disk activity associated with paging activity when memory is low.

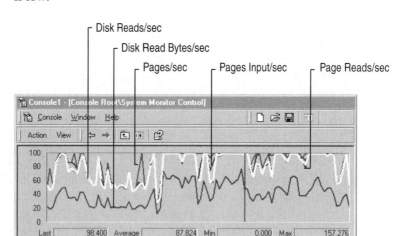

Figure 28.5 Disk and Paging Activity When Memory Is Low

Investigating User-Mode Memory Leaks

A memory leak occurs when applications allocate memory for use but do not free allocated memory when finished. As a result, available memory is used up over time, often causing the system to stop functioning properly. Therefore, it is important to investigate the causes of all memory leaks. This section describes how to identify memory leaks, including ones that affect the critical nonpaged memory pool, and where to find tools and information that can help reduce memory leaks.

Note It is sometimes possible to mistake an increase in system load for a memory leak. To distinguish between these conditions, observe the Memory and Process counters over a number of days. If you see the system first reach a steady state, then attain a level of increased load (usually achieved during some peak portion of the day), and then fall again, it is likely that you are seeing variations in load rather than a leak. On network computers, look at user sessions and throughput rates, such as transferred bytes per second, to eliminate workload as a factor.

Identifying a Memory Leak

The symptoms of a memory leak include the following:

- A gradually worsening response time.

- The appearance of an error message, shown in Figure 28.6, indicating that the system is low on virtual memory. (Another message box might precede this, indicating that virtual memory has been exceeded and that the system has increased the paging file size automatically.)

Figure 28.6   Out of Virtual Memory Error Message

- The appearance of error messages indicating that system services have stopped.

If you suspect that a particular application or service is causing a memory leak, investigate the memory use of your applications by using the following counters:

- **Memory\Available Bytes** reports available bytes; its value tends to fall during a memory leak.

- **Memory\Committed Bytes** reports the private bytes committed to processes; its value tends to rise during a memory leak.

- **Process(***process_name***)\Private Bytes** reports bytes allocated exclusively for a specific process; its value tends to rise for a leaking process.

- **Process(***process_name***)\Working Set** reports the shared and private bytes allocated to a process; its value tends to rise for a leaking process.

- **Process(***process_name***)\Page Faults/sec** reports the total number of faults (hard and soft faults) caused by a process; its value tends to rise for a leaking process.

- **Process(***process_name***)\Page File Bytes** reports the size of the paging file; its value tends to rise during a memory leak.

- **Process(***process_name***)\Handle Count** reports the number of handles that an application opened for objects it creates. Handles are used by programs to identify resources that they must access. The value of this counter tends to rise during a memory leak; however, you cannot rule out a leak simply because this counter's value is stable.

Monitor these counters over a period ranging from two hours to a few days. Logging is recommended, both because of the overhead of monitoring multiple instances of the Process counters and because leaks tend to manifest themselves slowly.

In addition, to isolate the problem and avoid unnecessary overhead, monitor from a remote computer, if possible. Network activity or interaction with other computers can interfere with the results.

Memory Leaks and the Nonpaged Pool

Although any leak is serious, memory leaks are of particular concern when they involve the nonpaged pool. Many system services allocate memory from the nonpaged pool because they need to reference it when processing an interrupt and cannot take a page fault at that time. To identify whether or not a leak affects the nonpaged pool, include the following counters in your monitoring:

- Memory\Pool Nonpaged Bytes
- Memory\Pool Nonpaged Allocs
- Process(*process_name*)\Pool Nonpaged Bytes

Note Because the internal counters used by Task Manager, Process Monitor, and System Monitor to measure the size of the nonpaged pool for each process are not precise, it is recommended that you monitor changes in the overall pool size over time (a few days, for example), rather than rely on the absolute, instantaneous values reported for each process. The counter values are estimates that count duplicate object handles as well as space for the object. Also, because the process pool size counts are rounded to page size, pool space is overestimated when a process uses only part of a page. In contrast, total pool size counts are precise. Therefore, the sum of pool sizes for each process might not equal the value for the whole system.

The counters on the Memory object monitor the total size of the nonpaged pool and the number of allocations of pool space for the whole system. The counter on the Process object monitors nonpaged pool space allocated to each process.

To use System Monitor to monitor the nonpaged pool for leaks, follow these steps:

- Record the size of the nonpaged pool when the system starts. Then log the Memory and Process objects for several days; a 10-minute update interval is sufficient.

- Review the log for changes in size of the nonpaged pool. Usually, you can associate any increases in the size of the pool, as indicated by Memory\Pool Nonpaged Bytes, with the start of a process, as indicated by Process\% Processor Time. Also look at individual Process object counters such as Process\Handle Count, Process\Private Bytes, Process\Nonpaged Pool Bytes, Process\Paged Pool Bytes, and Process\Threads. During a memory leak, you might also see rising values for these counters.

  When processes are stopped, you typically see a decrease in pool size. Any growth in the nonpaged pool is considered abnormal, and you need to distinguish which process is causing the change in pool size.

  You might also want to monitor the number of active threads before and after running the process (use the **Performance** tab in Task Manager or the Objects\Threads or Process(_Total)\Thread Count counters). A process that is leaking memory might be creating a large number of threads; these appear when the process starts and disappear when the process stops.

- Watch the value of Memory\Pool Nonpaged Bytes for an increase of 10 percent or more from its value at system startup to see whether a serious leak is developing.

The following additional tools provide information about the paged and nonpaged memory pools as listed in Table 28.2. These tools collect their data from the same sources.

Table 28.2   Tools That Provide Information About Memory Pools

Tool Name	Description	Location
Memsnap (memsnap.exe)[1]	Records system memory usage to a log file.	Windows 2000 Support Tools
Process Monitor (pmon.exe)[1]	Provides total and per process values for nonpaged and paged pool memory. Also monitors the committed memory values shown in the Pmon display for increases; the process with the leak typically has an increasing value reported under Commit Charge.	Windows 2000 Support Tools

[1] These tools are useful because they show allocations on a per-process basis.

For information about installing and using the Windows 2000 Support Tools and Support Tools Help, see the file Sreadme.doc in the \Support\Tools folder of the Windows 2000 operating system CD.

For a quick demonstration of a memory leak, start LeakyApp, a test tool on the *Windows 2000 Resource Kit* companion CD, and observe the values of the monitored counters. Notice the steady increase in the following counters: Memory\Pages/sec, Process(LeakyApp)\Working Set, and Process(LeakyApp)\Private Bytes.

Figure 28.7 illustrates counter activity during a memory leak generated by the LeakyApp tool.

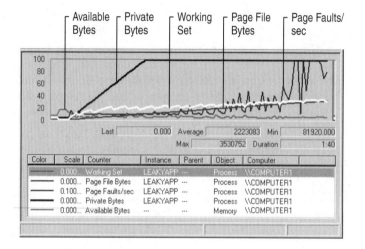

Figure 28.7   Process Memory Activity During a Memory Leak

Although the memory leak illustrated in Figure 28.8 has a systemic effect, the problem can be tracked to a single cause—the leaking application. If you have an application that exhibits similar behavior, it is recommended that you either modify it (if you have access to the source code) or replace it with another program.

Developer tools for analyzing and tuning memory usage by applications are available on the *Windows 2000 Resource Kit* companion CD. For more information about developer tools, see the MSDN link on the Web Resources page at http://windows.microsoft.com/windows2000/reskit/webresources.

The following tools optimize memory-intensive applications.

- **Application Monitor (ApiMon)** on the *Windows 2000 Resource Kit* companion CD monitors page faults caused by an application and reports them by using Microsoft® Win32® function calls.

- The **Working Set Tuner (WST)** on the Software Development Kit (SDK) analyzes the patterns of function calls in your application code and generates an improved function ordering to reduce physical memory usage. One objective of tuning your working set is to arrive at the smallest possible working set without causing page faults.

- **Virtual Address Dump (Vadump)** on the SDK creates a list that contains information about the memory usage of a specified process, including address size, total committed memory for the image, the executable file, each dynamic-link library (DLL), and heap usage.

The nonpaged pool size and the paged pool size are set by default during Windows 2000 Setup based on your memory configuration. The maximum nonpaged pool size is 256 MB. The maximum paged pool size is approximately 470 MB. The actual size varies depending on your configuration. More physical memory results in less paged pool because the virtual address space must instead be used to contain more critical memory-management structures. The pool sizes are defined in the registry in the HKEY_LOCAL_MACHINE\System \CurrentControlSet\Control\Session Manager\Memory Management subkey.

To extend the file system cache working set from 512 MB to 960 MB, set the value of the **PagedPoolSize** registry entry to 192000000, set **SystemPages** to 0, and make sure that the system is optimized for file sharing with **LargeSystemCache** set to 1. To make the maximum virtual address space available to the paged pool, set the **PagedPoolSize** registry entry to −1, provided your system is not using the **/3GB** Boot.ini switch.

Typically you do not need to set the **NonPagedPoolSize** entry because on systems with more than 1.2 GB of memory, the system automatically defaults to the maximum nonpaged pool size. If you need to set the **NonPagedPoolSize** value, set it to the value you want (in bytes); do not set it to −1.

Investigating Kernel-Mode Memory Leaks

Kernel-mode processes, such as device drivers, can also leak memory when bytes are allocated but not freed. Again, you typically track these over a period of several hours or days, but instead of relying on System Monitor counters, use Pool Monitor (Poolmon.exe). For information about Pool Monitor, see Windows 2000 Support Tools Help. For information about installing and using the Windows 2000 Support Tools and Support Tools Help, see the file Sreadme.doc in the \Support\Tools folder of the Windows 2000 operating system CD.

Pool Monitor (Poolmon.exe) shows the amounts of nonpaged and paged memory that were allocated and freed, calculates the difference between these, and associates the data with a function tag to help you identify the process involved. By default, Windows 2000 is configured not to collect pool information because of the overhead. To use Poolmon, you must enable the pool tag signal. Use Gflags.exe to make the change. In Gflags, select the **Enable Pool Tag** check box. For information about using Poolmon and Gflags, see Support Tools Help. For information about installing and using the Windows 2000 Support Tools and Support Tools Help, see the file Sreadme.doc in the \Support\Tools folder of the Windows 2000 operating system CD.

The pool tag is a mechanism for identifying the driver or other part of the kernel allocated to a particular portion of memory. These tags can be examined to reveal memory leaks and pool corruption, and the offending code component can be determined by finding which code component is allocated to which tag. Look for a tag with rapidly increasing byte counts that does not free as many bytes as it allocates, and verify that this tag corresponds to a function for which the increasing memory allocation might be appropriate. If it does not appear appropriate, it might be necessary to debug and tune the application to eliminate the leak.

Monitoring the Cache

The Windows 2000 file system cache is an area of memory into which the I/O system maps recently used data from disk. When processes need to read from or write to the files mapped in the cache, the I/O Manager copies the data from or to the cache, without buffering or calling the file system, as if it were an array in memory. Because memory access is quicker than a file operation, the cache provides an important performance boost to the processes.

Cache object counters provide information about data hits and misses and about file I/O operations that reflect how efficiently their applications access data in the file system cache. However, because the cache counters are based on the views mapped by the Cache Manager and not on data from the Virtual Memory Manager, the cache counter values do not provide definitive information about bottlenecks. In some cases, cache counters can report low rates of hits or high rates of misses, suggesting that the system is accessing the disk when, in fact, the requested data has been retrieved from memory. This can occur if virtual addresses mapped by the Cache Manager no longer exist, for example, because the file has closed. To obtain more accurate data on I/O bottlenecks, use the Memory\Pages Input/sec counter.

The cache itself can never really have a bottleneck because it is just a part of physical memory. However, when there is not enough memory to create an effective cache, the system must retrieve more data from disk, resulting in I/O operations that can impact overall performance. Such a shortage of cache space can be considered a cache bottleneck.

Cache bottlenecks are of greatest concern to users of Windows 2000 Professional–based computers running computer-aided design/computer-aided manufacturing (CAD/CAM) applications or large databases accessing large blocks of multiple files that rely on the cache. The cache counters can reveal that a small cache (based on a short supply of memory) is hurting system performance.

With memory-mapped file I/O, an entire file can be opened without actually being read into memory. Only the views (smaller portions of the file) are mapped into the process's address space just before I/O operations are performed. Memory-mapped I/O keeps the cache size small. For more information about memory-mapped I/O, see the Software Development Kit (SDK) link on the Web Resources page at http://windows.microsoft.com/windows2000/reskit/webresources.

Developers who want to understand how their programs use the cache for read and write operations might also want to monitor the cache. Data requested by an application is mapped to the cache and then copied from there. Data changed by applications is written from the cache to disk by the lazy writer system thread or by a write-through call from the application. The lazy writer thread in the system process periodically writes changed pages from the modified page list back to disk and flushes them from the cache. When a page is flushed from the cache, changed data is written from the page in the cache to the disk and the page is deleted from the cache. Thus, monitoring the cache is like watching your application I/O. Remember, however, that if an application uses the cache infrequently, cache activity has an insignificant effect on the system, on the disks, and on memory.

Understanding the Cache Counters

Use the following System Monitor Cache and Memory counters to measure cache performance.

Cache\Copy Read Hits %   Monitor this counter for hit rates and miss rates. Any value over 80 percent indicates that the application uses the cache very efficiently. Compare this counter against Cache\Copy Reads/sec to see how many hits you are really getting. Even though the hit percentage is small, if the rate of operations is high, this might indicate better cache effectiveness than a high percentage with a low rate of operations.

Note   For best results, monitor the Cache\Copy Read Hits % counter using the graph view rather than the report view. Hit percentage rates frequently appear as spikes that are hard to detect in a report.

Cache\Copy Reads/sec   Observe this counter to see the rate at which the file system attempts to find application data in the cache without accessing the disk. This is a count of all copy read calls to the cache, including hits and misses. Copy reads are the usual method by which file data found in the cache is copied into an application's memory buffers.

Cache\Data Flush Pages/sec   Review this counter for the rate at which both applications change pages of cached data and the pages are written back to disk. This includes pages that have been written by the system process when many changed pages have accumulated, pages that have been flushed so that the cache can be trimmed, and disk writes that are caused by an application write-through request.

Cache\Data Flushes/sec   Monitor this counter for the rate at which cache data is being written back to disk. This counter reports application requests to flush data from the cache and is an indirect indicator of the volume and frequency of application data changes.

Cache\Data Maps/sec   Examine this counter for the rate at which file systems map pages of a file into the cache for reading. This counter reports read-only access to file system directories, the file allocation table (FAT) in the FAT file system, and the Master File Table in the NTFS file system. This counter does not reflect cache use by applications.

Cache\Fast Reads/sec   Observe this counter for the rate at which applications bypass the file system and access data directly from the cache. A value over 50 percent indicates the application is behaving efficiently. Fast reads reduce processor overhead and are preferable to I/O requests.

Cache\Lazy Write Flushes/sec   Review this counter for the rate at which an application changes data, causing the cache to write to the disk and flush the data. If this value reflects an upward trend, memory might be becoming low. Lazy write flushes are a subset of data flushes. The lazy writer thread in the system process periodically writes changed pages from the modified page list back to disk and flushes them from the cache. This thread is activated more often when memory needs to be released for other uses. This counter counts the number of write and flush operations, regardless of the amount of data written.

Cache\Lazy Write Pages/sec   Examine this counter value for the rate at which pages are changed by an application and written to the disk. If the counter value is increasing, this can indicate that memory is becoming low. Cache\Lazy Write Pages are a subset of Data Flush Pages.

Cache\Read Aheads/sec   Use this counter to monitor the rate at which the Cache Manager detects that the file is being accessed sequentially. Sequential file access is a very efficient strategy in most cases. During sequential file access, the Cache Manager can read larger blocks of data into the cache on each I/O, thereby reducing the overhead per access.

Memory\Cache Bytes   Monitor this counter for growth or shrinkage of the cache. The value includes not only the size of the cache but also the size of the paged pool and the amount of pageable driver and kernel code. Essentially, these values measure the system's working set.

Memory\Cache Faults/sec   Observe this counter for the rate at which pages sought in the cache were not found there and had to be obtained elsewhere in memory or on the disk. Compare this counter against Memory\Page Faults/sec and Pages Input/sec to determine the number of hard page faults, if any.

Note   Performance Meter (Perfmtr.exe), a tool on the *Windows 2000 Resource Kit* companion CD and the SDK, lists among other statistics, data about the file system cache. For more information, see the *Windows 2000 Resource Kit* Tools Help (W2rktools.chm) or the SDK documentation.

Interpreting Changes in Cache Counter Values

Administrators need to watch for signs from the cache counters that low memory is causing insufficient cache size and consequently that cache usage is resulting in unnecessary disk I/O, which degrades performance. Monitor for the following conditions, using the counters as described. (Options for improving these conditions include defragmenting the disk and adding memory.)

Reduction in Cache Size

When memory becomes scarce and working sets are trimmed, the cache is trimmed as well. If the cache grows too small, cache-sensitive processes are slowed by disk operations. To monitor cache size, use the Memory\Cache Bytes and Memory\Available Bytes counters. Note that the effect of a smaller cache on applications and file operations depends on how often and how effectively applications use the cache.

Frequent Cache Flushing

Frequent cache flushing might occur if data is written to the disk frequently in order to free pages. Data flush counters reflect cache output. Monitor the Cache\Data Flushes/sec and Cache\Lazy Writes Flushes/sec counters.

Cache\Pin Reads/sec tells you how often the cache is reading data with the intention of writing it. A pin read occurs when data is mapped into the cache just to be changed and is then written back to disk. It is pinned in the cache to be sure the data being changed is not written to disk until the update is complete. Creating a file or changing its attributes results in a pin read. Changing file contents does not result in a pin read. Cache\Pin Reads/sec can predict flushing activity.

High Rates of Cache Misses

High cache miss rates indicate that requested data is not available in physical memory and must be retrieved from the disk. Monitor the Cache object counters that record hit percentages and hit rates (such as Cache\Copy Read Hits % and Cache\Copy Read Hits/sec).

Make sure to review both hit percentage and hit activity counters to ensure that your data gives an accurate picture of cache efficiency. For example, you might notice that your hit percentage is very high (90 percent on average), implying that the cache is highly efficient. However, when you examine hit activity, you might notice that only a few copy reads have occurred during the sample. In this case, relying on the percentages would have given you a false impression of cache effectiveness. Therefore, examining hit percentages over a range of activity rates is recommended.

High Rates of Cache Faults

Although you cannot tell from the Memory\Cache Faults/sec counter value alone, an increase in cache faults might mean that hard page faults are occurring, resulting in disk activity. Memory\Cache Faults/sec reports fault activity for the system working set, including hard and soft page faults. Because the cache counters do not provide conclusive information about this, you must monitor Memory\Pages Input/sec to determine whether hard page faults are occurring.

If Cache Faults/sec values increase and hit-percentage counter values decrease, it is likely there is not enough memory to create an efficient cache. When insufficient memory forces the system to maintain a small cache size, disk I/O tends to increase.

You can see the impact of cache and memory activity on the disk by adding Memory\Pages Output/sec to Cache\Data Flush Pages/sec. This total is approximately equal to the page equivalent of Disk Write Bytes/sec for the PhysicalDisk counters. As the Pages Output/sec and Data Flush Pages/sec counter values increase, so does the value of Disk Write Bytes/sec, reflecting the increasing disk writing activity. (Differences in values can be attributed to the sampling behavior of System Monitor.) Similarly, there is a corresponding read impact: look at Memory\Pages Input/sec; this needs to equal the number of bytes of memory reported under Disk Read Bytes/sec but expressed in pages for the PhysicalDisk counters as described in "Investigating Disk Paging" earlier in this chapter.

Resolving Memory and Cache Bottlenecks

While monitoring your memory and cache resources, you might discover memory and cache bottlenecks in your system. As a result, you might need to optimize cache usage, replace applications, or even add new memory. The following tips can assist you with your decision-making process.

Optimizing Cache Usage

Even though you cannot change the cache itself, there are a few things you can do to make the most of the cache:

- For applications that you develop or maintain, improve the locality of reference in your application's data structures. This improves its cache performance and minimizes its working set so that it uses less space in memory. In addition, it reduces disk access that can slow performance systemwide.

- Change the way work is distributed among workstations. Try dedicating a single computer to memory-intensive applications such as CAD/CAM and large database processors.

- Add memory. When memory is scarce, the cache is diminished and cannot do its job. After the new memory is installed, the Virtual Memory Manager expands the cache to use the new memory.

Resolving a Memory Bottleneck

Although adding memory is the easy solution to a memory bottleneck, it is not recommended as the first solution you undertake. Try the following, more cost-effective alternatives before spending money on additional memory. If you ultimately decide to add memory, note that the maximum amount of memory supported is 4 GB.

- Monitor your applications and replace or correct those that leak memory or use it inefficiently.

- Modify your application to improve the locality of reference. The Working Set Tuner, included in the Platform SDK, recommends an optimal organization of code functions. For more information, see the MSDN link on the Web Resources page at http://windows.microsoft.com/windows2000/reskit/webresources.

- Increase the size of the paging file. In general, the bigger you can make it, the better it is. You can also have multiple paging files, though it is recommended that you only have multiple paging files per physical drive when the drive is not partitioned into logical drives. Striped volumes can be used. This improves the read-write rates for the paging file because the work is distributed over multiple disks.

- Check the available space on your disks. If you are using a large paging file and space is not available, this can produce the symptoms of a memory bottleneck.

- To conserve memory, avoid using some display and sound features. Features that can drain memory include animated cursors, a large number of desktop icons, large-bitmap wallpaper, and some screen saver programs; removing or disabling them can offer some benefit on a memory-constrained system. Reducing display color depth and screen resolution can also save memory but to a lesser degree.

- To free memory, turn off services you do not use. Stopping services that you do not use regularly saves memory and improves system performance. However, make sure you understand the ramifications of stopping a service before you do so.

- Remove unnecessary protocols and drivers. Even idle protocols use space in the paged and nonpaged memory pools. Drivers also use memory. You can see how a driver uses memory by using Pool Monitor (Poolmon.exe).

- Replace 16-bit systems with 32-bit systems for better reliability and performance.

- If you have other computers that are underutilized, move memory-intensive applications to those computers.

Additional Resources

For more information about developer tools, see the MSDN link on the Web Resources page at http://windows.microsoft.com/windows2000/reskit/webresources.

C H A P T E R   2 9

Analyzing Processor Activity

A busy processor might efficiently handle all the work on your computer, or it might be overwhelmed. Examine processor activity to tell the difference. Use performance counters and *Microsoft® Windows® 2000 Resource Kit* tools to measure processing activity and to determine how to improve performance if necessary.

In This Chapter

Related Information in the Resource Kit

- For more information about using System Monitor graphs and counter logs, see "Overview of Performance Monitoring" in this book.

- For more information about implementing and optimizing multiprocessor systems, see "Measuring Multiprocessor System Activity" in the *Microsoft® Windows® 2000 Server Resource Kit Server Operations Guide*.

Quick Guide to Monitoring Processors

Use this quick guide to view the topics and tasks that you need to monitor your processor activity in Microsoft® Windows® 2000 Professional.

Get familiar with processor counters to understand the data they collect and how you can use it.

The Processor object counters report data about processor activity including processor use, requests queued for processor time, and more. It's important to understand the type of data these counters provide and what it tells you about processor performance.

- See "Overview of Processor Monitoring and Analysis"later in this chapter.

Establish a baseline for processor usage.

A performance baseline is the level of performance you can reliably expect during typical usage and workloads. When you have a baseline established, it becomes easier to identify when your system is experiencing performance problems, because counter levels are out of the baseline range.

- See "Establishing a Baseline for Processor Performance" later in this chapter.

Analyze utilization and queue data.

Typically a queue of several waiting processor requests combined with a high CPU utilization rate signals a processor bottleneck. Observing counters that report this data is important for detecting bottlenecks that might be reducing your system's ability to handle its workload.

- See "Recognizing a Processor Bottleneck" later in this chapter.

Identify inefficient applications by monitoring processor use and other data associated with processes and threads.

- See "Processes in a Bottleneck" later in this chapter.

Monitor thread activity and related data during bottlenecks to understand how applications are using processor resources.

See "Threads in a Bottleneck" later in this chapter.

Experiment with changing thread priority as a temporary cure for applications receiving little processor time.

The operating system is designed to schedule threads to run in an optimal fashion so that the user need not intervene to manually adjust thread scheduling by changing thread priority. However, if you find that certain threads are seldom able to run due to the activity of other threads, you can adjust the thread's priority in order to allow them to run. Doing so does not provide a long-term solution to a thread bottleneck but is a useful illustration of the effect of thread priority on thread activity.

See "Advanced Topic: Changing Thread Priority to Improve Performance" later in this chapter.

What's New

Users of Microsoft® Windows® 98 and Microsoft® Windows NT® 4.0 Workstation might notice a few changes in Windows 2000 with respect to processor resources and use. The following list provides a brief summary of the changes in features for these operating systems.

Dual processor support   Unlike Windows 98, which was uniprocessor-based, Windows 2000 Professional supports dual processors.

Optimal responsiveness for applications   Windows 2000 Professional's default configuration provides optimal responsiveness for applications. By default, it defines short, variable quanta for applications and gives a foreground application a priority boost. This is different from Windows NT 4.0 Workstation, which does not boost priority of the foreground application but only assigns a longer time slice (quantum) to the foreground thread. You can configure the setting by using System properties on both Windows NT Workstation and Windows 2000 Professional. Windows 98 does not provide a capability for configuring system responsiveness.

Changes in counters   In System Monitor under Windows 2000 Professional, the % Total Processor Time, % Total Privileged Time, % Total User Time, and Total Interrupts/sec counters have been removed from the System object. You now need to use the _Total instance with the % Processor Time, % Privileged Time, % User Time, or Interrupts/sec counters of the Processor object to collect similar data. In contrast, the System object in Performance Monitor (Windows NT 4.0 Workstation) provided counters for total processing time, total user time, total privileged time, and the total number of interrupts per second. Windows 2000 Professional also adds a new counter (Creating Process ID) to the Process object for identifying processes that open other processes, in addition to providing the new Job Object and Job Object Details objects. In Windows 98 System Monitor, the Kernel: Processor Usage (%) reports the amount of time that the processor is busy; the tool provides no other processor-specific items.

Overview of Processor Monitoring and Analysis

Uniprocessor monitoring and analysis involve many variables. The following steps summarize in-depth monitoring and analysis of processor activity.

- Establish a baseline for processor performance that reflects your system's typical workload. Perform this step to characterize your system's workload and identify how applications use the system.

- Examine overall processor usage by viewing processor queue length and processor utilization (also referred to as processor time). Perform this step to obtain an overview of how heavily your system uses its resources.

- Examine activity that adds to the processing load, such as high rates of interrupts and context switches. Perform this step to determine the efficiency of your system.

- Examine individual processes and their percentage of the overall processor time. Perform this step to learn about the processes on your system.

- Examine the threads—the units of work that make up a process—for each individual process and each thread's processor usage. Perform this step to learn about thread utilization on the system.

- Evaluate thread priorities and change them to see if this provides better performance. (Microsoft does not recommend this as a long-term solution, but suggests it for testing purposes.) Perform this step to learn how threads interact and to determine which threads are preempting other lower-priority threads.

Figure 29.1 illustrates the role of processor monitoring in overall system monitoring.

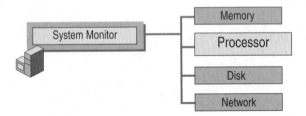

Figure 29.1   Role of Processor Monitoring in Overall Monitoring Sequence

Before you begin the monitoring process, become familiar with the counters designed to measure processor activity and the *Windows 2000 Resource Kit* tools that can give you more information about processor workload and performance. The following sections summarize these counters and tools.

Processor Counters

The System, Processor, Process, and Thread objects contain counters that provide useful information about the work of your processor. Examine the counters in Table 29.1 for details about computer processes.

Table 29.1   Processor Counters

Object	Counter	Description
System	Context Switches/sec	The average rate per second at which context switches among threads on the computer. High activity rates can result from inefficient hardware or poorly designed applications. Compare these counters with Processor\ % Privileged Time, Processor\ % User Time, and Processor\ % Interrupt Time. See "Monitoring Interrupts" and "Monitoring Context Switches" later in this chapter.
Processor	Interrupts/sec	The average rate per second at which the processor handles interrupts from applications or hardware devices. High activity rates can indicate hardware problems. Compare these counters with Processor\ % Privileged Time, Processor\ % User Time, and Processor\ % Interrupt Time. See "Monitoring Interrupts" and "Monitoring Context Switches" later in this chapter.
System	Processor Queue Length	An instantaneous count of threads that are in the processor queue. See "Observing Processor Queue Length" later in this chapter.
Processor	% Processor Time	The percentage of time the processor was busy during the sampling interval. This counter is equivalent to Task Manager's CPU Usage counter. See "Examining the Processor Time Counter" later in this chapter. For the value of total processor utilization systemwide, use the Processor(_Total)\ % Processor Time counter.
Process	% Privileged Time	The percentage of time a process was running in privileged mode. See "Processes in a Bottleneck" later in this chapter.
Process	% Processor Time	The percentage of time the processor was busy servicing a specific process.
Process	% User Time	The percentage of time a process was running in user mode.
Process	Priority Base	The base priority level of the process (can range from lowest to highest: Idle, Normal, High, or Real Time). Windows 2000 schedules threads of a process to run according to their priority. Threads inherit base priority from their parent processes.
Thread	Thread State	A numeric value indicating the execution state of the thread. The system numbers threads from 0 through 5; the states seen most often are 1 for ready, 2 for running, and 5 for waiting. Threads with a state of 1 are in the processor queue.
Thread	Priority Base	The base priority level (from 1 through 31) for the thread based on the priority class of the process. Windows 2000 schedules threads of a process to run according to their priority. Threads inherit base priority from their parent processes.

(continued)

Table 29.1   Processor Counters *(continued)*

Object	Counter	Description
Thread	Priority Current	The current priority level of a thread. This level can vary during operation.
Thread	Context Switches/sec	The average rate per second at which the processor switches context among threads. A high rate can indicate that many threads are contending for processor time. See "Threads in a Bottleneck" later in this chapter.
Thread	% Privileged Time	The percentage of time a thread was running in privileged mode.
Thread	% User Time	The percentage of time a thread was running in user mode.

Note Because System Monitor samples processor time, the values for processor time counters reported by the Processor, Process, and Thread objects might underestimate or overestimate the activity on your system that occurs before or after you collect the sample.

In addition to the preceding list of objects and counters, the Job Object and Job Object Details objects provide information about processor usage. These performance objects are installed by default for monitoring job object performance. The job object makes it possible for developers to manage groups of processes by their processor usage and other factors. For example, job objects make it possible for applications to restrict the amount of processor time a process consumes; this is called process throttling. Process throttling is useful in Web-based administration applications for limiting the amount of processor capacity a site uses over a defined interval, thus avoiding bottlenecks and freeing processor capacity for other tasks. You might also use the job object to manage sharing of CPU time among groups of jobs. In addition to supporting process throttling, job objects help developers control the active number of processes, process identifiers (IDs), priority classes, and processor affinity. For more information about creating applications by using the job object, see the Microsoft Platform Software Development Kit (SDK) link on the Web Resources page at http://windows.microsoft.com/windows2000/reskit/webresources. For a discussion of application support and job objects, see Getting Started in Windows 2000 Help.

Resource Kit Tools for Processor Monitoring

The *Windows 2000 Resource Kit* companion CD contains utilities to help you understand and experiment with processor performance. Table 29.2 lists these utilities.

Table 29.2   Performance Utilities

Utility Name	Description
CpuStress	Simulates processor workload.
Qslice	Provides a graphical display of processor usage by process.

Establishing a Baseline for Processor Performance

Begin your monitoring routine with an examination of processor usage under your normal workload. By doing so, you can begin to establish a baseline or reference point for processor usage. The baseline is generally not a single value, but a range within which processor usage can fluctuate and still provide acceptable performance. You can use the baseline to identify trends, such as increasing processor demands over time, or to recognize problems that arise from a sudden change.

Selecting Counters for Baseline Monitoring

To determine the baseline, use the following counters to create logs of processor usage over an extended period (from several weeks to a month).

- Processor\ % Processor Time
- System\Processor Queue Length

Be aware of the Idle process when monitoring processor usage. The Idle process runs a thread on each processor. This thread runs when the system is not already running the thread of an active user or system process. System Monitor and Task Manager both use the Idle process to calculate time when the processor is not busy. You can see processor time for the Idle process on the **Processes** tab in Task Manager (called the System Idle Process) or by tracking the Process(Idle)\ % Processor Time counter in System Monitor. Notice that the Total instance for this counter includes processor time for the Idle process. To measure the Idle process, use the Process(Idle)\ % Processor Time counter, or use the **Processes** tab in Task Manager. Zero idle time could mean that the processor is handling a lot of work, but it could also mean that the processor or central processing unit (CPU) is overloaded.

Selecting Times for Baseline Monitoring

To monitor processor activity, log the counters of the System, Processor, Process, Thread, PhysicalDisk, and Memory for at least several days at an update interval ranging from 15 minutes to an hour. (Use much shorter intervals for bottleneck detection.) Include network counters such as Bytes Total/sec (on the Network Interface object) if you suspect that network traffic might be interrupting the processor too frequently. Because excessive demand on memory and disk resources can cause bottlenecks that appear to affect your processor's performance, also include disk and memory counters in your monitoring configuration to help you determine the true source of any processor bottleneck.

If any applications running on the computer have counters, use these counters to monitor their activity and monitor these values along with system counter values.

Track the values reported at various times of day—for example, while users are logging on or off, while backups are being done, and so forth. As you are monitoring values for these counters, you might see occasional spikes. Typically, you can exclude these from your baseline; the range of values that appear consistently are the ones that constitute your baseline.

Note Keep in mind application overhead and disk-space usage when you set your monitoring frequency. Frequent updating demands more work and more file storage capacity from your computer. You can experiment with different update intervals to balance these considerations against the level of detail you require for your monitoring data. For more information about how to monitor performance, see Windows 2000 Professional Help.

The longer you log, the more accurate your baseline will be. Processor use might be a problem only at certain times of the day, week, or month, and you are likely to see patterns in your workload that are correlated with changes in processor activity if you log for a longer duration. You can even use the log service to schedule monitoring at critical times to determine whether your processor is operating efficiently. During these critical times, you might want to log intervals as short as every two seconds to get an accurate picture of processor usage on your system. This helps you isolate those applications that heavily stress your processor for further investigation and monitoring.

Recognizing a Processor Bottleneck

Processor bottlenecks occur when the processor is so busy that it cannot respond to requests for time. Although a high rate of processor activity might indicate an excessively busy processor, a long, sustained processor queue is a more certain indicator. As you monitor processor and related counters, you can recognize a developing bottleneck by the following conditions:

- Processor\ % Processor Time often exceeds 80 percent.
- System\ Processor Queue Length is often greater than 2 on a single-processor system.
- Unusually high values appear for the Processor(_Total)\ Interrupts/sec or System\ Context Switches/sec counters.

The most common causes for processor bottlenecks are insufficient memory or excessive numbers of interrupts from disk or network input/output (I/O). To investigate these possible causes, see the following chapters:

- "Evaluating Memory and Cache Usage" in this book
- "Disk Concepts and Troubleshooting" in this book

For more information about network performance, see "Monitoring Network Performance" in the *Server Operations Guide.*

Also, the Processor(_Total)\ Interrupts/sec counter value might rise dramatically if you've recently added many new applications or users. During periods of low activity the only source of interrupts might be the processor's timer ticks; these are periodic events that increment a processor hardware timer. These occur approximately every 10 to 15 milliseconds, or about 66 to 100 interrupts per second. Interrupt rates vary depending on system workload, including network packets per second and disk I/O operations per second. Watch for interrupt values that fall out of a normal range (expect these to be from 200 to 300 on Microsoft® Windows® 2000 Professional). If Processor\ % Interrupt Time exceeds 20 to 30 percent per processor, it might indicate that the system is generating more processor interrupts than it can handle. If this is the case, you might need to upgrade some of your components. For more information, see "Monitoring Network Performance" in the *Server Operations Guide.*

If a processor bottleneck does not exist but you are dissatisfied with system performance, and you have ruled out memory and other hardware factors, consider the following options to improve CPU response time or throughput:

- Schedule processor-intensive applications to run when the system load is low. Use **Scheduled Tasks** in Control Panel or the **at** command to do this.
- Upgrade to a faster processor. Upgrading to a higher-speed processor with a larger Level 2 (L2) cache expedites processing regardless of your system's workload.

  When upgrading to a faster processor, check with the chip vendor to ensure that you use the correct memory speed for the chip. Incompatible memory speed could cause a computer with a faster processor to appear to run more slowly than a computer with a slower processor.

Note Using multiple processors rather than switching to a faster one might not dramatically improve performance. For example, a 200-megahertz (MHz) dual-processor computer might not perform equally to a 400-MHz uniprocessor computer with all workloads because of overhead inherent in synchronization. Because scaling can incur some overhead, it is important to be aware of the factors involved and how to manage them. For more information, see "Measuring Multiprocessor System Activity" in the *Server Operations Guide.*

If conditions do not warrant immediate processor replacement, begin monitoring processor activity and system performance as described in the following sections.

Examining the Processor Time Counter

The Processor\ % Processor Time counter determines the percentage of time the processor is busy by measuring the percentage of time the thread of the Idle process is running and then subtracting that from 100 percent. This measurement is the amount of processor utilization. Although you might sometimes see high values for the Processor\ % Processor Time counter (70 percent or greater depending on your workload and environment), it might not indicate a problem; you need more data to understand this activity. For example, high processor-time values typically occur when you are starting a new process and should not cause concern.

Note   The value that characterizes high processor utilization depends greatly on your system and workload. This chapter describes 70 percent as a typical threshold value; however, you can define your target maximum utilization at a higher or lower value. If so, substitute that target value for 70 percent in the examples provided in this section.

To illustrate, consider that Windows 2000 allows an application to consume all available processor time if no other thread is waiting. As a result, System Monitor shows processor-time rates of 100 percent. If the threads have equal or greater priority, as soon as another thread requests processor time, the thread that was consuming 100 percent of CPU time yields control so that the requesting thread can run, causing processor time to lessen. For a discussion of thread priority and scheduling, see "Threads in a Bottleneck" later in this chapter.

If you establish that processor-time values are consistently high during certain processes, you need to determine whether a processor bottleneck exists by examining processor queue length data. Unless you already know the characteristics of the applications running on the system, upgrading or adding processors at this point would be a premature response to persistently high processor values, even values of 90 percent or higher. First, you need to know whether processor load is keeping important work from being done. You have several options for addressing processor bottlenecks, but you need to first verify their existence.

If you begin to see values of 70 percent or more for the Processor\ % Processor Time counter, investigate your processor's activity as follows:

- Examine System\ Processor Queue Length.
- Identify the processes that are running when Processor\ % Processor Time and System\ Processor Queue Length values are highest.

Observing Processor Queue Length

A collection of one or more threads that is ready but not able to run on the processor due to another active thread that is currently running is called the processor queue. The clearest symptom of a processor bottleneck is a sustained or recurring queue of more than two threads. Although queues are most likely to develop when the processor is very busy, they can develop when utilization is well below 90 percent. This can happen if requests for processor time arrive randomly and if threads demand irregular amounts of time from the processor. For more information about monitoring and adjusting thread scheduling, see "Threads in a Bottleneck" later in this chapter.

The System\ Processor Queue Length counter shows how many threads are ready in the processor queue but not currently able to use the processor. Figure 29.2 shows a sustained processor queue with utilization ranging from 60 to 90 percent. Notice that the default scale for the Processor Queue Length counter value is 10. Therefore, System Monitor graphs a queue that contains two threads as 20. You can change the scale factor by using the **Data** properties tab in System Monitor.

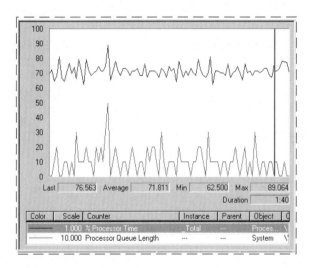

Figure 29.2   Sustained Processor Queue with Rising Processor Usage

In Figure 29.2, the line across the top represents Processor(_Total)\ % Processor Time. The lower line is System\ Processor Queue Length.

Figure 29.3 shows a sustained processor queue accompanied by processor use at or near 100 percent.

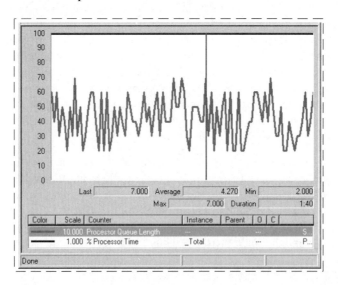

Figure 29.3   Sustained Processor Queue with Maximum Processor Usage

Figure 29.4 illustrates how a processor bottleneck interferes with your computer's performance. It shows that when a processor is already at 100 percent utilization, starting another process does not accomplish more work.

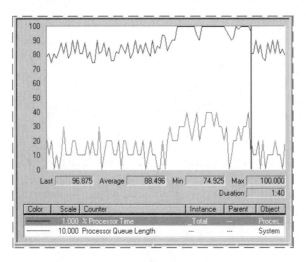

Figure 29.4   Saturated Processor

In Figure 29.4, the dark line running near the top of the graph is Processor(_Total)\ % Processor Time. The line below it is System\ Processor Queue Length. Midway through the sample interval, a process with three threads was started. The graph illustrates that the queue increased as a result of this added workload. Some of the threads of the added process might be in the queue, or they might be running, having displaced the threads of a lower-priority process. Nonetheless, because the processor was already at maximum capacity, it can accomplish no additional work.

If your system's counter values appear similar to those in Figure 29.4, this indicates a bottleneck. Over time, logging reveals any patterns associated with the bottleneck. For example, you might find that bottlenecks occur when certain processes are running or at a certain time of day. In this case, you might be able to eliminate the bottleneck by balancing the workload between computers—that is, running the process on another less-loaded computer.

However, if sustained queues appear frequently, you need to investigate the processes that are running when threads collect in the queue. To do this:

- Identify the processes that are consuming processor time. Determine whether a single process or multiple processes are active during a bottleneck. Running processes appear in the **Instance** box when you select the Process\ % Processor Time counter. For more information, see "Processes in a Bottleneck" later in this chapter.

- Scrutinize the processor-intensive processes. Determine how many threads run in the process and watch the patterns of thread activity during a bottleneck.

- Evaluate the priorities at which the process and its threads run. You might be able to eliminate a bottleneck merely by adjusting the base priority of the process or the current priorities of its threads. However, Microsoft does not recommend this as a long-term solution. Use Task Manager to find the base priority of the process.

Note   Different guidelines apply for queue lengths on multiprocessor systems. For busy systems (those having processor utilization in the 80 to 90 percent range) that use thread scheduling, the queue length should range from one to three threads per processor. For example, with Windows 2000 Server, on a four-processor system, the expected range of processor queue length on a system with high CPU activity is 4 to 12.

On systems with lower CPU utilization, the processor queue length is typically 0 or 1.

There are other objects that track processor queue length. The Server Work Queues\ Queue Length counter reports the number of requests in the queue for the processor on the selected server. For more information about monitoring the Server Work Queues object, see "Monitoring Network Performance" in the *Server Operations Guide*.

Monitoring Interrupts

Sharply rising counts for interrupts can affect your processor's performance, and you need to investigate their cause. The Processor\ Interrupts/sec counter reports the number of interrupts the processor is servicing from applications or hardware devices. You can expect interrupts to range upward from 100 per second for computers running Windows 2000 Professional. This interrupt rate is dependent on the rate of disk I/O operations per second and network packets per second. If your interrupt counter values are out of range, there might be hardware problems such as a conflict between the hard-disk controller and a network adapter. You can use System Information and Device Manager in the Computer Management console to check for problems with the disk controller or network adapter.

You might want to monitor interrupts along with I/O activity involving both disks and network adapters. Use the Disk Reads/sec or Disk Writes/sec counters on the PhysicalDisk object to monitor disk I/O as described in "Examining and Tuning Disk Usage" in this book. Use the network transmission counters to monitor network activity as described in "Monitoring Network Performance" in the *Server Operations Guide*. You can tell if interrupt activity is becoming a problem by determining the ratio of interrupts to I/O operations. An optimal ratio is one interrupt to four or five I/O operations. A one-to-one correspondence between these factors indicates poor performance and requires action.

If network or disk I/O is involved, you should consider upgrading to a controller and a driver that support interrupt moderation or interrupt avoidance. Interrupt moderation allows a processor to process interrupts more efficiently by grouping several interrupts to a single hardware interrupt. Interrupt avoidance allows a processor to continue processing interrupts without new interrupts being queued until all pending interrupts are complete. For more information about managing interrupts from network adapters, see "Monitoring Network Performance" in the *Server Operations Guide*.

High values for % Processor Time for threads of the System process can also indicate a problem with a device driver.

Monitoring Context Switches

A context switch occurs when the kernel switches the processor from one thread to another, for example, when a thread with a higher priority than the running thread becomes ready. Context switching activity is important for several reasons. A program that monopolizes the processor lowers the rate of context switches because it does not allow much processor time for the other processes' threads. A high rate of context switching means that the processor is being shared repeatedly, for example, by many threads of equal priority. A high context-switch rate often indicates that there are too many threads competing for the processors on the system.

Note The rate of context switches can also affect performance of multiprocessor computers. For more information about how to monitor and tune context-switch activity on multiprocessor systems, see "Measuring Multiprocessor System Activity" in the *Server Operations Guide*.

You can view context switch data in two ways:

- The System\ Context Switches/sec counter in System Monitor reports systemwide context switches.

- The Thread(_Total)\ Context Switches/sec counter reports the total number of context switches generated per second by all threads.

Although these counters might vary slightly due to sampling, generally they will be nearly equal.

Figure 29.5 plots System\ Context Switches/sec during a temporary bottleneck.

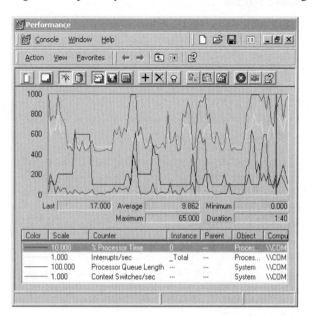

Figure 29.5   Systemwide Context Switches During a Processor Bottleneck

In Figure 29.5, Processor(_Total)\ % Processor Time jumps to about 60 percent during the sample interval. System\ Processor Queue Length (scaled by a factor of 10) shows that the queue varies from 2 to 6 with a mean near 4. System\ Context Switches (shown scaled by a factor of 10) reveals an average of about 750 switches per second. A rate of context switches from 500 to 2,000 per second might indicate that you have a problem with a network adapter or a device driver or that you are using an inefficient server-based application that spawns too many threads.

The Pviewer utility on the Windows 2000 operating system CD reports context switch data. For information about installing and using the *Windows 2000 Support Tools* and Support Tools Help, see the file Sreadme.doc in the Support\Tools folder of the Windows 2000 operating system CD.

Processes in a Bottleneck

After you have identified a processor bottleneck, you need to determine whether a single process is using the processor or whether many running processes are consuming the processor. To do this, log the processor time for each process that is running on your computer as follows:

- Select the Process object.
- Select the % Processor Time counter.
- Select each process instance.

Important   All processes that are running appear in the **Instance** box listed by the name of the associated executable program (for example, Windows Explorer appears as "explorer" in the **Instance** box). Note that if you are running multiple instances of the same executable program, System Monitor lists these under the identical name; thus, you need to track these by their process identifiers. You can find the process identifier by using the Process\ Process ID counter or by adding the process identifier (PID) column in Task Manager. For more information, see "Threads in a Bottleneck" later in this chapter.

For more information about MS-DOS-based and 16-bit Windows-based processes that appear differently in the user interface, see "Overview of Performance Monitoring" in this book and also see Windows 2000 Server Help.

Identifying Active Processes

To determine the processing load generated by your typical workload, include the instances for the processes that you normally run. If you find that you don't normally use some processes (such as background services) that are already running, stop these processes and measure the impact on your processing load. This might be an easy way to improve your computer's processing efficiency. However, before doing so, make sure you understand the possible effects. To stop a service, complete the following procedure.

▶ **To stop a service**

1. From the **Start** menu, point to **Programs** and **Administrative Tools**, and then click **Computer Management**.

2. In the Computer Management console, click **Services and Applications**.

3. Under **Services and Applications**, double-click **Services**.

4. Right-click the name of a service, and then click **Stop**.

Isolating Processor-Intensive Workloads

If the threads of a process are using a high percentage of CPU time, you need to analyze the process to determine if the application's performance can be optimized. For information about improving application performance, see the Microsoft Platform SDK link on the Web Resources page at http://windows.microsoft.com/windows2000/reskit/webresources. If optimization does not yield satisfactory results, you need to add processor resources.

Device driver problems can cause high % Processor Time values for the System process.

If a single process is using the processor, the chart line associated with that process is the highest one in the graph, such as in Figure 29.6, which is an actual histogram of a processor bottleneck caused by a single process. By running CpuStress, a utility on the *Windows 2000 Resource Kit* companion CD, you can produce the results shown in this example.

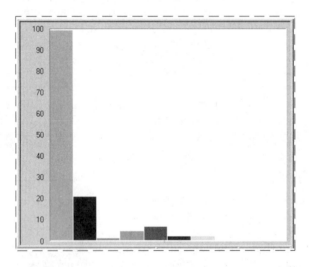

Figure 29.6   Processor Bottleneck Caused by a Single Process

This histogram shows that a single process (represented by the tallest bar) is highly active during a bottleneck; its threads are running for more than 90 percent of the sample interval. If this pattern persists and a long queue develops, it is reasonable to suspect that the application running in the process is causing the bottleneck.

Note that a highly active process is a problem only if a queue is developing. If you are not satisfied with response time and throughput, you can choose to upgrade to a faster processor to achieve better performance.

If you suspect that an application is causing a processor bottleneck, stop using the application for a few days or move it to a different computer. Another option is to schedule the process to run outside of peak operating hours. Then log processor use again. If the problem disappears, it is likely that the application caused it.

Reducing Single-Process Bottlenecks

If you cannot use another computer and you have access to the application source code, you can tune the application to increase efficiency. Start by using a profiler, an analysis tool that you can use to examine the run-time behavior of your programs. Profiling enables you to analyze how the application is spending processor time. The Platform SDK includes tools and methods for profiling and optimizing applications, including instructions for developing performance counters to monitor the inner workings of your application. To tune an application to be less CPU-intensive, use SDK utilities such as Call Attributed Profiler (CAP) or File I/O Synchronization Win32 API Profiler (FIOSAP). You can also use API Monitor (Apimon.exe) and Kernel Profiler (Kernprof.exe.), which are included on the *Windows 2000 Resource Kit* companion CD.

If tuning efforts do not reduce the application's load on your processor, or if you do not have access to the application source code, you can:

- Consider adding a processor or upgrading the one you have. If your application is multithreaded, adding a processor can alleviate a bottleneck because multithreaded applications can run on multiple processors. However, single-threaded applications do not benefit because the system cannot distribute their thread activity across processors; these applications need faster processors or need to run on a computer with extra processing capacity. Using a faster CPU will probably give you greater performance gain than installing additional processors because the management of the work performed by multiple CPUs also consumes processor time.

- Investigate the activity of threads in the process. For more information about examining thread behavior and changing thread scheduling patterns to ensure that the necessary processes get processor time, see "Threads in a Bottleneck" later in this chapter. This section also contains instructions for determining whether a process is single-threaded or multithreaded; this distinction is important in making an upgrade decision.

- If processor use continues to create a bottleneck even without the application that you first suspected, repeat the preceding steps and carefully monitor the processes that are active when the queues are longest.

- Consider replacing the application with one that has been optimized to run under Windows 2000.

Observing Processor Consumption by Multiple Processes

Figure 29.7 shows a histogram of processor time for many active processes. This example was produced by running two instances of CpuStress, which consumes processor cycles at the priority and activity levels that you specify.

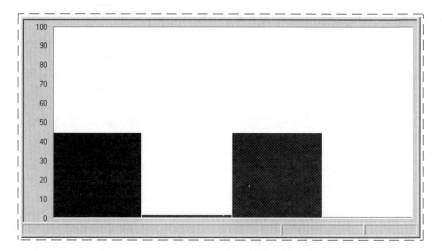

Figure 29.7   Processor Time for Multiple Active Processes

In this example, two processes are consuming the processor while sharing it nearly equally. Although each process is using only 45 percent of the processor, the result is the same as a single process using 90 percent of processor time.

Figure 29.8 shows System\ Processor Queue Length during this bottleneck.

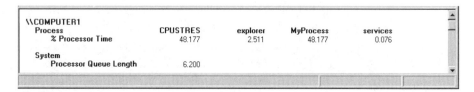

Figure 29.8   Processor Queue Length During Activity of Many Processes

In Figure 29.8, Processor\ % Processor Time for all processes is close to 100 percent during the sample interval. System\ Processor Queue Length reveals a long queue, averaging over six threads.

Figure 29.9 shows Task Manager during the same bottleneck. It shows that two CpuStress processes are each using about half of the time of the single processor on the computer. (Task Manager shows current values, so you need to watch the display to see changes in processor use for each process.)

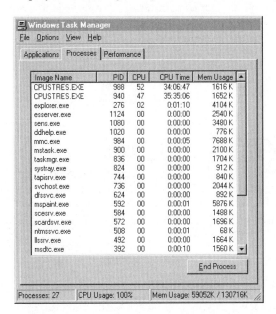

Figure 29.9   CPU Usage for Multiple Processes in Task Manager

At this point, you can choose to add a processor or upgrade the one you have, or you can investigate the activity further by researching thread behavior. Although a faster processor might help this situation somewhat, multiple-process bottlenecks are best resolved by adding another processor. Multithreaded processes, including multithreaded Windows 2000 services, benefit the most from additional processors because their threads can run simultaneously on multiple processors. You might want to partition the processes among the processors for optimal efficiency. For more information, see "Measuring Multiprocessor System Activity" in the *Server Operations Guide*.

To find out more about how a particular process uses the processor, examine the Process\ % User Time and Process\ % Privileged Time counters, followed by Thread object counters, as described in the following section.

For more information about determining if your application is multithreaded, see "Threads in a Bottleneck" later in this chapter. You might also want to find out whether all threads in a multithreaded process are active during bottlenecks. The benefit of adding processors depends on whether you have a lot of active threads. You could find, as a result of monitoring, that threads in a process are inactive most of the time, so adding a processor to handle these inactive threads is a waste of money and capacity.

For more information about the benefits of adding processors to manage a larger workload (called scaling) and how to determine whether scaling is appropriate, see "Measuring Multiprocessor System Activity" in the *Server Operations Guide*.

Threads in a Bottleneck

Investigate the individual thread or threads of the process or processes running during a bottleneck to understand more about the activity consuming the processor. Monitor the following factors to understand how thread activity is contributing to the problem and whether the cause is a single process or multiple processes:

- The number of threads in each process that is running during a bottleneck.
- The amount of processor time a thread is consuming.
- The priority level at which threads are scheduled to run.
- The amount of time the threads are using the processor in privileged mode.

You can use performance counters to analyze thread activity and adjust thread scheduling to allow more processor time for bottlenecked processes.

Apart from adjusting the thread's scheduling priority, you cannot alter thread behavior without changing the program code of the associated application. However, if you have access to application source code, you can write counters to monitor thread activity at a lower level. For more information, see the Microsoft Platform SDK link on the Web Resources page at http://windows.microsoft.com/windows2000/reskit/webresources.

Single vs. Multiple Threads in a Bottleneck

Bottlenecks can result from activity of multiple threads in a single process, single threads in multiple processes, or multiple threads in multiple processes. Because these problems require different solutions, you need to first distinguish their causes.

To study threads during a bottleneck, log counters of the Processor, Process, and Thread objects for several days at an update interval of 60 seconds. This allows you to look at thread activity during typical operating conditions and helps you associate that activity with processor usage.

Important   Performance counter values for threads are subject to error when threads are stopping and starting. Faulty values sometimes appear as large spikes in the data. For more information, see "Overview of Performance Monitoring" in this book.

▶ **To determine whether a process is single threaded or multithreaded**

1. Right-click the Windows task bar and then click **Task Manager**.

2. In **Task Manager**, click the **Processes** tab, and from the **View** menu, click **Select Columns**.

3. In the **Select Columns** check box, select **Thread Count**, and then click **OK**.

   This column shows the total number of threads associated with the process.

Figure 29.10 illustrates how Task Manager displays the number of threads running in a process and the name of the process.

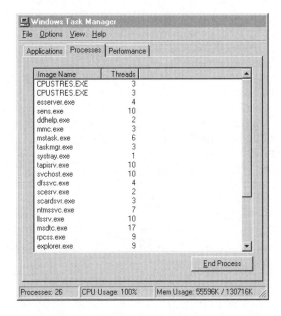

Image Name	Threads
CPUSTRES.EXE	3
CPUSTRES.EXE	3
esserver.exe	4
sens.exe	10
ddhelp.exe	2
mmc.exe	3
mstask.exe	6
taskmgr.exe	3
systray.exe	1
tapisrv.exe	10
svchost.exe	10
dfssvc.exe	4
scesrv.exe	2
scardsvr.exe	3
ntmssvc.exe	7
llssrv.exe	10
msdtc.exe	17
rpcss.exe	9
explorer.exe	9

Processes: 26   CPU Usage: 100%   Mem Usage: 55596K / 130716K

Figure 29.10   Number of Threads Initiated by a Process Shown in Task Manager

In System Monitor or in Counter Logs, select the Thread object and look at all instances listed in the **Instance** box. If there are several thread identifiers (IDs) listed, then the process is multithreaded. Figure 29.11 illustrates multiple threads of a process as they are listed in the **Instances** box in the System Monitor user interface.

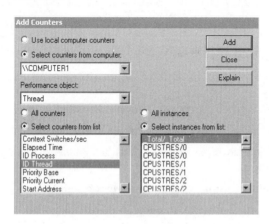

Figure 29.11   Thread Instances Shown When Adding Counters in System Monitor

System Monitor identifies threads by process name and thread number. The order in which the threads appear on the chart depends on the order in which you add them to your chart. The thread number shown in the **Instance** box represents the order in which the threads started, and it can change even as the process runs.

Thread identifiers are valid only during the lifetime of the thread; they are recycled when the thread terminates. Thread numbers can change while running, so it is best to monitor by thread identifier. The Task List Viewer (Tlist.exe) utility provides thread identifier information. For information about Tlist.exe, see Windows 2000 Support Tools Help. For information about installing and using the Windows 2000 Support Tools and Support Tools Help, see the file Sreadme.doc in the Support\Tools folder of the Windows 2000 operating system CD.

If a process is multithreaded, adding a processor improves performance. If it is single threaded, you can improve performance by using a faster processor. These solutions are more advanced and more relevant to developers who also might want to tune the problem applications.

Charting Processor Usage Per Thread

Observing processor time by threads in a process provides additional information about the activity of the processor during a bottleneck. System Monitor provides the Thread\ % Processor Time counter for monitoring processor usage for each thread in a running process. If you have determined that a process is single threaded, you do not need to track the processor time for the process's thread because it will be nearly identical (except for small variations due to sampling) to the processor time you recorded when tracking the process itself.

Figure 29.12 shows Thread\ % Processor Time for all initialized threads during a bottleneck. Each bar of the histogram represents the processor time of a single thread.

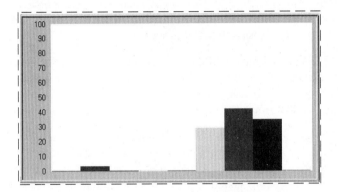

Figure 29.12   View of Threads and Processor Usage

Figure 29.12 shows that the three threads of the CpuStress process are dominating the pattern of processor use, although a few other threads are getting some processor time.

If your thread activity appears similar to the preceding figure and a long queue is developing, some applications on your system are probably not getting enough processor time to run as efficiently as you would like. To investigate the threads of the process and how they use the processor, monitor context switching and user-mode versus kernel-mode CPU usage, as described in the following sections.

Context Switches

The Thread\ Context Switches/sec counter in System Monitor provides another perspective on how the operating system schedules threads to run on the processor. A context switch occurs when the kernel switches the processor from one thread to another. A context switch might also occur when a thread with a higher priority than the running thread becomes ready or when a running thread must wait for some reason (such as an I/O operation). The Thread\ Context Switches/sec counter value increases when the thread gets or loses the time of the processor.

In the course of a context switch, at least two threads are changing their thread state. However, one of the threads might be the idle thread of a given processor. A careful examination of context switch data reveals the patterns of processor use for a thread and indicates how efficiently a thread shares the processor with other threads of the process or other processes.

The System\ Context Switches/sec counter that reports systemwide context switches must be close to, if not identical to, the value provided by the _Total instance of the Thread\ Context Switches/sec counter. Monitoring over time can help you determine the range by which the two counters' value might vary.

Interpret the data cautiously. A thread that is heavily using the processor lowers the rate of context switches because it does not allow much processor time for other processes' threads. A high rate of context switching means that the processor is being shared repeatedly—for example, by many threads of equal priority. It is a good practice to minimize the context switching rate by reducing the number of active threads on the system. The use of thread pooling, I/O completion ports, and asynchronous I/O can reduce the number of active threads. Consult your in-house developers or application vendors to determine if the applications you are running provide tuning features that include limiting the number of threads.

A context switching rate of 300 per second per processor is a moderate amount; a rate of 1000 per second or more is high. Values at this high level might be a problem.

You can determine whether context switching is excessive by comparing it with the value of Processor\ % Privileged Time. If this counter is at 40 percent or more and the context-switching rate is high, then you can investigate the cause for the high rates of context switches.

User Mode and Privileged Mode

You can determine the percentage of time that threads of a process are running in user and privileged mode. User mode is the processing mode in which applications run. Privileged or kernel mode is the processing mode that allows code to have direct access to all hardware and memory in the system. Developers might want to know how much time a process is spending in each mode and what function is using the processor in this way.

I/O operations and other system services run in privileged (kernel) mode; user applications run in user mode. Unless they are graphics-intensive or I/O-intensive (such as file and print services), most applications should not be processing much work in kernel mode.

System Monitor has % Privileged Time and % User Time counters on the System, Processor, Process, and Thread objects. These counters are described in "Processor Counters" earlier in this chapter. System Calls/sec is also a useful indicator of privileged time usage because application calls to the operating system are handled in privileged mode.

In the user time and privileged time counters, System Monitor displays the percentages of total processor time that the process is spending in user or privileged mode.

Figure 29.13 is a System Monitor report on the amount of user and privileged time for three processes.

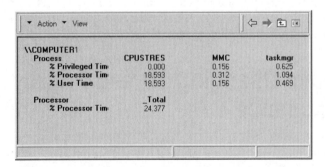

Figure 29.13   User and Privileged Time for Processes

In Figure 29.13, Microsoft® Management Console (MMC), the process in which System Monitor is running, is running mainly in privileged mode. Taskmgr.exe, the Task Manager process, is also running mainly in privileged mode , though this proportion varies significantly as the process runs. In contrast, Cpustres, the process for the CpuStress test program, runs entirely in user mode all of the time.

Figure 29.14 shows the amount of user and privileged time for each thread of the Task Manager process.

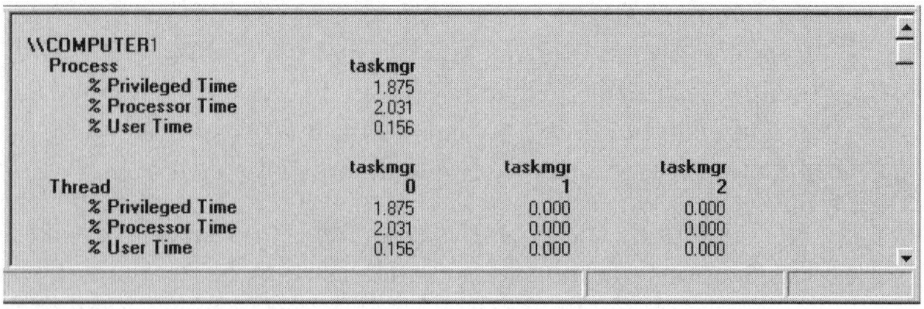

Figure 29.14   User and Privileged Time for a Process and Its Threads

The Process Viewer (Pviewer.exe) utility displays the amount of user time and privileged time for each running process and for each thread in the process. In Process Viewer, the user and privileged mode percentages for each process always total 100 percent because idle time is included. However, in System Monitor the percentages for each process reflect the amount of nonidle processor time actually used in each mode and instead total the amount of nonidle time. Therefore, the value for each process might not total 100 percent. To see the process times add up to 100 percent, combine the percentages for all processes including the Idle process.

For information about Pviewer.exe, see Windows 2000 Support Tools Help. For information about installing and using the Windows 2000 Support Tools and Support Tools Help, see the file Sreadme.doc in the Support\Tools folder of the Windows 2000 operating system CD.

Advanced Topic: Changing Thread Priority to Improve Performance

After observing the threads that use the greatest amount of processor time, monitor the dispatch states of the threads. This tells you which threads are running and which threads are ready. Most important, monitoring thread states on your system can help you identify which threads are piling up in the queue and which threads are actively running at various times.

The Thread\Thread State counter provided by System Monitor reports the current execution state (also known as dispatch state) of a thread. System Monitor reports thread state as a numeric value from 0 through 7, corresponding to whether the thread is ready, running, terminated, and so on.

Table 29.3 lists the typical thread states.

Table 29.3   Typical Thread States

Thread State	Description	Comments
0	Initialized	
1	Ready	The thread is prepared to run on the next available processor.
2	Running	
3	Standby	The thread is about to use the processor.
4	Terminated	
5	Waiting	The thread is not ready to run, typically because another operation (for example, involving I/O) must finish before the thread can run.
6	Transition	The thread is not ready to run because it is waiting for a resource (such as code being paged in from disk).
7	Unknown	The thread is in an unknown state.

To determine which threads are contending for the processor, track the states of all threads in the system by using System Monitor. Figure 29.15 shows a histogram. The vertical maximum for the chart is set to 10 to make it easier to see the values; an alternative for easier viewing is to display the thread-state values in a report view.

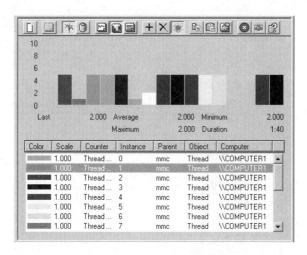

Figure 29.15   Display of Thread States

Notice that the preceding figure plots a thread of the MMC process with the steady value of **2** for running. This is the thread of the System Monitor snap-in that is collecting the data that you are monitoring. As long as System Monitor is running, one of its threads shows as running. Other threads' state values alternate between **1** for ready and **5** for waiting.

Plotting thread-state data in a chart rather than a histogram might make it easier to view the switching of thread states. Note in Figure 29.16 how a process's thread moves from the waiting state (plotted on the chart at 5) to the ready state (plotted on the chart at 1).

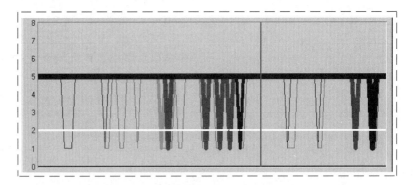

Figure 29.16   Changing Thread States

To find out how long each thread remains in a particular state, define log settings with a tab-separated (TSV) or comma-separated (CSV) file format and include Thread\ Thread State. When the log is completed, import the file into Microsoft® Excel. A sample log is shown in Figure 29.17.

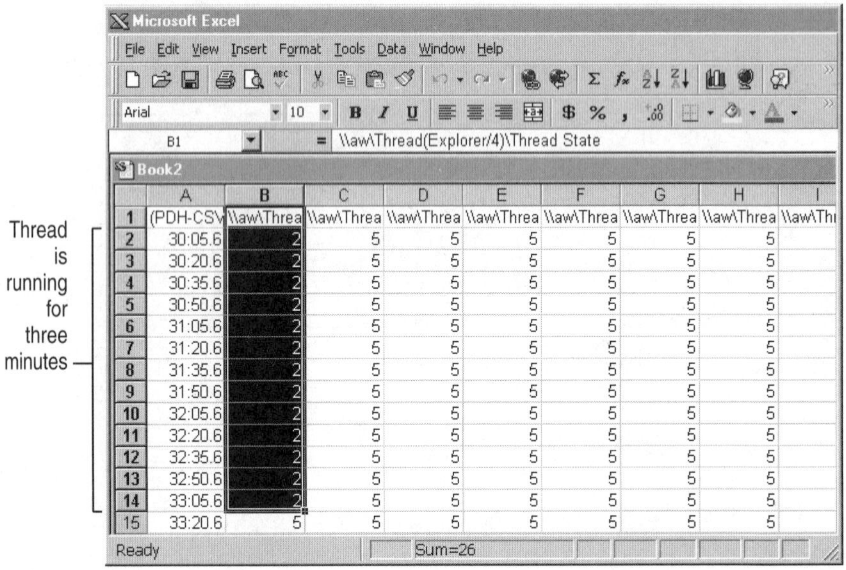

Figure 29.17   Sample Log Output Viewed in Microsoft Excel

By looking at log output, you can get an idea of the length of time that a thread remains in a state by determining the number of seconds that elapsed until the thread's state changed. However, it is important to note that, because sampling omits some data, you might not see all the state changes that occur.

In addition, the Thread\Thread Wait State counter and Perfmon4.exe on the *Windows 2000 Resource Kit* companion CD give you information about why a thread is in a waiting state.

The value reported for Thread Wait Reason is a code. The Counters Help file on the *Windows 2000 Resource Kit* companion CD provides descriptions for these codes.

Examining and Adjusting Thread Priority

Examining thread context switching and thread state gives you information about when threads in a bottleneck are being scheduled to run by the operating system and when threads are being held in the queue prior to running. Although the operating system is designed to optimize the scheduling of threads, you have some control over this behavior because you can adjust for situations in which scheduling behavior on your system is unsatisfactory. This section describes how you can determine a thread's scheduling priority and how you can adjust thread priority to reduce bottlenecks and allow blocked threads to run.

Important To ensure optimum performance on production systems, Microsoft recommends that you adjust priorities of processes first in a test environment. In addition, you should make these adjustments only if you have an in-depth understanding of priority settings and their effect on other processes and the operating system.

Priority Class and Priority

Under the preemptive multitasking strategy built into Windows 2000, threads and processes are assigned a priority for scheduling purposes. A thread's priority determines the order in which it is scheduled to run on the processor.

A thread's priority is based on the priority class of its parent process. The four process priority classes are:

Idle. Screen savers and other processes that periodically update the display typically use the Idle class.

Normal. The default priority class for a process is Normal.

High. Processes that run in the High priority class receive the majority of processor time.

Real Time. Many kernel-mode system processes, such as those that manage mouse and keyboard input and other device operations, run in the Real Time priority class.

Each process's priority class sets a range of priority values (between 1 and 31, where 1 is lowest and 31 is highest), and the threads of that process have a priority value that is within that range. (Priority 0 is reserved for system use.) If the priority class is Real Time (priorities 16 through 31), the thread's priority cannot change while the thread is running. If you have at least one priority 31 thread running, other threads cannot run.

On the other hand, threads running in all other priority classes are variable, meaning that the thread's priority can change while the thread is running. For threads in the Normal or High priority classes (priorities 1 through 15), the thread's priority can be raised or lowered by up to a value of 2 but cannot fall below its original, program-defined base priority. When the base priority is adjusted to optimize scheduling, the resulting value is called the thread's dynamic priority.

Table 29.4 associates each process priority class with relative thread priorities, ranked from highest priority to lowest. Notice that the highest priority class is Real Time and the lowest is Idle.

Table 29.4   Process Priority Classes with Relative Thread Priorities

	Process Priority Classes			
Thread Priorities	**Real Time**	**High**	**Normal**	**Idle**
Time critical	31	15	15	15
Highest	26	15	10	6
Above normal	25	14	9	5
Normal	24	13	8	4
Below normal	23	12	7	3
Lowest	22	11	6	2
Idle	16	1	1	1

Thread Scheduling

The scheduling routines of the operating system checks for the highest-priority thread that is in a ready state and runs it without interruption during a *quantum*. A quantum, also known as a time slice, is the maximum amount of time a thread can run before the system checks for another ready thread of the same priority to run. If a higher-priority thread becomes ready during the quantum, the lower-priority thread is interrupted and the higher-priority thread is run. Otherwise, threads with the same priority are scheduled to run in a round-robin fashion, and the operating system switches among those threads in order, allowing them to run until the quantum expires.

Windows 2000 always runs the highest-priority ready thread. However, there are optimization strategies built into the operating system to address situations in which the default scheduling methods would cause problems. The following sections describe these strategies.

Foreground Process Scheduling

The scheduler runs a foreground process at a higher priority, which means it tends to get more time slices than background processes. In addition, the scheduler ensures that those time slices are longer than the ones allocated to background processes. As a result, the foreground process is much more responsive than other processes because it runs more often, and it runs longer before being preempted. By default, Windows 2000 Professional defines short, variable time slices for applications and gives a foreground application a priority boost. On the other hand, Windows 2000 Server has longer, fixed time slices with no priority boost for foreground applications, allowing background services to run more efficiently. To see foreground process scheduling in action, monitor the processor time for a process and move its window to the bottom of the stack. Note that the time value allocated to that process falls immediately. Then move the process to the top of the stack and note that the processor time value rises immediately. See Figure 29.19 for an illustration.

Automatic Priority Boost

The operating system automatically boosts a thread's priority until it is high enough for a low-priority thread to complete its operation and release the resource. After raising a thread's dynamic priority, the scheduler reduces that priority by one level each time the thread completes a time slice (quantum), until the thread drops back to its base priority.

Determining and Tuning Priority

If a system has a high rate of CPU use, it is generally best to add processing power by upgrading to a faster processor or to add a processor for symmetric multiprocessing (SMP). However, if you find that a thread is consistently unable to get processor time, you can adjust its priority to allow it to run temporarily. Adjusting thread priority is not recommended as a long-term solution but is a useful illustration of the effect of thread priority on thread activity. Although this section explains how to elevate a priority to allow a process to run, you can also lower the priority of a process if you want it to run in the background while nothing else is running.

Windows 2000 and the Windows 2000 Support Tools include several utilities for monitoring the base priority of processes and threads and the dynamic priority of threads. They include:

- In Windows 2000: System Monitor and Task Manager.
- In Support Tools, which is on the Windows 2000 operating system CD: Pviewer.

Caution Changing priorities might destabilize the system. Increasing the priority of a process might prevent other processes, including system services, from running. Decreasing the priority of a process might prevent it from running, not merely force it to run less frequently. In addition, lowering priority does not necessarily reduce the amount of processor time a thread receives; this happens only if it is no longer the highest-priority thread.

System Monitor

System Monitor lets you watch and record—but not change—the base and dynamic priorities of threads and processes. System Monitor has priority counters on the Process and Thread objects:

- Process\ Priority Base
- Thread\ Priority Base
- Thread\ Priority Current

Figure 29.18 is a chart of the base priorities of several processes. The Idle process (the white line at the bottom of the chart) runs at a priority of Idle (0), so it never interrupts another process.

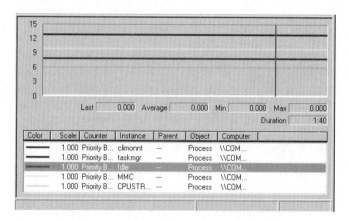

Figure 29.18   Processes and Their Base Priorities

Figure 29.19 is a chart of the dynamic priority of the single thread in the Paintbrush utility (Mspaint.exe) as it changes in response to user actions. The base priority of the thread is 8 (Foreground Normal). During this period of foreground use, the dynamic priority of the thread is 12, but drops to 8 when other processes need to run.

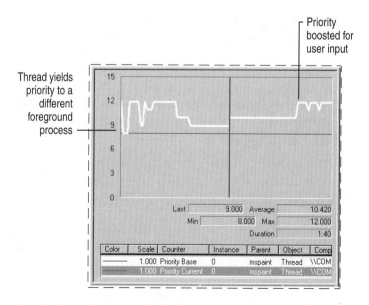

Figure 29.19   Processes Showing Base and Current Priorities

Task Manager

Task Manager presents and lets you change the base priority of a process, but it does not monitor threads. Base priorities that you change with Task Manager are effective only as long as the process runs. For more information, see Task Manager Help or see "Overview of Performance Monitoring" in this book.

Important To make this change, your user account must have permission to increase scheduling priority. By default, only user accounts in the Power User groups in Windows 2000 Professional have this permission.

▶ **To change the base priority of a process**

1. In Task Manager, click the **Processes** tab.

2. Right-click a process name and its menu appears.

3. Click **Set Priority**, and then click a new base priority.

Caution Problems can arise if multiple processes are running at the High priority class level. Avoid setting more than one process to run at this level.

The change in priority is effective at the next Task Manager update; you need not restart the process.

Process Viewer

Process Viewer (Pviewer.exe), one of the Support Tools on the Windows 2000 operating system CD, lets monitor process and thread priority and change the base priority class of a process. For information about installing and using the Windows 2000 Support Tools and Support Tools Help, see the file Sreadme.doc in the Support\Tools folder of the Windows 2000 operating system CD.

Start Command

When you begin processes from a command prompt by using the **start** command, you can specify a base priority for the processes for that run. To see all of the start options, type **start /?** at the command prompt.

You can change the priority class of a process to Real Time by using **start /realtime** at the command prompt or by using Task Manager. Note that changing the priority from **/normal** to **/high** or to **/realtime** can severely degrade the performance of other tasks.

Caution   Setting a processor-bound application to Real Time priority could cause the computer to stop responding.

Windows 2000 Configuration and Process Priority

Windows 2000 Professional is configured by default to assign variable, short time slices (quanta) to applications and to boost applications in the foreground. In contrast, Windows 2000 Server is configured to assign long, fixed quanta without any foreground boost to support the efficiency of background services. You can simulate the behavior of one type of operating system when the other type of system is installed—that is, simulate Windows 2000 Server behavior on a Windows 2000 Professional installation, or vice versa. Figure 29.20 shows the interface that you use for changing application response on an installation of Windows 2000 Professional.

▶   **To access the Performance Options dialog box**

1. In Control Panel, double-click **System**.

2. Click the **Advanced** tab, and then click **Performance Options**.

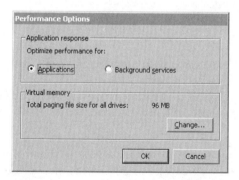

Figure 29.20   Performance Options Dialog Box in System Properties

It is easiest to see a change in thread priority as a result of resetting **Performance Options** if you shut down and then restart the computer. Changes in quantum type and length are so minute that they are often undetectable to the user.

Testing Priority Changes

The previous sections described changing thread priority so that, under bottleneck conditions, threads can run more efficiently. Unfortunately, when processor capacity is already stretched to its limit, boosting priorities of blocked threads might not eliminate or reduce processor bottlenecks. In such cases, it is best to add processor capacity.

Figure 29.21 shows threads of different priorities contending for processor time. It demonstrates the changing distribution of processor time among processes of different priorities as demand for processor time increases. (This test was conducted using the utility CpuStress.)

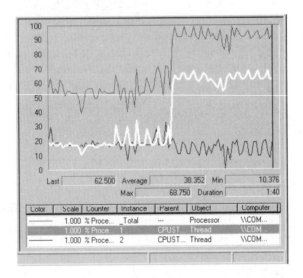

Figure 29.21   CPU Time Allocation to Threads Based on Priorities

This chart shows two threads of the same process running on a single-processor computer. Notice the values for processor time for the _Total instance and for threads 1 and 2.

Figure 29.22 shows two threads of the same process running on a single-processor computer. Figures 29.23, 29.24, and 29.25 provide more detail about how processor usage by threads of CpuStress changed in relation to each thread's priority.

In Figure 29.22, the two threads running CpuStress start out at the same low level of activity and run at the same priority—Normal.

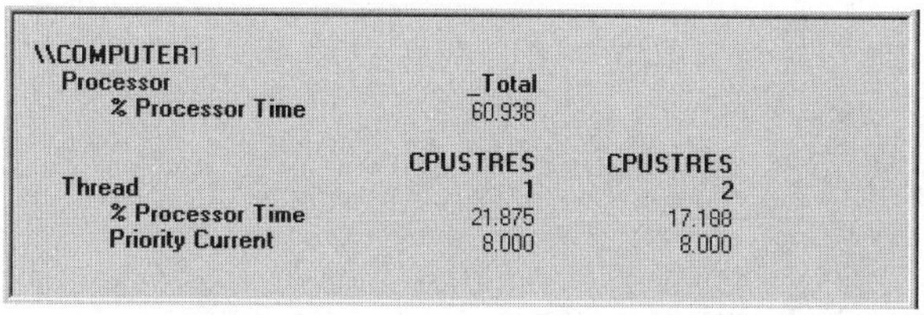

```
\\COMPUTER1
   Processor                    _Total
       % Processor Time          60.938

                          CPUSTRES       CPUSTRES
   Thread                     1              2
       % Processor Time       21.875        17.188
       Priority Current        8.000         8.000
```

Figure 29.22   Comparison of Threads at Normal Priority

Then, if you increase the priority of Thread 1 to Above Normal, and increase its activity level to moderate, you should notice a slight drop in CPU time for Thread 2, as shown in Figure 29.23.

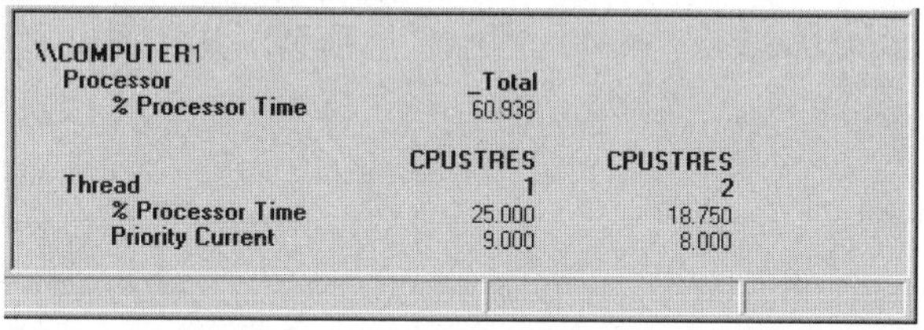

```
\\COMPUTER1
   Processor                    _Total
       % Processor Time          60.938

                          CPUSTRES       CPUSTRES
   Thread                     1              2
       % Processor Time       25.000        18.750
       Priority Current        9.000         8.000
```

Figure 29.23   Comparison of Threads at Normal and Above Normal Priority

Resetting priority for both threads to Normal while running at a higher rate of activity causes each process to consume a large share of processor time, as shown in Figure 29.24. Total processor usage is consistently and extremely high.

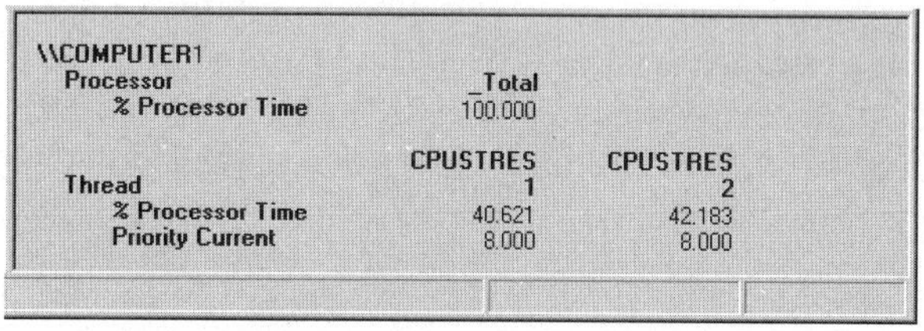

```
\\COMPUTER1
   Processor                    _Total
       % Processor Time         100.000

                          CPUSTRES       CPUSTRES
   Thread                     1              2
       % Processor Time       40.621        42.183
       Priority Current        8.000         8.000
```

Figure 29.24   Comparison of Normal-Priority Threads Under Slightly Different Loads

Finally, raising the priority level of Thread 1 to Above Normal while maintaining its heightened level of activity results in a much greater allocation of processor time to the higher-priority thread and a dramatic drop in processor time for Thread 2, as shown in Figure 29.25.

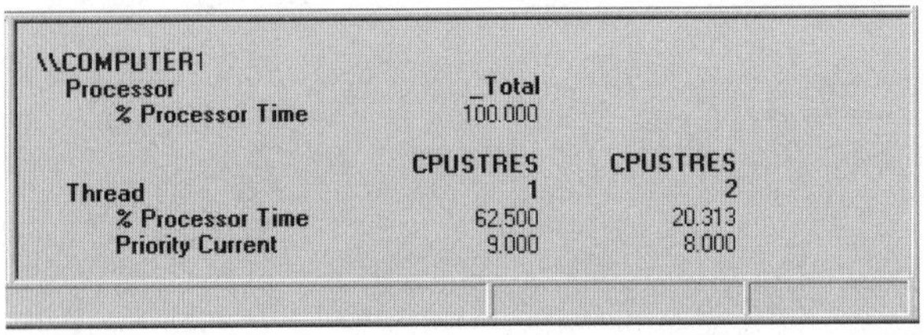

```
\\COMPUTER1
    Processor                      _Total
        % Processor Time           100.000

                            CPUSTRES    CPUSTRES
    Thread                        1            2
        % Processor Time         62.500      20.313
        Priority Current          9.000       8.000
```

Figure 29.25   Normal Threads Under Substantially Different Loads

These results demonstrate that when the processor has extra capacity, increasing the priority of one thread has little effect on the processor time allotted to each of the competing threads. However, when the processor is at its busiest, increasing the priority of one of the threads, even by one priority level, causes the higher-priority thread to get the vast majority of processor time.

In fact, when all processor time is consumed, Thread 2 might not have been scheduled at all were it not for priority boosts. Windows 2000 uses priority boosts to give processor time to lower-priority ready threads that would not otherwise be able to run. This is especially useful when a thread in low priority is waiting for an I/O operation.

Eliminating a Processor Bottleneck

If you determine that you do have a processor bottleneck, some of the following steps can shorten the processor queue and reduce the burden on your processor. Monitor processor usage and processor queue length after every change to determine the impact on resource usage and overall system operation.

- Upgrade to a faster processor. A faster processor improves response time and throughput for any type of workload.

  Make sure to use a processor with the largest processor cache that is practical. The size of the processor cache is important for your system's performance. You can typically choose from 512 KB to 2 MB for the L2 cache. (The primary cache is determined by what type of processor is installed.)

- Add another processor. If the process you are running has multiple, active threads that are processor-intensive, then it is a prime candidate for a multiprocessor system. It is important that most of the threads be active while the process is running; otherwise, the additional processing power might be wasted. To be certain the process will benefit from an additional processor, verify that most threads are active (that is, consuming a moderate to high amount of processor time). You can see this by monitoring thread state.

  For more information about upgrading to multiple processors, see "Measuring Multiprocessor System Activity" in the *Server Operations Guide*.

- Analyze the application and optimize it if necessary by using the performance utilities in the Platform SDK.

- Upgrade your network or disk adapters (32-bit intelligent adapters are recommended). Intelligent adapters provide better overall system performance because they allow interrupts to be processed on the adapter itself, relieving the processor of this work.

  Try to obtain adapters that have optimization features, such as interrupt moderation, and features for networking, such as card-based TCP/IP checksum support.

Additional Resources

- For more information about how Windows 2000 manages processes and threads, including a discussion of its scheduling strategies, see *Inside Windows NT* by David Solomon (Microsoft Press 1998, ISBN 1572316772).

C H A P T E R   3 0

Examining and Tuning Disk Performance

The disk system handles the storage and movement of programs and data on your system, giving it a powerful influence on your system's overall responsiveness. The Performance console provides disk-specific counters that enable you to measure disk activity and throughput, and instructs you on strategies to improve disk performance. In addition, it also covers tools found on the *Microsoft® Windows® 2000 Resource Kit* companion CD that can assist you in determining which programs are putting the greatest demand on your disk system.

In This Chapter

Related Information in the Windows 2000 Resource Kit

- For more information about disks and file systems, see "Disk Concepts and Troubleshooting" and "File Systems" in this book.

- For more information about system monitoring, see "Overview of Performance Monitoring" in this book.

- For more information about evaluating memory usage, see "Evaluating Memory and Cache Usage" in this book.

Quick Guide to Monitoring Disks

Use this quick guide to view the topics and tasks related to monitoring disk performance in Microsoft® Windows® 2000 Professional.

Tune registry settings and work with disk alignment tools to achieve better disk I/O performance.

To improve the system's performance, users of Windows 2000 Professional who choose to deploy the NTFS file system might want to reconfigure some default settings when using this file system.

In addition, developers using Windows 2000 Professional can experiment with Diskpar.exe, a sample program on the *Windows 2000 Resource Kit* companion CD, for insight into Windows 2000 APIs that can be used to reduce performance loss due to disk misalignment on disks with large track sizes and alignment optimizations.

- See "Configuring the Disk and File System for Performance" later in this chapter.

Review installed disk counters and activate LogicalDisk counters as needed.

Getting familiar with the PhysicalDisk counters that monitor the activity of physical disks including removable media drives is important for collecting the type of disk performance data that you want. You can use these counters to monitor disk space and efficiency, and to observe disk operations in detail. PhysicalDisk object counters are enabled on the operating system by default and appear in the Performance console user interface. If you want to obtain performance data on your logical volumes, use the **diskperf** command to enable the LogicalDisk performance counters. The LogicalDisk object counters do not appear in the user interface until enabled.

- See "Working with Disk Counters" later in this chapter.

Establish a baseline for disk performance.

A performance baseline is the level of performance you can reliably expect during typical usage and workloads. When you have a baseline established, it becomes easier to identify when your system is experiencing performance problems, because counter levels are out of the baseline range.

- See "Establishing a Baseline for Disk Usage" later in this chapter.

Analyze disk counter data that might suggest a disk bottleneck.

Specific disk counters provide data about disk paging activity, disk utilization, queuing of disk requests, and rates of throughput. Observing these counters helps you determine when a disk bottleneck is developing.

- See "Investigating Disk Performance Problems" later in this chapter.

Tune or upgrade disk resources as needed to improve disk performance.

When you have determined the cause of a disk bottleneck, you can undertake steps to correct the problem by changing disk-system configuration, defragmenting disks, upgrading hardware, or other tuning methods.

- See "Resolving Disk Bottlenecks" later in this chapter.

What's New

Users of Microsoft® Windows® 98 and Microsoft® Windows NT® Workstation 4.0 will notice a few changes in Microsoft® Windows® 2000 with respect to disk resources and utilization. The following list provides a brief summary of the changes in features for these operating systems.

- Disk defragmentation capability is built into Windows 2000 Professional. This was previously available in Windows 98 but not in Windows NT Workstation 4.0.

- Windows 2000 Professional updates the version of NTFS provided in Workstation NT 4.0. While continuing to support the FAT file system familiar from previous versions, Windows 2000 Professional adds the FAT32 file system format, available in Windows 98 and new to users of Windows NT Workstation 4.0.

- Users of Windows NT Workstation 4.0 might notice a change in how the disk performance counters operate. The PhysicalDisk object counters are now enabled by default; however, the LogicalDisk counters are not and must be manually enabled if needed. The data provided by the PhysicalDisk and LogicalDisk objects is similar to data supplied by the File System items in Windows 98 and offers additional information.

- Some performance counters related to disk and file system activity have changed from Windows NT Workstation 4.0. Windows 2000 Professional includes the new % Idle Time and Split IO/sec counters. In addition, the % Disk Time, % Disk Read Time, and % Disk Write Time have been modified to use a different counter type for greater precision. For file activity that can involve the disk subsystem, Windows 2000 Professional provides new Process object counters not available under Windows NT Workstation 4.0, such as IO Data Bytes/sec, IO Data Operations/sec, and so on.

Disk Monitoring Concepts

You need to observe many factors in determining the performance of a disk system. These include the level of utilization, the rate of throughput, the amount of disk space available, and whether a queue is developing for their disk systems. It is also important to monitor other types of activity that arise from disk operations, such as interrupts generated by the disk system and paging activity, because of their influence on other resources, such as processor or memory.

Figure 30.1 illustrates the importance of monitoring disk systems in relation to the overall performance of your system.

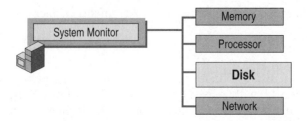

Figure 30.1   Role of Disk Monitoring in System Monitoring

Many of these factors are interrelated. For example, if utilization is high, transfer rates (*throughput*) might peak, and a queue might begin to form. These conditions might result in increased response time and cause performance to slow. Although disk space doesn't directly affect the disk's transfer rate, when extremely low, disk space can also have an influence on response time because applications that read and write data can't do so efficiently. Detect these performance issues through monitoring before they cause problems.

This chapter covers the following stages of a disk-monitoring strategy:

- Configuring the disk and file system for best performance
- Working with disk counters to monitor your disk space and disk efficiency
- Establishing a baseline for disk performance
- Investigating disk performance problems

Configuring the Disk and File System for Performance

The type of file system you are using affects your disk performance. The way in which the disk aligns tracks and sectors during format also affects performance. You need to configure the file system and the disk's track and sector alignment for optimal performance.

Configuring Your File System

The NTFS file system is the recommended file system because of its advantages in terms of reliability and security and because it is required for large drive sizes. However, these advantages come with some overhead. You can modify some functionality to improve NTFS performance as follows:

- Disable creation of short names. By default, NTFS generates the style of file name that consists of eight characters, followed by a period and a three-character extension for compatibility with MS-DOS and Microsoft® Windows® 3.*x* clients. If you are not supporting these types of clients, you can turn off this setting by changing the default value of the **NtfsDisable8dot3NameCreation** registry entry (in HKEY_LOCAL_MACHINE\SYSTEM\CurrentControlSet\Control \Filesystem)
  to 1.

- Disable last access update. By default NTFS updates the date and time stamp of the last access on directories whenever it traverses the directory. For a large NTFS volume, this update process can slow performance. To disable automatic updating, change the value of the **NtfsDisableLastAccessUpdate** registry entry (in HKEY_LOCAL_MACHINE\SYSTEM\CurrentContolSet \Control\Filesystem) to 1. If the entry is not already present in the registry, add it before setting the value.

- Reserve appropriate space for the master file table. Add the **NtfsMftZoneReservation** entry to the registry as a REG_DWORD in HKEY_LOCAL_MACHINE\SYSTEM\CurrentControlSet\Control \FileSystem. When you add this entry to the registry, the system reserves space on the volume for the master file table. Reserving space in this manner allows the master file table to grow optimally. If your NTFS volumes generally contain relatively few files that are typically large, set value of this registry entry to 1 (the default). Typically you can use a value of 2 or 3 for moderate numbers of files, and 4 (the maximum) if your volumes tend to contain a relatively large number of files. However, be sure to test any settings greater than 2 because these higher values cause the system to reserve a much larger portion of the disk for the master file table.

Caution Do not use a registry editor to edit the registry directly unless you have no alternative. The registry editors bypass the standard safeguards provided by administrative tools. These safeguards prevent you from entering conflicting settings or settings that are likely to degrade performance or damage your system. Editing the registry directly can have serious, unexpected consequences that can prevent the system from starting and require that you reinstall Windows 2000. To configure or customize Windows 2000, use the programs in Control Panel or Microsoft Management Console (MMC) whenever possible.

For information about changing the registry, see Windows 2000 Help.

Bypassing I/O Counts

By default, Task Manager continuously measures data for process I/O operations that you can select and display on the **Processes** tab in Task Manager. In a multiprocessor environment, this data is shared by the processors on which the process runs. When a process that generates considerable disk and network I/O, such as a database service, runs on several processors, updating the shared measurements of process I/O and global I/O operations can slow the system. You can improve the performance of I/O-intensive operations on SMP systems if you configure the system to bypass the global I/O counters and Task Manager process I/O counters. To do so, add the **CountOperations** entry to the registry as a REG_DWORD in HKEY_LOCAL_MACHINE\SYSTEM\CurrentControlSet \Control\Session Manager\I/O System. (If the I/O System subkey is not present, add it before creating the entry.) Set the entry value to 0. When so configured, Task Manager no longer provides per-process I/O measurements. For more information about Task Manager, see "Overview of Performance Monitoring" in this book.

Configuring Disk Alignment

Windows 2000 has an internal structure called the *master boot record* (MBR) that limits the maximum number of hidden sectors to 63. (For more information about the master boot record, see "Disk Concepts and Troubleshooting" in this book.) This characteristic of the MBR causes the default starting sector for disks that report more than 63 sectors per track to be the 64th sector. As a result, when programs transfer data to or from disks that have more than 63 sectors per track, misalignment can occur at the track level, with allocations beginning at a sector other than the starting sector. This misalignment can defeat system optimizations of I/O operations designed to avoid crossing track boundaries.

Additional disk-design factors make proper alignment even more difficult to achieve. For example, track information reported by disks is not always accurate. In addition, many disks have different numbers of sectors on different tracks (as might be the case with the outer bands versus the inner bands). Diskpar.exe, a sample program on the *Windows 2000 Resource Kit* companion CD, shows how you can use Windows 2000 APIs to obtain and set partition information. By applying the same functions used in this tool, you can avoid performance loss due to disk misalignment on disks with large track sizes and alignment optimizations. For more information about using Diskpar.exe, see *Microsoft® Windows® 2000 Resource Kit* Tools Help.

Working with Disk Counters

Windows 2000 includes counters that monitor the activity of physical disks (including removable media drives) and logical volumes. The PhysicalDisk object provides counters that report physical-disk activity; the LogicalDisk object provides counters that report statistics for logical disks and storage volumes. These counters measure disk throughput, queue length, usage, and other data. The interrelationships between different aspects of disk performance make it useful to monitor them simultaneously. The operating system enables a driver called Diskperf.sys to activate the disk monitoring counters. By default, the operating system activates only the PhysicalDisk performance counters. Users must activate the LogicalDisk counters manually using the **diskperf** command. See the following procedure for activating disk counters with the **diskperf** command.

▶ **To use the diskperf command to enable LogicalDisk object counters**

- At the command prompt, type **diskperf –yv**

The **diskperf** command takes the following syntax:

diskperf [**–y**[**d**|**v**] | **–n**[**d**|**v**]] [*computer_name*]

Use **−y** to enable counters and **−n** to disable counters. To specify the type of counters, include **d** for physical disk drives or **v** for logical disk drives or storage volumes. When the operating system starts up, it automatically sets the **diskperf** command with the **−yd** switch to activate physical disk counters. For more information about using the **diskperf** command, type **diskperf −?** at the command prompt.

The PhysicalDisk object counters provide data on activity for each of the physical disks in your system; the LogicalDisk object counters provide data on logical volumes in your system. The System Monitor user interface identifies physical disks by number starting with 0. If you are monitoring logical disks, it identifies these by drive letter. For logical disks consisting of multiple physical disks, the disk instances might appear as disk 0 C and disk 1 C, where logical drive C: consists of physical drives 0 and 1.

When monitoring logical volumes, remember that they might share a physical disk and your data might reflect contention between them. If you have a *spanned* volume or *striped* volume with disk controllers that support hardware-enabled redundant array of independent disks (RAID) volumes, the counters report physical disk data for all disks in the stripe as if they are a single disk. Software-enabled RAID-5 volumes are available only on computers running Microsoft® Windows® 2000 Server.

Use the counters described in Table 30.1 to measure disk space, disk throughput, and disk utilization.

Table 30.1   Performance Objects and Counters for Disk Monitoring

Counter	Description
LogicalDisk\% Free Space	Reports the percentage of unallocated disk space to the total usable space on the logical volume. When calculating the _Total instance, the %Free Space counters recalculate the sum as a percentage for each disk.
	There is no % Free Space counter for the PhysicalDisk object.
LogicalDisk\PhysicalDisk \Avg. Disk Bytes/Transfer	Measures the size of input/output (I/O) operations. The disk is efficient if it transfers large amounts of data relatively quickly.
	Watch this counter when measuring maximum throughput.
	To analyze transfer data further, use Avg. Disk Bytes/Read and Avg. Disk Bytes/Write.

(continued)

Table 30.1   Performance Objects and Counters for Disk Monitoring *(continued)*

Counter	Description
LogicalDisk|PhysicalDisk \Avg. Disk sec/Transfer	Indicates how fast data is being moved (in seconds). Measures the average time of each data transfer, regardless of the number of bytes read or written. Shows the total time of the read or write, from the moment it leaves the Diskperf.sys driver to the moment it is complete.
	A high value for this counter might mean that the system is retrying requests due to lengthy queuing or, less commonly, disk failures.
	To analyze transfer data further, use Avg. Disk sec/Read and Avg. Disk sec/Write.
LogicalDisk|PhysicalDisk \Avg. Disk Queue Length	Tracks the number of requests that are queued and waiting for a disk during the sample interval, as well as requests in service. As a result, this might overstate activity.
	If more than two requests are continuously waiting on a single-disk system, the disk might be a bottleneck. To analyze queue length data further, use Avg. Disk Read Queue Length and Avg. Disk Write Queue Length.
LogicalDisk|PhysicalDisk \Current Disk Queue Length	Indicates the number of disk requests that are currently waiting as well as requests currently being serviced. Subject to wide variations unless the workload has achieved a steady state and you have collected a sufficient number of samples to establish a pattern.
	An instantaneous value or snapshot of the current queue length, unlike Avg. Disk Queue Length, Avg. Disk Read Queue Length, and Avg. Disk Write Queue Length, that reports averages.
LogicalDisk|PhysicalDisk \Disk Bytes/sec	Indicates the rate at which bytes are transferred and is the primary measure of disk throughput.
	To analyze transfer data based on reads and writes, use Disk Read Bytes/sec and Disk Write Bytes/sec, respectively.
LogicalDisk|PhysicalDisk \Disk Transfers/sec	Indicates the number of read and writes completed per second, regardless of how much data they involve. Measures disk utilization.
	If value exceeds 50 (per physical disk in the case of a striped volume), then a bottleneck might be developing.
	To analyze transfer data based on reads and writes, use Disk Read/sec and Disk Writes/sec, respectively.
LogicalDisk\Free Megabytes	Reports the amount of bytes on the disk that are not allocated.
	There is no Free Megabytes counter for the PhysicalDisk object.

(continued)

Table 30.1   Performance Objects and Counters for Disk Monitoring *(continued)*

Counter	Description
LogicalDisk|PhysicalDisk \Split IO/sec	Reports the rate at which the operating system divides I/O requests to the disk into multiple requests. A split I/O request might occur if the program requests data in a size that is too large to fit into a single request or if the disk is fragmented. Factors that influence the size of an I/O request can include application design, the file system, or drivers. A high rate of split I/O might not, in itself, represent a problem. However, on single-disk systems, a high rate for this counter tends to indicate disk fragmentation.
LogicalDisk|PhysicalDisk \% Disk Time	Reports the percentage of time that the selected disk drive is busy servicing read or write requests. Because this counter's data can span more than one sample, and consequently overstate disk utilization, compare this value against % Idle Time for a more accurate picture.
	By default this counter cannot exceed 100 percent; however, you can reset the registry to allow System Monitor to display percentages exceeding 100 percent if appropriate. For information about this adjustment and other aspects of performance data collection and reporting, see "Performance Objects" in "Overview of Performance Monitoring" in this book.
LogicalDisk|PhysicalDisk \% Disk Write Time	Reports the percentage of time that the selected disk drive is busy servicing write requests.
LogicalDisk|PhysicalDisk \% Disk Read Time	Reports the percentage of time that the selected disk drive is busy servicing read requests.
LogicalDisk|PhysicalDisk \% Idle Time	Reports the percentage of time that the disk system was not processing requests and no work was queued. Notice that this counter, when added to % Disk Time, might not equal 100 percent, because % Disk Time can exaggerate disk utilization.

When working with the disk-time or disk-queue length counters, be aware of the following limitations that might yield unlikely counter values.

- The % Disk Read Time and % Disk Write Time counters can exaggerate disk time. This is because they report busy time based on the duration of the I/O request, which includes time spent in activities other than reading to or writing from the disk. It then sums up all busy time for all requests and divides it by the elapsed time of the sample interval. If multiple requests are in process at a time, the total request time is greater than the time of the sample interval; as a result, reported disk utilization can exceed actual utilization.

- Counter values that report sums can be misleading for multidisk systems. When you look at the _Total instance for the % Disk Time or disk-queue counters on a multidisk system, the counters report values totaled for all disks and do not divide these totals over the number of disks in use. Therefore, in a system with one idle disk and one disk that is 100 percent busy, it can appear as if all disks are 100 percent busy.

The following sections describe how you can use disk-monitoring counters to observe available space on the disk and to observe the efficiency of disk operations as you become acquainted with your system's disk performance.

Monitoring Disk Space

It is important to monitor the amount of available storage space on your disk because programs might fail due to an inability to allocate space. In addition, low disk space might make it impossible for your paging file to grow to support virtual memory. Fragmentation also has this effect. For information about setting the paging file size for optimal performance, see "Evaluating Memory and Cache Usage" in this book.

Use the % Free Space and Free Megabytes counters to monitor disk space. If the available space is becoming low, you might want to run Disk Cleanup in the **Disk Properties** dialog box, compress the disk, or move some files to other disks. Notice that disk compression incurs some performance loss.

Another option is Remote Storage, which enables you to create virtual disk storage out of tape or optical drives. When you use this service, infrequently accessed files are moved to tape or to other media storage. Remote Storage volumes are well suited for data that you need to access only at certain intervals, such as quarterly reports. Remote Storage service is available on computers running Windows 2000 Server. For more information about remote storage options, see "Removable Storage and Backup" in this book.

If you are using NTFS and you want to restrict the amount of space allocated by individual users, use the **Quota** tab in **Disk Properties**. Notice that using quotas results in a small performance loss. If you are not using NTFS, you can set an alert on the % Free Space counter to track dwindling disk space.

Even if you are not currently short on disk space, you need to be aware of the storage requirements for applications you are running. Complete the following procedure to determine whether your disk has adequate space for your needs.

▶ **To evaluate the adequacy of your system's disk capacity**

1. For best results, start with 1 GB (although the minimum disk size required to install the operating system might be lower).

2. Add the total size of all applications.

3. Add the size of the paging file (this depends on the amount of memory; this size needs to be at least twice that of system memory).

4. Add the amount of disk space budgeted per user (if a multiuser system), multiplied by the number of users.

5. Multiply by 1.3 (or take 130 percent) to allow room for expansion (this percentage can vary based on your expected growth).

The result is the size of disk you need.

Note Although not exactly a disk-storage issue, disk fragmentation slows the transfer rate and seek times of your disk system and you need to monitor for increasing disk fragmentation. On single-disk systems, you can use the Split IO/sec counter to determine the degree of fragmentation of your disks. Defragment the disk if this counter rate is consistently high and run Disk Defragmenter periodically to keep stored data organized for best performance.

Figure 30.2 shows a graph of disk counters including % Free Space. Notice that the % Free Space counter begins to rise approximately halfway through the graph. This illustration shows changes that result from deleting files on the disk.

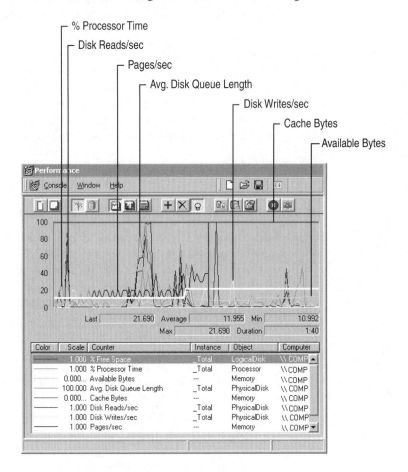

Figure 30.2   Increase in % Free Space Counter

Monitoring Disk Efficiency

Along with disk capacity, you need to consider disk throughput when evaluating your starting configuration. Use the bus, controller, cabling, and disk technologies that produce the best throughput that is practical and affordable. Most workstations perform adequately with the most moderately priced disk components. However, if you want to obtain the best performance, you might want to evaluate the latest disk components available.

If your configuration contains different types of disks, controllers, and buses, the differences in their designs can have an influence on throughput rates. You might want to test throughput using these different disk systems to determine if some components produce less favorable results overall or for certain types of activity, and replace those components as needed. In addition, the use of certain kinds of volume-set configurations can offer performance benefits. For example, using striped volumes can provide better performance because they increase throughput by enabling multiple disks to service sequential or clustered I/O requests. (Striped volumes are not fault tolerant.) System Monitor supports monitoring volume sets with the same performance objects and counters provided for individual disks. Notice that hardware-based RAID devices report all activity to a single physical disk and do not show distribution of disk operations among the individual disks in the array. For more information about using striped volumes, see Windows 2000 Help.

Be aware of the seek time, rotational speed, access time, and the data transfer rate of your disks by consulting manufacturer documentation. Also consider the bandwidth of cabling and controllers. The slowest component determines the maximum possible throughput, so be sure to monitor each component.

To compare the performance of different disks, monitor the same counters and activity on the disks. If you find differences in performance, you might want to distribute workload to the better performing disk or replace slower performing components.

Preparing for Comparison Testing

If you want to know more about the volume and rate of activity through the disk system, monitor the reading and writing activity as described in the following sections. Before you begin to test disk efficiency, complete the following steps to ensure valid results:

- When testing disk performance, log performance data to another physical disk or computer so that it does not interfere with the disk you are testing. If you cannot do this, log to another logical volume on the drive, or measure monitoring overhead during an idle period and subtract that overhead from your data to ensure your results include only disk-specific data and not overhead from other activity.

You might see some variations in the time it takes to read from or write to disk on standard disk configurations. For example, disks with fast write caches can complete write operations very quickly if there is sufficient idle time between random writes. Also, if reads are sequential, read operations might also occur very quickly, provided the disk has had time to prefetch data. Prefetching data is the process whereby data that is expected to be requested is read ahead into the onboard cache.

On striped volumes, reading is faster than writing. When you read, you read only the data; when you write, you read, modify, and write the *parity*, as well as the data. The exception to this rule is full-stripe writes. If entire stripes are being written, there is no need to read the old data or parity.

When you start writing to the disk during a read operation that you are monitoring, you will notice some dips in the curves of graphed data for read activity. This is because the application doing the reads must stop briefly to allow the write operation to proceed and then, when the write is finished, the read operation resumes. You can observe this as Performance Logs and Alerts service logs data.

Figure 30.4 shows the effect of writing on the efficiency of the reads. Notice how the increase of reading activity is accompanied by a slight decrease in writing.

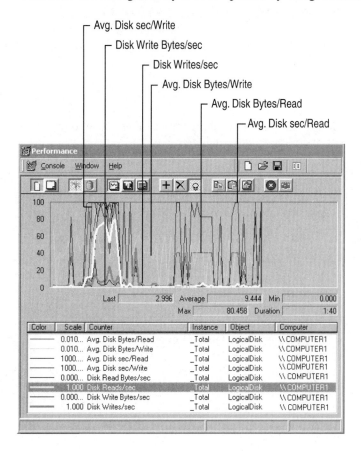

Figure 30.4   How I/O Operations Are Affected by Competing Activity

Establishing a Baseline for Disk Usage

Start your disk monitoring process by establishing a *baseline*, which is the level of performance you can expect during typical usage and workloads. Establishing a baseline consists of collecting and analyzing data about typical disk usage under typical disk load.

Data Collection

Monitor disk counters along with counters from other objects. The following is a list of recommended counters.

- LogicalDisk\% Free Space
- PhysicalDisk\Disk Reads/sec
- PhysicalDisk\Disk Writes/sec
- PhysicalDisk\Avg. Disk Queue Length
- Memory\Available Bytes
- Memory\Cache Bytes
- Memory\Pages/sec
- Processor(*All_Instances*)\% Processor Time
- System\Processor Queue Length

Figure 30.5 depicts a typical display for collecting overall system performance data.

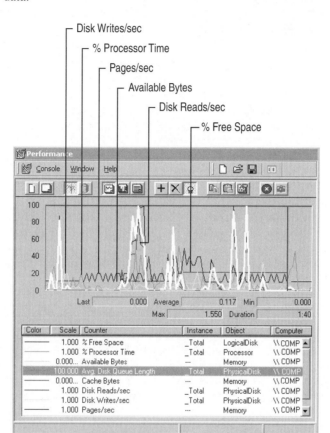

Figure 30.5   Counter Configuration for Baseline Monitoring

Observe activity at various times of day over a range of intervals, starting with one day, one week, one month, and so on. Over time a pattern develops, and you can see that the data tends to fall consistently within a particular range of values —that resulting range is your baseline.

You can monitor for short intervals such as two to five seconds, if your workload is characterized by random bursts of heavy activity. Otherwise 60-second intervals are adequate. If system demands fluctuate during the day, you might want to take shorter samples during periods of heaviest activity and longer samples when activity is tapering off.

For best results during monitoring, try to isolate the disk so that workload unrelated to your test does not affect your results. If you are logging performance to a disk that you are monitoring, values for the disk reflect a small amount of writing activity for that logging.

Data Analysis

While analyzing values at specific times, notice the type of work being performed on your system. Knowing the schedule and nature of your workload is important if you need to reschedule that work or distribute to other systems for better performance.

When interpreting log data, remember the limitations of the performance counters that report sums or that report disk time. The counters sum the totals rather than recalculate them over the number of disks. In addition, disk-time percentage counters cannot exceed 100 percent. Instead, use the Avg. Disk Queue Length, Avg. Disk Read Queue Length, and Avg. Disk Write Queue Length counters to display disk activity as a decimal, rather than a percentage, so that it displays values over 1.0 (100 percent). Then, remember to recalculate the values over the whole disk configuration.

Note   Although disk-time percentage counters cannot exceed 100 percent by default, you can reset the registry to allow System Monitor to display percentages exceeding 100 percent if appropriate. For information about this adjustment and other aspects of performance data collection and reporting, see "Performance Objects" in "Overview of Performance Monitoring" in this book.

You can exclude spiking values from your baseline, but make sure you understand what causes them. For example, if you run a weekly backup every Friday night, it is acceptable to see out-of-range disk values during that time. But it is important that you know why the spikes are happening. If the pattern starts to shift or you feel that the baseline performance is not satisfactory, use additional counters to monitor disk activity and usage as described in the following sections. You might need to upgrade resources as described in "Resolving Disk Bottlenecks" later in this chapter. If you have access to source code for applications that are in use, you might want to fine-tune these for more efficient data access.

When counter values fall outside the range established for your baseline, follow the instructions contained in "Investigating Disk Performance Problems" later in this chapter. If you encounter a problem or need information about how to improve performance, see "Resolving Disk Bottlenecks" later in this chapter.

Investigating Disk Performance Problems

Several conditions must exist in order for you to determine that a disk bottleneck exists. These are a sustained rate of disk activity well above your baseline, persistent disk queues longer than two per disk, and the absence of a significant amount of paging. Without this combination of factors, it is unlikely that you have a bottleneck. However, if you suspect a disk-specific performance problem, monitor the following types of counters:

- Paging counters (under the Memory object): Pages/sec, Page Reads/sec, Page Writes/sec
- Usage counters: % Disk Time, % Disk Read Time, % Disk Write Time, % Idle Time, Disk Reads/sec, Disk Writes/sec, Disk Transfers/sec
- Queue-length counters: Avg. Disk Queue Length, Avg. Disk Read Queue Length, Avg. Disk Write Queue Length, Current Disk Queue Length
- Throughput counters: Disk Bytes/sec, Disk Read Bytes/sec, Disk Write Bytes/sec

---

Note Although not reflected in disk activity, the rate of interrupt generation by your disk hardware can have a systemwide performance impact. Disk I/O can sometimes generate a sufficient number of interrupts to slow the performance of the processor. Although this does not constitute a "disk" bottleneck, it *is* a processor bottleneck caused by the disk system that can slow the responsiveness of the whole computer. For more information about monitoring disk interrupts and reducing their impact on system performance, see "Analyzing Processor Activity" in this book.

The following sections describe how you interpret the values of these counters to reveal or rule out a bottleneck.

Monitoring Paging

The symptoms of a memory shortage are similar to those of a disk bottleneck. When physical memory is scarce, the system starts writing the contents of memory to disk and reading in smaller blocks more frequently (this process is called *paging*). The less memory you have, the more the disk is used, resulting in a greater load on the disk system. Therefore, it's important to monitor memory counters along with disk counters when you suspect a performance problem with your disk system.

Monitor paging activity along with disk reading and writing, using the following counters:

- Avg. Disk Queue Length
- Disk Reads/sec
- Disk Writes/sec
- Memory\Pages/sec
- Memory\Page Reads/sec
- Memory\Page Writes/sec

Figure 30.6 shows how a memory shortage can cause disk counters to indicate a problem.

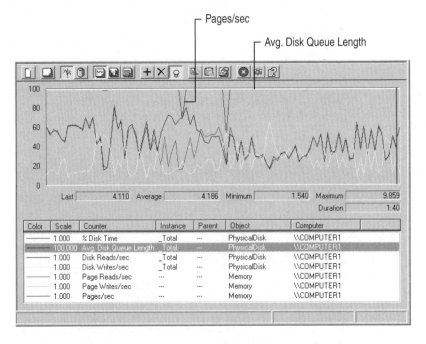

Figure 30.6   Paging Activity Compared with Disk Activity

Notice that this figure shows a long disk queue, accompanied by a high rate of paging. Compare the number of page reads against the number of disk reads to see how many times the system accessed the disk to retrieve pages that were not found in memory, or to write pages to free up memory for new data coming in from the disk. When these values are high, the system does not have sufficient memory. Without inclusion of the memory counters to reveal this behavior, you might have assumed that the disk was inadequate. Upgrading the disk in this situation would not have cured the problem.

For more information about measuring memory and identifying memory shortages, see "Evaluating Memory and Cache Usage" in this book.

Monitoring Usage

A high-performance disk is capable of about 50 to 70 random or up to 160 sequential I/O operations per second. The components you are using, as well as the request size, bus speed, and other factors, determine your system's capacity. Judge the maximum acceptable usage that your system can sustain based on your experience. Disk-time values must not consistently exceed the rate you've established as your baseline for performance. Consistent values in the 70 percent to 85 percent range are a definite cause for concern. However, if a queue is developing, lower percentages might indicate a disk that is unable to handle the load. If you see extremely high rates of disk usage, investigate the factors that might be responsible. Monitoring Disk Transfers/sec (a counter with values equal to the sum of Disk Reads/sec and Disk Writes/sec) or the individual counters Disk Reads/sec and Disk Writes/sec can show you the number of requests for service by the disk; the values of these counters provide a measure of disk demand.

If your workloads consist of random bursts of high activity, you might see high activity rates followed by long periods of idle time. If you only look at the average counter values with these types of workload, it can appear that your disk isn't busy even though it was bottlenecked during those bursts of high activity. To determine how well your disk system is handling these bursts, sample at short intervals when the activity occurs.

Note The disk time counters can yield inaccurate values when multiple disks are in use. You can compensate for this by monitoring % Idle Time and comparing its value with the values reported by the % Disk Time, % Disk Read Time, and % Disk Write Time counters.

Figure 30.7 depicts maximum disk usage and the development of a queue.

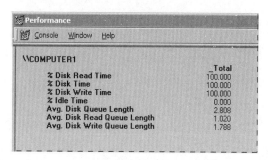

Figure 30.7   High Disk Time Values

Monitoring Queue Length

To determine the number of I/O requests queued for service, track Avg. Disk Queue Length for LogicalDisk or PhysicalDisk. Notice that this might overstate the true length of the queue, because the counter includes both queued and in-service requests. If the value of Avg. Disk Queue Length exceeds twice the number of spindles, then you are likely developing a bottleneck. With a volume set, a queue that is never shorter than the number of active physical disks indicates that you are developing a bottleneck.

Figure 30.8 shows a disk bottleneck with high disk usage and a long queue.

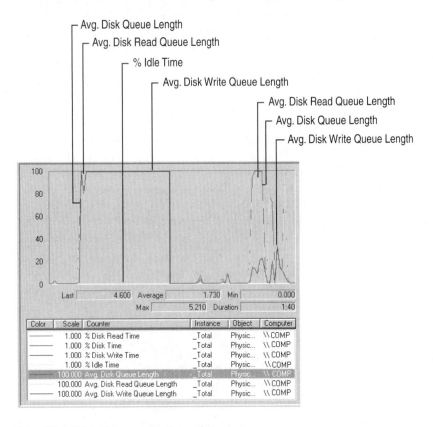

Figure 30.8   High Disk Usage and a Long Queue

Resolving Disk Bottlenecks

A disk that is developing a bottleneck might cause the entire system to slow. If you determine that disk resources are responsible for an overall decrease in system performance, you need to find a solution quickly. Although you might assume that installing another disk offers a quick fix, the right solution to your performance problem depends on the cause of the bottleneck.

Adding a disk is an appropriate solution if you can move files to a new disk, if you can create a striped volume, or if you are out of space. However, for disk-space problems only, you might want to compress your drive, provided that the processor has available cycle to handle the compression activity and that your disk requests are typically large. For a multiuser system, you can also implement disk quotas to restrict growth of user files.

If your disk system is too slow, consider the following alternative steps:

- Rule out a memory shortage. When memory is scarce, the Virtual Memory Manager writes more pages to disk, resulting in increased disk activity. Because low memory is a common cause of bottlenecks, make sure that this is not the source of the problem before adding hardware. Also, make sure to set the paging file to an appropriate size as described in "Evaluating Memory and Cache Usage" in this book.

- Defragment the disk using Disk Defragmenter. For information about using Disk Defragmenter, see Windows 2000 Help.

- Use Diskpar.exe on the *Windows 2000 Resource Kit* companion CD to reduce performance loss due to misaligned disk tracks and sectors.

- Use striped volumes to process I/O requests concurrently over multiple disks. The type you use depends on your data-integrity requirements. Implement striped volumes for fast reading and writing and improved storage capacity. When striped volumes are used, disk utilization per disk need to fall due to distribution of work across the volumes and overall throughput need to increase.

  When using striped volumes, make sure to use the optimal size of stripe for your workload. The stripe size needs to be a multiple of the size of the average request.

  If you find that there is no increased throughput when scaling to additional disks in a striped volume, you might be experiencing a bottleneck due to contention between disks for the disk adapter. You might need to add an adapter to better distribute the load.

- Place multiple drives on separate I/O buses, particularly if a disk has an I/O-intensive workload.

- Distribute workload among multiple drives. For example, for database applications, you might want to put transaction logs on a separate spindle from data. Notice that writing to a log file is a sequential operation and tends to be more efficient than the random operations typical of accessing data in a database.

  If you are unsure of a suitable distribution for network applications, track users and the files they work with in order to plan an efficient distribution by means of the auditing capability of the NTFS file system. This tells you which disks are getting the most usage and helps you determine whether you need to redistribute workloads. For more information about auditing, see Windows 2000 Professional Help.

- Limit your use of file compression or encryption. These features can add some overhead and you need to use them sparingly if not required by your enterprise and if performance is critical.

- When obtaining disk systems, use the most intelligent and efficient components available for your disk system, including controller, I/O bus, cabling, and the disk. Upgrade to faster-speed or wider-bandwidth components as necessary. These measures generally decrease transfer time and improve throughput. Use intelligent drivers that support interrupt moderation or interrupt avoidance to alleviate the interrupt activity for the processor due to disk I/O.

Evaluating Cache and Disk Usage by Applications

If you are an application developer, you might want to know if your programs read and write data efficiently to and from the disk, as well as how they utilize locality and manage the file-system cache. This section provides information to help you identify situations in which you can improve the I/O performance of applications.

Random and Sequential Data Access

Comparing random versus sequential operations is one way of assessing application efficiency in terms of disk use. Accessing data sequentially is much faster than accessing it randomly because of the way in which the disk hardware works. The seek operation, which occurs when the disk head positions itself at the right disk cylinder to access data requested, takes more time than any other part of the I/O process. Because reading randomly involves a higher number of seek operations than does sequential reading, random reads deliver a lower rate of throughput. The same is true for random writing. You might find it useful to examine your workload to determine whether it accesses data randomly or sequentially. If you find disk access is predominantly random, you might want to pay particular attention to the activities being done and monitor for the emergence of a bottleneck.

For workloads of either random or sequential I/O, use drives with faster rotational speeds. For workloads that are predominantly random I/O, use a drive with faster seek time.

For workloads that have high I/O rates, consider using striped volumes because they add physical disks, increasing the system's ability to handle concurrent disk requests. Notice, however, that striped volumes enabled in software can cause an increase in consumption of the processor. Hardware-enabled RAID volumes eliminate this impact on the processor but increase the consumption of processing cycles on the hardware RAID adapter.

Note   Even when an application reads records sequentially, if the file is fragmented throughout the disk or disks, the I/O will not be sequential. If the disk-transfer rate on a sequential or mostly sequential read operation deteriorates over time, run Disk Defragmenter on the disk and test again. When fragmentation occurs, data is not organized in contiguous clusters on the disk. Fragmentation slows performance because back-and-forth head movement is slow.

I/O Request Size

The size of requests and the rate at which they are sent are important for evaluating the way applications work with the disk. If you are an application developer, you can use the counters, such as Avg. Disk Bytes/Read, that reveal these types of information about I/O requests.

It is typically faster and more efficient to read a few large records than many small ones. However, transfer rates eventually peak due to the fact that the disk is moving blocks of data so large that each transfer occurs more slowly—although its total throughput is quite high. Unfortunately, it is not always easy to control this factor. However, if your system is used to transfer many small units of data, this inefficiency might help to explain, though not resolve, high disk use.

Requests need to be at least 8 kilobytes (KB), and, if possible, 64 KB. Sequential I/O requests of 2 KB consume a substantial amount of processor time, which affects overall system performance. However, if you can be sure that only 2 KB of data is necessary, doing a 2 KB I/O is the most efficient, because a larger I/O wastes *direct memory access (DMA)* controller bandwidth. As the record size increases, the throughput increases and the transfer rate falls because it takes fewer reads to move the same amount data.

Using 64 KB requests results in faster throughput with little processor time. Maximum throughput typically occurs at 64 KB, although some devices might have a higher maximum throughput size. When transferring data blocks greater than 64 KB, the I/O subsystem breaks the transfers into 64-KB blocks. Above 64 KB, the transfer rate drops sharply, and throughput levels off. Processor use and interrupts also appear to level off at 64 KB.

Investigating Disk Usage by Applications

Applications rarely read or write directly to disk. Instead, application code and data is typically mapped into the file system cache and copied from there into the working set of the application. When the application creates or changes data, the data is mapped into the cache and is then written back to the disk in batches. The disk is used only when an application requests a single write-through to disk or it instructs the file system not to use the cache at all for a file, usually because it is doing its own buffering. For this reason, tracking the cache and memory counters provides a way of investigating disk usage by your application. You can find information about monitoring cache and memory counters in "Evaluating Memory and Cache Usage" earlier in this book.

When monitoring disk usage by applications, you might find that applications that submit all I/O requests simultaneously tend to produce exaggerated values for the % Disk Time, % Disk Read Time, % Disk Write Time, and Avg. Disk sec/Transfer counters. Although throughput might be the same for applications that submit I/O requests intermittently, the values of counters that time requests will be much lower. It is important to understand your applications and factor their I/O methods into your analysis.

If you are writing your own tools to test disk performance, you might want to include the FILE_FLAG_NO_BUFFERING parameter in the open call for your test files. This instructs the Virtual Memory Manager to bypass the cache and go directly to disk.

PART 7

Troubleshooting

C H A P T E R   3 1

Troubleshooting Tools and Strategies

Troubleshooting computer problems can be a complex and arduous task. Microsoft® Windows® 2000 provides tools with which the user can resolve problems that might occur. This chapter details the most important troubleshooting tools, as well as troubleshooting strategies and procedures for some common problems.

In This Chapter

Related Information in the Resource Kit

- For more information about troubleshooting problems during Windows 2000 Setup and installation, see "Setup and Startup" in this book.

- For more information about troubleshooting disk problems and recovering from viruses, see "Disk Concepts and Troubleshooting" in this book.

- For more information about troubleshooting Stop errors, see "Windows 2000 Stop Messages" in this book.

Quick Guide to Troubleshooting

This chapter provides information about troubleshooting some of the more commonly encountered problems with using Microsoft® Windows® 2000 Professional, as well as tools that you can use to diagnose and treat problems. In addition, many chapters in this book discuss troubleshooting specific types of problems. Use this guide to determine where to find the information you need to maintain and troubleshoot your system.

You are having problems with your computer and don't know the cause.

Follow general troubleshooting procedures to isolate and repair the problem. Collect data along the way, in case you need to contact support personnel.

- See "General Troubleshooting Strategy" in this chapter.

Your computer does not start.

Startup problems can be caused by a variety of factors, such as viruses, disk corruption, or missing startup files. Some startup problems can be easily resolved; others might require that you perform emergency repair procedures or recovery operations.

- See "Startup and Recovery Tools" in this chapter.
- See "Troubleshooting Problems with System Startup and Shutdown" in this chapter.
- See "Disaster Recovery" in this chapter.
- See "Setup and Startup" in this book.
- See "Disk Concepts and Troubleshooting" in this book.

Your system experiences a failure and displays a "blue screen" error.

Stop errors, also referred to as "blue screens," are kernel-level errors. The Stop message provides information about the problem that caused the error and can be used by support personnel to fix the problem.

- See "Windows 2000 Stop Messages" in this book.

Your computer has been infected with a virus.

Viruses can infect the MBR or boot sector and cause problems such as preventing the system from starting up successfully. You can use tools to scan your computer for viruses and remove any that are found.

- See "Maintenance and Update tools" in this chapter.
- See "Disk Concepts and Troubleshooting" in this book.

You cannot connect to the Internet or local network.

If you are connecting to the Internet through a modem, check your hardware and dial-up configuration. If you are connected to the Internet or an intranet through a local area network (LAN), check that the server and client are correctly configured and working properly. Make sure that you have permission or a user account to access the network.

- See "Networking Tools" in this chapter.
- See "Using the Hardware Compatibility List" in this chapter.
- See "Telephony and Conferencing" in this book.
- See "Local and Remote Network Connections" in this book.

 Your network connection is slow or unreliable.

Slow or unreliable connections can have a wide range of causes, such as problems on the remote server, with the line you are using to access the network, or with the connection hardware or software you are using.

- See "Networking Tools" in this chapter.
- See "Using the Hardware Compatibility List" in this chapter.
- See "Telephony and Conferencing" in this book.
- See "Local and Remote Network Connections" in this book.

You are having name resolution problems.

The problem can be caused by a failure in host or NetBIOS name resolution. Check that parameters have been correctly configured.

- See "Networking Tools" in this chapter.
- See "TCP/IP in Windows 2000 Professional" in this book.

You are having IP addressing or routing problems.

Incorrect configurations on the client computer can cause problems with IP addressing, routing, IP security, and filtering. Also, check that the remote host or resource is available.

- See "Networking Tools" in this chapter.
- See "TCP/IP in Windows 2000 Professional" in this book.

You are connected to a non-Windows-based server, and are experiencing connection or printing problems.

Make sure that you have the correct software installed to connect to the network and that you have configured the client computers correctly.

- See "Networking Tools" in this chapter.
- See "Printing" in this book.
- See "Interoperability with NetWare" in this book.
- See "Interoperability with IBM Host Systems" in this book.
- See "Interoperability with UNIX" in this book.

 You cannot install a hardware device.

Make sure that you have installed devices correctly. If a device is not Plug and Play you need to configure it manually. Incompatible hardware devices or device drivers can also cause problems.

- See "System File and Driver Tools" in this chapter.
- See "Using the Hardware Compatibility List" in this chapter.
- See "Checking Hardware for Problems" in this chapter.
- See "Printing" in this book.
- See "Scanners and Cameras" in this book.
- See "Device Management" in this book.

 You cannot access a drive or other device attached to the computer.

Several problems can prevent devices from working properly. The connecting cables can become loose. A resource conflict can prevent a device from working. Missing or corrupted drivers can prevent the computer from recognizing devices that are installed. Incompatible hardware devices or device drivers can also cause problems.

- See "System File and Driver Tools" in this chapter.
- See "Using the Hardware Compatibility List" in this chapter.
- See "Checking Hardware for Problems" in this chapter.
- See "Device Driver Problems" in this chapter.
- See "Multimedia" in this book.
- See "Printing" in this book.
- See "Device Management" in this book.

You installed a second monitor, but there is no display, or the display is distorted.

Make sure that you have configured the monitors correctly and that your display adapters are compatible with Windows 2000 Professional.

- See "System File and Driver Tools" in this chapter.
- See "Using the Hardware Compatibility List" in this chapter.
- See "Device Management" in this book.

You cannot play audio, video, or multimedia files.

Problems with playing multimedia files can have a variety of causes, including missing or incorrectly installed sound cards, hardware or drivers that are not properly installed, or volume settings that are muted or turned down.

- See "System File and Driver Tools" in this chapter.
- See "Applications Tools" in this chapter.
- See "Multimedia" in this book.
- See "Device Management" in this book.

Your computer will not wake up from standby or sleep mode.

Make sure that you have configured the monitors correctly and that your display adapters are compatible with Windows 2000 Professional.

- See "Power Management" in this book.

You cannot print.

Printing problems can have a variety of causes, such as corrupted drivers or network problems (if you are printing to networked printer). Make sure that you have a driver installed for the printer that you are trying to access.

- See "Using the Hardware Compatibility List" in this chapter.
- See "Checking Hardware for Problems" in this chapter.
- See "Device Driver Problems" in this chapter.
- See "Printing" in this book.
- See "Device Management" in this book.

Your printed files are unreadable, or your print jobs take a long time.

If text is unreadable, there might be a problem with corrupted fonts, or a problem with the application from which you are printing, or the page settings might be incorrect. If you are printing graphics, you might need to use a different printer.

- See "Using the Hardware Compatibility List" in this chapter.
- See "Printing" in this book.
- See "Fonts" in this book.

 The desktop does not behave as expected, or it does not appear correctly.

Check that Group Policy has not been set so that you can customize your desktop. If you use a Web page as wallpaper, make sure that the Web page can be accessed.

- See "Customizing the Desktop" in this book.

General Troubleshooting Strategy

Record-keeping is essential to troubleshooting any complex system. Keep all records of all installed peripherals, the network layout (if applicable), cabling, previous problems and their solutions, upgrades, and hardware and software installation dates.

Many problems can be avoided with routine virus checks. Check for viruses before installing or upgrading to Windows 2000.

To troubleshoot a problem, follow these general guidelines:

- Analyze symptoms and factors.
- Check to see whether the problem is a common issue.
- Isolate the source of the problem.
- Define an action plan.
- Consult technical support resources.

Analyzing Symptoms

Start troubleshooting by gathering information. Develop a clear understanding of the symptoms and collect pertinent system information to understand the environment in which they occur. Precisely what is not working correctly? Under what conditions does the problem occur? Which aspects of the operating system control those conditions? Is the problem specific to an application, or is it specific to a subsystem (networks, video, and so on)? Try to narrow down exactly what you expect to have happen versus what is happening.

Consider the following:

- What is the issue? What do you expect to happen when the problem is resolved?
- Has the system or configuration ever worked? If so, what changed?
- Is the error condition reproducible or random?
- Is the error specific to a particular system, configuration, or application?
- What specific hardware and firmware are involved?
- When the problem occurs, are there any programs running other than those that automatically load when Windows 2000 is started?
- Does the error still occur in Safe Mode?
- Does it happen when another user is logged on to the computer?

Attempt to reproduce the symptom by using another application with similar functionality. If the problem is reproducible, it might be subsystem- or hardware-related. If the problem is not reproducible, investigate the application itself.

Has your task ever worked on this computer before? If so, something might have changed that affects it. Have you changed hardware or installed new software? Might another user have made changes that you do not know about?

If the task has never worked on this computer, compare the setup and configuration on this computer with another computer to identify differences.

Checking for Common Issues

Check to see whether the problem is a common issue by reviewing Windows 2000 Professional Help and other files included on the Windows 2000 operating system CD. For example, check Read1st.txt and Readme.doc in the root folder and the additional text files in the Setuptxt folder of the Windows 2000 operating system CD.

See the Windows 2000 Troubleshooters to diagnose and solve technical problems with the following system components and events:

- Client Service for NetWare
- Display
- Hardware
- Internet connections (ISP)
- Modem
- MS-DOS programs
- Multimedia and games
- Networking (TCP/IP)
- Print
- Remote access
- Sound
- System setup
- Windows 3.*x* programs

Isolating the Source of the Problem

Try to identify all variables that might affect the problem. Progressively eliminate these variables to isolate the cause of the issue. Record the effect of each action. If you eventually contact a support provider, your detailed notes are invaluable.

Eliminating variables helps determine the cause of a problem. Do symptoms occur when you run the system in Safe Mode? If not, check the programs that run when the system is started normally. Look at the shortcuts stored in the Startup group located in the folder Documents and Settings*username*\\Start Menu\\Programs \\Startup. Shortcuts to other programs run at system startup are located in the registry subkey **HKEY_LOCAL_MACHINE\\SOFTWARE\\Microsoft \\Windows\\CurrentVersion\\Run**.

Caution Do not use a registry editor to edit the registry directly unless you have no alternative. The registry editors bypass the standard safeguards provided by administrative tools. These safeguards prevent you from entering conflicting settings or settings that are likely to degrade performance or damage your system. Editing the registry directly can have serious, unexpected consequences that can prevent the system from starting and require that you reinstall Windows 2000. To configure or customize Windows 2000, use the programs in Control Panel or Microsoft Management Console (MMC) whenever possible.

If programs are run at startup that are not listed in either of these locations, your computer might be using policies. For more information about policies, see Windows 2000 Professional Help and the Group Policy Reference on the *Microsoft® Windows® 2000 Professional Resource Kit* companion CD.

If the computer is on a network, logon scripts or system management applications might also start programs on your computer. See your network administrator for assistance. If you have a local account on the system, log on to the local computer, to prevent network server–based policies and logon scripts from being carried out.

Windows 2000 only loads the minimum number of device drivers required to start the computer when it is run in Safe Mode. If you determine that the problem is not with software loading at startup, you can attempt to isolate the problem by disabling suspect devices' drivers. For more information about Safe Mode, see "Safe Mode" later in this chapter.

Caution   The Plug and Play specification allows an operating system to disable devices at the hardware level. For example, if you disable a COM port in Device Manager, you might be required to enter the CMOS or system setup to re-enable it.

For more information about Plug and Play and using Device Manager, see "Device Management" in this book.

If the problem is the result of a recent change to the system, undo that change. System Information lists installed device drivers. If a device fails and its driver has been recently updated, replace it with the original and retest.

If an update installed from the Windows Update Web site fails to meet your expectations, restore the original files by running **Update Wizard Uninstall**.

If the problem did not exist before the system was last started, restart the computer and press F8 at the Starting Windows screen. Choose **Last Known Good Configuration** to restore the system configuration to the last known working version.

Caution   Restoring a previous system configuration results in the loss of any changes made in the interim.

Defining an Action Plan

Try to identify all of the variables that might affect the problem. As you troubleshoot the problem, try to change only one of these variables at a time. Keep records of what you do and the effect of each action.

Develop your plan on paper. Decide what steps you want to take and the expected results of each step. Then complete the steps in order, and follow your plan.

If you see a result for which you have no plan:

- Return to the isolation phase.
- Identify what happens in similar situations.
- Define another plan.

Checking Technical Support Resources

Technical newsgroups offer peer support for common computer problems. You can post persistent problems on the appropriate online forum. Other users might have already reported similar problems. Suggestions from others can save you time and give you direction for your troubleshooting. For more information about technical support resources, see the Microsoft TechNet link on the Web Resources page at http://windows.microsoft.com/windows2000/reskit/webresources.

Windows 2000 Professional Help also contains information about online support.

Startup and Recovery Tools

Windows 2000 Professional offers tools to help you troubleshoot problems with starting your computer and recovering from disasters. Some of the most useful tools are detailed in this section, as shown in Table 31.1.

For more information about troubleshooting techniques for setting up your computer, see "Setup and Startup" in this book.

Table 31.1   Startup and Recovery Troubleshooting Tools

Tool	Description	How to Start
Safe Mode	A startup environment that limits the device drivers and system services that load for troubleshooting problems with starting and running Windows 2000.	**Windows 2000 Advanced Options Menu** at system startup
Recovery Console	A command-line startup environment that allows the system administrator access to the hard disk of computers running Windows 2000 for basic troubleshooting and system maintenance.	From **Repair** option of Setup or, if manually installed, from **Operating System** menu at startup
Emergency Repair Process	A process that can recover from problems such as damaged or deleted operating system files or a corrupted system volume boot sector.	From **Repair** option of Setup

Safe Mode

Safe Mode is a diagnostic tool for troubleshooting problems with starting and running Windows 2000. Safe Mode allows the user to specifically control how the computer starts Windows 2000.

If the computer fails to properly start up, restart Windows 2000 in Safe Mode to troubleshoot the problem. To do this, press F8 while the message "For troubleshooting and advanced startup options for Windows 2000, press F8" is displayed. Once the **Windows 2000 Advanced Options Menu** is displayed, you can start the computer in Safe Mode or press ESC to return to the normal startup menu.

Table 31.2 describes the **Windows 2000 Advanced Options Menu** options.

Table 31.2   Windows 2000 Advanced Options Menu Options

Start Menu Option	Description
Safe Mode	Loads the minimum required basic device drivers and system services to start the system. Programs located in the Startup Program group are not started.
Safe Mode with Networking	Similar to standard Safe Mode, but also adds essential services and drivers needed to start networking. Safe Mode with Networking allows Group Policy to be implemented, including those implemented by the server during the logon process and those configured on the local computer.
Safe Mode with Command Prompt	Similar to standard Safe Mode but loads the command interpreter instead of Explorer.exe as the user shell.
Enable Boot Logging	Creates a log file, Ntbtlog.txt in the %SystemRoot% folder, during normal startup, which logs the name and status of all drivers loaded into memory.
Enable VGA Mode	Starts the computer in basic VGA mode in cases of corruption or incompatibility of currently installed video driver.
Last Known Good Configuration	Reverts to the last successfully started system configuration.
Directory Services Restore Mode	Only applies to Windows 2000 domain controllers. Displays system information such as the number of processors, amount of main memory, Service Pack status, and build number during startup.

(continued)

Table 31.2   Windows 2000 Advanced Options Menu Options *(continued)*

Start Menu Option	Description
Debugging Mode	Starts Windows 2000 in kernel debug mode, which allows a debugger to break into the kernel for troubleshooting and system analysis.
Boot Normally	Starts Windows 2000, loading all normal startup files and registry values.

Note A boot log file, Ntbtlog.txt, is automatically created every time the computer is started in Safe Mode. If a boot log file using that name already exists, the new data is appended to the existing file.

Use Safe Mode in the following situations:

- If Windows 2000 Professional stalls for an extended period of time.
- If Windows 2000 Professional does not work correctly or has unexpected results.
- If your video display does not work correctly.
- If your computer suddenly slows down.
- If you need to test an intermittent error condition.
- If you have recently installed a new device driver or software and your system no longer starts.

Unlike Microsoft® Windows® 98, Windows 2000 does not automatically initiate Safe Mode after the system startup has failed. You need to manually access the **Windows 2000 Advanced Options Menu** to access Safe Mode.

When starting Windows 2000 in Safe Mode, only essential drivers and system services are loaded, including the mouse, keyboard, CD-ROM, standard VGA device drivers, the Event Log, Plug and Play, Remote Procedure Call (RPC), and Logical Disk Manager system services. Safe Mode also bypasses programs referenced in Startup Program group folders (including the user's profile, the All Users profile, and the Administrator profile), programs referenced in the registry to automatically run, and all local group policies (which might also enforce the automatic start of an application). This makes Safe Mode useful for isolating and resolving error conditions caused by faulty automatically started applications, system services, and device drivers.

Safe Mode provides access to the Windows 2000 configuration files so you can make configuration changes, and then restart Windows 2000 Professional normally.

Note Safe Mode with Command Prompt loads the basic VGA video driver and a graphical user interface with a command prompt.

After you are in Safe Mode, you can disable or delete a system service, a device driver, or automatically started application that is preventing the computer from starting normally.

Note Your computer can take substantially longer to start up and shut down when running in Safe Mode because all disk caching is disabled.

For more information about using Safe Mode, see "Troubleshooting Problems with System Startup and Shutdown" later in this chapter.

Recovery Console

The Recovery Console is a startable text-mode command interpreter environment separate from the Windows 2000 command prompt that allows the system administrator access to the hard disk of computer running Windows 2000 Professional, regardless of the file format used, for basic troubleshooting and system maintenance tasks. Since Windows 2000 does not need to be running to use Recovery Console, it is most useful when a Windows 2000–based computer does not start properly or cannot start at all.

The Recovery Console allows you to obtain limited access to NTFS file system, file allocation table (FAT) 16, and FAT32 volumes without starting the graphical interface. The Recovery Console allows administrators to manage files and folders, start and stop services, and repair the system. It can also be used to repair the master boot record (MBR) and boot sectors and to format volumes. The Recovery Console also prevents unauthorized access to volumes by requiring the user to enter the system administrator password before using the console.

Starting the Recovery Console

To start the Recovery Console, start the computer from the Windows 2000 operating system CD or the Windows 2000 Setup floppy disks. If you do not have Windows 2000 Setup floppy disks and your computer cannot start from the CD, use another Windows 2000–based computer to create the setup disks. For information about creating the Windows 2000 Setup floppy disks, see Windows 2000 Professional Help.

Note The Recovery Console can also be installed to the local hard disk and accessed from the Windows 2000 startup menu. However, if the MBR or system volume boot sector have been damaged, you need to start the computer from either the Setup floppy disks or the Windows 2000 Professional operating system CD to access the Recovery Console.

To add the Recovery Console to existing installations of Windows 2000, carry out the following command from the Windows 2000 operating system CD in the **Run** dialog box:

```
d:\I386\Winnt32.exe /cmdcons
```

where *d:* represents the CD-ROM drive. This installation requires approximately 7 megabytes (MB) of disk space on your system volume.

This only works correctly if your computer does not contain a mirrored volume. To install the Recovery Console on a computer that contains a mirrored volume, first break the mirror. After the Recovery Console is installed, you can re-establish the mirrored volume. For more information, see the Microsoft Knowledge Base link on the Web Resources page at http://windows.microsoft.com/windows2000/reskit/webresources.

Start the computer from either the Windows 2000 Setup disks or the operating system CD, and then enter Windows 2000 Setup. Press ENTER at the "Setup Notification" screen to go to the "Welcome to Setup" screen. Press R to repair a Windows 2000 installation, and then press C to use the Recovery Console.

The Recovery Console displays valid Windows 2000 installations and prompts you select the installation to repair. To access the disk with the Recovery Console, press the number key for the Windows 2000 installation that you want to repair, and then press ENTER. If you press ENTER without typing a number, the Recovery Console quits and restarts the computer.

Note The Recovery Console might show installations of Microsoft® Windows NT®. However, the results of attempting to access a Windows NT installation from the Recovery Console can be unpredictable. Only use the Recovery Console to fix Windows 2000 installations.

Mirrored volumes appear twice in the Recovery Console startup menu, but each entry uses the same drive letter, indicating a reference to the same disk.

The Recovery Console then prompts you for the local administrator account password. If you do not enter the correct password after three attempts, Recovery Console refuses access to the local disks and restarts the computer.

Note If the registry is corrupted or missing or no valid installations are found, the Recovery Console starts in the root of the startup volume without requiring a password. You cannot access any folders, but you can carry out commands such as **chkdsk**, **fixboot**, and **fixmbr** for limited disk repairs.

After the password is validated, you can access the following folders on your computer:

- The root folder of any volume.
- %SystemRoot% and subfolders of the Windows 2000 installation on which you are currently logged on.
- \Cmdcons and subfolders (if they exist).
- Folders on removable media disks, such as CD-ROM and floppy disks.

By default, the Recovery Console prevents access to other folders such as Program Files or Documents and Settings, and folders containing other installations of Windows 2000. This can be changed by using local Group Policy settings. For more information about using Group Policy to change the default behavior of the Recovery Console, see the procedure on setting the policy later in this section. For access to other Windows 2000 installation folders, restart the Recovery Console, and select that installation.

Using the Recovery Console

You cannot copy a file from the local hard disk to a floppy disk. However, you can copy a file from a floppy disk or a CD-ROM to any hard disk, and from one hard disk to another. The Recovery Console displays an "Access is denied" error message when it detects invalid commands.

You cannot run any programs or commands other than the supported commands listed later in this section. The Recovery Console contains no editing capabilities.

Important The **set** command makes use of Recovery Console environment variables to enable, among other options, disk write access to floppy disks. To enable the user to modify the restricted default Recovery Console environment variables, a Group Policy setting must be made. For more information about enabling the **set** command in Recovery Console, see the procedure at the end of this section.

The Recovery Console buffers previously entered commands and makes them available to the user by means of the UP ARROW and DOWN ARROW keys. To edit a previously entered command, use BACKSPACE to move the cursor to the point where you want to make the edit and rekey the remainder of the command.

To quit and restart the computer, at the command prompt, type:

exit

Important The Recovery Console might not map disk volumes with the same drive letters found in Windows 2000. If you are having trouble locating files to copy make sure that the drive mappings for both the source and the target locations are correct. If not, examine other drive letters for the file you are seeking. In addition, some volumes might not have drive letters assigned to them, such as volumes formatted with NTFS and grafted onto the folder structure of another volume by the use of volume mount points. Use the **map** command to confirm which drive letters and unnamed volumes correspond to which local volumes on the system. For more information about volume mount points, see "File Systems" in this book.

Several of the Recovery Console commands are not fully functional to users who have converted to dynamic disk. For more information about dynamic disks, see "Disks Concepts and Troubleshooting" in this book.

Supported Commands

Table 31.3 lists the commands that are supported by the Recovery Console.

Table 31.3   Available Recovery Console Commands

Command	Explanation
Attrib	Changes the attributes of a file or folder. Syntax: `attrib -|+[c][h][r][s] filename` `+` Sets an attribute. `-` Clears an attribute. `c` Compressed file attribute. `h` Hidden file attribute. `r` Read-only file attribute. `s` System file attribute. At least one attribute must be set or cleared. To view attributes, use the **dir** command. You can set multiple attributes simultaneously. To change multiple attributes in a like manner, use either enable/disable switch (+/-) and all the attribute letters to be changed, as in the following syntax: **+chr**. To change multiple attributes in a dissimilar manner, use the enable switch (+) and all the attribute letters to be enabled, followed immediately by the disable switch (-) and all the attribute letters to be disabled, as in the following syntax: **+ch-r**. Do not separate attribute switches with spaces.
Batch	Carries out commands specified in a text file. Syntax: `batch inputfile [outputfile]` `inputfile` Specifies the text file that contains the list of commands to be executed. `outputfile` Contains the output of commands listed in inputfile. If no outputfile is specified, the command output is displayed on the screen. Batch cannot be one of the commands included in the inputfile.

(continued)

Table 31.3   Available Recovery Console Commands *(continued)*

Command	Explanation
| **Cd or Chdir** | Displays the current volume and directory or changes to the folder specified. Syntax:<br><br>```
cd [path]|[..]|[drive:]
chdir [path]|[..]|[drive:]
```<br><br>```
path     Changes to the specified folder on the same volume.
..       Changes to the parent folder.
drive:   Displays the active folder of the volume specified.
Using no switches displays the current volume and folder.
```<br><br>**Cd** treats spaces as delimiters, requiring that a space precede all arguments, including the use of double periods. Use quotation marks to enclose a path or file name that contains a space. |
| **Chkdsk** | Checks a disk and, if needed, repairs or recovers the volume. **Chkdsk** also marks bad sectors and recovers readable information. Syntax:<br><br>```
chkdsk [drive:] [/p]|[/r]
```<br><br>```
drive:   Specifies the volume to check.
/p       Forces check if volume is not identified as bad.
/r       Locates bad sectors and recovers readable information (/p is
         automatic).
```<br><br>**Chkdsk** can be used without switches, and when no disk is specified the current volume is implied. **Chkdsk** requires that Autochk.exe be installed in the System32 folder or be available from the Windows 2000 operating system CD. |
| **Cls** | Clears the screen. |

(continued)

Table 31.3   Available Recovery Console Commands *(continued)*

Command	Explanation

Copy	Copies a single file to a specified location. Syntax:
	
	`copy source [target]`
	
	`source   Specifies the file to be copied.`
	`target   Specifies the destination folder and/or filename for the new file.`
	
	The use of wildcard characters (* and ?) is not permitted. If the target is not specified, it defaults to the current folder. If the file already exists, you are prompted to overwrite it. Compressed files from the Windows 2000 operating system CD are automatically decompressed as they are copied.

Del or Delete	Deletes one file. Syntax:
	
	`del [drive:][path]filename`
	`delete [drive:][path]filename`
	
	`drive:   Specifies the volume on which the file to be deletes resides.`
	`path     Specifies the location within the folder structure of the file`
	`         to be deleted.`
	`filename Specific file to be deleted.`
	
	The use of wildcard characters (* and ?) in file names is not permitted.

Dir	Displays a list of files and folders within a folder. Syntax:
	
	`dir [drive:][path][filename]`
	
	`drive:   Specifies the volume on which the files to be displayed`
	`         reside.`
	`path     Specifies the location within the folder structure of the`
	`         files to be displayed.`
	`filename Specific file to be displayed.`
	
	Dir lists all folders and files, including hidden and system files. Each listing can have any of the following attributes:
	
	`a   Archive` `h   Hidden`
	`c   Compressed` `p   Reparse point`
	`d   Directory` `r   Read-only`
	`e   Encrypted` `s   System file`
	
	The use of wildcard characters (* and ?) is permitted.

(continued)

Table 31.3   Available Recovery Console Commands *(continued)*

Command	Explanation

Disable	Disables a Windows 2000 system service or driver. Syntax:
	
	`disable servicename`
	
	`servicename   Name of the service or driver to be disabled.`
	
	Use the **listsvc** command to display all services or drivers that can be disabled. **Disable** prints the previous START_TYPE of the service before resetting it to SERVICE_DISABLED. Because of this, make sure that you record the previous START_TYPE, in case it is necessary to re-enable the service. The START_TYPE values that the **disable** command displays are:
	
	`SERVICE_DISABLED`
	`SERVICE_BOOT_START`
	`SERVICE_SYSTEM_START`
	`SERVICE_AUTO_START`
	`SERVICE_DEMAND_START`

Diskpart	Manages the partitions on your hard disk. Syntax: `diskpart[/add|/delete] [device-name|drive-name|partition-name] [size]`

<table>
<tr><td><code>/add</code></td><td>Create a new partition.</td></tr>
<tr><td><code>/delete</code></td><td>Delete an existing partition.</td></tr>
<tr><td><code>device-name</code></td><td>Device name for creating a new partition (such as \Device\HardDisk0).</td></tr>
<tr><td><code>drive-name</code></td><td>Drive-letter based name for deleting an existing partition (such as D:).</td></tr>
<tr><td><code>partition-name</code></td><td>Partition-based name for deleting an existing partition and can be used in place of the drive-name argument (such as \Device\HardDisk0\Partition1).</td></tr>
<tr><td><code>size</code></td><td>Size of the new partition, in megabytes.</td></tr>
</table>

If no arguments are used, a user interface for managing your partitions appears.

Warning

This command can damage your partition table if the disk has been upgraded to dynamic disk. Do not modify the structure of dynamic disks unless you are using the Disk Management tool.

(continued)

Table 31.3   Available Recovery Console Commands *(continued)*

Command	Explanation

Enable	Enables a Windows 2000 system service or driver. Syntax:
	
	`enable servicename [start_type]`
	
	`servicename` Name of the service or driver to be enabled.
	`start_type` How the service or driver is scheduled to be started. Valid values include:
	      `SERVICE_BOOT_START`
	      `SERVICE_SYSTEM_START`
	      `SERVICE_AUTO_START`
	      `SERVICE_DEMAND_START`
	
	Use the **listsvc** command to display all eligible services or drivers to enable. The **enable** command prints the previous START_TYPE of the service before resetting it to the new value. Note the previous value, in case it is necessary to restore the START_TYPE of the service. If you do not specify a new START_TYPE, **enable** prints the previous START_TYPE.

Exit	Quits the Recovery Console and restarts your computer.

Expand	Expands a compressed file stored on the Windows 2000 operating system CD or from within a CAB file on the Windows 2000 operating system CD and copies it to a specified destination. Syntax:
	
	`expand source [/f:filespec] [target] [/y]`
	`expand source [/f:filespec] /d`
	
	`source` Specifies the file to be expanded. May not include wildcard (* and ?) characters.
	`target` Specifies the destination folder and/or file name for the new file.
	`/y` Do not prompt before overwriting existing file.
	`/f:filespec` If source contains more than one file, this parameter is required to identify the specific file(s) to be expanded. May use wildcards.
	`/d` Do not expand—only display a folder of the files which are contained in the source.
	
	If target is not specified, the default is the current folder. If the file already exists, you are prompted to overwrite it unless the **/y** switch is used. The target file cannot be read-only. Use **attrib** to remove the read-only attribute.

Fixboot	Rewrites the boot sector code on the hard disk. This is useful for repairing corrupted boot sectors. Syntax: `fixboot [drive:]` `drive:` Specifies the volume on which to rewrite a new boot sector. If drive: is not specified, the default is the system boot volume.

(continued)

Table 31.3   Available Recovery Console Commands *(continued)*

Command	Explanation
Fixmbr	Rewrites the master boot code of the master boot record (MBR) of the startup hard disk. This command is useful for repairing corrupted MBRs. Syntax:

```
fixmbr [device-name]
```

```
device-name    Specifies the name of device needing a new MBR (such as
               \Device\HardDisk1).
```

If device-name is not specified, the default is disk 0. If disk 0 is not the device needing repair, the device-name of other disks can be obtained by using **map**.

If **fixmbr** detects an invalid or nonstandard partition table signature, it prompts you for permission before rewriting the MBR.

Warning
This command can damage your partition table if a virus is present, if you have a third-party operating system installed, if you have a non-standard MBR, or if a hardware problem exists and causes volumes to become inaccessible. It is recommended that you run antivirus software before using this command.

Important
Running **fixmbr** overwrites only the master boot code, leaving the existing partition table intact. If corruption in the MBR affects the partition table, running **fixmbr** might not resolve the problem.

Format   Formats the specified volume to the specified file system. Syntax:

```
format [drive:] [/q] [/fs:file_system]
```

```
drive:             Specifies the volume to format.
/q                 Performs a quick format.
/fs:file_system    Specifies the file system use. Valid values for
                   file_system include FAT, FAT32, and NTFS.
```

If no file system is specified, NTFS is used by default. Choosing FAT formats a volume as FAT16. FAT16 volumes *cannot* be larger than 4 gigabytes (GB) and *should* not be larger than 2 GB to maintain compatibility with Microsoft® MS-DOS®, Microsoft® Windows® 95, and Windows 98. Windows 2000 can format FAT32 volumes up to 32 GB. Larger volumes should be formatted as NTFS.

(continued)

Table 31.3   Available Recovery Console Commands *(continued)*

Command	Explanation

Help	Shows help display for commands within the Recovery Console. Syntax:
	
	`help [command]`
	
	`command    Any Recovery Console command.`
	
	If command is not specified, all of the commands supported by the Recovery Console are listed. The command argument is used to see help for any specific command.

Listsvc	Lists all available services, drivers, and their START_TYPES for the current Windows 2000 installation. Used in conjunction with the **disable** and **enable** commands. The information listed by this command is extracted from the registry file System in the folder %SystemRoot%\System32\Config. If System is damaged or missing, results can be unpredictable.
Logon	Lists all detected installations of Windows 2000 and Windows NT, and then requests the local administrator password. If more than three attempts to log on fail, the Recovery Console quits, and the computer restarts.

Map	Lists all drive letters, file system types, volume sizes, and mappings to physical devices that are currently active. Syntax:
	
	`map [arc]`
	
	`arc    Forces the use of Advanced RISC Computing (ARC) specification name`
	`       paths instead of Windows device paths. This can be used in`
	`       recreating the Boot.ini file.`
	
	Important
	The **map** command might not work correctly with systems using dynamic disk.

Md or Mkdir	Creates a directory. Syntax:
	
	`md [drive:]path`
	`mkdir [drive:]path`
	
	`drive:   Specifies the volume on which to create a folder.`
	`path     Specifies the name of the folder to be  created.`
	
	Wildcard characters (* and ?) are not allowed.
	
	Note
	This command might not display all of the volumes on disk or the correct volume sizes if the disk has been upgraded to dynamic disk.

(continued)

7. In the **Add/Remove Snap-in** dialog box, click **OK**.

8. Expand **Local Computer Policy**.

9. Expand **Computer Configuration**, **Windows Settings**, **Security Settings**, and **Local Policies**.

10. Click **Security Options**.

11. Double-click the policy **Recovery Console: Allow floppy copy and access to all volumes and folders**.

12. In the **Local Security Policy Setting** dialog box, select **Enabled**, and then click **OK**.

Important If you are using computers running Windows 2000 Professional on a Microsoft® Windows® 2000 Server–based network, use Group Policy from the server to control this functionality. It is more efficient to set this policy in one place and have the workstations automatically implement it when logging on to the network than to implement it on each workstation.

Note You can also use the Group Policy snap-in to enable the policy **Recovery Console: Allow automatic administrative logon**, allowing you to bypass the logon process when the Recovery Console is started. Activating this policy eliminates a security barrier used to protect your computer against intruders. You should only enable this policy on systems that have controlled access to the console, such as those in rooms that can be locked.

Both of the settings available in the Group Policy snap-in can also be made through the Security Configuration and Analysis snap-in.

For more information about setting up, starting, and using Group Policy, see "Customizing the Desktop" in this book.

Using the Recovery Console to Restore the Registry

If you know your registry is damaged, or some of your registry files are corrupted or have been deleted, you might be able to use the Recovery Console to restore your registry. However, this procedure can only work if you regularly create an Emergency Repair Disk (ERD) and you choose the option to back up your registry to the repair directory. For more information about backing up the registry when creating the ERD, see "Emergency Repair Process" later in this chapter.

When you create an ERD and you choose this option, the current version of your registry files are copied from the %SystemRoot%\System32\Config folder to the %SystemRoot%\Repair\RegBack folder. Since both of these folders are accessible through the Recovery Console, you can use the **copy** command to restore the files.

▶   **To restore the Registry by using the Recovery Console**

> **Warning**   Only use this procedure if you are certain which registry file needs to be restored, and you are certain that the restoration will not cause other damage to your computer. Restoring registry files improperly can prevent your system from starting and can cause you to lose data.

1. Start the Recovery Console and log on to the Windows 2000 installation containing the registry that you want to restore.

2. To copy the files you want from %SystemRoot%\Repair\RegBack to %SystemRoot%\System32\Config, type:

   cd repair\regback

   and:

   copy *file_name drive_letter:\system_root***system32\config**

   where *file_name* is the registry file you want to restore, *drive_letter* is the drive letter where your system is installed (for example, C), and *system_root* is the system installation folder (for example, Winnt).

> **Note**   As a precaution, first rename the existing file in the Config folder that you intend to restore from backup. If a problem arises from the restoration attempt, you can restore the renamed file to return your system to its original condition.

   To restore your entire registry, you need to copy the files Default, Sam, Security, Software, and System.

3. To exit the Recovery Console, type:

   exit

Emergency Repair Process

The Emergency Repair Process is a text-mode tool that you can use to repair or recover a system that cannot properly start. It helps you repair problems caused by damaged or deleted operating system files or a corrupted system volume boot sector.

The Emergency Repair Process can repair system files and re-enable the system to start up—it does not back up any files or programs.

The Emergency Repair Process can perform the following tasks:

- Inspect and repair the startup environment.
- Verify and replace system files.

- Replace the system volume boot sector.
- Replace the registry if it is missing or badly corrupted.

Important   Using the Emergency Repair Process to repair registry problems is not recommended. The copy of the registry that the Emergency Repair Process restores is the original registry created during Setup. To back up the current registry in Windows 2000, you have one of two options using Backup:

1. Perform a backup of the System State data. This backs up the registry, the Component Services class registration database, and all system startup files.

2. Create a new ERD, and then back up the registry at the same time.

As a result of either action, the registry files are copied to the %SystemRoot%\Repair\RegBack folder. The registry files backed up with these processes are not the ones restored by the Emergency Repair Process. The Emergency Repair Process refers to the registry files stored in the %SystemRoot%\Repair folder. To use these backup registry files for system restoration, use the Recovery Console to copy the backed up registry files to the %SystemRoot%\System32\Config folder. For more information about restoring backed up registry files by using the Recovery Console, see "Recovery Console" earlier in this chapter.

To prepare for the Emergency Repair Process, create an Emergency Repair Disk (ERD).

▶ **To create an ERD**

1. From the **Start** menu, click **Programs**, **Accessories**, **System Tools**, and **Backup**.

2. On the **Welcome** tab, click **Emergency Repair Disk**.

3. Insert an empty, high-density 3.5-inch floppy disk into the floppy disk drive.

4. When the process is complete, remove the disk, label it "Emergency Repair Disk," and then store it in a safe location.

Note   Windows 2000 does not include the Rdisk.exe program that was used in Microsoft® Windows NT® version 4.0 and earlier versions to create an ERD.

When the ERD is created, the files listed in Table 31.4 are copied from the %SystemRoot%\Repair folder to a floppy disk.

Table 31.4   Contents of the ERD

File Name	Contents
Autoexec.nt	A copy of %SystemRoot%\Repair\Autoexec.nt, which is used to initialize the MS-DOS environment.
Config.nt	A copy of %SystemRoot%\Repair\Config.nt, which is used to initialize the MS-DOS environment.
Setup.log	A copy of %SystemRoot%\Repair\Setup.log, which lists the files installed by Setup as well as their cyclic redundancy check (CRC) data for use during the Emergency Repair Process.

Note   The Emergency Repair Process relies on data saved in the %SystemRoot%\Repair folder. Do not change or delete this folder.

The registry in Windows 2000 is too large to fit on a floppy disk, and the registry entries are no longer included on the ERD.

To restore your system with the Emergency Repair Process, use the Windows 2000 operating system CD or the Windows 2000 Setup disks and the ERD. During the restore process, press F1 for more information about your options.

Note   You must use the correct CD-ROM for repairs. You cannot use setup CDs for different languages or incorrect versions.

▶   **To restore your system with the Emergency Repair Process**

1. Use the Windows 2000 Professional operating system CD to start your computer. If you have a computer that cannot start up from a CD-ROM, use the Windows 2000 Setup disks instead.

2. At the Setup Notification screen, press ENTER to continue.

3. At the Welcome to Setup screen, press R to select the option to repair a Windows 2000 installation.

4. When prompted to choose the type of repair or recovery option required, press R to repair a Windows 2000 installation by using the Emergency Repair Process.

5. Choose the type of repair option you want to use:

   ▪ Press M for Manual Repair.

   ▪ Press F for Fast Repair.

6. Follow the instructions that appear and insert the ERD when prompted. If you have the original Windows 2000 operating system CD, you can have Setup check your disk for corruption.

Important Because missing or corrupted files are replaced with files from the Windows 2000 operating system CD, changes made after the original installation are lost. Any Service Pack or hotfix installations must be reapplied after using the Emergency Repair Process to restore system files.

If you choose Fast Repair, all repair options are automatically performed, including examination of the registry files. If the registry files are corrupted or missing, Fast Repair automatically replaces them with the copies stored in %SystemRoot%\Repair.

Manual Repair allows you to select from the following three options:

Inspect Startup Environment. Inspect Startup Environment verifies that the Windows 2000 files in the system volume are the correct ones. If any of the files that are needed to start Windows 2000 are missing or corrupted, Repair replaces them from the Windows 2000 operating system CD. If Boot.ini is missing, it is recreated.

Note The replacement Boot.ini only contains information for the current installation. If your system was configured as a multiple-boot system, the nondefault entries in Boot.ini are not recreated.

Verify Windows 2000 System Files. Verify Windows 2000 System Files uses a checksum to verify that each installed file is good and that it matches the file that was installed from the Windows 2000 operating system CD. If the recovery process determines that a file on the disk does not match what was installed, it displays a message that identifies the file and asks whether you want to replace it. The Emergency Repair Process also verifies that startup files, such as Ntldr, Ntdetect.com, and Ntoskrnl.exe, are present and valid.

Inspect Boot Sector. Inspect Boot Sector verifies that the boot sector on the system volume references Ntldr, and replaces it if it does not. The Emergency Repair Process can only replace the boot sector for the system volume on the first hard disk.

If the Emergency Repair Process was successful, your computer automatically restarts, and you likely have a working system.

Tip Make a copy of the ERD and store it in a secure location, perhaps off-site.

There are a couple of points to consider about maintaining and using the ERD:

- Be sure to maintain a copy of your current ERD.
- The ERD is not a replacement for backups.

If any of the files that Windows 2000 installs on the system volume are missing or corrupted, you cannot start your computer. You can restore any of the files listed in Table 31.5 by using the ERD.

Table 31.5   Additional Files Restored by the ERD

File	Folder
Ntldr	C:\
Ntdetect.com	C:\
Boot.ini	C:\
Ntbootdd.sys (only applies to systems using SCSI disks)	C:\
Hal.dll	%SystemRoot%\System32

For more information about creating and using the ERD, see Windows 2000 Professional Help.

Maintenance and Update Tools

Windows 2000 provides tools that you can use to maintain and update your system. Some of the most useful of these tools are detailed in this section, as shown in Table 31.6.

Table 31.6   Maintenance and Update Troubleshooting Tools

Tool	Overview	Location
Check Disk (Chkdsk.exe)	Scans for and repairs physical problems, such as bad blocks, as well as logical structure errors, such as lost clusters, cross-linked files, or directory errors, on volumes on the hard disk.	%SystemRoot%\System32
Disk Defragmenter (Dfrg.msc)	Rearranges files, folders, programs, and unused space on the hard disk to optimize disk performance.	%SystemRoot%\System32
AVBoot (Makedisk.bat)	Scans for and removes MBR and boot sector viruses from the computer's memory and disk.	\VALUEADD\3RDPARTY\CA_A NTIV on the Windows 2000 operating system CD

(continued)

Table 31.6   Maintenance and Update Troubleshooting Tools *(continued)*

Tool	Overview	Location
Windows Update (Wupdmgr.exe)	Serves as an online extension of Windows 2000. It provides a central location to find customized files and product enhancements, including Service Packs, system files, device drivers, and new Windows 2000 features.	%SystemRoot%\System32

Chkdsk

Chkdsk is a command-line tool that scans and repairs volumes on the hard disk for physical problems, such as bad blocks, and logical structure errors, such as lost clusters, cross-linked files, or directory errors.

Run Chkdsk from a command prompt rather than from Windows Explorer to see the resulting display.

Chkdsk Syntax

The command-line syntax for Chkdsk is as follows:

```
chkdsk [volume[[path]filename]]] [/f] [/v] [/r] [/x] [/i] [/c]
       [/l[:size]]
```

Used without parameters, Chkdsk displays the status of the disk in the current volume.

Chkdsk Switches

Table 31.7 lists all Chkdsk command-line switches.

Table 31.7   Chkdsk Switches

Switch	Effect
filename	FAT only. Specifies the file or set of files to check for fragmentation. Wildcard characters (* and ?) are allowed.
path	FAT only. Specifies the location of a file or set of files within the folder structure of the volume.
size	NTFS only. Changes the log file size to the specified number of kilobytes. Must be used with the **/l** switch.
volume	FAT only. Specifies the drive letter (followed by a colon), mount point, or volume name.
/c	NTFS only. Skips checking of cycles within the folder structure.

(continued)

Table 31.7   Chkdsk Switches *(continued)*

Switch	Effect
/f	Fixes errors on the volume. The volume must be locked. If Chkdsk cannot lock the volume, it offers to check it the next time the computer starts.
/i	NTFS only. Performs a less vigorous check of index entries.
/l	NTFS only. Displays current size of the log file.
/r	Locates bad sectors and recovers readable information (implies **/f**). If Chkdsk cannot lock the volume, it offers to check it the next time the computer starts.
/v	On FAT. Displays the full path and name of every file on the volume.
	On NTFS. Displays cleanup messages, if any.
/x	NTFS only. Forces the volume to dismount first, if necessary. All opened handles to the volume are then invalid (implies **/f**).
/?	Displays this list of Chkdsk switches.

Note FAT refers to volumes formatted with FAT12, FAT16, or FAT32.

Using the **/i** or **/c** switch skips certain checks of the NTFS volume and reduces the amount of time required to run Chkdsk.

Use Chkdsk occasionally on each volume to check for errors. You must be logged on as a member of the Administrators group.

Chkdsk Reports

Chkdsk creates and displays a status report for a volume, based on the file system used. Chkdsk also lists and corrects errors on the volume.

The following are sample Chkdsk reports for volumes using each hard disk file system supported by Windows 2000. Each of these tests were run using the **/f** switch, although no errors were reported on any of the volumes.

Following is an example Chkdsk report from an NTFS volume:

```
The type of the file system is NTFS.

CHKDSK is verifying files (stage 1 of 3)...
File verification completed.
CHKDSK is verifying indexes (stage 2 of 3)...
Index verification completed.
CHKDSK is verifying security descriptors (stage 3 of 3)...
Security descriptor verification completed.
Windows has checked the file system and found no problem.

   4096543 KB total disk space.
    639500 KB in 3206 files.
       692 KB in 113 indexes.
         0 KB in bad sectors.
     26427 KB in use by the system.
     22544 KB occupied by the log file.
   3429924 KB available on disk.

      4096 bytes in each allocation unit.
   1024135 total allocation units on disk.
    857481 allocation units available on disk.
```

An example of a Chkdsk report from a FAT32 volume:

```
The type of the file system is FAT32.
Volume FAT32 created 8/7/1999 11:19 AM
Volume Serial Number is 1067-3B1C
Windows is verifying files and folders...
File and folder verification is complete.
Windows has checked the file system and found no problem.

2,618,732,544 bytes total disk space.
      286,720 bytes in 29 hidden files.
      401,408 bytes in 86 folders.
  307,101,696 bytes in 2,179 files.
2,310,938,624 bytes available on disk.

        4,096 bytes in each allocation unit.
      639,339 total allocation units on disk.
      564,194 allocation units available on disk.
```

An example of a Chkdsk report from a FAT16 volume:

```
The type of the file system is FAT.
Volume FAT16 created 8/7/1999 11:23 AM
Volume Serial Number is 0CE5-DBB4
Windows is verifying files and folders...
File and folder verification is complete.
Windows has checked the file system and found no problem.

1,340,538,880 bytes total disk space.
    1,933,312 bytes in 50 hidden files.
    3,407,872 bytes in 103 folders.
  705,921,024 bytes in 3,158 files.
  629,276,672 bytes available on disk.


       32,768 bytes in each allocation unit.
       40,910 total allocation units on disk.
       19,204 allocation units available on disk.
```

Note A sample Chkdsk report from FAT12 is not shown because it is only supported on floppy disks and volumes less than 16 MB in size.

Chkdsk only runs on local floppy disks, hard disks, and removable, read/writable disks. It does not support CD-ROM and DVD-ROM disks.

If errors exist on the volume, Chkdsk alerts you by using a message and, if the **/f** switch was used, corrects the errors.

Correcting Problems by Using Chkdsk

Chkdsk cannot correct found errors when there are open files on the volume because Chkdsk cannot lock the volume. In this case, Chkdsk offers to check the volume automatically the next time the computer is started. This is typical behavior for the boot volume. When the boot volume is checked, the computer is automatically restarted after the volume check is completed.

Because some repairs, such as correcting lost clusters (also knows as allocation units) or cross-linked files, change a volume's file allocation table and can cause data loss, Chkdsk first prompts you with a confirmation message similar to the following:

```
10 lost allocation units found in 3 chains.
Convert lost chains to files?
```

If you press N, Windows 2000 fixes the errors on the volume but does not save the contents of the lost clusters. If you press Y, Windows 2000 attempts to identify the folder to which they belong. If the folder is identified, the lost cluster chains are saved there as files. If the folder cannot be identified or if the folder does not exist, it saves each chain of lost clusters in a folder called Found.*xxx*, where *xxx* is a sequential number starting with 000. If no folder Found.000 exists, one is created at the root. If one or more sequential folders called Found.*xxx* (starting at 000) exists, one using the next number in the sequence is created.

After the storage folder has been identified or created, one or more files with a name in the format File*nnnn*.chk (the first saved file is named File0000.chk, the second is named File0001.chk, and so on in sequence) are saved. When Chkdsk finishes, you can examine the contents of these files with a text editor to see whether they contain any needed data (if the converted chains came from corrupted binary files, they are of no value). You can delete the CHK files after you have saved any useful data.

Note Be careful to delete only files using the file name extension CHK from the Found.*xxx* folders. Other programs might create and use files with that extension.

If you do not use the **/f** switch, Chkdsk alerts you if it detects a file that needs to be fixed by indicating that it needs to be rerun with the **/f** switch to fix the errors.

If you use the **/f** switch on an extremely large volume (for example, 70 GB) or a volume with a very large number of files (in the millions), Chkdsk can take a long time (perhaps days) to complete. The volume is not available during this time, since Chkdsk does not relinquish control until it is done. If the system volume is being checked during the startup process, the computer is not be available until the Chkdsk process is complete.

Bad sectors reported by Chkdsk were marked when your volume was first prepared for operation. The fact that they are marked as bad means that the system prevents the disk from using them, so previously identified bad sectors pose no danger to your data.

Disk Defragmenter

Disk Defragmenter is a Windows-based tool that rearranges files, folders, programs, and unused space on your computer's hard disk. This is occasionally necessary because of the way files are stored on disk.

When files are edited and outgrow their original space on the disk, the file is broken into fragments, with latter fragments stored in open spots elsewhere on disk. In addition, when files are deleted on FAT16 and FAT32 volumes, only the entries in the file allocation table itself are deleted. The formerly occupied space is marked as open and can be used by other files. When other files use the empty space, if it is not large enough to accommodate the remaining data of the file, the file is again broken up with the remainder stored in another open space on disk. This process occurs with every new and edited file that is stored to disk.

While this process makes storage faster and more efficient when the file is saved, it takes much longer to read and write fragmented files than unfragmented files. Creating new files and folders also takes longer because the space available on the volume is scattered. Windows must then save new files and folders to various locations on the volume. When many files on disk become badly fragmented, performance notably suffers.

Running Disk Defragmenter

Disk Defragmenter remedies this problem by rewriting the files on disk back into contiguous segments. To start Disk Defragmenter, from the **Start** menu, point to **Programs**, **Accessories**, and **System Tools**, and then click **Disk Defragmenter**.

You can analyze the volume to see how many fragmented files and folders there are and then decide whether or not to defragment the volume.

The amount of time that the defragmentation process takes to run depends on several factors, including the size of the volume, the number of files on the volume, the amount of fragmentation, and the available local system resources.

Disk Defragmenter defragments volumes formatted with FAT16, FAT32, and NTFS.

Disk Defragmenter Results

The Disk Defragmenter tool display is split into two main areas, as shown in Figure 31.1. The upper portion lists the volumes on the local computer. The lower portion shows how fragmented the volume is. The colors indicate the condition of the volume:

- Red areas show fragmented files.
- Blue areas show contiguous (unfragmented) files.

- White areas show free space on the volume.

- Green areas show system files, which cannot be moved by Disk Defragmenter. These system files are not part of the Windows operating system but include files belonging to NTFS (when applicable) and the system paging file.

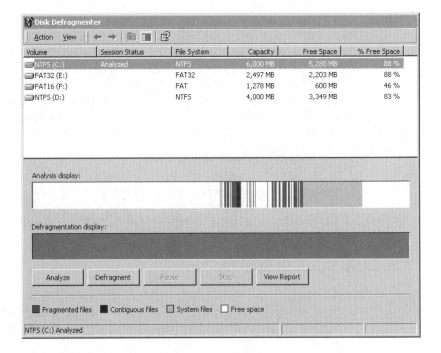

Figure 31.1   Disk Defragmenter

By comparing the **Analysis Display** band to the **Defragmentation Display** band, you can see the improvement in your volume after defragmenting. Always analyze volumes before defragmenting them. After the analysis is complete, a dialog box tells you if you need to defragment the volume.

You can defragment local file system volumes only, and you can only run one Disk Defragmenter console at a time. In addition, you must be logged on as an administrator or a member of the Administrators group. If your computer is connected to a network, network policy settings might also prevent you from completing this procedure.

AVBoot

InoculateIT Antivirus AVBoot version 1.1 is a command-line tool that scans the computer's memory and all locally-installed disk drives for MBR and boot sector viruses. If a virus is found, AVBoot can remove the virus. AVBoot is located in the \VALUEADD\3RDPARTY\CA_ANTIV folder of the Windows 2000 operating system CD.

▶ **To create an AVBoot startup disk**

1. Insert the Windows 2000 operating system CD into the CD-ROM drive.

2. Insert an empty, high-density 3.5–inch floppy disk into the floppy disk drive.

3. From the **Start** menu, click **Run**.

4. Browse the CD-ROM drive in the **Look in** list box, and navigate to the \VALUEADD\3RDPARTY\CA_ANTIV folder.

5. Double-click **Makedisk.bat**, and then click **OK**.

6. When the process is complete, remove the floppy disk, label it "AVBoot," and then store it in a safe location. Record the creation date in a log book.

Makedisk.bat is used to create a startup floppy disk that runs AVBoot.

To run AVBoot, insert the AVBoot startup floppy disk and restart the computer. AVBoot automatically starts when the computer has completed the startup process from the floppy disk.

Note On many computers, an option in the CMOS setup program allows the user to set the sequence of installed disks that the system searches for the startup files. If drive C is set to be searched before drive A, the AVBoot disk is not loaded.

When the AVBoot menu appears, press 1. It displays a report showing the version number and the date of the installed virus-scanning engine and the data or antivirus signature files. The next line displays the results of a virus scan in memory. Below that, a Boot Sector Summary report is displayed, showing the results of the scan on the installed floppy disk drives and all hard disks. If a second floppy disk drive or hard disk is not installed, the report states "Not Installed". Press any key to return to the AVBoot menu. Following is an example:

```
InoculateIT AntiVirus Avboot V1.1
Copyright 1997-99 Computer Associates International, Inc.
 and/or its subsidiaries. All Rights Reserved.
```

Table 31.8   Device and Driver Troubleshooting Tools

Tool	Overview	Location
System File Checker (Sfc.exe)	As part of Windows File Protection, scans protected system files and replaces files overwritten with correct versions provided by Microsoft.	%SystemRoot%\System32
Driver Verifier (Verifier.exe)	Runs a series of checks in the Windows 2000 kernel to help readily expose errors in kernel mode drivers.	%SystemRoot%\System32
Driver Signing (Sigverif.exe)	Verifies that device drivers have passed a series of rigorous tests administered by the Windows Hardware Quality Lab (WHQL).	%SystemRoot%\System32

System File Checker

System File Checker (SFC) is a command-line tool that scans protected system files and replaces files overwritten with the correct system files provided by Microsoft. It is part of the Windows File Protection feature of Windows 2000.

Windows File Protection

The Windows File Protection (WFP) feature protects your system files with two mechanisms. The first runs in the background: WFP is implemented when it is notified that a file in a protected folder is modified. After this notification is received, WFP determines which file was changed, and if it is protected, looks up the file signature in a catalog file to determine if the new file is the correct Microsoft version or if the file is digitally signed. If it is not, a replacement file is retrieved from either the %SystemRoot%\System32\Dllcache folder or the Windows 2000 operating system CD. By default, WFP displays the following message to an administrator and logs it to the System event log:

```
A file replacement was attempted on the protected system file <file
name>. To maintain system stability, the file has been restored to the
correct Microsoft version. If problems occur with your application,
please contact the application vendor for support.
```

The second WFP mechanism is SFC, which allows an administrator to scan all protected files to verify their versions. SFC also checks and repopulates the Dllcache folder. If the Dllcache folder becomes damaged or unusable, use SFC with the **/purgecache** switch to repair its contents. Most SYS, DLL, EXE, TTF, FON and OCX files on the Windows 2000 operating system CD are protected. However, for disk space considerations, maintaining cached versions of all of these files in the Dllcache folder is not always preferable on computers with limited available storage space.

SFC also checks all catalog files used to track correct file versions. If any catalog files are missing or damaged, WFP renames the affected catalog file and retrieves a cached version of that file from the Dllcache folder. If a cached copy of the catalog file is not available, WFP requests that you insert the Windows 2000 operating system CD to retrieve a new copy of the catalog file.

SFC Syntax

The command-line syntax for SFC is as follows:

```
sfc [/scannow] [/scanonce] [/scanboot] [/cancel] [/enable] [/purgecache]
    [/cache size=x] [/quiet]
```

SFC Switches

The SFC switches are listed in Table 31.9.

Table 31.9   SFC Switches

Switch	Description
/scannow	Scans all protected system files immediately.
/scanonce	Scans all protected system files at the next system start.
/scanboot	Scans all protected system files at every start.
/cancel	Cancels all pending scans of protected system files.
/enable	Enables WFP for normal operation.
/purgecache	Purges the file cache and scans all protected system files immediately.
/cachesize=*x*	Sets the file cache size, in megabytes.
/quiet	Replaces incorrect file versions without prompting the user.
/?	Displays this list.

Driver Verifier

Driver Verifier is a Windows-based tool that runs a series of checks in the Windows 2000 kernel to expose errors in kernel-mode drivers. It can gather statistics from the kernel, which are displayed by the GUI or logged in a file.

Driver Verifier can be run as a Windows 2000 application (called the "Driver Verifier Manager"), as a command-line tool, or as a debugger option in the system debugger WinDbg.

Driver Verifier Syntax

The command-line syntax for Driver Verifier is as follows:

```
verifier [/flags value [/iolevel level]] /all
verifier [/flags value [/iolevel level]] /driver name [name ...]
verifier /volatile /flags value
verifier /reset
verifier [/query]
verifier /log log_file_name [/interval seconds]
```

Driver Verifier Switches

The **Run** dialog box switches of **Driver Verifier** are listed in Table 31.10.

Table 31.10   Driver Verifier Command-Line Switches

Switch	Description
/all	Verifies all installed drivers.
/driver	Verifies the driver specified in the **name** argument.
/flags	Runs the checks specified in the **/value** argument.
/interval	Records log file entries in x second increments. The default interval is 30 seconds.
/iolevel	Specifies the level of I/O verification.
level	Specifies between a high-level scan and a full scan: 1 Only detects problems that will immediately cause the computer to fail. 2 A superset of level 1, it also detects problems that will cause failures from which the system can likely recover. This is the recommended setting.
/log	Creates a log file to hold memory, Interrupt Request Level (IRQL), and spin lock information.
/query	Causes the current data to be displayed on the screen. Data includes a count of memory allocations, IRQL raises, spin locks, and other data relevant to Driver Verifier options.
/reset	Erases all the current Driver Verifier settings.
/volatile	Used to change the Driver Verifier settings without restarting the system. Any new settings are lost when the system is restarted.
log_file_name	Name of the log file.
name	Name of the driver file. Multiple driver files can be listed in sequence, separated by spaces, but wildcards (* and ?) are not supported.

(continued)

Table 31.10   Driver Verifier Command-Line Switches *(continued)*

Switch	Description
seconds	Number of seconds in the interval.
value	A decimal combination of bits representing the available flags:
	0x01 Special pool checking
	0x02 Force IRQL checking
	0x04 Low resources simulation
	0x08 Pool tracking
	0x10 I/O checking
	Bits can be freely combined. The default is 3.
/?	Displays this list.

Running Driver Verifier with no command-line switches starts Driver Verifier Manager which uses a tabbed dialog box to separate the options it offers for testing device drivers, as shown in Figure 31.2.

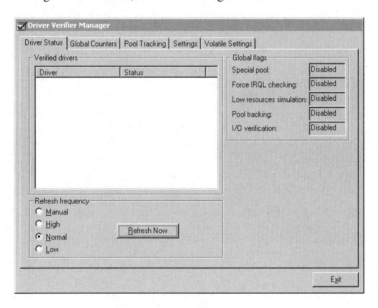

Figure 31.2   Driver Verifier Manager

Driver Verifier Manager

The following list shown in Table 31.11 contains a description of each tab in the **Driver Verifier Manager** dialog box:

Table 31.11   Driver Verifier Manager Dialog Box Tabs

Tab	Definition
Driver Status	Displays which drivers are loaded and being verified, and which Driver Verifier options are active.
Global Counters	Displays statistics that assist in monitoring Driver Verifier actions.
Pool Tracking	Displays information about paged and nonpaged pool allocations (both current amounts and peak amounts).
Settings	Lists the drivers that are loaded and can be verified, as well as **Verification type** options available for use.
Volatile Settings	Provides a list of verified drivers and a list of Verification type options used for each driver.

▶ **To set up a driver to be tested by Driver Verifier Manager**

1. Open Driver Verifier Manager.
2. Click the **Driver Status** tab, and then select the driver that you want to verify.

   Note   You can verify multiple drivers at the same time, but to simplify the process, it is strongly recommended that you verify one driver at a time.

3. Check the verification techniques that you want to enable in **Verification Type**. It is recommended that you enable all techniques for general testing.
4. Click **Apply** and **Exit,** and then restart the computer for the changes to take effect.
5. Reopen Driver Verifier Manager and make sure that the driver you want to test is shown in the **Driver Status** tab.
6. Start an application that uses the device driver that you want to test.

Run a series of tests that use the full capability of the device driver in question.

If the Windows 2000 kernel detects any driver errors during startup or during the user tests, it generates a Stop message and displays information useful to support personnel on the screen and the kernel debugger host (if one is connected).

If no errors are found, reset the Driver Verifier Manager so it does not continue to test the drivers.

▶   **To reset the Driver Verifier Manager**

1. Reopen Driver Verifier Manager.

2. In the **Additional Drivers** text box, enter the driver's full file name and file name extension (without its path; if multiple drivers were tested, separate file names by using spaces).

3. Clear all options in **Verification Type**.

4. Click **Apply** and **Exit,** and then restart the computer.

Driver Signing

Driver signing is a multifaceted process in which device drivers are verified through a series of tests administered by the Windows Hardware Quality Lab (WHQL). Drivers that earn this certification are more robust and cause fewer problems with Windows 2000. Microsoft digitally signs drivers that pass the WHQL tests so they are recognized natively by Windows 2000 Professional. Devices covered include:

- Keyboard
- Hard disk controller
- Multimedia device
- Video display
- Modem
- Mouse
- Network adapters
- Printer
- SCSI adapter
- Smart card reader

The system files provided with Windows 2000 have a Microsoft digital signature, which indicates that the files are original, unaltered system files and that they have been approved by Microsoft for use with Windows 2000.

Windows 2000 Professional can warn or prevent users from installing unsigned code. If a file has not been digitally signed and resides in one of the mentioned device driver classes, a message alerts the user, and asks if they want to continue.

All drivers included with Windows 2000 are digitally signed by Microsoft. You can verify that third-party drivers have met the WHQL standards and that they have not been modified since they were tested. To ensure that device drivers are compatible with Windows 2000, look for vendors offering drivers signed by Microsoft.

Checking for Digital Signatures

Windows 2000 includes the File Signature Verification tool and Signature Checking to identify files that have been signed.

The File Signature Verification tool determines whether a file is signed and allows you to do the following:

- View the certificates of signed files to ensure that the file has not been tampered with after being certified.
- Search for signed files in a specific location.
- Search for unsigned files in a specific location.

To run the File Signature Verification tool, from the **Start** menu, click **Run**, and then type:

sigverif

To customize the behavior of the File Signature Verification tool, in the **File Signature Verification** dialog box, click **Advanced**. The **Advanced File Signature Verification Settings** dialog box provides the following options:

- The **Search** tab allows you to search all drivers or specify the name and location of your driver search.
- The **Logging** tab saves the program's results as a log file, in which you can specify the file name, whether to overwrite or append to an existing file, and view the existing log.

The log file, Sigverif.txt, is stored in the %SystemRoot% folder by default, and records the following information about the files it scans:

- Name
- Modification date
- Version number
- Signed status
- Location

Signature Checking

Signature Checking can be enabled by system administrators to ensure that Windows 2000 inspects files for digital signatures whenever drivers are installed.

Signature Checking has three levels:

- Level 0 disables digital signature checking. The dialog box that identifies a digitally signed driver does not appear, and all drivers are installed whether they are signed or not.

- Level 1 determines whether the driver has passed WHQL testing. A message appears whenever a user tries to install a driver that fails the signature check.

- Level 2 blocks installation of a driver that fails the signature check. The user is notified that the driver cannot be installed because it is not digitally signed.

You can start the Signature Checking feature by using the **Hardware** tab of the **System Properties** dialog box.

Drivers

Drivers is a command-line tool that lists all of the drivers currently running on the computer from the %SystemRoot%\System32\Drivers folder. You can use this tool to identify a driver that might be causing problems due to corruption or because it is missing, not loaded, or outdated.

Drivers is part of the Resource Kit Tools collection on the *Windows 2000 Professional Resource Kit* companion CD. For more information about Drivers, see Rktools.chm in the folder C:\Program Files\Resource Kit.

Run Drivers from a command prompt, rather than from Windows Explorer, to see the resulting display. Drivers has no command-line switches.

Tip Run Drivers when the system is working properly and save the output to a file. You can use these results as a comparison later if the system has problems with missing or corrupted drivers. To save the drivers list to a file, redirect the screen output to a file with the following command-line syntax:

drivers > drivers_*M-D-Y*.txt

where *M* is the numerical month, *D* is the day, and *Y* is the year that the report was run. Keep this file in a safe location or print it and record the date on the page.

Table 31.12 describes the output from the Drivers tool. The most important field is **Module Name**, which is the name of the component.

Table 31.12   Column Names and Descriptions of the Drivers Tool Output

Column	Definition
ModuleName	The driver's file name.
Code	The nonpaged code in the image.
Data	The initialized static data in the image.
Bss	The uninitialized static data in the image. This is data that is initialized to 0.
Paged	The size of the data that is paged.
Init	Data not needed after initialization.
LinkDate	The date that the driver was linked.

The following is a sample portion of a Drivers output:

```
ModuleName    Code    Data    Bss   Paged     Init          LinkDate
-------------------------------------------------------------------------
ntoskrnl.exe  423680  61952    0   730432   136448   Sun Aug 22 14:47:30 1999
    hal.dll    33536   5536     0    31648    15488   Sat Aug 21 12:39:25 1999
BOOTVID.dll     6048   2464     0        0      448   Sat Aug 21 12:34:13 1999
    pci.sys    12128   1536     0    30816     4576   Fri Aug 20 15:36:35 1999
  isapnp.sys   14432    832     0    23200     2080   Wed Aug 18 18:29:07 1999
intelide.sys    1760     32     0        0      128   Sun Aug 22 14:17:56 1999
PCIIDEX.SYS     4512    480     0    10848     1632   Sun Aug 22 14:17:56 1999
MountMgr.sys    1088      0     0    22496     2176   Mon Aug 02 17:26:33 1999
  ftdisk.sys    4640     32     0    95776     3392   Sun Aug 22 14:18:00 1999
Diskperf.sys    1440     32     0     2016      992   Sun Aug 22 14:17:59 1999
 WMILIB.SYS      480      0     0     1152      192   Sat Jul 31 11:29:42 1999
  dmload.sys    2848     64     0        0      608   Fri Aug 20 14:29:47 1999
...
   ntdll.dll   282624  16384    0    16384        0   Sun Aug 22 14:57:40 1999
-------------------------------------------------------------------------
    Total    3831648  306848    0  2966016   403552
```

Applications Tools

Windows 2000 offers tools to gather information about and manage application issues. Some of the most useful tools, which are shown in Table 31.13, are detailed in this section.

Table 31.13   Applications Troubleshooting Tools

Tool	Overview	Location
System Information (Msinfo32.exe)	Collects and displays system configuration information about hardware, system components, and the software environment.	Program Files\Common Files\Microsoft Shared\Msinfo
DirectX Diagnostics (Dxdiag.exe)	Presents information about installed components and drivers of the Microsoft® DirectX® API; tests sound, graphics output, and DirectPlay service providers; and disables some hardware acceleration features.	%SystemRoot%\System32
Registry Editor (Regedt32.exe)	An advanced editing tool for adding and changing settings and creating subkeys in the registry.	%SystemRoot%\System32
Registry Editor (Regedit.exe)	An advanced editing tool for searching, adding, and changing settings and creating subkeys in the registry.	%SystemRoot%

System Information

System Information is a Windows-based tool that collects and displays configuration information to help diagnose and correct problems. This tool can quickly find the required data to resolve problems, about the following categories:

- **System Summary** displays basic information about the system, such as version number of the operating system, the NetBIOS computer name, the manufacturer and model number, the installation folder of Windows 2000, locale and time zone information, as well as information about the amount of installed physical memory and virtual memory.

- **Hardware Resources** displays hardware resource settings such as direct memory access (DMA), interrupt requests (IRQs), I/O addresses, and memory addresses.

- **Components** displays information about the Windows 2000 configuration and determines the status of peripheral devices, ports, and universal serial bus (USB) connections.

- **Software Environment** displays a snapshot of drivers, environment variables, tasks, and services loaded into computer memory. This information can be used to check whether a process is still running or to check version information.

- **Internet Explorer 5** displays a list of configuration settings related to Internet Explorer, including install location, cipher strength, build number, a list of associated files and version numbers, and settings for connectivity, file caching, and security zones.

- **Applications** displays a list of installed Microsoft applications that support System Information. Microsoft® Office 2000 applications are currently supported. Additional Microsoft applications might be included in the future.

The **Tools** menu in System Information also provides links to several tools used for troubleshooting, including the following:

- Disk Cleanup
- Dr. Watson for Windows 2000
- DirectX Diagnostic Tool
- Add/Remove Hardware wizard
- Network and Dial-up Connections
- Backup
- File Signature Verification Tool
- Update Wizard Uninstall
- Windows Report Tool

To use System Information, from the **Start** menu, click **Run**, and then type:

msinfo32

System Information categories are displayed in a tree structure, as shown in Figure 31.3.

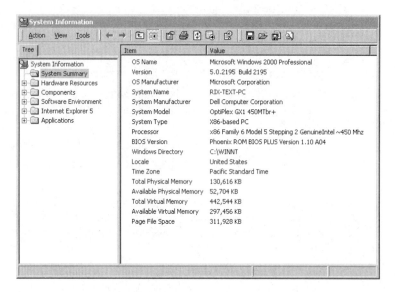

Figure 31.3   System Information

You can print or save System Information to a text file to send to support personnel. These files are stored in the My Documents folder by default.

Note A full System Information report printout can total more than 80 pages depending on the hardware and software installed.

System Summary

System Summary provides a general profile of the system, including the version of Windows, the installation folder, virtual memory, locale and local time zone, and system hardware, such as BIOS, CPU, memory, and other system resources. Use this information at the beginning of the troubleshooting process to develop a basic picture of the environment in which the problem occurs.

Hardware Resources

Hardware Resources, as shown in Table 31.14, displays hardware-specific settings, such as assigned or used IRQs, DMA channels, I/O addresses, and memory addresses.

Table 31.14   Hardware Resources

Section	Definition
Conflicts/Sharing	Identifies resource conflicts between multiple Industry Standard Architecture (ISA) devices or Peripheral Component Interconnect (PCI) devices. Use this information to identify hardware conflicts or troubleshoot a nonworking device.
DMA	Reports the DMA channels in use, the devices using them, and those free for use.
Forced Hardware	Lists hardware devices that have user-specified resources, as opposed to system-specified resources. This information is useful when troubleshooting Plug and Play resource conflicts.
I/O	Lists all I/O port ranges in use and the devices using each range.
IRQs	Summarizes IRQ usage, by identifying the devices using the IRQs and showing free IRQs.
Memory	Lists memory address ranges in use by devices.

Components

Components displays information about your Windows 2000 system configuration, as shown in Table 31.15. The Components view includes information about the status of peripheral devices, ports, and USB connections. There is also a summary of problem devices.

Table 31.15   Components

Section	Definition
Multimedia	Lists sound card information, audio and video codecs loaded, and the drive letter and model of the CD-ROM drive. With a data CD-ROM in the drive, System Information performs a data transfer test.
Display	Lists video card information and current video configuration.
Infrared	Lists infrared device information.
Input	Lists keyboard and pointer device information.
Modem	Lists modem information.
Network	Lists network adapter, protocol, and Winsock information.
Ports	Lists serial and parallel port information.
Storage	Lists information about hard disks, floppy disk drives, removable storage, and controllers.
Printing	Lists installed printers and printer drivers.
Problem Devices	Lists devices with problems. Each device flagged in Device Manager is displayed, with the corresponding status information.
USB	Lists USB controllers and drivers installed.

Software Environment

Software Environment, as shown in Table 31.16, displays the software loaded in computer memory.

Table 31.16   Software Environment

Section	Definition
Drivers	Lists all installed drivers, whether they are currently running, and their status.
Environment Variables	Lists all system environment variables and their values.
Jobs	Lists all open jobs, including print jobs.
Network Connections	Lists all mapped network connections.
Running Tasks	Lists all processes currently running on the system.
Loaded Modules	Lists loaded system-level DLLs and programs, along with their version numbers, size, and file date and path. Useful for debugging software problems, such as application faults.
Services	Lists all available system services, showing current run status and start mode.
Program Groups	Lists all existing program groups for all known users of the system.
Startup Programs	Lists programs started automatically either from the registry, the Startup program group, or the Win.ini file.
OLE Registration	Lists OLE file associations controlled by the registry.

Internet Explorer 5

Internet Explorer 5, as shown in Table 31.17, displays configuration information for Internet Explorer 5.

Table 31.17   Internet Explorer 5

Section	Definition
Summary	Lists a summary of Internet Explorer 5 information, such as the version and build numbers, installation path, cipher strength, and so on.
File Versions	Lists all files associated with Internet Explorer 5, as well as version numbers, file sizes, file dates, installation paths, and manufacturer.
Connectivity	Lists all the connectivity settings used by Internet Explorer 5.
Cache	Lists a general summary of cache settings and of cached objects.
Content	Identifies whether Content Advisor is enabled and lists all installed personal certificates, other people certificates, and their publishers.
Security	Lists the settings for Internet security zones.

Applications

Applications, as shown in Table 31.18, displays configuration information about the installed applications that are compatible with System Information.

Table 31.18   Applications

Section	Definition
Microsoft® Word 2000	Lists information about the active document, the number of fields used, installed file converters, available fonts, headers and footers, number of hyperlinks, mail merge information, number of sections and page numbering schemes used, page setup data, styles used, Word settings, and number of tables.
Microsoft® Excel 2000	Lists information about the active workbook, installed add-ins, and charts in the active workbook.
Microsoft® PowerPoint® 2000	Lists information about the active presentation.
Microsoft® Outlook® 2000	Lists summary information about Outlook 2000.
Microsoft® Access 2000	Lists summary information about Access 2000.
Microsoft® Publisher 2000	Lists summary information about Publisher 2000.
Microsoft® FrontPage® 2000	Lists information about the active Web project, the active Web page, installed Component Object Model (COM) add-ins, and installed themes.
Microsoft® Office Environment	Lists information about the last Web connection error, installed local Web server extensions, installed data transport technologies, installed open database connectivity (ODBC) drivers, and OLE DB providers.

Note   The Applications module is installed into System Information whenever any version of Office 2000 is installed. By default, this module lists all of the applications included in the Microsoft® Office 2000 Premium Edition, regardless of whether any particular application listed is installed.

Other than the Summary pages, the data fields for the configuration information of the individual applications in Office 2000 are not populated unless the particular application is running at the time that System Information is active.

DirectX Diagnostic Tool

The DirectX Diagnostic Tool (DXDiag) is a Windows-based DirectX tool that presents information about the components and drivers of the DirectX application programming interface (API) installed on your system. Administrators or users can test sound and graphics output and DirectPlay service providers, and disable some hardware acceleration features. You can use DXDiag to gather information during a support call or to send an e-mail message.

To start DXDiag, from the **Start** menu, click **Run**, and then type:

dxdiag

Note Some information displayed in DXDiag, such as the amount of memory on a display card, might be approximate.

DXDiag uses a tabbed dialog box format to separate the sections of reports, as shown in Figure 31.4.

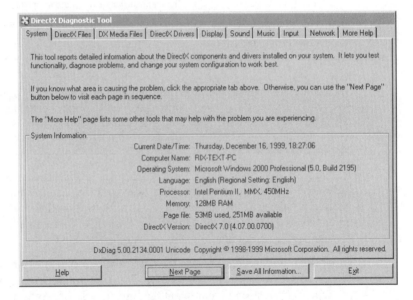

Figure 31.4   DXDiag Dialog Box

Table 31.19, describes each tab in the **DirectX Diagnostic Tool** dialog box.

Note If a DirectX problem is detected on a particular tab, a warning message is displayed in the Notes box.

Table 31.19   DXDiag Dialog Box Tabs

Tab	Definition
System	Provides system information about your computer and specifies the version of DirectX installed on your computer.
DirectX Files	Lists the file name, version number, date, and size for each DirectX file installed on your computer.
DX Media Files	Lists the file name, version number, date, and size for each DirectX media file installed on your computer.
DirectX Drivers	Lists the file name, version number, date, and size for each DirectX driver file installed on your computer.
Display	Lists your current display settings, and allows you to disable hardware acceleration and test DirectDraw® and Direct3D®.
Sound	Displays current sound settings, and allows you to test DirectSound.
Music	Lists installed music ports, displays current Musical Instrument Digital Interface (MIDI) settings, and allows you to test the DirectMusic component of DirectX.
Input	Lists the input devices and drivers installed on your computer.
Network	Lists the registered DirectPlay service providers and the registered lobbyable DirectPlay applications installed on your computer and allows you to test the DirectPlay component of DirectX.
More Help	If you cannot resolve your DirectX by issue using the previous tabs, you can use the **More Help** tab to continue troubleshooting the issue. Click **MSInfo** to start System Information. For more information about using System Information, see "System Information" earlier in this chapter. Click **Override** to change the DirectDraw refresh rate. This is not recommended as a general troubleshooting step.

What to Look For

If you are experiencing problems when running DirectX applications, DXDiag can help you find the source of the trouble. The following are issues to look for:

Incorrect versions of DirectX components. In the Notes section of the DirectX Files page, look for warnings about beta and debug files.

Uncertified drivers. In the file list on the DirectX Drivers page, look for drivers that are marked as uncertified. Other problems might be shown in the Notes section of the Display, Sound, and Input pages. Uncertified drivers have not been tested by Microsoft for full compatibility with the latest version of DirectX.

Lack of hardware acceleration. Some programs run slowly or not at all unless DirectDraw or Direct3D hardware acceleration is available. On the Display page, under DirectX Features, check whether DirectDraw, Direct3D, or AGP Support is marked "Not available." If so, consider upgrading your hardware.

Device not connected. If a joystick or other input device fails to respond, it might not be properly set up. Make sure the device is accounted for on the Input page of DXDiag. If not, add the device by using the Game Controllers icon in Control Panel.

Testing DirectX Components

You can test DirectDraw and Direct3D on each monitor attached to your system, DirectSound on each WAV output device, and DirectMusic on each music port.

Click **Test**, read any messages that appear, and watch or listen to the tests. Let each test run until you see a message asking whether the test was successful. If you respond **No**, no more tests are run.

There is a single test for DirectMusic. Click **OK** when you are satisfied that the music is or is not playing correctly.

You can also test DirectPlay functionality on any available service provider.

▶   **To test DirectPlay on two connected computers**

1. On Computer A on the Network page, click **Test DirectPlay**. In the **DirectPlay Test** dialog box, type a user name and choose a service provider. Select **Create New Session**, and then click **OK**. If you have chosen a modem connection, in the **Modem Connection** dialog box click **Answer** to put the modem in autoanswer mode.

2. Run DXDiag on Computer B to establish the selected connection with Computer A. Click **Test DirectPlay**, type in a different user name, choose the same service provider, select **Join Existing Session**, and then click **OK**. For some types of connections, you might be asked to provide more information, such as a telephone number. For a TCP/IP connection on a local network, you can leave the text box blank.

3. A session list is displayed on Computer B, containing the name of the session that you created on Computer A. Select the name of the session, and then click **OK**.

Both computers display a chat dialog box. Type a message in the input box on one computer, and then click **Send**. The message appears in the scrolling area of the chat dialog box on both computers.

Overriding Default Settings

On the Sound page, you can set a different level of hardware acceleration by moving the slider. This level remains in effect after you have closed DXDiag.

On the Display page for each installed display device, you can disable hardware acceleration for DirectDraw or Direct3D and AGP Support (if such options are available) by clicking **Disable**. These features remain disabled after you close DXDiag, and are not available to any applications. To re-enable a disabled feature, click **Enable**.

Note   Disabling DirectDraw acceleration also disables acceleration for Direct3D.

You can also override the monitor refresh rate set by DirectDraw full-screen applications. Do this only if you are experiencing display problems with certain applications and have good reason to believe that the application is setting an invalid refresh rate.

▶ **To set an override refresh rate**

1. On the More Help page, click **Override**.

2. In the **Override DirectDraw Refresh Behavior** dialog box, select the **Override Value** text box and type a valid refresh rate for your monitor. The **Override Value** option is automatically selected.

▶ **To cancel the override refresh rate**

1. On the More Help page, click **Override**.

2. In the **Override DirectDraw Refresh Behavior** dialog box, select **Default**.

Restoring Drivers

On some configurations, DXDiag allows you to restore older audio and video drivers. This can be the best way of solving problems with incompatible drivers.

If a **Restore** button appears on the More Help page, click it to run the DirectX Setup program.

DirectX Setup has two buttons labeled **Restore Audio Drivers** and **Restore Display Drivers**. Clicking either of these buttons restores drivers that were replaced when DirectX was installed on your system. If a button is disabled, you do not have older drivers to which to revert. Contact the hardware manufacturer for the newest drivers.

Saving Information

To save information gathered by DXDiag, click **Save All Information**.
Information from all the pages is saved in a file under a name and in a location
you choose.

Registry Editors

Windows 2000 contains two registry editors (Regedit and Regedt32) that you can
use to change settings in your system registry, which stores information about
how the hardware and software on your computer runs. Windows 2000 stores its
configuration information in a set of database files, organized into subtrees, keys,
and subkeys, and displayed in a tree format by the registry editors. Although the
registry editors enable you to inspect and modify the registry, normally you do not
need to do so, and making incorrect changes can damage your system. An
advanced user who is prepared to edit and restore the registry can use a registry
editor for tasks such as eliminating duplicate entries, deleting entries for programs
that have been uninstalled or deleted, verifying options and settings, or
configuring options that are not accessible through the normal user interface.

If there is an error in your registry and your computer ceases to function properly,
you can restore the registry to its state when you last successfully started your
computer by starting the computer using the **Last Known Good Configuration**.
For more information on the Last Known Good Configuration option, see "Safe
Mode" earlier in this chapter.

Warning Do not use a registry editor to edit the registry directly unless you have
no alternative. The registry editors bypass the standard safeguards provided by
administrative tools. These safeguards prevent you from entering conflicting
settings or settings that are likely to degrade performance or damage your system.
Editing the registry directly can have serious, unexpected consequences that can
prevent the system from starting and require that you reinstall Windows 2000. To
configure or customize Windows 2000, use the programs in Control Panel or
Microsoft Management Console (MMC) whenever possible.

Before the registry is changed, it is highly recommended that you backup the
registry files. For more information about backing up the registry, see
"Emergency Repair Process" earlier in this chapter.

The five subtrees, through which all registry keys, subkeys, and assigned values
are accessed, are defined in Table 31.20.

Table 31.20   Predefined Registry Subtrees

Key	Definition
HKEY_CURRENT_USER	Contains the root of the configuration information for the user who is currently logged on. The user's folders, screen colors, and Control Panel settings are stored here. This information is referred to as a user's profile.
HKEY_USERS	Contains the root of all user profiles on the computer. HKEY_CURRENT_USER is an alias for a subkey in the HKEY_USERS subtree.
HKEY_LOCAL_MACHINE	Contains configuration information particular to the computer (for any user).
HKEY_CLASSES_ROOT	A subkey of HKEY_LOCAL_MACHINE\Software. The information stored here ensures that the correct program opens when you open a file by using Windows Explorer.
HKEY_CURRENT_CONFIG	Contains information about the hardware profile used by the local computer at system startup.

Differences Between the Registry Editors

The registry editors included with Windows 2000 include Regedt32 and Regedit. Each registry editor has advantages and disadvantages. You can perform most tasks with either registry editor, but certain tasks are easier with one registry editor.

The following are advantages of Regedt32:

- Using the **Security** menu, you can check for and apply access permissions to subtrees, keys, and individual subkeys.

- Each subtree is displayed in its own dedicated window, reducing clutter.

- You can set an option to work in read-only mode.

- You can edit values longer than 256 characters.

- You can easily edit REG_MULTI_SZ entry values.

- You can load multiple registry files at the same time.

> **Note** From the **Registry** menu, select **Load hive** and open any registry file on disk. You can have more than one registry file open at one time. This feature is particularly useful when a computer with multiple installations of Windows 2000 cannot start from one of the installations due to a registry problem. If the cause of the problem is known, the user can start the computer from the secondary installation. Using Regedt32, the registry files from the primary installation can be loaded, edited, and saved, resolving the problem with the primary installation.

Figure 31.5 shows the Regedt32 interface.

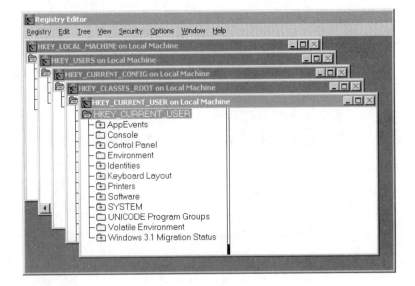

Figure 31.5   Regedt32

The following are advantages of Regedit:

- Regedit has more powerful search capabilities.
- All the keys are visible in one Windows Explorer–like window.
- You can bookmark favorite subkeys for fast access later on.
- Regedit reopens to the subtree that was last edited.
- You can export the registry to a text file.
- You can import a registry file from the command line.

> **Note** To import a registry file from the command line, type
>
> **regedit /s** *regfile*
>
> where *regfile* is the full path and file name of the registry file to be imported.

Figure 31.6 shows the Regedit interface.

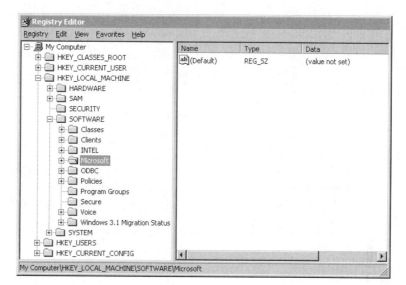

Figure 31.6   Regedit

Important   Regedit cannot display registry values larger then 256 characters. Values that contain a larger number of characters are ignored and not shown. These values can only be edited by Regedt32.

Using the Registry Editors

Folders represent subtrees, keys, and subkeys and are shown in the navigation pane. In the topic pane, the registry entries in a subkey are displayed. When you double-click a registry entry, it opens an editing dialog box.

Within the registry editors, you can assign entries to new subkeys or alter the entries assigned to a currently selected subkey. Entries appear in the registry as strings that consist of three components separated by colons. For example, in the following registry entry:

```
RefCount : REG_DWORD : 0x1
```

RefCount is the entry name, REG_WORD is the data type, and 0x1 is the value of the entry.

For more information about using the registry editors for tasks such as saving a subtree, key, or subkey as a file, printing, importing, and exporting registry data, see Windows 2000 Professional Help and the Technical Reference to the Windows 2000 Registry (Regentry.chm) on the *Windows 2000 Resource Kit* companion CD.

Regedt32 provides the following ways to update registry display:

- **Auto Refresh** (on the **Options** menu) automatically updates the registry when any change is made to registry data.
- **Refresh All** (on the **View** menu) updates all of the information in all windows.
- **Refresh Active** (on the **View** menu) updates only the information in the active window.

Note When **Auto Refresh** is in effect, a check mark appears next to the command and **Refresh All** and **Refresh Active** are unavailable.

You cannot use **Auto Refresh** while viewing a remote registry. If you click **Auto Refresh** while displaying a remote registry, the manual refresh options (**Refresh All** and **Refresh Active**) are not available. Although **Auto Refresh** appears to work, the contents of the remote registry window are not automatically refreshed.

Networking Tools

Windows 2000 provides a large collection of networking client tools to optimize and troubleshoot network performance. Several of the most useful tools, shown in Table 31.21, are discussed in this section.

Table 31.21   Networking Troubleshooting Tools

Tool	Overview	Location
Network Diagnostics (Netdiag.exe)	Helps isolate networking and connectivity problems by performing a series of tests to determine the state of your network client and whether it is functional.	Support Tools on the Windows 2000 operating system CD
IP Configuration (Ipconfig.exe)	Displays the current configuration of the installed IP stack on a networked computer using TCP/IP.	%SystemRoot%\System32
NetBT Statistics (Nbtstat.exe)	Displays protocol statistics and current TCP/IP connections using NetBIOS over TCP/IP (NetBT), including NetBIOS name resolution to IP addresses.	%SystemRoot%\System32
Path Ping (Pathping.exe)	A route tracing tool that sends packets to each router, and then computes results based on the packets returned from each hop.	%SystemRoot%\System32
IP Security Monitor (Ipsecmon.exe)	Confirms whether your secured communications are successful by displaying the active security associations on local or remote computers.	%SystemRoot%\System32

NetDiag

NetDiag is a command-line, diagnostic tool that helps isolate networking and connectivity problems by performing a series of tests to determine the state of your network client and whether it is functional. These tests and the network status information they expose help network administrators and support personnel identify and isolate network problems. Moreover, because this tool does not require parameters or switches, you can focus on analyzing the output, rather than training users on tool usage.

NetDiag diagnoses network problems by checking all aspects of a client computer's network configuration and connections. Beyond troubleshooting TCP/IP issues, it also examines a client computer's Internet Packet Exchange (IPX) and NetWare configurations.

NetDiag is part of the Support Tools collection on the Windows 2000 operating system CD. For information about NetDiag, see Windows 2000 Support Tools Help. For information about installing and using the Windows 2000 Support Tools and Support Tools Help, see the file Sreadme.doc in the Support\Tools folder of the Windows 2000 operating system CD.

Run NetDiag from a command prompt rather than from Windows Explorer to see the results upon completion of the tests. Because the results fill more than one normal command prompt screen, use the **/l** switch to log the results to the text file NetDiag.log. The tests take a few minutes to complete.

NetDiag Syntax

The command-line syntax for NetDiag is as follows:

```
netdiag [[/q|/v|/debug][/l][/d:DomainName][/fix][/dcaccountenum]
        [/test:TestName|/skip:TestName]]
```

No switches or syntax need to be specified, but several are available, primarily to increase or decrease the level of detail in NetDiag reports. These switches are shown in the Table 31.22.

Table 31.22   NetDiag Switches

Switch	Name	Function
/q	Quiet output	Lists only tests that return errors.
/v	Verbose output	Lists more detail from test data as tests are performed.
/debug	Most verbose output	Lists the most detail from of test data with reasons for success or failure.

(continued)

Table 31.22   NetDiag Switches *(continued)*

Switch	Name	Function
/l	Log output	Stores output in NetDiag.log, in the current folder.
/d:*DomainName*	Find DC	Finds a domain controller in the specified domain.
/fix	Fix DNS problems	Only applies to domain controllers.
/DCAccountEnum	Domain Controller Account Enumeration	Enumerates domain controller computer accounts.
/test:	Perform single test	Runs only the specified test.
/skip:	Skip one test	Skips the specified test.
TestName	Test name	Test specified. For a complete list, see Table 31.23.
/?	Help	Displays this list.

NetDiag prints the string [FATAL] when it detects a condition that needs to be fixed immediately. The string [WARNING] signals a failure condition that does not require immediate attention.

NetDiag Tests

Run NetDiag whenever a computer is having network problems. The tool tries to diagnose the problem and can even flag problem areas for closer inspection.

NetDiag examines DLL files, output from other tools, and the system registry to find potential problem spots. It checks which network services or functions are enabled and then runs the network configuration tests listed in Table 31.23, in the order presented.

Note If the computer is not running one of the network troubleshooting tools listed in Table 31.23, that test is skipped and no results are displayed, not even an acknowledgement that the test was skipped.

Table 31.23   NetDiag Tests

Test Name	Function	Details
NDIS	Network Adapter Status	Lists the network adapter configuration details, including the adapter name, configuration, media, globally unique identifier (GUID), and statistics. If this test shows an unresponsive network adapter, the remaining tests are aborted.
IPConfig	IP Configuration	Provides most of the TCP/IP information normally obtained from carrying out the **ipconfig /all** command, pings the DHCP and WINS servers, and checks that the default gateway is on the same subnet as the local computer's IP address.
Member	Domain Membership	Confirms details of the primary domain, including computer role, domain name, domain GUID. Checks that NetLogon service is started, adds the primary domain to the domain list, and queries the primary domain security identifier (SID).
NetBTTransports	Transports Test	Lists NetBT transports managed by the redirector. Prints error information if no NetBT transports are found.
Autonet	Autonet Address	Checks whether any interface is using Automatic Private IP Addressing (APIPA).
IPLoopBk	IP Loopback Ping	Pings the IP loopback address of 127.0.0.1.
DefGw	Default Gateway	Pings all the default gateways for each interface.
NbtNm	NetBT Name Test	Similar to the **nbtstat -n** command. It checks that the workstation service name <00> equals the computer name. It also checks that the messenger service name <03>, and server service name <20> are present on all interfaces and are not in conflict.
WINS	WINS Service Test	Sends NetBT name queries to all the configured WINS servers.
Winsock	Winsock Test	Uses Windows Sockets WSAEnumProtocols() function to retrieve available transport protocols.
DNS	DNS Test	Checks whether DNS cache service is running, and whether the computer is correctly registered on the configured DNS servers. If the computer is a domain controller, DNS Test checks to see whether all the DNS entries in Netlogon.dns are registered on the DNS server. If the entries are incorrect and the **/fix** option is on, it tries to reregister the domain controller record on a DNS server.

(continued)

Table 31.23   NetDiag Tests *(continued)*

Test Name	Function	Details
Browser	Redirector and Browser Test	Checks whether the workstation service is running. Retrieves the transport lists from the redirector and the browser. Checks whether the NetBT transports are in the list from NetBT transports test. Checks whether the browser is bound to all the NetBT transports and whether the computer can send mailslot messages. Tests both via browser and redirector.
DsGetDc	DC Discovery Test	Finds a generic domain controller from directory service, finds the primary domain controller, and then finds a Windows 2000 domain controller. If the tested domain is the primary domain, checks whether the domain GUID stored in Local Security Authority (LSA) is the same as the domain GUID stored in the domain controller. If not, the test returns a fatal error; if the **/fix** option is used, DsGetDC tries to fix the GUID in LSA.
DcList	DC List Test	Gets a list of domain controllers in the domain from the directory service on an active domain controller. If there is no domain controller information for this domain, tries to get an active domain controller from the directory service (similar to DsGetDc test). Gets the domain controller list from the target domain controller and checks the status of each domain controller. Adds them all the to the list of the tested domain. If the preceding sequence fails, uses the browser to obtain the domain controllers, checks their status, and adds them to the list. If the **DcAccountEnum** registry entry option is enabled, NetDiag tries to get a domain controller list from Security Accounts Manager (SAM) on the discovered domain controller.
Trust	Trust Relationship Test	Tests trust relationships to the primary domain only if the computer is a member workstation, member server, or domain controller. Checks that the primary domain SID is correct and contacts an active domain controller. Connects to the SAM server on the domain controller and uses the domain SID to open the domain to verify that the domain SID is correct. Queries information of the secure channel for the primary domain. If the computer is a backup domain controller, reconnects to the primary domain controller. If the computer is a member workstation or server, sets a secure channel to each domain controller listed for this domain.

(continued)

Table 31.23   NetDiag Tests *(continued)*

Test Name	Function	Details
Kerberos	Kerberos Test	Tests Kerberos protocols only if the computer is a member computer or domain controller and the user is not logged on to a Windows 2000 domain account and not logged on to a local account. Connects to LSA and looks up the Kerberos package. Gets the ticket cache of the Kerberos package and checks whether the Kerberos package has a ticket for the primary domain and the local computer.
LDAP	Lightweight Directory Access Protocol (LDAP) Test	Run only if the domain controller is running directory services and the computer is a member or domain controller. Tests LDAP on all the active domain controllers found in the domain and creates an LDAP connection block to the domain controller, then searches in the LDAP directory with three types of authentication: "unauthenticated," NTLM, and "Negotiate." If the /v (verbose) switch is on, prints the details of each entry retrieved.
Route	Route test	Prints the static and persistent entries in the routing table, including a Destination Address, Subnet Mask, Gateway Address, Interface, and Metric.
NetStat	NetStat test	Similar to NetStat tool. Displays statistics of protocols and current TCP/IP network connections.
Bindings	Bindings test	Lists all bindings, including interface name, lower module name, upper module name, whether the binding is currently enabled, and the owner of the binding.
WAN	WAN test	Displays the settings and status of current active remote access connections.
Modem	Modem test	Retrieves all available line devices. Displays the configuration of each line device.
NetWare	NetWare test	Determines whether NetWare is using the directory tree or bindery logon process, determines the default context if NetWare is using the directory tree logon process, and finds the server to which the host attaches itself at startup.
IPX	IPX test	Examines the network's IPX configuration, including frame type, Network ID, RouterMTU, and whether packet burst or source routing are enabled.
IPSec	IP Security test	Checks the current status of the IP Security Policy Agent service. It also reports which IPSec policy (if any) is currently active for the computer.

IPConfig

IPConfig is a command-line tool that displays the current configuration of the installed IP stack on a networked computer using TCP/IP.

Run IPConfig from a command prompt rather than from Windows Explorer to see the resulting display.

IPConfig Syntax

The command-line syntax for IPConfig is as follows:

```
ipconfig [/?|/all|/release [adapter]|/renew [adapter]
         |/flushdns|/registerdns|/showclassid adapter
         |/setclassid adapter [classidtoset]]

adapter    Full name or pattern with '*' and '?' to 'match', * matches
           any character, ? matches one character.

The default is to display only the IP address, subnet mask and default
gateway for each adapter bound to TCP/IP.

For /release and /renew, if no adapter name is specified, then the IP
address leases for all adapters bound to TCP/IP will be released or
renewed.

For SetClassID, if no class ID is specified, then the ClassID is
removed.
```

IPConfig Switches

Table 31.24 lists the IPConfig command-line switches.

Table 31.24   IPConfig Switches

Switch	Effect
/all	Produces a detailed configuration report for all interfaces.
/release *<adapter>*	Releases the IP address for a specified adapter. If no adapter name is specified, releases the DHCP leases for all adapters bound to TCP/IP.
/renew *<adapter>*	Renews the IP address for the specified adapter. If no adapter name is specified, renews the DHCP leases for all adapters bound to TCP/IP.
/flushdns	Removes all entries from the DNS Resolver Cache.
/registerdns	Refreshes all DHCP leases and reregisters DNS names.
/displaydns	Displays the contents of the DNS Resolver Cache.

(continued)

Table 31.24   IPConfig Switches *(continued)*

Switch	Effect
/showclassid *adapter*	Displays all the DHCP class IDs allowed for the specified adapter.
/setclassid *adapter*	Modifies the DHCP class ID for the specified adapter.
/?	Displays this list.

Caution It is recommended that only a network administrator or support personnel use many of the advanced features of IPConfig. Using these commands incorrectly can cause problems with the client system's connection to the server.

Run IPConfig to check the status of a computer's TCP/IP configuration. When used with the **/all** switch, it displays a detailed configuration report for all interfaces, including any configured WAN miniports (typically used for remote access or virtual private network [VPN] connections). The following is a sample report:

```
Windows 2000 IP Configuration

        Host Name . . . . . . . . . . . . : TESTPC1
        Primary Domain Name . . . . . . . : reskit.com
        Node Type . . . . . . . . . . . . : Hybrid
        IP Routing Enabled. . . . . . . . : No
        WINS Proxy Enabled. . . . . . . . : No
        DNS Suffix Search List. . . . . . : ntcorpdc1.reskit.com
                                            dns.reskit.com
                                            reskit.com

Ethernet adapter Local Area Connection:

        Connection-specific DNS Suffix  . : dns.reskit.com
        Description . . . . . . . . . . . : Acme XL 10/100Mb Ethernet NIC
        Physical Address. . . . . . . . . : 00-CC-44-79-C3-AA
        DHCP Enabled. . . . . . . . . . . : Yes
        Autoconfiguration Enabled . . . . : Yes
        IP Address. . . . . . . . . . . . : 172.16.245.111
        Subnet Mask . . . . . . . . . . . : 255.255.248.0
        Default Gateway . . . . . . . . . : 172.16.240.1
        DHCP Server . . . . . . . . . . . : 172.16.248.8
        DNS Servers . . . . . . . . . . . : 172.16.55.85
                                            172.16.55.134
                                            172.16.55.54
        Primary WINS Server . . . . . . . : 172.16.248.10
        Secondary WINS Server . . . . . . : 172.16.248.9
        Lease Obtained. . . . . . . . . . : Friday, March 05, 1999 2:21:40 PM
        Lease Expires . . . . . . . . . . : Sunday, March 07, 1999 2:21:40 PM
```

NBTStat

NBTStat is a command-line tool for troubleshooting NetBIOS name over TCP/IP (NetBT) resolution problems. It displays protocol statistics and current TCP/IP connections using NetBT.

When a network is functioning normally, NetBT resolves NetBIOS names to IP addresses. It uses several options for NetBIOS name resolution, including local cache lookup, WINS server query, broadcast, Lmhosts lookup, Hosts lookup, and DNS server query.

Run NBTStat from a command prompt rather than from Windows Explorer to see the resulting display.

NBTStat Syntax

The command-line syntax for NBTStat is as follows:

```
nbtstat [-a RemoteName] [-A IP address] [-c] [-n]
        [-r] [-R] [-RR] [-s] [-S] [interval]
```

RemoteName   Remote host machine NetBIOS name.
IP address   Dotted decimal representation of the IP address.
interval   Redisplays selected statistics, pausing interval seconds
             between each display. Press Ctrl+C to stop redisplaying
             statistics.

NBTStat Switches

NBTStat removes and corrects preloaded entries using case-sensitive switches as shown in Table 31.25.

Table 31.25   NBTStat Switches

Switch	Name	Function
-a *<NetBIOS name>*	Adapter status by NetBIOS name	Returns the NetBIOS name table and media access control (MAC) address of the address card for the specified computer name.
-A *<IP address>*	Adapter status by IP address	Lists the same information as **-a** when given the target's IP address.
-c	Cache	Lists the contents of the NetBIOS name cache.
-n	Names	Displays the names registered locally by NetBIOS applications such as the server and redirector.
-r	Resolved	Displays a count of all names resolved by broadcast or WINS server.
-R	Reload	Purges the name cache and reloads all #PRE entries from LMHosts.

(continued)

Table 31.25   NBTStat Switches *(continued)*

Switch	Name	Function
-RR	Release Refresh	Sends name release packets to the WINS server and starts a refresh, reregistering all names with the name server.
-s	Sessions by NetBIOS names	Lists the NetBIOS sessions table converting destination IP addresses to computer NetBIOS names.
-S	Sessions by IP address	Lists the current NetBIOS sessions and their status, with the IP addresses.
[*Number*]	Interval	Redisplays selected statistics at intervals specified in seconds, pausing between each display. Press CTRL+C to stop redisplaying statistics.
-?	Help	Displays this list.

NBTStat output is in the form of a table. For example, **nbtstat -S** lists the current NetBIOS sessions by IP address, including status, as in the following example:

```
Local Area Connection:
Node IpAddress: [172.16.0.142]  Scope Id: []

          NetBIOS Connection Table

    Local Name     State      In/Out   Remote Host     Input   Output
    ------------------------------------------------------------------

    TESTPC1  <00>  Connected  Out      172.16.210.25    6MB     5MB
    TESTPC1  <00>  Connected  Out      172.16.3.1      108KB   116KB
    TESTPC1  <00>  Connected  Out      172.16.3.20     299KB    19KB
    TESTPC1  <00>  Connected  Out      172.16.3.4      324KB    19KB
    TESTPC1  <03>  Listening
```

The following example shows a sample NetBIOS name table for a client running Windows 2000 Professional on a Windows 2000 Server–based network, using the **nbtstat -n** command. This example shows the sixteenth byte for special names, plus the type of NetBIOS name (unique or group).

```
Local Area Connection:
Node IpAddress: [192.168.17.41] Scope Id: []

          NetBIOS Local Name Table

        Name            Type      Status
    ---------------------------------------------

        WIN2KPROF  <00>  UNIQUE    Registered
        NOAM       <00>  GROUP     Registered
        WIN2KPROF  <03>  UNIQUE    Registered
        WIN2KPROF  <20>  UNIQUE    Registered
        NOAM       <1E>  GROUP     Registered
        USER1      <03>  UNIQUE    Registered
```

In this example, the following NetBIOS special names are identified:

- *computer*\0x00 (shown as <00> in the example) indicates the computer name associated with the Workstation service.

- *domain*\0x00 indicates the domain to which this computer belongs.

- *computer*\0x03 indicates the computer name associated with the Messenger service.

- *computer*\0x20 indicates the computer name associated with the Server service.

- *domain*\0x1E indicates that this computer can serve as a backup browser in this domain.

- *username*\0x03 displays the user name of the account currently logged on to the computer.

Possible NetBIOS special names found in NBTStat are described in Table 31.26.

Table 31.26   Samples of NetBIOS Special Names

Special Name	Description
Registered unique user name:	
<USERNAME><03>	Registers the name of the user currently logged on in the WINS database so **net send** commands can be sent to specified user names.
Registered unique computer names:	
<COMPUTER><00>	Used by Microsoft networking workstations to receive second-class mailslot requests. This is the computer name registered for workstation services by a WINS client and is needed to receive mailslot requests.
<COMPUTER><03>	The computer name registered for the Messenger service on a WINS client.
<COMPUTER><20>	The name registered for the Server service on a Windows 2000–based WINS client.
<COMPUTER><BE>	The unique name registered when the Network Monitor agent is started on the computer.
<COMPUTER><BF>	The group name registered when the Network Monitor agent is started on the computer. If this name is not 15 characters in length, it is padded with plus (+) symbols.
<COMPUTER><1F>	The unique name registered for network dynamic data exchange (NetDDE) when the NetDDE service is started on the computer.

(continued)

Table 31.26 Samples of NetBIOS Special Names *(continued)*

Special Name	Description
Registered group names:	
<01><02>MSBROWSE<02><01>	Used by master browser servers to periodically announce their domain on a local subnet. This announcement contains the domain name and the name of the master browser server for the domain. In addition, master browser servers receive the domain announcements sent to this name and maintain them in their internal browse list with the announcer's computer name.
<DOMAIN><00>	Used by workstations and servers to process server announcements to support NTLM. Servers running Microsoft® Windows® for Workgroups, Windows 95, Windows 98, Windows NT, and Windows 2000 do not broadcast this name unless the **LMAnnounce** option is enabled in the server's properties.
<DOMAIN><1B>	Used to identify the domain master browser name, which is a unique name that only the domain controller can add. The domain controller processes GetBrowserServerList requests on this name. WINS assumes that the computer that registers a domain name with the <1B> character is the domain controller. The **1B** entry is resolved when the **NetGetDcName** function is called.
<DOMAIN><1C>	Used for the internet group name, which the domain controllers register. The internet group name is a dynamic list of up to 25 computers that have registered the name. This is the name used to find a Windows 2000 domain controller for pass-through authentication. The **1C** entry is resolved when the **NetGetAnyDcName** function is called.
<DOMAIN><1D>	Used to identify a segment master browser (not a domain master browser). The master browser adds this name as a unique NetBIOS name when it starts. Workstations announce their presence to this name so that master browsers can build their browse list.
<DOMAIN><1E>	Used for all domain-wide announcements by browser servers in a Windows 2000–based server domain. This name is added by all browser servers and potential servers in the workgroup or domain. All browser election packets are sent to this name.

PathPing

PathPing is a command-line route tracing tool that combines features of the tools Ping and TraceRt with additional information that neither provides. PathPing sends packets to each router on the way to a final destination over a period of time, and then computes results based on the packets returned from each hop. Since PathPing shows the degree of packet loss at any specified router or link, you can pinpoint which routers or links might be causing network problems.

Run PathPing from a command prompt rather than from Windows Explorer to see the resulting display.

PathPing Syntax

The command-line syntax for PathPing is as follows:

```
pathping [-n] [-h maximum_hops] [-g host-list] [-p period]
         [-q num_queries] [-w timeout] [-T] [-R] target_name
```

PathPing Switches

A number of switches are available, as shown in Table 31.27.

Table 31.27   PathPing Switches

Switch	Name	Function
-n	Host names	Does not resolve addresses-to-host names.
-h *<max_hops>*	Maximum hops	Maximum number of hops to search for target. The default is 30.
-g *<host list>*	Host list	A loose source route along host-list from host to target system. Type in a series of router IP addresses separated by spaces for testing.
-p *<milliseconds>*	Period	Time, in milliseconds, to wait between pings. The default is 250 milliseconds.
-q *<num_queries>*	Number of queries	Number of queries per hop. The default is 100.
-w *<milliseconds>*	Time out	Time, in milliseconds, waited for each reply. The default is 3000 milliseconds.
-T	Layer-2 Priority	Test connectivity to each hop with Layer-2 priority tags.
-R	RSVP	Test whether each hop is RSVP-aware.
-?	Help	Display this list.

PathPing Reports

The following is a sample PathPing report. Note that the compiled statistics that follow the hop list indicate packet loss at each router.

```
Tracing route to testpc1.dns.reskit.com [7.54.1.196]
over a maximum of 30 hops:
  0  172.16.87.35
  1  172.16.87.218
  2  192.168.52.1
  3  192.168.80.1
  4  7.54.247.14
  5  7.54.1.196

Computing statistics for 125 seconds...
                Source to Here   This Node/Link
Hop  RTT    Lost/Sent = Pct   Lost/Sent = Pct  Address
  0                                             172.16.87.35
                                0/ 100 =  0%   |
  1  41ms      0/ 100 =  0%     0/ 100 =  0%   172.16.87.218
                               13/ 100 = 13%   |
  2  22ms     16/ 100 = 16%     3/ 100 =  3%   192.168.52.1
                                0/ 100 =  0%   |
  3  24ms     13/ 100 = 13%     0/ 100 =  0%   192.168.80.1
                                0/ 100 =  0%   |
  4  21ms     14/ 100 = 14%     1/ 100 =  1%   7.54.247.14
                                0/ 100 =  0%   |
  5  24ms     13/ 100 = 13%     0/ 100 =  0%   7.54.1.196

Trace complete.
```

When PathPing is run, the first results you see list the route as it is tested for problems. This is the same path shown by TraceRt. PathPing then displays a busy message while it gathers information from all the routers previously listed and the links between them. At the end of this period, it displays the test results.

The columns "This Node/Link Lost/Sent = Pct" and "Address" contain the most useful information. In the preceding sample report, the link between 172.16.87.218 (hop 1), and 192.168.52.1 (hop 2) is dropping 13 percent of the packets. All other links are working normally. The routers at hops 2 and 4 also drop packets addressed to them, but this loss does not affect their forwarding path.

The loss rates displayed for the links (marked as a "|" in the rightmost column) indicate losses of packets being forwarded along the path. This loss indicates link congestion. The loss rates displayed for routers (indicated by their IP addresses in the rightmost column) indicate that their CPUs or packet buffers might be overloaded. These congested routers might also be a factor in end-to-end problems, especially if packets are forwarded by software routers.

IP Security Monitor

The IP Security Monitor (IPSecMon) is a Windows-based tool used to confirm whether your secured, IP-based communications are successful by displaying the active security associations on local or remote computers.

For example, you can use IPSecMon to determine whether there has been a pattern of authentication or security association failures, possibly indicating incompatible security policy settings.

IPSecMon can be run locally or remotely if you have a network connection to the remote computer. From the **Start** menu, click **Run**, and then type:

ipsecmon *<computer name>*

An entry is displayed for each active security association, as shown in Figure 31.7. The information contained in each entry includes the name of the active IPSec policy, the active Filter Action and IP Filter List (including details of the active filter), and the tunnel endpoint (if one was specified in the active IPSec policy).

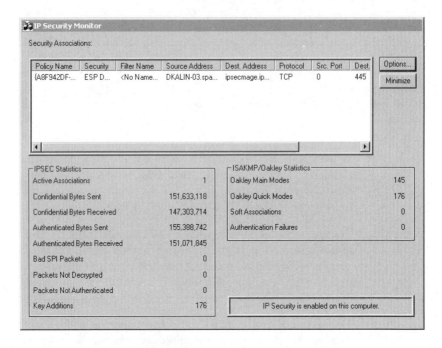

Figure 31.7   IP Security Monitor

Entry information can also provide statistics for tuning and troubleshooting, including the following:

- The number and type of active security associations.

- The total number of master and session keys (Main and Quick modes). Successful IPSec security associations initially cause one master key and one session key. Subsequent key regenerations are shown as additional session keys.

- The total number of confidential (Encapsulating Security Payload or ESP) or authenticated (ESP or Authentication Header — AH) bytes sent or received.

Note Because ESP provides authenticity and confidentiality, both counters are incremented.

- The total number of soft associations.

The refresh rate is the only configurable option in IPSecMon. By default, the statistics update every 15 seconds and are accumulated with each communication that uses IPSec.

A Bad SPI (Security Parameters Index) error might occur if a key lifetime value is set too low, or if the security agent has expired but the sender continues to transmit data. To determine and correct the problem, run IPSecMon, and then examine the number of rekeys.

If the number of rekeys is very large compared to the amount of time the connections have been active, set the key lifetimes in the policy longer. Good values for high-traffic Ethernet connections are greater than 50 MB and longer than five minutes.

This is likely to significantly reduce bad SPIs.

For more information about IPSec, see "Internet Protocol Security" in the *Microsoft® Windows® 2000 Server Resource Kit TCP/IP Core Networking Guide*.

Troubleshooting Procedures

This section provides basic instructions for troubleshooting problems that might occur when running Windows 2000.

For troubleshooting information related to topics not found in this chapter, see the related chapter in this book. Use the Quick Guide at the beginning of this chapter to determine which chapter contains the troubleshooting information you are looking for.

Using the Hardware Compatibility List

The most common cause of hardware problems is using hardware that is not compatible with Windows 2000. The Hardware Compatibility List (HCL) outlines the hardware components that have been tested for use with Windows 2000. It is especially important to refer to the HCL if you plan to use modems, tape backup units, and SCSI adapters.

If several different models of a device are available from one manufacturer, only those models included in the HCL are supported; a slightly different model might cause problems. Where special criteria are required for a model to be supported (for example, a particular version of driver), this information is described in the HCL.

The HCL is a Web-based searchable database which is updated as additional hardware is tested and approved. For more information about supported hardware devices, see the HCL link on the Web Resources page at http://windows.microsoft.com/windows2000/reskit/webresources.

Checking Hardware for Problems

If your hardware components are listed on the HCL, and you still have problems, try the following:

1. Ensure that all physical connections are secure, that expansion cards are fully inserted in their slots, and that cables are tight. You might also try using new cables or moving a card to a different slot.
2. Check that resources, such as IRQs, DMA channels, and I/O addresses, are properly assigned and configured. For instances of device conflicts, reassign a configurable device to use an available resource.
3. Check with the manufacturer for possible updated Windows 2000 drivers or for known issues and workarounds.

If you are using a SCSI device, check its termination.   Even if you are sure that the termination is correct, open the computer case and check again. Use active rather than passive SCSI terminators whenever possible.

Note   Terminators provide the correct impedance at the end of a cable. If the impedance is too high or too low, internal signal reflections can occur. These echoes represent noise on the cable and can corrupt subsequent signals, resulting in degraded performance or data loss.

Passive terminators are resistors with the appropriate resistance value for the characteristic impedance of the cable. Active terminators can better maintain the correct impedance necessary to eliminate signal reflection.

Verify that the SCSI cables are not longer than necessary. If a two-foot cable is long enough to connect the device to the controller, do not use a three-foot cable just because one is available. The acceptable lengths vary depending on factors such as whether you are using basic SCSI, SCSI-2, wide SCSI, ultra-wide SCSI, or differential SCSI; the quality of the termination; and the quality of the devices being used. Consult your hardware documentation for more information.

Check your hardware configuration. I/O and interrupt conflicts that went unnoticed with other operating systems must be resolved with Windows 2000. Likewise, pay close attention to CMOS and EISA BIOS configuration parameters when using Windows 2000, such as ensuring the **Plug and Play OS BIOS** parameter setting is set to **No** or **Disabled**, and enabling Advanced Configuration and Power Interface (ACPI) support on ACPI-compatible systems. For more information, see your motherboard or system manual documentation.

Check the Knowledge Base for information about hardware problems.

There are several articles about memory problems, memory parity errors, SCSI problems, and other hardware information in the Knowledge Base. For information about these issues, see the Knowledge Base link on the Web Resources page at
http://windows.microsoft.com/windows2000/reskit/webresources.

Troubleshooting Problems with System Startup and Shutdown

Problems which prevent the computer from completing startup or shut down can be frustrating. However, there are several techniques that you can use to isolate and solve these problems.

Startup Problems

If a computer fails to complete the Windows 2000 startup process, note whether any new hardware or software has been added since the last startup. If so, remove the new component to see whether this resolves the problem.

If nothing has been added or changed on the system, restart the computer in Safe Mode. If successful, you might be able to resolve the problem from within Safe Mode. Starting Windows 2000 in Safe Mode can help you resolve issues that occur when you start Windows 2000 normally, including (but not limited to):

- Setup freezes during the first restart.
- Error messages are displayed.
- The system stops responding.
- You lose functionality.

Starting Windows 2000 in Safe Mode bypasses the current configuration and loads a minimal configuration, enabling only basic Windows 2000 device drivers and system services.

If the startup failure does not occur in Safe Mode, you might have a conflict with hardware settings or system resources; incompatibilities with Windows programs, services, or drivers; or registry damage.

In Safe Mode, use the following tasks to find a startup problem. Many of these steps require changes to system configuration files. The changes are to isolate the conflict that is causing the problem and are not intended to be permanent. For more information about Safe Mode, see "Safe Mode" earlier in this chapter.

▶ **To troubleshoot startup problems in Safe Mode**

1. To enter Safe Mode, restart the computer, and then press F8 when the screen displays the prompt "For troubleshooting and advanced startup options for Windows 2000, press F8."

2. On the **Windows 2000 Advanced Options Menu,** select **Safe Mode**, and then press ENTER. Determine whether the startup failure is resolved. If not, check for hardware problems such as defective devices, improper installation, cabling, or connector problems. Remove any newly added hardware to see whether the problem is resolved.

   If you cannot complete the startup process and you suspect your computer might have corruption in the registry, restart the computer, press F8, and on the **Windows 2000 Advanced Options Menu**, select **Last Known Good Configuration**. Press ENTER.

3. If you can complete the startup process in Safe Mode, start System Information. Open the **Run** dialog box, and then type:

   msinfo32

   For more information about System Information, see "System Information" earlier in this chapter.

4. Within System Information, check the **Conflicts/Sharing** section under **Hardware Resources** and the **Problem Devices** section under **Components** for known issues. Address any issues found by reconfiguring or disabling the devices in conflict, and then restart the computer.

   If you disabled a device to resolve the problem, check that the device is listed on the HCL and that it was installed correctly; or check it on another computer to see whether the device might be defective. Try using Windows Update to see whether any updated drivers are available. If not, try visiting the manufacturer's Web site to see whether an updated driver is available.

5. If there were no conflicting devices reported in System Information, under **Software Environment,** check the **Startup Programs** section for programs that are automatically started when the computer is started. Disable these programs and restart the system.

Note Links to startup programs can be in a variety of places, including in the registry under the following subkeys:

HKEY_LOCAL_MACHINE\SOFTWARE\Microsoft\Windows\CurrentVersio n\Run

HKEY_LOCAL_MACHINE\SOFTWARE\Microsoft\Windows\CurrentVersio n\RunOnce

HKEY_USERS\.DEFAULT\Software\Microsoft\Windows\CurrentVersion\Ru nOnce

HKEY_CURRENT_USER\Software\Microsoft\Windows\CurrentVersion\Run Once

Also look for startup programs in C:\Documents and Settings*logon_name*\Start Menu\Programs\Startup and in C:\Documents and Settings\All Users\Start Menu\Programs\Startup. If the user is a member of the local administrators group, check C:\Documents and Settings\Administrator\Start Menu\Programs\Startup.

If the problem is resolved by disabling the startup programs, re-enable them one at a time, and restart the computer each time to determine which program causes the startup failure.

6. If disabling the Startup Programs does not resolve the problem, check the boot log file, %SystemRoot%\Ntbtlog.txt. Rename this file to indicate that it is a Safe Mode boot log file, and compare its contents to a recently saved boot log file from a normally started session. If a normal boot log does not exist, create one by restarting the computer, pressing F8 at the "Starting Windows" screen to display the **Windows 2000 Advanced Options Menu**, selecting **Enable Boot Logging**, and then pressing ENTER. The normal boot log file can indicate which driver file did not load properly.

Note Some startup problems occur so early in the startup process that they prevent the system from saving the boot log file to disk.

Examine the Safe Mode version of the boot log file to see which drivers were not loaded. This list of skipped drivers is a good starting place to look for the driver that is causing the startup process to fail.

If the problem is a Stop message (also known as a blue screen), see the troubleshooting tips in the chapter "Windows 2000 Stop Messages" in this book.

Shutdown Problems

The Windows 2000 shutdown process involves sending messages to the installed devices, system services, and applications to notify them that Windows is preparing to shut down. The system waits for responses from open applications to make sure that they shut down properly, and save unsaved data to disk. Each running device, system service, and application usually respond to the shutdown message, indicating that it can be closed.

Typical causes for problems with Windows 2000 shutdown include:

- Device drivers not responding correctly, if at all.
- System services not responding or sending busy request messages to the system.
- Applications not responding, particularly 16-bit Windows programs.

To resolve problems with shutdown, try the following suggestions:

- Check that the system properly shuts down in Safe Mode. If so, check the boot log file. Note the services that were disabled under Safe Mode, stop them one at a time in normal mode, and then shut down to see whether the system works properly. After the problem driver or service is identified, if the file is corrupted, either reinstall it, search for an update, or uninstall it until the problem can be resolved.
- Press CTRL+SHIFT+ESC to start Task Manager and see which applications are currently running. Manually quit the applications before shutting down to see whether that resolves the problem.
- Check with your computer manufacturer to be sure that you have the latest BIOS update for the system.

If the problem occurs immediately after a change to the system, such as installing or upgrading applications, system services, or hardware with device drivers, undo the last change made to the system and test the system.

Using Windows File Protection

Earlier operating systems did not prevent shared system files from being overwritten by program installations, causing unpredictable performance results, such as program errors or an unstable operating system. This problem affected files such as dynamic-link libraries (DLLs) and executable (EXE) files. Windows 2000 includes a feature called Windows File Protection (WFP) that prevents the replacement of certain protected system files and significantly minimizes file version mismatches.

WFP uses the digital file signatures and catalog files generated by code signing to verify whether protected system files are the correct Microsoft versions. WFP does not generate signatures.

WFP is notified when a file in a protected folder is modified. WFP determines which file was changed, and if the file is protected, WFP compares the digital file signature of the replacement file to those in the catalog files to determine whether the new file has been certified by Microsoft. If it has not, the original file is restored from the %SystemRoot%\System32\Dllcache folder (if it is located in the Dllcache folder) or from the Windows 2000 operating system CD.

Checking for Correct File Versions

You can use the System File Checker (SFC) tool to scan for system files that have been changed by applications and alert you to discovered changes. If necessary, SFC prompts you to restore the original file from the Windows 2000 operating system CD.

For more information about using SFC, see "System File Checker" earlier in this chapter.

Updating System Files and Drivers

Windows Update lets you update system files and device drivers specific to your computer. Any new system files downloaded by using Windows Update are automatically registered with WFP.

For more information about updating your computer's Windows 2000 installation, see "Windows Update" earlier in this chapter.

Checking Whether a Required File Is Missing or Damaged

If a particular hardware device or system service fails to work properly after starting the computer, especially after encountering problems with disk corruption, it is possible that the driver file did not properly load when the computer was started. To determine whether failures when loading driver files are the problem, restart the computer and enable boot logging. For information about how to enable boot logging, see "Safe Mode" earlier in this chapter.

▶ **To check for driver files that did not load at system startup**

1. Restart the computer.

2. At the Starting Windows screen, at the prompt "For troubleshooting and advanced startup options for Windows 2000, press F8" press F8 to display the **Windows 2000 Advanced Options Menu**.

3. Select **Enable Boot Logging**, and then press ENTER.

4. After the computer has completed the startup process, start Windows Explorer and navigate to the %SystemRoot% folder. Locate the file Ntbtlog.txt and double-click it to open it in Notepad.

The log file lists a long series of drivers that the computer loaded or attempted to load. Files that were loaded are preceded by the phrase "Loaded driver," followed by the path and file name of the specific driver. Files that did not load are preceded by the phrase "Did not load driver." A quick scan for these listings can help you identify the location and names of files that might be missing or corrupted. For more information about the choices in the **Windows 2000 Advanced Options Menu**, see "Safe Mode" earlier in this chapter.

If a file that is needed to load or run Windows 2000 becomes corrupted or is deleted, the system typically displays an error message and might generate information in the event log. You can use this information to find the problem.

On rare occasions an executable file or DLL does not report missing or corrupted files. If there is no indication of an error, but you think some component did not start correctly due to a required file that is missing or corrupted, you can run a few tests to attempt to resolve the problem.

Check to see whether all of the Windows 2000 system files exist and appear to be uncorrupted. Symptoms of file corruption can be unpredictable, but include a file being an unusual size (for example, zero bytes or larger than its original size) or having a date or time that does not match the installation date. Compare files in %SystemRoot%\System32 and its subfolders with files in these folders on another computer running the same Windows 2000 version and Service Packs. Run SFC to inspect all installed system files. Also, run an antivirus program designed to work with Windows 2000 to scan for virus corruption.

If you think that you might be having a problem with a missing Windows 2000 system file, you can run Windows 2000 Setup and repair the installation by running the Fast Repair process. For more information about the Fast Repair process, see "Emergency Repair Process" earlier in this chapter.

Device Driver Problems

Corrupted or faulty device drivers and system services can cause problems such as hardware peripheral device or system feature failure and startup failures. To troubleshoot these problems, you need to isolate the cause.

Checking Device Configuration

Conflicts between devices that are trying to use the same system resources can cause errors. You can view your device configuration by using either System Information or Device Manager.

System Information collects information such as devices installed or device drivers loaded, and displays the associated system topics. Device Manager provides a central place where you can verify that devices are configured correctly, and to change device resource settings.

▶ **To check for resource conflicts among devices**

1. Open System Information.

2. Expand the **Components** category, and then select **Problem Devices**. Devices with hardware conflicts are identified.

3. To determine the resource in conflict, expand the **Hardware Resources** category and select **Conflicts/Sharing**. If neither of the devices are listed under **Problem Devices**, they are probably sharing the resource.

   Note   Peripheral Component Interconnect (PCI) devices can share resources.

4. If necessary, change the devices' resource settings by using Device Manager. To open **Device Manager**, in Control Panel click **System**, click the **Hardware** tab, and then click **Device Manager**.

   Note   If you use multiple hardware profiles, first select the appropriate configuration by using the list in the device's Resource properties page.

For more information about using System Information to check for device conflicts, see "System Information" earlier in this chapter. For more information about Device Manager and troubleshooting problems with devices, see "Device Management" in this book. For more information about troubleshooting problems related to device detection, see "Setup and Startup" in this book.

Identifying a Problem Driver

If you can log on to your computer, use the Drivers tool on the *Windows 2000 Professional Resource Kit* companion CD to display information about the device drivers that are currently loaded. If you have previously printed the output from the Drivers tool (by redirecting the output to a printer or a file), you can compare it to your current output. You can also run the Drivers tool on a similar computer and compare the results.

It might also be helpful to look at System Information's display on Drivers and Problem Devices. For more information about System Information, see "System Information" earlier in this chapter.

Identifying a Service That Does Not Start

Some services are configured to start automatically on Windows 2000. The specific services depend on your computer configuration, and which network services and protocols you are using.

You can use the **Services** option in Administrative Tools to view which services are set to start automatically and which did not start, as seen in Figure 31.8.

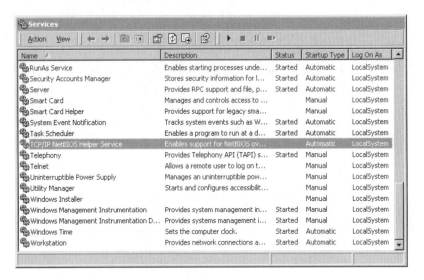

Figure 31.8   System Services Window

In Figure 31.8, TCP/IP NetBIOS Helper Service is configured to start automatically, but it did not start.

Try to manually start the service or change the startup type status by double-clicking it to open the **Service Properties** dialog box, shown in Figure 31.9.

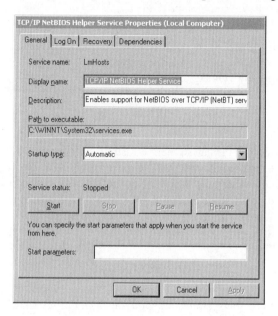

Figure 31.9   Service Properties Dialog Box

Note   You must have administrator privileges to change the startup type of a service.

Saving Output from Troubleshooting Tools

Most of the command line–based troubleshooting tools produce useful information in the form of reports, but lack a command-line switch that offers to save their reports to disk.

When using these tools, you can redirect the display output to a text file that can be viewed in Notepad. At the command prompt, type:

Toolname /switch > Toolname.txt

Use the standard command-line syntax to produce the report you want to save, including any optional command-line switches to produce the specific results you need. The redirector, the greater-than sign (>), transfers the screen output to the text file specified at the end of the command.

Note Unless directed otherwise, the output file is stored in the current folder by using the preceding syntax.

Disaster Recovery

Disaster recovery is primarily used to restore your system in the event that your hard disk fails and you have to replace or reformat it. You can also restore your system if critical system files have been accidentally erased or have become corrupted and you need to reformat your hard disk. Disaster recovery is for use only after you have attempted to repair your system using Safe Mode, Recovery Console, and the Emergency Repair Process, described earlier in this chapter.

Preparing for Disaster Recovery

To perform a complete disaster recovery you need a recent backup of your entire system, including the system state data, the system files, and your data files. The system state data includes the registry, the Component Services class registration database, and the system files required to start your computer (also known as the boot files).

The Backup tool provides two methods for backing up your entire system, including the system components mentioned earlier: the first method relies on the Backup Wizard to select files and folders and set backup options; the second method gives you maximum control over the backup process because it relies on you to set backup options and select the files and folders to back up.

Important You must be a member of the Backup Operators group or a member of the Administrators group on the local computer to back up the system state.

▶ **To prepare for disaster recovery by using the Backup Wizard**

1. Start Backup. From the **Start** menu, click **Programs**, **Accessories**, **System Tools**, and **Backup**.

2. On the **Welcome** tab, click **Backup Wizard**.

3. At the "Welcome to the Windows 2000 Backup and Recovery Tools" screen, click **Next**.

4. Click **Back up everything on my computer**, and then click **Next**.

5. Select a **Backup media type**, select **Backup media or file name**, and then click **Next**.

6. Click **Advanced** to set advanced backup options, including backup type, data verification, hardware compression, media labels and ownership, and scheduling. Otherwise, the Backup Wizard sets the following options by default:

- Backup type: normal.
- Migrated Remote Storage data: do not back up.
- Data verification: none.
- Hardware compression: on (if backing up to tape); off (if backing up to file).
- Ownership/permissions: not set.
- Overwrite/append data to media: overwrite.
- Backup and media labels: set to time and date that Backup is performed.
- Schedule: Not set (runs Backup immediately).

7. Click **Finish** to start the backup operation.

The advanced backup options that appear when you run the Backup Wizard are a subset of the options you can set in the Backup tool. To prepare for disaster recovery and configure other options, use the following procedure.

▶ **To manually prepare for disaster recovery**

1. Start Backup.

2. On the **Backup** tab, select the volumes, files, and folders to back up. Select **System State** or you cannot use the backup set for disaster recovery.

3. In the **Backup destination** list box, choose the type of media to which to back up, and then choose **Backup media or file name**.

4. On the **Tools** menu, click **Options** to configure backup options, and then click **OK**.

5. Click **Start Backup**, and then make any changes you want to the **Backup Job Information** dialog box.

6. Click **Advanced** to set advanced backup options, and then click **OK**.

7. Click **Schedule** to add the backup operation to the Task Scheduler so that it runs automatically at some time in the future.

8. Click **Start Backup** to start the backup operation.

Because can only back up the system state data on the computer that is running Backup, you cannot prepare remote computers for disaster recovery. However, you can indirectly automate a remote system backup of each computer on a network by scheduling regular file backups of the System State data on each computer and then backing up those backup files by making a regular network backup of each computer. The procedure is described below.

Note   You can use third-party software to remotely back up the system state data.

▶   **To perform a complete system backup on a remote computer**

1. Log on as an Administrator or a Backup Operator to the remote computer, and then start the Backup Wizard.

2. At the "Welcome to the Windows 2000 Backup and Recovery Tools" screen, click **Next**.

3. Select **Only back up the System State data**, and then click **Next**.

4. Under **Backup media type**, select **File**. Under **Backup media or file name**, enter the path and file name for the backup. The file must have the .bkf file name extension. Save it in a shared folder on the local computer or on a network share for which you have write permission. Click **Next**.

5. Click **Advanced**, and then follow the instructions to set advanced backup options and schedule the backup to run unattended. You do not need to back up migrated Remote Storage data and you do not need to set the backup type because the System State data is always treated as a Copy backup type. Also, schedule the backup to run on a regular basis (for example, weekly or monthly). Click **Finish** to add the backup job to the task scheduler and finish setting up the remote computer.

Note   The remote computer must have the logon account used on the computer running the backups listed in either the Administrator or Backup Operator local groups to gain access to volumes on the remote computer. It is recommended that you use the administrative shares, such as C$, to back up the contents of the volumes.

6. Log on as an Administrator or a Backup Operator, and then start Backup.

7. On the **Backup** tab, select the shared folder containing the System State backup file you scheduled.

8. Select all of the shared volumes for the remote computer.

9. Click **Start Backup**, and on the **Backup Job Information** dialog box, click **Schedule** to schedule the backup. Schedule the backup to run *after* the backup job you scheduled to run on the remote computer has completed.

10. Click **Start Backup** to add the backup job to the task scheduler.

There are several backup options that you can set. For more information about Backup, including backup and restore options, see "Removable Storage and Backup" in this book.

Performing Disaster Recovery

The disaster recovery process typically begins after you have installed a new hard disk or reformat your existing disk. If you installed a new hard disk, you need at least as much storage capacity as the original hard disk. Also, it must have the same volumes as the original hard disk, including volume drive letter, volume size, and file system, or disaster recovery might not succeed.

To start the disaster recovery process, install a new version of Windows 2000 and run Backup to restore (recover) your system and data files. The installation folder for the new system must be in the same location as the installation folder of your original system. This applies to the drive letter and the folder name. If your original system was installed to the default Setup location (C:\Winnt), you can simply install a fresh copy of Windows 2000, and then begin the disaster recovery process. However, if your original system was installed in a different location, for example at D:\Windows, your new system must be installed at D:\Windows.

Note Backup allows you to restore files to an alternate location, but does not restore the System State data in a form that recovers your system. When you restore or recover a system you need to restore all files, including the System State data, to the original location.

The Windows Setup program does not prompt you for the installation folder unless Winnt already exists on the volume that you intend to use for the installation. To perform disaster recovery on a computer that did not use the default Windows 2000 installation volume and folder name, create a Winnt folder on the installation volume before you run Setup. You can do this by using either the Recovery Console or a startup disk for MS-DOS, Windows 95 or Windows 98. Both methods are discussed in the following sections.

Note You can designate a different installation folder during an unattended installation by specifying the folder name in the "TargetPath=" parameter in the answer file. For more information about unattended installations, see "Customizing and Automating Installations" in this book.

Using the Recovery Console to Create a Winnt Folder on a Volume

You can use the Recovery Console to create a Winnt folder on an unformatted volume. If the disk has not been partitioned, you can also use the Recovery Console to create volumes. To perform this procedure you need access to a computer with a text editing program (for example, Notepad) and a floppy disk drive. If you do not have access to a computer with a text editor and a floppy drive, see the next section.

▶ **To create a Winnt folder on an empty volume by using the Recovery Console**

1. Open the Recovery Console by using either the four Windows 2000 Setup disks or the Windows 2000 operating system CD. Choose the repair option by pressing R when prompted, and then press C to choose the Recovery Console. You do not need to log on as the Recovery Console starts because there is no system installed.

2. If there are no volumes on your disk, use the **diskpart** command to create an installation volume on your hard disk (type **diskpart** with no switches to start a user interface for managing volumes). The volume must have the same drive letter and be at least as large as the installation volume that was on your hard disk when it was last backed up. You might need to create more than one volume to reach the appropriate drive letter. For example, if the original installation was on drive D, create drive C first, and then create drive D.

3. Use the **format** command to format the volumes you created in step 2. Format the new installation volume with the same file system the original installation volume or you can lose data and other file and folder features. For example, if your original installation volume was drive C and it was formatted with NTFS, type the following command:

   format c: /q /fs:ntfs

4. Use the **map** command to display the Advanced RISC Computing (ARC) path for the new installation volume. Write this information down. It is needed for step 6. On drive C, the ARC path typically looks similar to the following:

   \Device\Harddisk0\Partition1.

5. On another computer, use a text editor to create a file called Setup.log and save it to a floppy disk. Be sure the file ends with the file name extension .log and not .txt.

6. Add the following information to the Setup.log file and save it. After TargetDevice= and SystemPartition= you must type the ARC path you wrote down in step 4. The ARC path must be inside double quotes. For example:

```
[Paths]
TargetDirectory = "\WINNT"
TargetDevice = "arc_path_information"
SystemPartitionDirectory = "\"
SystemPartition = "arc_path_information"
[Signature]
Version = "WinNt5.0"
[Files.SystemPartition]
NTDETECT.COM = "NTDETECT.COM","11f1b"
ntldr = "ntldr","3aae6"
arcsetup.exe = "arcsetup.exe","3036c"
arcldr.exe = "arcldr.exe","33a86"
[Files.WinNt]
```

7. Restart your computer from the Windows 2000 operating system CD or the four Windows 2000 Setup disks to run the Setup program. When you are prompted, press R, and then press R again to choose the Emergency Repair Process.

8. Select the Manual Repair option by pressing M. This displays a screen with three manual repair options. Clear all of the options except **Verify Windows 2000 System files**. When you are finished, select **Continue (perform selected tasks)**, and then press ENTER.

9. When you are prompted for the Emergency Repair Disk, insert the disk you created in steps 5 and 6, and then press ENTER. This creates a Winnt folder on your installation volume.

Note The Recovery Console offers an **md** command, but by default, you cannot create a folder at the root folder. You can change the default behavior of Recovery Console to allow this type of action with local Group Policy settings, but because the hard disk does not yet have an installation of Windows 2000 on it, you cannot implement policies or change the default behavior for Recovery Console.

Using a Windows 98 Startup Disk to Create a Winnt Folder on a Volume

You can create a Winnt folder on an unformatted volume by using a Windows 98 startup floppy disk.

When you use a Windows 98 startup disk to create a Winnt folder, you can only format the volume with the FAT16 or FAT32 file systems. If your original installation volume was formatted with NTFS, and you want to restore your system to the same file system, you can use this procedure to create a Winnt folder on your volume. Use the Windows 98 disk partitioning tool Fdisk to create the volume to the original size, then format the volume with FAT32. If the original volume used NTFS, use the **convert** command to convert the FAT volume to NTFS *after* you create the Winnt folder and install a fresh copy of Windows 2000, but *before* you restore your system from backup.

Note The Windows 98 startup disk must contain the files Fdisk.exe and Format.exe from the C:\Windows\Command folder in Windows 98 to complete this procedure.

▶ **To create a Winnt folder on a volume using a Windows 98 startup disk**

1. Start your computer by using a Windows 98 startup disk.

2. If your disk does not have an installation volume, use the **fdisk** command to create a primary DOS partition with the same drive letter as the original installation volume. It must also be at least as large as the original installation volume.

   Make the partition active to be able to use it as an installation volume. You might need to create more than one volume to reach the drive letter your original installation used. Once **fdisk** is finished, the computer restarts. If your hard disk already has a formatted installation volume, skip to step 5.

3. Restart your computer by using the Windows 98 Startup disk.

4. Use the **format** command to format the volumes created in step 2.

Note The Format tool cannot format FAT16 volumes made by Windows 98 that are larger than 2 GB. Format larger volumes using FAT32.

---

5. Use the **md** command to create a Winnt folder on the volume in which you want to install Windows 2000.

Installing a Fresh Version of Windows 2000

Before you can recover your system and your data files, you must install a fresh copy of Windows 2000. If your original installation folder used the default volume and folder name (C:\Winnt) and no other volumes exist on the disk, simply restart your computer with the Windows 2000 operating system CD or the four Windows 2000 Setup disks, and follow the instructions on your screen.

If you have more than one usable volume, Setup asks you to choose the volume on which to install Windows 2000. Choose the volume whose drive letter matches that of the original installation. If the original installation was on drive D but used the default folder name, Setup automatically begins the installation by using the default folder name (Winnt) unless you already created a Winnt folder on that volume. If there is a folder named Winnt on the volume, Setup prompts you for the name of the installation folder.

▶ **To install a fresh version of Windows 2000 during disaster recovery**

1. Start your computer by using the Windows 2000 operating system CD or the Windows 2000 Setup disks.

2. If prompted, select a volume to use for the installation.

3. When asked whether to format the volume or leave it as it is, choose **Leave the current file system intact (no changes)**. This preserves the Winnt folder on the installation volume. If you format the disk, the Winnt folder is erased.

4. If your original installation used the default installation folder name, proceed to Windows 2000 Setup and skip the remaining steps in this procedure.

5. If you manually created a Winnt folder on your installation volume, Setup prompts you to confirm whether or not you want to use the Winnt folder for this installation. Create the folder name you originally used.

6. When you are warned that there is a Winnt folder already on your computer, press ESC to choose a different installation folder. Enter a new installation folder, press ENTER, and then follow the instructions that appear.

If you installed Windows 2000 on a FAT16 or FAT32 volume, and your original installation volume was formatted to use NTFS, convert the new installation volume to NTFS before you restore the system. When the installation finishes, log on as the local administrator, and use the **convert** command. From the command prompt, type

convert *drive_letter:* **/fs:ntfs**

where *drive_letter* is the installation volume.

Restoring the System and Data Files

To finish the disaster recovery process, restore your system from the most recent backup. To fully recover your system, restore the following:

- System files
- Data files
- System State data

Use the Restore function of Backup to restore these components to their original locations. This is especially critical when you restore the System State. After you finish restoring your files and system data, restart the computer. Your fully-restored system is in the same state it was in when you backed it up.

C H A P T E R   3 2

Disk Concepts and Troubleshooting

Understanding the organizational structure of information on hard disks, as well as being familiar with disk terminology, is key to diagnosing and troubleshooting disk problems. When troubleshooting system problems, you can refer to this chapter for detailed descriptions of the *master boot record* (MBR) and *boot sector*, two disk sectors that are critical to the startup process.

In This Chapter

Related Information in the Resource Kit

- For more information about startup, see "Setup and Startup" in this book.

- For more information about file systems, see "File Systems" in this book.

- For more information about preparing for and performing recovery, see "Troubleshooting Tools and Strategies" in this book.

Quick Guide to Disk Concepts

Understanding disk structures is critical to maintaining your hard disks and troubleshooting disk-related problems. Use this guide to find the information you need to understand Windows 2000 disk configurations and how these configurations affect your fault tolerance and disaster recovery strategies.

Determine whether to configure your hard disks as basic or dynamic.

Understand the differences between basic and dynamic disks. Determine the advantages and restrictions of each type of disk and which of these configurations best meets your needs.

- See "Basic and Dynamic Disks" in this chapter.

Understand how disk sectors are used during system startup.

The master boot record (MBR) and the boot sector are critical to starting your computer. Review the structure of these sectors and how they affect the startup and use of your computer to help you troubleshoot a variety of disk problems.

- See "Disk Sectors Critical to Startup" in this chapter.

Troubleshoot problems affecting your hard disks.

Disk structures, such as the MBR and boot sector, can become corrupted by viruses and other causes. Depending on the severity of the problem, you might need to run antivirus tools or repair or restore the MBR and boot sector.

- See "Troubleshooting Disk Problems" in this chapter.

Basic and Dynamic Disks

Microsoft® Windows® 2000 offers two types of disk storage configurations: basic disk and dynamic disk. Basic disk is similar to the disk structures used in Microsoft® Windows NT®. Dynamic disk is new to Windows 2000. By default, Windows 2000 initializes hard disks as basic disk.

The Disk Administrator tool found in Microsoft® Windows NT® version 4.0 and earlier has been replaced in Windows 2000 with the Disk Management snap-in for the Microsoft Management Console (MMC). Disk Management supports both basic and dynamic disks. You can use the upgrade wizard in Disk Management to convert basic disks to dynamic disks.

You can use both basic and dynamic disks on the same computer system, and with any combination of file systems (*file allocation table* [FAT], including FAT16 and FAT32, and NTFS file system). However, all volumes on a physical disk must be either basic or dynamic.

You can upgrade from basic to dynamic storage at any time. Any changes made to your disk are immediately available in Windows 2000—you do not need to quit Disk Management to save them or restart your computer to implement them. However, if you upgrade the startup disk to dynamic, or if a volume or partition is in use on the disk that you are upgrading, the computer must be restarted for the upgrade to succeed.

Terms

To help you understand the differences between basic disk and dynamic disk, a set of definitions are provided.

Basic Disk

A *basic disk* is a physical disk that contains primary partitions and/or extended partitions with logical drives used by Windows 2000 and all versions of Windows NT. Basic disks can also contain volume or striped sets that were created using Windows NT 4.0 or earlier. As long as a compatible file format is used, basic disks can be accessed by Microsoft® MS-DOS®, Microsoft® Windows® 95, Microsoft® Windows® 98, and all versions of Windows NT.

Since Windows 2000 automatically initializes disks as basic, you can troubleshoot partitions and volumes using the same methods as in Windows NT.

Note FAT32 is new in Windows 2000. Disk troubleshooting tools from Windows NT will likely not recognize FAT32 boot sectors and may cause problems with FAT32-formatted volumes. If FAT32 is used on your computer, be sure to use a disk troubleshooting tool designed for Windows 2000 that recognizes this file format.

New or empty disks can be initialized as either basic or dynamic after the hardware installation is complete.

Basic Volume

A *basic volume* is a volume on a basic disk. Basic volumes include primary partitions, logical drives within extended partitions, as well as volume or striped sets created using Windows NT 4.0 or earlier. You cannot create basic volumes on dynamic disks.

Note Creating new fault-tolerant (FT) sets, such as mirrored and redundant array of independent disks (RAID) Level 5 (also known as striped with parity) volumes, is only available on computers running Windows 2000 Server. The disk must be upgraded to dynamic disk before these volumes can be created. You can, however, use a computer running Windows 2000 Professional to create mirrored and RAID-5 volumes on a remote computer running Windows 2000 Server.

Dynamic Disk

A *dynamic disk* is a physical disk that has been upgraded by and is managed with Disk Management. Dynamic disks do not use partitions or logical drives. They can contain only dynamic volumes created by Disk Management. Only computers running Windows 2000 can access dynamic volumes.

Note Disks that have been upgraded from basic to dynamic disk still contain references to partitions in the *partition table* of the MBR. However, the MBR's reference to these partitions identifies the partition types as dynamic, indicating to Windows 2000 that the disk configuration data is now maintained in the disk management database at the end of the disk. Furthermore, any new changes made to the disk, such as deleting existing or creating additional volumes, are not recorded in the partition table.

Dynamic disks use dynamic volumes to subdivide physical disks into one or more drives enumerated by letters of the alphabet.

Note Volumes formatted with NTFS can also be represented as volume mount points. For more information about volume mount points, see "File Systems" in this book.

Disk configuration data is contained in a disk management database stored in the last 1 megabyte (MB) of space at the end of the disk. Since dynamic disks do not use the traditional disk organization scheme of partitions and logical volumes, they cannot be directly accessed by MS-DOS, Windows 95, Windows 98, or any versions of Windows NT. Shared folders on dynamic disks, however, are available to computers running all of these operating systems.

Dynamic Volume

A *dynamic volume* is a logical volume that is created on a dynamic disk using Disk Management. Dynamic volume types include simple, spanned, and striped, although Windows 2000 Server also supports the FT volume types (mirrored and RAID-5). You cannot create dynamic volumes on basic disks. Dynamic volumes are not supported on portable computers or removable media.

Note Dynamic volumes that were upgraded from basic disk partitions cannot be extended. This specifically includes the system volume, which contains hardware-specific files needed to start Windows 2000, and the boot volume, which contains the Windows 2000 system files required for startup. Only volumes created after the disk was upgraded to dynamic can be extended.

Partitions and Volumes

When you upgrade to dynamic disk, existing partitions and logical volumes are converted into dynamic volumes. Table 32.1 illustrates the translation of terms between basic and dynamic disk structures.

Table 32.1   Translation of Terms Between Basic and Dynamic Disk

Basic Disk Organization	Dynamic Disk Organization
Primary partition	Simple volume
System and boot partitions	System and boot volumes
Active partition	Active volume
Extended partition	Volume and unallocated space
Logical drive	Simple volume
Volume set	Spanned volume
Stripe set	Striped volume

Features of Basic Disk

You can use partitions on a basic disk just as you did with Microsoft® Windows NT® Workstation version 4.0, but you do not need to commit changes to save them or to restart your computer to make the changes effective. Changes made by Disk Management are implemented immediately. Unless you are making a change that affects existing files on the disk, the system executes your change without confirmation.

You can create up to four partitions in the free space on a physical hard disk; one of these can be an extended partition. You can use the free space in the extended partition to create one or more logical drives. You cannot use basic disk to create any kind of multiple volume sets or FT volumes.

You can perform the following tasks only on a basic disk:

- Create and delete primary and extended partitions.
- Create and delete logical drives within an extended partition.
- Format a partition and mark it as active.
- Delete volume, striped, mirror, or stripe sets with parity.

Certain legacy functions are no longer available on basic disks because multiple-disk storage systems need to use dynamic disks. Disk Management supports legacy volume sets and striped sets, but it does not allow you to create new ones. For example, you cannot create volume or striped sets or extend volumes and volume sets on a basic disk.

While you cannot create new multiple disk sets on basic disks, you can delete them. Be sure to back up all the information on the set before you delete it.

To establish a new spanned or striped volume, first upgrade the disk to dynamic disk. To convert an existing volume or striped set, upgrade the physical disks on which the set resides to dynamic disk.

Features of Dynamic Disk

Disk Management is very flexible. The number of volumes that you can create on a physical hard disk is limited only by the amount of available free space on the disk. You can also create volumes that span two or more disks and that, if you are running Windows 2000 Server, are fault tolerant.

You can perform the following tasks only on a dynamic disk:

- Create and delete simple, spanned, and striped volumes.
- Extend a simple or spanned volume.
- Reactivate a missing or offline disk.

Dynamic disks are not supported on portable computers. If you are using a portable computer and right-click a disk in the graphical or list view in Disk Management, you will not see the option to upgrade the disk to dynamic.

Note On some older and non-Advanced Configuration and Power Interface (ACPI)–compliant portable computers, you might be able to upgrade to dynamic disk, but it is neither recommended nor supported. Dynamic disk is not supported on removable disks, nor on disks using Universal Serial Bus (USB) or IEEE 1394 (also called FireWire) interfaces.

The limitations of dynamic volumes occur in the following situations:

When installing Windows 2000 If a dynamic volume is created from unallocated space on a dynamic disk, you cannot install Windows 2000 on that volume.

The setup limitation occurs because Windows 2000 Setup uses BIOS calls that only recognize volumes listed in the partition table. Only basic disk partitions, as well as simple volumes of dynamic disk that were upgraded from basic disk partitions, appear in the partition table. Dynamic disk does not use the partition table to manage its volumes, so new dynamic volumes are not registered in the partition table as they are created. Windows 2000 must be installed on a volume that is correctly represented in the partition table.

When extending a volume You cannot extend either the system volume or the boot volume in dynamic disk. Neither can be part of a spanned volume, since Windows 2000 considers extended volumes to be the same as spanned volumes.

Windows 2000 cannot extend any dynamic volume that existed as a basic volume before the dynamic disk upgrade, and the system and boot volumes (which might be one and the same) are likely the same volumes that existed under basic disk. Upgraded simple volumes in dynamic disk are still hard-linked to the partition table and must match the listing found there. Extending a dynamic volume changes its size, but since dynamic disk does not record volume changes to the partition table, upgraded volumes cannot be modified in this manner. The only dynamic volumes that can be extended are simple volumes created after the disk was upgraded to dynamic disk. If you want to extend an upgraded non-boot or non-system volume, delete the upgraded volume and recreate it under dynamic disk. You can use Windows 2000 Backup to save all the data on the volume and restore it after the volume has been recreated. Use Disk Management to assign the new volume the same drive letter or volume mount point as the original volume to ensure that all drive letter connections continue to work after the change.

Features Common to Both Basic and Dynamic Disks

You can perform the following tasks on both basic and dynamic disks:

- Check disk properties such as capacity, available free space, and current status.
- View volume and partition properties such as size, drive-letter assignment, label, type, and file system.
- Establish drive-letter assignments for disk volumes or partitions, and for CD-ROM devices.
- Establish disk sharing and security arrangements for a volume or partition.
- Upgrade a basic disk to dynamic or revert a dynamic disk to basic.

Note You can upgrade a basic disk to dynamic disk without loss of data. However, reverting a dynamic disk back to basic disk requires that you remove all volumes prior to the conversion. If you want to keep your data, you must back it up or move it to another volume. Once the volume is reverted back to basic disk, you can create a new partition using the same drive letter or volume mount point that was used with the dynamic volume and restore the data.

Disk Sectors Critical to Startup

The two sectors critical to starting your computer are the master boot record (MBR), which is always located at sector 1 of cylinder 0, head 0, the first sector of a hard disk, and the boot sector, which resides at sector 1 of each volume. These sectors contain both executable code and the data required to run the code.

Note The use of basic or dynamic disk does not affect where the MBR is located on disk and only minor differences exist between the two for how the partition table is configured. However, as the Disk Management database contains the information where dynamic volumes begin and end, the method of walking, or navigating, partition tables to find the start and end of partitions and logical volumes, as well as finding volume boot sectors, does not work on dynamic disks. Disk editing tools, such as DiskProbe and third-party tools, can walk the partitions as expected with basic disks. Also, many disk editor tools that work with Windows NT and NTFS are not currently compatible with FAT32 boot sectors and volumes.

Master Boot Record

The MBR, the most important data structure on the disk, is created when the disk is partitioned. The MBR contains a small amount of executable code called the master boot code, the disk signature, and the partition table for the disk. At the end of the MBR is a 2-byte structure called a signature word or end of sector marker, which is always set to 0x55AA. A signature word also marks the end of an *extended boot record* (EBR) and the boot sector.

The disk signature, a unique number at offset 0x01B8, identifies the disk to the operating system. Windows 2000 uses the disk signature as an index to store and retrieve information about the disk in the registry subkey HKEY_LOCAL_MACHINE\SYSTEM\MountedDevices.

Master Boot Code

The *master boot code* performs the following activities:

1. Scans the partition table for the active partition.
2. Finds the starting sector of the active partition.
3. Loads a copy of the boot sector from the active partition into memory.
4. Transfers control to the executable code in the boot sector.

If the master boot code cannot complete these functions, the system displays one of the following error messages:

- `Invalid partition table.`
- `Error loading operating system.`
- `Missing operating system.`

Note There is no MBR on a floppy disk. The first sector on a floppy disk is the boot sector. Although every hard disk contains an MBR, the master boot code is used only if the disk contains the active, primary partition.

For more information about troubleshooting MBR problems, see "Damaged MBRs and Boot Sectors" later in this chapter.

Partition Table

The partition table, a 64-byte data structure used to identify the type and location of partitions on a hard disk, conforms to a standard layout independent of the operating system. Each partition table entry is 16 bytes long, with a maximum of four entries. Each entry starts at a predetermined offset from the beginning of the sector, as follows:

- Partition 1   0x01BE (446)
- Partition 2   0x01CE (462)
- Partition 3   0x01DE (478)
- Partition 4   0x01EE (494)

Note Only basic disk makes use of the partition table in Windows 2000. Dynamic disk uses the Disk Management database located at the end of the disk for disk configuration information. The partition table is not updated when volumes are deleted or extended after the dynamic disk upgrade, or when new dynamic volumes are created.

The following example shows a partial printout of an MBR revealing the partition table from a computer with three partitions. When there are fewer than four partitions on a disk, the remaining partition table fields are set to the value 0.

```
000001B0:                                      80 01              ..
000001C0: 01 00 07 FE BF 09 3F 00  - 00 00 4B F5 7F 00 00 00    ......?...K. ...
000001D0: 81 0A 07 FE FF FF 8A F5  - 7F 00 3D 26 9C 00 00 00    ........ .=&....
000001E0: C1 FF 05 FE FF FF C7 1B  - 1C 01 D6 96 92 00 00 00    ..............
000001F0: 00 00 00 00 00 00 00 00  - 00 00 00 00 00 00          ..............
```

Table 32.2 describes the fields in each entry in the partition table. The sample values correspond to the first partition table entry shown in this example. The Byte Offset values correspond to the addresses of the first partition table entry. There are three additional entries whose values can be calculated by 10h to the byte offset value specific for each additional partition table entry (for example, add 20h for partition table entry 3 and 30h for partition table entry 4).

Table 32.2   Partition Table Fields

Byte Offset	Field Length	Sample Value	Field Name and Definition
0x01BE	BYTE	0x80	**Boot Indicator**. Indicates whether the volume is the active partition. Legal values include: 00. Do not use for booting. 80. Active partition.
0x01BF	BYTE	0x01	**Starting Head**.
0x01C0	6 bits	0x01 *	**Starting Sector**. Only bits 0-5 are used. The upper two bits, 6 and 7, are used by the Starting Cylinder field.
0x01C1	10 bits	0x00 *	**Starting Cylinder**. Uses 1 byte in addition to the upper 2 bits from the Starting Sector field to make up the cylinder value. The Starting Cylinder is a 10-bit number, with a maximum value of 1023.
0x01C2	BYTE	0x07	**System ID**. Defines the volume type. See Table 32.3 for sample values.
0x01C3	BYTE	0xFE	**Ending Head**.
0x01C4	6 bits	0xBF *	**Ending Sector**. Only bits 0-5 are used. The upper two bits, 6 and 7, are used by the Ending Cylinder field.
0x01C5	10 bits	0x09 *	**Ending Cylinder**. Uses 1 byte in addition to the upper 2 bits from the Ending Sector field to make up the cylinder value. The Ending Cylinder is a 10-bit number, with a maximum value of 1023.

(continued)

Table 32.2   Partition Table Fields *(continued)*

Byte Offset	Field Length	Sample Value	Field Name and Definition
0x01C6	DWORD	0x3F000000	**Relative Sectors**. The offset from the beginning of the disk to the beginning of the volume, counting by sectors.
0x01CA	DWORD	0x4BF57F00	**Total Sectors**. The total number of sectors in the volume.

A BYTE is 8 bits, a WORD is 16 bits, a DWORD is 32 bits, and a LONGLONG is 64 bits. Sample values marked with an asterisk (*) do not accurately represent the value of the fields, because the fields are either 6 bits or 10 bits and the data is recorded in bytes.

Numbers larger than one byte are stored in little endian format, or reverse-byte ordering. Little endian format is a method of storing a number so that the least significant byte appears first in the hexadecimal number notation. For example, the sample value for the **Relative Sectors** field in the previous table, 0x3F000000, is a little endian representation of 0x0000003F. The decimal equivalent of this little endian number is 63.

Boot Indicator Field

The first element of the partition table, the **Boot Indicator** field, indicates whether or not the volume is the active partition. Only one primary partition on the disk can have this field set.

It is possible to have different operating systems and different file systems on different volumes. By using disk configuration tools such as the Windows 2000-based Disk Management or the MS-DOS-based Fdisk to designate a primary partition as active, the **Boot Indicator** field for that partition is set in the partition table.

System ID Field

Another element of the partition table is the **System ID** field. It defines which file system, such as FAT16, FAT32, or NTFS, was used to format the volume and the FT characteristics of the volume. The **System ID** field also identifies an extended partition, if one is defined. Windows 2000 uses the **System ID** field to determine which file system device drivers to load during startup. Table 32.3 identifies the values for the **System ID** field.

Table 32.3   System ID Values

Partition Type	ID Value
0x01	FAT12 primary partition or logical drive (fewer than 32,680 sectors in the volume)
0x04	FAT16 partition or logical drive (32,680–65,535 sectors or 16 MB–33 MB)
0x05	Extended partition
0x06	BIGDOS FAT16 partition or logical drive (33 MB–4 GB)
0x07	Installable File System (NTFS partition or logical drive)
0x0B	FAT32 partition or logical drive
0x0C	FAT32 partition or logical drive using BIOS INT 13h extensions
0x0E	BIGDOS FAT16 partition or logical drive using BIOS INT 13h extensions
0x0F	Extended partition using BIOS INT 13h extensions
0x12	EISA partition
0x42	Dynamic disk volume
0x86	Legacy FT FAT16 disk *
0x87	Legacy FT NTFS disk *
0x8B	Legacy FT volume formatted with FAT32 *
0x8C	Legacy FT volume using BIOS INT 13h extensions formatted with FAT32 *

Partition types denoted with an asterisk (*) indicate that they are also used to designate non-FT configurations such as striped and spanned volumes.

When a mirrored or RAID-5 volume is created in Windows NT 4.0 or earlier, the high bit of the **System ID** field byte is set for each primary partition or logical drive that is a member of the volume. For example, a FAT16 primary partition or logical drive that is a member of a mirrored or RAID-5 volume, has a **System ID** value of 0x86. A FAT32 primary partition or logical drive has a **System ID** value of 0x8B, and an NTFS primary partition or logical drive has a **System ID** value of 0x87. Partitions that have the high bit set can only be directly accessed by Windows 2000 and Windows NT. Shared folders on FT disks, however, are also available to computers running MS-DOS, Windows 95, and Windows 98.

Note   MS-DOS can only access volumes that have a **System ID** value of 0x01, 0x04, 0x05, or 0x06. However, you can delete volumes that have the other values listed in Table 32.3 using MS-DOS tools such as Fdisk. If you use a low-level disk editor, such as DiskProbe, you can read and write to any sector, including ones that are in NTFS volumes.

Starting and Ending Cylinder, Head, and Sector Fields

The **Starting** and **Ending Cylinder**, **Head**, and **Sector** fields (collectively known as the **CHS** fields) are additional elements of the partition table. These fields are essential for starting the computer. The master boot code uses these fields to find and load the boot sector of the active partition. The **Starting CHS** fields for non-active partitions point to the boot sectors of the remaining primary partitions and the EBR of the first logical drive in the extended partition as shown in Figure 32.1

Knowing the starting sector of an extended partition is very important for low-level disk troubleshooting. If your disk fails, you need to work with the partition starting point (among other factors) to retrieve stored data.

Note To have a written record of the starting and ending sectors of the partitions on your hard disk, as well as other useful disk configuration data, use the DiskMap tool. For more information about DiskMap, see the documentation provided on the *Windows 2000 Resource Kit* companion CD.

Figure 32.1 shows the MBR, partition table, and boot sectors on a disk with four partitions. The definitions of the fields in the partition table and the extended partition tables are the same.

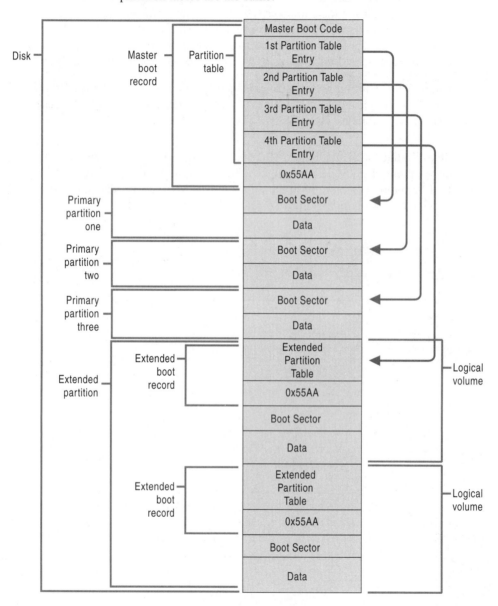

Figure 32.1   Detail of a Basic Disk with Four Partitions

The **Ending Cylinder** field in the partition table is 10 bits long, which limits the number of cylinders that can be described in the partition table to a range of 0–1,023. The **Starting Head** and **Ending Head** fields are each one byte long, which limits the field range to 0–255. The **Starting Sector** and **Ending Sector** fields are each six bits long, which limits the range of these fields to 0–63. However, the enumeration of sectors starts at 1 (not 0, as for other fields), so the maximum number of sectors per track is 63.

Because all hard disks are low-level formatted with a standard 512-byte sector, the maximum disk capacity described by the partition table is calculated as follows:

```
Maximum capacity = sector size x cylinders (10 bits) x heads (8 bits) x
sectors per track (6 bits)
```

Using the maximum possible values yields:

```
512 x 1024 x 256 x 63 (or 512 x 2^24) = 8,455,716,864 bytes or 7.8 GB
```

The calculation results in a maximum capacity of slightly less than 8 gigabytes (GB). Before BIOS INT 13h extensions drive geometry translation (also known as *logical block addressing*, or LBA) were introduced, the active, primary partition could not exceed 7.8 GB, regardless of the file system used.

Important   When using the standard 512-byte sector, the maximum cluster size that you can use for FAT16 volumes while running Windows 2000 is 64 kilobytes (KB). Therefore, the maximum size for a FAT16 volume is 4 GB.

If you use a multiple-boot configuration with Windows 95, Windows 98, or MS-DOS, FAT16 volumes must be limited to 2 GB to be accessed from these operating systems. In addition, a Macintosh computer that accesses volumes on a computer running Windows 2000 cannot access a FAT16 volume that is larger than 2 GB. If you try to use a FAT16 volume larger than 2 GB when running MS-DOS, Windows 95, or Windows 98, or try to access such a volume from a Macintosh computer, you might get a message that zero bytes are available.

The maximum FAT16 volume size that you can use on a computer depends on the disk geometry and the maximum values that fit in the partition table entry fields. Table 32.4 shows the typical FAT16 volume size when LBA is enabled or disabled. The number of cylinders in both cases is 1,024 (0–1,023). When a primary partition or logical drive extends beyond the 1,023rd cylinder, all fields described in this section contain the maximum values.

Table 32.4   FAT16 Volume Size When LBA Is Enabled or Disabled

Translation Mode	Number of Heads	Sectors per Track	Maximum Size for System or Boot Partition
Disabled	64	32	1 GB
Enabled	255	63	4 GB

Warning Do not change the LBA setting on any hard disk containing data. You can adversely affect the process in which the system translates the disk attributes for storing data and corrupt all the files and partitions on the physical disk. Refer to your computer owner's manual before modifying this BIOS setting.

To accommodate sizes larger than 7.8 GB, Windows 2000 ignores the values in the **Starting** and **Ending Sector** fields of the partition table in favor of the **Relative Sectors** and **Total Sectors** fields.

Relative Sectors and Total Sectors Fields

The **Relative Sectors** field represents the offset from the beginning of the disk to the beginning of the volume, counting by sectors, for the volume described by the partition table entry. The **Total Sectors** field represents the total number of sectors in the volume.

Using the **Relative Sectors** and **Total Sectors** fields (resulting in a 32-bit number) provides eight more bits than the CHS scheme to represent the total number of sectors. This allows partitions containing up to 2^{32} sectors to be defined. With a standard sector size of 512 bytes, the 32 bits used to represent the **Relative Sectors** and **Total Sectors** fields translates into a maximum partition size of 2 terabytes (or 2,199,023,255,552 bytes).

This addressing scheme is only used in Windows 2000 with NTFS and FAT32.

Note In addition, the Format tool of Windows 2000 limits the maximum size of FAT32 volumes it can create to 32 GB. However, Windows 2000 can directly access larger FAT32 volumes created by Windows 95 OSR2 or Windows 98.

Windows 2000 uses the fields in the partition table entries to access all partitions. A partition that is formatted while Windows 2000 is running puts data into the **Starting** and **Ending CHS** fields to have compatibility with MS-DOS, Windows 95, and Windows 98, and to maintain compatibility with the BIOS INT 13h for startup.

Extended Boot Record

An EBR, which consists of an *extended partition table* and the signature word for the sector, exists for each logical drive in the extended partition. It contains the only information on the first side of the first cylinder of each logical drive in the extended partition. The boot sector in a logical drive is usually located at either Relative Sector 32 or 63. However, if there is no extended partition on a disk, there are no EBRs and no logical drives.

Note This information applies only to disks configured with basic disk.

The first entry in an extended partition table for the first logical drive points to its own boot sector. The second entry points to the EBR of the next logical drive. If no further logical drives exist, the second entry is not used and is recorded as a series of zeroes. If there are additional logical drives, the first entry of the extended partition table for the second logical drive points to its own boot sector. The second entry of the extended partition table for the second logical drive points to the EBR of the next logical drive. The third and fourth entries of an extended partition table are never used.

As shown in Figure 32.2, the EBRs of the logical drives in the extended partition are a linked list. The figure shows three logical drives on an extended partition, illustrating the difference in extended partition tables between preceding logical drives and the last logical drive.

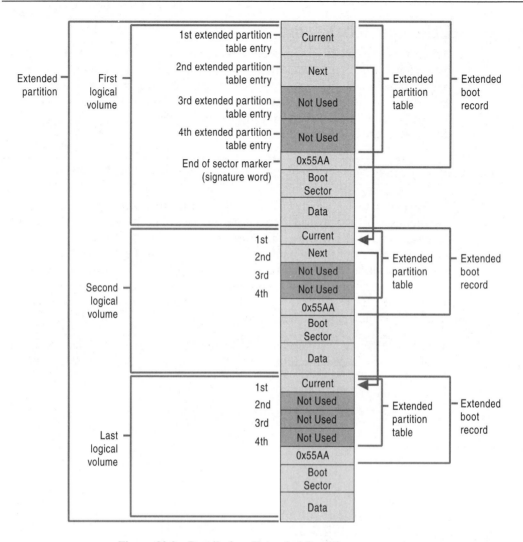

Figure 32.2   Detail of an Extended Partition

With the exception of the last logical drive on the extended partition, the format of the extended partition table, described in Table 32.5, is repeated for each logical drive: the first entry identifies the logical drive's own boot sector and the second entry identifies the next logical drive's EBR. The extended partition table for the last logical drive has only its own partition entry listed. The second through fourth entries of the last extended partition table are not used.

Table 32.5   Contents of Extended Partition Table Entries

Extended Partition Table Entry	Entry Contents
First	Information about the current logical drive in the extended partition, including the starting address for data.
Second	Information about the next logical drive in the extended partition, including the address of the sector that contains the EBR for the next logical drive. If no further logical drives exist, this field is not used.
Third	Not used
Fourth	Not used

The fields in each entry of the extended partition table are identical to the MBR partition table entries. See Table 32.2 for more information about partition table fields.

The **Relative Sectors** field in an extended partition table entry shows the number of bytes that are offset from the beginning of the extended partition to the first sector in the logical drive. The number in the **Total Sectors** field refers to the number of sectors that make up the logical drive. The value of the **Total Sectors** field equals the number of sectors from the boot sector defined by the extended partition table entry to the end of the logical drive.

Because of the importance of the MBR and EBR sectors, it is recommended that you run disk-scanning tools regularly as well as regularly back up all your data files to protect against losing access to a volume or an entire disk.

Boot Sector

The boot sector, located at sector 1 of each volume, is a critical disk structure for starting your computer. It contains executable code and data required by the code, including information that the file system uses to access the volume. The boot sector is created when you format a volume. At the end of the boot sector is a two-byte structure called a signature word or end of sector marker, which is always set to 0x55AA. On computers running Windows 2000, the boot sector on the active partition loads into memory and starts Ntldr, which loads the operating system.

The Windows 2000 boot sector consists of the following elements:

- An *x*86-based CPU jump instruction.
- The *original equipment manufacturer* identification (OEM ID).
- The *BIOS parameter block (BPB)*, a data structure.

Following the OEM ID is the BPB, which provides information that enables the executable boot code to locate Ntldr. The BPB always starts at the same offset, so standard parameters are in a known location. Disk size and geometry variables are encapsulated in the BPB. Because the first part of the boot sector is an x86 jump instruction, the BPB can be extended in the future by appending new information at the end. The jump instruction needs only a minor adjustment to accommodate this change. The BPB is stored in a packed (unaligned) format.

FAT16 Boot Sector

Table 32.6 describes the boot sector of a volume formatted with the FAT16 file system.

Table 32.6   Boot Sector Sections on a FAT16 Volume

Byte Offset	Field Length	Field Name
0x00	3 bytes	Jump Instruction
0x03	LONGLONG	OEM ID
0x0B	25 bytes	BPB
0x24	26 bytes	Extended BPB
0x3E	448 bytes	Bootstrap Code
0x01FE	WORD	End of Sector Marker

The following example illustrates a hexadecimal printout of the boot sector on a FAT16 volume. The printout is formatted in three sections:

- Bytes 0x00–0x0A are the jump instruction and the OEM ID (shown in bold print).
- Bytes 0x0B–0x3D are the BPB and the extended BPB.

- The remaining section is the bootstrap code and the end of sector marker (shown in bold print).

```
Physical Sector: Cyl 0, Side 1, Sector 1
00000000: EB 3C 90 4D 53 44 4F 53 - 35 2E 30 00 02 40 01 00   .<.MSDOS5.0..@..
00000010: 02 00 02 00 00 F8 FC 00 - 3F 00 40 00 3F 00 00 00   ........?.@.?...
00000020: 01 F0 3E 00 80 00 29 A8 - 8B 36 52 4E 4F 20 4E 41   ..>..)..6RNO NA
00000030: 4D 45 20 20 20 20 46 41 - 54 31 36 20 20 20 33 C0   ME    FAT16   3.
00000040: 8E D0 BC 00 7C 68 C0 07 - 1F A0 10 00 F7 26 16 00   ....|h......&..
00000050: 03 06 0E 00 50 91 B8 20 - 00 F7 26 11 00 8B 1E 0B   ....P.. ..&.....
00000060: 00 03 C3 48 F7 F3 03 C8 - 89 0E 08 02 68 00 10 07   ...H........h...
00000070: 33 DB 8F 06 13 02 89 1E - 15 02 0E E8 90 00 72 57   3.............rW
00000080: 33 DB 8B 0E 11 00 8B FB - 51 B9 0B 00 BE DC 01 F3   3.......Q.......
00000090: A6 59 74 05 83 C3 20 E2 - ED E3 37 26 8B 57 1A 52   .Yt... ...7&.W.R
000000A0: B8 01 00 68 00 20 07 33 - DB 0E E8 48 00 72 28 5B   ...h. .3...H.r([
000000B0: 8D 36 0B 00 8D 3E 0B 02 - 1E 8F 45 02 C7 05 F5 00   .6...>....E.....
000000C0: 1E 8F 45 06 C7 45 04 0E - 01 8A 16 24 00 EA 03 00   ..E..E.....$....
000000D0: 00 20 BE 86 01 EB 03 BE - A2 01 E8 09 00 BE C1 01   . ..............
000000E0: E8 03 00 FB EB FE AC 0A - C0 74 09 B4 0E BB 07 00   .........t......
000000F0: CD 10 EB F2 C3 50 4A 4A - A0 0D 00 32 E4 F7 E2 03   .....PJJ...2....
00000100: 06 08 02 83 D2 00 A3 13 - 02 89 16 15 02 58 A2 07   .............X..
00000110: 02 A1 13 02 8B 16 15 02 - 03 06 1C 00 13 16 1E 00   ................
00000120: F7 36 18 00 FE C2 88 16 - 06 02 33 D2 F7 36 1A 00   .6........3..6..
00000130: 88 16 25 00 A3 04 02 A1 - 18 00 2A 06 06 02 40 3A   ..%.......*...@:
00000140: 06 07 02 76 05 A0 07 02 - 32 E4 50 B4 02 8B 0E 04   ...v....2.P.....
00000150: 02 C0 E5 06 0A 2E 06 02 - 86 E9 8B 16 24 00 CD 13   ............$...
00000160: 0F 83 05 00 83 C4 02 F9 - CB 58 28 06 07 02 76 11   .........X(...v.
00000170: 01 06 13 02 83 16 15 02 - 00 F7 26 0B 00 03 D8 EB   ..........&.....
00000180: 90 A2 07 02 F8 CB 42 4F - 4F 54 3A 20 43 6F 75 6C   ......BOOT: Coul
00000190: 64 6E 27 74 20 66 69 6E - 64 20 4E 54 4C 44 52 0D   dn't find NTLDR.
000001A0: 0A 00 42 4F 4F 54 3A 20 - 49 2F 4F 20 65 72 72 6F   ..BOOT: I/O erro
000001B0: 72 20 72 65 61 64 69 6E - 67 20 64 69 73 6B 0D 0A   r reading disk..
000001C0: 00 50 6C 65 61 73 65 20 - 69 6E 73 65 72 74 20 61   .Please insert a
000001D0: 6E 6F 74 68 65 72 20 64 - 69 73 6B 00 4E 54 4C 44   nother disk.NTLD
000001E0: 52 20 20 20 20 20 20 00 - 00 00 00 00 00 00 00 00   R       ........
000001F0: 00 00 00 00 00 00 00 00 - 00 00 00 00 00 00 55 AA   ..............U.
```

Tables 32.7 and 32.8 illustrate the layout of the BPB and the extended BPB for FAT16 volumes. The sample values correspond to the data in this example.

Table 32.7   BPB Fields for FAT16 Volumes

Byte Offset	Field Length	Value	Field Name and Definition
0x0B	WORD	0x0002	**Bytes Per Sector**. The size of a hardware sector. Valid decimal values for this field are 512, 1024, 2048, and 4096. For most disks used in the United States, the value of this field is 512.
0x0D	BYTE	0x40	**Sectors Per Cluster**. The number of sectors in a cluster. Because FAT16 can track only a limited number of clusters (up to 65,536), large volumes are supported by increasing the number of sectors per cluster. The default cluster size for a volume depends on the volume size. Valid decimal values for this field are 1, 2, 4, 8, 16, 32, 64, and 128. Values that lead to clusters larger than 32 KB (**Bytes Per Sector * Sectors Per Cluster**) can cause disk and software errors.
0x0E	WORD	0x0100	**Reserved Sectors**. The number of sectors preceding the start of the first FAT, including the boot sector. The value of this field is always 1.
0x10	BYTE	0x02	**Number of FATs**. The number of copies of the FAT on the volume. The value of this field is always 2.
0x11	WORD	0x0002	**Root Entries**. The total number of 32-byte file and folder name entries that can be stored in the root folder of the volume. On a typical hard disk, the value of this field is 512. One entry is always used as a Volume Label, and files and folders with long names use multiple entries per file. The largest number of file and folder entries is typically 511, but entries run out before you reach that number if long file names are used.
0x13	WORD	0x0000	**Small Sectors**. The number of sectors on the volume represented in 16 bits (< 65,536). For volumes larger than 65,536 sectors, this field has a value of zero and the **Large Sectors** field is used instead.
0x15	BYTE	0xF8	**Media Descriptor**. Provides information about the media being used. A value of 0xF8 indicates a hard disk and 0xF0 indicates a high-density 3.5-inch floppy disk. Media descriptor entries are a legacy of MS-DOS FAT16 disks and are not used in Windows 2000.
0x16	WORD	0xFC00	**Sectors Per FAT**. The number of sectors occupied by each FAT on the volume. The computer uses this number and the number of FATs and hidden sectors, to determine where the root directory begins. The computer can also determine where the user data area of the volume begins based on the number of entries in the root directory (512).
0x18	WORD	0x3F00	**Sectors Per Track**. Part of the apparent disk geometry used on a low-level formatted disk.
0x1A	WORD	0x4000	**Number of Heads**. Part of the apparent disk geometry used on a low-level formatted disk.
0x1C	DWORD	0x3F000000	**Hidden Sectors**. The number of sectors on the volume before the boot sector. This value is used during the boot sequence to calculate the absolute offset to the root directory and data areas.
0x20	DWORD	0x01F03E00	**Large Sectors**. If the value of the **Small Sectors** field is zero, this field contains the total number of sectors in the FAT16 volume. If the value of the **Small Sectors** field is not zero, the value of this field is zero.

Table 32.8   Extended BPB Fields for FAT16 Volumes

Byte Offset	Field Length	Value	Field Name and Definition
0x24	BYTE	0x80	**Physical Drive Number**. Related to the BIOS physical drive number. Floppy drives are identified as 0x00 and physical hard disks are identified as 0x80, regardless of the number of physical disk drives. Typically, this value is set prior to issuing an INT 13h BIOS call to specify the device to access. The value is only relevant if the device is a boot device.
0x25	BYTE	0x00	**Reserved**. FAT16 volumes are always set to zero.
0x26	BYTE	0x29	**Extended Boot Signature**. A field that must have the value 0x28 or 0x29 to be recognized by Windows 2000.
0x27	DWORD	0xA88B3652	**Volume Serial Number**. A random serial number created when formatting a disk, which helps to distinguish between disks.
0x2B	11 bytes	NO NAME	**Volume Label**. A field once used to store the volume label. The volume label is now stored as a special file in the root directory.
0x36	LONGLONG	FAT16	**File System Type**. A field with a value of either FAT, FAT12 or FAT16, depending on the disk format.

FAT32 Boot Sector

Table 32.9 describes the boot sector of a volume formatted with the FAT32 file system.

Note   The FAT32 boot sector is structurally very similar to the FAT16 boot sector, but the FAT32 BPB contains additional fields. The FAT32 extended BPB uses the same fields as FAT16, but the offset addresses of these fields within the boot sector are different than those found in FAT16 boot sectors. Drives formatted in FAT32 are not readable by operating systems that are incompatible with FAT32.

Table 32.9   Boot Sector Sections on a FAT32 Volume

Byte Offset	Field Length	Field Name
0x00	3 bytes	Jump Instruction
0x03	LONGLONG	OEM ID
0x0B	53 bytes	BPB
0x40	26 bytes	Extended BPB
0x5A	420 bytes	Bootstrap Code
0x01FE	WORD	End of Sector Marker

The following example illustrates a hexadecimal printout of the boot sector on a FAT32 volume. The printout is formatted in three sections:

- Bytes 0x00–0x0A are the jump instruction and the OEM ID (shown in bold print).

- Bytes 0x0B–0x59 are the BPB and the extended BPB.

- The remaining section is the bootstrap code and the end of sector marker (shown in bold print).

```
Physical Sector: Cyl 878, Side 0, Sector 1
00000000: EB 58 90 4D 53 44 4F 53 - 35 2E 30 00 02 08 20 00   .X.MSDOS5.0... .
00000010: 02 00 00 00 00 F8 00 00 - 3F 00 FF 00 EE 39 D7 00   ........?....9..
00000020: 7F 32 4E 00 83 13 00 00 - 00 00 00 00 02 00 00 00   2N..............
00000030: 01 00 06 00 00 00 00 00 - 00 00 00 00 00 00 00 00   ................
00000040: 80 00 29 8B 93 6D 54 4E - 4F 20 4E 41 4D 45 20 20   ..)..mTNO NAME
00000050: 20 20 46 41 54 33 32 20 - 20 20 33 C9 8E D1 BC F4     FAT32   3.....
00000060: 7B 8E C1 8E D9 BD 00 7C - 88 4E 02 8A 56 40 B4 08   {......|.N..V@..
00000070: CD 13 73 05 B9 FF FF 8A - F1 66 0F B6 C6 40 66 0F   ..s......f...@f.
00000080: B6 D1 80 E2 3F F7 E2 86 - CD C0 ED 06 41 66 0F B7   ....?.......Af..
00000090: C9 66 F7 E1 66 89 46 F8 - 83 7E 16 00 75 38 83 7E   .f..f.F..~..u8.~
000000A0: 2A 00 77 32 66 8B 46 1C - 66 83 C0 0C BB 00 80 B9   *.w2f.F.f.......
000000B0: 01 00 E8 2B 00 E9 48 03 - A0 FA 7D B4 7D 8B F0 AC   ...+..H...}.}...
000000C0: 84 C0 74 17 3C FF 74 09 - B4 0E BB 07 00 CD 10 EB   ..t.<.t.........
000000D0: EE A0 FB 7D EB E5 A0 F9 - 7D EB E0 98 CD 16 CD 19   ...}....}.......
000000E0: 66 60 66 3B 46 F8 0F 82 - 4A 00 66 6A 00 66 50 06   f`f;F...J.fj.fP.
000000F0: 53 66 68 10 00 01 00 80 - 7E 02 00 0F 85 20 00 B4   Sfh.....~.... ..
00000100: 41 BB AA 55 8A 56 40 CD - 13 0F 82 1C 00 81 FB 55   A..U.V@........U
00000110: AA 0F 85 14 00 F6 C1 01 - 0F 84 0D 00 FE 46 02 B4   .............F..
00000120: 42 8A 56 40 8B F4 CD 13 - B0 F9 66 58 66 58 66 58   B.V@......fXfXfX
00000130: 66 58 EB 2A 66 33 D2 66 - 0F B7 4E 18 66 F7 F1 FE   fX.*f3.f..N.f...
00000140: C2 8A CA 66 8B D0 66 C1 - EA 10 F7 76 1A 86 D6 8A   ...f..f....v....
00000150: 56 40 8A E8 C0 E4 06 0A - CC B8 01 02 CD 13 66 61   V@............fa
00000160: 0F 82 54 FF 81 C3 00 02 - 66 40 49 0F 85 71 FF C3   ..T.....f@I..q..
00000170: 4E 54 4C 44 52 20 20 20 - 20 20 20 0D 0A 4E 54 4C   NTLDR      ..NTL
00000180: 44 52 20 69 73 20 6D 69 - 73 73 69 6E 67 FF 0D 0A   DR is missing...
00000190: 44 69 73 6B 20 65 72 72 - 6F 72 FF 0D 0A 50 72 65   Disk error...Pre
000001A0: 73 73 20 61 6E 79 20 6B - 65 79 20 74 6F 20 72 65   ss any key to re
000001B0: 73 74 61 72 74 0D 0A 00 - 00 00 00 00 00 00 00 00   start...........
000001C0: 00 00 00 00 00 00 00 00 - 00 00 00 00 00 00 00 00   ................
000001D0: 00 00 00 00 00 00 00 00 - 00 00 00 00 00 00 00 00   ................
000001E0: 00 00 00 00 00 00 00 00 - 00 00 00 00 00 00 00 00   ................
000001F0: 00 00 00 00 00 00 00 00 - 00 7B 8E 9B 00 00 55 AA   .........{....U.
```

Tables 32.10 and 32.11 illustrate the layout of the BPB and the extended BPB for FAT32 volumes. The sample values correspond to the data in this example.

Table 32.10   BPB Fields for FAT32 Volumes

Byte Offset	Field Length	Value	Field Name and Definition
0x0B	WORD	0x0002	**Bytes Per Sector**. The size of a hardware sector. Valid decimal values for this field are 512, 1024, 2048, and 4096. For most disks used in the United States, the value of this field is 512.
0x0D	BYTE	0x08	**Sectors Per Cluster**. The number of sectors in a cluster. Because FAT32 can only track a finite number of clusters (up to 4,294,967,296), extremely large volumes are supported by increasing the number of sectors per cluster. The default cluster size for a volume depends on the volume size. Valid decimal values for this field are 1, 2, 4, 8, 16, 32, 64, and 128. The Windows 2000 implementation of FAT32 allows for the creation of volumes only up to a maximum of 32 GB. However, larger volumes created by other operating systems (Windows 95 OSR2 and later) are accessible in Windows 2000.
0x0E	WORD	0x0200	**Reserved Sectors**. The number of sectors preceding the start of the first FAT, including the boot sector. The decimal value of this field is typically 32.
0x10	BYTE	0x02	**Number of FATs**. The number of copies of the FAT on the volume. The value of this field is always 2.
0x11	WORD	0x0000	**Root Entries (FAT12/FAT16 only)**. For FAT32 volumes, this field must be set to zero.
0x13	WORD	0x0000	**Small Sectors (FAT12/FAT16 only)**. For FAT32 volumes, this field must be set to zero.
0x15	BYTE	0xF8	**Media Descriptor**. Provides information about the media being used. A value of 0xF8 indicates a hard disk and 0xF0 indicates a high-density 3.5-inch floppy disk. Media descriptor entries are a legacy of MS-DOS FAT16 disks and are not used in Windows 2000.
0x16	WORD	0x0000	**Sectors Per FAT (FAT12/FAT16 only)**. For FAT32 volumes, this field must be set to zero.
0x18	WORD	0x3F00	**Sectors Per Track**. Contains the "sectors per track" geometry value for disks that use INT 13h. The volume is broken down into tracks by multiple heads and cylinders.
0x1A	WORD	0xFF00	**Number of Heads**. Contains the "count of heads" geometry value for disks that use INT 13h. For example, on a 1.44-MB, 3.5-inch floppy disk this value is 2.
0x1C	DWORD	0xEE39D700	**Hidden Sectors**. The number of sectors on the volume before the boot sector. This value is used during the boot sequence to calculate the absolute offset to the root directory and data areas. This field is generally only relevant for media that are visible on interrupt 13h. It must always be zero on media that are not partitioned.

(continued)

Table 32.10   BPB Fields for FAT32 Volumes *(continued)*

Byte Offset	Field Length	Value	Field Name and Definition
0x20	DWORD	0x7F324E00	**Large Sectors**. Contains the total number of sectors in the FAT32 volume.
0x24	DWORD	0x83130000	**Sectors Per FAT (FAT32 only)**. The number of sectors occupied by each FAT on the volume. The computer uses this number and the number of FATs and hidden sectors (described in this table), to determine where the root directory begins. The computer can also determine where the user data area of the volume begins based on the number of entries in the root directory.
0x28	WORD	0x0000	**Extended Flags (FAT32 only)**. The value of the bits in this two-byte structure are:
			Bits 0–3: Number of the active FAT (starting count at 0, not 1). It is only valid if mirroring is disabled.
			Bits 4–6: Reserved.
			Bit 7: A value of 0 means the FAT is mirrored at runtime into all FATs. A value of 1 means only one FAT is active (referenced in bits 0-3).
			Bits 8–15: Reserved.
0x2A	WORD	0x0000	**File System Version (FAT32 only)**. The high byte is the major revision number, whereas the low byte is the minor revision number. This field supports the ability to extend the FAT32 media type in the future with concern for old FAT32 drivers mounting the volume. If the field is non-zero, back-level Windows versions will not mount the volume.
0x2C	DWORD	0x02000000	**Root Cluster Number (FAT32 only)**. The cluster number of the first cluster of the root directory. This value is typically, but not always, 2.
0x30	WORD	0x0100	**File System Information Sector Number (FAT32 only)**. The sector number of the File System Information (FSINFO) structure in the reserved area of the FAT32 volume. The value is typically 1. A copy of the FSINFO structure is kept in the Backup Boot Sector, but it is not kept up-to-date.
0x34	WORD	0x0600	**Backup Boot Sector (FAT32 only)**. A non-zero value indicates the sector number in the reserved area of the volume in which a copy of the boot sector is stored. The value of this field is typically 6. No other value is recommended.
0x36	12 bytes	0x000000000 00000000000 0000	**Reserved (FAT32 only)**. Reserved space for future expansion. The value of this field should always be zero.

Table 32.11   Extended BPB Fields for FAT32 Volumes

Byte Offset	Field Length	Value	Field Name and Definition
0x40	BYTE	0x80	**Physical Drive Number**. Related to the BIOS physical drive number. Floppy drives are identified as 0x00 and physical hard disks are identified as 0x80, regardless of the number of physical disk drives. Typically, this value is set prior to issuing an INT 13h BIOS call to specify the device to access. It is only relevant if the device is a boot device.
0x41	BYTE	0x00	**Reserved**. FAT32 volumes are always set to zero.
0x42	BYTE	0x29	**Extended Boot Signature**. A field that must have the value 0x28 or 0x29 to be recognized by Windows 2000.
0x43	DWORD	0xA88B3652	**Volume Serial Number**. A random serial number created when formatting a disk, which helps to distinguish between disks.
0x47	11 bytes	NO NAME	**Volume Label**. A field once used to store the volume label. The volume label is now stored as a special file in the root directory.
0x52	LONGLONG	FAT32	**System ID**. A text field with a value of FAT32.

NTFS Boot Sector

Table 32.12 describes the boot sector of a volume formatted with NTFS. The bootstrap code for an NTFS volume is longer than the 426 bytes, as shown in Table 32.12. When you format an NTFS volume, the format program allocates the first 16 sectors for the boot sector and the bootstrap code.

Table 32.12   Boot Sector Sections on an NTFS Volume

Byte Offset	Field Length	Field Name
0x00	3 bytes	Jump Instruction
0x03	LONGLONG	OEM ID
0x0B	25 bytes	BPB
0x24	48 bytes	Extended BPB
0x54	426 bytes	Bootstrap Code
0x01FE	WORD	End of Sector Marker

On NTFS volumes, the data fields that follow the BPB form an extended BPB. The data in these fields enables Ntldr to find the *master file table* (MFT) during startup. On NTFS volumes, the MFT is not located in a predefined sector, as on FAT16 and FAT32 volumes. For this reason, the MFT can be moved if there is a bad sector in its normal location. However, if the data is corrupted, the MFT cannot be located, and Windows 2000 assumes that the volume has not been formatted.

Troubleshooting Disk Problems

There are various causes of disk problems and means of recovering from them. The following are tools that you can use to troubleshoot disk problems:

- DiskProbe can be used to examine and change information on individual disk sectors.
- DiskMap can be used to display the layout of partitions and logical volumes on your disk.

Neither of these tools is designed for use with dynamic disks because they cannot read the dynamic Disk Management database. DiskProbe can change the values of individual bytes in any sector on a dynamic disk, but it cannot navigate the structure of a dynamic disk, so it might be impossible to find the sector that you want to view or edit. Therefore it is generally recommended that these tools only be used on basic disks.

DiskProbe is part of the Support Tools collection in the \Support\Tools folder on the Windows 2000 product CD. For more information about using DiskProbe, see the document Dskprtrb.doc in the C:\Program Files\Support Tools folder.

DiskMap is one of the Resource Kit tools on the *Windows 2000 Resource Kit* companion CD. For more information about using DiskMap, see the document Diskmap.doc, installed with the Resource Kit tools into the C:\Program Files\Resource Kit folder.

Warning Be extremely cautious about making any changes to the structures of your hard disk! DiskProbe does not validate the proposed changes to records. Incorrect values in key data structures can render the hard disk inaccessible or prevent the operating system from starting.

You can easily make changes that have serious consequences, resulting in the following error messages:

- You cannot start any operating system.
- A volume is no longer accessible.
- You have to recreate and reformat all of the partitions and logical volumes.

DiskProbe displays a messages asking you to verify any change that you want recorded to disk. Please carefully consider any changes before accepting them.

With careful use of such disk tools as DiskProbe, you can solve problems whether they occur through human error, hardware problems, power outages, or other events. It is a good idea to familiarize yourself with these tools in a test situation. Testing is especially important if your configuration has legacy spanned or striped sets.

Note   Using DiskProbe, you can save, restore, find, examine, and change the bytes of any sector on the disk, including the MBR and the boot sector. The MBR of disk 0 is used to start Windows 2000–based computers, and the system and boot volumes of disk 0 must be defined in the partition table, making the boot sectors easily located, regardless of the disk configuration used. As a result, DiskProbe can be used to back up and restore these disk structures on computers using dynamic disk.

Viruses

It is always important to take precautions to protect your computer and the data on it from viruses. Many computer viruses exploit the disk structures that your computer uses to start up by replacing, redirecting, or corrupting the code and data that start the operating system.

MBR Viruses

MBR viruses exploit the master boot code that runs automatically when the computer starts up. MBR viruses are activated when the BIOS activates the master boot code, before the operating system is loaded.

Many viruses replace the MBR sector with their own code and move the original MBR to another location on disk. Once the virus is activated, it stays in memory and passes the execution to the original MBR so that startup appears to function normally. Some viruses do not relocate the original MBR, causing all volumes on the disk to become inaccessible. If the active, primary partition's listing in the partition table is destroyed, the computer cannot start. Other viruses relocate the MBR to the last sector of the disk; if that sector is not protected by the virus, it might be overwritten during normal use of the computer, preventing the system from being restarted.

Boot Sector Viruses

As with the master boot code, the boot sector's executable code also runs automatically at startup, creating another vulnerable spot exploited by viruses. Boot sector viruses are activated before the operating system is loaded and run when the master boot code in the MBR identifies the active, primary partition and activates the executable boot code for that volume.

Many viruses update the boot sector with their own code and move the original boot sector to another location on disk. Once the virus is activated, it stays in memory and passes the execution to the original boot sector so that startup appears normal. Some viruses do not relocate the original boot sector, making the volume inaccessible. If the affected volume is the active, primary partition, the system cannot start. Other viruses relocate the boot sector to the last sector of the disk. If that sector is not protected by the virus, it might be overwritten by normal use of the computer, rendering the volume inaccessible or preventing the system from restarting, depending upon which volume was affected.

How MBR and Boot Sector Viruses Affect Windows 2000

A computer can contract an MBR or boot sector virus by one of two common methods: by starting up from an infected floppy disk; or by running an infected program, causing the virus to drop an altered MBR or boot sector onto the hard disk.

The function of an MBR or boot sector virus is typically contained once Windows 2000 has started. If a payload is not run during system startup and the virus preserved the original MBR or boot sector, Windows 2000 prevents the virus from self-replicating to other disks.

Windows 2000 is immune to viruses infecting these disk structures during normal operation, because it only accesses physical disks through protected mode disk drivers. Viruses typically subvert the BIOS INT 13h disk access routines, which are ignored once Windows 2000 has started. However, Windows 2000 computers that are multiple-booted with MS-DOS, Windows 95, or Windows 98 can become infected when Windows 2000 is not running the computer.

If a multiple-boot computer on which Windows 2000 has been installed becomes infected by an MBR or boot sector virus while running another operating system, Windows 2000 is vulnerable to damage.

Once the protected mode disk drivers have been activated, the virus cannot copy itself to other hard disks or floppy disks because the BIOS mechanism on which the virus depends is not used for disk access. However, viruses that have a payload trigger that executes during startup are a threat to computers that are running Windows 2000 because the trigger process is initiated before the control during the computer startup process passes to Windows 2000.

Treating an MBR or Boot Sector Virus Infection

To remove a virus from your computer, use a current, well-known, commercial antivirus program designed for Windows 2000, and update it regularly. In addition to scanning the hard disks in your computer, be sure to scan all floppy disks that have been used in the infected computer, in any other computers, or with other operating systems in an infected multiple-boot computer. Scan them even if you believe they are not infected. Many infections recur because one or more copies of the virus were not detected.

If the computer is already infected with a boot sector virus when Windows 2000 is installed, standard antivirus programs might not completely eliminate the infection because Windows 2000 copies the original MS-DOS boot sector to a file called Bootsect.dos and replaces it with its own boot sector. The Windows 2000 installation is not infected, but if the user chooses to start MS-DOS, Windows 95, or Windows 98, the infected boot sector is reapplied to the system, reinfecting the computer. Antivirus tools that are not specifically designed for Windows 2000 do not know to check Bootsect.dos for viruses.

AVBoot

Microsoft provides a customized antivirus tool that can be used for these types of viruses. AVBoot is located in the \Valueadd\3rdparty\Ca_antiv folder of the Windows 2000 Setup CD. Insert an empty, high-density, 3.5-inch floppy disk, and use Windows 2000 Explorer to locate and double-click Makedisk.bat to create a startup floppy disk that automatically runs AVBoot.

AVBoot scans the memory as well as the MBR and all boot sectors of every locally installed disk. If a virus is found, it offers to remove the virus.

Important   Whether you use a third-party antivirus program or AVBoot, be sure to regularly update the virus signature files. Once you install an antivirus program, immediately update the signature files, usually through an Internet connection. Check with the software manufacturer's documentation for specific instructions. AVBoot includes update instructions in the installation folder and on the AVBoot floppy disk.

It is extremely important that you regularly update your antivirus program. In most cases, antivirus programs are unable to reliably detect and clean viruses of which they are unaware. False negative reports can result when using an out-of-date virus scanner. Most commercial antivirus software manufacturers offer monthly updates. Take advantage of the latest download to ensure that your system is protected with the latest virus defenses.

Fdisk /mbr command

Do not depend on the MS-DOS command **Fdisk /mbr**, which rewrites the MBR on the hard disk, to resolve MBR infections. Many newer viruses have the properties of both file infector and MBR viruses, and restoring the MBR does not solve the problem if the virus immediately reinfects the system. In addition, running **Fdisk /mbr** in MS-DOS on a system infected by an MBR virus that does not preserve or encrypt the original MBR partition table permanently prevents access to the lost partitions. If the disk was configured with a third-party disk management program, running this command eliminates the program overlay control and you cannot start up from the disk.

Important Running **Fdisk /mbr** in MS-DOS overwrites only the first 446 bytes of the MBR, the portion known as the master boot code, leaving the existing partition table intact. However, if the signature word, the last two bytes of the MBR, has been deleted, the partition table entries are overwritten with zeroes. If an MBR virus overwrites the signature word, access to all partitions and logical volumes is lost.

Fixmbr command

The Recovery Console, a new troubleshooting tool in Windows 2000, offers a feature called **Fixmbr**. However, it functions identically to the **Fdisk /mbr** command, replacing only the master boot code and not affecting the partition table. For this reason, it is also unlikely to help resolve an infected MBR.

For more information about the Recovery Console, see "Troubleshooting Tools and Strategies" in this book.

Damaged MBRs and Boot Sectors

When you start a computer from the hard disk, the system BIOS code identifies the startup disk and reads the MBR. The master boot code in the MBR searches for the active, primary partition on the hard disk. If the first hard disk on the system does not contain an active partition, or if the master boot code cannot locate the system partition's boot sector to start the operating system, the MBR displays one of the following error messages:

- `Invalid partition table.`
- `Error loading operating system.`
- `Missing operating system.`

There might not be an active partition on the hard disk that you want to use to start the computer, or the wrong partition might be identified as the active partition. In this case, use an MS-DOS startup floppy disk to start the computer and use the MS-DOS tool Fdisk to set or change the active partition.

Note Fdisk can only set primary partitions as the active partition. If MBR corruption prevents Fdisk from setting or changing the active partition, you might need to use a third-party, low-level disk editor that can work under MS-DOS to make this change manually. The partition table field that needs to be changed is the **System ID** field. For more information about the fields in the partition table, see "Master Boot Record" earlier in this chapter.

Restoring the MBR

Occasionally the MBR can becomecorrupted. This can be caused by human error, hardware problems, power fluctuations, viruses, and other factors.

Replacing the MBR with a Disk Editor

You need to replace the MBR if it becomes corrupted and you can no longer access any volumes on that disk. If you have backed up the MBR using a tool such as DiskProbe, you can use it to restore the MBR on a non-startable disk. Restoring the backup MBR rewrites the entire sector, including the partition table. However, DiskProbe only runs under Windows 2000 and Windows NT. It does not run under MS-DOS, Windows 95, or Windows 98.

If the MBR on the startup disk is corrupted, you will likely not be able to start Windows 2000 or DiskProbe. For more information about restoring backed up MBRs with DiskProbe, see the document Dskprtrb.doc in the folder C:\Program Files\Support Tools.

If DiskProbe is not available to you, you can use an MS-DOS–based, third-party, low-level disk editor to restore the backup MBR.

Replacing the MBR with the Recovery Console

You can also use the Recovery Console to rewrite the MBR to resolve a corrupted MBR on a startup disk.

To start the Recovery Console, start the computer from the Windows 2000 Setup CD or the Windows 2000 Setup floppy disks. If you do not have Windows 2000 Setup floppy disks and your computer cannot start from the CD, use another Windows 2000–based computer to create the setup disks. For information about creating the Windows 2000 Setup floppy disks, see Windows 2000 Professional Help.

Start the computer and enter Windows 2000 Setup. Press ENTER at the **Setup Notification** screen to go to the **Welcome to Setup** screen. Press R to repair a Windows 2000 installation, and then press C to use the Recovery Console.

The Recovery Console displays all valid installations of Windows 2000 on the computer. To access the hard disk, press the number key representing the Windows 2000 installation you that want to repair (typically represented as 1: C:\WINNT), and then press ENTER.

Note If you press ENTER without typing a number, the Recovery Console quits and restarts the computer.

The Recovery Console may also show valid installations of Windows NT. However, the results of attempting to access a Windows NT installation can be unpredictable.

The Recovery Console then prompts you for the Administrator password.

Note To access the hard disks with Recovery Console, you must know the password for the local Administrator account. If you do not have the correct password, or if the security database for the installation of Windows 2000 you are attempting to access is corrupted, Recovery Console does not allow access to the local disks.

To replace the MBR, at the Recovery Console command prompt, type:

fixmbr

Verify if you want to proceed. Depending upon the location and the cause of the corruption within the damaged MBR, this operation can cause the data on the hard disk to become inaccessible. Press Y to proceed, or N to cancel.

Important Running **Fixmbr** overwrites only the master boot code, leaving the existing partition table intact. If the corruption in the MBR affects the partition table, running **Fixmbr** might not resolve the problem.

Last Resort Alternatives

As a last resort, using a disk editor tool, you can try to copy an MBR from another disk. However, since the partition table is part of the MBR, the new MBR is not likely match the existing partition scheme of the original MBR. If you used DiskMap to save a record of the original partition table, you might be able to manually recreate the partition table in the new MBR.

When you have copied an MBR from another computer of the same type (for example, another computer made by the same manufacturer with identical disk controllers), use a disk editor tool, such as DiskProbe, to edit the partition table information. Verify your work carefully.

Caution   Overwriting the existing MBR with one from another system and manually recreating the partition table is only recommended for the most advanced users. The likelihood for permanently losing data is very high.

After you have replaced the MBR and edited the partition table, check that it is now functional. If the MBR is still not functional after you have verified that the edits were correct, the problem might be caused by either a hardware problem, such as incorrect SCSI termination or disk controller error, or by a virus.

Replacing the Boot Sector

You need to replace the boot sector if it becomes corrupted. The procedure you follow depends upon whether the corrupted boot sector is from the boot volume.

Replacing the Boot Sector with a Disk Editor

If the boot sector is not from the boot volume on the hard disk, there are several methods that can be used to replace it. If you backed up the boot sector with DiskProbe, restoring it with DiskProbe is the fastest method.

For NTFS volumes, there is another alternative. When you create or reformat an existing volume as an NTFS volume, NTFS writes a duplicate of the boot sector at the end of the volume (on volumes formatted with Windows 2000 and Windows NT 4.0) or at the logical center of the volume (on disks formatted with Windows NT 3.51 and earlier). You can use DiskProbe to locate and copy this sector to the beginning of the volume. There are also third-party MS-DOS-based disk tools that you can use to locate and copy this backup boot sector to the primary boot sector on the volume.

For specifically replacing corrupted boot sectors from boot volumes, DiskProbe is not always an available option. Unless you have created a Windows 2000 startup floppy disk, you cannot start Windows 2000, which is required by DiskProbe. You can use an MS-DOS–based, third-party, low-level disk editor to restore the backup up boot sector.

Replacing the Boot Sector with the Emergency Repair Process

If the boot sector cannot find Ntldr, Windows 2000 cannot start. This condition can be caused by moving, renaming, or deleting Ntldr, corruption of Ntldr, or corruption of the boot sector. Under these circumstances, the computer might not respond to input or might display one of the following error messages:

- `A disk read error occurred.`
- `NTLDR is missing.`
- `NTLDR is compressed.`

If Ntldr is damaged or missing, or if the boot sector is corrupted, you can resolve either problem by starting the Emergency Repair Process and following the prompts for repairing the installation using the Emergency Repair Disk (ERD). For more information about running the Emergency Repair Process and using the ERD, see "Troubleshooting Tools and Strategies" in this book..

Replacing the Boot Sector with the Recovery Console

You can also use the Recovery Console to replace the corrupted boot sector. To replace the boot sector.

If you do not specify a particular drive, the Recovery Console replaces the boot sector of the boot partition. If another volume's boot sector is corrupted, enter the **Fixboot** command, followed by a space, and then specify the drive letter with a colon.

For more information about starting the Recovery Console, see "Replacing the MBR with the Recovery Console" earlier in this chapter. For more detailed information about the Recovery Console, see "Troubleshooting Tools and Strategies" in this book.

Checking for Disk Corruption

If key operating system data structures are damaged, they can prevent system startup. These structures include the MBR, the boot sector, and the core operating system files.

Caution   Back up key data files before performing any disk repair operations. Do not run any disk tools that are not specifically designed for Windows 2000. Earlier versions of disk repair tools may not work properly. To prevent possible data loss, use a disk tool that is specifically designed for Windows 2000, such as Chkdsk.

▶ **To check for disk corruption with Chkdsk**

- From the command prompt, type:

  chkdsk c: /r

You can substitute drive C in the example for any locally installed read/writable drive in the computer.

Note Chkdsk cannot correct errors if there are open files on the volume because Chkdsk cannot lock the volume for exclusive access. In this case, Chkdsk offers to check the volume automatically the next time the computer restarts. This is typical behavior with the boot volume. When the boot volume is checked, the computer is automatically restarted after the volume check is completed.

If corruption is detected, you might need to replace system files. For more information about using Chkdsk and replacing system files, see "Troubleshooting Tools and Strategies" in this book.

Other Disk Problems

Disk problems can occur that do not involve the MBR, partition table, extended partition table, or boot sector. Typically, the Windows 2000 disk tools cannot be used to troubleshoot these disk problems.

Stop 0x0000007B — Inaccessible Boot Device

This Stop message, also known as Stop 0x7B, indicates that Windows 2000 lost access to the system partition during the startup process.

This error can be caused by a number of factors, including the failure of the boot device driver to initialize, the installation of an incompatible disk or disk controller, an incompatible device driver, disk cabling problems, disk corruption, viruses, or incompatible logical block addressing (LBA).

The system BIOS allows access to fixed disks that use fewer than 1024 cylinders. Many later disks, however, exceed 1024 cylinders. LBA is used to provide support for these disks. Such support is often built into the system BIOS. However, there are potential problems with LBA, such as:

- If partitions are created and formatted with LBA disabled, and LBA is subsequently enabled, a STOP 0x7B can result. The partitions must be created and formatted while LBA is enabled.

- Some LBA schemes are not compatible with Windows 2000. Check with your vendor.

Warning   Changing LBA modes from one scheme to another can force you to recreate and reformat the partitions.

For more information about Stop message 0x7B, see "Windows 2000 Stop Messages" in this book.

Volume Displays as Unknown

If you create and format a volume with NTFS, FAT16, or FAT32, but you cannot access files on it, and Disk Management displays the volume as Unknown, the boot sector for the volume might be corrupted. For NTFS volumes, there are two other possible causes for a volume to display as Unknown:

- Permissions for the volume have been changed.
- The master file table (MFT) is corrupted.

The boot sector can be corrupted by viruses. For more information about cleaning an infected computer, see "Viruses" earlier in this chapter.

Permission problems can occur when you perform the following tasks:

- Create a second volume.
- Remove the group Everyone from the *access control list* (ACL).
- Grant access to a specific user.

The single user has normal access, but if other users log on, or if Windows 2000 is reinstalled, Disk Management shows the drive as Unknown. To correct this problem, log on as an administrator and take ownership of all folders, or return full control to the group Everyone.

If the MFT file is corrupted, there is no general solution, and you need to contact Microsoft Product Support Services.

CMOS Problems

The CMOS typically stores configuration information about the basic elements of the computer, including RAM, video, and storage devices. If the CMOS is damaged or incapable of retaining its configuration data, the computer might be unable to start.

Each manufacturer and BIOS vendor can decide what a user can configure on the CMOS, and what the standard configuration is. You can access the CMOS by using either a keyboard sequence at startup or a software tool, depending on the manufacturer's specifications. It is recommended that you record or print all CMOS information.

The computer uses the CMOS checksum to determine if any CMOS values have been changed other than by using the CMOS Setup program. If the checksum is not correct, the computer cannot start.

After the CMOS is correctly configured, any CMOS problem is usually caused by one of the following problems:

- A weak battery, which can happen when the computer has been turned off for a long time.
- A loose or faulty connection between the CMOS and the battery.
- A damaged CMOS caused by static electric discharge.

Cables and Connectors

Another source of disk problems can be cabling and connectors. Cables can go bad, but if the cable works initially, it is likely to work for a long time. When new disks are added to the computer, check for cabling problems. New problems might stem from a previously unused connector on an existing cable or from a faulty, longer cable used to connect all the disks that might have replaced the working original. Also check the connections to the disk themselves. If the cables are tightly stretched, one or more connectors may work themselves loose over time, resulting in intermittent problems with the disks.

If your system has *small computer system interface* (SCSI) adapters, contact the manufacturer for updated Windows 2000 drivers. Try disabling **sync negotiation** in the SCSI BIOS, checking the SCSI identifiers of each device, and confirming proper termination. For *enhanced integrated drive electronics* (EIDE) devices, define the onboard EIDE port as **Primary only**. Also, check each EIDE device for the proper master, slave, or stand-alone setting. Try removing all EIDE devices except for hard disks.

To make sure that any new disks and disk controllers are supported, see the Microsoft Windows 2000 Hardware Compatibility List (HCL) link on the Web Resources page at http://windows.microsoft.com/windows2000/reskit/webresources.

CHAPTER 33

Windows 2000 Stop Messages

When Microsoft® Windows® 2000 detects an error condition from which it cannot recover, it generates a variety of system messages including Stop messages and hardware malfunction messages, commonly referred to as blue screen messages. Interpreting the meaning of various Stop messages and taking appropriate action to resolve the problems that generated the errors are critical skills in a production environment. In addition, it is vital that technical support personnel and power users know how to handle system hardware failure correctly. This chapter contains general information and troubleshooting tips about these types of errors as well as specific information about the 12 most common Stop messages seen by callers to Microsoft Product Support Services.

In This Chapter

System Messages

The two types of system messages generated by Windows 2000 depend on the event being reported. Both are generated in character mode.

Stop messages occur when the Windows 2000 kernel detects a condition from which it cannot recover.

Hardware malfunction messages occur when the processor detects a hardware condition from which the system cannot recover.

These messages were created to cover everything that might happen to halt the system, so you are unlikely to see most of them. For example, the Stop message 0x0000003E, or "Multiprocessor Configuration Not Supported," is displayed only if multiple but asymmetric central processing unit (CPU) types, such as a Pentium and a Pentium III, are installed on the same system.

To diagnose and resolve Stop messages, many users also need technical assistance from a person who has been trained to support Windows 2000. In some circumstances, running a kernel debugger on the faulty system might be required.

Stop Messages

Stop messages are always displayed on a full screen in character mode, as shown in Figure 33.1, rather than in a window. Each message is uniquely identified by a hexadecimal number and a string indicating the error's symbolic name. In addition, Stop messages are usually followed by a series of up to four additional hexadecimal numbers, shown in parentheses, which identify error parameters, as shown in the following example:

```
*** STOP: 0x0000001E (0xC0000005, 0xFDE38AF9, 0x00000001, 0x7E8B0EB4)
KMODE_EXCEPTION_NOT_HANDLED ***
```

To a trained support technician, the content of the symbolic name string might suggest which part of the system is affected by the error that left the kernel no recourse but to stop. However, it is also possible that the cause might be in another part of the system. Figure 33.1 is an example of a complete Stop message screen generated by Windows 2000.

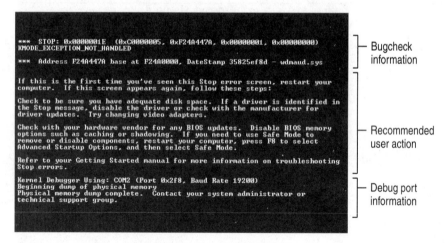

Figure 33.1   Stop Message Screen

Stop Message Screen Sections

As shown in Figure 33.1, a Windows 2000 Stop message screen contains three major sections: bugcheck information, recommended user action, and debug port information. Whenever a Stop message is displayed, first examine the bugcheck information section for assistance with troubleshooting. Second, examine the recommended user action section for troubleshooting information; Windows 2000 now incorporates troubleshooting tips, including some custom tips relevant to the particular error detected. Finally, check the debug port information section to see whether or not a memory dump file was saved for later use by a debugger.

Bugcheck Information

The bugcheck information section includes the Stop error code, also known as the bugcheck code, which contains up to four developer-defined parameters, enclosed in parentheses, and the symbolic name of the error. In Figure 33.1, the Stop error code is 0x0000001E and its symbolic name is KMODE_EXCEPTION_NOT_HANDLED.

The bugcheck information section frequently, but not always, includes a line that lists the specific hexadecimal memory address of the problem's source, along with the name of the particular driver or device in question. The type of problem detected determines whether or not this information is displayed.

Under some conditions, the kernel displays only the first line of the Stop message. This can occur if vital services needed for the display have been affected by the error.

Recommended User Action

The recommended user action section provides a list of suggestions for recovering from the error. In some cases, a simple restart might be all that is necessary because the problem is not likely to recur. In other cases, even after restarting, the Stop message returns and you are faced with getting back to an operable state. Often, this means either backing out of a recent change or, in the case of Windows 2000 setup, pinpointing and eliminating the source of the problem.

Tip A generic list of troubleshooting tips is displayed when no specific text for a Stop message exists. For some Stop messages, tips specific to the problem are listed.

Debug Port Information

The debug port information section provides confirmation of the communications parameters (COM port and bits-per-second data transmission rate) used by the kernel debugger on the computer, if the kernel debugger is enabled. It also indicates whether a memory dump file was saved (the dump file indicator is displayed only if that feature is enabled).

Types of Stop Messages

Stop messages generally fall into one of four categories:

- Messages that appear during general use of Windows 2000.
- Messages that appear during the installation of Windows 2000.
- Messages that appear only during the relatively short Phase 4 period of the Windows 2000 Executive initialization sequence.
- Messages that can be traced to a software condition, called a *software trap*, detected by the processor.

General Stop Messages

The most common Stop messages are generated during regular operations. Even in a complex and robust operating system such as Windows 2000, catastrophic problems sometimes cause the system to stop responding and display a Stop message. In Windows 2000, a driver or the file system can generate a Stop message by introducing an unhandled error (exception) in the code or by performing some illegal operation.

For information about troubleshooting Stop messages, including detailed information about the most common errors, see "Troubleshooting Stop Messages" later in this chapter.

For the most comprehensive list of Stop messages in Windows 2000, along with useful information about diagnosing and troubleshooting these messages, see the Microsoft Knowledge Base article Q103059, titled "Descriptions of Bug Codes for Windows NT."

Stop Messages During Installation

An unsuccessful attempt to install Windows 2000 can result in a Stop message. When this happens, first check that the computer and all of its peripheral hardware are compatible with Windows 2000. To do this, refer to the latest Windows 2000 Hardware Compatibility List (HCL). Microsoft compiles the HCL through rigorous component and compatibility testing of computers and peripheral hardware to determine if they work well with Windows 2000. For more information about the HCL, see "Additional Resources" at the end of this chapter.

If the hardware you use is not included on the Windows 2000 HCL, contact the hardware manufacturer as a first-line resource for available information, newly tested hardware, and Basic Input/Output System (BIOS) and firmware revisions. Reducing the number of hardware components by removing nonessential peripherals and devices can help you pinpoint installation conflicts as well.

Stop Messages That Occur Only at Executive Initialization

Some Stop messages occur only during the relatively short Phase 4 period of the Windows 2000 startup sequence. Initialization of the *Windows 2000 Executive*, a family of software components that provides basic operating system services, is one step during Phase 4. Executive initialization can be further broken down into two phases: Phase 0 and Phase 1. During Phase 0, interrupts are disabled and only a few Executive components, such as the hardware abstraction layer (HAL), are initialized. During Phase 1 of Executive initialization, the system is fully operational, and the Windows 2000 subcomponents go through a full initialization.

Phase 0 Initialization Stop Messages

If you receive one of the Phase 0 initialization Stop messages listed in Table 33.1, run the hardware diagnostics provided by your system manufacturer.

Note In many situations, hardware failures manifest themselves as errors that generate Stop messages. This is why troubleshooting many of the Stop messages includes running hardware diagnostics on the system.

If no hardware problems are found, reinstall Windows 2000 and try to initialize it again. If you get the same message, contact a support technician.

Table 33.1   Phase 0 Initialization Stop Messages

Message ID	Symbolic Name
0x31	PHASE0_INITIALIZATION_FAILED
0x5C	HAL_INITIALIZATION_FAILED
0x5D	HEAP_INITIALIZATION_FAILED
0x5E	OBJECT_INITIALIZATION_FAILED
0x5F	SECURITY_INITIALIZATION_FAILED
0x60	PROCESS_INITIALIZATION_FAILED

Phase 1 Initialization Stop Messages

If you receive one of the Phase 1 initialization Stop messages listed in Table 33.2, reinstall Windows 2000 and try to initialize it again. If you get the same message, contact a support technician.

Table 33.2   Phase 1 Initialization Stop Messages

Message ID	Symbolic Name
0x32	PHASE1_INITIALIZATION_FAILED
0x61	HAL1_INITIALIZATION_FAILED
0x62	OBJECT1_INITIALIZATION_FAILED
0x63	SECURITY1_INITIALIZATION_FAILED
0x64	SYMBOLIC_INITIALIZATION_FAILED
0x65	MEMORY1_INITIALIZATION_FAILED
0x66	CACHE_INITIALIZATION_FAILED
0x67	CONFIG_INITIALIZATION_FAILED
0x68	FILE_INITIALIZATION_FAILED
0x69	IO1_INITIALIZATION_FAILED
0x6A	LPC_INITIALIZATION_FAILED
0x6B	PROCESS1_INITIALIZATION_FAILED
0x6C	REFMON_INITIALIZATION_FAILED
0x6D	SESSION1_INITIALIZATION_FAILED
0x6E	SESSION2_INITIALIZATION_FAILED
0x6F	SESSION3_INITIALIZATION_FAILED
0x70	SESSION4_INITIALIZATION_FAILED
0x71	SESSION5_INITIALIZATION_FAILED

Stop Messages Caused by Software Traps

Erroneous software conditions detected by the processor, called software traps, can also generate Stop messages. A software trap occurs when a processor detects a problem with executing an instruction, which causes it to stop. For example, a processor does not carry out an instruction whose variables contains invalid data types.

When you receive one of these messages, first write down the information displayed in the bugcheck information section of the Stop message, and then restart the computer. If the message recurs, you have four options for diagnosing the Stop error, all of which need to be handled by a trained support technician at your own site:

- Diagnose the problem by using the information and troubleshooting tips displayed in the Stop message. For more information see "Troubleshooting Stop Messages" later in this chapter and in the Windows 2000 Error and Event Messages Help, where message explanations and recommended user actions for the most common Stop messages are listed. This file is located on the *Microsoft® Windows® 2000 Resource Kit* companion CD.

- Contact your own or another technical support group to discuss the information in the Stop message. They might recognize a familiar pattern in the information and be able to offer assistance.

Important If you use either of the following options, be sure Windows 2000 is in debug mode before you restart your computer.

- Set up the Windows 2000 kernel debugger to gather more information about the problem.
- Contact your own or another technical support group for assistance in the remote use of the Windows 2000 kernel debugger.

Troubleshooting Stop Messages

Many problems can be resolved through troubleshooting procedures, such as verifying instructions, reinstalling key components, and verifying file dates. Also, diagnostic tools, such as Winmsd and Network General Sniffer and those found on the *Windows 2000 Resource Kit* companion CD, might isolate and resolve these issues.

Generic Troubleshooting Procedures

For general troubleshooting of Windows 2000 Stop messages, follow these suggestions:

- If new hardware has been added to the system recently, remove it or replace it to see if that resolves the error. Also, try running hardware diagnostics supplied by the system manufacturer. Check with the manufacturer to see if an updated system BIOS or firmware is available. Make sure that any expansion boards are properly seated and all cables are completely connected.

- Confirm that any new hardware is listed on the Windows 2000 Hardware Compatibility List (HCL). For more information about the HCL, see "Additional Resources" at the end of this chapter.

- If new device drivers or system services have been added recently, remove them or update them to see if the problem is resolved. You need to use Safe Mode to remove or disable components, because Safe Mode loads only the minimum required drivers and system services during the startup of Windows. To enter Safe Mode, restart your computer, and press F8 at the character-mode screen that displays the prompt "For troubleshooting and advanced startup options for Windows 2000, press F8." On the resulting **Windows 2000 Advanced Options** menu, choose **Safe Mode**. For more information about safe mode, see "Troubleshooting Tools and Strategies" in this book.

- Check the computer with an up-to-date virus scanner program that is compatible with Windows 2000. Viruses can infect all types of Windows-formatted hard disks, and resulting disk corruption can generate system stop messages. Make sure the virus scanner checks the master boot record for infections.

- Verify that any recently added software is listed as compatible with Windows 2000. If it is not, check with the manufacturer to see if an update or a patch is available. Otherwise, remove the program to see if this resolves the error.

- Verify that the system has the latest Service Pack installed. To check which Service Pack, if any, is installed on your system, click **Start**, click **Run**, type **winver,** and then press ENTER. The **About Windows 2000** dialog box displays the Windows version number and the version number of the Service Pack, if one has been installed. For information about downloading the latest Service Packs, see "Additional Resources" at the end of this chapter.

- Disable BIOS memory options such as caching or shadowing.

- Check the System Log and Application Log in Event Viewer to see if any additional error messages have been logged recently. These might pinpoint the cause of the error.

- Check the Microsoft Knowledge Base link using the keywords **winnt** and the full Stop error code, such as the example in Figure 33.1, **0x0000001E**. For information about the Microsoft Knowledge Base link, see "Additional Resources" at the end of this chapter.

Kernel debugging is especially helpful when other troubleshooting techniques have failed, or when a problem repeats often. In these cases, it is possible to pinpoint the failing code in a driver or an application by using a kernel debugger. For kernel debugging, it is important to capture the exact text in the bugcheck information section of the error message. Also, in order to isolate a complex problem and develop a viable workaround or a program replacement, it is essential to record the exact steps leading to the failure.

Troubleshooting Common Stop Messages

For the most commonly encountered Stop messages, troubleshooting tips and recommendations have been gathered together to help you resolve the problem on your own. If the error persists after you have tried all of the recommendations listed both here and within the Stop message display, contact your technical support group for further assistance.

Stop 0x0000000A or IRQL_NOT_LESS_OR_EQUAL

This Stop message, also known as Stop 0xA, indicates that a kernel-mode process attempted to access a portion of memory at an Interrupt Request Level (IRQL) that was too high. A kernel-mode process can only access other processes that have an IRQL lesser than or equal to its own.

Interpreting the Message

The four parameters listed in the Stop 0xA message are defined in order of appearance as follows:

1. Memory address referenced
2. IRQL
3. Type of access (0 = read operation, 1 = write operation)
4. Address that referenced memory in parameter 1

If the third parameter is the same as the first parameter, a special condition exists in which a system worker routine, executed by a worker thread to handle background tasks known as work items, returned at a raised IRQL. In that case, the parameters are defined as follows:

1. Address of the worker routine
2. IRQL

3. Address of the worker routine

4. Address of the work item

Resolving the Problem

Buggy device driver, system service, or BIOS. The error that generates Stop 0xA usually occurs after the installation of a buggy device driver, system service, or BIOS. To resolve it quickly, restart your computer, and press F8 at the character-mode screen that displays the prompt "For troubleshooting and advanced startup options for Windows 2000, press F8." On the resulting **Windows 2000 Advanced Options** menu, choose the **Last Known Good Configuration** option. This option is most effective when only one driver or service is added at a time.

Incompatible device driver, system service, virus scanner, or backup tool. If you encounter Stop 0xA while upgrading to a newer version of Windows, it might be caused by a device driver, a system service, a virus scanner, or a backup tool that is incompatible with the new version. If possible, remove all third-party device drivers and system services and disable any virus scanners prior to upgrading. Contact the software manufacturers to obtain updates of these tools.

For additional error messages that might help pinpoint the device or driver that is causing the error, check the System Log in Event Viewer. Disabling memory caching of the BIOS might also resolve this error. You also need to run hardware diagnostics supplied by the system manufacturer, especially the memory scanner. For details on these procedures, see the owner's manual for your computer.

If your system has small computer system interface (SCSI) adapters, contact the adapter manufacturer to obtain updated Windows 2000 drivers. Try disabling sync negotiation in the SCSI BIOS, checking the cabling and the SCSI IDs of each device, and confirming proper termination. For enhanced integrated drive electronics (EIDE) devices, define the onboard EIDE port as Primary only. Also, check each EIDE device for the proper master/slave or stand-alone setting. Try removing all EIDE devices except for hard disks.

If the message appears during an installation of Windows 2000, make sure that the computer and all installed peripherals are listed on the Microsoft Windows 2000 Hardware Compatibility List (HCL). For more information about the HCL, see "Additional Resources" at the end of this chapter.

Microsoft periodically releases a package of product improvements and problem resolutions called a Service Pack. Because many problems are resolved by installing the latest Service Pack, it is recommended that all users install them as they become available. To check which Service Pack, if any, is installed on your system, click **Start**, click **Run**, type **winver,** and then press ENTER. The **About Windows 2000** dialog box displays the Windows version number and the version number of the Service Pack, if one has been installed. For information about installing the latest Service Pack, see "Additional Resources" at the end of this chapter.

Occasionally, remedies to specific problems are developed after the release of a Service Pack. These remedies are called hotfixes. Microsoft does not recommend that you install a post–Service Pack hotfix unless the specific problem it addresses has been encountered. Service Packs include all of the hotfixes released since the release of the previous Service Pack. The status of hotfix installations is not indicated in the **About Windows 2000** dialog box. For information about downloading hotfixes and Service Packs, see "Additional Resources" at the end of this chapter.

For more troubleshooting information about the 0xA Stop message, refer to the Microsoft Knowledge Base link, using the keywords **winnt** and **0x0000000A**. For information about this resource, see "Additional Resources" at the end of this chapter.

Stop 0x0000001E or KMODE_EXCEPTION_NOT_HANDLED

This Stop message, also known as Stop 0x1E, indicates that a kernel-mode process tried to execute an illegal or unknown processor instruction. This error handler is a default error handler that catches errors not associated with other specific error handlers.

Interpreting the Message

The four parameters listed in the message are defined in order of appearance as follows:

1. Exception code that was not handled

2. Address at which the exception occurred

3. Parameter 0 of the exception

4. Parameter 1 of the exception

The first parameter is a Windows 2000 error code, which is defined by the type of error encountered in the file Ntstatus.h of the Microsoft® Windows 2000 Device Driver Development Kit (DDK). For information about the DDK, see "Additional Resources" at the end of this chapter. The second parameter identifies the address of the module in which the error occurred. Frequently, the address points to an individual driver or piece of faulty hardware, which is generally listed on the third line of the Stop message. Always make a note of this address, as well as the link date of the driver or image that contains it. The last two parameters vary, depending upon the exception that has occurred. You can typically find a description of the parameters that are included with the name of error code in Ntstatus.h. If the error code has no parameters, the last two parameters are listed as 0x00000000.

Resolving the Problem

Hardware incompatibility. First, make sure that any new hardware installed is listed on the Windows 2000 Hardware Compatibility List (HCL). For more information about the HCL, see "Additional Resources" at the end of this chapter.

Buggy device driver or system service. In addition, a buggy device driver or system service might be responsible for this error. Hardware issues, such as memory conflicts and interrupt request (IRQ) conflicts, can also generate this error.

If a driver is listed by name within the Stop message, disable or remove that driver. Disable or remove any drivers or services that were recently added. If the error occurs during the startup sequence, restart the computer using Safe Mode to rename or delete the file. If the driver is used as part of the system startup process in Safe Mode, you need to start the computer by using the Recovery Console to access the file. For more information about Safe Mode and the Recovery Console, see "Troubleshooting Tools and Strategies" in this book.

If the problem is associated with Win32k.sys, the source of the error might be a third-party remote control program. If such software is installed, the service can be removed by starting the system using the Recovery Console and disabling the offending system service.

Check the System Log in Event Viewer for additional error messages that might help pinpoint the device or driver that is causing Stop 0x1E. Disabling memory caching of the BIOS might also resolve the error. You also need to run hardware diagnostics, especially the memory scanner, supplied by the system manufacturer. For details on these procedures, see the owner's manual for your computer.

One type of this kind of error displays exception code 0x80000003. This error indicates a hard-coded breakpoint or assertion was hit, but the system was started with the /NODEBUG switch. This problem rarely occurs. If it occurs repeatedly, make sure a kernel debugger is connected and the system is started with the /DEBUG switch.

The error that generates this message can occur after the first restart during Windows 2000 Setup, or after setup is finished. A possible cause of the error is lack of disk space for installation and system BIOS incompatibilities. For problems during Windows 2000 installation that are associated with a lack of disk space, reduce the number of files on the target hard disk. Check for and delete any unneeded temporary files, Internet cache files, application backup files, and CHK files containing saved file fragments from disk scans. You can also use another hard disk with more free space for the installation. BIOS problems can be resolved by upgrading the system BIOS version.

For more troubleshooting information about the 0x1E Stop message, refer to the Microsoft Knowledge Base link, using the keywords **winnt** and **0x0000001E**. For information about this resource, see "Additional Resources" at the end of this chapter.

Stop 0x00000024 or NTFS_FILE_SYSTEM

This Stop message, also known as Stop 0x24, indicates that a problem occurred within Ntfs.sys (the driver file that allows the system to read and write to NTFS drives).

Interpreting the Message

The four parameters listed in the message are defined in order of appearance as follows:

1. Source file and line number.
2. A non-zero value contains the address of the exception record.
3. A non-zero value contains the address of the context record.
4. A non-zero value contains the address where the original exception occurred.

All Stop messages due to problems with the file system have encoded in their first parameter the source file and the line number within the source file that generated the Stop. The high 16 bits (the first four hexadecimal digits after the 0x) identify the source file number, while the lower 16 bits (the last four hexadecimal digits of the parameter) identify the source line in the file where the stop occurred.

Resolving the Problem

Disk Corruption. Corruption in the NTFS file system or bad blocks (sectors) on the hard disk can induce this error. Corrupted SCSI and EIDE drivers can also adversely affect the system's ability to read and write to disk, thus causing the error.

Check Event Viewer for error messages from SCSI and FASTFAT (System Log) or Autochk (Application Log) that might help pinpoint the device or driver that is causing the error. Try disabling any virus scanners, backup programs, or disk defragmenter tools that continually monitor the system. You also need to run hardware diagnostics supplied by the system manufacturer. For details on these procedures, see the owner's manual for your computer. Run **Chkdsk /f /r** to detect and resolve any file system structural corruption. You must restart the system before the disk scan begins on a system partition. If you cannot start the system due to the error, use the Recovery Console and run **Chkdsk /r**. For more information about the Recovery Console, see "Troubleshooting Tools and Strategies" in this book.

Warning If your system partition is formatted with the file allocation table (FAT16) file system, the long file names used by Windows 2000 can be damaged if Scandisk or another MS-DOS-based hard disk tool is used to verify the integrity of your hard disk from an MS-DOS prompt. (An MS-DOS prompt is typically derived from an MS-DOS startup disk or from starting MS-DOS on a multiboot system.) Always use the Windows 2000 version of Chkdsk on Windows 2000 disks.

Depletion of nonpaged pool memory. If you create a Services for Macintosh volume on a large partition (7 gigabytes or larger) with a large number of files (at least 100,000) while the AppleTalk driver Apf.sys is loaded, the indexing routine consumes a large amount of nonpaged pool memory. If the nonpaged pool memory is completely depleted, this error can stop the system. However, during the indexing process, if the amount of available nonpaged pool memory is very low, another kernel-mode driver requiring nonpaged pool memory can also trigger this error. To resolve this error, either increase the amount of installed random access memory (RAM), which increases the quantity of nonpaged pool memory available to the kernel, or reduce the number of files on the Services for Macintosh volume.

Microsoft periodically releases a package of product improvements and problem resolutions called a Service Pack. Because many problems are resolved by installing the latest Service Pack, it is recommended that all users install them as they become available. To check which Service Pack, if any, is installed on your system, click **Start**, click **Run**, type **winver,** and then press ENTER. The **About Windows 2000** dialog box displays the Windows version number and the version number of the Service Pack, if one has been installed.

Occasionally, remedies to specific problems are developed after the release of a Service Pack. These remedies are called hotfixes. Microsoft does not recommend that you install a post–Service Pack hotfix unless the specific problem it addresses has been encountered. Service Packs include all of the hotfixes released since the release of the previous Service Pack. The status of hotfix installations is not indicated in the **About Windows 2000** dialog box. For more information about Service Packs and hotfixes, see "Additional Resources" at the end of this chapter.

For more troubleshooting information about the 0x24 Stop message, refer to the Microsoft Knowledge Base link, using the keywords **winnt** and **0x00000024**. For information about this resource, see "Additional Resources" at the end of this chapter.

Stop 0x0000002E or DATA_BUS_ERROR

This message, also known as Stop 0x2E, typically indicates that a parity error in system memory has been detected. This error is almost always caused by a hardware problem—a configuration issue, defective hardware, or incompatible hardware. The exception is when a device driver has accessed an address in the 0x8xxxxxxx range that does not exist (that is, does not have a physical address mapping).

Interpreting the Message

The four parameters listed in the message are defined in order of appearance as follows:

1. Virtual address that caused the fault
2. Physical address that caused the fault
3. Processor status register (PSR)
4. Faulting instruction register (FIR)

Resolving the Problem

Hardware problem. The most common cause of this error is a hardware problem, usually related to defective RAM, Level 2 (L2) RAM cache, or video RAM.

Stop 0x2E usually occurs after the installation of faulty hardware or when existing hardware fails. If hardware has recently been added to the system, remove it to see if the error recurs. If existing hardware has failed, remove or replace the faulty component. You need to run hardware diagnostics supplied by the system manufacturer to determine which hardware component has failed. For details on these procedures, see the owner's manual for your computer. Check that all the adapter cards in the computer, including memory modules, are properly seated. Use an ink eraser or an electrical contact treatment, available at electronics supply stores, to ensure adapter card contacts are clean. Be sure to wipe the cleaned contacts off, removing all cleaning debris, before reinstalling the adapter card into the computer. If compressed air is available, use it to clear out the adapter card slot.

If the problem occurs on a newly installed system, check the availability of updates for BIOS revisions on the motherboard, SCSI controllers, or network cards. Updates of this kind are typically available on the Web site or BBS of the hardware manufacturer.

If the error occurs after installing a new or updated device driver, the driver needs to be removed or replaced. If, under this circumstance, the error occurs during startup, restart the computer using Safe Mode to rename or delete the file. If the driver is used as part of the system startup process in Safe Mode, you need to start the computer using the Recovery Console in order to access the file. For more information about Safe Mode and the Recovery Console, see "Troubleshooting Tools and Strategies" in this book.

For additional error messages that might help pinpoint the device or driver that is causing the error, check the System Log in Event Viewer. Disabling memory caching of the BIOS might also resolve this error. In addition, check the system for viruses, using any up-to-date, commercial virus scanning software that examines the Master Boot Record of the hard disk. All Windows 2000 file systems can be infected by viruses.

Disk corruption. This error can also be a result of hard disk corruption. Run **Chkdsk /f /r** on the system partition. You must restart the system before the disk scan begins. If you cannot start the system due to the error, use the Recovery Console and run **Chkdsk /r**. For more information about the Recovery Console, see "Troubleshooting Tools and Strategies" in this book.

Warning If your system partition is formatted with the FAT16 file system, the long file names used by Windows 2000 can be damaged if Scandisk or another MS-DOS-based hard disk tool is used to verify the integrity of your hard disk from an MS-DOS prompt. (An MS-DOS prompt is typically derived from an MS-DOS startup disk or from starting MS-DOS on a multiboot system.) Always use the Windows 2000 version of Chkdsk on Windows 2000 disks.

Microsoft periodically releases a package of product improvements and problem resolutions for Windows 2000 called a Service Pack. Because many problems are resolved by installing the latest Service Pack, it is recommended that all users install them as they become available. To check which Service Pack, if any, is installed on your system, click **Start**, click **Run**, type **winver,** and then press ENTER. The **About Windows 2000** dialog box displays the Windows version number and the version number of the Service Pack, if one has been installed.

Occasionally, remedies to specific problems are developed after the release of a Service Pack. These remedies are called hotfixes. Microsoft does not recommend that you install a post–Service Pack hotfix unless the specific problem it addresses has been encountered. Service Packs include all of the hotfixes released since the release of the previous Service Pack. The status of hotfix installations is not indicated in the **About Windows 2000** dialog box. For more information about Service Packs and hotfixes, see "Additional Resources" at the end of this chapter.

Finally, if all the above suggestions fail to resolve the error, take the system motherboard to a repair facility for diagnostic testing. A crack, a scratched trace, or a defective component on the motherboard can also cause this error.

For more troubleshooting information about the 0x2E Stop message, refer to the Microsoft Knowledge Base link, using the keywords **winnt** and **0x0000002E**. For information about this resource, see "Additional Resources" at the end of this chapter.

Stop 0x00000050 or PAGE_FAULT_IN_NONPAGED_AREA

This Stop message, also known as Stop 0x50, occurs when requested data is not found in memory. The system generates a fault, which normally indicates that the system looks for data in the paging file. In this circumstance, however, the missing data is identified as being located within an area of memory that cannot be read to disk. The system faults, but cannot find, the data and is unable to recover. Faulty hardware, a buggy system service, antivirus software, and a corrupted NTFS volume can all generate this type of error.

Interpreting the Message

The four parameters listed in the message are defined in order of appearance as follows:

1. Virtual address that caused the fault

2. Type of access (0 = read operation, 1 = write operation)

3. If not zero, the instruction address that referenced the address in parameter 1

4. Opaque information about the stop, interpreted by the kernel

Resolving the Problem

Faulty hardware. Stop 0x50 usually occurs after the installation of faulty hardware or in the event of failure of installed hardware (usually related to defective RAM, be it main memory, L2 RAM cache, or video RAM). If hardware has been added to the system recently, remove it to see if the error recurs. If existing hardware has failed, remove or replace the faulty component. You need to run hardware diagnostics supplied by the system manufacturer. For details on these procedures, see the owner's manual for your computer.

Buggy system service. Often, the installation of a buggy system service is a culprit. Disable the service and confirm that this resolves the error. If so, contact the manufacturer of the system service about a possible update. If the error occurs during system startup, restart your computer, and press F8 at the character-mode screen that displays the prompt "For troubleshooting and advanced startup options for Windows 2000, press F8." On the resulting **Windows 2000 Advanced Options** menu, choose the **Last Known Good Configuration** option. This option is most effective when only one driver or service is added at a time.

Antivirus software. Antivirus software can also trigger this error. Disable the program and confirm that this resolves the error. If it does, contact the manufacturer of the program about a possible update.

Corrupted NTFS volume. A corrupted NTFS volume can also generate this error. Run **Chkdsk /f /r** to detect and repair disk errors. You must restart the system before the disk scan begins on a system partition. If you cannot start the system due to the error, use the Recovery Console and run **Chkdsk /r**. For more information about the Recovery Console, see "Troubleshooting Tools and Strategies" in this book. If the hard disk is a SCSI disk, check for problems between the SCSI controller and the disk.

Warning If your system partition is formatted with the FAT16 file system, the long file names used by Windows 2000 can be damaged if Scandisk or another MS-DOS-based hard disk tool is used to verify the integrity of your hard disk from an MS-DOS prompt. (An MS-DOS prompt is typically derived from an MS-DOS startup disk or from starting MS-DOS on a multiboot system.) Always use the Windows 2000 version of Chkdsk on Windows 2000 disks.

Finally, check the System Log in Event Viewer for additional error messages that might help pinpoint the device or driver that is causing the error. Disabling memory caching of the BIOS might also resolve this error.

Microsoft periodically releases a package of product improvements and problem resolutions for Windows 2000 called a Service Pack. Because many problems are resolved by installing the latest Service Pack, it is recommended that all users install them as they become available. To check which Service Pack, if any, is installed on your system, click **Start**, click **Run**, type **winver,** and then press ENTER. The **About Windows 2000** dialog box displays the Windows version number and the version number of the Service Pack, if one has been installed.

Occasionally, remedies to specific problems are developed after the release of a Service Pack. These remedies are called hotfixes. Microsoft does not recommend that you install a post–Service Pack hotfix unless the specific problem it addresses has been encountered. Service Packs include all of the hotfixes released since the release of the previous Service Pack. The status of hotfix installations is not indicated in the **About Windows 2000** dialog box. For more information about Service Packs and hotfixes, see "Additional Resources" at the end of this chapter.

For more troubleshooting information about the 0x50 Stop message, refer to the Microsoft Knowledge Base link, using the keywords **winnt** and **0x00000050**. For information about this resource, see "Additional Resources" at the end of this chapter.

Stop 0x00000077 or KERNEL_STACK_INPAGE_ERROR

This Stop message, also known as Stop 0x77, indicates that the requested page of kernel data from the paging file could not be read into memory.

Interpreting the Message

The four parameters listed in the message are defined in order of appearance as follows:

1. 0 (zero)
2. Value found in stack where signature should be
3. 0 (zero)
4. Address of signature on kernel stack

The first set of definitions applies only if the first and third parameters are both zero. Otherwise, the following definitions are applicable:

1. Status code
2. I/O status code
3. Page file number
4. Offset into page file

Frequently, the cause of this error can be determined from the second parameter, the I/O status code. Examples include:

- 0xC000009A, or STATUS_INSUFFICIENT_RESOURCES, is caused by lack of nonpaged pool resources.
- 0xC000009C, or STATUS_DEVICE_DATA_ERROR, is generally due to bad blocks (sectors) on the hard disk.
- 0xC000009D, or STATUS_DEVICE_NOT_CONNECTED, indicates defective or loose cabling, termination, or the controller not seeing the hard disk.
- 0xC000016A, or STATUS_DISK_OPERATION_FAILED, is also caused by bad blocks (sectors) on the hard disk.
- 0xC0000185, or STATUS_IO_DEVICE_ERROR, is caused by improper termination or defective cabling on SCSI devices, or two devices attempting to use the same IRQ.

These codes are the most common ones for which specific causes have been determined. For information about other possible status codes that can be returned, see the file Ntstatus.h of the Windows 2000 Device Driver Development Kit (DDK). For information about the DDK, see "Additional Resources" at the end of this chapter.

Resolving the Problem

Bad block. Stop 0x77 is caused by a bad block (sector) in a paging file or a disk controller error. In extremely rare cases, it is caused when nonpaged pool resources run out.

If the first and third parameters are zero, the stack signature in the kernel stack was not found. This error is caused by defective hardware. If the I/O status is C0000185 and the paging file is on a SCSI disk, the disk cabling and SCSI termination needs to be checked for problems.

Viruses. In addition, check your computer for viruses using any up-to-date, commercial virus scanning software that examines the Master Boot Record of the hard disk. All Windows 2000 file systems can be infected by viruses.

An I/O status code of 0xC000009C or 0xC000016A normally indicates that the data could not be read from the disk due to a bad block (sector). If you can restart the system after the error, Autochk runs automatically and attempts to map the bad sector to prevent its further use. If Autochk does not scan the hard disk for errors, you can manually start the disk scanner. Run **Chkdsk /f /r** on the system partition. You must restart the system before the disk scan begins. If you cannot start the system due to the error, use the Recovery Console and run **Chkdsk /r**. For more information about the Recovery Console, see "Troubleshooting Tools and Strategies" in this book.

Warning If your system partition is formatted with the FAT16 file system, the long file names used by Windows 2000 can be damaged if Scandisk or another MS-DOS-based hard disk tool is used to verify the integrity of your hard disk from an MS-DOS prompt. (An MS-DOS prompt is typically derived from an MS-DOS startup disk or from starting MS-DOS on a multiboot system.) Always use the Windows 2000 version of Chkdsk on Windows 2000 disks.

Failing RAM. Another common cause of this error message is failing RAM. You need to run hardware diagnostics supplied by the system manufacturer, especially the memory scanner. For details on these procedures, see the owner's manual for your computer.

Also, check that all the adapter cards in the computer, including memory modules, are properly seated. Use an ink eraser or an electrical contact treatment, available at electronics supply stores, to ensure adapter card contacts are clean. Be sure to wipe the cleaned contacts off, removing all cleaning debris, before reinstalling the adapter card into the computer. If compressed air is available, use it to clear out the adapter card slot.

In addition, check the System Log in Event Viewer for additional error messages that might help pinpoint the device that is causing the error. Disabling memory caching of the BIOS might also resolve this error.

Finally, if all the above steps fail to resolve the error, take the system motherboard to a repair facility for diagnostic testing. A crack, a scratched trace, or a defective component on the motherboard can also cause this error.

For more troubleshooting information about the 0x77 Stop message, refer to the Microsoft Knowledge Base link, using the keywords **winnt** and **0x00000077**. For information about this resource, see "Additional Resources" at the end of this chapter.

Stop 0x00000079 or MISMATCHED_HAL

This message, also known as Stop 0x79, is displayed when the hardware abstraction layer (HAL) and the kernel or the computer type do not match. This error most often occurs when single-processor and multiprocessor configuration files are mixed on the same system.

Interpreting the Message

The types of mismatch parameters are defined in order of appearance in the sets as follows. The first parameter determines which set is applicable.

1. If this parameter is 1, the processor control block (PRCB) release levels mismatch (that is, something is out of date).

2. Major PRCB level of Ntoskrnl.exe.

3. Major PRCB level of Hal.dll.

4. 0 (zero).

   –Or–

1. If this parameter is 2, the build types mismatch.

2. Build type of Ntoskrnl.exe.

3. Build type of Hal.dll.

4. 0 (zero).

   (Build Types: 0 = free, multiprocessor-enabled build; 1 = checked, multiprocessor-enabled build; and 2 = free, single-processor build)

Resolving the Problem

Stop 0x79 can occur if either the Ntoskrnl.exe or Hal.dll files have been manually updated. The error can also indicate that one of those two files is out-of-date (that is, the HAL is designed for Microsoft® Windows NT® version 4.0 and the kernel is for Windows 2000). Additionally, the computer might erroneously have a multiprocessor HAL and a single-processor kernel installed, or vice versa.

The kernel file Ntoskrnl.exe is for single-processor systems and Ntkrnlmp.exe is for multiprocessor systems. However, these file names correspond to the files on the installation media; after Windows 2000 has been installed, the file is renamed Ntoskrnl.exe, regardless of the source file used. The HAL file also uses the name Hal.dll after installation, but there are several possible HAL files on the installation media.

To resolve this error, restart the computer using either the product CD or the four Setup disks and enter Windows 2000 Setup. Press ENTER at the **Setup Notification** screen to go to the **Welcome to Setup** screen. Press R to repair a Windows 2000 installation, and then press C to use the Recovery Console. Use the **Copy** command to copy either the correct HAL or kernel file from the original CD into the appropriate folder on the hard disk. The **Copy** command detects whether the file to be copied is in the Microsoft compressed file format. If so, it automatically expands the file copied on the target drive, although you need to specify the correct file name extension as part of the command. These files can also be located within the Driver.cab file. If so, use the **Expand** command to extract them from the CAB and copy them to the hard disk. For more information about the Recovery Console, see "Troubleshooting Tools and Strategies" in this book.

For more troubleshooting information about the 0x79 Stop message, refer to the Microsoft Knowledge Base link, using the keywords **winnt** and **0x00000079**. For information about this resource, see chapters under "Additional Resources" at the end of this chapter.

Stop 0x0000007A or KERNEL_DATA_INPAGE_ERROR

This Stop message, also known as Stop 0x7A, indicates that the requested page of kernel data from the paging file could not be read into memory.

Interpreting the Message

The four parameters listed in the message are defined in order of appearance as follows:

1. Lock type that was held (value 1, 2, 3, or Page Table Entry [PTE] address).
2. I/O status code.
3. Current process (virtual address for lock type 3, or PTE).
4. Virtual address that could not be read into memory.

For information about all possible status codes that might be returned, see the file Ntstatus.h of the Windows 2000 Device Driver Development Kit (DDK). For information about the DDK, see "Additional Resources" at the end of this chapter.

Resolving the Problem

Stop 0x7A is usually caused by a bad block (sector) in a paging file, a virus, a disk controller error, or failing RAM. In rare cases, it is caused when nonpaged pool resources run out. It is also caused by defective hardware.

SCSI problems. If the I/O status is C0000185 and the paging file is on a SCSI disk, check the disk cabling and SCSI termination for problems.

Viruses. Check your computer for viruses, using any up-to-date, commercial virus scanning software that examines the Master Boot Record of the hard disk. Any Windows 2000 file system can be infected by viruses.

Bad block. An I/O status code of 0xC000009C or 0xC000016A normally indicates the data cannot be read from the disk due to a bad block (sector). If you can restart the system after the error, Autochk runs automatically and attempts to map out the bad sector. If Autochk does not scan the hard disk for errors, you can manually launch the disk scanner. Run **Chkdsk /f /r** on the system partition. You must restart the system before the disk scan begins. If you cannot start the system due to the error, use the Recovery Console and run **Chkdsk /r**. For more information about the Recovery Console, see "Troubleshooting Tools and Strategies" in this book.

Warning If your system partition is formatted with the FAT16 file system, the long file names used by Windows 2000 can be damaged if Scandisk or another MS-DOS-based hard disk tool is used to verify the integrity of your hard disk from an MS-DOS prompt. (An MS-DOS prompt is typically derived from an MS-DOS startup disk or from starting MS-DOS on a multiboot system.) Always use the Windows 2000 version of Chkdsk on Windows 2000 disks.

Failing RAM. Another common cause of this error message is failing RAM. Run hardware diagnostics supplied by the system manufacturer, especially the memory scanner. For details on these procedures, see the owner's manual for your computer.

Also, check that all the adapter cards in the computer, including memory modules, are properly seated. Use an ink eraser or an electrical contact treatment, available at electronics supply stores, to ensure adapter card contacts are clean. Be sure to wipe the cleaned contacts off, removing all cleaning debris, before reinstalling the adapter card into the computer. If compressed air is available, use it to clear out the adapter card slot.

Check the System Log in Event Viewer for additional error messages that might help pinpoint the device that is causing the error. Disabling memory caching of the BIOS might also resolve it.

Microsoft periodically releases a package of product improvements and problem resolutions for Windows 2000 called a Service Pack. Because many problems are resolved by installing the latest Service Pack, it is recommended that all users install them as they become available. To check which Service Pack, if any, is installed on your system, click **Start**, click **Run**, type **winver,** and then press ENTER. The **About Windows 2000** dialog box displays the Windows version number and the version number of the Service Pack, if one has been installed.

Occasionally, remedies to specific problems are developed after the release of a Service Pack. These remedies are called hotfixes. Microsoft does not recommend that you install a post–Service Pack hotfix unless the specific problem it addresses has been encountered. Service Packs include all of the hotfixes released since the release of the previous Service Pack. The status of hotfix installations is not indicated in the **About Windows 2000** dialog box. For more information about Service Packs and hotfixes, see "Additional Resources" at the end of this chapter.

Finally, if all the above steps fail to resolve the error, take the system motherboard to a repair facility for diagnostic testing. A crack, a scratched trace, or a defective component on the motherboard can also cause this error.

For more troubleshooting information about the 0x7A Stop message, refer to the Microsoft Knowledge Base link, using the keywords **winnt** and **0x0000007A**. For information about this resource, see "Additional Resources" at the end of this chapter.

Stop 0x0000007B or INACCESSIBLE_BOOT_DEVICE

This Stop message, also known as Stop 0x7B, indicates that Windows 2000 lost access to the system partition during the startup process. This error always occurs while the system is starting and cannot be debugged because it generally occurs before the operating system has loaded the debugger.

Interpreting the Message

The four parameters listed in the message are defined in order of appearance as follows:

1. Address of a Unicode string data structure representing the Advanced RISC Computing (ARC) specification name of the device from which the startup was being attempted.

2. Pointer to ARC name string in memory.

3. 0 (zero).

4. 0 (zero).

The first parameter typically contains two separate pieces of data. For example, if the parameter is 0x00800020, 0x0020 is the actual length of the Unicode string and 0x0080 is the maximum name string length. The next parameter contains the address of the buffer. This address is in system space, so the high-order bit is set.

If the file system that is supposed to read the boot device failed to initialize or simply did not recognize the data on the boot device as a file system structure, the following parameter definition applies:

1. Address of the device object that could not be mounted.

2. 0 (zero).

3. 0 (zero).

4. 0 (zero).

The value of the first argument determines whether the argument is a pointer to an ARC name string (ARC names are a generic method of identifying devices within the ARC environment) or a device object, because a Unicode string never has an odd number of bytes, and a device object always has a Type code of 0003.

Resolving the Problem

Failed boot device. During I/O system initialization, the boot device driver might have failed to initialize the boot device (typically a hard disk). File system initialization might have failed because it did not recognize the data on the boot device.

Also, repartitioning the system partition or installing a new SCSI adapter or disk controller might induce this error. If this happens, the Boot.ini file must be edited. For additional information about the Boot.ini file, see "Additional Resources" at the end of this chapter.

Incompatible disk hardware. If the error occurred at the initial setup of the system, the system might have been installed on an unsupported disk or SCSI controller. Some controllers are supported only by drivers that are in the Windows Driver Library (WDL), which requires the user to use a custom driver during installation. If upgrading the computer to Windows 2000, you might see a prompt to press F6 to use a custom driver. If doing a clean installation of Windows 2000, press F6 when the message "Setup is inspecting your computer's hardware configuration…" is displayed. You will be prompted later for the new driver. If Setup autodetected the controller, you might need to skip detection and use a specific manufacturer's diskette to load the driver. Also, check the availability of updates for the system BIOS and SCSI controller firmware. Updates of this kind are typically available on the Web site or BBS of the hardware manufacturer.

Remove any recently added hardware, especially hard disks or controllers, to see if the error is resolved. If the offending piece of hardware was a hard disk, the disk firmware version might be incompatible with Windows 2000. Contact the manufacturer for updates. If the removal of another piece of hardware resolved the error, IRQ or I/O port conflicts likely exist. Reconfigure the new device according to the manufacturer's instructions.

Confirm that all hard disks, hard disk controllers, and SCSI adapters are listed on the Microsoft Windows 2000 Hardware Compatibility List (HCL). For more information about the HCL, see "Additional Resources" at the end of this chapter.

If a driver was recently added, restart your computer, and press F8 at the character-mode screen that displays the prompt "For troubleshooting and advanced startup options for Windows 2000, press F8." On the resulting **Windows 2000 Advanced Options** menu, choose the **Last Known Good Configuration** option. This option is most effective when only one driver or service is added at a time.

In addition, check your computer for viruses using any up-to-date, commercial virus scanning software that examines the Master Boot Record of the hard disk. All Windows 2000 file systems can be infected by viruses.

This error can also be a result of hard disk corruption. Run **Chkdsk /f /r** on the system partition. You must restart the system before the disk scan begins. If you cannot start the system due to the error, use the Recovery Console and run **Chkdsk /r**. For more information about the Recovery Console, see "Troubleshooting Tools and Strategies" in this book.

Warning If your system partition is formatted with the FAT16 file system, the long file names used by Windows 2000 can be damaged if Scandisk or another MS-DOS-based hard disk tool is used to verify the integrity of your hard disk from an MS-DOS prompt. (An MS-DOS prompt is typically derived from an MS-DOS startup disk or from starting MS-DOS on a multiboot system.) Always use the Windows 2000 version of Chkdsk on Windows 2000 disks.

If your system has SCSI adapters, contact the adapter manufacturer to obtain updated Windows 2000 drivers. Try disabling sync negotiation in the SCSI BIOS, checking the cabling and the SCSI IDs of each device, and confirming proper termination. For EIDE devices, define the onboard EIDE port as Primary only. Also check each EIDE device for the proper master/slave/stand-alone setting. Try removing all EIDE devices except for hard disks.

For more troubleshooting information about the 0x7B Stop message, refer to the Microsoft Knowledge Base link, using the keywords **winnt** and **0x0000007B**. For information about this resource, see "Additional Resources" at the end of this chapter.

Stop 0x0000007F or UNEXPECTED_KERNEL_MODE_TRAP

This Stop message, also known as Stop 0x7F, means that one of two types of problems occurred in kernel-mode, either a kind of condition that the kernel is not allowed to have or catch (a *bound trap*), or a kind of error that is always fatal. Occasionally, this message can be caused by software problems, but the most common cause is hardware failure.

Interpreting the Message

The four parameters listed in the message are defined in order of appearance as follows:

1. Processor exception code
2. 0 (zero)
3. 0 (zero)
4. 0 (zero)

The first and most important parameter (0x0000000x) can have several different values. The cause of this error can vary, depending on the value of this parameter. All conditions that cause a Stop 0x7F can be found in any x86-based microprocessor reference manual because they are specific to the x86-based platform. Here are some of the most common exception codes:

- 0x00000000, or Divide by Zero Error, is caused when a DIV instruction is run and the divisor is 0. Memory corruption, other hardware problems, or software failures can cause this error.

- 0x00000004, or Overflow, occurs when the processor executes a call to an interrupt handler when the overflow (OF) flag is set.

- 0x00000005, or Bounds Check Fault, is generated when the processor, while executing a BOUND instruction, finds that a variable's assigned value exceeds the specified limits. A BOUND instruction is used to ensure that a signed array index is within a certain range.

- 0x00000006, or Invalid Opcode, is generated when the processor attempts to run an invalid instruction. This is generally caused when the instruction pointer has become corrupted and is pointing to the wrong location. The most common cause of this is hardware memory corruption.

- 0x00000008, or Double Fault, is when an exception occurs while trying to call the handler for a prior exception. Normally, the two exceptions can be handled serially. However, there are several exceptions that cannot be handled serially, and in this situation the processor signals a double fault. This is almost always caused by hardware problems.

Other exception codes are defined as follows:

- 0x00000001—A system-debugger call.

- 0x00000003—A debugger breakpoint.

- 0x00000007—A hardware coprocessor instruction with no coprocessor present.

- 0x0000000A—A corrupted Task State Segment.

- 0x0000000B—An access to a memory segment that was not present.

- 0x0000000C—An access to memory beyond the limits of a stack.

- 0x0000000D—An exception not covered by some other exception; a protection fault that pertains to access violations for applications.

Resolving the Problem

Hardware failure or incompatibility. Stop 0x7F usually occurs after the installation of faulty or mismatched hardware (especially memory) or in the event that installed hardware fails. If hardware was recently added to the system, remove it to see if the error recurs. If existing hardware has failed, remove or replace the faulty component. Run hardware diagnostics supplied by the system manufacturer, especially the memory scanner, to determine which hardware component has failed. For details on these procedures, see the owner's manual for your computer. Check that all the adapter cards in the computer, including memory modules, are properly seated. Use an ink eraser or an electrical contact treatment, available at electronics supply stores, to ensure adapter card contacts are clean. Be sure to wipe the cleaned contacts off, removing all cleaning debris, before reinstalling the adapter card into the computer. If compressed air is available, use it to clear out the adapter card slot.

If the error appears on a newly installed system, check the availability of updates for BIOS revisions on the motherboard, SCSI controllers, or network cards. Updates of this kind are typically available on the Web site or BBS of the hardware manufacturer.

Confirm that all hard disks, hard disk controllers, and SCSI adapters are listed on the Windows 2000 Hardware Compatibility List (HCL). For more information about the HCL, see "Additional Resources" at the end of this chapter.

If the error occurred after the installation of a new or updated device driver, the driver needs to be removed or replaced. If, under this circumstance, the error occurs during the startup sequence, restart the computer using Safe Mode to rename or delete the file. If the driver is used as part of the system startup process in Safe Mode, you need to start the computer using the Recovery Console in order to access the file. For more information about Safe Mode and the Recovery Console, see "Troubleshooting Tools and Strategies" in this book.

Also try restarting your computer, and press F8 at the character-mode screen that displays the prompt "For troubleshooting and advanced startup options for Windows 2000, press F8." On the resulting **Windows 2000 Advanced Options** menu, choose the **Last Known Good Configuration** option. This option is most effective when only one driver or service is added at a time.

Overclocking. Setting the CPU to run at speeds above the rated specification (known as *overclocking* the CPU) can cause this error. If this has been done to the computer experiencing the error, return the CPU to the default clock speed setting.

Check the System Log in Event Viewer for additional error messages that might help pinpoint the device or driver that is causing the error. Disabling memory caching of the BIOS might also resolve it.

If you encountered this error while upgrading to Windows 2000, it might be caused by a device driver, a system service, a virus scanner, or a backup tool that is incompatible with the new version. If possible, remove all third-party device drivers and system services and disable any virus scanners prior to upgrading. Contact the software manufacturer to obtain updates of these tools.

Microsoft periodically releases a package of product improvements and problem resolutions for Windows 2000 called a Service Pack. Because many problems are resolved by installing the latest Service Pack, it is recommended that all users install them as they become available. To check which Service Pack, if any, is installed on your system, click **Start**, click **Run**, type **winver,** and then press ENTER. The **About Windows 2000** dialog box displays the Windows version number and the version number of the Service Pack, if one has been installed.

Occasionally, remedies to specific problems are developed after the release of a Service Pack. These remedies are called hotfixes. Microsoft does not recommend that you install a post–Service Pack hotfix unless the specific problem it addresses has been encountered. Service Packs include all of the hotfixes released since the release of the previous Service Pack. The status of hotfix installations is not indicated in the **About Windows 2000** dialog box. For more information about Service Packs and hotfixes, see "Additional Resources" at the end of this chapter.

Finally, if all the above steps fail to resolve the error, take the system motherboard to a repair facility for diagnostic testing. A crack, a scratched trace, or a defective component on the motherboard can also cause this error.

For more troubleshooting information about the 0x7F Stop message, refer to the Microsoft Knowledge Base link, using the keywords **winnt** and **0x0000007F**. For information about this resource, see "Additional Resources" at the end of this chapter.

Stop 0xC000021A or STATUS_SYSTEM_PROCESS_TERMINATED

This Stop message occurs when a user-mode subsystem, such as Winlogon or the Client/Server Runtime Subsystem (CSRSS), is fatally compromised and security can no longer be guaranteed. The operating system switches into kernel-mode and generates this error. Because Windows 2000 cannot run without Winlogon or CSRSS, this is one of the few situations where the failure of a user-mode service can bring down the system. Running the kernel debugger is not useful in this situation because the actual error occurred in a user-mode process.

Interpreting the Message

The first three parameters listed in the message are defined in order of appearance as follows:

1. Status code
2. 0 (zero)
3. 0 (zero)

For information about all possible status codes that might be returned, see the file Ntstatus.h of the Windows 2000 Device Driver Development Kit (DDK). For information about the DDK, see "Additional Resources" at the end of this chapter.

Resolving the Problem

Device drivers, system services, and third-party applications. Because Stop 0xC000021A occurs in a user-mode process, the most common culprits are third-party applications. If the error occurred after the installation of a new or updated device driver, system service, or third-party application, the new software needs to be removed or disabled. Contact the manufacturer of the software about a possible update.

If the error occurs during system startup, restart your computer, and press F8 at the character-mode screen that displays the prompt "For troubleshooting and advanced startup options for Windows 2000, press F8." On the resulting **Windows 2000 Advanced Options** menu, choose the **Last Known Good Configuration** option. This option is most effective when only one driver or service is added at a time. If this does not resolve the error, try manually removing the offending software by restarting the computer in Safe Mode and renaming or uninstalling the faulty software. If the faulty software is used as part of the system startup process in Safe Mode, you need to start the computer using the Recovery Console in order to access the file. For more information about Safe Mode and the Recovery Console, see "Troubleshooting Tools and Strategies" in this book. If a newly installed piece if hardware is suspected, remove it to see if this resolves the issue.

Try running the Emergency Recovery Disk (ERD) and allow the system to repair any errors that it detects. For more information about the ERD, see "Troubleshooting Tools and Strategies" in this book.

Mismatched system files. Mismatched system files can also cause this error. If you can successfully start the computer using Safe Mode, try using the System File Checker (SFC) to correct the problem. Open up the **Run** dialog box, type **sfc /scannow**, and then press ENTER. For more information about System File Checker and Safe Mode, see "Troubleshooting Tools and Strategies" in this book. If SFC does not correct the problem, running a full system restore from tape might generate this error (some restore programs might skip restoring system files they determine are in use). Check to see if there is an updated version of the Backup/Restore program available from the manufacturer.

Microsoft periodically releases a package of product improvements and problem resolutions for Windows 2000 called a Service Pack. Because many problems are resolved by installing the latest Service Pack, it is recommended that all users install them as they become available. To check which Service Pack, if any, is installed on your system, click **Start**, click **Run**, type **winver,** and then press ENTER. The **About Windows 2000** dialog box displays the Windows version number and the version number of the Service Pack, if one has been installed.

Occasionally, remedies to specific problems are developed after the release of a Service Pack. These remedies are called hotfixes. Microsoft does not recommend that you install a post–Service Pack hotfix unless the specific problem it addresses has been encountered. Service Packs include all of the hotfixes released since the release of the previous Service Pack. The status of hotfix installations is not indicated in the **About Windows 2000** dialog box. For more information about Service Packs and hotfixes, see "Additional Resources" at the end of this chapter.

For more troubleshooting information about the 0xC000021A Stop message, refer to the Microsoft Knowledge Base link, using the keywords **winnt** and **0xC000021A**. For information about this resource, see "Additional Resources" at the end of this chapter.

Stop 0xC0000221 or STATUS_IMAGE_CHECKSUM_MISMATCH

This Stop message indicates that a driver or a system DLL has been corrupted. Typically, the name of the damaged file is displayed as part of the message.

Resolving the Problem

To resolve this error, restart the computer using either the product CD or the four Setup disks and enter Windows 2000 Setup. Press ENTER at the **Setup Notification** screen to go to the **Welcome to Setup** screen. Press R to repair a Windows 2000 installation, then press R to start the Emergency Repair Process, and then press F to run the Fast Repair option. You will be prompted for the Emergency Recovery Disk (ERD). Allow the system to repair or replace the missing or damaged driver file on the system partition. For more information about the ERD, see "Troubleshooting Tools and Strategies" in this book.

If you can successfully start the computer using Safe Mode, try using the System File Checker (SFC) to correct the problem. Open up the Run dialog box, type **sfc /scannow** and press ENTER. For more information about System File Checker and Safe Mode, see "Troubleshooting Tools and Strategies" in this book.

If a specific file was identified in the Stop message as being corrupted, you can try replacing that individual file manually. Restart the system, then press F8 at the character-mode screen that displays the prompt "For troubleshooting and advanced startup options for Windows 2000, press F8." On the resulting **Windows 2000 Advanced Options** menu, choose **Safe Mode with Command Prompt**. From there, copy a fresh version of the file from the original source onto the hard disk. If the file is used as part of the system startup process in Safe Mode, you need to start the computer using the Recovery Console in order to access the file. For more information about Safe Mode and the Recovery Console, see "Troubleshooting Tools and Strategies" in this book. If these methods fail, try reinstalling Windows 2000 and then restoring the system from a backup.

Note Some files are located in the Driver.cab located on the Windows 2000 operating system CD or in the %SystemRoot%\Driver cache\I386 folder. Files inside the CAB file need to be extracted before they can be used. If you can successfully start the computer with Safe Mode, they can be extracted by double-clicking the CAB file in Explorer and copying the files to the target location. If you cannot start the computer, use the Recovery Console. Use the **Expand** command to extract them from the CAB and copy them to the hard disk. If the original file from the product CD is not in a CAB file but has a file name extension ending in an underscore, the file needs to be uncompressed before it can be used. The Recovery Console's **Copy** command automatically detects compressed files and expands them as they are copied to the target location, although you need to specify the correct file name extension as part of the command. For more information about the Recovery Console, see "Troubleshooting Tools and Strategies" in this book.

Disk errors can be a source of file corruption. Run **Chkdsk /f /r** to detect and resolve any file system structural corruption. You must restart the system before the disk scan begins on a system partition. If you cannot start the system due to the error, use the Recovery Console and run **Chkdsk /r**. For more information about the Recovery Console, see "Troubleshooting Tools and Strategies" in this book.

Warning If your system partition is formatted with the FAT16 file system, the long file names used by Windows 2000 can be damaged if Scandisk or another MS-DOS-based hard disk tool is used to verify the integrity of your hard disk from an MS-DOS prompt. (An MS-DOS prompt is typically derived from an MS-DOS startup disk or from starting MS-DOS on a multiboot system.) Always use the Windows 2000 version of Chkdsk on Windows 2000 disks.

If the error occurred immediately after RAM was added to the system, the paging file might be corrupted or the new RAM itself might be either faulty or incompatible.

▶ **To determine if newly added RAM is causing a Stop message**

1. Return the system to the original RAM configuration.

2. Use the Recovery Console to access the partition containing the paging file and delete the file Pagefile.sys. For more information about the Recovery Console, see "Troubleshooting Tools and Strategies" in this book.

3. While still in the Recovery Console, run **Chkdsk /r** on the partition that contained the paging file.

4. Restart the system.

5. Set the paging file to an optimal level for the amount of RAM added.

6. Shut down the system and add your RAM.

   The new RAM must meet the system manufacturer's specifications for speed, parity, and type (that is, fast page mode [FPM] versus extended data out [EDO] versus synchronous dynamic random access memory [SDRAM]). Try to match the new RAM to the existing installed RAM as closely as possible. RAM can come in many different capacities, and more importantly, in different formats (single inline memory modules [SIMMs] or dual inline memory modules [DIMMs]). The electrical contacts can be either gold or tin, and it is not wise to mix these contact types.

If you experience the same error message after reinstalling the new RAM, run hardware diagnostics supplied by the system manufacturer, especially the memory scanner. For details on these procedures, see the owner's manual for your computer.

When you can log on to the system again, check the System Log in Event Viewer for additional error messages that might help pinpoint the device or driver that is causing the error. Disabling memory caching of the BIOS might also resolve this error.

For more troubleshooting information about the 0xC0000221 Stop message, refer to the Microsoft Knowledge Base link, using the keywords **winnt** and **0xC0000221**. For information about these resources, see "Additional Resources" at the end of this chapter.

Hardware Malfunction Messages

Hardware malfunction messages are another form of Stop messages. Like Stop messages, they are character-mode messages. They are caused by a hardware condition detected by the processor. The first one or two lines of the hardware malfunction message on one computer might differ from those on a different computer, even with the same failed component, depending upon the hardware abstraction layer (HAL) that is loaded at startup. However, these lines always convey the same idea, as shown in the following example:

```
Hardware malfunction.
Call your hardware vendor for support.
```

The installed HAL also determines how additional lines in each system's message differ in format and content. Therefore, before doing what the hardware malfunction message recommends, contact a support technician within your own organization to run hardware diagnostics on your computer. The information provided after the first two lines in the message helps your support technician decide which hardware diagnostics to run. For example, for ISA bus computers, this information indicates whether it is a memory-parity error or a bus-data error. On EISA computers, if the hardware problem is in an adapter, the adapter slot number on the system board is displayed.

Important In many situations, hardware failures first manifest themselves as Stop errors. Software using the failing hardware can detect problems because of unexpected results before the hardware itself has been identified as faulty. This is why troubleshooting many of the Stop messages includes running hardware diagnostics on the system.

Under rare circumstances, hardware malfunction messages can be generated by software bugs—specifically driver problems. For example, if a problematic driver writes to the wrong I/O port, the actual device at the targeted port might generate a hardware malfunction message. However, most errors of this sort are detected and debugged before the software is released to the public.

If you need help from outside your organization to interpret the information on the screen, contact the hardware manufacturer for your specific brand of computer, adapter, or peripheral device.

Additional Resources

- For more information about individual Stop messages, see the Microsoft Knowledge Base link on the Web Resources page at http://windows.microsoft.com/windows2000/reskit/webresources.

- For more information, see the Hardware Compatibility List link on the Web Resources page at http://windows.microsoft.com/windows2000/reskit/webresources.

- The latest Service Packs and hotfixes for Windows 2000 are available from Windows Update. Click **Start,** and then click **Windows Update** to see a list of components, if any, that are available as downloads for your system.

- For more information about Windows 2000 status code definitions in the file Ntstatus.h of the Windows 2000 Device Driver Development Kit (DDK), see the Device Driver Development Kit (DDK) link on the Web Resources page at http://windows.microsoft.com/windows2000/reskit/webresources.

PART 8

Appendixes

In This Part

APPENDIX A

Accessibility for People with Disabilities

The Microsoft Corporation is dedicated to making its products and services accessible and usable for everyone. Microsoft® Windows® 2000 includes new and enhanced accessibility features that benefit all users. These features make it easier to customize the computer and give users with disabilities better access to the applications they need to do their work.

In This Appendix

Related Information in the Resource Kit

- For more information about using accessibility features on the Internet, see "Accessibility Features and Functionality" in the *Microsoft® Windows® 2000 Server Resource Kit Internet Explorer Resource Guide.*

- For more information about deployment planning for accessibility features, see the appendix "Accessibility for People with Disabilities" in the *Microsoft® Windows® 2000 Server Resource Kit Deployment Planning Guide.*

Quick Guide to Accessibility for People with Disabilities

Use this quick guide to learn about the features of Microsoft® Windows® 2000 Professional that are important to accessibility for users with disabilities. The following summaries of tasks and planning issues map you to related sections in the appendix.

Set up the computer for maximum accommodation of accessibility features.

Use administrative options in **Accessibility Wizard** or Control Panel and customize the computer for user profiles for multiple users. Set new personalized accessibility feature settings, and preserve previous settings.

- See "Customizing Computers for Accessibility" in this chapter.

Choose options according to the type of disability.

Set accessibility and other options to suit individual categories of disabilities and the user's personal needs.

- See "Setting Accessibility Options by Type of Disability" in this chapter.

Configure accessibility features by using Windows 2000 Professional options.

Set accessibility options by using Control Panel, Utility Manager, and **Accessibility Wizard**.

- See "Configuring Accessibility Features" in this chapter.

Add third-party assistive devices.

Choose from a wide range of assistive technology to combine built-in Windows 2000 features with non-Microsoft add-on devices for all categories of disabilities for better control of the computer.

- See "Adding Third-Party Products and Services" in this chapter.

Overview of Accessibility in Windows 2000 Professional

Accessibility means equal access to computer software for everyone, including people with cognitive, hearing, physical, or vision disabilities. Cognitive disabilities can mean learning impairments, Down syndrome, dyslexia, or language impairments such as illiteracy. Users with hearing disabilities include people who are deaf or hard-of-hearing. Physical disabilities include cerebral palsy, tremors, seizures from epilepsy, lack of limbs or digits, and paralysis. Vision impairments include blindness and various kinds of low vision, such as colorblindness and tunnel vision. For Windows 2000, accessibility means making computers more usable through a flexible, customizable user interface (UI), alternative input and output methods, and better visibility of screen elements.

Accessibility Enhancements in Windows 2000 Professional

Several built-in Windows 2000 Professional technologies and Windows Explorer options are available for administrators and users to configure their computers with the accessibility features they need. Many of these features have added functionality beyond Microsoft® Windows® 98 and Microsoft® Windows NT® operating systems. New technologies and features in Windows 2000, as well as significantly enhanced existing features described in this appendix allow users and administrators to perform the functions described in the following sections.

What's New and Enhanced

Override defaults for multiple-user customized settings. Administrators can set a wider range of accessibility and other options for groups using Control Panel, **Accessibility Wizard**, and Utility Manager.

Quickly and easily navigate Windows 2000. Special features, such as hot keys and Active Desktop™, facilitate access to objects on the desktop, Windows Explorer, other servers on the network, or Internet Explorer. These features also give quick access to Windows 2000 and help users open folders and create their individualized settings.

Use a wider range of assistive technology. With Microsoft® Active Accessibility®, applications work more effectively with system extensions, applications, devices, and other third-party add-on accessibility aids, such as speech recognition products. Invisible to the user, Active Accessibility is integrated into the Windows 2000 operating system.

Customize input methods. Expanded configurations of keyboards, including On-Screen Keyboard, special mouse settings, and other options, allow users to customize their UI schemes.

Configure options through a single entry point. Located from the **Start** menu, **Accessibility Wizard** is a tool that allows administrators and users to set up their computers quickly with the most commonly used features to suit individual needs.

Magnify a portion of the screen for an enlarged display. Several built-in limited-use features, such as Magnifier, make it possible for users to work away from their customary add-on assistive devices.

Maneuver within Windows 2000. Utility Manager, personalized keyboard options, and keyboard shortcuts assist users with their work in applications.

Set sound options to suit individualized hearing needs. In addition to customizable features, such as volume adjustment and multimedia options, several accessibility features, such as ShowSounds and SoundSentry, give people with hearing impairments control of their audio environment.

Set options for users with vision requirements. Specialized features include Narrator, a text-to-speech tool that is built into Windows 2000; ToggleKeys, a feature that gives audio cues when the user presses certain locking keys; and event cues under **Sounds and Multimedia** in Control Panel.

Use keyboard filters to customize keys to aid various cognitive, hearing, mobility, and vision needs.
The FilterKeys feature adjusts keyboard response time and ignores accidental pressing of keys.

Assign contrast, color, timing, and sizing schemes for screen elements.
Expanded ranges of screen elements, such as high-visibility mouse pointers, high-contrast color schemes, and **Accessibility Wizard** give users options that suit their needs and preferences.

Active Accessibility

Active Accessibility is a developer technology that improves the way programs and the operating system work with accessibility aids. As an underlying technology, it is invisible to users. With Active Accessibility, software developers can make their programs more compatible with accessibility aids, and accessibility aid developers can make more reliable and more robust aids. It also can expand the capabilities of testing tools and other specialized utilities. Ultimately, Active Accessibility increases options for people who depend on accessibility aids in order to use computers.

Customizing Computers for Accessibility

Windows 2000 installs accessibility options automatically. Users cannot delete built-in accessibility options from the operating system after they are installed, including those options available in **Accessibility Wizard** or Control Panel.

Note Even if all of an individual user's data and applications are stored centrally, some user settings are stored on the local computer. When you perform a clean installation, these settings and data must be preserved and reapplied to the system after the installation.

Windows Installer

Windows Installer is a Windows 2000 technology that allows the operating system to install, maintain, and remove software on client computers. The service includes self-repairing applications. If an application is missing or damaged, Windows Installer reinstates the missing files the next time the user tries to open them. The self-repairing feature can alter selected options upon reinstallation. By using Group Policy settings, you can modify Windows Installer to prevent the self-repairing feature from altering options you have customized for accessibility purposes.

For more detailed information about Windows Installer, see "Custom and Automated Installations" in this book.

Group Policy

Group Policy is important to administrators who support users with disabilities because you can ensure that accessibility features and settings are available. You can publish applications for groups of users who have assistive needs. And you can verify that the Group Policy settings that are applied to your users or computers allow a flexible UI and include compatibility with external software tools.

For more detailed information about Group Policy, see "Group Policy" in the *Microsoft® Windows® 2000 Server Resource Kit Distributed Systems Guide*.

User Profiles

A user profile is a user-environment setting that users with disabilities can change to suit their accessibility needs. For accessibility purposes, it is important to consider setup options that maintain individual user profiles.

Automatic Logon

For many users, the step that requires pressing CTRL+ALT+DEL before logging on to a computer is difficult, if not impossible. Some users select the StickyKeys option to allow them to use CTRL+ALT+DEL. But others might prefer to log on without this step. The automatic logon feature allows users to bypass this keyboard shortcut and go directly to the logon process, which requires the correct name and password. An administrator can customize the computer to allow a user to log on without using CTRL+ALT+DEL.

▶ **To change the default option for CTRL+ALT+DEL before logging on to a Windows 2000 Professional computer**

1. In Control Panel, double-click **Users and Passwords**.

2. Click the **Advanced** tab.

3. Click the **Require users to press CTRL+ALT+DEL before logging on** check box to clear it.

Multiple User Profiles

You can use **Accessibility Wizard** to set multiple user profiles. The next user to log on to Windows 2000 can change the settings without deleting the previous settings. Individual settings are restored the next time a user logs on. This feature allows users or administrators to set the user's preferences. Windows 2000 automatically presets features to default for other users. When accessibility features are turned off, users who do not need them do not notice that the features are installed, so that people who require assistance and people who do not can use the computer. Multiple users of the same computer can use their logon and password information to set preferences and desktop settings, including any accessibility features that they need.

Note In both **Accessibility Wizard** and Control Panel, it is not a requirement to set multiple user profiles. You can specify public use or hot keys to open a feature at the logon prompt. All predefined settings are automatically reinstated the next time the user logs on.

Administrative Options

You can set administrative options for several features by using **Accessibility Wizard** or **Accessibility Options** in Control Panel. Settings you can make in both include automatic time-out, automatic reset, and default accessibility settings. However, to use settings on another computer, you must save settings to a file by using **Accessibility Wizard**. The time-out feature turns off accessibility functionality after the computer has been idle for a specified period of time. The operating system then returns to its default configuration.

Note The automatic reset and automatic time-out features do not turn off the SerialKeys feature.

Customizing the Desktop

Desktop elements such as menus, toolbars, shortcuts, and status indicators are important to accessibility for users who must customize many features for daily operation. In Windows 2000 Professional, you can customize the desktop to create an uncluttered arrangement of needed navigational elements for quick access of applications and folders. To create customizable desktop schemes, in Control Panel, double-click the **Display** icon, and then click the **Appearance** tab.

Personalized Menus

Windows 2000 tracks which programs you frequently use and, by default, hides, the associated commands for any programs that you have not used for six days. Programs that are hidden are still accessible from the **Start** menu by pointing to **Programs** and then clicking the chevron-shaped down arrow at the bottom of the **Programs** menu.

▶ **To turn off Personalized Menus**

1. From the **Start** menu, point to **Settings**, and then click **Taskbar & Start Menu**.

2. Click the **General** tab, then click the **Use Personalized Menus** check box to clear it.

Desktop Toolbars

Users can create their own desktop toolbars so that the toolbars contain frequently used commands and buttons. The ability to create custom desktop toolbars is most useful for people who prefer to use the mouse rather than the keyboard. Users who prefer the keyboard usually also prefer to add commands to the **Start** menu. Users can create desktop toolbars in the following ways:

- Putting a toolbar in a handier place on a desktop or taskbar.
- Using Drag and Drop or SHIFT+F10 to move frequently used files and programs for quick access.
- Adding an address bar to the taskbar or to the desktop to give the user the ability to type an Internet address without first opening the browser.

▶ **To create a custom desktop toolbar**

1. Create a folder with the appropriate documents, shortcuts, or programs.

2. Display the shortcut menu for the taskbar by right-clicking the taskbar.

   –Or–

   Press CTRL+ESC, ESC, and then TAB, TAB. Then press SHIFT+F10.

3. Point to **Toolbars**, and then click **New Toolbar**.

4. Type the path to the appropriate folder, or select the folder from the displayed list. To display all the folders in a branch, a user can press the Right Arrow key. The new toolbar appears on the taskbar.

Start Menu Options

You can customize the **Start** menu and add shortcuts to programs to make the menu more efficient. To change **Start** menu options, point to **Settings,** then click **Taskbar & Start Menu**; and then click the **Advanced** tab. To add a shortcut to the **Start** menu, in **Taskbar and Start Menu Properties**, click **Add**, then follow the instructions in the Create Shortcut wizard. To add **Start** menu options, drag and drop program icons onto the **Start** button.

System Status Indicators

The ability to use the TAB key to move to the status indicators on the system status area of the taskbar (sometimes called the "system tray") is new in Windows 2000. These indicators, or icons, show the user whether MouseKeys or FilterKeys are active and the status of specified other programs or products. These status indicators replace the status indicator feature of Microsoft® Windows NT® 4.0 and earlier.

For more detailed information about customizing the desktop, see "Customizing the Desktop and Working with Files and Folders" in this book.

Active Desktop

In addition to displaying intranet and Internet content, a user can personalize almost everything on the desktop with Active Desktop.

▶ **To turn on Active Desktop**

- In Control Panel, double-click **Folder Options**, click the **General** tab, and then select the **Enable Web content on my desktop** check box in the Active Desktop menu.

  –Or–

  Right-click a blank area on the desktop, point to Active Desktop, and then select the **Show Web content** check box.

  –Or–

  In **Control Panel**, double-click **Display**, click the **Web** tab, and then select the **Show Web Content on My Active Desktop** check box.

You can use Active Desktop to add Web pages that contain active content to a desktop. To change desktop schemes, double-click the **Display** icon in Control Panel and then click the **Appearance** tab. In Active Desktop, navigation by using TAB and SHIFT+TAB from the **Start** button, selection rotates in the following order: **Start**, Quick Launch bar, Taskbar, desktop icons, channel bar, and then **Start** again.

Windows Explorer

Windows Explorer allows the user to navigate through desktop elements, such as taskbar icons, files, shortcut icons, and other objects that are on the network. This feature provides a consistent interface for all categories of objects and, for some users, can be an easier way to navigate to objects on the desktop than by using the mouse.

For a list of Active Desktop and other shortcuts, see "Essential Keyboard Shortcuts" later in this appendix.

Utility Manager

Utility Manager allows faster access to some accessibility tools and also displays the status of the tools or devices that it controls. Utility Manager saves users time because an administrator can designate features to open when Windows 2000 starts. Utility Manager includes three built-in accessibility tools: Magnifier, Narrator, and On-Screen Keyboard.

Although only administrators can customize Utility Manager, users can start or stop the tools. Users with administrator access can also set up additional applications or run programs that install an add-on device. A third-party vendor must supply the installer for the add-on device. For related, detailed information about third-party devices, refer to the specific third-party documentation.

Although administrators have access to Utility Manager through the **Start** menu (under **Programs/Accessories/Accessibility**), it is also possible to use the WINDOWS LOGO key+U shortcut keys. Network policy settings might prevent opening Utility Manager through the **Start** menu if the computer is connected to a network.

▶ **To have Utility Manager open when Windows 2000 starts**

1. Open Utility Manager.

2. In the Name column, select the program.

3. Select **Start automatically when Windows starts** in the **Options** list box.

These options allow the administrator to designate immediate access for users who must have Narrator, Magnifier, or On-Screen Keyboard to operate the computer. This procedure can also open third-party devices when Windows starts if the vendor has supplied the installer for them.

Setting Accessibility Options by Type of Disability

You can configure most accessibility options in either Control Panel or **Accessibility Wizard**. However, several options are configurable in only one of these modes. In some instances, there are different names for the same, or similar, features. Table A.1 describes such variances.

Table A.1   Variances in Accessibility Wizard and Control Panel Features

Start Menu/Programs or Accessibility Wizard	Start Menu/Settings/ Control Panel	Description
UI elements and schemes organized by category of disability	UI elements and schemes organized by feature	In **Accessibility Wizard**, most key settings are arranged by category of disability rather than by UI element.
Magnifier	No Magnifier	Feature is available from **Start** menu only.
Narrator	No Narrator	Feature is available from **Start** menu only.

(continued)

Table A.1   Variances in Accessibility Wizard and Control Panel Features
(continued)

Start Menu/Programs or Accessibility Wizard	Start Menu/Settings/ Control Panel	Description
Utility Manager	No Utility Manager	Feature is available from **Start** menu or WINDOWS LOGO key+U.
No SerialKeys	SerialKeys	SerialKeys is available in Control Panel only.
On-Screen Keyboard	No On-Screen Keyboard	Feature is available from **Start** menu only.
No customizable keyboard	Dvorak keyboard	Customizable keyboard layout is available in Control Panel only.
BounceKeys	FilterKeys (SlowKeys only)	In **Accessibility Wizard**, basic FilterKeys is called BounceKeys.
All Mouse options in **I have trouble using a keyboard** option, in Mouse options menu	Mouse options in **Mouse** properties and **Accessibility Options**	In Control Panel, Mouse options are in **Mouse** properties. MouseKeys options are in the **Mouse** property sheet in **Accessibility Options**.
Personalized menus	No personalized menu options	You can create personalized menus from the **Start** menu.

Creating custom interfaces gives users with disabilities control of their computing environment so that they can succeed in their work. A simplified UI is a necessity for reducing the amount of navigation. The Windows 2000 features and techniques discussed in the following sections allow users and administrators to customize computers according to their specific needs and preferences. These options are grouped by category of disability.

Accessibility Options for Users with Cognitive Disabilities

Cognitive disabilities include developmental disabilities, such as Down syndrome; learning disabilities; dyslexia; illiteracy; attention deficit disorder; memory loss; and perceptual difficulties, such as slow response time. In addition to third-party assistive devices, such as voice-input utilities, some built-in Windows 2000 features can be especially helpful to people with cognitive disabilities. Examples of built-in features include AutoCorrect, AutoComplete, and Automatic Spell Checking.

You can customize AutoComplete to include only the information that users need. For some users, these features facilitate their work considerably. However, for other users, with some features—such as AutoComplete or certain sound schemes—it is advantageous for users with cognitive disabilities to clear, rather than to select these options. Such features can cause distractions, especially if the user is working with a text-to-speech utility. There are two types of AutoComplete that affect use of Windows Explorer and the **Run** box. One is an automatic suggestion, with a drop-down list of Web sites with the same letters the user has typed. The other AutoComplete feature, called Inline AutoComplete, automatically completes a line if the user has typed it before. The first feature is turned on by default, but Inline AutoComplete is not. To change these defaults, perform the following steps:

▶ **To disable the site-address AutoComplete feature**

1. In Control Panel, double-click **Internet Options**, and then click the **Content** tab.

2. Click **AutoComplete**.

3. Click the **Web Addresses** check box to clear it.

▶ **To activate the inline AutoComplete feature**

1. In Control Panel, double-click **Internet Options**, and then click the **Advanced** tab.

2. Select the **Use Inline AutoComplete** check box.

Keyboard Filters

Several Windows 2000 accessibility features, found in **Accessibility Wizard** or Control Panel, can be useful to people with cognitive disabilities. The FilterKeys feature allows users to adjust keyboard response time, forgive accidental pressing of keys, and slow response time. Users who are familiar with Windows NT 4.0 or earlier need to know that special keyboard filters have been rearranged in Windows 2000. In both **Accessibility Wizard** and Control Panel, users can adjust keyboard response time to ignore accidental pressing of keys and slow response time. FilterKeys includes RepeatKeys and SlowKeys. Through RepeatKeys, the user can choose to ignore keyboard repeat or to slow down the keyboard repeat rate. SlowKeys requires keys to be held down for a specified period of time before it accepts a keystroke. In **Accessibility Wizard**, the **FilterKeys** option that ignores keystrokes that are faster than a set period of time is called BounceKeys.

1.1.1.2 Keyboard Shortcuts

Other options that are useful to people with cognitive disabilities are hot keys and other keyboard shortcuts, such as Narrator, Active Desktop, Quick Launch bar, status indicators on the system status area of the taskbar that show which features are on, and sound options found in **Accessibility Wizard** and in Control Panel. Also, sound schemes can help draw attention to, or provide additional feedback for, tasks as the user does them. For a more extensive list of keyboard shortcuts and procedures for using them, see the section "Accessibility Options for Users with Physical Disabilities" later in this chapter.

Accessibility Options for Users with Hearing Impairments

Users who are deaf or hard-of-hearing or who have limited ability to distinguish sounds might find the following options useful. These features incorporate sound scheme adjustments and visual media as substitutes for sound.

Customizable Sound Schemes

Users who are hard-of-hearing or who work in a noisy environment can adjust the pitch and timbre of sounds, as well as the volume associated with various on-screen events, to make them easier to distinguish. The sounds are customizable either by using **Accessibility Wizard** or by using Control Panel. Windows 2000 provides sounds that users can associate with many events. These can be events that Windows 2000 or programs generate. If users have difficulty distinguishing between the default sounds, such as the beep to signal an inoperative keystroke, they can choose a new sound scheme or design their own scheme to make the sounds easier to identify. In Windows 2000, users can turn off the default downloading of sound files.

If the computer has a sound card, users can adjust the volume for all of the Windows sounds by using the **Volume Control** property sheet under **Sounds and Multimedia** in Control Panel. They can also adjust the sound volume by using the speaker icon on the taskbar.

Some users require visual feedback instead of sound. Such users are likely to be interested in customizable sounds and closed captioning. The following Windows 2000 features are useful to people who are deaf or hard-of-hearing.

ShowSounds   ShowSounds, a feature under **Accessibility Options** in Control Panel, instructs programs that are closed-caption-enabled to display visual feedback in the form of closed captioning. In Windows 2000, users can choose to display closed captioning in programs with audiovisual content.

SoundSentry This feature for deaf users tells Windows 2000 to send a visual cue, such as a blinking title bar or screen flash, whenever the system generates a sound. Enabling this feature allows users to see when the computer is generating sounds and to be aware of messages that they might not have heard.

In Windows 2000, to enable the SoundSentry feature, double-click **Accessibility Options** in Control Panel, then click the **Sound** tab. This feature allows users to change settings for visual warnings, a blinking title bar or a screen flash when the computer generates a sound. To select a visual cue, select the **Warning for Windowed Programs** option. You can also choose to have no visual cue.

Note If you choose to flash the active window's title bar, a visual cue might not be visible if the active window has no title bar. Some displays do not have a flashing border, so there is no visual cue with this option on incompatible display hardware. This is true of some liquid crystal displays typically found on portable computers.

In Windows 2000, the SoundSentry feature supports only those sounds the computer's internal speaker generates, but it cannot detect sounds that are made using multimedia sound cards. If the computer has a multimedia sound card, you might need to disable this hardware to force the computer's built-in speaker to relay the sounds. To disable the multimedia sound card, double-click **Sounds and Multimedia** in Control Panel, then click the **Audio** tab.

Figure A.1 illustrates the sound options in Control Panel, **Accessibility Options** under **Sounds**.

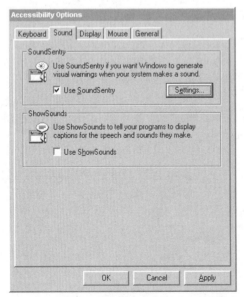

Figure A.1   Sound Features in Control Panel Accessibility Options Menu

Other Alternatives to Sound in Control Panel

Users with hearing impairments often rely on indicators, such as lights, to replace sound. If the indicator lights for the locking keys NUM LOCK, CAPS LOCK, or SCROLL LOCK are not on, it can mean that the user selected the ToggleKeys feature in the **Accessibility Options** property sheet under **Keyboard** in Control Panel. To re-activate the indicator lights, click the **ToggleKeys** check box to clear it.

Accessibility Options for Users with Physical Disabilities

Some users are unable to perform certain manual tasks, such as using a mouse or typing two keys at the same time. Others tend to hit multiple keys or bounce their fingers off keys. Physical disabilities, or mobility impairments, include paralysis, repetitive stress injuries, cerebral palsy, erratic motion tremors, quadriplegia, or lack of limbs or fingers. Many users need keyboard and mouse functions adapted to their particular needs, or they rely exclusively on an alternative input device. A large number of input devices are available to users, including keyboard filters, voice-input utilities for controlling the computer with the user's voice, on-screen keyboards, smaller or larger keyboards, eye-gaze pointing devices, and sip-and-puff systems that the user operates by breath control. For more information about assistive devices and a catalog of third-party accessibility aids, see the Microsoft Accessibility link on the Web Resources page at http://windows.microsoft.com/windows2000/reskit/webresources.

The following options include some of the Windows 2000 accessibility features that are useful to people with mobility impairments.

Keyboard Options

Impaired dexterity can make it difficult for a person to use a standard keyboard. However, keyboard filters built into Windows 2000 compensate somewhat by correcting for erratic motion tremors, slow response time, and similar conditions. Other kinds of keyboard filters include typing aids, such as word prediction and abbreviation expansion tools and add-in spelling checkers.

The following sections describe input devices and features that are different from the standard keyboard. These features include alternative keyboard layouts, keyboard shortcuts, and specialized keyboard filters that operate on the standard keyboard but carry options that tailor the behavior of keys to specific accessibility needs.

Note In most cases, it is not possible to apply the same keyboard behavior corrections to pointing devices, such as the mouse. This limitation might affect the use of the mouse for users with impaired dexterity.

On-Screen Keyboard

Some users have difficulty with both the mouse and the keyboard. However, they might be able to use an on-screen keyboard with another input device, such as a pointing device or a joystick that connects to the serial port, or use the keyboard space bar as a switch device. An on-screen keyboard is a utility that allows users to select keys by using an alternative input mode, as shown in Figure A.2.

Note To use switch modes, see your switch manufacturer for the custom cables they require.

Users can set up and customize the Windows 2000 On-Screen Keyboard by going to **Accessibility Options** from the **Start** menu. The On-Screen Keyboard can also be run through Utility Manager. Many users with physical disabilities need an alternative keyboard with a higher functionality for daily use. For a list of other Windows-based on-screen keyboard tools, see the Microsoft Accessibility Web site at http://windows.microsoft.com/windows2000/reskit/webresources.

Note The On-Screen Keyboard, illustrated in Figure A.2, is meant to be used as a temporary solution and not as a day-to-day alternative keyboard in lieu of a third-party on-screen keyboard.

Figure A.2   Microsoft On-Screen Keyboard

Dvorak Keyboard

The Dvorak keyboard makes the most frequently typed characters on a keyboard more accessible to people who have difficulty typing on the standard QWERTY layout. There are three Dvorak layouts: one for people who use two hands to type, one for people who type with their left hand only, and one for people who type with their right hand only. Dvorak layouts reduce the degree of motion required to type common English text. This feature might help avoid some kinds of repetitive strain injuries that are associated with typing. You can either add the Dvorak keyboard as part of the setup or add it later. To configure the Dvorak Keyboard, double-click the **Keyboard** icon in Control Panel.

Keyboard Shortcuts

Keyboard shortcuts are keyboard-driven commands that allow a user to navigate and enter commands without using a mouse. Keyboard shortcuts are important to users with disabilities, and they cover nearly all categories of disabilities. Through the use of ALT commands and CTRL keys, a user can navigate and enter commands without the mouse. Even without configuring accessibility features, the user can use the TAB key in dialog boxes to move the focus and then use the arrow keys to select options in a list. In property sheets that have multiple tabs, the user can press CTRL+TAB to select each property sheet in order from left to right. Or the user can press the TAB key until the focus is on the tab for the current property sheet and then press an arrow key to select the next sheet. In Active Desktop, the user can add shortcut keys to the **Start** menu.

By default, Windows 2000 does not underline keyboard navigation indicator letters. There are three ways to override this default and reinstate the underlines.

▶ **To reinstate the underlines for keyboard navigation**

- In Control Panel, double-click the **Display** icon. Click **Effects**, and then click the **Hide keyboard navigation indicators until I use the ALT key** check box to clear it. With this step, the underlines are always visible. (If you select the **Hide keyboard navigation indicators until I use the ALT key** check box and then press the ALT key, the system displays the underlines, but only temporarily. The next time that you click using the mouse, that action hides the underlines again.)

  –Or–

  In Control Panel, double-click **Accessibility Options**. Click the **Keyboard** tab, and then select the **Show extra keyboard help in programs** check box.

  –Or–

  In **Accessibility Wizard**, select the **I have difficulty using the keyboard or mouse** check box, and then select the **Do you want extra keyboard help...?** check box.

For a comprehensive list of keyboard shortcuts, see Windows 2000 Professional Help. Look for the entry "Shortcut Keys" in the index. For accessibility-specific keyboard shortcuts, see the Microsoft Enable Web site in the following resource. For general keyboard-only commands, accessibility shortcuts, and Microsoft natural keyboard keys, see the Microsoft Accessibility Web site at http://windows.microsoft.com/windows2000/reskit/webresources.

For detailed information about keyboard shortcuts, see "Keyboard Shortcuts" in Windows 2000 Professional Help.

Hot Keys for Emergency Use

The hot keys feature is designed for accessibility as an immediate method of activating accessibility features for people who cannot use the computer without first having accessibility features in effect. Hot keys, which are a type of shortcut, allow the user to turn on a specific feature temporarily. Then, after a feature has been turned on, users can open **Accessibility Wizard** or double-click **Accessibility Options** in Control Panel to adjust the feature to their own preferences or to turn on the feature permanently. The same hot key temporarily turns off the feature if it gets in the way or if another person wants to use the computer without this feature.

Hot keys are unique key combinations that should not conflict with keys that programs use. If such a conflict does arise, the user can turn the hot keys off and still use the feature as needed. In a typical installation of Windows 2000, the accessibility hot keys are inactive to prevent them from conflicting with other programs. Except for the high-contrast feature, which is inactive by default, hot keys are active by default until a user or administrator de-activates them.

You can assign hot keys to frequently used programs, documents, or folders, and then use a hot key to open the object or make it the active window. To turn on the hot key for a feature, double-click **Accessibility Options** in Control Panel. Then click **Settings** for the feature, and select the **Use Shortcut** check box.

As a precaution against accidental use, if the sound features for StickyKeys are turned on, pressing an accessibility hot key causes special tones to sound (a rising tone for activating and a falling tone for de-activating). A confirmation dialog box then appears, which briefly explains the feature and how it was turned on. By pressing the hot key unintentionally, the user can cancel the feature's activation at this time. The confirming dialog box also provides a quick path to more detailed help and to Control Panel settings for the hot key feature, in case the user wants to turn off the hot key permanently.

▶ **To assign a hot key to start a program**

1. Create a shortcut to the object on the desktop or on the **Start** menu.

2. Display the properties for the shortcut by right-clicking the shortcut icon or name and then clicking **Properties** or by using SHIFT+F10.

3. Click the **Shortcut** tab, and then type the key combination that you want to assign to this object in the **Shortcut Key** box.

When a shortcut is placed on the desktop or on the **Start** menu, the user can press the hot key for the program at any time, and Windows 2000 opens that window. Or, if the program is not running, the hot key starts it.

Essential Keyboard Shortcuts

Tables A.2, A.3, A.4, A.5, A.6, A.7, A.8, and A.9 list essential keyboard shortcuts for the user who has difficulty using the mouse or other input methods and must rely on the keyboard to maneuver through Windows 2000. Some configurations may vary in what the shortcut letter designates. In such situations, when users navigate, they must also use directional arrows, the tab key, or repeat the same letter to arrive at the icon they want.

Table A.2   Emergency Hot Keys

To enable Emergency Hot Keys	Keyboard Shortcut
Switch FilterKeys on or off.	RIGHT SHIFT for 8 seconds
Set **SlowKeys** and **RepeatKeys** in **FilterKeys** to most conservative values.	RIGHT SHIFT for 12 seconds
Switch High Contrast on and off.	LEFT ALT+LEFT SHIFT+PRINT SCREEN
Switch MouseKeys on and off.	LEFT ALT+LEFT SHIFT+NUM LOCK
Switch StickyKeys on and off.	SHIFT 5 times
Switch ToggleKeys on and off.	NUM LOCK for 5 seconds

Table A.3   Help Shortcuts

Accessibility Topics in HELP	Key Sequence
Display accessibility table of contents in Help.	CTRL+ESC, H, Alt C
Select "Accessibility for People with Disabilities."	Down Arrow repeatedly to topic, ENTER
Enter topic content area.	F6
Select a link.	TAB repeatedly, ENTER
Return to Help table of contents (move between panes).	F6
Close Help.	ALT+SPACEBAR, C

Table A.4   Active Desktop Navigation Shortcuts

Shortcut Keys to Use Active Desktop	Key Sequence
From the **Start** menu; go to Settings and then to Control Panel.	CTRL+ESC, S, C (or if another icon in the **Start** menu begins with S, you may need to use the right arrow key to expand the Settings menu)
Open **Folder Options.**	F until **Folder Options** has the focus, then ENTER (or TAB or arrows to reach icon)
Open **Active Desktop**.	TAB, Up/Down Arrows
Open **Enable Web content on my desktop**.	TAB, Up/Down Arrows
Or, on a blank area of the desktop, select **Show Web content** check box.	SHIFT+F10
Or, go to Control Panel, then open **Display**.	Arrows to Web tab, TAB, then spacebar to select the **Show Web Content on My Active Desktop** check box
Minimize windows for Active Desktop use.	WINDOWS LOGO key+D

Table A.5   Accessibility Wizard Shortcuts

Accessibility Wizard	Key Sequence
Start Accessibility Wizard.	CTRL + ESC, P, A, Down Arrow, A, ENTER
Select setting.	Up/Down Arrows, or TAB, SPACEBAR for setting
Go to next screen or save settings.	ENTER
Close Accessibility Wizard.	ALT+F4

Table A.6   Magnifier Shortcuts

Magnifier	Key Sequence
Start Magnifier.	CTRL+ESC, P, A, Right Arrow, M, ENTER
Invert colors.	TAB, Up/Down Arrow, or SPACEBAR
Start Magnifier by using Utility Manager.	WINDOWS LOGO key+U

Table A.7   Narrator Shortcuts

Narrator	Key Sequence
Start Narrator.	CTRL+ESC, P, A, right ARROW, N, ENTER
Invert colors.	TAB, Up/Down Arrow, or SPACEBAR
Start Narrator through Utility Manager.	WINDOWS LOGO key+U

Table A.8   Control Panel Accessibility Shortcuts

Control Panel Accessibility Options	Key Sequence
Go to **Start** menu.	CTRL+ESC
On the **Start** menu, go to Settings and then to Control Panel.	S, C (or if another icon in the **Start** menu begins with S, you may need to use the right arrow key to expand the Settings menu or use the tab key or directional arrows to reach icon)
Select **Accessibility Options**.	A, ENTER
Select settings.	TAB, Up/Down Arrows to desired setting
Check/clear settings.	SPACEBAR
Save settings.	ENTER
Close Control Panel window.	ALT+F4

Table A.9   Control Panel Standard Shortcuts

Other Control Panel Options for Greater Accessibility	Key Sequence
Go to **Start** menu.	CTRL+ESC
On the **Start** menu, go to Settings and then to Control Panel.	S, C (or if another icon in the **Start** menu begins with S, you may need to use the right arrow key to expand the Settings menu)
Go to icon (**Mouse**, **Display**, **Keyboard**, or **Sounds and Multimedia**).	M, D, K, or S, until icon has the focus, then ENTER (or TAB or arrows to reach icon)
Move focus to tab (if present).	CTRL+TAB
Move focus to dialog box.	TAB
Display predefined schemes (if present).	Down Arrow
Navigate in dialog box.	TAB and SPACEBAR
Respond to **Save the previous scheme?** dialog box query (if present).	"Y" for "Yes," "N" for "No," or ESC to close the dialog box without saving changes

(continued)

Table A.9   **Control Panel Standard Shortcuts** *(continued)*

Other Control Panel Options for Greater Accessibility	Key Sequence
Save settings.	ENTER
Close Control Panel window.	ALT+F4
Move slider bars right or left.	CTRL+RIGHT or Left Arrow

For more detailed information about keyboard shortcuts, see the Microsoft Accessibility Web site at http://windows.microsoft.com/windows2000 /reskit/webresources.

StickyKeys for One-Finger or Mouthstick Typing

Many software programs require the user to press two or three keys at a time. For people who type using a single finger or a mouthstick, that process is not possible. StickyKeys allows the user to press one key at a time and instructs Windows to respond as if the keys are pressed simultaneously. StickyKeys is especially useful when a user must press CTRL+ALT+DEL to log on to the computer. If StickyKeys is not turned on, then the user can use hot keys.

▶   **To activate the StickyKeys feature**

1. In Control Panel, double-click the **Accessibility Options** icon.

2. Click the **Keyboard** tab.

3. Select the StickyKeys options that you want.

    –Or–

    To activate StickyKeys from the keyboard, use hot keys, press SHIFT five times.

The following are tips for using StickyKeys:

- When StickyKeys is on, pressing any modifier key (SHIFT, CTRL, WINDOWS LOGO, or ALT) latches that key down until the user presses a key that is not a modifier key. If the StickyKeys sound features are on, you hear a short low-pitched beep and then a high-pitched beep. When the next nonmodifier key is pressed, the modifier key(s) are released.

- Pressing a modifier key twice in a row locks the key down until it is tapped a third time. If the StickyKeys sound features are on, you hear a short low-to-high sound after the first tap and a single high-pitched beep after the second tap. After a modifier key is locked, it stays locked until it is pressed a third time.

- Any and all of the modifier keys (SHIFT, CTRL, WINDOWS LOGO, and ALT) can be latched or locked in combination.

- For shared computers, there is an optional feature to keep other users from being confused when StickyKeys is left on. If the option **Turn StickyKeys Off If Two Keys Are Pressed at Once** is activated and two keys are held down simultaneously, StickyKeys automatically turns off.

- Some people do not like to have keyboard sounds, although others find them useful. To turn feedback sounds on or off, select the **StickyKeys** check box; then either select the **Make Sounds When Modifier Key Is Pressed** check box to activate the feature or click the check box to clear it if the feature is already activated and you do not want it on.

- To turn off the StickyKeys Locked mode, make sure the **Press Modifier Key Twice to Lock** check box is cleared.

- To turn StickyKeys off, press SHIFT five times. This process triggers a high-to-low series of tones.

- To turn StickyKeys on, also press SHIFT five times. This process triggers a low-to-high series of tones.

Figure A.3 illustrates the options under **Keyboard** in Control Panel.

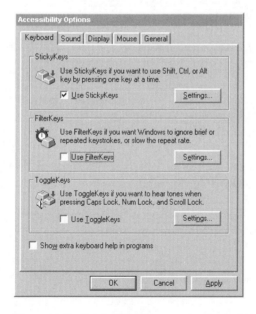

Figure A.3   StickyKeys Feature in Control Panel Accessibility Options Menu

FilterKeys for Users with Impaired Manual Dexterity

Windows 2000 includes keyboard filters that work separately or in combination to make input easier for users who have difficulty with the keyboard because of slow response time, erratic motion tremors, or a tendency to repeat the keys inadvertently. These special keys, grouped in Control Panel in the FilterKeys properties, are named RepeatKeys and SlowKeys.

FilterKeys can perform the following functions:

- RepeatKeys allows the user to adjust the repeat rate or ignore the key repeat function on the keyboard, which compensates for a tendency to hold a key down too long. Most keyboards allow the user to repeat a key just by holding it down. Although this automatic repeat feature can be convenient for some people, it poses a problem for individuals who cannot lift their fingers off the keyboard quickly. This feature can also compensate for a tendency to press the wrong key accidentally.

- SlowKeys also instructs the computer to disregard keystrokes that are repeated quickly. This allows a user to brush against keys without any effect. By placing a finger on the proper key, the user can hold the key down until the character appears on the screen.

In Control Panel, the **Keyboard Speed** option also allows users to alter character repeat rates.

Note For RepeatKeys, SlowKeys, or BounceKeys, you must define the acceptance delay, which allows you to adjust the amount of time that you must hold a key down before the computer accepts it.

Another useful FilterKeys feature is the option **Beep When a Key Is Pressed**. If this option is on and any FilterKeys functions are active, you hear a beep when you press the key or when the key repeats. For example, if SlowKeys is active, you hear a sound when the key is pressed and also when the computer accepts the key. This feature can be useful when the keyboard is set to respond differently than usual.

▶ **To adjust key repeat delay and speed:**

1. In Control Panel, double-click the **Keyboard** icon.

2. Click the **Speed** tab, then drag a slider bar to adjust keyboard behavior:

   To adjust how long you must hold down a key before it begins repeating, drag the **Repeat Delay** slider.

   To adjust how fast a key repeats when you hold it down, drag the **Repeat Rate** slider.

ToggleKeys for Users Who Inadvertently Brush Against the Lock Keys

ToggleKeys instructs Windows to play a high beep or a low beep when the lock keys NUM LOCK, CAPS LOCK, or SCROLL LOCK are on. This sound signals to the user that one of these keys has been turned on.

Mouse Options

Users with mobility impairments can now choose among options for size, color, and animation schemes. To adjust mouse properties to increase the pointer's visibility, double-click the **Mouse** icon in Control Panel. Then click the **Pointers** tab, and select the **Scheme** check box. This customizable feature is also useful for users with vision impairment.

Note To use High-Contrast mode for pointers under **Mouse** options in Control Panel, you must first turn off the default hot keys for input locales.

Adjusting Mouse Properties

To make the mouse pointer automatically move to the default button (such as **OK**, or **Apply**) in dialog boxes and to reverse the buttons so that the right mouse (index finger) button is the primary button, click the **Mouse** icon in Control Panel. Users can adjust other mouse settings, such as pointer rate of speed and acceleration, left-right orientation, size, color, shape, time allowed between clicks, or animation. By selecting **I am blind or have difficulty seeing things on screen** and **I have difficulty using the keyboard or mouse**, users can also set several mouse options in **Accessibility Wizard**.

MouseKeys for Keyboard-only Input

Although Windows 2000 is designed so that users can perform all actions without a mouse, some programs might still require one; and a mouse might be more convenient for some tasks. MouseKeys in Control Panel is also useful for graphic artists and others who must position the pointer with great accuracy. A user does not need a mouse to use this feature. With MouseKeys, users can control the mouse pointer with one finger or a mouthstick by using the numeric keypad to move the mouse pointer. In this way, users can click, double-click, and move objects with both mouse buttons. To use hot keys to turn the MouseKeys on or off select the **Use Shortcut** check box in the **Settings for MouseKeys** dialog box or click this check box to clear it.

Figure A.4 illustrates the numeric keypad used as MouseKeys.

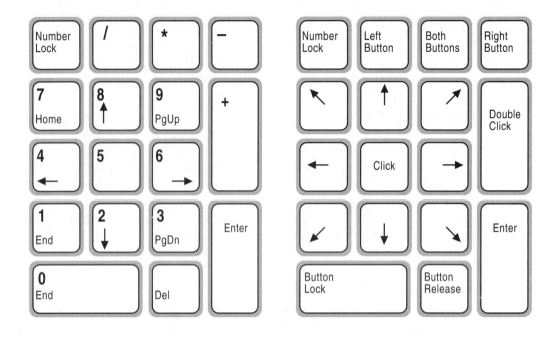

Numeric Keypad   **MouseKeys**

Figure A.4   MouseKeys Feature for Users Who Have Difficulty Using a Mouse

▶   **To turn on MouseKeys from the keyboard**

  ▪ Press left ALT+left SHIFT+NUM LOCK.

When MouseKeys is on, it emits a rising tone if sounds are turned on. If a user is using only one finger or a mouthstick to operate the computer, the easiest way to activate MouseKeys is first to activate StickyKeys by tapping the SHIFT key five times. The user can then press the three keys in sequence rather than simultaneously.

Note   If FilterKeys is active, all the MouseKeys control keys respond according to the setting for FilterKeys.

When MouseKeys is on, use the following keys to move the pointer on the screen:

  ▪ On the numeric keypad, press any of the numbered keys immediately surrounding the 5 key (also called the "arrow keys") to move the pointer in the direction that is indicated by the arrows.

- Use the 5 key on the numeric keypad for a single mouse-button click and the PLUS SIGN (+) key for a double-click.

- To drag and release an object, place the pointer on the object and then press the INS KEY to begin dragging. Move the object to its new location, and then press DEL to release it.

You can use the NUM LOCK key to toggle the MouseKeys control pad back to the numeric keypad and vice versa. This is especially useful with a portable computer that lacks a separate numeric keypad. On these computer keyboards, the numeric keypad is usually overlaid on top of the standard QWERTY keyboard. For example, if you are using the numeric keypad for number entry before starting MouseKeys, when you toggle out of MouseKeys by using the NUM LOCK key, you can enter numbers with the numeric keypad. If you are using the numeric keypad as a cursor keypad before starting MouseKeys, when you toggle out of MouseKeys by using the NUM LOCK key, you have a cursor keypad.

Note If the MouseKeys feature is on but NUM LOCK is toggled to the opposite setting, the MouseKeys icon in the taskbar shows that MouseKeys is off.

It can be useful to combine MouseKeys and a physical mouse. For example, a user can use the standard mouse to move quickly around the screen and then use MouseKeys to move more precisely (unit by unit) to the insertion point. Some people cannot use the standard mouse and simultaneously hold down the mouse button. Such users can use MouseKeys to lock down the currently active mouse button, move the mouse pointer by using MouseKeys or the standard mouse, and then release the mouse button by using MouseKeys.

Accessibility Options for Users Who Have Seizures

Users who have seizures, including those with epilepsy, can adjust screen elements, such as timing, color and contrast, and sound by using **Accessibility Wizard** or Control Panel. The range and selection in many of these features are expanded in Windows 2000. Users can also limit the number of fonts to one or more specified favorites. Customizing the following accessibility features can be helpful to people who have seizures.

Timing Options

Timing patterns can affect users in many adverse ways. Users who have seizures might be sensitive to screen refresh rates and blinking or flashing images. Settings in Control Panel can prevent the default loading of animations and videos. Users or administrators can adjust the rate at which most objects flash to select a frequency that is less likely to trigger seizures. You can alter the insertion point indicator (sometimes called "caret") blink rate, and can link it to flashing events for users who are sensitive to screen refresh rates. Or, you can turn off blinking or flashing images.

Sound Schemes

In addition to users with hearing impairments or users in crowded or noisy environments, users who have seizures can also be susceptible to specific sounds. Settings in Windows 2000 can prevent the default loading of animations, videos, and sounds. By using Control Panel, users can also assign custom sounds to any event. The ability to customize sound schemes, whether turning sound on or off or adjusting the volume up or down, is becoming more important for users and takes many forms in Windows 2000 in support of people with various kinds of disabilities and requirements.

Color and Contrast Settings

By using **Accessibility Options** in Control Panel, and with Magnifier, users can adjust color and contrast settings. New to Windows 2000 is an expanded spectrum of color schemes, customizable to suit a user's individual needs. For more detailed information about color and contrast settings, see the following section on vision impairments.

Accessibility Options for Users with Vision Impairments

The following accessibility features are useful to people who are blind or have low vision, colorblindness, tunnel vision, or other vision impairments: Text-to-speech tools, such as Narrator; keyboard shortcuts; Magnifier; and customizable features, such as mouse pointer, color and contrast schemes, and other UI elements.

Microsoft Narrator

Narrator is a minimally featured text-to-speech tool that is included with Windows 2000. This new feature works through Active Accessibility to read objects on the screen, their properties, and their spatial relationships. Narrator automatically reads some information to the user when it changes on the screen. The benefit of Narrator is that it is always available to the user and allows the user to log on initially and then install any alternative device or other features the user might need. It is also available for the user who is working on a different computer.

Narrator has a number of options that allow a user or administrator to customize the way a device reads screen elements. The **Voice** option allows you to adjust the speed, volume, or pitch of the voice. The **Reading** option allows you to select the typed characters you want the device to read aloud, such as DELETE, ENTER, printable characters, or modifiers. The **Mouse Pointer** option causes the mouse pointer to follow the active object on the screen. The **Announce events on screen** option allows you to order the device to announce any of the following components when it displays them: new windows, menus, or shortcut menus.

You can run Narrator through the **Start** menu by pointing to Programs, Accessories, and then the Accessibility Options menu, or through Utility Manager. Many users with low vision need a text-to-speech utility with a higher functionality for daily use. For a list of other Windows-based text-to-speech tools, see the Microsoft Accessibility Web site at http://windows.microsoft.com /windows2000/reskit/webresources.

Note Narrator is a temporary aid and is not intended as a replacement for the full-featured text-to-speech utilities that are available from other software companies.

Keyboard Audio Cues

People with vision impairments might not be able to see the lights on the keyboard that indicate CAPS LOCK, NUM LOCK, and SCROLL LOCK status. ToggleKeys provides audio cues—high and low beeps—to tell the user whether these keys are active or inactive. If ToggleKeys is on, when you press one of these keys and it turns on, you hear a high-pitched beep. When you press one of these keys and it turns off, you hear a beep an octave lower. To adjust ToggleKeys settings double-click **Accessibility Options** in Control Panel or select **I have trouble using a keyboard or a mouse** in **Accessibility Wizard**.

▶ **To turn ToggleKeys on or off by using an emergency hot key**

- Press and then hold down the NUM LOCK key for eight seconds.

  When ToggleKeys turns on, you hear a rising series of beeps if sound is on. When it is off, the sound is a descending series of beeps.

ToggleKeys is especially useful for people who accidentally press the CAPS LOCK key instead of the TAB key because it provides immediate feedback when they do so. ToggleKeys also functions with keyboards that do not have the status indicator lights for the CAPS LOCK, NUM LOCK, and SCROLL LOCK keys.

Note FilterKeys in Control Panel and BounceKeys in **Accessibility Wizard** include the option **Do you want Windows to beep when it accepts a keystroke?** Select the option check box, or use the appropriate hot keys shortcut.

Microsoft Magnifier

Magnifier is a screen enlarger that magnifies a portion of the display of Windows 2000 to make the screen easier to read for people with slight vision impairments or whenever magnifying screen elements might be useful, such as during graphic editing. Magnifier displays an enlarged portion of the screen in a separate window. Many users with low vision need a magnification utility with a higher functionality for daily use. For a list of other Windows–based magnification tools, see the Microsoft Accessibility Web site at http://windows.microsoft.com/windows2000/reskit/webresources.

Note Magnifier is a temporary solution and is not intended as a replacement for the full-featured screen-enlargement utilities that are available from other software companies.

Using Magnifier, you can do the following:

- Magnify an area of the screen up to nine times the standard display size.
- Follow the mouse pointer, the keyboard focus, the text editing focus, or any combination of these three.
- Invert colors for contrast.
- Toggle High Contrast mode display for the entire screen.
- Resize and relocate the Magnifier display area.

When Magnifier is on, the magnified area is merely a display and is not itself an active area. The active focus for cursor, keyboard, and other input devices is always in the unmagnified area. To run Magnifier through the **Start** menu, point to **Programs**, **Accessories**, and **Accessibility Options**, and then click **Magnifier**; or use the WINDOWS LOGO key+U to run Utility Manager. If **Magnifier** is already running, select its button on the taskbar to open the dialog box. You can set tracking options to follow the mouse pointer, the keyboard focus, or text editing.

▶ **To change the size of the magnification window**

1. Move the mouse pointer over the edge of the magnification window. The pointer becomes a double-pointed arrow.
2. Drag the magnification window border to resize the window.

▶ **To change the position of the magnification window**

1. Place the mouse pointer inside the magnification window.

2. Drag the window to the desired area on the desktop.

You can dock the magnification window to the top, bottom, or side of the display, or you can position the window anywhere within the desktop area. Reposition the windows by using the arrow key.

Customizing Fonts

You can add or remove fonts and also restrict font sizes by removing all TrueType customizable fonts and leaving only raster fonts. TrueType fonts are device-independent fonts that are stored as outlines and that can be scaled to produce characters in varying sizes. Raster fonts are created with a printer language that is based on bitmap images for greater visibility. Removing fonts does not delete them from the hard disk drive. Users can easily reinstall the fonts for later use. To add or remove fonts, in Control Panel, double-click **Fonts**.

Note Limiting fonts also limits the number of fonts available to applications. This operation affects the display of documents on the screen and how they are printed and should be used with caution.

▶ **To limit the system to a single font**

1. Create a new folder on the desktop or hard disk, and give it a name such as Other Fonts.

2. In Control Panel, double-click **Fonts**.

3. Select all the fonts in the **Fonts** folder, and then move them to the new folder named Other Fonts. (The system font is not listed, so it remains even when you delete all other fonts.)

4. Shut down, and then restart the computer.

▶ **To restore the fonts**

1. Move or copy the fonts from the Other Fonts folder that you have created to Control Panel, **Fonts**.

2. Shut down, and then restart the computer.

You can change text sizes in Windows messages in **Accessibility Wizard** or Control Panel. Set custom options in **Custom Font Size** by choosing **Other** in the **Font Size** list and then either selecting one of the percentage options in the drop-down list or clicking the ruler and dragging the pointer to specify a font size. If you install new fonts, you must restart your computer to apply any changes. The font size you specify in Control Panel affects all video adapters on your system. To change font settings for individual window objects, double-click **Display** in Control Panel, and then click the **Appearance** tab. To add a new font, in Control Panel, double-click **Fonts**.

▶ **To add OpenType, TrueType, or raster fonts from a network drive without using disk space**

- In the **Add Fonts** dialog box, check the **Copy Fonts to Fonts Folder** check box to clear it, and then select the **Install New Font** check box.

Size and Color Schemes

In the Windows 2000 **Accessibility Wizard** and in Control Panel, users can adjust the size and color of most screen elements, such as window text, menus, mouse pointer, fonts, and caption bars. This capability can make the system easier to use and can reduce eyestrain. In **Accessibility Wizard**, users can change icon size, mouse pointer size, and text size. In Control Panel, font options are unavailable for properties that do not contain text.

The following are some points to take into consideration when you adjust the color settings:

- Settings that display a large number of colors require a large amount of computer processor resources.
- A High Color setting (16-bit) includes more than 65,000 colors. A True Color setting (24-bit) includes more than 16 million colors.
- The monitor and display adapter determine the maximum number of colors that can appear on the screen.
- To change settings for another monitor in a multiple-monitor system, you must select the **Extend My Windows Desktop onto this Monitor** check box to change the settings for the other monitor. You can make color settings for each installed monitor.

▶ **To adjust window size using the keyboard**

1. Press ALT+SPACE to select the window's control menu, and then select the **Size** check box.

2. Press an arrow key to select the top, bottom, left, or right border to resize. The mouse pointer moves to the corresponding window edge.

3. Press the arrow keys to move the selected window edge, and then press ENTER when you are finished. Or you can press ESC to cancel.

To change the border width of windows, including command prompt windows, double-click **Display** in Control Panel, and then click the **Appearance** tab to select the preferred scheme. Users can also resize a window by using the keyboard instead of the mouse, or in **Accessibility Wizard** by selecting **I am blind or have difficulty seeing things on screen**.

High-Contrast Color Schemes

This feature, new to Windows 2000, is a built-in and expanded library of color schemes for users with low vision who require a high degree of contrast between foreground and background objects to distinguish the objects. An example is those users who cannot easily read black text on a gray background or text drawn over a picture. By selecting a high-contrast display scheme, users can now instruct Windows 2000 and programs to display information with a high degree of contrast. Activating High Contrast mode automatically selects the user's preferred color scheme. Ready-to-use appearance schemes make it easier to see screen objects.

Built-in, and no longer in Control Panel alone, the high-contrast color schemes feature for users with various kinds of vision needs has an expanded selection. Through the **Magnifier** dialog box, users can invert the colors of the magnification window or display the screen in high contrast. It can take a few seconds for High Contrast Mode to take effect. Customizing contrast and color can make the system easier to use and can reduce eyestrain.

New Mouse Pointers

Customized through **Accessibility Wizard** or Control Panel, new mouse pointers allow the user to select the most visible one. Pointers now include three sizes—large and extra-large in addition to the default size—and a white or black pointer or an inverted pointer that reacts to screen colors and changes to a color that contrasts with the background. Users can now set the following characteristics to improve the visibility of the mouse pointer:

▪ Pointer size

▪ Pointer color

▪ Speed of the pointer

- Visible trails of pointer movement
- Animation of the pointer

Another option for users who have difficulty seeing the mouse pointer is to use MouseKeys. For a description of this feature, please see "Options for Users with Physical Disabilities" earlier in this appendix.

Insertion Point Indicator Blink Rate

For users with low vision, you can increase the visibility of the insertion point indicator (sometimes called a "caret") by changing the rate at which it flashes. You can change the insertion point indicator blink rate by going to Control Panel and then double-clicking the **Keyboard** icon.

Configuring Accessibility Features

Custom interfaces allow users with disabilities to control their computing environment so that they can succeed in using the software they need to perform their work. Depending on each person's specific needs, users might find challenges with different aspects of Windows. Although accessibility features install automatically with Windows 2000, in a complete installation, previously configured options and settings must be reconfigured—and new customized options must be configured for individual users.

Table A.10 describes some of the user aids that are built into the Windows 2000 operating system to make it more accessible. Because some features can apply to several disabilities, they are listed by particular difficulty, rather than by any one category of disability. For descriptions of features by category of disability, see the section "Setting Options by Type of Disability" later in this appendix.

Table A.10 Common User Difficulties and Solutions

If user has difficulty...	Windows 2000 Solutions
Customizing settings in a multiple user network.	**Accessibility Wizard**, Control Panel.
Doing the following: • Opening Windows or applications. • Navigating through desktop elements and windows.	Hot keys; Utility Manager; Narrator; On-Screen Keyboard; Active Desktop, keyboard shortcuts.
Remembering what accessibility features are activated.	**Show Status on Screen** option in Control Panel, status indicators on the system status area of the taskbar, Utility Manager.

(continued)

Table A.10   Common User Difficulties and Solutions *(continued)*

If user has difficulty...	Windows 2000 Solutions
Finding a needed feature.	Options listed by disability in **Accessibility Wizard**; Windows Help.
Remembering keyboard navigation indicators (underlined access keys).	**I have difficulty using the keyboard or mouse,** then **Do you want extra keyboard help...?** options in **Accessibility Wizard**.
	Display, **Effects**, then clear **Hide keyboard navigation indicators until I use the ALT key** options in Control Panel (temporary).
	Accessibility Options, **Keyboard,** then **Show extra keyboard help in programs** options in Control Panel.
Spelling words correctly.	Automatic Spell Checker, AutoComplete feature, AutoCorrect feature, keyboard shortcuts.
Hearing, such as in the following situations: ■ Hearing sound prompts. ■ Distinguishing sounds. ■ Hearing audible cues. ■ Working in a noisy environment.	ShowSounds, SoundSentry in Control Panel; customizable sound schemes in **Accessibility Wizard** and in Control Panel.
Using standard keyboard configurations.	Dvorak keyboards, On-Screen Keyboard, MouseKeys in **Accessibility Wizard** and in Control Panel; third-party alternative keyboards.
Using keyboard due to slow response time.	RepeatKeys and StickyKeys in Control Panel; **Keyboard Options** in Control Panel.
Using keyboard due to inadvertent repeating of keys.	BounceKeys in **Accessibility Wizard**; RepeatKeys, SlowKeys, and ToggleKeys in **Accessibility Wizard** and in Control Panel.
Holding down two or more keys at the same time.	StickyKeys in Control Panel.
Using standard UI methods, including using the standard mouse and keyboard.	Narrator; On-Screen Keyboard on the **Start** menu, MouseKeys, Utility Manager, third-party utilities.
Manipulating a mouse.	MouseKeys in **Accessibility Wizard** and in Control Panel; keyboard shortcuts.

(continued)

Table A.10   Common User Difficulties and Solutions *(continued)*

If user has difficulty…	Windows 2000 Solutions
Working with flashing events and other schemes that trigger seizures.	Timing, color, contrast, and sound schemes in **Accessibility Wizard** and in Control Panel.
Seeing or following the mouse pointer.	Mouse options in **Accessibility Wizard** and **Accessibility** and **Mouse Options** in Control Panel.
Seeing keyboard status lights.	ToggleKeys in **Accessibility Wizard** and in Control Panel; Narrator
Seeing screen elements.	Narrator and Magnifier on the **Start** menu, Utility Manager; size, color, and contrast schemes in **Accessibility Wizard** and **Accessibility** and **Display Options** in Control Panel.
Functioning well with built-in accessibility features; needs add-on devices.	SerialKeys in Control Panel for third-party assistive devices.
Finding third-party assistive devices and other accessibility information.	Microsoft Accessibility Web site. (See "Additional Resources" for details.)

Users and administrators can use **Accessibility Options** in Control Panel to customize many of the accessibility features in Windows 2000. However, you can also configure many popular accessibility features using **Accessibility Wizard**. For example, you can customize display, keyboard, mouse, and sound options for the user's own particular needs by using either Control Panel or **Accessibility Wizard**. The two ways to configure options are described in the following sections.

Configuring Accessibility Options by Using Accessibility Wizard

Accessibility Wizard makes it easier to set up accessibility preferences in accordance with the particular needs a user might have, instead of by numeric value changes or by Control Panel settings. Available from the **Start** menu, the wizard provides a single entry point for many frequently used features. The user can also save settings to a file to use on other computers. Some of the options the wizard controls are sound and screen options, such as volume and font sizes, several keyboard options, such as BounceKeys and MouseKeys, and the ability to set administrative options. Figure A.5 illustrates these option settings.

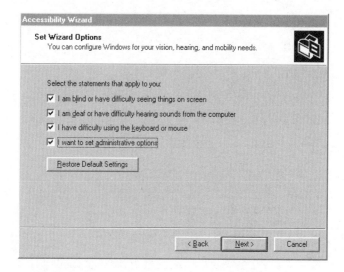

Figure A.5   Options Menu in Accessibility Wizard

▶   **To start Accessibility Wizard**

- On the **Start** menu, point to **Programs**, **Accessories**, and **Accessibility,** and then click **Accessibility Wizard**.

Configuring Accessibility Options by Using Control Panel

The **Accessibility Options** icon in Control Panel allows users to customize many of the accessibility features in Windows 2000. Users can turn accessibility features on or off and can customize keyboard, sound, and mouse operations for the user's particular needs. **Accessibility Options** gives users access to the following features: StickyKeys, FilterKeys, ToggleKeys, SoundSentry, ShowSounds, MouseKeys, and SerialKeys.

▶ **To enable Accessibility Options**

1. In Control Panel, double-click **Accessibility Options**.

2. In the **Accessibility Options** dialog box, select the check boxes for the features you want to enable.

3. To change the feature options, click **Settings**.

Figure A.6 illustrates the Control Panel **Accessibility Options** property sheet.

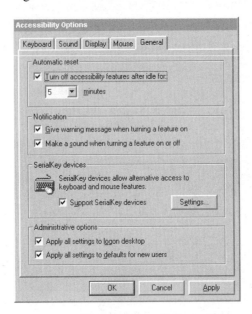

Figure A.6   Accessibility Options Properties in Control Panel

In addition to options for users with disabilities in **Accessibility Options**, Control Panel offers other ways to modify settings in a in a Windows 2000 Professional–based computer. Users can modify settings in **Display**, **Keyboard**, **Mouse**, **Sounds and Multimedia**, and other properties. The following sections describe many other general features as well as features that are designed specifically for users with disabilities.

Adding Third-Party Products and Services

Although the accessibility tools that are included with Windows 2000 provide some functionality for users with special needs, many users with disabilities might need assistive tools with a higher functionality for daily use. With the use of hardware and software available through ISVs, people with disabilities can enhance their use of the Windows 2000 operating system.

"Certified for Microsoft Windows" Logo

Throughout the computer industry, hardware and software developers and vendors are collaborating to bring about accessible products for all computer users. The Certified for Microsoft Windows Specification now applies to Windows 2000. The specification promotes accessible design and includes a set of requirements and a checklist for application developers. The specification addresses such requirements as closed captioning in place of sound to convey information, visibility of the insertion point indicator (sometimes called a "caret"), and the ability to control the mouse and keyboard and to turn off animations. The major goal of this collaborative effort is to ensure quality and consistency in products that work on the Windows 2000 operating system for users with disabilities.

For more information about the "Certified for Microsoft Windows" Logo, including application specifications, see the Application Specification Download link on the Web Resources page at http://windows.microsoft.com/windows2000/reskit/webresources.

Add-on Assistive Devices

Microsoft works with independent manufacturers to produce compatible software and hardware for users with disabilities. One of the purposes of the Active Accessibility technology is to provide an infrastructure that aids the operating system and applications in understanding each other for greater compatibility with these important devices. By using Utility Manager, which is a new feature in Windows 2000, vendors are now able to add their products for easier access.

Independent vendors that manufacture specialized assistive devices help people with disabilities to make better use of Windows 2000. Products available from third-party vendors are many and varied and make it possible for people with disabilities to use computers. Some of the kinds of products that are available are the following:

- Hardware and software tools that modify the behavior of the mouse and keyboard.
- Add-on technology, such as the following alternative input devices:
    - Head-pointer. A device for users who are unable to use standard input devices, such as a mouse or a keyboard. A head-pointer device allows a user to pause the pointer over the command for a specified length of time.
    - Mouthstick. A keyboard input device operated by the mouth that allows a user to activate commands by pressing one key at a time.

- Single-switch. A device, such as a voice activation, that allows a user to scan or select options or text by using a single switch.

- Eye-gaze pointer. A device that operates by vision to control an on-screen cursor that allows a user to press on-screen UI elements, such as buttons in dialog boxes, to choose menu options, and to select cells or text.

- Sip-and-puff device. A device that allows a user to operate a computer by breath control.

- Voice-activation device. A type of speech recognition device that allows users with disabilities to control computers with their voices instead of with a mouse or keyboard.

- Alternative keyboards, such as on-screen keyboards, or variously sized or shaped keyboards.

- Devices that provide synthesized speech or that print information on the screen by using Braille-embossed printers for people who are blind or have difficulty reading.

- Word or phrase prediction software that helps users type more quickly and with fewer keystrokes.

- Closed-captioning devices for users with hearing impairments.

- Devices that enlarge or alter the color of information on the screen.

Important Most third-party accessibility aids are compatible with specific versions of an operating system. Some add-on utilities can be intrusive because they depend on file formats and programming interfaces to interpret data accurately to the user. Such dependencies change with each new operating system. Therefore, before you decide to upgrade, it is important to take inventory and perform compatibility testing with the new operating system and the applications you plan to use. For more information about emerging technologies and compatibility, see the Microsoft Accessibility link on the Web Resources page at http://windows.microsoft.com/windows2000/reskit/webresources.

Using SerialKeys for Add-on Hardware and Software

The SerialKeys feature is designed for people who are unable to use a standard UI method, such as a keyboard or a mouse. However, SerialKeys also allows an augmentative device to work with the local keyboard and mouse. Users who can point, but not click, can use pointing devices or Morse-code input systems. The interface device sends coded command strings through the computer's serial port to specify keystrokes and mouse events, which are then treated as typical keyboard or mouse input. To enable SerialKeys, double-click **Accessibility Options** in Control Panel, then click the **General** tab.

If the user is using SerialKeys and the aid stops sending keys successfully, try to do the following:

- Make sure that any necessary periods in the key names are included.

- Send three null (nondisplaying) characters.

- Reset both the aid and SerialKeys to 300 baud. (If there is a communication difficulty, SerialKeys might automatically reset itself to 300 baud, which makes it unable to communicate with the aid if the aid is ending at a different rate.)

- SerialKeys uses hardware handshaking (DTR/RTS) and software handshaking (XON/XOFF) to control the flow of characters from the aid. Characters might be lost if the aid ignores these handshaking signals.

Check your hardware vendor's manual for more detailed information.

Additional Resources

In addition to the standard printed forms of documentation, many Microsoft documents are also available in other formats to make them more accessible to users with disabilities. Material available on Microsoft Web sites might include information that was not ready when the product or resource kit was released. For more information about accessibility for users with disabilities, including technical support, documentation, and information related to accessibility, see the http://windows.microsoft.com/windows2000/reskit/webresources.

Microsoft provides a catalog of a wide range of accessibility aids—such as those listed in the previous paragraph—that can be used with Windows 2000. Additional information is available about support services and documentation for users who are deaf or hard-of-hearing, and users who have difficulties reading or handling printed materials. This information and the catalog are available from the Microsoft Accessibility Web site address: http://windows.microsoft.com /windows2000/reskit/webresources, by voice telephone at 1 +(800) 426-9400, by telephone to receive faxed-back materials at 1 +(800) 727-3351, or by writing to the Microsoft Sales Information Center, One Microsoft Way, Redmond, Washington 98052-6393.

APPENDIX B

Sample Answer Files for Windows 2000 Professional Setup

Unattended Setup in Microsoft® Windows® 2000 Professional uses an answer file, which is a type of ASCII text file, to automatically supply data that you would otherwise type in manually when installing Windows 2000 Professional. The answer file is specified using either the Winnt.exe or Winnt32.exe command line when the Unattended Setup option is used. Answer files can be either fully unattended or can have limited user interaction

This appendix contains sample answer files that can be used during common installation configurations. You can customize the default answer file (Unattend.txt) that comes with Windows 2000 or write a new one based on the samples provided.

In This Appendix:

Related Information in the Resource Kit

- For more information about Setup commands, see "Custom and Automated Installations" in this book.

Answer File Format

An answer file consists of section headers, keys, and the values for each key. Most of the section headers are predefined, but some can be user defined. You do not need to specify all the possible keys in an answer file; your installation does not require them. Invalid key values generate errors or can cause incorrect behavior after Setup has completed. The file format is as follows.

Section headers are enclosed with brackets on both ends. The following is an example:

```
[section_name]
```

Sections contain keys and the corresponding values for those keys. The following is an example:

```
key = "value"
```

Some sections have no keys and merely contain a list of values. The following is an example:

```
[OEMBootFiles]
    Txtsetup.oem
```

Note Keys are typically indented four spaces to enhance the readability of the file. Indentation, however, is not required.

Comment lines start with a semicolon and typically precede the key they reference.

```
; This is an example of a comment line.
```

Answer File Keys and Values

Every key in an answer file must have a value assigned to it. However, some keys are optional, and some keys have default values that are used if the key is omitted.

Key values are strings of text unless a numeric value is specified. If a numeric value is specified, the value is decimal unless otherwise noted.

Note Keys are not case sensitive; they can be uppercase or lowercase.

For more information about answer file keys and values, see the Unattend.doc file on the Windows 2000 operating system CD. The Unattend.doc file is part of the Deploy.cab file in the Support\Tools folder. In Microsoft® Windows® 98 or Windows 2000, use Windows Explorer to extract this document.

Sample Answer Files

The sample answer files provided in this section show the more common installation configurations of the keys typically used in those configurations. These sample files can be modified as appropriate for your organization. The following examples do not reflect fully unattended installations or upgrades. In these cases the End User License Agreement (EULA) must be manually accepted by the user.

Sample 1- Default Unattend.txt

The following answer file is the default Unattend.txt file that is provided on the Windows 2000 CD.

```
; Microsoft Windows 2000 Professional, Server, Advanced Server and
; Datacenter
; (c) 1994 - 1999 Microsoft Corporation. All rights reserved.
;
; Sample Unattended Setup Answer File
;
; This file contains information about how to automate the installation
; or upgrade of Windows 2000 Professional and Windows 2000 Server so the
; Setup program runs without requiring user input.
;

[Unattended]
    UnattendMode = "FullUnattended"
    OemPreinstall = "NO"
    TargetPath = "WINNT"
    FileSystem = "LeaveAlone"

[UserData]
    FullName = "Your User Name"
    OrgName = "Your Organization Name"
    ComputerName = "COMPUTER_NAME"

[GuiUnattended]
; Sets the Time Zone to the Pacific Northwest
; Sets the Admin Password
; Turn AutoLogon ON and login once
    AdminPassword = "Password"
    AutoLogon = "Yes"
    AutoLogonCount = "1"
    TimeZone = "004"
```

```
[Display]
    BitsPerPel = "8"
    XResolution = "800"
    YResolution = "600"
    VRefresh = "75"


[Networking]


[Identification]
    JoinWorkgroup = "Workgroupname"
```

Sample 2 - Windows 95 or Windows 98 Upgrade

This sample Unattend.txt file upgrades a Microsoft® Windows® 95 or
Windows 98 operating system to Windows 2000 Professional and migrates users
of Windows 95 or later to the Power Users group on Windows 2000 Professional.

```
[Unattended]
    FileSystem = "LeaveAlone"
; This key will signal the answer file to upgrade the OS from Windows 95
; or Windows 98 to Windows 2000 Professional, otherwise it would be a
; clean install.
    Win9xUpgrade = "YES"


; This section specifies the keys for an unattended upgrade from
; Windows 95 or Windows 98. These keys are not valid on any other
; upgrade path
[Win9xUpg]
; Causes Setup to add all accounts that it creates during migration to
; the Power Users group, giving accounts more permissions than those in
; the Users group, but fewer permissions than users in the
; Administrators group. For more information about group-level security
; settings, see Windows 2000 Help.
    MigrateUsersAsPowerUser = "YES"


[Networking]


[Identification]
    DomainAdmin = "Accountname"
; If DomainAdminPassword is not specified, you will be prompted for one.
; If one is specified, for security reasons, this value will be deleted
; from the file on the computer after Setup has finished.
    DomainAdminPassword = "Password"
    JoinDomain = "Domainname"
```

Sample 3 - Novell Network Environment

This sample file installs Windows 2000 Professional in a Novell environment by using the NWlink and TCP/IP protocol and then setting the preferred server name to a server named "NWServer."

```
[Unattended]
    OemPreinstall = "NO"

[GuiUnattended]
    AdminPassword = "Password"
    OEMSkipRegional = "1"
    OEMSkipWelcome = "1"
    TimeZone = "004"

[UserData]
    ComputerName = "COMPUTER_NAME"
    FullName = "Your User Name"
    OrgName = "Your Organization Name"

[Display]
    BitsPerPel = "8"
    VRefresh = "75"
    XResolution = "800"
    YResolution = "600"


[TapiLocation]
    AreaCode = "425"
    CountryCode = "1"
    Dialing = "Tone"

[Networking]

[Identification]
    JoinWorkgroup = "Workgroupname"

[NetAdapters]
    Adapter1 = "params.Adapter1"

[params.Adapter1]
    InfID = "*"

[NetProtocols]
    MS_NWIPX = "params.MS_NWIPX"
    MS_TCPIP = "params.MS_TCPIP"
```

```
[params.MS_TCPIP]
    UseDomainNameDevolution = "NO"
    EnableLMHosts = "YES"
    AdapterSections = "params.MS_TCPIP.Adapter1"

[params.MS_TCPIP.Adapter1]
    SpecificTo = "Adapter1"
    DHCP = "YES"
    WINS = "NO"
    NetBIOSOption = "0"

[params.MS_NWIPX]
    VirtualNetworkNumber = "0"
    AdapterSections = "params.MS_NWIPX.Adapter1"

[params.MS_NWIPX.Adapter1]
    SpecificTo = "Adapter1"
    PktType = "FF"

[params.MS_MSClient]

[NetClients]
    MS_NWClient = "params.MS_NWClient"

[params.MS_NWClient]
    LogonScript = "NO"
    PreferredServer = "NWServer"

[NetServices]
    MS_Server = "params.MS_SERVER"

[Data]
; These keys are required when initiating an unattended installation
; from the CD-ROM
    AutoPartition = "1"
    MsDosInitiated = "0"
    UnattendedInstall = "YES"
```

Sample 4 - Setup Using [GuiRunOnce] Option

This sample file installs Windows 2000 Professional using the GuiRunOnce option.

```
[Unattended]
    OemPreinstall = "YES"
    UnattendMode = "FullUnattended"
```

```
[GuiUnattended]
    AdminPassword = "Password"
    OEMSkipRegional = "1"
    OEMSkipWelcome = "1"
    TimeZone = "004"

[UserData]
    ComputerName = "COMPUTER_NAME"
    FullName = "Your User Name"
    OrgName = "Your Organization Name"

[GuiRunOnce]
    "c:\myfolder\myprogram.exe"

[Display]
    BitsPerPel = "24"
    VRefresh = "85"
    XResolution = "1024"
    YResolution = "768"

[TapiLocation]
    CountryCode = "1"
    Dialing = "Tone"
    AreaCode = "425"
    LongDistanceAccess = "9"

[Networking]

[Identification]
    JoinWorkgroup = "Workgroupname"

[Data]
; These keys are required when initiating an unattended installation
; from the CD-ROM
    AutoPartition = "1"
    MsDosInitiated = "0"
    UnattendedInstall = "YES"
```

Sample 5 - Install and Configure Windows 2000 and Configure Microsoft Internet Explorer with Microsoft Proxy Settings

The following answer file installs Windows 2000 Professional and configures Microsoft® Internet Explorer with MS Proxy settings.

```
[Unattended]
    FileSystem = "LeaveAlone"
    OemPreinstall = "YES"
    TargetPath = "Winnt"
    UnattendMode = "FullUnattended"

[GuiUnattended]
    AdminPassword = "Password"
    AutoLogon = "YES"
    AutoLogonCount = "1"
    OEMSkipRegional = "1"
    OEMSkipWelcome = "1"
    TimeZone = "004"

[UserData]
    ComputerName = "COMPUTER_NAME"
    FullName = "Your User Name"
    OrgName = "Your Organization Name"

[Proxy]
; This section contains custom proxy settings for Microsoft
; Internet Explorer. If these settings are not present, the default
; settings are used. If proxysrv:80 is not accurate for your
; configuration, be sure to replace the proxy server and port number
; with your own keys.
    HTTP_Proxy_Server = "http://proxysrv:80"
    Proxy_Enable = "1"
    Proxy_Override = "<local>"
    Use_Same_Proxy = "1"

[URL]
; This section contains custom URL settings for Microsoft
; Internet Explorer. If these settings are not present, the
; default settings are used. Specifies the URL for the
; browser's default home page. For example, you might use the
; following: Home_Page = "http://www.microsoft.com"
    Home_Page = "http://www.windows.com"
; Specifies a shortcut URL in the link folder of Favorites.
    Quick_Link_1 = "http://www.microsoft.com"
; Specifies a shortcut name in the link folder of Favorites.
    Quick_Link_1_Name = "Microsoft Home Page"
```

```
[Branding]
; This section brands Microsoft Internet Explorer with custom
; properties from the Unattended answer file.
    BrandIEUsingUnattended = "YES"

[Display]
    BitsPerPel = "8"
    VRefresh = "75"
    XResolution = "800"
    YResolution = "600"

[TapiLocation]
    AreaCode = "425"
    CountryCode = "1"
    Dialing = "Tone"
    LongDistanceAccess = "9"

[Components]
; Installs the optional networking components under the
; [NetOptionalComponents] section.
    netoc = "ON"

[Networking]

[Identification]
    JoinDomain = "Domainname"
    DomainAdmin = "Accountname"
    DomainAdminPassword = "Password"

[NetOptionalComponents]
; This section contains a list of the optional network components to
; install. 1 = ON, 0 = OFF.
NETMONTOOLS = "1"

[Data]
; These keys are required when initiating an unattended installation
; from the CD-ROM
    AutoPartition = "1"
    MsDosInitiated = "0"
    UnattendedInstall = "YES"
```

Sample 6 - Install and Configure Windows 2000 Professional with Two Network Adapters

The following answer file installs Windows 2000 Professional with two network adapters. One adapter uses Dynamic Host Configuration Protocol (DHCP) and the other uses static information.

```
[Unattended]
    Filesystem = "ConvertNTFS"
    TargetPath = "Winnt"
    UnattendMode = "FullUnattended"

[GuiUnattended]
    AdminPassword = "Password"
    AutoLogon = "YES"
    AutoLogonCount = "1"
    TimeZone = "004"

[UserData]
    ComputerName = "COMPUTER_NAME"
    FullName = "Your User Name"
    OrgName = "Your Organization Name"

[Display]
    VRefresh = "75"
    BitsPerPel = "8"
    XResolution = "800"
    YResolution = "600"

[Networking]

[Identification]
    DomainAdmin = "Accountname"
    DomainAdminPassword = "Password"
    JoinDomain = "Domainname"

[NetAdapters]
; In this example, there are two network adapters, Adapter01
; and Adapter02. Note that the adapter specified here as 01 is not
; always local area network (LAN) connection 1 in the user interface.
    Adapter01 = "params.Adapter01"
    Adapter02 = "params.Adapter02"
```

```
[params.Adapter01]
; Specifies which adapter is number one. Note that the InfID key
; must match a valid PNP ID in the system. For example, a valid
; PNP ID might look like the following: InfID = "pci\ven_0e11&dev_ae32"
    InfID = "Your_PNP_ID_for_Adapter01"
; If you have two cards with the same PnP ID, you can specify the MAC
; address of each network adapter with the NetCardAddress value.

[params.Adapter02]
; Specifies which adapter is number two. Note that the InfID key ;must
; match a valid PNP ID in the system. For example, a valid PNP ID
; might look as follows: InfID = "pci\ven_8086&dev_1229&subsys_00018086"
    InfID = "Your_PNP_ID_for_Adapter02"

 [NetProtocols]
; Installs only the TCP/IP protocol.
    MS_TCPIP = "params.MS_TCPIP"


[params.MS_TCPIP]
; This section configures the TCP/IP properties.
  AdapterSections = "params.MS_TCPIP.Adapter01,
params.MS_TCPIP.Adapter02"


[params.MS_TCPIP.Adapter01]
; Adapter01 uses DHCP server information.
    SpecificTo = "Adapter01"
    DHCP = "YES"
    WINS = "YES"


[params.MS_TCPIP.Adapter02]
; Adapter02 uses static TCP/IP configuration.
    SpecificTo = "Adapter02"
    IPAddress = "1.1.1.1"
    SubnetMask = "255.255.248.0"
    DefaultGateway = "2.2.2.2"
    DHCP = "NO"
    WINS = "NO"

[NetClients]
; Installs the Client for Microsoft Networks.
    MS_MSClient = "params.MS_MSClient"
```

```
[params.MS_MSClient]

[NetServices]
; Install File and Print services.
    MS_Server = "params.MS_Server"

[Data]
; These keys are required when initiating an unattended installation
; from the CD-ROM
    AutoPartition = "1"
    MsDosInitiated = "0"
    UnattendedInstall = "YES"
```

Additional Resources

- For more information about the answer file keys, see the Unattend.doc file, on the Microsoft® Windows® 2000 Professional operating system CD in Support\Tools\Deploy.cab,

APPENDIX C

Hardware Support

Microsoft® Windows 2000 Professional supports a broad range of hardware, including many new devices not previously supported in Microsoft® Windows® 95, Microsoft® Windows® 98, or Microsoft® Windows NT® 4.0. Windows 2000 also includes enhanced support for older devices. Newly supported system buses, such as Universal Serial Bus (USB) and Institute of Electrical and Electronics Engineers (IEEE) 1394, further enhance hardware support functionality in Windows 2000 Professional.

In This Appendix

Related Information in the Professional Resource Kit

- For more information about installing and troubleshooting hardware devices, see "Device Management" in this book.

- For more information about troubleshooting hardware devices, see "Troubleshooting Tools and Strategies" in this book.

Overview of Hardware Support

Windows 2000 Professional supports a broader set of hardware than any version of Windows NT. Windows 2000 supports more than 7,000 devices, including expanded support for many devices not previously supported by Windows NT 4.0. Windows 2000 Professional also features new and enhanced support for a variety of devices, such as digital audio devices, DVD, Human Interface Devices (HIDs), still-image devices, and video capture devices.

Windows 2000 Professional provides support for the Universal Serial Bus (USB) and the IEEE 1394 bus.

The Universal Serial Bus (USB) is an external bus that supports Plug and Play installation. With USB, you can connect and disconnect devices without shutting down or restarting your computer. You can use a single USB port to connect up to 127 peripheral devices, including speakers, telephones, CD-ROM drives, joysticks, tape drives, keyboards, scanners, and cameras.

IEEE 1394 is a high-speed, Plug and Play-capable bus that is designed to complement USB. It functions as a bridge to bring computers and consumer electronics together. For example, you can use a digital VCR both for viewing movies and for storing computer data. Because of the very high data transfer rates that IEEE 1394 can handle, it is ideal for storing, printing, and high-resolution scanning; for consumer audio and video components; and for portable devices.

Comparison of Hardware Features

Table C.1 compares the hardware features of Windows 2000 Professional with older Windows platforms.

Table C.1   Hardware Feature Comparison

Feature	Windows 2000 Professional	Windows 95	Windows 98	Windows NT 4.0 Workstation
Plug and Play	Yes	Yes	Yes	No
Universal Serial Bus (USB), IEEE 1394, Accelerated Graphics Port (AGP)	Yes	No	Yes	No
Driver Signing	Yes	No	Yes	No
Windows Driver Model (WDM)	Yes	No	Yes	No
Multiprocessor	Yes	No	No	Yes

Universal Serial Bus

Universal Serial Bus (USB) is a standard-based, external bus for the computer that brings the Plug and Play capability of hardware devices (such as keyboards, pointing devices, and hard drives) outside the computer, eliminating the need to install internal cards into dedicated computer slots and reconfigure the system. Using USB technology, you can configure hardware devices as soon as they are physically attached — without the need to restart or run a set up sequence. USB is supported by the Windows Driver Model (WDM) under Windows 2000 Professional.

USB has the following significant advantages over older I/O standards:

- All USB devices use the same type of I/O connector, eliminating the need for different cables and connectors.
- You can plug multiple USB devices into a single USB port.
- USB supports *hot plugging*, which means that you can install or remove a USB device while the computer is running, and the operating system automatically reconfigures itself accordingly.

There are many different types of USB devices that you can purchase. Table C.2 categorizes the types of USB devices that are available, and points you to additional information available in this Resource Kit.

Table C.2   USB Device Categories

Category	Devices	See the chapter in this book entitled:
Input	Keyboards, joysticks, and pointing devices	"Multimedia"
Storage	Disk drives, CD-ROM drives, and removable media	"Data Storage and Management"
Communications	Modems, ISDN adapters, and network adapters	"Local and Remote Networking"
Output	Monitors, printers, and audio devices	"Device Management"
Imaging	Scanners and digital cameras	"Multimedia"

USB Topology

As illustrated in Figure C.1, USB uses a tiered topology, allowing you to attach up to 127 devices to the bus simultaneously. USB currently supports up to five tiers, and each device can be located up to five meters from its hub.

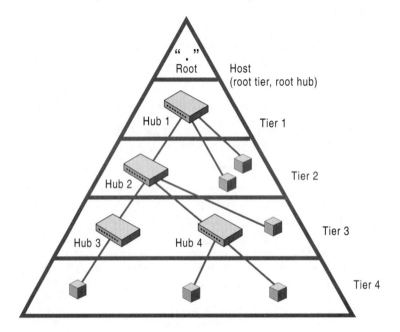

Figure C.1   Example of the USB topology

The three types of USB components are:

- *Host*. Also known as the *root*, the *root tier*, or the *root hub*, the host is built into the motherboard or installed as an adapter card in the computer. The host controls all traffic on the bus and can also function as a hub.

- *Hub*. Provides a point, or *port,* to attach a device to the bus. Hubs are also responsible for detecting devices which are attached or detached from them and for providing power management for devices attached to them. Hubs are either *bus-powered*, drawing power directly from the bus, or *self-powered*, drawing power from an external source. You can plug a self-powered device into a bus-powered hub. You cannot connect a bus-powered hub to another bus-powered hub or support more than four downstream ports. You cannot connect a bus-powered device that draws more than 100 milliamperes (mA) to a bus-powered hub.

- *Device*. A USB-capable device, which is attached to the bus through a port. USB devices can also function as hubs. For example, a USB monitor can have ports for attaching a USB keyboard and a mouse. In this case, the monitor is also a hub.

> **Note**   When you plug a device into a particular port for the first time,
> Windows 2000 Professional must go through the detection and *enumeration*
> process with that device. In the enumeration process, Plug and Play devices are
> identified by the operating system.

USB Functions

A *function* is a USB device that is able to transmit or receive data or control
information over the bus. A function is typically implemented as a separate
peripheral device, with a cable that plugs into a port on a hub. However, it is
possible to implement multiple functions and an embedded hub with a single USB
cable. This is known as a compound device. A compound device appears to the
host as a hub with one or more permanently attached USB devices.

Each function contains configuration information that describes its capabilities
and resource requirements. Before you can use a function, it must be configured
by the host. This configuration includes allocating USB bandwidth and selecting
function-specific device configurations.

Choosing Devices Supported by USB

You can connect the following USB devices to your computer: monitor controls,
audio I/O devices, telephones, modems, speakers, keyboards, mouse devices,
joysticks, scanners, printers, low-bandwidth video devices, digital still-image
cameras, data gloves, and digitizers. For computer-telephony integration, USB
provides an interface for Digital Subscriber Line (DSL), Integrated Services
Digital Network (ISDN), and digital Private Branch Exchanges (PBXs).

For USB, the computer host controller is implemented through the Open Host
Controller Interface (OHCI) standard or the Universal Host Controller Interface
(UHCI) standard. To work with USB, the host controller must comply with one of
these standards.

USB Connector and Cable

The USB specification defines a standard connector, socket, and cable, which all
USB devices can use. This single standard eliminates the confusion caused by the
current mixture of connector and cable types required for hardware devices.

Data Transfer Rates Supported by USB

USB supports two data transfer modes: *isochronous* and *asynchronous*. An isochronous transfer requires a constant bandwidth within certain time constraints. A constant bandwidth is required to support the demands of multimedia applications and devices. Unlike asynchronous transfers, no handshaking occurs and delivery is not guaranteed. By contrast, asynchronous transfers employ a handshaking system and allow data streams to be broken at random intervals.

There are three variants of the asynchronous mode: interrupt, control, and bulk. Each mode applies to the *endpoints* of the same name and has unique characteristics. In the USB architecture, the term endpoint refers to a USB logical device.

Interrupt   Interrupt endpoints reserve bandwidth and are guaranteed access to transfer data at the established rate. This mode is used when a device transfers unsolicited data to a host.

Control   The control mode is used to transfer specific requests. It is generally used during device configuration.

Bulk   A bulk transfer is used to transfer large blocks of data that have no periodic or transfer rate requirement. Printing uses bulk transfers.

The USB host determines the data transfer rate and the priority assigned to a data stream. USB supports the following maximum data transfer rates, depending on the amount of bus bandwidth a device requires:

- 1.5 megabits per second (Mbps) for devices that do not require a large amount of bandwidth, such as pointing devices and keyboards.

- 12 Mbps isochronous transfer rate for higher bandwidth devices, such as telephones, modems, speakers, scanners, video devices, and printers.

USB Support for Plug and Play

Windows 2000 Professional supports Plug and Play configuration of USB devices by using the following methods.

Hot Plug-in Capability   You can plug a USB device into the system anytime. The USB hub driver enumerates the device and notifies the system that the device is present.

Persistent Addressing   USB devices use descriptors to identify the device, its capabilities, and the protocols it uses. A descriptor contains a Vendor ID (VID) and Product ID (PID) that tell the computer exactly which drivers to load. An optional serial number differentiates one device from another of the same type. Older devices might have a Plug and Play ID, which can also be used to identify the device type and subtype.

Power Options Support   USB supports three power modes: On, Suspend, and Off.

USB Driver Interface

Windows 2000 Professional supports USB by allowing USB device drivers to communicate with the USB driver stack. The USB Driver Interface (USBDI) is between the drivers for USB devices (such as keyboards, mice and joysticks) and the USB driver stack. In Windows 2000 Professional, communication through the USBDI takes place in the Windows Driver Model (WDM) architecture.

Windows 2000 Professional can recognize a USB device once the client device driver communicates with the USB driver stack. This requires that a WDM I/O request packet (IRP) be issued to pass information across the USBDI between the client device driver and the USB driver stack.

For more information about how device drivers communicate with the USB through the use of I/O Request Packets (IRPs), see Driver Development Kits link on the Web Resources page at http://windows.microsoft.com/windows2000 /reskit/webresources

IEEE 1394

Windows 2000 Professional supports the IEEE 1394 bus, which is designed for high-bandwidth devices, such as digital camcorders, digital cameras, digital VCRs, and storage devices. IEEE 1394 is a serial protocol supporting speeds ranging from 100 to 400 megabits per second (Mbps), depending on the implementation. It provides a high-speed Plug and Play-capable bus that eliminates the need for peripheral devices to have their own power supply, and provides support for isochronous data transfer.

You can connect up to 63 devices to one IEEE 1394 bus and interconnect up to 1023 buses to form a very large network with over 64,000 devices. Each device can have up to 256 terabytes of memory addressable over the bus. A built-in mechanism ensures equal access to the bus for all devices.

Choosing Devices Supported by IEEE 1394

Windows 2000 Professional supports IEEE 1394 by allowing IEEE 1394 device drivers to communicate with the IEEE 1394 bus class driver. In accordance with the Open Host Controller Interface (OHCI) standard, Windows 2000 Professional currently includes the IEEE 1394 bus class driver with hardware-specific minidriver extensions for add-on and motherboard-based host controllers.

Important Windows 2000 Professional does not support IEEE 1394 devices that are not OHCI-compatible, such as Adaptec 1394 cards, which predate OHCI. Other implementations which are pre-OHCI are Sony Tin-Tin and TI-lynx. While Sony has a driver that allows their older Tin-Tin to work, Microsoft does not support it. Sony has since moved to the OHCI standard.

IEEE 1394 Bus Connector and Cable

The IEEE 1394 specification defines a standard connector and socket. An IEEE 1394 bus cable contains two pairs of twisted pair cabling to accommodate the needs of the serial bus. The specification actually defines three interfaces: 6-pin connector and cable, 4-pin connector and cable, and a 6-pin-to-4-pin connector and cable.

Data Transfer Rates Supported by IEEE 1394

The IEEE 1394 specification currently supports the following bus transfer rates:

- S100 (98.304 Mbps)
- S200 (196.608 Mbps)
- S400 (393.216 Mbps)

Higher transfer rates are under development.

You can freely interconnect devices with different data rates; communication automatically takes place at the highest rate supported by the lowest-rate device.

IEEE 1394 supports two data transfer protocols: *isochronous* and *asynchronous*. An isochronous transfer requires a constant bandwidth within certain time constraints. A constant bandwidth is required to support the demands of multimedia applications and devices. Unlike asynchronous transfers, no handshaking occurs and delivery is not guaranteed. By contrast, asynchronous transfers employ a handshaking system and allow data streams to be broken at random intervals.

IEEE 1394 Support for Plug and Play

Windows 2000 Professional supports hot plugging of nodes; you can plug an IEEE 1394 device into the system anytime.

IEEE 1394 Support for A/V Devices

Windows 2000 Professional supports only audio-video devices that are compliant with the Open Host Controller Interface (OHCI).

IEEE 1394 Support for Storage Devices

Support for IEEE 1394 storage devices, printers, and scanners is implemented through the Serial Bus Protocol (SBP-2) protocol. Small Computer System Interface (SCSI) class drivers can use SBP-2 to connect and use IEEE 1394 devices.

Supporting Other Buses

The following sections describe how the buses supported by previous versions of Windows function under Windows 2000 Professional.

Note Windows 2000 Professional does not support the Micro Channel™ bus. The Micro Channel architecture is found mainly in older IBM PS/2 computers.

PCI Bus

The *Peripheral Component Interconnect (PCI) bus* is a high-performance bus well suited for transferring data between hardware devices, adapters, and other bus circuit boards. Almost all computers ship with a PCI bus.

Because of its high bandwidth, the PCI bus is capable of high-performance data transfers. The PCI bus is usually connected to the host CPU and main memory through a bridge device that controls the data transfers between the CPU, cache, and main memory. This bridge also provides the major interface, and controls the data transfer between main memory and all the other devices on the PCI bus.

▶ **To calculate the maximum transfer rate on the PCI bus**

1. Multiply the bus clock rate by the bus width in bits.

2. Divide by the number of clock cycles it takes for each data transfer (1 cycle for the PCI bus).

For example, if the clock rate is 33 MHz and the width is 32 bits, then the maximum transfer rate is 1.06 gigabytes per second (Gbps). This is higher than the maximum IEEE 1394 bus rates (98.304, 196.608, and 393.216 Mbps) and considerably higher than the maximum USB rate (12 Mbps).

Note This calculation is an approximation of the maximum transfer rate. Not every PCI bus cycle is used to transfer data, and the calculation does not include latency or guarantees of isochronous transfers.

PC Card and CardBus

Windows 2000 Professional supports the new features of products designed for the PC Card standard, formerly known as the Personal Computer Memory Card International Association (PCMCIA) standard. These products include multifunction cards, 3.3-V cards, and 32-bit PC Cards.

Windows 2000 Professional supports *CardBus*, a combination of PC Card 16 and PCI, also known as PC Card 32. CardBus brings 32-bit performance and the benefits of the PCI bus to the PC Card architecture. CardBus allows portable computers to perform high-bandwidth functions such as capturing video.

SCSI Bus

The *Small Computer Standard Interface (SCSI)* is used with such devices as hard disks, CD-ROM drives, and scanners. Each device on the bus is connected in a daisy-chained topology. SCSI devices that are Plug and Play–capable support dynamic changes to the adapter and automatic configuration of device ID and termination.

ISA Bus

The *Industry Standard Architecture (ISA) bus* is specified for the IBM PC/AT. Plug and Play ISA devices can be used on existing computers, because Plug and Play does not require any change to ISA buses. Standard ISA cards can coexist with Plug and Play ISA cards on the same computer.

EISA Bus

The *Enhanced Industry Standard Architecture (EISA) bus* is specified for *x*86-based computers by an industry consortium. The EISA bus can use cards made for both EISA and ISA buses, and standard EISA cards can coexist with Plug and Play–capable EISA cards on the same computer.

For more information about support for the device types listed here, see "Device Management" in this book.

New and Enhanced Hardware Support

Windows 2000 Professional supports standards for the following types of hardware devices: Human Interface Device (HID); DVD; digital audio; still image; multiple display support; video capture; and Accelerated Graphics Port (AGP). Much of this support is either new or significantly improved from what was offered in previous versions of Windows. The following sections describe the hardware device standards supported by Windows 2000 Professional.

Human Interface Devices

Windows 2000 Professional supports devices compliant with the *Human Interface Device (HID)* firmware specification, the new standard for input devices, such as keyboards, mouse and pointing devices, joysticks, game pads, and other types of game controllers. HIDs also include a variety of controls for vehicle simulation, virtual reality, sports equipment, and appliances. Support is based on the specification developed by the USB Implementers' Forum and is meant for devices connecting through USB. Windows 2000 Professional also includes HID support for devices connected through older interfaces.

The HID-compliant device is self-describing; it indicates its type and provides usage information when plugged into the host system.

For more information about the USB Implementers Forum and HID usage, see the USB link on the Web Resources page at http://windows.microsoft.com /windows2000/reskit/webresources.

Windows 2000 Professional provides support for HIDs through WDM. The operating system supplies the HID class driver, the HID minidriver, and the HID parser. Windows 2000 Professional includes complete support for the following types of standard HID input devices:

- Keyboards and keypads
- Mouse and pointing devices
- Joysticks and game pads

You can plug these types of HID devices into the system and use them immediately. They do not require installation of additional software drivers.

The generality of the HID specification opens up the opportunity for new kinds of input devices. For example, HID use is defined for the following types of devices:

- Simulation devices (for example, automobiles, planes, tanks, spaceships, and submarines)

- Virtual reality devices (for example, belts, body suits, gloves, head trackers, head-mounted displays, and oculometers)

- Sports-equipment devices (for example, golf clubs, baseball bats, rowing machines, and treadmills)

- Consumer appliance devices (for example, audio and video appliances, and remote controls)

- Advanced game controllers (for example, 3-D game controllers and pinball devices)

Support for Plug and Play and power management for USB/HID devices takes place within the USB driver stack that is part of the new WDM-based architecture.

From the perspective of a computer program, any HID device can be accessed either through HID APIs exposed by Hid.dll, or through DirectInput Component Object Model (COM) methods. DirectInput, which is part of Microsoft® DirectX® multimedia architecture, includes support for HID devices.

Windows 2000 Professional also supports HID devices that connect to the system through ports or buses other than those of Hidusb.sys. For example, the IEEE 1394 bus can be developed and supplied by vendors.

For more information about developing minidrivers and filter drivers, see the Driver Development Kits link on the Web Resources page at http://windows.microsoft.com/windows2000/reskit/webresources. For more information about supporting HID devices, see "Device Management" in this book.

DVD

Digital Versatile Disk (DVD) provides digital data storage that encompasses audio, video, and computer data, and therefore has the potential for replacing current technologies for business data storage, laser disc, audio CD, CD-ROM, VHS videotape, and dedicated game technologies. DVD was designed for multimedia applications, with the goal of storing full-length feature movies.

The DVD Consortium has defined two major compression technologies, MPEG-2 and AC-3 (also called Dolby Digital), which you can use to store over two hours of video and audio on a single DVD disk. The quality of the stored video and audio is higher than that found on laser disks and CDs.

DVD Support

Windows 2000 Professional supports DVD as follows:

DVD Movie Playback   If the proper decoding hardware or software is present, Windows 2000 Professional supports playback of DVD video. This support is especially important for entertainment computers, but it is also important for any multimedia platform meant to provide good quality support for the playback of movies. This support includes the full range of interactivity and high-quality playback found on a standard DVD Video player. Because computers are capable of better image quality than television, playing DVDon a computer running Windows 2000 Professional can produce an image of better quality than standard DVD video player devices connected to a television set.

DVD as a Storage Device   You can use DVD as a storage device on most computers that support DVD. While most first-generation DVD-ROM drives do not read CD-Recordable (CD-R) disks, all second-generation drives do. DVD-ROM discs and devices provide cost-effective storage for large data files. There are a number of competing formats for rewritable DVD, such as DVD-RAM, DVD-RW, and DVD+RW. However, there is no single drive that is capable of reading all of these different types of media.

Figure C.2 shows the support architecture for existing DVD technologies that use Windows 2000 Professional.

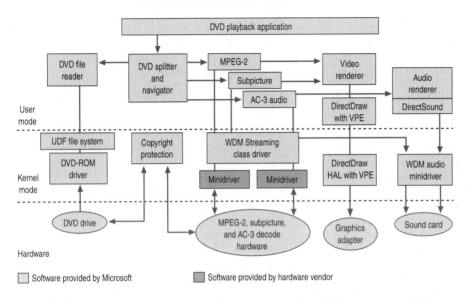

Figure C.2   Implementation of the DVD support architecture

DVD Movie Playback Components

The following components comprise support for DVD movie playback under Windows 2000 Professional:

DVD-ROM Class Driver   DVD-ROM has its own industry-defined command set, supported through an updated CD-ROM class driver. This driver provides the ability to read data sectors from a DVD-ROM drive.

UDF File System   Support for Universal Disk Format (UDF) ensures support for UDF-formatted DVD discs. UDF takes advantage of packet writing and is the industry standard for compact disc storage. As with File Allocation Table (FAT) and FAT32 file systems, Windows 2000 Professional provides installable file systems for UDF.

WDM Stream Class Driver   The WDM Stream class driver supports streaming data types, and MPEG-2 and AC-3 (Dolby Digital) hardware decoders. Hardware vendors must write only a small amount of interface code in a minidriver to ensure that the specific features in their hardware are supported. This allows most DVD decoders to work without user intervention.

DirectShow   Microsoft® DirectShow® (formerly ActiveMovie) proxy filters and related support include a DVD Navigator/Splitter, proxy filters for video streams, a video mixer, and a video renderer. The proxy filters allow programs written to the DirectShow API to control kernel mode filters.

DirectDraw Hardware Abstraction Layer (HAL) with Video Port Extensions (VPE)

Decoded video streams are huge — possibly too large even for the PCI bus on a computer. Manufacturers have solved this problem by creating dedicated buses to transfer decoded video streams from an MPEG-2 decoder to the display card. Microsoft provides software support for these interfaces using the DirectDraw HAL with VPE.

Copyright Protection   Copyright protection for DVD is established when key sectors on a disk are encrypted , then decrypted before the sectors are decoded. The encryption scheme used is called the Content-Scrambling System (CSS). Microsoft provides support for both software and hardware decrypters using a software module that enables authentication between the decoders and the DVD-ROM drives in a computer.

Regionalization   As part of the copyright protection scheme used for DVD, the DVD Consortium has defined six worldwide regions. Disks are playable on DVD devices in some or all of the regions according to regional codes set by the content creators. Microsoft provides software that responds to the regionalization codes as required by the DVD Consortium and as part of the decryption licenses.

DVDPlay   Microsoft provides a DVD movie playback application, which you can replace with another DVD playback application written to DirectShow2.

DVD-ROM Storage Device

Under Windows 2000 Professional, DVD-ROM is simply a large storage medium, much like CD-ROM. To enable DVD-ROM as a read-only device, Microsoft provides support for DVD-ROM devices in Windows 2000 Professional and support for UDF as an installable file system. Using DVD-ROM device drivers, a DVD-ROM drive is treated as another peripheral, using industry-defined methods to access DVD disks and handle encrypted content.

DVD and Streaming Data

A program produces *streaming* data when it delivers large amount of data in a constant load, or stream, over time. The program never loads the data completely into memory; the data file might be too large, and the operations on the data file are typically sequential. The best example of this for DVD is an MPEG-2 video stream. When a computer plays an MPEG-2 file, a program loads and streams the MPEG-2 data through the computer for decoding and displaying. The data might enter and exit the host processor and bus of the computer several times during this process. In addition, an MPEG-2 stream starts out at approximately 5 to 10 Mbps. After the stream is decoded, the data transfer rate can easily exceed 100 Mbps. A single data stream this large can saturate and overwhelm a computer's PCI bus, so an alternate path might be required for the raw, decoded video data.

A single stream demands a potentially large and constant load on a computer, over what can be considered a long time in computer terms. DVD is even more demanding because the system must be able to independently manage and decode at least four separate streams:

- MPEG-2 video
- AC-3 or MPEG-2 audio
- Subpicture
- Navigation

This independent processing of streams is necessary to ensure that the streams are totally synchronized when they reach their final destinations, with no dropped frames or degraded video. This requires precision in load balancing, synchronization, and processing.

The WDM Stream class driver can deal with these problems because it is optimized to work with any devices that use streamed data. This includes devices that encode data (for example, video capture devices), and those that decode data (for example, DVD hardware decoders that decode MPEG-2 streams for playing DVD movies). This class driver uses the WDM layered architecture for interconnecting device drivers to optimize data flow within the Windows 2000 Professional kernels.

For more information about DVD, see "Multimedia" in this book.

Digital Audio

Because Windows 2000 Professional supports USB and the IEEE 1394 bus, it can support digital audio. USB and IEEE 1394 have the bandwidth necessary to support digital audio and have mechanisms to provide synchronization between an audio source and an audio sink. Both provide different forms of isochronous and asynchronous services that distributed audio systems can use.

In Windows 2000 Professional, digital audio is supported by WDM, which enables it to handle multiple streams of audio simultaneously. This means that two applications can play sound at the same time, and you can hear both. Windows 2000 Professional can also redirect audio output. Redirecting audio output to external USB and IEEE 1394 devices has two significant advantages:

- *Higher fidelity.* Unlike internal audio devices, external devices are not subject to signal degradation due to high levels of radio-frequency noise.

- *Device visibility.* While Plug and Play can configure an internal audio device, it cannot guarantee that the speakers are connected to it. With USB speakers however, Plug and Play can *see* that they are in fact connected.

How USB Supports Digital Audio

The attributes of USB that allow it to accommodate digital audio devices are as follows:

Capacity   With a total transfer rate of 12 Mbps, USB has enough capacity for consumer audio but is inappropriate for multitrack audio production. Adding nodes to a USB network does not add to the total data-carrying capacity of the network, unlike IEEE 1394.

Synchronization   Although USB uses a 1 millisecond (ms) master clock for synchronization, the burden of synchronization is placed on the host computer. USB provides the following three modes of synchronization:

- Asynchronous nodes have independent clocks. It is the responsibility of code in the host to add or delete samples to keep a source and data sink synchronized.

- Synchronous nodes synchronize to the master clock in the host. Two synchronized nodes can communicate without host intervention. The host might need to perform sample rate conversions but can assume that clocks on both devices are synchronized relative to one another.

- Adaptive nodes derive their clock from the data stream. For example, in an Internet telephone conversation, the nominal data rate might be 8,000 samples per second, but the remote party's sound card might be running at 8,002 samples per second. Every millisecond the computer is expected to send eight samples to the local USB audio device, but because the remote device is sending data faster, the network telephony program can compensate by sending an extra sample every half second. Adaptive nodes can deal with this sort of variance without problems.

Digital Signal Processing (DSP) Capability   With USB, DSP must take place in the end nodes or in the host. For example, if a DVD drive and a home stereo are connected to a host, and the user wants to play an AC-3 audio-encoded stream, the AC-3 decoding can take place in either the host or in the stereo set, but not in an intermediate DSP *dongle* (a device, attached to a computer's I/O port, that adds hardware capabilities). The USB requirement for DSP connection is in contrast to the IEEE 1394 bus requirement, in which DSPs can also be connected as interior members of the daisy-chain or tree.

USB Device Classes   If a device conforms to a defined USB device class, you can use Plug and Play methods to identify the device and load a device driver. This eliminates the need for device manufacturers to ship driver disks with their products.

Appliances as computer peripherals with USB Open Standards   Not only is USB designed for standard devices, such as joysticks, keyboards, printers, and mouse devices, but because of its low production cost and relatively simple implementation, USB enables a wide class of devices to become computer peripherals. For example, a postage meter containing microcontrollers can have a USB port added for a small increase in cost. Connected to a computer, the meter can become part of a company-wide cost-tracking system. Adding voice output to the postage meter for use by a sight impaired user requires connecting the postage meter to a computer containing USB audio hardware. A programmer can add audio by using application programming interfaces (APIs) under Windows 2000 Professional.

If the postage meter conforms to the HID class, Plug and Play support ensures that the device is recognized as soon as it is plugged into the computer. When that occurs, Windows 2000 Professional loads a device driver, configures the device, and makes it available to end-user software. This is particularly useful for telephones. A telephone is both an HID (the keypad) and an audio USB device. It might also include a conventional, ISDN, or high-speed cable modem. If a telephone answering/fax machine has a USB port, the device works well in a stand-alone mode, but when it is plugged into a computer, it becomes a modem, scanner, printer, or more intelligent answering machine.

Home entertainment   The home stereo system is another consumer device that contains a microcontroller and can be easily upgraded to connect to a computer running Windows 2000 Professional with USB. Except for the audio data rates, a stereo system is not much different from a telephone with USB. When equipped with a USB interface, a stereo system becomes a USB audio class device and an HID class device. The microcontroller inside a stereo system is not much different from the microcontroller inside a keyboard. The stereo system microcontroller spends most of its time polling buttons, waiting for the user to change the volume or tone controls.

IEEE 1394 Bus Support for Digital Audio

The attributes of the IEEE 1394 bus that allow it to accommodate digital-audio devices are as follows:

Capacity and Synchronization   With the IEEE 1394 bus, it is possible to put a CD drive on one node and a digital-to-analog converter (DAC) on another node. The clocks of both devices can be synchronized to the master clock on the bus. Because the IEEE 1394 bus is designed to handle video data (a transfer rate of 400 Mbps), handling multiple tracks of audio is a much simpler task. IEEE 1394 networks can be configured using multiple buses and filtering bridges in a leaf-node configuration so many devices can play in parallel without passing data over the same segment of the bus.

DSP capability   Arbitrary amounts of DSP power can be applied to streams of audio by means of IEEE 1394 dongles. DSPs inside a computer are limited by the total memory of the system and must compete with the CPU for this resource. On the IEEE 1394 bus, signals can be passed between nodes containing DSPs. Each DSP node increases delay to the processing time, but the IEEE 1394 bus can string many DSPs together.

Supporting Still Image Devices

Windows 2000 Professional supports *still image* (STI) devices under the WDM architecture. WDM supports SCSI, IEEE 1394, USB digital still image, and serial devices. Support for infrared and serial still image devices, which are connected to standard COM ports, comes from the existing infrared and serial interfaces. Image scanners and digital cameras are examples of STI devices.

Figure C.3 illustrates the STI architecture.

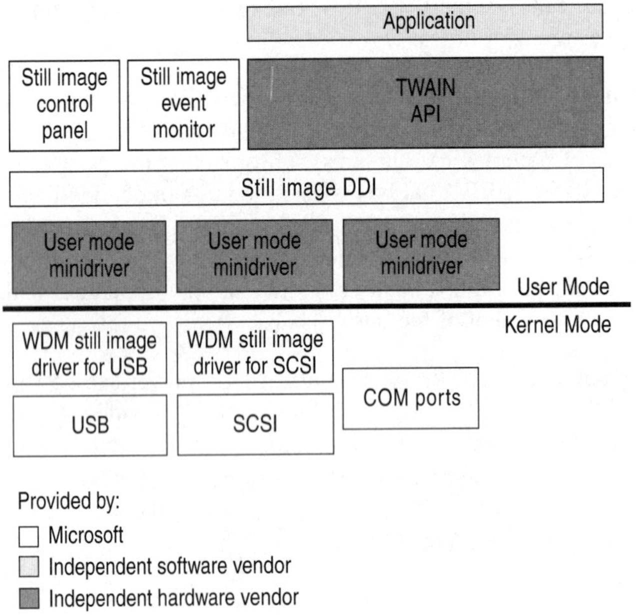

Figure C.3   STI architecture

The following describes the components shown in Figure C.3:

Application   Two primary types of applications use still images. One type is for the editing of image data. Examples of this type are Adobe PhotoShop and Microsoft® PictureIt!® The other type is for authoring documents that include image data, but that do not focus on editing that image data. Examples of this type are word processing and page layout applications, such as Microsoft® Word, or a presentation application, such as Microsoft® PowerPoint®.

Still Image APIs   TWAIN, ISIS, and Adobe Acquire are the common API interfaces in use today. Currently, a hardware vendor must supply a device-specific component that implements a driver for each supported API.

Color Management   This interface and implementation maintains device color profiles and provides for color-space conversion. All color output from scanners must be defined. To accomplish this, a scanner must either create Red, Green, Blue (RGB) output or embed the International Color Consortium (ICC) profile for the scanned image into the image file to identify the color-space information for that image.

Still Image Control Panel In Windows 2000 Professional, Scanners and Cameras in Control Panel gives you access to the following options for installed STI devices:

- List of the installed STI devices
- Addition and removal of STI devices that are not Plug and Play
- Test of the validation of a selected device
- Optional device-specific configuration
- Control of the association between specific device events and the applications to be notified of these events.

The Scanners and Cameras icon appears in Control Panel when Windows 2000 Professional detects a Plug and Play STI device, or when you install a non Plug and Play STI device through the Add New Hardware Wizard.

For more information about the Add New Hardware Wizard, see "Device Management" in this book.

Still Image Event Monitor This application (provided by Microsoft) supports push-model behavior by detecting events coming from installed STI devices, and dispatching a set of those events to an application. From Control Panel, you can configure which Still Image-compliant applications are invoked.

Still Image Device Driver Interface (DDI) You use the Still Image Device Driver Interface (DDI) to communicate with a particular device. The Still Image APIs, Control Panel, and the Event Monitor use the Still Image DDI. This DDI uses the color management system as a repository for the color profile supplied for a specific device. The DDI provides interfaces for the following:

- Enumeration
- Device information (primitive capabilities and status)
- Test activation
- Data and command I/O
- Notification for device events, including polling for device activity
- Retrieval of an Image Color Management (ICM) color profile and other auxiliary information associated with a device

User-Mode Minidrivers These vendor-written modules are small components used to implement device-specific DDI functionality (test, status, and data I/O).

Still Image Kernel-Mode Drivers These modules, provided by Microsoft, package a command or data for delivery on a specific bus type. All new kernel-mode drivers provided by Microsoft are WDM-based, although kernel-mode drivers generally need not be. Vendors must supply their own kernel-mode drivers for devices that are not designed to use the standard Microsoft kernel-mode drivers for a specific bus. Currently, kernel mode drivers for SCSI and USB are provided specific to still image devices.

Bus drivers. These modules, provided by Microsoft, are used to communicate with the STI device. Examples are the USB driver stack and drivers for the serial and parallel ports.

Video Capture

Video Capture under Windows 2000 Professional is based on the WDM Stream class driver. Windows 2000 Professional provides minidrivers for USB and IEEE 1394 cameras, as well as PCI and videoport analog video devices. Support includes DirectShow filters for WDM video capture interfaces, and for compatibility with previous interface versions, a Video for Windows (VFW)-to-WDM mapper. The mapper, also called the VFWWDM mapper, allows WDM video capture devices to take advantage of existing 32-bit VFW applications, using the AVICap interfaces.

Capturing video with WDM has the following advantages:

- Compatibility with Windows 98
- Synergy with Microsoft® DirectShow® and Connection and Streaming Architecture
- Single class driver architecture for hardware (such as video ports and chip sets) that is shared between video capture devices and DVD or MPEG devices
- Television tuner, input selection, and support for fields, vertical blanking interval (VBI), and video port extensions

Capture applications have been developed using both DirectShow and VFW. A sample DirectShow capture application (Amcap.exe) is included in the DirectShow Software Development Kit.

Vidcap32.exe is a sample Video for Windows (VFW) capture application included in the Win32 SDK. It allows you to capture video sequences and images from a VCR, videodisc player, or video camera. Video Capture provides two modes for capturing video sequences:

- Real-time capture
- Step-frame capture

Using Real-Time Capture

Real-time capture processes a video sequence and audio as the events occur naturally or as the video source plays without interruption. A video source for real-time capture (such as a video camera or videodisc) provides an uninterrupted stream of information to the capture hardware. The capture hardware copies each frame of the video sequence (and each portion of audio) and transfers it to the hard disk before the next frame of data enters the capture hardware. A video frame contains one image of the video sequence.

Real-time capture demands a fast computer and hard disk. The computer must process and store each incoming video frame before the next frame is received in the capture board. If the system lags during capture, frames of video data are lost.

Using Step-Frame Capture

Step-frame capture pauses the video source as it collects each frame (image) of data. If audio is also selected, this capture mode rewinds the media in the video source and collects audio data as the video source plays a second time. Step-frame capture collects video frames from a video sequence in a series of steps. Frames are captured one at a time, generally from a paused video device. You can perform step-frame capture manually, advancing the video source using the controls on the video device. Video Capture also provides automatic step-frame capture for video devices that support the Media Control Interface. With this method, Video Capture issues frame-advance commands to the source device and captures the sequence frame-by-frame. When Video Capture finishes capturing the current frame, it advances the video source to the next capture point.

Step-frame capture provides an alternative for systems that cannot process a video sequence in real time. Because the system can fully process a video frame before contending with the next frame, you can use larger frame sizes and color formats, and you can compress the video sequence during capture. When a step-frame capture is complete, you can capture the audio segment associated with the video frames by playing the source video a second time.

Smart Cards

Smart Card technology is fully integrated into Windows 2000 Professional, and is an important component of the operating system's public-key infrastructure security feature. It allows Windows 2000 Professional to authenticate users using the private and public key information stored on a card, and enables single sign-on to the enterprise.

A *smart card* is a small electronic device, approximately the size of a credit card, that contains an embedded integrated circuit. Smart cards are used to securely store public and private keys, passwords, and other personal information such as medical records.

Smart cards provide:

- Tamper-resistant storage for protecting private keys and other forms of personal information.

- Isolation of security-critical computations involving authentication, digital signatures, and key exchange from other parts of the system that do not have a "need to know"

- Portability of credentials and other private information between computers at work, home, or on the road

The Smart Card subsystem on Windows 2000 Professional supports industry standard Personal Computer/Smart Card (PC/SC) recommendations, and provides drivers for commercially available Plug and Play smart card readers. Windows 2000 Professional does not support non PC/SC-compliant or non–Plug and Play smart card readers. Some manufacturers might provide drivers for non–Plug and Play smart card readers that work with Windows 2000 Professional; however, it is recommended that you purchase only Plug and Play PC/SC-compliant smart card readers.

Windows 2000 Professional automatically detects Plug and Play-compliant smart card readers and installs them using the Hardware Wizard. Once the reader is installed, you only need to configure a dial-up network connection to use a pre-configured smart card. In the **Security** tab of the connection **Properties** box, select **Use smart card** in the **Validate my identity as follows** list.

Note Non-Plug and Play smart card readers are not recommended on the Windows 2000 platform. If you use a non-Plug and Play reader, you must obtain installation instructions including associated device driver software directly from the manufacturer of the smart card reader. Microsoft does not support nor recommend using non-Plug and Play smart card readers.

For information about Windows 2000-compatible smart card readers see the Windows Hardware Compatibility List link on the Web Resources page at http://windows.microsoft.com/windows2000/reskit/webresources

---

To log on with a smartcard in Windows 2000 Professional, you need a Smart Card Cryptographic Provider (SCCP). As an option, Smart Card Service Providers (SCSPs), are provided by the smart card supplier or issuer. These service providers pertain to non-cryptographic and cryptographic services.

For more information about Smart Card technology, see "Security" in this book. For smart card installation procedures, see Windows 2000 Professional Help.

Note   To develop a device driver or service provider, see the Windows 2000 SDK. For more information, see SDK information in the MSDN™ Library link on the Web Resources pages at http://windows.microsoft.com/windows2000 /reskit/webresources

Smart card readers typically come with set up instructions about how to connect cables, if there are any. If your reader has instructions, follow them. If you do not have instructions, then use the following general procedure.

▶ **To install a smart card reader**

1. Shut down your computer.

2. Attach your reader to an available serial port or insert the PC Card reader into an available PCMCIA Type II slot.

3. If your serial reader has a supplementary PS/2 cable/connector, attach your keyboard or mouse connector to it and plug it into your computer's keyboard or mouse port. Many new smart card readers take power from the keyboard or mouse port because power is not always provided by RS-232 ports and a separate power supply can be expensive and cumbersome.

4. Start up your computer and log on.

If your smart card reader is Plug and Play-compliant, the Hardware Wizard detects it and installs the correct device driver.

To install a smart card reader driver, follow the Hardware Wizard's directions for installing device driver software. This requires that you either use the Windows 2000 Professional CD or media from the smart card reader manufacturer which contains the appropriate device driver.

Troubleshooting Hardware Support Components

This section contains troubleshooting examples for the Windows 2000 Professional hardware management components.

For more information about troubleshooting problems with devices, see "Device Management" and "Troubleshooting Tools and Strategies" in this book.

Troubleshooting System Buses

This section contains procedures for troubleshooting the system buses supported by Windows 2000 Professional.

Troubleshooting USB

Because of the nature of USB devices, there are no resource settings that can cause a USB device to function improperly or fail.

▶ **To resolve problems with USB speakers**

- Most speakers are available in two modes: digital and audio. If you use USB speakers and don't receive a signal, make sure the speakers are in digital mode.

▶ **To resolve most other problems involving a USB device**

1. If only one device fails, reconnect that device to another USB port. If the device works, the original port is faulty and should be repaired. If the device does not work when connected to the new port, the device is probably faulty and should be repaired or replaced.

2. If the bus configuration is multi-tiered, make sure the configuration adheres to the following guidelines:

   - You cannot connect a bus-powered hub to another bus-powered hub.

   - Bus-powered hubs cannot support more than four downstream ports.

   - Bus-powered hubs cannot support bus-powered devices that draw more than 100 milliamperes (mA).

   - The bus cannot exceed five tiers.

3. Uninstall the USB host controller from Device Manager and restart the computer. This allows Windows 2000 Professional to redetect and reinstall the entire bus.

Troubleshooting the IEEE 1394 Bus

If you want to connect two computers on the IEEE 1394 bus, make sure you use the correct cable. This cable is not supplied with the bus and must be purchased separately.

Additional Resources

- For more information about device support, and hardware development see the Hardware Development link on the Web Resources page at http://windows.microsoft.com/windows2000/reskit/webresources

- For more information about WDM and developing drivers for Windows 2000 Professional, see DDK information in the MSDN Library link on the Web Resources page at http://windows.microsoft.com/windows2000/reskit/webresources

- For more information about WDM, see *Programming the Microsoft Windows Driver Model* by Walter Oney, 1999, Microsoft Press.

- For more information about hardware design, see the *PC 99 System Design Guide* link on the Web Resources page at http://windows.microsoft.com/windows2000/reskit/webresources

Glossary

3

3270 A class of IBM Systems Network Architecture terminal and related protocol used to communicate with IBM mainframe host systems.

5

5250 A class of IBM Systems Network Architecture terminal and related protocol used to communicate with AS/400 host systems.

8

802.1p A protocol that supports the mapping of RSVP signals to Layer 2 signals using 802.1p priority markings to enable the prioritization of traffic across Layer 2 devices, such as switches, on a network segment. IEEE 802 refers to the Layer 2 technology used by LANs including the data-link layer and the media access control layer.

8mm cassette A tape cartridge format used for data backups, similar to that used for some video cameras except that the tape is rated for data storage. The capacity is 5 GB or more of (optionally compressed) data.

A

AC-3 The coding system used by Dolby Digital. A standard for high quality digital audio that is used for the sound portion of video stored in digital format.

Accelerated Graphics Port (AGP)
A type of expansion slot that is solely for video cards. Designed by Intel and supported by Windows 2000, AGP is a dedicated bus that provides fast, high-quality video and graphics performance.

access control entry (ACE) An entry in an access control list (ACL) containing the security ID (SID) for a user or group and an access mask that specifies which operations by the user or group are allowed, denied, or audited. See also access control list; access mask; security descriptor.

access control list (ACL) A list of security protections that apply to an entire object, a set of the object's properties, or an individual property of an object. There are two types of access control lists: discretionary and system. See also access control entry; discretionary access control list; security descriptor; system access control list.

access mask A 32-bit value that specifies the rights that are allowed or denied in an access control entry (ACE) of an access control list (ACL). An access mask is also used to request access rights when an object is opened. See also access control entry.

access token A data structure containing security information that identifies a user to the security subsystem on a computer running Windows 2000 or Windows NT. An access token contains a user's security ID, the security IDs for groups that the user belongs to, and a list of the user's privileges on the local computer. See also privilege; security ID.

accessibility The quality of a system incorporating hardware or software to engage a flexible, customizable user interface, alternative input and output methods, and greater exposure of screen elements to make the computer usable by people with cognitive, hearing, physical, or visual disabilities.

accessibility status indicators Icons on the system status area of the taskbar of the Windows desktop that let the user know which accessibility features are activated.

Accessibility Wizard An interactive tool that makes it easier to set up commonly used accessibility features by specifying options by type of disability, rather than by numeric value changes.

ACPI See Advanced Configuration and Power Interface.

Active Accessibility A core component in the Windows operating system that is built on COM and defines how applications can exchange information about user interface elements.

Active Directory The directory service included with Windows 2000 Server. It stores information about objects on a network and makes this information available to users and network administrators. Active Directory gives network users access to permitted resources anywhere on the network using a single logon process. It provides network administrators with an intuitive hierarchical view of the network and a single point of administration for all network objects. See also directory; directory service.

ActiveX A set of technologies that enables software components to interact with one another in a networked environment, regardless of the language in which the components were created.

administrator See system administrator.

Advanced Configuration and Power Interface (ACPI)
An open industry specification that defines power management on a wide range of mobile, desktop, and server computers and peripherals. ACPI is the foundation for the OnNow industry initiative that allows system manufacturers to deliver computers that will start at the touch of a keyboard. ACPI design is essential to take full advantage of power management and Plug and Play in Windows 2000. Check the manufacturer's documentation to verify that a computer is ACPI-compliant. See also Plug and Play.

Advanced Power Management A software interface (designed by Microsoft and Intel) between hardware-specific power management software (such as that located in a system BIOS) and an operating system power management driver.

advertisement In Systems Management Server, a notification sent by the site server to the client access points (CAPs) specifying that a software distribution program is available for clients to use. In Windows 2000, the Software Installation snap-in generates an application advertisement script and stores this script in the appropriate locations in Active Directory and the Group Policy object.

allocation unit In file systems an allocation unit is the smallest amount of disk space that can be allocated to hold a file. All file systems used by Windows 2000 organize hard disks based on allocation units. The smaller the allocation unit size, the more efficiently a disk stores information. If no allocation unit size is specified during formatting, Windows 2000 chooses default sizes based on the size of the volume and the file system used. These defaults are selected to reduce the amount of space lost and the amount of fragmentation on the volume. Also called cluster.

American Standard Code for Information Interchange (ASCII)
A standard single byte character encoding scheme used for text-based data. ASCII uses designated 7-bit or 8-bit number combinations to represent either 128 or 256 possible characters. Standard ASCII uses 7 bits to represent all uppercase and lowercase letters, the numbers 0 through 9, punctuation marks, and special control characters used in U.S. English. Most current x86 systems support the use of extended (or "high") ASCII. Extended ASCII allows the eighth bit of each character to identify an additional 128 special symbol characters, foreign-language letters, and graphic symbols. See also Unicode.

answer file A text file that you can use to provide automated input for unattended installation of Windows 2000. This input includes parameters to answer the questions required by Setup for specific installations. In some cases, you can use this text file to provide input to wizards, such as the Active Directory Installation wizard, which is used to add Active Directory to Windows 2000 Server through Setup. The default answer file for Setup is known as Unattend.txt.

API See application programming interface.

APM See Advanced Power Management.

application media pool A data repository that determines which media can be accessed by which applications and that sets the policies for that media. There can be any number of application media pools in a Removable Storage system. Applications create application media pools.

application programming interface (API)
A set of routines that an application uses to request and carry out lower-level services performed by a computer's operating system. These routines usually carry out maintenance tasks such as managing files and displaying information.

assistive technology System extensions, programs, devices, and utilities added to a computer to make it more accessible to users with disabilities.

asynchronous communication A form of data transmission in which information is sent and received at irregular intervals, one character at a time. Because data is received at irregular intervals, the receiving modem must be signaled to inform it when the data bits of a character begin and end. This is done by means of start and stop bits.

Asynchronous Transfer Mode (ATM)
A high-speed connection-oriented protocol used to transport many different types of network traffic.

ATM See Asynchronous Transfer Mode.

attribute (object) In Active Directory, an attribute describes characteristics of an object and the type of information an object can hold. For each object class, the schema defines what attributes an instance of the class must have and what additional attributes it might have.

auditing To track the activities of users by recording selected types of events in the security log of a server or a workstation.

authentication A basic security function of cryptography. Authentication verifies the identity of the entities that communicate over the network. For example, the process that verifies the identity of a user who logs on to a computer either locally, at a computer's keyboard, or remotely, through a network connection. See also cryptography; confidentiality; integrity; Kerberos authentication protocol; nonrepudiation; NTLM authentication protocol.

Authentication Header (AH) A header that provides authentication, integrity, and anti-replay for the entire packet (both the IP header and the data payload carried in the packet).

authoritative In the Domain Name System (DNS), the use of zones by DNS servers to register and resolve a DNS domain name. When a DNS server is configured to host a zone, it is authoritative for names within that zone. DNS servers are granted authority based on information stored in the zone. See also zone.

automated installation An unattended setup using one or more of several methods such as Remote Installation Services, bootable CD, and Sysprep.

automatic caching A method of automatically storing network files on a user's hard disk drive whenever a file is open so the files can be accessed when the user is not connected to the network.

Automatic Private IP Addressing (APIPA) A feature of Windows 2000 TCP/IP that automatically configures a unique IP address from the range 169.254.0.1 to 169.254.255.254 and a subnet mask of 255.255.0.0 when the TCP/IP protocol is configured for dynamic addressing and a Dynamic Host Configuration Protocol (DHCP) is not available.

available state A state in which media can be allocated for use by applications.

averaging counter A type of counter that measures a value over time and displays the average of the last two measurements over some other factor (for example, PhysicalDisk\Avg. Disk Bytes/Transfer).

B

B-tree A tree structure for storing database indexes. Each node in the tree contains a sorted list of key values and links that correspond to ranges of key values between the listed values. To find a specific data record given its key value, the program reads the first node, or root, from the disk and compares the desired key with the keys in the node to select a subrange of key values to search. It repeats the process with the node indicated by the corresponding link. At the lowest level, the links indicate the data records. The database system can thus rapidly search through the levels of the tree structure to find the simple index entries that contain the location of the desired records or rows.

backup A duplicate copy of a program, a disk, or data, made either for archiving purposes or for safeguarding valuable files from loss should the active copy be damaged or destroyed. Some application programs automatically make backup copies of data files, maintaining both the current version and the preceding version.

backup operator A type of local or global group that contains the user rights needed to back up and restore files and folders. Members of the Backup Operators group can back up and restore files and folders regardless of ownership, access permissions, encryption, or auditing settings. See also auditing; global group; local group; user rights.

backup types A type that determines which data is backed up and how it is backed up. There are five backup types: copy, daily, differential, incremental, and normal. See also copy backup; daily backup; differential backup; incremental backup; normal backup.

bad block A disk sector that can no longer be used for data storage, usually due to media damage or imperfections.

bandwidth In analog communications, the difference between the highest and lowest frequencies in a given range. For example, a telephone line accommodates a bandwidth of 3,000 Hz, the difference between the lowest (300 Hz) and highest (3,300 Hz) frequencies it can carry. In digital communications, the rate at which information is sent expressed in bits per second (bps).

bar code A machine-readable label that identifies an object, such as physical media.

base file record The first file record in the master file table (MFT) for a file that has multiple file records. The base file record is the record to which the file's file reference corresponds.

baseline A range of measurements derived from performance monitoring that represents acceptable performance under typical operating conditions.

basic disk A physical disk that contains primary partitions or extended partitions with logical drives used by Windows 2000 and all versions of Windows NT. Basic disks can also contain volume, striped, mirror, or RAID-5 sets that were created using Windows NT 4.0 or earlier. As long as a compatible file format is used, basic disks can be accessed by MS-DOS, Windows 95, Windows 98, and all versions of Windows NT.

basic input/output system (BIOS)

The set of essential software routines that tests hardware at startup, assists with starting the operating system, and supports the transfer of data among hardware devices. The BIOS is stored in read-only memory (ROM) so that it can be executed when the computer is turned on. Although critical to performance, the BIOS is usually invisible to computer users.

basic volume A volume on a basic disk. Basic volumes include primary partitions, logical drives within extended partitions, as well as volume, striped, mirror, or RAID-5 sets that were created using Windows NT 4.0 or earlier. Only basic disks can contain basic volumes. Basic and dynamic volumes cannot exist on the same disk.

batch program An ASCII (unformatted text) file containing one or more Windows NT or Windows 2000 commands. A batch program's filename has a .BAT extension. When you type the filename at the command prompt, the commands are processed sequentially. "Script" is often used interchangeably with "batch program" in the Windows NT and Windows 2000 environment.

Bidirectional communication Communication that occurs in two directions simultaneously. Bidirectional communication is useful in printing where jobs can be sent and printer status can be returned at the same time.

binding A process by which software components and layers are linked together. When a network component is installed, the binding relationships and dependencies for the components are established. Binding allows components to communicate with each other.

binding order The sequence in which software components, network protocols and network adapters are linked together. When a network component is installed, the binding relationships and dependencies for the components are established.

BIOS See basic input/output system.

BIOS parameter block (BPB) A series of fields containing data on disk size, geometry variables, and the physical parameters of the volume. The BPB is located within the boot sector.

boot sector A critical disk structure for starting your computer, located at sector 1 of each volume or floppy disk. It contains executable code and data that is required by the code, including information used by the file system to access the volume. The boot sector is created when you format the volume.

bootable CD An automated installation method that runs Setup from a CD-ROM. This method is useful for computers at remote sites with slow links and no local IT department. See also automated installation.

bottleneck A condition, usually involving a hardware resource, that causes the entire system to perform poorly.

BounceKeys A keyboard filter that assists users whose fingers bounce on the keys when pressing or releasing them.

bound trap In programming, a problem in which a set of conditions exceeds a permitted range of values that causes the microprocessor to stop what it is doing and handle the situation in a separate routine.

browsing The process of creating and maintaining an up-to-date list of computers and resources on a network or part of a network by one or more designated computers running the Computer Browser service. See Computer Browser service.

bulk encryption A process in which large amounts of data, such as files, e-mail messages, or online communications sessions, are encrypted for confidentiality. It is usually done with a symmetric key algorithm. See also encryption; symmetric key encryption.

C

cable modem A modem that provides broadband Internet access in the range of 10 to 30 Mbps.

cache For DNS and WINS, a local information store of resource records for recently resolved names of remote hosts. Typically, the cache is built dynamically as the computer queries and resolves names; it helps optimize the time required to resolve queried names. See also cache file; naming service; resource record.

cache file A file used by the Domain Name System (DNS) server to preload its names cache when service is started. Also known as the "root hints" file because resource records stored in this file are used by the DNS service to help locate root servers that provide referral to authoritative servers for remote names. For Windows DNS servers, the cache file is named Cache.dns and is located in the %SystemRoot%\System32\Dns folder. See also authoritative; cache; systemroot.

caching The process of storing recently-used data values in a special pool in memory where they are temporarily held for quicker subsequent accesses. For DNS, the ability of DNS servers to store information about the domain namespace learned during the processing and resolution of name queries. In Windows 2000, caching is also available through the DNS client service (resolver) as a way for DNS clients to keep a cache of name information learned during recent queries. See also caching resolver.

caching resolver For Windows 2000, a client-side Domain Name System (DNS) name resolution service that performs caching of recently learned DNS domain name information. The caching resolver service provides system-wide access to DNS-aware programs for resource records obtained from DNS servers during the processing of name queries. Data placed in the cache is used for a limited period of time and aged according to the active Time To Live (TTL) value. You can set the TTL either individually for each resource record (RR) or default to the minimum TTL set in the start of authority RR for the zone. See also cache; caching; expire interval; minimum TTL; resolver; resource record; Time To Live (TTL).

callback number The number that a RAS server uses to call back a user. This number can be preset by the administrator or specified by the user at the time of each call, depending on how the administrator configures the user's callback status. The callback number should be the number of the phone line to which the user's modem is connected.

CardBus A 32-bit PC Card.

cartridge A unit of media of a certain type, such as 8mm tape, magnetic disk, optical disk, or CD-ROM, used by Removable Storage.

Central Processing Unit (CPU) The part of a computer that has the ability to retrieve, interpret, and execute instructions and to transfer information to and from other resources over the computer's main data-transfer path, the bus. By definition, the CPU is the chip that functions as the "brain" of a computer.

certificate A digital document that is commonly used for authentication and secure exchange of information on open networks, such as the Internet, extranets, and intranets. A certificate securely binds a public key to the entity that holds the corresponding private key. Certificates are digitally signed by the issuing certification authority and can be issued for a user, a computer, or a service. The most widely accepted format for certificates is defined by the ITU-T X.509 version 3 international standard. See also certification authority; private key; public key.

Certificate Services The Windows 2000 service that issues certificates for a particular CA. It provides customizable services for issuing and managing certificates for the enterprise. See also certificate; certification authority.

certification authority (CA) An entity responsible for establishing and vouching for the authenticity of public keys belonging to users (end entities) or other certification authorities. Activities of a certification authority can include binding public keys to distinguished names through signed certificates, managing certificate serial numbers, and certificate revocation. See also certificate; public key.

Certified-for-Windows Logo A specification that addresses the requirements of computer users with disabilities to ensure quality and consistency in assistive devices.

Challenge Handshake Authentication Protocol (CHAP)
A challenge-response authentication protocol for PPP connections documented in RFC 1994 that uses the industry-standard Message Digest 5 (MD5) one-way encryption scheme to hash the response to a challenge issued by the remote access server.

change journal   A feature new to Windows 2000 that tracks changes to NTFS volumes, including additions, deletions, and modifications. The change journal exists on the volume as a sparse file.

changer   The robotic element of an online library unit.

CHAP   See Challenge Handshake Authentication Protocol.

child object   An object that is the immediate subordinate of another object in a hierarchy. A child object can have only one immediate superior, or parent, object. In Active Directory, the schema determines what classes of objects can be child objects of what other classes of objects. Depending on its class, a child object can also be the parent of other objects. See also object; parent object.

CIM (COM Information Model) Object Manager
A system service that handles interaction between network management applications and providers of local or remote data or system events. CIM (COM Information Model) Object Manager is also known as CIMOM.

ciphertext   Text that has been encrypted using an encryption key. Ciphertext is meaningless to anyone who does not have the decryption key. See also decryption; encryption; encryption key; plaintext.

client   Any computer or program connecting to, or requesting services of, another computer or program. See also server.

cluster   A group of independent computer systems known as nodes or hosts, that work together as a single system to ensure that mission-critical applications and resources remain available to clients. A server cluster is the type of cluster that the Cluster service implements. Network Load Balancing provides a software solution for clustering multiple computers running Windows 2000 Server that provides networked services over the Internet and private intranets. In file systems a cluster is the smallest amount of disk space that can be allocated to hold a file. All file systems used by Windows 2000 organize hard disks based on clusters. The smaller the cluster size, the more efficiently a disk stores information. If no cluster size is specified during formatting, Windows 2000 chooses default sizes based on the size of the volume and the file system used. These defaults are selected to reduce the amount of space lost and the amount of fragmentation on the volume. Also called allocation units.

cluster remapping   A recovery technique used when Windows 2000 returns a bad sector error to NTFS. NTFS dynamically replaces the cluster containing the bad sector and allocates a new cluster for the data. If the error occurs during a read, NTFS returns a read error to the calling program, and the data is lost. If the error occurs during a write, NTFS writes the data to the new cluster, and no data is lost.

code page   A page that maps character codes to individual characters. Different code pages include different special characters, typically customized for a language or a group of languages. The system uses code pages to translate keyboard input into character values for non-Unicode based applications, and to translate character values into characters for non-Unicode based output displays.

COM   See Component Object Model.

COM port   Short for communications port, the logical address assigned by MS-DOS (versions 3.3 and higher) and Microsoft Windows (including Windows 95, Windows 98, Windows NT and Windows 2000) to each of the four serial ports on an IBM Personal Computer or a PC compatible. COM ports are also known as the actual serial ports on a PC's CPU where peripherals, such as printers, scanners, and external modems, are plugged in.

commit a transaction   To record in the log file the fact that a transaction is complete and has been recorded in the cache.

Common Internet File System (CIFS)
A protocol and a corresponding API used by application programs to request higher level application services. CIFS was formerly known as SMB (Server Message Block).

Compact Disc File System (CDFS)
A 32-bit protected-mode file system that controls access to the contents of CD-ROM drives in Windows 2000.

compact disc-recordable (CD-R)   A type of CD-ROM that can be written on a CD recorder and read on a CD-ROM drive.

complementary metal-oxide semiconductor (CMOS)
The battery-packed memory that stores information, such as disk types and amount of memory, used to start the computer.

Component Object Model (COM)   An object-based programming model designed to promote software interoperability; it allows two or more applications or components to easily cooperate with one another, even if they were written by different vendors, at different times, in different programming languages, or if they are running on different computers running different operating systems. COM is the foundation technology upon which broader technologies can be built. Object linking and embedding (OLE) technology and ActiveX are both built on top of COM.

Computer Browser service   A service that maintains an up-to-date list of computers and provides the list to applications when requested. The Computer Browser service provides the computer lists displayed in the My Network Places, Select Computer, and Select Domain dialog boxes and (for Windows 2000 Server only) in the Server Manager window.

confidentiality   A basic security function of cryptography. Confidentiality provides assurance that only authorized users can read or use confidential or secret information. Without confidentiality, anyone with network access can use readily available tools to eavesdrop on network traffic and intercept valuable proprietary information. For example, an Internet Protocol security service that ensures a message is disclosed only to intended recipients by encrypting the data. See also cryptography; authentication; integrity; nonrepudiation.

console tree   The tree view pane in a Microsoft Management Console (MMC) that displays the hierarchical namespace. By default it is the left pane of the console window, but it can be hidden. The items in the console tree (for example, Web pages, folders, and controls) and their hierarchical organization determines the management capabilities of a console. See also Microsoft Management Console (MMC); namespace.

container object An object that can logically contain other objects. For example, a folder is a container object. See also noncontainer object; object.

copy backup A backup that copies all selected files but does not mark each file as having been backed up (that is, the archive bit is not set). A copy backup is useful between normal and incremental backups because copying does not affect these other backup operations. See also daily backup; differential backup; incremental backup; normal backup.

CPU See Central Processing Unit.

cryptography The art and science of information security. It provides four basic information security functions: confidentiality, integrity, authentication, and nonrepudiation. See also confidentiality; integrity; authentication; nonrepudiation.

D

daily backup A backup that copies all selected files that have been modified the day the daily backup is performed. The backed-up files are not marked as having been backed up (that is, the archive bit is not set). See also copy backup; differential backup; incremental backup; normal backup.

data confidentiality A service provided by cryptographic technology to assure that data can be read only by authorized users or programs. In a network, data confidentiality ensures that data cannot be read by intruders. Windows 2000 uses access control mechanisms and encryption, such as DES, 3DES and RSA encryption algorithms, to ensure data confidentiality.

Data Encryption Standard (DES) An encryption algorithm that uses a 56-bit key, and maps a 64-bit input block to a 64-bit output block. The key appears to be a 64-bit key, but one bit in each of the 8 bytes is used for odd parity, resulting in 56 bits of usable key.

data integrity A service provided by cryptographic technology that ensures data has not been modified. In a network environment, data integrity allows the receiver of a message to verify that data has not been modified in transit. Windows 2000 uses access control mechanisms and cryptography, such as RSA public-key signing and shared symmetric key one way hash algorithms, to ensure data integrity.

Data Link Control (DLC) A protocol used primarily for IBM mainframe computers and printer connectivity.

data packet A unit of information transmitted as a whole from one device to another on a network.

deallocate To return media to the available state after they have been used by an application.

decommissioned state A state that indicates that media have reached their allocation maximum.

decryption The process of making encrypted data readable again by converting ciphertext to plaintext. See also ciphertext; encryption; plaintext.

default gateway A configuration item for the TCP/IP protocol that is the IP address of a directly reachable IP router. Configuring a default gateway creates a default route in the IP routing table.

defragmentation The process of rewriting parts of a file to contiguous sectors on a hard disk to increase the speed of access and retrieval. When files are updated, the computer tends to save these updates on the largest continuous space on the hard disk, which is often on a different sector than the other parts of the file. When files are thus fragmented, the computer must search the hard disk each time the file is opened to find all of the parts of the file, which slows down response time. In Active Directory, defragmentation rearranges how the data is written in the directory database file to compact it. See also fragmentation.

dependent client For Message Queuing, a computer that requires synchronous access to a Message Queuing server to perform all standard message queuing operations, such as sending and receiving messages and creating queues. See also independent client; Message Queuing server.

desktop The on-screen work area in which windows, icons, menus, and dialog boxes appear.

destination directory The directory (or folder) to which files are copied or moved. See also source directory.

destination queue The queue on a target computer where messages sent from a source computer are delivered to and stored. As they traverse a Message Queuing network, the messages can be stored temporarily on intermediary Message Queuing routing servers. See also Message Queuing; Message Queuing routing; Message Queuing routing server; Message Queuing service.

device driver A program that allows a specific device, such as a modem, network adapter, or printer, to communicate with Windows 2000. Although a device can be installed on a system, Windows 2000 cannot use the device until the appropriate driver has been installed and configured. If a device is listed in the Hardware Compatibility List (HCL), a driver is usually included with Windows 2000. Device drivers load (for all enabled devices) when a computer is started, and thereafter run invisibly. See also Hardware Compatibility List (HCL).

Device Manager An administrative tool that can be used to manage the devices on your computer. Use Device Manager to view and change device properties, update device drivers, configure device settings, and remove devices.

Device Tree A hierarchical tree that contains the devices configured on the computer.

differential backup A backup that copies files created or changed since the last normal or incremental backup. It does not mark files as having been backed up (that is, the archive bit is not set). If you are performing a combination of normal and differential backups, restoring files and folders requires that you have the last normal as well as the last differential backup. See also copy backup; daily backup; incremental backup; normal backup.

digital audio tape (DAT) A magnetic medium for recording and storing digital audio data.

digital certificate See certificate.

digital linear tape (DLT) A magnetic medium for backing up data. DLT can transfer data faster than many other types of tape media.

digital signature A means for originators of a message, file, or other digitally-encoded information to bind their identity to the information. The process of digitally signing information entails transforming the information, as well as some secret information held by the sender, into a tag called a signature. Digital signatures are used in public key environments and they provide nonrepudiation and integrity services. See also public key cryptography.

digital subscriber line (DSL) A special communication line that uses modulation technology to maximize the amount of data that can be sent over copper wires. DSL is used for connections from telephone switching stations to a subscriber rather than between switching stations.

direct hosting A feature that allows Windows 2000 computers using Microsoft file and print sharing to communicate over a communications protocol, such as TCP or IPX, bypassing the NetBIOS layer.

direct memory access (DMA) Memory access that does not involve the microprocessor. DMA is frequently used for data transfer directly between memory and a peripheral device, such as a disk drive.

directory An information source that contains information about computer files or other objects. In a file system, a directory stores information about files. In a distributed computing environment (such as a Windows 2000 domain), the directory stores information about objects such as printers, applications, databases, and users.

directory service Both the directory information source and the service that make the information available and usable. A directory service enables the user to find an object given any one of its attributes. See also Active Directory; directory.

disable To make a device nonfunctional. For example, if a device in a hardware profile is disabled, the device cannot be used while using that hardware profile. Disabling a device frees the resources that were allocated to the device.

discretionary access control list (DACL) The part of an object's security descriptor that grants or denies specific users and groups permission to access the object. Only the owner of an object can change permissions granted or denied in a DACL; thus access to the object is at the owner's discretion. See also access control entry; object; security descriptor; system access control list.

disk bottleneck A condition that occurs when disk performance is reduced to the extent that overall system performance is affected.

disk quota The maximum amount of disk space available to a user.

dismount To remove a removable tape or disc from a drive. See also library.

distinguished name A name that uniquely identifies an object by using the relative distinguished name for the object, plus the names of container objects and domains that contain the object. The distinguished name identifies the object as well as its location in a tree. Every object in Active Directory has a distinguished name. An example of a distinguished name is CN=MyName,CN=Users,DC=Reskit,DC=Com.

This distinguished name identifies the "MyName" user object in the reskit.com domain.

Distributed file system (Dfs) A Windows 2000 service consisting of software residing on network servers and clients that transparently links shared folders located on different file servers into a single namespace for improved load sharing and data availability.

distribution folder The folder created on the Windows 2000 distribution server to contain the Setup files.

DMA See direct memory access.

DNS See Domain Name System.

DNS server A computer that runs DNS server programs containing name-to-IP address mappings, IP address-to-name mappings, information about the domain tree structure, and other information. DNS servers also attempt to resolve client queries.

DNS zone In a DNS database, a zone is a contiguous portion of the DNS tree that is administered as a single separate entity, by a DNS server. The zone contains resource records for all the names within the zone.

domain In Windows 2000 and Active Directory, a collection of computers defined by the administrator of a Windows 2000 Server network that share a common directory database. A domain has a unique name and provides access to the centralized user accounts and group accounts maintained by the domain administrator. Each domain has its own security policies and security relationships with other domains and represents a single security boundary of a Windows 2000 computer network. Active Directory is made up of one or more domains, each of which can span more than one physical location. For DNS, a domain is any tree or subtree within the DNS namespace. Although the names for DNS domains often correspond to Active Directory domains, DNS domains should not be confused with Windows 2000 and Active Directory networking domain.

domain controller For a Windows NT Server or Windows 2000 Server domain, the server that authenticates domain logons and maintains the security policy and the security accounts master database for a domain. Domain controllers manage user access to a network, which includes logging on, authentication, and access to the directory and shared resources.

domain local group A Windows 2000 group only available in native mode domains that can contain members from anywhere in the forest, in trusted forests, or in a trusted pre-Windows 2000 domain. Domain local groups can only grant permissions to resources within the domain in which they exist. Typically, domain local groups are used to gather security principals from across the forest to control access to resources within the domain.

domain name In Windows 2000 and Active Directory, the name given by an administrator to a collection of networked computers that share a common directory. For DNS, domain names are specific node names in the DNS namespace tree. DNS domain names use singular node names, known as "labels," joined together by periods (.) that indicate each node level in the namespace. See also Domain Name System (DNS); namespace.

Domain Name System (DNS) A hierarchical naming system used for locating domain names on the Internet and on private TCP/IP networks. DNS provides a service for mapping DNS domain names to IP addresses, and vice versa. This allows users, computers, and applications to query the DNS to specify remote systems by fully qualified domain names rather than by IP addresses. See also domain; Ping.

domain tree In DNS, the inverted hierarchical tree structure that is used to index domain names. Domain trees are similar in purpose and concept to the directory trees used by computer filing systems for disk storage. See also domain name; namespace.

dongle A device that attaches to a computer to control access to a particular application. Dongles provide the most effective means of copy protection. Typically, the dongle attaches to a computer's parallel port.

DOT4 See IEEE 1284.4

DSL See digital subscriber line.

dual boot A computer configuration that can start two different operating systems. See also multiple boot.

DVD decoder A hardware or software component that allows a digital video disc (DVD) drive to display movies on your computer screen. See also DVD disc; DVD drive.

DVD disc A type of optical disc storage technology. A digital video disc (DVD) looks like a CD-ROM disc, but it can store greater amounts of data. DVD discs are often used to store full-length movies and other multimedia content that requires large amounts of storage space. See also DVD decoder; DVD drive.

DVD drive A disk storage device that uses digital video disc (DVD) technology. A DVD drive reads both CD-ROM and DVD discs; however, a DVD decoder is necessary to display DVD movies on your computer screen. See also DVD decoder; DVD disc.

Dvorak keyboard An alternative keyboard with a layout that makes the most frequently typed characters more accessible to people who have difficulty typing on the standard QWERTY layout.

dynamic disk A physical disk that is managed by Disk Management. Dynamic disks can contain only dynamic volumes (that is, volumes created by using Disk Management). Dynamic disks cannot contain partitions or logical drives, nor can they be accessed by MS-DOS. See also dynamic volume; partition.

Dynamic Host Configuration Protocol (DHCP) A networking protocol that provides safe, reliable, and simple TCP/IP network configuration and offers dynamic configuration of Internet Protocol (IP) addresses for computers. DHCP ensures that address conflicts do not occur and helps conserve the use of IP addresses through centralized management of address allocation.

dynamic priority The priority value to which a thread's base priority is adjusted to optimize scheduling.

dynamic volume A logical volume that is created using Disk Management. Dynamic volumes include simple, spanned, striped, mirrored, and RAID-5 volumes. Dynamic volumes must be created on dynamic disks. See also dynamic disk; volume.

dynamic-link library (DLL) A feature of the Microsoft Windows family of operating systems and the OS/2 operating system. DLLs allow executable routines, generally serving a specific function or set of functions, to be stored separately as files with .dll extensions, and to be loaded only when needed by the program that calls them.

E

EAP See Extensible Authentication Protocol.

EIDE See Enhanced Integrated Drive Electronics.

embedded object Information created in another application that has been pasted inside a document. When information is embedded, you can edit it in the new document by using toolbars and menus from the original program. When you double-click the embedded icon, the toolbars and menus from the program used to create the information appear. Embedded information is not linked to the original file. If you change information in one place, it is not updated in the other. See also linked object.

emergency repair disk (ERD) A disk, created by the Backup utility, that contains copies of three of the files stored in the %SystemRoot%/Repair folder, including Setup.log that contains a list of system files installed on the computer. This disk can be used during the Emergency Repair Process to repair your computer if it will not start or if your system files are damaged or erased.

encapsulating security payload (ESP)
An IPSec protocol that provides confidentiality, in addition to authentication, integrity, and anti-replay. ESP can be used alone, in combination with AH, or nested with the Layer Two Tunneling Protocol (L2TP). ESP does not normally sign the entire packet unless it is being tunneled. Ordinarily, just the data payload is protected, not the IP header.

Encrypting File System (EFS) A new feature in Windows 2000 that protects sensitive data in files that are stored on disk using the NTFS file system. It uses symmetric key encryption in conjunction with public key technology to provide confidentiality for files. It runs as an integrated system service, which makes EFS easy to manage, difficult to attack, and transparent to the file owner and to applications.

encryption The process of disguising a message or data in such a way as to hide its substance.

encryption key A bit string that is used in conjunction with an encryption algorithm to encrypt and decrypt data. See also public key; private key; symmetric key.

Enhanced Integrated Drive Electronics (EIDE)
An extension of the IDE standard, EIDE is a hardware interface standard for disk drive designs that houses control circuits in the drives themselves. It allows for standardized interfaces to the system bus, while providing for advanced features, such as burst data transfers and direct data access.

Enterprise Resource Planning (ERP)
A software system designed to support and automate the processes of an organization, including manufacturing and distribution, accounting, project management and personnel functions.

environment variable A string consisting of environment information, such as a drive, path, or filename, associated with a symbolic name that can be used by Windows NT and Windows 2000. Use the System option in Control Panel or the set command from the command prompt to define environment variables.

ERD See emergency repair disk.

Ethernet An IEEE 802.3 standard for contention networks. Ethernet uses a bus or star topology and relies on the form of access known as Carrier Sense Multiple Access with Collision Detection (CSMA/DC) to regulate communication line traffic. Network nodes are linked by coaxial cable, fiber-optic cable, or by twisted-pair wiring. Data is transmitted in variable-length frames containing delivery and control information and up to 1,500 bytes of data. The Ethernet standard provides for baseband transmission at 10 megabits (10 million bits) per second.

exabyte Approximately one quintillion bytes, or one billion billion bytes.

expire interval For DNS, the number of seconds that DNS servers operating as secondary masters for a zone use to determine if zone data should be expired when the zone is not refreshed and renewed. See also zone.

explicit trust relationship A trust relationship from Windows NT in which an explicit link is made in one direction only. Explicit trusts can also exist between Windows NT domains and Windows 2000 domains, and between forests.

export In NFS, to make a file system available by a server to a client for mounting.

Extended Industry Standard Architecture (EISA)
A 32-bit bus standard introduced in 1988 by a consortium of nine computer-industry companies. EISA maintains compatibility with the earlier Industry Standard Architecture (ISA) but provides for additional features.

extended partition A portion of a basic disk that can contain logical drives. To have more than four volumes on your basic disk, you need to use an extended partition. Only one of the four partitions allowed per physical disk can be an extended partition, and no primary partition needs to be present to create an extended partition. You can create extended partitions only on basic disks. See also basic disk; logical drive; partition; primary partition; unallocated space.

Extensible Authentication Protocol (EAP)
An extension to PPP that allows for arbitrary authentication mechanisms to be employed for the validation of a PPP connection.

Extensible Markup Language (XML)
A meta-markup language that provides a format for describing structured data. This facilitates more precise declarations of content and more meaningful search results across multiple platforms. In addition, XML will enable a new generation of Web-based data viewing and manipulation applications.

F

FAT See file allocation table.

FAT32 A derivative of the file allocation table file system. FAT32 supports smaller cluster sizes than FAT in the same given disk space, which results in more efficient space allocation on FAT32 drives. See also file allocation table (FAT); NTFS file system.

fault tolerance The assurance of data integrity when hardware failures occur. On the Windows NT and Windows 2000 platforms, fault tolerance is provided by the Ftdisk.sys driver.

FDDI See Fiber Distributed Data Interface.

Fiber Distributed Data Interface (FDDI)
A type of network media designed to be used with fiber-optic cabling. See also LocalTalk; Token Ring.

file allocation table (FAT) A file system based on a file allocation table (FAT) maintained by some operating systems, including Windows NT and Windows 2000, to keep track of the status of various segments of disk space used for file storage.

file record The row in the master file table (MFT) that corresponds to a particular disk file. The file record is identified by its file reference.

file system In an operating system, the overall structure in which files are named, stored, and organized. NTFS, FAT, and FAT32 are types of file systems.

file system cache An area of physical memory that holds frequently-used pages. It allows applications and services to locate pages rapidly and reduces disk activity.

File Transfer Protocol (FTP)   A protocol that defines how to transfer files from one computer to another over the Internet. FTP is also a client/server application that moves files using this protocol.

filter   In IPSec, a rule that provides the ability to trigger security negotiations for a communication based on the source, destination, and type of IP traffic. See also search filter.

FilterKeys   A Windows 2000 accessibility feature that allows people with physical disabilities to adjust keyboard response time. See also BounceKeys; RepeatKeys; SlowKeys.

firewall   A combination of hardware and software that provides a security system, usually to prevent unauthorized access from outside to an internal network or intranet. A firewall prevents direct communication between network and external computers by routing communication through a proxy server outside of the network. The proxy server determines whether it is safe to let a file pass through to the network. A firewall is also called a security-edge gateway.

folder redirection   A Group Policy option that allows you to redirect designated folders to the network.

foreground boost   A mechanism that increases the priority of a foreground application.

forest   A collection of one or more Windows 2000 Active Directory trees, organized as peers and connected by two-way transitive trust relationships between the root domains of each tree. All trees in a forest share a common schema, configuration, and Global Catalog. When a forest contains multiple trees, the trees do not form a contiguous namespace.

fragmentation   The scattering of parts of the same disk file over different areas of the disk. Fragmentation occurs as files on a disk are deleted and new files are added. It slows disk access and degrades the overall performance of disk operations, although usually not severely. See also defragmentation.

free media pool   A logical collection of unused data-storage media that can be used by applications or other media pools. When media are no longer needed by an application, they are returned to a Free media pool so that they can be used again. See also media pool; Removable Storage.

G

gatekeeper   A server that uses a directory to perform name-to-IP address translation, admission control and call management services in H.323 conferencing.

gateway   A device connected to multiple physical TCP/IP networks, capable of routing or delivering IP packets between them. A gateway translates between different transport protocols or data formats (for example, IPX and IP) and is generally added to a network primarily for its translation ability. See also IP address; IP router.

Global Catalog   A domain controller that contains a partial replica of every domain directory partition in the forest as well as a full replica of its own domain directory partition and the schema and configuration directory partitions. The Global Catalog holds a replica of every object in Active Directory, but each object includes a limited number of its attributes. The attributes in the Global Catalog are those most frequently used in search operations (such as a user's first and last names) and those attributes that are required to locate a full replica of the object. The Global Catalog enables users and applications to find objects in Active Directory given one or more attributes of the target object, without knowing what domain holds the object. The Active Directory replication system builds the Global Catalog automatically. The attributes replicated into the Global Catalog include a base set defined by Microsoft. Administrators can specify additional properties to meet the needs of their installation.

global group   For Windows 2000 Server, a group that can be used in its own domain, in member servers and in workstations of the domain, and in trusting domains. In all those places a global group can be granted rights and permissions and can become a member of local groups. However, a global group can contain user accounts only from its own domain. See also group; local group.

globally unique identifier (GUID)   A 16-byte value generated from the unique identifier on a device, the current date and time, and a sequence number. A GUID is used to identify a particular device or component.

Graphical Identification and Authentication (GINA)   A DLL loaded during the Windows 2000 Winlogon process, which displays the standard logon dialog box, collects and processes user logon data for verification.

graphical user interface (GUI)   A display format, like that of Windows, that represents a program's functions with graphic images such as buttons and icons. GUIs allow a user to perform operations and make choices by pointing and clicking with a mouse.

group   A collection of users, computers, contacts, and other groups. Groups can be used as security or as e-mail distribution collections. Distribution groups are used only for e-mail. Security groups are used both to grant access to resources and as e-mail distribution lists. In a server cluster, a group is a collection of resources, and the basic unit of failover. See also domain local group; global group; native mode; universal group.

Group Identification (GID)   A group identifier that uniquely identifies a group of users. UNIX uses the GID to identify the group ownership of a file, and to determine access permissions.

group memberships   The groups to which a user account belongs. Permissions and rights granted to a group are also provided to its members. In most cases, the actions a user can perform in Windows 2000 are determined by the group memberships of the user account to which the user is logged on. See also group.

Group Policy   An administrator's tool for defining and controlling how programs, network resources, and the operating system operate for users and computers in an organization. In an Active Directory environment, Group Policy is applied to users or computers on the basis of their membership in sites, domains, or organizational units.

Group Policy object A collection of Group Policy settings. Group Policy objects are the documents created by the Group Policy snap-in. Group Policy objects are stored at the domain level, and they affect users and computers contained in sites, domains, and organizational units. Each Windows 2000-based computer has exactly one group of settings stored locally, called the local Group Policy object.

H

H.323 The ITU-T standard for multimedia communications over networks that do not provide a guaranteed quality of service. This standard provides specifications for workstations, devices, and services to carry real-time video, audio, and data or any combination of these elements. See also QoS.

hardware abstraction layer (HAL)
A thin layer of software provided by the hardware manufacturer that hides, or abstracts, hardware differences from higher layers of the operating system. Through the filter provided by the HAL, different types of hardware all look alike to the rest of the operating system. This allows Windows NT and Windows 2000 to be portable from one hardware platform to another. The HAL also provides routines that allow a single device driver to support the same device on all platforms. The HAL works closely with the kernel.

Hardware Compatibility List (HCL)
A list of the devices supported by Windows 2000, available from the Microsoft Web site.

hardware malfunction message A character-based, full-screen error message displayed on a blue background. It indicates the microprocessor detected a hardware error condition from which the system cannot recover.

hardware profile A set of changes to the standard configuration of devices and services (including drivers and Win32 services) loaded by Windows 2000 when the system starts. For example, a hardware profile can include an instruction to disable (that is, not load) a driver, or an instruction not to connect an undocked laptop computer to the network. Because of the instructions in this subkey, users can modify the service configuration for a particular use while preserving the standard configuration unchanged for more general uses.

hardware type A classification for similar devices. For example, Imaging Device is a hardware type for digital cameras and scanners.

heartbeat thread A thread initiated by the Windows NT Virtual DOS Machine (NTVDM) process that interrupts every 55 milliseconds to simulate a timer interrupt.

hop In data communications, one segment of the path between routers on a geographically dispersed network. A hop is comparable to one "leg" of a journey that includes intervening stops between the starting point and the destination. The distance between each of those stops (routers) is a communications hop.

Hosts A local text file in the same format as the 4.3 Berkeley Software Distribution (BSD) UNIX/etc/hosts file. This file maps host names to IP addresses. In Windows 2000, this file is stored in the \%SystemRoot%\System32\Drivers\Etc folder.

hot keys A Windows feature that allows quick activation of specified accessibility features through a combination of keys pressed in unison.

HTML See Hypertext Markup Language.

HTML+Time   A new feature in Microsoft Internet Explorer 5 that adds timing and media synchronization support to HTML pages. Using a few Extensible Markup Language (XML)-based elements and attributes, you can add images, video, and sounds to an HTML page, and synchronize them with HTML text elements over a specified amount of time. In short, you can use HTML+TIME technology to quickly and easily create multimedia-rich, interactive presentations, with little or no scripting.

HTTP   See Hypertext Transfer Protocol.

Human Interface Device (HID)   A firmware specification that is a new standard for input and output devices such as drawing tablets, keyboards, USB speakers, and other specialized devices designed to improve accessibility.

Hypertext Markup Language (HTML)
A simple markup language used to create hypertext documents that are portable from one platform to another. HTML files are simple ASCII text files with embedded codes (indicated by markup tags) to indicate formatting and hypertext links. HTML is used for formatting documents on the World Wide Web.

Hypertext Transfer Protocol (HTTP)
The protocol used to transfer information on the World Wide Web. An HTTP address (one kind of Uniform Resource Locator [URL]) takes the form: http://www.microsoft.com.

I

I/O request packet (IRP)   Data structures that drivers use to communicate with each other.

ICM   See Image Color Management.

IDE   See Integrated device electronics.

IEEE 1284.4   An IEEE specification, also called DOT4, for supporting multi-function peripherals (MFPs). Windows 2000 has a driver called DOT4 is a driver that creates different port settings for each function of an MFP, enabling Windows 2000 print servers to simultaneously send data to multiple parts of an MFP.

IEEE 1394 Firewire   A standard for high-speed serial devices such as digital video and digital audio editing equipment.

IIS   See Internet Information Services.

ILS   See Internet locator service.

Image Color Management (ICM)   The process of image output correction. ICM attempts to make the output more closely match the colors that are input or scanned.

impersonation   A circumstance that occurs when Windows NT or Windows 2000 allows one process to take on the security attributes of another.

import media pool   A repository where Removable Storage puts media when it recognizes the on-media identifier (OMID), but does not have the media cataloged in the current Removable Storage database.

in-routing server (InRS)   A Message Queuing routing server that provides session concentration by acting as a gateway for all incoming messages for one or more Message Queuing independent clients. Message Queuing independent clients can be configured to use an InRS. See also Message Queuing; Message Queuing routing; Message Queuing routing server; Message Queuing server; session concentration.

incremental backup A backup that copies only those files created or changed since the last normal or incremental backup. It marks files as having been backed up (that is, the archive bit is set). If a combination of normal and incremental backups is used to restore your data, you need to have the last normal backup and all subsequent incremental backup sets. See also copy backup; daily backup; differential backup; normal backup.

independent client For Message Queuing, a computer running Windows 2000 Professional that can create queues and store messages locally without synchronous access to a Message Queuing server. Independent clients can also use Message Queuing servers to provide efficient message routing. See also dependent client; Message Queuing server; routing services.

independent software vendors (ISVs)
A third-party software developer; an individual or an organization that independently creates computer software.

Industry Standard Architecture (ISA)
A bus design specification that allows components to be added as cards plugged into standard expansion slots in IBM Personal Computers and IBM compatible computers. Originally introduced in the IBM PC/XT with an 8-bit data path, ISA was expanded in 1984, when IBM introduced the PC/AT, to permit a 16-bit data path. A 16-bit ISA slot consists of two separate 8-bit slots mounted end-to-end so that a single 16-bit card plugs into both slots. An 8-bit expansion card can be inserted and used in a 16-bit slot (it occupies only one of the two slots), but a 16-bit expansion card cannot be used in an 8-bit slot. See also Extended Industry Standard Architecture (EISA).

infrared (IR) Light that is beyond red in the color spectrum. While the light is not visible to the human eye, infrared transmitters and receivers can send and receive infrared signals. See also Infrared Data Association; infrared device; infrared port.

Infrared Data Association (IrDA) A networking protocol used to transmit data created by infrared devices. Infrared Data Association is also the name of the industry organization of computer, component, and telecommunications vendors who establish the standards for infrared communication between computers and peripheral devices, such as printers. See also infrared; infrared device; infrared port.

infrared device A computer, or a computer peripheral such as a printer, that can communicate using infrared light. See also infrared.

infrared port An optical port on a computer that enables communication with other computers or devices by using infrared light, without cables. Infrared ports can be found on some portable computers, printers, and cameras. See also infrared device.

input/output (I/O) port A channel through which data is transferred between a device and the microprocessor. The port appears to the microprocessor as one or more memory addresses that it can use to send or receive data.

insert/eject (IE) port IE ports, also called "mailslots," offer limited access to the cartridges in a library managed by Removable Storage. When an administrator adds cartridges to a library through an IE port, the cartridges are placed in the IE port and then the library uses the transport to move the cartridges from the IE port to a slot. Some libraries have no IE ports; others have several. Some IE ports handle only one cartridge at a time; others can handle several at one time.

instantaneous counter A type of counter that displays the most recent measurement taken by the Performance console.

Institute of Electrical and Electronics Engineers (IEEE)
An organization of engineering and electronics professionals that are notable for developing standards for hardware and software.

integrated device electronics (IDE)
A type of disk-drive interface in which the controller electronics reside on the drive itself, eliminating the need for a separate adapter card. IDE offers advantages such as look-ahead caching to increase overall performance.

Integrated Services Digital Network (ISDN)
A type of phone line used to enhance WAN speeds. ISDN lines can transmit at speeds of 64 or 128 kilobits per second, as opposed to standard phone lines, which typically transmit at 28.8 kilobits per second. An ISDN line must be installed by the phone company at both the server site and the remote site. See also wide area network (WAN).

integrity A basic security function of cryptography. Integrity provides verification that the original contents of information have not been altered or corrupted. Without integrity, someone might alter information or the information might become corrupted, but the alteration can go undetected. For example, an Internet Protocol security property that protects data from unauthorized modification in transit, ensuring that the data received is exactly the same as the data sent. Hash functions sign each packet with a cryptographic checksum, which the receiving computer checks before opening the packet. If the packet-and therefore signature-has changed, the packet is discarded. See also cryptography; authentication; confidentiality; nonrepudiation.

IntelliMirror A set of Windows 2000 features used for desktop change and configuration management. When IntelliMirror is used in both the server and client, the users' data, applications, and settings follow them when they move to another computer.

inter-site routing The process of routing Message Queuing messages between Windows 2000 sites. See also intra-site routing; Message Queuing; Message Queuing routing; Message Queuing routing server; Message Queuing server.

interactive logon A network logon from a computer keyboard, when the user types information in the Logon Information dialog box displayed by the computer's operating system.

Internet A worldwide public TCP/IP internetwork consisting of thousands of networks, connecting research facilities, universities, libraries, and private companies.

Internet Control Message Protocol (ICMP)
A required maintenance protocol in the TCP/IP suite that reports errors and allows simple connectivity. ICMP is used by the Ping tool to perform TCP/IP troubleshooting.

Internet Information Services (IIS)
Software services that support Web site creation, configuration, and management, along with other Internet functions. Internet Information Services include Network News Transfer Protocol (NNTP), File Transfer Protocol (FTP), and Simple Mail Transfer Protocol (SMTP). See also File Transfer Protocol (FTP); Network News Transfer Protocol (NNTP); Simple Mail Transfer Protocol (SMTP).

Internet Key Exchange (IKE) A protocol that establishes the security association and shared keys necessary for two parties to communicate with Internet Protocol security.

Internet locator service (ILS) An optional component of Microsoft Site Server that creates a dynamic directory of videoconferencing users.

Internet Printing Protocol (IPP) The protocol that uses the Hypertext Transfer Protocol (HTTP) to send print jobs to printers throughout the world. Windows 2000 supports Internet Printing Protocol (IPP) version 1.0.

Internet Protocol (IP) A routable protocol in the TCP/IP protocol suite that is responsible for IP addressing, routing, and the fragmentation and reassembly of IP packets.

Internet Protocol security (IPSec)
A set of industry-standard, cryptography-based protection services and protocols. IPSec protects all protocols in the TCP/IP protocol suite and Internet communications using L2TP. See also Layer Two Tunneling Protocol (L2TP).

Internet service provider (ISP) A company that provides individuals or companies access to the Internet and the World Wide Web. An ISP provides a telephone number, a user name, a password and other connection information so users can connect their computers to the ISP's computers. An ISP typically charges a monthly and/or hourly connection fee.

Internetwork Packet Exchange (IPX)
A network protocol native to NetWare that controls addressing and routing of packets within and between LANs. IPX does not guarantee that a message will be complete (no lost packets). See also Internetwork Packet Exchange/Sequenced Packet Exchange (IPX/SPX).

Internetwork Packet Exchange/Sequenced Packet Exchange (IPX/SPX)
Transport protocols used in Novell NetWare and other networks.

interrupt A request for attention from the processor. When the processor receives an interrupt, it suspends its current operations, saves the status of its work, and transfers control to a special routine known as an interrupt handler, which contains the instructions for dealing with the particular situation that caused the interrupt.

interrupt request (IRQ) A signal sent by a device to get the attention of the processor when the device is ready to accept or send information. Each device sends its interrupt requests over a specific hardware line, numbered from 0 to 15. Each device must be assigned a unique IRQ number.

intra-site routing The process of routing Message Queuing messages within a Windows 2000 site. See also inter-site routing; Message Queuing; Message Queuing routing; Message Queuing routing server; Message Queuing server.

intranet A network within an organization that uses Internet technologies and protocols, but is available only to certain people, such as employees of a company. An intranet is also called a private network.

IP See Internet Protocol.

IP address A 32-bit address used to identify a node on an IP internetwork. Each node on the IP internetwork must be assigned a unique IP address, which is made up of the network ID, plus a unique host ID. This address is typically represented with the decimal value of each octet separated by a period (for example, 192.168.7.27). In Windows 2000, the IP address can be configured manually or dynamically through DHCP. See also Dynamic Host Configuration Protocol (DHCP); node.

IP router A system connected to multiple physical TCP/IP networks that can route or deliver IP packets between the networks. See also packet; router; routing; Transmission Control Protocol/Internet Protocol.

IPP See Internet Printing Protocol.

IPSec See Internet Protocol security.

IPSec driver A driver that uses the IP Filter List from the active IPSec policy to watch for outbound IP packets that must be secured and inbound IP packets that need to be verified and decrypted.

IPSec filter A part of IPSec security rules which make up an IPSec security policy. IPSec filters determine whether a data packet needs an IPSec action and what the IPSec action is, such as permit, block, or secure. Filters can classify traffic by criteria including source IP address, source subnet mask, destination IP address, IP protocol type, source port, and destination port. Filters are not specific to a network interface. See also IPSec security rules.

IPSec security rules Rules contained in the IPSec policy that govern how and when an IPSec is invoked. A rule triggers and controls secure communication when a particular source, destination, or traffic type is found. Each IPSec policy may contain one or many rules; any of which may apply to a particular packet. Default rules are provided which encompass a variety of clients and server-based communications or rules can be modified to meet custom requirements.

IPX See Internetwork Packet Exchange.

IrDA See Infrared Data Association.

IRP See I/O request packet.

IRQ See Interrupt Request.

IrTran-p A protocol that transfers images from cameras to Windows 2000 computers using infrared transmissions, making a physical cable connection unnecessary.

isochronous Time dependent. Refers to processes where data must be delivered within certain time constraints. Multimedia streams require an isochronous transport mechanism to ensure that data is delivered as fast as it is displayed, and to ensure that the audio is synchronized with the video.

J

job object A feature in the Win32 API set that makes it possible for groups of processes to be managed with respect to their processor usage and other factors.

K

Kerberos authentication protocol
An authentication mechanism used to verify user or host identity. The Kerberos v5 authentication protocol is the default authentication service for Windows 2000. Internet Protocol security and the QoS Admission Control Service use the Kerberos protocol for authentication. See also Internet Protocol security (IPSec); NTLM authentication protocol; QoS Admission Control Service.

kernel The core of layered architecture that manages the most basic operations of the operating system and the computer's processor for Windows NT and Windows 2000. The kernel schedules different blocks of executing code, called threads, for the processor to keep it as busy as possible and coordinates multiple processors to optimize performance. The kernel also synchronizes activities among Executive-level subcomponents, such as I/O Manager and Process Manager, and handles hardware exceptions and other hardware-dependent functions. The kernel works closely with the hardware abstraction layer.

key A secret code or number required to read, modify, or verify secured data. Keys are used in conjunction with algorithms to secure data. Windows 2000 automatically handles key generation. For the registry, a key is an entry in the registry that can contain both subkeys and entries. In the registry structure, keys are analogous to folders, and entries are analogous to files. In the Registry Editor window, a key appears as a file folder in the left pane. In an answer file, keys are character strings that specify parameters from which Setup obtains the needed data for unattended installation of the operating system.

keyboard filters Special timing and other devices that compensate for erratic motion tremors, slow response time, and other mobility impairments.

Korn shell (ksh) A command shell which provides the following functionality: file input and output redirection; command line editing using vi; command history; integer arithmetic; pattern matching and variable substitution; command name abbreviation (aliasing); built-in commands for writing shell programs.

L

L2TP See Layer Two Tunneling Protocol.

LAN See local area network.

Last Known Good Configuration A hardware configuration available by pressing F8 during startup. If the current hardware settings prevent the computer from starting, the Last Known Good Configuration can allow the computer to be started and the configuration to be examined. When the Last Known Good Configuration is used, later configuration changes are lost.

layer 2 forwarding (L2F) Permits the tunneling of the link layer of higher-level protocols. Using these tunnels, it is possible to separate the location of the initial dial-up server from the physical location at which the dial-up protocol connection is terminated and access to the network is provided. See also L2TP; tunnel.

Layer two Tunneling Protocol (L2TP)
A tunneling protocol that encapsulates PPP frames to be sent over IP, X.25, Frame Relay, or ATM networks. L2TP is a combination of the Point-to-Point Tunneling Protocol (PPTP) and Layer 2 Forwarding (L2F), a technology proposed by Cisco Systems, Inc.

legend The area of the System Monitor graph or histogram display that shows computer name, object name, counter name, instances, and other information as a reference to the lines in the graph or the bars in the histogram.

library A data-storage system, usually managed by Removable Storage. A library consists of removable media (such as tapes or discs) and a hardware device that can read from or write to the media. There are two major types of libraries: robotic libraries (automated multiple-media, multidrive devices) and stand-alone drive libraries (manually operated, single-drive devices). A robotic library is also called a jukebox or changer. See also Removable Storage.

library request A request for an online library or stand-alone drive to perform a task. This request can be issued by an application or by Removable Storage.

Lightweight Directory Access Protocol (LDAP)
A directory service protocol that runs directly over TCP/IP and the primary access protocol for Active Directory. LDAP version 3 is defined by a set of Proposed Standard documents in Internet Engineering Task Force (IETF) RFC 2251. See also Lightweight Directory Access Protocol application programming interface (LDAP API).

Lightweight Directory Access Protocol application programming interface (LDAP API)

An API for experienced C programmers who want to enable new or existing applications to connect to, search, and update LDAP servers. You can use the LDAP API to write directory-enabled applications that allow LDAP client applications to search for and retrieve information from an LDAP server. LDAP API enables the modification of directory objects, where such modifications are permitted. There are also functions that provide access control for servers, by allowing clients to authenticate themselves.

The LDAP API is delivered with Windows 2000 and is found in the Wldap32.dll file. The Microsoft LDAP API is compatible with both version 2 and version 3 of the LDAP standard.

Line Printer A connectivity tool that runs on client systems and is used to print files to a computer running an LPD server. See also Line Printer Daemon (LPD).

Line Printer Daemon (LPD) A service on the print server that receives documents (print jobs) from line printer remote (LPR) tools running on client systems. See also Line Printer Remote (LPR).

Line Printer Port Monitor A port monitor that is used to send jobs over TCP/IP from the client running Lprmon.dll to a print server running an LPD (Line Printer Daemon) service. Line Printer Port Monitor can be used to enable Internet printing, UNIX print servers, or Windows 2000 print servers over a TCP/IP network.

Line Printer Remote (LPR) See Line Printer.

linked object An object that is inserted into a document but still exists in the source file. When information is linked, the new document is updated automatically if the information in the original document changes. See also embedded object.

local area network (LAN) A communications network connecting a group of computers, printers, and other devices located within a relatively limited area (for example, a building). A LAN allows any connected device to interact with any other on the network. See also wide area network (WAN).

local computer A computer that can be accessed directly without using a communications line or a communications device, such as a network adapter or a modem. Similarly, running a local program means running the program on your computer, as opposed to running it from a server.

local group For computers running Windows 2000 Professional and member servers, a group that is granted permissions and rights from its own computer to only those resources on its own computer on which the group resides. See also global group.

Local Security Authority (LSA) A protected subsystem that authenticates and logs users onto the local system. In addition, the LSA maintains information about all aspects of local security on a system (collectively known as the local security policy), and provides various services for translation between names and identifiers.

local user profile A computer-based record maintained about an authorized user that is created automatically on the computer the first time a user logs on to a computer running Windows 2000.

localmon.dll The standard print monitor for use with printers connected directly to your computer. If you add a printer to your computer using a serial or parallel port (such as COM1 or LPT1), this is the monitor that is used.

LocalTalk The Apple networking hardware built into every Macintosh computer. LocalTalk includes the cables and connector boxes to connect components and network devices that are part of the AppleTalk network system. LocalTalk was formerly known as the AppleTalk Personal Network.

locator service In a distributed system, a feature that allows a client to find a shared resource or server without providing an address or full name. Generally associated with Active Directory, which provides a locator service.

logical drive A volume created within an extended partition on a basic disk. You can format and assign a drive letter to a logical drive. Only basic disks can contain logical drives. A logical drive cannot span multiple disks. See also basic disk; basic volume; extended partition.

logical volume A volume created within an extended partition on a basic disk. You can format and assign a drive letter to a logical drive. Only basic disks can contain logical drives. A logical drive cannot span multiple disks. See also basic disk; basic volume; extended partition.

logon script Files that can be assigned to user accounts. Typically a batch file, a logon script runs automatically every time the user logs on. It can be used to configure a user's working environment at every logon, and it allows an administrator to influence a user's environment without managing all aspects of it. A logon script can be assigned to one or more user accounts. See also batch program.

long file name (LFN) A folder name or file name on the FAT file system that is longer than the 8.3 file name standard (up to eight characters followed by a period and an extension of up to three characters). Windows 2000 supports long file names up to the file-name limit of 255 characters. Macintosh users can assign long names to files and folders on the server and, using Services for Macintosh, long names to Macintosh-accessible volumes can be assigned when created. Windows 2000 automatically translates long names of files and folders to 8.3 names for MS-DOS and Windows 3.*x* users. See also name mapping.

loopback address The address of the local computer used for routing outgoing packets back to the source computer. This address is used primarily for testing.

M

MAC See media access control.

magazine A collection of storage locations, also called "slots," for cartridges in a library managed by Removable Storage. Magazines are usually removable.

magneto-optic (MO) disk A high-capacity, erasable storage medium which uses laser beams to heat the disk and magnetically arrange the data.

Magnifier A screen enlarger that magnifies a portion of the screen in a separate window for users with low vision and for those who require occasional screen magnification for such tasks as editing art.

manual caching A method of manually designating network files and folders so they are stored on a user's hard disk and accessible when the user is not connected to the network.

Master Boot Record (MBR) The first sector on a hard disk, this data structure starts the process of booting the computer. It is the most important area on a hard disk. The MBR contains the partition table for the disk and a small amount of executable code called the master boot code.

master file table (MFT) The database that tracks the contents of an NTFS volume. The MFT is a table whose rows correspond to files on the volume and whose columns correspond to the attributes of each file.

maximum password age The period of time a password can be used before the system requires the user to change it.

media The physical material on which information is recorded and stored.

media access control A sublayer of the IEEE 802 specifications that defines network access methods and framing.

media label library A dynamic-link library (DLL) that can interpret the format of a media label written by a Removable Storage application.

media pool Logical collections of removable media that have the same management policies. Media pools are used by applications to control access to specific tapes or discs within libraries managed by Removable Storage. There are four media pools: Unrecognized, Import, Free, and application-specific. Each media pool can only hold either media or other media pools. See also Removable Storage.

media states Descriptions of conditions in which Removable Storage has placed a cartridge that it is managing. The states include Idle, In Use, Mounted, Loaded, and Unloaded.

memory leak A condition that occurs when applications allocate memory for use but do not free allocated memory when finished.

Message Queuing A messaging queuing service that allows Message Queuing-based applications running at different times to communicate across heterogeneous networks and systems that might be temporarily offline. Applications send messages to Message Queuing, and Message Queuing uses queues to ensure that the messages eventually reach their destination. Message Queuing provides guaranteed message delivery, efficient routing, security, and priority-based messaging.

Message Queuing routing A direct connection (or session) established by Message Queuing) using the underlying protocol if possible. When a direct connection is not possible or not allowed, Message Queuing uses its own routing system. Message Queuing routing occurs when one or more of the following conditions exist: A session cannot be established between the sender and the receiver (for example, when the target computer is offline). In-routing servers (InRSs) or out-routing servers (OutRSs) are defined for the sender or receiver. Messages must travel between two sites. See also In-routing servers (InRSs); Message Queuing; Message Queuing server; out-routing servers (InRSs).

Message Queuing routing server Supports dynamic routing and intermediate store-and-forward message queuing. Message Queuing routing servers allow computers that use different protocols to communicate. If configured to do so, Message Queuing routing servers can provide session concentration. See also Message Queuing; Message Queuing routing; Message Queuing routing server; Message Queuing server; session concentration.

Message Queuing server For Message Queuing, a computer that can provide message queuing, routing, and directory services to client computers. Message Queuing servers can be used to provide message routing and session concentration for independent clients, provide message routing between sites over routing links, create queues and store messages for dependent clients and Access information in Active Directory (if installed on a Windows 2000 domain controller). See also Active Directory; dependent client; independent client; routing link; routing services; session concentration.

Message Queuing service The Message Queuing component that provides core Message Queuing functionality. This service runs on all Message Queuing servers and independent clients. See also Message Queuing; Message Queuing server.

metric A number used to indicate the cost of a route in the IP routing table to enable the selection of the best route among possible multiple routes to the same destination.

MFP See multi-function peripherals

Microsoft Challenge Handshake Authentication Protocol version 1 (MS-CHAP v1)
An encrypted authentication mechanism for PPP connections similar to CHAP. The remote access server sends a challenge to the remote access client that consists of a session ID and an arbitrary challenge string. The remote access client must return the user name and a Message Digest 4 (MD4) hash of the challenge string, the session ID, and the MD4-hashed password.

Microsoft Challenge Handshake Authentication Protocol version 2 (MS-CHAP v2)
An encrypted authentication mechanism for PPP connections that provides stronger security than CHAP and MS-CHAP v1. MS-CHAP v2 provides mutual authentication and asymmetric encryption keys.

Microsoft Indexing Service Software that provides search functions for documents stored on disk, allowing users to search for specific document text or properties.

Microsoft Internet Directory A Web site provided and maintained by Microsoft used by applications such as NetMeeting to locate people to call on the Internet. The Microsoft Internet Directory is operated through an ILS server.

Microsoft Management Console (MMC)
A framework for hosting administrative consoles. A console is defined by the items on its console tree, which might include folders or other containers, World Wide Web pages, and other administrative items. A console has one or more windows that can provide views of the console tree and the administrative properties, services, and events that are acted on by the items in the console tree. The main MMC window provides commands and tools for authoring consoles. The authoring features of MMC and the console tree might be hidden when a console is in User Mode. See also console tree.

Microsoft Point-to-Point Encryption (MPPE)
A 128/40-bit encryption algorithm using RSA RC4. MPPE provides for packet security between the client and the tunnel server and is useful where IPSec is not available. The 40-bit version addresses localization issues based on current export restrictions. MPPE is compatible with Network Address Translation. See also IPSec.

Microsoft Tape Format (MTF) The data format used for tapes supported by the Backup application in Windows 2000. There are three major components to MTF: a Tape Data Block (Tape DBLK), otherwise known as the tape header; one or more Data Sets; and On Tape Catalog Information (On Tape Catalog Inf).

Minidrivers Relatively small, simple drivers or files that contain additional instructions needed by a specific hardware device, to interface with the universal driver for a class of devices.

minimum TTL A default Time To Live (TTL) value set in seconds for use with all resource records in a zone. This value is set in the start of authority (SOA) resource record for each zone. By default, the DNS server includes this value in query answers to inform recipients how long it can store and use resource records provided in the query answer before they must expire the stored records data. When TTL values are set for individual resource records, those values will override the minimum TTL. See also Time To Live (TTL).

mirrored volume A fault-tolerant volume that duplicates data on two physical disks. The mirror is always located on a different disk. If one of the physical disks fails, the data on the failed disk becomes unavailable, but the system continues to operate by using the unaffected disk. A mirrored volume is slower than a RAID-5 volume in read operations but faster in write operations. Mirrored volumes can only be created on dynamic disks. In Windows NT 4.0, a mirrored volume was known as a mirror set. See also dynamic disk; dynamic volume; fault tolerance; redundant array of independent disks (RAID); volume.

mixed mode The default mode setting for domains on Windows 2000 domain controllers. Mixed mode allows Windows 2000 domain controllers and Windows NT backup domain controllers to co-exist in a domain. Mixed mode does not support the universal and nested group enhancements of Windows 2000. You can change the domain mode setting to Windows 2000 native mode after all Windows NT domain controllers are either removed from the domain or upgraded to Windows 2000. See also native mode.

Mode Pruning A Windows 2000 feature that can be used to remove display modes that the monitor cannot support.

mount To place a removable tape or disc into a drive. See also library.

MouseKeys A feature in Microsoft Windows that allows use of the numeric keyboard to move the mouse pointer.

MP3 Audio compressed in the MPEG1 Layer 3 format

MPEG-2 A standard of video compression and file format developed by the Moving Pictures Experts Group. MPEG-2 offers video resolutions of 720 x 480 and 128 x 720 at 60 frames per second, with full CD-quality audio.

MS-CHAPv2 See Microsoft Challenge Handshake Authentication Protocol version 2.

Multicast IP IP packets sent from a single destination IP address but received and processed by multiple IP hosts, regardless of their location on an IP internetwork.

multicasting The process of sending a message simultaneously to more than one destination on a network.

multihomed computer A computer that has multiple network adapters or that has been configured with multiple IP addresses for a single network adapter.

multiple boot A computer configuration that runs two or more operating systems. For example, Windows 98, MS-DOS, and Windows 2000 operating systems can be installed on the same computer. When the computer is started, any one of the operating systems can be selected. See also dual boot.

N

name devolution A process by which a DNS resolver appends one or more domain names to an unqualified domain name, making it a fully qualified domain name, and then submits the fully qualified domain name to a DNS server.

namespace A set of unique names for resources or items used in a shared computing environment. The names in a namespace can be resolved to the objects they represent. For Microsoft Management Console (MMC), the namespace is represented by the console tree, which displays all of the snap-ins and resources that are accessible to a console. For Domain Name System (DNS), namespace is the vertical or hierarchical structure of the domain name tree. For example, each domain label, such as "host1" or "example," used in a fully qualified domain name, such as "host1.example.microsoft.com," indicates a branch in the domain namespace tree. For Active Directory, namespace corresponds to the DNS namespace in structure, but resolves Active Directory object names.

naming service A service, such as that provided by WINS or DNS, that allows friendly names to be resolved to an address or other specially defined resource data that is used to locate network resources of various types and purposes.

Narrator A synthesized text-to-speech utility for users who have low vision. Narrator reads aloud most of what the screen displays.

native mode The condition in which all domain controllers within a domain are Windows 2000 domain controllers and an administrator has enabled native mode operation (through Active Directory Users and Computers). See also mixed mode.

NDIS miniport drivers A type of minidriver that interfaces network class devices to NDIS.

nested groups A Windows 2000 capability available only in native mode that allows the creation of groups within groups. See also domain local group; forest; global group; trusted forest; universal group.

NetBEUI See NetBIOS Extended User Interface.

NetBIOS Extended User Interface (NetBEUI) A network protocol native to Microsoft Networking, that is usually used in local area networks of one to 200 clients. NetBEUI uses Token Ring source routing as its only method of routing. It is the Microsoft implementation of the NetBIOS standard.

NetBIOS over TCP/IP (NetBT) A feature that provides the NetBIOS programming interface over the TCP/IP protocol. It is used for monitoring routed servers that use NetBIOS name resolution.

NetWare Novell's network operating system.

network adapter Software or a hardware plug-in board that connects a node or host to a local area network.

network basic input/output system (NetBIOS) An application programming interface (API) that can be used by applications on a local area network or computers running MS-DOS, OS/2, or some version of UNIX. NetBIOS provides a uniform set of commands for requesting lower level network services.

Network Control Protocol (NCP) A protocol within the PPP protocol suite that negotiates the parameters of an individual LAN protocol such as TCP/IP or IPX.

Network Driver Interface Specification (NDIS)
A software component that provides
Windows 2000 network protocols a common
interface for communications with network
adapters. NDIS allows more than one transport
protocol to be bound and operate simultaneously
over a single network adapter card.

network file system (NFS) A service for
distributed computing systems that provides a
distributed file system, eliminating the need for
keeping multiple copies of files on separate
computers.

Network Information Service (NIS)
Formerly known as Yellow Pages, NIS is a
distributed database service that allows for a
shared set of system configuration files on UNIX-
based systems, including password, hosts, and
group files.

Network News Transfer Protocol (NNTP)
A member of the TCP/IP suite of protocols, used
to distribute network news messages to NNTP
servers and clients, or news-readers, on the
Internet. NNTP is designed so that news articles
are stored on a server in a central database, and
the user selects specific items to read. See also
Transmission Control Protocol/Internet Protocol
(TCP/IP).

Network security administrators Users who
manage network and information security.
Network security administrators should
implement a security plan that addresses network
security threats.

node In tree structures, a location on the tree that
can have links to one or more items below it. In
local area networks (LANs), a device that is
connected to the network and is capable of
communicating with other network devices. In a
server cluster, a server that has Cluster service
software installed and is a member of the cluster.
See also local area network (LAN).

noncontainer object An object that cannot
logically contain other objects. A file is a
noncontainer object. See also container object;
object.

nonrepudiation A basic security function of
cryptography. Nonrepudiation provides assurance
that a party in a communication cannot falsely
deny that a part of the communication occurred.
Without nonrepudiation, someone can
communicate and then later deny the
communication or claim that the communication
occurred at a different time. See also
cryptography; authentication; confidentiality;
integrity.

nonresident attribute A file attribute whose value
is contained in one or more runs, or extents,
outside the master file table (MFT) record and
separate from the MFT.

nontransitive trust relationship A type of trust
relationship that is bounded by the two domains
in the relationship. For example, if domain A
trusts domain B and domain B trusts domain C,
there is no trust relationship between domain A
and domain C. A nontransitive trust relationship
can be a one-way or two-way relationship. It is
the only type of trust relationship that can exist
between a Windows 2000 domain and a
Windows NT domain or between Windows 2000
domains in different forests. See also trust
relationship; transitive trust relationship.

normal backup A backup that copies all selected
files and marks each file as backed up (that is, the
archive bit is set). With normal backups, only the
most recent copy of the backup file or tape is
needed to restore all of the files. A normal backup
is usually performed the first time a backup set is
created. See also copy backup; daily backup;
differential backup; incremental backup.

Novell Directory Services (NDS) On networks running Novell NetWare 4.*x* and NetWare 5.*x*, a distributed database that maintains information about every resource on the network and provides access to these resources.

NT-1 (Network Terminator 1) A device that terminates an ISDN line at the connection location, commonly through a connection port.

NTFS file system A recoverable file system designed for use specifically with Windows NT and Windows 2000. NTFS uses database, transaction-processing, and object paradigms to provide data security, file system reliability, and other advanced features. It supports file system recovery, large storage media, and various features for the POSIX subsystem. It also supports object-oriented applications by treating all files as objects with user-defined and system-defined attributes.

NTLM A security package that provides authentication between clients and servers. See also NTLM authentication protocol.

NTLM authentication protocol A challenge/response authentication protocol. The NTLM authentication protocol was the default for network authentication in Windows NT version 4.0 and earlier. The protocol continues to be supported in Windows 2000 but no longer is the default. See also authentication.

NWLink An implementation of the Internetwork Packet Exchange (IPX), Sequenced Packet Exchange (SPX), and NetBIOS protocols used in Novell networks. NWLink is a standard network protocol that supports routing and can support NetWare client/server applications, where NetWare-aware Sockets-based applications communicate with IPX/SPX Sockets-based applications. See also Internetwork Packet Exchange (IPX); network basic input/output system (NetBIOS).

O

object An entity, such as a file, folder, shared folder, printer, or Active Directory object, described by a distinct, named set of attributes. For example, the attributes of a File object include its name, location, and size; the attributes of an Active Directory User object might include the user's first name, last name, and e-mail address. For OLE and ActiveX objects, an object can also be any piece of information that can be linked to, or embedded into, another object. See also attribute; child object; container object; noncontainer object; parent object.

object linking and embedding (OLE) A method for sharing information among applications. Linking an object, such as a graphic, from one document to another inserts a reference to the object into the second document. Any changes you make in the object in the first document will also be made in the second document. Embedding an object inserts a copy of an object from one document into another document. Changes you make in the object in the first document will not be updated in the second unless the embedded object is explicitly updated. See also ActiveX.

offline media Media that are not connected to the computer and require external assistance to be accessed.

on-media identifier (OMID) A label that is electronically recorded on each medium in a Removable Storage system. Removable Storage uses on-media identifiers to track media in the Removable Storage database. An application on-media identifier is a subset of the media label.

on-screen keyboard A utility that displays a virtual keyboard on a computer screen and allows users with mobility impairments to type using a pointing device or joystick.

OnNow See Advanced Configuration and Power Interface (ACPI).

open database connectivity (ODBC)

An application programming interface (API) that enables database applications to access data from a variety of existing data sources.

Open Host Controller Interface (OHCI)

Part of the IEEE 1394 standard. In Windows 2000 Professional, only OHCI-compliant host adapters are supported.

OpenType fonts Outline fonts that are rendered from line and curve commands, and can be scaled and rotated. OpenType fonts are clear and readable in all sizes and on all output devices supported by Windows 2000. OpenType is an extension of TrueType font technology. See also font; TrueType fonts.

operator request A request for the operator to perform a task. This request can be issued by an application or by Removable Storage.

original equipment manufacturer (OEM)

The maker of a piece of equipment. In making computers and computer-related equipment, manufacturers of original equipment typically purchase components from other manufacturers of original equipment and then integrate them into their own products.

out-routing server (OutRS) A Message Queuing routing server that provides session concentration by acting as a gateway for all outgoing messages for one or more independent clients. Message Queuing independent clients can be configured to use an OutRS. See also Message Queuing; Message Queuing server; session concentration.

overclocking Setting a microprocessor to run at speeds above the rated specification.

P

package An icon that represents embedded or linked information. That information can consist of a complete file, such as a Paint bitmap, or part of a file, such as a spreadsheet cell. When a package is chosen, the application used to create the object either plays the object (if it is a sound file, for example) or opens and displays the object. If the original information is changed, linked information is then updated. However, embedded information needs to be manually updated. In Systems Management Server, an object that contains the files and instructions for distributing software to a distribution point. See also embedded object; linked object; object linking and embedding (OLE).

packet A transmission unit of fixed maximum size that consists of binary information. This information represents both data and a header containing an ID number, source and destination addresses, and error-control data.

packet assembler/disassembler (PAD)

A connection used in X.25 networks. X.25 PAD boards can be used in place of modems when provided with a compatible COM driver.

PAD See packet assembler/disassembler.

page fault An error that occurs when the requested code or data cannot be located in the physical memory that is available to the requesting process.

page-description language (PDL)

A computer language that describes the arrangement of text and graphics on a printed page. See also printer control language (PCL); PostScript.

paging The process of moving virtual memory back and forth between physical memory and the disk. Paging occurs when physical memory limitations are reached and only occurs for data that is not already "backed" by disk space. For example, file data is not paged out because it already has allocated disk space within a file system. See also virtual memory.

paging file A hidden file on the hard disk that Windows 2000 uses to hold parts of programs and data files that do not fit in memory. The paging file and physical memory, or RAM, comprise virtual memory. Windows 2000 moves data from the paging file to memory as needed and moves data from memory to the paging file to make room for new data. Also called a swap file. See also random access memory (RAM); virtual memory.

PAP See Password Authentication Protocol.

Parallel connection A connection that simultaneously transmits both data and control bits over wires connected in parallel. In general, a parallel connection can move data between devices faster than a serial connection.

Parallel device A device that uses a parallel connection.

Parallel ports The input/output connector for a parallel interface device. Printers are generally plugged into a parallel port.

parent object The object that is the immediate superior of another object in a hierarchy. A parent object can have multiple subordinate, or child, objects. In Active Directory, the schema determines what objects can be parent objects of what other objects. Depending on its class, a parent object can be the child of another object. See also child object; object.

partition A logical division of a hard disk. Partitions make it easier to organize information. Each partition can be formatted for a different file system. A partition must be completely contained on one physical disk, and the partition table in the Master Boot Record for a physical disk can contain up to four entries for partitions.

password authentication protocol (PAP) A simple, plaintext authentication scheme for authenticating PPP connections. The user name and password are requested by the remote access server and returned by the remote access client in plaintext.

path A sequence of directory (or folder) names that specifies the location of a directory, file, or folder within the Windows directory tree. Each directory name and file name within the path must be preceded by a backslash (\). For example, to specify the path of a file named Readme.doc located in the Windows directory on drive C, type C:\Windows\Readme.doc.

PC Card A removable device, approximately the size of a credit card, that can be plugged into a PCMCIA (Personal Computer Memory Card International Association) slot in a portable computer. PCMCIA devices can include modems, network adapters, and hard disk drives.

PCI See Peripheral Component Interconnect.

PCNFS Daemon (PCNFSD) A program that receives requests from PC-NFS clients for authentication on remote machines.

peer-to-peer network See workgroup.

performance counter In System Monitor, a data item associated with a performance object. For each counter selected, System Monitor presents a value corresponding to a particular aspect of the performance that is defined for the performance object. See also performance object.

performance object In System Monitor, a logical collection of counters that is associated with a resource or service that can be monitored. See also performance counter.

peripheral A device, such as a disk drive, printer, modem, or joystick, that is connected to a computer and is controlled by the computer's microprocessor.

peripheral component interconnect (PCI) A specification introduced by Intel Corporation that defines a local bus system that allows up to 10 PCI-compliant expansion cards to be installed in the computer.

permission A rule associated with an object to regulate which users can gain access to the object and in what manner. Permissions are granted or denied by the object's owner. See also access control list; object; privilege; user rights.

physical location The location designation assigned to media managed by Removable Storage. The two classes of physical locations include libraries and offline media physical locations. The offline media physical location is where Removable Storage lists the cartridges that are not in a library. The physical location of cartridges in an online library is the library in which it resides.

physical media A storage object that data can be written to, such as a disk or magnetic tape. A physical medium is referenced by its physical media ID (PMID).

physical object An object, such as an ATM card or smart card used in conjunction with a piece of information, such as a PIN number, to authenticate users. In two factor authentication, physical objects are used in conjunction with another secret piece of identification, such as a password, to authenticate users. In two factor authentication, the physical object might be an ATM card which is used in combination with a PIN to authenticate the user.

Ping A tool that verifies connections to one or more remote hosts. The ping command uses the ICMP Echo Request and Echo Reply packets to determine whether a particular IP system on a network is functional. Ping is useful for diagnosing IP network or router failures. See also Internet Control Message Protocol (ICMP).

pinning To make a network file or folder available for offline use.

plaintext Data that is not encrypted. Sometimes also called clear text. See also ciphertext; encryption; decryption.

Plug and Play A set of specifications developed by Intel that allows a computer to automatically detect and configure a device and install the appropriate device drivers.

Point and Print A way of installing network printers on a user's local computer. Point and Print allows users to initiate a connection to a network printer and loads any required drivers onto the client's computer. When users know which network printer they want to use, Point and Print greatly simplifies the installation process.

point of presence (POP)   The local access point for a network provider. Each POP provides a telephone number that allows users to make a local call for access to online services.

Point-to-Point Protocol (PPP)   An industry standard suite of protocols for the use of point-to-point links to transport multiprotocol datagrams. PPP is documented in RFC 1661.

Point-to-Point Tunneling Protocol (PPTP)
A tunneling protocol that encapsulates Point-to-Point Protocol (PPP) frames into IP datagrams for transmission over an IP-based internetwork, such as the Internet or a private intranet.

Portable Operating System Interface for UNIX (POSIX)
An IEEE (Institute of Electrical and Electronics Engineers) standard that defines a set of operating-system services. Programs that adhere to the POSIX standard can be easily ported from one system to another. POSIX was based on UNIX system services, but it was created in a way that allows it to be implemented by other operating systems.

POST   See power-on self test.

PostScript   A page-description language (PDL) developed by Adobe Systems for printing with laser printers. PostScript offers flexible font capability and high-quality graphics. It is the standard for desktop publishing because it is supported by imagesetters, the high-resolution printers used by printing services for commercial typesetting. See also printer control language (PCL); page-description language (PDL).

power-on self test (POST)   A set of routines stored in read-only memory (ROM) that tests various system components such as RAM, the disk drives, and the keyboard, to see if they are properly connected and operating. If problems are found, these routines alert the user with a series of beeps or a message, often accompanied by a diagnostic numeric value. If the POST is successful, it passes control to the bootstrap loader.

PPTP   See Point-to-Point Tunneling Protocol.

primary partition   A volume created using unallocated space on a basic disk. Windows 2000 and other operating systems can start from a primary partition. As many as four primary partitions can be created on a basic disk, or three primary partitions and an extended partition. Primary partitions can be created only on basic disks and cannot be subpartitioned. See also basic disk; dynamic volume; extended partition; partition.

printer control language (PCL)   The page-description language (PDL) developed by Hewlett Packard for their laser and inkjet printers. Because of the widespread use of laser printers, this command language has become a standard in many printers. See also page-description language (PDL); PostScript.

priority   A precedence ranking that determines the order in which the threads of a process are scheduled for the processor.

priority inversion   The mechanism that allows low-priority threads to run and complete execution rather than being preempted and locking up a resource such as an I/O device.

private branch exchange (PBX) An automatic telephone switching system that enables users within an organization to place calls to each other without going through the public telephone network. Users can also place calls to outside numbers.

private key The secret half of a cryptographic key pair that is used with a public key algorithm. Private keys are typically used to digitally sign data and to decrypt data that has been encrypted with the corresponding public key. See also public key.

privilege A user's right to perform a specific task, usually one that affects an entire computer system rather than a particular object. Privileges are assigned by administrators to individual users or groups of users as part of the security settings for the computer. See also access token; permission; user rights.

privileged mode Also known as kernel mode, the processing mode that allows code to have direct access to all hardware and memory in the system.

process throttling A method of restricting the amount of processor time a process consumes, for example, using job object functions.

processor queue An instantaneous count of the threads that are ready to run on the system but are waiting because the processor is running other threads.

protocol A set of rules and conventions by which two computers pass messages across a network. Networking software usually implements multiple levels of protocols layered one on top of another. Windows NT and Windows 2000 include NetBEUI, TCP/IP, and IPX/SPX-compatible protocols.

proxy server A firewall component that manages Internet traffic to and from a local area network and can provide other features, such as document caching and access control. A proxy server can improve performance by supplying frequently requested data, such as a popular Web page, and can filter and discard requests that the owner does not consider appropriate, such as requests for unauthorized access to proprietary files. See also firewall.

public key The non-secret half of a cryptographic key pair that is used with a public key algorithm. Public keys are typically used to verify digital signatures or decrypt data that has been encrypted with the corresponding private key. See also private key.

public key cryptography A method of cryptography in which two different but complimentary keys are used: a public key and a private key for providing security functions. Public key cryptography is also called asymmetric key cryptography. See also cryptography; public key; private key.

public switched telephone network (PSTN)
Standard analog telephone lines, available worldwide.

Q

QoS See Quality of Service.

QoS Admission Control Service A software service that controls bandwidth and network resources on the subnet to which it is assigned. Important applications can be given more bandwidth, less important applications less bandwidth. The QoS Admission Control Service can be installed on any network-enabled computer running Windows 2000.

Quality of Service (QoS) A set of quality assurance standards and mechanisms for data transmission, implemented in Windows 2000.

quantum Also known as a time slice, the maximum amount of time a thread can run before the system checks for another ready thread of the same priority to run.

quarter-inch cartridge (QIC) An older storage technology used with tape backup drives and cartridges. A means of backing up data on computer systems, QIC represents a set of standards devised to enable tapes to be used with drives from different manufacturers. The QIC standards specify the length of tape, the number of recording tracks, and the magnetic strength of the tape coating, all of which determine the amount of information that can be written to the tape. Older QIC-80 drives can hold up to 340 MB of compressed data. Newer versions can hold more than 1 GB of information.

R

RAID-5 volume A fault-tolerant volume with data and parity striped intermittently across three or more physical disks. Parity is a calculated value that is used to reconstruct data after a failure. If a portion of a physical disk fails, you can recreate the data that was on the failed portion from the remaining data and parity. Also known as a striped volume with parity.

raster fonts Fonts that are stored as bitmaps; also called bit-mapped fonts. Raster fonts are designed with a specific size and resolution for a specific printer and cannot be scaled or rotated. If a printer does not support raster fonts, it will not print them.

rate counter Similar to an averaging counter, a counter type that samples an increasing count of events over time; the change in the count is divided by the change in time to display a rate of activity.

read-only memory (ROM) A semiconductor circuit that contains information that cannot be modified.

recoverable file system A file system which ensures that if a power outage or other catastrophic system failure occurs, the file system will not be corrupted and disk modifications will not be left incomplete. The structure of the disk volume is restored to a consistent state when the system restarts.

Recovery Console A startable, text-mode command interpreter environment separate from the Windows 2000 command prompt that allows the system administrator access to the hard disk of a computer running Windows 2000, regardless of the file format used, for basic troubleshooting and system maintenance tasks.

redundant array of independent disks (RAID) A method used to standardize and categorize fault-tolerant disk systems. Six levels gauge various mixes of performance, reliability, and cost. Windows 2000 provides three of the RAID levels: Level 0 (striping) which is not fault-tolerant, Level 1 (mirroring), and Level 5 (striped volume with parity). See also fault tolerance; mirrored volume; RAID-5 volume; striped volume.

registry In Windows 2000, Windows NT, Windows 98, and Windows 95, a database of information about a computer's configuration. The registry is organized in a hierarchical structure and consists of subtrees and their keys, hives, and entries.

relative ID (RID) The part of a security ID (SID) that uniquely identifies an account or group within a domain. See also security ID.

remote access server A Windows 2000 Server--based computer running the Routing and Remote Access service and configured to provide remote access.

remote procedure call (RPC) A message-passing facility that allows a distributed application to call services that are available on various computers in a network. Used during remote administration of computers.

Removable Storage A service used for managing removable media (such as tapes and discs) and storage devices (libraries). Removable Storage allows applications to access and share the same media resources. See also library.

reparse points New NTFS file system objects that have a definable attribute containing user-controlled data and are used to extend functionality in the input/output (I/O) subsystem.

RepeatKeys A feature that allows users with mobility impairments to adjust the repeat rate or to disable the key-repeat function on the keyboard. (See FilterKeys)

Request for Comments (RFC) A document that defines a standard. RFCs are published by the Internet Engineering Task Force (IETF) and other working groups.

resident attribute A file attribute whose value is wholly contained in the file's file record in the master file table (MFT).

resolver DNS client programs used to look up DNS name information. Resolvers can be either a small "stub" (a limited set of programming routines that provide basic query functionality) or larger programs that provide additional lookup DNS client functions, such as caching. See also caching, caching resolver.

resource publishing The process of making an object visible and accessible to users in a Windows 2000 domain. For example, a shared printer resource is published by creating a reference to the printer object in Active Directory.

resource record (RR) Information in the DNS database that can be used to process client queries. Each DNS server contains the resource records it needs to answer queries for the portion of the DNS namespace for which it is authoritative.

response time The amount of time required to do work from start to finish. In a client/server environment, this is typically measured on the client side.

RGB The initials of red, green, blue. Used to describe a color monitor or color value.

roaming user profile A server-based user profile that is downloaded to the local computer when a user logs on and is updated both locally and on the server when the user logs off. A roaming user profile is available from the server when logging on to any computer that is running Windows 2000 Professional or Windows 2000 Server.

ROM See read-only memory.

route table See routing table

router A network device that helps LANs and WANs achieve interoperability and connectivity and that can link LANs that have different network topologies, such as Ethernet and Token Ring.

routing The process of forwarding a packet through an internetwork from a source host to a destination host.

Routing Information Protocol (RIP)
An industry standard distance vector routing protocol used in small to medium sized IP and IPX internetworks.

routing link For Message Queuing, a communications link established between Windows 2000 sites for routing messages. Specially configured Message Queuing servers with routing services enabled are used to create a routing link between sites. See also Message Queuing; routing services; routing-link cost.

routing services For Message Queuing, a service on a Message Queuing server that provides message routing services. If so configured, this feature can be used on a Message Queuing server to, enable computers that use different network protocols to communicate, reduce the number of sessions by acting as a gateway for all incoming or outgoing messages for independent clients and route messages between sites over a routing link. See also Message Queuing server; routing link; independent client.

routing table A database of routes containing information on network IDs, forwarding addresses, and metrics for reachable network segments on an internetwork.

routing-link cost For Message Queuing, a number used to determine the route that messages can take between two sites. This number represents the relative monetary cost of communication over a link. A routing link has a default routing-link cost of 1 and should not be changed unless you have multiple routing links between two sites and you want to enforce message routing over a specific routing link. See also intersite routing; routing link.

RPC See Remote Procedure Call.

rules An IPSec policy mechanism that governs how and when an IPSec policy protects communication. A rule provides the ability to trigger and control secure communication based on the source, destination, and type of IP traffic. Each rule contains a list of IP filters and a collection of security actions that take place upon a match with that filter list.

S

Safe Mode A method of starting Windows 2000 using basic files and drivers only, without networking. Safe Mode is available by pressing the F8 key when prompted during startup. This allows the computer to start when a problem prevents it from starting normally.

screen-enlargement utility A utility that allows the user to magnify a portion of the screen for greater visibility. (Also called a screen magnifier or large-print program.)

script A type of program consisting of a set of instructions to an application or utility program. A script usually expresses instructions by using the application's or utility's rules and syntax, combined with simple control structures such as loops and if/then expressions. "Batch program" is often used interchangeably with "script" in the Windows environment.

SCSI See Small Computer System Interface.

SCSI connection A standard high-speed parallel interface defined by the X3T9.2 committee of the American National Standards Institute (ANSI). A SCSI interface is used to connect microcomputers to SCSI peripheral devices, such as many hard disks and printers, and to other computers and local area networks.

search filter An argument in an LDAP search that allows certain entries in the subtree and excludes others. Filters allow you to define search criteria and give you better control to achieve more effective and efficient searches.

Secure Sockets Layer (SSL) A proposed open standard developed by Netscape Communications for establishing a secure communications channel to prevent the interception of critical information, such as credit card numbers. Primarily, it enables secure electronic financial transactions on the World Wide Web, although it is designed to work on other Internet services as well.

Security Accounts Manager (SAM)
A protected subsystem that manages user and group account information. In Windows NT 4.0, both local and domain security principals are stored by SAM in the registry. In Windows 2000, workstation security accounts are stored by SAM in the local computer registry, and domain controller security accounts are stored in Active Directory.

security association (SA)   A set of parameters that defines the services and mechanisms necessary to protect Internet Protocol security communications. See also Internet Protocol security (IPSec).

security descriptor   A data structure that contains security information associated with a protected object. Security descriptors include information about who owns the object, who may access it and in what way, and what types of access will be audited. See also access control list; object.

security event types   Different categories of events about which Windows 2000 can create auditing events. Account logon or object access are examples of security event types.

security ID (SID)   A data structure of variable length that uniquely identifies user, group, service, and computer accounts within an enterprise. Every account is issued a SID when the account is first created. Access control mechanisms in Windows 2000 identify security principals by SID rather than by name. See also relative ID; security principal.

security method   A process that determines the Internet Protocol security services, key settings, and algorithms that will be used to protect the data during the communication.

Security Parameters Index (SPI)   A unique, identifying value in the SA used to distinguish among multiple security associations existing at the receiving computer.

security principal   An account-holder, such as a user, computer, or service. Each security principal within a Windows 2000 domain is identified by a unique security ID (SID). When a security principal logs on to a computer running Windows 2000, the Local Security Authority (LSA) authenticates the security principal's account name and password. If the logon is successful, the system creates an access token. Every process executed on behalf of this security principal will have a copy of its access token. See also access token; security ID; security principal name.

security principal name   A name that uniquely identifies a user, group, or computer within a single domain. This name is not guaranteed to be unique across domains. See also security principal.

seek time   The amount of time required for a disk head to position itself at the right disk cylinder to access requested data.

Serial Bus Protocol (SBP-2)   A standard for storage devices, printers, and scanners that is a supplement to the IEEE 1394 specification.

Serial connection   A connection that exchanges information between computers or between computers and peripheral devices one bit at a time over a single channel. Serial communications can be synchronous or asynchronous. Both sender and receiver must use the same baud rate, parity, and control information.

Serial device   A device that uses a serial connection.

SerialKeys   A Windows feature that uses a communications aid interface device to allow keystrokes and mouse controls to be accepted through a computer's serial port.

server   A computer that provides shared resources to network users.

Server Message Block (SMB) A file-sharing protocol designed to allow networked computers to transparently access files that reside on remote systems over a variety of networks. The SMB protocol defines a series of commands that pass information between computers. SMB uses four message types: session control, file, printer, and message.

service access point A logical address that allows a system to route data between a remote device and the appropriate communications support.

Service Pack A software upgrade to an existing software distribution that contains updated files consisting of patches and fixes.

Service Profile Identifier (SPID) A 14-digit number that identifies a specific ISDN line. When establishing ISDN service, your telephone company assigns a SPID to your line. See also ISDN.

service provider In TAPI, a dynamic link library (DLL) that provides an interface between an application requesting services and the controlling hardware device. TAPI supports two classes of service providers, media service providers and telephony service providers.

session concentration For Message Queuing, a feature that typically reduces network bandwidth within a site, and the number of sessions between sites. Specially configured Message Queuing servers with routing services provide session concentration. See also Message Queuing server; routing services.

session key A key used primarily for encryption and decryption. Session keys are typically used with symmetric encryption algorithms where the same key is used for both encryption and decryption. For this reason, session and symmetric keys usually refer to the same type of key. See also symmetric key encryption.

Sfmmon A port monitor that is used to send jobs over the AppleTalk protocol to printers such as LaserWriters or those configured with AppleTalk or any AppleTalk spoolers.

shared folder permissions Permissions that restrict a shared resource's availability over the network to certain users. See also permission.

Shiva Password Authentication Protocol (SPAP) A two-way, reversible encryption mechanism for authenticating PPP connections employed by Shiva remote access servers.

shortcut key navigation indicators Underlined letters on a menu or control. (Also called access keys or quick-access letters.)

ShowSounds A global flag that instructs programs to display captions for speech and system sounds to alert users with hearing impairments or people who work in a noisy location such as a factory floor.

Simple Mail Transfer Protocol (SMTP) A protocol used on the Internet to transfer mail. SMTP is independent of the particular transmission subsystem and requires only a reliable, ordered, data stream channel.

Simple Network Management Protocol (SNMP) A network management protocol installed with TCP/IP and widely used on TCP/IP and Internet Package Exchange (IPX) networks. SNMP transports management information and commands between a management program run by an administrator and the network management agent running on a host. The SNMP agent sends status information to one or more hosts when the host requests it or when a significant event occurs.

Single Sign-On Daemon (SSOD) A program installed on a UNIX-based system to handle password synchronization requests.

single-switch device An alternative input device, such as a voice activation program, that allows a user to scan or select using a single switch.

slot Storage locations for cartridges in a library managed by Removable Storage.

SlowKeys A Windows feature that instructs the computer to disregard keystrokes that are not held down for a minimum period of time, which allows the user to brush against keys without any effect. See also FilterKeys.

Small Computer System Interface (SCSI)
A standard high-speed parallel interface defined by the X3T9.2 committee of the American National Standards Institute (ANSI). A SCSI interface is used for connecting microcomputers to peripheral devices, such as hard disks and printers, and to other computers and local area networks.

Small Office/Home Office (SOHO)
An office with a few computers that can be considered a small business or part of a larger network.

smart card A credit card-sized device that is used with a PIN number to enable certificate-based authentication and single sign-on to the enterprise. Smart cards securely store certificates, public and private keys, passwords, and other types of personal information. A smart card reader attached to the computer reads the smart card. See also authentication; certificate; nonrepudiation.

SNA Server Client Software that allows workstations to communicate through SNA Server and support SNA Server advanced host integration features. SNA Server Client software also provides application programming interfaces (APIs) that are used by third-party vendors to gain access to IBM host systems and applications.

SNA Server Manager A graphical Microsoft Management Console (MMC) snap-in that supports simultaneous monitoring, diagnosis, and management of SNA Server resources and services.

SNMP See Simple Network Management Protocol.

software trap In programming, an event that occurs when a microprocessor detects a problem with executing an instruction, which causes it to stop.

SoundSentry A Windows feature that produces a visual cue, such as a screen flash or a blinking title bar instead of system sounds.

source directory The folder that contains the file or files to be copied or moved. See also destination directory.

SPAP See Shiva Password Authentication Protocol.

sparse file A file that is handled in a way that requires less disk space than would otherwise be needed by allocating only meaningful non-zero data. Sparse support allows an application to create very large files without committing disk space for every byte.

speech synthesizer An assistive device that produces spoken words, either by splicing together prerecorded words or by programming the computer to produce the sounds that make up spoken words.

stand-alone drive An online drive that is not part of a library unit. Removable Storage treats stand-alone drives as online libraries with one drive and a port.

status area The area on the taskbar to the right of the taskbar buttons. The status area displays the time and can also contain icons that provide quick access to programs, such as Volume Control and Power Options. Other icons can appear temporarily, providing information about the status of activities. For example, the printer icon appears after a document has been sent to the printer and disappears when printing is complete.

StickyKeys An accessibility feature built into Windows that causes modifier keys such as SHIFT, CTRL, WINDOWS LOGO, or ALT to stay on after they are pressed, eliminating the need to press multiple keys simultaneously. This feature facilitates the use of modifier keys for users who are unable to hold down one key while pressing another.

Stop error A serious error that affects the operating system and that could place data at risk. The operating system generates an obvious message, a screen with the Stop message, rather than continuing on and possibly corrupting data. Also known as a fatal system error. See also Stop message.

Stop message A character-based, full-screen error message displayed on a blue background. A Stop message indicates that the Windows 2000 kernel detected a condition from which it cannot recover. Each message is uniquely identified by a Stop error code (a hexadecimal number) and a string indicating the error's symbolic name. Stop messages are usually followed by up to four additional hexadecimal numbers, enclosed in parentheses, which identify developer-defined error parameters. A driver or device may be identified as the cause of the error. A series of troubleshooting tips are also displayed, along with an indication that, if the system was configured to do so, a memory dump file was saved for later use by a kernel debugger. See also Stop error.

streaming media servers Software (such as Microsoft Media Technologies) that provides multimedia support, allowing you to deliver content by using Advanced Streaming Format over an intranet or the Internet.

streams A sequence of bits, bytes, or other small structurally uniform units.

striped volume A volume that stores data in stripes on two or more physical disks. Data in a striped volume is allocated alternately and evenly (in stripes) to these disks. Striped volumes offer the best performance of all volumes available in Windows 2000, but they do not provide fault tolerance. If a disk in a striped volume fails, the data in the entire volume is lost. You can create striped volumes only on dynamic disks. Striped volumes cannot be mirrored or extended. In Windows NT 4.0, a striped volume was known as a stripe set. See also dynamic disk, dynamic volume, fault tolerance, volume.

subkey In the registry, a key within a key. Subkeys are analogous to subdirectories in the registry hierarchy. Keys and subkeys are similar to the section header in .ini files; however, subkeys can carry out functions. See also key.

subnet A subdivision of an IP network. Each subnet has its own unique subnetted network ID.

subnet mask A 32-bit value expressed as four decimal numbers from 0 to 255, separated by periods (for example, 255.255.0.0). This number allows TCP/IP to determine the network ID portion of an IP address.

subnet prioritization The ordering of multiple IP address mappings from a DNS server so that the resolver orders local resource records first. This reduces network traffic across subnets by forcing computers to connect to network resources that are closer to them.

Subpicture A data stream contained within a DVD. The Subpicture stream delivers the subtitles and any other add-on data, such as system help or director's comments, which can be displayed while playing multimedia.

symmetric key A single key that is used with symmetric encryption algorithms for both encryption and decryption. See also bulk encryption; encryption; decryption; session key.

symmetric key encryption An encryption algorithm that requires the same secret key to be used for both encryption and decryption. This is often called secret key encryption. Because of its speed, symmetric encryption is typically used rather than public key encryption when a message sender needs to encrypt large amounts of data.

Synchronization Manager In Windows 2000, the tool used to ensure that a file or directory on a client computer contains the same data as a matching file or directory on a server.

syntax The order in which a command must be typed and the elements that follow the command.

system access control list (SACL)
The part of an object's security descriptor that specifies which events are to be audited per user or group. Examples of auditing events are file access, logon attempts, and system shutdowns. See also access control entry (ACE); discretionary access control list (DACL); object; security descriptor.

system administrator A person that administers a computer system or network, including administering user accounts, security, storage space, and backing up data.

system files Files that are used by Windows to load, configure, and run the operating system. Generally, system files must never be deleted or moved.

system media pool A pool used to hold cartridges that are not in use. The free pool holds unused cartridges that are available to applications, and the unrecognized and import pools are temporary holding places for cartridges that have been newly placed in a library.

system policy In network administration, the part of Group Policy that is concerned with the current user and local computer settings in the registry. In Windows 2000, system policy is sometimes called software policy and is one of several services provided by Group Policy, a Microsoft Management Console (MMC) snap-in. The Windows NT 4.0 System Policy Editor, Poledit.exe, is included with Windows 2000 for backward compatibility. That is, administrators need it to set system policy on Windows NT 4.0 and Windows 95 computers. See also Microsoft Management Console (MMC); registry.

System Policy Editor The utility Poledit.exe, used by administrators to set system policy on Windows NT 4.0 and Windows 95 computers.

system state data A collection of system-specific data that can be backed up and restored. For all Windows 2000 operating systems, the System State data includes the registry, the class registration database, and the system boot files.

system volume The volume that contains the hardware-specific files needed to load Windows 2000. The system volume can be (but does not have to be) the same volume as the boot volume. See also volume.

systemroot The path and folder name where the Windows 2000 system files are located. Typically, this is C:\Winnt, although a different drive or folder can be designated when Windows 2000 is installed. The value %systemroot% can be used to replace the actual location of the folder that contains the Windows 2000 system files. To identify your systemroot folder, click Start, click Run, and then type %systemroot%.

Systems Management Server A part of the Windows BackOffice suite of products. Systems Management Server (SMS) includes inventory collection, deployment, and diagnostic tools. SMS can significantly automate the task of upgrading software, allow remote problem solving, provide asset management information, manage software licenses, and monitor computers and networks.

Systems Network Architecture (SNA)
A communications framework developed by IBM to define network functions and establish standards for enabling computers to share and process data.

T

taskbar The bar that contains the Start button and appears by default at the bottom of the desktop. You can use the taskbar buttons to switch between the programs you are running. The taskbar can be hidden, moved to the sides or top of the desktop, or customized in other ways. See also desktop; taskbar button; status area.

taskbar button A button that appears on the taskbar when an application is running. See also taskbar.

TCP/IP See Transmission Control Protocol/Internet Protocol.

Tcpmon.ini The file that specifies whether a device supports multiple ports. If the Tcpmon.ini file indicates that a device can support multiple ports, users a prompted to pick which port should be used during device installation.

Telephony API (TAPI) An application programming interface (API) used by communications programs to communicate with telephony and network services. See also Internet Protocol.

Telnet 3270 (TN3270) Terminal emulation software, similar to Telnet, that allows a personal computer to log on to an IBM mainframe over a TCP/IP network.

Telnet 5250 (TN5250) Terminal emulation software, similar to Telnet, that allows a personal computer to log on to an IBM AS/400 host system over a TCP/IP network.

terabyte Approximately one trillion bytes, or one million million bytes.

Terminal Services Software services that allow client applications to be run on a server so that client computers can function as terminals rather than independent systems. The server provides a multisession environment and runs the Windows-based programs being used on the clients. See also client.

third-party accessibility aids Non-Microsoft add-on, augmentative hardware and software devices, such as accessibility products that assist users with disabilities.

thread A type of object within a process that runs program instructions. Using multiple threads allows concurrent operations within a process and enables one process to run different parts of its program on different processors simultaneously. A thread has its own set of registers, its own kernel stack, a thread environment block, and a user stack in the address space of its process.

thread state A numeric value indicating the execution state of the thread. Numbered 0 through 5, the states seen most often are 1 for ready, 2 for running, and 5 for waiting.

throughput For disks, the transfer capacity of the disk system.

Time To Live (TTL) A timer value included in packets sent over TCP/IP-based networks that tells the recipients how long to hold or use the packet or any of its included data before expiring and discarding the packet or data. For DNS, TTL values are used in resource records within a zone to determine how long requesting clients should cache and use this information when it appears in a query response answered by a DNS server for the zone.

timer bar The colored bar that moves across the screen according to the frequency of the data-collection update interval.

ToggleKeys A Windows feature that beeps when one of the locking keys (CAPS LOCK, NUM LOCK, or SCROLL LOCK) is turned on or off.

Token Ring A type of network media that connects clients in a closed ring and uses token passing to allow clients to use the network. See also Fiber Distributed Data Interface (FDDI).

total instance A unique instance that contains the performance counters that represent the sum of all active instances of an object.

transitive trust relationship The trust relationship that inherently exists between Windows 2000 domains in a domain tree or forest, or between trees in a forest, or between forests. When a domain joins an existing forest or domain tree, a transitive trust is automatically established. In Windows 2000 transitive trusts are always two-way relationships. See also domain tree; forest; nontransitive trust relationship.

Transmission Control Protocol/Internet Protocol (TCP/IP)
A set of software networking protocols widely used on the Internet that provide communications across interconnected networks of computers with diverse hardware architectures and operating systems. TCP/IP includes standards for how computers communicate and conventions for connecting networks and routing traffic.

Transmitting Station ID string (TSID)
A string that specifies the Transmitter Subscriber ID sent by the fax machine when sending a fax to a receiving machine. This string is usually a combination of the fax or telephone number and the name of the business. It is often the same as the Called Subscriber ID.

Transport Layer Security (TLS) A standard protocol that is used to provide secure Web communications on the Internet or intranets. It enables clients to authenticate servers or, optionally, servers to authenticate clients. It also provides a secure channel by encrypting communications.

transport protocol A protocol that defines how data should be presented to the next receiving layer in the Windows NT and Windows 2000 networking model and packages the data accordingly. The transport protocol passes data to the network adapter driver through the network driver interface specification (NDIS) interface and to the redirector through the Transport Driver Interface (TDI).

TrueType fonts Fonts that are scalable and sometimes generated as bitmaps or soft fonts, depending on the capabilities of your printer. TrueType fonts are device-independent fonts that are stored as outlines. They can be sized to any height, and they can be printed exactly as they appear on the screen. See also font.

trust relationship A logical relationship established between domains that allows pass-through authentication in which a trusting domain honors the logon authentications of a trusted domain. User accounts and global groups defined in a trusted domain can be granted rights and permissions in a trusting domain, even though the user accounts or groups do not exist in the trusting domain's directory. See also authentication; domain; two-way trust relationship.

trusted forest A forest that is connected to another forest by explicit or transitive trust. See also explicit trust relationship; forest; transitive trust relationship.

TSID See Transmitting Station ID string.

tunnel The logical path by which the encapsulated packets travel through the transit internetwork.

TWAIN An acronym for Technology Without An Interesting Name. An industry-standard software protocol and API that provides easy integration of image data between input devices, such as scanners and still image digital cameras, and software applications.

two-way trust relationship A link between domains in which each domain trusts user accounts in the other domain to use its resources. Users can log on from computers in either domain to the domain that contains their account. See also trust relationship.

type 1 fonts Scalable fonts designed to work with PostScript devices. See also font; PostScript.

U

UART See Universal Asynchronous Receiver/Transmitter.

unallocated space Available disk space that is not allocated to any partition, logical drive, or volume. The type of object created on unallocated space depends on the disk type (basic or dynamic). For basic disks, unallocated space outside partitions can be used to create primary or extended partitions. Free space inside an extended partition can be used to create a logical drive. For dynamic disks, unallocated space can be used to create dynamic volumes. Unlike basic disks, the exact disk region used is not selected to create the volume. See also basic disk; dynamic disk; extended partition; logical drive; partition; primary partition; volume.

Unicode A fixed-width, 16-bit character-encoding standard capable of representing the letters and characters of the majority of the world's languages. Unicode was developed by a consortium of U.S. computer companies.

UniDriver The UniDriver (or Universal Print Driver) carries out requests (such as printing text, rendering bitmaps, or advancing a page) on most types of printers. The UniDriver accepts information from a printer specific minidriver and uses this information to complete tasks.

Uniform Resource Locator (URL)
An address that uniquely identifies a location on the Internet. A URL for a World Wide Web site is preceded with http://, as in the fictitious URL http://www.example.microsoft.com/. A URL can contain more detail, such as the name of a page of hypertext, usually identified by the file name extension .html or .htm. See also HTML; HTTP; IP address.

Universal Asynchronous Receiver/Transmitter (UART)
An integrated circuit (silicon chip) that is commonly used in microcomputers to provide asynchronous communications. The UART does parallel-to-serial conversion of data to be transmitted and serial-to-parallel conversion of data received. See also asynchronous communication.

Universal Disk Format (UDF) A file system defined by the Optical Storage Technology Association (OSTA) that is the successor to the CD-ROM file system (CDFS). UDF is targeted for removable disk media like DVD, CD, and Magneto-Optical (MO) discs.

universal group A Windows 2000 group only available in native mode that is valid anywhere in the forest. A universal group appears in the Global Catalog but contains primarily global groups from domains in the forest. This is the simplest form of group and can contain other universal groups, global groups, and users from anywhere in the forest. See also domain local group; forest; Global Catalog.

Universal Naming Convention (UNC)
A convention for naming files and other resources beginning with two backslashes (\), indicating that the resource exists on a network computer. UNC names conform to the \\SERVERNAME \SHARENAME syntax, where SERVERNAME is the server's name and SHARENAME is the name of the shared resource. The UNC name of a directory or file can also include the directory path after the share name, with the following syntax: \\SERVERNAME\SHARENAME \DIRECTORY\FILENAME.

Universal Serial Bus (USB) A serial bus with a bandwidth of 1.5 megabits per second (Mbps) for connecting peripherals to a microcomputer. USB can connect up to 127 peripherals, such as external CD-ROM drives, printers, modems, mice, and keyboards, to the system through a single, general-purpose port. This is accomplished by daisy chaining peripherals together. USB supports hot plugging and multiple data streams.

UNIX A powerful, multi-user, multitasking operating system initially developed at AT&T Bell Laboratories in 1969 for use on minicomputers. UNIX is considered more portable—that is, less computer-specific—than other operating systems because it is written in C language. Newer versions of UNIX have been developed at the University of California at Berkeley and by AT&T.

unrecognized pool A repository for blank media and media that are not recognized by Removable Storage.

upgrade When referring to software, to update existing program files, folders, and registry entries to a more recent version. Upgrading, unlike performing a new installation, leaves existing settings and files in place.

URL See Uniform Resource Locator.

USB See Universal Serial Bus.

user account A record that consists of all the information that defines a user to Windows 2000. This includes the user name and password required for the user to log on, the groups in which the user account has membership, and the rights and permissions the user has for using the computer and network and accessing their resources. For Windows 2000 Professional and member servers, user accounts are managed by using Local Users and Groups. For Windows 2000 Server domain controllers, user accounts are managed by using Microsoft Active Directory Users and Computers. See also domain controller; group; user name.

User Identification (UID) A user identifier that uniquely identifies a user. UNIX-bases systems use the UID to identify the owner of files and processes, and to determine access permissions.

user mode The processing mode in which applications run.

user name A unique name identifying a user account to Windows 2000. An account's user name must be unique among the other group names and user names within its own domain or workgroup.

user principal name (UPN) A friendly name assigned to security principals (users and groups) that is shorter than the distinguished name and easier to remember. The default user principal name is composed of the security principal name for the user and the DNS name of the root domain where the user object resides.

user principal name (UPN) (continued)
For example, user "MyName" in the tree for microsoft.com might have a user principal name of "MyName@microsoft.com". The user principal name is the preferred logon name for Windows 2000 users and is independent of the distinguished name, so a User object can be moved or renamed without affecting the user's logon name. See also distinguished name.

user profile   A file which contains configuration information for a specific user, such as desktop settings, persistent network connections, and application settings. Each user's preferences are saved to a user profile that Windows NT and Windows 2000 use to configure the desktop each time a user logs on.

user rights   Tasks a user is permitted to perform on a computer system or domain. There are two types of user rights: privileges and logon rights. An example of a privilege is the right to shut down the system. An example of a logon right is the right to log on to a computer locally (at the keyboard). Both types are assigned by administrators to individual users or groups as part of the security settings for the computer. See also permission; privilege.

user rights policy   Security settings that manage the assignment of rights to groups and user accounts.

Utility Manager   A function of Windows 2000 that allows administrators to review the status of applications and tools and to customize features and add tools more easily.

V

value bar   The area of the System Monitor graph or histogram display that shows last, average, minimum and maximum statistics for the selected counter.

Vector fonts   Fonts rendered from a mathematical model, in which each character is defined as a set of lines drawn between points. Vector fonts can be cleanly scaled to any size or aspect ratio.

vertical blanking interval (VBI)   The part of a TV transmission that is blanked, or left clear of viewable content, to allow time for the TV's electron gun to move from the bottom to the top of the screen as it scans images. This blank area is now being used to broadcast closed captioned and HTML-formatted information.

Video for Windows (VfW)   A format developed by Microsoft for storing video and audio information. Files in this format have an .avi extension. AVI files are limited to 320 x 240 resolution at 30 frames per second, neither of which is adequate for full-screen, full-motion video.

Video Port Extensions (VPE)   A DirectDraw extension to support direct hardware connections from a video decoder and autoflipping in the graphics frame buffer. VPE allows the client to negotiate the connection between the MPEG or NTSC decoder and the video port. VPE also allows the client to control effects in the video stream, such as cropping, scaling, and so on.

Virtual Device Driver (VxD)   Software for Windows that manages a hardware or software system resource. The middle letter in the abbreviation indicates the type of device; x is used where the type of device is not under discussion.

virtual memory   The space on the hard disk that Windows 2000 uses as memory. Because of virtual memory, the amount of memory taken from the perspective of a process can be much greater than the actual physical memory in the computer. The operating system does this in a way that is transparent to the application, by paging data that does not fit in physical memory to and from the disk at any given instant.

virtual private network (VPN)   The extension of a private network that encompasses links across shared or public networks, such as the Internet.

virus scanner   Software used to scan for and eradicate computer viruses, worms, and Trojan horses. See virus.

volume A portion of a physical disk that functions as though it were a physically separate disk. In My Computer and Windows Explorer, volumes appear as local disks, such as drive C or drive D.

volume mount points New system objects in the version of NTFS included with Windows 2000 that represent storage volumes in a persistent, robust manner. Volume mount points allow the operating system to graft the root of a volume onto a directory.

W

WDM Streaming class The means by which Windows 2000 Professional supports digital video and audio. Enables support for such components as DVD decoders, MPEG decoders, video decoders, tuners, and audio codecs.

wide area network (WAN) A communications network connecting geographically separated computers, printers, and other devices. A WAN allows any connected device to interact with any other on the network. See also local area network (LAN).

Windows 2000 MultiLanguage Version
A version of Windows 2000 that extends the native language support in Windows 2000 by allowing user interface languages to be changed on a per user basis. This version also minimizes the number of language versions you need to deploy across the network.

Windows File Protection (WFP) A Windows 2000 feature that runs in the background and protects your system files from being overwritten. When a file in a protected folder is modified, WFP determines if the new file is the correct Microsoft version or if the file is digitally signed. If not, the modified file is replaced with a valid version.

Windows Internet Name Service (WINS)
A software service that dynamically maps IP addresses to computer names (NetBIOS names). This allows users to access resources by name instead of requiring them to use IP addresses that are difficult to recognize and remember. WINS servers support clients running Windows NT 4.0 and earlier versions of Windows operating systems. See also Domain Name System (DNS).

Windows Update A Microsoft-owned Web site from which Windows 98 and Windows 2000 users can install or update device drivers. By using an ActiveX control, Windows Update compares the available drivers with those on the user's system and offers to install new or updated versions.

WINS See Windows Internet Name Service.

Winsock An application programming interface standard for software that provides TCP/IP interface under Windows. Short for Windows Sockets. See also TCP/IP.

work queue item A job request of an existing library, made by an application that supports Removable Storage, which is placed in a queue and processed when the library resource becomes available.

workgroup A simple grouping of computers, intended only to help users find such things as printers and shared folders within that group. Workgroups in Windows 2000 do not offer the centralized user accounts and authentication offered by domains.

working set For a process, the amount of physical memory assigned to a process by the operating system.

Index

T

Get a **Free**
e-mail newsletter, updates,
special offers, links to related books,
and more when you

register on line!

Register your Microsoft Press® title on our Web site and you'll get a FREE subscription to our e-mail newsletter, *Microsoft Press Book Connections.* You'll find out about newly released and upcoming books and learning tools, online events, software downloads, special offers and coupons for Microsoft Press customers, and information about major Microsoft® product releases. You can also read useful additional information about all the titles we publish, such as detailed book descriptions, tables of contents and indexes, sample chapters, links to related books and book series, author biographies, and reviews by other customers.

Registration is easy. Just visit this Web page and fill in your information:

http://www.microsoft.com/mspress/register

Microsoft®

Proof of Purchase

Use this page as proof of purchase if participating in a promotion or rebate offer on this title. Proof of purchase must be used in conjunction with other proof(s) of payment such as your dated sales receipt—see offer details.

Microsoft® Windows® 2000 Professional Resource Kit
1-57231-808-2

CUSTOMER NAME

Microsoft Press, PO Box 97017, Redmond, WA 98073-9830

Ready
solutions
for the
IT administrator

Keep your IT systems up and running with ADMINISTRATOR'S COMPANIONS from Microsoft Press. These expert guides serve as both tutorial and reference for critical deployment and maintenance tasks for Microsoft products and technologies. Packed with real-world expertise, hands-on numbered procedures, and handy workarounds, ADMINISTRATOR'S COMPANIONS deliver ready answers for on-the-job results.

MICROSOFT LICENSE AGREEMENT

Microsoft Windows 2000 Professional Resource Kit CD

SOFTWARE PRODUCT LICENSE

OR RESALE AS ON-LINE CONTROL EQUIPMENT IN HAZARDOUS ENVIRONMENTS REQUIRING FAIL-SAFE PERFOR-MANCE, SUCH AS IN THE OPERATION OF NUCLEAR FACILITIES, AIRCRAFT NAVIGATION OR COMMUNICATION SYSTEMS, AIR TRAFFIC CONTROL, DIRECT LIFE SUPPORT MACHINES, OR WEAPONS SYSTEMS, IN WHICH THE FAILURE OF JAVA TECHNOLOGY COULD LEAD DIRECTLY TO DEATH, PERSONAL INJURY, OR SEVERE PHYSICAL OR ENVIRONMENTAL DAMAGE.

DISCLAIMER OF WARRANTY

NO WARRANTIES OR CONDITIONS. MICROSOFT EXPRESSLY DISCLAIMS ANY WARRANTY OR CONDITION FOR THE SOFTWARE PRODUCT. THE SOFTWARE PRODUCT AND ANY RELATED DOCUMENTATION ARE PROVIDED "AS IS" WITHOUT WARRANTY OR CONDITION OF ANY KIND, EITHER EXPRESS OR IMPLIED, INCLUDING, WITHOUT LIMITATION, THE IMPLIED WARRANTIES OF MERCHANTABILITY, FITNESS FOR A PARTICULAR PURPOSE, OR NONINFRINGEMENT. THE ENTIRE RISK ARISING OUT OF USE OR PERFORMANCE OF THE SOFTWARE PRODUCT REMAINS WITH YOU.

LIMITATION OF LIABILITY. TO THE MAXIMUM EXTENT PERMITTED BY APPLICABLE LAW, IN NO EVENT SHALL MICROSOFT OR ITS SUPPLIERS BE LIABLE FOR ANY SPECIAL, INCIDENTAL, INDIRECT, OR CONSEQUENTIAL DAMAGES WHATSOEVER (INCLUDING, WITHOUT LIMITATION, DAMAGES FOR LOSS OF BUSINESS PROFITS, BUSINESS INTERRUP-TION, LOSS OF BUSINESS INFORMATION, OR ANY OTHER PECUNIARY LOSS) ARISING OUT OF THE USE OF OR INABILITY TO USE THE SOFTWARE PRODUCT OR THE PROVISION OF OR FAILURE TO PROVIDE SUPPORT SERVICES, EVEN IF MICROSOFT HAS BEEN ADVISED OF THE POSSIBILITY OF SUCH DAMAGES. IN ANY CASE, MICROSOFT'S ENTIRE LIABIL-ITY UNDER ANY PROVISION OF THIS EULA SHALL BE LIMITED TO THE GREATER OF THE AMOUNT ACTUALLY PAID BY YOU FOR THE SOFTWARE PRODUCT OR US$5.00; PROVIDED, HOWEVER, IF YOU HAVE ENTERED INTO A MICROSOFT SUPPORT SERVICES AGREEMENT, MICROSOFT'S ENTIRE LIABILITY REGARDING SUPPORT SERVICES SHALL BE GOV-ERNED BY THE TERMS OF THAT AGREEMENT. BECAUSE SOME STATES AND JURISDICTIONS DO NOT ALLOW THE EXCLUSION OR LIMITATION OF LIABILITY, THE ABOVE LIMITATION MAY NOT APPLY TO YOU.

MISCELLANEOUS

This EULA is governed by the laws of the State of Washington USA, except and only to the extent that applicable law mandates governing law of a different jurisdiction.

Should you have any questions concerning this EULA, or if you desire to contact Microsoft for any reason, please contact the Microsoft subsidiary serving your country, or write: Microsoft Sales Information Center/One Microsoft Way/Redmond, WA 98052-6399.

PN 097-0002297

System Requirements

To use the Microsoft Windows 2000 Professional Resource Kit compact disc, you need a computer equipped with the following minimum configuration:

- PC with Pentium II 233-MHz or higher processor

- Microsoft Windows 2000 Professional

- 64 MB RAM minimum; 128 MB RAM recommended

- 30 MB of available hard disk space minimum; 100 MB recommended

- Super VGA monitor; 256-color display card recommended

- CD-ROM or DVD-ROM drive

- Microsoft Mouse or other compatible pointing device